THE ELIZABETHAN NEW YEAR'S GIFT EXCHANGES
1559–1603

Elizabeth I by an Unknown Artist, c.1590–92 (Toledo Art Museum)

RECORDS OF SOCIAL AND ECONOMIC HISTORY
NEW SERIES 51

THE ELIZABETHAN NEW YEAR'S GIFT EXCHANGES 1559–1603

Edited by

JANE A. LAWSON

Published for THE BRITISH ACADEMY
by OXFORD UNIVERSITY PRESS

Oxford University Press, Great Clarendon Street, Oxford OX2 6DP

© The British Academy 2013
Database right The British Academy (maker)

First edition published in 2013

British Library Cataloguing in Publication Data
Data available

Library of Congress Cataloging in Publication Data
Data available

Typeset by
New Leaf Design, Scarborough, North Yorkshire
Printed in Great Britain
on acid-free paper by
CPI Antony Rowe Limited
Chippenham, Wiltshire

ISBN 978–0–19–726526–0

Foreword

Historians and social scientists have shown a longstanding interest in gift exchanges as expressions of social bonding and reciprocity. The survival of a large number of gift lists recording both gifts given to and received by Queen Elizabeth I on New Year's Day and distributed over the full extent of her reign from 1559 to 1603, provides a remarkable body of information of significant scholarly value. Jane Lawson's formidable efforts have enabled her to prepare a full edition of 24 extant lists and from a variety of other sources she has reconstituted a 25th list. The relevant manuscripts are currently located in 11 different libraries or archive repositories located in England, the United States and Switzerland. From these lists we know the names of over 1200 persons who were responsible for over 4,000 gifts given to and 4,800 gifts received from Elizabeth. Such lists enable identification of those persons who were closest to the Queen and mattered most in her court. Nonetheless while high-ranking members of the nobility and Church dominate the lists, the names also include more minor gentry, London merchants other officials outside the court as well as the occasional menial household servant. The changing composition of that list is of obvious interest to political historians who desire to know who formed the inner circle of her court and contacts at different points in time. However, the most valuable evidence yielded by the lists concerns the gifts themselves and their often detailed descriptions which certainly cast much light on many aspects of the material culture, particularly associated with valuable objects, among the predominantly elite group with whom Elizabeth interacted. Many of the gifts were customary with coin looming large among gifts received from earls and countesses while gifts of plate were given in turn to such persons with their weights carefully recorded. However the gifts also reveal an enormous array of items, including for instance clothing, gloves, scarves, hats, muffs, musical instruments, medicines, spices, books and paintings and sweet meats, even in one case a two-year old lion that Elizabeth received in 1559.

Jane Lawson provides, in a series of valuable appendices, indexes of the offices and occupations of persons appearing and the types and descriptions of gifts given and their custody. In addition, following a careful analytical introduction the reader will encounter very useful biographical sketches of all those named persons appearing in the lists and a glossary of terms which are indispensable for effective use of the edition.

We are especially grateful to Jane Lawson for the enormous care with which she has undertaken this task. Thanks must also go to Joanna Innes who, while a member of the committee, acted as the principal link with Jane Lawson while the edition was being prepared.

October 2012

Richard Smith
Chairman
Records of Social and Economic History Committee

Contents

List of Illustrations

Preface

The idea for this project began with a simple task I began about 1983: to collect and organize the names of all those who exchanged New Year's gifts with Queen Elizabeth as an aid to identifying courtier poets. The first database contained biographical information and noted the years of the donors' participation. I based my research on the gift list bibliography in A. J. Collins's *Jewels and Plate of Queen Elizabeth I* (1955) to locate both primary and secondary sources of information. Collins cited extant gift rolls, only six of which had been edited in whole or part at that time, five of them in John Nichols's *The Progresses and Public Processions of Queen Elizabeth* (1823). As I searched for additional sources of gift list participation, I discovered as Collins did, that little had been done to make the mass of information found on these rolls available to anyone who wanted to study the Elizabethan court. My edition is based on all the sources located in Collins's book plus three additional rolls that have not heretofore been subject to scholarly analysis: the 1571 roll in the collection of his Grace the Duke of Buccleuch and Queensberry, the 1594 roll at the Dallas Public Library, and the 1597 roll at the Pierpont Morgan Library. My aim has been to provide a reliable text of these original documents with fully-indexed control over their principal contents. To that end, each entry on the rolls is uniquely identified with its sequential number within a given year. Accordingly, appendices can be used to locate the wide variety of gifts received by the Queen and given by her in return, and to identify all but a handful of the participants named.

Acknowledgements

I am grateful to Steven W. May for bringing the gift lists to my attention and pointing out one way the wealth of information they contain can be used for scholarly purposes. My on-going research is greatly indebted to the expertise and helpful advice of the professional staffs of the British Library, Dallas Public Library, Eton College, Folger Shakespeare Library, the Public Record Office at Kew, John Rylands Library, University of Manchester, Society of Antiquaries, Sheffield City Archives, Somerset Heritage Centre, Surrey Record Office, and the Tower of London. I especially thank the staffs of the John Rylands Library and The Morgan Library & Museum for hosting me while they were in the midst of major renovations to their facilities and were working out of temporary quarters.

This project could not have been completed without research funding and support provided by the Records of Social and Economic History (RSEH) Committee of the British Academy, the Doreen Yarwood Award of the Costume Society, and Emory University. His grace, the late Walter Francis John Scott, 9th Duke of Buccleuch, 11th Duke of Queensberry, graciously provided access to the manuscript at Boughton House, a courtesy also extended to me by his son, Richard John Walter Scott, 10th Duke of Buccleuch, 12th Duke of Queensberry, who has continued his interest in this edition. I have profited greatly from discussing the project, often at some length, with scholars in the many disciplines touched upon by the gift rolls, especially Peter Beal, Alan Bryson, Susan Cerasano, Mary Hill Cole, Marion Colthorpe, Katherine Duncan-Jones, Lucas Erne, Gareth Fitzpatrick, Maria Hayward, Joanna Innes, Grace Ioppolo, Sybil Jack, Kate Jarman, Jennifer Lee, Hilton Kelliher, Declan Kelly, Charles Lister, Michael Meredith, Alan Nelson, Julian Pooley, Gerit Quealy, Nigel Ramsay, Danielle Shields, Pam Porter, Stella Revard, Emma Stuart, Heather Wolfe, Henry Woudhuysen, Letitia Yeandle, Robert Yorke, Anne Young, and Georgianna Ziegler. I owe special gratitude and appreciation to Nigel Ramsay, Heather Wolfe and Marion Colthorpe for bringing to my attention manuscripts I would not otherwise have discovered. I appreciate also the exchange of ideas from time to time with others whose names I have not properly recorded here.

Abbreviations

BDECM	Ashbee, A. and D. Lasocki, ed., *A Biographical Dictionary of English Court Musicians, 1485–1714*
BL	British Library, London
Bindoff	Bindoff, B., ed., *The House of Commons, 1509–1558*
CPR	*Calendar of the Patent Rolls Preserved in the Public Record Office: Elizabeth I*
CSP Domestic	*Calendar of State Papers, Domestic, of the Reigns of Edward VI, Mary, Elizabeth, James I*
CSP Foreign	*Calendar of State Papers, Foreign Series, of the Reign of Elizabeth; Preserved in the State Paper Department of Her Majesty's Public Record Office*
CSP Ireland	*Calendar of State Papers Relating to Ireland, of the Reigns of Henry VIII, Edward VI, Mary, and Elizabeth*
CSP Scotland	*Calendar of the State Papers Relating to Scotland and Mary, Queen of Scots, 1547–1603: Preserved in the Public Record Office, the British Museum, and Elsewhere in England*
CSP Spanish	*Calendar of Letters and State Papers Relating to English Affairs: Preserved Principally in the Archives of Simancas: Elizabeth, 1558–[1603]*
CSP Venetian	*Calendar of State Papers, Relating to English Affairs, Preserved Principally at Rome, in the Vatican Archives and Library*
Hasler	P. W. Hasler, ed., *The House of Commons, 1558–1603*
HMC Ancaster	Great Britain. Royal Commission on Historical Manuscripts. *Report on the Manuscripts of the Earl of Ancaster Preserved at Grimsthorpe*
HMC Hastings	Great Britain. Royal Commission on Historical Manuscripts. *Report on the Manuscripts of the Late Reginald Rawdon Hastings*
HMC De L'Isle	Great Britain. Royal Commission on Historical Manuscripts. *Report on the Manuscripts of Lord De L'Isle and Dudley*
HMC Rutland	Great Britain. Royal Commission on Historical Manuscripts. *The Manuscripts of his Grace the Duke of Rutland*
HMC Salisbury	Great Britain. Royal Commission on Historical Manuscripts. *Calendar of the Manuscripts of the Most Honourable the Marquess of Salisbury*
GEC, *Peerage*	G. E. Cokayne, ed., *Complete Peerage of England, Scotland, Ireland, Great Britain and the United Kingdom*

Index to Privy Bills	W. P. W. Phillimore, ed., *An Index to Bills of Privy Signet: Commonly Called Signet Bills, 1584 to 1596 and 1603 to 1624, with a Calendar of Writs of Privy Seal, 1601 to 1603*
LP Henry VIII	*Letters and Papers, Foreign and Domestic, of the Reign of Henry VIII*
ODNB	*Oxford Dictionary of National Biography*
OED	*Oxford English Dictionary*
STC	A. W. Pollard and G. R. Redgrave, ed., *A short-title catalogue of books printed in England, Scotland and Ireland, and of English books printed abroad 1475–1640.*
PCC	*Index to Administrations in the Prerogative Court of Canterbury and Now Preserved in the Principal Probate Registry, Somerset House, London*
PRO	Public Record Office at the National Archives at Kew
RECM	A. Ashbee, ed., *Records of English Court Music*
VCH	Victoria County Histories
Visitations	Harleian Society, *The Visitations of the Heralds*

Introduction

The records of Queen Elizabeth's New Year's gift exchanges convey a wealth of information about the late Tudor court. The Queen presided over forty-five such exchanges during her reign as well as others during the reigns of her father, Henry VIII and her siblings, Edward VI and Mary I. This royal tradition, in one form or another, stretches back in English history to at least the thirteenth century. Twenty-four gift rolls survive from her reign, each transcribed on vellum and listing by name or title every participant in the ceremony. I have reconstructed a twenty-fifth exchange for 1582 from contemporary Jewel House documents. The documents record Elizabeth's first (1559) and last (1603) gift exchanges as Queen, with the remaining rolls fairly evenly spaced throughout her reign.[1] The extant rolls name more than 1,200 persons, about one third of whom are women. Each entry describes, often in great detail, what these participants gave the Queen and what they received from her in return. In all, these documents list more than 4,400 gifts presented to Elizabeth in the course of twenty-five New Year's exchanges, plus more than 4,800 royal gifts that she gave to these and other persons.

The gift rolls convey important information on a broad range of topics, including Elizabethan biography, language, and social and economic conditions, as well as the age's costume, jewellery, and plate, yet they remain largely unstudied by scholars in the many disciplines that would benefit from such evidence. During the eighteenth and nineteenth centuries, members of the Society of Antiquaries discussed on occasion the nature of individual rolls displayed at their meetings, and published notes about these artefacts in *Archaeologia*. In 1736, for instance, George Holmes exhibited the 1552 roll of Edward VI (present location unknown), and the 1559 Elizabethan roll, while Charles Lyttelton, Bishop of Carlisle, displayed the 1585 gift roll at the Society in 1756.[2] John Nichols transcribed gift rolls, collected other information about the gift exchanges, and published his results between 1788 and 1823.[3] Subsequent attention to the rolls has taken the form of popular articles about the gift exchanges as part of the holiday celebrations at court; these studies all derive from Nichols's work on the subject, often without

---

[1] I refer to the rolls as vellum in the generic sense of animal skins. The rolls may be composed largely of parchment (made from the skins of sheep and goats) rather than vellum (calfskin). See pp. 000–000 for descriptions and the locations of the extant gift rolls.

[2] 'Minutes of the Society of Antiquaries', BL MS Egerton 1041, f. 151; C. Lyttelton, 'Queen Elizabeth's New Year's Gifts, A.1584–5', *Archaeologia*, 1 (1770), pp. 9–11.

[3] J. Nichols, *The Progresses and Public Processions of Queen Elizabeth* (3 vols, London, 1823). Nichols edited five gift rolls in these volumes: the 1562 roll, vol. 1, pp. 108–30; 1578, vol. 2, pp. 65–91; 1579, vol. 2, pp. 249–75; 1589, vol. 3, pp. 1–26; and 1600, vol. 3, pp. 445–67. F. W. Joy transcribed most of the 1559 roll in 'Queen Elizabeth's New Year's Gifts', *Notes and Queries*, ns 9 (March 29, 1884), pp. 241–2. The 1584 roll was edited by J. L. Nevinson, 'New Year's Gifts to Queen Elizabeth I', *Costume* 20 (1975), pp. 27–31.

acknowledgment.[4] A. Jeffries Collins, the first scholar to undertake a comprehensive analysis of the rolls, lamented more than a half-century ago how little use had been made of them by professional historians: 'The neglect is the more to be deplored in that the rolls afford guidance of a kind unobtainable from any other source'.[5] A few later studies have drawn on at least a majority of these documents for their conclusions. Janet Arnold regularly used the rolls' detailed descriptions of articles of clothing in her contributions to the history of costume during the period, notably in her monumental *Queen Elizabeth's Wardrobe Unlock'd.*[6] In *Records of English Court Music* and A Biographical *Dictionary of English Church Musicians*, Andrew Ashbee and David Lasocki combed the rolls to identify court musicians, and cited representative examples of the gifts presented by and to them.[7] Steven W. May found the New Year's gift rolls among the most useful criteria for identifying courtiers in his study of poetry at the Elizabethan court. May analyzed the personnel involved in twenty-four Elizabethan New Year's exchanges, describing them as 'persons who were, with a few exceptions, actually known to the Queen', whether or not they achieved courtier status.[8] Otherwise, Elizabethan studies rarely cite the substantial and varied information found in these documents, and even that use has been almost wholly restricted to the seven New Year's rolls edited in whole or part to date.[9]

More widespread study of the gift rolls has been hampered by the fact that these manuscripts are housed in eleven widely-scattered libraries and archival collections in England, the United States, and Switzerland. This edition opens up their use to scholars by providing complete transcriptions of the twenty-four extant rolls, plus a detailed reconstruction of the 1582 ceremony. These texts are complemented by several appendices including biographical sketches of participants with cross references to their titles, a table of court offices with details of

---

[4] See for example, Z. Cocke, 'A Queen's Christmas Gifts', *St Nicholas*, 301 (1902/03), pp. 236–37; W. G. Benham, 'New Year Presents in Queen Elizabeth's Court', *The Essex Review*, 44 (1935), pp. 1–6 ; M. C. Draper, 'The New Year's Gifts of Queen Elizabeth', *National Review*, 108 (1937), pp. 76–81.

[5] A. J. Collins, *Jewels and Plate of Queen Elizabeth I: The Inventory of 1574* (London, 1955), pp. 3 n. 3, 237–9.

[6] J. Arnold, *Queen Elizabeth's Wardrobe Unlock'd* (Leeds, 1988).

[7] A. Ashbee, ed., *Records of English Court Music* (9 vols, Aldershot, 1986–1996) ; A. Ashbee and D. Lasocki, ed., *A Biographical Dictionary of English Court Musicians, 1485–1714* (2 vols, Aldershot, 1988).

[8] S. W. May, *The Elizabethan Courtier Poets* (Columbia, 1991), p. 22.

[9] E.g. Lisa M. Klein analyzes the function of embroidered gifts in the Tudor exchanges based on data supplied by Nichols and Arnold, in 'Your Humble Handmaid: Elizabethan Gifts of Needlework', *Renaissance Quarterly*, 50 (1997), pp. 459–93. Patricia Fumerton, 'Exchanging Gifts: The Elizabethan Currency of Children and Poetry', *English Literary History*, 53 (1986), pp. 241–78, and L. A. Montrose 'Gifts and Reasons: The Contexts of Peele's Araygnement of Paris', *English Literary History*, 47 (1980), pp. 433–61, discuss Elizabethan gift-giving without benefit of primary evidence from the gift rolls. Natalie Zemon Davis does not cite the rolls, in 'Beyond the Market: Books as Gifts in Sixteenth-Century France', *Transactions of the Royal Historical Society*, 33 (1983), p. 83, n. 30. In *Selfish Gifts: The Politics of Exchange and English Courtly Literature*, 1580–1628 (Madison, 2006), Alison V. Scott makes no mention of the New Year's gift exchanges at court.

participants' offices and occupations, a listing of gift terms and descriptors, and a glossary of unusual or obsolete words found on the rolls.

I. History of the New Year's Ceremony

The exchanging of gifts is widely acknowledged as a practice central to social and cultural cohesiveness; it bestows benefits on both the giver and the recipient. Frans de Waal has demonstrated that reciprocity in gift giving is practised by chimpanzees as well as humans.[10] The motives and results of the custom in human society have been analyzed in studies ranging from Seneca's *De Beneficiis* to a host of modern essays (many centred on Renaissance gift giving) in dialogue with the classic twentieth-century works of Marcel Mauss and Claude Lévi-Strauss.[11] European customs for including gift exchanges with New Year celebrations mingled pagan and Christian influences. The ancient Greeks did not celebrate the New Year, partly because no one day was singled out for the beginning of their year. In Rome, observance of the January *calends* (*kalends*) as the beginning of a new year evolved into a major ceremony, with both official and private festivities that included elaborate gift-giving and the swearing of allegiance to the emperor. The early Christian church merged the *calends* festival with the celebration of Christmas. In 567, the Council of Tours prolonged the observance of Christmas by instituting the festive cycle of the Twelve days from the Nativity to the Epiphany, absorbing the New Year celebration. The Romano-Christian observance of New Year's became associated with what Gregory of Tours described as the *ars donandi*, a flair for giving the right gift at the right moment. This was compatible with the Germanic tradition that used gift giving to forge the social contract based on mutually binding obligations.[12] Thus gift giving at New Year's, firmly embedded in the celebration of Christmas and the beginning of the new year, spread throughout Christian Europe during the Middle Ages.

Some form of New Year's gift-giving at the English court is documented by the mid thirteenth-century, although the practice is no doubt much older. It is important to distinguish, however, between 'rewards' bestowed by the sovereign on court servants at New Year's time, and the development of a formal, royal exchange of gifts that involved peers, courtiers, and favoured personal servants. Evolution of the latter practice, the one recorded by the Tudor gift rolls, is of uncertain antiquity. In 1249, Henry III demanded such excessive New Year's gifts from the citizens of London that Matthew Paris in his *Chronica Majora* condemned the king's greed. But sovereigns also gave New Year's gifts by this time (and prob-

---

[10] F. de Waal, *Tree of Origin: What Primate Behavior Can Tell Us about Human Social Evolution* (Cambridge, MA, 2001).

[11] M. Mauss, *The Gift: The Form and Reason for Exchange in Archaic Societies* (New York, 1967); C. Lévi-Strauss, 'The Principle of Reciprocity', in A. Komter, ed., *The Gift: An Interdisciplinary Perspective* (Amsterdam, 1996), pp. 18–26; A. Komter, 'Gifts and Social Relations: The Mechanisms of Reciprocity', *International Sociology*, 22 (2007), p. 93.

[12] B. Buettner, 'Past Presents: New Year's Gifts at the Valois Courts, ca. 1400', *Art Bulletin*, 84 (2001), pp. 598–625; J. Hirschbiegel, Étrennes: *Untersuchungen zum Hofischen Geschenkverkehr im Spätmittelalterlichen Frankreich der Zeit König Karls VI* (1380–1422) (München, 2003).

ably much earlier), for the household and wardrobe accounts of Henry's Queen, Eleanor of Provence, include New Year's gifts among other expenditures for the years 1251–3. It is not clear at what social levels, however, this royal largesse was distributed. If merely to court servants (or from the oppressed Londoners to King Henry), the gift-giving was of a different kind from the reciprocal Tudor exchanges.[13] The ceremony in which sovereigns gave as well as received gifts at the new year may have reached England from France, where it was a well-established ritual at the Valois court during the reign of Charles VI (1368-1422).[14] By the mid fourteenth-century, gift exchanges among peers at the English court were apparently so well-established that the Pearl Poet in *Sir Gawain and the Green Knight* described them as a New Year's ritual dating back to King Arthur's time:

> Wyle Nw Yer was so yep that it was nwe cummen,
> …
> Nowel nayted onewe, nevened ful ofte;
> And sithen riche forth runnen to reche hondeselle,
> Yeyed yeres yiftes on high ...
>
> (With New Year so young it still yawned and stretched
> …
> "Noel," they cheered, then "Noel, Noel,"
> "New Years Gifts!", the knights cried next
> as they pressed forwards to offer their presents ...)[15]

The New Year's gift exchange was certainly a well-defined royal custom by the time of the first Tudor sovereign, Queen Elizabeth's grandfather, Henry VII. A detailed description survives for the ceremony of 1494:

> Alsoe, for New Yeares Day in the morninge, the King when hee cometh to his foot-sheete, an usher of the chamber shall bee readie at the doore, and say, There is a new yeare's gift come from the Queene; then the King shall say, Sir, lett it come in; then the usher shall lett in the messenger with the guifte, and soe after the great estates servants, as they come, each one after other, as they bee of estate; and after that donne, all lordes and ladies after their estate; and all the season the Kinge shall sitt still in his footesheete; then that donne, the chamberlaine to send for the treasurer of the chamber, and charge him to give the messenger that came from the Queen, if he bee a knight, x marks; if hee bee an esquire, viij marks; or at least C shillings ; and those which come from the King's brother and sisters; everie of them vj marks; and to everie Duke and Duchesse's servant or messenger, v markes; and everie Earle and

---

[13] J. Noorthouck, *A New History of London, Including Westminster and Southwark* (London, 1773), pp. 37–56; M. Paris, *Matthæi Parisiensis, Monachi Sancti Albani, Chronica Majora*, ed. H. R. Luard, Rerum *Britannicarum Medii Aevi Scriptores*; no. 57 (7 vols, London, 1876–83), vol. 3, p. 47; BL MS Additional 24510, f. 87, no. 7.
[14] Buettner, p. 600.
[15] I. Gollancz, ed., *Sir Gawain and the Green Knight*, (London, 1966), p. 3, lines 60, 68–70; S. Armitage, ed., *Sir Gawain and the Green Knight: A New Verse Translation* (New York, 2007), pp. 24–25, lines 60, 68–70.

Countesse' servant, each of them xl shillings; these are the rewards of them that bring the giftes'.[16]

Prince Henry, the future King Henry VIII, would have participated in this exchange by sending his servant to deliver gifts to his parents. The servant would have returned with a present to the three-year-old prince along with his reward for delivering the prince's present.

Prince Henry maintained the New Year's gift exchange tradition when he succeeded his father as Henry VIII in 1509. At New Year, 1510 he received gifts from the bishops, his household officers, and from courtiers, including the blind poet Bernard André and the young Charles Brandon.[17] Henry's first household book, covering the years 1509–18, records the New Year's exchanges until the ninth year of his reign (BL MS Additional 21481). The accounts list rewards to the servants who delivered the gifts, as well as non-reciprocal gifts that the king bestowed on his own servants. A New Year's account for 1528 describes only gifts given by the king (PRO E 101/420/4). The earliest extant royal New Year's gift roll divided into lists of donors (the 'By list') and what they received from the sovereign (the 'To list') survives on six paper sheets (originally formatted as a roll) documenting the 1532 ceremony (PRO E 101 420/15). Similar paper rolls survive for Henrician exchanges in 1534 (PRO E 101/415/13) and 1539 (Folger MS Z.d.11). The gifts of money presented by the clergy and religious 'in a very generous and liberal manner' to the King for 24 Henry VIII (1533) are listed in Strype's *Ecclesiastical Memorials*.[18] By 1532 at latest, however, Henry's gift-giving ceremony had evolved significantly from his father's practice of receiving the gifts in his bedchamber. The donors now brought their gifts to a specially prepared gift chamber in the royal palace. Building accounts for 1532 at Greenwich record payments for both 'trestles and boards for the King's New Year gifts to stand upon' and 'a great hooped double stock lock for the chamber door where the King's New Year gifts was set.'[19] John Hussey described the gift exchange ritual at Greenwich Palace at New Year's, 1538, when he presented Lord and Lady Lisle's gift to the king:

> Pleaseth it your lordship to be advertised that I delivered on New Year's Day your gift to the King's Majesty in his own hands; and as soon as I was within the Chamber of Presence, going to present the same as accustomed, my Lord Privy Seal [Thomas Cromwell] smiled and said to the King's Grace, 'Here cometh my Lord Lisle's man'; and the King spake merrily unto him again, but what his Highness said I cannot tell. So that, after I had done my duty, his Grace received it of me smiling, and thanking your lordship did ask heartily how you and my lady did. His Grace spake few words that day to those that came. As far as I could perceive he spake to no man so much as he did unto me, which was no more words but this: 'I thank my lord. How does

---

[16] *A Collection of Ordinances and Regulations for the Government of the Royal Household, made in Divers Reigns* (London, 1790), p. 120.

[17] J. P. Carley, *The Books of King Henry VIII and his Wives* (London, 2004), pp. 53, 55.

[18] J. Strype, *Ecclesiastical Memorials* (3 vols, London, 1721), vol. 1, pp. 137–8. For a transcription and discussion of the Folger Shakespeare Library MS Z.d.11, see M. A. Hayward, 'Gift Giving at the Court of Henry VIII: The 1539 New Year's Gift Roll in Context', *Antiquaries Journal*, 85 (2006), pp. 125–75.

[19] D. Starkey, ed., *Henry VIII: A European Court in England* (London, 1991), p. 126.

my lord and my lady? Are they merry?' It was greatly done of my Lord Privy Seal to have your lordship in remembrance, setting the matter so well forward. The King stood leaning against the cupboard, receiving all things; and Mr Tuke [Sir Brian Tuke, Treasurer of the Chamber] at the end of the same cupboard, penning all things that were presented; and behind his Grace stood Mr Kingston and Sir John Russell, and beside his Grace stood the Earl of Hertford and my Lord Privy Seal.[20]

The importance attached to the giving of New Year's gifts in court society is witnessed by the fact that the king's children also gave and received New Year's gifts virtually from birth. Princess Mary was not yet two years old at the New Year 1518, when she received among other presents a gold spoon from Lady Devonshire, a primer from Lady Norfolk, two smocks from Lady Mountjoy, and a gold pomander from the French Queen, Mary Tudor, now the wife of Charles Brandon, Duke of Suffolk. As an adult, Princess Mary managed her own New Year's gift-giving, bestowing in 1539 on her half-brother, Prince Edward, for example, an embroidered coat of crimson satin, and to the Princess Elizabeth, a kirtle of yellow satin.[21] Princess Elizabeth's ambitious participation in the custom of gift-giving at New Year's has been carefully studied and emphasizes, again, the ceremony's significance in the life of the court. As early as New Year 1544, and regularly thereafter, she personally wrote out a number of works in manuscript to present to members of the royal family. In addition, Elizabeth embroidered canvas covers for these books, working the recipients' initials into the embroidery.[22] In 1548, she apologized to Prince Edward for not sending him her usual translation work as a New Year's gift, explaining that she had been ill. Another reason for the lack of a gift was Lord Protector Somerset's proposed ban on the giving of New Year's gifts, on the ground that they were part of the superstitions of the Catholic Church. However, gift rolls, now lost, are recorded for 1552 and 1553, showing that this ban was short-lived, although no details of later New Year's gift translations by Elizabeth have come to light.[23] Her household expenses for 1551, however, include the purchase of over seventy-four ounces of gold for distribution as New Year's gifts, purchased from Thomas Crocock, goldsmith, for £32 3s. 10d.[24]

Subsequent records confirm the continuance of the New Year's gift ritual under King Edward VI and Queen Mary. Edward's 'Boke of Receiptes and

---

[20] M. St. C. Byrne, ed., *The Lisle Letters* (6 vols, Chicago, 1981), vol. 5, p. 10, letter 1086.

[21] F. Madden, ed., *Privy Purse Expenses of Princess Mary* (London, 1831), pp. xxi–xxii, lxxxiii. The lists of gifts given to Prince Edward in 1539 and 1540 are found in BL MS Royal Appendix 89, 'Certeyn Neweyeres Gyftes Gevon vnto the Prynce Grace', and in BL MS Additional 11301.

[22] See M. H. Swain, 'A New Year's Gift from the Princess Elizabeth', *Connoisseur*, 183 (1973), pp. 258–66; M. Perry, *The Word of a Prince: A Life of Elizabeth I from Contemporary Documents* (Woodbridge, 1990), pp. 34–40; M. Shell, *Elizabeth's Glass* (Lincoln, Nebraska, 1993); F. Teague, 'Princess Elizabeth's Hand in *The Glass of the Sinful Soul*', *English Manuscript Studies*, 9 (2000), pp. 33–48; Klein, pp. 476–7.

[23] D. Starkey, *Elizabeth, The Struggle for the Throne* (New York, 2001), pp. 85–6; Collins, p. 249.

[24] P. E. F. W. S. Strangford, ed., 'Household Expenses of the Princess Elizabeth during her Residence at Hatfield October 1, 1551 to September 30, 1552', in *Camden Miscellany* volume the second (London, 1853), p. 36.

Paymentes' mentions New Years' gift expenses in 1547 and 1548.[25] The earliest references to vellum rolls concern the missing 1552 and 1553 gift rolls from the last two years of Edward VI's reign. The transfer of these records from the Henrician paper rolls to vellum is significant. While the keeping of systematic records of the New Years' exchanges is a Tudor innovation, nearly all classes of official documents introduced under this regime were kept on paper.[26] The upgraded format of the gift exchange records from paper to the more expensive vellum no later than 1552 underscores the importance of these court rituals in maintaining close personal ties between subjects and their sovereign. Both the exchanges and their recording on vellum rolls continued under Mary I, although only a single Marian gift roll survives, that for 1557 (now BL MS Additional 62525, with photocopy, BL RP 294, v.2).

II. The Elizabethan New Year's Rolls

The Elizabethan New Year's rolls are composed of between four and five vellum membranes attached at the ends to produce rolls measuring from twelve to about fifteen feet in length. Each is transcribed on both sides in the handwriting of a professional scribe. Donors' names with descriptions of the gifts they gave the Queen appear on one side, each name being preceded with 'By', or 'By the' (thus, the 'By list'). On the verso, the record of the Queen's gifts to these donors is likewise preceded with 'To', or 'To the' (the 'To list'). Thereafter on every complete Elizabethan roll occurs a section of gifts given by her Majesty at 'Sundry Times' (a heading also found on the extant Marian roll). These 'Sundry Gifts' were presented outside of the New Year's ceremony that dominates the roll, usually covering events and visitors of the preceding year. They tend to record a greater range of royal gifts than appears on the 'To list' for, in contrast with the great variety of gifts Elizabeth received at New Year's, she almost always gave gilt plate in return.

The physical condition of the extant rolls varies considerably, from the near-pristine condition of the 1571 roll to four rolls that have sustained significant damage. Signatures excised from the 1563 roll have also removed some text from the 'Sundry Gifts' section on the opposite side. The 1575 roll (Folger MS Z.d.14) was reassembled during the last century from fragments, one of which was formerly BL MS Harley 6257.[27] This roll's 'By list' lacks the heading; its text, begins with Margaret, Countess of Derby. Also missing are the names of more than thirty individuals between Baroness Dacre of the South and Sir Owen Hopton, as well as all Gentlemen after John Dudley, Sergeant of the Pastry. The first readable name on the 'To list' is the Countess of Warwick. This side of the roll also lacks the heading and over twenty participants from the Marquesses and Duchesses,

[25] PRO E 101/426/5; also BL MS Royal 7 C XVI and PRO E 315/439 (which records expenses for April–December 1547 only); Edward VI, *Literary Remains of King Edward the Sixth*, ed. J. G. Nichols (London, 1857).

[26] L. C. Hector, *Palaeography and Forgery* (London, 1959), p. 16.

[27] Folger Shakespeare Library, correspondence from A. J. Collins, to the Folger, dated 20 June 1947, regarding the manuscript acquisition from Maggs Brothers (London). I am grateful to Heather Wolfe, Curator of Manuscripts, for allowing me access to these files.

Earls, and Countesses categories, with about sixty participants missing between Baroness Chandos and Archdeacon Carew. Two other Folger rolls, those for 1564 and 1565, are also incomplete. The 1564 'By list' is complete, but more than ninety persons are missing from the 'To list', including all categories down to the Knights. The 1565 'By list' skips approximately sixty-nine names to begin with Ladies. Thirty-odd names are missing from the 'To list' as well, from the 'Gentlemen' through 'Free Gifts,' nor do the Maids of Honour or the Sundry Gifts appear on this roll. After the 1589 roll had been drawn up, it was discovered that the names of ten gentlemen were missing from both lists. They were added on a separate vellum leaf signed on both sides by the Queen and her Jewel House staff (who also subscribed their names to the 'By' and 'To' lists). A fifth sign manual is found at the top of the 'By' list, but not in its corresponding place on the 'To' list.

Elizabethan gift giving at the New Year followed the same general pattern observed by her grandfather. Letters patent issued on 6 July 1559 to her first Treasurer of the Chamber, Sir John Mason, specify how he shall make payments 'for the accustomed rewards to bringers of New Year's gifts' along with rewards to the Queen's officers at other times.[28] Throughout the reign, the Treasurer of the Chamber's accounts list cash rewards paid to household servants in addition to their salaries at New Year's and Easter, with a lump-sum total of the rewards given to servants who delivered New Year's gifts for the Queen.[29] The rewards to household servants, however, were 'one-way' transactions entirely separate from the royal gift exchange. And, while anyone could offer a New Year's gift to the Queen, only favoured individuals were admitted to the exchange ceremony and received a gift from her in return. The lists of those who participated in the exchanges are dominated by high-ranking members of the nobility and Church, although names of a fairly diverse range of gentlefolk, including London merchants, out-of-court royal officers, and even rather menial household servants also appear on the rolls.[30] Participation in the exchange was apparently an obligation of office or social rank for some, a privilege for others. Within the peerage, husbands and wives both participated; however, among the knights, ladies, gentlemen, and gentlewomen, participation by one spouse did not automatically include the other. The criteria that governed admission to the ceremony are unclear and may have been rather elastic, with this exception, that no one manifestly in disgrace with the Queen is known to have participated in the exchange regardless of office or rank.

The contents of the Elizabethan rolls are organized in the same way as those of the later Henrician exchanges and for Queen Mary's new year as recorded on the 1557 roll. Thomas Cromwell apparently standardized this format during the reign of Henry VIII.[31] It remained quite stable throughout Elizabeth's reign and

---

[28] *Calendar of the Patent Rolls Preserved in the Public Record Office 1558–1582* (9 vols, London, 1939–86), p. 96.

[29] E.g. PRO E 351/542, m. 1 lists rewards 'to diuerse of her officers and servantes, as also to the Servauntes of the Nobilitie and others for bringinge of Neweyeres giftes at Neweyerestyde'.

[30] For an analysis of the social spectrum represented on the rolls see May, *Elizabethan Courtier Poets*, pp. 22–6.

[31] Collins, *Jewels and Plate*, p. 247.

is found as well on the extant rolls from the reigns of James I and Charles I. Each roll begins with a title indicating the regnal year and the palace in which the exchange took place. The headings which follow group the participants in peerage order. The orderly listings of donors and recipients under each subheading that follows, with the gifts exchanged, are individually designated in this edition by year and location on the rolls. Thus, 64.120 refers to the participant, Dorothy Broadbelt, whose name occurs in the 120th place on the 1564 roll along with the gift she presented.

Following the title of each roll is a short list of donors that is never introduced with a marginal heading. I designate these as 'Primary' donors, not only because their names begin every list but because they are all either Elizabeth's blood relatives on her father's side or her highest ranking state officers. No more than six persons appeared in this category on any one roll during her reign, and a total of only sixteen different names are recorded between 1559 and 1603. These include two daughters of the sisters of Henry VIII who were living when Elizabeth ascended the throne: Frances Brandon, Duchess of Suffolk, and Margaret Douglas, Countess of Lennox. Margaret Clifford, Lady Strange, and Lady Mary Grey, both the Queen's first cousins once removed, appear here, while Mary's sister, Lady Catherine Grey, appears under the Maids of Honour heading on the 1559 roll. Close cousins from her mother's side are regular participants in Elizabeth's gift exchanges but never achieve 'Primary' status. The last appearance on the rolls of a royal cousin, Margaret, Countess of Derby, occurs in 1582 (although she neither gave nor received a gift on that occasion). Elizabeth never exchanged New Year's gifts with her cousin, Mary Queen of Scots, nor with Mary's son James, later King James I.[32] The remaining primary participants are familiar figures in Elizabethan politics and government: the Lord Keeper of the Great Seal, or Lord Chancellor, and the Lord High Treasurer. The highest ranking male peers round out the list: the Duke of Norfolk, Marquess of Winchester, and Marquess of Northampton. Successive Paulets, Marquesses of Winchester, participated in every surviving exchange from 1559 to 1603, as the title passed to four men, three of them named William.

The next categories of participants are introduced by headings based on social rank or title, then listed, for the most part, in descending order of precedence. In a number of instances, however, royal favour trumped seniority. During the 1570s, for instance, Elizabeth's great favourite, the Earl of Leicester, though Master of the Horse, always precedes the Earl of Sussex, holder of a far older earldom who also held the superior court office of Lord Chamberlain of the royal household. Category titles are recorded in the left-hand margins of each roll, with some spacing before and after each section. Additionally, the first entry of a category is usually written with a larger engrossed capital to designate it as the beginning of a section. Marquesses, earls, and viscounts follow the Primary donors, followed by duchesses, lady marquesses, countesses, and viscountesses, the bishops (lords

---

[32] However, both Mary and James have entries in the Biographical Sketches because the rolls record the christening gift given to Mary on the occasion of James' birth in 1566 (67.362) and gifts presented to James's envoys in 1579 and 1585 (79.450, 84.413, 85.414, 85.415).

spiritual), then lords (barons), baronesses, ladies (knights' wives), knights, gentle-women, chaplains, and gentlemen. The ordering of these classifications received only minor alterations during Elizabeth's reign. Bishops preceded the duchesses and countesses on the rolls from 1559 to 1567, while the countesses et al. precede the bishops for the remainder of the reign. The Queen's chaplain was appended to the end of the knights' list in 1584, 1585, 1588, and 1589; thereafter, this category disappears from the records. The ladies (knights' wives) were appended to the baronesses' group between 1559 and 1571, becoming a separate group from 1575 onward to 1603.

Gift roll naming practices often complicate identification of the donors, especially with regard to mutations in the names of titled women, and donors who are listed only by their given names. Mistress Catherine Knyvett, for example, became Baroness Paget when she married Henry Paget, Lord Paget. Her second marriage, to Sir Edward Carey, led to her gift list designation as Baroness Paget Carey. Similarly Elizabeth Stafford became Lady Drury when she married Sir William Drury, but after her second marriage to Sir John Scott, she is designated on the rolls as Lady Drury Scott and Lady Scott. Douglas Howard appears first on the gift rolls as a maid of honour, becoming Baroness Sheffield on her first marriage to John Sheffield, Lord Sheffield. She was the dowager baroness when she married Edward Stafford in 1579 and was listed as Baroness Sheffield Stafford from the mid-1590s to the end of the reign, probably to distinguish her from her daughter-in-law Ursula, the junior Baroness Sheffield. Donors who are listed only by their given names can also be hard to trace. Some of these listings denote persons so well-known at court that they needed no further designation, or whose foreign names challenged the scribes' capacity for spelling. Blanche Parry, chief gentlewoman of the Privy Chamber, is frequently listed as Mistress Blanche. John Baptist Castilion and his wife Margaret née Compagni, were known simply as Master and Mistress Baptist. Guilio Borgarucci and his wife appear on the rolls as Doctor and Mistress Julio. 'Mark Anthony' refers to several of the Italian musicians (surnamed Galliardello, Bassano, and Peacock), and the merchant Erizo. 'George' designated both John George Henrick (84.416) and George Schuavenius (88.407, 89.400), while 'Dennys' refers to Dionysius Burreus (62.380). Other foreign envoys appear in the 'Sundry Gifts' under variations of their titles, such as Frederic Perrenot, Sieur de Champagney, who is described as 'Gouerner of Anwarp' (Governor of Antwerp, 76.425).

In addition to the changing surnames of women through marriage, their peerage titles were also subject to a variety of changes on the rolls. An earl's unmarried daughter could appear on the gift rolls under either the category of 'baroness' or 'lady'. When an earl's daughter married, she took her husband's rank, if equal to or higher than her own. If she married someone of lesser rank, however, she kept her status and title as at birth, using her husband's surname instead of her maiden name. Two daughters of the Duke of Somerset, for instance, the Seymour sisters, Lady Mary and Lady Elizabeth, are consistently listed by their maiden surnames but with the further identifications on the gift rolls as 'Mr Roger's wife' and 'alias Knightley'. Two earl's daughters, however, Lady Anne Clinton and Lady Catherine Neville, appear on the rolls under the surnames of their untitled husbands as Lady Anne Askew and Lady Catherine Constable. In a third variation, Lady Catherine Wriothesley, daughter of Thomas, Earl of Southampton, married the groom porter, Thomas Cornwallis, yet her gift roll title is Baroness Cornwallis. The 'Baroness' enjoyed special privileges countenanced by the Queen, including the celebration of mass in her own home and the grant of a monopoly to her husband which she retained after his death.[33]

The 'To lists' include two categories of 'Free Gifts' recipients which do not appear on the 'By lists'. The Maids of Honour category comprises the six Maids themselves (or fewer when there were vacancies) and the Mother of the Maids. Many of these young women continued as courtiers and reappeared on the rolls under their married names. Among the Maids, Mary Radcliffe served the longest tenure as a Maid of Honour (about twenty-five years) and was the only one who continued at Court unmarried, becoming a Gentlewoman of the Privy Chamber. The Mothers of the Maids supervised the Maids and experienced a high rate of turnover, probably due to 'burn out' from the strain of supervising their charges. Each Maid's usual reward was about ten ounces of plate, the amount still being bestowed on the Maids of Honour by Queen Henrietta Maria in 1626.[34] The Mother of the Maids was usually included with the Maids as the last entry in that category, receiving the same ten or so ounces of plate. It was possible for a Mother of the Maids to be included with the gentlewomen and to give the Queen a gift. In 1597 Catherine Bromfield is listed among the gentlewomen with the designation, 'Mother of the Maids'. Elizabeth Wingfield seems to have held that position from 1597 until 1600, where she is also listed among the gentlewomen, but is described as 'Mother of the Maids.' Both 'Mothers' gave gifts to the Queen as well as receiving gilt plate weighing between sixteen and twenty-one ounces, about double the amount usually given by the Queen to the Mother of the Maids. In 1603, the Mother of the Maids, Mrs Brydges, is listed with the Maids and does not give a gift to the Queen.

The other group of 'Free Gifts' comprises the Jewel House staff, including the Master, Clerk, Grooms, and Yeoman, the Grooms of the Privy Chamber, and the Yeoman of the Robes. These names appear throughout the rolls among those to whom the gifts were delivered. There were only two Masters of the Jewel House during the entire reign. John Astley was appointed Master of the Jewel House and Treasurer of the Queen's Jewels and Plate in 1558 and held that combined position until 1595, when he was succeeded by Sir Edward Carey, another Groom of the Privy Chamber. Everyone named in these categories received gifts from the Queen, but did not reciprocate. The 'Free Gifts' normally occurred as the final category of recipients on the 'To lists', where the category is also found on the Marian roll. This category of recipients produced a few 'double dippers'; in 1581, for instance, Thomas Knyvett exchanged gifts with Elizabeth in his capacity as Keeper of Westminster Palace, but also received a free gift as a Groom of the Privy Chamber. And each list of 'Free Gifts' on the rolls of 1598, 1599, 1600, and

---

[33] *HMC Salisbury*, vol 8, p. 541; W. H. Price, *The English Patents of Monopoly* (New York, 1906), pp. 147, 149, 151–2.
[34] Somerset Heritage Centre DD\MI/19/39.

1603 names Sir Edward Carey twice: as Master of the Jewels and Plate, and as Groom of the Privy Chamber. Elizabeth therefore gave a greater number of New Year's gifts than she received, due to the number of unreciprocated gifts among those in the immediate circle of her household servants.

The complete rolls conclude with a category of important and often very detailed information, the gifts given by her Majesty at 'Sundry Times'. Because the 'To list' was less detailed than the 'By list' in its descriptions of gifts from the Queen, the extra space after the 'Free Gifts' was used to accommodate these additional entries. In this section, scribes recorded primarily the royal gifts presented to ambassadors or as christening gifts, marriage gifts, and gifts bestowed during the summer progresses. Each roll's account of these 'Sundry Gifts' usually covers a calendar year as calculated from Lady Day, 25 March. Thus the 1562 roll records 'Guiftes delyuerid at sundry tymes' between 3 April 1561 and 1 May 1562. In 1597 the heading reads, 'Guiftes giuen by her Matie to Soundry persons and deliuered at sondry tymes', with dates between 3 July 1596 and 30 December 1597. A few other entries under this heading also fall outside the two regnal years spanned by this March-to-March system of reckoning; for instance, the Queen's present at the marriage of Thomas Astley's daughter with Edward Darcy (31 July 1579), was recorded among the 'sundry gifts' on the 1581 roll. I have added brief descriptions of the occasions for 'Gifts Given at Sundry Times' to the biographical information of each person listed in the Sundry Gifts category.

In addition to the wealth of biographical data about those who gave the Queen gifts or received gifts from her, the rolls shed light on management within the royal household by specifying who took custody of each New Year's gift. In the right margin of each roll, scribes recorded the person or title of the household officer to whom the gift was delivered (in the edited text, these custody notations are justified to the right under the item or group of items to which they apply). Predictably, Ralph Hope, Yeoman of the Wardrobe, collected articles of clothing, while Lucy Hyde, Gentlewoman of the Bedchamber, was responsible for gloves, scarves, hats, snufkins, ruffs, and other accessories. Royal musicians Thomas Lichfield and Mathias Mason took charge of musical instruments. Blanche Parry was Elizabeth's first keeper of the royal jewels. She was joined in 1573 by Lady Catherine Carey Howard, whose inventory of the jewels is now BL MS Sloane 814. Mary Radcliffe took over the post in 1587; two copies of her inventory for the years 1587-1603 have survived (BL MSS Royal Appendix 68 and Additional 5751A. ff. 212–285). These inventories provide valuable supplementary information about participants in the exchanges and exactly what they gave the Queen in years for which no rolls survive. Another custodian of New Year's gifts, Henry Seckford, succeeded John Tamworth as Keeper of the Privy Purse in 1569; by the end of the reign he had taken responsibility for more of the New Year's offerings than anyone else: over 1,000 gifts of coin, nearly a quarter of all the gifts recorded on the extant 'By lists'. In a few instances, a custody space on the rolls was left blank, as was that for the two-year old lion given by George Rotheridge and Robert Kingston in 1559 (59.218). Presumably the lion was taken to the menagerie at the Tower of London, but there was, perhaps, some understandable reluctance about this assignment. The gift roll notes only that it was 'Delivered to' followed by a space. Generally, however, custody assignments are recorded for each gift on the rolls (see Appendix IV for a list of Custodians, and 'Custody of Gifts' as a category in Appendix V, Biographical Sketches).

Custodians were held strictly responsible for the gifts entrusted to them. John Tamworth, for example, collected more than 300 gifts of money and other valuables given to the Queen between 1562 and 1568. The executors of his will provided an accounting of all the amounts he received (unfortunately, without naming the persons who gave the gifts).[35] Similarly, John Astley, Master and Treasurer of her Majesty's Jewels and Plate, was responsible for all silver and gold plate received from and distributed to the donors of New Year's gifts. His accounts itemize the plate down to weights of one-eighth of an ounce. His 1574 inventory, now BL MS Stowe 555, lists 'all suche parcelles of the Quenis Majesties Juelles, plate and other stuff as remaine . . . in the custodie and chardge of John Asteley'. Astley's second wife and widow, Margaret Lenton, alias Grey, was responsible for procuring a discharge for all the valuables in his account at his death.[36] The Crown's insistence on accountability explains why gifts damaged at the time of delivery were carefully noted on the gift rolls. In 1575, for instance, the Earl of Warwick gave the Queen a black velvet girdle, but with 'the buckle and studs of gold broken' (75.14), while the gift from his brother, the Earl of Leicester, was missing 'one of the smaller Diamondes' (75.5). Other damaged items include a jewel 'lacking a Fyshe' (79.97) and, from 'abeeste of Ophalles' (a beast of opals), 'one horne Lackyng' (81.12). Of three dozen gold buttons given by Mildred Cecil in 1579, one, the scribe noted, was broken (79.78).

As official financial records, the gift rolls convey other kinds of information as well. Many of them include auditors' marks, essentially notations indicating that the item had been located and matched the description on the roll (I have not attempted to reproduce these marks in my transcription). Auditors of the royal Exchequer accounted for every shilling, penny, and ounce of plate down to the eighth of an ounce, given and received by the Queen. Each roll is certified as an approved record with the Queen's signature (sign manual) at the head and foot of both sides of the roll, along with signatures of the principal officers of the Jewel House at the foot of the 'To list', after the 'Sundry Gifts.' Most but not all the rolls also specify the goldsmiths from whom the Crown purchased the plate distributed on the 'To lists' and the 'Sundry Gifts'. Five goldsmiths produced the majority of gilt plate in these categories between 1559 and 1603: Robert Raynes (a carry-over from Mary's reign, 1559 only), Affabel Partridge (1559–1577), Robert Brandon (1559-1581), Hugh Keall (1574–1603), and Richard Martin (1578–1603).[37]

The gilt plate procured from the goldsmiths and received as gifts to the Queen went to the Jewel Tower under the custody of the Master of the Jewel House, who also was responsible for keeping the completed gift exchange rolls and related documents. The Jewel Tower should not be confused with the Tower of London.

---

[35] BL MS Harley Roll AA 23.

[36] Collins, *Jewels and Plate*, p. 223; PRO AO 1/1533/2, Roll 2; E 351/1954.

[37] Other goldsmiths are identified in Appendix III.

Neither should the 'jewels and plate' be confused with the Crown Jewels which have been kept at the Tower of London since 1303. These Jewels have long been a tourist destination in London. In 1606 James I brought his brother-in-law Christian IV of Denmark to the Tower where they viewed the rare and richest jewels.[38] Most of the royal regalia was melted down during the Commonwealth, but was replaced in 1660 upon the Restoration of Charles II. Some of the jewels from the original regalia were recovered and set into the newer pieces.[39]

The Jewel House is a stone tower at Westminster near the Abbey (Plate 6), built in 1363 during the reign of Edward III and still standing today. Abbot Nicholas Litlyngton (Litlington)[40] oversaw completion of the rebuilding of the Abbot's house and the Jerusalem Chamber, and the construction of the South and West Corridors of Westminster Abbey, including the Jewel Tower. The Tower's original groined vaults with moulded ribs and carved bosses exhibit the same work as the cloisters and other vaulted sub-structures of Abbot Litlyngton's renovations. The Tower was sold to the Crown in 1377 and functioned as the Jewel House until 1649. From the mid-seventeenth century until 1864, the Tower served as a repository for Parliamentary records, until the new Victoria Tower was completed and the records were transferred there. Between 1869 and 1938 the Jewel Tower was used as the Office of the Standards, the repository of official weights and measures.[41]

III. The Elizabethan Gift Exchange Ceremony

Too little is known about how the Edwardian and Marian New Year's ceremonies were carried out to compare them with the practice under Elizabeth. As in her father's time, a gift chamber was set up at New Year's in whatever palace Elizabeth celebrated the Christmas season. This chamber was equipped with display tables for the gifts, as described in these entries from the Treasurer of the Chamber's accounts:

1574 Dec:	The Office of Works set up 'tables for the banquet and for her Majesty's New Year gifts'.
1584 Dec:	Works: 'Making New Year's gift boards'.
1585 Dec:	Two Jewel-house officers 'for their attendance at the Tower to provide, set out and deliver her Highness's New Year gifts'.
1586 Dec:	Works: 'Setting up a table 40 foot long in the Privy Gallery to lay the New Year's gifts for her Majesty to see them ...'

---

[38] J. Nichols, *Progresses, Processions, and Magnificent Festivities of King James the First* (4 vols, London, 1828), vol. 2, p. 78.

[39] J. Britton and E. W. Brayley, *Memoirs of the Tower of London* (London, 1830), p. 285.

[40] B. F. Harvey, 'Litlyngton , Nicholas (b. before 1315, d. 1386)', ODNB (Oxford, 2004; online edn, Jan 2008).

[41] A. P. Stanley, *Historical Memorials of Westminster Abbey* (3 vols, London, 1889), vol. 2, pp. 197–8; R. Widmore, *A History of the Church of St Peter, Westminster* (London, 1751), pp.174, 231; G. G. Scott, *Gleanings from Westminster Abbey* (London, 1863), pp. 226–7; B. Weinreb and C. Hibbert, ed., *The London Encyclopaedia* (London, 1984), p. 429.

1596 Dec:	Works: 'Setting up long tables for the New Year gifts'.
1599 Dec:	Richard Coningsby made ready 'the New Year's gift chamber'.
1602 Dec:	Anthony Abington made ready 'the New Year's gift chamber'.
	Works: 'Setting up boards for the banquet in the Great Chamber and Presence [chamber] after Christmas'.[42]

Although the poet George Gascoigne fancifully depicted himself kneeling to present a New Year's gift to the Queen, such face-to-face, sovereign-to-donor exchanges were not part of the ceremony, nor was Gascoigne ever admitted to it.[43] Instead, the donors' servants delivered their presents to the gift chamber in the manner described by Hussey in 1538. A uniquely detailed list in the Treasurer of the Chamber's accounts records the sums paid to servants who delivered gifts for the Queen in 1582 (BL MS Harley 1644). This list parallels the normal format of the rolls by recording payments to the servants of 'Marquesses and Earles', 'Busshopps', 'Barrons and Lordes', and so forth, but with a few variations. No category of primary donors appears on this list. Male peers precede their female counterparts in this document (but not on the vellum rolls), and the standard 'Ladies' heading is replaced by 'Knights' wives'. As a result, the daughters of earls, ladies by virtue of their birth, are promoted to the category of 'Baronesses'. The servants, unnamed on this list, received variable rewards for carrying out their duties: those who brought presents from lords (spiritual and temporal) received 20 shillings; servants of knights and ladies, 13 shillings, 4 pence, and of gentlewomen and gentlemen, 6 shillings 8 pence. The procedure they followed can be tentatively reconstructed from an account of the Jacobean exchange. Late in 1604, the Earl of Huntingdon gave these instructions for delivering his New Year's gift in 1605:

> You must buy a new purse of about v s. price, and put thereinto xx pieces of new gold of xx s. a piece, and go to the Presence-chamber, where the Court is, upon New-yere's day, in the morninge about 8 a clocke, and deliver the purse and the gold unto my Lord Chamberlin, then you must go down to the Jewell-House for a ticket to receive xviii s. vj d. as a gift to your paines, and give v d. there to the box for your ticket; then go to Sir William Veall's office, and shew your ticket, and receive your xviii s. vi d. Then go to the Jewell-House again, and make [choice of] a peece of plate of xxx ounces waight, and marke it, and then in the afternoone you may go and fetch it away, and then give the Gentleman who delivers it you xl s. in gold, and give to the box ii s. and to the porter vj d'.[44]

This account indicates that the servants not only received rewards but in turn provided honoraria for the Jewel House staff. Under Elizabeth, gifts to the Queen were not always delivered by the donors' servants, for the Earl of Leicester's

---

[42] PRO E 351; A banquet was a light meal, and it seems only to be mentioned by the Works in relation to New Year. I am grateful to Marion Colthorpe for providing me with these references (letter dated 20 Nov 2006).

[43] Gascoigne's drawing is reproduced in G. Gascoigne, *The Complete Works of George Gascoigne*, ed. J. W. Cunliffe (2 vols, New York, 1969), vol. 2, p. 472.

[44] Nichols, *Progresses of King James*, vol. 1, p. 471.

'Disbursement Book' records on 6 January 1585 rewarding Henry Seckford with a cup and £20 'for presenting the Quenes New Yeres gefte'.[45] As under James, however, the Lord Chamberlain, the officer in charge of court ritual, no doubt supervised the Elizabethan exchanges; moreover, the Jewel House staff who signed the gift rolls reported to him. A scribe or scribes must have written down the names of the donors whose servants delivered the presents, along with the detailed descriptions of the presents that appear on the final rolls. But how was this diverse mass of information marshalled into the highly organized listings in order of precedence under earls, bishops, countesses, and so forth that appear on the rolls? The answer is found in a unique document at the Somerset Heritage Centre in Taunton among papers of the Mildmay family, two of whose members served as Master and Groom of the Jewels and Plate under the early Stuarts.

Somerset Heritage Centre DD\MI/19/1 is a quarto paper booklet of sixty-nine pages, damaged by damp, dated twenty-four Elizabeth (1582), and entitled 'Newyeres Guiftes geven by the Quenes Maiestie. . .' The list begins, 'To the Lady margret Countes of Darbe', and continues with names and titles engrossed by a professional scribe who left such wide spacing between the entries as to average only seven names per page. This series of entries includes a page entitled 'The maides', and the 'Fre guiftes' to the officers of the Jewel House and Grooms of the Privy Chamber. A new heading occurs on p. 35, 'Newyeres Guiftes geuen to the Quenis Maiestie. . .', introducing the 'By list' in the same format as the preceding 'To list'. This booklet is in effect a blank form that organizes in advance the 1582 gift exchange, drawn up with the names of the anticipated donors, but with plenty of space left to describe the gifts, into whose custody they were entrusted, and to add donors' names as needed. The relevant details have been filled in throughout in a different hand from that of the scribe who first drafted the document, showing that this was the actual record compiled at the time of the exchange. The first scribe apparently copied the engrossed names from the 1581 gift roll as the best available predictor of who would participate in the 1582 exchange. Thus Baroness 'Riche' is listed on pp. 15 and 51 because Lady Elizabeth Rich took part in the 1581 exchange. But the hand that literally filled in the blanks in this manuscript added 'doger' (dowager) above the line after her name to distinguish her from 'Riche junior', a new addition at the foot of the page. The latter entry denotes Penelope Devereux, who became Lady Rich junior when she married Lady Elizabeth's son, Robert, Lord Rich, on 1 November 1581, just two months before the 1582 ceremony. Finally, the second scribe numbered in sequential order each participant within each donor category. This numbering appears on none of the vellum rolls, but was apparently added to this draft manuscript as an aid to drawing up the final account.

The Somerset booklet's 'To list' also provides unique insight into the conditions under which the Jewel House staff accounted for the presents given and received. Clearly, they were often working at top speed in the busy environment

[45] S. Adams, ed., *Household Accounts and Disbursement Books of Robert Dudley, Earl of Leicester, 1558–1561, 1584–1586*, Royal Historical Society, Camden Fifth Series, vol. 6 (Cambridge, 1995), pp. 209–10.

of the gift chamber and the Jewel House. The penmanship falters and there are numerous crossings-out. Abbreviations proliferate as servants crowd in, eager to be on their way: a gift of 'A guilt bolle Keall' (a gilt bowl purchased from Keall, the goldsmith) for the Countess of Rutland (82.261) is later rendered, 'A g bolle K' for Sir Owen Hopton (82.359). After 'Fraunces Walsingham principall Secretary', Thomas Wilson's name is followed by 'esquier,' after which the scribe attempted to write 'also Secretary'. Three letters into 'also', however, he transformed this into the hybrid 'alsquire'. He added 'also', then crossed out the entire entry as Wilson was a non-participant, having died in 1581 (unnumbered entry between 82.313 and 82.314). The weights of gilt plate on the 'To list' are totalled on each page of the account, with more than a dozen entries having been corrected, suggesting that each piece was weighed twice to insure accuracy. Many names of gift custodians have also been crossed out and replaced. Accordingly, this document not only reveals the scribal mechanism that allowed the final rolls to be compiled in descending order of royal favour, social rank, and office, it gives us a unique view of the Jewel House staff recording all this complicated data in the confused rush of the exchange ceremony at court. Above all, the Somerset manuscript permits a detailed reconstruction of the lost 1582 roll from this, its immediate documentary ancestor.

Other anomalies in the New Year's manuscripts suggest that accurate record keeping during the exchange was often difficult to manage. There was much to record, as servants delivered gifts, received rewards, and collected plate, while a variety of household servants assisted the Ladies, Gentlewomen, and Grooms of the Privy Chamber in taking custody of the gifts. Each of these transactions was supposed to be documented, although there is ample evidence of lapses in the system. For instance, eleven names are struck through on the Somerset manuscript or lack any mention of a gift, although the servants of these donors were rewarded for delivering gifts on their behalf according to BL MS Harley 1644. In 1584 Elizabeth received two quite elegant gifts totaling twenty pairs of 'longe aglettes of gold', but the roll states, 'no report made who gave them' (84.126–27). In Lady Howard's inventory, the phrase 'from an unknown' occurs several times. Even so important a 'primary' donor as Lady Mary Grey presented a gift to the Queen in 1563 (63.1) but is not named on the 'To list'. Similarly, the renowned miniaturist Nicholas Hilliard gave the Queen a painting in 1584 (84.190), but apparently received nothing in return, while Benedict Spinola received a very generous seventy-seven ounces of gilt plate from the Queen in 1576, but does not appear on the 'By list' (76.382). Clement Adams, Schoolmaster to the (disbanded) Henchmen, received forty shillings in 1562–64 and 1567, yet no gift is recorded from the Queen in either 1565 or 1568, although Adams gave her something in both years (65.98, 68.167). These irregularities more likely reflect failures of record keeping than violations of the reciprocal exchange tradition.

The New Year's gift rolls identify the personnel who mattered at court and to the Queen personally. Some allowance must be made, however, for Elizabeth's first New Year's exchange as sovereign, which occurred less than two months after her accession to the throne, 17 November 1558. Its participants were, understandably, a mixture of the new Queen's household servants and favourites with those of her predecessor. Many of those listed on the 1559 roll never participated in the exchange again. The rolls for 1560 and 1561 are missing, so that we cannot tell how quickly and drastically the makeup of court society changed. Predictably, those named on the next documented exchange in 1562 are markedly different from Elizabeth's first exchange in two categories of donors. First, the Catholic bishops who participated in 1559 were replaced by the reformed prelates listed on subsequent rolls. Fourteen of the sixteen bishops named only once on the extant rolls appear on this first such record of the Queen's reign. Second, the 1559 list of gentlemen is inflated with a number of menial household servants and court outsiders who appear only on this roll, among them the poet Thomas Phaer, Thomas Doughtie, bitmaker, and John Greene, Queen Mary's coffermaker, who retained his post under Elizabeth but was apparently excluded from later New Year's ceremonies. Thereafter, the list of annual participants became sufficiently stable that the Jewel House staff could draft in advance their names and titles, as witnessed by the draft for the exchange of 1582.

While the exchanges centred on a stable core of donors, a considerable range of participation necessarily developed during the course of the reign. Six participants appeared on every extant roll between 1559 and 1603: Edward Seymour, Earl of Hertford; Anne Carey, Lady Hunsdon (wife of the first Lord Hunsdon); Lady Mary Cheke, widow of Sir John Cheke and wife of Henry Mackwilliam; Henry Seckford; Lucy Penne, later Barley; and Douglas Howard, Baroness Sheffield Stafford. Other favourites and servants began their court careers under Henry VIII and continued with Elizabeth, while others served Elizabeth and continued their court careers under James I. Peter Vannes exchanged gifts with at least four monarchs, beginning with Henry VIII and ending with Elizabeth. Sir Edward Carey served as Groom of the Privy Chamber and Master of the Jewel House under both Elizabeth and James. On the other hand, and for a variety of reasons, many persons other than the Catholic bishops already cited appeared only once on the rolls. Foreign visitors to the court delivered gifts from time to time without being admitted to the exchange. In 1568, for example, an unnamed 'Frencheman' presented Elizabeth with an elaborate 'Deuice made of silke Nuttemegges and Cloues of thistory of Pirramus and Tysbey' (68.169), but he remained unidentified and received nothing from her majesty in return. In 1584 the Jewel House staff noted that one 'Ogier Bellehache,' probably a Huguenot refugee from Caen, presented the Queen with a book of Latin verses (84.198), but again, she did not reciprocate. John Anthony Fenotus, alias Joannes Anthonius Phenotus, submitted a cure for a particularly severe toothache that afflicted the Queen in 1578. As part of his reward, she admitted him to the 1579 exchange (79.203) , his only appearance on the lists.[46] It is possible that his gift of 'a smale booke in Italian meter' was related to his work, *Alexipharmacum, sive antidotus apologetica*, ... published in 1575. For his pains he received a gilt bowl weighing just over seven ounces (79.416).

---

[46] J. Strype, *Historical Collections of the Life and Acts of the Right Reverend Father in God, John Aylmer, Lord Bishop of London in the Reign of Queen Elizabeth* (Oxford, 1821), pp. 192–3.

A few donors cannot be identified because, as noted above, the Jewel House staff simply lost track of who delivered what on behalf of whom. In some cases the scribes perhaps found it difficult to learn or recall the names of participants who were not regulars at court. The 'Gentleman vnknowne' who gave the Queen a fan in 1589 (89.160) may be John Chudleigh, who first appeared on the rolls in 1588. He belonged to a seafaring family from Devon with ties to the interconnected Ralegh, Gilbert, and Drake families of that shire. The unknown gentleman of 1589 appears in exactly the same place on both the 'By' and 'To' lists, as did Chudleigh in 1588. If this was Chudleigh's second exchange, however, he was destined never to appear on the rolls again. In the following August he set out on a voyage of circumnavigation, but died in the Straits of Magellan.[47] Other names on the rolls are so common or undifferentiated by office or title, that they remain unidentified in the Biographical Sketches (e.g. Mistress Britten, 1597, Mistress Harman, 1577, William Bursch 1603). The 'Lady Carey Sir Lawrens wife' who appears on the 1564 roll is probably Elizabeth Norwich, lady of the Privy Chamber and Sir Gawain Carew's third wife (64.81). Lady Carew is regularly listed from 1562 through 1589 except for 1564, but this identification assumes a scribal substitution of 'Lawrens' for Gawain.

On one occasion the Queen apparently intervened to disguise the identity of a participant in the exchange. The last entry in the 'Knights' category of the 1597 'By list' records, 'By my Skimskine for my pantables one Snuskyn of blacke veluet imbroadered all ouer like bee hives and bees of seede pearles' (97.138). 'Pantables' (pantofles) are variously a type of indoor slipper or high-heeled shoes. 'Snufkin' refers to a close-fitting muff to warm the hands and 'skimskin' seems to be another term for muff. The OED includes an entry for snufkin and its variant of snoskin, but no mention is yet made of skimskin or skinskin. This 1597 entry thus seems to describe a gift from 'my skimskin' and Elizabeth's reciprocating gift to one of her favourites. Elizabeth gave pet names to a number of her favourite courtiers, but no 'skimskin' appears among them.[48] She reciprocated, however, with a respectable 20⅜ ounces of gilt plate 'To my Skuvskyne for my Pantaples' (97.334).

Although Elizabeth did not supervise the delivery of New Year's gifts as did her father, she certainly reviewed them and routinely interrupted their consignment to the appropriate custodians. Gifts that caught the Queen's eye remained 'with the Queen'. For example, the bejewelled 'Earepyke' Lord Strange offered in 1575 remained 'with her Matie' (75.74), as did the jewel she received from the Earl of Northumberland in 1588 (88.15). Other gifts were put to immediate use by being delivered directly into the Privy Chamber, such as the 'xxx glasses for wyne and Beare' given by Jacomo Manucci (88.177), and the 'faier bounde' Bible given by Robert Barker the royal printer (03.177). Elizabeth frequently 'recycled' gifts. At New Year's 1564, for instance, John Astley presented her with 'a very fayer Cup of siluer guilt made like a Gourde' (64.130). On 5 March following, the

---

[47] K. R. Andrews, *English Privateering Voyages to the West Indies, 1588–1595* (Cambridge, 1959), chap. 3, 'The Voyage of John Chidley, 1589'.

[48] May, *Elizabethan Courtier Poets*, pp. 196–7, argues that the donor was Sir Robert Sidney.

Queen bestowed this cup as a christening gift for the child of Dr. Richard Master, one of her physicians in ordinary (64.220). After the 1581 exchange, Elizabeth presented Mistress Anne West with an elaborate jewel she had just received from Lady Sheffield (81.89, 81.143). In 1598 Lady Elizabeth Leighton participated in the exchange as usual, but then received from the Queen as an additional gift the bejewelled necklace given by her fellow Lady of the Privy Chamber, Margaret Hawkins (98.96, 98.107).

Elizabeth could predict much of what she would receive from one New Year's exchange to the next because gifts from many individuals and even from whole classes of donors were already customary or became standardized early in the reign. From the reign of Henry VIII, if not earlier, the bishops and, with few exceptions, the higher ranking nobility (duchesses, marquesses, earls, and countesses), gave purses filled with coins. The debased state of English coinage early in Elizabeth's reign is reflected in the mixture of coins she received at New Year's, including Flemish angels, French crowns, Spanish pistolets, and Portuguese portingales. In 1565, for example, Sir Edward Warner, Lieutenant of the Tower, gave a crimson velvet purse containing 'a portugue a doble Duckett thre olde angelles and two Dimy soueraignes', valued at £6 13 s. 4 d. (65.38). By the 1570s the exotic array of foreign coins had been largely replaced by English crowns, sovereigns, and demi-sovereigns.[49] A son succeeding to an earldom normally gave the same amount in gold at New Year's as had his father, a pattern also applicable when women succeeded to the higher titles of nobility through either marriage or death of their predecessors.

While the gift of choice for most earls, countesses and bishops was cash, the lords and ladies of the rank of baron gave a greater variety of gifts, opting for clothing and jewellery as well as cash. The diversity of gifts increased down the social scale, from knights to gentlewomen to the Queen's nearest Privy Chamber servants. From her musicians, for example, she frequently received 'sweet' (perfumed) gloves, but she also received a pair of virginals (77.195), a nocturnal dial (79.206), a basket of masks (59.178), lutes, bandores, and gitterns. Her royal physicians and apothecaries chose hippocras, orange flowers, candied ginger and preserves. A gentlewoman of the Privy Chamber, Elizabeth Snowe, née Cavendish, specialized in gold toothpicks, while Levina Teerlinc, née Benninck, presented a series of miniature portraits of the Queen that she herself had painted. Most of the books and manuscripts the Queen received from year to year also came from the lower ranks of donors.[50] These patterns of gift giving appear to be based on the donors' personal preferences or they were regulated, at most, by the force of custom. Collins's systematic study of the plate received at the New Year reveals, however, a gradual decline in the popularity of this kind of gift on the 'By lists' during the reign. By the 1580s only three or four pieces of plate at most were

---

[49] I am grateful to Sybil Jack for her observations on coinage and auditing techniques in relation to the gift rolls.

[50] For an analysis of these gifts, see J. A. Lawson, 'This Remembrance of the New Year: Books Given to Queen Elizabeth as New Year's Gifts', in P. Beal and G. Ioppolo, ed., *Elizabeth I and the Culture of Writing* (London, 2007), pp. 133–71.

PLATE 1

John Astley (c.1507–1596), Master of the Jewel House, by an Unknown Flemish artist 1555, National Portrait Gallery, London

PLATE 2

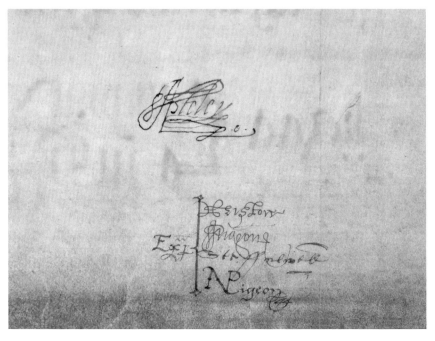

Signature of John Astley, Master of the Jewel House, with other Jewel House officers, Nicholas Bristow, John Pigeon, Stephen Fulwell, and Nicholas Pigeon, 1589 31 Elizabeth, Folger Shakespeare Library, MS Z.d.16

PLATE 3

Portion of the Gift Roll: 1571 13 Elizabeth, Collection of the Duke of Buccleuch and Queensberry, K. T., Boughton House

PLATE 4

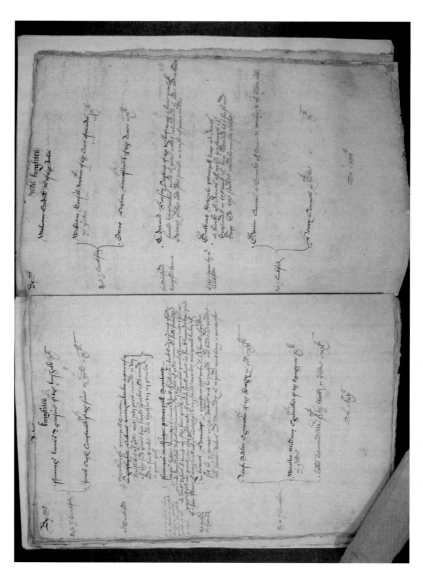

PLATE 5

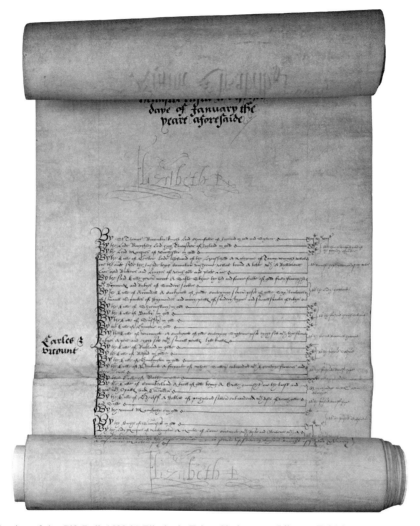

Portion of the Gift Roll: 1589 31 Elizabeth, Folger Shakespeare Library, Z.d.16

PLATE 6

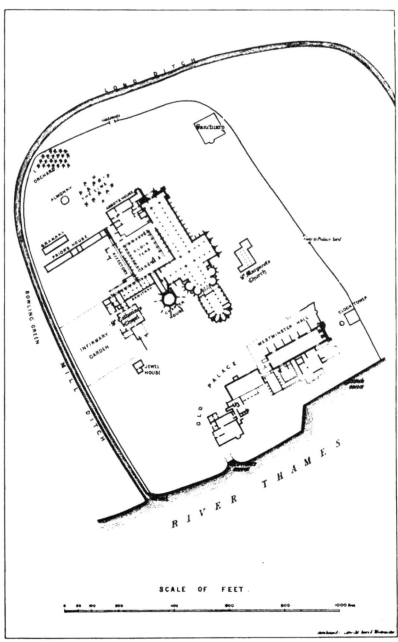

WESTMINSTER ABBEY & ITS PRECINCT.
·ABOUT A.D 1535·

Plan of the Palace of Westminster and its Precincts about A.D. 1535 Showing the Location of the Jewel Tower

PLATE 7

Exterior of the Jewel Tower at the Palace of Westminster, London, © English Heritage

presented to the Queen at the New Year, and in some years (1588, 1600, 1603), none at all. Yet Collins estimates that the gift exchanges supplied the Crown with about one quarter of all the plate brought in between 1574 and 1594.[51]

Elizabeth's reciprocal gifts were also fairly predictable, title by title and class by class, throughout the reign, although we do not know how or when she decided to bestow these amounts of plate on individual donors. The archbishops of Canterbury and York, for instance, received about forty and thirty ounces of plate respectively. Knights averaged twenty to thirty ounces. Significant variations in the standard amounts thus stand out as signs of particular favour. Even so valued a servant as William Cecil, Lord Burghley, never received more than $40\frac{7}{8}$ ounces, while the Queen's beloved Helena, Lady Marquess of Northampton, received between 42 and 44 ounces annually. Accordingly, the 103 ounces bestowed on Ambrose Dudley, Earl of Warwick, the 132 ounces given to the Earl of Leicester, and the 400 ounces given to Sir Christopher Hatton reveal the Queen's exceptional regard for these high-ranking courtiers. And while the amounts of gilt plate given by Elizabeth within each category of donor were fairly stable, fewer details of their descriptions on the rolls were provided. Before 1581 the rolls record both the types of plate and their weights. Bowls and cups, with or without covers, were the most popular gifts, with basins, casting bottles, chandeliers, cruses, hanse pots, pepper boxes, and tankards mentioned regularly during the first half of the reign. After about 1580 the procedure was simplified to record only the weights of gilt plate given.

As with Elizabethan court life generally, the New Year's gift exchanges were social functions within an adult community. There is no evidence that children, even if royal wards, were 'brought up at court' in any meaningful sense of that phrase during the Queen's reign. The youngest participants in the annual exchanges were the maids of honour, who were usually appointed in their early teens and received their 'free gifts' from the Queen during tenure. Young men occasionally began to attend court as early as their teens. Francis Wolley, for example, participated in the 1597 ceremony at age fourteen. Ferdinando Stanley, Lord Strange, first appeared on the rolls in 1575, aged sixteen, and Robert Devereux, Earl of Essex, was nineteen at the time of his first exchange in 1584, although he next appeared on the rolls in 1587. Accordingly, special interest attaches to three entries that clearly involve children. The heading on the 1571 roll regarding the free gifts bestowed on the maids of honour is amended to 'Fre Guiftes to the Maides of Honor and others' in order to accommodate nine-year-old Elizabeth Brooke, daughter of William Brooke, Lord Cobham and his wife, Frances Brooke, née Newton. The Queen presented Elizabeth with the bejewelled golden angel she had just received *eodem die* from Blanche Parry (71.322, 71.119). Presumably, young mistress Cobham was brought to court for the New Year festivities, caught the Queen's eye, and was admitted to the New Year's exchange as a special favour. Similarly eight-year-old Elizabeth Howard, daughter of Charles, Lord Howard and his wife, Baroness Catherine Howard, née Carey was presented

---

[51] Collins, *Jewels and Plate*, p. 102.

with a red and white rose jewel also given to the Queen by Blanche Parry in 1572.[52] Five-year-old Frances Drury, daughter of Sir William Drury and his wife, Elizabeth (later Scott, née Stafford), not only received a gift from the Queen in the 1582 exchange (a regifting of Charles Smith's present to her 'gevon to Mrs Fraunces Drury by Mrs Newtons report', 82.193), she gave the Queen in return 'a forke of corrall' garnished with gold (82.162).

The overall nature of Elizabethan New Year's gift-giving must be reconstructed from a variety of documents other than the vellum rolls. The missing 1582 roll has been fully reconstructed from the Somerset Heritage Centre booklet. The names of scores of donors from missing rolls can be retrieved from the accounts of Lady Howard's and Mary Radcliffe's inventories of the Queen's jewels. Howard's account, BL MS Sloane 814, is edited in Nichols's *Progresses* with the note, 'this list will be found in its proper date at the end of every year till 1593/94 inclusive';[53] it is the most detailed supplemental source of New Year's gifts given to the Queen, for it includes both descriptions of the jewels and the names of the donors.

Other documents illustrate, consistently, that those who were admitted to the New Year's exchanges took their participation very seriously. In a letter of 28 December 1578, the Earl of Shrewsbury authorized his Countess, Bess of Hardwick, to spend the considerable sum of £100 on the Queen's New Year's gift. An interesting omission from the 1576 gift list also concerns Lady Shrewsbury and her preparations for the exchange. In October 1575 Anthony Wingfield, gentleman usher, advised the Countess, his sister-in-law, to give the Queen a watchet (light blue) or peach-coloured cloak and safeguard. Wingfield had consulted with both the Countess of Sussex and Lady Cobham, who informed him that such a cloak and safeguard would best please the Queen because 'she hath no garment off that collor att all'.[54] Both watchet and peach colours made their first appearance in the gift exchanges in 1576, but no cloaks are listed among them. Not until 1585 did the Queen receive a peach-coloured cloak, the gift of Michael Stanhope, while no watchet cloaks appear on any of the extant rolls. Instead, at the 1576 exchange Lady Shrewsbury gave Elizabeth a kirtle and a doublet of yellow satin, cut and lined with black sarsenet (76.26). In the following year she presented Elizabeth with a gown of tawny satin laid with a pasmane lace of Venice gold and buttons of the same lined with yellow sarsenet (77.31). The Countess probably did not give the Queen a watchet or peach-coloured cloak despite Wingfield's enquiries on her behalf.[55] Janet Arnold proposed that the cloak and safeguard described in Wingfield's letter were made by the royal tailor Walter Fish as a 'rush job', given that, from the time he could have received the countess's instructions,

---

[52] BL MS Sloane 814, f. 2v.

[53] Lady Howard's edited jewel inventory (BL MS Sloane 814) is transcribed in Nichols, *Progresses*, vol. 1, pp. 294–6, 323–4, 379–81, 412–3; vol. 2, pp. 1–2, 52–3, 289–90, 300–2, 387–9, 419–20, 426–7, 451–2, 498–500, 528–9; and vol. 3, pp. 26, 38, 74, 124, 227, 252. References to MS Sloane 814 in the Biographical Sketches denote gift exchange participants named in this document.

[54] Folger Shakespeare Library, MS X.d.428 (127, 128).

[55] J. A. Lawson, 'Rainbow for a Reign: The Colours of a Queen's Wardrobe', *Costume*, 41 (2007), p. 35.

he had only two and a half weeks to create this lavish garment. However, Arnold found no documentation for Fish's work.[56] It seems more likely that Bess made do with a kirtle and doublet more readily at hand.

On a number of occasions the gift rolls reveal that members of the court collaborated to assemble coordinated outfits to give the Queen. Sir Henry Guildford and Lady Elizabeth Somerset, his wife, aligned their gifts in both 1598 and 1599. In the first instance they each presented the Queen with part of a clay-coloured kirtle lined with lawn cutwork flourished with Venice silver (98.93, 98.133), and the next year with two parts of a clay-coloured satin petticoat embroidered with branches and owes (99.90, 99.125). In 1597 Sir John Scudamore and his wife, Mary Scudamore née Shelton, gave two parts of a loose gown of pink-coloured taffeta (97.101, 97.126). It seems likely that the orange-tawny satin kirtle cut and lined with white sarsenet, presented by the Countess of Lennox in 1581, was meant to be worn with the white satin gown with ash sleeves and a tawny ground guard given by her mother, the Countess of Shrewsbury, in the same year (81.36, 81.23). Clothing with similar embroidery patterns, motifs, and colours can sometimes be traced to members of the same family or to gentlewomen of the Privy Chamber, suggesting that they had coordinated their gifts, although the duplications may simply reflect current fashions or what tailors and embroiderers had in stock at the time. The white satin doublet given by Elizabeth Carey, Lady Hunsdon in 1600 (00.78) was perhaps intended to match the white satin petticoat Lady (Ursula) Walsingham gave the Queen that same year (00.107). The former was embroidered with 'flyes and leaves of venyce silver,' the latter with 'flyes & branches'. Were these garments intended as a single outfit, or are their similarities coincidental? In any event, most of Elizabeth's New Year's gifts were chosen by donors who were in frequent and sometimes intimate contact with her. What they gave undoubtedly reflected her tastes and foibles as well as general tastes and fashions, year by year, at the apex of Elizabethan society.

The Queen, too, sometimes split her reciprocal gift of gilt plate between two of her subjects. Sir William Cecil and his wife Mildred, née Cooke, for instance, each received one part of a pair of flagons in 1562 (62.266, 62.282), as did Sir Francis Knollys and his wife Catherine in 1568 (68.247, 68.268). Thomas and Anne Heneage shared a basin and matching lair (a pitcher with a wide spout) in 1564 (64.173, 64.191), and in 1582 they received, respectively, a gilt bowl with a cover (82.297, 82.314). Sir Edward Bray shared the office of almoner at the coronation in 1559 and received an alms dish as payment (59.459). He refused to share this plate with the two other honorary almoners on the grounds that it was not easily divisible.[57] It is not clear how individuals like John Tamworth, John Smithson, and Edward Bashe managed to take away their parts of a bowl, hanse pot, and tankard (64.206, 68.320, 75.224), unless they received only broken fragments of these vessels; there is no indication that the other parts of these items went to other donors.

---

[56] Arnold, *Queen Elizabeth's Wardrobe*, p. 95; Klein, p. 470, likewise assumes that the Queen's enthusiastic response to the countess's gift in 1576 concerned this non-existent cloak.
[57] Hasler, vol. 1, p. 481; PRO C 3/76/82.

Gift exchange participants were understandably curious as to how the Queen reacted to their gifts. After the 1576 exchange, for instance, Elizabeth Wingfield assured Bess of Hardwick that the Queen greatly admired 'the color and strange triminge' of her gift, but without specifying the garment or its colour.[58] Similarly, a court correspondent informed Philip Howard, Earl of Surrey, that the girdle he had given the Queen at New Year 1579 (79.21), so delighted her 'that she wold haue worne it to daye' but could not because she was already wearing the girdle and matching head attire presented to her by Christopher Hatton. The same letter also mentions that the Earl of Oxford 'gaue the Quene a greatt new yers gifft this yere' and that Lord Henry Howard was disappointed that by 3 o'clock his gift for the Queen had not yet arrived. Oxford's gift was 'afeyer Juell of golde wherein is ahelmet of golde', garnished with diamonds and rubies (79.13). Howard's gift finally arrived and is duly noted as 'a Juell of golde being adedtre [a dead tree] with mystiltow set at the rote with Sparkes of Diamondes & Rubyes' (79.77).[59]

Participants in the exchange were, of course, pleased when the Queen responded favourably to their gifts. In 1599, the London merchant Thomas Ferrers gave Elizabeth 'one guilte Cuppe with a Couer stayned with sondry colores & some siluer leaves' (99.195). Ferrers wrote to his brother, Sir Humphrey, that in an audience with Elizabeth on 12 January, she remarked of the gift, 'I doe estime ytt greattley, and doe kepe ytt for myne owne vse ... But I estime the giver much more'.[60] The Queen also expressed her high regard for Ferrers through the exchange itself, giving him 14¾ ounces of gilt plate (99.396) in return for the cup he had given her, which weighed only 11¾ ounces.

Elizabeth did not respond favourably to everything she received at New Year's. In 1578, Lady Mary Vere presented her with a purple taffeta forepart 'set with Roses of white sipers and cheynes betweene of venice golde with a brode pasmane of golde vnlyned and vnmade' (78.99). This elegant garment was designed to be fitted and lined before the Queen wore it. Ralph Hope of the Robes took it into custody, but it apparently languished, neglected, in the Great Wardrobe where it is listed on the inventory of 1600, unmade and unworn.[61] Elizabeth probably rejected this gift because scarcely two months after the New Year's exchange Lady Vere and Peregrine Bertie were married by March 1578—a match opposed by two great courtiers, Peregrine's mother, the Duchess of Suffolk, and Mary's brother Edward, Earl of Oxford.

Many of the nobility and, no doubt, most Elizabethan bishops managed their annual gift exchanges with the Queen in absentia. In a letter of 7 January 1574, Roger Woode reported in detail to Edward Manners, Earl of Rutland, how he had carried out the exchange on behalf of his lordship and his countess. He delivered to Lord Chamberlain Sussex two purses, each containing £10 in gold, as their respective New Year's gifts. This was on the advice of Roger Manners, Lord

[58] Folger Shakespeare Library, MS X.d.428 (130).
[59] Folger Shakespeare Library, MS L.d.880. I am grateful to Heather Wolfe, Curator of Manuscripts at the Folger Shakespeare Library, for locating and transcribing this and the following letter.
[60] Folger Shakespeare Library, MS L.e.514.
[61] Arnold, *Queen Elizabeth's Wardrobe*, pp. 94, 295.

Rutland's uncle and one of the Queen's Esquires for the Body. Not until 7 January, however (the day of his letter) did Woode receive two gilt cups with covers, the Queen's gifts to the Earl and Countess. Woode reminded his master that he had not yet rewarded the servants who brought him the cups, 'but they are very desirous to have their reward'.[62]

Meanwhile, following a custom that no doubt long predates the Tudor era, the nobility and gentry carried out a considerable volume of New Year's gift giving of their own, quite separate from the ceremony at court. Account books of substantial households parallel those of the royal household by listing rewards to servants at the New Year, and records of gifts sent to and received from friends and family members.[63] A considerable amount of wealth changed hands during these yearly exchanges. In 1564, Edwin Sandys, Bishop of Worcester, sent Sir William Cecil a clock that had belonged to King Edward VI.[64] On 7 December 1587, Thomas Screven wrote to John Manners, Earl of Rutland (who had acceded to his brother Edward's title earlier that year), regarding his New Year's obligations. They included a £20 gift to the Queen on behalf of the Earl and Countess, plus gifts worth a total of £78 for Lord Treasurer Burghley, the Earl of Leicester, and Secretary Walsingham, with additional presents for Lady Stafford and Mistress Radcliffe of the Privy Chamber.[65] Julius Caesar, judge of the Admiralty Court, and one of the Masters of Requests, did not participate in any of the extant royal exchanges, but there survive copies of his letters that accompanied his New Year's gifts in 1590 to Burghley, Lord Chancellor Hatton, Lord Admiral Charles Howard, the Earl of Essex, and the Countess of Nottingham.[66]

A detailed list of New Year's gifts given by and presented to Robert Dudley in 1564 although mostly concerned with exchanges outside the formal court ceremony, may restore details about the court exchange missing from the incomplete 1564 gift roll (Folger MS X.d.12). This document lacks an account of the gifts given to peers ranking before the knights. Leicester's name is missing from the 'By' list, but his private account book states that he presented Elizabeth with jewels worth some £324, described as 'a little puppet, two pendants called ear rings, a dial set with Rubies and diamonds, a great jewel with a looking glass set with diamonds and rubies'. She gave him in return 'A Carkenet set with diamonds & rubies, a George set with diamonds with a pearl pendant, ten dozen of buttons set

---

[62] *HMC Rutland*, vol. 1, pp. 102–3.

[63] E.g. Roger Lord North's household account book (BL MS Stowe 774) lists charges for New Year's gifts given and received between 1576–1589. The Earl of Northumberland's accounts mention, among other gift entries, twenty shillings paid to Fulke Greville's servant for delivering a New Year's gift for either 1586 or 1587 (H. Percy, *The Household Papers of Henry Percy, Ninth Earl of Northumberland*, ed. G. R. Batho (London, 1962), p. 48. Sir Thomas Egerton's household account book for 1596–97 (Bodleian Library, MS Rawlinson D.406), records the 'rewards for newyers giftes brought this last newyeares tyde £16 xij s. x d.' (f. 19v). Sir Robert Cecil's New Year's gifts for 1602 are recorded in *HMC Salisbury*, vol.12, 1602, pp. 527–8.

[64] BL MS Lansdowne 6, no. 88.

[65] *HMC Rutland*, vol. 1, p. 232.

[66] BL MS Lansdowne 157, no.1, ff. 1, 5.

with Diamondes and perle'.[67] The Duchess of Suffolk does not appear as a participant in the 1562 gift exchange although her account books record the payments to four goldsmiths for the making of the Queen's New Year's gift which included several gold chains and a chessboard with a set of men.[68] Perhaps Walter Ralegh also observed the New Year's ritual with the Queen informally, for his name never appears on the rolls during the years of his greatest royal favour between 1583 and 1589; Ralegh's only listing on the extant rolls occurs for that of Elizabeth's last exchange in 1603.

Tantalizing references to New Year's exchanges not represented by the extant rolls occur in various other documents. The Spanish ambassador described a curious political statement incorporated into the jewel given by the Earl of Leicester in 1571: on it, 'the Queen was represented on a great throne with the queen of Scotland in chains at her feet, begging for mercy, whilst the neighboring countries of Spain and France were as if covered by the waves of the sea, and Neptune and the rest bowing to this Queen'.[69] Was Leicester's gift omitted from the 'By' list in 1571 because of the inflammatory political statement made by this jewel, or was this another instance of a hurried scribe omitting a donor and a description? Certainly, the donor was well enough known at court and the gift was distinctive enough, that the scribe was obligated to fill in this information under normal circumstances. BL MS Additional 5756 and CSP Domestic (12 July 1590, Nov 1596 and 23 May 1597) list warrants for payments to goldsmiths for the making of plate at New Year during the years for which no gift rolls survive. A manuscript at Corpus Christi College, Cambridge (MS Parker 105, p. 220, no. 13) includes a list of some sundry gifts from the 1566 exchange, 'Coppied oute of the rolle of newyeres guiftes signed with the Quenes hande' (c.1560–1580). In addition to the 1582 account book, the Mildmay Family Muniments at Somerset Heritage Centre include several seventeenth-century warrants for New Year's gifts.[70] DD\MI/19/2 in this collection duplicates many entries among the 'sundry gifts' on the extant rolls by listing royal gifts to ambassadors and at christenings for 30-45 Elizabeth (1588–1603).[71] A draft warrant from 1592 provides a similar list of gifts for christenings and marriages along with payments to goldsmiths (BL RP 7288, from the original in a private collection).

---

[67] BL MS Additional 78172, ff. 1–2v. A partial list of gifts given and received by Leicester at New Year's 1582 can be found in a household inventory, BL MS Additional 78177, ff. 4–5, 21, 25, 27.

[68] Great Britain. Royal Commission on Historical Manuscripts. *Report on the Manuscripts of the Earl of Ancaster Preserved at Grimsthorpe* (Dublin, 1907), p. 466.

[69] Dispatch of Guerau de Spes to Zayas, 9 January 1571. *CSP Spanish, 1568–1579*, p. 290, no. 231. Another report from Mendoza describes the gift of Francis Drake to the Queen in 1581. *Calendar of State Papers, Spain (Simancas)*, Volume 3: 1580–1586 (1896), vol.3, pp. 71–82, I –LVI

[70] Warrant to Sir Henry Carey, Master of the Jewels, Somerset Heritage Centre DD\MI/19/19–20; warrants to Sir Henry Mildmay, Master of the Jewels, Somerset Heritage Centre DD\MI/19/21–24, DD\MI/19/28–31, DD\MI/19/34–46.

[71] J. A. Bennett, 'Account of Papers Relating to the Royal Jewel-House in the Sixteenth and Seventeenth Centuries', *Archaeologia*, 48 (1884), pp. 204–6.

IV. Later Fortunes of the Gifts and Gift Rolls

Of more than nine thousand gifts presented to and by the Queen and described in detail on these rolls, almost none have survived or can be identified today. Perishables—pies, marzipans, quinces, preserved citrus fruit, and other edibles—were, of course, consumed. Clothing and accessories were refashioned, worn out, or given away. Some of the books and manuscripts remained in the royal library until George II donated most of it to the British Museum in 1757. The rest were dispersed, with only a few now identifiable in other archives and private collections.[72] Many items were regifted to courtiers who kept them as heirlooms or gave them to others. Bridget Chaworth, gentlewoman of the Privy Chamber, for example, gave George Tenecre an ash-coloured scarf she had received from the Queen. Tenecre singled out this item in his will, listing it among his jewels as an heirloom 'that was the Queen's that Mrs. Chaworth gave me'.[73]

The royal jewels and plate were sold off en masse on several occasions, beginning in 1600 when Elizabeth divested herself of broken and damaged jewellery and plate to finance the war in Ireland.[74] From the first year of his reign, Charles I authorized a series of sales of the royal gold and jewellery.[75] Additional treasure was sold or melted down between 1626 and 1649.[76] Finally, in August 1649, Parliament seized both the Jewel Tower at Westminster and the Jewel House in the Tower of London, completing the dissolution of what remained of the collection of jewels and plate accumulated by the Crown through the centuries.[77] Collins's account of the dispersal of both collections concludes rather forlornly with regard to Elizabeth's plate that a single 'Royal Gold Cup ... remains in our time the one witness to the magnificence of her table and the sole relic of the treasure-hoard of Tudor England'.[78]

The survival of the New Year's gift rolls is closely linked to the fate of the Queen's jewels and plate. The office of Master of the Jewels and Plate passed under the Stuarts from Sir Edward Carey (1595–1618), to joint office with his son, Sir Henry Carey (1603–1618), and then to Sir Henry Mildmay (1618–1649). Mildmay was turned out of his office by Parliament in 1649 after its officers carried off the remaining treasure in October of that year. However, subsequent orders from Parliament as late as November, 1652, addressed to both Sir Henry Mildmay and Sir Carew Harvey Mildmay, his cousin and a groom of the Jewels and Plate, indicate that many 'Jewel-house books' and papers remained in their hands. Others, perhaps including some or all of the New Year's rolls, had been

---

[72] Lawson, 'Remembrance', pp. 170–1.

[73] Lawson, 'Rainbow', p. 32.

[74] The valuables sacrificed for this cause are listed on six rolls in PRO E 407/4.

[75] R. Strong, *Lost Treasures of Britain* (London, 1990), pp. 79–80.

[76] Somerset Heritage Centre DD\MI/19/32, 'An Account of the Plate Appointed to be Sold at the Tower'; DD\MI/19/56, 'Plate Sold to Pay Debts'; DD\MI/19/82, 'List of Plate That Was Melted in 1644'; DD\MI/19/95, 'A Particular of Plate Delivered Out of the Office of Jewelhouse'.

[77] *Archaeologia*, 15 (1770), p. 277; Collins, *Jewels and Plate*, chap. 4, provides a detailed account of the dispersal of the royal collection of plate and jewels.

[78] Collins, *Jewels and Plate*, p. 198.

carried off by Parliamentary troops billeted in the Jewel Tower. A memorandum among the Mildmay family papers states that 'Many office books and papers are missinge[,] for in these tymes the office was common to all sorts, it being made a suckling house[79] for the Souldery at their first coming to London: and had they knowne of any Plate of the King within the office noe question but it would have been judged good plunder'.[80]

The earliest subsequent references I have found to the gift rolls occur in the eighteenth century and are all connected with the Society of Antiquaries. Fellows like George Holmes, Charles Lyttelton, and John Nichols were prominent among those who acted to preserve the rolls. By 1825, Nichols and his son, John Bowyer Nichols, owned at least five of these manuscripts, including the 1594 roll that vanished after the auction of the Nichols family collection in 1874.[81] This roll has now been located in the Dallas Public Library, donated by a Dallas family in 1984.

By the end of the last century, four institutions had acquired multiple Elizabethan gift rolls: seven rolls and two high-quality photocopies of two more rolls are housed at the British Library, six were acquired by the Folger Shakespeare Library in Washington, DC, four are among the records of Chancery in the Public Record Office at the National Archives, Kew, and two are at the Society of Antiquaries. The remaining seven extant rolls are found at six locations in England, the United States, and Switzerland. The locations and /or existence of the other manuscripts remain a mystery.

The most recent migrations of the Elizabethan documents are traced through two auctions held in 1968 and in 1969. The 1968 Christie's (London) auction included the 1600 roll, purchased by Harry Levinson, a California book dealer and sold in 1969 to Martin Bodmer. This manuscript is displayed in the Bodmer Fondation museum as an 'autograph signature "Elizabeth R" on [New-year's gift roll]'.[82] The same Christie's auction included the 1557 Mary roll which was also purchased by Levinson who then sold it to the British Library (BL MS Additional 62525). The reserved photocopies (BL RP 294, 2 vols) of these two rolls in the BL manuscript collection indicate that both manuscripts were prepared for export from England to California. In 1797 these two manuscripts were owned by William Herrick of Beaumanor Park, Leicestershire whose family had probably acquired them at the time of the dispersal of the Jewel House records. The Sotheby's (London) auction of 14 March 1967 included the 1596 roll as lot 201, described as 'the property of Mrs. E. Dudley Smith' which was purchased by Mrs. Hutton who donated the manuscript to the Morgan Library and Museum, New

---

[79] A satiric jibe at the Roundheads; a suckling house is 'a house or hut in which young calves or lambs are brought up' (OED).
[80] Somerset Heritage Centre DD\MI/19/106, Box 19 of the Mildmay Family Muniments; quoted in Bennett, pp. 215–6.
[81] Private collection; I am grateful to Julian Pooley for this reference.
[82] Collins, *Jewels and Plate*, pp. 248–52; H. A. Levinson, *History, Literature, Sciences, Scholarship Before 1700* (Catalogue 60) (Beverly Hills, California, 1968–1971) pt 3, p. 241; M. Crum, *English and American Autographs in the Bodmeriana*, (Cologny-Genève, 1977), p. 87.

York in 1972.[83] BL Facs 672 is a photocopy of this manuscript. No other rolls are known to have been offered at auction or sale since 1969.

The aim of this edition is to make all the information in these scattered manuscripts readily available for further research and analysis; they have much to tell us about the Elizabethan court, its culture, and its personnel.

---

[83] I am grateful to Declan Keily, Curator of Literary and Historical Manuscripts at the Morgan Library and Museum for providing this provenance.

Editorial Procedures

Both sides of each roll (the 'By lists' and 'To lists') begin with titles indicating the date and place of the New Year's celebration. The membranes of the extant rolls are unnumbered, so that it is ambiguous whether the side listing the gifts given to the Queen or the side listing the gifts she gave her courtiers was considered the 'beginning' of the account. I have begun each year's transcription of the rolls with the 'By' list in order to keep the 'Free Gifts' and 'Gifts given at sundry times' at the end of each year's record. To maintain a consistent ordering of the gifts, I have begun the transcription of the paginated Somerset MS with the 'By list' (p. 35), although this document begins on p. 1 with the 'To list'. Throughout this edition, each entry is accompanied in the left margin with a wholly editorial citation of its year and gift number (e.g. 85.111 for gift 111 on the 1585 roll). These citations provide orientation within the text of each document and allow for ready and accurate location of text entries from the various cross indexes of their contents. I provide modernized dates for the headings to each roll; otherwise, dates are recorded as they appear in the manuscripts, so that the years cited for dates between January 1 and March 25 are always, in Elizabethan practice, one behind the current reckoning.

The text is a semi-diplomatic transcription that reproduces the layout of the manuscript as closely as possible. I retain the original spelling and punctuation except that, for clarity's sake, I have changed 'i'/'I' to 'j'/'J' where a form of the letter 'j' is required in modern spelling. The gift roll scribes, however, following normal Elizabethan practice, used 'j' in place of 'i' as the final digit in Roman numerals, a convention I have retained. I also change initial majuscule 'ff' to its modern equivalent, 'F.' The letters 'u' and 'v', however, have not been transliterated when they represent their opposite in modern spelling, so that initial 'v' often stands for modern 'u,' and medial 'u' for modern 'v.' Scribes commonly combined words, such as 'thother' for the other, creating such potentially obscure formations as 'alouer' for all over, 'adedtre' for a dead tree, and 'thendes' for the ends.

Abbreviations and contractions are transcribed literatim except for silent expansion of the various contractions formed with the letter 'p' (per, par, pro, pre), wth or wt (for 'with'), the thorn (ye, yt, yr for 'the', 'that', 'their', etc.), the abbreviations for 'er', 'ar', 'ir', 'ieur', etc., formed with an ascending curved line or loop, and the terminal loops standing for a final 'es' or 'is'. Macrons (tildes) above words and letters often add a superfluous 'm' or 'n' and have been silently expanded only when they add a letter necessary for identifying the word in modern spelling. I use ellipses [...] to indicate illegible or missing text. Bracketed words or letters enclose hypothetical readings and interpolations. Egregious scribal errors or eccentricities are noted with '[sic]'. The scribes often left spaces between names in the manuscripts, probably intending to fill in missing information at a later date. This missing information is indicated with '[blank]'. 'Sr' is expanded to

'Sir', but I retain the familiar 'Mr' and 'Mrs' with the caution that during the Renaissance these abbreviations stood for 'Master' and 'Mistress'. Goldsmiths responsible for providing plate were often abbreviated to the first initial(s) of their surname; e.g., P or Par stands for Affabel Partridge. Regarding the confusion between Westminster and Whitehall Palaces, I follow Janet Backhouse and editors of the inventory of Henry VIII who treat them as synonymous.[84]

Five appendices enable the users of this edition to locate the varied kinds of data it records. Appendix I, Gift Descriptions and Motifs, is a catalogue of individual items, motifs incorporated into the gifts, and key terms used to describe the gifts. It is meant as a finding aid for information in the text, not as a catalogue of the individual gifts. These terms are arranged alphabetically in normalized spelling with the year and gift number of each instance of usage. I have used the term '*passim*' (e.g. for 'gold') to indicate that the descriptor appears too frequently to warrant individual indexing of every occurrence.

Appendix II, Glossary, defines words according to their sixteenth-century meanings and includes the year and roll locations of their earliest usage. A number of these usages pre-date the entries in the Oxford English Dictionary. This appendix also includes regularly appearing abbreviations and variant spellings of terms. Some abbreviations which have the appearance of words have been included in the Glossary to help the reader decipher the most unfamiliar and frequently used forms found on the rolls. Elizabethan spelling was largely and loosely phonetic. The same scribe might routinely spell the same word, even proper nouns, several different ways in the same manuscript. Where spelling deviates radically from modern usage, it is often helpful to say the word aloud in order to hear, for example, that 'estridge' is ostrich, and 'abrycocke' means apricot.

Appendix III is composed of two sections. The first part provides an overview of the Principal Officers of State including Officers and Divisions of the Royal Household. This table has been compiled from extant contemporary documents and includes some offices whose holders never participated in the Gift Exchanges. The table of household departments in this appendix shows the variety of positions required to maintain the Elizabethan court.[85] The names of many individuals who performed their duties within these household departments are recorded, but little more is known about many of them. Many household office holders were never in a position of close proximity to the Queen and did not qualify to participate in the gift exchange. A few offices carried over from the courts of Henry VIII, Edward VI, and Mary I. The Master of the Henchmen, for example, became in Elizabeth's court a mere sinecure. This table does not pretend to be

---

[84] J. Backhouse, 'Sir Robert Cotton's Record of a Royal Bookshelf', *British Library Journal*, 18 (1992), pp. 44–51; D. Starkey, *The Inventory of King Henry VIII: Society of Antiquaries MS 129 and British Library MS Harley 1419* (London, 1998).

[85] Other lists of the royal household offices are found in: A. F. Kinney, *Titled Elizabethans* (Hamden, Connecticut, 1973); Nichols, *Progresses*, vol. 2, pp. 42–8; E. K. Chambers, *The Elizabethan Stage* (4 vols, Oxford, 1961), vol. 1, pp. 27–70; G. E. Aylmer, *The King's Servants* (New York, 1961); BL Additional MSS 30198, 33378, Lansdowne MS 3; for Mary I's household, Sheffield City Archives WWM Str. P33; J. Haydn, *Book of Dignities* (London, 1851); J. C. Sainty, ed., *Office Holders in Modern Britain* (12 vols, London, 1972–1998); D. L. Loades, *The Tudor Court* (London, 1986).

exhaustive as the Court. Much remains to be learned about the structure of the Elizabethan court and its personnel.

The second part of Appendix III lists the offices and occupations which are recorded in the Elizabethan gift rolls. Gift roll entries sometimes fail to record the offices an individual held (e.g. Sir Edward Rogers was Captain of the Guard in 1559, but is listed on that roll as Vice Chamberlain, 59.110). This list also includes offices held by gift roll participants, even if that particular office is not named in the rolls. The individuals holding these titles participated in the gift exchanges or took charge of the gifts. For more details about an individual's role at Court, see the biographical entry in Appendix V.

Appendix IV, Custody of Gifts, lists names and department affiliations of those individuals who took charge of the gifts. Gifts delivered to the Queen were placed in the custody of various household officers who were held accountable for the gifts placed in their custody. Some gifts were taken to a specific household office with no named custodian while other gifts lack any distribution information. A select group of individuals were responsible for certain types of gifts. Others took custody of one or two items on a seemingly ad hoc basis. Many of the custodians included in this appendix appear only because they were named in the Somerset draft document of 1582. This is the only record known to record the names of persons who received the gifts given to the Queen in the gift chamber and those who then delivered the gifts to their various royal custodians. Their biographical entry for an individual notes their participation in the exchange under the heading, 'Custody of Gift'. The gift rolls in final draft do not retain the details of these internal workings of the court.

Appendix V, Biographical Sketches, identifies all participants in the extant Elizabethan New Year's gift exchanges, both those who gave and received gifts along with the many others named in the manuscripts. The biosketches provide basic identifications of the participants and list sources of additional information about them. These sources are included in the Bibliography and Abbreviations. Dates of birth and/or death are given for each participant if known; otherwise, fl. (flourished) indicates years when known to be alive. For each entry, I include that person's children and siblings who participated in the New Year's exchanges, but I do not attempt to include all the children and siblings of participants. Relatives of those named in the biosketches who also participated in the New Year's exchanges are indicated with an asterisk (*). I have included other relevant relationships among participants.

I have standardized the spelling of proper names in the Biographical Index to assist in locating the individuals and I have cross referenced erratic spellings as necessary. 'Catherine' is the default spelling for all forms of this name in the indexes, as scribes spelled it with initial 'K' or 'C' interchangeably, though referring to the same person. Men are entered under their surnames at birth, while women are listed under the surname by which they are most frequently referred to in the gift rolls. Women frequently appeared at court first under their family surname, and later under one or more married surnames. I have provided cross-references among the multiple surnames of the women participants, as well as variant spellings. To assist in locating married women who are included in spouse or off-spring entries, I have included the name under which their entry is filed in parenthesis, e.g. Nazareth Newton, mar 1st Southwell, then Paget is listed as Nazareth Newton (Paget*) under two husbands and a child. Where two or more persons share the same given and surnames, they are differentiated in the Biographical Index with Roman numerals, e.g. Henry [I] Neville, Henry [II] Neville. These identifiers are assigned in birth order for these individuals. Peerage titles are included in the Biographical Index, cross referenced to the surnames under which the title holders are identified. The dates included with cross-references for peers, both temporal and spiritual, refer to the term they held that title. Only peers who participated in the gift exchange are included in these cross references. The 'Gift List Category' indicates how the persons are listed on the gift rolls, not necessarily their actual titles. (For example, 'Mothers' of the maids of honour are usually listed in the 'Maids of Honour' category.) Additional details are offered about the reasons gifts were given for those listed under Sundry Gifts. The order of information, as relevant, included for each individual is:

Surname, Given Name, Peerage Title (Birth Year-Death Year or Flourished Date) Offices. Family Connections including Parentage, Siblings, Spouse(s), Children, Other Relevant Relationships, particularly Relationship to the Queen. Sources of biographical information.
Gift List Category: Years and locations on the rolls

Extant Elizabethan New Year's Gift Rolls

Year	Regnal	Location	Manuscript Shelf Mark
1559	1 Eliz	John Rylands Library, Manchester	MS Eng 117
1562	4 Eliz	British Library, London	Harley Roll V.18
1563	5 Eliz	The National Archives, Public Record Office at Kew	C 47/3/38
1564	6 Eliz	Folger Shakespeare Library, Washington	MS Z.d.12
1565	7 Eliz	Folger Shakespeare Library, Washington	MS Z.d.13
1567	9 Eliz	British Library, London	MS Additional 9772
1568	10 Eliz	Society of Antiquaries, London	MS 538
1571	13 Eliz	Duke of Buccleuch & Queensberry	private collection
1575	17 Eliz	Folger Shakespeare Library	MS Z.d.14
1576	18 Eliz	British Library, London	MS Additional 4827
1577	19 Eliz	The National Archives, Public Record Office at Kew	C 47/3/39
1578	20 Eliz	Society of Antiquaries, London	MS 537
1579	21 Eliz	Folger Shakespeare Library, Washington	MS Z.d.15
1581	23 Eliz	Eton College, Eton	MS 192
1582	24 Eliz	Somerset Heritage Centre, Taunton	DD\MI/19/1
		British Library, London	Harley 1644
1584	26 Eliz	British Library, London	MS Egerton 3052
1585	27 Eliz	Folger Shakespeare Library, Washington	MS Z.d.16
1588	30 Eliz	British Library, London	MS Additional 8159
1589	31 Eliz	British Library, London	Lansdowne Roll 17
1594	36 Eliz	Dallas Public Library, Dallas	MS 524
1597	39 Eliz	Morgan Library & Museum, New York	MA 3199
		British Library	Facs 672
1598	40 Eliz	The National Archives, Public Record Office at Kew	C 47/3/40
1599	41 Eliz	Folger Shakespeare Library, Washington	MS Z.d.17
1600	42 Eliz	Fondation Martin Bodmer, Geneva	shelfmark unknown
		British Library	RP 294, vol.1
1603	45 Eliz	The National Archives, Public Record Office at Kew	C 47/3/41

Anno Regni Regine
Elizabeth Primo

Neweyeres guiftes Geuon
to the Quenis Maiestie by thiese
persones whose names hereafter ensue, The First of January
The yere abouesaide

Elizabeth R
[sign manual]

59.1 By the Duches of Suff[olk] oone faire Cusshion allouer richly enbrauderid and
sett with pearle and oone booke couerid with purple vellat garnisshid and
clasped with Siluer and guilt of Ecclesiastes
The Cusshion delyuerid to Dauid Vincent
keper of the standing Guarderobe at hamptonnecorte
The book with the Quene
59.2 By the Lady Margret Lennex in a purse of Tyssue in haulf Soueraignes . . . xx li
59.3 By the Lady Margret Strainge in golde. . . . . .vj li xiij s
with the Quene
59.4 By the Duke of Norff[olk] oone faire Standing Cup with a Couer of
Siluer and guilt weing . . . . lix oz
ex et oner
deliuered in to thoffice of Juelles and plate
59.5 By the marquis of Winchester Lorde Treasurer of Englande in a Redde vellat
purse in newe Aungelles. . . . . xx li
59.6 By the Marquis of Northampton in a purse of Red silke and golde in
Aungelles . . . . xx li
with the Quene
And more oone mounte of siluer ower in a Case of Lether
the mounte deliuerid to George Bredeman
keper of the pallace at Westminster

Earls

59.7 By the Earle of Arundell Lorde Stewarde in a purse of Taphata couerid
with a cawle of golde and Siluer in golde . . . . xxx li
59.8 By Therle of Shrewisbury in a Satten purse in golde . . . . xx li
59.9 By Therle of Darbye in a purse of cloth of golde in Demy Soueraignes. . . . xx li
59.10 By Therle of Huntingdon in a red vellat purse in haulf Soueraignes . . . . . . xv li
59.11 By Thearle of Westmarlande in a purse of red silke and siluer knit in
haulf Soueraignes . . . . x li
59.12 By Thearle of Oxfourde Lorde great Chamberlen in a purse of blake
silke and golde knet in haulf Soueraignes. . . . . x li

59.13 By Thearle of Rutlande in a purse of Red silke and siluer knett in haulf
Souferaignes. . . . . x li
59.14 By Thearle of Penbrouke in a red Satten purse in Aungelles . . . . xxx li
59.15 By Thearle of Lennex in a purse of Tyssue in golde . . . . .xiij li vj s
59.16 By Thearle of Bedfurde in a red silke purse knet in haulfe Soueraignes . . . . xx li
59.17 By Thearle of Bathe in a purse of blake silke and gold in golde . . . . x li
59.18 By Thearle of Sussex in a blake silke purse in golde. . . . . x li
59.19 By Thearle of Northumberlande in a purse of blake silke and golde knett
in haulf Soueraignes . . . . x li
59.20 By Thearle of Cumberlande in a purse of purple silke and siluer in haulf
Soueraignes . . . . xx li
with the Quene
59.21 By Thearle of Hartfourde oone partlet and a peire of Ruffes and Sleues
wrought with golde Siluer and Silke
deliuered to Mrs Newton
59.22 By Countie Ferre a Cup or leire with a handell and Spoute of Christall
with a Couer in a Case of blake lether with smale Claspes of Siluer xxiij oz di
ex et oner
deliuered in chardge to the office of the Juells and plate
59.23 By Vicounte Mountegue fourtie pistelattes. . . . . .xij li vj s viij d
with the Quene

Bussoppes

59.24 By the Arche Bussop of Yorke in a red purse in haulf Soueraignes . . . . .xl li
59.25 By the Bussop of Duresmye in a red Satten purse in haulf Soueraignes . . . . . .l li
59.26 By the Bussop of Exetor in a redde purse in new Aungelles . . . . x li
59.27 By the Bussop of London in a red purse in haulf Soueraignes . . . . xx li
59.28 By the Bussop of Lichefelde and Coventrye in a red purse . . . . . . xiij li vj s viij d
59.29 By the Bussop of Worcester in a red purse in haulf Soueraignes. . . . . xx li
59.30 By the Bussop of Lincolne in a vellat purse in haulf Soueraignes. . . . . xx li
59.31 By the Bussop of Bathe in a red purse in haulf Soueraignes . . . . xx li
59.32 By the Bussop of Peterborough in a red purse in golde . . . . xiij li vj s viij d
59.33 By the Bussop of Chester in golde . . . . x li
59.34 By the Bussop of Carlell in a Red Satten purse in haulf Soueraignes . . . . x li
59.35 By the Bussop of St Davies in golde and Siluer . . . . xiij li vj s viij d
59.36 By the Bussop of Winchester in haulf Soueraignes and Aungelles . . . . .l li
with the Quene

Ducheses Marques and Countesses

59.37 By the Duches of Norff[olk] in a purse of blake silke and Siluer knytte
in olde Aungelles . . . . xx li
with the Quene
59.38 By the Duches of Somerset oone Smoke wrought with blake silke and golde
59.39 By the Lady Marques of Northampton oone Lye potte of golde
poz . . . . x oz iij qrt
the Smock deliuered to Mrs Newton and also the lye pott

59.40	By the Countes of Surreye in golde .... v li
59.41	By the Countes of Penbrouke in a Red Satten purse in Aungelles......... xv li
59.42	By the Countes of Bedfourde Dowager in Aungelles and haulf
59.43	Soueraignes .... xx li
59.44	By the Countes of Bedfourde in golde of diuers coynes ....ix li xix s x d
	By the Countes of Oxfourde in a silke purse knett in haulf Soueraignes .... v li
59.45	By the Countes of Shrewisbury Dowager in a purse of blewe silke and
	siluer knytte in Aungelles..................................... xij li
59.46	By the Countes of Huntingdon in golde............................. x li
59.47	By the Countes of Sussex in a blake purse in Aungelles.................. v li
59.48	By the Countes of Rutlande in golde .... x li
59.49	By the Countes of bathe in a purse of blake cloth of golde in golde....... viij li
59.50	By the Countes of Worcester dowager Syxe Double Souferaignes ....ix li
59.51	By the Vicounte Hereforde dowager in a litell Cofer of Crimsen Satten
	enbr with venice golde in Crusadowes twentie .... vj li xiij s iiij d
59.52	By the Vicountes Mountague Twentie and fyve pistelattes ...... vij li xiij s ij d
	with the Quene

Lords

59.53	By the Lorde keper of the grate Seale in a purse of red silke and golde
	knett in Aungells .... x li
59.54	By the Lorde Pagett in a purse of purple silke and siluer knett in di
	soueraignes.. xx li
59.55	By the Lorde William Howarde Lorde Chamberlen in a vellat purse xv
	Duckettes .... x li
59.56	By the Lorde Clinton Lorde Admyrall in a vellat purse in Aungelles .... x li
59.57	By the Lorde Williams of Tame in haulf Soueraignes .... xx li
59.58	By the Lorde Riche in a Red silke purse twentie Soueraignes .... xx li
59.59	By the Lorde Hastinge of Loughborowe in a blake vellat purse in
	golde..xiij li vj s
59.60	By the Lorde Staffourde in a red purse in golde........................ v li
59.61	By the Lorde Windsour in a red silke purse in haulf Soueraignes.......... x li
59.62	By the Lorde John Graye one Cup of mother of pearle garnisshed with
	siluer and guilt weing..xxxv oz
59.63	By the Lorde Northe in a purse of red silke and golde in golde .... xx li
59.64	By the Lorde Barkeley in a red Satten purse......................... x li
59.65	By the Lorde of St Johns in a Taphata purse twentie and sixe olde
	Royalles and oone Angell .... xx li
	with the Quene
59.66	By the Lorde Ambrose Dudley a Remnaunte of blake Satten
	deliuered John Roynon yeoman of the Robes
59.67	By the Lorde Thomas Howarde a Saulte of Christall garnisshed with
	Siluer and guilt weing .... xxviij oz di
	ex et oner
	deliuered to the office of the Juelles and plate

59.68 By the Lorde Mounteioye in a purse of cloth of golde in haulf
       Soueraignes . . . . x li

59.69 By the Lorde Burgaveny in a red Satten purse in golde . . . . v li
                                         with the Quene

59.70 By the Lorde Scrowp a partelet Lynyng Sleueis and Ruffes wrought
     with golde siluer and red Silke
                                deliuered to Mrs Newton

59.71 By the Lorde Shandowes oone handkercher wrought with golde and
     Silke with a purse therin and twelue olde Royalles and two Aungelles . . . . x li
                                      with the Quene

59.72 By the Lorde Hastinges oone loking glasse in a table and on thotherside
     a Globe
                        deliuered to the said george Bredeman

59.73 By the Lorde Graye of Wilton a Ringe with a Diamond

59.74 By the Lorde Robt Dudley Mr of the Horse a faire Cheine set with pearle

59.75 By the Lorde Lumley oone Cup of golde with a Couer poz . . . . x oz di qrt
                                      with the Quene

Ladyes

59.76 By the Lady Pagett in a purse of silke and Siluer knette in golde . . . . x li

59.77 By the Lady Howarde in a vellat purse in Aungelles . . . . x li

59.78 By the Lady Clenton in a rounde purse of blake vellat in golde . . . . x li

59.79 By the Lady Anne Graye in a purse of red silke and gold knet in gold &
     siluer. . . . . Lxj s

59.80 By the Lady Audley in a purse of blake silke and golde in haulf
     soueraignes. . . . . vij li
                                      with the Quene

59.81 By the Lady Shandowes oone handkercher edged with gold with a purse
     therin and in Aungelles . . . . v li
                                  deliuered to Mrs Newton

59.82 By the Lady Butler Twentie Frenche Crownes . . . . vj li vj s viij d
                                      with the Quene

59.83 By the Lady Ratlyf a Smoke wrought with blewe silke and two swete bags
                                  deliuered to Mrs Newton

59.84 By the Lady Masone in haulf soueraignes . . . . v li
                                      with the Quene

59.85 By the Lady Yorke a Combe case of Ibonett furnisshed and a vane wrought
     with silke and a glass to the same
                                deliuered to Mrs Newton

59.86 By the Lady Catesbye in olde Aungelles. . . . . iiij li

59.87 By the Lady Barkeley Sir Mores barkeleyes wif in a purse of silke and
     gold in Aungelles . . . . v li

59.88 By the Lady Lane in Aungelles . . . . v li
                                      with the Quene

59.89 By the Lady Darrell a partelet with a Ruffe wrought with silke & siluer

59.90   By the Lady Hennyngham oone Cusshion cloth of Camrike frenged buttoned
    and tasseled with golde siluer and silke
                              deliuered to Mrs Newton

59.91   By the Lady Cheeke in a purse of red silke and golde in golde . . . . iiij li
                                 with the Quene

59.92   By the Lady Dudley the Lorde Ambrose Dudlyes wif a peire of Sleuis and a
    partelett wrought with golde and siluer
                         with the Quene by Mrs Newton

59.93   By Lady Throgmorton two flaundours Smockes wrought with white worke
                              deliuered to Mrs Newton

59.94   By Lady Cycell in newe Aungelles. . . . . v li

59.95   By Lady Buckeler in golde . . . . v li
                                 with the Quene

59.96   By Lady Mary Sydney oone hole pece of purple vellat
                    deliuered to the said John Roynon

59.97   By Lady Tailboyes Sir Peter Carowes wif in a purse of blake silke and
    Siluer in Aungelles . . . . x li
                                 with the Quene

59.98   By Lady Knowles oone Smoke wrought with gold siluer and silk
                              dd to Mrs Newton

59.99   By Lady Parre a haunce potte with a handle thinner parte glasse finly
    wrought with Siluer parcell guilt weing. . . . . xxxij oz

59.100 By Lady Barkeley in a red satten purse. . . . . v li
                                 with the Quene

59.101 By Lady Lister oone Clocke and six handkercheves edged with
    passamayne of golde

59.102 By the Lady Chamberlen oone Cusshencloth and a Smoke faire wrought
    with golde and silke
                the Cloke dd to Mrs Blaunche Appary the handkercheves
                Cusshen cloth and Smoke dd to Mrs Newton

59.103 By Lady Latemer in a purse of blake silke and siluer in Angelles . . . . v li

59.104 By Lady MontJoy in a silke purse in frenche Crownes. . . . . v li

59.105 By Lady Burgavenye in a Redde Satten purse in golde. . . . . v li

59.106 By Lady Poynes a partelet and a peire of Ruffes wrought with golde and
59.107 Silke
    By Lady Caree in a blake purse in golde. . . . . v li

59.108 By Lady Clerke six handercheves edged with gold and silk
                               with the Quene

Knights

59.109 By Sir Thoms Parrye Comptrowler Two muske Cattes with Liams and
    Collers of silke and golde
             delivered to John Frankwell gent vssher the keper at Hamptonne Courte

59.110 By Sir Edwarde Rogers Vicechamberlen in Soueraignes . . . . vij li

59.111 By Sir William Cicell Secretarie in Aungelles . . . . x li

59.112	By Sir William Peeter in Aungelles	x li
59.113	By Sir Ambrose Cave in olde Royalles . . . . .vij li x s
		with the Quene
59.114	By Sir Richard Sackevile oone rounde perfume of Siluer poz	Lx oz di
59.115	By Sir John Masone in Angelles . . . . .viij li
59.116	By Sir Walter Myldemay in a Crymsen Silke purse in golde . . . . v li
59.117	By Sir Christopher Haydon in a purse of Crymsen silke & siluer . . . . v li
59.118	By Sir Fraunces Inglefelde in golde. . . . . xij li
59.119	By Sir Edwarde Wauldgraue in a Taphata purse in haulf soueraigns . . . . x li
		with the Quene
59.120	By Sir Henry Jernigan a Cup with a Couer of Silver & guilt . . . . .xxx oz
	Gevon to the Lorde Robert Dudley Mr of thorse the same daye	
59.121	By Sir Edmunde Peckham in a purse of Russet silke and gold knet . . . . x li
59.122	By Sir Richarde Southwell in a blewe Satten purse in Angelles . . . . x li
59.123	By Sir John Yorke in haulf Soueraignes . . . . x li
59.124	By Sir Thomas Joslen in a red Satten purse in haulf soueraignes . . . . .vj li
59.125	By Sir Edwarde Warner oone Grediron of Siluer poz . . . . xxxiij oz
59.126	By Sir William Cordall in a litell silke purse in haulf Soueraignes . . . . x li
59.127	By Sir John Thynne in a blake silke purse in Soueraignes . . . . x li
59.128	By Sir William Dansell Twelve olde Royalles . . . . .ix li
59.129	By Sir George Howarde in a lether purse . . . . .ob
59.130	By Sir Thomas Smyth in a knett purse . . . . .vj li
59.131	By Sir James Bullen in golde of Sundry Coynes. . . . . xx li
59.132	By Sir Gawen Carowe Two Portagues. . . . . vij li
59.133	By Sir Thomas Benger oone Ringe of golde with a diamonde	
		with the Quene

Chaplains

59.134	By the Deane of the Chappell archeDeacon carow in soueraignes . . . . x li
59.135	By Doctour Bylle Amner in Aungelles . . . . lxx s
59.136	By Peter Vanne Deane of Salisbury in french Crownes . . . . xij li xiij s iiij d
		with the Quene

Gentlewomen

59.137	By Maistres Ashlye oone partelet and apeire of Ruffes wrought with silk	
59.138	By Mrs Semer widowe oone Spone of mother of pearle with a Steele of	
	Siluer and guilt poz . . . . iij qrt di	
		with the Quene
59.139	By Mrs Penne widowe Sixe handkercheves edged with passamayne of gold	
		dd to Mrs Newton
59.140	By Mrs Pawne oone Cusshion of cloth of golde with workes the baksid	
	of baudken	
59.141	By Mrs Chapell oone Cusshion of purple vellat allouer enbrauderid with	
	Clothe of golde	
		dd to the saide James Harman

59.142　By Mrs Haynes a Smocke wrought with Siluer and blake Silke
dd to the said Mrs Newton

59.143　By Mrs Marven a Smoke wrought with blake Silke
with the Queen by Baptest

59.144　By Mrs Hennage a Smocke wrought with golde siluer and silke purled
　　　with pipes of golde
dd to the said Mrs Newton

59.145　By Zynzans wif oone peire of gloues

59.146　By Mrs Penne Nurse to King Edwarde oone peire of swete Gloues

59.147　By Mrs Bacone of Northhaule a faire purse of red silke & golde knette
dd to Mrs blaunche Appare

59.148　By Mrs Blaunche A parry nine Rooles of golde and siluer
with the Quene by Mr Sackforde

59.149　By Mrs Levina Terling the Quenis picture finly painted vpon a Card
with the Quene by Mrs Newton

59.150　By Mrs Vincent oone Lowe Stowle of waulnuttre Couerid with Cloth of
　　　golde
In the previe Chamber

59.151　By Mrs Frankewell two greate and twentie & foure smale swet bages
with the Quene by Mrs Marbery

59.152　By Mrs Margret Fawkenstone a Marchepane
[blank]

59.153　By Mrs Hunynges Sixe handkercheuers edged with golde
with the Quene by Mrs Dorothye

59.154　By Anes Bylliarde a barrel of Oranges and oone disshe of Marchepanes
[blank]

Gentlemen

59.155　By Mr Astely Maister and threasouror of the Quenis maiesties Juelles
　　　and plate oone portegue . . . . Lxx s
with the Quene

59.156　By Mr North a riche bande and Ruffes with a paire of Sleves alouer
　　　enbrauderid with golde and silke
dd to the said Mrs Newton

59.157　By Mr Thomas Hennage oone Caule wrought with golde siluer and
　　　silke in a bagge of Crymsen Taphata enbrauderid with siluer golde
　　　and pearle
dd to the said Mrs Newton

59.158　By Mr Thoms Hobbye oone longe haunce pott the Inner parte Glasse
　　　couerid with Siluer and parcell guilt weing together. . . . . .xxxv oz
dd in to the said office of Juelles and Plate *ex et oner*

59.159　By Spynolla a Straunger oone foreparte of a kirtell and a peire of sleues
　　　wrought all ouer with golde and silke like vnto a Cawle vpon Crymsen
　　　Satten with a partelet of like worke / oone Lawne for the hedde of
　　　Callacowe Clothe wrought with golde and silke, Two Vanes to holde

in oones Hande of Silke And oone Riding rodde garnisshed with Golde
Silke and pearle all in a Case of wodde couerid with grene vellat
enbrauderid with Siluer

The foreparte dd to the said John Roynon
The rest dd to the said Mrs Newton

59.160 By Bartholomew Campaine oone pece of Clothe of Siluer stained with the
          haulf picture of king Henry theight with a border of blake vellat enbr with
          golde and lined with grene vellat

dd to the said George Bredeman

59.161 By Thomas Stanly in a red purse in Angelles . . . . vj li

with the Quene

59.162 By Docter Wendy Two pottes of Surropes and a boxe of Drogge
59.163 By Docter Maister two pottes of Surropes and oone of Comfettes

with the Quene by Sackeforde

59.164 By Watsone Marchaunte oone guilt Cup with a Couer poz. . . . . xxij oz di

Gevon toThomas Marowe
eodem die

59.165 By Thomas Marowe an Ouche of golde cont fyve Diamondes and iiij
          perles . . . . j oz di di qrt

with the Quene

59.166 By Marke Anthony Erizo two peire of parfumed Gloves

with the Quene

59.167 By Armygell Wade oone Table of Ebonet wherin is a loking glasse and
          Certeine Verses

dd to the said George Bredeman

59.168 By John Younge a book of certeigne Deuises for the Avauncement of
          the state of a Realme couerid with blake vellat edged with siluer
          passamayne

with the Quene

59.169 By Dane Merchaunte oone faire hatt of blake vellat enbrauderid with
          venice golde and damaske golde and laide with passamayne

dd to the said Mrs Newton

59.170 By Robert Robotham a Table painted

with the Quene

59.171 By John Frankewell Gent Vssher oone peire of Swete gloues

with the Quene by Mrs Marbery

59.172 By Phillip Manwaring two peire of gloues wrought with silk Lowpes
59.173 By Whitchurche thre bokes oone of the commen Preier couerid with
          Crimsen vellat another of the Homelyes couered with Lether the
          thirde of a letter couerid with Lether

dd to the said Mrs Blaunche Apparye

59.174 By Aylesworth Two Tables thone of king Henry theight theother of king
          Edwarde the Sixthe

dd to the said George Bredeman

59.175 By Riche Pottecary oone Swetebagge of white Satten

59.176 By John Baptist and his brethrene two bottelles of muskewater and oone
Loking glass couerid with Chrymsen Satten enbrauderid
dd to the said Mrs Newton

59.177 By Thomas Kentt a Songe booke
dd to Mr Lichefelde

59.178 By Tholde Sagbuttes oone basket of Visardes
dd to the said Bredeman

59.179 By Mr Belmaine late schole Mr to King Edward a booke finly printed
De la Vie de la Morte couerid with Crimsen Satten allouer enbrauderid
with golde
dd to the said Mrs Blaunche Apparye

59.180 By Jugge printer oone Mappe Ptholomeis Tables in Italion
The mappe dd to the said georg bredeman

59.181 By Smalwod grocer a boxe of Nutmegges and Gynger wth a boundell
of Sinamond
with the Quene by Mr Sackeford

59.182 By Harres fruterer oone Basket of Apples Wardons and oone glas of
Cheries preseruid
[blank]

59.183 By Lawrence Shrif grocer oone pounde of large Sinnamon oone pounde
of Nutmegges / oone pounde of Cased Gynger oone Sugerlof foure
grate pomegranettes and twentie swete Orainges
with the Quene by Mr Sakford

59.184 By Thomas Browne oone faire Lewte
dd to Mr Lichefelde

59.185 By Smyth Customer oone boult of Camricke

59.186 By Laurence Ball oone dosen of Handkercheves edged with golde
dd to the said Mrs Newton

59.187 By John Grene Cofermaker oone Cofer couerid with Crymsen vellat
edged with passamayne of golde
with the Quene

59.188 By Laurence Brodshawe Suruoire of the workes two Rolles of Camrike
dd to the said Mrs Newton

59.189 By Nicolsone glasseyere two Tables painted vpon glasse
dd to the said George Bredeman

59.190 By Thomas Phaire a booke written of Eneados in Englesh verses
with the Quene

59.191 By John Cavely Thirtene Songe bookes couerid with lether of diuers
makinges
dd to the said Mrs Blaunche Appare

59.192 By Anthony Anthony oone faire purse of passamayne golde and siluer
and in another Litell purse in Angelles . . . . Lx s
with the Quene

59.193 By White Sewer oone peire of perfumed gloues with buttones of golde
with the Quene by Mrs Blaunche Apparye

59.194 By Richarde Holfourde oone peire of perfumed gloues cuffed with
    Crymsen vellat enbrauderid with golde

Gevon to Mrs Newton

59.195 By John Soda pottecary oone potte of Quinces in surrope and oone boxe
    of Alcorses

[blank]

59.196 By Doughtie Bytmaker two byttes for Horses

dd to the Mr of the Horse

59.197 By Alexaunder Zynzan and Robt Zynzan two peire of gloues

59.198 By Robt Kinge oone paire of gloves allouer wrought with silke

59.199 By Cawodde printer Josephus in Greeke

dd to Mrs Blaunche Apparye

59.200 By George Comy musitian two Rounde Globes of Asia and Europa

with the Quene by Baptest

59.201 By Partrige goldsmyth oone pere of guilt Snuffers poz . . . . vj oz

with the Quene

59.202 By John Roose oone Chest with thre Getternes in it

with the Quene by Mr Lichfild

59.203 By Thomas Gemenye two pictures of the Quenis Maistie

[blank]

59.204 By Guillyam Threasouer oone peire of Virgenalls

in the previe Chamber

59.205 By Burnell a Deske of wodde of diuers colores pesed

59.206 By John Keyme Smythe oone faire peire of Aundirons of Irone

dd to the said George bredeman

59.207 By Edwarde Atkensone yeoman purvier of wine Twentie and foure Englesh
    bookes of Sundrey writers vpon the Scripture

59.208 By Nicholas Vrsue oone faire square Clocke guilt

dd to the said Mrs Blaunche

59.209 By Robert Newport gent usher Fesauntes Partriges & Quailes

Gevon to Mr Secretary

59.210 By William St Barbe a Crosbowe

59.211 By Allen Crosbowe maker a Crosbowe

dd to Giles Churchell yeoman of the Crosbowes

59.212 By Nicholas Luzarde a Table painted of the history of Assuerus

dd to the said George Bredeman

59.213 By Pigott the Quenis Mr Cooke a Marchepane being a chessebourde

59.214 By the Sergaunt of the Pastrey a pye of Quinces

with the Quene

59.215 By William Bayarde a Table painted of a king with certeigne Scriptures
    belonging to the same

dd to the said George bredeman

59.216 By the Violandes one boxe of Flowers and smale bottel of swett water

59.217 By Launcellot Stronge a peire of gloues lined with Taphata wrought

with the Quene

59.218 By George Rotherige portingale and Robt Kingeston oone faire Lion of
   Thage of two yeres

                   dd [blank]

59.219 By Rayne Wolfe Printer one bible couerid with Crymsen vellat

             dd to the said Mrs Blaunche

59.220 By Hunynges a Standishe couerid with Crymsen vellat with an Inke pott
   and a Dustbox of Siluer and guilt a penknif thauft of siluer and guilt
   and a penne thande[l] garnisshed with venice golde

     with the Quene by Thomas Astleye grome of the privie Chamber

59.221 By Everade Everdice a Ringe of golde made like Anegles foote with a
   pointed Diamond sett therein with owte the foyle

                 with the Quene

Elizabeth R
[sign manual]

                   Jo Asteley

        Sum – iij m CCl xxiiij li x s viij d ob

Anno Regni Regine
Elizabeth Primo

Newe yeres guiftes geuon by
the Quene her maiestie to those
persones whose names hereafter ensue The First of
January the yere aboue saide
That is to saye

Elizabeth R
[sign manual]

59.222 To the Ladye Fraunces Duches of Suff[olk] oone guilt Cup with a couer
   Branden and Partrige weing . . . . .xxx oz qrt

59.223 To the Lady Margret Lynnex oone guilt Cup with a couer Branden &
   partrige. . . . . xxxviij oz qrt

59.224 To the Lady Margret Straunge oone guilt Cup with a couer B. P
   poz . . . . xvj oz di qrt

59.225 To the Duke of Norff[olk] oone guilt bolle with a Couer Branden and
   Partrige weing . . . . xlvj oz di

59.226 To the Marques of Winchester Lorde Threasorour of Englande one guilt
   Cup with a Couer Branden and Partige weing . . . . .xxxij oz iij qrt

59.227 To the Marques of Northampton oone guilte Cup with a Couer Branden
   and Partrige weing. . . . . xxxvij oz di di qrt

Earls

59.228	To the Earle of Arundell Lorde Stewarde a guilt Cup with a couer Branden and Partrige weing . . . . xlviij oz di
59.229	To the Earle of Shrewisbury a guilt Cup with a couer Branden & Partrige. . . . . xxviij oz iij qrt di
59.230	To the Earle of Darbye oone guilt Cup with a couer Branden & Partrige. . . . . xxviij oz di di qrt
59.231	To the Earle of Huntingdon oone guilt Cup with a couer Raines . . . . xix oz
59.232	To the Earle of Westmerlaunde one guilt Cup with a Couer Branden and Partrige weing. . . . . xviij oz
59.233	To the Earle of Oxfourde Lorde greate Chamberlen oone guilte Cup with a Couer Branden and Partrig weing . . . . xvij oz iij qrt di
59.234	To the Earle of Rutlande oone guilt Cup Branden and Partrige . . . . . .xvij oz qrt
59.235	To the Earle of Penbrouke oone guilt Cup with a Couer B. P poz . . . . xlvij oz di
59.236	To the Earle of Lennex oone guilt Cup with a couer B. P poz. . . . . xxij oz
59.237	To the Earle of Bedfourde oone guilt Cup with a Couer Branden & partrige. . . . . .xxx oz qrt di
59.238	To the Earle of Bathe oone guilt Cup with a Couer Branden & partrige. . . . . .xx oz iij qrt
59.239	To the Earle of Sussex oone guilt bolle Raines weing . . . . xix oz
59.240	To the Earle of Northumberland oone guilt Cup with a couer B. P poz . . . . xxj oz di
59.241	To the Earle of Cumberlande oone guilt Cup Branden and Partrige. . . . . xxix oz iij qrt
59.242	To the Earle of Hartfourde oone guilt Cup Partrige and Branden . . .xxvij oz qrt
59.243	To the Countie Ferre a guilt Cup with a couer Partrige and Brandon weing . . . . xlviij oz di
59.244	To the Vicount Mountegue oone guilt Cup Branden and Partrige . . . .xxij oz qrt

Busshoppes

59.245	To the Arche Busshop of yorke oone guilt bolle with a couer P. B poz . . . . xxviij oz di di qrt
59.246	To the Busshop of Duresme oone guilt bolle B. P weing . . . . xxxij oz di qrt
59.247	To the Busshop of Exetor oone guilt Cruse B. P weing . . . . xvj oz di di qrt
59.248	To the Busshop of Londone oone guilt Cruse Branden and Partrige weing . . . . xix oz iij qrt
59.249	To the Busshop of Lichfelde and Couentrye oone guilt Cruse B. P weing . . . . xvij oz di
59.250	To the Busshop worchester oone guilt bolle Raynes weing . . . . .xxij oz qrt
59.251	To the Busshop of Lincolne oone guilt Cruse Raynes weing. . . . . xx oz
59.252	To the Busshop of Bathe a bolle with a couer guilt Branden & Partrige poz . . . . xxij oz di
59.253	To the Busshop of Peterborough oone guilt Cup Branden and Partrige. . . . . xxj oz di qrt

59.254	To the Busshop of St Dauies oone guilt bolle Branden and partrige	
	weing . . . . xviij oz iij qrt di
59.255	To the Busshop Chester oone guilt bolle Branden and Partrige	
	weing . . . . xvj oz di di qrt
59.256	To the Busshop of Carlell oone guilt Cup with a Couer Branden and	
	Partrige weing . . . . xvj oz
59.257	To the Busshop of Winchester oone guilt bolle with a Couer B P	
	weing . . . . .xxxij oz qrt

Ducheses, Marques, and Countesses

59.258	To the Duches of Norff[olk] oone guilt Cup Brandon and Partrige . xxxiiij oz di
59.259	To the Duches of Somersett oone guilt Cup Brandon and Partrige . . .xvij oz qrt
59.260	To the Lady Marques of Northampton thre guilt bolles with a couer	
	Rayns . . . . lij oz
59.261	To the Countes of Surrey oone hans pott guilt Brandon and	
	Partrige. . . . . xij oz di qrt
59.262	To the Countes of Penbrouke oone guilt Jug Brandon and Partrige . . . xxx oz di
59.263	To the Countes of Bedforde dowager oone guilt bolle B P	
	weing . . . . xxiiij oz di di qrt
59.264	To the Countes of Bedforde oone guilt Cup Brandon and Partrige . xxj oz iij qrt
	To the Countes of Oxfourde oone guilt Cruse Brandon and	
59.265	Partrige. . . . . xj oz iij qrt di
	To the Countes of Shrewisbury Dowager oone guilt Cup B P poz . . . xviij oz qrt
59.266	To the Countes of Huntingdon oone guilt Cruse Brandon & Partrige . . xix oz di
59.267	To the Countes of Sussex oone hans pott guilt Brandon and	
59.268	Partrige. . . . . xiiij oz iij qrt di
	To the Countes of Rutlande oone guilte Cruse Brandon and	
59.269	Partrige. . . . . xviij oz qrt
	To the Countes of Bathe oone hans pott guilt Brandon and Partrige . . . xvj oz di
59.270	To the Countes of Worcester oone hans pot guilt Brandon and	
59.271	Partrige. . . . . .xvj oz di
	To the Vicountes Hereforde oone hans pott guilt Brandon and Partrige	
59.272	weing . . . . xiiij oz qrt di
	To the Vicountes Mountegue oone hance pott guilt Brandon and partrige	
59.273	poz . . . . xiiij oz qrt

Lords

59.274	To the Lorde Keper of the greate Seale oone guilt Jug Raynes weing . . . xxiiij oz
59.275	To the Lorde Paget oone guilt Cup Brandon and Partrige weing . . . . . . xxvij oz
59.276	To the Lorde William Howarde Lorde Chamberlen oone guilt Cup	
	B P . . . . xxvj oz qrter
59.277	To the Lorde Clynton Lorde Admyrall oone guilt Cup B. P . . .xxj oz iij qtrers di
59.278	To the Lorde Williams of Thame oone oone [sic] guilt Cup Raynes	
	weing . . . . .xxviij oz iij qrt di
59.279	To the Lorde Riche oone guilt Cup Raynes weing . . . . xxvj oz qrt
59.280	To the Lorde Hastinges of Loughborowe oone guilt Cup B P poz . . . . xxj oz

59.281   To the Lorde Staffourde oone hans pott guilt Brandon and
Partrige. . . . . xij oz di qrt

59.282   To the Lorde Windsor oone guilt bolle Brandon and Partrige
weing . . . . .xx oz iij qrt

59.283   To the Lorde John Graye oone guilt bolle Raynes weing. . . . . .xxxv oz

59.284   To the Lorde Northe oone guilt cup Brandon and partrige weing . . . xxvij oz di

59.285   To the Lorde Barkeley oone guilt Cruse Brandon and Partrige. . . . . xix oz di

59.286   To the Lorde of St Johns oone guilt Cup Brandon and Partrige. . . . . .xxv oz qrt

59.287   To the Lorde Ambrose Dudley oone guilt Cruse Brandon and
Partrige. . . . . xvij oz di di qrt

59.288   To the Lorde Thomas Howarde oone guilt Salte Raynes weing . . . . . .xvij oz qrt

59.289   To the Lord MounteJoye oone guilt Cruse Brandon and
Partrige. . . . . xix oz iij qrt di

59.290   To the Lorde Burgavenye oone guilt Salte Brandon and Partrige . . . . xj oz di

59.291   To the Lorde Scrowpe oone guilt Cruse Brandon and Partrige . . xvij oz di di qrt

59.292   To the Lorde Shandowes oone guilt Cruse B. P weing. . . . . xix oz iij qrt di

59.293   To the Lorde Hastinges oone guilt Salte Brandon and Partrig . . . . . . x oz iij qrt

59.294   To the Lorde Robt Dudley Mr of the Horse oone guilte bolle Gevon
to the Quene by Sir Henry Jernegan the same Daye. . . . . .xxx oz

59.295   To the Lorde Lumley oone guilt bolle with a couer B P weing . . xxxj oz iij qrt di

Ladyes

59.296   To the Lady Pagett oone Hans pott guilt Brandon and Partrige . . . . xvj oz qrt di

59.297   To the Lady Howarde oone Magdaline Cup guilt B. P weing . . . .xxj oz iij qrters

59.298   To the Lady Clynton oone guilt Cup Brandon and Partrige poz. . xxiiij oz qrt di

59.299   To the Lady Anne Gray oone guilt Cruse Brandon and Partrige . . . . xj oz qrt di

59.300   To the Lady Audley oone hans pott guilt Brandon and Partrige. . . . . . xiiij oz di

59.301   To the Lady Shandowes oone hans pott guilt B. P weing. . . . . xiiij oz qrt

59.302   To the Lady Butler oone guilt Cruse Brandon and Partrige . . . . .xvij oz qrt

59.303   To the Lady Ratlif oone guilt Cruse Brandon and Partrige poz . .xiij oz iij qrters

59.304   To the Lady Mason oone hans pott guilt Brandon and Partrige. . . . xiij oz di qrt

59.305   To the Lady Yorke oone guilt Salte Brandon and Partrige poz . . . . xj oz

59.306   To the Lady Catesbye oone guilt Cruse Brandon and Partrige .viij oz iij qrters di

59.307   To the Lady Barkeley Sir Mores barkeleys wif a hans pott guilt Brandon
and Partrige weing . . . . xiiij oz di qrt

59.308   To the Lady Lane oone guilt Cruse Brandon and Partrige poz . . . . xiij oz qrt

59.309   To the Lady Dorrell oone guilt Cup Brandon and Partrig weing . . . . .xxj oz

59.310   To the Lady Henyngham oone guilt Salte Brandon and Partrige . . . viij oz qrt di

59.311   To the Lady Cheeke oone guilt Salte Brandon and Partrige weing . xj oz iij qrt di

59.312   To the Lady Dudley the Lorde Ambrose Dudleyes wif oone guilt Cup
Brandon and Partrige weing . . . . xv oz di di qrt

59.313   To the Lady Throgmorton oone guilte Cup Brandon and Partrige. . . . xiij oz qrt

59.314   To the Lady Cycell oone hans pott guilt Brandon and Partrige. . . . . . . .xv oz qrt

59.315   To the Lady Buckeley oone guilt Salte Brandon and Partrige . . . . x oz iij qrtes di

59.316   To the Lady Mary Sydney oone guilt Cruse B. P . . . . .xxiij oz iij qrt

59.317   To the Lady Carewe Sir Peter Carewis wif oone guilte Cup Brandon and
Partrige weing . . . . xxiiij oz iij qrt di

59.318   To the Lady Parrye oone guilt Cup Brandon and Partrige . . . . . . xxiiij oz di qrt

59.319   To the Lady Barkeley the Lorde Barkelyes wif oone guilte Cruse
Brandon and Partrige . . . . xiij oz iij qrt di

59.320   To the Lady Lyster oone guilt Cruse Brandon & Partrige . . . . ix oz iij qrt

59.321   To the Lady Chamberlen oone hans pott guilt Brandon and
Partrige. . . . . xv oz di qrt

59.322   To the Lady Lattemer oone guilt Cup Brandon and Partrige weing . xiij oz di qrt

59.323   To the Lady MounteJoye oone guilt Cup Brandon and Partrige
weing . . . . xxj oz iij qrt

59.234   To the Lady Burgaveny oone guilt Salte Raynes poz . . . . xij oz qrt

59.235   To the Lady Poynes oone guilt bolle Brandon and Partrige weing . . . . . xxj oz di

59.236   To the Lady Caree oone guilt Cup Brandon and Parterige weing . . . . xvj [oz] qrt

59.237   To the Lady Clerke oone guilte Saulte Brandon and Parterige poz. . . xj oz iij qrt

Knights

59.328   To Sir Thomas Parrye Comptroller two hans pottes guilt B. P
poz . . . . xxviij oz di di qrt

59.329   To Sir Edwarde Rogers oone hans pott guilt Brandon and
Partrige. . . . . xvij oz iij qrt

59.330   To Sir William Cycell Secretary oone guilt Cup with a couer B. P
weing . . . . xxvj oz di

59.331   To Sir William Peeter oone guilt bolle Raynes weing . . . . xix oz di

59.332   To Sir Ambrouse Cave oone hans pott guilt Brandon and Partrige. . . xiiij oz qrt

59.333   To Sir Richarde Sackevile oone guilt Cup Brandon and Partrige . xxviij oz iij qrt

59.334   To Sir John Mason oone guilt Jug Raynes poz. . . . . xix oz iij qrt

59.335   To Sir Waulter Myldemay oone hans pott guilt Brandon and P . . . . xvj oz iij qrt

59.336   To Sir Christopher Haydon oone Tankerde Brandon and Partrige . . . . xx oz

59.337   To Sir Fraunces Inglefelde oone guilt Cruse Brandon and Partrige
poz . . . . xvij oz di di qrt

59.338   To Sir Edwarde Wauldgraue oone hance pott Brandon and
Partrige. . . . . xvj oz di di qrt

59.339   To Sir Henry Jernegam oone guilt Cruse Brandon and Partrige
weing . . . . xviij oz iij qrt di

59.340   To Sir Edmunde Pecham oone guilt Cruse Brandon and Partrige
weing . . . . xvij oz di qrt

59.341   To Sir Richard Southwell oone hans pott guilt Brandon and
Partrig . . . . xvj oz di qrt

59.342   To Sir John Yorke oone guilt Cup Brandon and Partrige weing . . xx oz iij qrt di

59.343   To Sir Thomas Jostelen oone guilt Cruse Brandon and Partrige
weing . . . . xiiij oz iij qrt di

59.344   To Sir Edwarde Warner oone hans pott guilt Brandon and Partrig. . . . . xix oz di

59.345   To Sir William Cordall oone guilt Cruse Brandon and Partrige poz. . . xvij oz di

59.346   To Sir John Thynne oone guilt Cup Brandon and Partrige poz. . . . . xxij oz

59.347   To Sir William Dansell oone guilt bolle Brandon and Partrige . . xxij oz iij qrt di

59.348   To Sir George Howard oone magdaline Cup guilt Raynes weing . . . . xxij oz

59.349   To Sir Thomas Smyth oone hans pott guilt Brandon and Partrige
      weing . . . . xv oz di qrt

59.350   To Sir James Bullen oone guilt Cup Brandon and Partrige weing. . . . xxvj oz qrt

59.351   To Sir Gowen Carew oone hans pott guilt Brandon and Partrige
      weing . . . . xvj oz qrt

59.352   To Sir Thomas Benger oone guilt Cup Brandon and Partrige weing. . . .xv oz qrt

Chaplains

59.353   To the Deane of the Chappell Arche Deacon Carow oone guilt Cup
      Brandon and Partrige weing . . . . xxij oz

59.354   To Doctor Bylle Amner oone guilt Salte brandon and Partrige . . . . . ix oz qrt di

59.355   To Peter Vanne Deane of Salisbury oone guilt bolle Raynes weing. . xxj oz qrt di

Gentlewomen

59.356   To Maistres Astelye oone guilte Tankerd B P weing – xx oz qrt di / And
      oone guilt Cruse Brandon and Partrige weing – xxij oz di di qrt weing
      togethers. . . . . xliij oz

59.357   To Mrs Blaunch Apparrye oone guilt Salte Raynes weing. . . . . xv oz

59.358   To Mrs Hennage oone guilt bolle Brandon and Partrige weing. . . xxiiij oz qrt di

59.359   To Mrs Frankenwell oone guilt Cruse Brandon and Partrige weing . . x oz iij qrt

59.360   To Mrs Levina Terling oone Casting bottell guilt Raynes weing . . . . . ij oz iij qrt

59.361   To Mrs Vincent oone guilt Salte Raynes weing . . . . xiiij oz di qrt

59.362   To Mrs Penne Late nurse to King Edwarde a guilt Cruse B & P
      poz . . . . x oz di di qrt

59.363   To Mrs Bacone of Northhaule two guilt Spones B P weing. . . . . iiij oz

59.364   To Mrs Seymour widdowe oone guilt Salte Raynes weing. . . . . . . viij oz iij qrt di

59.365   To Mrs Penne widdowe a hans pott guilt Brandon and Partrige
      weing . . . . xij oz di qrt

59.366   To Mrs Hunnynges oone guilt Cruse Raynes poz. . . . . viij oz

59.367   To Mrs Pawne oone guilt Salt Brandon and Partrige weing . . . . iiij oz iij qrt

59.368   To Mrs Chappell oone guilt Salte Brandon and Partrige weing . . . . . ix oz di qrt

59.369   To Mrs Heynes oone guilt Cruse Brandon and Partrige weing . . . . x oz

59.370   To Mrs Marven oone guilt Salte Raynes poz . . . . xvij oz di di qrt

59.371   To Zynzans wif for her and her two Sonnes thre guilt Spones B. P poz . . . . vj oz

59.372   To Anes Byllyarde oone guilt Spone Brandon and Partrige poz . . . . ij oz

Freguiftes

59.373   To the Lady Kateryne Graye oone of the Quenes maydes oone guilte
      Cruse Brandon and Partrige weing. . . . . x oz di

59.374   To the Lady Jane Seymer oone other of the maides oone guilt Cruse
      Brandon and Partrige weing . . . . x oz qrt di

59.375   To the Lady Jane Howarde oone guilt Cruse Brandon and Partrige . . . . .x oz qrt

59.376   To Mrs Mary Howarde one of the maides oone guilt Cruse B. P weing . .x oz qrt

59.377   To Mrs Douglas Howarde a maide oone guilt Cruse B. P weing . . . . .x oz qrt

59.378	To Mrs Mary Manxell a maide oone guilt Cruse B. P weing . . . . x oz di qrt
59.379	To Mrs Morys mother of the maides oone guilt Cruse B. P weing . . . x oz di qrt

Gentlemen

59.380	To Maistre Astely Mr of the Juelles and Plate oone guilt Cruse B P . . . . xvij oz iij qrt
59.381	To Mr Roger North oone guilt Cruse Brandon and Partrige weing . xix oz iij qrt
59.382	To Mr Thomas Hobbye oone guilt Cup Brandon and Partrige weing . . . . .xv oz iij qrt
59.383	To Spynulla oone guilt bolle Brandon and Partrige weing. . . . . xxix oz di qrt
59.384	To Bartholomew Compane oone guilt Cruse B P weing . . . . xij oz
59.385	To Thomas Stanlye oone guilt Cruse Brandon and Partrige weing . . xij oz qrt di
59.386	To Doctour Wendie oone guilt Cruse Brandon and Partrige weing . . x oz di qrt
59.387	To Doctor Maister oone guilt Cruse Brandon and Partrige weing . . . . . .x oz qrt
59.388	To Watsone Merchaunte oone guilt bolle Brandon and Partrige weing . xxiiij oz
59.389	To Thomas Marowe oone guilt Cup gevon by Watsone Merchaunte
59.390	the same daye weing. . . . . xxij oz di
	To Armygell Wadde oone guilt Cruse Brandon and Partrige weing . . . . .v oz qrt
59.391	To Mark Anthony Erizo oone guilt Bolle Brandon and Partrige weing . . . . vij oz iij qrt di
59.392	To John Younge oone Casting bottell guilt Raynes . . . . vij oz qrt
59.393	To John Frankewell gent. vssher oone guilt Salte Brandon and Partrige . . iiij oz
59.394	To Philip Manwaring oone guilt Cup Raynes weing . . . . x oz qtr di
59.395	To Rayne Wolf oone guilt Cruse Brandon and Partrige weing . . . . . . xj oz di qrt
59.396	To Whitchurche Printer oone guilt Salte Brandon and Partrige weing . . . . .iij oz iij qrt di
59.397	To Aylworth oone guilt Cruse Brandon and Partrige weing . . . . viij oz iij qrt
59.398	To Riche Pottecary oone guilt Salte Brandon and Partrige weing. . . . .j oz qrt di
59.399	To John Baptest basson musition oone guilt Salt Brandon and Partrige. . . . . ij oz di di qrt
59.400	To Augustine Basson / Anthony Basson Jasper Basson and John basson musitions foure guilt Spones Brandon and Partrige weing. . . . . .viij oz
59.401	To Thomas Kent oone guilt Cruse Brandon and Partrige weing. . . . . .viij oz
59.402	To the olde Sagbuttes Anthony Mary Edward Device John Pecoke and Nicolas Androwe oone peper boxe guilt Raynes poz . . . . .vj oz di
59.403	To Jugge prenter oone guilt Salte Raynes poz . . . . .vj oz di di qrt
59.404	To Belmayne oone guilt Casting bottell Raynes poz . . . . .vj oz qrt di
59.405	To Smalwodd grocer oone guilt Cruse Brandon and Partrige weing. . . . vij oz di
59.406	To Harres Fruterer thre guilt Spones Brandon and Partrige weing . . . . .vj oz
59.407	To Laurence Sheryffe oone guilt Salte Brandon and Partrige weing . . v oz qrt di
59.408	To Thomas Browne oone hans pott Brandon and Partrige weing. . . . . .xv oz qrt
59.409	To Smyth Customer oone guilt Cruse Raynes weing . . . . .xiij oz di
59.410	To Laurence Ball oone guilt Salte Brandon and Partrige weing . . . . .iiij oz
59.411	To John Grene cofermaker oone guilt Cruse B and P poz. . . . . x oz di di qrt
59.412	To Hunnynges oone guilt Cruse Raynes poz . . . . x oz
59.413	To Bradshawe Surueire of the Workes oone hans pott B P poz. . . . . .xiij oz

59.414	To Nicolsone Glasyere oone guilt Spone Brandon and Partrige	ij oz
59.415	To Thomas Phaire oone Casting bottell guilt B P weing	v oz di
59.416	To Cawuelye two guilt Spones Brandon and Partrige weing	iiij oz
59.417	To Anthony Anthony oone guilt Tankerd B P weing	xiij oz iij qrt di
59.418	To White Sewer oone guilt Salte Brandon and Partrige weing	iij oz di qrt
59.419	To Richard Holferde oone guilt Salte Brandon and Partrige poz	iij oz qrt
59.420	To John Soda oone guilt Cruse Brandon and Partrige	viij oz
59.421	To Doughtie two guilt Spones Brandon and Partrige weing	iiij oz
59.422	To Robt King oone guilt Spone Raynes weing	ij oz
59.423	To Cawodde Printer two guilt Spones Raynes poz	iiij oz
59.424	To George Comy a guilt Salte Brandon and Partrige weing	ij oz di di qrt
59.425	To Partrige Goldsmyth oone guilt Salte Brandon and Partrige weing	vj oz
59.426	To John Roose oone guilt Tankerd Brandon and Partrige weing	xiij oz iij qrt di
59.427	To Thomas Gemeny oone guilt Salte Brandon and Partrige weing	ij oz iij qrt
59.428	To Guilham Threasouror oone guilt Cruse Brandon and Partrige	x oz di di qrt
59.429	To Burnell thre guilt Spones Raynes weing	vj oz
59.430	To Keyme Smyth oone guilt Cruse Brandon and Partrige weing	ix oz iij qrt di
59.431	To Edward Atkynsone oone guilt Spone Raynes weing	ij oz
59.432	To Nicholas Vrsue oone guilt cruse Brandon and Partrige weing	xj oz
59.433	To William St barbe oone guilt Tankerde Brandon and Partrige	viiij oz
59.434	To Allen Crosbowe maker oone guilt Tankerde Brandon and Partrige	xiij oz iij qrt
59.435	To Nicholas Luzarde painter oone guilt Cruse Brandon and Partrige	viij oz qrt di
59.436	To Robert Robotham oone guilt bolle with a couer Brandon and Partrige	viij oz di qrt
59.437	To Pigott the Quenis Mr Cooke oone guilt Salt B P weing	vij oz
59.438	To the Sergaunte of the Pastry oone guilt Salte B P weing	ij oz di di qrt
59.349	To William Bayarde a Painter oone guilt Salte Raynes poz	iij oz qrt di
59.440	To Albert Devenice Ambrose de Myllayne Fraunces De Venice Marke Anthony Gayardell / Peter Gayardell / and Innocent Come Violandes foure guilt Spones Raynes weing	viij oz qrt
59.441	To Launcellot stronge oone guilt Spone Rayne weing	ij oz
59.442	To Evererd Everdice oone guilt Cruse Brandon and pertridge weing	xvj oz di

Freeguiftes

59.443	To Mr Drewe Drewery oone guilt Salt Raynes weing	xij oz qrt di
59.444	To John Roynon Yeomane of the Roobes oone guilt Cruse B P poz	xj oz iij qrt di
59.445	To Thomas Asteley grome of the previe Chamber oone guilt Salt B P	v oz
59.446	To Henry Sackefourde grome also a guilt Salt B P weing	v oz
59.447	To Baptest also a grome oone guilt Salte B P weing	v oz
59.448	To Nicholas Bristowe Clerke of the office of the Juelles and plate oone guilt Cruse Raynes weing	x oz iij qrt di

59.449   To John Kyrkeby yeoman of same Office oone guilt Cruse Raynes
       weing . . . . x oz iij qrt di

59.450   To Edmund Pigeon yeoman also oone guilt Cruse Brandon and
       Partrig . . . . x oz iij qrt di

59.451   To John Pigeon Grome of the saide Office oone guilt Cruse Raynes
       weing . . . . x oz iij qrt di

59.452   To John Tamworth oone of the gromes of the previe Chamber guilt salt . . . v oz

Taken for fees at our Coronation

59.453   The Lorde Ambrose Dudle
       Taken by the Lorde Ambrose Dudley being Cheefe pantler oone
          Standing Trencher of Siluer and guilt of the Chardge of
          Richard Wilbraham deceassed . . . . xxviij oz *ex per oer*
       Item more oone Spone of golde with a wrethen Steele and the
          Quenes Armes enamelid at thend of the chardge of Richard
          Wilbraham weing. . . . . ij oz di *ex per oer*
       Item oone Salte of Syluer and guilt with a Couer enamelid of
          Thistorye of Joobe of the saide Chardge weing . . . . xlviij oz *ex per oer*
       Item oone brode knif and oone Carving knif Thaftes of Siluer and
          guilt of the said Chardge of Richard Wilbraham. . . . . *ex per oer*
       Item oone smale knif thaft of siluer enamelid of the said chardge . . *ex per oer*
       Item oone Strayner of Siluer guilt of the saide chardge poz . . . . viij oz di
          charged in the book of charges but . . . . vij oz
       Item oone Forke with a Spoone at thende of Siluer and guilte of the
          chardge of the said Richard Wilbraham poz . . . . .j oz qrt *ex per oer*

59.454   The Earle of Oxforde
       Item taken by the Earle of Oxfourde Chef Ewer oone peire of Couerid
          basones guilt of the chardge of the said Richard Wilbraham
          poz . . . . CCxj oz *ex per oer*
       Item oone guilt Cup of assaye of the said Chardge poz. . . . . . vij oz *ex per oer*

59.455   Sir Robert Dymoke
       Item taken by Sir Robert Demoke Champion oone Cup of golde with
          a couer newemade of an Ingott of golde of the saide Chardge
          weing . . . . xviij oz iij qrt di *ex per oer*

59.456   The Maire of London
       Item taken by the mayer of London oone Cup of golde with a couer
          newemade of the saide Ingott poz. . . . . xv oz iij qrt di *ex per oer*

59.457   Sir Giles Allington
       Item taken by Sir Gyles Allington knight oone Cup of Siluer and guilt
          with a couer bought of the Late Cardenall his Executors
          weing . . . . xxv oz qrt *ex per oer*

59.458   Geuon at the Christeni[n]g of the L. Williams of Tame his Doughter
       Item Gevon by our commandement at the Christening of the lorde
          Williams of Tame his Doughter the xxiiij[th] of Januerry Anno Regne
          regine primo oone guilt Cup with a Couer parcell of the Chardge
          of the saide Richard Wilbraham poz . . . . xxvij oz iij qrt di *ex per oer*

59.459   Mr Braye amner

Item taken by Maister Braye chefe Amner oone Sheppe of Siluer and
guilt of the Chardge of the said Richarde Wilbraham weing
. . . . CCCv oz di *ex per oer*

Elizabeth R
[sign manual]

J Asteley

Anno Regni Reginae Elizabethae Quarto

Neweyeur's Giftes geuon
to the Queene her Majestie by those persons whose
Names hereafter ensue the first of January the
Yere above written
viz

Elizabeth R
[sign manual] . . . .

62.1 By the Lady Margaret Strainge a litle rounde Mounte of golde to conteyne a
      pomaunder in it

                                              with the Quene her majestie

Dukes Marquesses and Earles

62.2 By the Duke of Norfolke in a purse of purple silke and golde knitt in
      sundry coynes of golde . . . . xx li
62.3 By the Marques of Wynchester highe Threasourer of Englande in a purse
      of crymsen Satten in Angelles . . . . xx li
62.4 By the Marques of Northampton in a purse of crymsen silke and golde
      knytt in Dimy Soueraignes . . . . xx li
62.5 By the Earle of Arundell Lorde Stewearde in a paper in Angelles. . . . . xxx li
62.6 By the Earle of Shrewisburye in a red silke purse in Dimy Soueraignes . . . . xx li
62.7 By the Earle of Darbye in a purse of crymsen Satten enbrauderid with
      golde in Dimy soueraignes. . . . . xx li
62.8 By the Earle of Pembroke in a purse of blak silke and siluer knytt in new
      Angelles . . . . xxx li
62.9 By the Earle of Bedforde in a purse of blak silke and golde knytt in Dimy
      Soueraignes . . . . xx li
62.10 By the Earle of Rutlande in a purse of red silke and golde knytt in Dimy
      soueraignes & Angelles . . . . xx li
62.11 By the Earle of Huntingdon in a red silke purse in Angelles . . . . xv li
62.12 By the Earle of Westmerlande in a red silke purse in Dimy soueraignes . . . . . x li
62.13 By the Earle of Oxforde in a red silke purse in Dimy soueraignes. . . . . x li
62.14 By the Earle of Northumberlande in a purse of blak silke and siluer
      knytt in Angelles . . . . x li

                                              with the Quene her highnes
62.15 By the Earle of Warwicke a Smocke wrought with blak silke, a peire of
      Slevis and a partelett wrought with golde siluer and blak silke

                                              Delyverid to the Lady Cobham
62.16 By the Viscounte Mountague in a purse of cloth of golde in Dimy
      soueraignes. . . . . x li

                                              with her said Matie

Busshopps

62.17 By the Archebusshop of Cavnterbury in a red silke purse in Dimy
       Soueraignes . . . . xl li
62.18 By the Archebusshop of Yorke in soueraignes . . . . xxx li
62.19 By the Busshop of Duresme in a purse of crymsen silke and golde knytt
       in Angelles . . . . xxx li
62.20 By the Busshop of Elye in a red vellat purse in Angelles . . . . xxx li
62.21 By the Busshop of Wynchester in a purse of crymsen silke and golde
       knytt and sett with pearle in Angelles . . . . xx li
62.22 By the Busshop of London in a red Satten purse in Dimy Soueraignes . . . . xx li
62.23 By the Busshop of Salisbury in a red Satten purse in Dimy Soueraignes . . . xx li
62.24 By the Busshop of Worcester in a blak vellat purse in Dimy Soueraignes. . . xx li
62.25 By the Busshop of Lyncolne in a red purse in Dimy Soueraignes . . . . xx li
62.26 By the Busshop of Chichester in a red purse in Dimy Soueraignes . . . . x li
62.27 By the Busshop of Norwiche in a blewe silke purse . . . . xiij li vj s viij d
62.28 By the Busshop of Hereforde in a grene silke purse in Dimy soueraignes. . . . x li
62.29 By the Busshop of Lytchfilde and Coventrye in a red Satten purse in
       Angelles . . . . xiij li
62.30 By the Busshop of Rochester in a red purse in golde . . . . xiij li vj s viij d
62.31 By the Busshop of Ste Davies in a red silke purse in Angelles . . . . x li
62.32 By the Busshop of Bathe in a purse of red silke in Angelles . . . . x li
62.33 By the Busshop of Exetor in a blewe silke purse in Angelles . . . . x li
62.34 By the Busshop of Peterborowe in a red purse in Dimy soueraignes. . . . . x li
62.35 By the Busshop of Chester in a red purse in Angelles and soueraignes. . . . . . x li
                                                                with her said majestie

Duches and Countes

62.36 By the Duches of Norfolke in a purse of crymsen silke and golde knytt
       in Angelles . . . . xx li
62.37 By the Duches of Somersett in a purse of siluer and blak silke in Royalles
       and Duckettes . . . . xiiij li
62.38 By the Countes of Surrey in a purse of tawny silke and golde in Dimy
       soueraignes. . . . . C s
62.39 By the Countes of Pembroke in a cherry bag of crymsen Satten in new
       Angelles . . . . xv li
62.40 By the Countes of Bedforde in a purse of crymsen silke and siluer knytt
       in Dimy soueraiges . . . . x li
62.41 By the Countes of Darbye in a purse of crymsen Satten enbrauderid with
       golde in Dimy soueraignes. . . . . x li
62.42 By the Countes of Oxford in a red purse in Dimy soueraignes . . . . C s
62.43 By the Countes of Shrewisbury Dowager a purse of blak silke and golde
       knytt in Dimy soueraignes. . . . . xij li
62.44 By the Countes of Shrewisbvry in a red silke purse knytt in Dimy
       Soueraignes . . . . x li

62.45 By the Countes of Huntingdon Dowager in a red purse in Dimy
Soueraignes . . . . x li
62.46 By the Countes of Huntingdon in a red purse in Angelles. . . . . x li
62.47 By the Countes of Northumberlande in a purse of blak silke and siluer
knytt in Angelles . . . . x li
62.48 By the Countes of Rutlande in a red purse in Dimy Soueraignes . xiij li vj s viij d
with her said majestie

Viscountes

62.49 By the Viscountes Hereforde Dowager sixe hankercheves edgid with golde
Delyuerid to the said Lady Cobham
62.50 By the Viscountes Montague in a purse of cloth of golde in Dimy
Soueraignes . . . . x li
with her said majestie

Lordes

62.51 By the Lorde keper of the greate Seale Bacon in a purse of siluer knytt in
Angelles . . . . xiij li vj s viij d
62.52 By the Lorde William Howarde Lorde Chamberlen in a purse of crymsen
silke and golde knytt in Dimy Soueraignes. . . . . x li
62.53 By the Lorde Pagett in a greene purse in Dimy Soueraignes . . . . . xiij li vj s viij d
62.54 By the Lorde Clynton Lorde Admyrall in golde. . . . . x li
62.55 By the Lorde Riche in a red Satten purse in Dimy Soueraignes. . . . . xx li
62.56 By the Lorde North in a purse of purple silke and siluer in Dimy
soueraignes. . . . . xx li
62.57 By the Lorde Lumley in a paper in Angelles . . . . xx li
62.58 By the Lorde Hastinges of Lougheborowe in a red silke purse in Frenche
Crownes . . . . .xiij li
62.59 By the Lorde Stafforde in a red purse in Dimy Soueraignes . . . . C s
62.60 By the Lorde Windsor in a purse of crymsen silke and golde knytt in Dimy
Soueraignes . . . . x li
with her said Matie
62.61 By the Lorde John Graye a haunce pott of Allablaster garnesshid with siluer
guilte

ex et oner

Delyuerid in chardge to John Asteley esquier Mr and
Threasourer of her highnes Juelles and plate
62.62 By the Lorde Barkeley in a red purse in golde . . . . x li
62.63 By the Lorde Movntejoye in a red purse in Dimy soueraignes . . . . x li
62.64 By the Lorde Aburgavennye in a purse of red silke in Dimy soueraignes . . . . C s
62.65 By the Lorde Scrowpe in a purse of blak silke and siluer knytt in Angelles . . x li
62.66 By the Lorde Caree of Hundesdon in a purse of crymsen silke in doble
Duckettes . . . . xiij li vj s viij d
62.67 By the Lorde Strainge in a purse of red silke and golde in Dimy
soueraignes. . . . . C s

62.68 By the Lorde Darcey of Chichey in a red purse in Dimy soueraignes . . . . x li
62.69 By the Lorde Shefilde in a red silke purse in golde . . . . x li
62.70 By the Lorde Shandowes in a blak silke purse in Angelles . . . . x li
                                                                    with her said majestie

Ladyes

62.71 By the Lady Howarde in a purse of crymsen silke and golde knytt in Dimy
          Soueraignes . . . . x li
                                                                    with her said Matie

62.72 By the Lady Clinton a peire of Sleevis of golde pulled out with Lawne
                                                         Delyuerid to the said Lady Cobham
62.73 By the Lady Pagett in golde . . . . vj li xiij s iiij d
62.74 By the Lady Barkeley Lorde Barkeleyes wief in golde . . . . C s
62.75 By the Lady Mountejoye in a red silke purse in Angelles . . . . x li
62.76 By the Lady Aburgavenny in a red Satten purse in Dimy soueraignes . . . . C s
62.77 By the Lady Caree of Hundesdon in a blak purse knytt in Angelles . . . . x li
62.78 By the Lady Taylboyes Sir Peter Carewes wyf in a purse of blak silke and
          siluer in Dimy soueraignes . . . . x li
                                                                    with her said majestie

62.79 By the Lady Cobham a partelett and a peire of slevis of sypers wrought
          with siluer & blak silke
                                                                    redelyverid to her self
62.80 By the Lady Dakers a warmyng Ball of golde poz . . . . iij oz di
                                                                    with her said majestie
62.81 By the Lady Shefilde a peire of Slevis wrought with frenges of blak silke
          and lozenges of gold
                                                         Delyuerid to the said Lady Cobham
62.82 By the Lady Scrowpe in a purse of blak silke and siluer in Angelles . . . . vij li
                                                                    with her said majestie
62.83 By the Lady Shandowes a peire of Sleves and a partelett of golde & siluer
          knytt cawle facon
                                                         Delyuerid to the said Lady Cobham
62.84 By the Lady Knowlles a feyre Carpett of nedleworke chevernde frengid
          and buttoned with gold and silke
                                          Delyuerid to John Tameworth grome of the pryvye Chamber
62.85 By the Lady Butler in a litle white purse in frenche Crownes . . . . vj li
                                                                    with her said majestie
62.86 By the Lady Radlyef a peire of slevis of Cameryk allouer sett with purle
          and two swete baggs
                                                         Delyuerid to the said Lady Cobham
62.87 By the Lady Mason in a purse of blak silke and golde knytt in
          soueraignes . . . . vj li
                                                                    with her said majestie
62.88 By the Lady Yorke thre sugar loves and a barrell of suckett
                                                               Delyuerid to Mrs Asteley

62.89 By the Lady Cycell a partelett and a peire of Sleves wrought with
    Roundells of golde frenge and drawen owte with Syphers
62.90 By the Lady Lane sixe handkercheves foure of them blak silke and golde
    & two of red silke
62.91 By the Lady Henningham sixe handekercheves garnesshid with golde siluer
    and silke
                           Delyuerid to the said Lady Cobham
62.92 By the Lady Cheeke in a russett silke purse . . . . iiij li
62.93 By the Lady Pallat in a cherry bag of crymsen Satten in Angelles . . . . C s
                                 with her said Matie
62.94 By the Lady Stlowe oone peire of Sleves of fyne Cameryke enbrauderid
    with Goldesmythes worke of siluer guilt and a pece of purle vpon a
    paper to edge them
62.95 By the Lady Woodehouse a partelett and a peire of Slevis wrought with
    golde and silke, tuffed owte with Cameryk
62.96 By the Lady Carewe a Smock wrought with blak silke and collor & ruffes with
    golde & silke
62.97 By the Lady Jobson oone Smock allover wrought with blak silke the slevis
    wrought with golde
                            dd to the said Lady Cobham
62.98 By the Lady Sackevile in a purse of red silke and golde knytt in
    soueraignes. . . . . C s
                                with her said majestie
62.99 By the Lady Fitzwilliams widowe oone Petycoate of purple Satten cutt
    Vpon golde sarceonett with two borders enbrauderid with golde and
    siluer and frengid with golde siluer and silke
                      Delyuerid in chardge to John Roynon
                       and Rauf Hoope yeomen of the Roobes
62.100 By the Lady Gresham a Boxe with foure swete baggs in it
                      Delyuerid to the said Lady Cobham

Knightes

62.101 By Syr Edwarde Rogers Comptroller of the Howseholde in a purse of
62.102   crymsen silke and siluer knytt in Dimy Soueraignes and oone Angell. . . . . C s
By Syr William Cycell Secretary A Standishe garnesshid with siluer guilt
    and mother of pearle with an Inkepott of like siluer guilt, and a glasse of
    Chrystall in the couer the base plated with like siluer guilt cont therin two
    boxes for Duste and xxiiij Counters of siluer guilt with ballaunce weightes
    and a beame of siluer guilt / A penknyf thafte of siluer guilt / and a Seale
    of bone typped with siluer guilt
62.103 By Sir Frauncis Knowlles vicechamberlen in a purse of blewe silke and
    golde knytt in Dimy Soueraignes . . . . x li
62.104 By Sir Ambrose Caue Chauncellor of the Duchie of Lancaster in a purse of
    crymsen silke and golde knitt in Dimy Soueraignes . . . . x li

62.105 By Sir Richarde Sackevile vnderthreasourer of Englande in a purse of red
silke and golde in Soueraignes. . . . . x li
with her said majestie

62.106 By Sir John Mason Threasourer of the Chamber a smale Collog of
serpentyne garnesshid with siluer guilt And two Bookes
Delyuerid to the said John Asteley *ex per oer*

62.107 By Sir William Peter in a red purse in Dimy soveraignes . . . . x li

62.108 By Sir Walter Myldemaye Chauncellor of the Exchequer in a purse of red
silke and golde knytt in Dimy Angelles. . . . . C s

62.109 By Sir Edmunde Peckeham highe Threasourer of the Mynts in a chery bag
in Dimy soueraignes . . . . ix li

62.110 By Sir Christopher Heydon in a red silke purse in Angelles. . . . . x li

62.111 By Sir Henry Jernegham in golde . . . . x li

62.112 By Sir Edwarde Warner Levetenaunte of the Tower of London in sundry
coynes of golde . . . . vj li xviij s iiij d

62.113 By Sir William Cordall Master of the Rolles in a white Satten purse in
Angelles . . . . x li

62.114 By Sir Richarde Sowthewell in a red Satten purse in Angelles. . . . . x li

62.115 By Sir Moryce Dennyce oone rounde Dyall of golde sett with stone and pearle

62.116 By Sir Thomas Josleyne in a purse of blewe silke in Dimy soueraignes. . . . . . vj li

62.117 By Sir John Thynne in Dimy soueraignes. . . . . C s

62.118 By Sir William Damsell Receyvor of the Court of Wardes in a russett
silke purse in Dimy soueraignes . . . . x li

62.119 By Sir Thomas Benger Master of the Revelles a Ring with a smale poynted
Diamonde
with her said majestie

62.120 By Sir Gowen Carew Master of the Henchemen a Deske couered with
purple vellat enbr with golde
Delyuerid to Mrs blaunche apparry

62.121 By Sir Peter Carew in a purse of blak silke and golde in Dimy soueraignes . . x li

62.122 By Sir Roger North in a purse of red silke and gold knytt in frenche
Crownes . . . . vj li

62.123 By Sir Thomas Gresham in a purse of blak silke and siluer knytt in
Angelles . . . . x li
with her said majestie

62.124 By Sir William [sic, i.e. Gilbert] Dethyk King at Armes a booke of the
Armes of the Knightes of the Garter now being, couered with Tyncell

62.125 By Sir John Alee a Cofer of wodde carved paynted and guilt with Combes
glasses & balls
Delyuerid to the said Mrs Blaunche

62.126 By Sir George Howarde a Booke cont thoffice of the Armery couerid with
blak vellat & bounde with passamayne of siluer with two plates of siluer
Delyuerid to Sir William Cecill knight Secretarye

62.127 By Sir James Stumpe two Greyhoundes a fallow and a blak pyed
Delyuerid to John Coxe yeoman of the Leashe

Chapleyns

62.128 By Archedeacon Carew Deane of The Chappell in a purse of yellowe silke
and siluer knytt in frenche Crownes and Dimy Soueraignes . . . . x li
62.129 By Doctor Wotton Deane of Caunterbury in a red Satten purse in Dimy
soueraignes. . . . . x li
62.130 By Peter Vanne Deane of Salisbury in a red purse in frenche Crownes. . . . . xij li
with her said majestie

Gentlewomen

62.131 By Mysteris Asteley chief gentilwoman of the privy Chamber twelve
handkercheves edgid with golde and siluer
Delyuerid to the said Lady Cobham
62.132 By Mrs Blaunche Appary a square pece of vnshorne vellat edgid with
siluer lase
dd to the said Tameworth
62.133 By Mrs Skypwyth a Cusshion cloth wrought with blak silke and frengid with
golde and purple silke with a Pynpillowe enbrauderid
62.134 By Mrs Marven a Smock wrought with blak silke with a highe coller
edgid with golde & silke
62.135 By Mrs Harington a Smock allouer wrought with blak silke
62.136 By Mrs Hennage a fayre Smocke allouer wrought with blak silke and a
standing collor and Ruffes wrought with golde
62.137 By Mrs Dorothy Brodebelte a peire of Slevis of Cameryk nettid with golde
62.138 By Mrs Sandes sixe handkercheves wrought with red silke edgid with golde
62.139 By Mrs Marbery a Cawle and thre forehedclothes of Cameryk nettyd with
golde
62.140 By Mrs Arundell sixe handkercheves wrought with flowers of silke & golde,
edgid with golde
62.141 By Mrs Katheryn Caree sixe handekercheves edgid with golde siluer and
silke
62.142 By Mrs Baptest two Cawles thone of golde thother of siluer knytt
Delyuerid to the said Lady Cobham
62.143 By Mrs Penne a peire of silke knytt hoose
Delyuerid to Mrs Marberye
62.144 By Mrs Dane a pece of Cameryk in a boxe
dd to the said Mrs Blaunche
62.145 By Mrs Barley alias Penne sixe handekerchevs edgid with golde
dd to the said Lady Cobham
62.146 By Mrs Snowe widowe in Angelles . . . . C s
62.147 By Mrs Levina Terling the Quenis personne and other personages in a boxe
fynely paynted
with her said majestie
62.148 By Mrs Amy Shelton sixe handekercheves edgid with siluer and buttoned
dd to the said Lady Cobham

62.149 By Mrs Elizabeth Shelton a Standishe couerid with crymsen Satten allouer
enbr with venice gold & silke

dd to the said Mrs Blaunche

62.150 By Mrs Randell alias Smallepage six handekercheves edgid with golde
62.151 By Mrs Huggens oone pillowebeere and six faire handekercheves wrought
with silke & golde

dd to the said Lady Cobham

Gentlemen

62.152 By Maister John Asteley Master and Threasourer of the Quenis Juelles
and plate oone feire guilt bolle or Spice plate with a couer poz . . . . . . xxxj oz

Given to the Earle
of Penbrok eodem die

62.153 By Mr Thomas Hennage oone hower glasse garnesshid with golde poz with
glasse sand and all In a Case of blak vellat enbrauderid with siluer . . . . . v oz

with her said majestie

62.154 By Mr Harrington a peire of Sleves and a partelett enbr with golde &
siluer sett with pearle

dd to the said Lady Cobham

62.155 By Mr Bashe in Soueraignes . . . . x li
62.156 By Mr Thomas Standley in a red purse in Dimy Soueraignes . . . . vj li

with her said Matie

62.157 By Mr John Younge a Table paynted in a frame of walnuttre and certeyne
verses aboute it of money / And a round pece of siluer

The Table dd in chardge to George
Bredeman keper of the pallace at Westminster
The pece of siluer with the Quene

62.158 By Mr Doctor Maister two potts thone of Nvttemegges thother of
gynger condit
62.159 By Mr Doctor Hewycke two pottes thone of grene gynger, thother of
oring flowers

dd to the Gromes of the prevye Chamber

62.160 By Mr William Huggyns a greate swete bagge of tapheta with a zypher
and a border of Roses and Spheres enbrauderid with venice golde and
pearle

dd to the said Mrs Blaunche

62.161 By Benedick Spinulla one hoole pece of purple vellat

dd to the said Lady Cobham

62.162 By Robert Robatham two peire of silke hoose knytt

dd to the said Mrs Marbery

62.163 By Revell Svrveior of the workes a Marchepane with the Modell of
Powles churche and steeple in past
62.164 By George Mantle a neckercheve and a peire of Slevis allover wrought
with blak silke

dd to the said Lady Cobham

62.165 By Smyth Customer a pece of fyne Cameryk
dd to the said Mrs Blaunche
62.166 By Armygell Wade thre fyne glasses in a wycker baskett
dd to the said Lady Cobham
62.167 By Blomefilde Levetennante of thordennance a feire Darte of brasell
garnesshid and tassellid with siluer and blak silke the hedde Damaskyne
Gevon to the Lord Robt Mr of the Horse
62.168 By John Hemyngway Poticary a pott of Oring condytt a box of pyne
Cumfetts musked, A boxe of Manus Christi and lozenges
62.169 By Lawrence Shref grocer a Suger lof, a boxe of gynger, A boxe of
Nvtmegges, and a pounde of Synamon
dd to the foresaid Gromes
62.170 By Adams Scholemaister to the Henchemen a patron of a peire of Slevis
62.171 By Fraunces Chamberlen of Wodstock a boxe full of Gaernesey hoose &
slevis knytt
dd to the said Lady Cobham
62.172 By William Stbarbe a feire Crosbow with a Gaffle
dd to the Lorde Chamberlen
62.173 By Marke Anthony Eryzo a Combecase allouer enbrauderid and sett
with pearle and furnesshid with Combes glasses, and other necessaryes
dd to John baptest grome of
the pryvy Chamber
62.174 By Anthony Anthony a Cabonett full of Tylles
62.175 By Trayforde cheif Clerke of the Spicery Pomegranettes aples, boxes of
Confittes &c
62.176 By Richarde Hickes yeoman of the Chamber a very fayre Marchepane
made like a Tower with men and sundry Artillery in it
[blank]
62.177 By Modeno the half picture of Patche king henry theightes foole
dd to the forenamed G bredman
62.178 By Richarde Mathew Cutler a peir of knyves with a shethe couered
with purple vellat
with the Quene her Matie
62.179 By George Webster Master Cooke a Marchepane being a Chessebourde
62.180 By John Bettes Serjaunte of the Pastrye oone pye of Quinces
[blank]

Elizabeth R
[sign manual]

J Asteley

Ex[aminatio] per Ed. Pigeon

Anno Regni Reginae Elizabeth Quarto

Neweyere Giftes
geuon by the Queen her Majestie to those
Parsons whose names hereafter ensue, the
First of Januarye, the yere abouewrytten

Elizabeth R
[sign manual]
viz

62.181   To the Lady Margaret Strainge oone guilte Bolle with a couer
poz . . . . xvj oz iij qrt di

Dukes Marquesses and Earles

62.182   To the Duke of Norfolke oone guilte Cup with a couer poz . . . . xlij oz di
62.183   To the Marques of Winchester Highe Threasourer of Englande one guilt
Cup with a couer poz. . . . . xxxiij oz qrt
62.184   To the Marquis of Northampton oone guilt Cup with a couer
poz . . . . xxxviij oz iij qrt
62.185   To the Earle of Arundell Lorde Stewarde thre guilt Bolles with thre
couers weing xvij oz di qrt the pece in toto .Lj oz qrt di
62.186   To the Earle of Shrewisburye oone guilt Cup with a couer poz. . xxix oz iij qrt di
62.187   To the Earle of Darby oone guilt Bolle with a couer poz. . . . . xxxj oz qrt di
62.188   To the Earle of Pembroke oone guilt Bolle or Spice plate with a couer
gevon to the Quene her Matie by Mr John Asteley Mr and Threasourer
of her Juelles and plate poz – xxxj oz And oone guilt Cup with a couer
poz xviij oz di in toto . . . . xlix oz di
62.189   To the Earle of Bedfourde oone guilt Cup with a couer poz . . . . .xxxij oz qrt
62.190   To the Earle of Warwyk oone guilt Cup with a couer poz. . . . . xlij oz qrt
62.191   To the Earle of Rutlande oone guilt Cup with a couer poz . . . . xxxij oz
62.192   To the Earle of Huntingdon one guilt Cup with a cover poz. . . . xxxiiij oz iij qrt
62.193   To the Earle of Westmerlande one guilt Cup with a cover poz . . . xx oz iij qrt di
62.194   To the Earle of Oxfourde oone guilt Cup with a cover poz . . . . xxj oz qrt di
62.195   To the Earle of Northumberlande one guilt Cup with a couer poz. . . . .xx oz qrt

Vicounte

62.196   To the Vicounte Mountague oone guilt Cup with a couer poz . . . . xxiij oz qrt di

Busshop

62.197   To the Archebusshop of Canterbury one guilt Cup with a couer of the
Quene her Maties store of the chardge of the said John Asteley
poz . . . . .xl oz *ex per oer*
62.198   To the Archebusshop of Yorke oone guilt Goblett with a couer
poz . . . . xxxvij oz di

62.199 To the Busshop of Elye o oone guilt Cup with a couer poz . . . . xxxvj oz

62.200 To the Busshop of Duresme a guilt Cup with a couer of the said store
and chardge poz . . . . xxxiij oz qrt poz *ex per oer*

62.201 To the Busshop of Wynchester oone guilt cup with a couer poz . . . . . xxvij oz di

62.202 To the Busshop of London oone guilt Cup with a couer poz . . . . xxviiij oz

62.203 To the Busshop of Salisbury oone guilt Cup with a couer poz . xxxij oz iij qrt di

62.204 To the Busshop of Worcester one guilt Cup with a couer poz . . . . xxvij oz

62.205 To the Busshop of Lyncolne oone guilt Cup with a couer poz . . . . xxvij oz

62.206 To the Busshop of Chycester one guilt Cup with a couer poz . . . . xviij oz

62.207 To the Busshop of Norwiche one guilt Cup with a couer poz . . . . . . xx oz qrt di

62.208 To the Busshop of Herforde oone guilt Cup with a couer poz . . . . . . xviiij oz qrt

62.209 To the Busshop of Lichefilde and Coventrye oone hance pott guilt poz . . . xx oz

62.210 To the Busshop of Rochester oone guilte Salte with a couer poz . . . xxj oz iij qrt

62.211 To the Busshop of St Davies oone guilte Bolle withowt a couer
poz . . . . xviiij oz di di qrt

62.212 To the Busshop of Bath oone haunce pott guilt poz . . . . xx oz

62.213 To the Busshop of Exetor oone haunce pott guilt poz . . . . xviiij oz di di qrt

62.214 To the Busshop of Peterborowe oone haunce pott guilt poz . . . . xviiij oz di di qrt

62.215 To the Busshop of Chester one haunce pott guilt poz . . . . xvij oz di

Duchesses and Countesses

62.216 To the Duches of Norfolke oone guilt Cup with a couer poz . . . . . . .xxxij oz qrt

62.217 To the Duches of Somersett oone guilt Cup with a couer poz . . . . . xxxj oz di qrt

62.218 To the Countes of Surrey oone guilt Cup with a couer poz . . . . . . xij oz di di qrt

62.219 To the Countes of Pembroke oone guilt Cup with a couer poz . . . . . .xxvij oz qrt

62.220 To the Countes of Bedforde oone guilt Cup with a couer poz . . . . . . xxj oz qrt di

62.221 To the Countes of Darby oone guilt Cup with a couer poz . . . . . xxiij oz di di qrt

62.222 To the Countes of Oxforde one guilt Cup with a couer poz . . . . . xij oz di di qrt

62.223 To the Countes of Shrewisbury Dowager oone guilt Cup with a couer
poz . . . . xxij oz di

62.224 To the Countes of Shrewisbury oone guilt Cup with a couer poz . xix oz iij qrt di

62.225 To the Countes of Huntingdon Dowager oone guilt Cup with a couer
poz . . . . .xviiij oz di di qrt

62.226 To the Countes of Huntingdon oone guilt Cup with a couer poz . . . . . .xxxvij oz

62.227 To the Countes of Northumberlande oone guilt Bolle with a couer
poz . . . . xx oz di qrt

62.228 To the Countes of Rutland oone guilt Cup with a couer poz . . . . xxix oz qrt

Viscountesses

62.229 To the Viscountes Hereforde Dowager oone guilt Cup with a couer
poz . . . . xij oz qrt

62.230 To the Viscountes Mountague oone guilt Cup with a couer poz . . . . . . xviiij oz di

Elizabethan New Year's Gift Exchanges

Lordes

62.231	To the Lorde keper of the greate Seale Bacon oone guilt Cup with a couer poz	xxxvij oz iij qrt
62.232	To the Lorde William Howarde Lorde Chamberlen oone guilt Cup with a couer poz	xxvij oz qrt
62.233	To the Lorde Caree of Hundesdon oone guilt Cup with a couer poz	xxxvj oz di
62.234	To the Lorde Pagett oone guilt Cup with a couer poz	xxv oz di di qrt
62.235	To the Lorde Clinton Lorde Admirall oone guilt Cup with a couer poz	xxv oz qrt
62.236	To the Lorde Ryche oone guilt Cup with a couer poz	xxxiij oz qrt di
62.237	To the Lorde North oone guilt Cup with a couer poz	xxx oz iij qrt
62.238	To the Lorde Lumley oone guilt Cup with a couer poz	xxx oz iij qrt di
62.239	To the Lorde Hastinges of Lougheborowe oone guilt Cup with a couer poz	xxv oz iij qrt
62.240	To the Lorde Stafforde oone guilt Cup with a couer poz	xiij oz qrt
62.241	To the Lorde Windesor oone guilt Cup with a couer poz	xxj oz di di qrt
62.242	To the Lorde John Greye oone guilt Cup with a couer poz	xxvj oz qrt
62.243	To the Lorde Barkeley oone guilt Haunce potte poz	xx oz qrt
62.244	To the Lorde Mountejoye oone guilt Cup with a couer poz	xxxiij oz
62.245	To the Lorde Aburgavennye oone guilt Cup with a couer poz	xij oz iij qrt
62.246	To the Lorde Scrowpe oone guilt Cup with a couer poz	xxiij oz
62.247	To the Lorde Strainge one guilt Cup with a couer poz	xij oz di
62.248	To the Lorde Darcy of Cheche oone haunce pott guilt poz	xx oz
62.249	To the Lorde Shefilde oone haunce pott guilt poz	xx oz di qrt
62.250	To the Lorde Shandowes one haunce pott guilt poz	xix oz iij qrt

Ladyes

62.251	To the Lady Howarde oone guilt Cup with a couer poz	xxj oz
62.252	To the Lady Caree of Hundesdon oone guilt Cup with a couer poz	xxiij oz
62.253	To the Lady Clynton oone guilt Cup with a couer poz	Liij oz
62.254	To the Lady Cobham oone guilt Cup with a couer poz	xxxix oz qrt
62.255	To the Lady Paget one guilt Cup with a couer of the said store and chardge poz	xv oz iij qrt di
62.256	To the Lady Barkeley the Lorde Barkeleyes wyef oone guilt Cup with a couer poz	xij oz di qrt
62.257	To the Lady Mountjoye oone haunce pott guilt poz	xix oz di
62.258	To the Lady Aburgavennye oone guilt Cup with a couer poz	xij oz iij qrt di
62.259	To the Lady Dakers oone guilt Bolle with a couer poz	xv oz qrt di
62.260	To the Lady Tayleboyes Sir Peter Carewes wief oone guilt Salte with a couer poz	xxv oz quart di
62.261	To the Lady Shefilde oone haunce pot guilt poz	xiij oz iij qrt
62.262	To the Lady Scrowpe oone guilt Bolle with a couer poz	xviij oz
62.263	To the Lady Shandowis oone guilt haunce pott poz	xiiij oz qrt
62.264	To the Lady Knowlles thre guilt Bolles with a couer poz	Lxv oz di
62.265	To the Lady Carowe oone guilt Bolle with a couer poz	xxxv oz qrt

62.266	To the Lady Cicell parte of a peir of guilt Flagons poz . . . . xl oz
62.267	To the Lady Butler oone haunce pott guilt poz . . . . xvj oz di di qrt
62.268	To the Lady Ratlif oone guilt Cup with a couer poz . . . . xiij oz di
62.269	To the Lady Mason oone guilt Cup with a couer poz . . . . xv oz qrt di
62.270	To the Lady Yorke oone guilt Cup with a couer poz . . . . xij oz di di qrt
62.271	To the Lady Lane oone guilt Stoope with a couer poz. . . . . ix oz iij qrt
62.272	To the Lady Hennyingham one guilt Stoope with a couer poz . . . . xij oz
62.273	To the Lady Cheeke oone Tankerd guilt poz . . . . xiiij oz
62.274	To the Lady Pallett one guilt Stoope with a couer poz. . . . . xiij oz
62.275	To the Lady StLowe oone guilt Cup with a couer poz. . . . . xxvj oz iij qrt
62.276	To the Lady Wodhouse one guilt Bolle with a couer poz. . . . . xxvij oz di
62.277	To the Lady Jobson oone guilt Cup with a couer poz . . . . xxij oz di qrt
62.278	To the Lady Sackevile oone guilt Stoope with a couer poz . . . . xj oz iij qrt
62.279	To the Lady Fytzwilliams oone guilt Bolle with a couer poz . . . . xix oz iij qrt
62.280	To the Lady Gresham oone guilt Cup with a couer poz. . . . . xj oz di qrt

Knightes

62.281	To Syr Edwarde Rogers Comptroller of the householde oone guilt Bolle with a couer poz. . . . . xix oz di di qrt
62.282	To Sir William Cycell Se[c]retary parte of a peire of guilt Flagones poz. . xliiij oz
62.283	To Sir Fraunces Knowlles vicechamberlen oone guilt Cup with a couer poz . . . . xxiij oz iij qrt
62.284	To Sir Ambrose Cave Chaunncellor of the Duche of Lancaster one guilt Cup with a couer poz. . . . . xxiij oz iij qrt di
62.285	To Sir Richarde Sackevile vnderthreasourer of England oone guilt Cup with a couer poz. . . . . xxiij oz iij qrt
62.286	To Sir John Mason Threasourer of the Chamber one venecian Cup of the said store and Chardge poz . . . . .xx oz qrt
62.287	To Sir William Peter oone guilt Cup with a couer poz – xix oz qrt di and two guilt Spones poz – iij oz iij qrt di in toto . . . . xxiij oz qrt
62.288	To Sir Walter Myldemaye Chaunncellor of the Exchequer oone guilt Cup with a couer of the said store and chardge poz . . . . xiiij oz di
62.289	To Sir Edmonde Peckeham highe threasourer of the Mynte oone guilt Cup with a couer poz. . . . . xvij oz di di qrt
62.290	To Sir Christopher Heydon oone guilt Cup with a couer poz . . . . . xxvj oz iij qrt
62.291	To Sir Henry Jernegham oone guilt Tankerde poz . . . . xxj oz
62.292	To Sir Edwarde Warner Levetennaunte of the Tower of London oone haunce pott guilt poz. . . . . xix oz di
62.293	To Sir William Cordall Mr of the Rolles oone guilt Tankerd poz . . . . xxj oz
62.294	To Sir Richard Sowthewell oone haunce pott guilt poz . . . . xx oz qrt di
62.295	To Sir Thomas Jostelen oone guilt cup with a couer poz . . . . xiiij oz
62.296	To Sir John Thynne oone guilt Stowpe with a couer poz . . . . xiij oz qrt di
62.297	To Sir William Damsell Receyvor of corte of wardes oone guilt Cup with a couer poz. . . . . .xxij oz qrt
62.298	To Sir Thomas Benger Mr of the Revelles oone haunce pott guilt poz. . xix oz di

62.299	To Sir Gowen Carewe Mr of the Henchemen oone guilt Cup with a couer	
	poz . . . . .xxxv oz	
62.300	To Sir Peter Carewe oone guilt Cup with a couer poz . . . . xxiij oz qrt di	
62.301	To Sir Roger North oone guilt Bolle with a couer poz. . . . . xv oz	
62.302	To Sir Thomas Gresham oone guilt Cup with a couer poz . . . . xxiiij oz	
62.303	To Sir William [sic, i.e. Gilbert] Dethyk king at Armes oone guilt Cup	
	with a couer poz. . . . . xv oz	
62.304	To Sir John Alee one guilt Stowpe with a couer poz . . . . x oz iij qrt	
62.305	To Sir Morryce Dennyce thre guilt Bolles with a couer poz. . . . . Lxxvij oz iij qrt	
62.306	To Sir James Stumpe oone guilt Cup with a couer of the said store and	
	chardge poz . . . . x oz di di qrt	
62.307	To Sir George Howarde oone guilt Tankerd poz . . . . xxj oz qrt	

Chapleyns

62.308	To Archedeacon Carew Deane of the Chappell oone guilt Tankerd poz—	
	xix oz di and two guilt Spones poz iiij oz in toto . . . . .xxiij oz di	
62.309	To Doctor Wotten Deane of Caunterbury oone guilt Tankerd	
	poz . . . . xxij oz iij qrt	
62.310	To Peter wannes Deane of Salisbury one guilt Bolle with a couer	
	poz . . . . xxij oz di qrt	

Gentlewomen

62.311	To Maisteris Asteley chief gentilwoman of the prevy Chamber two guilt	
	Bolles withowt a couer poz—xxxij oz di / oone guilt Salte with a couer	
	poz—vj oz qrt / oone guilt Spone poz—j oz di di qrt / And oone guilt	
	peper boxe poz—v oz di qrt in toto . . . . xlv oz di	
62.312	To Mrs Blaunche Appary oone guilt Stowpe with a couer poz . . . . . xvj oz di qrt	
62.313	To Mrs Skypwith oone guilt Salte with a couer poz. . . . . xv oz iij qrt di	
62.314	To Mrs Marven oone guilt Bolle with a couer poz. . . . . xv oz di di qrt	
62.315	To Mrs Harrington oone guilt Bolle with a couer poz. . . . . .xv oz qrt	
62.316	To Mrs Hennage oone guilt Bolle with a couer poz—xvij oz iij qrt di and	
	two guilt Spones poz—iiij oz di in toto. . . . . xxij oz qrt di	
62.317	To Mrs Dorothy Brodebelt oone haunce pott guilt poz. . . . . xiij oz qrt di	
62.318	To Mrs Sandes oone guilt Bolle with a couer poz—xij oz iij qrt di / And	
	one guilt Spone poz – one ounce in toto. . . . . .xiij oz iij qrt di	
62.319	To Mrs Marbery one guilte Cup with a couer poz . . . . xiij oz qrt	
62.320	To Mrs Arundell oone guilt Bolle with a couer poz. . . . . xv oz qrt di	
62.321	To Mrs Katheren Caree oone guilt Stowpe with a couer poz—xj oz di qrt /	
	and two guilt Spones poz—iiij oz di qrt in toto . . . . .xv oz qrt	
62.322	To Mrs Bapteste oone guilt Bolle with a couer poz . . . . xvj oz di qrt	
62.323	To Mrs Penne Eight guilt Spones poz. . . . . xvj oz qrt di	
62.324	To Mrs Dane oone guilt Cup with a couer poz . . . . xviij oz qrt di	
62.325	To Mrs Barley alias Penne oone guilt Stowpe with a couer poz. . . . x oz iij qrt di	
62.326	To Mrs Snowe widowe oone guilt Stowpe with a couer poz . . . . xiij oz di	
62.327	To Mrs Randall alias Smalepage oone guilt Salte with a couer poz . . vj oz di qrt	

62.328	To Mrs Huggens oone guilt Salte with a couer poz . . . . xx oz
62.329	To Mrs Levina Terling oone guilt Salte with a couer poz. . . . . .v oz qrt
62.330	To Mrs Amy Shelton oone guilt Cup with a couer poz . . . . xiiij oz di di qrt
62.331	To Mrs Elizabeth Shelton one guilt Cup with a couer poz. . . . . .xiij oz di

Maydens of Honor

62.332	To Mrs Mary Howarde oone guilt Cup with a couer poz . . . . xj oz qrt di
62.333	To Mrs Mary Manxwell oone guilt Cup with a couer poz. . . . . xj oz di qrt
62.334	To Mrs Katheryn Knevett oone guilt Owle poz . . . . xj oz
62.335	To Mrs Anne Wyndesor oone guilt Cup with a couer poz. . . . . xj oz
62.336	To Mrs Mary Ratlyef oone guilt Cup with a couer poz. . . . . .x oz qrt
62.337	To Mrs Fraunces Mewthevs one guilt Cup with a couer poz. . . . . . . x oz qrt di
62.338	To Mrs Eglandby Mother of the Maydens oone guilt Cup with a couer poz . . . . .xj oz di

Gentlemen

62.339	To Maister John Asteley Mr and Threasourer of the Quenis Juelles and plate oone guilt Cup with a couer poz . . . . Liiij oz
62.340	To Mr Thomas Hennage oone guilt Cup with a couer poz . . . . xl oz iij qrt
62.341	To Mr Harrington thre guilt Bolles with a couer poz. . . . . .Lix oz di
62.342	To Mr Bashe oone guilt Cup with a couer poz. . . . . xxiiij oz
62.343	To Mr Thomas Stanley oone guilt Bolle with a couer poz. . . . . xv oz di
62.344	To Mr John Yonge oone guilt Bolle with a couer poz . . . . .xxx oz qrt di
62.345	To Mr Doctor Master oone guilt haunce pott poz. . . . . xvj oz qrt di
62.346	To Mr Doctor Hewyk oone guilt haunce pott poz. . . . . xvj oz iij qrt di
62.347	To Mr William Huggyns oone guilt Bolle with a couer poz. . . . . xxix oz di
62.348	To Blomefilde Levetennavnte of thordnaunce oone guilt Cruse with a couer poz . . . . ix oz iij qrt di
62.349	To Benedicke Spynulla one guilt Cup with a couer poz . . . . xxiiij oz qrt di
62.350	To Robert Robotham oone guilt Stowpe with a couer poz . . . . .xiij oz
62.351	To Revell Svrueior of the workes oone haunce pott guilt poz . . . . xj oz qrt
62.352	To George Mantle rewarded in money payed by the Threasourer of the Chamber . . . . x li
62.353	To Smyth Custmer one guilt Cruse with a couer poz. . . . . .xv oz qrt
62.354	To Armygell Wade oone guilt Casting Bottle poz . . . . vij oz di di qrt
62.355	To John Hemyngewaye oone guilt Bolle withowt a couer poz. . . . . x oz di di qrt
62.356	To Lawrence Shreff Grocer oone guilt Salte with a couer poz. . . . . vij oz
62.357	To Adams Scholemaster to the Henchemen rewarded and payed vt supra. . . . . .xl s
62.358	To Fraunces Chamberlen oone guilt Cruse with a couer poz. . . . . xiij oz iij qrt di
62.359	To William Stbarbe oone haunce pott guilt poz. . . . . .xiij oz qrt di
62.360	To Marke Anthony Eryzo oone guilt Stowpe with a couer poz. . . xiij oz di di qrt
62.361	To Anthony Anthony oone guilt Cruse with a couer poz. . . . . xiij oz qrt
62.362	To Henry Trayforde oone guilt Salte with a couer poz. . . . . ix oz di qrt
62.363	To Richarde Hickes Yeoman of the Chamber rewarded and payed vt svpra. . . . . lxvj s viij d

62.364	To Modeno rewarded and payed vt svpra................................	xl s
62.365	To Richarde Matthewe Cutler rewarded and payed vt svpra.........	xiij s iiij d
62.366	To George Webster Mr Cooke oone guilt Tankerd poz	xiij oz
62.367	To John Bettes Seraunte of the Pastrye two guilt Spones poz	iiij oz

[Free Gifts]

62.368	To Mr John Tamworthe Grome of the prevye chamber oone guilt Cup with a couer poz	xxxv oz iij qrt
62.369	To Mr Thomas Asteley grome &c. oone guilt Cruse with a couer poz	viij oz
62.370	To Mr Henry Sackeforde grome &c. oone guilt Cruse with a couer poz...	viij oz
62.371	To Mr John Bapteste grome &c. oone guilt Cruse with a couer poz	viij oz
62.372	To Mr George [sic, i.e. Edward] Caree grome &c. oone guilt Cruse with a couer poz	viij oz
62.373	To John Roynon yeoman of the Robes oone guilt Salte with a couer poz	xij oz di
62.374	To Nicholas Bristow Clerke of the Juells and plate oone guilt Cruse with a couer poz...	x oz iij qrt di
62.375	To Edmunde Pigeon yeoman of the said Juells and plate oone guilt cruse with a couer poz	x oz iij qrt di
62.376	To John Pigeon yeoman of the said Juells and plate oone guilt cruse with a couer poz...	x oz iij qrt di
62.377	To Stephen Fulwell grome of the said Juells and plate ut supra oone guilt Cruse with a couer poz	x oz iij qrt di

Guiftes delyuerid at sundry

tymes in mannor and fourme folowyng.

viz

62.378	Mounsieur Saulte
	Geuon by the Quene her Matie the thirde of Apriell Anno iij^{tio} &c. / To Mounsieur Saulte Frenche Ambassator / Oone Bason and Ewer guilt poz – iiij^{xx} xvij oz di / Item oone peire of guilt Pottes poz— Clxiij oz / Item thre guilt Bolles with a couer poz – lxiij oz di and oone guilt Salte with a couer poz – xxij oz di / bought of the goldesmythes in toto .... CCCxlvj oz di
62.379	Sir William Cycell
	Item geuon by her Matie the xxjth of Apriell Anno predicto at the Christenynge of Sir William Cycell knight principall Secretary to her highnes his Childe oone guilt Cup with a couer poz........ xxviij oz iij qrt bought of the goldesmythes
62.380	Mounsieur Dennys
	Item geuon by her Matie the vth of Maye Anno predicto to Mounsieur Dennyce Ambassator from the King of Swetheland Oone Bason and Ewer guilt poz – lx oz di / Item one peire of guilt pottes poz— lxxxij oz / and oone guilt Cup with a couer poz—xlix oz qrt bought of the Goldesmythes in toto .... Ciiij^{xx} xj oz iij qrt

62.381   Vitzcount Mountague
    Item geuon by her Matie the xxvij^th of Maye Anno predicto to the
    Chrystenyng of the vicounte Mountague his Doughter oone guilt
    Cup with a couer poz – xxvij oz bought of the goldesmythes . . . . . xxvij oz
62.382   Copley
    Item geuon by her Matie the xviij^th of June Anno predicto to the
    chrystenyng of [blank] Copley his childe oone guilt Cup with a
    couer poz – xx oz iij qrt bought of the goldesmythes . . . . .xx oz iij qrt
62.383   Lorde Oraily
    Item geuon by her Matie the xix^th of June Anno predicto to the
    Lorde Oraily of Ireland Oone coller of Esses of golde poz—
    xvj oz bought of the goldesmythes . . . . xvj oz
    Item geuon by her Matie to the said Lorde one crownett of siluer
    guilt poz – viij oz iij qrt bought of the said Goldesmythes. . . . . viij oz iij qrt
62.384   Lorde Odonerle
    Item geuon by her Matie the xix^th of June Anno predicto to the
    Lorde Odonerle of Ireland Oone coller of Esses of golde poz—
    xvj oz / bought of the Goldesmythes. . . . . xvj oz
    Item geuon by her Matie to the said Lorde Oone crownett of siluer
    guilt poz – viij oz di di qrt bought of the goldesmythes . . . . . viij oz di di qrt
62.385   Lorde Barcley
    Item geuon by her Matie the xxvj^th of June Anno predicto to the
    Chrystenyng of the Lorde Barcle his Childe oone guilt Bolle with
    a couer poz – xxvij oz qrt bought of the goldesmythes . . . . .xxvij oz qrt
62.386   Ipolitan
    Item geuon by her Matie the xiij^th of July Anno predicto to the
    Chrystenynge of Ipolitan the Tartarian Oone Cheine of golde
    poz—iiij oz di and two penny weight / And also oone Tablett of
    golde poz – j oz iij qrt di bought of the goldesmythes in toto
    . . . . vj oz qrt ij wts golde
62.387   Sir William [sic, i.e. Gilbert] Dethyk
    Item geuon by her Matie the xv^th of July Anno predicto to the
    chrystenyng of Sir William [sic, i.e. Gilbert] Dethyk alias Garter
    king at Armes his Childe Oone guilt Cup with a couer poz—
    xix oz qrt di bought of the Goldesmythes. . . . . xix oz qrt di
62.388   Lorde MounteJoye
    Item geuon by her Matie the xxx^th of July Anno predicto to the
    chrystenyng of the Lord Mountejoye his Childe oone guilt Cup
    with a couer poz – xxviij oz di qrt bought of the Goldesmythes
    . . . . xxviij oz di qrt
62.389   Lorde Shefilde
    Item geuon by her Matie the xxvj^th of September Anno predicto to
    the chrystenyng of the Lorde Shefilde his childe oone guilt Cup
    with a couer poz – xxviij oz di qrt bought vt supra. . . . . xxviij oz di qrt

62.390   Thomas Sackeuile
          Item geuon by her Matie the xxiiij^th of November Anno iiij^to predicto
          to the chrystenyng of Mr Thomas Sackevile his childe oone guilt
          Cup with a couer poz – xx oz quart di bought, vt supra. . . . . . . xx oz qrt di

62.391   Mounsieur Morett
          Item geuon by her Matie the xxj^th of January Anno iiij^to predicto to
          Mounsieur Morrett Ambassator to the Duke of Savoye / Oone Bason
          and Ewer guilt poz – lxxij oz di / And oone peire of guilt Pottes poz—
          lxxij oz iij qrt / And thre guilt Bolles with a couer poz—liiij oz /
          bought of the goldesmythes in toto. . . . . .Ciiij xx xix oz di

62.392   Mounsieur Seure
          Item geuon by her Matie the last of February Anno predicto to
          Mounsieur De Sevre liger Ambassator from the French kinge Oone
          Bason and Ewer guilt poz—Cxxj oz di / Item oone peire of Flagons
          guilte poz—Cl oz di / Item oone peire of guilt Pottes poz—iiij^xx ix
          oz iij qrt / Item oone peire of lesser guilt Pottes poz—lvj oz qrt /
          Item thre guilt Bolles with a couer poz—lxvj oz / Item thre other
          guilt Bolles with a couer poz—lix oz di / Item oone guilt Cup with a
          couer poz—xxxij oz di qrt / And two guilt Saltes with a couer poz
          —xxxvj oz iij qrt di bought of the Goldesmythes in toto. . . . . . Dcxiij oz di

62.393   Mr Nicholas Guildensterne
          Item geuon by her Matie the last of Marche Anno predicto to Maister
          Nicholas Guldensterne Ambassator ligier from the king of Swethland
          at his departure Oone Bason and Ewer guilt poz—Clj oz di / Item
          oone peire of pottes guilt poz—CCviij oz di / Item oone peire of guilt
          Flagons poz—Ciiij^xx oz di / Item oone peire of lesse Flagons poz—
          iiij^xx xij oz di / Item thre guilt Bolles with a couer poz—lxiiij oz /
          Item thre mo guilt Bolles with a couer poz—lxiiij oz iij qrt / Item
          oone guilt Cup with a couer poz—liij oz / Item oone other guilt
          Cup with a couer poz—lij oz qrt / Item two guilt Saltes with couer
          poz—xlvij oz iij qrters di bought of the Goldesmythes in toto
          . . . . ix^C xiij oz iij qrt di

62.394   Countie Russey
          Item geuon by her Matie the first of Maye Anno predicto to Countie
          Russey Ambasator from the Frenche King oone Cheine of golde
          bought of the Goldesmythes poz . . . . .xxxiij oz qrt di of golde

Elizabeth R
[sign manual]

J Astley
Ex[aminatio] per Ed. Pigeon

Anno regni
Regine Elizabeth quinto

Neweyere guiftes geuon
to the Quene her majestie by those persones
whose names hereafter ensue. The First of
January the yere abouesaid
viz

[sign manual cut out of manuscript]

63.1 By the Lady Mary Graie a peire of perfumed Gloves sett with smale
buttons of golde

Delyuerid to the Lady Cobham

63.2 By the Lady Margaret Strainge a spone and a Fork of golde the steales
being alabaster . . . . iij oz

Delyuerid in chardge to Mr John Asteley Mr and
Threasorer of her highnes Juelles & plate *ex et oner*
Duke Marquisses and Earles

63.3 By the Duke of Norfolke in a purse of red silke and golde knytt in Dimy
Soueraignes . . . . xx li

63.4 By the Marques of Northampton in a purse of blak silke & siluer knytt in
di soueraignes . . . . xx li

63.5 By the Marques of Winchester Highe Threasourer of Englande in a purse
of crymsen Satten in olde Soueraignes and one half soueraigne . . . . xx li

63.6 By the Earle of Arundell Lorde Stewearde in a paper in dimy
soueraignes. . . . . xxx li

63.7 By the Earle of Northumberlande in a purse of blake silke and golde
knytt in dimy Soueraignes . . . . x li

63.8 By the Earle of westmerlande in a purse of blak silke and siluer in
Angelles . . . . x li

63.9 By the Earle of Shrewisburye in a red Satten purse in newe Soueraignes . . . xx li

63.10 By the Earle of Darbye in a purse of crymsen Satten enbr with golde in
dimy soueraignes . . . . xx li

63.11 By the Earle of Rutlande in a purse of red silke and golde knytt in Di
soueraignes & Angelles . . . . xx li

63.12 By the Earle of Huntingdon in a purse of blak silke in golde and siluer in
olde Angelles . . . . xv li

63.13 By the Earle of Bedforde in a purse of red silke and golde knytt in Dimy
soueraignes. . . . . xx li

63.14 By the Earle of Pembroke in a purse of blak silke and golde knytt in Dimy
soueraignes. . . . . xxx li

With her Matie

63.15 By the Vicounte Mountague in a purse of golde Tyncell in Dimy
soueraignes. . . . . x li

With her Matie

Busshoppes

63.16 By the Arche Busshop of Caunterby in a purse of cloth of golde tyssued
with siluer in new Soueraignes . . . . .xl li

63.17 By the Arche Busshop of Yorke in a purse of red Satten in Dimy
Soueraignes . . . . xxx li

63.18 By the Busshop of Durisme in a purse of red Satten in olde Angelles . . . . xxx li

63.19 By the Busshop of Elye in a purse of crymsen vellat in dimy
Soueraignes . . . . xxx li

63.20 By the Busshop of Wynchester in a purse of red Satten in Dimy
Soueraignes . . . . xx li

63.21 By the Busshop of London in a purse of red Satten in Dimy Soueraignes . . xx li

63.22 By the Busshop of Salisbury in a purse of crymsen vellat in Dimy
Soueraignes . . . . xx li

63.23 By the Busshop of worcester in a purse of crymsen Satten in Dimy
Soueraignes . . . . xx li

63.24 By the Busshop of Lincolne in a purse of carnacon silke and siluer knytt
in Di soueraignes and Angelles . . . . xx li

63.25 By the Busshop of Chichester in a purse of red Satten in Dimy soueraignes . x li

63.26 By the Busshop of Norwiche in a purse of red silke knyt in Dimy
soueraignes. . . . . xx li

63.27 By the Busshop of Herefourde in a purse of golde tyssue in dimy
soueraignes. . . . . x li

63.28 By the Busshop of Lichfilde and Couentry in a paper in golde and
siluer. . . . . xiij li vj s viij d

63.29 By the Busshop of Rochester in a purse of red Satten in Dimy soueraignes
and one Cruseado . . . . xiij li vj s viij d

63.30 By the Busshop of St Davies in a purse of red silke and golde knytt in Di
Soueraignes . . . . x li

63.31 By the Busshop of Bathe in a purse of red Satten in Dimy Soueraignes. . . . . x li

63.32 By the Busshop of Exeter in a purse of red silke and siluer in Di
Soueraignes . . . . x li

63.33 By the Busshop of Peterbourowe in a purse of red Satten in Di
Soueraignes . . . . x li

63.34 By the Busshop of Chester in a purse of red silke and siluer in Di
Soueraignes . . . . x li

63.35 By the Busshop of Glocester in a purse of new making vellatt reyzid
with golde in Di soueraignes . . . . x li

With her Matie

Duchesses Marques and Countesses

63.36 By the Duches of Norforlke in a purse of crymsen silke and golde knytt
          in Di soueraignes . . . . xx li
                                                                                                       With her Matie

63.37 By the Duches of Suffolke two Slevis allouer wrought with golde and fyne
          Lawne
                                                                                       Delyuerid to the said L. Cobham

63.38 By the Duches of Somersett in olde Royalles and doble
          Duckettes . . . . xiiij li iij s iiij d
                                                                                                       With her Matie

63.39 By the Marques of Northampton a Snayle of golde sett with Diamontes
                                                                                       With the Quene her Matie

63.40 By the Countes of Surrey in a Satten purse enbr with golde in
          Di soueraignes . . . . C s

63.41 By the Countes of Oxfourde in a purse of grene taphata in Dimy
          Soueraignes . . . . C s

63.42 By the Countes of Northumberlande in a purse of blak silke & golde knytt
          in Di soueraignes . . . . x li

63.43 By the Countes of Rutland in a purse of red silke and golde in Soueraignes
          Angelles & a crusado . . . . xiij li vj s

63.44 By the Countes of Shrewisbury Dowager in a purse of red silke & golde
          knytt in presse Di Soueraignes . . . . xij li

63.45 By the Countes of Shrewisbury in a purse of blewe Satten in newe
          Soueraignes . . . . x li

63.46 By the Countes of Darbye in a purse of crymsen Satten enbr in Di
          Soueraignes . . . . x li

63.47 By the Countes of Huntingdon Dowager in a purse of blak silke & golde
          knytt in Di soueraignes . . . . x li

63.48 By the Countes of Huntingdon in a purse of blak silke & siluer in Angelles . x li

63.49 By the Countes of Pembroke in a purse of blak silke and golde in newe Di
          soueraignes. . . . . xv li
                                                                                                       With her said Matie

Vicountes

63.50 By the Vicountess Hereforde Lorde wylloughbyes wyef six handekercheves
          thre wrought with golde and crymsen silke thother thre wrought with
          blewe silke and siluer
                                                                                       Delyuerid to Mrs Dorothy Brodbelt

63.51 By the Vicountess Mountague in a purse of Tyncell in Dimy soueraignes . . . x li
                                                                                                       With her Matie

Lordes

63.52 By the Lorde keper of the greate Seale Bacon in a purse of blak silke and
          siluer knytt in Dimy soueraignes and one Crusado . . . . xiij li vj s viij d

63.53 By the Lorde william Howarde Lorde Chamberlayne in a purse of red
    silke knytt in Di Soueraignes. . . . . x li

63.54 By the Lorde Pagett in a purse of grene silke knytt in Di soueraignes
    . . . . xiij li vj s viij d

63.55 By the Lorde Clinton Lorde Admyrall in a purse of blak silke in Angelles . . x li

63.56 By the Lorde Riche in a litle purse of red vellat in Di soueraignes . . . . xx li

63.57 By the Lorde North in a purse of red silke and golde in Soueraignes Di
    soueraignes Angelles and half Angelles . . . . xx li
                                                    With her Matie

63.58 By the Lorde Lumley a Ring of golde with fyve poynted Diamondes and
    two smale table Diamondes sett therin
                                                    With her majestie

63.59 By the Lorde Hastinges of Lougheborowe in a purse of red Satten and
    golde knytt in golde & siluer . . . . xiij li vj s viij d

63.60 By the Lorde Stafford in a purse of red taphata in Angelles . . . . C s
                                                    With her Matie

63.61 By the Lorde windesor a Table enbrauderid with Paris Juno Diana and
    Venis
                     Delyuered in chardge to George Bredeman
                          keper of the pallace at westminster

63.62 By the Lorde John Grey a Cup of siluer guilt peare fasson poz . . . . xiij oz qrt di
                    Delyuerid to the said John Asteley &c *ex et oner*

63.63 By the Lorde Barkeley in a purse of crymsen silke and siluer knytt in Di
    Soueraignes . . . . x li

63.64 By the Lorde Mountejoye in a purse of grene silke and siluer in Di
    Soueraignes . . . . x li

63.65 By the Lorde Aburgauenny in a purse of red silke and siluer in Di
    Soueraignes . . . . C s

63.66 By the Lorde Scrowpe in a purse of blak silke and siluer in Angelles . . . . x li
                                                    With her Matie

63.67 By the Lorde Caree of Hunsdon a Combecase couerid with crymsen vellat
    allouer enbr with golde & set with perle furnishid with glasses combes
    and other necessaryes &c
                            Delyuerid to the said Mrs Dorothye

63.68 By the Lorde Strainge in a purse of red silke and siluer knytt in Di
    Soueraignes . . . . vj li

63.69 By the Lorde Darcye in a purse of red Satten in Di Soueraignes . . . . v li
                                                    With her Matie

Ladies

63.70 By the Lady Howarde in a purse of red silke knytt in Dimy Soueraignes . . . . x li
                                                   With her Matie

63.71 By the Lady Clinton two Rayles wrought with golde
                             Delyuerid to Mrs Dorothy

63.72 By the Lady Pagett in a Dimy Soueraignes. . . . . vj li xiij s iiij d

63.73 By the Lady Barkeley in a purse of red silke and golde knytt in Di
   Soueraignes . . . . .vj li

63.74 By the Lady Mountejoye in a purse of red silke in Dimy Soueraignes . . . . . . x li

63.75 By the Lady Aburgavennye in a purse of red silke and siluer. . . . . C s

63.76 By the Lady Caree of Hunsdon in a purse of crimsen silke & golde in
   Angelles & a Georg Nobil . . . . .ix li xviij s

63.77 By the Lady Taylboyes Sir Peter Carowes wief in a purse of blake silke &
   siluer in Angelles . . . . x li
   With her Matie

63.78 By the Lady Cobham one Cup of Assaye of golde poz . . . . iiij oz qrt
   Delyuerid to the said John Asteley *ex et oner*

63.79 By the Lady Dakers a Petycoate of crymsen Satten cutt allouer and
   enbrauderid with purles of Damaske siluer and thre borders of like
   Damaske purle frengid &c
   Delyuerid to Rauf Hoope yeoman of the Roobes

63.80 By the Lady williams of Tame Mr Drewrye his wief in a purse of blak silke
   and siluer knytt in Angelles . . . . x li
   With her Matie

63.81 By the Lady Knowlles a partelett and a peire of Slevis feyre wrought with
   siluer & blak silke
   With the Quene

63.82 By the Lady Butler in a paper in Dimy Soueraignes . . . . .vj li
   With her Matie

63.83 By the Lady Ratclyef a Smocke wrought with siluer and bone lase with
   two swete Bagges all in a Bag of Cameryke edgid with bone lase
   dd to Mrs Dorothye

63.84 By the Lady Mason in a purse of tawny silke and golde knytt in Angelles . . . vj li
   With her Matie

63.85 By the Lady Yorke six Sugerloues a Glasse of oring water and certeyne
   sewinge silke

63.86 By the Lady Cicell a wastecoate of white Satten allouer enbr like a cheverne
   of siluer & silke
   Delyuerid to the Lady Cobham

63.87 By the Lady Lane a feire Smocke allouer wrought with blak worke

63.88 By the Lady heningham Six handekercheves wrought with blak silke edgid
   with golde & siluer
   dd to Mrs Dorothye

63.89 By the Lady Cheeke a peire of Slevis wrought with blak silke
   Delyuerid to the Lady Cobham

63.90 By the Lady Pallat in a purse of golde knytt in Angelles . . . . C s
   With her Matie

63.91 By the Lady St lowe a peire of Slevis & a partelett wrought with blak silke
   dd to the Lady Cobham

63.92   By the Lady wodhowse two peire of silke Hoose knytt and a Cusshionett sett
     with seede perle

The hoose dd to Mrs Dorothy and the
Cusshionet to the Lady Cobham

63.93   By the Lady Carowe Sir Gowines wief a peire Slevis striped with gold and
     blak silke

dd to the said Lady Cobham

63.94   By the Lady Jobson a Smocke wrought with blak silke golde and siluer

dd to Mrs Dorothye

63.95   By the Lady Sackevile in a purse of blak silke and siluer knytt in Angelles .. C s

With her Matie

63.96   By the Lady Gresham Sixe bagges of white and blak taphata and two paire
     of perfume Gloves

dd to the Lady Cobham

63.97   By the Lady Throgemorton a Boxe couerid with golde siluer and silke
     nedleworke with A Partelett and a peire of Slevis of white worke knytt
     & vj playne white handekerches

The boxe & sleves dd to the said L. Cobham
The handekercheves to Mrs Dorothy

63.98   By the Lady Stafford widowe a Cawle and a peire of Slevis wrought with
     blak silk & golde

dd to the Lady Cobham

Knightes

63.99   By Syr Edwarde Rogers Comptroller in a purse of red silke and golde
     knytt in Di soueraignes . . . . vij li

With her Matie

63.100   By Syr william Cicell Secretary a faire Booke of Prayers and many other
     things in it couerid with siluer enamuled with the Quenis and her Maties
     Mothers Armes on both sides of golde garnesshid and clasped with
     golde sett with Garnettis and Turquisses

With her majestie

63.101   By Syr Fraunces Knolles vicechamberlayne in a purse of red silke & siluer
     in Di Soueraignes. . . . . x li

63.102   By Syr Ambrose Cave Chauncellor of the Duchey of Lancaster in a purse
     of silk & golde in Dukettes . . . . xiij li vj s viij d

With her Matie

     And eight smale Mappes in frames of wod of Castelles within the said
       Duchey

Delyuerid to the said George Bredeman

63.103   By Syr Richard Sackevile underthreasourer of England in a purse of blak
     silke & siluer in Angelles . . . . x li

With her Matie

63.104   By Syr John Mason Threasourer of the Chamber A Case of siluer guilt
     with thre hower glasses

Delyuerid to the said John Asteley *ex et oner*

And two Bookes of St Augustynes worke

Delyuerid to Mrs Blaunche Apparye

63.105 By Syr william Peter in a purse of purple silke and siluer knytt in Doble soueraines & Di souerans . . . . x li

63.106 By Syr walter Mildemaye Chauncellor of the Exchequer in a purse of crymsen striped with golde knytt in half Angelles . . . . C s

63.107 By Syr Edmonde Peckeham highe Threasourer of the Myntes in a chery bag of blewe in new Angeles . . . . x li

63.108 By Syr Christofer Haydon in a purse of blew silke and golde knytt in olde Angelles . . . . x li

63.109 By Syr Henry Jernegham in a red chery bag in newe Di Soueraignes . . . . x li

63.110 By Syr Edwarde warner in a red chery bag in golde of sundri coynes
. . . . vj li xviij s iiij d

63.111 By Syr william Cordall Mr of the Rolles in a purse of white Satten in Angelles . . . . x li

63.112 By Syr Richarde Sowthewell in a red silke purse knytt in Angeles and Di soueraignes. . . . . x li

63.113 By Syr John Thynne in a purse of red Satten in Di soueraignes . . . . C s

63.114 By Syr william Damsell in a purse of grene silke and siluer knytt in Di Soueraignes . . . . x li

With her Matie

63.115 By Syr Thomas Benger a Ringe of golde with a table Diamonde sett therin

With her Matie

63.116 By Syr Gower Carowe a Smocke wrought with golde and blak silke

dd to the said Dorothye

63.117 By Syr Peter Carowe in a purse of blak silke and siluer knytt in di soueraignes. . . . . x li

63.118 By Syr Roger North in a lether purse of golde and siluer . . . . vj li xiij s iiij d

With her Matie

63.119 By Syr Thomas Gresham in a purse of blak silke and siluer knytt in Soueraignes . . . . x li

With her Matie

63.120 By Syr Gylbert Dethick kinge at Armes a Booke of Armes of all the Lordes as they sytt in perliament coueird with tyssue

With her Matie

Chapleynes

63.121 By Archedeacon Carew Deane of the Chappell in a chery bag of chaungeable taphata in Angelles . . . . x li

63.122 By Doctor Wotton Deane of Caunterburye in a purse of red Satten in Dimy soueraignes . . . . x li

63.123 By Peter Vanne Deane of Salisbury in a purse of red Satten in Dimy soueraignes. . . . . xij li

With her Matie

Gentlewomen

63.124 By Maisteris Asheley chief gentlewoman of prevye Chamber a Cawle And a
        night Rayle wrought with blak silke

                                                    The Cawle with her Matie
                                                    The Rayles dd to Mrs Dorothye

63.125 By Mrs Blaunche Appary sixe handekercheves wrought with golde siuer
        and silke of sundry facons And a Cawle wrought with golde and siluer

                                            The handkercheves dd to the said
                                            Mrs Dorothye / the Cawle with her self

63.126 By Mrs Skypwith a night Smocke wrought with blak silke

                                                    dd to the said Mrs Dorothye

63.127 By Mrs Harington thre partelettes of golde siuer and silke of sundry
        makinges

                                                    dd to the Lady Cobham

63.128 By Mrs Hennage a Smocke wrought with blake silke

63.129 By Mrs Dorothy Brodebelt a Pyllowebere wrought with blak silke and
        siluer

                                                    dd to Mrs Dorothye

63.130 By Mrs Marberye a night Rayle and a Coyphe wrought with blak silke &
        siluer striped

                                                    With her self

63.131 By Mrs katheryn Caree a Cawle wrought with Damaske golde siuer and
        blak silke

                                                    dd to the Lady Cobham

63.132 By Mrs winkefilde a Booke of the Psalter in latten couerid with
        nedleworke of golde Siluer and blewe silke

                                                    With her Matie

63.133 By Mrs Baptest two Partelertes wrought with golde and siluer

                                                    dd to the Lady Cobham

63.134 By Mrs Penne sixe handekercheves edgid with golde

                                                    dd to Mrs Dorothye

63.135 By Mrs Dane a pece for a Tablecloth and a pece for Napkins of Dyaper

                                                    dd to Mrs blaunche

63.136 By Mrs Snowe in a purse of blak silke and siluer in Angelles . . . . C s

                                                    With her Matie

63.137 By Mrs Levina Terling a Carde with the Quenis Matie & many other
        personages

                                                    with her Matie

63.138 By Mrs Amy Shelton sixe handekercheves wrought with blak silke and
        golde

                                                    dd to Mrs Dorothy

63.139 By Mrs Elizabeth Shelton foure peire of Sockes wrought with blak silke
        And a Cusshionett of crymsen vellat enbrauderid with golde

                                            The Sockes dd to Mrs Dorothye
                                            The Cusshionet to the Lady Cobham

63.140 By Mrs Smalepage als Randall foure handkercheves edgid with a freinge
of golde and siluer

63.141 By Mrs Huggens a Cawle and a night Rayle wrought with golde and blak
silke

63.142 By Ipolita the Tartarian A handekercheve wrought with golde siluer and
silke with buttons and tasselles

Delyuerid to Mrs Dorothye

Gentlemen

63.143 By Maister John Asteley Mr and Threasourer of the Quenis Jeuells and
plate Oone guilt Cup with a couer faire wrought poz – xxv oz And one
guilt Cup of Assay poz – vj oz. . . . . xxxj oz

With her Matie

63.144 By Mr Thomas Hennage oone Remnant of blak striped newmaking
vellat enbr cont . . . . .ix yardes

dd to Rauf Hoope &c

63.145 By Mr Harington a peire of Slevis and a partelett of lawne wrought with
pipes of golde

dd to the Lady Cobham

63.146 By Mr Bashe in a purse of red silke and golde knytt in Angelles. . . . . x li

63.147 By Mr Staneley in a purse of red Satten in doble Soueraignes . . . . .vj li

With her Matie

63.148 By John Younge A feire Table paynted of a Story of Poetry

In the pryvy Chamber

63.149 By Doctor Master two pottes of conservasses

63.150 By Doctor Hewyke two pottes of conservasses

With her Matie

63.151 By Mr william Huggens two greate swete Bagges of crymsen taphata
faire enbr

dd to the Lady Cobham

63.152 By Benedicke Spinula a Boxe couerid with crimsen Satten wherein are A
Cusshion cloth wrought with golde and red silke two partelettes wrought
with golde and silke and two wrought with siluer a peire of Slevis of
golde two peire of wasshed Gloves playne twelve flowers wrought with
golde siluer and silke A glasse of swete powder. And a turquey
handkerchev

The Cusshion cloth dd to Mrs Dorothie
The rest dd to the Lady Cobham

63.153 By Robert Robotham two peire of blak silke hoose knytt

dd to Mrs Dorothye

63.154 By George Mantell a partelett and a peire of Sleves wrought with golde
siluer and blake silke

dd to the Lady Cobham

63.155 By Smyth Custmer A Bolte of Cameryck in a Case of white Damaske
edgid with crymsen silke and golde frenge

dd to Mrs Blaunche

63.156   By Armygell wade A Glasse of byrrall with a couer in a case of wyker

63.157   By John Hemawaye a Pott of Conser[ves] and a Boxe of Comfittis

With her Matie

63.158   By Lawrence Shref groser a Suger lof a boxe of Nutmegg and Synamon

With her Matie

63.159   By Adams Schole Mr to the henchemen a Drawght vpon fyne cloth for a
     peir of sleves

dd to the Lady Cobham

63.160   By Chamberlen of wodstock foure waistecoates of Guarnesey making

With her Matie

63.161   By Anthony Anthony a Candlesticke of siluer guilt the shank christall
     with a peire of Snoffers of siluer guilte poz togethers . . . . xxj oz iij qrt

dd to the said John Asteley

63.162   By Traford Chief clerke of the Spicery two dysshes of Aples Oringes
     Pomegranettes Lemons and Chessenuttes

63.163   By George Webster Mr Cooke a Marchepayne of suger plate like a
     Castle

63.164   By John Bettis Seriaunte of the Pastrye a Quince Pye

[blank]

63.165   By Marke Anthony A Bason and Ewer of Byrrall

dd to the said John Asteley *ex et oner*

63.166   By Anthony of Myllen a Smale Cusshion Cofer to putt necessaryes in
     couerid with blak vellat layed with passamayne of siluer

dd to Mrs Dorothye

63.167   By Alen Bandenson Crosbowemaker oone feyre Crosbowe with a Gaffle

63.168   By Lewis Byllyard crosbowemaker oone feyre Crosbowe with a Gaffle

dd to Robt Childre yeoman of the Crosbowes

63.169   By william Mvge a Booke callid the Acidence of Armes

dd to Mrs blaunche

63.170   By Robert Cooke als Chester Herrald a Booke cont the Armes of all the
     Gentilmen in Lyncolneshire couerid with purple vellat

With her Matie

63.171   By Alen Marchaunte two half Boltes of Camryck in a Case of
     Cr[imson] Satten

dd to Mrs blauche

63.172   By Richard Mathew cutler a peire of knyves the sheth couerid with
     crymsen vellat with a lase and tasselles of crymsen silke and golde

dd to the said Mrs blaunche

63.173   By John Fitzwilliams oone glasse Cup of Chrystall of the Mountayne
     with a couer and foote of siluer guilte

dd to Mr Tameworth

Elizabeth R
[sign manual]

Anno Regni
Regine Elizabeth Quinto

Neweyeres guiftes
gueft by the Quene her Matie
to those parsones whose names here after ensue, The first of January.
The yere abouesaied
viz

Elizabeth R
[sign manual]

63.174 To the Lady Margeret Strainge oone guilt Cup with a Couer poz. . . xix oz qrt di

Duke Marquesses and Earles

63.175 To the Duke of Norfolke thre guilt Bolles with a couer poz . . . . xlj oz qrt
63.176 To the Marques of Northampton oone guilt Cup with a couer
        poz . . . . xxxviij oz iij qrt
63.177 To the Marquis of wynchester highe Threasourer of England oone guilt
        Bolle with a couer poz . . . . xxxiiij oz di
63.178 To the Earle of Arundell Lorde Stewarde oone guilt Cup with a couer
        poz . . . . .Lxj oz iij qrt
63.179 To the Earle of Northumberlande oone guilt Bolle with a couer poz . . . xxj oz di
63.180 To the Earle of westmerlande oone guilt Bolle with a couer poz. . . xxij oz di qrt
63.181 To the Earle of Shrewisburye one guilt Bolle with a couer poz . . xxxj oz di di qrt
63.182 To the Earle of Darbye oone guilt Bolle with a couer poz. . . . . .xxix oz di
63.183 To the Earle of Rutlande oone guilt Cup with a couer poz . . . . xxxj oz di qrt
63.184 To the Earle of Huntingdon oone guilt Bolle with a couer
        poz . . . . xxvij oz di di qrt
63.185 To the Earle of Bedfourde oone guilt Bolle with a couer poz . . . . . . .xxxij oz qrt
63.186 To the Earle of Pembroke oone guilt Cup with a couer poz . . . . .Lj oz di

Vicounte

63.187 To the vicounte Mountague oone guilt Cup with a couer poz. . . . . . xxj oz qrt di

Busshop

63.188 To the Archebusshop of Caunterbury oone guilt Bolle with a couer
        poz . . . . xlj oz di di qrt
63.189 To the Arche Busshop of Yorke oone guilt Bolle with a couer poz
        . . . . xxxvj oz qrt di
63.190 To the Busshop of Durisme two guilt Bolles with owte a couer poz
        . . . . xxxvj oz di
63.191 To the Busshop of Elye thre guilt Bolles with a couer poz. . . . . . . xxxvj oz qrt di
63.192 To the Busshop of winchester oone guilt Bolle with a couer poz . . xxix oz iij qrt

63.193   To the Busshop of London oone guilt Bolle with a couer poz . . . . xxviij oz
63.194   To the Busshop of Salisbury oone guilt Bolle with a couer poz . . . . . . xxxj oz di
63.195   To the Busshop of worcester oone guilt Salte with a couer
        poz . . . . xxviij oz iij qrt di
63.196   To the Busshop of Lincolne oone guilt Cup with a couer poz . . xxvij oz iij qrt di
63.197   To the Busshop of Chichester oone hanse pott guilt poz . . . . xviij oz di qrt
63.198   To the Busshop of Norwiche oone guilt Bolle with a couer
        poz . . . . xxvij oz qrt di
63.199   To the Busshop of Hereforde oone guilt Bole poz . . . . xxviij oz qrt
63.200   To the Busshop of Lichefilde and Coventry oone guilt Cup with a couer
        poz . . . . xxiiij oz iij qrt
63.201   To the Busshop of Rochester oone guilt Bolle with a couer poz . . xx oz di di qrt
63.202   To the Busshop of St Davies oone hans pott guilt poz . . . . xviij oz di di qrt
63.203   To the Busshop of Bathe oone guilt Cup with a couer poz . . . . xviij oz di
63.204   To the Busshop of Exetor oone haunce pott guilt poz . . . . xviij oz di
63.205   To the Busshop of Peterborowe oone guilt Cup with a couer poz . . . . xviij oz
63.206   To the Busshop of Chester oone guilt Cup with a couer poz . . . . . . xviij oz qrt di
63.207   To the Busshop of Glochester one guilt Cup with a couer poz—
        xvj oz iij qrt, And a guilt Spone poz oone ounce iij qrt in toto . . . . . xviij oz di

Duchesses Marques and Countesses

63.208   To the Duches of Norfolke oone guilt Bolle with a couer poz . . . . . . xxxvj oz qrt
63.209   To the Duches of Suffolke thre guilt Bolles with a couer poz . . . iiij^{xx} vj oz iij qrt
63.210   To the Duches of Somersett oone guilt Cup with a couer poz. . . . xxviij oz iij qrt
63.211   To the Marques of Northampton oone guilt Cup with a couer
        poz . . . . xxviij oz iij qrt
63.212   To the Countes of Surrey oone guilt Cup with a couer poz . . . . xij oz
63.213   To the Countes of Oxforde oone guilt Cup with a couer poz . . . . xij oz qrt
63.214   To the Countes of Northumberlande oone guilt Cup with a couer poz . xx oz di
63.215   To the Countes of Shrewisbury Dowager oone guilt Cup with a couer
        poz . . . . .xxij oz qrt
63.216   To the Countes of Shrewisbury oone guilt Cup with a couer poz . . . . . . xxj oz di
63.217   To the Countes of Darbye oone guilt Cup with a couer poz . . . . . xxj oz di di qrt
63.218   To the Countes of Rutlande oone guilt Cup with a couer poz. . . . . .xxx oz
63.219   To the Countes of Huntingdon Dowager oone guilt Cup with a couer
        poz . . . . xix oz iij qrt di
63.220   To the Countes of Huntingdon oone guilt Cup with a couer
        poz . . . . xxxiiij oz di qrt
63.221   To the Countes of Pembroke oone guilt Cup with a couer poz
        . . . . xxvij oz di di qrt

Vicountesses

63.222   To the vicountes Hereforde L. willowebyes wyef oone guilt Cup with a
        couer poz . . . . xij oz
63.223   To the vicountes Montague oone guilt Cup with a couer poz . . . xviij oz di di qrt

Lordes

63.224   To the Lorde keper of the great Seale Bacon two guilt Saltes with a couer
         poz . . . . xxxv oz di

63.225   To the Lorde william Howarde Lorde Chamberlayne one guilt Cup with
         a couer poz. . . . . .xxvij oz qrt

63.226   To the Lorde Caree of Hunsdon oone guilt Bolle with a couer poz
         . . . . xxxvj oz di qrt

63.227   To the Lorde Clynton Lorde Admirall oone guilt Bolle with a couer
         poz . . . . xxv oz di di qrt

63.228   To the Lorde Pagett oone guilt Bolle with a couer poz . . . . .xxv oz qrt di

63.229   To the Lorde Riche oone guilt Cup with a couer poz—xxj oz di di qrt ,
         And a guilt Bolle with a Couer poz—xiij oz qrt di in toto. . . . . .xxxv oz

63.230   To the Lorde North oone guilt Bolle with a couer poz . . . . xxxij oz di di qrt

63.231   To the Lorde Lumley oone guilt Bolle with a couer poz . . . . .xxix oz di

63.232   To the Lorde Hastinges of Lougheborowe oone guilt Bolle with a couer
         poz . . . . xxiiij oz di di qrt

63.233   To the Lorde Stafforde oone guilt Cup with a couer poz. . . . . xij oz di qrt

63.234   To the Lorde Barkeley oone guilt Cup with a couer poz . . . . .xxj oz di

63.235   To the Lorde windesore oone guilt Cup with a couer poz . . . . .xix oz di

63.236   To the Lorde John Grey oone guilt Cup with a couer poz. . . . . xxiiij oz di

63.237   To the Lorde Mountejoye oone guilt Cup with a couer poz . . . . .xx oz iij qrt

63.238   To the Lorde Aburgavennye oone guilt Cup with a couer poz. . . . . xij oz

63.239   To the Lorde Scrowpe oone guilt Cup with a couer poz . . . . xix oz di di qrt

63.240   To the Lorde Strainge oone guilt Cup with a couer poz. . . . . .xv oz qrt

63.241   To the Lorde Darcye oone guilt Cup with a couer poz . . . . xix oz qrt

Ladies

63.242   To the Lady Howarde oone guilt Cup with a couer poz. . . . . .xxiij oz

63.243   To the Lady Clinton oone guilt Cup with a couer poz. . . . . xxviij oz iij qrt

63.244   To the Lady Caree of Hunsden oone guilt Cup with a couer poz . . . . . . .xxiij oz

63.245   To the Lady Barkeley oone guilt Cup with a couer poz. . . . . xv oz di qrt

63.246   To the Lady Mountejoye oone guilt Cup with a couer poz . . . . xx oz qrt di

63.247   To the Lady Aburgavennye oone guilt Cup with a couer poz . . . . . . xij oz di qrt

63.248   To the Lady Pagett oone guilt Bolle with a couer poz . . . . xv oz di qrt

63.249   To the Lady Tayleboyes Sir Peter Carowe his wife oone guilt Tankerd
         poz . . . . .xxj oz di qrt

63.250   To the Lady Cobham oone guilt Cup with a couer poz—xxxix ounces
         And oone guilt Bolle poz—xxvij di di qrt. . . . . lxvj oz di di qrt

63.251   To the Lady Dakers oone guilt Cup with a couer poz . . . . xix oz qrt

63.252   To the Lady williams of Tame oone guilt Cup with a couer poz . . xx oz di di qrt

63.253   To the Lady Knowlles Oone bason and a Layer guilt poz . . . . . .iiij^{xx} vij oz iij qrt

63.254   To the Lady Carewe Sir Gawens wief parte of a guilt Cup with a couer
         poz . . . . .xxxv oz qrt di

63.255   To the Lady Cheeke oone guilt Cup with a couer poz . . . . xiiij oz qrt di

63.256   To the Lady wodehouse oone guilt Cup with a couer poz . . . . xxvj oz qrt

63.257	To the Lady Jobson oone guilt Cup with a couer poz . . . . xxx oz di
63.258	To the Lady Stafford oone guilt Cup with a couer poz . . . . xx oz di
63.259	To the Lady Cecill oone guilt Bolle with a couer poz. . . . . xxvij oz di di qrt
63.260	To the Lady Mason parte of a peire of guilt Flagons poz . . . . xv oz di di qrt
63.261	To the Lady Bulter one hans pott guilt poz . . . . xvj oz iij qrt
63.262	To the Lady Lane oone guilt Cup with a couer poz . . . . xx oz di di qrt
63.263	To the Lady Heningham parte of a guilt Cup with a couer poz . . . . xiiij oz
63.264	To the Lady Ratlyf oone guilt Bolle with a couer poz . . . . xiij oz iij qrt di
63.265	To the Lady Sackevyle oone guilt hauns pott poz . . . . xij oz qrt di
63.266	To the Lady Pallat oone hans pott guilt poz. xij oz di qrt
63.267	To the Lady Seyntlowe oone guilt Cup with a couer poz. . . . . xxvj oz
63.268	To the Lady Yorke oone guilt Salte with a couer poz. . . . . xij oz
63.269	To the Lady Gresham oone guilt Bolle with a couer poz. . . . . xiij oz di di qrt
63.270	To the Lady Throgmorton oone guilt Salte with a couer poz . . . . xj oz di qrt
63.271	To the Lady Elenor Nevelle oone guilt Cup with a couer of the chardge
	of John Asteley Mr and Threasourer of the Quenis Juells and plate
	poz . . . . xv oz qrt *ex et oner*

Knightes

63.272	To Syr Edwarde Rogers Comptroller oone guilt Bolle with a couer poz . . . xx oz
63.273	To Sir william Cecill oone peire of guilt Flagons poz. . . . . Liiij oz di di qrt
63.274	To Sir Frauncis Knowlles vicechamberlayne one Casting Bottle guilt
	poz—vij oz iij qrt and parte of a Bason and a Layer guilt poz—
	xvj oz in toto . . . . xxiij oz iij qrt
63.275	To Sir Ambrose Cave Chauncellor of the Duchye of Lancaster one
	guilt Cup with a couer poz . . . . xxvj oz di
63.276	To Sir Richard Sackevile vnderthreasourer of Englande one guilt Cup
	with a couer poz. . . . . xxiiij oz qrt
63.277	To Sir John Mason Threasourer of the Chamber parte of a parre of guilt
	Flagons poz . . . . .xx oz iij qrt
63.278	To Sir william Peter oone guilt Cup with a couer poz . . . . xxiiij oz iij qrt
63.279	To Sir walter Myldemaye Chauncellor of thexchequer one guilt Bolle
	with a couer poz. . . . . xvij oz di qrt
63.280	To Sir Edmonde Peckeham high Threasourer of the Mynte one guilt
	Cup with a couer poz. . . . . xxj oz di qrt
63.281	To Sir Christofer Haydon oone guilt Cup with a couer poz. . . . . xxvj oz qrt
63.282	To Sir Henry Jernegham oone guilt Cup with a couer poz . . . . xxj oz
63.283	To Sir Edwarde warner oone guilt Cup with a couer poz. . . . . xix oz
63.284	To Sir william Cordall Mr of the Rolles oone guilt Bolle with a couer
	poz . . . . xxj oz di di qrt
63.285	To Sir Richarde Sowthewell oone guilt Bolle with a couer poz . . . . xxj oz qrt
63.286	To Sir John Thynne oone guilt Stowpe with a couer poz . . . . xiiij oz di
63.287	To Sir william Damsell oone guilt Cup with a couer poz. . . . . xxj oz qrt
63.288	To Sir Thomas Benger one guilt Cup with a couer poz . . . . xxiiij oz di di qrt
63.289	To Sir Gowyn Carowe parte of a guilt Cup poz – vj oz and one guilt
	Bolle with a Couer poz – xxix oz di qrt in toto. . . . . . xxxv oz di qrt *ex et oner*

63.290	To Sir Peter Carowe oone guilt Bolle with a couer poz . . . . xxviij oz di
63.291	To Sir Roger North oone guilt Cup with a couer poz . . . . xv oz di di qrt
63.292	To Sir Thomas Gressham oone guilt Cup with a couer poz. . . . . xxij oz di
63.293	To Sir Gilbert Dethyck kinge at Armes oone guilt Cup with a couer poz . . . . xvj oz qrt

Chapleynes

63.294	To Archedeacon Carow Deane of the Chapell oone guilt Cup with a couer poz . . . . xxiij oz
63.295	To Doctor wotten Deane of Caunterburye oone guilt Cup with a couer poz . . . . xxiij oz
63.296	To Peter Vanne Deane of Salisbury oone guilt Cup with a couer poz. . . xxiiij oz

Gentlewomen

63.297	To Maisteris Asteley chief gentilwoman of prevy Chamber Onne guilt Salte with a couer poz—xiij oz di qrt / Another guilt Salte poz— iiij oz di qrt and viij guilt Spones poz—xvj oz di and another guilt Salte poz—iiij oz di qrt in toto. . . . . .xxxvij oz iij qrt
63.298	To Mrs Blaunche Apparye oone guilt Cup with a couer poz. . . . . .xvij oz qrt
63.299	To Mrs Skypwithe oone guilt Cup with a couer poz . . . . xv oz di di qrt
63.300	To Mrs Harington oone guilt Cup with a couer poz . . . . .xv oz qrt
63.301	To Mrs Henneage oone guilt Salte with a couer poz . . . . xxj oz iij qrt
63.302	To Mrs Dorothy Brodelt oone guilt Cup with a couer poz . . . . xvij oz qrt di
63.303	To Mrs Marberye oone guilt Cup with a couer poz. . . . . xiij oz iij qrt
63.304	To Mrs katheryn Caree oone guilt Cup with a couer poz . . . . .n[il]. li
63.305	To Mrs wingfilde oone guilt Cup with a couer poz . . . . .xv oz qrt
63.306	To Mrs Baptest oone guilt Cup with a couer poz. . . . . xvj oz qrt
63.307	To Mrs Dane oone guilt Cup with a couer poz . . . . xviij oz qrt di
63.608	To Mrs Bareley als Penne oone guilt Cup with a couer poz. . . . . xj oz qrt
63.609	To Mrs Snowe widowe oone guilt Cup with a couer poz . . . . xiij oz di qrt
63.610	To Mrs Levina Terling two guilt Spones poz . . . . v oz iij qrt di
63.611	To Mrs Anne Shelton oone guilt Cup with a couer poz—x oz iij qrt / And a guilt Spone poz—one ounce iij qrt di in toto. . . . . xij oz di di qrt
63.612	To Mrs Elizabeth Shelton oone guilt Salte with a couer poz . . . . xiij oz qrt di
63.313	To Mrs Smalepage als Randall two guilt Spones poz. . . . . vj oz
63.314	To Mrs Huggens oone guilt Bolle with a couer poz . . . . xxj oz iij qrt

Maydens of Honor

63.315	To Mrs Marye Howarde oone guilt Cup with a couer poz . . . . xj oz iij qrt di
63.316	To Mrs Anne wyndesor oone guilt Bolle with a couer poz . . . . xj oz qrt di
63.317	To Mrs Mary Manxwell oone guilt Bolle with a couer poz . . . . xj oz qrt di
63.318	To Mrs katheryn knevett oone guilt Bolle withowte a couer poz. . . . . . . .xj oz di
63.319	To Mrs Mary Ratclyef oone guilt Stowpe with a couer poz . . . . xj oz qrt
63.320	To Mrs Frauncis Mewtax oone guilt Stowpe with a couer poz . . . . xj oz qrt
63.321	To Mrs Egloesbye Mother of the Maydens oone guilt Bolle . . . . xj oz

Gentlemen

63.322	To Maister John Astely Mr and Threasourer of the Quenis Juelles and plate Oone guilt Cup with a couer poz . . . . xxvij oz
63.323	To Mr Hennage thre guilt Bolles with a couer poz. . . . . xl oz
63.324	To Mr Harington iij g. bolles poz . . . . lix oz di
63.325	To Mr Bashe oone guilt Cup with a couer poz. . . . . xxij oz iij qrt di
63.326	To Mr Standley oone guilt Bolle with a couer poz. . . . . xiiij oz iij qrt
63.327	To Mr John Yonge oone Salte with a couer guilte poz. . . . . xxj oz
63.328	To Doctor Master oone guilt Hans pott poz . . . . .xv oz qrt
63.329	To Doctor Hewicke oone guilt Bolle. . . . . xiiij oz di
63.330	To Huggens oone guilt Cup with a couer poz. . . . . .xxx oz di qrt
63.331	To Benedick Spinula oone guilt Cup with a couer poz. . . . . .xxv oz iij qrt
63.332	To Robotham oone guilt Cruse poz . . . . xiij oz
63.333	To George Mantle rewarded in money payed by the Threasourer of the Chambre . . . . x li
63.334	To Smyth Custumer oone guilt Cup with a Couer poz . . . . xv oz di qrt
63.335	To Armygell wade two guilt Spones poz. . . . . v oz qrt di
63.336	To John Hemewaye oone guilt Stowpe with a couer poz . . . . x oz di di qrt
63.337	To Lawrence Shref Grocer thre guilt Spones poz. . . . . .vj oz di
63.338	To Clement Adames schole Mr to the henchmen rewarded and payed ut supra . . . . xl s
63.339	To Frauncis Chamberlen oone guilt Salte with a couer poz. . . . . xij oz
63.340	To Anthony Anthony oone Hauns Pott guilt poz. xvj oz
63.341	To Traforde chief Clerke of the Spicery two guilt Spones poz. . . . . v oz iij qrt di
63.342	To George webster Mr Cooke oone guilt Cruse poz . . . . viij oz
63.343	To John Bettes Serjaunte of the Pastry two guilt Spones poz . . . . iiij oz
63.344	To Marke Anthony oone guilt Salte with a couer poz . . . . xij oz di
63.345	To Anthony of Myllen oone guilt peper Boxe poz. . . . . v oz iij qrt
63.346	To Allen Crosbowemaker oone guilt Salte with a couer poz . . . . xij oz qrt
63.347	To Lewis Billyard Crosbowemaker oone guilt Salte with a couer poz xj oz qrt di
63.348	To william Monge rewarded in money & payed ut supra. . . . . .xx s
63.349	To Robert Cooke als Chester oone guilt Salte with a couer poz . . . . x oz
63.350	To Alen Marchaunte oone guilt Cup with a couer poz . . . . xx oz di di qrt
63.351	To Richarde Mathewe rewarded in money and payed by the said Threasourer . . . . xl s

Free Guiftes

63.352	To Mr Tamworth oone of the Gromes of the privy Chamber oone guilt Boll poz . . . . viij oz di qrt
63.353	To Mr Thomas Asteley grome &c. oone guilt Cruse poz. . . . . viij oz
63.354	To Mr Henry Sackeford grome &c. oone guilt Cruse poz . . . . viij oz
63.355	To Mr John Baptiste grome &c. oone guilt Cruse poz . . . . viij oz
63.356	To Mr Edwarde Carye oone of the said Gromes one guilt Cruse poz. . . . . viij oz
63.357	To Rauf Hoope yeoman of the Roobes oone guilt Cruse poz. . . . xij oz iij qrt di

63.358   To Nicholas Bristowe Clerke of the Juelles and plate oone guilt Cruse
poz . . . . x oz iij qrt di

63.359   To Edmunde Pigeon yeoman of the said Juelles and plate one guilt
Cruse poz . . . . x oz iij qrt di

63.360   To John Pigeon yeoman of the said Juelles and plate oone guilt Cruse
poz . . . . x oz iij qrt di

63.361   To Stephen Fulwell grome of the said Juelles and plate one guilt Cruse
poz . . . . x oz iij qrt di

Guiftes delyuered at
Sundrye tymes in mannor & fourme
folowyng
viz.

63.362   Syr Frauncis Knolles
Gevon by the Quene her Matie this xviij of Maye Anno quarto Regni
Regine Elizabeth at the Christeninge of Syr Frauncis Knowlles his
Doughter Thre guilt Bolles with a couer bought of the Goldesmythes
poz . . . . xlvj oz di

63.363   Lorde Leuyngton
Item gevon the vjth of July Ao iiij^{to} predicto to the Lorde Leuyngton
Ambassetor of Scotland Oone Bason and oone Ewer guilte poz—
lxxv oz di / Item oone peir of guilte Pottes poz—iiij^{xx} xj oz di /
Item oone peire of guilte Flagons poz – iiij^{xx} ix oz / And thre guilte
Bolles with a couer poz – lxxij oz di all bought of the goldesmithes
in toto. . . . . .CCCxxviij oz

63.364   Mounseur Velleville
Item gevon the xvijth of August Ao iiij^{to} predicto to Mounseur
Velleville Ambassator from the Frenche kinge Oone peire of guilte
Pottes poz – iiij^{xx} x oz qrt / Item oone peire of guilte Flagons poz—
Cxix oz iij qrt / Item thre guilte Bolles with a couer poz—liiij oz /
Item oone Bason and oone Ewer guilte poz – lxvij oz / And two
guilte Saltes with a couer poz – xliij oz di di qrt all bought of the
goldesmythes in toto . . . . .CCClxxiiij oz di di qrt

63.365   Thomas Asteley
Ite[m gevon the ixth of Septem]ber Ao iiij^{to} predicto at the Christening
of Mr Thomas Ast[eley his Childe a guilt C]up with a couer bought
of the Goldesmythes
poz [...] . . . . xxiiij oz qrt

63.366   Lorde Hunsdon
Item gevon the xxvjth of December Ao v^{to} Regne Regine Elizabeth
at the Christeninge of the Lorde of Hunsden his Childe thre guilt
Bolles with a couer bought of the Goldesmythes poz . . . . . . iiij^{xx} j oz iij qrt

63.367   vicounte Hereforde
          Item gevon the iij^de of February Ao vto predicto at the Christeninge
          of the vicount Hereforde his Childe oone guilt Cup with a couer
          bought of the Goldesmythes poz . . . . xlv oz
63.368   Syr Thomas Chamberleyne
          Item gevon the vij^th of Marche Anno predicto at the Christeninge of
          Syr Thomas Chamberlen his Doughter Oone guilt Bolle with a
          couer bought of the Goldesmythes poz . . . . xxvij oz di di qrt

Anno Regni
Regine Elizabeth Sexto

Newe yeris guiftes geuon to
the Quene her majestie by these persons whose
names hereafter ensue. The First of Januarye
the yere abouesaide
viz.

Elizabeth R
[sign manual]

64.1   By the Lady Mary Graye a Spone and a Forke of siluer guilte poz . . . . j oz

ex et oner

Deluyerid in chardge to John Asteley esquire Mr &
Threasourer of her Maties Juelles & plate

64.2   By the Lady Margarett Strainge a Hatte of vellat enbrauderid with golde
and siluer with a Fether, and a Skarfe of sipers with a frenge of venice golde
and siluer

Deluyerid to the Lady Cobham

Duke Marquesses and Earles

64.3   By the Duke of Norfolke in a purse of crymsen silke and golde in golde . . . xx li
64.4   By the Marques of Northampton in a purse of blake silke and siluer in
Dimy Soueraignes . . . . xx li
64.5   By the Marques of Wyntchester Highe Threasourer of Englande in a purse
of crymsen Satten in Dimy Soveraignes . . . . xx li
64.6   By the Earle of Arundell lorde Stewarde in a paper in Dimy Soueraignes . xxx li
64.7   By the Earle of Northumberlande in a purse of russett silke and siluer in
Di soueraignes . . . . x li
64.8   By the Earle of Westemerlande in a purse of purple silke and golde in
Angelles . . . . x li
64.9   By the Earle of Shrewisburye in a purse of crymsen vellat in Dimy
Soueraignes . . . . xx li
64.10   By the Earle of Darbye in a purse of russett silke in Dimy Soueraignes . . . . xx li
64.11   By the Earle of Huntingdon in a purse of purple silke and siluer in golde . . . x li
64.12   By the Earle of Bedfourde in a purse of crymsen silke & siluer in Dimy
Soueraignes . . . . xx li
64.13   By the Earle of Pembrocke in a purse of blake silke and golde in Dimy
Soueraignes . . . . xxx li

Delyuerid to the Quenis Matie by thandes of John Tameworth esquire one of
the gromes of her highnes pryvy Chamber the xxj of July Ao vj^{to} pred

64.14   By the Earle of Warwicke a paire of Sleues a partelett and a Cawle enbossed
with venice golde and siluer

Delyuerid to the said Lady Cobham

Viscounte

64.15   By the Viscounte Mountague in a purse of blewe silke in Dimy
        Soueraignes . . . . x li
                Delyuerid to her said Matie by thandes of the said John Tameworth &c

Busshoppes

64.16   By the Archebusshoppe of Caunterburye in a purse of crymsen taphata in
        Dimy Soueraignes . . . . .xl li
64.17   By the Archebusshoppe of Yorke in a purse of crymsen satten in Dimy
        Soueraignes . . . . xxx li
64.18   By the Busshop of Duresme in a purse of Tynsell in Angelles. . . . . xxx li
64.19   By the Busshop of Ely in a litell taphata purse in Dimy Soueraignes . . . . . xxx li
64.20   By the Busshop of Wyntchester in a purse of baudeken in Dimy
        Soueraignes . . . . xx li
64.21   By the Busshop of London in a white Satten purse in Dimy Soueraignes . . xx li
64.22   By the Busshop of Worseter in a chery bag of crymsen taphata silke in
        Dimy Soueraignes . . . . xx li
64.23   By the Busshop of Lincolne in a purse of blake silke in Dimy
        Soueraignes . . . . xx li
64.24   By the Busshop of Norwiche in a purse of blake Tynsell in Dimy
        Soueraignes . . . . xx li
64.25   By the Busshop of Rochester Amner in a purse of blake silke in Dimy
        Soueraignes . . . . xiij li vij s
                Deliuyered to her said Matie by thande of the said John Tamworth &c
                And a Booke of thexposition of the newe Testament in latten
                                        Deluyerid to Blaunche Apparry
64.26   By the Busshop of Lichefilde and Couentrye in a paper in Dimy
        Soureraignes. . . . . xiij li vj s viij d
64.27   By the Busshop of Chitchester in a purse of baudeken in Dimy
        Soueraignes . . . . x li
64.28   By the Busshop of Herforde in a purse of crymsen silke in Dimy
        Soueraignes . . . . x li
64.29   By the Busshop of St Dauies in a purse of crymsen silke & siluer in Dimy
        Soueraignes . . . . x li
64.30   By the Busshop of Bathe in a paper in Dimy Soueraignes. . . . . x li
64.31   By the Busshop of Exetor in a purse of red silke and golde in Dimy
        Soueraignes . . . . x li
64.32   By the Busshop of Peterborowe in a purse of crymsen satten in Dimy
        Soueraignes . . . . x li
64.33   By the Busshop of Chester in a purse of grene silke in Angelles . . . . x li
64.34   By the Busshop of Gloucester in a purse of tawny vellat in golde Dimy
        Soueraignes . . . . xx li
64.35   By the Busshop of Salisbury in a purse of crymsen Satten in Dimy
        Soueraignes . . . . xx li
                Deliuyered to her said Matie by thande of the said John Tamworth &c.

Duchesses Marques & Countesses

64.36   By the Duches of Norfolke in a purse of crymsen silke and golde in
golde. . . . . xx li

64.37   By the Duches of Suffolke in a purse of blewe silke in Dimy Soueraignes . . xv li

64.38   By the Duches of Somersett in a purse of silke and siluer in
golde. . . . . xiiij li iij s iiij d

                     Delyuerid to her said Matie by thande of the said John Tameworth &c.

64.39   By the Lady Marques of Northampton a Petycoate of crymsen clothe of
golde lyned with doble crymsen taphata garded with a brode garde of
crymsen vellat layed on with thre passamayne laces of golde & frengid
with crymsen silke and golde

                 Delyuerid in chardge to Rauf Hoope yeoman of the Roobes

64.40   By the Countes of Surrey in a purse of carnacion silke in Angelles . . . . C s

64.41   By the Countes of Oxfourde in a purse of blewe silke in Angelles . . . . C s

64.42   By the Countes of Northumberlande in a purse of blake silke & golde in
Dimy Soueraignes . . . . x li

64.43   By the Countes of Shrewesburye dowager in a purse of blake silke &
siluer in Dimy Soueraignes . . . . xij li

64.44   By the Countes of Shrewesburye in a purse of crymsen vellat in Dimy
Soueraignes . . . . x li

64.45   By the Countes of Darbye in a purse of russett silke in Dimy Soueraignes . . x li

64.46   By the Countes of Rutlande in a purse of crymsen silke & golde in golde
& siluer. . . . . xiij li vj s viij d

64.47   By the Countes of Huntingdon dowager in a paper in Dimy Soueraignes . . . x li

64.48   By the Countes of Huntingdon in a purse of blewe silke in Angelles . . . . x li

64.49   By the Countes of Pembrouke in a purse of red silke and golde in Dimy
Soueraignes . . . . xv li

Delyuered to the Quene her Matie by thande of the said Jo. Tameworth ut supra

Vicountesses

64.50   By the Vicountes Hertforde a Smocke with a square coller and a Rayle
wroughte with blake silke and golde

                     Delyuerid to Dorothe Brodbelt

64.51   By the Vicountes Mountague in a purse of blewe silke in Dimy
soueraignes. . . . . x li

            Delyuerid to her said Matie by thandes of the said John Tameworth

Lordes

64.52   By the Lorde keper of the greate Seale Bacon in a purse of blewe silke and
siluer in Dimy Soueraignes and one Crusado. xiij li vj s

64.53   By the Lorde William Howarde Lorde Chamberlayne in a purse of blewe
silke and siluer in Dimy Soueraignes. . . . . x li

64.54   By the Lorde Aburgavenny in a purse of crymsen silke and siluer in Di
Soueraignes . . . . C s

64.55   By the Lorde Clinton Lorde Admirall in a purse of blak silke and siluer . . . . x li

64.56 By the Lorde Strainge in a purse of crymsen silke . . . . C s

64.57 By the Lorde Barkeley in a paper in Dimy soueraignes . . . . x li

64.58 By the Lorde Scrowpe in a paper in Angelles . . . . x li

64.59 By the Lorde Lumley in a purse of crymsen silke . . . . xx li

64.60 By the Lorde Mountejoye in a purse of blewe silke in golde . . . . . ix li xiij s iiij d

64.61 By the Lorde Wyndesore in a purse of crymsen silke & siluer in Dimy
Soueraignes . . . . x li

64.62 By the Lorde Riche in a purse of crymsen vellat in Dimy Soueraignes . . . . . xx li

64.63 By the Lorde Pagett in a very fayer purse in Dimy Soueraignes . . . . xx li

64.64 By the Lorde Darcey of Chichey in a purse of Baudeken . . . . x li

64.65 By the Lorde North in a paper in Dimy Soueraignes . . . . xx li

64.66 By the Lorde Hastinges of Loughborowe in a paper in golde and siluer
. . . . xiij li vj s viij d

64.67 By the Lorde Hunsdon in a purse of crymsen silke and golde in Dimy
Soueraignes . . . . x li

> Delyuerid to her Matie by thandes of the said John Tameworth

64.68 By the Lorde John Graye a Spiceboxe with a Spone a peperBoxe & a
Salte of siluer guilt poz . . . . xxiij oz di

> Delyuerid in chardge to the said John Asteley

Ladyes

64.69 By the Lady Aburgauenny in a purse of crymsen silke in Dimy Soueraignes . . C s

> Delivered to her said Matie by thandes of the said Jo. Tameworth

64.70 By the Lady Clinton a peire of Sleues and a partelett of stoleworke drawne
owte with blake Sipers

> Delyuerid to the said Lady Cobham

64.71 By the Lady Barckeley in a paper in Dimy Soueraignes . . . . C s

64.72 By the Lady Dakers of the Southe in a purse of blake silke in Angelles . . . . . x li

> Delyuerid to her said Matie by the handes of the said John Tameworth

64.73 By the Lady Cobham a Remnaunte of crymsen Taphata rewid with golde

> With her self

64.74 By the Lady Mountejoye in a purse of blewe silke in golde . . . . . . ix li xiij s iiij d

64.75 By the Lady Howarde in a purse of russett silke & siluer in Dimy
Soueraignes . . . . x li

64.76 By the Lady Hunsdon in a purse of crymsen silke and golde in Dimy
Soueraignes . . . . x li

> Delyuerid to her said Matie ut supra

64.77 By the Lady Knowlles a partelett a peire of sleues and a Cawle of golde and
siluer with golde and siluer sarceonett to lyne them

> Delyuerid to the Lady Cobham

64.78 By the Lady Cecille in a purse of crymsen silke in Dimy Soueraignes . . . . x li

64.79 By the Lady Taylboyes Sir Peter Carewes wief in a purse of blak silke in
golde . . . . x li

64.80 By the Lady Williams of Thame in a purse of blak silke and siluer in dimy
soueraignes . . . . x li

> Delyuerid to her said Matie by thande of the said John Tomeworth

64.81 By the Lady Carey Sir Lawrens [sic Gawain] wief a partelett and a Cawle
wrought with blake silke and edged with siluer

Deluyerid to the Lady Cobham

64.82 By the Lady Wodhouse in a purse of russett silke and golde in Dimy
Soueraignes . . . . x li

64.83 By the Lady Jobson in a purse of crymsen silke and golde in Angelles . . . . . . x li

Delyuerid to her said Matie by thandes of the said John Tomeworth &c.

64.84 By the Lady Stafforde a very fayre partelett and a peire of Sleues of Lawne
lowped ouer with golde

Delyuerid to the Lady Cobham

64.85 By the Lady Mason in a purse of blewe silke and siluer in Dimy
Soueraignes . . . . vj li

64.86 By the Lady Butler in frenche Crownes . . . . vj li

Delyuerid to her said Matie by thandes of the said Jo. Tomeworth

64.87 By the Lady Heningham sixe handekercheues wrought with blak silke edgid
with a purle of golde

64.88 By the Lady Ratclyf a Cusshencloth allouer wrought with blak silke and
a swete bagge

Deluyerid to the said Dorothye Brodbelt

64.89 By the Lady Sackevile in a purse of grene silke in Angelles . . . . C s

64.90 By the Lady Pallet in a paper in Angelles . . . . C s

Delyuerid to her said Matie by thandes of the said John Tameworth

64.91 By the Lady Gresham a Horse

In the Stable

64.92 By the Lady Grey a peire of Sleues and a partelett allouer enbrauderid with
golde and siluer the grounde like Tyncell

Delyuerid to the Lady Cobham

Knightes

64.93 By Sir Edwarde Rogers Comptroller in a purse of crymsen silke in Di
Soueraignes . . . . vij li

64.94 By Sir Frauncis Knowles Vice Chamberlayne in a purse of crymsen silke
and golde in Di soueraignes . . . . x li

64.95 By Sir William Cicell Secretarye in a purse of blewe silke & siluer in Dimy
Soueraignes . . . . xx li

64.96 By Sir Ambrose Caue Chauncellor of the Duche in a purse of crymsen
silke & gold . . . . xv li

64.97 By Sir Richarde Sackeuile vnder Threasourer in a purse of blake silke &
golde in Angelles . . . . x li

64.98 By Sir John Mason Threasorer of the Chamber in a purse of crymson
silke & golde. . . . . viij li

Delyuerid to her said Matie by the handes of the said John Tomeworth
And a Booke in Greeke

Deluyerid to the saide blaunch Apparry

64.99 By Sir William Peter Chauncellor of the Garter in a chery bag of taphata
in Angelles . . . . x li

64.100	By Sir Walter Myldemaye Chauncellor of the Exchequer in a paper in Dimy soueraignes . . . . C s
64.101	By Sir Edmunde Peckeham high Threasourer of the Myntes in a purse of red taphata . . . . x li
64.102	By Sir Christopher Haydon in a purse of blak silke and golde in Angelles. . . x li
64.103	By Sir Edwarde Warner in a purse of crymsen Satten in golde . . . vj li xiij s iiij d
64.104	By Sir William Cordall Mr of the Rowles in a blake chery bagge in Angelles . . . . x li
64.105	By Sir Richarde Southewell in a paper in Dimy Soueraignes. . . . . x li
64.106	By Sir John Thynne in a very litell chery bag in Dimy Soueraignes. . . . . C s
64.107	By Sir William Damsell in a purse of blak taphata in Dimy Soueraignes . . . . x li
	Delyuerid to her said Matie by thande of the said John Tomeworth
64.108	By Sir Thomas Benger oone smale Ringe of golde with a table Diamounte in it
	with her Matie
64.109	By Sir Gowen Carowe a Smocke wrought with blak silke the coller wrought with gold & siluer
	dd to the said Dorothye
64.110	By Sir Peter Carowe in a purse of blake silke and siluer in Dimy Soueraignes . . . . x li
64.111	By Sir Roger Northe in a paper in golde and siluer . . . . vj li xiij s iiij d
64.112	By Sir Thomas Gresham in a purse of blak silke and siluer in Dimy Soueraignes . . . . x li
	Delyuerid to her said Matie by thandes of the said Jo. Tameworth &c.
64.113	By Sir Gilbert Dethicke oone Booke of thearmes of the Garter couered with blak vellat and edgid with passamayne of siluer
	Delyuerid to the said Blaunche Apparrye

Chaplaines

64.114	By Archedeacon Carowe Deane of the Chappell in a paper in Dimy soueraignes. . . . . x li
64.115	By Doctor wotton Deane of Caunterbury in a purse of crymsen silke & siluer in Dimy Souereraignes. . . . . x li
	Delyuerid to her said Matie by the handes of the said John Tomeworth

Gentlewomen

64.116	By Maistres Asteley chief gentilwoman of the preuy Chamber A Smocke wrought with blake silke onely with a square coller
	Delyuerid to the said Dorothye
64.117	By Mrs Blaunche Parye a peire of perfumed Gloues sett with buttons of golde & pearles
	Delyuerid to the Quene by Elizabeth Marbery
	And six handekercheues edgid with siluer and silke of sundry colores
64.118	By Mrs Skipworth a Smocke the sleues allouer wrought with blake silke
	Delyuerid to the said Dorothye

64.119   By Mrs Hennage a very fayre peire of Sleues a Partelett and a Cawle of
       Camerycke allouer wrought with golde and siluer

Delyuerid to the Lady Cobham

64.120   By Mrs Dorothy Brodebelte a Rayle of Lawne wrought with golde
64.121   By Mrs Kathryn Howarde a peire of Pillowebeeres wrought with blake
       silke
64.122   By Mrs Marberye a Smocke wrought with red silke & edgid with a
       passamayne of siluer

Delyuerid to the said Dorothy

64.123   By Mrs Sackefourde a peire of Sleues of lynen cloth enbrauderid with
       golde & siluer

Delyuerid to the Lady Cobham

64.124   By Mrs Barlye als Penne sixe handekercheues edgid with passamayne of golde
       and buttons of golde

Delyuerid to the said Dorothye

64.125   By Mrs Leuina Terling a certayne Journey of the Quenis Matie and the Trayne
       fynely wrought vpon a Carde

[blank]

64.126   By Mrs Amy Shelton sixe handekerchures edgid with golde and siluer
64.127   By Mrs Elizabeth Shelton oone Cusshen clothe wrought with red silke
       and a passamayne of golde and buttoned and tasselled with red silke
       and golde

Delyuverid to the said Dorothye

64.128   By Mrs Huggens one Pillowebeere wrought with hoopes & flowers of red
       silke And one greate swete Bagge of taphata enbrauderid with a hoope
       of golde / And sixe smaule sweete Bagges of changeable taphata

dd to the Lady Cobham

64.129   By Mrs Smytheson, Laundres oone Pillowebeere wrought with red silke

dd to the said Dorothye

Gentlemen

64.130   By Maister John Asteley Maister and Threasourer of the Quene her Maties
       Juelles and plate a very fayer Cup of siluer guilt made like a Gourde
       poz . . . . xviij oz qrt

Delyuerid to himself in chardge

64.131   By Mr Thomas Hennage a Ringe of golde made like a Yoake sett full of
       sparkes of Diamondes with this worde in it Iugum necessitatis

with the Quene by the said Marbery

64.132   By Mr Bashe in a purse of blake silke and golde in Dimy Soueraignes. . . . . . x li
64.133   By Mr Stanlye in a purse of crymsen silke and siluer in Dimy
       Soueraignes . . . . vj li

Delyuerid to her said Matie by the hande of the said John Tameworth

64.134   By Doctor Maister two Pottes of Concerues
64.135   By Doctor Hewicke two Pottes of Concerues

Delyuerid to Henry Sackforde

64.136 By Benedicke Spinola a huole pece of purple vellat with Satten grounde
                                        Delyuerid to the Lady Cobham
64.137 By Robotham two peires of blake knytt hoose
                                        dd to the said Marbery
64.138 By Smyth Customer a bolte of fayre Camerycke in a case of damaske
                                        Delyuerid to the said Blaunche Apparrye
64.139 By John Hemenwaye Poticary two cases Concerues and a square boxe
          of Manus Christi
                                        Delyuerid to the said Sackforde
64.140 By Clement Adames a peire of Sleues of fyne hollande Drawne fynely with a
          worke vnwrought
                                        Delyuerid to the said Dorothye
64.141 By Traifourde Clerke of the Spicerye thre boxes of Comfittes, with Lemons,
          Orinages, and other frute
                                        dd to the said Sackforde
64.142 By George Webster Mr Cooke a Marche pane
64.143 By John Bettes serjaunte of the Pastrye a Quince Pye
64.144 By Gardener Serjaunte of the Seller a Bottell of Ipocras
                                        [blank]
64.145 By Petrus vbaldinis florentinus a Booke conteigning the seremonyes of the
          Coronation of Themperors
                                        Delyuerid to the said Blaunche Apparrye
64.146 By William Huggens oone Cusshion cloth wroughte with Hoopes and Raspes
          frengid with golde and red silke
                                        dd to the said Dorothye

Summa totalis of the money Gevon to her Matie ut supra
. . . . m mcclvij li viij s viij d

Elizabeth R
[sign manual]

                                        J Asteley
                                        Edm Pigeon

[Anno regni regine Elizabeth Sexto]

[Newe yeres guiftes geuen by]
[the Quene her majesties to those persones whose]
[names hereafter ensue The First of Januarye]
[the year abovesaide]
[viz]

[Incomplete Roll – Begins with "To Knights" Does not list Earls, Duchesses & Countesses, Bishops, Lordes, Baronesses and Ladies.]

Knightes

64.147 To Sir Edwarde Rogers Comptroller oone guilt Bolle with a couer poz . . . xx oz

64.148 To Sir William Cicell Secretary oone guilt Bolle with a couer poz. . . . . . xxxvj oz

64.149 To Sir Frauncis Knowles vicechamberlaine one guilt Cup with a couer poz. xxiij oz di

64.150 To Sir Ambrose Caue Chauncellor of the Duchye one guilt Cup with a couer poz . . . . .xxv oz qrt

64.151 To Sir Richarde Sackuile vnder Threasourer oone guilt Cup with a couer poz . . . . xxiiij oz

64.152 To Sir John Mason Threasourer of the Chamber oone haunce pott guilt poz . . . . xxj oz

64.153 To Sir William Peter Chauncellor of the Garter oone guilt Cup with a couer poz . . . . xxiiij oz di qrt

64.154 To Sir Walter Myldemaye Chauncellor of thexchequer oone guilt Cup with a couer poz. . . . . .xvij oz qrt

64.155 To Sir Edmunde Peckeham highe Threasourer of the Myntes one guilt Bolle with a couer poz . . . . xx oz

64.156 To Sir Christopher Haydon oone guilt Salte with a couer poz. . . . . xxvj oz iij qrt

64.157 To Sir Edwarde Warner oone guilt Cup with a couer poz . . . . . . xviij oz iij qrt di

64.158 To Sir William Cordall Mr of the Rowles oone guilt Bolle with a couer poz . . . . xx oz di di qrt

64.159 To Sir Richarde Southewell one guilt Bolle with a couer poz . . . . xx oz iij qrt di

64.160 To Sir John Thynne oone guilt Cup with a couer poz . . . . xiiij oz

64.161 To Sir William Damsell oone guilt Bolle with a couer poz. . . . . xxj oz

64.162 To Sir Thomas Benger oone guilt Cup with a couer poz . . . . xxiiij oz qrt di

64.163 To Sir Gowen Carowe parte of a guilt Bolle with a couer poz. . . . . .xxxv oz

64.164 To Sir Peter Carowe oone guilt Cup with a couer poz . . . . xxviij oz qrt

64.165 To Sir Roger Northe oone guilt Bolle with a couer poz . . . . xx oz

64.166 To Sir Thomas Gresham oone guilt Bolle with a couer poz. . . . . xxj oz di qrt

64.167 To Sir Gilbert Dethicke oone guilt Bolle with a couer poz. . . . . .xvj oz di

Chaplaynes

64.168 To Archedeacon Carowe Deane of the Chappell oone guilt Cup with a couer poz . . . . xxiiij oz di di qrt

64.169 To Doctor Wotton Deane of Caunterbury oone guilt Cup with a couer poz . . . . xxiiij oz iij qrt

Gentlewomen

64.170 To Mrs Asteley chief gentilwoman of the preuye Chamber Oone guilt Bolle with a couer poz—xxviij oz di And a guilt Cup with a couer poz —x oz qrt di in toto. . . . . xxxiij oz iij qrt di

64.171 To Mrs Blaunche Pary oone guilte peper Boxe poz—iiij oz di qrt and a
guilt Cup with a couer poz—xiij oz in toto . . . . xvij oz di qrt

64.172 To Mrs Skipworth oone guilt Bolle withowte a couer poz . . . . xv oz di

64.173 To Mrs Hennage parte of a Bason and a Leyer poz—lviij oz qrt thereof
for her guifte—xviij oz qrt And one guilt Spone poz—ij oz qrt in
toto . . . . xx oz di

64.174 To Mrs Dorothey Brodebelte oone guilt Bolle with a couer poz . . . . xvj oz iij qrt

64.175 To Mrs Marberye oone guilt Salte with a couer poz . . . . xiij oz di qrt

64.176 To Mrs Barlye als Penne oone guilt Cup with a couer poz . . . . xj oz di qrt

64.177 To Mrs Leuina Terling oone guilt Casting Bottell poz . . . . v oz iij qrt di

64.178 To Mrs Amye Shelton oone guilt Salte with a couer poz . . . . xij oz di

64.179 To Mrs Elizabeth Shelton oone guilt Cup with a couer poz . . . . . xij oz di di qrt

64.180 To Mrs Huggans oone guilt Cup with a couer poz . . . . xx oz di

64.181 To Mrs Sackefourde oone guilt Bolle with a couer poz . . . . xix oz di qrt

64.182 To Mrs Smytheson, Laundres oone guilt Salte with a couer poz . . . . vij oz iij qrt

Maydens of Honor

64.183 To Mrs Marye Howarde parte of thre guilt Bolles with a couer poz . . xj oz qrt di

64.184 To Mrs Anne Wyndesor parte of a stone Jug garnesshid with siluer guilt
poz . . . . xj oz iij qrt di

64.185 To Mrs Katheryn Kneuett oone guilt Cup with a couer poz . . . . . . xj oz iij qrt di

64.186 To Mrs Marye Ratclief oone guilt Bolle with a couer poz . . . . xj oz qrt

64.187 To Mrs Frauncis Mewtas oone guilt Bolle with a couer poz . . . . xj oz qrt

64.188 To Mrs Katheryn Cooke oone guilt Bolle with a couer poz . . . . xj oz qrt

64.189 To Mrs Eglombe, Mother oone guilte Bolle with owte a couer poz . vij oz iij qrt

Gentlemen

64.190 To Mr John Asteley Maister and Threasourer of the Quene her Ma[ties]
Juelles and plate oone guilte Cup with a couer poz . . . . .xxvij oz iij qrt

64.191 To Mr Thomas Hennage parte of a Bason and a leyer guilt poz . . . . xl oz

64.192 To Mr Stanley oone guilt Cup with a couer poz . . . . xiiij oz di di qr

64.193 To Mr Bashe parte of a guilt Bolle with a couer poz . . . . xxiij oz iij [qrt] di

64.194 To Mr Doctor Maister oone guilte Cup with a couer poz . . . . xv oz

64.195 To Mr Doctor Hewicke parte of a guilte Bolle poz . . . . xv oz

64.196 To Benedicke Spinula oone guilt Bolle with a couer poz . . . . xxvij oz di

64.197 To Robotham oone guilt Cup with a couer poz . . . . .xiij oz

64.198 To Smyth Customer oone guilt Bolle with a couer poz . . . . xiiij oz iij qrt

64.199 To John Hemawaye Poticarye oone guilt Bolle with owte a couer poz . . . . . x oz

64.200 To Clement Adames rewarded in money by the Threasourer of the
Chamber . . . . .xl s

64.201 To Traifourde Clearke of the Spicerye oone guilt Casting Bottell
poz . . . . vj oz di qrt

64.202 To George Webster Mr Cooke oone haunce pott guilt poz . . . . viij oz

64.203 To John Bettes serjaunte of the Pastrye parte of a guilt Bolle poz . . iiij oz iij qrt

64.204 To Petrus vbaldinus florentinus oone Casting Bottell guilt poz . . . . vj oz di
64.205 To William Huggens oone guilt Cup with a couer poz. . . . . xxxj oz di

Free Guiftes
64.206

64.207 To Mr John Tamworthe oone of the Gromes of the preuye Chamber parte
        of a guilte Bolle poz . . . . viij oz iij qrt di
64.208 To Mr Thomas Asteley oone other Grome oone guilt Cruse with a
        couer poz . . . . viij oz
64.209 To Mr Henry Sackefourde oone other Grome oone guilt Cruse with a
        couer poz . . . . viij oz
64.210 To Mr John Bapteste oone other Grome oone guilt Cruse with a couer
        poz . . . . viij oz
64.211 To Mr Edwarde Carye oone other Grome oone guilt Cruse with a couer
        poz . . . . viij oz
64.212 To Rauf Hoope yeoman of the Roobes oone guilt Jug with a couer poz . . . .
        xij oz iij qrt di
64.213 To Nicholas Bristowe clearke of the Juelles and plate oone guilt Cruse
        poz . . . . x oz iij qrt di
64.214 To Edmunde Pigeon yeoman of the said Juelles oone guilt Cruse
        poz . . . . x oz iij qrt di
64.215 To John Pigeon one other yeoman of the said Juelles oone guilt Cruse
        poz . . . . x oz iij qrt di
        To Stephen Fulwell Grome of the said Juelles and plate oone guilt Cruse
        poz . . . . x oz iij qrt di

Guiftes delyuerid at sundry
tymes; in manner and fourme folowing.
viz

64.216 Doctor Hewick
        Geuon by the Quene her Matie the xxix^th of Maye Anno Regine
            Elizabeth quinto, At the Christeninge of Doctor Hewicke his
            Doughter oone guilt Cup with a couer prouided for by the
            Goldesmythes poz . . . . xviij oz qrt
64.217 Countye Arco
        Item geuon by her said Matie the iiij^th of June Anno predicto to
            Countye Arco Italian Oone Cup of golde with a couer with Diuers
            flowers enameled and in the top of the couer a blewe Saphier poz—
            xxvj oz iij qrt of the chardge of John Asteley esquire Mr and
            Threasourer of her Maties Juelles and plate, And oone Salte of
            golde with a couer in the toppe thereof the Quenis Armes crowned
            holden by a lyon and a Dragon poz – xvij oz qrt of the said chardge
            in toto. . . . . xliiij oz golde *ex et oner*

64.218   **Lorde Ludington**

Item geuon by her said Matie the xxth of June Anno v^{to} predicto to the Lorde of Ludington Ambassador from the Quene of Skottes Oone Bason and a Layer guilt poz—iiij^{xx} iij oz di Oone payer of guilt Pottes poz—Cxj oz iij qrt : Thre guilt Bolles with a couer— Liiij oz iij qrt di : Oone guilt Salte with a couer poz—xvj oz di qrt : Oone guilt Cup with a couer poz—xlv oz qrt di. And oone other guilt Cup with a couer poz—xxxiiij oz di qrt, all whiche plate prouided for by the said Goldesmythes in toto . . . . CCCxxxix oz iij qrt

64.219   **Mounsieur Teligny**

Item geuon by her said Matie the xxiijth of Februarye Anno v^{to} predicto to Mounsieur Teligny sent from the Admirall of Fraunce Oone Cheyne of golde prouided for by the said Goldesmythes poz

. . . . .xxij oz qrt golde

64.220   **Doctor Master**

Item geuon by her said Matie Ao vj^{to} Regine suae At the Christeninge of Doctor Master his chylde the vth of Marche Oone guilt Cup with a couer made like a gourde geuon to her highnes primo January Anno p.d. by Mr John Asteley Mr and Threasourer of her highnes Juelles and plate poz . . . . xviij oz qrt

64.221   **Sir Nicholas Throgmourton**

Item geuon by her said Matie the xviijth day of Aprell Anno vj^{to} predicto at the Christening of Sir Nicholas Throgmorton his childe Oone guilt Cup with a couer of her highnes store of the chard[g]e of the said John Asteley poz. . . . . xxvij oz iij qrt^{*ex et oner*}

64.222   **Mounsieur Maluisiere**

Item geuon by her said Matie the xxvijth day of Aprell Anno vj^{to} predicto to Mounsieur Maluisiere sent from the Frenche kinge Oone Cheyne of crowne golde bought of the said goldesmythes poz . . . . lxiiij oz iij qrt golde

64.223   **Sir Morice Barkeley**

Item geuon by her said Matie the [blank] at Christening of Sir Morice Barkeley his Childe Oone guilt Cup with a couer bought of the said goldesmythes poz. . . . . xxviij oz

64.224   **Mounsieur Frauncis Halewyn**

Item Geuon by her said Matie the ixth daye of Maye Anno vj^{to} predicto to Mounsieur Frauncis Halewyn Segneor Zveneghen ambassador owte of Flaunders Oone Cheyne of golde bought of the said goldesmythes poz . . . . xxij oz di golde

64.225   **Mounsieur Carovacant, Marchante**

Item geuon by her said Matie the first of June Anno predicto to Mounseur Carovacant, Marchante Oone Cheine of golde bought of the said goldesmythes poz. . . . . xviij oz golde

64.226   Frenche Kinge

Item gevon by her said Matie the xxix^th day of Maye Anno vj^to predicto
to the Frenche Kinge Oone Coller of thorder of the Garter with a
George of golde borowed of the Lorde Robert Dudley Mr of the Horse
poz—xxx oz qrt di et allouer Item oone feyer Garter with buckelles
pendauntes & lettres of goldesmithes worke the buckell and pendaunte
sett with fowre rocke Rubyes and fyue table Diamountes sett between
the wordes with CCiiij^xx iij seede pearles sett in thedge of the garter
bought of Affabell Partridge goldesmythe poz vellat stone pearle and
golde – iij oz di di qrt Item oone George of golde enameled and sett
with nyne Diamondes and thre pearles pendaunte bought of Euerad
Euerdice poz – j oz good in toto . . . . xxxv oz   golde

64.227   Mounsieur Gonnort

Item geuon by her said Matie the xij^th of June Anno predicto to
Mounsieur Gonnorte Ambassador from the Frenche Kinge Oone
Bolle of golde with a couer borowed of the saide Lorde Robert
Dudley poz. . . . . lv oz iij qrt   gold
Item geuon to the said Ambassador Thre guilt Bolles with a couer
poz—Clxiij oz qrt Item one guilte Bolle with a couer poz—Lxiiij
oz Item two peire of guilt Pottes poz—CCCiiij^xx iiij oz iij qrt Item
two peire of guilt Flagons poz—CCCCviij oz di qrt Item thre guilt
Cuppes with thre couers poz—Ciiij^xx v oz iij qrt Item two guilt
Layers poz—xlix oz. Item two guilt Basons and two Ewers guilt
poz—CCxlij oz di. Item two guilt Saltes with oone couer poz—
lxxix oz qrter bought of the said goldesmythes. Item fore guilt
Candlestickes of her Maties store of the chardge of the said John
Asteley poz—Clij oz iij qrt et allouer . . . . mdccxxix oz qrt di

64.228   Mr Charles Howarde

Item geuon by her said Matie the xxiiij^th of June Anno predicto at
the Christeninge of Mr Charles Howarde his doughter Oone guilt
Bolle with a couer bought of the said goldesmythes poz . . . . xxxij oz

64.229   Mr Mackwilliams

Item geuon by her said Matie the xxvij^th of June Anno predicto at the christeninge of Mr Mackwilliams his doughter Oone guilt Cup with
a couer bought of the said goldesmythes poz . . . . xx oz di

64.230   Sir William Cecill

Item geuon by her said Matie the vj^th day of Julye Anno vjto predicto
at the christeninge of Sir William Cicel knight principall Secretarye
his child doughter Oone guilt Cup with a couer bought of the said
goldesmythes poz. . . . . .xxxiiij oz qrt

64.231   Sir William Cecill

Item Delyuerid to her said Matie by the Lady Marques of Northampton
the iij^de of Marche Anno iiij^to Regni sui Oone karkanett of golde

bought of the goldesmythe by the said Lady Marques / and geuon
by the Quenis highnes the same tyme to oone of [the] Doughters of
the said Sir William Cecill poz .... oone oz iij qrt di   golde

Elizabeth R
[sign manual]

> J Astleley
> ex[aminatio] per Edm: Pigeon

[Newe yeris Gyftes gevon]
[to her maiestie by those parsonnes whose]
[names hereafter ensue the first of January]
[the yere aforesaied:]
[that is to saye:]

[Incomplete Roll – Begins with "By Ladyes" Does not list Earls, Duchesses & Countesses, Bishops, Lordes, Baronesses]

Ladyes

65.1 By the Lady Burgaveny in a red Satten purse in Di soueraignes . . . . C s
Delyurid to the said John Tameworth

65.2 By the Lady Clinton two pullinges owte of blake Sipers wrought with
venice golde And two Ruffes of camerike edgid with pipes of venice
golde and siluer
Deluyerid to the said Dorothye

65.3 By the Lady Barteley in a paper in Di Soueraignes . . . . C s
Delyuerid to the said John Tameworth

65.4 By the Lady Dakers of the Sowth a wastecoate of purple Satten allover
enbrauderid with venice Siluer
Delyuerid to the said Dorothye

65.5 By the Lady Dakers of the North in a purse of red silke and siluer in Di
soueraignes. . . . . vj li

65.6 By the Lady Mountjoye in a purse of blake silke and siluer knytt in Di
soueraignes. . . . . x li

65.7 By the Lady Howarde in a purse of red silke and golde knytt in Di
soueraignes. . . . . x li

65.8 By the Lady of Hunsdon in Di Soueraignes. . . . . x li

65.9 By the Lady Tailboyes Sir peter Carowes wief in a purse of blake silke and
siluer in Di soueraignes . . . . x li
Delyuerid to the said John Tameworth

65.10 By the Lady Knolles a Cloake & A Saufgarde of golde taphata in dentid
rounde aboute and bounde with narrowe passamayne of venice golde
Delyuerid to the said Rauf Hope

65.11 By the Lady Cicell a Remnent of crymsen vellat striped with siluer
cont . . . . viij yerdes
Delyuerid to the said Rauf Hope

65.12 By the Lady Wodhowse lxxiiij flowers made for pullinges owte for a peire
of sleves wrought with venice golde and silke

65.13   By the Lady Carowe Sir Gowins wief a partelet a coyf and a peire of Ruffes wrought with venice golde and blake silke

Delyuerid to the said Dorothye

65.14   By the Lady Jobson in a purse of red silke and golde in Di soueraignes . . . . . x li

Delyuerid to the said John Tameworth

65.15   By the Lady Staffourde alitle tablett of golde ennamuled there in sett fyve Diamondes and foure Rubyes with a pearle pendaunte

with the Quene her Matie

65.16   By the Lady Mason in a purse of blake silke and siluer knytt in Di soueraignes. . . . . C s

65.17   By the Lady Butler in a paper in Di Soueraignes . . . . vj li

65.18   By the Lady Heningham in a purse of red silke and golde knytt in Di soueraignes. . . . . C s

Delyuerid to the said John Tamworth

65.19   By the Lady Ratlif one standishe of Siluer and guilt poz . . . . xij oz

Delyuerid in to chardge to Mr Asteley
esquire Mr and Threasourer of her Juells and plate *ex et oner*

65.20   By the Lady Sackevile in a purse of cloth of golde in Angelles . . . . C s

65.21   By the Lady Pallett in a purse of blewe silke and siluer knytt in Di soueraignes. . . . . C s

Delyuerid to the said John Tameworth

65.22   By the Lady Gresham two peire of Swete gloves playn

65.23   By the Lady Fitzwillams widowe two Cusshion clothes thone wrought with grene and yellowe silke and thother with crymsen silke

Delyuerid to the said Dorethye

65.24   By the Lady Parrye in a Duckett cont xx Duckettes poz—cij oz qrt value

. . . . vj li xiij s iiij d

Delyuerid to the said John Tameworth

65.25   By the Lady Cheeke a peire of slevis a partelett and a Cawle of Camerycke crossed allouer with black silke and venice golde

Delyuerid to the said Dorothye

65.26   By the Lady Throgmorton a turquey purse of golde siluer and silke with a nedle case having two nedles of golde and foure nedles of siluer therin

with her Matie

65.27   By the Lady Cheyney a hatt wrought alouer with venice gold siluer and sede pearles And a Scarff of purple Sipers wrought with venice golde siluer and silke and garnisshed with seede perle

Delyuerid to Rauf Hoope &c.

65.28   By the Lady Cobham oone Remnent of new making crymsen vellat rewid with golde cont . . . . vij yerdes

Delyuerid to Rauf Hope

Knightes

65.29   By Sir Edwarde Rogers Comptroler in a purse of red silke and golde knytt in Di Soueraignes. . . . . vij li

65.30   By Sir William Cicell Secretary in a purse of crymsen taphata in Di
      soueraignes. . . . . xx li

65.31   By Sir Fraunces Knowles Vicechamberlayne in a purse of red silke . . . . x li

65.32   By Sir Ambrose Cave Chauncellor of the Duchy in a purse of blake silke
      siluer knytt two portugues and two Doble soueraignes of xxx s the pece . . x li

65.33   By Sir Richarde Sackevill vnder Threasourer in a purse of tawny silke and
      golde knytt in Angelles . . . . x li

65.34   By Sir John Mason Threasourer of the Chamber in a purse of blake silke
      and siluer knytt xxx of frenche Crownes. . . . . .ix li

                      Delyuerid to the said John Tameworth

  And two bookes thone is *Vita Plutarchi* thother is *Resp. Gallie Platonis*
     Venitie et TH: Mori

                      Delyuerid to the said Blaunche

65.35   By Sir William Peter in a chery bage of taphata in Di souveraignes . . . . x li

65.36   By Sir Walter Mildemaye Chauncellor of the Exchequer in a purse of
      russett silke and siluer in Di Souveraynes. . . . . C s

65.37   By Sir Christopher Haydon in a purse of red silke and siluer in Angelles. . . . x li

65.38   By Sir Edwarde Warner in a crymsen vellat purse a portugue a doble
      Duckett thre olde angelles and two Dimy soueraignes. . . . . vj li xiij s iiij d

65.39   By Sir William Cordall Mr of the Rowles in a chery bag of purple taphata
      in Angells. . . . . x li

65.40   By Sir John Thynne in a red satten purse in di Soueraignes. . . . . C s

65.41   By Sir William Damsell in a purse of red silke and siluer knytt in Di
      soueraignes. . . . . x li

                      Delyuerid to the said John Tameworth

65.42   By Sir Thomas Benger a flower being a Roose wherin is sett a Ballas or a
      garnett

                      Delyuerid to the said Blaunche

65.43   By Sir Gowen Carowe a fayer Smock wrought with venice golde and blake
      silke

                      Delyuerid to the said Dorothye

65.44   By Sir Peter Carowe in a purse of blake silk and siluer in Di soueraignes. . . . x li

65.45   By Sir Thomas Gresham in a purse of blake silke and siluer in Di
      soueraignes. . . . . x li

                      Delyuerid to the said Tameworth

65.46   By Sir Gilbert Dethike a booke of all tharmes of the knyghtes made since
      the beginnyng of her Highnes Reigne

                      With her Matie by John Baptist

65.47   By Sir Nicholas Throgmorton a peticoate of crymsen wrought vellatt
      enbroidered with a fayer border of venice siluer frengid with like siluer

                      Delyuerid to the said Rauf Hope

65.48   By Sir Fraunces Jobson in a purse of blake silke and siluer. . . . . x li

65.49   By Sir Henry Jarnyngham in a purse of Satten enbrauderid in Di
      Soueraignes . . . . x li

65.50   By Sir Henry Cromeell in a fayer purse of crymsen silke venice golde and
       siluer knytt in olde Royalles. . . . . xv li
                                Delyuerid to the said John Tameworth

Chaplaines

65.51   By Archedeacon Carowe Deane of the Chappell in an olde purse of red
       silke and golde knytt in Di soveraignes . . . . x li
65.52   By Docter Wottone Deane of Caunterbury in a red Satten purse in Di
       Soveraignes . . . . x li
                                Delyuerid to the said John Tameworth

Gentlewomen

65.53   By Mrs Asteley cheif Gentelwoman of the Privey Chamber alowe square
       Stowle of walnuttre the seate coverid with yellowe silke nedleworke and
       knottes of venice siluer and grene silke fringid with siluer and silke
                    Delyuerid in chard[g]e to James Harmon keper of the
                              standing Guarderobe at Westminster
65.54   By Mrs Blaunch Apparry a tablet of gold sett with fyve Diamondes two
       Rubyes and a pearle pendaunte poz . . . . di oz
                       Gevon to Elizabeth Knowles eodem die
65.55   By Mrs Skipwith a peire of pillowebeers allouer wrought with blake silke
                           Delyuerid to the said Dorothye
65.56   By Mrs Howarde a Chest of Ebony garnisshed with Copper and guilt
            Delyuerid to George Bredeman keper of the Palloice at Westminster
65.57   By Mrs Hennage a Carpett of Englishemaking the colores moast grene
       cont . . . . iiij yerdes scant
65.58   By Mrs Arundell an open partelet of venice siluer and golde purle
65.59   By Mrs Knolles a peire of Slevis and a partlet of white lawne netted
65.60   By Mrs Doretie Brodbelt thre partelettes two of them wrought with venice
       golde and the thirde with venice siluer vpon lawne
                           Delyuerid to the said Dorothye
65.61   By Mrs Marbery a Rayle a Coyphe and a peire of Ruffes edgid with blake
       silke and golde
                             With the Quene by herself
65.62   By Mrs Newton a cusshioncloth wrought with blake silke
65.63   By Mrs Barlye als Penne vj handekercheves edgid with venice golde
                           Delyuerid to the said Dorothy
65.64   By Mrs Levena Terling a howse paynted and theraboute certeyne
       parsonages in a case of walnuttree
                               with the Quene
65.65   By Mrs Amye Shelton sixe handekercheves wrought with an indentid
       frenge of venice golde
                           Delyuerid to the said Dorothye
65.66   By Mrs Elizabeth Shelton two Regesters with laces of blake silke in a boxe of
       grene vellatt
                     with the Quene by Thomas Asteley

65.67 By Mrs Huggans a fayer Sheete allouer wrought with hopes and
 heythornes of red silke frengid and tassellid with venice golde
65.68 By Mrs Dane lx flowers – for pullinges owte of cameryke wrought with
 venice golde and siluer with a partelet and a Coller wrought with like
 golde & siluer
65.69 By Mrs Lucretia an Italion a fayre handekercheve wrought with red silke
 and golde
65.70 By Mrs Smythson launderis one night Rayle wrought with blake silke
65.71 By Mrs Baptest a partelet and a Cawle wrought with venice golde & siluer
65.72 By Mrs Swigo a Cusshioncloth enbrauderid with venice golde siluer and
 silke

Delyuerid to the said Dorothye

65.73 By Mrs Snowe one hownde of siluer being a Cup to Drinke in weyeng ... xij oz

Delyuerid to the said John Asteley *ex et oner*

65.74 By Mrs Wingfelde one Coyphe wrought with venice golde siluer and silke

Delyuerid to the said Dorothye

Gentlemen

65.75 By Mr John Asteley Master and Threasovror of the Quene her Maties
 Juelles and plate one Tankerd of siluer guilt fayre wrought and sett
 with thre Camewis headdes poz .... xxxiiij oz

with her Matie

65.76 By Mr Thomas Henage a peire of bracellettes of golde ennamiled with
 Tortyses and Crabbes

with her said Matie

65.77 By Mr Haryngton twoo Candlestickes of christall garnisshid with siluer
 and guilt poz .... lxv oz

Delyuerid to the said John Asteley *ex et oner*

65.78 By Mr Bashe in a purse of blake silke and siluer in olde golde .... x li
65.79 By Mr Stanlye in a satten purse in di soueraignes .... xj li

Delyuerid to the said John Tameworth

65.80 By Mr Doctor Hewike a pott of grene ginger and another of floweres of
 oringes
65.81 By Mr Doctor Master a pott of grene ginger and a pott of flowrs of Citron

with her Matie by the saide Thomas Asteley

65.82 By Benodicke Spinola oone greate Cusshion and two lesser of purple
 Satten enbrauderid with venice gold siluer and silke cont sweete bagges
 in them garnisshed with pearle and garnettes in a boxe couerid with
 carnation vellat with a Cusshioncloth of nettecloth wrought with
 bordors of silke

Delyuerid to the said Dorothy

65.83 By Robotham two peire of blake silke hose knytt

with her Matie by Richarde Todde

65.84 By William Huggans twelve sweete bagges of taphata enbrauderid with flowers
 of venice golde and siluer

Delyuerid to the said Dorothy

65.85   By Smyth Customer two boltes of Cameryke

Delyuerid to the said Blaunche

65.86   By John Hemyngway apothecary a pot of quinces a boxe of colliander
comfettes musked and a boxe of Cordialles Manus Christi

65.87   By John Soda foure boxes of Lozenges and Suger plate

with her Matie by the said Thomas Asteley

65.88   By George Webster Master Cooke a Marchpane

65.89   By John Bettes Sergaunte of the Pastry a pye of Quinces

65.90   By Allen Merchaunte two boltes of Cameryke

65.91   By Marke Anthony Violan a looking glasse of Christall of the mountayne
sett in Ebony

65.92   By Petrucio baldini an Italion a booke of the seven Psalmes in latten coverid
with blewe satten

Delyuerid to the said Blaunche

65.93   By Armygell Wade a half picture of mettall of Sigismend king of Polo sett
in wod

65.94   By Lewis Stockwell Surveior of the workes one table paynted of the Tombe
for king Henry theight

Delyuerid to the said George Brydeman

65.95   By John Baptest oone venice Lute

Delyuerid to Thomas Lychefelde

65.96   By Robert Cooke als Chester one petygree of the Quenis Matie from
William Conquerer

65.97   By Henry Kyllegrewe a Trencher boxe with thre Dossen of ringes of golde of
sundry devises

with her said Matie by the said John Tameworth

65.98   By Clement Adams Scholemaster to the henchemen one Modyle of a peire of
Steyers

Delyuerid to the said George Brydeman
ex[aminatio] per Edm Pigeon

Summa Totalis of the money gyven to her Matie and delyuerid for Newe
Yeres gyftes . . . . iij^m CLxxvij li iij s. iiij d.

Anno Regni
Regine Elizabeth vij^{mo}

Newe yeris Giftes geuon
by her maiestie to those parsonnes whose
names hereafter ensue the first of January
the yere aforesaied:

That is to Saye.
Elizabeth **R**
[sign manual]

110

65.99 To the Lady Margret Lennex one nest of bolles with a couer poz—Lx
oz qrt and a salt with a peperboxe in the top poz – xvj oz qrt . . . . . Lxxvj oz di
65.100 To the Lady Margret Straunge a guilt Cup with a couer poz. . . . . . . xix oz iij qrt
65.101 To the Lady Mary Graye one guilt Cup with a couer poz . . . . xix oz qrt

Duke Marques Earles

65.102 To the Duke of Norff one guilt Bolle with a Couer poz . . . . xl oz
65.103 To the Marques of Winchester high Threasouror of Englande one guilt
Bolle with a couer poz. . . . . .xxxv oz iij qrt
65.104 To the Marques of Northampton one guilt bolle poz . . . . xxxvj oz iij qrt
65.105 To the Earle of Arundell oone guilt Cup with a couer poz . . . . Lij oz qrt di
65.106 To the Earle of Northumberlande one guilt bolle with a couer
poz . . . . xxj oz iij qrt
65.107 To the Earle of Westmerlande one guilt bolle with a couer poz. . . . . xxj oz iij qrt
65.108 To the Earle of Shrewesbury oone guilt bolle with a couer poz. . . . . xxxij oz
65.109 To the Earle of Darbye oone guilt bolle with a couer poz . . . . .xxxij oz qrt
65.110 To the Earle of Comberlande oone guilt bolle with a couer poz
. . . . xxvij oz iij qrt di
65.111 To the Earle of Sussex oone guilt Bolle with a couer poz . . . . xxj oz qrt
65.112 To the Earle of Huntingdon oone guilt Bolle with a couer poz. . . . . xxij oz
65.113 To the Earle of Bedfourde oone guilt Bolle with a couer poz . . xxxij oz di di qrt
65.114 To the Earle of Penbrouke oone guilt Cup with a couer poz. . . . . .Lj oz di
65.115 To the Earle of Warwike a fayre Double Cup garnisshed with Christall
with Diuers parcelles in it poz – Cxxix oz and a peire of guilt pottes
poz—iiij^xx oz iij qtr toto. . . . . CCix oz iij qrt

Vicounte

65.116 To the Vicounte Mountague oone guilt Bolle with a couer poz. . . . . xxj oz di

Busshoppes

65.117 To the Arche Busshoppe of Caunterbury two guilt hauns pottes poz. . . . xliij oz
65.118 To the Arche Busshoppe of Yorke oone guilte Bolle with a couer
poz . . . . .xxxv oz iij qrt
65.119 To the Busshoppe of Durisme oone guilt Ewer poz. . . . . xxxvj oz
65.120 To the Busshoppe of Elye oone guilt bolle with a couer poz . . . . . .xxxv oz iij qrt
65.121 To the Busshoppe of London oone guilt bolle with a Couer poz
. . . . .xxviij oz di di qrt
65.122 To the Busshoppe of Winchester oone guilt Cup with a couer
poz . . . . xxxj oz iij qrt
65.123 To the Busshoppe of Salisbury oone guilt Bolle with a couer poz
. . . . xxxij oz di di qrt
65.124 To the Busshoppe of Worseter oone guilt Bolle with a couer poz . . . xxviij oz qrt
65.125 To the Busshoppe of Lyncolne oone guilt Salte with a couer poz
. . . . xxxij oz di di qrt
65.126 To the Busshoppe of Norwiche oone guilt Cup with a couer poz . . . . xxviij oz di

65.127	To the Busshoppe of Rochester Amner oone guilt bolle with a couer poz . . . . xxij oz
65.128	To the Busshoppe of Lichefelde and Coventry oone guilt Cup with a couer poz . . . . xxij oz
65.129	To the Busshoppe of Chetchester oone guilt hans pott poz . . . . . xxij oz iij qrt di
65.130	To the Busshoppe of Herforde oone guilt hans pott poz . . . . xviij oz di di qrt
65.131	To the Busshoppe of St Dauies oone guilt hauns pott poz . . . . xviij oz di
65.132	To the Busshoppe of Bathe oone guilt hauns pott poz. . . . . xviij oz
65.133	To the Busshoppe of Exetor oone guilt Cup with a couer poz . . . xxj oz di di qrt
65.134	To the Busshoppe of Peterborowe oone guilt Cup with a couer poz. . .xvij oz qrt
65.135	To the Busshoppe of Chester oone guilt hans pott poz . . . . xvij oz iij qrt di
65.136	To the Busshoppe of Glocester oone guilt hans pott poz. . . . . xvij oz iij qrt

Duchesses Marques & Countesses

65.137	To the Duches of Suffolk oone guilt bolle with a couer poz . . . . . . xxxj oz di qrt
65.138	To the Duches of Somersett oone guilt bolle with a couer poz . . . . .xxx oz qrt di
65.139	To the Lady Marques of Northampton oone guilt bolle with a Couer And a guilt Cup with a couer poz together. . . . . lxxv oz
65.140	To the Countes of Surrey oone guilt bolle with a couer poz . . . . . xij oz di di qrt
65.141	To the Countes of Oxfourde oone guilt hans pott poz. . . . . .xj oz di di qrt
65.142	To the Countes of Northumberlande oone guilt hans pott poz. . . . . xx oz di qrt
65.143	To the Countes of Westmereland oone guilt bolle with a couer poz . . . . xxiij oz qrt
65.144	To the Countes of Shrewisbery Douger oone guilt hans pott poz. . . . . . xxj oz di
65.145	To the Countes of Shrewisbery oone guilt hans pott poz. . . . . .xx oz iij qrt
65.146	To the Countes of Darby oone oone [sic] guilt hans pott poz . . . . xx oz di
65.147	To the Countes of Rutlande oone guilt bolle with a couer poz . . . .xxxij oz iij qrt
65.148	To the Countes of Sussex oone guilt bolle with a couer poz . . . . xx oz di
65.149	To the Countes of Huntingdon Douger oone guilt bolle with a Couer poz . . . . xx oz di
65.150	To the Countes of Huntingdon oone guilt bolle poz with a couer poz . . . . xxxvj oz iij qrt
65.151	To the Countes of Penbrouke oone guilt bolle with a couer poz . . . . xxvj oz
65.152	To the Vicountes Mountague oone guilt Bolle with a Couer poz . . . xix oz qrt di

Lordes

65.153	To the Lorde keper of the greate Seale Sir Nicholas Bacon oone guilt Bolle with a couer poz . . . . xxxiiij oz qrt di
65.154	To the Lorde William Howarde Lorde Chamberlayne oone guilt bolle with a couer poz. . . . . xxvij oz iij qrt di
65.155	To the Lorde of Burgaveny oone guilt Cup with a couer poz . . . . .xj oz di
65.156	To the Lorde Clinton Lorde Admyrall oone guilt bolle with a couer poz . . . . xxiiij oz di qrt
65.157	To the Lorde Straunge oone guilt bolle with a couer poz . . . . xv oz iij qrt
65.158	To the Lorde Barkeley oone guilt bolle with a couer poz. . . . . xx oz iij qrt di

65.159	To the Lorde Dakers of the North oone guilt bolle with a couer
	poz . . . . .xx oz iij qrt
65.160	To the Lorde Scrowpe oone guilt Cup with a couer poz . . . . xix oz iij qrt di
65.161	To the Lorde Lumley oone guilt bolle with a couer poz. . . . . xxix oz di
65.162	To the Lorde Mountjoye oone guilt Cup with a couer poz . . . . xix oz iij qrt
65.163	To the Lorde Windsour oone guilt Cup with a couer poz . . . . xix oz di
65.164	To the Lorde Riche oone guilt Bolle with a couer poz. . . . . xxxij oz di di qrt
65.165	To the Lorde Darcye of Chitchey oone guilt Cup with a couer poz . . . . . . xxj oz
65.166	To the Lorde Hastinges of Loughborowe oone guilt bolle with a couer
	poz . . . . xxiij oz
65.167	To the Lorde Hunsdone oone guilt Cup with a couer poz. . . . . xxxvj oz di

Ladyes

65.168	To the Lady Aburgaveny oone guilt Cup with a couer poz . . . . xj oz iij qrt
65.169	To the Lady Clinton oone guilt Bolle with a couer poz . . . . .xxvij oz qrt
65.170	To the Lady Barkeley oone guilt Cup with a couer poz . . . . xj oz iij qrt
65.171	To the Lady Dakers of the Sowth oone guilt Cup with a couer
	poz . . . . xvij oz iij qrt
65.172	To the Lady Dakers of the North oone guilt Bolle with a couer
	poz . . . . xiij oz iij qrt
65.173	To the Lady Mountjoye oone guilt Cup with a couer poz . . . . xxj oz qrt di
65.174	To the Lady Howarde oone guilt Bolle with a couer poz. . . . . xxiij oz qrt
65.175	To the Lady of Hounsdon oone guilt Cup with a couer poz . . . . . . xxiij oz iij qrt
65.176	To the Lady Tailboyes Sir Peter Carowes wiefe oone guilt bolle with a
	couer poz . . . . xxj oz qrt
65.177	To the Lady Knowlles oone peire of guilt pottes poz. . . . . iiij^{xx} vj oz di
65.178	To the Lady Cycell oone guilt Bolle with a couer poz . . . . .xxv oz qrt
65.179	To the Lady Carowe Sir Gowins wief oone guilt Bolle with a couer
	poz . . . . .xxxv oz di di qrt
65.180	To the Lady Wodhowse oone guilt bolle with a couer poz. . . . . . . xxiiij oz qrt di
65.181	To the Lady Jobson oone guilt bolle with a couer poz. . . . . . . xxviij oz iij qrt di
65.182	To the Lady Staffourde oone guilt Bolle with a couer poz. . . . . . . xxix oz di qrt
65.183	To the Lady Mason oone guilt Cup with a couer poz . . . . .xv oz qrt
65.184	To the Lady Butlar oone guilt bolle with a couer poz . . . . xv oz iij qrt di
65.185	To the Lady Heningham oone guilt Cup with a couer poz . . . . xj oz qrt di
65.186	To the Lady Ratlif oone guilt Cup with a couer poz . . . . xij oz qrt
65.187	To the Lady Sackeville oone guilt Cup with a couer poz . . . . xj oz iij qrt di
65.188	To the Lady Pallett oone guilt Cup with a couer poz. . . . . xj oz iij qrt
65.189	To the Lady Gresham oone guilt Cup with a couer poz. . . . . x oz iij qrt
65.190	To the Lady Fitzwillms olde widowe oone guilt bolle with a couer
	poz . . . . xvj oz iij qrt di
65.191	To the Lady Parrye oone guilt Cup with a couer poz. . . . . .xxxij oz iij qrt
65.192	To the Lady Cheeke oone guilt bolle with a couer poz. . . . . xiij oz
65.193	To the Lady Throgmorton oone guilt bolle with a couer poz . . . . .xxij oz qrt
65.194	To the Lady Cheyney oone guilt bolle with a couer poz . . . . xxxj oz iij qrt di
65.195	To the Lady Cobham two guilt saltes poz. . . . . lxvj oz

Knightes

65.196   To Sir Edwarde Rogers Comptroler oone guilt Cup with a couer
poz . . . . xix oz iij qrt di

65.197   To Sir Fraunces Knowles Vicechamberlayne oone guilt bolle with a couer
poz . . . . xxiiij oz

65.198   To Sir William Cicell Secretary oone guilt bolle with a couer poz . . . . . . xxxvj oz

65.199   To Sir Ambrose Caue Chauncellor of the Duche oone guilt bolle with a
couer poz . . . . xx oz qrt di

65.200   To Sir Richarde Sackevill vnder Threasouor oone guilt bolle with a couer
poz . . . . xxij oz

65.201   To Sir John Mason Threasouror of the Chamber parte of a peire of guilt
pottes poz. . . . . xxj oz di qrt

65.202   To Sir William Peter oone guilt bolle with a couer poz . . . . xxij oz di di qrt

65.203   To Sir Walter Mildemaye Chauncellor of the Exchequer a hans pott
guilt poz . . . . xvij oz qrt di

65.204   To Sir Christopher Haydon oone guilt Salte poz . . . . xxv oz iij qrt

65.205   To Sir Edwarde Warner oone guilt hans pott poz. . . . . .xvij oz qrt

65.206   To Sir William Cordall Master of the Rowlles oone guilt bolle with a
couer poz . . . . xxiij oz iij qrt

65.207   To Sir John Thynne a hans pott guilt poz. xj oz di di qrt

65.208   To Sir William Damsell a hans pott guilt poz. . . . . xxij oz di qrt

65.209   To Sir Thomas Benger oone guilt Cup with a couer poz . . . . xxvj oz di qrt

65.210   To Sir Gowen Carowe oone guilt Bolle with a couer poz. . . . . xxxvj oz qrt

65.211   To Sir Peter Carowe oone guilt Bolle with a couer poz . . . . xxv oz iij qrt di

65.212   To Sir Thomas Gresham oone guilt Bolle with a couer poz. . . . . xxij oz iij qrt di

65.213   To Sir Gilbert Dethike oone guilt Cup with a couer poz . . . . xv oz

65.214   To Sir Nicholas Throgmorton oone Bason and Ewer guilt poz. . . . . . .lxvj oz qrt

65.215   To Sir Fraunces Jobson oone guilt Bolle with a couer poz. . . . . xxiij oz

65.216   To Sir Henry Jarnengham a guilt Bolle with a couer poz. . . . . xxiij oz qrt

65.217   To Sir Henry Cromewell oone guilt Bolle with a couer poz . . . . xxxiij oz di di qrt

Chaplains

65.218   To Archedeacon Carowe Deane of the Chappell oone guilt Cup with a
couer poz . . . . xxij oz qrt di

65.219   To Doctor Wotten Deane of Caunterbury oone guilt hans pott poz. . .xxij oz qrt

Gentlewomen

65.220   To Mrs Asteley Chefe Gentelwoman of the prevey Chamber oone guilt
Salt with a couer poz – ij oz di di qrt another guilt Salt with a couer poz
—ij oz qrt and oone other like Salt poz—ij oz qrt A casting bottle poz
—v oz iij qrt two Spones poz—iiij oz di di qrt a hans pott poz—xiij oz
qrt and a guilt Cup with a couer viij oz di poz . . . . xxxix oz qrt

65.221   To Mrs Blaunche Apparry oone guilt Bolle with a couer poz . . . . .xvij oz qrt

65.222   To Mrs Skypwith one guilt bolle poz—viij oz qrt di and thre guilt spones
poz—vj oz iij qrt di poz all . . . . .xv oz qrt

65.223	To Mrs Hennage oone guilt Cup with a couer poz.	xx oz
65.224	To Mrs Arundell oone guilt Cup with a couer poz.	xv oz di qrt
65.225	To Mrs Elizabeth Knowlles a Tablet of gold sett with fyve Dyamondes two Rubyes and a pearle pendaunt gevon by Mrs Blaunche Apparry eodem die	
65.226	To Mrs Dorothy Brodebelt oone guilt Salt poz	xvj oz di di qrt
65.227	To Mrs Marbery oone guilt Cup with a couer poz.	xiij oz iij qrt di
65.228	To Mrs Newton one guilt hans pott poz.	xiij oz qrt di
65.229	To Mrs Barley oone guilt hans pott poz	xj oz qrt
65.230	To Mrs Levyna Terlyng oone guilt Cup with a couer poz	vj oz di qrt
65.231	To Mrs Amy Shelton oone guilt hans pott poz.	xiij oz qrt
65.232	To Mrs Elizabeth Shelton oone guilt Bolle with a cover poz	xij oz
65.233	To Mrs Huggans oone guilt Cup with a couer poz.	xx oz di
65.234	To Mrs Dane oone guilt Cup with a couer poz	xviij oz qrt di
65.235	To Mrs Smythson laundres oone guilt Cup with a couer poz	vij oz qrt
65.236	To Mrs Baptest oone guilt Bolle with a cover poz	xvj oz di qrt
65.237	To Mrs Swigo oone guilt Bolle with a couer poz	xiiij oz iij qrt di
65.238	To Mrs Snowe oone guilt Cup with a couer poz.	x oz qrt di
65.239	To Mrs Wingfelde oone guilt Bolle with a couer poz	xiiij oz di di qrt
65.240	To Mrs Lucretia an Italion oone guilt Salte with a couer poz	vj oz qrt

[Incomplete Roll – Ends after "To Gentlewomen" – Does not list Gentlemen, Maids of Honor, and Free Gifts, Does not list gifts given at Sundry Times]

Anno Regni Regine
Elizabeth nono

Newe yeris Guiftes geuon to the
Queine her majestie by those
parsonnes whose names hereafter ensue
The First of Januarye the yere
abouewritten

Elizabeth R
[sign manual]

67.1 By the Lady Margarett Strainge a fayre Cawle a Partelett and a peire of
Ruffes wrought with venice golde and siluer
Delyuerid to Dorothy Broadbelt one of her Maties pryuye Chamber

67.2 By the Lorde keper of the greate Seale in a purse of blewe silke and siluer
knytt in golde . . . . .xiij li vj s
Delyuerid to John Tameworth Grome of the
priuy chamber to her Maties vse

67.3 By the Duke of Norffolke in a red silke purse knytt in Dimy Soueraignes . . xx li
Delyuerid to the said John Tameworth

67.4 By the Marques of Wyntchester highe Threasourer of Englande in a grene
silke Purse knytt in Dimy soueraignes. . . . . xx li
Delyuerid to the said John Tameworth

67.5 By the Marques of Northampton a litell Cheste of Christall garnisshid
with golde with foure Pillers of Agath therin are fyve flowers of
nedleworke the christall and golde poz togethers . . . . xx oz
Delyuerid to Blaunche Parry of her Maties
pryuye Chamber to her Maties use

Earles

67.6 By the Earle of Northumberlande in a blak silke purse knytt in Dimy
soueraignes. . . . . x li

67.7 By the Earle of Westmerelande in a grene silke purse knytt in Dimy
soueraignes and Angelles. . . . . x li

67.8 By the Earle of Shewisburye in a cherry Bagge of purple Satten in Dimy
soueraignes and one olde Noble . . . . .xix li xix s ij d

67.9 By the Earle of Darbye in a paper in Dimy soueraignes . . . . xx li

67.10 By the Earle of Sussex in a red silke purse in Angelles. . . . . x li

67.11 By the Earle of Huntingdon in a blewe silke purse in Dimy soueraignes . . . . x li

67.12 By the Earle of Bedfourde in a purse of red silke and siluer knytt in Dimy
soueraignes. . . . . xx li

67.13 By the Earle of Pembrowke in a crymsen Satten purse . . . . xxx li
Delyuerid to the said John Tameworth

67.14 By the Earle of Warwicke a fayre Flower of golde of thistorye of Charitye
sett with small Diamondes and small Rubies and one Emeralde with fyue
Pearles pendaunte
Delyuerid to the said Blaunche Parrye

67.15 By the Earle of Ormounde a fayer Bason and a Layer of flaunders worke
poz . . . . CClij oz
Delyuerid in chardge to John Astley esquire
Master and Threasuror of the Juelles and plate

67.16 By the Viscounte Mountague in a red silke purse knytt in Dimy
soueraignes. . . . . x li
Delyuerid to the said John Tameworth

Bysshoppes

67.17 By the Archebysshop of Caunterburye in a red silke purse knytt in dimy
soueraignes. . . . . .xl li

67.18 By the Archebysshop of Yorke in a purse of red silke and siluer knytt in
golde. . . . . xxx li

67.19 By the Bysshop of Duresme in a blak silke purse knytt in Angelles thone
being flemyshe at—vij s vj d . . . . .xxix li xvij s vj d
Delyuerid to the said John Tameworth

67.20 By the Bysshop of Elye in a purse of red silke and siluer knytt in Dimy
soueraignes. . . . . xxx li

67.21 By the Bysshop of London in a white Satten purse knytt in Dimy
soueraignes. . . . . xx li

67.22 By the Bysshop of Wynchester in a red Satten purse in Dimy soueraignes. . xx li

67.23 By the Bysshop of Salysburye in a crymsen Satten purse in Dimy
soueraignes. . . . . xx li

67.24 By the Bysshop of Worcester in a blewe silke purse knytt in Dimy
soueraignes. . . . . xx li

67.25 By the Bysshop of Lyncolne in a purse of bawdkyn in Dimy soueraignes . . xx li

67.26 By the Bysshop of Norwich in a red silke purse in Dimy soueraignes. . . . . . xx li
Geuon by her Matie the same daye and yere to the
Earle of Ormounde as parcell of CCxx li
put in a Cup of siluer & guilte

67.27 By the Bysshop of Rochester in a blak silke purse knytt in Dimy
soueraignes and a frenche crowne. . . . . .xiij li vj s

67.28 By the Bysshop of Lychefilde and Couentrye in a purse of blewe silke
in golde and siluer . . . . xiij li vj s viij d
Delyuerid to the said John Tameworth

67.29 By the Bysshop of Chichester in a red Satten purse in Dimy soueraignes. . . . x li

67.30 By the Bysshop of Hereforde in a grene silke purse in Dimy soueraignes. . . . x li
Geuon to the said Earle of Ormounde &c.

67.31 By the Bysshop of Sayncte Dauyes in a blak silke purse in Angelles. . . . . x li
Deliverid to the said John Tameworth

67.32 By the Bysshop of Bath in a red Satten purse in Dimy soueraignes . . . . x li

67.33　By the Bysshop of Exetor in a red Satten purse in Dimy soueraignes . . . . x li

67.34　By the Bysshop of Peterborowe in a red Satten purse in Dimy soueraignes . . x li

67.35　By the Bysshop of Chester in a red Satten purse in Dimy soueraignes . . . . . . x li

67.36　By the Bysshop of Glouchester in a purse of red silke and siluer knytt in
　　　　Dimy soueraignes . . . . x li

> Geuon by her Matie to the saide Earle of Ormounde
> making the said full Summ of CCxx li

Duchesses and Countesses

67.37　By the Duches of Suffolke in a grene silke purse knytt in Dimy
　　　　soueraignes. . . . . xiiij li

> Delyuerid to the said John Tameworth

67.38　By the Duches of Somersett a fayer Hatt of crymsen Satten allouer
　　　　wrought with pipes of venice siluer and golde and sett with pearles

> Delyuerid to Rauf Hope yeoman of the Robes

67.39　By the Countes of Surrey in a blak silke purse knytt in Angelles . . . . C s

67.40　By the Countes of Oxforde dowager in a red satten purse in Angelles . . . . . . C s

67.41　By the Countes of Northumberlande in a red silke purse knytt in Dimy
　　　　soueraignes. . . . . x li

67.42　By the Countes of Westmerlande in a blewe silke purse in Dimy
　　　　soueraignes. . . . . x li

67.43　By the Countes of Shrewisburye dowager in a purse of purple silke &
　　　　golde knitt in Di soueraignes. . . . . xij li

67.44　By the Countes of Shrewisburye in a cherry bag of purple Satten in golde
　　　　one being a flemyshe Angell at—vij s vj d. . . . . xv li

67.45　By the Countes of Darbye in a paper in Dimy soueraignes. . . . . x li

> Delyuerid to the said John Tameworth

67.46　By the Countes of Bedforde a fayer Petycoate of tyncell rewid with siluer
　　　　and golde with thre borders of grene vellat layed with golde lase

> Delyuerid to the said Rauf Hope

67.47　By the Countes of Sussex in a blak silke purse knytt in Dimy soueraignes. . . x li

67.48　By the Countes of Huntingdon dowager in a carnation purse knytt in
　　　　Dimy soueraignes . . . . x li

67.49　By the Countes of Huntingdon in a red silke purse knytt in Dimy
　　　　soueraignes. . . . . viij li

64.50　By the Countes of Pembroke in a red Satten purse . . . . xv li

> Delyuerid to the said John Tameworth

67.51　By the Countes of Warwicke a fayer Flower of golde and mother of
　　　　Pearle of Orpheus and sundry Beastes, garnisshed with foure Rubies
　　　　a Diamonde and a Pearle pendaunte

> Delyuerid to the said Blaunche Parrye

67.52　By the Viscountes Mountague in a red silke purse in Dimy soueraignes. . . . . x li

> Delyuerid to said John Tameworth

67.53　By the Viscountes Hereforde a Coyphe a Cawle, a Partelett / a peire of
　　　　Ruffes and a peire of Sleuis wrought with venice golde and blewe silke

> Delyuerid to the said Dorothy Broadbelt

Lordes

67.54 By the Lorde William Howarde Lorde Chamberlayne in Dimy
soueraignes. . . . . x li
67.55 By the Lorde Aburgeyney in a blewe silke purse knytt in golde and siluer . . . C s
67.56 By the Lorde Clinton L. Admyrall in a purse of grene silke knytt in Dimy
soueraignes. . . . . x li
67.57 By the Lorde Strainge in a red silke purse knytt in Dimy soueraignes. . . . . . C s
67.58 By the Lorde Barkley in a blak silke purse in Dimy soueraignes . . . . x li
67.59 By the Lorde Scrowpe in a purse of grene silke knytt in Dimy
soueraignes. . . . . x li
67.60 By the Lorde Lomeley in a purse of purple silke and siluer knytt in
golde. . . . . xv li
67.61 By the Lorde Wyndesore in a purse of red silke and siluer knytt in Dimy
soueraignes. . . . . x li
67.62 By the Lorde Riche in a red silke purse knytt in Dimy soueraignes. . . . . xx li
67.63 By the Lorde Darcye of Chichey in a taphata purse in Dimy soueraignes . . . x li
Delyuerid to the said John Tameworth
67.64 By the Lorde Hastinges of Loughborowe in a red satten purse in golde
and siluer . . . . xiij li vj s viij d
67.65 By the Lorde Hunsden in a purse of blewe silke in Crownes of the Roose . . . x li
67.66 By the Lorde North in a purse of red silke and siluer knytt in Angelles . . . . . x li
67.67 By the Lorde Pagett in a purse of golde siluer and silke knytt in Dimy
soueraignes. . . . . x li
Delyuerid to the said John Tameworth

Ladyes

67.68 By the Lady Clynton a fayre Cawle of venice and Damaske golde knotted
allouer and garnesshid with Pearle
Delyuerid to the said Blaunche Parry
67.69 By the Lady Aburgeyney in a red silke Purse knytt in golde . . . . C s
67.70 By the Lady Barkeley in a blewe silke Purse knytt in Dimy soueraignes . . . . . C s
67.71 By the Lady Dakers of the North widowe in a purse of red silke & golde
knytt in Dimy souer. . . . . x li
Deluyerid to the said John Tameworth
67.72 By the Lady Dakers of the South a Peticoate of grene vellat layed with
foure bone laces of golde and siluer and frengid with like golde siluer
and silke
Delyuerid to the said John Tameworth
67.73 By the Lady Mountejoye A Boxe full of Englishe silke sleued
Delyuerid to the Lady Knolles
67.74 By the Lady Howarde in Dimy soueraignes . . . . x li
67.75 By the Lady Hunsden in a paper in frenche Crownes and siluer . . . . x li
67.76 By the Lady Talboyes Sir Peter Carewis wief in a red Satten purse in Dimy
soueraignes. . . . . x li
Delyuerid to the said John Tameworth

67.77   By the Lady Cobham a litle Cloake of crymsen Satten allouer enbrauderid
with venice golde and silke lyned with white vellat pinked blak like
powderid Armyones

                                      Delyuerid to the said Rauf Hope

67.78   By the Lady Cromewell the Lorde Cromewelles wief a Partelett wrought
with blak silke and venice siluer

67.79   By the Lady Sheffilde a Combecase of Ebonye garnisshid with siluer
furnesshid with Combes

                                      Delyuerid to the said Rauf Hope

67.80   By the Lady Knolles in a purse of blewe silke and siluer knytt in dimy
soueraignes. . . . . xx li

67.81   By the Lady Sackevile in a purse of blewe silke and golde knytt in Angelles . x li

67.82   By the Lady Pawlett in a grene silke purse in Dimy soueraignes . . . . C s

                                     Delyuerid to the said John Tameworth

67.83   By the Lady Cecill a Partelett wrought with blewe silke and venice golde

                                      dd to the said Dorothy Brodbelt

67.84   By the Lady Wodhowse a feyre Peticoate of single tyncell rewid with a
great brode border of crymsen Satten allouer enbrauderid with
damaske & venice siluer, frengid with like siluer and silke

                                      Delyuerid to the saied Rauf Hope

67.85   By the Lady Carewe Sir Gawen Carewis wief a Rayle and a peire of
Ruffes wrought with venice siluer and silke

                                      Delyuerid to Dorothy Brodbelt

67.86   By the Lady Stafforde a litle Osterige of golde enameled standing vpon
a Base wherein is a pomaunder poz alltogether . . . . oone ounce qrter

                                      dd to the said Blaunch Parrye

67.87   By the Lady Jobson a Smock wrought with blak silke and venice golde

                                      delyvered to the said Dorothy Brodbelt

67.88   By the Lady Butler in a paper in golde and siluer . . . . vj li

67.89   By the Lady Hennyngham in a purse of blak silke in Angelles thone being
flemyshe at—vj s vj d. . . . . iiij li xvij s vj d

                                      Delyuerid to the said John Tameworth

67.90   By the Lady Ratclyff twelue handekercheues of Lawne fayre wrought
with blak silke

67.91   By the Lady Cheeke a Partelett and a peire of Sleuis of Lawen tufte with
venice golde and siluer

67.92   By the Lady Gresham one peire of Sleuis wrought allouer with venice
siluer knytt

67.93   By the Lady Throgmorton one Canapye of carnation silke of knytt worke
wrought with venice golde and siluer and two Curtens of sipers of the
same worke to hange ouer a Cusshioncloth

                                      Delyuerid to the said Dorothy Brodbelte

67.94   By the Lady Cheyney a feyre Petycoate of yellow vellat enbrauderid with
two borders of oken leaues of golde siluer and silke and frengid with
golde and siluer

                                      Delyuerid to the said Rauf Hope

67.95   By the Lady St loo a Smock a Rayle and a Cawle allouer lowped with
     blak silke cutt

> Delyuerid to the said Dorothy Brodbelt

67.96   By the Lady Wilforde two litle flagons of Agate garnesshid with siluer
     guilt sett with stones poz alltogether . . . . xvij oz di

> Delyuerid in chardge to the said John Asteley *ex et oner*

67.97   By the Lady Yorke a Barrell of Suckett, and foure Sugerloues

> Delyuerid to the said Dorothy Brodbelt

67.98   By Madame Horsey a Flower of golde made like a knott sett with small
     Diamondes and Rubies

> Delyuerid to the [said] Blaunche Parry

Knightes

67.99   By Syr Edwarde Rogers Comptroller of her Maties howseholde in a red
     Satten purse in Dimy soueraignes . . . . vij li

67.100   By Sir Frauncis Knolles vicechamberlen &c. in a purse of red silke &
     golde knytt in Dimy soueraignes . . . . x li

67.101   By Sir William Cecill principall Secretarye in a red Satten purse in Dimy
     soueraignes . . . . xx li

67.102   By Sir Ambrose Caue Chauncellor of the Duchye in a red silke purse in
     olde Royalles . . . . xv li

67.103   By Sir William Peter Chauncellor of the Order in a chery bag of purple
     Satten in Dimy souer . . . . x li

67.104   By Sir Walter Myldemaye Chauncellor of the Exchequer in a red silke
     purse in Crownes . . . . x li

67.105   By Sir William Cordall Mr of the Rolles in a chery bag of taphata in
     Angelles . . . . x li

67.106   By Sir Henry Cromewell in a purse of crymsen silke golde and siluer knytt
     in Dimy soueraignes . . . . xv li

67.107   By Sir Christopher Heydon in a red Satten purse in Dimy soueraignes . . . . . x li

67.108   By Sir John Thynne in a purse of russett silke in Angelles . . . . C s

67.109   By Sir William Damsell in a red silke purse knytt in Dimy soueraignes . . . . . x li

67.110   By Sir Peter Carewe in Dimy soueraignes . . . . x li

67.111   By Sir Frauncis Jobson in a siluer purse knytt in Angelles . . . . x li

67.112   By Sir Henry Jernegham in a chery bag of sarceonett in half soueraignes
     & frenche crownes . . . . x li

> Delyuerid to the sayid John Tameworth

67.113   By Sir Gawen Carew Mr of the Henchemen a Smocke allouer wrought
     with carnation silke the coller and ruffes wrought with venice siluer

> Delyuerid to the said Dorothy Brodbelt

67.114   By Sir William Pickeringe a feyre Rynge of golde with a Diamonde in
     the middes and small Diamondes on eache side

> Delyuerid to the said Blaunch Parry

67.115   By Sir Thomas Benger Mr of the Reuelles a Ryng of golde with an
     Emerald in it

> Delyuerid to the sayd Blaunch Parrye

67.116 By Sir Thomas Gresham a Cloake of lether perfumed garnisshid with
     fayre borders of pipes of venice golde and damaske golde knytt lyned
     with crymsen vellat vnshorne
                Delyuerid to the said Rauf Hope

67.117 By Sir Nicholas Throgmorton one Cusshioncloth wrought with red silke
     and venice golde, And one Combecase of Ebonye furnesshid with
     combes & other necessaryes
              Delyuerid to the said Dorothy Brodbelt

67.118 By Sir Gylbert Dethyk a Booke of Armes of the Order of knyghtes of the
     Garter enstalled by king Edwarde the iijde couerid with crymsen vellat
     edgid with passamayne of venice golde
              Delyuerid to the said Blaunche Parrye

Chaplaynes

67.119 By Doctor Wotton Deane of Caunterburye in a purse of red and white
     silke rewid in Dimy soueraignes . . . . x li
67.120 By Archedeacon Carewe Deane of the Chapell in Dimy soueraignes . . . . x li
67.121 By Doctor Newton Deane of Wyntchester in a paper in Dimy soueraignes . . x li
              Delyuerid to the said John Tameworth

Gentlewomen

67.122 By Mysteris Blaunche Pary a Juell with an Agath hedde garnesshid with
     foure Rubies and a cluster of foure Pearles pendaunte
               Delyuerid to herself in chard[g]e
67.123 By Mrs Katheryn Howarde wief in a blewe silke purse knytt . . . . C s
              Delyuerid to the said John Tameworth
67.124 By Mrs Elizabeth Knolles a Partelett and a peire of Sleuis wrought with
     venice golde and blewe silke
67.125 By Mrs Caue a Partelett a peire of Sleuis a foreparte of a kyrtle and a
     Cawle of knytt worke of siluer
              Delyuerid to the said Dorothy Brodbelt
67.126 By Mrs Hennage a Hatt fayre wrought with venice golde siluer and silke
     And a Cusshioncloth wrought with blewe silke and venice siluer
            The hatt delyuerid to Rauf Hope aforesaid
          The Cusshioncloth to the said Dorothy Brodbelt
67.127 By Mrs Arundell a Pillowe couerid with white cloth allouer wrought with
     a trayle of knottes of silke
67.128 By Mrs Anne Wingfilde a Pillowebeere of holland allouer wrought with
     blak silke
67.129 By Mrs Dorothey Brodebelt one Partelett and a peire of Ruffes of
     knyttworke wrought with venice golde and red silke
67.130 By Mrs Marbery a Rayle and a peire of Ruffes wrought with red silke &
     venice siluer
               Delyuerid to Dorothy Brodbelt
67.131 By Mrs Sowthewell a feyre Hatt of crymsen Satten allouer enbrauderid
     with venice golde / And a Skarff of chaungeable silke edgid with a

passamayne of venice golde and siluer / and two buttons with tasselles
of like golde and siluer

> The hatt delyuerid to the said Rauf Hope aforesaid
> The Skarff to the said Dorothy Brodbelt

67.132 By Mrs Edmundes a Rayle and a peire of Ruffes wrought with blewe
silke & venice golde

67.133 By Mrs Maruen a feyre Smock wrought with blak silke and venice golde
and siluer like Oken leaues

67.134 By Mrs Smytheson Laundres a Rayle and a peire of Ruffes wrought with
blewe silke and venice golde

> Deluyerid to the said Dorothy Brodbelt

67.135 By Mrs Leuyna Terlyng the Picture of the Quene her Maties whole stature
drawne vpon a Carde paynted

> Delyuerid to Elizabeth Knolles

67.136 By Mrs Amy Shelton Sixe handekercheues edgid with bone lase of venice
silver & silke

67.137 By Mrs Elizabeth Shelton Sixe handekercheues wrought with blak silke
and edgid with bone lase of silke and venice siluer and buttoned with
the same

67.138 By Mrs Huggens of Hamptoncorte a Sheete fayre wrought with borders
of blewe silke and venice golde frengid buttoned and tassellid with like
golde and silke

67.139 By Mrs Dane a fayre Cusshioncloth of fyne holland vallaunced at thendes,
and allouer enbrauderid with venice golde and silke frengid with like
silke and golde

67.140 By Mrs Ipolita a handkercheue and a Cusshionett wrought with venice gold
siluer & silke

67.141 By Mrs Huggens of Norff[olk] a feyre Smock wrought with blak silke and
venice golde

67.142 By Mrs Heynes a Rayle and a peire of Ruffes wrought with silke and
edgid with purles of venice golde and siluer

67.143 By Mrs Elizabeth Wyngefilde a feyre peire of Sleuis wrought with carnation
silke and venice golde

67.144 By Mrs Baptist two fayre Cusshionclothes wrought with red silke

67.145 By Mrs Ellen a frowe a Cawle a partelett and a peire of Ruffes allouer
wrought with blewe silke and siluer

67.146 By Mrs Bareley Sixe handekercheues thre edgid with bone lace of venice
golde and thother thre with siluer

> Delyuerid to the said Dorothy Brodbelt

Gentlemen

67.147

By Mr Thomas Hennage a litle Juell like a flagon of Agath garnesshid
with golde sett with small Diamondes and Rubies with a Cheyne of
golde likewise garnesshid with litell Diamondes

> Delyuerid to the said Blaunch Parrrye

67.148 By Mr John Harington a lawmpe of siluer & guilt with a Christall in it
  poz alltogether . . . . xxiiij oz qrter
            Deluyerid in chardge to the said John Asteley

67.149 By Mr Thomas Sackeuile in a purse of blak silke & golde knytt in Di
  soueraignes. . . . . x li

67.150 By Mr Chamberleyne of Garnesey in a blewe silke purse knytt in Dimy
  soueraignes. . . . . vj li

67.151 By Mr Edwarde Bashe in a blak silke purse knytt in Angelles . . . . x li

67.152 By Mr Thomas Stanley Threasourer of the Mynte in a taphata purse in
  Dimy soueraignes . . . . vj li
            Deluyerid to the said John Tameworth

67.153 By Mr William Drewery a Chessebourde with chessemen in a boxe all of
  bone
                     with her Matie

67.154 By Mr William Huggens Twentie swete Bagges of white taphata
  enbrauderid with a flower with venice golde and blewe silke edgid
  with like golde and silke

67.155 By Mr Doctor Hewyck two Pottes of Oringe Flowers and candy Gynger

67.156 By Mr Doctor Maister two like Pottes of oringe Flowers and candy Gynger
            Deluyerid to the said Dorothy Brodbelt

67.157 By Benedicke Spinula a feyre Petycoate of crymsen Satten netted allouer
  with venice golde with a border enbrauderid with venice golde and
  sett with Stones
             Deluyerid to the said Rauf Hope

67.158 By Robert Robotham Two peire of blak silke hoose knytt
           Deluyerid to the said Elizabeth Marbery

67.159 By Smyth customer Two boltes of Cameryk

67.160 By Allen a Marchaunte a fyne pece of Cameryke in a Case of crymsen
  Satten
             Delyuerid to the said Blaunch Parrye

67.161 By Treyforde Clerke of the Spicerye Pomegranettes Rootes of Spayne
  A Cheese in a Case, Twoo small Tapnettes of Figges and thre boxes of
  comfettes

67.162 By John Hemyngwaye Two Boxes of lozenges and Manus Christi and a
  Pott of Sidona

67.163 By John Soda a Boxe of synamon Comfettes and another boxe of Corsili
            Delyuerid to the said Dorothy Brodbelt

67.164 By Marke Anthony a fayre Cytrene with a Stone like an Emeraulde in the
  sounde of the bellye
             Deluyerid to Thomas Lychefilde

67.165 By George Webster Mr Cooke to the Quene a Chessebourde being made
  of Suger with the Quenis Armes

67.166 By John Battes Serjaunte of the Pastrye a Pye of Quinces

67.167 By Patritio Baldino a Glasse of swete water with certeyne other
  Instrumentes for Teethe &c.
                  with the Quene

67.168	By Adams a peire of Pilloweberres of camerik drawen to be wrought
67.169	By Dunston Ames Grocer thre Sugerloues

Delyuerid to the said Dorothy Brodbelt

67.170	By Roberte Cooke als Chester A Booke of Armes of the Quenis Maties
	progenitors Tytle to the Crowne of Englande and Fraunce

with the Quene

Summa totalis / of the money / geuon to her Matie as aforesaid
. . . . M Cxlj li xvij s

wherof gevon / to the Earle of / Ormound as aforesaid / CC xx li / and delyuerid to John Tameworth as is aforedeclared ix C xxj li xvij s

Elizabeth R
[sign manual]

J Asteley
Ex[aminatio] per
Edm Pigeon
J Pigeon
Ste Fulwell

Anno Regne Regine
Elizabeth nono

Newyeres Guiftes geuon by
the Quenis hir maiestie to those
parsones whose names hereafter
ensue. The First of January the
yere abouewritten

Elizabeth R
[sign manual]

67.171	To the Lady Margarett Strainge oone guilt Bolle with a couer P. poz . . .xx oz qrt
67.172	To the Lorde keper of the greate Seale oone guilt Cup with a couer B.
	poz . . . . xxxviij oz qrter
67.173	To the Duke of Northfolke oone guilt Cup with a couer P. poz . . . . xlj oz di
67.174	To the Marques of Wyntchester oone guilt Cup with a couer B. poz
	. . . . .xxxiiij oz qrt
67.175	To the Marques of Northampton thre Bolles with a couer B. poz . . xxxvj oz qrt

Earles

67.176 To the Earle of Northumberlande one guilt Bolle with a couer P.
poz . . . . xix oz di di qrt

67.177 To the Earle of Westmerlande one guilt Bolle with a couer P. poz . . xix oz iij qrt

67.178 To the Earle of Shrewisburye one guilt Cup with a couer B. poz. . . xxxj oz di qrt

67.179 To the Earle of Darbye one guilt Cup with a couer B. poz . . . . xxix oz iij qtr

67.180 To the Earle of Sussex one guilt Bolle with a couer P. poz. . . . . xix oz iij qrt

67.181 To the Earle of Huntingdon one guilt Cup with a couer B. poz . . . xxij oz di qrt

67.182 To the Earle of Bedfourde one guilt Cup with a couer B. poz . . . xxx oz di di qrt

67.183 To the Earle of Pembroke one guilt Cup with a couer B. poz . . . . lv oz di qrt

67.184 To the Earle of Warwick one guilt Basen and a Layer P. poz . . . . . .Cvj oz di qrt

67.185 To the Earle of Ormewode one doble Bolle guilte B. poz . . . . xxvij oz
And also putt into the said Bolle In dimy soueraignes which were geuon to
her Matie by sundry persones eodem die et Anno . . . . .CCxx li

67.186 To the Viscounte Mountague one guilt Bolle with a couer P. poz . . . . . .xx oz qrt

Bysshoppes

67.187 To the Archebysshop of Caunterburye one guilt Cup with a couer P. poz
—xxvj oz di di qrt: And a guilt Bolle with a couer P. poz—xviij oz
di in toto. . . . . xlv oz di qrt

67.188 To the Archebysshop of Yorke one Tankerd B. poz—xvj oz qrt di And
another Tankerd B. poz – xvj oz di qrt in toto . . . . xxxiiij oz di

67.189 To the Bysshop of Duresme one guilt Bolle with a couer B. poz. . . . xxxiiij oz di

67.190 To the Bysshop of Elye parte of a Bason and a Layer guilt B.
poz . . . . xxxvj oz qrt di

67.191 To the Bysshop of London one guilt Bolle with a couer B. poz. . . . xxix oz iij qrt

67.192 To the Bysshop of Wyntchester thre guilt Bolles with a couer B. poz . . . . xxxj oz

67.193 To the Bysshop of Salisburye one Hans pott guilt P. poz—xv oz
di qrt / And parte of another Hans pott guilt P. poz—xvij oz qrt
Di in toto . . . . xxxij oz di

67.194 To the Bysshop of Worcester one guilt Salte with a couer P. poz. . . . . . . xxvij oz

67.195 To the Bysshop of Lyncolne two guilt Bolles withoute a couer Brandon
poz . . . . xxvij oz di qrt

67.196 To the Bysshop of Norwich one guilt Bolle with a couer B. poz . . . . xxviij oz qrt

67.197 To the Bysshop of Rochester one guilt Bolle with a couer P. poz . . . . xxij oz

67.198 To the Bysshop of Lychefilde and Couentrye one guilt Salte with a couer
P. poz . . . . .xxj oz di

67.199 To the Bysshop of Chichester one Hans pott guilt B. poz . . . . xvij oz di qrt

67.200 To the Bysshop of Hereforde one Hans pott guilt B. poz . . . . xvj oz di di qrt

67.201 To the Bysshop of Saynt Dauyes one Hans pott guilt B. poz . . . . xvj oz di

67.202 To the Bysshop of Bath one Hans pott guilt B. poz. . . . . xvj oz qrt di

67.203 To the Bysshop of Exetor one Hans pott guilt P. poz . . . . xvj oz qrt di

67.204 To the Bysshop of Peterboroughe one guilt Salte with a couer P.
poz . . . . .xx oz iij qrt

67.205 To the Bysshop of Chester one guilt Hans pott P. poz. . . . . xvj oz di di qrt

67.206 To the Bysshop of Glouchester one guilt Bolle withoute a couer

P. poz . . . . xvij oz di qrt

Duchesses and Countesses

67.207 To the Duches of Suff[olk] oone guilt Cup with a couer P. poz . . . . xxx oz qrt

67.208 To the Duches of Somersett one guilt Bolle with a couer B. poz. xxx oz di di qrt

67.209 To the Countes of Surrey one guilt Bolle with a couer P. poz . . . . xj oz di

67.210 To the Countes of Oxforde dowager one guilt Bolle with a couer P. poz. . . xij oz

67.211 To the Countes of Northumberlande one guilt Bolle with a couer B.

poz . . . . xxj oz qrt

67.212 To the Countes of Westmerlande one guilt Bolle with a couer B.

poz . . . . xxj oz di qrt

67.213 To the Countes of Shrewisburye dowager one guilt Cup with a couer P.

poz . . . . xxiij oz qrt

67.214 To the Countes of Shrewisburye one guilt Bolle with a couer B.

poz . . . . xxj oz di di qrt

67.215 To the Countes of Darby one guilt Bolle with a couer B. poz . . . . xxj oz

67.216 To the Countes of Bedforde one guilt Bolle with a couer B. poz. . . . xxx oz iij qrt

67.217 To the Countes of Sussex one guilt Bolle with a couer B. poz . . . . xx oz qrt

67.218 To the Countes of Huntingdon Dowager one guilt Bolle with a couer

B poz . . . . xix oz qrt Di

67.219 To the Countes of Huntingdon one guilt Bolle with a couer P. poz . xxxvj oz qrt

67.220 To the Countes of Pembroke one guilt Bolle with a couer P. poz . . . . xxvj oz

67.221 To the Countes of Warwyck one peire of guilt Flagons P. poz . . . . . . C oz qrt di

67.222 To the Viscountes Hereforde one Bolle with a couer P. poz . . . . xxx oz di

67.223 To the Viscountes Mountague one guilt Bolle with a couer P. poz . . xix oz qrt di

Lordes

67.224 To the Lorde William Howarde Lorde Chamberlayne one guilt Cup

with a couer P. poz. . . . . xxvij oz di di qrt

67.225 To the Lorde Aburgeyney one guilt Bolle with a couer P. poz . . . . vij oz qrt

67.226 To the Lorde Clynton Lorde Admyrall one guilt Bolle with a couer P.

poz . . . . xxiij oz iij qrt

67.227 To the Lorde Strainge one guilt Bolle with a couer P. poz . . . . xij oz qrt

67.228 To the Lorde Barkeley one guilt Bolle with a couer P. poz. . . . . . . xx oz di di qrt

67.229 To the Lorde Scrowpe one guilt Bolle with a couer B. poz. . . . . xix oz qrt

67.230 To the Lorde Lumley one guilt Bolle with a couer B. poz . . . . xxiiij oz qrt

67.231 To the Lorde Wyndesor one guilt Bolle with a couer B. poz . . . . xxj oz iij qrt

67.232 To the Lorde Riche one guilt Bolle with a couer B. poz. . . . . xxxj oz di

67.233 To the Lorde Darcye of Chichey one guilt Bolle with a couer B.

poz . . . . xix oz di qrt

67.234 To the Lorde Hastinges of Loughborowe one guilt Bolle with a couer

B. poz . . . . xxiiij oz qrt

67.235 To the Lord Hunsden one guilt Bolle with a couer B. poz . . . . xxxvj oz di

67.236 To the Lorde North one guilt Bolle with a couer P. poz. . . . . xviij oz iij qrt

67.237 To the Lorde Pagett one guilt Cup with a couer B. poz . . . . xx oz qrt

Ladies

67.238	To the Lady Clynton one doble Cup B. poz – xlvij oz. And a casting Bottell guilt poz – vj oz Di di qrt P. In toto. . . . . liij oz di di qrt
67.239	To the Lady Aburgany one guilt Bolle with a couer P. poz . . . . xij oz qrt
67.240	To the Lady Barkeley, one Hans pott guilt B. poz . . . . xj oz iij qrt
67.241	To the Lady Dakers of the North one guilt Tankerd P. poz. . . . . . xx oz di di qrt
67.242	To the Lady Dakers of the South one guilt Bolle with a couer B. poz. . . . xvij oz
67.243	To the Lady Mountejoye one guilt Tankard P. poz . . . . xx oz di di qrt
67.244	To the Lady Howarde one guilt Bolle with a couer P. poz . . . . xxiiij oz
67.245	To the Lady Hunsden one guilt Bolle with a couer B. poz. . . . . xxiiij oz di di qrt
67.246	To the Lady Taylboyes Sir Peter Carewis wief one guilt Tankerd B. poz. . . xxj oz
67.247	To the Lady Cobham one guilt Cup with a couer P. poz . . . . lij oz
67.248	To the Lady Crumwell L. Cromewelles wief oone guilt Cup with a couer P. poz . . . . xviij oz iij qrt di
67.249	To the Lady Sheffilde one guilt Bolle with a couer P. poz . . . . xij oz di
67.250	To the Lady Knolles one guilt Cup with a couer B. poz—xx oz qrt. And thre guilt Candlestickes B. poz—lxvj oz in toto . . . . iiij xx vj oz qrt
67.251	To the Lady Sackeuile one guilt Tankerd P. poz. . . . . xxj oz qrt
67.252	To the Lady Pawlett one guilt Bolle with a couer P. poz . . . . xj oz di di qrt
67.253	To the Lady Cecill one guilt Bolle with a couer P. poz. . . . . .xxv oz di qrt
67.254	To the Lady Wodhouse one guilt Bolle with a couer P. poz . . . . xxiij oz di
67.255	To the Lady Carewe Sir Gawen Carewis wief one guilt Bolle with a couer P. poz . . . . .xxxv oz
67.256	To the Lady Staffarde one guilt Bolle with a couer P. poz . . . . .xxx oz qrt
67.257	To the Lady Jobson one guilt Bolle with a couer B. poz . . . . . . xxiiij oz di di qrt
67.258	To the Lady Butler parte of thre guilt Bolles with a couer B. poz . xv oz iij qrt di
67.259	To the Lady Hemyngham one guilt Cup with a couer B. poz . . . . . . xij oz di qrt
67.260	To the Lady Ratclyff one guilt Salte with a couer B. poz. . . . . xj oz qrt
67.261	To the Lady Cheeke one guilt Bolle with a couer P. poz. . . . . xiij oz iij qrt
67.262	To the Lady Gresham one guilt Cup with a couer B. poz . . . . xij oz di di qrt
67.263	To the Lady Throgmorton one guilt Bolle with a couer B. poz . . . . . . xxvij oz di
67.264	To the Lady Cheyney one guilt Bolle with a couer B. poz . . . . .xxvij oz qrt
67.265	To the Lady St loo one guilt Bolle with a couer P. poz. . . . . xviij oz iij qrt
67.266	To the Lady Willforde one guilt Cup with a couer B. poz . . . . xij oz
67.267	To the Lady Yorke one Hans pott guilt B. poz . . . . xiij oz di qrt
67.268	To Madam Horsey thre guilt Bolles with a couer P. poz . . . . lxxj oz di di qrt

Knightes

67.269	To Syr Edwarde Rogers Comptroller of her Maties howseholde one guilt Bolle with a couer P. poz . . . . xix oz iij qrt di
67.270	To Sir Frauncis Knolles vichamberlene &c. one guilt Bolle with a couer B. poz . . . . xxvj oz iij qrt
67.271	To Sir William Cicell principall secretarye one guilt Bolle with a couer B. poz . . . . xxxvj oz qrt

67.272	To Sir Ambrose Caue Chauncellor of the Duchye one guilt Cup with a couer P. poz . . . . xxviij oz
67.273	To Sir William Peter Chauncellor of the Order one guilt Bolle with a couer P. poz . . . . xxj oz di
67.274	To Sir Walter Myldemaye Chauncellor of thexchequer one guilt bolle with a couer P. poz . . . . xxvj di
67.275	To Sir William Cordall Mr the Rolles one guilt Bolle with a couer P. poz . . . . xxij oz iij qrt
67.276	To Sir Henry Cromewell one guilt Cup with a couer P. poz. . . . . . xxviij oz iij qrt
67.277	To Sir Christofer Haydon one guilt Bolle with a couer P. poz . . . . xxiiij oz iij qrt
67.278	To Sir John Thynne one guilt Cup with a couer B. poz . . . . x oz di qrt
67.279	To Sir William Damsell one guilt Bolle with a couer P. poz. . . . . . xx oz iij qrt di
67.280	To Sir Peter Carewe one guilt Cup with a couer B. poz . . . . xx oz di
67.281	To Sir Frauncis Jobson one guilt Bolle with a couer P. poz . . . . . xviij oz iij qrt di
67.282	To Sir Henry Jernegham one guilt Bolle with a couer P. poz . . . . xviij oz di di qrt
67.283	To Sir Gowen Carewe Mr of the Henchemen one guilt Bolle with a couer P. poz. . . . . .xxxv oz iij qrt
67.284	To Sir William Pickeringe thre guilt Bolles with a couer B. poz. . . . . . . liiij oz qrt
67.285	To Sir Thomas Benger Mr of the Reuelles one guilt Bolle with couer P. poz . . . . xxvj oz qrt
67.286	To Sir Thomas Gresham one guilt Bason and a Leyer guilt P. poz . . xxiiij oz qrt
67.287	To Sir Nicholas Throgmorton one guilt Bolle with a couer B. poz . . . xxix oz qrt
67.288	To Sir Gylbert Dethyck one guilt Bolle with a couer B. poz . . . . xiij oz di qrt

Chapleynes

67.289	To Doctor wootton Deane of Caunterburye one guilt Bolle with a couer B. poz . . . . xxiij oz di qrt
67.290	To Archedeacon Carewe Deane of the Chapell one guilt Bolle with a couer B. poz To Mystris Blaunche Pary one guilt Bolle with a couer B. poz . . . . xvij oz di di qrt
67.293	To Mrs Katheryn Howarde wief one guilt Bolle with a couer B. poz xv oz di qrt
67.294	To Mrs Elizabeth Knolles Rewarded by the Quene
67.295	To Mrs Caue one guilt Bolle with a couer B. poz. . . . . .xv oz iij qrt
67.296	To Mrs Hennage one guilt Leyer B. poz . . . . .xx oz qrt
67.297	To Mrs Arundell one guilt Bolle with a couer P. poz . . . . .xv oz iij qrt
67.298	To Mrs Anne Wingefilde one Hans pott guilt P. poz . . . . xv oz di
67.299	To Mrs Dorothey Brodebelte Eight guilt spones B. poz. . . . . xvj oz
67.300	To Mrs Marberye one guilt Bolle with a couer P. poz . . . . xiij oz iij qrt
67.301	To Mrs Southewell one guilt Tankerd B. poz . . . . xvj oz iij qrt
67.302	To Mrs Edmundes one guilt Bolle with a couer P. poz. . . . . xiij oz iij qrt
67.303	To Mrs Maruen one guilt Hans pott B. poz . . . . xiiij oz iij qrt
67.304	To Mrs Smytheson Launderes one guilt Cup with a couer P. poz . . . vij oz di qrt
67.305	To Mrs Leuyna Terlyng one guilt Cup with a couer P. poz . . . . vj oz
67.306	To Mrs Amy Shelton one guilt Bolle with a couer B. poz . . . . xj oz di qrt

67.307 To Mrs Elizabeth Shelton one guilt Bolle with a couer B. poz. . . . . xj oz di di qrt
67.308 To Mrs Huggens of Hamptoncorte one guilt Bolle with a couer P. poz . . . xxj oz
67.309 To Mrs Dan e one guilt Bolle with a couer P. poz . . . . xviij oz di
67.310 To Mrs Ipolita two guilt spones B. poz. . . . . iiij oz
67.311 To Mrs Huggens of Norff one guilt Salte with a couer B. poz . . . . xiij oz qrt
67.312 To Mrs Heynes one guilt Salte with a couer B. poz . . . . xij oz
67.313 To Mrs Elizabeth Wyngefilde one guilt Salte with a couer Ca. poz . . . . xij oz qrt
67.314 To Mrs Baptist one guilt Tankerde B. poz . . . . xvj oz qrt
67.315 To Mrs Ellen a frowe one guilt Salte with a couer P. poz. . . . . xiij oz di
67.316 To Mrs Bareley one guilt Salte with a couer B. poz . . . . xij oz

Maydens of Honour

67.317 To Mrs Mary Howarde one guilt Cup with a couer B. poz . . . . x oz iij qrt
67.318 To Mrs Ann Wyndesor one guilt Cup with a couer B. poz . . . . x oz iij qrt
67.319 To Mrs Katheryne Kneuett one guilt Cup with a couer B. poz . . . . x oz di
67.320 To Mrs Mary Ratclyff one guilt Cup with a couer B. poz . . . . x oz di qrt
67.321 To Mrs Dorothey Brooke one guilt Cup with a couer B. poz . . . . x oz di qrt
67.322 To Mrs Eglandby Mother of the Madens of Honor one guilt Cup with
a couer B. poz . . . . xij oz iij qrt

Gentlemen

67.323 To Mr Thomas Hennage one guilt Bason B. poz . . . . lij oz di
67.324 To Mr John Harrington one guilt Cup with a couer B. poz. . . . . xlv oz
67.325 To Mr Thomas Sackeuile one guilt Bolle with a couer B. poz . . . . . . .xx oz iij qrt
67.326 To Mr Chamberleyne of Garnesey one Hans pott guilt B. poz . . . . xiiij oz iij qrt
67.327 To Mr Edward Bashe one guilt Bolle with a couer B. poz . . . . .xx oz iij qrt
67.328 To Mr Thomas Stanley Threasourer of the Mynt one guilt Cup with a
couer B. poz. . . . . xiiij oz iij qrt
67.329 To Mr William Drewery one guilt Bolle with a couer B. poz. . . . . . xj oz iij qrt di
67.330 To Mr William Huggens one guilt Bolle with a couer Ca. poz . . . . xxxj oz di qrt
67.331 To Mr Doctor Hewyck one guilt Tankerd P. poz . . . . xiiij oz di di qrt
67.332 To Mr Doctor Maister one guilt Bolle withoute a couer P. poz. . . . . xiij oz
67.333 To Benedicte Spinula one guilt Bolle with a couer B. poz . . . . xxvj oz
67.334 To Roberte Robotham one guilt Cup with a couer B. poz. . . . . xij oz
67.335 To Smyth Customer one guilt Cup with a couer B. poz. . . . . xv oz qrt di
67.336 To Allen a Marchaunte one Hans pott guilt B. poz . . . . .xv oz iij qrt
67.337 To Trayforde Clarke of the Spicerye one guilt Cup with a couer P. poz . . . viij oz
67.338 To John Hemyngwaye Eight percell guilt spones B. poz . . . . xiij oz iij qrt
67.339 To John Soda Thre guilt Spones B. poz . . . . vj oz
67.340 To Marke Anthony one guilt Cup with a couer B. poz . . . . xij oz qrt
67.341 To George Webster Mr Cooke one guilt Cup with a couer B. poz. . . . . . viij oz di
67.342 To John Bettis Serjaunte of the Pastrye one guilt Cup B. poz . . . . iiij oz di
67.343 To Petro vbaldicio one peper Boxe guilt P. poz. . . . . iiij oz iij qrt

67.344	To Clement Adams Rewarded in Money by the Threasourer of the Chamber . . . . xl s
67.345	To Dunston Ames Rewarded in Money by the Threasourer of the Chamber . . . . .xx s
67.346	To Robert Cooke als Chester one guilt Bolle with a couer P. poz . . . . x oz iij qrt

Free Giftes

67.347	To Mr John Asteley Mr of the Juelles and plate oone guilt Cup with a couer P. poz . . . . xviij oz qrt
67.348	To Mr Thomas Asteley grome of her Maties preuy Chamber one guilt Cup P. poz . . . . .viij oz di
67.349	To Mr John Tamworth one other Grome &c. one guilt Cup B. poz . . . . viij oz qrt di
67.350	To Mr Henry Sackeforde one other grome &c. one guilt Cup P. poz. . . . viij oz di
67.351	To Mr John Baptiste one other grome &c. one guilt Cup P. poz . . . . viij oz di
67.352	To Mr Edwarde Cary one other grome &c. one gult Cup B. poz. . . . . . . viij oz di
67.353	To Rauf Hoope yeoman of the Roobes one guilt Cup with a couer B. poz. . . . . xij oz qrt di
67.354	To Nicholas Bristowe Clarke of the Juelles and Plate one guilt Cruse B. poz. . . . . x oz iij qrt di
67.355	To Edmunde Pigeon yeoman of the said office one guilt Cruse B. poz . . . . x oz iij qrt di
67.356	To John Pigeon one other yeoman one guilt Cruse B. poz. . . . . x oz iij qrt di
67.357	To Stephen Fullwell Grome of the said office one guilt Cruse B. poz . . . . x oz iij qrt di

Summa totalis of all the said plate geuon by her Matie as aforesaide . . . . mmmm Clj oz

Guiftes geuon by her majestie
and delyuerid owte of the Office of her
highnes Juellis and Plate in maner and fourme
following
viz

| 67.358 | Lady Cecillia |
| | Geuon by her Matie and Delyvered the xxvj^{th} of Apriell Anno viij^{no} Regine Elizabeth To the Lady Cicillia, Syster to the king of Sweethlande at her departure owte of Englande Oone Bolle of golde bought of Robert Brandon and Affabell Partrige her Maties goldesmythes poz. . . . . .Cxxxiij oz di |

67.359 Mounsier de Foiex

Geuon by her Matie and Delyvered the xxiiij^th of Maye Anno viij^no
pred to Mounsier de foiex Ambassator liger of Fraunce at his
departure owte of Englande Oone Bason and Ewer guilt Brandon
poz—lxxviij oz qrt . Item one other Bason and Layer guilt B. poz—
lxxij oz. Item one peire of guilt Flagons B. poz—Ciiij^xx viij oz qrt.
Item one other peire of guilt Flagons Partrige poz—Cxlij oz iij qrt.
Item one peire of guilt Pottes P. poz—Cxiij oz di di qrt. Item one
peire of guilt Pottes B. poz—lxxix oz iij qrt. Item thre guilt Bolles
with a couer B. poz—iiij^xx vj oz qrt / Item three mo guilte Bolles
with a couer P. poz—iiij^xx iiij oz iij qrt di. Item oone guilt Cup
with a couer B. poz—xxxviij oz di di qrt. Item one other guilt
Cup with a couer B. poz—xxxviij oz. And two guilt Saltes with
oone cover P. poz—xlv oz di. In toto . . . . .ix^C lviij oz iij qrt di

67.360 Mr James Meluen

Geuon by her Matie and Delyverid the xxvij^th of June Anno pred to
Mr James Meluen sent from the Quene of Scottes one Cheyne of
golde bought of the said Robert Brandon and Affabell Partridge
poz . . . . xvij oz di golde

67.361 Lady Hobbye

Geuon by her hignes and delyvered the xvij^th of Septembr Anno pred
at the christenyng of the Lady Hobby her Childe one guilt Bolle
with a couer bought of Partrige poz . . . . xxv oz di

67.362 Quene of Scottes

Geuon by her Matie at the Christenynge of the Quene of Scottes Sonne
Oone Funte of golde with a couer garnesshid with sundry curious
peces of golde enameled poz—CCCxxxiij oz which was made of a
Cxxxiij oz di of golde bought of the said Robert Brandon and
Affabell Partrige. And of – Ciiij^xx xix oz di of golde Delyverid to
the said Brandon and Partrige by the said John Asteley owte of his
custody and chardge being the weight of the cleare gold that came
of sundry percelles of golde plate of the said John Asteleyes chardge
broken and molten by her Maties expresse commaundement towardes
the making of the said Founte / which percelles of golde plate are
playnely and perticulerly expressed in a booke datid the first of
August Anno viij^no pred and subscribed with the handes of the
said Robert Brandon Affabell Partige Edmunde Pigeon and
William [sic, i.e. Richard] Marten . . . . CCCxxxiij oz golde

67.363 Mr Markham

Geuon by her Matie and delyverid the ij^de of December Anno ixno
Regine Elizabeth &c. to the christenynge of Mr Markeham his
childe one guilt bolle with a couer bought of Brandon poz . . . . . xxiij oz qrt

67.364 Countys de Arco

Geuon by her highnes and Delyverid the xvj[th] of January Anno ix[no] pred To Counte de Arco one Cheyne of golde bought of Affabell Partrige and Robert Brandon poz...................... xxxiij oz qrt di

Elizabeth R
[sign manual]

J Asteley
ex[aminatio] per
Edm Pigeon
J Pigeon
Ste Fulwell

Anno Regni Regine
Elizabethae Decimo

Newyeris Guiftes geuon to the Quene
her Maiestie by those parsonnes whose Names
hereafter ensue. The first of Januarye The
yere above written

Elizabeth R
[sign manual]

68.1   By the Lady Margerett the Earle of Lenys wief In Dimy soueraignes and
siluer. . . . . xiij li vj s viij d
Delyuerid to John Tamworth Grome
of the preuy Chamber to her Maties vse

68.2   By the Lady Margerett the Lorde Strainge his wief A Cawle and a
partelett of venice golde knytt with knottes. And a peire of Sleuis
and partelett of fyne Lawne wrought with venice golde grene &
crymsen silke like Rooses vnmade
Delyuerid to Dorothey Abingdon
one of her Maties preuy Chamber

68.3   By the Lorde keper of the greate Seale in a purse of blak silke venice
golde and siluer knitt In golde & siluer. xiij li vj s viij d

68.4   By the Duke of No[r]ffolke in a blewe silke purse knytt In Dimy
soueraignes. . . . . xx li

68.5   By the Marques of Wyntchester in a yellowe silke purse in Dimy
soueraignes. . . . . xx li
Delyuerid to the said John Tamworth

68.6   By the Marques of Northampton A feyer Jug of Christall the foote lypp
and cover garnesshid with golde
Delyuerid in chardge to John Astley Mr and Threasourer of
the Juelles and Plate *ex et oner* / poiz – x oz

Earles

68.7   By the Earle of Pembroke Lorde Stewarde of her Majesties howseholde
in a purse of crymsen satten in Di souer. . . . . xxx li
68.8   By the Earle of Arundell in a paper in Dimy soueraignes . . . . xxx li
68.9   By the Earle of Northumberlande in a red silke purse in Dimy soueraignes. . x li
68.10 By the Earle of Westmerlande in a red silke purse in golde . . . . x li
68.11 By the Earle of Shrewisburye in a red silke purse in golde. . . . . xx li
68.12 By the Earle of Darbye in a red silke purse knytt in newe soueraignes
Dimy . . . . xx li
68.13 By the Earle of Huntingdon in a red satten purse in Angelles and
soueraignes. . . . . x li

68.14   By the Earle of Bedforde in a purse of red silke and venice siluer knitt in Dimy
          soueraignes. . . . . xx li
                                                            Delyuerid to John Tamworthe
68.15   By the Earle of Warwicke Oone Cheyne of golde sett with sparkes of
          Rubies and Pearles
                                                Delyuerid to Blaunche Pary gentillwoman
                                                          of her highnes preuy Chamber
          And a handekercheue of turqueyworke wrought with silke
                                                      Delyverid to the said Mrs Abingdon
68.16   By the Earle of Ormonde a Hatt of blewe taphata allouer enbrauderid
          with venice golde & siluer. With a Brouche of golde sett with Diamondes
          like a Starre
                                                      The Hatt Delyuerid to Rauf Hope
                                                              yeoman of the Roobes
                                          The Brouche Delyuerid to the said Blaunch Pary
          And a Remnaunte of blewe cloth of siluer tyncel prented
          conteignynge . . . . vij yerdes iij qrt
                                                            Delyuerid to the said Rauf Hope
68.17   By the Earle of Lennys in a purse of grene silke and siluer in Angelles . . . . xx li
68.18   By the Viscounte Mountague in a red silke purse knitt in Dimy
          soueraignes. . . . . x li
                                                        Delyuerid to the said John Tamworth
                                                                  Duchesses & Countesses
68.19   By the Duches of Suffolke one pece of Murrey vellat with workes
          Conteignynge. . . . . xvj yerdes iij qrt
                                                            Delyuerid to the said Rauf Hope
68.20   By the Duches of Somersett a feyer loking Glasse sett in Steele Damaskyned
          and garnesshid with counterphett Stones and Pearles
                                                      Delyuerid to the said Blaunch Parry
68.21   By the Countes of Surrey in a red silke purse knytt in golde . . . . C s
68.22   By the Countes of Oxford Dowager in a litell red silke purse in Dimy
          soueraignes. . . . . C s
68.23   By the Countes of Northumberlande in a grene silke purse in Dimy
          soueraignes. . . . . x li
                                                        Delyuerid to the said John Tamworth
68.24   By the Countes of Shrewisburye Oone foreparte of a kyrtell and a
          placarde of blak vellat allouer enbrauderid with pipes and purles of
          Damaske golde
                                                      Delyuerid to said Rauf Hope
68.25   By the Countes of Darbye in a red silke purse knytt in English Crownes . . . . x li
68.26   By the Countes of Huntingdon Dowager in a red silke purse knitt in Dimy
          soueraignes. . . . . x li
68.27   By the Countes of Huntingdon in a chery bag of red Satten in Dimy
          soueraignes and Angelles. . . . . viij li

68.28 By the Countes of Pembroke in a crymsen Satten chery bag in Dimy
 soueraignes. . . . . xv li
                                          Delyuerid to said John Tamworth
68.29 By the Countes of Bedforde a peire of Bracelettes of golde cont tenne
 Rubies & xx pearles vpon them
68.30 By the Countes of Warwicke a Flower of golde garnesshid with stone &
 pearle with a litell Byrde standinge before a Sonne
                                          Delyuerid to said Blaunche Pary
68.31 By the Viscountes Mountague in a red silke purse in Dimy soueraignes. . . . . x li
                                          Delyuerid to the said John Tamworth

Bysshoppes

68.32 By the Archebysshop of Caunterburye in a red silke purse knitt in Dimy
 soueraignes. . . . . .xl li
68.33 By the Archebysshop of Yorke in a red lether purse in Dimy
 soueraignes. . . . . xxx li
68.34 By the Bysshop of Duresme in a chery bag of crymsen satten in
 Angelles . . . . xxx li
68.35 By the Bysshop of Elye in a taphata purse in Dimy soueraignes. . . . . xxx li
68.36 By the Bysshop of London in a white Satten purse in Dimy soueraignes . . . xx li
68.37 By the Bysshop of Wynchester in a red Satten purse in Angelles and Dimy
 soueraignes. . . . . xx li
68.38 By the Bysshop of Salisburye in a red silke purse in Dimy soueraignes . . . . xx li
68.39 By the Bysshop of Worcester in a red Satten purse in Dimy soueraignes
 and Angelles. . . . . xx li
68.40 By the Bysshop of Lincolne in a red Satten purse in Angelles and Dimy
 soueraignes. . . . . xx li
68.41 By the Bysshop of Norwich in a red silke purse knytt in Angelles one
 being a Flemyshe Angell . . . . .xix li xvij s vj d
68.42 By the Bysshop of Rochester in a blak silke purse knytt in golde . . . . . .xiij li vj s
68.43 By the Bysshop of Lychefilde and Couentrye in a red silke purse in
 golde and siluer . . . . xiij li vj s viij d
68.44 By the Bysshop of Chichester in a red Satten purse in golde. . . . . x li
68.45 By the Bysshop of Hereforde in a red silke purse knytt in Dimy
 soueraignes. . . . . x li
68.46 By the Bysshop of St Dauyes in a blewe silke purse knytt in Angelles . . . . . . x li
68.47 By the Bysshop of Bath in a red Satten purse in golde. . . . . x li
68.48 By the Bysshop of Exeter in a purse of yellowe cloth of golde in
 soueraignes. . . . . x li
68.49 By the Bysshop of Peterborowe in a red silke purse in Dimy soueraignes. . . . x li
68.50 By the Bysshop of Chester in a red Satten purse in Angelles. . . . . x li
68.51 By the Bysshop of Glocester in a blewe silke purse in Dimy soueraignes
 and Angelles. . . . . x li
                                          Delyuerid to the said John Tamworth

Lordes

68.52 By the Lorde William Howarde Lorde Chamerlayne of her Maties
honorable Chamber in a purse of red silke and venice golde in Dimy
soueraignes and Angelles. . . . . x li

68.53 By the Lorde Burgauenny in a yellowe silke purse in Dimy soueraignes . . . . . C s

68.54 By the Lorde Clynton Lorde Admirall of Englande in a silke purse in
Dimy soueraignes . . . . x li

68.55 By the Lorde Strainge in a red silke purse in Dimy soueraignes . . . . C s

68.56 By the Lorde Barkeley in a purse of red silke and venice golde in Angelles . . x li

68.57 By the Lorde Scrowpe in a paper in Dimy soueraignes . . . . x li

68.58 By the Lorde Lumley in a paper in Dimy soueraignes . . . . xv li

68.59 By the Lorde Wyndesor in a red silke purse in Dimy soueraignes . . . . x li

68.60 By the Lorde Riche in a red satten purse in Dimy soueraignes . . . . x li

68.61 By the Lorde Darcye of Chichey in a red taphata purse in golde . . . . x li

68.62 By the Lorde Shandowes in a purse of red silke and venice golde knytt
in Dimy soueraignes . . . . x li

68.63 By the Lorde Hastinges of Lougheborowe in a red silke purse knitt in
golde and siluer . . . . xiij li vj s viij d

68.64 By the Lorde Pagett in a red silke purse in Dimy soueraignes . . . . x li

68.65 By the Lorde Hunsdon in a purse of red silke and venice golde knitt in
Dimy soueraignes . . . . x li

68.66 By the Lorde Buckhurste in a blewe silke purse in newe Dimy soueraignes . . x li
Delyuerid to the said John Tamworth

Ladyes

68.67 By the Lady Clynton two Cusshionclothes of fyne Camerik fayer wrought
with red silke & venice gold layedworke
Delyuerid to the said Mrs Abingdon
And a Loking Glasse of Christall sett in steele Damaskyned garnesshid with
counterphett stone and Pearle
Delyuerid to the said Blanch Parry

68.68 By the Lady Burgauennye in a paper in Dimy souevaignes . . . . C s

68.69 By the Lady Barcley in a purse of red silke and venice golde in Angelles . . . . C s

68.70 By the Lady Dakers of the South in a purse of crymsen silke and venice
siluer knytt in Angelles . . . . x li
Delyuerid to the said John Tamworth

68.71 By the Lady Cobham a foreparte of a kyrtell of white Satten allouer
enbrauderid with venice golde like Roundelles
Delyuerid to the said Rauf Hope

68.72 By the Lady Tayleboyes Sir Peter Carewis wief In a silke purse in Dimy
soueraignes. . . . . x li
Delyuerid to the said John Tamworth

68.73 By the Lady Cromwell the Lorde Cromwelles wief a partelett and a peire
of Sleuis of Lawne wroughte allouer with Trowtes of silke
Delyuerid to the said Rauf Hope

68.74   By the Lady Howarde in a purse of red silke and venice golde knytt in
Dimy soueraignes . . . . x li
Delyuerid to the said John Tamworth

68.75   By the Lady Shandowes two Cusshionettes of lynen cloth allouer
wroughte with venice golde siluer and silke of Diuers colors
Delyuerid to the said Mrs Abingdon

68.76   By the Lady Hunsden in a purse of red silke and venice golde knytt in
Dimy soueraignes . . . . x li

68.77   By the Lady Pagett in a blak silke purse in Dimy soueraignes . . . . x li

68.78   By the Lady Knolles in a purse of blewe silke and venice golde knytt in
Dimy soueraignes . . . . xx li
Delyuerid to the said John Tamworth

68.79   By the Lady Stafforde a Rynge of golde sett with foure small Diamondes
and foure small Rubies
with her majestie

68.80   By the Lady Cicell a Cawle of venice golde knytt with Rooses of Pearle.
And fyue Spanyshe handkerches wroughte with silke of sundry colors
Delyuerid to the said Mrs Abingdon

68.81   By the Lady Wodhowse one foreparte of a kyrtell of golde and siluer
sackecloth allouer sett with spangelles of siluer and guilt with a brode
border of carnation Satten allouer enbrauderid with spangelles of siluer
guilt and siluer guilt like flowers with foure leaues and frengid with silke
and golde
Delyuerid to the said Rauf Hope

68.82   By the Lady Carewe two Pillowis thone couerid with red silke and venice
golde thother with blak silke edgid with passamayne of like golde and
buttoned and tasselid

68.83   By the Lady Jobson a fayre Smocke allover wrought with venice golde and
blak silke
Delyuerid to the said Mrs Abingdon

68.84   By the Lady Butler in a paper in Golde . . . . vj li

68.85   By the Lady Hemyngham in a purse of blak silke and venice siluer in
Angelles . . . . C s

68.86   By the Lady Sackevile in a purse of murrey silke knytt in Soueraignes . . . . . . x li

68.87   By the Lady Paulett in a purse of blewe silke and venice golde in Angelles . . C s
Delyuerid to the said John Tamworth

68.88   By the Lady Ratclyff a Rayle and a peire of Sleuis of Lawne wrought
with oring tawnye silke edgid with passamayne of venice golde and
siluer. And two swete Bagges
Delyuerid to the said Mrs Abingdon

68.89   By the Lady Cheeke in a purse of red silke and venice golde knytt in Dimy
soueraignes. . . . . C s

68.90   By the Lady Gresham in a blak silke purse knytt in Angelles . . . . x li
Delyuerid to the said John Tamworth

68.91   By the Lady Throgmorton a night Rayle and peire of Ruffes wrought with
venice golde siluer and blewe and carnation silke

138

68.92   By the Lady Cheyney a partelett and a peire of Sleuis of venice golde
     with hoopes and buttons drawen out with Lawne
                                     Delyuered to the said Mrs Abingdon

68.93   By the Lady Wilforde in a purse of yellow silke knytt A wedge of golde
     poz . . . . vij oz di qrt
                                  Delyuerid to the said John Tamworth

68.94   By the Lady Yorke Six small Suger loues and two small Barelles of Suckett

68.95   By the Lady Stoner a Cawle wrought with pipes of venice golde and siluer
     pulled oute with Lawne

68.96   By the Lady Norrys two Cawles of Lawne wrought with venice golde and
     siluer knytt And certeyne frewtes in silke wounde

68.97   By the Lady Vane one peire of Gloues perfumed the Cuffes sett with sixtene
     Buttons of golde garnesshid with thre Pearles the pece
                                     Delyuerid to the said Mrs Abingdon

Knights
68.98

By Sir Edwarde Rogers Comptroller of her Maties howseholde in a chery
68.99   bag of crymsen Satten in Dimy soueraignes . . . . vij li

By Sir Fraunces Knollys vicechamberlen &c. in a purse of blewe silke and
68.100   venice siluer knytt in Dimy soueraignes . . . . x li

By Sir William Cicell principall Secretarye in a purse of red silke and
68.101   siluer knytt in newe Di soueraignes . . . . xx li

By Sir Ambrose Caue Chauncellor of the Duchye in a purse of greene
68.102   silke and siluer in olde Royalles . . . . xv li

By Sir William Peter Chauncellor of the Order in a purse of blak silke
68.103   and golde knitt in new Di soueraignes . . . . x li

By Sir Walter Myldemaye Chauncellor of the Eschequer in a purse of
68.104   russett silke & siluer knitt in Di soueraignes . . . . x li

By Sir William Cordall Mr of the Rolles in a litell red Satten purse in
68.105   Dimy soueraignes . . . . x li

68.106   By Sir Christopher Heydon in a yellowe silke purse in Dimy soueraignes . . . x li

68.107   By Sir Henry Jernengham in a purse of Tyncell in Dimy Soueraignes . . . . . . x li

68.108   By Sir Peter Carewe in a silke purse in Dimy soueraignes . . . . x li

68.109   By Sir William Damsell in a red silke purse knytt in Dimy soueraignes . . . . . x li

By Sir Fraunces Jobson in a litell purse of venice siluer knytt in new
68.110   Dimy soueraignes . . . . x li

By Sir Henry Cromewell in a purse of venice siluer and silke knytt in
68.111   Dimy soueraignes . . . . xv li

By Sir John Thynne in a yellowe silke purse in Dimy soueraignes . . . . C s
68.112   Delyuerid to the said John Tamworth

By Sir Gowen Carewe a Smock the coller and handewristes wrought
     with venice golde and siluer therest wrought with purple silke
68.113   Delyuerid to the said Mrs Abingdon

By Sir Thomas Benger a Ring of golde with a small table Rubie in it
                               Delyuerid to the said Blaunch Pary

68.114   By Sir Thomas Gresham in a red silke purse knytt in Dimy soueraignes .... x li
                                                        Delyuerid to the said John Tamworth
68.115   By Sir Nicholas Throgmorton a Cawle wrought with venice golde
                                                        Delyuerid to the said Mrs Abingdon
          And a Rynge of golde with a stone called an Opall
                                                        Delyuerid to the said Blaunch Parry
68.116   By Sir William Pyckeringe one Remnaunte of blak cloth of golde
          tyncell prented conteignyng.............................. x yerdes iij qrt
                                                        Delyuerid to the said Rauf Hope
68.117   By Sir Gylbert Dethyck a Booke of tharmes of all the knightes of the
          Garter that were in kynge Richarde the ijde his tyme couerid with
          crymsen vellat with a passamayne of golde
68.118   By Sir Henry Sydney Lorde Deputye of Irelande a feyre payer of knyues
          the Sheethe and haftes of golde garnesshid with Rubies Diamondes and
          Emerodes
                                                        Delyuerid to the said Blaunch Pary

Gentilwomen

68.119   By Misteris Blaunche Pary a Flower of golde conteignynge thre sparckes
          of Diamondes thre sparkes of Rubies, and a litell pearle pendaunte
          being thistory of Justice
                                                        Delyuerid to the said Blaunche Pary
68.120   By Mrs Katheryn Howarde wief a partelett and a Coyphe of fine lawne
          wrought with borders of silke spanyshe worke
68.121   By Mrs Elizabeth Knollys a partelett and a peire of Sleuis of Lawne
          allouer wrought with venice golde and silke: And two Cusshionettes of
          crymsen and blewe taphata allouer embr with venice gold & siluer
68.122   By Mrs Caue a Smock wrought with blak silke edgid with venice golde
                                                        Delyuerid to the said Mrs Abingdon
68.123   By Mrs Hennage a Remnaunte of crymsen cloth of golde tyncell rewid
          conteignynge ....vj yerdes
                                                        Delyuerid to the said Rauf Hope
68.124   By Mrs Edmundes a Rayle and a peire of Ruffes wrought with venice golde
          siluer and blak silke
68.125   By Mrs Maruen a Smock wrought in ye coller and handwristes with venice
          golde therest with red silke
68.126   By Mrs Abingdon a partelett & a peire of sleuis of Lawne nettid with knottes of
          venice gold & siluer
68.127   By Mrs Marberye a partlett and a peire of Ruffes of nettworke in colors
68.128   By Mrs Ellene Wolf a Rayle & a peire of Ruffes of sipers wrought with
          venice siluer blak & carnacon silke
68.129   By Mrs Baptest a Cusshioncloth fayer wrought with a border of red silke
          & venice golde layed worke
68.130   By Mrs Huggens of Hamptoncorte two fayer Cusshionclothes of fyne
          holland wrought with fayer borders of venice golde siluer and blewe
          silke, fringid buttoned and tasselid with like golde and silke

68.131 By Mrs Huggens of Norff a Smocke wrought with venice golde siluer
and grene silke

62.132 By Mrs Elizabeth Wyngefilde two Cawles thone wrought with venice golde
thother with siluer & blak silke
Delyuerid to the said Mrs Abingdon

68.133 By Mrs Dane a feyer Cusshion of Arras frengid buttoned and tassellid with
venice golde and silke lyned with grene Taphata. And a pece of Lawne
Delyuerid to Richard Todde keper of the Guarderobe at hamptoncorte
The Lawne Delyuerid to the said Blaunche Pary

68.134 By Mrs Smytheson Laundres a Coyphe of Lawne cheuernid with venice siluer
Delyuerid to the said Mrs Abingdon

68.135 By Mrs Leuina Terling a paper paynted with the Quenis Matie and the
knightes of thorder
Delyuerid to the said Blaunch Pary

68.136 By Mrs Amy Shelton Sixe handkercheues edgid with passamayne lase of
venice golde
Delyuerid to the said Mrs Abingdon

68.137 By Mrs Elizabeth Shelton a litell Boxe couerid with stooleworke of
venice golde and silke and therein two Regesters of golde with theire
laces of venice golde and silke
Delyuerid to the said Blaunch Pary

68.138 By Ipolita the Tartarian a Coyphe wrought with venice golde siluer and
silke

68.139 By Mrs Loo a flower like an Eare of Barley and wylde Ootes wrought of
venice golde

68.140 By Mrs Bareley Sixe handekercheues edgid with passamayne lase of venice
golde
Delyuerid to the said Mrs Abingdon

Chaplaynes

68.141 By Archedeacon Carewe Deane of the Chapell in a purse of red silke &
venice golde knitt in Di soueraignes . . . . x li

68.142 By Doctor Newton Deane of Wyntchester in a purse of blewe silke &
venice siluer knitt in Di soueraignes . . . . x li
Delyuerid to the said John Tamworth

68.143 By Parson Dorrell a small square Cheyne of golde hauing hanging therat
a Roose of Rubies with a litell pearle pendaunte . . . . iij qrt of an oz
Delyuerid to the said Blaunch Pary

Gentlemen

68.144 By Maister John Asteley Mr and Threasourer of her Majesties Juelles and
Plate a Table of Towchestone folding garnesshid with siluer guilt with
theese wordes Loue God aboue all thinges and thy Neighbor as thy self
. . . . xxxviij oz qrt
ex et oner
Delyuerid in chardge to the said John Asteley

141

68.145   By Mr Thomas Hennage a Fanne of Fethers with a handell of golde enameled

68.146   By Mr John Harington a Juell of golde wherein is a Clocke garnesshid with sixe sparkes of Rubies poz. . . . . one oz di
Delyuerid to the said Blaunch Pary

68.147   By Mr Chamberlen of Garnesey in a red silke purse in frenche crownes . . . . vj li

68.148   By Mr Edwarde Bashe in a red satten purse in Angelles . . . . x li

68.149   By Mr Thomas Stanley in a litell silke purse in Angelles . . . . x li
Delyuerid to the said John Tamworth

68.150   By William Huggens two fayer longe swete Bagges of blewe taphata fayer enbrauderid with hoopes & thees wordes aboute a burnynge Torche. Res mihi iam crux est quae fuit ante Salus. fayer buttoned tassellid & frengid with venice golde and silke

68.151   By Benedicke Spinula Two Pillowis and a Cusshioncloth wrought allouer with venice gold siluer & silk turkemaking
Delyuered to the said Mrs Abingdon

68.152   By Smyth Custumer two Boltes of Camerike

68.153   By Allen Marchaunte two Boltes of Camerike
Delyuerid to the said Blaunch Pary

68.154   By Doctor Hewicke a Pott of gynger conditt / Another of oringe Flowers condite

68.155   By Doctor Maister two like Pottes

68.156   By John Hemyngwaye appoticary certeyne Boxes of Marmelade and Corserueres

68.157   By John Soda appoticary certeyne Boxes of conseruees & Marmelades & a glasse of conserued barberyes
Delyuerid to the said Mrs Abingdon

68.158   By Robert Robotham Oone peire of blak silke hoose knytt
Delyuerid to Elizabeth Marbery

68.159   By George Webster Mr Cooke Two suger leeches
[blank]

68.160   By Ambrose a violan a Standishe like a Cusshionett couerid allouer with grene vellat layed with a brode passamayne of venice golde and siluer
Delyuerid to the said Mrs Abingdon

68.161   By Jaques Greuen a litell Booke written in Frenche couerid with parchement
Delyuerid to the said Blaunche Pary

68.162   By Marke Anthony a Bolle of glasse with a couer guilded
Delyuerid to the said John Asteley

68.163   By Adams Scolemaster to the henchemen two patrons for Sleuis drawen vpon Cameryke
Delyuerid to the said Mrs Abingdon

68.164   By Anthony Marye a booke in Italian called *Caualarie della citta di ferrara* coverid with parchement paynted & gilt
Delyuerid to the said Blaunche Pary

68.165   By John Bettes serjaunte of the Pastrye a Pye of Quinces
[blank]

68.166   By Petricio Vbaldino a peire of writing Tables the claspes and corners
      garnesshid with siluer

Delyuerid to the said Blaunch Pary

68.167   By Baptista Bassani two peire of Gloues thone wrought with venice
      golde & silke, thother with silke onely

Delyuerid to the said Mrs Abingdon

68.168   By James Bellott a Booke conteignynge certeyne wordes and rules of the
      Frenche Tonge

Delyuerid to the said John Tamworth

68.169   By [blank] a Frencheman a Deuice made of silke Nuttemegges and Cloues of
      thistory of Pirramus and Tysbey

Delyuerid in charge to George Brydeman
keper the Palloice of Westminster

Summa totalis of
the Money Geuon to her   ex[aminatio] per
Matie as aforesaid . . . . m li Cliij li xs ij d

Delyuerid to the said John Tamworth as aforesaid

Elizabeth R
[sign manual]

J Asteley
Edm Pigeon
Ste Fulwell
ex[aminatio] per

Anno Regni Regine
Elizabethae Decimo

Newyeris Guiftes geuon by the
Queine her maiestie to those parsons
whose names hereafter ensue, The
first of Januarye The yere abovewritten.

Elizabeth R
[sign manual]

68.170   To the Lady Margerett the Earle of Lennys wief One guilt Cup with a
      couer B. poz . . . . xxxiij oz di

68.171   To the Lady Margerett the Lorde Strainge his wief One guilt Cup with a
      couer B. poz . . . . xix oz di

68.172   To the Lorde keper of the greate Seale of Englande One guilt Bolle with
      a couer P. poz . . . . xxxiiij oz

68.173   To the Ducke of Norffolke one guilt Bolle with a couer P. poz . . . xlj oz iij qrt di

68.174   To the Marques of Wyntchester one guilt Bolle with a couer P. poz . . . .xxxv oz

68.175   To the Marques of Northampton one guilt Bolle with a couer P. poz

. . . . .xxxv oz di di qrt

Earles

68.176   To the Earle of Pembroke Lorde Stewarde of Her Maties howseholde thre

guilt Bolles with a couer B. poz . . . . L oz

68.177   To the Earle of Arundell one guilt Bolle with a couer P. poz . . . . Lij oz di

68.178   To the Earle of Northumberlande one guilt Bolle with a couer P.

poz . . . . xx oz qrt di

68.179   To the Earle of Westmerlande one guilt Bolle with a couer poz P. . . xx oz qrt di

68.180   To the Earle of Shrewisburye one guilt Bolle with a couer P. poz . . . . . xxx oz di

68.181   To the Earle of Darbye one guilt Bolle with a couer B. poz . . . . . . xxix oz iij qrt

68.182   To the Earle of Huntingdon one guilt Bolle with a couer P poz . . . . xxij oz

68.183   To the Earle of Bedfourde one guilt Bolle with a couer P. poz . . . . xxxj oz iij qrt

68.184   To the Earle of Warwicke one peire of guilt Pottes P. poz . . . . . Cxij oz iij qrt di

68.185   To the Earle of Ormonde one peire of guilt Pottes P. poz—lxix oz di

di qrt: Thre guilt Bolles with a couer B. poz—lxiij [oz] di di qrt.

And a guilt Bolle with a couer B. poz—xxv oz iij qrts in toto . . . . . Clix oz qrt

68.186   To the Earle of Lennys One guilt Bolle with a couer P. poz . . . . xxx oz di di qrt

68.187   To the Vicounte Mountague one guilt Bolle with a couer B. poz . . . xx oz di qrt

Duchesses and Countesses

68.188   To the Duches of Suff[olk] one guilt Bolle with a couer B. poz . . . . xxxj oz

68.189   To the Duches of Somersett one guilt Cup with a couer P. poz . . xxix oz di di qrt

68.190   To the Countes of Surrey one guilt Cup with a couer B. poz . . . . xij oz qrt

68.191   To the Countes of Oxford Dowager one guilt Cup with a couer B.

poz . . . . xj oz iij qrt

68.192   To the Countes of Northumberlande one guilt Bolle with a couer P.

poz . . . . xx oz di di qrt

68.193   To the Countes of Shrewisbury one guilt Cup with a couer B. poz . . . . . . xxiij oz

68.194   To the Countes of Darby one guilt Bolle with a couer P. poz . . . . . . xx oz qrt di

68.195   To the Countes of Huntingdon Dowager one guilt Bolle with a couer

P. poz . . . . xx oz di

68.196   To the Countes of Huntingdon one guilt Bolle with a couer P.

poz . . . . .xxxv oz di di qrt

68.197   To the Countes of Pembroke one guilt Bolle with a couer. P poz

. . . . xxviij oz di qrt

68.198   To the Countes of Bedforde Thre guilt Bolles with a couer B. poz

. . . . xxxiij oz di di qrt

68.199   To the Countes of Warwick Thre guilt Bolles with a couer P. poz. . . . . . . xlix oz

68.200   To the Vicountes Mountague one guilt Bolle with a couer P. poz

. . . . xix oz di di qrt

Bysshoppes

68.201	To the Archebysshop of Caunterbury one guilt Cup with a couer B. poz . . . . .xlij oz di di qrt
68.202	To the Archebysshop of Yorke one guilt Bolle with a couer P. poz . . . . xxxiiij oz di di qrt
68.203	To the Bysshop of Duresme Thre guilt Bolles with a couer B. poz . . . . .xxxvij oz qrt
68.204	To the Bysshop of Elye one guilt Bolle with a couer B. poz. . . . . xxxiiij oz qrt di
68.205	To the Bysshop of London one guilt Salte with a couer B. poz. . . . . .xxx oz
68.206	To the Bysshop of Wynchester one guilt Salte with a couer B. poz . . . . xxxj oz Di di qrt
68.207	To the Bysshop of Salisburye Two hans Pottes guilt B. thone poz— xvij oz qrt. thother poz – xiiij oz iij qrt . . . . xxxij oz
68.208	To the Bysshop of Worcester one guilt Bolle with a couer P. poz . . . . xxix oz qrt di
68.209	To the Bysshop of Lyncolne one guilt Bolle with a couer B. poz . . . . xxxj oz iij qrt di
68.210	To the Bysshop of Norwiche one guilt Bolle with a couer P. poz . . . . .xxviij oz di di qrt
68.211	To the Bysshop of Rochester one guilt Cup with a couer B. poz . . . . . .xxij oz qrt
68.212	To the Bysshop of Lychefilde and Couentrye one Bolle with a couer guilt B. poz. . . . . .xxj oz di qrt
68.213	To the Bysshop of Chichester one guilt Bolle with a couer B. poz . . . . xvij oz di
68.214	To the Bysshop of Herfourde one guilt Bolle with a couer B. poz. . . . . xvij oz di
68.215	To the Bysshop of Saynt Dauyes one guilt Bolle with a couer B. poz . . xvij oz di
68.216	To the Bysshop of Bath one guilt Bolle with a couer B. poz . . . . . . xvij oz qrt di
68.217	To the Bysshop of Exetor one guilt Bolle with a couer B. poz. . . . . xvij oz
68.218	To the Bysshop of Peterborowe one guilt Boll with a couer B. poz. . xvj oz iij qrt
68.219	To the Bysshop of Chester one guilt Cup with a couer B. poz. . . . . xvij oz
68.220	To the Bysshop of Glocester one guilt Bolle with a couer B. poz . . xviij oz qrt di

Lordes

62.221	To the Lorde William Howarde Lorde Chamberlen of her Maties Honorable Chamber one guilt Bolle with a couer P. poz . . . . xxvj oz iij qrt
68.222	To the Lorde Aburgauenny one guilt Bolle with a couer P. poz. . . . . xij oz di
68.223	To the Lorde Clynton Lorde Admirall of Englande one guilt Cup with a couer B. poz . . . . xxiiij oz qrt
68.224	To the Lorde Strainge one guilt Bolle with a couer P. poz . . . . xij oz qrt di
68.225	To the Lorde Barcley one guilt Bolle with a couer P. poz. . . . . xx oz di di qrt
68.226	To the Lorde Scrowpe one guilt Bolle with a couer P. poz. . . . . xx oz di
68.227	To the Lorde Lomeley one guilt Bolle with a couer B. poz . . . . xxiiij oz
68.228	To the Lorde Wyndesor one guilt Bolle with a couer P. poz. . . . . .xx oz iij qrt
68.229	To the Lorde Riche one guilt Bolle with a couer P. poz . . . . xx oz iij qrt di
68.230	To the Lorde Darcey of Chechey one guilt Bolle with a couer P. poz . . . . .xx oz iij qrt

68.231 To the Lorde Hastinges of Loughborow one guilt Bolle with a couer P. poz . . . . xxiij oz qrt

68.232 To the Lorde Pagett one guilt Bolle with a couer P. poz . . . . xxj oz di di qrt

68.233 To the Lorde Shandowes one guilt Bolle with a couer B. poz . . . . xxj oz qrt

68.234 To the Lorde Hunsden one hans pott guilt P. poz—xxij qrt di. And parte of another P. poz—xiij oz iij qrt di . . . . xxxvj oz qrt

68.235 To the Lorde Buckehurst one guilt Bolle with a couer B. poz . . . . xix oz di

Ladyes

68.236 To the Lady Clynton one guilt Cup with a couer B. poz—xiiij oz di and one guilt Bolle with a couer P. poz – xl oz. . . . . Liiij oz di

68.237 To the Lady Aburgauenney one guilt Bolle with a couer P. poz . . . . . . xij oz qrt

68.238 To the Lady Barcley one guilt Bolle with a couer P. poz . . . . xj oz

68.239 To the Lady Dakers of the Sowth one guilt Tankerd B. poz . . . . xxj oz di qrt

68.240 To the Lady Cobham one guilt Cup with a couer P. poz . . . . Lij oz

68.241 To the Lady Tayleboies Sir Peter Carewis wief one guilt Bolle with a couer P. poz . . . . xx oz iij qrt di

68.242 To the Lady Cromewell one guilt Cup with a couer P. poz . . . . . xviij oz di di qrt

68.243 To the Lady Pagett one guilt Bolle with a couer P. poz . . . . xix oz

68.244 To the Lady Howarde one guilt Bolle with a couer B. poz. . . . . xxvj oz

68.245 To the Lady Shandowes one guilt Cup with a couer B. poz. . . . . . xxj oz di di qrt

68.246 To the Lady Hunsdon one guilt Bolle with a couer B. poz—xv oz iij qrt di and parte of a hans pott P. poz—vij oz di qrt . . . . xxiij oz

68.247 To the Lady Knolles parte of a peire of guilt Flagons P. poz—Lxxvij oz iij qrts. and a guilt Bolle P. poz—viij oz di di qrt . . . . iiij^{xx} vj oz qrt di

68.248 To the Lady Stafford Two guilt Cuppes with couers B. poz bothe . . . . xxxj oz qrt di

68.249 To the Lady Cecill one guilt Bolle with a couer B. poz. . . . . .xxv oz di qrt

68.250 To the Lady Wodhowse one guilt Cup with a couer P. poz . . . . xxiij oz

68.251 To the Lady Carew one guilt Bolle with a couer P. poz . . . . .xxxv oz qrt

68.252 To the Lady Jobson one guilt Bolle with a couer B. poz . . . . xxij oz di

68.253 To the Lady Butler one guilt Bolle with a couer P. poz . . . . xiiij oz di di qrt

68.254 To the Lady Hemyngham one guilt hans pott P. poz . . . . xij oz iij qrt

68.255 To the Lady Sackevile one guilt Bolle with a couer P. poz . . . . xx oz di

68.256 To the Lady Pawlett one guilt Bolle with a couer P. poz . . . . x oz iij qrt di

68.257 To the Lady Ratclyff parte of hans pott guilt B. poz . . . . xij oz qrt di

68.258 To the Lady Cheeke one hans pott guilt B. poz . . . . xiij oz di di qrt

68.259 To the Lady Greshem one guilt Tankarde B. poz. . . . . xx oz di

68.260 To the Lady Throgmorton one guilt Bolle with a couer P. poz—xij oz di di qrt / and guilt Tankard B. poz—xiiij oz di di qrt . . . . .xxvij oz qrt

68.261 To the Lady Cheyney one guilt Bolle with a couer P. poz . . . . xxv oz di

68.262 To the Lady Wilforde one guilt Bolle with a couer B. poz . . . . . xxviij oz iij qrt di

68.263 To the Lady Yorke one guilt Bolle with a couer B. poz . . . . ix oz

68.264 To the Lady Stoner one guilt Salt with a couer B. poz. . . . . .xv oz qrt

68.265 To the Lady Norris one guilt Cup with a couer P. poz . . . . xviij oz iij qrt di

68.266 To the Lady Vane one guilt Bolle with a couer P. poz . . . . xvj oz qrt di

Knyghtes

68.267	To Syr Edwarde Rogers Comptroller of her Maties howseholde one guilt Bolle with a couer P. poz . . . . xix oz qrt
68.268	To Sir Fraunces Knolles vicechamberlen &c parte of a peire of guilt Flagons P. poz . . . . xxvj oz
68.269	To Sir William Cecill principall Secretarye thre guilt Bolles with a couer B. po . . . . xxxvj oz
68.270	To Sir Ambrose Caue Chauncellor of the Duchye one guilt Bolle with a couer B. poz . . . . xxviij oz qrt
68.271	To Sir William Peter Chauncellor of the Order one Cup with a couer guilt B. poz . . . . xx oz di qrt
68.272	To Sir Walter Myldemaye Chauncellor of the Eschequer one guilt Bolle with a couer P. poz . . . . xxv oz di di qrt
68.273	To Sir William Cordall Mr of the Rolles one guilt Bolle with a couer P. poz . . . . xxj oz
68.274	To Sir Christopher Heydon one guilt Bolle with a couer P. poz. . . . xxij oz iij qrt
68.275	To Sir Peter Carew one guilt Bolle with a couer P. poz . . . . .xx oz iij qrt
68.276	To Sir William Damsell one hans pott guilt B. poz . . . . xx oz iij qrt di
68.277	To Sir Fraunces Jobson one hans pott guilt B. poz . . . . xx oz di di qrt
68.278	To Sir Henry Jernegham one guilt Tankard P. poz. . . . . xix oz qrt di
68.279	To Sir Henry Cromewell one guilt Bolle with a couer B. poz. . xxvij oz iij [qrt] di
68.280	To Sir John Thynne one guilt Bolle with a couer P. poz . . . . x oz di di qrt
68.281	To Sir Gowen Carew one guilt Bolle with a couer B. poz . . . . .xxxiiij oz qrt
68.282	To Sir Thomas Benger one guilt Bolle with a couer P. poz. . . . . xxvj oz qrt
68.283	To Sir Thomas Gresham one guilt Bolle with a couer P. poz. . . . . .xx oz qrt
68.284	To Sir Nicholas Throgmorton one guilt Tankard B. poz—xvij oz di di qrt, and a guilt Bolle P. poz—ix oz di di qrt . . . . .xxvij oz qrt
68.285	To Sir William Pickering Two guilt Bolles with a couer P. poz. . . . . Lv oz
68.286	To Sir Gylbert Dethyck one hans pott guilt B. poz . . . . xiij oz di
68.287	To Sir Henry Sydney Lorde Deputye of Irelande one guilt Bason and a Leyer B. poz. . . . . Clij oz

Gentlewomen

68.288	To Mysteris Blaunche Pary one guilt Bolle with a couer P. poz. . . . xviij oz iij qrt
68.289	To Mrs Katheryn Howard wief one guilt Tankerd B. poz . . . . xv oz di qrt
68.290	To Mrs Caue one guilt Bolle with a couer P. poz . . . . xv oz di
68.291	To Mrs Hennage one guilt Leyer B. poz. . . . . xx oz di
68.292	To Mrs Edmundes one guilt Cup with a couer B. poz . . . . xiiij oz di
68.293	To Mrs Maruen one guilt Bolle with a couer B. poz . . . . xiiij oz di
68.294	To Mrs Abingdon one guilt Bolle with a couer B. poz. . . . . .xv oz iij qrt
68.295	To Mrs Marbery one guilt Salte with a couer B. poz . . . . xiij oz iij qrt
68.296	To Mrs Ellen Wolf one guilt Bolle with a couer P. poz. . . . . xiij oz di
68.297	To Mrs Baptist one guilt Bolle with a couer B. poz . . . . xvj oz iij qrt di
68.298	To Mrs Huggens of Hamptoncourte one guilt Cup with a couer B. poz . . . . xxj oz di

68.299	To Mrs Huggens of Norff[olk] one guilt Bolle with a couer P. poz . . . . xiij oz
68.300	To Mrs Elizabeth Winkefilde one guilt Bolle with a couer P. poz . . . . xiij oz
68.301	To Mrs Dane one guilt Cup with a couer B. poz . . . . xvij oz di qrt
68.302	To Mrs Smythson Laundres one guilt Casting Bottell B. poz . . . . vij oz qrt
68.303	To Mrs Leuina Terling one guilt Casting Bottell B. poz. . . . . vj oz di
68.304	To Mrs Amy Shelton one guilt Cup with a couer B. poz . . . . xj oz di
68.305	To Mrs Elizabeth Shelton one guilt Cup with a couer B. poz . . . . xj oz qrt
68.306	To Ipolita Two guilt Spones B. poz . . . . iiij oz qrt
68.307	To Mrs Bareley one guilt Salte with a couer P. poz . . . . xij oz di di qrt

Maydens of Honour

68.308	To Mrs Mary Howarde one guilt Cup with a couer B. poz . . . . x oz iij qrt
68.309	To Mrs Anne Wyndesore one guilt Cup with a couer B. poz. . . . . x oz di
68.310	To Mrs Mary Ratclyf one guilt Salte with a couer B. poz . . . . .x oz qrt
68.311	To Mrs Dorothey Browke one guilt Bolle with a couer P. poz. . . . . . . x oz iij qrt
68.312	To Mrs Agabell Hemyngham one guilt Bolle with a couer P. poz . . . . x oz di
68.313	To Mrs Eglambye Mother of the Maydens of honor one guilt Bolle with
	a couer P. poz. . . . . xij oz di di qrt

Chaplaynes

68.314	To Archedeacon Carewe Deane of the Chapell one hans pott guilt P.
	poz . . . . xx oz di qrt
68.315	To Doctor Newton Deane of Wyntchester one hans pott guilt P. poz . . . . xx oz

Gentlemen

68.316	To Maister John Asteley Mr and Threasourer of her Maties Juelles and
	plate one guilt Cup with a couer B. poz . . . . xxxvj oz
68.317	To Mr Thomas Hennage one guilt Bason B. poz – xlv oz and Sixe guilt
	Spones B. poz – v oz di di qrt in toto . . . . L oz di di qrt
68.318	To Mr John Harrington one guilt Cup with a couer B. poz. . . . . .xl oz
68.319	To Mr Chamberlen of Garnesey one hans pott guilt B. poz . . . . . . xiiij oz di qrt
68.320	To Mr Edwarde Bashe parte of a hans pott guilt B. poz . . . . xxj oz
68.321	To Mr Thomas Stanley one guilt Tankarde P. poz. . . . . xix oz di di qrt
68.322	To William Huggens one guilt Bolle with a couer P. poz . . . . xxxj oz
68.323	To Benedicke Spinula one guilt Bolle with a couer P. poz . . . . . . xxvj oz di di qrt
68.324	To Smyth Custumer one guilt Cup with a couer B. poz. . . . . xv oz
68.325	To Allen Marcheaunte one guilt Bolle with a couer P. poz . . . . xvj oz di qrt
68.326	To Doctor Hewicke one guilt Bolle with a couer P. poz. . . . . xiiij oz qrt di
68.327	To Doctor Maister one guilt Salte with a couer B. poz . . . . xiiij oz qrt
68.328	To John Hemmyngwaye one guilt Cup with a couer P. poz . . . . x oz di di qrt
68.329	To John Soda one guilt Salte with a couer B. poz. . . . . vj oz iij qrt di
68.330	To Robert Robotham one guilt Bolle with a couer P. poz . . . . .ix oz di
68.331	To George Webster Mr Cooke one guilt Tankerd B. poz. . . . . viij oz iij qrt di
68.332	To Marke Anthony one guilt Bolle with a couer P. poz . . . . viij oz iij qrt di
68.333	To John Bettis Serjaunte of the Pastrye Two guilt Spones B. poz . . . . . . iiij oz di
68.334	To Petro Vbaldino one guilt Salte with a couer B. poz. . . . . iiij oz iij qrt

Free Gifts

68.335 To Thomas Asteley Grome of the preuy Chamber one guilt Cruse P.
poz . . . . viij oz iij qrt di

68.336 To John Tamworth one other Grome &c one guilt Cruse B. poz. . viij oz iij qrt di

68.337 To Henry Sackeforde Grome &c one guilt Cruse P. poz. . . . . viij oz di

68.338 To John Baptist Grome &c one guilt Cruse B. poz. . . . . viij oz di

68.339 To Edwarde Carey Grome &c one guilt Cruse B. poz . . . . viij oz di

68.340 To Rauf Hope yeoman of the Roobes one guilt Cup with a couer B.
poz . . . . xij oz iij qrt di

68.341 To Nicholas Bristowe Clarke of the Juelles and plate one guilt Cruse
B. poz. . . . . x oz iij qrt di

68.342 To Edmunde Pigeon yeoman of the said Juelles and plate one guilt
Cruse P. poz . . . . x oz iij qrt di

68.343 To John Pigeon yeoman of the said office one guilt Cruse B poz . . x oz iij qrt di

68.344 To Stephen Fullwell Grome of the said Juells and plate one guilt Cruse
P poz . . . . x oz iij qrt di

Summa total / of all the said plate / Geuen by her Matie as /
aforesaid. . . . . .mmmm Ciiij^{xx} v oz di

Guyftes geuon by her majestie and delyuerid
owte of the Office of her highnes Juellis and Plate In
Manner and fourme folowing
viz

68.345 Seignior Anthony
Geuon by her Matie and Delyuerid the xv^{th} of June Anno nono
Regni Regine Elizabeth &c. To Seignior Anthony Musician Italion
one Cheine of golde bought of Affabell Partriche her Maties
Goldesmythe . . . . x oz   gold

68.346 Mr Robert Meluen
Item gevon by her Matie and Delyuerid the xxiij^{th} of June Ao ix^{no}
pred To the Mr Robert Meluen gent to the Quene of Scottes One
Cheine of golde bought of the said Affabell Parteriche goldesmythe
poz . . . . .xix oz iij qrt di one pennyweight golde

68.347 Count of Stobridge
Item gevon by her Matie and Delyuerid the xxv^{th} of June Ao ix^{no} pred
To the Count of Stobridge Ambassador from the Emperor One Bason
and a Leyer guilt poz—Cxxviij oz qrt di : One peire of guilt Pottes
poz—CCiiij oz : One peire of Vases guilt poz—CClxx oz : One nest
of Bowles with a couer guilt – Cxxiiij oz : And one peire of guilt
Saltes with a couer poz – iiij xx viij oz qrt di bought of the said
Affabell Partriche In toto. . . . . .DCCCxiiij oz iij qrt

149

68.348 Mounsieur Mandeghene
    Item gevon by her Matie and Delyuerid To Mounsieur Mandeghene
      also Ambassador from Themperor One Bason and a Leyer guilt poz—
      iiij^{xx} ix oz : One peire of guilt Vases poz—Cxix oz qrt : One peire of
      guilt Pottes poz—iiij^{xx} iiij oz iij qrt : One Nest of Bowles with a couer
      guilt poz—lxxij oz di : and one peire of guilt Saltes with a couer poz—
      lj oz di qrt. all bought of Robert Brandon and Affabell Partriche
      In toto . . . . CCCCxvj oz di di qrt

68.349 Sir Henry Norris
    Item gevon by her Matie and Delyuerid the xxij^{th} of July Ao ix^{no}
      predicto To the Christenynge of Sir Henry Norris knight his Sonne
      Oone guilt Cup with a couer bought of Robert Brandon
      goldesmythe poz . . . . xxxj oz di qrt

68.350 Mr Thomas Southewell
    Item gevon by her Matie and Delyuerid the ij^{de} of October Ao ix^{no}
      predicto To the Christeninge of Mr Thomas Sowthewell his
      Doughter One guilt Cup with a couer bought of Robert Brandon
      goldesmythe poz . . . . xxviij oz iij qrt

68.351 Sir Donolde Oconor Slego
    Item geuon by her Highnes and Delyuerid the xxvj^{th} of January
      Anno decimo Regni Regine Elizabeth To Sir Donolde Oconor
      Slego knight One Cheyne of golde bought of Affabell Partrich
      poz . . . . xxxiij oz di   gol[d]

Elizabeth R
[sign manual]

                                         J Asteley
                                     Edm Pigeon
                     Ex[aminatio] per Ste Fullwell

Anno Regni Regine
Elizabeth Decimo tertio

Newyeres guiftes geuon to the
Quene her maiestie by those Parsones
whose names here after ensue the First of January the yere aboue
written

Elizabeth R
[sign manual]

71.1 By the Lady Margerete the Earle of Lennex his wif a rounde kirtell with a
paire of bodyes loose of golde and siluer tyncell striped borderid with
two gardes of blacke vellat enbrauderid with pipes and spangles of
venice silver

71.2 By the Lady Margerett the Lorde Straunge his wif a Peticoate of golde Tincell
garded with two brode gardes of blewe vellat and enbrauderid with venice
golde and siluer in pipes and fringed with venice golde siluer and silke
                    Deliuerid to Raulf Hoope yeoman of her maiesties Roobes

71.3 By the Lorde keeper of the greate Seale in ared silke purse in golde and
silver . . . . xiij li vj s viij d

71.4 By the Lorde Marques of Winchester high Threasouror of Englande in
a red Satten purse in Dimy Soueraignes . . . . xx li
                    deliuerid to Henry Sackeforde grome of her Maties
                    privye Chamber to her highnes vse

71.5 By the Lorde Marques of Northamptone a Flower of golde with a white
Roose sette with Rubyes and a redde Rose sette with Diamondes thre
sparkes of Rubyes a table Sapher and two ragged pearles
                    With the Quene by Mr Kneuet

Earles

71.6 By the Earle of Arundell in a redde Satten purse in Dimy Soueraignes . . . xxx li
71.7 By the Earle of Shrewisbury in a blacke silke purse in Di soueraignes . . . . . xx li
71.8 By the Earle of Darbye in a red silke purse in Di soueraignes . . . . xx li
71.9 By the Earle of Sussex in a blewe silke purse in Di soueraignes . . . . x li
71.10 By the Earle of Huntingdon in a red silke purse in Di soueraignes . . . . x li
                    Deliuerid to the saide Henry Sackefourde vt supra
71.11 By the Earle of Warwike a Juell of golde being a Mounster of the Sea
garnisshed with Diamondes
                    Deliuerid to Mrs Blaunche
71.12 By the Earle of Bedfourde in a yellowe satten purse in Di soueraignes . . . . . xx li
71.13 By the Earle of Penbrouke in a purse of red silke and venice golde in Di
soueraignes . . . . xx li

71.14 By the Earle of Southamptone in a purse wrought with venice golde siluer and silke in Crownes . . . . xv li

71.15 By the Earle of Rutlande in a Taphata purse in Aungelles. . . . . x li

71.16 By the Vicount Mountigew in a red silke purse in di soueraignes . . . . x li
Deliuerid to the saide Henry Sackefourde vt supra

Duchesses and Countesses

71.17 By the Duches of Souffolke in a red silke purse in Dimy soueraignes . . . . . . xv li
Deliuerid to the saide Henry Sackefourde vt supra

71.18 By the Duches of Somerset a Cusshion of nedleworke the grounde Red and wrought with flowers grene and yellowe and venice siluer sett also with spangles of venice golde sette with pearles the backeside of tuft Taphata fringed buttoned and Tasselled with crymsen silke and venice siluer
Deliuerid to Richarde Todde keper of
standing Guarderobe at Hamptoncorte

71.19 By the Countes of Surrey in a litell purse of venice golde and silver knet in Angelles . . . . C s

71.20 By the Countes of Shrewisbury in Angelles . . . . xx li
Deliuerid to the saide Henry Sackeforde vt supra

71.21 By the Countes of Darbye oone Remnant of blewe clothe of golde straked & prented cont . . . . v yerdes iij qrt
Deliuerid to the saide Raulf Hoope vt supra

71.22 By the Countes of Huntingdon Dowger in a blacke silke purse in Di soueraignes. . . . . x li
Deliuerid to the saide Henry Sackeforde vt supra

71.23 By the Countes of Huntingdon a Snaile of mother of pearle garnisshed with golde and smale Diamondes and with a flower wherein are fyve sparkes of Rubyes and two smale Diamondes Lozanged with a pearle pendaunt

71.24 By the Countes of Warwike oone Gurdell of golde cont xxx knottes sett with Rubyes and pearles with a smale sparke Ruby in the middest of the pearles
Deliuerid to the said Mrs Blaunche

71.25 By the Countes of Penbrouke Dowger in a purse of red silke in Di soueraignes. . . . . xij li

71.26 By the Countes of Penbrouke in a purse of red silke and venice siluer in Di soueraignes . . . . x li
Deliuerid to the saide Henry Sackeforde vt supra

71.27 By the Countes Bedfourde a Frenche kirtell of Carnation clothe of golde tyncell with a border of crymsen vellat enbrauderid with venice golde and siluer
Deliuerid to the saide Raulf Hoope vt supra

71.28 By the Countes of Southamptone Dowger in a crymsen vellat purse in Di soueraignes. . . . . xx li

71.29 By the Countes of Southamptone in a purse of Venice golde and siluer in Crownes . . . . xv li

| 71.30 | By the Countes of Sussex in a blewe silke purse knytt in Di soueraignes .... x li |

Deliuerid to the saide Henry Sackeforde vt supra

| 71.31 | By the Vicountes Mountegue in a red silke purse in Di soueraignes .... x li |

Deliuerid to the saide Henry Sackeforde vt supra

Busshopes

71.32 By the Arche Busshope of Caunterbury in a purse of Red silke and venice
siluer knyt in Di Soueraignes. . . . . .xl li

71.33 By the Arche Busshope of Yorke in a white satten Cherrye bagge in
golde. . . . . xxx li

71.34 By the Busshop of Duresme in a grene silke purse in Angelles good and
badde lacking in the hoole of x oz a quarter of an oz. and farthing
golde weight. . . . . xxx li

71.35 By the Busshop of Elye in a purse of clothe of golde in Di soueraignes. . . xxx li

71.36 By the Busshop of London in a grene silke purse in Di soueraignes. . . . . . . xx li

71.37 By the Busshop of Winchester in a lether purse in Di soueraignes . . . . xx li

71.38 By the Busshop of Salisbury in a red satten purse in Di soueraignes . . . . . . xx li

71.39 By the Busshop of Lincolne in Angelles. . . . . xx li

71.40 By the Busshop of Norwiche in a skewid purse grene in Di soueraignes . . . xx li

71.41 By the Busshop of Rochester Amner in a blacke silke purse in Di
soueraignes and a Crusado with a longe Crose . . . . .xiij li vi s

71.42 By the Busshop of Lichefelde and Couentrye in a blewe silke purse in
golde and siluer . . . . xiij li vj s viij d

71.43 By the Busshop of Hereforde in a litell red silke purse in Di soueraignes . . . . x li

71.44 By the Busshop of St Dauyes in a blewe silke purse in Di soueraignes . . . . . . x li

71.45 By the Busshop of Bathe in a Crymsen silke purse in Di soueraignes. . . . . . . x li

71.46 By the Busshop of Chester in a red Satten purse in Di soueraignes . . . . x li

71.47 By the Busshop of Peterborow in a red Satten purse in Di soueraignes . . . . . x li

71.48 By the Busshop of Glocester in a red Satten purse in Di soueraignes. . . . . . . x li

71.49 By the Busshop of Chichester in a purse wrought with venice golde siluer and
silke in Angelles . . . . x li

Deliuerid to the said Henry Sackforde vt supra

Lordes

71.50 By the Lorde William Howarde Lorde Chamberlen of her Maiesties
honorable Chamber in a purse of blewe silke in haulf Soueraignes . . . . . . x li

71.51 By the Lorde Burgavenye in a red silke purse in Di soueraignes . . . . C s

71.52 By the Lorde Clyntone Lorde Admyrall in a blacke silke purse in Di
soueraignes. . . . . x li

71.53 By the Lorde Strainge in a red Satten purse in Angelles . . . . C s

71.54 By the Lorde Barcley in a blacke silke purse in Di soueraignes . . . . x li

71.55 By the Lorde Lumley in a purse of Crymsen silke in Di soueraignes . . . . . . xv li

71.56 By the Lorde Ryche in a red silke purse in Di soueraignes. . . . . x li

Deliuerid to the saide Henry Sackforde vt suBy the Lorde Cobham a bolle of

71.57 Christall with a couer crased the foote slightly garnisshed with a ryme of golde; another about the shanke and the knop of the Couer of like golde enamelid poz . . . . xiij oz

ex et oner

Deliuerid in chardge to John Astley Mr and

Threasoror of her highnes Juelles and plate to her use

71.58 By the Lorde Darcye of Chetchey in a blacke silke purse in Di soueraignes

. . . . x li

71.59 By the Lorde Shandoyes in a blewe purse in Angelles . . . . x li

71.60 By the Lorde Hastinges of Loughbrowe in a blewe silke purse in gold and siluer . . . . xiij li vj s viij d

Deliuerid to the saide Henry Sackforde vt supra

71.61 By the Lorde Hunsdon a Cranes of golde garnisshed with Diamondes

Deliuerid to Mrs Blaunche

71.62 By the Lorde Buckehurst in a yellowe satten Chery bagge in Di soueraignes . . . . C s

71.63 By the Lorde Northe in a blacke purse in Di soueraignes . . . . x li

71.64 By the Lorde Pagett in a red silke purse in Di soueraignes . . . . x li

71.65 By the Lorde Windsor in a tawny lether purse in Di soueraignes . . . . x li

Deliuerid to the said Henry Sackforde vt supra

71.66 By the Lorde Staffourde oone Ringe of golde with a poynted lozainged Diamonde and with sparkes of Diamondes about the same and on eitherside a Rubye

Deliuerid to Mrs Blaunche

Ladyes

71.67 By the Lady Clyntone oone Remnant of blacke clothe of golde Tyncell cont . . . . x yeardes

Deliverid to the said Raulf Hoope

71.68 By the Lady Burgavenye in a red silke purse in Di soueraignes . . . . C s

Deliuerid to the saide Henry Sackefourde vt supra

71.69 By the Lady Dakers of the Southe a partlet and a paire of Sleues and Ruffes of networke white and blacke

Deliuerid to Mrs Habingdon

71.70 By the Ladye Cobham a Peticote of blewe Satten striped with golde with two brode borders of blacke vellat cutte like clowdes fourmid with venice golde and sette with spangles of like golde and frenged with a fringe of like golde and silke

Deliuered to Raulf Hoope yeoman of the Robes

by thandes of Waulter Fysshe

71.71 By the Lady Sheffilde oone partelet and a paire of Sleues and a lyning knitt with Venice gold & threde

Deliuerid to Mrs Habingdon

71.72 By the Lady Taulboys Sir Peter Carowes wif in a red satten purse in Di soueraignes . . . . x li

71.73   By the Lady Howarde in a grene silke purse in Di soueraignes . . . . x li
                                  Deliuerid to the saide Henry Sackeforde vt supra
71.74   By the Lady Shandoyes two partelettes and two paire of Sleues of nette
              worke of venice golde siluer and silke of sundrye collors
71.75   By the Lady Mary Sydney a partelet and a paire of Sleues of Camerike
              faire wrought all ouer with venice golde siluer and blacke silke
                                                        Deliuered to Mrs Habingdon
71.76   By the Lady St John Pawlat in a purse of blacke silke in Angelles. . . . . x li
                                  Deliuerid to the saide Henry Sackeforde vt supra
71.77   By the Lady Paget thre vales of blacke, Carnation and Murre two of
              them edged with venice siluer and the thirde with blacke silke and
              buttons and tasselles to the same
                                                          Deliuerid to Mrs Knowles
71.78   By the Lady Buckehurst in a yellowe chery bagge with her hosbande. . . . . . . C s
                                  Deliuerid to the saide Henry Sackeforde vt supra
71.79   By the Lady Staffourde a partelet and a paire of Sleues of blacke Sipers
              and venice golde edged with like golde
71.80   By the Lady Cycell a paire of Sleues and a partelet of Lawne wrought with
              venice golde and edged with bone lace of golde
71.81   By the Lady Wodhouse a partelet of nette worke of venice golde and blacke
              silke with a Cawle and a paire of Sleues to the same
                                                        Deliuerid to Mrs Habingdon
71.82   By the Lady Carewe a Rayle and a paire of Ruffes of Camerike wrought
              with blacke silke and edged with venice golde
                                                      Deliuerid to Mrs Staffourde
71.83   By the Lady Butler in Di soueragines . . . . vj li
                                  Deliuerid to the saide Henry Sackefourd vt supra
71.84   By the Lady Hennyngham a Skarfe of blacke Sipers edged with a brode
              passamayne of venice golde and siluer
                                                          Deliuered to Mrs Knowles
71.85   By the Lady Pawlet in a purse of blewe silke and venice siluer in Angelles . . . C s
                                  Deliuerid to the saide Henry Sackfourd vt supra
71.86   By the Lady Ratlif a night Rayle and a paire of Ruffes of lawne wrought
              with blacke silke and edged with venice siluer and silke / a Swette bagge,
              and six Touthe pickes of Quilles garnisshed with silke
                                                      The Sleues dd to Mrs Staffourde
                                                  The Sweetebagge dd to Mrs Habingdon
                                                    The touthpickes to Mrs Knowles
71.87   By the Lady Cheeke a hawthorne flower of golde garnisshed with two
              smale Rubyes oone smale Emeraude / six smale Diamondes and fyve
              smale pearles
                                                          Deliuered to Mrs Blaunche
71.88   By the Lady Gresham in a purse of red silke with her housbande in
              golde . . . . x li
                                  Deliuerid to the said Henry Sackefourd vt supra

71.89 By the Lady Throgmortone a Cannapye to hange over a Cussion clothe of grene vellat enbr all ouer with flowers of venice silver with two Curtens of Taphata chaungable white and grene

With her Matie by Mr Middellmore

71.90 By the Lady Cheynye a Cloke of perfumed lether laied with a garde of six smale borders enbrauderid with venice golde and silke

ex et oner

Deliuerid to Raulf Hoope yeoman of the Roobes vt supra

71.91 By the Lady Wilfourde a Salte with a couer of Caulsidon garnisshed with golde poz . . . . xv oz di

ex et oner

Deliuerid to the saide John Asteley

71.92 By the Lady Yorke six muske sugerloues and two barrelles of Suckett

Deliuered to Mrs Habingdon

71.93 By the Lady Stoner a night raile of lawne rewid with brode passamaine of venice golde and siluer

Deliuerid to Mrs Staffourde

71.94 By the Lady Fraunces Cumpton a faire loking glasse of Christall in a case garnisshed with venice golde and set with stoone and pearle and an hower glasse cased in a case of like worke

Deliuerid to the saide Rycharde Todde vt supra

71.95 By the Lady Cromwell in Di soueraignes golde . . . . C s

Deliuerid to the saide Henry Sackfourd

71.96 By the Lady Norres a litell cabonet couered with crymson vellat garnisshed guilt with boxis in it of Ebonye sett with pictures of Alablaster and two nette partelettes

The Cabonet dd to Mrs Knowles

The partelettes with the Quene by Mrs Habingdon

71.97 By the Lady Barcley the Lorde Barcleyes wif in Di soueraignes . . . . C s

Deliuerid to the saide Henry Sackforde

Knights

71.98 By Sir Fraunces Knowlles Threasouror of her Maties housholde in a purse of grene silke in golde . . . . .xl li

71.99 By Sir James Acroftes Coumptrolor in a purse of crymsen satten in Di soueraignes. . . . . x li

Deliuerid to the saide Henry Sackforde

71.100 By Sir William Cycell principall Secretary a laire of Cristall crased garnisshed with siluer guilt poz togethers . . . . .xlij oz

ex et oner

Deliuerid to the saide John Astley vt supra

71.101 By Sir Raulf Sadler Chauncellor of the Duchey in a purse of blacke silke and siluer . . . . xv li

71.102 By Sir William Peeter Chauncellor of thorder in a purse of red silke in Di soueraignes . . . . x li

71.103 By Sir Waulter Mildmay Chauncellor of the Eschequer in a blewe purse
in Di soueraignges . . . . x li
71.104 By Sir William Cordall Mr of the Rolles in a white satten chery bagge in
Angelles . . . . x li
71.105 By Sir Christoher Haidone in a red silke purse in Di soueraignes . . . . x li
71.106 By Sir Henry Jernegham in a red silke purse in Di soueraignes . . . . x li
71.107 By Sir Peter Carowe in a red satten purse in Angelles and Di soueraignes . . . x li
71.108 By Sir Willm Dansell in a red silke purse in Di soueraignes . . . . x li
71.109 By Sir Fraunces Jobsone in a blacke silke purse in Di Soueraignes . . . . x li
71.110 By Sir Henry Cromell in a purse of blewe silke and gold in Di
soueraignes . . . . xv li
71.111 By Sir John Thynne in a yellowe and red silke purse in Di soueraignes . . . . . . C s
Deliuerid to the saide Henry Sackforde vt supra
71.112 By Sir Gawin Carowe a Smocke of Cameryk wrought with blacke silke and
edged with venice golde
Deliuerid to Mrs Stafforde
71.113 By Sir Thomas Benger oone litell Casting bottell rounde with oute
Chaine of siluer guilt . . . . v oz di qrt
ex et oner
Deliuerid to the saide John Asteley
71.114 By Sir Nicholas Throgmortone oone littell Clocke sette in Eliotropye and
garnisshed with golde
Deliuerid to Mrs Blaunche
71.115 By Sir William Pyckeringe oone Remnant of blacke clothe of golde
Tyncell cont . . . . x yerdes
Deliuerid to the saide Raulf Hoope
71.116 By Sir Guilbart Dethicke a booke of tharmes of the knightes of the
garter made in in the tyme of king Henry the Fyft couered with
crymsen vellat and garnisshed with passamen lase of venice golde
Deliuered to Mrs Blaunche
71.117 By Sir Thomas Gresham in a purse of red silke in Di soueraignes . . . . x li
71.118 By Sir Owen Hoptone Levetenant of the Tower xxx peces of golde with
the quenis Phisnamy on thone side and a Tower on thother poz—
iiij oz valued at . . . . x li
Deliuerid to the saide Henry Sackfurde vt supra

Gentelwomen

71.119 By Maisteris Blaunche Parrye a Juell being an Angell of Golde garnisshed
with smale Diamondes and an Emeralde
Geveon by her maiestie to Mrs Elizabethe browke
the Lorde Cobhams Doughter eodem die by Mr Middlemore
71.120 By Mrs Katerine Howarde Charles Howarde wief a partelet and a paire of
Sleues wrought with venice golde and silke loope wise
71.121 By Mrs Fraunces Howarde a partelet and a peire of Sleues of lawne wrought
with Rooses of venice golde siluer and blacke silke
Deliuerid to Mrs Habingdon

71.122   By Mrs Elizabeth Knowles a scarf of blacke and grene knotted with
venice siluer and frengid with like siluer

Deliuerid to her self

71.123   By Mrs Caue Sixe handkercheues wrought with blacke silke and edged
with a narrowe passamain of venice golde with buttons of like venice
golde

71.124   By Mrs Southwell two Cussion clothes of Camerike wrought with Diuers
colored silke

Deliuerid to Mrs Staffourde

71.125   By Mrs Hennage a hans potte of pied marble garnisshed in the foote
mouthe Couer and handell with siluer guilte poz stone and all . . . . . . xxvij oz

ex et oner
Deliuered to the said John Asteley vt supra

71.126   By Mrs Anne Wingfelde thre lyninges of knytworke very fine

Deliuerid to Mrs Habington

71.127   By Mrs Edmundes a Drinking glasse with a handell the foote lyppe and
Couer of siluer guilt enamelid poz glass and all . . . . xj oz di

ex et oner vt parcell omnis [...] priuato Camer
With the Quene by the saide John Asteley

71.128   By Mrs Maruen in a purse of Red silke in Di soueraignes . . . . C s
deliuered to the saide Henry Sackefourde

71.129   By Mrs Habingdon a paire of Sleues and a partelet wrought with venice
golde and white nettworke
deliuerid to herself

71.130   By Mrs Marbery two night Coyphes wrought with blacke silke

71.131   By Mrs Elizabeth Staffourde a pillowe with a bere of Hollande allouer
wrought with silke of sundrey collors and venice golde

71.132   By Mrs Marye Shelton six handkercheues wrought with silke of sundrey
collors edged with venice golde and silke

Deliuerid to Mrs Staffourde

71.133   By Mrs Ellen Wolf a partelet and a paire of Sleues and a lyning of Lawne
wroght with blacke silke

Deliuerid to Mrs Habingdon

71.134   By Mrs Snowe six handkercheues of Camrike wrought with blacke silke
and edged with bone lace of venice golde and siluer and tassellid with the
same

71.135   By Mrs Baptest a Cusshion clothe of fine hollande enbrauderid with
venice golde and blacke silke

71.136   By Mrs Sackefourde a litell Cusshion or sweete bagge faire wrought with
venice golde & siluer

71.137   By Mrs Huggans of Hamptone Courte Sixe handkercheues wrought with
silke of Diuers coullors and edged with bone lace of venice golde and
siluer with six swete bagges

Deliuerid to Mrs Staffourde

71.138 By Mrs Dane fower peces of Arras two bigger and two lesser of thistory of
 Susanna vnlyned, and a Couer pane of Diaper frenged with venice golde
 The peces of Arras dd to Mrs Blaunche
 The couerpane to Mrs Habington

71.39 By Mrs Smythsone Laundres foure handkercheues wrought with black
 edged and fringed with venice golde and siluer
 Deliuerid to Mrs Staffourde

71.140 By Mrs Leuina Terling a Carde wheron is painted the Quene with many
 other personages
 Deliuerid to Mrs Blaunche

71.141 By Mrs Anne Shelton sixe handkercheues of Camrike edged with a lace of
 venice golde of silke buttoned and tasselid
 Deliuerid to Mrs Staffourde

71.142 By Mrs Mountague a Partelet and lining and a paire of Sleues and fyve
 Ruffes vnmade of white knitworke
 Deliuerid Mrs Habingdon

71.143 By Mrs Barlye sixe handkercheues edged with passamayne of venice golde
 and buttoned

71.144 By Mrs Lucretia a night Coyfe wrought with red silke and white threde
 vpon Lawne
 Deliuerid to Mrs Staffourde

71.145 **Chaplaynes**

71.146 By Arche Deacone Carowe Deane of the Chappell in a red satten purse
 in Di soueraignes . . . . x li
 By Doctour Newtone Deane of winchester in a red silke purse in Di
 soueraignes. . . . . x li
 Deliuerid to the saide Henry Sackefourde

71.147 **Gentelmen**

71.148 By Mr Thomas Hennage Threasouror of the Chamber a Flower of golde
 enameled grene and sette with sundrey Diamondes
 deliuerid to Mrs Blaunche

71.149 By Mr John Haringtone oone pece of tawny vellat with workes stayned
 in sundrey places cont . . . . xxvj yerdes di

71.150 Deliuerid to the said Raulf Hoope
 By Mr Edwarde Basshe in a blacke silke purse in Angelles . . . . x li

71.151 By Stanlye Threasouror of the mynte in a red silke purse in Angelles. . . . . . . x li
 Deliuerid to the saide Henry Sackeforde

71.152 By Mr Horsey a Juell of golde enamelid of Allexaundor Magnus of Agathe
 with iiij smale Rubyes and iiij smale pearles and a pearle pendaunt
 By Mr Dyer a faire Juell of golde fully garnisshed with Rubyes and
 Diamondes with a pearle pendaunt wherin is a Clocke

71.153   By Mr Hattone a faire Juell of golde with a man lying vpon a wheele garnisshed with a sparkes of Diamondes and fully garnisshed with Diamondes Rubyes and Emeraudes on bothe sides, with a scotteshe pearle pendaunt and having a Diall therin

deliuerid to the said Mrs Blaunche

71.154   By Benodicke Spinnulla a pece of blacke Lawne knotted / A vaile of purple Laune striped with venice golde and bounde with like venice golde, and thre peces of edginges of venice golde siluer and silke and thre laces to teye Cawles of like venice golde siluer and silke

The Lawne and vaile deliuered to the said Raulf Hoope
The edginges and Lace deliuered to Mrs Knowles

71.155   By Smythe Customer two boltes of Camerike

Deliuerid to Mrs Blaunche

71.156   By Doctour Hewicke oone potte of grene Gynger and a pott of Oringe flowers

71.157   By Doctour Maister oone potte of grene gynger and a potte of Orange flowers

71.158   By John Hemingwaye Poticarye oone potte of Condment peares oone boxe of fenell seede Coumfettes oone boxe of Cordiall lozanges and manus Christie

71.159   By John Soda Potocary oone boxe of Sinamon Comfettes / oone boxe of fenell seede Comfettes, thre boxes of Codinia

Delyuerid to Mrs Habyngdon

71.160   By George Webster Mr Cooke a marche pane being a Chesse bourde

71.161   By John Dudley Sergaunt of the pastrey a pye of Quinces or wardons

[blank]

71.162   By Charles Smythe page of the Roobes xij poyntes of silke tagged with aglettes of gold

Deliuered to the said Rauf Hoope

71.163   By William Huggans a greate sweete bagge of white serceonet enbrauderid with two Spheres the backeside of Carnation Satten edged and fringed with venice golde and xiiij sweete bagges made of Divers colorid serceonet

Deliuered to Mrs Staffourde

71.164   By Mark Anthony, a Drinking Glasse with a Couer grene painted and guilte in a case of red lether

ex et oner
Deliuered to the saide John Asteley

71.165   By Ambrosio violan two glasses of sweete water and vij Cakes of venice Soope

Deliuered to Mrs Knowles

71.166   By Edward Skeetes page of the Chamber a Salte of siluer guilt the foote a branch of Currall poz with the Currall. . . . . v oz di

ex et oner ut [...] h th [...] v oz iij qrters
Deliuered to the said John Asteley

71.167 By Petricio Vbaldino a table painted with the picture of a woman and
        certeigne verses

Deliuerid to the said Rychard Todde

71.168 By Anthony County, violan a boxe with two glasses of swete water and two
        garters of silke

Deliuerid to Mrs Knowles

71.169 By Wodde a Dogge Collor for a hounde of purple vellat enbrauderid with
        venice golde and siluer with a liame of purple silke

Deliuerid to the said Rauf Hoope

Summa totalis of all the mony / geuon to her Matie and deliuerid as
aforesaide is . . . . m li lj li vj s

Elizabeth R
[sign manual]

J Asteley
Edm Pigeon
Ste Fulwell
ex[aminatio] per J Pigeon

Anno Regni Regine
Elizabeth Decimo tertio

Newyeres Guiftes geuon by
the Quene her maiestie at her Honor
of Hampton Corte to those persones whose names here after ensue
the first of January the yere abuue written.
That is to saye

Elizabeth R
[sign manual]

71.170 Too the Lady Margeret the Earle of Lennex his wif oone Basone and an
        Ewer guilt Partrige weing—lxiiij oz iij qrt di / And a guilt Cup with a
        Couer partrige poz—xxiiij oz qrt di in toto . . . . iiij^{xx} ix oz qrt
71.171 To the Lady Margeret the Lorde Strainge his wif oone guilt Cup with a
        Couer brandon poz . . . . .xx oz qrt
71.172 To the Lorde keper of the greate Seale thre guilt bolles with a Couer
        Brandon poz . . . . xxxiiij oz iij qrt
71.173 To the Lorde Marques of Winchester high Threasouror of Englande oone
        guilt Bolle with a Couer Partrige poz . . . . xxxiiij oz di
71.174 To the Lorde Marques of Northampton oone paire of guilt pottes
        Brandon poz . . . . Clxxiiij oz

161

Earles

71.175   To the Earle of Leciter oone guilt Cup with a Couer Brandon poz . . . Cxxxij oz

71.176   To thearle of Arundell oone guilt Cup with a Couer Partrige poz . . . . Lij oz qrt

71.177   To thearle of Shrewisbury oone guilt bolle with a Couer Brandon poz . . . . .xxx oz qrt di

71.178   To thearle of Darbye oone guilt Cup with a Couer Partrige poz. . . . . . xxxj oz di

71.179   To thearle of Sussex oone guilt bolle with a Couer Partrige poz . . . . xxj oz

71.180   To thearle of Huntingdon oone guilt Cup with a Couer Brandon poz . . . . xx oz iij qrt di

71.181   To thearle of Warwike oone paire of guilt pottes Partrige poz . . . . Cxij oz

71.182   To thearle of Bedfourde oone guilt Cup with a Couer Partrige poz . . . xxxj oz di

71.183   To thearle of Penbroke oone guilt Bolle with a Couer Brandon poz . . . . xxx oz di di qtr

71.184   To thearle of Southampton oone guilt Bolle with a Couer Brandon poz . . . . xxvij oz iij qtr di

71.185   To thearle of Rutlande oone guilt Cup with a Couer Partrige poz . . . . xxj oz

71.186   To the Vicount Mountegue oone guilt Cup with a Couer Partrige poz. . . . xxj oz

Duchesses and Countesses

71.187   To the Duchess of Suffolke oone guilt Cup with a Couer Brandon poz . . . . xxxij oz di di qrt

71.188   To the Duches of Somerset thre guilt bolles with a Couer Brandon poz . . . . xxxj oz iij qrt di

71.189   To the Countes of Surrey oone guilt bolle with a Couer Partrige poz . . . . xij oz di qrt

71.190   To the Countes of Shrewisbury thre guilt bolles with a Couer Brandon poz . . . . .xxx oz qrt di

71.191   To the Countes of Darbye oone guilt bolle with a Couer Partrige poz . . . . xx oz di di qrt

71.192   To the Countes of Huntingdon Dowger oone guilt bolle with a Couer Partrige poz . . . . xx oz iij qrt

71.193   To the Countes of Huntingdon oone guilt Cup with a Couer partrige poz . . . . xlj oz qrt

71.194   To the Countes of Warwike oone guilt Cup with a Couer Partrige poz . . xlvij oz

71.195   To the Countes of Penbroke Dowger oone guilt bolle with a Couer Partrige poz . . . . xxviij oz qrt di

71.196   To the Countes of Penbroke oone guilt bolle with a Couer Partrige poz . . . . xx oz iij [qrt] di

71.197   To the Countes of Bedfourde oone guilt Cup with a Couer Brandon poz . . . . .xxxiij oz di qtr

71.198   To the Countes of Sowthamptone Dowger oone guilt bolle with a couer Partrige poz . . . . xxxij oz

71.199   To the Countes of Sowthamptone oone guilt bolle with a Couer Brandon poz . . . . xvj oz iij qtr

71.200 To the Countes of Sussex oone guilt bolle with a Couer Partrige
        poz . . . . xxj oz di qrt
71.201 To the Vicountes Mountague oone guilt bolle with a Couer Partrige
        poz . . . . xxj oz di qtr

Busshopes

71.202 To the Arche Busshop of Caunterbury thre guilt bolles with a Couer
        Brandon poz . . . . xlij oz qtr di
71.203 To the Arche Busshop of Yorke oone guilt Cup with a Couer Brandon
        poz . . . . xxxvj oz di
71.204 To the Busshop of Durham oone guilt bolle with a Couer Brandon
        poz . . . . xxxvj oz di di qrt
71.205 To the Busshop of Elye oone guilt bolle with a Couer Brandon poz. . . . xxxvj oz
71.206 To the Busshop of London a guilt Salte with a Couer Partrige
        poz . . . . .xxx oz qtr di
71.207 To the Busshop of Winchester a guilt Salte with a Couer Partrige
        poz . . . . xxxj oz di qtr
71.208 To the Busshop of Salisbury two hans pottes guilt Partrige
        poz . . . . xxxj oz di di qtr
71.209 To the Busshop of Lincolne thre guilt bolles with a Couer Brandon
        poz . . . . xxxij oz
71.210 To the Busshop of Norwiche thre guilt bolles with a Couer Brandon
        poz . . . . xxvij oz di qtr
71.211 To the Busshop of Rochester oone guilt bolle with a Couer Brandon
        poz . . . . xxij oz di qtr
71.212 To the Busshop of Lichfelde and Couentrye a guilt Tankerde Brandon
        poz . . . . xix oz iij qtr di
71.213 To the Busshop of Hereforde oone guilt bolle with a Couer Brandon
        poz . . . . xvij oz di
71.214 To the Busshop of St Dauyes oone guilt bolle with a Couer Partrige
        poz . . . . .xviij oz
71.215 To the Busshop of Bathe oone hans potte guilt Brandon poz . . . . . xvij oz qtr di
71.216 To the Busshop of Chester oone guilt bolle with a Couer Brandon
        poz . . . . xvij oz qtr di
71.217 To the Busshop of Peterborowe oone hans potte guilt Brandon
        poz . . . . xvij oz di qtr
71.218 To the Busshop of Glocester oone guilt Tankerde Brandon poz . . . . . . xviij oz di
71.219 To the Busshop of Chycester oone guilt bolle with a Couer Partrige
        poz . . . . xvij oz iij qtr di

Lordes

71.220 To the Lorde William Howarde Lord Chamberlen oone guilt Cup with a
        Couer Partrige poz . . . . xxvij oz di qtr
71.221 To the Lorde Burgaveny oone guilt bolle with a Couer Partrige poz . . . xij oz di

71.222 To the Lorde Clynton oone guilt Cup with a Couer Brandon poz . . . . . xxiiij oz
71.223 To the Lorde Strainge oone guilt bolle with a Couer Partrige poz . . . . . xij oz di
71.224 To the Lorde Barcley oone guilt Cup with a Couer Brandon poz . . . xxj oz di qtr
71.225 To the Lorde Lumley oone guilt Cup with a Couer Brandon poz . . . xiij oz iij qtr
71.226 To the Lorde Ryche oone guilt Cup with a Couer Brandon poz . . xx oz iij qtr di
71.227 To the Lorde Cobham oone guilt Salte with a Couer Partrige poz . . . . . .xxxv oz
71.228 To the Lorde Darcye of Chetchey oone guilt Cup with a Couer
        Brandon poz . . . . xx oz di di qtr
71.229 To the Lorde Shandoyes oone guilt Cup with a Couer Brandon
        poz . . . . xx oz di di qtr
71.230 To the Lorde Hastinges of Loughborowe oone guilt bolle with a
        Couer Brandon poz . . . . xxiij oz
71.231 To the Lorde Hunsdon thre guilt bolles with a Couer brandon poz . . . . .xxxv oz
71.232 To the Lorde Buckehurst oone guilt bolle with a Couer Partrige poz . . . xiij oz di
71.233 To the Lorde Northe oone guilt bolle with a Couer Brandon poz. . . . . .xx oz qtr
71.234 To the Lorde Pagett oone guilt bolle with a Couer Brandon poz . . . .xx oz iij qtr
71.235 To the Lorde Staffourde oone guilt bolle with a Couer Brandon
        poz . . . . .xxiij oz iij qtr di
71.236 To the Lorde Windsore oone guilt Cup with a Couer Brandon poz
        . . . . xx oz iij qtr di

Ladyes

71.237 To the Lady Clynton oone guilt Cup with a Couer Brandon poz . . . . liij oz
71.238 To the Lady Burgavenye oone guilt bolle with a Couer Partrige poz. . . xij oz qtr
71.239 To the Lady Dakers of the Southe oone guilt Cup with a Couer Brandon
        poz . . . . .xviij oz di di qtr
71.240 To the Lady Cobham oone guilt Cup with a Couer Partrige poz . . . . .lij oz
71.241 To the Lady Sheffilde oone guilt Bolle with a Couer Partrige
        poz . . . . .xiij oz di di qtr
71.242 To the Lady Taulboyes oone guilt Cup with a couer Partrige poz. . . . . . . .xxj oz
71.243 To the Lady Howarde oone guilt Cup with a Couer Brandon poz . . . . . . xiiij oz
71.244 To the Lady Shandoyes oone guilt bolle with a Couer Partrige
        poz . . . . .xviij oz di qtr
71.245 To the Lady Mary Sydney oone guilt Cup with a Couer Partrige
        poz . . . . .xxix oz iij qtr di
71.246 To the Lady St John Paulet oone guilt bolle with a Couer Brandon
        poz . . . . .xxj oz di qtr
71.247 To the Lady Pagett Dowager thre bolles with a Couer Brandon poz
        . . . . .xxvj oz qtr
71.248 To the Lady Buckehurst oone guilt bolle with a Couer Partrige poz. . . . xij oz di
71.249 To the Lady Staffourde oone guilt bolle with a Couer Brandon
        poz . . . . .xxxj oz di di qtr
71.250 To the Lady Cycell oone guilt bolle with a Couer Brandon poz . . . .xxv oz qtr di
71.251 To the Lady Wodhouse oone guilt Cup with a Couer Brandon poz . . xxiiij oz di
71.252 To the Lady Carowe oone guilt potte Brandon poz . . . . .xxxv oz
71.253 To the Lady Butler oone guilt Cup with a Couer Partrige poz . . . . xvj oz

71.254 To the Lady Hemyngham oone guilt bolle with a Couer Partrige poz . . . . xij oz qtr

71.255 To the Lady Paulet oone guilt bolle with a Couer partrige poz . . . . xij oz qtr

71.256 To the Lady Ratlyf oone guilt bolle with a Couer Partrige poz . . . . xij oz qtr

71.257 To the Lady Cheeke oone guilt bolle with a Couer Brandon poz . . . . xxvj oz

71.258 To the Lady Gresham oone guilt bolle with a Couer Brandon poz . . . . xix oz qtr di

71.259 To the Lady Throgmorton oone guilt Cup with a Couer Brandon poz . . . . .xxv oz iij qtr

71.260 To the Lady Chayne oone guilt Cup with a Couer Brandon poz . . . . xxiiij oz di di qtr

71.261 To the Lady Wilfourde oone bolle with a Couer Brandon poz . . . . xxv oz di di qtr

71.262 To the Lady Yorke oone guilt bolle with a Couer Partrige poz . . . . .x oz qtr

71.263 To the Lady Stoner oone guilt bolle with a Couer Partrige poz . . . . .xiij oz iij qtr di

71.264 To the Lady Frauncis Cumpton oone guilt bolle with a Couer Partrige poz . . . . xxj oz di qtr

71.265 To the Lady Cromell oone guilt bolle with a Couer Partrige poz . . . xij oz qtr di

71.266 To the Lady Norres oone guilt Cup with a Couer Partrige poz . . . . . xvj oz di qtr

71.267 To the Lady Barcley the Lorde Barcleyes wif oone guilt bolle with a Couer Brandon poz . . . . xij oz qtr di

Knightes

71.268 To Sir Frauncis Knowles thre guilt bolles with a Couer Brandon poz . . . . xxvj oz iij qtr

71.269 To Sir James A Croftes oone guilt Cup with a Couer Brandon poz . . . xxvj oz di

71.270 To Sir William Cycill thre guilt Bolles with a Couer Partrige poz . . . . .xxxv oz iij qrt

71.271 To Sir Raulf Sadler oone guilt Cup with a Couer Brandon poz . . . . . . xxx oz di

71.272 To Sir William Peeter oone guilt bolle with a Couer Partrige poz . . . xxj oz di qtr

71.273 To Sir Waulter Mildmay oone guilt Cup with a Couer Partrige poz . . . xxvj oz di

71.274 To Sir William Cordell oone guilt bolle with a Couer Partrige poz . . xxj oz di qtr

71.275 To Sir Christopher Haidone oone guilt bolle with a Couer Partrige poz . . . . xxj oz di qtr

71.276 To Sir Henry Jernigham oone guilt bolle with a Couer Partrige poz . . . . xxj oz qtr di

71.277 To Sir Peter Carowe oone guilt Cup with a Couer Partrige poz . . . . .xxj oz

71.278 To Sir William Dansell oone guilt Salte with a Couer Brandon poz . . . . xx oz iij qtr di

71.279 To Sir Frauncis Jobsone oone guilt Cup with a Couer Partrige poz . . . . xxj oz iij qtr di

71.280 To Sir Henry Cromell oone guilt bolle with a Couer Brandon poz . . . . .xxj oz di

71.281 To Sir John Thynne oone guilt bolle with a Couer Partrige poz . . . . xij oz qtr di

71.282 To Sir Gawin Carowe oone guilt potte Brandon poz . . . . .xxxv oz di di qtr

71.283   To Sir Thomas Benger oone guilt Cup with a Couer Brandon
poz . . . . xxvj oz qtr di

71.284   To Sir Nicholas Throgmortone oone guilt Cup with a couer Partrige
poz . . . . xxvij oz

71.285   To Sir William Pickering thre guilt bolles with a Couer Partrige poz . . . . . Lv oz

71.286   To Sir Gulbert Dethicke oone hanse potte guilt brandon poz . . . . . . xiij oz di qtr

71.287   To Sir Thomas Gresham two guilt bolles with a Couer Partrige
poz . . . . .xx oz iij qtr

71.288   To Sir Owen Hoptone two guilt bolles with a Couer Partrige poz. . . . . . . xxij oz

Gentelwomen

71.289   To Mrs Blaunche Parrye oone guilt Tankerde Partrige poz . . . . xviij oz di

71.290   To Mrs Katerine Howarde oone guilt Salte with a Couer Brandon
poz . . . . .xv oz qrt

71.291   To Mrs Frauncis Howarde oone guilt bolle with a Couer Brandon
poz . . . . xiiij oz iij qrt di

71.292   To Mrs Elizabeth Knowles oone guilt bolle with a Couer Brandon
poz . . . . xiiij oz di

71.293   To Mrs Caue oone guilt Cup with a Couer partrige poz . . . . xv oz di qrt

71.294   To Mrs Southwell oone guilt bolle with a Couer Partrige poz. . . . . . xv oz di qrt

71.295   To Mrs Hennage two guilt bolles with a Couer Partrige poz. . . . . xx oz

71.296   To Mrs Anne Wingfelde oone hans potte guilt Partrige poz . . . . .xv oz iij qrt

71.297   To Mrs Edmundes oone guilt Cup with a Couer Brandon poz . . . xv oz di di qrt

71.298   To Mrs Maruen oone guilt Cup with a Couer Brandon poz . . . . . xiij oz iij qrt di

71.299   To Mrs Abingdon oone guilt Cup with a Couer Brandon poz . . xvij oz iij qtr di

71.300   To Mrs Marberye oone guilt bolle with a Couer Partrige poz. . . . . . xiij oz iij qtr

71.301   To Mrs Elizabeth Staffourde oone guilt Cup with a Couer Brandon
poz . . . . xiij oz iij qtr

71.302   To Mrs Mary Shelton oone guilt Tankerde Brandon poz . . . . xiij oz di di qrt

71.303   To Mrs Ellen Wolf oone guilt Tancarde Brandon poz . . . . xvj oz

71.304   To Mrs Snowe oone guilt Bolle with a Couer Partrige poz . . . . xvj oz di

71.305   To Mrs Baptest oone guilt bolle with a Couer Partrige poz. . . . . . . xvj oz qtr di

71.306   To Mrs Sackefourde oone guilte bolle withe a Couer Partrige poz . . . . . xix oz di

71.307   To Mrs Huggans of Hamptonecourt oone guilt bolle with owte a
Couer Partrige poz. . . . . xx oz di di qtr

71.308   To Mrs Dane a guilt Cup with a Couer Brandon poz . . . . xviij oz

71.309   To Mrs Smythsone Laundres oone Casting Bottell guilt Brandon
poz . . . . vij oz iij qtr di

71.310   To Mrs Leuina Terling oone guilt bolle with owte a Couer Partrige
poz . . . . .vj oz qrt di

71.311   To Mrs Anne Shelton oone guilt bolle with a Couer partrige poz. . . . x oz qrt di

71.312   To Mrs Mountague oone guilt bolle with a Couer Brandon poz . . . . xij oz

71.313   To Mrs Barlye oone guilt Cup with a Couer Brandon poz . . . . xij oz di

71.314   To Mrs Lucretia thre guilte Spones Brandon poz . . . . vj oz

Fre Guiftes to the Maides of Honor and others

71.315 To the Lady Hastinges oone guilt bolle with a Couer Partrige poz . . . . x oz

71.316 To the Lady Susan Bowser oone guilt bolle with a Couer Partrige
poz . . . . x oz di qrt

71.317 To Mrs Mary Howarde oone guilt bolle with a Couer Partrige poz . . . . .x oz qrt

71.318 To Mrs Abagell Henyngham oone guilt bolle with a Couer Partrige
poz . . . . x oz di qrt

71.319 To Mrs Mary Ratlif oone guilt Cruet with a Couer Brandon poz . . . . . .x oz qrt

71.320 To Mrs Isabell Holcroft oone hans potte guilt Partrige poz . . . . x oz di qrt

71.321 To Mrs Harvye mother of the maides oone guilt bolle with a Couer
Partrige poz . . . . xij oz di qrt

71.322 To Mrs Elizabethe Browke Doughter to the Lorde Cobham a Juell being
an angell of golde garnisshed with smale Diamondes and oone
Emeraude

gevon by Mrs Blaunche parry the same Daye

Chaplaines

71.323 To Arche Deacone Carowe Deane of the Chappell a guilt Cup Brandon
poz . . . . xx oz iij qtr di

71.324 To Doctor Newton deane of Winchester oone guilt bolle with a Couer
Brandon poz . . . . .xviij oz qrt di

Gentelmen

71.325 To Maister Hennaige oone guilt Cuppe with a Couer Partrige poz. . . xlviij oz di

71.326 To Mr Harington oone guilt Cup with a Couer Brandon poz . . . . xl oz

71.327 To Mr Basshe oone guilt Cup with a Couer Brandon poz . . . . xx oz iij qrt di

71.328 To Mr Stanlye oone guilt Cup with a Couer Brandon poz . . . . xx oz di

71.329 To Mr Horsey oone guilt Salte with a Couer Brandon poz . . . . xx oz di qrt

71.330 To Mr Dier oone basone and an Ewer guilt Partrige poz . . . . .Cj oz qrt di

71.331 To Mr Hattone oone basone and an Ewer guilt Partrige poz . . Cxxx oz di di qrt

71.332 To Benodike Spenolla oone guilt bolle with a Couer Partrige
poz . . . . xxvij oz iij qtr di

71.333 To Smythe Coustomer oone guilt Cup with a Couer Partrige poz . . . . xv oz

71.334 To Doctour Hewike oone guilt bolle withowte a Couer Partrige poz . . xiiij oz di

71.335 To Doctour Maister oone guilte bolle with owte a couer Partrige
poz . . . . xiiij oz di

71.336 To John Hemyngwaye oone guilt bolle with a Couer Brandon poz . . . . viij oz di

71.337 To John Sooda oone guilt bolle with owte a Couer Brandon poz . . . vij oz di qtr

71.338 To William Huggans oone guilt Cup with a Couer Brandon poz . . . . . xxxj oz di

71.339 To George Webster oone guilt bolle with owte a Couer Brandon
poz . . . . viij oz qtr di

71.340 To John Dudlye two guilt Spones Partrige poz. . . . . iiij oz iij qtr

71.341 To Marke Anthonye thre guilt Spones Partrige poz. . . . . vj oz qtr

71.342 To Ambroso Lupo two guilt Spones Brandon poz . . . . iiij oz di qtr

71.343   To Edwarde Skeetes oone guilt bolle with owte a Couer Brandon
poz . . . . vj oz qtr

71.344   To Petricho Vbaldino two guilt Spones Brandon poz . . . . iiij oz di qtr

71.345   To Charles Smythe oone guilt Salte with a Couer Partrige poz . . . . viij oz

71.346   To Anthony De Countie in Rewarde. . . . . xl s

71.347   To Wodde in Rewarde . . . . xx s

Freguiftes

71.348   To John Asteley Mr and Threasouror of her highnes Juelles and plate
oone guilte Cup with a Couer Partrige poz. . . . . xviij oz iij qrt di

71.349   To Thomas Asteley oone of the Gromes of her highnes privye Chamber oone
guilt Cruse Partrige poz. . . . . viij oz iij qrt di

71.350   To Henry Sackefourde oone other of the gromes of the saide privye
Chamber oone guilt Cruse Brandon poz . . . . viij oz iij qrt di

71.351   To John Baptest oone other of the saide Gromes oone guilt Cruse partrige
poz . . . . viij oz di di qrt

71.352   To Edwarde Care oone of the gromes also oone guilt Cruse Brandon
poz . . . . viij oz di

71.353   To Thomas Kneuett also a grome oone guilt Cruse Brandon poz. . . . . viij oz

71.354   To William [sic Henry] Middlemore likewise a grome &c oone guilt
Cruse Partrige poz. . . . . viij oz

71.355   To Rauf Hoope yeoman of the Roobes oone guilt bolle with a couer
Brandon poz . . . . xij oz iij qrt di

71.356   To Nicholas Bristowe Clerke of the Juelles and plate oone guilt Cruse
Partrige poz . . . . x oz iij qrt di

71.357   To Edmunde Pigeon yeoman of the said Juelles and plate oone guilt
Cruse Partrige poz . . . . x oz iij qrt di

71.358   To John Pigeon another yeoman of the same Office oone guilt Cruse
Brandon poz . . . . x oz iij qrt di

71.359   To Stephan Fullwell grome of the same Office oone guilt Cruse Brandon
poz . . . . x oz iij qrt di

Guiftes geuon and deliuerid at
sundrey tymes in maner and fourme folowing

71.360   Mr Haruye
Geuon by her maiestie the last of Maye Anno Regni sue xj oone guilt
tankarde poz – xvij oz iij qrt di to the Christening of Henry Haruye
Esquire oone of the gent Pentioners his Childe bought of the
Goldsmythes And Deliuerid to thandes of Anthony Light gent
vssher . . . . xvij oz iij qrt di

71.361   Jane Newton
Item gevon by her Matie the xxix^th of Maye Anno Regni sue xij° at
the mariage of Mrs Jane Newtone sister to the Lady Cobham oone
Cup of Siluer guilt with a Couer bought of Robt Brandon poz . . . . . liij oz

71.362 Euan Grigorey wiche Ambassatour from Themperour of Russhia
Item Gevon by her maiestie and Deliuerid the xxvth of Maye Anno xij°
predicto to Euan Grigorye wiche Ambassator from the Emperour of
Muscovya at his Departure owte of Englande Oone paire of guilt
pottes Brandon poz—Cxij oz di / Item oone basone and an Ewer
guilt Brandon poz—Ciiij oz / Item thre bolles with a Couer guilt
Brandon poz—lxxvij oz qrt di / Item two guilt Cuppes with Couers
Partrige poz—lxxvij oz qrt / Item two guilt Saltes with a Couer
Brandon poz—xlviij oz qrt di / All bought of the saide Brandon
and Partrige summa totalis . . . . CCCCxix oz di

71.363 Mounsieur Vidam his Doughter
Item Gevon by her maiestie and Deliuerid the vth of July Anno xij°
predicto at the Christening of Monsieur Vidam his Doughter oone
Basone and a Laier guilt Partrige poz – Cxli oz iij qrt di / Item thre
guilt Bolles with a Couer Brandon poz – iiij^{xx} j oz iij qrt di / Item
oone Cuppe with a Couer guilt Brandon poz – xl oz in toto
. . . . CClxiij oz iij qrt

71.364 Sir Bryan Mack Folomy Captaine in Irelande
Item gevon by her maiestie and Deliuerid the xiijth of September Anno
predicto to Sir Bryan Mackfolomye knight A Capitaine in Irelande,
Thre bolles with a Couer guilt Partrige poz – liiij oz / Item oone Cup
with a Couer guilt Partrige poz - xl oz iij qrt in toto. . . . . Ciiij oz iij qrt

71.365 Lorde of Hunsdon
Item taken by the Lorde of Hunsdon in the presence of her Matie from
of the Cupbourd in her highnes privy Chamber one stone Jug trymmed
with siluer and guilte Ribbes poz all togethers . . . . xxvj oz di *ex et oner*

Elizabeth R
[sign manual]

J Asteley
Bristow
E Pigeon
J Pigeon

[Newyeres Guiftes geuon to the Quene her]
[Maiestie by those Persones whose names hereafter]
[ensue The first of Januarye The yere abouewritten]

75.1 [By the Ladye Margret Countes of Darbie...] venice golde and Siluer [....]
[dd to Mrs Skydmore]
75.2 [By Sir Nicholas Bacon Kni]ght Lorde keper of the greate Seale of
Inglande in golde in a purse . . . . xx li
75.3 By the Lord Burleigh Lorde High Threausoror of Inglande in golde in a
purse. . . . . xx li
75.4 By the Lorde Marquis of Winchester in golde in a purse . . . . xx li
[dd to Henry Seckford grome of the privie chamber]

[Erl]es & Vicount

75.5 By therle of Leycetor Mr of the Horses aFeyer Gowne of black Taphata
with a feyer border of venice golde and Siluer Lyned with white
Sarceonet / a kirtill of White Satten cut with alyke border Lyned with
Lyke Sarceonet and a Dublet of white Satten garnesshed with golde of
Goldesmythes worke and set with Eightene verey Feyer Clapses of
golde of goldesmythes worke euery peyce set with Fyve Diamondes and
Eight Rubyes one Diamond in every peyer loped bigger then threste one
of the smaller Diamondes Lackyng and afeyer pasamane Lace of
Damaske golde and Siluer
Delivered to the Lady Howarde
75.6 By therle of Arundell in golde in a purse . . . . xxix li
Delivered to Henry Sackford
75.7 By therle of Oxforde a verey fayer juell of golde conte a woman holdinge
a Ship of sparkes of Dyamonds vpon her knee the same fully garnesshed
with Sparkes of Dyamondes iiij feyer rubyes one large Dyamonde &
sundry smaller Dyamondes & iij perles pendant with thre small cheynes
of golde set with sparkes of Dyamondes poz all . . . . vj oz iij qrt
dd to the Lady Howarde
75.8 By therle of Shrewesbury in golde in a purse . . . . xx li
75.9 By therle of Darby in golde in apurse. . . . . xx li
75.10 By therle of Sussex in golde in apurse. . . . . xx li
75.11 By therle of Lincoln Lorde Admirall in golde in a purse. . . . . x li
75.12 By therle of Rutlande in golde in a purse . . . . x li
75.13 By therle of Huntyngdon in golde in a purse . . . . x li
dd to Henry Sackford

75.14   By therle of Warwyck awast Gyrdill of black vellate the buckyll and
        Studdes of golde broken the same guyrdill set with fyfteen Emeraldes
        and vnto euery of them iij pearles in colletes of golde
                                          Delyuered to the Lady Howarde
75.15   By therle of Bedforde one Cup of Christall with a couer the glasse fasshen
        garnisshed with golde poz . . . . xix oz iij qrt
                              dd in charge to Mr Asteley Mr of the Juells & plate
75.16   By therle of Pembrocke in golde in a purse . . . . xx li
75.17   By therle of Northumberland in golde in a purse . . . . x li
75.18   By therle of Southampton in golde in a purse . . . . xv li
75.19   By the Vicounte Mountague [in gold in a purse] . . . . x li

Duchesses Marquiss and Countises

75.20   By the Duches of Suffolk in golde in a paper . . . . xv li
                                  Delyuered to the foresaid H Sackforde
75.21   By the Lady Marques of Northampton a Trayne gowne of fyne Launde
        the bodyes and Sleves the midest edged with thre smale Drawne pasamane
        laces of venice golde
                                          dd to the foresaid Mrs Skydmore
75.22   By the Lady Marques of Winchester in golde in a purse . . . . x li
75.23   By the Countes of Surrey in golde in a purse . . . . v li
                                      dd to the foresaid H Sackforde
75.24   By the Countes of Shrewesbury a lytill Tray or bull of golde set vppon iiij
        smale battes of golde a Lyon graven in the myddest thereof
        weynge . . . . xj oz qrt
                              dd in charge to Mr Asteley Mr of the Juells & plate
75.25   By the Countes of Huntyngdon Doager in golde in a purse . . . . x li
75.26   By the Countes Huntyngdon Junior in golde in a paper . . . . viij li
                                          dd to the foresaid H Sackford
75.27   By the Countes Warwicke acap of blacke vellate cheyned alouer with smale
        cheynes of golde with paunses and set with buttons of golde and agathe
        heddes / in number xlvj with six Torteses of golde eche of there backes
        halfe perle
                                      Delyuered to the foresaid Rauf Hope
75.28   By the Countes of Oxforde a kyrtill with apeyre of lose boddyes of blacke
        networke with Cheyne worke of venice golde and set full of spangilles
        with a border of leaves of venice golde and sylke thedge Indented Lyned
        with whyte Taphata
                                      Delyuered to the said Rauf Hope
75.29   By the Countes of Sussex in golde in a purse . . . . x li
75.30   By the Countes of Penbroke Dowager in golde in apurse . . . . xij li
75.31   By the Countes of Penbroke Junior in golde in apurse . . . . x li
                                          dd to the foresaid H Sackford

75.32   By the Countes of Bedford a very feyre peyre of Tabilles of Ebonet alouer
        plated and xxx pleyinge men of lyke stufe with armes / and a large peyre
        of Dyce of Siluer all in a case of grene vellate with a smale pasmayn lace
        of golde

                                            dd in charge to Richard Tod

75.33   By the Countes of Northumberland in golde in a purse . . . . x li
75.34   By the Countes of Southampton in golde in a purse . . . . x li

                                            Delyuered to the said H Sackford

75.35   By the Countes of Lincoln a Remnent of clothe of Tynsell stryped
        wroughte wythe branches of Golde and Syluer the grounde Russett
        cont . . . . .iij yerdes iij qrt di

                                            dd to foresaid Rauf Hope

75.36   By the Countes of Essex a wastecote of whyte Satten alouer enbraudred
        with venice golde and siluer

                                            Delyuered to Mrs Abingdon

75.37   By the Countes of Rutlande in golde in a purse . . . . x li

                                            dd to the foresaid H Sackford

75.38   By the Countes of Kent Dowager a cosshenclothe of hollan bordered with
        networke with flowers, and a smale sweete bage of crymsen satten
        enbrawderid with venice silke and siluer

                                            dd to the foresaid Mrs Skydmore

Vicecountis

75.39   By the Vicountes Mountague in golde in a purse . . . . x li

Busshopes

75.40   By the Arche Busshop of Canterburye in golde in a purse . . . . .xl li
75.41   By the Arche Busshop of yorke in gold in a purse . . . . xxx li
75.42   By the Busshop of Durham in golde in a purse . . . . xxx li
75.43   By the Busshop of Ely in golde in a purse . . . . xxx li
75.44   By the Busshop of London in golde in a purse . . . . xx li
75.45   By the Busshop of Wynchester in golde in a purse. xx li
75.46   By the Busshop of Salysburye in golde in a purse . . . . xx li
75.47   By the Busshop of Lincoln in golde in a purse. . . . . xx li
75.48   By the Busshop of Worcetor in golde in a purse . . . . xx li
75.49   By the Busshop of Rochester in golde in a purse . . . . x li
75.50   By the Busshop of Lichefelde and coventrye in golde in a purse. . xiij li vj s viij d
75.51   By the Busshop of Hereford in golde in a purse. . . . . x li
75.52   By the Busshop of St Davys in golde in a purse. . . . . x li
75.53   By the Busshop of Exetor in golde in a purse. . . . . x li
75.54   By the Busshop of Bathe in golde in a purse . . . . x li
75.55   By the Busshop of Chester in golde in a purse. . . . . x li
75.56   By the Busshop of Peterboroughe in golde in a purse . . . . x li
75.57   By the Busshop of Gloster in golde in a purse . . . . x li
75.58   By the Busshop of Chichester in golde in a purse . . . . x li

Lordes

75.59 By the Lorde of Burgevenny in golde in a purse . . . . v li

75.60 By the Lorde Barkeley in golde in a purse . . . . x li

75.61 By the Lorde Ryche in golde in a paper . . . . x li

75.62 By the Lorde Darcy in golde in a purse . . . . x li

dd to the foresaid H Sackford

75.63 By the Lorde Hawarde a Juell of golde conteynyng a Woman Sapeint
Victrix garnesshed with Dyuers Stones wherein the Top is an Emeralde
/ and in the bottom is a Ruby and furnesshed with Dyuers other Stones
and meane perles

Delyuered to the Lady Hawarde

75.64 By the Lorde Shandowes in golde in a purse . . . . vj li xiij s iiij d

75.65 By the Lorde of Hynnesdon in golde in a purse . . . . x li

75.66 By the Lorde Sturton in golde in a purse . . . . x li

75.67 By the Lorde of Bokehurst in a paper in golde . . . . x li

75.68 By the Lorde Northe in golde in a purse . . . . x li

75.69 By the Lorde Paget in golde in a paper . . . . x li

75.70 By the Lorde Stafford in golde in a purse . . . . x li

75.71 By the Lorde Compton in golde in a purse . . . . x li

75.72 By the Lorde of Rycote in golde in a purse . . . . x li

75.73 By the Lorde Lumley in a purse in golde . . . . x li

dd to the foresaid H Sackeford

75.74 By the Lorde Strange one Earepyke of golde ennamuled garnesshed with
Sparkes of Rubyes blewe Saphers and seede perle poz . . . . di oz di qrt

with her Matie

75.75 By the Lorde Cobham in golde in a purse . . . . x li

75.76 By the Lorde Dudley in golde in apaper . . . . x li

Baronesses

75.77 By the Barrownes Burgevenny in golde in a purse . . . . v li

75.78 By the Barrownes Barkeley in golde in a purse . . . . v li

dd to the foresaid H Sackford

75.79 By the Barrownes Hawarde agreyhownde of golde garnesshed with thre
Diamondes and thre Rubyes with acollor abought his neck garnesshed
with Sparkes of Rubys with a small perle pendant poiz . . . . j oz di qrt

dd to the same Lady Hawarde

[Missing section of manuscript]

[Ladies]

75.80 By the Lady Dakers a Cloke of Cammeryck alouerwrought with nedilwork of
Murry Silke & venice siluer edgid with pasamayne Lace of Siluer

Deyuvered to Mrs Skydmore

[Missing section of manuscript]

[Knightes]

75.81   By Sir Owen Hopton in golde in a purse . . . . x li
75.82   By Sir John Thyn in golde in a purse . . . . v li
                                    dd to the foresaid H Sackford
75.83   By Sir Gilbert Dethick king at armes a booke of Armes of the knightes of
           the gartier made in the tyme of king Henry theight couered with crymsen
           vellat & pasamaynn lace of gold
                                    dd to Mrs Blanche aparry
75.84   By Sir Henry Lee the Facying of agowne a partelet a peyer of Sleves and a
           Call of cameryk alover enbrawdered with venice golde Siluer and Sylke
           of sundry collors / and edged with a feyer pasamayne Lace of venice
           golde
                                    dd to the foresaide Mrs Skydmore
75.85   By Sir Richard a Lee averey feyer loking glasse of Cristall set in alarge
           Frame of walnuttre guylte with ix muses feyer wrought owte of
           Allablaster & piloers of marble
                                    hanged in the gallery at hampton corte

Gentilwomen

75.86   By Blanche a Parry a Flower of golde ennamuled grene hauyng thre litle
           white roses in euery of them a Sparcke of Rubyes and aFly in the myddes
           thereof with a small cheyne of golde to hange it by poz all . . . . di oz qrt
                                    dd to the foresaid La Hawarde
75.87   By Fraunces Hawarde iiij peces of Facynges for gownes of Lawnde wrought
           with white worke
75.88   By Elizabeth Knowles avale of Networke with aborder of whiteworke edged
           with cordantes of venice syluer
                                    dd to the foresaid Mrs Skydmore
75.89   By Hennage asmall picture of Stone plated ouer with athyn plate of golde in a
           litle rounde case of woode
                                    dd to the Lady Hawarde
75.90   By Caue vj handekercheres wrought with blackworke and edged with avery feyre
           pasmayne lace of venice golde and buttoned with Lyke golde
75.91   By Edmundes acusshincloth of Lawnde networke wrought with murry sylke
           checkered with golde and sylke with afeyre pasmayn lace at both thendes
           of golde & sylke and asmaller pasmayn at the sides
                                    dd to the foresaid Mrs Skydmore
75.92   By Abington apettycote of changeable Taphata quylted and lyned with
           white Bayes
                                    dd to the foresaid Rauf Hope
75.93   By Skydmore awaiscote of white Satten stryped with venice golde lyned
           with orenge colored sarceonet
                                    dd to Mrs Skydmore

75.94 By Elizabeth Drury a Call of Heere with buttons of Corrall Lapped on
    seede peerles

                                                           dd to Mrs Elizabeth Knowles

75.95 By Snowe Six litle tothe pykes of gold and Six verey small tothe clothes
    edged with black sylke

                                                        with her Matie

75.96 By Bapteste Six Feyre handekerchers thre wrought with feyer borders of
    blewe silke and thother thre with crymsen Sylke and edged with
    pasmayn of golde Syluer and Sylke

75.97 By west the facyng of a gowne and apeyer of Sleves of Lawnde wrought with
    white worke

                                                           dd to Mrs Skydmore

75.98 By Sackford a Feyer cusshion of crymsen vellat enbrawdred in the myddes
    with Flowers and Roses / in the myddes of the Leaves is alyon with
    Dyuers other beastes / and Foure verey feyer buttons and Tasselles of
    venice golde Siluer and Sylke lyned with grene Satten

                                                                     [blank]

75.99 By Huggans one night Rayle and a coyfe of black worke

                                                          dd to Mrs Skydmore

75.100 By Katheryn paston two Cawles of here, one garnisshed with venice Siluer
    and gold and thother Garnisshed with Knottes of venice goulde

                                                 dd to Mrs Elizabeth knowles

75.101 By Dane acusshenet verye feyer enbrawdered with Dame Flora in the myddes
    and half a pece of lawnde

                                      the cusshenet dd to Mrs Skydmore
                                        & the Lawnde dd to Mrs Blanch aparye

75.102 By Smythsone Laundrys a Raile of Sypers edged with a pasmayn Lace of golde

                                                          dd to Mrs Skydmore

75.103 By Levina Terlinge a carte paynted vpon a carde of Her Matie and dyuers
    other personages

75.104 By Amy Shelton Six handekercheres with pasmayn lace of golde

75.105 By Mountague a feyre night Rayle and a Coyfe of camericke wrought
    alover with Flowers & Spyders of black silke edged with pasmayne
    Lace of blacke silke

75.106 By Barley Sixe verey feyre handekercheres edged averey fayre pasamayn
    Lace of venice golde and likewyse buttoned

                                                      dd to saide Mrs Skydmore

75.107 By Lichefelde two peyre of swete gloves, two very feyer handekercheres
    white lopeworke iiij breddes of Ruffes with pasmayn lace black and
    white / And iiij peces of lawnde loope worke sett withe spangels of silver

                              the gloves dd to Mrs E Knolles & threst to Mrs Skydmore

75.108 By Winkefelde a partelett and a night Rayle of camerycke wrought with
    flowers of gren and black sylke edged with apasmayn lace of lyke sylke

75.109 By Crokeson a feyer partelett & a peyre of sleves of networke whyte and
    blacke flowers set with spangilles of Syluer

                                                  dd to the foresaide Mrs Skydmore

75.110   By Townesend a cheyne of golde ennamuled grene with two Nuttmegges
         lyke ennamuled poz . . . . ij oz iij qrt di
                                                                    dd to the La Haward
75.111   By Notte Six very feyre handekercheres garnesshed with very feyer
         pasmayn of venice golde
75.112   By Marbery three small Say pillowbyeres of blackworke edged with
         pasmayn of golde & silver
75.113   By Hampton thre boxes one of Sytherons and thother of marmelade
                                                         dd to the foresaide Mrs Skydmore

Chaplyns

75.114   By Arch Carew in golde in a purse . . . . x li
                                                              dd to the foresaid H Sackford
75.115   By Doctor Wylson Mr of Requestes thre Sewtes of Ruffes of whyte worke
                                                              dd to the foresaid Mrs Skydmore

Gentilmen

75.116   By Thomas Henage treausorer of the Chamber apeyre of braslettes of
         golde withe seven rounde Agathes and perles in eche of them sett in
         roses of golde ennamuled white and vij troches of raged perle
75.117   By Hatton Captayne of the garde a very feyr Juell of golde beinge abirde
         in the brest thereof ys a Feyre Dyamonde lozenged benethe ys afeyre
         Rubye above is thre Emeraldes and all the rest of the Juell winges and
         all is garnesshed with sparkes of Dyamondes and Rubies with a blewe
         Sapher pendant and a pomander in the bottome thereof poz all . . . . vj oz
                                                                    dd to the Lady Hawarde
75.118   By Edwarde Basshe in golde in a purse. . . . . x li
                                                              dd to the foresaid H Sackford
75.119   By William Huggans xij Swete Bagges of Sarceonet of sondrye Coullors
         and alarge swete bag verey feyre embrawdered with aquene havinge the
         sonne in her hande the Beames spredding a broade
                                                              dd to the foresaide Mrs Skydmore
75.120   By Smythe Customer two halfe boltes of Camerycke
                                                              dd to Mrs Blanche aparry
75.121   By Benedicke Spinela two Smockes two pillowbyres a Shete and a night
         coyf all Cameryke with silke of sondry Collors
75.122   By Doctor Huycke one pot of orenge flowers, and a pot of gynger
         candydyd
75.123   By Doctor Maister one pot of orenge flowers and a pot of gynger candydyed
75.124   By Docter Julyo Six Bookes of Italian prynted
                                                                       with her Matie
75.125   By John Hemaway a pot of peares coundet and a box of lozenges
75.126   By Ryche a box of peches of Janoa and a box of plummes of Bruner

75.127   By Layton two feyr handekerchers of cameryke wrought with blacke sylke
          and iiij bredes of Lawnde openworke Thedging vpon work blacke and
          whyte in a paynted box

                                          dd to the foresaide Mrs Skydmore

75.128   By Taylor Mr Cooke one faire marchepayne
75.129   By John Dudley Serjaunt of the Pastery a pye of Quinces

[manuscript cut]

75.130   [By Churchyard] .... with a couer in a case of painted woode

[Missing heading – manuscript cut]

                            [Anno Regni Regine]
                            [Elizabeth xvij]

                    [Newyeres Guiftes geuon by the Quene her]
                    [Maiestie to those Persones whose names hereafter]
                    [ensue The first of Januarye The yere abouewritten]

[Duchesses, Marquisses, Countisses]

[manuscript cut]

          [To the Duches of Suffolk]
          [To the Lady Marques of Northampton]
          [To the Lady Marques of winchester]
          [To the Counties of Surrey]
75.131   [To the Counties of Shrewesbury] . . . . xxxj oz di
75.132   [To the Counties of Huntindon Dowager] partrige poz . . . . xx oz qrt di
75.133   [To the Counties of Huntingdon Junior] in partrige poz . . . . xxxix oz di qrt
75.134   To the Counties of Warwycke in sondry parcelles . . . . xliij oz di di qrt
75.135   To the Counties of Oxforde a guylt bolle with acouer partryge poz . . . .xx oz qrt
75.136   To the Countyes of Penbrocke dowager a guylte Cup with a couer Br
          poz . . . . xxvj oz iij qrt
75.137   To the Counties of Sussex a guylte Cup with a couer Br poz . . . . xx oz iij qrt di
75.138   To the Countyes of Penbrocke Junior one guilte bole with a couer partr
          poz . . . . xx oz di qrt
75.139   To the Counties of Bedford a guilte Cup with a couer Br poz. . . . . .Lj oz
75.140   To the Counties of Northumberlande a guilte Cup with a couer Br
          poz . . . . xx oz di di qrt
75.141   To the Counties of Southampton a guylte bole with a couer partrydge
          poz . . . . .xxv oz qrt
75.142   To the Counties of Lyncoln a cup with a couer partr poz . . . . L oz iij qrt

                                    177

75.143 To the Counties of Essex thre guylte bolles with a couer partrydge
poz . . . . .xxxij oz qrt

75.144 To the Counties of Rutlande a guilte cup with a couer partrydge
poz . . . . xix oz iij qrt di

75.145 To the Counties of Kent a guilte boll with a couer partr poz . . . . . . xx oz di qrt

75.146 To the Counties Mountgomery a boll with a couer guilte
partrydge . . . . xxxj oz di di qrt

Vicecount

75.147 To the Vice Counties Mountague one guilte boll with a couer partrydge
poz . . . . xx oz qrt di

Busshops

75.148 To the Arche Busshop of Caunt iij guilte bolles partrydge
poz . . . . .xlij oz iij qrt di

75.149 To the Arche Busshopp of yorke ij guilte bolles without couers
poz . . . . .xxxvij oz qrt di

75.150 To the Busshop of Durhem a guylte cup with a couer Br poz. . . . xxxvj oz iij qrt

75.151 To the Busshop of Ely in guylte plate partridge poz . . . . .xxxv oz

75.152 To the Busshop of Lundon thre guylte bolles with a couer Br
poz . . . . .xxx oz iij qrt

75.153 To the Busshopp of Wynchester one guylte goblete Br poz. . . . . . . xxxj oz qrt di

75.154 To the Busshopp of Salysburye one guilte cup with a couer Keyle
poz . . . . xxvij oz iij qrt di

75.155 To the Busshopp of Lincoln a boll with a couer guilte Br poz. . . . . . . .xxx oz qrt

75.156 To the Busshopp of Worcetor two Tancardes guilte Bran poz. . . . . . . xxxj oz qrt

75.157 To the Busshopp of Rochester one guilte Salte with a couer partrydge
poz . . . . .xxvij oz iij qrt

75.158 To the Busshopp of Lychefeld and Coven[try] one guilte Tankerde Keyle
poz . . . . .xx oz qrt

75.159 To the Busshopp of Hereforde in sondry parcelles Br and partridge
poz . . . . xviij oz qrt

75.160 To the Busshopp of St Davies one hans pot gilte Keyle poz . . . . . . xvij oz di qrt

75.161 To the Busshopp of Exeter one hans pot gylte Keyle poz . . . . xvj oz qrt

75.162 To the Busshopp of bathe one hans pot guylt Keyle poz. . . . . xvj oz iij qrt di

75.163 To the Busshopp of Chester a Tankerde guilte Brd. poz . . . . xvij oz iij qrt

75.164 To the Busshopp of Peterborowghe one guilte salte Jp poz. . . . . xx oz di

75.165 To the Busshopp of Gloceter one guylte Tankerde br poz. . . . . xix oz qrt di

75.166 To the Busshopp of Chicester a guilte bole with a couer Keyle poz . . . . xix oz di

Lordes

75.167 To the Lorde Burgaveny a guilt boll with a couer partridg poz . . . . x oz di di qrt

75.168 To the Lorde Barcley a guilte cup with a couer Br poz . . . . .xx oz qrt

75.169 To the Lorde Riche a guilte cup with a couer Br poz. . . . . xx oz qrt di

75.170 To the Lorde Darcie of Chichey a guilte cup with a couer Br poz. . . xx oz qrt di
75.171 To the Lorde Howarde in sondrye parcelles partrydge—Lvij oz di di qrt
and Brandon—xlix oz di qrt in toto . . . . Cvj oz iij qrt
75.172 To the Lord Shandois a guilte Tankerde br poz . . . . xvj oz iij qrt
75.173 To the Lorde Hunsdon a guilte boll with a couer br poz . . . . .xxxv oz iij qrt
75.174 To the Lorde Sturton a guilt Salte Br poz. . . . . xix oz di qrt
75.175 To the Lorde Buckhurste a guilte cup with a couer Keyle poz. . . . . .xj oz di
75.176 To the Lorde Northe a guilte bole with a Couer partrydge poz. . . . . . . .xx oz qrt
75.177 To the Lorde Pagett a guilte bolle with a Couer partrydge poz . . . . .xx oz qrt
75.178 To the Lorde Stafforde a guilte cup with a Couer br poz. . . . . .xx oz iij qrt
75.179 To the Lorde Compton a guilte cup with a Couer partridge poz. . . . . . .xx oz qrt
75.180 To the Lorde Ricott a guilte bolle with a Couer par poz . . . . xx oz qrt di
75.181 To the Lorde Lumley a guilt cup with a Couer Br poz. . . . . xx oz di
75.182 To the Lorde Strange a guilte bolle with a couer poz. . . . . .x oz qrt
75.183 To the Lorde Cobham in guilte plate in sondry parcelles par . . . . .xx oz qrt
75.184 To the Lorde Dudley a guilte hanse pott with a couer Br . . . . xix oz di

Barronesses

75.185 To the Barronesse Burgaueny a guilte bole with a Couer par poz . . . . .xj oz
75.186 To the barronesse Barckley a guilte cup with a Couer br poz . . . . x oz di qrt
75.187 To the barronesse Dakers of the southe a gilt hanse pot poz par xvj oz iij [qrt] di
75.188 To the barronesse Cobbham a guilte cup with a couer br poz . . . . Lij oz
75.189 To the barronesse Hunsdon guilte bole with a couer br poz . . . . . . xxij oz di qrt
75.190 To the barronesse Tayleboyes a guilt cup with a Couer par poz . . . . xx oz qrt di
75.191 To the barronesse Hawarde Dowager a guilte bole with a Couer bran poz xxj oz
75.192 To the barronesse Hawarde Junior in guilt plate in sondry parcelles br
poz . . . . .xxiij oz iij qrt
75.193 To the barronesse Shandowes Dowager a guilte cup with a couer br
poz . . . . xx oz di di qrt
75.194 To the baronesse St John of bletezo a guilt bole with a Couer par
poz . . . . xij oz qrt di
75.195 To the barronesse Pagett Care a guilt boule with a Couer br poz . . . . xxvij oz di
75.196 To the barronesse Burleye a guilte cup with a Couer br poz . . . . xxv oz iij qrt di
75.197 To the barronesse Pagett Lorde Pagettes wife a guilt cup with acouer
br poz. . . . . .xviij oz di qrt
75.198 To the baronesse Cheyney a guilte bole with a couer br poz . . . . xliiij oz j qrt
75.199 To the baronesse Shandowes Junior a guilt cup with a couer Keyle
poz . . . . xij oz di qrt

[Missing section of manuscript]

Chaplyns

75.200 To Archedeacon Carow a guylte Tankerde br poz . . . . xix oz di qrt
75.201 To Doctor Wylson a guylte Salte par poz. . . . . xiiij oz

Maydes of Honour

75.202 To the Ladye Susan bowser a guylte boule with a couer br poz. . . . . .x oz qrt

75.203 To Mrs Marye Rattlife a boule with a couer br poz. . . . . x oz

75.204 To Mrs Ellon Brydges a guilte boule with a couer par poz . . . . x oz

75.205 To Mrs Katherin Howarde a guilt boule with a couer K. poz . . . . x oz di qrt

75.206 To Mrs Elizabeth Garrett a guilt bole with acouer par poz . . . . x oz qrt di

75.207 To Mrs Mary Burroughe a guilte boule with a couer par poz . . . . .x oz qrt

75.208 To Mrs Hyde Mother a guilt Salte with a couer K. poz. . . . . xij oz iij qrt

Gentilmen

75.209 To Mr Hatton Capitayn of the garde in guilt plate par . . . . CCLxxxvij oz

75.210 To Mr Hennaige a guilte boule with a couer par poz. . . . . xlviij oz

75.211 To Benedic Spinola in guilte plate Brandon . . . . .Lxxviij oz

75.212 To Clere a guilt Tankerde br poz. . . . . xix oz qrt di

75.213 To Stanhop a guilt salte with a couer par poz . . . . .x oz qrt

75.214 To Drewry a guilt boule with a couer br poz . . . . xvij oz

75.215 To Edward Basshe a guilt Tankerde K. poz . . . . xx oz

75.216 To William Huggans a guilt cup with a couer br poz. . . . . .xxx oz

75.217 To Smythe Customer a guylte Cup with a couer br poz. . . . . xv oz

75.218 To Doctor Hewicke a guilte Cup with a couer br poz . . . . xiiij oz iij qrt

75.219 To Dr Maister a guilte Tankerde bra poz . . . . xiiij oz di

75.220 To Dr Julyo a guilte boule Brandon poz. . . . . xiiij oz

75.221 To John Hemigway a guilte boul without a couer par poz. . . . . vij oz iij qrt

75.222 To Riche potycarye a cup with a couer K. poz. . . . . vij oz di

75.223 To Captayne Laighton a guilt Cup with a couer br poz. . . . . xxi oz iij qrt di

75.224 To Smythson Mr Cooke parte of a guilte Tankerde br poz . . . . viij oz qrt

75.225 To John Dudley Sergeant of the pastery in guilt plate br poz . . . . . . iiij oz iij qrt

75.226 To Marke Anthony violano a guilte salte par poz . . . . v oz di

75.227 To Ambrosu Lupo violano a guilte salte par poz. . . . . iiij oz di

75.228 To Petro Vbaldyno in guilt spones br poz. . . . . v oz iij qrt

75.229 To Charles Smythe a guilte boule par poz . . . . xxj oz qrt di

75.230 To Clarentius [sic Garter] Kyng at Armes a guylte salte br poz. . . . xiiij oz iij qrt

75.231 To Edwarde Skeetes a cup with a Couer br poz . . . . x oz qrt di

75.232 To Wylliam Skeetes a guylt Tankerd bran poz . . . . xvj oz di qrt

75.233 To Bassony the brethern in gylte plate partrige . . . . iiij oz

75.234 To Churchyerd a cruse of Siluer and gilte Brandon poz . . . . vj oz qrt

Freguiftes

75.235 To John Asteley Esquire Mr of the Juelles & plate a cup with a couer guilt
        bra poz. . . . . xviij oz iij qrt

75.236 To Thomas Asteley grome of the previe chamber one guilt cruse br
        poz. . . . . .viij oz iij qrt di

75.237 To Henry Sackeforde an other grome there one guilt cruse par
        poz. . . . . .viij oz iij qrt di

75.238 To John Bapteste another grome there one guilte cruse par poz
.... viij oz iij qrt di

75.239 To Edwarde Care another grome there one guilt cruse par poz..... viij oz iij qrt

75.240 To Thomas Knevett another grome there one guilt cruse Br poz ...... viij oz di

75.241 To William [sic Henry] Middlimore another grome there one guilt
cruse par poz .... viij oz di

75.242 To Thomas Gorge another grome there one guilte cruse par poz
.... viij oz di di qrt

75.243 To Kyllygrave another grome there, one guilte Cruse Br .... viij oz di

75.244 To Rauffe Hoope yoman of the Roobes one guilte Cruse par poz
.... xij oz iij qrt di

75.245 To Nicholas Brystow Clerk of the Juelles and plate one cruse guilte
br poz... x oz iij qrt di

75.246 To John Pigeon yoman of the same, one cruse guilte part poz .... x oz iij qrt di

75.247 To Stephen Fulwell an other yoman there, one Cruse guilte par
poz .... x oz iij qrt di

75.248 To Rycharde Dysteley [sic Asteley] grome there, one guilte Cruse par
poz .... x oz iij qrt

Summa totalis of all the
plate giuen as aforesaid .... m li m li m li m li m li CCiiij oz

Guiftes giuen and delyuered at sundrye
tymes in maner & fourme followinge
viz

75.249 Mr Gray
First gevon by her Matie the last Daye of July at the christenyng of
Mr Henry Grayes childe one double Cup of Siluer and gilte
goldesmithes making bought of Aphabel Partrige goldsmith
weyng .... xxviij oz di qrt

75.250 Don Ferdinand
Item gevon by her Matie and Delyvered xxv Daye of January Anno
predicto to Don Ferdinando de Mendoz ambassador from the kyng
of Spayne a cheyne of golde which Cxxiij oz iij qtr weight bought of
goldsmiths principall in charge of the said Ambassador .... Lxxj oz

75.251 Lady Shandoys
Item gevon by her Matie the x Daye of January anno predicto at the
christening of Lady Shandos childe [hole in ms] Siluer and gilte
bought of Aphabel Partrige goldsmith weyng .... xl oz iij qtr

75.252 Mr Drury
Item given by her Matie the xiiij Daye of February anno predicto
at the christening of Mr William Drurys childe one pere of p[ottes]
[hole in ms] Siluer and gilte bought of the foresaid Aphabel Partige
poz .... lxv oz iij qtr di

Elizabeth R
[sign manual]

John Asteley
Ex[aminatio] per
Bristow
J Pigeon
Ste Fulwell
Richarde Asteley

Anno Regni Regine
Elizabeth Decimo octauo

Newyeres Guiftes geuon to the Quene her
Maiestie by those Persones whose names hereafter
ensue The first of Januarye The yere abouewritten

Elizabeth R
[sign manual]

76.1 By the Ladye Marye Gray oone longe Cussion of purple vellot faire
wrought with pearle and spangles Lined with Crymsen vellat with
foure tasselles contaigning in length oone yerde and thre nailes, and in
breadth haulf a yerde

Deliuered in chardge to Richarde Todde
keper of the standing Guarderobe at Hampton Courte

76.2 By the Ladye Margret Countes of Darbie a Peticoate of cloth of Siluer
striped with golde garded with foure gardes of blacke vellat lined with
blewe serceonet frenged with venice golde and blewe silke with two peeces
of blewe silke with Aglettes of golde

Deliuered in chardge to Rauf Hoope Yeoman of the Roobes

76.3 By Sir Nicholas Bacone Knight Lorde Keeper of the greate Seale of
Englande in a purse of grene silke and golde knit in golde . . . . xiij li vj s viij d

76.4 By the Lorde Burghley Lorde High Threasouror of Englande in a purse
of crymsen silke and siluer in Newe Angelles . . . . xx li

76.5 By the Lorde Marques of Winchester in a purse of crymsen silke and siluer
in Angelles . . . . xx li

Deliuered to Henry Sackeforde grome of the preuie Chamber

Earles

76.6 By the Earle of Leicester Master of the Horse a juell being a Crosse of
golde conteigning sixe very fayre Emeraldes wherof two being bigger
than the rest thone of them Crased and thre large perles pendaunt poz
all together . . . . viij oz

Deliuered to the Lady Howarde

76.7 By the Earle of Arundell in a paper in Angelles . . . . xxx li

76.8 By the Earle of Shrewesbury in a blewe purse in Di souereignes . . . . xx li

76.9 By the Earle of Darbie in a purse of Crymsen Satten and embrodered in
golde . . . . xx li

76.10 By the Earle of Sussex Lorde Chamberlen in a purse of Crymsen silk in
Angelles . . . . xx li

76.11 By the Earle of Lincolne Lorde Admirall of Englande in a paper in
golde . . . . x li

76.12 By the Earle of Surrey in a purse in golde . . . . x li

76.13   By the Earle of Huntingdon in a purse of Red silke in Di souereignes . . . . . . x li
                               Deliuered to the said Henry Sackforde

76.14   By the Earle of Warwicke A Gowne of blacke wrought vellat with Russet
        grounde garnisshed with Fethers and buttons of Damaske golde and
        siluer fased with vnshorne vellat
                                 Deliuered to the said Rauf Hoope

76.15   By the Earle of Bedforde in a purse of blewe silke in Angelles . . . . xx li

76.16   By the Earle of Pembrouke in a Crymsen purse knit in Angelles . . . . xx li

76.17   By the Earle of Northumberlande in a purse of Crymson silke in
        Angelles . . . . x li
                                Deliuerid to the said Henry Sackford

76.18   By the Earle of Hereforde a lute of white bone in a Case of grene vellat
        garnisshid with a brodelace of siluer and grene silke
            Deliuered in chardge to Thomas Lichfilde of her Maties previe Chamber

76.19   By the Earle of Southampton in a purse of blewe silke and siluer in Di
        souereignes. . . . . xx li
                               Deliuered to the said Henry Sackeforde

76.20   By the Earle of Essex oone whole pece of blake vellat the grounde whyt
        Satten fringed with blake knottis conteigyning. . . . . vij yerdes di
                                Deliuerid to the said Rauf Hoope

76.21   By the Vicount Mountague in a Red purse in Angelles . . . . x li
                                Deliuerid to the said Henry Sackforde

Duchesses, Marques, and Countesses

76.22   By the Duches of Suffolke oone Cusshion vnstuffed of nedleworke with
        storie of musike lined with grene vellat with a passmayne lace in the
        same frengid and buttoned with grene silke stripes and tassseled with
        venice golde cont in length . . . . one yerdes di qrt and in bredth di

76.23   By the Duches of Somerset a litell Cofer or deske with Diuers tilles in the
        same couerid with Crymsen vellat in the lidde is sette a Steele glasse and
        in the same cofer is diuers other things vide Comes, Touthpickes, Sisers
        &c and also in it is a Snusken of Nedleworke of venice golde siluer and
        silke lyned with vnshorne vellat and frenged at bothe endes, And a swet
        bagge of blewe Taphata enbrauderid
                                Deliuerid to the said Richarde Todde

76.24   By the Lady Marques of Winchester in a grene silke purse in Angelles . . . . . x li

76.25   By the Countes of Surrey in golde . . . . v li
                                Deliuerid to the said Sackeforde

76.26   By the Countes of Shrewisbury a kirtell and a Doublett of yellowe Satten
        cut lined with blake Serceonet wrought allouer with shorte Staues of
        purlid Siluer with a like passamaine
                                Deliuerid to the said Rauf Hoope

76.27   By the Countes of Huntingdon Douger in a purse of blake wrought vellat
        in Angelles . . . . x li

76.28   By the Countes of Huntingdon in a purse in Angelles. . . . . viij li
                                Deliuerid to the said Henry Sackeforde

76.29 By the Countes of Oxfourde a Doublet and a kirtell of peache colored
Tincell lined with white Serceonet edged with a passamaine of siluer
and set with spangles of like siluer

76.30 By the Countes of Warwicke a fore parte of a kirtell of white Tincell
allouer wrought with whit Rooses of Lawne with a passamaine of
purlid golde and siluer vpon blewe lined with white Taphata And a
rounde kirtell and a Doublet of Russet Satten cut and laide with a
Compas Lace of venice golde siluer and Carnation silke Lined with
Carnation Taphata with xviij buttons of golde

Deliuerid to the said Rauf Hoope

76.31 By the Countes of Sussex in a purse of Crymsen silke in golde. . . . . x li

76.32 By the Countes of Penbrouke Douger in a Crymsen purse in new
Angelles . . . . vij li

76.33 By the Countes of Penbrouke in a red knit purse in Angelles . . . . x li

Deliuerid to the said Sackeforde

76.34 By the Countes of Bedfourde a Cheyne of golde in a boxe couerid with
grene Satten poz. . . . . ix oz iij qtr di

Deliuerid to the said Lady Howarde

76.35 By the Countes of Northumberlande in a purse of red silke in Angelles . . . . x li

76.36 By the Countes of Southampton in a purse of Crymsen silke and siluer in
Di soueraignes . . . . x li

Deliuerid to the said Henry Sackforde

76.37 By the Countes of Lincolne a Girdell of golde set with xvj Agath heddes
and xv Troches of pearle two in a troche

Deliuerid to the said La Hawarde

76.38 By the Countes of Essex a foreparte of a kirtle a paire of Sleues and a
partelet of grene Satten castouer with networke the grounde of the
Sleues grene sipers

Deliuerid to the said Mrs Skidmor oone of her Maties Chamberers

76.39 By the Countes of Rutlande in a purse of red silke in golde . . . . x li

Deliuerid to the said Sackforde

76.40 By the Countes of Kente Douger two Smockes of fine Holland wrought
with open white worke And two swete bagges of Crymsen Taphata
edged with a smale passamaine of venice golde

76.41 By the Countes Mongomere two pilloweberes of Lawne networke florisshid
allouer with silke of diuers collores with a brode passamaine of golde
and silke / And a bande of Lawne edged with bone Lace of white
worke

Deliuerid to Mrs Skidmore vt supra

76.42 By Mademisell Bewfourde Doughter to the saide Countes Mongomerie
oone Lace for a necke of networke

Deliuerid to Mrs Eliza. Knowles

76.43 By the Viscountes Mountague in a grene silke purse in Angelles. . . . . x li

Deliuerid to the said H Sackeforde vt supra

Busshoppes

76.44	By the Arche Busshop of Yorke in a white purse in Di soueraignes	xxx li
76.45	By the Busshop of Durehym in a purse of crymsen silke in Angelles	xxx li
76.46	By the Busshop of Eleye in a blewe purse in golde.	xxx li
76.47	By the Busshop of London in a purse of grene silke in Angelles.	xx li
76.48	By the Busshop of Winchester in a purse of grene silke in Di soueraignes	
	. . . .	xx li
76.49	By the Busshop of Salisbury in a blacke silke purse in Angelles	xx li
76.50	By the Busshop of Lincolne in a paper in Di soueraignes	xx li
76.51	By the Busshop of Worster in a red silke purse in golde	xx li
76.52	By the Busshop of Norwiche in a purse of red silke in Di soueraignes	
	. . . . xiij li x s	
76.53	By the Busshop of Lichfelde and Couentrie in a purse in golde and	
	siluer. . . . . xiij li vj s viij d	
76.54	By the Busshop of Herford in a purse in golde	x li
76.55	By the Busshop of St Dauies in a purse of red silke and siluer knit in	
	Angelles	x li
76.56	By the Busshop of Exetor in a red purse in Di soueraignes.	x li
76.57	By the Busshop of Bathe in a purse in golde	x li
76.58	By the Busshop of Chester in a purse in golde.	x li
76.59	By the Busshop of Peterborowe in a purse in Angelles	x li
76.60	By the Busshop of Gloster in a paper in golde.	x li
76.61	By the Busshop of Chichester in a blewe purse in Angelles.	x li
	Deliuerid to the saide Henry Sackeforde vt supra	

Lordes

76.62	By the Lorde Burgavenie in a purse in golde	v li
76.63	By the Lorde Riche in a purse in golde.	x li
76.64	By the Lorde Darcy of Chichey in a red purse in Angelles	x li
	Deliuerid to the said Sacford vt supra	
76.65	By the Lorde Howarde a Juell of golde being a shippe sett with a table	
	Dyamonde of fyve sparcks of Dyamondes and a smale perle pendaunte	
76.66	By the Lorde Hunsdon a Juell of mother of pearle garnisshid with golde	
	and set with two sparcks of Dyamondes and vj sparcks of Rubyes and	
	two Dyamondes pendaunte	
	Deliuerid to the saide Lady Howarde vt supra	
76.67	By the Lorde Shandowes in a purse in golde and siluer.	vj li xiij s iiij d
76.68	By the Lorde Stourton in a purse of crymsen satten and siluer in	
	Angelles	x li
76.69	By the Lorde Buckehurst in a purse in Angelles.	v li
76.70	By the Lorde Northe in a purse of grene silke in Di soueraignes	x li
76.71	By the Lorde Lumley in a purse of blewe & siluer silke in golde.	x li
76.72	By the Lorde Paget in a purse of blewe silke and golde in Angelles	x li
76.73	By the Lorde Stafford in a purse of Crymsen silke in Di soueraignes	x li
76.74	By the Lorde Compton in a purse of venice golde in Angelles	x li

76.75 By the Lorde Rycotte in a paper in golde . . . . x li
76.76 By the Lorde Taulbot a mount of siluer guylte [...] width and bredth of
    j [...] . . . . vij oz
Deliuerid to the said Henry Sackford vt supra

76.77 By the Lorde Cobham a foreparte of a kirtle of white Clothe of Siluer
    garded with venice golde and siluer and edged with a smale frenge of
    venice golde and siluer
Deliuerid to the said Rauf Hope

76.78 By the Lord Straunge A Juell of golde being a Squyrrell set with thre
    smale Dyamondes thre smale emerodes and thre pearles pendaunt
Deliuerid to the said Lady Howarde

Baronesses

76.79 By Burgaueny in golde . . . . v li
76.80 By the Lady Barkeley in a paper in Angelles . . . . x li
76.81 By the Lady Hunsdon in a purse in golde. . . . . x li
76.82 By the Lady Howard Dowager in a purse of blewe silke in Angelles. . . . . x li
76.83 By the Lady Ste John of Bletzo in a purse in golde . . . . x li
76.84 By the Lady Paget Cary in a purse of blewe silke in Angelles . . . . x li
76.85 By the Lady Shandowes Junior in a purse of Crimsen silke in Angelles . . . . . v li
76.86 By the Lady Buckehurst in golde . . . . v li
76.87 By the Lady Norres in a purse in golde . . . . x li
76.88 By the Lady Taileboyes in a paper in Angelles . . . . x li
Delyuerid to the saide Henry Sackeforde vt supra

76.89 By the Lady Howarde a paire of Braslettes of golde garnisshed with iiij
    jacentes and iiij agathes the paire
Deliuerid to the saide Lady Howard vt supra

76.90 By the Lady Shandowes Douger a faire Chaire of Nedleworke of
    Damask of silke venice golde and siluer and frengid with venice golde
    siluer and silke
Deliuerid to the saide Richarde Todde vt supra

76.91 By the Lady Dakers of the Southe a peticoat of white Satten lyned with
    Serceonet and bordered with a faire border of smale passamayne lace
    of venis golde frengid with white silke [...]
76.92 By the Lady Cobham A kirtell of white Satten cut and lined with yellow
    sercenet striped Downeside with a passamayne of venice golde and
    siluer
76.93 By the Lady Paget the Lorde pagettes wief a Dublet and a kirtell of
    white Satten allouer couerid with cutworke florisshed
dd to the said Rauf Hoope

76.94 By the Lady Burghley a smale Cofer of Mother of pearle garnisshed
    with wodworke guilt with Eight bookes in it
With the Quene by thande of Goodyere page

76.95 By the Lady Cheynie a Gowne of Murrey Taphata sarceonet couerid
    allouer with networke florisshed allouer with golde and siluer with a
    passamaine Lace of gold and siluer

76.96 By the Lady Taulbot A Doublet of gingercolorid Satten cut, with smale
       flowers and spangelles of venice siluer lined with white sarceonet
76.97 By the Lady Gray of Pirgo a [kyrtell of] frengid Satten with networke and
       florisshid with golde and Siluer and [silke of sundrey collors]
76.98 By the Lady Russell a swettebagge enbrouderid with Rooses and flowers of
       venice golde and siluer lined with white Taphata
                              Deliuerid to the said Rauf Hope vt supra
76.99 By the Lady Sheffeld a scarf of tawnye silke wrought allouer with silke
       of sundrey collers knotted with a brode passamaine of venice golde and
       siluer lined wadget colored Taphata
                    Deliuerid to the Countes of Lincolne by thandes of William Norres her
                       servant to be eyred because it was made in a house enfected
76.100 By the Lady Cromwell the Lorde Cromwell his weif a bande and Ruffes of
       Lawne wrought with blacke worke and [...]
76.101 By the Lady [willobie of warrike] a Caule alouer [garnesshid and flouresshid]
       with venice golde
76.102 By the Lady [Mountjoy ...] and a peire of Sleeues of networke [...] rances
       of golde and siluer and sondrey collers
76.103 By the Lady Mary Vere vj handkercheres of Camerike wrought with
       blacke silke edged fethers and Taphata with a passamane lase of
       blacke silke [...]
                              Deliuerid to the saide Mrs Skidmore vt supra

Ladies

76.104 By the Lady Mary Sidney oone sault of siluer guilt squared with foure
       pillers and Two bolles of Cristall poz together . . . . iiij^{xx} j oz
                              Deliuered in the chardge to John Asteley, Esquier Mr and
                                 Threasouror of her highnes Juells and plate
76.105 By the Lady Stafford a payre of braceletts of golde set with agathe heddes
       & other stones grauen
                                     Deliuerid to the said Lady Haworde
76.106 By the Lady Carowe a fayre bagge of Camerike the one side allouer
       wrought with [silke of sondery collors] thother side of venice golde
       and blacke silke and at euery corner a button and [a tassell of venice
       silver and silke]
76.107 By the Lady Ratlife a payre of sleeues of Lawne edged with golde
76.108 By the Lady Cheeke a partlet of Lawne edged with a small passamane of
       silke
76.109 By the Lady Butler a cusshion and a Coueringe of lawne openworke
                                     Deliuerid to the said Mrs Skidmor
76.110 By the Lady Paulet a cusshioncloth of networke wrought with blake silke
       and edged with a brode passamane of blacke silke, two swetebagges of
       Taphata, twelue tothpickes and a Litle nosegaye of flowers of silke
       thendes trimed with pearle
                           The tothepickes & nosegaye with the Quene by Richard Todde
                           / The Cusshion cloth and bagges to the saide Mrs Skidmore

76.111 By the Lady Wodhouse a Doublet of murrey Taphata netted ouer with
blake silke wrought with flowers of golde and siluer with a passamaine
lace of siluer

Deliuerid to the said Ralf Hoope

76.112 By the Lady Frogmortone a longe Cusshion of nedleworke wrought with
Diuers flowers of sundry colores the backe side of murre Satten with
foure tasselles netted ouer with blacke silke [...] qtr in length one yerde
Di qrt in bredth di yerde qrt

dd to the said Todde

76.113 By the Lady [Wil]ford in a paper in golde . . . . vj li
76.114 By the Lady Marven in a purse of blewe silke and siluer in Angelles . . . . v li
76.115 By the Lady Cromwell Sir Henryes wif in Angelles . . . . v li
76.116 By the Lady Gresham in a purse in french soueraignes . . . . v li

Deliuerid to the saide Henry Sackefore vt supra

Knightes

76.117 By Sir Fraunces Knolles knight Threasouror of the Householde in a
purse of crymsen in Angelles. . . . . x li
76.118 By Sir James Crofte Comptroller of the same in a purse in golde . . . . x li
76.119 By Sir Thomas Smyth principall secretarie in a Chere bag in golde . . . . x li

Deliuerid to the saide Henry Sackeforde vt supra

76.120 By Mr Fraunces Walsingham esquire also Secretary oone Coller of golde
being two Sarpentes [the hedds being Ophall] a pendaunt of small
Dyamondes in the toppe therof a Strawberie [with a rocke Rubye] in
it poz . . . . v oz di

Deliuerid to the saide Lady Howarde vt supra

76.121 By Sir Rauf Sadler Chaunceller of the Duchie of Lancaster in golde . . . . . xv li
76.122 By Sir Walter Myldmay Chauncellor of the Eschequer in a paper in Di
souveraignes. . . . . x li
76.123 By Sir William Cordell Mr of the Rolles in a white satten purse in golde . . . . x li
76.124 By Sir Christofer Hayden in a purse in golde . . . . x li
76.125 By Sir William Damsell Receuor of the Corte of wardes in a red purse in
golde. . . . . x li
76.126 By Sir Henry Cromwell in a purse in Di soueraignes . . . . x li
76.127 By Sir Thomas Gresham in a paper in golde . . . . x li
76.128 By Sir Owen Hopton Leiutenent of the Tower in a blewe purse in new
Angelles . . . . x li
76.129 By Sir John Thynne in golde . . . . v li

Deliuerid to the saide Henry Sackeforde vt supra

76.130 By Sir Henry Lee a booke of golde Enameled full of leaues of paper and
parchement printed with serteign devises poz togethers. . . . . viij oz

Deliuerid to the saide Lady Hawarde

76.131 By Sir Gawen Carowe a Smoke of Camrike the bodie wrought with blake
silke the Sleeuis and edges wrought with venis golde and blake silke

Deliuerid to the saide Mrs Skidmore

76.132   By Sir Gilbert Dethick Alias Garter chef kinge at Armes oone booke of
Armes cont thistorie of the Knights of the Garter made in the Tymes
of king Edwarde the sixthe and Queen Mary couered with Crymsen
vellat and edged with a passamaine of golde

Deliuerid to Mrs Blaunche Aparie

Gentelwomen

76.133   By Maistres Blaunche Parrie A Juell being a Christall sett in golde with
Stories in it appering on both sides / with a pearle pendaunt

76.134   By Elizabeth Knowles A girdill of wadget colorid Taphata edged at thendes
with a brode passamaine lace of venice golde and siluer with a Flower of
golde vpon it and with garnettes & two roses of siluer in it and pendaunt
with lozenged ballaces in it and a butterflye of golde enameled

Deliuerid to the said Lady Howard

76.135   By Mrs Frances Howarde a partelet and a peire of Sleves of lawne wrought with
blake silke and siluer and spangled with bugles

76.136   By Mrs Hennage twoo smale Cusshions of Satten of sundrey collores
enbrauderid with venice siluer

76.137   By Mrs Edmundes viij Ruffes of Lawne wrought with blake silke and
edged with a passamaine of blacke silke Likewise edged

76.138   By Mrs Elizabeth Drurie a paire of Sleues of yellow Satten cut laide with a
passamaine of siluer and spangles

dd to the said Hoope

76.139   By Mrs Skidmore a Canope of white woorke wrought with silke of
sundrey collors with two Curtens of the same to hange And a cusshion
edged as a passamaine of golde and silke

dd to the said skidmor

76.140   By Mrs Abingdon a peticoate of sarceonet quilted lined with white
Flannell and frenged with venice golde and blewe silke

dd to the said Rauf Hoope

76.141   By Mrs Katerin Paston a peire of sleues and a partelet of Lawne wrought with
open worke

76.142   By Mrs Marburey Sixe handkercheues of Camrike wrought with blak silke

76.143   By Mrs Jane Brusselles alis Hawkes a partelet and a peire of Ruffes of lawne
wrought with blake silke and siluer, set with spangles

Deliuerid to the said Mrs Skydmore

76.144   By Mrs Mary Bridges a Doublet of strawecolorid taphata couerid allouer
with a caule of whit with buttons and a smale passamaine of venice siluer
lined with white serceonet

Deliuerid to the said Hoope

76.145   By Mrs Caue two litell pillowberes of Camrike thone side allouer wrought
with blake silke

76.146   By Mrs Baptest six handkercheues of Lawne wrought with silke of
sundrey collors and edged with a faire passamaine of venice golde siluer
and silke

Deliuerid to Mrs Skydmore

76.147   By Mrs Snowe foure touthpickes of golde and Sixe touth clothes wrought
      with blake silke and golde

76.148   By Mrs West iiij hower glasses in a case of Mother of pearle, in a box
      or case of Crymsen silke faire enbrauderid with venice golde and
      siluer

                                  The tothe clothes dd to Mrs Skydmore
                    the tothepickes and houerglasse dd to the said John Asteley

76.149   By Mrs Sackforde a Doublet of murrey Satten cut and lined with
      serceonet laide with a passamaine of siluer and murrey silke
                                      Deliuerid to the said Rauf Hoope

76.150   By Mrs Tounsend a Girdell of grene sarceonet powderid with spangles
      and a border at the endes enbrauderid and a smale Ringe of golde with
      a phenix in it garnisshed a bout with a Roose of eight Rubies
                   Delivered to Mrs Eliz. Knolles by thandes of Mr Baptest

76.151   By Mrs Lichfilde thre Ruffes and two handkercheves of cut white worke
      allouer wrought with the nedle And oone paire of swete gloves
                              Deliuerid to the said Mrs Skidmore

76.152   By Mrs Wingfilde theonside of a Cusshion of purple Satten allouer
      enbrauderid with flowers of cloth of golde and siluer cut in length j
      yerdes and oone naile and in bredth di yerdes and oone naile
                                          dd to the said Tod

76.153   By Mrs Digbie two pillowes of Camrike allouer wrought with silke of
      Diuers collors stuffed with Downe

76.154   By Mrs Hampton two boxes of sweete meates

76.155   By Mrs Smithson late laundres a paire of Ruffes and a partelet of lawne

76.156   By Amy Shelton sixe handkercheues with a faire passamaine of golde and
      siluer

76.157   By Mrs Allenn a Smocke of fine hollande the sleues and bodie ritchly
      wrought with blake silke and the coller and handes wrought with
      Damaske and venice golde and blake silke
                              Deliuerid to the said Mrs Skidmore

76.158   By Mrs Dane in a purse of Crymsen silke in Di soueraignes. . . . . v li
                              Deliuerid to the said Sackeford

76.159   By Mrs Mountague the Quenis silkewoman a Doublet of Networke of
      golde siluer and silke lined with silke Tinsell and the lining white serconet
      edged with smale passamaine lase of venice golde and set with buttons of
      golde and silke
                                Deliuerid to Mrs Eliza Drury

76.160   By Mrs Crocson A Tire for the Quenis hedde of Networke set full of
      Spangles

76.161   By Mrs Barley sixe handkercheves of Camrike edged with a passamaine of
      venice golde

76.162   By Mrs Noote sixe handkercheues of Camrike edged with a passamaine of
      venice golde
                              Deliuerid to the said Mrs Skidmor

76.163   By Mrs Mary Sidney a Jeull of golde being two Cheries and a butterflie of Opalles

Deliuerid to the said Lady Howard

76.164   By Mrs Huggans sixe handkercheues of Camerike the borders wrought with openworke & garnisshid with silke and golde and xviij smale bagges of sercenet of sundrey collores

76.165   By Ipolita late oone handkerchef of hollande with a brode border of openworke

76.166   By Mrs Laundres Twist two handkercheues and iiij totheclothes trimmed with gold & silke

76.167   By Mrs Lucretia a faire handkerchef of Camrike wrought with silke of sundrey collors edged with two faire passamaines of venice golde and siluer and a smale swete bagge of grene Taphata

Deliuerid to the said Mrs Skidmor

76.168   By Leuina Terlyng the Quenis picture vpon a Carde

with the Quene by Mr Baptest

Chaplaine

76.169   By Arche Deacon Carowe Deane of the Chappell in a red purse in Angelles . . . . x li

Deliuerid to the said Sackeforde

Gentelmen

76.170   By Mr Hatton captaine of the Garde A Riche Juell being a Clocke of golde garnisshed with Diamondes Rubies Emeraudes and pearles with one very faire Rubye in the bottome and a faire Emeraude pendaunt set in golde and two mene perles pendaunt poz all togethers . . . . . . ix oz iij qtr

dd to the said La Howard vt supra

76.171   By Mr Heneage Threasurer of the Chamber A Juell of Agath sett with two Diamondes and xvj sparcks of rubyes with a pendaunte of golde enamuled redd and sparcks of smale Rubyes and a flye of ophall upon it

Deliuered to the said La howard

76.172   By Mr John Harrington A Saulte of Agath garnisshed with golde steeple fation / in the toppe a Jasper with v smale pearles sette and iiij pendaunte poz togethers

dd to the said La Howard vt supra

76.173   By Mr Cleere in a paper in golde . . . . v li

dd to the said H Sackforde

76.174   By Mr Captaine Horsey Captaine of Thisle of Wight a peece of grene Satten cont . . . . .xviij yerdes

dd to the said Rauf Hoope

76.175   By Mr Captaine Leighton Captaine of Garnsey A Sewtt of lawne wrought with silke

dd to Mrs Skidmore

76.176 By Mr Skidmore a Doublet of Changeable yellowe Taphata with a Caule allouer set with spangles

76.177 By Mr William Drurie a Hatte of Russet Taphata allouer enbraudered with flowers and curles [... ms torn] of seed pearle with a Fether of Orange collor

76.178 By Mr Robinson A Doublet and a kirtell of Lawne nettedouer with flowers of golde and set with spangles guilt and edged with a passamaine lace of golde lined with strawecollorid serceonet the kirtell frenged with venice golde and yellowe silke

Deliuerid to the said R Hoope

76.179 By Mr Basshe vitler of the Quenes Navie in a purse of grene silke in new Angelles . . . . x li

Deliuerid to the saide Sackforde

76.180 By Mr Fulke Greuell a Canapie cloth for a Cusshion and a Couerpane allouer enbraudered with a worke of silke and golde of sundrey collors, And Two coyphes allouer wrought with blak silke

the Cannopie dd to Tod the rest to Mrs Skidmore

76.181 By Mr Smyth Customer ij boltes of Camrike

76.182 By Mr Allan Sixe very fayre handkercheues wrought with silke of sundrey collors and edged with a fayre passamane of venice golde and buttones of the same

76.183 By Alphontius a night Smocke of fine hollande the Coller handes and skertes wrought with cutworke and edged with a brode passmayne

Deliuerid to the said Mrs Skidmore

76.184 By Laneson Mynt Master A Juell cont iiij Emeraudes garnisshid with golde set with vij smale pearles the Emeraudes shewing bothewaise

dd to the said Lady Howard

76.185 By Doctor Hewicke A potte of Orainge Flowers & a pot of Ginger condit

76.186 By Doctor Masters two other like pottes

76.187 By Doctor Julio two other like pottes as aforesaide

76.188 By John Hemyngwaye Potecarie a box of peares condite & a box of Lozanges

76.189 By Riche Potycarie a box of plomes of Genoway and another of Peches

76.190 By Smithson alias Tailor Mr Cooke a marchepane made like a Chestbourde

76.191 By John Dudley Sergeant of the Pastrie a pie of Quinces

76.192 By Mark Anthony violin foure glasses with a Couer guilt in a Case of Lether

Deliuerid to the said Mrs Skidmore

76.193 By Ambrose Lupo violin a litell Cofer of Lether guilt with a swete bagge in it of Changable Taphata

Deliuerid to the Lady Howard vt supra

76.194 By Petrucho Vbaldino A booke of Italian written of viij Englishe Ladies

Deliuerid to Mr Baptest

76.195 By William Huggans oone fayre swete bagge of white Satten enbrauderid
in the middest within a roundell of Damaske golde veetus edged with a
passamaine lace of venice golde buttoned and tasseled with grene silke
curled with venice golde

Deliuerid to the said Mrs Skidmore

Summa totalis of all / the mony geuon to her Maiestie and
Deliuerid in Manner and forme after / declared is . . . . m li xxvij li xvj s viij d

Elizabeth R
[sign manual]

Anno Regni Regine
Elizabeth Decimo octauo

Newyeres Guiftes geuon by the Quenes
Maiestie at her Highnes Honor of Hampton
Court to theise Persones whose names hereafter
ensue The First of January the yere abouesaid

Elizabeth R
[sign manual]

76.196 Too the Lady Mary Graye a guilt bolle with a Couer Brandon poz . . . . . xviij oz
76.197 To the Lady Margret Countes of Darbie oone guilt Cup with a Couer
brandon poz. . . . . L oz di di qtr
76.198 To Sir Nicholas Bacone knight Lorde keper of the greate Seale of
Englande oone guilte bolle with a Couer Brandon poz . . . . xxxiij oz
76.199 To the Lorde Burghley Lorde Highe Threasouror of Englande oone
guilt Cup with a couer Partrige weing. . . . . xl oz iij qtr di
76.200 To the Lorde Marques of Winchester oone guilt Cup with a Couer
partrige poz . . . . xxxj oz qtr di

Earles

76.201 To the Earle of Leictor Mr of the Horse oone guilt Cup with a Couer
partrige poz . . . . C oz iij qtr
76.202 To the Earle of Arundell oone guilt Cup with a Couer, partrige poz . . . . . .Lj oz
76.203 To the Earle of Shrewisbury a Frenche bolle with a Couer Brandon
poz. . . . . xxxj oz qtr
76.204 To the Earle of Darby a guilt bolle with a Couer Partrige poz . . xxx oz di di qtr
76.205 To the Earle of Sussex Lord Chamberlen oone guilt Cup with a Couer
Brandon poz . . . . .xxxv oz iij qtr
76.206 To the Earle of Lincoln Lorde Admiral oone guilt Cup with a Couer
Partrige poz . . . . xxiiij oz iij qtr di
76.207 To the Earle of Rutland oone guilt bolle with a Couer Partrige poz . . . .xx oz qtr

76.208 To the Earle of Huntingdon oone guilt bolle with a Couer Partridge
poz . . . . .xx oz qtr

76.209 To the Earle of Warwike a payre of guilt Flagons Partrige poz—Cv oz
iij qtr And a Casting bottell Partrige poz – viij oz in toto . . . . .Cxiij oz qtr

76.210 To the Earle of Bedfourde oone guilt Cup with a Couer partrige
poz . . . . .xxxij oz qtr

76.211 To the Earle of Penbrouke oone guilt bolle with a Couer Brandon
poz . . . . xxx oz di di qtr

76.212 To the Earle of Northumberlande oone guilt bolle with a Couer partrige
poz . . . . xx oz

76.213 To the Earle of Southampton oone guilt bolle with a Couer partrige
poz . . . . xxix oz

76.214 To the Earle of Hereford oone guilt Cup with a Couer partrige poz xxj oz di qtr

76.215 To the Earle of Essex oone guilt bolle with a Couer partridge poz . . . . . . xxix oz

76.216 To the Vicount Mountague a payre of guilt bolles with a Couer partridge
poz . . . . xx oz di qtr

Duches Countes and Marques

76.217 To the Duches of Suffolke oone guilte Cup with a Couer partrige
poz . . . . xlj oz di qtr

76.218 To the Duches of Somerset oone guilt bolle with a Couer partridge
poz . . . . xxx oz di

76.219 To the Lady Marques of Wynchester oone guilt bolle with a Couer partrige poz
. . . . xx oz qtr di

76.220 To the Countes of Surrye a guilt bolle with a Couer partridge poz. . xij oz di qtr

76.221 To the Countes of Shrewisburye oone guilte bolle with a Couer partridge
poz . . . . .xxx oz iij qtr

76.222 To the Countes of Huntingdon Douger oone guilt bole with a Couer
partridge poz . . . . xv oz qrt di

76.223 To the Countes of Huntington oone guilt bolle with a Couer Partridge
poz . . . . xlj oz

76.224 To the Countes of Oxfourde oone guilt bolle with a Couer partridge
poz . . . . .xxj oz di di qtr

76.225 To the Countes of Warwike in guilt plate Brandon poz. . . . . xliij oz qtr

76.226 To the Countes of Sussex oone guilt bolle with a Couer Brandon
poz . . . . xxij oz iij qtr di

76.227 To the Countes of Penbrouke Douger oone guilt bolle with a Couer
Brandon poz . . . . xxvij oz di

76.228 To the Countes of Penbrouke oone guilt bolle with a Couer Partridge
poz . . . . .xx oz qtr

76.229 To the Countes of Bedfourde oone guilt Cup with a Couer partridge
poz . . . . .Lj oz di

76.230 To the Countes of Northumberland oone guilt Cup with a Couer Brandon
poz . . . . .xx oz iij qtr

76.231 To the Countes of Southampton a guilt Sault with a Couer Brandon
poz . . . . xx oz

76.232	To the Countes of Lincolne in guilt plate Brandon poz . . . . L oz di di qtr
76.233	To the Countes of Essex oone guilt bolle with a Couer Brandon poz . . . . xxix oz qtr di
76.234	To the Countes of Rutlande oone guilt Cup with a Couer Partridge poz . . xx oz
76.235	To the Countes of Kent Douger oone guilt bolle with a Couer Brandon poz . . . . .xx oz qtr
76.236	To the Countes Mongomore oone guilt Cup with a Couer Brandon poz . . . . xxx oz di di qtr
76.237	To Madamisell Bewforde Doughter to the said countes Mongomere a guilt bolle Partrige poz . . . . xx oz qtr di
76.238	To the Vicountes Mountague oone guilt Cup with a Couer Brandon poz . . . . .xx oz qtr

Busshoppes

76.239	To the Arche Busshop of Yorke oone guilt Cup with a Couer Brandon poz . . . . .xxxvij oz di qtr
76.240	To the Busshop of Durham oone guilt Cup with a Couer Brandon poz . . . . xxxvj oz iij qtr
76.241	To the Busshop of Elye thre guilt bolles with a Couer Brandon poz . . . . .xxxv oz
76.242	To the Busshop of London thre guilt bolles with a Couer Partridg poz . . . . xxxj oz iij qtr
76.243	To the Busshop of Winchester oone guilt Cup with a Couer Brandon poz . . . . xxxj oz qtr
76.244	To the Busshop of Salisbury oone guilt Salt with a Couer Brandon poz . . . . xxvij oz di
76.245	To the Busshop of Lyncolne oone guilt Salt with a Couer Brandon poz . . . . .xxxj oz di
76.246	To the Busshop of Worcester oone guilt bolle with a Couer Brandon poz . . . . xxxj oz qtr
76.247	To the Busshop of Norwiche oone guilt Salt with a Couer Brandon poz . . . . xxiij oz qtr
76.248	To the Busshop of Lichfelde and Couentrie oone guilt bolle Brandon poz . . . . xx oz di qtr
76.249	To the Busshop of Herfourde oone guilt Tankerde brandon poz . . xvij oz qtr di
76.250	To the Busshop of St Dauies oone guilt Salte with a Couer Brandon poz . . . . xvij oz iij qtr
76.251	To the Busshop of Exetor oone guilt Salte Brandon poz . . . . xvj oz qtr di
76.252	To the Busshop of Bathe oone Hans potte guilt Brandon poz . . . . . xvj oz di qtr
76.253	To the Busshop of Chester oone guilt bolle with a Couer Brandon poz . . . . xvij oz iij qtr di
76.254	To the Busshop of Peterborowe oone guilt Stope partridg poz . . . . xvij oz iij qtr
76.255	To the Busshop of Gloster oone Hans pott guilt Brandon poz . . . xix oz di di qtr
76.256	To the Busshop of Chitchester oone guilt Stope partridg poz . . . . xviij oz

Lordes

76.257 To the Lorde Burgaveny oone guilt Sault with a Couer partridg poz
.... xj oz di qtr
76.258 To the Lorde Howarde in guilt plate Partridg poz .... Ciiij oz
76.259 To the Lorde Lumley oone guilt Cup Brandon poz .... xx oz iij qtr di
76.260 To the Lorde Cobham oone guilt Cup Brandon poz .... xx oz iij qtr di
76.261 To the Lorde Riche oone guilt Cup with a Couer Brandon poz .... xx oz qtr
76.262 To the Lorde Northe oone guilt Sault with a Couer Brandon poz ..... xx oz qtr
76.263 To the Lorde Hunsdon in guilt plate Partridg poz .... xxxv oz
76.264 To the Lorde Staffourde oone guilt bolle with a Couer Brandon poz ... xx oz di
76.265 To the Lorde Paget oone guilt bolle with a Couer Brandon poz .... xx oz qtr
76.266 To the Lorde Taulbot oone guilt Sault Partridg poz .... xj oz qtr
76.267 To the Lorde Sturton oone guilt bolle with a Couer Brandon poz
.... xviij oz iij qtr
76.268 To the Lorde Darcie of Chitchey oone guilt Tankerd Brandon
poz .... xix oz di di qtr
76.269 To the Lorde Shandows oone guilt Tankerd Brandon poz......... xiij oz di qtr
76.270 To the Lorde Buchurst oone guilt bolle with a Couer Partridg poz.... xij oz qtr
76.271 To the Lorde Compton oone guilt bolle with a Couer Brandon
poz .... xx oz di qtr
76.272 To the Lorde Ricott oone guilt Tankerde brandon poz .... xx oz qtr di
76.273 To the Lorde Strainge oone guilt Sault partrid poz .... x oz iij qtr

Baronesses

76.274 To the Lady Burgaueny oone guilt Cup with a Couer Partridg
poz .... xj oz di qtr
76.275 To the Lady Burghly oone guilt Cup with a Couer Partridg poz
.... xxv oz di di qtr
76.276 To the Lady Cobham oone guilt Cup with a Couer Partridg poz .... Lj oz
76.277 To the Lady Hunsdon in guilt plate partridg poz........... xxvij oz di di qtr
76.278 To the Lady Howarde Douger oone guilt Cup with a Couer Brandon
poz .... xxj oz di
76.279 To the Lady Howarde Junior in guilt plate Brandon and Partridg
poz .... xxiiij oz di
76.280 To the Lady Paget Care oone guilt Cup with a Couer Partridg poz .. xxvj oz qtr
76.281 To the Lady Paget the Lorde Pagetes wif oone guilt Tankerd Brandon
poz .... xix oz qtr
76.282 To the Lady Shandoies Douger oone hans potte guilt Brandon poz
.... xx oz iij qtr
76.283 To the Lady Shandoies Junior oone guilt bolle Partridg poz......... xij oz qtr
76.284 To the Lady Barkley oone guilt Cup with a Couer Brandon poz ...... xx oz qtr
76.285 To the Lady Dakers of the South oone guilt bolle with a Couer Brandon
poz .... xvj oz
76.286 To the Lady Taileboyes oone Hans potte guilt Partridg poz .... xx oz
76.287 To the Lady Chaney oone guilt bolle Partridg poz............... xxx oz iij qtr

76.288 To the Lady St John Bletzo oone guilt bolle with a Couer Partridg
        poz . . . . xvij oz iij qtr
76.289 To the Lady Taulbot oone guilt Salt with a Couer Brandon poz . . . . . . xiiij oz di
76.290 To the Lady Buckhurst oone guilt bolle with a Couer Partridg poz . . . xij oz qtr
76.291 To the Lady Norres oone Hans potte guilt Brandon poz . . . . xx oz di
76.292 To the Lady Cromwell oone guilt bolle with a Couer Partridg poz . . . . xij oz qtr
76.293 To the Lady Sheffilde oone Hans potte guilt Brandon poz . . . . xviij oz
76.294 To the Lady Gray of Pirgo oone guilt bolle with a Couer partridg
        poz . . . . xij oz qtr di
76.295 To the Lady Russell oone Spoute potte guilt Partridg poz . . . . xxij oz di qtr
76.296 To the Lady Willobie oone guilt bolle with a Couer Partridg poz . . . . . xij oz qtr
76.297 To the Lady Mountjoye oone guilt Cup with a Couer Partridg poz
        . . . . xxxiiij oz di di qtr
76.298 To the Lady Mary Veare oone guilt Cup with a Couer Partridg
        poz . . . . xviij oz di qtr

Ladies

76.299 To the Lady Mary Sidney oone Double bolle guilt Partridg poz . . . . . . xxxj oz di
76.300 To the Lady Staffourde in guilt plate Brandon poz . . . . .xxx oz qtr
76.301 To the Lady Carowe in guilt plate Partridg poz . . . . .xxxv oz
76.302 To the Lady Wodhouse oone guilt bolle with a Couer partridg
        poz . . . . xxiiij oz qtr di
76.303 To the Lady Cheeke oone guilt bolle with a Couer Brandon poz . . .xxv oz di qtr
76.304 To the Lady Butler oone guilt bolle Brandon poz . . . . xvj oz qtr di
76.305 To the Lady Pawlet oone guilt bolle with a Couer Brandon poz . . . . xij oz qtr di
76.306 To the Lady Gresham oone oone [sic] guilt Tankerde Brandon poz . xx oz qtr di
76.307 To the Lady Cromwell Sir Henry Cromwelles wif oone guilt bolle
        Partridg poz . . . . xij oz qtr
76.308 To the Lady Ratlif oone guilt Sault Partridg poz . . . . .xiij oz di di qtr
76.309 To the Lady Frogmorton oone guilt Tankerde Partridg poz . . . . . . xxiij oz qtr di
76.310 To the Lady Woolforde oone guilt Tankerd Brandon poz . . . . xix oz di qtr
76.311 To the Lady Marven oone guilt bolle with a couer Brandon poz
        . . . . xiiij oz di qtr

Knightes

76.312 To Sir Fraunces Knoles Knight Threasoror of Thousholde oone guilt
        Cup with a Couer Partridg poz . . . . xxv oz di
76.313 To Sir James Croughtes Comptrollor of the same oone guilt Cup with a
        couer Brandon poz . . . . .xxv oz qtr di
76.314 To Sir Thomas Smyth her majesties Secretarye oone guilt Cup with a
        couer Brandon poz . . . . xxiiij oz di di qtr
76.315 To Mr Fraunces Walsingham esquire also Secretarye a guilt Cup with a
        couer Brandon poz . . . . .Lxij oz di

76.316	To Sir Rauf Sadler Chauncellor of the Duchye oone guilt bolle with a couer Partridg poz . . . . xxx oz di
76.317	To Sir Walter Mildemaye Chancellor of the Exchequer a guilt Cup partridg poz . . . . xxvj oz di qtr
76.318	To Sir William Cordall Mr of the Rolles oone guilt Bolle Brandon poz . . . . xxij oz
76.319	To Sir Christopher Haydon oone guilt Salte with a Couer Partridg poz . . . . xx oz
76.320	To Sir William Damsell Receuor of the Court of wardes oone guilt Cup Partridg poz . . . . .xx oz iij qtr
76.321	To Sir Gawen Carowe in guilt plate partridge poz . . . . xxxiiij oz di di qtr
76.322	To Sir Henry Cromwell oone guilt Tankerde Brandon poz . . . . xix oz di
76.323	To Sir Henry Lee thre guilt bolles with a Couer Brandon poz. . . . . . . xlix oz di
76.324	To Sir Thomas Gresham oone Hans potte guilt Brandon poz. . . . . xix oz di
76.325	To Sir Owen Hopton Leuetennant of the Tower oone guilt Bolle Partridg poz . . . . xxj oz iij qtr di
76.326	To Sir John Thynne oone guilt Sault with a Couer Partridg poz . . . . xj oz di
76.327	To Sir Guilbert Dethycke chefe king at Armes oone guilt Sault partridg poz . . . . xiij oz di di qtr

Gentlewomen

76.328	To Maistres Blaunche Parre nine Spones Brandon poz . . . . xviij oz iij qtr
76.329	To Mrs Fraunces Howarde oone guilt Saulte with a Couer Brandon poz . . . . xiij oz di qtr
76.330	To Mrs Elizabeth Knowles oone guilt Tankerd Brandon poz . . . . xv oz di di qtr
76.331	To Mrs Hennage oone guilt Cup Partridg poz . . . . xx oz di
76.332	To Mrs Edmondes oone guilt bolle with a Couer partridg poz . . . . xv oz
76.333	To Mrs Abingdon vij guilt Spones Brandon poz . . . . .xvij oz qtr
76.334	To Mrs Skidmor oone guilt Cup Partridg poz . . . . xv oz
76.335	To Mrs Eliz Drurie oone guilt Tankerd Brandon poz . . . . xvj oz qtr
76.336	To Mrs Katherine Paston oone guilt Tankerd Brandon poz . . . . xv oz
76.337	To Mrs Jane Brisselles oone guilt Saulte Brandon poz. . . . . xij oz di
76.338	To Mrs Bridges oone guilt Cup Brandon poz. xiij oz di
76.339	To Mrs Caue oone guilt bolle with a Couer Brandon poz . . . . xv oz di di qtr
76.340	To Mrs Mountagewe a guilt Tankerd Brandon poz . . . . xvj oz qtr
76.341	To Mrs Dane oone guilt Tankerd Brandon poz . . . . xiiij oz di di qtr
76.342	To Mrs Digbye one guilt Cup without a Couer Brandon poz . . . . .xv oz qtr
76.343	To Mrs Marbery one guilt Cup with a Couer Brandon poz. . . . . .xv oz iij qtr
76.344	To Mrs Tounsend oone guilt bolle with a Couer Brandon poz . . . xxviij oz qtr di
76.345	To Mrs Allenn oone guilt bolle with a Couer Partridg poz . . . . xij oz qtr di
76.346	To Mrs Lichfelde oone guilt bolle with a Couer Partridg poz . . . . xvj oz qtr
76.347	To Mrs Hampton oone guilt bolle with a Couer Brandon poz . . . . vij oz qtr
76.348	To Mrs Mary Sidney oone guilt bolle with a Couer Brandon poz . . . . xiij oz di di qtr
76.349	To Mrs Baptest oone guilt Cup with a Couer Partridg poz . . . . xvj oz
76.350	To Mrs Sackford oone guilt bolle with a Couer Partridge poz . . . . xxij oz

76.351	To Mrs Snowe oone guilt Salte Brandon poz	xx oz iij qtr di
76.352	To Mrs Weste thre guilt bolles with a Couer Partridg poz	xij oz qtr di
76.353	To Mrs Croxson oone guilt Salt Brandon poz	ix oz di qtr
76.354	To Mrs Wingfeld oone guilt bolle with a Couer Partridg poz	xij oz qtr di
76.355	To Mrs Smithson late Laundres oone guilt Tankerd Brandon poz	vij oz di qtr
76.356	To Mrs Amy Shelton oone guilt Cup Brandon poz	x oz di qtr
76.357	To Mrs Note oone guilt bolle with a Couer Partridg poz	xiij oz
76.358	To Mrs Barlye oone guilt Cup Partridg poz	xij oz di
76.359	To Mrs Huggens oone guilt Bolle Partridg poz	xx oz
76.360	To Mrs Laundres Twist thre guilt Spones Brandon poz	iiij oz qtr
76.361	To Lucretia thre guilt Spones Brandon poz	vj oz di qtr
76.362	To Lauina Terling thre guilt Spones Brandon poz	vj oz di di qtr
76.363	To Ipolita Late thre guilt Spones Brandon poz	iiij oz di

Chaplaine

76.364	To Arche Deacone Carowe oone guilt Cup Brandon poz	xxij oz qtr

Free guiftes to the Maides of Honour

76.365	To the Lady Susan Bowser oone guilt bolle with a Couer Brandon poz	x oz qtr
76.366	To Mrs Mary Ratlif oone guilt bolle with a Couer Partridg poz	x oz di qtr
76.367	To Mrs Ellen Bridges oone guilt bolle with a Couer Patridg poz	x oz di qtr
76.368	To Mrs Katerin Howarde oone guilt bolle with a Couer Partridg poz	x oz qtr di
76.369	To Mrs Elizabeth Garrett oone guilt bolle with a Couer Partridg poz	x oz qtr
76.370	To Mrs Mary Borowe oone guilt Bolle Brandon poz	x oz qtr
76.371	To Mrs Hide mother oone guilt Cup with a Couer Brandon poz	xiij oz

Gentlemen

76.372	To Maister Hattone Captaine of the Garde in guilt Plate Partridg poz	CCiiij^{xx} xij oz
76.373	To Mr Hennage Threasuror of the Chamber in guilt plate Partridg poz	xlviij oz
76.374	To Mr Stanhop oone guilt Tankerd Brandon poz	xxj oz di
76.375	To Mr William Drurie oone guilt Saulte with a Couer Brandon poz	xviij oz
76.376	To Mr Robinsen oone guilt Tankerde Brandon poz	xxj oz di qtr
76.377	To Mr Harington thre guilt bolles with a Couer Keele poz	xl oz
76.378	To Mr Cleere oone guilt bolle with a Couer Brandon poz	xxj oz qtr di
76.379	To Mr Basshe oone guilt Bolle Partridge poz	xvj oz qtr
76.380	To Captain Leighton oone guilt Cup with a Couer Partridg poz	xvj oz di di qtr
76.381	To Capitaine Horsey oone guilt bolle with a Couer Brandon poz	xxij oz
76.382	To Benedik Spenolla in guilt plate Brandon and Partridg poz	Lxxvij oz qtr
76.383	To Smith Costomer oone guilt Cup with a Couer Partridg poz	xv oz
76.384	To Allen oone guilt bolle with a Couer Brandon poz	xij oz
76.385	To Alphontious oone guilt Sault with a Couer Brandon poz	ix oz iij qtr di

76.386   To Laneson oone guilt Cup with a couer Brandon poz . . . . xxij oz di

76.387   To Doctor Hewike oone guilt Tankerd Brandon poz. . . . . xiiij oz iij qtr

76.388   To Doctor Maisters oone guilt bolle with owte a Couer Partridg
           poz . . . . .xiij oz qtr di

76.389   To Doctor Julio oone guilt Cup with a Couer Brandon poz . . . . xiiij oz

76.390   To John Hemingway Potecarie oone guilt Cup with owte a couer
           Brandon poz . . . . vij oz di qtr

76.391   To John Riche Potecarie oone guilt bolle with owte a Couer Partridg
           poz . . . . vij oz di

76.392   To William Huggens two guilt Bolles with a Couer partridg poz . . . . .xxx oz qtr

76.393   To Smithsone Mr Cooke oone guilt Tankerd Brandon poz. . . . . .viij oz

76.394   To John Dudley Sergeaunt of the pastrie oone guilt Sault Brandon
           poz . . . . iiij oz iij qtr

76.395   To Mark Anthony oone guilt Sault partridg poz . . . . v oz di

76.396   To Ambrose Lupo oone guilt Sault partridg poz . . . . v oz di

76.397   To Petrucho Vboldino thre guilt Spones Brandon poz . . . . iiij oz di

Freguiftes

76.398   To Sir George Howarde gent vsher of the previe Chamber a guilt bolle
           Brandon poz . . . . xij oz di

76.399   To Mr John Asteley Mr and Threasouror of her Maties Juelles and plate
           a guilt Cup partridg poz . . . . .xviij oz iij qtr di

76.400   To Mr Thomas Asteley grome of the saide previe Chamber a guilt cup
           Partridg poz. . . . . viij oz iij qtr di

76.401   To Mr Care also a grome of the said previe Chamber oone guilt Sault
           Brandon poz . . . . viij oz iij qtr

76.402   To Mr Sackforde likewise a grome predicto oone guilt Cup Partridg
           poz . . . . viij oz iij qtr di

76.403   To Mr Baptest also grome &c oone guilt bolle Brandon poz. . . . . viij oz iij qtr di

76.404   To Middlemor also grome &c oone guilt Sault Partridge poz . . . . .viij oz di

76.405   To Kneuett also oone of the gromes of the same Chamber a guilt Cup
           Brandon poz . . . . viij oz iij qtr di

76.406   To Mr Gorges grome also &c oone guilt Cruse Partridg poz. . . . . viij oz di di qtr

76.407   To Killegrewe also a grome &c oone guilt Sault Brandon poz. . . . . .viij oz di

76.408   To Rauf Hoope yeoman of the Roobes oone guilt Cup Partridg poz
           . . . . xij oz iij qtr di

76.409   To Nicholas Bristowe Clerke of her Maties Juelles and plate oone guilt
           Cruse par poz. . . . . x oz iij qtr di

76.410   To John Pigeon oone of the yeoman of the same Office oone guilt Cruse
           Br poz. . . . . x oz iij qtr di

76.411   To Stephen Fulwell oone other yeoman of the same Office a guilt Cruse
           Br poz. . . . . x oz iij qtr di

76.412   To Richard Asteley grome of the same Office oone guilt Cruse Brandon
           poz . . . . x oz iij qtr di

Summa totalis of all / the plate geuon in maner
and Fourme aforesaide is : . . . . v m Cix oz qrter di

Guiftes geuon by her saide Matie
and Deliuerid at sundry tymes in maner and
Fourme folowing. That is to saye

76.413   Mounseur de la Chastre

First Geuon by her saide maiestie and deliuerid the vij of Apriell Anno
xvij Regni sui to Mounseur de la Chastre Ambassator From the
Frenche king oone Cheine of golde poz – iiij^{xx} xix oz and fyve
graines being of the goodnes of twentie and oone karrettes and thre
graines bought of the saide Robt Brandon and Affabell Partridge and
paide for by spetiall warrant . . . . .iiij^{xx} xix oz v graines golde

76.414   The erle of oxfordes Doughter

Item more geuon by her saide Matie and Deliuerid the xiiijth of July
Anno pred at the Christeing of the Earle of Oxfourdes Doughter
oone Basone and a Laire guilt poz -- Ciij oz di qtr / And one Standing
Cup guilt with a Couer of Flaundors making poz – Liij oz di both
bought of the said Robt Brandon in toto . . . . Clvij oz di di qtr

76.415   Mrs Weston

Item more geuon by her Matie and Deliuered the xvjth of July Anno
predicto To Mrs Westone Late wif vnto Judge westone at whose house
her Matie Laye going on her progres the same somer oone Cup with a
Couer of siluer guilt bought of the said Partridg . . . . xxvij oz iij qtr di

76.416   The Lo Barcleis Chylde

Item more gevon by her maiestie and Deliuered the xxth of July Anno
pred at the Christeing of the Lorde Barcleyes Childe oone Basone
and a Laire guilt bought of the saide Affabell Partridg poz . . . . .Lxvj oz

76.417   Mr Wainans Childe

Item more gevon by her saide Matie and Deliuerid the saide xxth of
July Anno pred at the Christeing of Mr Wainmans Childe oone Cup
with a Couer of siluer guilt bought of the saide Partridg poz
. . . . xxiij oz iij qtr

76.418   Monseur Boyschotte

Item more gevon by her maiestie and deliuered the vijth of September
Anno pred to Monsieur Boish Ambasators resiant from the Lowe
countrie of Flaunders oone Cheyne of golde being of the goodnes
of xxj karrettes two graines and a haulf bout of the saide Brandon
and Partridg poz . . . . .xlv oz qtr   j penie weite   golde

71.419   To Monsieur de la Mothe

Item more gevon by her Matie and deliuerid the xiiijth of September
Anno pred to Mons[ieur] De la Mothe Late Ambassator Leger
From the Frenche king at his Departure owte of Englande oone
Basone and a Laire guilt Partridge poz—Cxvij oz / oone guilt Cuppe

with a Couer Partridg poz—Cxxiij oz iij qrt / oone other guilt Cup
with a Couer Brandon poz—Ciiij^{xx} viij oz qrt / oone paire of guilt
pottes Brandon poz—Cliij oz qrt / oone paire of guilt Flagons
Brandon poz—Cxxiij oz di / Thre guilt bolles with a Couer Par poz
—xxx oz di di qrt / Two guilt Laires Partridg poz—Cl oz / two guilt
Saultes with a Couer Brandon poz—xxxj oz di / one Basone and a
laire guilt Brandon poz—Clxiij oz / oone paire of guilt pottes
Partridg poz—Cxxiij oz qrt di / oone peire of guilt Flagons Partridg
poz—xxij oz qrt di / Thre guilt Bolles with a Couer Brandon poz—
xlix oz iij qtr di / oone paire of guilt Laires Brandon poz—Cxlij
oz / two guilt Cuppes partridge poz—lxj oz di qrt / And two guilt
Saultes with a Couer Partridg poz – xliij oz qrt in toto
. . . . .M v^{c} lxiij oz iij qrt di

76.420   to the Lo Russelles Chylde
Item more gevon by her saide Matie and deliuered the xxvijth of
October Anno pred oone guilt Cuppe with a Couer at the Christeing
of the lorde Russelles Doughter bought of Affabell Partridg poz
. . . . .Lxxviij oz di di qrt

76.421   to Therle of Rutlandes Chylde
Item more gevon by her Matie and deliuered the vijth of January Anno
xviij at the Christeing of the Earle of Rutlandes chylde oone paire of
guilte pottes bought of the saide Partridg poz . . . . Lxvij oz qrt

76.422   to Monsieur de la Mothe
Item more gevon by her Matie and deliuered the vijth of February Anno
xviij pred[ict]o to monsieur de la mothe Ambassator from the Frenche
king oone Chaine of golde being of the goodnes of xxij karrettes and
oone qrt of a graine bought of the saide Robt Brandon and Affabell
Partridg poz . . . . Lij oz qrt   golde

76.423   to monseur de la Port
Item more gevon by her saide Matie the saide Daie and yere to
Monsieur de la Port likewise Ambassator of Fraunce oone Chaine
of golde being of the goodnes of xxij karrettes and qrt of a graine
bought as afore said poz . . . . .xlj oz di ij d wait & ij graines   golde

76.424   Mr Marbery
Item more gevon by her saide Matie and deliuered the first of Marche
anno xviij Anno pd to Mr John Marberie esquire being her highnes
godsone At his mariage oone guilt bolle with a Couer bought of the
saide Affabell Partridg poz . . . . xxxiij oz qtr

76.425   To the Gouerner of Anwarp
Item more Gevon by her saide Matie and deliuered the xxiijth of March
afore saide To the Gouernor of Anwarpe Oone Cheine of golde made
of two peces wherof thone pece poz – xlij oz di being of the goodnes
of xxj karrittes two graines di / And threst being of the goodnes of xxj
karrittes thre graines and a qrter of a graine bought of the saide Robt
Brandon and Affabell Partridge poz togethers
. . . . .iiij^{xx} j oz iij qtr di   ij d wait   golde

Elizabeth R
[sign manual]

J Asteley
Ex[aminatio] per
Bristow
J Pigeon
Ste Fulwell
Rich. Asteley

Anno Regni Regine
Elizabeth decimo nono

Newyeres giuft giuen to the Quene Her
maiestie by those persones whose names hereafter
ensue the First of January the yere aforesade

Elizabeth R
[sign manual]

77.1   By the Lady Margret Leneox a dublet and kyrtell of carnation Satten
enbrawdred with golde lopes with alace of Fyne golde and spangells
>> Delyuered in charge to Rauf Hoope yoman of the robes

77.2   By the Lady Mary Gray a cusshion of crymson Satten alouer enbrawdred
with pasmayn Lace of venice golde the same being a swete bag to put the
quene Matie night gere in and two pere of garters
>> Delyuered to Mrs Skydmore

77.3   By the Lady Margret Countes of Derby a night gowne of Murry Satten
enbrawdred with venice golde and sylke of sundry colors
>> dd to Rauf Hoope by Charles Smith

77.4   By Sir Nicholas Bacon knight Lorde keper of the greate Seale of Inglande
in golde. . . . . xiij li vj s viij d

77.5   By the Lorde Burleigh Lorde High Treausoror of Inglande in golde . . . . . . xx li

77.6   By the Lorde Marques of winchester in gold . . . . xx li
>> dd to henry Sakford grome of the Chamber

Earles

77.7   By therle of Leycetor Mr of the Horses a collor of golde cont xiij peces
with great Emeraldes xiij peces with Troches of perle v in euery troche
and in euery pece iiij small Rubies
>> Delyuered to the Lady Haward

77.8   By therle of Arondell in apurse of Lether in golde . . . . xxx li

77.9   By therle of Sussex Lorde chamberleyn in golde . . . . xx li
>> dd to henry Sakford

77.10   By therle of Surr[ey] a Juell of golde being an oyster with iiij small Rubies
one Diamond & a ophal
>> the Juewel to the Lady Haward

77.11   By therle of Shrewesbury in golde . . . . xx li

77.12   By therle of Darby in golde. . . . . xx li

77.13   By therle of Lincoln Lorde Admirall of Inglande in golde . . . . x li
>> dd to henry Sakford

77.14   By therle of Warwyk Six Dosen of buttons of golde, whereof thre Dosen
being men / and thre Dosen Fysshes in abox couered with black vellat
and edged with pasmayne of Syluer

77.15   By therl of Bedford a Juell of golde being a Dove wherein is thre Emeraldes
the biggest of them pendant without Foyle two table rubyes two table
Diamondes & threst garneshed with iiij small Rubyes

77.16   By therle of Kyldare apeir of Braselettes of golde cont xx peces of gold
goldesmythesworke ennamuled whereof x peces in euery pece arubye
and x more peces in euery of them two perles

            dd to the La Haward

77.17   By therle of Rutlande in golde . . . . x li

77.18   By therle of Huntingdon in golde. . . . . x li

77.19   By therle of Penbrooke in golde . . . . xx li

77.20   By therle of Northumberlande in golde . . . . x li

            dd to henry Sakford

77.21   By therle of Hertf[ord] apeir of Braselettes of golde being xx peces
whereof xvj set with black stones and iiij with small perle v in a troche

77.22   By therle of Ormonde a feyre Juell of golde with iij personages in it standing
vnder a tree garneshed with small Diamondes in the myddes is a large
Ruby and bynethe it is a les rock ruby with aragged perle pendant

            dd to La Haward

77.23   By therle of Southampton in golde. . . . . xx li

77.24   By the vicounte Mountague in golde . . . . x li

            dd to henry Sakford

77.25   By the vicounte Gormarstone a cheyne of golde garneshed with small
perle poz. . . . . xj oz di qrt

            dd to the Lady Haward

Duchesses, Marquesses, Countesses

77.26   By the Duches of Suff[olk] one pece of murry vellat cont . . . . xxj yerdes qrt

            dd to Rauf hoope

77.27   By the Duches of Somerset in golde. . . . . xiij li vj s viij d

            dd to h Sakford

77.28   By the Lady marques of Northampton avale of white Networke set
alouer with Spangilles

            dd to Mrs Abingdon

77.29   By the Lady marques of Winchester Dowager in golde. . . . . x li

77.30   By the Countes of Surr[ey] in golde . . . . v li

            dd to henry Sakford

77.31   By the countes of Shrewesbury a gowne of tawny Satten Leyed with
apasmayn lace of venice golde and buttons of the same lyned with
yelow Serceonet

            dd to Rauf hope

77.32   By the countes of Sussex in golde. . . . . x li

77.33   By the countes of Huntingdon in golde . . . . viij li

            dd to henry Sakford

77.34   By the countes of Lincoln a Carcanet and apeir of Brascelettes of golde
set with Amatistes and camew heddes the carcanet cont xviij peces and
the Braslettes xvj peces

77.35 By the countes of Warwyk thre Dosen of buttons of golde being
Acornes

dd to Lady Haward

77.36 By the countes of Bedford a feyer foreparte of akyrtill of purple Satten
alouer enbrawdred with venice golde cut Diamonde fashon drawen owte
with Lawnde set with sede perle / and lyned with yelow taphata

dd to Rauf hoope

77.37 By the countes of Northumberland in golde . . . . x li
77.38 By the countes of Southampton in golde . . . . x li
77.39 By the countes of Rutlande in golde. . . . . x li

dd to henry Sakford

77.40 By the countes of Essex the foreparte and boddyes of akyrtill of Asshcollor
couered with a Net of sylke and golde Lyned with crymsen serceonet

dd to Rauf hope

77.41 By the countes of kent avale of white networke pyncked and set with
Spangilles of Siluer

dd to Mrs Abington

77.42 By the countes of kent Dowager two cusshyn clothes of fyne hollande
with borders of fyne open worke lyned with murrey Taphata and a small
swete bag of purple Satten enbrawdred with venice golde and set with
seede perle

dd to Mrs Skydmore

77.43 By the countes Dowager of Penbroke in golde. . . . . xij li

dd to henry Sakford

77.44 By the countes of Oxford a Juell being an Agathed garnesshed with golde
/ and a lawrell garlonde garnesshed abought with Sperckes of Rubyes
and apendant with viij Sparckes of rubys & ahophall in the mydes

dd to the Lady Haward

77.45 By the vicecountes Mountague in golde . . . . x li

dd to henry Sakford

Busshops

77.46 By the Arche Busshopp of Canterbury in golde. . . . . xl li
77.47 By the Busshopp of Elye in golde . . . . xxx li
77.48 By the Busshopp of London in golde . . . . xx li
77.49 By the Busshopp of Winchester in golde . . . . xx li
77.50 By the Busshopp of Salisbury in golde . . . . xx li
77.51 By the Busshopp of Lincolne in golde . . . . xx li
77.52 By the Busshopp of Norwiche in golde . . . . xx li
77.53 By the Busshopp of Lychfild & Coventry in golde & siluer . . . . . . xiij li vj s viij d
77.54 By the Busshopp of Rochester in golde . . . . x li
77.55 By the Busshopp of Hereforde in golde . . . . x li
77.56 By the Busshopp of St Davyes in golde . . . . x li
77.57 By the Busshopp of Exetor in golde . . . . x li
77.58 By the Busshopp of Bathe in golde. . . . . x li
77.59 By the Busshopp of Chester in golde . . . . x li

77.60	By the Busshopp of Peterborow in golde	x li
77.61	By the Busshopp of Gloster in golde	x li
77.62	By the Busshopp of Chitchester in golde	x li

dd to h Sakford

Lordes

77.63 By the Lorde Howarde a Gowne with a Trayn of Carnation Cloth of
siluer layed with a Passamayne of golde and blacke silke

77.64 By the Lorde of Hunsdon a Doublet & a foreparte of a kirtel of Mury
Satten embrawdored allouer with white worke with a passamaine of
venice golde

dd to Rauf hoope

77.65 By the Lorde Burgaveny in golde . . . . v li

dd to henry Sakford

77.66 By Henry Hawarde a Doublet of Orenge collor satten allouer wrought
with venice siluer with buttons of Like siluer Lyned with Asshe collor
serceonett

dd to Rauf hoope

77.67	By the Lorde Ryche in golde	x li
77.68	By the Lorde Darcye of Chitchey in golde	x li
77.69	By the Lorde Shandowes in golde & siluer	vj li xiij s iiij d
77.70	By the Lorde Buchurste in golde	v li
77.71	By the Lorde Northe in golde	x li
77.72	By the Lorde Pagett in golde	x li
77.73	By the Lorde Stafforde in golde	x li
77.74	By the Lorde Compton in golde	x li
77.75	By the Lorde Rycott in golde	x li

dd to henry Sakford

77.76 By the Lorde Cobham aforeparte of a kyrtle of white satten allouer embr
with Flowers of venice golde & a fayre border of the same stuff Lyned
with whyte serceonett

dd to Rauf hoope

77.77	By the Lorde Lumley in golde	x li
77.78	By the Lorde Wharton in golde	x li

dd to henry Sakford

77.79 By the Lord Henry Seymer a Jug of Chrystall garn with siluer guilt with a
phenix in the topp with in a Crowne

dd in charge to Jo Asteley Esquier Mr and Treausoror of the Juelles &c

Baronesses

77.80 By Lady Barrones Burleigh a Juell of golde being an Agath of Nepthew
with vj Rubyes ij small Diamond & iij corsse perles Neptune

dd to the Lady Haward

77.81 By the Lady Bvrgaveny in golde . . . . v li

dd to h Sakford

77.82   By the Lady Howarde a frenche kyrtle with bodyes & trayne of Mvry
          Clothe of golde Layed with a passamayne of golde and siluer
77.83   By the Lady Cobham a Pettycoate of yellow satten Layed with siluer lace
          lyke waves and bordred bout the skirte with the same lyned with blew
          serceonete
                                                                    dd to Rauf hoope
77.84   By the Lady Hunsdon in golde . . . . x li
77.85   By the Lady Barkeley in golde . . . . x li
                                                                    dd to henry Sakford
77.86   By the Lady Dakers of the southe a Pettycote of peche collor
                                                                    dd to Raff hoope
77.87   By the Lady Taylboyes in golde. . . . . x li
77.88   By the Lady Howarde Dowager in golde . . . . x li
                                                                    dd to henry Sakford
77.89   By the [Lady] Shandowes Dowager a peire of blacke Sipers allouer trailed
          with buttons of nedle worke of golde and silk cont . . . . v yardes qrt di
                                                                    dd to Rauf Hoope
77.90   By the Lady Shandowes Junior a vaile of networke allouer wrought with
          white worke
                                                                    dd to Mrs Abingdon
77.91   By the Lady St John Bletzo in golde . . . . x li
                                                                    dd to henry Sakford
77.92   By the Lady Paget Care a sute of lawne allouer wrought with blacke &
          white cont v pieces
                                                                    dd to Mrs Skydmore
77.93   By the Lady Paget the Lorde Paggettes wief a peice of Crymsen Satten
          striped withe siluer & golde cont viij yardes .viij yardes
                                                                    dd to Rauf hoope
77.94   By the Lady Cheyney a Petycoat of Clothe of siluer with v yardes of
          grene satten embr with knottes and purles of Damask golde & sett
          with seede perle & frenged withe golde siluer and silke and lyned withe
          Crymsen Taphata
77.95   By the Lady Audley a doblet of Asshecollor Satten allouer embr with a
          smale cordaunt of venice golde with xiiij like pointes with small
          Aglettes of golde & lyned with yellow serceonet
                                                                    dd to Rauf hoope
77.96   By the Lady Buckhurste in golde . . . . v li
77.97   By the Lady Norres in golde . . . . x li
                                                                    dd to henry Sakford
77.98   By the Lady Cromwell the lord Cromwelles wiefe a Bande & peyre of
          Ruffes of fyne white networke
                                                                    dd to Jane Brisselles
77.99   By the Lady Sheffeilde a Doblet of Asshecollor layed ouer with net worke
          of blacke silke florisshed ouer with buttons or roses of venice golde
                                                                    dd to Rauf hoope

77.100 By the Lady Mary Veere a Cusshion Clothe of fyne holland allouer
wrought with golde siluer & silke of sondry collores edgid with a
passamaine of venice golde

dd to Mrs Skydmore

77.101 By the Lady Willowby of warwickeshere a faire smocke of fine holland
wrought with black silke edged with a passamaine of venice golde the
sleves allouer wroughte with black silke

dd to Mrs Skydmore

77.102 By the Lady Lattemer a Combecase of clothe of golde very feyre embr &
sett with seede perle full garnisshed with Combes glasses & other
Instrumentes of siluer beinge vj the Corners of the same case sett with
sparkes of Emeraldes and Rubyes in Collettes of golde

dd to Mrs Abingdon

Ladyes

77.103 By the Lady Mary Sydney two sootes of Ruffes of lawne thone white
worke set with small seede perle & spangles of golde Thother cut worke
with spangles of siluer & a sweate bag of purple satten embr wyth venice
golde

dd to Jane Brisselles

77.104 By the Lady Stafforde a nighte gowne of blacke tufte taphata edged with
passamayne lace of siluer The sleves laid thicke with the same Lace &
furred thorough with blacke Coneye

dd to Rauf hoope

77.105 By the Lady Carew a Cusshion clothe of holland wrought with snayles
& butterflyes of black silke

dd to Mrs Skydmore

77.106 By the Lady Woodhouse a Dublet of mvrrey networke with a passamayne
Lace of golde & siluer

dd to Rauf hoope

77.107 By the Lady Mary Seymer iiij^or peces of Ruffes of Camerycke faire
wrought with open worke edgid wyth purles and spangles

with the La Drury

77.108 By the Lady Cheeke a Toothe & Eare picke of golde beinge a Dolphin
enamvled with a perle pendaunt with xvj smale Rubyes beinge but
sparckes & v sparkes of Dyamondes

dd to the Lady Howard

77.109 By the Lady Butler in golde . . . . .vj li

dd to henry Sakford

77.110 By the Lady Drury a Dublett of blacke satten cut with a passamayne lace
& buttons of venice golde & the saide buttons & loopes set with seade
perle lyned with white serceonett

dd to Rauf hoope

77.111 By the Lady Pawlett in golde. . . . . v li
77.112 By the Lady Gressham in golde . . . . x li

77.113　By the Lady Cromwell Sir Henryes wife in golde . . . . v li
　　　　　　　　　　　　　　　　　　　　　　　　　　dd to henry Sakford
77.114　By the Lady Ratlyff two sutes of Ruffes thone blacke thother white Six
　　　　handkerchefes of Camerycke whereof iij wroughte with blacke with
　　　　passamayne of siluer & thother iij wrought with flowers of blacke silke
　　　　with a passamayne lace of blacke silke & siluer and v sweate bages of
　　　　striped silke
　　　　　　　　　　　　　　　　　　　dd the vj handkerchers to Mrs Skydmore
　　　　　　　　　　　　　　　　　　　and the Ruffes to Jane Brisselles
77.115　By the Lady Frogmorton a night Rayle & a Coife of lawne allouer wrought
　　　　with whyte worke the coyf & forehead clothe set with a edge of rounde
　　　　perle & one playne night coyfe of lawne
　　　　　　　　　　　　　　　　　　　　　　　　　dd to Mrs Skydmore
77.116　By the Lady Arundell a Dublet of white Satten cut lyned with grene
　　　　serceonett laid allouer with lace off golde and grene silke
　　　　　　　　　　　　　　　　　　　　　　　　　　dd to Rauf hoope
77.117　By the Lady Wylforde a scarf of grene serceonett with a passamaine lace
　　　　of venice golde & siluer
　　　　　　　　　　　　　　　　　　　　　dd to Mrs Elizabeth Knowlles
77.118　By the Lady Marven a peyre of Doblett sleves of Straw collor Satten
　　　　allouer embr with a smale Cordaunt of venice siluer with a passamaine
　　　　of venice siluer at the hande
　　　　　　　　　　　　　　　　　　　　　　　　　　dd to Rauf hoope

Knights

77.119　By Sir Frances Knowelles Threasor of the house in golde . . . . x li
77.120　By Sir James Croftes Comptroler of the same in golde . . . . x li
77.121　By Sir Thomas Smyth principall Secretary in golde . . . . x li
　　　　　　　　　　　　　　　　　　　　　　　　　dd to henry Sakford
77.122　By Mr Fraunces Walsingham also secretary a Cloake of Tufte taphata the
　　　　tufte blake the grounde yellowe with buttons & lopes of venice siluer
　　　　with a passamaine rounde aboute of venice siluer
　　　　　　　　　　　　　　　　　　　　　　　　　　dd to Rauff hoope
77.123　By Sir Raulf Sadler Chancellor of the Duchy in golde . . . . xv li
77.124　By Sir Waulter Myldemay Chauncellor of the Exchequer in golde . . . . x li
77.125　By Sir William Cordall Mr of the Rolles in golde . . . . x li
77.126　By Sir Christopher Haydon in golde . . . . x li
77.127　By Sir William Damsell Receivor of the Courte of Wardes in golde . . . . x li
77.128　By Sir Henry Cromwell in golde . . . . x li
　　　　　　　　　　　　　　　　　　　　　　　　　dd to henry Sakford
77.129　By Sir Gawon Carow a smocke of fyne holland wrought with blacke
　　　　worke of honysockles the Ruffes edgid with a passamayne of venice
　　　　golde & blacke silke
　　　　　　　　　　　　　　　　　　　　　　　　　　dd to Mrs Skydmore
77.130　By Sir Thomas Gressham in golde . . . . x li
77.131　By Sir Owen Hopton Lievetenant of the Tower in golde . . . . x li

77.132   By Sir John Thynne in golde . . . . v li

dd to henry Sakford

77.133   By Sir Gilbert Dethicke alias Garter a booke of Tharmes of the garter
since the tyme of the Qs Matie

dd to Mrs Blanche Parry

77.134   By Sir Henry Lee a coife of vellate with xlviij peces of golde / havinge
camew heddes

77.135   By Sir William Drury a foreparte of murry vellate wrought with Estrices
feathers of venice golde

dd to Rauf hoope

Gentlewomen

77.136   By Mrs Blaunch Parre a Juell of golde wherein is set a white Agathe & set
with iiij^{or} smale sparkes of Rubies and a smale perle pendaunte

dd to the Lady Hawarde

77.137   By Mrs Hennage a Ringe of golde with vj Opalles & very smale Rubies

dd to the said La Hawarde

77.138   By Mrs Fraunces Howard a night coif and a sute of ruffes of lawne
wrought with blake & white

dd to Mrs Eliz Knowles

77.139   By Mrs Elizabeth Knowles a Doublet of neteworke set with spangles of
siluer

dd to Rauf hoope

77.140   By Mrs Edmondes a vaile of fyne neteworke edgid with a smale pasamaine
lace and spangles of golde and siluer

dd to Mrs Abingdon

77.141   By Mrs Abingdon a wastcoate of satten allouer embr

dd to Mrs Skydmore

77.142   By Mrs Skydmore a foreparte of a kyrtle of oreng collor satten embr with
blacke silke & siluer Lyned with blacke serceonate

77.143   By Mrs Wallsingham a savegarde of tufte Taphata the ground yellow and
the tufte blacke with a pasamaine, Lopes & buttons of venice siluer

dd to Rauf hoope

77.144   By Mrs Snowe vj tothe pickes of golde, and vj smale clothes to wype Teeth
wrought with black silke

dd the vj tothpickes to the La Hawarde
and the clothes to Mrs Skydmore

77.145   By Mrs Babteste a cusshion Clothe of lawne wrought with golde & silke of
sondry collors and edgid with a fayre pasamayne of venice golde

dd to Mrs Skydmore

77.146   By Mrs Weste a Doublate of tawny satten embr with networke of white
and yellowe silke Lyned with Tawney serceonate

dd to Rauf hope

77.147   By Mrs Katherin Paston a Juell of golde beinge a pomaunder / on eche
side a smale poynted dyamonde and a smale perle pendaunt

dd to the La Howarde

77.148 By Mrs Marbery a pillow peere of holland wrought allouer with Roses
braunches and Burdes of silk of sundry collores
dd to Mrs Skydmore

77.149 By Mrs Digbye a Couering of a gowne of lawne playne edgid with a smale
lace of siluer
dd to Rauf hoope

77.150 By Mrs Mary Sydney a foreparte & a payre of bodyes of networke with
tuftes of browne silke
dd to Mrs Skydmore

77.151 By Mrs Jane Brysselles alias Hawkes a partelet and a peyre of Ruffes
dd to Mrs Skydmore

77.152 By Mrs Townesende one Juell of golde beinge a litle bell enamvled and
set with sparkes of Rubyes and the clapper beinge a corse perle
dd to the La Haward

77.153 By Mrs Caue one peyre of pillo peeres [sic] of fyne holland allouer wrought
with blacke silke and a passmayne of like blacke silke
dd to Mrs Skydmore

77.154 By Mrs Lichfield a forparte of a partelet & a payre of sleves of Sipres
wrought with gold siluer and silke of sundry collers very feyre wroughte

77.155 By Mrs Sackeforde a smocke of fyne holland wroughte with blacke worke
in the Sleaves Collor & Ruffes

77.156 By Mrs Wingfeild a Cusshion Clothe of nedleworke the grownde red
allouer wrought with oke leaves of grene silke and venice gold & siluer
with a bordre of roses of like stuf

77.157 By Mrs Harman a partlett & a peyre of sleves of lawne with open worke
of siluer and edgid with a passamaine Lace and spangles
dd to Mrs Skydmore

77.158 By Mrs Allen a peyre of Doublet sleves of yellow Satten cutt & lyned with
mvrrey serceonett
dd to Rauf hoope

77.159 By Mrs Twiste laundrys Six smale Tothe clothes wrought with black
silke and edgid with a smale border of black silke siluer & golde and
a smale Cusshionet of purple Satten embr & L[...] with vellatt

77.160 By Mrs Taylor a nyght aprone of fyne holland wrought with flowers of
black worke & venice golde & edgid with a passamayne of venice
golde

77.161 By Mrs Noot Sixe handkercheves with a passamaine Lace of venice golde

77.162 By Mrs Barley Sixe handerkercheves with a passamayne of venice golde
& siluer

77.163 By Mrs Mountague a night Rayle of Camerycke allouer wrought with black
silke and edgid with a passamayne of blacke silke & whyte thred
dd to Mrs Skydmore

77.164 By Mrs Dane iij peces of fyne Camericke
dd to Mrs Blanche Parry

77.165 By Mrs Croxson a night Apron of fyne Camericke wrought very feyre
with flowers of red silke & Gold beinge pomegranettes

77.166	By Mrs Amy Shelton vj handkerchefes edgid with a passamaine of blacke silke & golde
77.167	By Mrs Huggans xxiiij smale swete bages of Taphata of sundry collors & vj handkercheifes of fine holland wrought with black silke iij edgid with a passamayne of golde & iij with siluer
77.168	By Mrs Lucretia a handkerchefe of Camericke wrought with a bordre of Acornes & other flowers of golde siluer & silke of sondry collores & edgid with a like passamaine

dd to Mrs Skydmore

77.169	By Mrs Dale a Standisshe of siluer guilt with thre boxes for Incke Dust & Counters all off Siluer guilt weyinge .xxxvij oz qrt

dd in charge to Mr Asteley Mr of the Juelles as aforesaid

Chaplens

77.170	By Archdeacon Carow Deane of the chapple in golde . . . . x li

dd to henry Sakford

Gentlemen

77.171	By Mr Thomas Hennaige Threasoror of the Chamber a Juell of golde being a Tablett thereon a Salamaunder of Opalles gar[nished] with xviij smale Dyamondes and a pendaunt with Opalles and Rubies
77.172	By Mr Christopher Hatton Captayne of the garde a peyre of brasselettes which may serue for a Carckenet fully gar[nished] with Opalles & Rubyes & very fayre enamvled with a Opall pendaunt

dd to the La Hawarde

77.173	By Mr John Harrington two pillowberes of fyne Camericke wrought with white cutworke

dd to Mrs Skydmore

77.174	By Mr Edward Care a scarf of Carnation Taphata allouer wrought with networke of golde & siluer set with spangles / Awhole piece of wrought Lawne And a caule of golde & siluer with burdes & Flowers sett with seede perle

dd the Skarf & Caule to Mrs E Knolles
and the Lawnde with Mrs Abingdon

77.175	By Mr Edward Cleere in golde . . . . x li

dd to henry Sakford

77.176	By Mr Captayne Laighton a Chaine of pomaunders slightly garn with golde

dd to the La Hawarde

77.177	By Mr Edward Basshe in golde . . . . x li

dd to henry Sakford

77.178	By Mr Stanhop a sute of Ruffes sleves & paretlett of networke Florisshed ouer with venice golde & spangles

dd the ruffes to Jane Brisselles
the partlet & sleves to Mrs Skydmore

77.179 By Mr Jerningham a Doublate of yellow satten garn with a passamaine
lace of blacke Satten and venice siluer lyned with Asshe collor
serceonett

dd to Rauf hoope

77.180 By Mr Alfonsus an Italian booke wrytten

with Kylligrave

77.181 By Mr Smythe Customer two boltes of Camericke

dd to Mrs Blanche Parry

77.182 By Benedicke Spinula a peticoat of Carnation Satten allouer embr with
venice golde & siluer sett with spangles frenged with a smale frenge of
like golde & siluer lyned with grene serceonett

dd to Rauf hoope

77.183 By Foulke Grevell a peyre of Tawney silke hosen a peyre of garters of
white Sipers bordred with nedle worke & a peyre of showes & Pantables
of lether embr

dd to Mrs Skydmore

77.184 By Lanysen ment Mr a Juell of golde being an Aungell furnysshed with
smale Rubyes & Dyamondes & a perle pendaunt

dd to the La Haward

77.185 By Doctor Huycke ij pottes of Ginger

77.186 By Doctor Maister ij pottes of ginger

77.187 By John Hemingway a pott of peeres Conduit

77.188 By John Ryche in a box vj Glasses with Conserves

dd to Mrs Skydmore

77.189 By John Smythson Mr Cooke for the Q. a marche pane made like a
Tower

77.190 By John Dudley Sergeaunte of the Pastry a pye of Quinces & Orenges
very fare made

[blank]

77.191 By William Huggans a smale square Cusshion of white satten embr with
a Tree and serteine personages Carrieng braunches from yt

dd to Mrs Skydmore

77.192 By Marke Anthony a fayre Drinking glasse guilt in a case of lether guilt

with Mr Knyvett

77.193 By Ambroseo Lupo a smale Cheste Couerid with leather guilt & a peyre
of perfumed gloves therein

dd the chest to Mr Sakford the gloves to Mrs Skydmore

77.194 By Petrucio a booke wrytten in Italian fayre

with Mr Bapteste

77.195 By Edward Skeetes a smale peyre of virginalles

with her Matie of the saide Skydmore

77.196 By Charles Smythe a hat of blacke vellat with abande sett with seede perle
and edgid with a smale passamaine of venice golde and siluer

dd to Rauf Hoope

77.197 By Henry Gyrtens an Englisshe boke in verse beinge a Story translated

[blank]

Summa totalis of all the money giuen to her Matie
Deliuered in manner and Fourme aboue declared

ix^C Lviij li viij s iiij d

Elizabeth R
[sign manual]

J Asteley
ex[aminatio] per
N Bristow
Pigeon
Ste Fulwell
Richard Asteley

Anno Regni Regine
Elizabeth decimo nono

Newe yers guift geuon by the Quenes
Maiestie at her highnes Honor of Hampton
courte to these persones whose names hereafter
ensue the First of January the yere abouesaid

Elizabeth R
[sign manual]

77.198	Too the Lady Margeret Leneox in guilte plate Keyle poz . . . . . iiij^xx x oz iij qrt di
77.199	To the Lady Mary Gray in guilte plate Keyle poz . . . . xviij oz iij qrt di
77.200	To the Lady Margerett countes of Darby in guilte plate Brandon
	poz . . . . L oz iij qrt
77.201	To Sir Nicholas Bacon knight Lorde keper of the greate Seale of
	Englande in guilt plate Brandon poz. . . . . xxxiiij oz di di qrt
77.202	To the Lorde Burliegh Lorde High Threasoror of Englande in guilt plate
	K. poz. . . . . xl oz di qrt
77.203	To the Lorde marques of Winchester in guilt plate K. poz . . . . xxxj oz qrt

Earles

77.204	To the Erle of Leycetor Mr of the horses three guilt boles with acouer of
	the Charge of John Asteley Esquire Mr of the Juelhouse and parcell of
	iiij^m ounces of guilte plate appoynted for lyke purposes poz – iiij^xx xvij
	oz qrt di and a guilte Spone K poz – iij oz – in toto . . . . C oz qrt di
77.205	To Therle of Arundell in guilt plate Keyle poz. . . . . L oz iij qrt di
77.206	To Therle of Sussex Lorde Chamberlyen in guilt plate K poz . . . . .xxxv oz di qrt
77.207	To Therle of Surrey in guilt plate K poz. . . . . xvj oz qrt

77.208	To Therle of Shrewesbury in guilt plate K poz . . . . xxx oz di di qrt
77.209	To Therle of Darby in guilt plate Br poz . . . . .xxx oz di qrt
77.210	To Therle of Lincoln in guilt plate K poz . . . . .xxiij oz iij qrt di
77.211	To Therle of Warwyke a peire of gilte pottes K poz—iiij^{xx} xiij oz qrt /
	and a guilt bowle wythe a couer Brandon poz—xix oz—in toto . . . Cxii oz qrt
77.212	To Therle of Bedford in guilt plate K poz . . . . xxxj oz qrt di
77.213	To Therle of Kyldare in guilt plate Br poz . . . . xxxj oz qrt di
77.214	To Therle of Rutlande in guilte plate Ke poz . . . . xx oz
77.215	To Therle of Huntingdon in guilte plate Br poz . . . . xx oz di
77.216	To Therle of Penbroke in guilte plate poz . . . . .xxx oz
77.217	To Therle of Northumberland in guilte plate poz . . . . .xxv oz di qrt
77.218	To Therle of Hertf[ord] in guilt plate K poz . . . . xx oz di
77.219	To Therle of Southampton in guilte plate Br poz . . . . .xxx oz
77.220	To Therle of Ormonde in guilt plate Ke poz . . . . Ciiij^{xx} iij oz qrt
77.221	To the Vicounte Mountague in guilt plate Br poz . . . . xx oz di qrt
77.222	To the Vicounte Gormanstone in guilt plate K poz . . . . .xxviij oz qrt di

Duchesses Marquesses and Countesses

77.223	To the Duches of Suff[olk] in guilte plate K poz . . . . xxxix oz di
77.224	To the Duches of Somerset in guilte plate K poz . . . . xxvj oz qrt
77.225	To the Lady Marques of Northampton in guilte plate K poz . . . . .xlij oz
77.226	To the Lady Marques of Wynchester Dowager in guilt plate Br poz . . . . . . xxj oz
77.227	To the Counties of Surrey Dowager in guilt plate K poz . . . . xij oz qrt
77.228	To the Counties of Shrewesbury in guilte plate K poz . . . . .xxx oz qrt
77.229	To the Counties of Sussex in guilte plate K poz . . . . xxj oz
77.230	To the Counties of Lincoln in guilte plate parcell of the foresaid iiij^{m} oz
	poz—xxvij [oz] di qrt and in guilte plate Brandon poz—xxij oz qrt in
	toto . . . . xlix oz qrt di
77.231	To the Counties of Warwicke in guilt plate Br poz xxxv oz qrt & in guilt
	plate Ke ix oz in toto . . . . .xliiij oz qrt
77.232	To the Counties of Bedford in guilt plate K—xxiiij oz qrt in guilte plate
	Br—xvij oz di qrt & in guilte plate Brandon—ix oz di—in toto
	. . . . L oz iij qrt di
77.233	To the Counties of Hunt[ingdon] in guilte plate Ke poz . . . . xxxvj oz di qrt
77.234	To the Counties of Oxforde in guilte plate Ke poz . . . . .xx oz qrt
77.235	To the Counties of Penbroke Doger in guilte plate Ke poz . . . . .xxvij qrt di
77.236	To the Counties of Northumberlande in guilte plate Ke poz . . . . xix oz qrt
77.237	To the Counties of Southampton in guilte plate Ke poz . . . . xx oz di qrt
77.238	To the Counties of Essex in guilte plate parcell of the foresaid iiij^{m} oz
	poz . . . . xviij oz iij qrt
77.239	To the Counties of Rutlande in guilt plate Ke poz . . . . .xx oz iij qrt
77.240	To the Counties of Kente Dowager in guilte plate parcell of the said iiij^{m}
	oz poz . . . . xx oz qrt di
77.241	To the Counties of Kente in guilt plate parcell of the same poz . . . . xx oz
77.242	To the Vicountes of Mountague in guilte plate Ke poz . . . . .xx oz qrt

217

Busshops

77.243	To the Archbusshopp of Canterbury in guilte plate Br poz . . . . xl oz di
77.244	To the Busshop of Elye in guilte plate parcell of the forsaid iiij^m oz
	poz . . . . xxxvj oz di qrt
77.245	To the Busshop of London in guilte plate Ke poz . . . . xxx oz iij qrt di
77.246	To the Busshop of Winchester in guilte plate Br poz . . . . xxx oz di
77.247	To the Busshop of Salisbury in guilt plate parcell of the saide iiij^m oz
	poz . . . . xxxvij di qrt
77.248	To the Busshop of Lincoln in guilte plate Br poz . . . . xxxj oz qrt
77.249	To the Busshop of Norwich in guilte plate Ke poz . . . . xxij oz iij qrt di
77.250	To the Busshop of Lichefeild & Coventry in guilte plate Ke poz . . xx oz di di qrt
77.251	To the Busshop of Hereforde in guilte plate Ke poz . . . . xvij oz
77.252	To the Busshop of St Davyes in guilte plate Ke poz . . . . xvij oz
77.253	To the Busshop of Exetor in guilte plate Ke poz . . . . xvj oz di
77.254	[hole in ms] To the Busshop of Bathe in guilte plate Ke poz . . . . . xvij oz di qrt
77.255	To the Busshop of Chester in guilte plate Ke poz . . . . xviij oz di qrt
77.256	To the Busshop of Peterborow in guilte plate Ke poz . . . . xvj oz qrt
77.257	To the Busshop of Glocetor in guilte plate Ke poz . . . . xviij oz iij qrt di
77.258	To the Busshop of Chichester in guilte plate Ke poz . . . . xvj oz qrt
77.259	To the Busshop of Rochester in guilte plate Ke poz . . . . xviij oz di

Lordes

77.260	To the Lorde Howarde in guilte plate Br poz . . . . Ciij oz
77.261	To the Lorde of Hunesdon in guilte plate parcell of the saide iiij^m oz
	po . . . . xxxij oz qrt
77.262	To the Lord of Burgevenay in guilte plate Ke poz . . . . .x oz qrt
77.263	To the Lord Henry Howarde in guilte plate Br poz . . . . xv oz di qrt
77.264	To the Lorde Ryche in guilte plate parcell of the saide iiij^m oz poz . . . . xx oz
77.265	To the Lorde Darcy in guilte plate Ke poz . . . . xviij oz iij qrt di
77.266	To the Lorde Shandowes in guilte plate parcell the said iiij^m oz poz
	. . . . xiij [oz] di di qrt
77.267	To the Lorde of Boockurste in guilte plate parcell of the same iiij^m
	oz . . . . xj oz di
77.268	To the Lorde Northe in guilte plate Ke poz . . . . xvj oz qrt di
77.269	To the Lorde Paget in guilte plate Ke poz . . . . xx oz di di qrt
77.270	To the Lorde Stafford in guilte plate Ke poz . . . . xx oz di qrt
77.271	To the Lorde Compton in guilte plate Ke poz . . . . xx oz qrt di
77.272	To the Lorde Norryes in guilte plate Ke poz . . . . xx oz di di qrt
77.273	To the Lorde Cobham in guilte plate Br xv oz & in guilte plate Ke iiij
	oz qrt di in toto . . . . xix oz qrt di
77.274	To the Lorde Wharton in guilte plate parcell of the iiij^m oz poz . . . . xix oz
77.275	To the Lorde Henry Seymor in guilte plate Ke poz . . . . xx oz iij qrt
77.276	To the Lord Lumley in guilte plate Ke poz . . . . xv oz qrt di

Baronesses

77.277 To the Lady Burleigh in guilte plate parcell of the said iiij^m oz poz . . . xxiiij oz di

77.278 To the Lady Burgavenny in guilt plate Ke poz . . . . x oz di qrt

77.279 To the Lady Howarde in guilte plate Br poz . . . . xxiiij oz

77.280 To the Lady Cobham in guilte plate Br poz . . . . L oz qrt di

77.281 To the Lady Hunsedon in guilte plate parcell of the iiij^m oz poz . . . . .xxv oz

77.282 To the Lady Barkely in guilt plate Ke poz . . . . xviij oz iij qrt

77.283 To the Lady Dacres of the Southe in guilte plate Br poz . . . . xvj oz

77.284 To the Lady Taylboyes in guilte plate Ke poz . . . . xx oz

77.285 To the Lady Howard Dowager in guilt plate Br poz . . . . xx oz

77.286 To the Lady Shandowes Dowager in guilte plate Ke poz . . . . .xx oz qrt

77.287 To the Lady Shandowes in guilte plate Ke poz . . . . xj oz iij qrt di

77.288 To [the Lady] St John of Bletteslowe in guilte plate Br poz . . . . xviij qrt

77.289 To the Lady Pagett Care in guilte plate Br poz . . . . xxv oz di

77.290 To the Lady Paget in guilt plate Br poz . . . . xviij oz di qrt

77.291 To the Lady Cheyny in guilt plate Br poz . . . . L oz iij qrt di

77.292 To the Lady Audley in guilte plate Br poz . . . . xvj oz di di qrt

77.293 To the Lady Bookhurste in guilt plate Ke poz . . . . ix oz iij qrt

77.294 To the Lady Norrys in guilte plate parcell of the iiij^m oz aforesaid poz . . xx oz di

77.295 To the Lady Crvmwell in guilte plate Br poz . . . . xij oz qrt

77.296 To the Lady Sheffild in guilte plate Ke poz . . . . xvij oz di

77.297 To the Lady Wyllowby of Warwickeshere in guilt plate Ke poz. . . . . xij oz qrt di

77.298 To the Lady Mary Veere in guilt plate Br poz . . . . xviij oz qrt

77.299 To the Lady Latymer in guilt plate Ke poz . . . . .xxij oz qrt

Ladyes

77.300 To the Lady Mary Sydney in guilte plate Ke poz . . . . xxxj oz qrt

77.301 To the Lady Stafforde in guilte plate Ke—xv oz qrt & Br in guilte plate
poz—xv oz—in toto . . . . .xxx oz qrt

77.302 To the Lady Carow in guilte plate parcell of the foresaid iiij^m oz poz
. . . . .xxxv oz di qrt

77.303 To the Lady Woodhouse in guilt plate Br poz . . . . xxij oz qrt di

77.304 To the Lady Mary Seymor in guilte plate Br poz . . . . xiij oz iij qrt

77.305 To the Lady Cheke in guilte plate Br poz . . . . xxiiij oz di di qrt

77.306 To the Lady Butler in guilte plate Ke poz . . . . xvj oz qrt di

77.307 To the Lady Drury in guilte plate Ke poz . . . . xvj oz iij qrt

77.308 To the Lady Pawlett in guilt plate parcell of the said iiij^m oz poz. . . . . xj oz qrt di

77.309 To the Lady Gressham in guilt plate parcell of the same iiij^m oz poz
. . . . xx oz di di qrt

77.310 To the Lady Crumwell sir Henrys wyf in guilte plate Br poz. . . . . xij oz qrt

77.311 To the Lady Ratclif in guilt plate Ke poz . . . . xiij oz qrt di

77.312 To the Lady Frogmerton in guilt plate Ke poz . . . . xxij oz qrt di

77.313 To the Lady Arondell in guilte plate Ke poz . . . . .xv oz qrt

77.314 To the Lady Wilford in guilte plate Ke poz. . . . . xix oz di
77.315 To the Lady Marvyn in guilte plate Br poz. . . . . xiiij oz di

Knights

77.316 To Sir Fraunces Knowllys Treasoror of the householde in guilt plate Ke
     poz . . . . xxiiij oz di qrt
77.317 To Sir James Croffes Comptroller of the same house in guilte plate parcell
     of the iiij^m oz aforesaid poz . . . . .xxv oz
77.318 To Sir Thomas Smythe principall Secretary in guilte plate Ke poz . . . xxiiij oz di
77.319 To Mr Fraunces Walsingham Esquire thother Secretary in guilte plate
     parcell of the sayde iiij^m oz poz—Lvij oz and a peper box g. Ke poz—
     iiij oz iij qrt di in toto. . . . . Lxij oz
77.320 To Sir Rauf Sadler Knight chauncellor of the Duchy in guilte plate Ke
     poz . . . . .xxx oz qrt di
77.321 To Sir Walter Myldemaye Chauncellor of the exchequire in guilte plate
     Ke poz . . . . xxvij oz iij qrt di
77.322 To Sir William Cordell Mr of the Rolles in guilte plate Ke poz. . . . . xxj oz
77.323 To Sir Xperfer Haydon in guilte plate Ke poz . . . . .xv di di qrt
77.324 To Sir William Damsell in guilt plate Ke poz. . . . . xix oz qrt
77.325 To Sir Henry Crumwell in guilt plate Ke poz. . . . . .xx oz qrt
77.326 To Sir Gawen Carow in guilt plate Br poz . . . . xxxv oz di
77.327 To Sir Thomas Gresham in guilte plate parcell of the iiij^m oz aforesaid
     poz . . . . xix oz iij qrt
77.328 To Sir Owen Hopton in guilte plate Ke poz . . . . xxij oz di qrt
77.329 To Sir John Thynn in guilte plate Br poz . . . . ix oz qrt
77.330 To Sir Gilberte Dethicke in guilt plate parcell of the saide iiij^m oz
     . . . . xiij oz di di qrt
77.331 To Sir Henry Lee in guilte plate Ke poz . . . . Lij oz di qrt
77.332 To Sir William Drury in guilte plate Br poz . . . . xvij oz di di qrt

Gentlewomen

77.333 To Mrs Blanche Parry in guilt plate Ke poz . . . . .xviij oz di di qrt
77.334 To Mrs Hennage in guilte plate Ke poz . . . . xx oz
77.335 To Mrs Fraunces Howarde in guilte plate K poz . . . . xiiij oz qrt
77.336 To Mrs Elizabeth Knowelles in guilt plate Ke poz . . . . xv oz di
77.337 To Mrs Edmondes in guilte plate Ke poz . . . . xv oz di
77.338 To Mrs Abingdon in guilt plate Ke poz . . . . xvj oz iij qrt di
77.339 To Mrs Skydmore in guilte plate Ke poz . . . . xv oz
77.340 To Mrs Walsingham in guilte plate Ke poz. xvj oz di qrt
77.341 To Mrs Snowe in guilte plate Ke poz . . . . xiiij oz qrt
77.342 To Mrs Bapteste in guilte plate Ke poz. . . . . xvj oz
77.343 To Mrs Weste in guilt plate Br poz . . . . .xiiij qrt di
77.344 To Mrs Katheryn Paston in guilt plate Ke poz. xv oz
77.345 To Mrs Marborow in guilt plate Br poz . . . . xiij oz di qrt
77.346 To Mrs Digby in guilt plate Ke poz . . . . xv oz di
77.347 To Mrs Mary Sydney in guilte plate Bra poz . . . . xv oz

77.348	To Mrs Jane Bryselles als Hawkes in guilte plate Ke poz	xv oz
77.349	To Mrs Townesende in guilt plate parcell of the foresaid iiij^m oz	

77.348 To Mrs Jane Bryselles als Hawkes in guilte plate Ke poz . . . . xv oz

77.349 To Mrs Townesende in guilt plate parcell of the foresaid iiij^m oz
poz . . . . xxviij oz qrt

77.350 To Mrs Cave in guilt plate parcell of the same iiij^m oz poz. . . . . . . xv oz iij qrt di

77.351 To Mrs Lychefeld in guilt plate Br poz . . . . xvj oz qrt di

77.352 To Mrs Sackeford in guilt plate Ke poz . . . . xxij oz

77.353 To Mrs Wynkefeld in guilt plate Br poz . . . . xij oz qrt

77.354 To Mrs Harman in guilt plate parcell of the foresaid iiij^m oz poz
. . . . vij oz di di qrt

77.355 To Mrs Allen in guilte plate Ke poz . . . . xij oz di

77.356 To Mrs Smythson Laundrys in guilt plate Ke poz . . . . vij oz

77.357 To Mrs Twyste Lawnderys in guilt plate Ke poz . . . . v oz

77.358 To Mrs Note in guilt playte Ke poz . . . . xiij oz

77.359 To Mrs Barley in guilte plate Ke poz . . . . xij oz di

77.360 To Mrs Mountague in guilte plate Ke poz . . . . xij oz qrt

77.361 To Mrs Dane in guilte plate Ke poz . . . . .xx oz iij qrt

77.362 To Mrs Croxson in guilte plate Ke poz. . . . . ix oz di

77.363 To Mrs Huggans in guilte plate Br poz. . . . . xx oz di

77.364 To Mrs Amy Shelton in guilte plate Ke poz . . . . x oz di

77.365 To Mrs Lucrecia in guilte plate Br poz . . . . vij oz

77.366 To Mrs Dale in guilte plate parcell of the said iiij^m oz poz. . . . . xxiiij oz

Chaplens

77.367 To ArchDeacon Carow Dene of the Chapell in guilt plate Ke poz . xxij oz di qrt

Fre Guift to the Maydes of Honor

77.368 To the Lady Susan Boughser in guilte plate Br poz . . . . x oz di qrt

77.369 To Mrs Katheryn Howard in guilt plate parcell of the iiij^m oz poz . . . . x oz

77.370 To Mrs Ellyn Brydges in guilte plate parcell of the same poz . . . . x oz di qrt

77.371 To Mrs Mary Ratclyf in guilt plate parcell of the same poz . . . . .x oz qrt

77.372 To Mrs Elizabeth Garrett in guilte plate parcell of the same poz . . . . x oz di qrt

77.373 To Mrs Mary Borough in guilt plate Ke poz . . . . .x oz qrt

77.374 To Mrs Hyde mother of the Maydes in guilte plate Ke poz. . . . . .xij di di qrt

Gentlemen

77.375 To Mr Hatten capten of the gard in guilte plate K poz . . . . .CCCiiij^{xx} xij oz

77.376 To Mr Thomas Henage Treausor of the chamber in guilt plate Ke poz . xlviij oz

77.377 To Mr John Harrington in guilte plate Ke poz. . . . . .xl oz

77.378 To Mr Edward Clere in guilte plate parcell of the saide iiij^m oz poz
. . . . xx oz di di qrt

77.379 To Mr Basshe in guilte plate parcell of the saide iiij^m oz poz. . . . . . . .xx oz iij qrt

77.380 To Mr Captayn Layton in guilte plate parcell of the same iiij^m oz poz
. . . . .Lxxiij oz di di qrt

77.381 To Mr Stanhop in guilte plate Ke poz. . . . . xxj oz qrt

77.382 To Mr Jernyngham in guilte plate Ke poz. . . . . .xiij oz iij qrt di

77.383 To Mr Smythe Custumer in guilte plate Br poz . . . . xv oz

77.384	To Benedike Spinula in guilte plate Ke xxxj oz qrt di in guilte plate parcell of the saide iiij^m oz xlv oz qrt in toto . . . . .Lxxvj oz di di qrt
77.385	To Mr of the Mynt in guilte plate Ke poz . . . . xxiiij oz di
77.386	To Doctor Huyke in guilte plate Ke poz . . . . xiiij oz iij qrt
77.387	To Doctor Maister in guilt plate Ke poz . . . . xiiij oz iij qrt
77.388	To John Hemaway in guilte plate Br poz . . . . vij oz qrt
77.389	To John Rych apottycary in guilte plate parcell of the iiij^m oz poz . . . . . vij oz di
77.390	To John Smythson alias Taylor Mr Cooke in guilte plate Ke poz . . . . .viij oz
77.391	To John Dudley Sergeante of the pastry in guilt plate Br poz . . . . . . iiij oz iij qrt
77.392	To William Huggans in guilt plate Br poz . . . . .xxx oz
77.393	To Alphoncius in guilt plate parcell of the said iiij^m oz poz . . . . vij oz qrt
77.394	To Mark Anthony in guilte plate Br poz . . . . v oz di
77.395	To Ambroso Lupo in guilt plate Br poz . . . . .v oz qrt
77.396	To Petruccio in guilt plate Ke poz . . . . iiij oz di di qrt
77.397	To Charles Smith in guilte plate Ke poz . . . . .xx oz iij qrt
77.398	To Fulke Grevill in guilte plate Ke poz . . . . xiij oz qrt
77.399	To Henrie Gitten for a Rewarde . . . . xl s

Fre Guiftes

77.400	To Sir George Haward gent ussher of the privey Chamber in guilte plate Ke poz . . . . xij oz di di qrt
77.401	To John Astelye Esquire Mr and Treasoror of the Juelles & plate in guilte plate Ke poz . . . . .xviij oz iij qrt di
77.402	To Thomas Asteley grome of the privey Chamber in guilte plate Ke poz . . . . viij oz iij qrt di
77.403	To Edward Care another grome in guilte plate Ke poz . . . . viij oz iij qrt
77.404	To Henry Sackeford a nother grome in guilte plate Ke poz . . . . . . viij oz iij qrt di
77.405	To John Baptest another grome in guilte plate Ke poz . . . . viij oz iij qrt
77.406	To Henry Myddlemore a nother grome in guilte plate Br poz . . . . .viij oz di
77.407	To Thomas Knevet a nother grome in guilte plate Br poz . . . . .viij oz di
77.408	To Thomas Gorges another grome in guilte plate Ke poz . . . . . . .viij oz di di qrt
77.409	To William Killegrewe another grome in guilte plate Br poz . . . . .viij oz di
77.410	To Raufe Hoope yeoman of the Roobes in guilte plate Ke poz . . . xij oz iij qrt di
77.411	To Nicholas Bristow a Clerk of the Juelles in guilte plate Br poz . . x oz iij qrt di
77.412	To John Pigeon another Offycer there in guilte plate Br poz . . . . . . x oz iij qrt di
77.413	To Stephen Fultor [sic] another Offycer there in guilte plate Br poz . . . . x oz iij qrt di
77.414	To Richard Asteley grome there in guilte plate—ij oz qrt di parcell of the iiij^m oz aforesaid in guilt plate Brandon—iij oz di and in guilte plate Ke—v oz in toto . . . . x oz iij qrt di

Summa totalis of all the / plate Giuon in maner &
fourme aforesaid is . . . . v^m ccc xlix oz di di qrt

Guiftes geuon by her said Matie and deliuered
in maner & fourme Following that is to say

77.415 Mr Sauage
First given by her Matie & Deliuered the laste day of Aprell the xviij^th^
yere of the quenes Maties Regne at the Maryage of Mrs Savage the
Mr of the Rolles kynneswoman in guilte plate of the iiij^m^ oz afore
expressed poz . . . . xxxiiij oz iij qrt

77.416 Sir George Care
Item given by her Matie & Delivered the xj^th^ day of June Ao predicto
at the christeninge of Sir George Cares Daughter one Bason & leyre
guilt parcell of the said iiij^m^ oz poz . . . . Cj oz

77.417 Le Generall Le Portall a french man
Item gyven by her Matie & Delivered the xxvij^th^ of June anno predicto
To Le generall Le Portall a frenche man one Cheyne of golde poz—
xx oz being of the goodnes of xxij kar iij qrt le grayn / x oz thereof
being parcell of iiij^m^ oz iiij dweight of gold of the charge of the said
John Asteley / & the rest bought of Hugh Keyle in toto . . . . xx oz in golde

77.418 Mr Tramane
Item gyven by her Matie & Delivered the vth of September Anno
predicto to Mr Tramayn one of the Clerkes of the privey Counsaile
at his marage a cup siluer gilte with a couer parcell of the foresaid
iiij^m^ oz poz . . . . L oz qrt

77.419 Mr Frogmerton
Item given by her said Matie & Delyvered the vj^th^ of Septembre
Anno predicto to Arthure Frogmerton goinge into Fraunce with
Mr Amyas Pawlett Ambassador ledger there a Cheyne of gold beinge
of the goodnes of xxij kar & one gr parcell of the forsaide Ciiij^xx^
oz iij d weight of gold of the charge of the said John Asteley poz
. . . . viij oz qrt   vj gr   in gold

77.420 Henry Knowlles
Item gyven by her saide Matie & Delivered the xxij^th^ of Octobre Anno
predicto at the Christening of Mr Henrye Knowles childe one guilt
bolle with acouer of the charge of the said John Asteley as parcell of
the saide iiij^m^ oz poz . . . . xxiij oz di di qrt

77.421 Mr Bridges
Item given by her said Matie & Delivered the xix^th^ of December Anno
xix° Regine Eliz at the Cristeninge of William Bridges esquire his
chyld / one Bolle of Siluer and guilte with acouer of the charge of
the saide John Asteley and parcell of the said iiij^m^ oz poz . . . . xxiij oz di qrt

77.422 Mounsieur Gastell
Item given by her saide Matie & Deliuerid the xxvj^th^ of January Anno
xix° predicto to Mounsieur Gastell gentleman sent from Senior don
John de Austria one cheyne of golde being of the goodnes of xxij kar
j gr of the Charge of the said John Asteley & parcell of the foresaid
Ciii^xx^ oz iiij d weight poz . . . . xxxiiij oz in golde

77.423   Mounsieur Maluesyer

Item given also by her saide Matie & Delivuered the xxvij^th of January
Anno predicto To Mounsieur Maluesyer Ambassador lyger from the
french kinge at the Christeninge of his child one bason & leyer guilte
of the Charge of the said John Asteley parcell of the said iiij^m oz poz –
Cxxxij oz iij qrt and a Duble cup guilt of the Almayne making poz—
lxij oz di / also of the charge of the said John Asteley but no parte
of the said iiij^m oz in toto . . . . Ciiij^xx xv oz qrt

77.424   Mounsieur de Fainine

Item more given by her saide Matie and Deliuerd the vij^th of Marche
Anno predicto to Mounsieur De Fainine a messenger sent from the
prince of Orange a Cheyne of golde poz – xx oz di qrt of the goodnes
of xxij kar one gr parcell of the foresaid Ciiij^xx oz iiij d weighte of
golde . . . . xx oz di qrt

Elizabeth R
[sign manual]

                           J Astley
                           Bristow
                        John Pigeon
                        Ste Fulwell
                    Richard Asteley

Anno Regni Regine
Elizabethae} vicesimo

Newyers guifts giuen to her Maiestie
at her honor of Hampton corte by these
Persons whose Names do whereat ensue
the first day of January
the Yere aforesaid

Elizabeth R
[sign manual]

78.1   By the Lady Margret Lineox acasting bottell of Agathe garnesshed with
golde and set with stone poiz

Deliuered to the Lady Howard

78.2   By the Lady Mary Gray ij peir of swete gloves with fower Dosen buttons
of golde in euery one asede perle

Deliuered to Mrs Eliz Knowlles

78.3   By the Lady Margret Countes of Darby apetticote of white Satten reysed
and edged with a brode enbrawdery of Diuers collours

dd to Rauf hoope yoman of the Roobes

78.4   By Sir Nichas Bacon knyght Lorde keper of the greate Seale of Inglande
in golde . . . . xiij li vj s viij d

78.5   By the Lorde Burligh Lorde Treausoror of Inglande in golde . . . . xx li

78.6   By the Lorde Marques of Winchester in golde . . . . xx li

dd to henry Sakford grome of the previe Chamber

Earles & Vicount

78.7   By therle of Leycetor Mr of the Horses acarcanet of golde ennamuled
nyne peces whereof are garnesshed with Sparkes of Diamondes and
rubyes and euery one of them a pendant of golde ennamuled garnesshed
with small Sparkes of Rubyes and Ophall in the myddes / and tenne other
peces of golde lykewyse ennamuled euery of them garnesshed with verey
small Diamondes two Large ragged perles set in a rose of Sparkes of
Rubyes / and two lesser perles pendant / and a pendant of golde in euery
of them asmall Diamonde lozenged and a small Rubye / and in the
myddes alarge pendant of golde garnesshed with meane Rubyes an
Ophall and ameane perle pendant / And Six Dosen of Buttons of
golde lykewyse ennamuled euery button garnesshed with small Sparkes
of Rubyes in euery of them alarge ragged perle

dd to the said Lady Howarde

78.8   By therle of Arondell in golde . . . . xxx li

78.9   By therle of Sussex Lorde Chamberleyn in golde . . . . xx li

78.10   By therle of Lincoln High Admirall of Inglande in golde . . . . x li

78.11   By therle of Bedford in golde . . . . xx li

78.12   By therle of Shrewesbury in golde . . . . xx li

78.13   By therl of Darby in golde . . . . xx li

78.14 By therle of Huntingdon in golde . . . . x li
dd to henry Sakford

78.15 By therle of Warwick agowne with Hanging sleves of black vellat alouer
with small wyer of golde Lyke Scallop Shelles set with Spangilles
enbrawdred with agarde with sondry byrdes and Flowers enbossed with
golde Siluer and Silke / set with seede perle
dd to Rauf hoope

78.16 By therle of Rutlande in golde . . . . x li

78.17 By therle of Penbroke in golde . . . . xx li

78.18 By therle of Northumberlande in golde . . . . x li

78.19 By therle of Southampton in golde. . . . . xx li
dd to henry Sakford

78.20 By therle of Hertford A Juell being a Ship of mother of perle garnesshed
with small rubys & iij small diamondes and small Diamondes

78.21 By therle of Ormonde a fayer Juell of golde being a phenex / the winges
fully garnesshed with Rubyes and small Diamondes / and at the fete thre
feyer Diamondes and two smaller in the top abranche garnesshed with
Six small Diamondes thre small Rubyes & iij very meane perle and in the
bottome thre perles pendant
dd to the said Lady Howarde

78.22 By the vicounte Mountague in golde . . . . x li
dd to henry Sakford

Duchesses Marquess and Countesses

78.23 By the Duches of Suffolke a feyer Cusshyn of purple vellat verey feyerly
enbrawdred of the story of Truth slaing lion set with garnettes and sede
perle the baksyde purple Satten frynged & tasselles of venice golde &
sylke
dd to Richard Tod keper of the Warderobe

78.24 By the Duches of Somerset in golde. . . . . xiij li vj s viij d
dd to henry Sakford

78.25 By the Marques of Northampton a kyrtill of white Satten enbrawdred
with purles of golde Like Clowdes and Leyed rownde aboughly with
abone Lace of venice golde
dd to Rauf hoope

78.26 By the Lady Marques of winchester Dowager in golde . . . . x li
dd to henry Sakford

78.27 By the Lady Marques of Winchester asmock of Cameryck wrought with
Tawny Sylke & Black the Ruffes and collor edged with abone Lace of
Siluer
dd to the Mrs Skydmore

78.28 By the Countes of Sussex in golde . . . . x li
dd to henry Sakford

78.29 By the Countes of Lincoln a Dublet with Doble Sleves Asshcollor vpon
Tyncell Leyed with pasmane Lace of golde and Siluer Lyned with
yelowe serceonet

78.30 By the Countes of Warwyck a foreparte and apeir of Sleves of white
       Satten enbrawdred with branches and trees of Damaske golde / two
       gardes of black vellat vpon the foreparte enbrawdred with golde Siluer
       and Sylke set with seede perle and lyned with tawney Sarceonet
78.31 By the Countes of Shrewesbury agowne of white Satten Leyed ouer with
       pasmane of golde chevernewyse Lyned with Strawe collored Sarceonet
                                                         dd to Rauf hoope
78.32 By the Countes of Huntingdon in golde. . . . . .viij li
                                                         dd to henry Sakford
78.33 By the Countes of Oxford a Dublet of white Satten alouer enbrawdred
       with Flowers of golde / and Lyned with Strawe collored Serceonet
                                                         dd to Rauf hoope
78.34 By the Countes of Essex Ruffes of Lawnde white worke edged with sede
       perle / and ayelo here and another like black
                                              dd here to Mrs Eliz Knowlles
                                          and the ruffs to Mrs Jane Breselles
78.35 By the Countes of Penbroke Dowagier in golde. . . . . xij li
                                                         dd to henry Sakford
78.36 By the Countes of Penbroke a Dublet of Lawne enbrowdred alouer with
       golde Siluer & sylke of Diuers collors and lyned with yelow Taphata
78.37 By the Countes of Bedford a Dublet and aforeparte of murry Satten
       enbrawdred with Flowers of golde siluer and Sylke / and lyned with
       orenge tawny Taphata
                                                         dd to Rauf Hoope
78.38 By the Countes of Northumberlande in golde . . . . x li
78.39 By the Countes of Southampton in golde . . . . x li
78.40 By the countes of Rutlande in golde. . . . . x li
                                                         dd to henry Sakford
78.41 By the Countes of Kent a Remnent of white Satten prented cont. . . . . xix yds di
                                                         dd to Rauf Hoope
78.42 By the Countes of Kent Dowager a Fan of Flowers of Sylke of sundry
       collors the handill of an Inbrawdry worke set with small sede perle
                                                    dd to Mrs Eliz Knowlles
78.43 By the countes of Cumberlande aforeparte of Lawnde cutworke wrought
       with black and white vnmade
                                                         dd to Mrs Skydmore

Vicecountess

78.44 By the viscountess Mountague in golde . . . . x li
                                                         dd to henry Sakford

Busshopps

78.45 By tharchebusshop of yorke in golde . . . . xxx li
78.46 By the Busshop of Ely in golde. . . . . xxx li
78.47 By the Busshop of Dureham in golde. . . . . xxx li
78.48 By the Busshop of London in golde . . . . xx li

78.49	By the Busshop of winchester in golde	xx li
78.50	By the Busshop of Salisbury in golde	xx li
78.51	By the Busshop of Lincoln in golde	xx li
78.52	By the Busshop of Norwiche in golde	xx li
78.53	By the Busshop of worcetor in golde	xx li
78.54	By the Busshop of Lichfelde and Couentrie in golde	xiij li vj s viij d
78.55	By the Busshop of Hereford in golde	x li
78.56	By the Busshop of St Dauid in golde	x li
78.57	By the Busshop of Carlill in golde	x li
78.58	By the Busshop of Exetor in golde	x li
78.59	By the Busshop of Bathe in golde	x li
78.60	By the Busshop of Peterborowe in golde	x li
78.61	By the Busshop of Glocetor in golde	x li
78.62	By the Busshop of Chichester in golde	x li

dd to henry Sakford

Lordes

78.63 By the Lorde of Hunesdon a Juell of golde being a Swan of mother of
perle on thoneside thother syde ennamuled / white thone of her wynges
garnesshed with small Diamondes / and one small Diamonde towardes
the tayle / and a nother pece of mother of perle being alilly pot garnysshed
with small Diamondes & Rubys

dd to the said Lady howard

78.64 By the Lorde Haward a foreparte of white cutworke enbrawdred with
golde vnlyned

dd to Rauf hoope

78.65	By the Lorde Burgevenny in golde	v li
78.66	By the Lorde Ryche in golde	x li
78.67	By the Lorde Darcy of Chyche in golde	x li
78.68	By the Lorde Shandowes in golde	vj li xiij s iiij d
78.69	By the Lorde of Bokehurst in golde	v li
78.70	By the Lorde Northe in golde	x li
78.71	By the Lorde Pagett in golde	x li
78.72	By the Lorde Stafforde in golde	x li
78.73	By the Lorde Cumpton in golde	x li
78.74	By the Lorde Norreys of Ricote in golde	x li
78.75	By the Lorde Lumley in golde	x li
78.76	By the Lorde Wharton in golde	x li

dd to henry Sakford

78.77 By the Lorde Cobham a petticote of yelow Satten Leyed alouer with a
pasmane of Siluer and tawnye sylke frenged with Siluer and sylke and
lyned with tawny Serceonet

dd to Rauf hoope

78.78 By the Lorde Russell a Ringe of golde set vij small Diamondes & rounde
abowte with small rubyes & ij sparkes of ophall

dd to the said Lady howarde

78.79 By the Lorde Cheny a foreparte and apeir of boddys of aFrenche kyrtill
    of blewe cloth of Siluer enbrawdred alouer with venice golde with asmall
    garde of black vellat enbrawdred with venice golde & Siluer and lyned
    with black Sarceonet

                                       dd to Rauf hoope

Baronesses

78.80 By the La Burley a round kyrtill of cloth of Siluer with a garde of black
    vellat enbrawdred with Flowers of golde & siluer & lyned with black
    serceonet

                                       dd to Rauf hoope

78.81 By the Lady of Hunesdon in golde.................................... x li

78.82 By the Lady Hawarde Dowager in golde .... x li

78.83 By the Lady Tayleboyes in golde.................................... x li

                                  dd to henry Sakford

78.84 By the Lady Cobham a Petticote of white Satten lyned with carnacion
    Serceonet Leyed over with a Siluer Lace lyke waves and carnacion Silke
    and frynged with Siluer and carnacon sylke

                                       dd to Rauf hoope

78.85 By the Lady Seint John of Bletteslowe in golde....................... x li

78.86 By the Lady Audeley in golde .... vj li

78.87 By the Lady of Bookehurst in golde............................... v li

78.88 By the Lady Norrys in golde..................................... x li

78.89 By the Lady Barckley in golde .... x li

                                  dd to henry Sakford

78.90 By the Lady Cheny the trayne of aFrench kyrtill of blewe cloth of Siluer
    enbrawdred alouer with venice golde with a small garde of blac vellat
    enbrawdred with golde and Siluer & lyned with blac sercenet

78.91 By the Lady Hawarde Junior a foreparte of Networke changeable
    enbrawdred with Flowers Like Roses of golde Siluer and Sylke / and
    Lyned with crymsen Taphata

78.92 By the Lady Dacres of the South apettycote of Tawny Satten reysed with
    iiij borders of enbrawdery Siluer and golde with Hoopes Lyned with
    orenge collored Serceonet

                                         dd to Rauf hope

78.93 By the Lady Shandowes Dowager a Dublet of peche collored Satten
    alouer couered with white cutworke and Leyed with alace of venice
    gold / Lyned with orange collored serceonet / and aswete bag of
    crymson Taphata enbrawdred with venice golde and Spangilles

                              the Dublet dd to Rauf hoope
                            the swete bag dd to Mrs Skydmore

78.94 By the Lady Shandowes Junior a cusshynclothe of Lawne wrought with
    whiteworke of branches and trees edged with white bone worke wrought
    with Crownes

                                         dd to Mrs Skydmore

78.95 By the Lady Paget the Lord Pagettes wif a Gascone coate of black vellat
 alouer Leyed with Pasmane of Siluer / and lyned with white serceonet
 dd to Rauf hoope

78.96 By the Lady Paget Care agarlande of golde ennamuled with apendant of
 golde like aswerde and a man of golde ennamuled grene hang at a small
 cheyne
 dd to the said Lady howard

78.97 By the Lady Talbot a Skarf of Networke flowresshed with golde and
 Siluer edged at thendes with a abrode pasmane of venice golde & Siluer
 / and at the sides a narrow Lyned with Russet serceonet
 dd to Mrs Eliz Knowlles

78.98 By the Lady Sheffeld a Dublet of Sad tawny satten couered with white
 cutworke enbrawdred with Flowers of Siluer and Spangilles / and
 Lyned with white serceonet

78.99 By the Lady Mary Vere aforeparte of purple Taphata set with Roses of
 white sipers and cheynes betweene of venice golde with abrode pasmane
 of golde vnlyned and vnmade
 dd to Rauf hoope

Ladies

78.100

By the Lady Mary Sydney one peire of perfumed gloues with xxiiij small
 buttons of golde in euery of them asmall Diamond

78.101 dd to Mrs Eliz Knowlles

By the Lady Mary Semor wif of Mr Rogers / alynyng apeir of Sleues &
 iij Ruffes of Lawne cutworke of Flowers

78.102 dd to Mrs Skydmore

By the Lady Stafford a nyghtgowne of tawny Satten edged with apasmane
 of venice golde / and furred with black conny

78.103 dd to Rauf hoope

By the Lady Carewe a cusshyncloth of Fyne cameryk with byrdes &
 bestes of black silke edged with bone lace of venice Siluer

78.104 dd to Mrs Skydmore

By the Lady Woodehouse apeir of Braslettes of golde cont xxiiij peces
 of goldesmythes worke / in xij of them Agathes and in thother xij two
 perles apece poiz . . . . ij oz iij qrt

78.105 dd to Mrs Skidmore

By the Lady Cheke a foreparte of a kyrtill of white networke floresshed
 with Siluer with asmall pasmann Lace & lyned with white sercenet

78.106 dd to Rauf hoope

78.107 By the Lady Butler in golde . . . . vj li

78.108 By the Lady Pawlet in golde . . . . v li

78.109 By the Lady Gresham in golde . . . . x li

By the Lady Crumwell in golde. . . . . v li
 dd to henry Sakford

78.110   By the Lady Drury aforeparte and apeir of Sleves of white Satten set with
            Spangilles and lyned with tawney Sarceonet

                                                                dd to Rauf hoope

78.111   By the Lady Hennage a Juell being adolphyn of mother of perle garnesshed
            with small sparkes of Rubyes and Ophalles

                                                        dd to the said Lady Howard

78.112   By the Lady walsingham two pillowbiers of Cameryck wrought with sylke
            of Diuers collors cut

78.113   By the Lady willowbye sir Fraunces willowbyes wyf alynyng for acollor &
            apeir of sleves networke floresshed with siluer & golde

                                                            dd to Mrs Skydmore

78.114   By the Lady Ratclif v crippins of Lawne garnesshed with golde and siluer
            purle two swete bagges of sylke and anightcoyf of white cutworke
            floresshed with Siluer and set with Spangilles / and v tothe pykes
            beinge quilles

                                the Crepyns dd to Mrs Blanch threst to Mrs Skydmor

78.115   By the Lady Frogmerton akyrtill of yelow Satten alouer with venice siluer
            with roses of twistes of siluer lyned with serceonet

                                                                dd to Rauf hoope

78.116   By the Lady Arondell a Ring of golde with one small Diamonde with
            small sparkes of Diamondes and rubys abowte it

                                                        dd to the said Lady Howard

78.117   By the Lady wylford aforeparte of Lawne cutworke white

78.118   By the Lady Marvyn two Partelettes of Networke thone floresshed with
            golde / thother with Siluer

                                                            dd to Mrs Skydmor

78.119   By the Lady Croftes afeyer cusshyn enbrawdred with Silke of sundry collors
            with thistory of Icorus Lyned with changeably Taphata and iiij buttons
            with Tassells of Silke of sondry collors

                                                            dd to Richard Tod

78.120   By the Lady Sowche Sir John Sowches wyf a Smock of Camerick the Sleves
            and parte of the boddy wrought with black silke and golde / the ruffes and
            collor edged with abone Lace of golde

                                                            dd to Mrs Skydmor

Knights

78.121   By Sir Fraunces Knowlles knight Treausoror of the householde in golde. . . . x li
78.122   By Sir James Croftes knight Comptroller of the housholde in golde. . . . . . . x li

                                                            dd to henry Sakford

78.123   By Sir Christofer Hatton knight vicechamberleyn and capitane of the
            garde afeyer Juell of golde being acrosse of Diamondes fully garnesshed
            with small Diamondes / and a/feyer perle pendaunt and a Juell of golde
            wherein is a Dog leding aman ouer abrid[g]e the boddy fully garnesshed
            with small Diamondes and rubys / and thre small perles pendant

                                                        dd to the said Lady Howard

231

78.124 By Sir Rauf Sadlier knight Chauncellor of the Duchy of Lancaster in
golde . . . . xv [li]
dd to henry Sakford

78.125 By Sir Fraunces walsingham knight principall Secretary a Gowne of
blewe Satten with rewes of golde / and two small pasmane Laces of
venice golde Faced with powdred Armyns
dd to Rauf hoope

78.126 By Thomas wylson Esquir Secretary acup of Agathe garnesshed with
golde and set with Stone
dd in charge to the Mr of the Juelles

78.127 By Sir walter Myldemey knight Chauncellor of thexchequire in golde . . . . . . x li
78.128 By Sir william Cordell Mr of the Rolles in golde . . . . x li
78.129 By Sir Christofer Haydon knight in golde . . . . x li
78.130 By Sir William Damsell knight receyvor of the Courte of wardes in golde. . . x li
78.131 By Sir Henry Crumwell knight in golde . . . . x li
78.132 By Sir Thomas Gresham knight in golde . . . . x li
78.133 By Sir Owen Hopton liutenant of the Tower in golde . . . . x li
78.134 By Sir John Thynn in golde . . . . v li
dd to henry Sakford

78.135 By Sir Gawen Carowe a Smock of Camerick wrought with black Sylke
in the collor and sleves the square and ruffes wrought with venice golde /
and edged with a small bonelace of venice golde
dd to Mrs Skydmor

78.136 By Sir Gilbert Dethick alias Garter principall king at Armes Abooke of
the States in king william conquerors tyme
dd to Mrs Blanche

78.137 By Sir henry Lee knight a Juell being a Garlande of golde with Leaves /
and thre walnuttes in the myddes with a butterfly pendant of Sparkes
of Ophalles and Rubyes
dd to said said Lady Howard

78.138 By Sir Thomas Henage knight Treausoror of the chamber acloke of black
vellat set with xvj greate buttons of golde being Dolphyns / and edged
with a small pasmane Lace of golde / and Lyned with Serceonet

78.139 By Sir william Drury a foreparte of Asshecollored Satten enbrawdred with
Clowdes and wormes of golde and Siluer lyned with yelowe Serceonet
dd to Rauf hoope

78.140 By Sir Edwarde Horsey knight aCheyne of Pomaunder with verey small
ragged perle
dd to the said Lady Howard

Gentilwomen

78.141 By Blanche aParry alitill Box of golde to put in cumphettes and a litill
spone of golde weying all . . . . j oz iij qrt
dd to the said La howard

78.142 By Fraunces Hawarde alitill vale of Networke set with Spangilles of Siluer
dd to Mrs Eliz Knowlles

78.143 By Elizabeth Knowles a foreparte boddies and partelet of Sipers Cryppen
     worke

78.144 By Edmundes a Dublet of white networke floresshed alouer with Siluer &
     Spangilles / lyned with white taphata

78.145 By Skydmore a foreparte and apeir of Sleves of peche collored Satten with
     acordant of golde and sylke and set with Spangilles / Lyned with yelow
     sercenet with two pasmane laces of golde abowte the border

                                    dd to Rauf hoope

78.146 By Snowe vj handekerchers wrought with silke of sundry collors and
     edged with pasmane lace of golde

           ij with the Lady Stafford & iiij with Mrs Skydmor

78.147 By Baptest vj handekerchers of Cameryck with abrode border of black
     sylke & edged with pasmane of golde

                                   dd to Mrs Skydmor

78.148 By West a Fan of Fethers of sundry collors with a handill of Siluer

                                   dd to Mr Myddilmore

78.149 By katheryn Paston a pettycote of white Satten alouer with pasman of
     golde & siluer lyned with yelow sercenet

                                   dd to Rauf hoope

78.150 By Marbury two small Pillowbyers wrought with silke of Diuers collors

78.151 By Digby vj handekerchers wrought with black / and edged with abone
     Lace black and white

                                   dd to Mrs Skydmor

78.152 By Jane Brysselles a partelet apeir of ruffes and apeir of cuffes of
     Lawne wrought with black sylke and Siluer and the partelet floresshed
     with golde and Siluer set with Spangilles

                                   dd to herself

78.153 By Townesende a rownde kyrtill of Tawny vellat edged with abrode
     bonelace of Siluer & golde set with spangilles

                                   dd to Rauf hoope

78.154 By Cave vj handekerchers wrought with blackworke with aborder of venice
     golde & siluer pasmane lace

                                   dd to Mrs Skydmor

78.155 By Lichefelde two peir of gloves perfumed a sute of Ruffes / iij peces of
     very feyer cutworke wrought with golde and sylke / and a Feyer
     Handekercher

                    the gloves dd to Mrs Knolles the Ruffes
              to Mrs Jane & the handkercher to Mrs Skydmor

78.156 By Sackford a Skrene of Serceonet enbrawdred with venice golde with a white
     Falkon bering a Septor

                                   dd to Mr Sakford

78.157 By Elizabeth Hawarde a Collor and apeir of Ruffes of cutworke garnesshed
     with siluer blakwork & spangilles

                             dd to Mrs Jane Briselles

78.158 By wynkefelde apece of plate guilte poz . . . . vj oz di
                                in charge with the Mr of the Juelles

78.159   By Harman a sute of Lawne floresshed black with byrdes and beastes edged with abonelace white and black

78.160   By Twyst Lawndrys iij handekerchers wrought with blac spanysshworke and edged with abonelace of venice golde and iiij totheclothes of corse hollande wrought with black sylke / and edged with bonelace of Siluer & black sylke

78.161   By Taylor a night coyf of lynnen alouer enbrawdred with venice golde and Silke of sundry collors

78.162   By Note vj handekerchers of Cameryck edged with bone lace of golde and Siluer

78.163   By Barley vj handekerchers of Cameryck edged with pasmane Lace of golde

78.164   By Mountague a peir of Sleves of Cameryck wrought with Roses and buddes of black Sylke

dd to Mrs Skydmor

78.165   By Dane thre peces of Lawne

dd to Mrs Blanche

78.166   By Croxson anight coyf of cameryk cutworke & spangilles with a forehedcloth and anight border of cutwork with bonelace

78.167   By Amy Shelton vj handekerchers of Camerik edged with pasmane of golde and Siluer

78.168   By Huggans vj handekerchers of sundry sortes one wrought with murry sylke and threst of other collors

dd to Mrs Skydmor

78.169   By Dale a foreparte of a kyrtill & adublet of strawe collered Satten netted alouer with Flowers trees and borders of Syluer and black Sylke / Lyned with orenge collered Taphata

dd to Rauf hoope

78.170   By Julio a Cusshyncloth and apyllowbere of Cameryk wrough[t] with blackworke of Sylke

dd to Mrs Skydmor

Chaplyns

78.171   By ArchDeacon Carowe Deane of the Chapell in golde . . . . x li

dd to henry Sakford

78.172   By Absolon Mr of the Savoy a Bible couered with cloth of golde garnesshed with Siluer & gilte & ij plates with the quenes armes

dd to John of the Closet

Gentilmen

78.173   By John Harrington Esquire a Remnant of black clothe of Siluer rewed cont . . . . vj yards qrt di

dd to Rauf hoope

78.174   By Rauf Bowes acap of purple vellat set with viij dosen and Six buttons of golde / with white Fether

78.175   By Edwarde Clere in golde . . . . x li
                                              dd to henry Sakford

78.176   By Phillp Sydney a Smock of Camerick the Sleves and collor wrought
      with blacworke / and edged with asmall bone lace of golde and Siluer /
      and asute of Ruffes cutworke floresshed with golde & siluer & set with
      spangillg [sic] cont iiij peces
                           dd to Mrs Skydmor the Smocke
                       the Ruffes to Mrs Jane briselles

78.177   By Edwarde Basshe in golde . . . . x li
                                                dd to henry Sakford

78.178   By Dyer a foreparte of akyrtill of Lawne enbrawdred with Flowers of golde
      sylke & siluer of sundry collors lyned with sercenet
                                    dd to Rauf hoope

78.179   By Stanhop asmall Juell of golde with an ophall in the myddes set abowte
      with small Rubyes and aperle pendant
                             dd to the said La howarde

78.180   By Fowlke Grevell a Smock of Camerick wrought abowte the Coller and
      Sleves of Spanysshe worke of Roses and Letteres / and anight coyf with
      aforehedclothe of the same worke
                                   dd to Mrs Skydmor

78.181   By Benedic Spynnala a petticote of Watchet Satten Leyed alouer with
      pasmann Lace of golde and syluer and Flowers / with viij gardes of
      pasmann of golde and Siluer rownde abowte it lyned with yelo Taphata
                                    dd to Rauf hoope

78.182   By Newton acup of Siluer guilt being aporanger with a snayle in the top
      standing vpon an oken Leaf poiz . . . . [no weight given]
                      with the Quene by John Wyneard

78.183   By Doctor Hewyk a pot of grene gynger and another of Orenge Flowers
78.184   By Doctor Maister apot of grene ginger and a nother of Orenge Flowers
78.185   By Julio a pot of grene ginger and another of Orenge Flowers
78.186   By John Hemmawey a pot of wardyns condite and manus i
78.187   By Ryche abox of peches of Jennowey
                                   dd to Mrs Skydmor

78.188   By Smythsonne Mr Cooke a feyer Marchepane
78.189   By Dudley Sergeaunt of the Pastry a greate pye of Quynses and wardyns
      guilte
                                       [blank]

78.190   By William Huggans agrete swete bag of purple Taphata enbrawdred /
      and xix small bagges of sercenet
                                   dd to Mrs Skydmor

78.191   By Marke Antony a vyall
                                      dd to Mr Baptest

78.192   By Ambroso Lupo a box of Lute Strynges
78.193   By Putricio two pictures thone of Judith and holyfernus / thother of Jula
      and Sectra
                                    dd to Mr Baptest

78.194   By Charles Smyth a cheyne of Pomaunder, with buttons of Siluer betwene
                                 dd to the said Lady Howard

78.195   By Christofer Gyles a Cutler / a meate knyf with a feyer hafte of white
      bone aconceyte in it
                                 dd to Mrs Skydmor

78.196   By Morgan a potticary thre boxes one of gynger candy / another grene
      gynger / & the thirde oringes cundit
                                 dd to Mr Sakford

78.197   By Smyth Custumer two Boltes of Cameryck
                                 dd to Mrs Blanche

           Juelles brought into the Neweyeres guift chamber without reporte
                         made by whom they were given

78.198   Item a Juell of golde being awoman ennamuled called virtute / standing
      vpon a Raynebowe the boddy garnesshed with sparkes of Diamondes
      and Rubyes brought into the Newyers guift chamber by Henry Sakford
      But no reporte made who gave it to her Matie

78.199   Item a Juell of golde being a Fawcon and aphesaunt garnesshed with
      Rubys Diamondes Emeraldes and perles Lykewyse brought by the said
      Sackforde making no reporte who gave it

78.200   Item a Juell being alampe with aharte in a Flame of Fyer garnesshed with
      two Saphers Diamondes Rubyes and Ophalles and a Sarpent of Ophall
      with a Ruby pendant set with Six small perles and one perle pendant
      brought into the said Chamber by Kyllegrave without reporte made
      who gave it

78.201   Item a Juell being a lylly of golde with a Butterflye in the same and a
      Secrabe garnesshed with small Ophalles Rubys and Diamondes / with
      Rooses of mother of perle and Sparkes of Rubyes brought in to the said
      Chamber by Mrs Skydmore without Reporte made by whom it was
      given
                                dd to the saide Lady Howarde

Summa totalis of all the / money giuen to her
Matie & delured / ut supra . . . . ix^C iiij^xx xiij li xiij s iiij d

Elizabeth R
[sign manual]

                                         J Asteley
                              Ex[aminatio] per
                                           Bristow
                                       J Pigeon
                                   Ste Fulwell
                                 Richard Asteley

Anno Regni Regine
Elizabeth } Vicesimo

Newyers Guiftes giuen by her Matie
at her Honor of Hamptoncorte to thise persones whose names
Doo Hereafter ensue the First Day of January the yere
aforesaid

Elizabeth R
[sign manual]

78.202	To the Lady margret Lineox thre guilte boolles with acouer of the store of the charge of John Asteley Esquire Maister and Treausoror of our Juelles and plate and parcell of iiij^m oz by vs appoynted to be in areddynes for like purposes . . . . .iiij^xx vij oz di
78.203	To the Lady Mary Gray acup with a cover Brandon poz. . . . . xviij oz
78.204	To Sir Nicholas Bacon knight keper of the greate Seale of Inglande one Doble Booll of Siluer and guilte Keell poz . . . . xxxiiij oz iij qrt di
78.205	To the Lady Margret Countes of Darby one Doble Boole guilte Brandon poz . . . . L oz
78.206	To the Lorde Burley Lorde High Treausoror of Inglande a Duble Boll of Siluer and guilte Keele poz . . . . xl oz iij qrt di
78.207	To the Lorde Marques of winchester a Boole of Siluer and guilte Brandon poz . . . . .xxx oz iij qrt

Earles

78.208	To therle of Leycetor Mr of the horses one Boole of Siluer and guilte Keele poz . . . . C oz di
78.209	To therle of Arondell a Duble Boole of Siluer and guilte Keele poz . . . . L oz
78.210	To therle of Sussex Lorde Chamberleyn a Doble Boole of Siluer and guilte Brandon poz . . . . .xxxv oz
78.211	To therle of Lincoln Lorde Admirall one Boole of Siluer and guilte with acouer Brandon poz . . . . xxij oz iij qrt
78.212	To therle of Warwyck in guilte plate Keele poz . . . . Cxij oz di di qrt
78.213	To therle of Bedford agilte cup with acouer Keele poz . . . . xxxj oz di
78.214	To therle of Shrewesbury aBoole of Siluer and guilte with acouer Keele poz . . . . .xxx oz qrt di
78.215	To therle of Darby thre Booles with acouer of Siluer and guilte of our store aforesaid poz . . . . .xxx oz
78.216	To therle of Huntingdon a Boole of Siluer and guilte with acouer Brandon poz . . . . xx oz
78.217	To therle of Rutlande one Boole with acouer guilte Brandon poz. . . . . xx oz
78.218	To therle of Penbroke one Boole of Siluer and guilte Keele poz . . . . xxx oz iij qrt di
78.219	To therle of Northumberlande one Boole of Siluer and guilte with acouer Keele. . . . . xx oz

78.220 To therle of Hertford one Boole of Siluer and guilte with acouer Keele
. . . . xix oz iij qrt di

78.221 To therle of Southampton a Boole of Siluer and guilte with acouer
Brandon poz . . . . xxx oz di di qrt

78.222 To therle of Ormunde one peir of Flagonnes of Siluer and guilte parcell
of our store ut supra – iiij^{xx} xv oz iij qrt and thre Booles of Siluer and
guilte with acouer Keele poz in toto . . . . Clxj oz

78.223 To the vicounte Mountaque in guilte plate Keele. . . . . xix oz iij qrt di

Duchesses Marquises & Countisses

78.224 To the Duches of Suff[olk] a Doble Boole of Siluer and guilte Keele
. . . . xxxix oz iij qrt di

78.225 To the Duches of Somerset one cup of Siluer and guilte with acouer
Brandon poz . . . . .xxv oz qrt di

78.226 To the Lady Marques of Northampton in guilte plate Keele poz . . . . xlij oz

78.227 To the Lady Marques of winchester Dowager in guilte plate Keele poz
. . . . xxj oz

78.228 To the Lady Marques of winchester the younger in guilte plate Keele
. . . . .xviij oz iij qr di

78.229 To the Countes of Sussex one Boll of Siluer and guilte with acouer
Brandon poiz. . . . .
xx oz di qr

78.230 To the Countes of Lincoln in guilte plate Keele . . . . xlix oz iij qrt di

78.231 To the Countes of warwick in guilte plate Brandon—xxxiij oz qrt di / in
guilte plate Keele—iiij oz and one cup of Siluer and guilte of our store
ut supra—vij oz di qrt in toto . . . . xliiij oz di

78.232 To the Countes of Shrewesbury a Boole of Siluer and guilte Brandon
poz . . . . .xxx oz iij qrt

78.233 To the Countes of Huntingdon a Doble Boole of Siluer and guilte
Brandon poi. . . . . .xxxv oz

78.234 To the Countes of Oxford a Boole of Siluer and guilte Brandon poz
. . . . xx oz di qrt

78.235 To the Countes of Essex a Stope of Siluer and guilte Keele poz
. . . . xxviij oz di di qrt

78.236 To the Countes of Penbroke Dowager one Boole of Siluer & guilte with
acouer of our store ut supra poz. . . . . .xxvj oz di di qrt

78.237 To the Countes of Penbroke the younger one Boole of Siluer and guilte
Brandon poz . . . . xxiiij oz di di qrt

78.238 To the Countes of Bedford in guilte plate Keele poz . . . . L oz di

78.239 To the Countes of Northumberlande in guilte plate Keele oz . . . . .xx oz qrt

78.240 To the Countes of Southampton in guilte plate Brandon poz. . . . xix oz di di qrt

78.241 To the Countes of Rutlande one Boole of Siluer and guilte with acouer
Brandon poz . . . . .xx oz qrt

78.242 To the Countes of Kent Dowager a cup of Siluer and guilte with acouer
Brandon poz . . . . xviij oz di di qrt

78.243 To the Countes of Kent Junior a cup of Siluer and guilte Keele poz
.... xx oz qrt di

78.244 To the Countes of Commerlande a cup of Siluer and guilte with a couer
Keele poz .... ix oz di di qrt

Viccount

78.245 To the Vicecountes Montague acup of Siluer and gilte with acouer Brandon
poz .... xx oz di

Busshopps

78.246 To the Archebusshop of yorke a Boll of Siluer and guilte with acouer
Keele poz .... xxxv oz

78.247 To the Busshop of Ely a tankerd of Siluer and guilte Keele poz .... xxxvj oz

78.248 To the Busshop of Dureham a boll of Siluer and guilte with acouer
Keele poz .... xxxiiij oz di

78.249 To the Busshop of London a Salte of Siluer and guilte Keele poz
.... xxviij oz iij qrt

78.250 To the Busshop of wynchester in guilte plate Keele poz .... xxx oz di qrt

78.251 To the Busshop of Salisbury in guilte plate Brandon poz .... xxviij oz di qrt

78.252 To the Busshop of Lincolne in guilte plate Brandon poz............. xxxj oz

78.253 To the Busshop of Norwiche one guilte Boole of our store ut supra
poz .... xxiiij oz di qrt

78.254 To the Busshop of worcetor one guilte cup of our store ut supra
poz .... xxiij oz di qrt

78.255 To the Busshop of Lichfield and Coventry in guilte plate Kee poz
.... xx oz qrt

78.256 To the Busshop of Hereford in guilte plate Keele poz .... xvj oz qrt

78.257 To the Busshop of St Davis in guilte plate Keele poz............... xvij oz qrt

78.258 To the Busshop of Karlile in guilte plate Keele poz .... xv oz di di qrt

78.259 To the Busshop of Excetor in guilte plate Keele poz .... xvj oz

78.260 To the Busshop of Bathe in guilte plate Keele poz............... xvj oz qrt di

78.261 To the Busshop of Peterborough in guilte plate Brandon poz.... xv oz iij qrt di

78.262 To the Busshop of Glocetor one guilte pot of our store poz .... xviij oz qrt

78.263 To the Busshop of Chichester in guilte plate Brandon poz .... xvj oz qrt

Lordes

78.264 To the Lorde of Hunesdon one Doble Boole of Siluer and guilte Brandon
poiz.. xxxj oz di di qrt

78.265 To the Lorde Hawarde in guilte plate Keele poz.............. Ciiij oz iij qrt di

78.266 To the Lorde of Burgevenny in guilte plate of our store as aforesaid
poz .... ix oz qrt di

78.267 To the Lord Ryche in guilte plate Keele poz..................... xix oz iij qrt

78.268 To the Lorde Darcy of Chytte in guilte plate Brandon poz .... xix oz di

78.269	To the Lorde Russell in guilte plate Brandon poz.	xx oz qrt di
78.270	To the Lorde Shandowes in guilte plate Keele poz	xiij oz di qrt
78.271	To the Lorde Bokehurst in guilte plate Brandon poiz	x oz di qrt
78.272	To the Lorde Northe in guilte plate Keele poiz	xx oz qrt di
78.273	To the Lorde Paget in guilte plate Kele poz	xx oz qrt di
78.274	To the Lorde Stafford in guilte plate Brandon poz.	xx oz iij qrt
78.275	To the Lorde Compton in guilte plate Brandon poz	xx oz di qrt
78.276	To the Lorde Norreys of Ricot in guilte plate Keele poiz	xxj oz
78.277	To the Lorde Cobham in guilte plate Keele poiz	xx oz
78.278	To the Lorde Lumley in guilte plate Brandon poiz	xx oz qrt
78.279	To the Lorde Wharton in guilte plate Keele poz.	xix oz
78.280	To the Lorde Cheyny in guilte plate Keele poiz	xxj oz di qrt

Barronesses

78.281	To the Barronesse Burleigh in guilte plate Keele poz	xxiiij oz
78.282	To the Barronesse Hawarde Dowager in guilte plate Keele poz.	xx oz
78.283	To the Barronesse Hawarde Junior in guilte plate of our store ut supra poz.	xxiiij oz qrt
78.284	To the Barronesse Cobham a Doble boole of siluer & guilte Ke poz	L oz
78.285	To the Barronesse Hunesdon thre guilte Booles with acouer Keele poiz.	xxv oz qrt di
78.286	To the Barronesse Dacres of the South in guilte plate Brandon	xvj oz qrt di
78.287	To the Barronesse Tayleboyes in guilte plate Keele poz	xx oz iij qrt
78.288	To the Barronesse Shandowes Dowager in guilte plate Brandon poz	xx oz di
78.289	To the Barronesse Shandowes Junior in guilte plate Keele poz	xj oz qrt di
78.290	To the Barronesse St John of Bletslow in guilte plate of our store ut supra.	xvij oz di
78.291	To the Barronet Paget the Lorde Pagettes wyf in guilte plate of our store ut supra	xix oz di
78.292	To the Barronesse Paget Care in guilte plate Keele poiz.	xxv oz qrt
78.293	To the Barronesse Cheyney in guilte plate Brandon poiz.	xl oz iij qrt di
78.294	To the Barronesse Audeley in guilte plate Keele poz	xij oz di qrt
78.295	To the Lady Talbot in guilte plate Keele poiz.	xiij oz
78.296	To the Barronesse Bokehurst in guilte plate Keele poz.	ix oz di
78.297	To the Barronesse Norres in guilte plate Brandon poz.	xx oz qrt
78.298	To the Barronesse Sheffelde in guilte plate Keele poz	xvj oz qrt di
78.299	To the Barronesse Barkley in guilte plate Keele poz.	xviij oz qrt di
78.300	To the Lady Mary Veere in guilte plate of our store ut supra	xvj oz qrt

Ladies

78.301	To the Lady Mary Sydney in guilt plate Keele poiz	xxx oz iij qrt di
78.302	To the Lady Mary Semer wyf to Mr Rogers in guilte plate Brandon poiz.	xiij oz di di qrt
78.303	To the Lady Stafford in guilte plate Brandon poiz	xxx oz iij qrt di

78.304	To the Lady Carowe in guilte plate Keele poz	xxxv oz qrt
78.305	To the Lady woodehouse in guilte plate Keele poz.	xxiij oz di di qrt
78.306	To the Lady Cheke in guilte plate Brandon poz	xxiiij oz iij qrt di
78.307	To the Lady Butler in guilte plate Keele poz.	xvj oz qrt di
78.308	To the Lady Hennage in guilte plate Keele poz	xxij oz
78.309	To the Lady walsingham in guilte plate Brandon poz	xvj oz iij qrt
78.310	To the Lady Drury in guilte plate Keele poz.	xvj oz
78.311	To the Lady Pawlet in guilte plate Keele poz	xj oz di qrt
78.312	To the Lady willowby Sir Fraunces wif in guilte plate Brandon poz	xij oz di qrt
78.313	To the Lady Gresham in guilte plate Keele poz	xix oz
78.314	To the Lady Crumwell in guilte plate Brandon poz	xij oz
78.315	To the Lady Ratclyff in guilte plate Keele poz	xiiij oz
78.316	To the Lady Frogmerton in guilte plate Brandon poz	xxij oz qrt
78.317	To the Lady Arondell in guilte plate Brandon poiz	xv oz
78.318	To the Lady wylforde in guilte plate Brandon poz	xix oz
78.319	To the Lady Marvyn in guilte plate Keele poz	xiiij oz iij qrt di
78.320	To the Lady Croftes in guilte plate Brandon poz	xx oz
78.321	To the Lady Sowche in guilte plate Brandon poiz	xiij oz di qrt

Knightes

78.322	To Sir Fraunces Knowlles knight Treausoror of the house in guilte plate Keele poiz.	xxv oz
783.23	To Sir James Croftes Comptroller of the same in guilte plate Brandon poz	xxiiij oz iij qrt di
78.324	To Sir Christofer Hatton knight vicechamberleyn and capitane of the garde in guilte plate Keele poiz	iiij^C oz
78.325	To Sir Rauf Sadlier Chaunçellor of the Duchy in guilte plate Brandon poz	xxx oz iij qrt
78.326	To Sir Fraunces Walsingham knight principall Secretary in guilte plate Keele poiz.	Lx oz di
78.327	To Sir Walter Myldemey Chauncellor of thexchequire in guilt Brandon poz	xxvij oz qrt
78.328	To Thomas Wilson Esquire another Secretary in guilte plate Brandon poz	xxv oz
78.329	To Sir Thomas Hennage knight Treausoror of the Chamber in guilte plate Keele poz	xlviij oz
78.330	To Sir William Cordell knight Mr of the Rolles in guilte plate Brandon poiz.	xx oz iij qrt di
78.331	To Sir Christofer Haydon knight in guilte plate Keele poz	xxij oz
78.332	To Sir William Damsell knight Receyvor of the Courte of Wardes in guilte plate Keele poz.	xxj oz di di qrt
78.333	To Sir Henry Crumwell knight in guilte plate Brandon poz	xx oz iij qrt
78.334	To Sir Gawen Carowe knight in guilte plate Keele poz	xxxv oz di
78.335	To Sir Thomas Gresham knight in guilte plate of our store ut supra poz	xx oz iij qrt

241

78.336   To Sir Owen Hopton knight liutenant of the Tower in guilte plate of or
        store poiz . . . . xxij oz qrt

78.337   To Sir John Thynn knight in guilte plate Brandon poiz . . . . xj oz

78.338   To Sir Gilbert Dethyck knight in guilte plate Keele poz . . . . xij oz iij qrt di

78.339   To Sir Henry Lee knight in guilte plate Keele poiz . . . . xlix oz iij qrt

78.340   To Sir William Drury knight in guilte plate Keele poz . . . . xvij oz

78.341   To Sir Edwarde Horsey knight a guilte boole of our store ut supra
        poz . . . . xxxj oz qrt

Gentilwomen

78.342   To Mrs Blanche Parry in guilte plate Keele poz . . . . xviij oz di

78.343   To Mrs Elizabeth Knowlles in guilte plate Keele poz . . . . xv oz

78.344   To Mrs Fraunces Hawarde in guilte plate Brandon poz . . . . xiiij oz qrt di

78.345   To Mrs Edmundes in guilte plate Keele poz . . . . xv oz di qrt

78.346   To Mrs Skydmore in guilte plate Ke poz . . . . xv oz

78.347   To Mrs Snowe in guilte plate Keele poz . . . . xiij oz qrt

78.348   To Mrs Baptest in guilte plate Keele poz . . . . xvj oz

78.349   To Mrs West in guilte plate Keele poiz . . . . xv oz di di qrt

78.350   To Mrs Katheryn Pastone in guilte plate of our store ut supra . . . . xv oz

78.351   To Mrs Marbury in guilte plate Brandon poz . . . . xiij oz qrt

78.352   To Mrs Digby in guilte plate of our store ut supra . . . . xvj oz di di qrt

78.353   To Mrs Jane Brisselles in guilte plate Brandon poz . . . . xv oz

78.354   To Mrs Townesende in guilte plate Keele poz . . . . xxix oz

78.355   To Mrs Cave in guilte plate Keele poz . . . . xv oz iij qrt di

78.356   To Mrs Lychefelde in guilte plate Keele poz . . . . xvj oz qrt

78.357   To Mrs Sackforde in guilte plate Keele poz . . . . xxij oz

78.358   To Mrs Elizabeth Hawarde in guilte plate Keele poz . . . . xiiij oz qrt

78.359   To Mrs Dale in guilte plate of our store ut supra poz . . . . xxiiij oz di di qrt

78.360   To Mrs Wynkefelde in guilte plate Brandon poz . . . . xij oz qrt di

78.361   To Mrs Harman in guilte plate Keele poz . . . . ix oz qrt di

78.362   To Mrs Smythson in guilte plate Brandon poz . . . . vij oz qrt

78.363   To Mrs Twyst Lawndris in guilte plate Keele poz . . . . v oz

78.364   To Mrs Note in guilte plate Keele poz . . . . xiij oz

78.365   To Mrs Barley in guilte plate Keele poz . . . . xij oz di

78.366   To Mrs mountague in guilde plate of our store ut supra poz . . . . xiij oz di qrt

78.367   To Mrs Dane in guilte plate Keele poz . . . . xx oz

78.368   To Mrs Huggans in guilte plate Brandon poz . . . . xx oz

78.369   To Amy Shelton in guilte plate of our store ut supra . . . . xj oz di qrt

78.370   To Mrs Julio in guilte plate Brandon poz . . . . xj oz qrt

78.371   To Mrs Crokeson in guilte plate of our store ut supra . . . . ix oz

Maydes of Honour

78.372   To the Lady Susan in guilte plate Brandon poz . . . . x oz di di qrt

78.373   To Mrs Mary Ratclyf in guilte plate Brandon poz . . . . x oz di qrt

78.374   To Mrs Katheryn Hoowarde in guilte plate Brandon poz . . . . x oz qrt di

78.375   To Mrs Elyn Bridges in guilte plate Keele poz . . . . x oz di di qrt

78.376	To Mrs Elizabeth Garret in guilte plate Brandon poiz . . . . x oz di di qrt
78.377	To Mrs Martha Hawarde in guilte plate Keele poz . . . . x oz di di qrt
78.378	To Mrs Hyde mother of the maydes in guilte plate Brandon poz
	. . . . xij oz di di qrt

Chaplyns

78.379	To Archedeacon Carowe Deane of the chapell in guilte plate Keele
	poz . . . . .xxij oz qrt
78.380	To Absolyn Mr of the Savoy in guilte plate Keele poz . . . . v oz

Gentilmen

78.381	To John Haring[t]on in guilte plate Keele poz . . . . xl oz
78.382	To Rauf Bowes in guilte plate Keele poz . . . . xxiiij oz di
78.383	To Edward Clere in guilte plate Keele poz . . . . xvij oz iij qrt
78.384	To Phillip Sydney in guilte plate Brandon poz . . . . xxij oz di di qrt
78.385	To Edwarde Basshe in guilte plate of our store ut supra poz . . . . xxj oz
78.386	To Dyer in guilte plate Keele poz . . . . xvj oz di qrt
78.387	To Stanhop in guilte plate Keele poiz . . . . xxj oz iij qrt di
78.388	To Fowlke Grervell in guilte plate Brandon poz . . . . xiij oz qrt di
78.389	To Smyth Custumer in guilte plate Brandon poz . . . . xv oz
78.390	To Benedic Spyinnala in guilte plate Brandon poz—Lj oz / and in guilte
	plate Keele poz—xxix oz—in toto . . . . iiij^{xx} oz
78.391	To Newton in guilte plate of our store ut supra—vj oz iij qrt / and in
	guilte plate Keele poiz—viij oz qrt—in toto . . . . xv oz
78.392	To Doctor Hewick in guilte plate Kele poiz . . . . xiiij oz iij qrt
78.393	To Doctor Maister in guilte plate Brandon poiz . . . . xiiij oz iij qrt
78.394	To Julio in guilte plate Brandon poz . . . . xiiij oz di di qrt
78.395	To John Hemawey in guilte plate Keele poz . . . . vj oz di
78.396	To John Ryche in guilte plate Keele poz . . . . vj oz di
78.397	To John Smythson al Taylor Mr Cooke in guilte plate Brandon poz
	. . . . viij oz qrt
78.398	To John Dudley Sergeant of the pastry in guilte plate Keele poiz
	. . . . iiij oz iij qrt di
78.399	To William Huggans in guilte plate brandon poz .xxx oz
78.400	To Morgan Potticary in guilte plate Keele poz .v oz qrt
78.401	To Marke Anthony in guilte plate Keele poz . . . . v oz di
78.402	To Ambroso Lupo in guilte plate of our store ut supra poiz . . . . .v oz qrt
78.403	To Petricio in guilte plate Keele poz . . . . iiij oz di
78.404	To Charles Smyth in guilte plate Keele poz . . . . xx oz iij qrt di
78.405	To Christofer Gyles Cutlier in guilte plate Keele poz . . . . ij oz qrt

Fre Guiftes

78.406	To Sir George Haward knight gent vssher of our privey Chamber in
	guilte plate Keell poz . . . . xij oz di
78.407	To Mr John Asteley Mr and Treausoror of our Juelles and plate in gulte
	plate Keele poz . . . . xviij oz iij qrt di

78.408   To Mr Thomas Asteley grome of our privey Chamber in guilte plate
          Brandon poz . . . . viij oz iij qrt di
78.409   To Mr. Edwarde Care grome of our said privy chamber in guilte plate Br
          poz . . . . viij oz iij qrt
78.410   To Mr Henry Sackford another grome of our said Chamber in guilte plate
          Ke poiz. . . . . viij oz iij qrt
78.411   To Mr John Baptest another grome in guilte plate Keele. . . . . viij oz iij qrt
78.412   To Mr Henry Myddilmore another grome in guilte plate Keele poiz
          . . . . viij oz iij qrt
78.413   To Mr Knevet another grome in guilte plate Brandon poz . . . . viij oz di
78.414   To Mr Thomas Gorges likewyse grome in guilte plate Keele poz
          . . . . viij oz di di qrt
78.415   To William Killegrave another grome in guilte plate Brandon poz . . . . . viij oz di
78.416   To Rauf Hoope yoman of our Roobes in guilte plate Brandon
          poz . . . . xij oz iij qrt di
78.417   To Nicholas Bristow clerc of our Juelles and plate in guilte plate
          Brandon poz . . . . x oz iij qrt di
78.418   To John Pigeon yoman of the same in guilte plate Brandon poiz . . x oz iij qrt di
78.419   To Stephen Fulwell another yoman there in guilte plate Brandon
          poz . . . . x oz iij qrt di
78.420   To Richard Asteley grome of the same in guilte plate of our store—
          one oz iij qrt and in guilte plate Br – ix oz di qrt in toto . . . . x oz iij qrt di

          Summa totalis of all the plate
          giuen awey as aforesaid . . . .}v^m CCC xxxij oz

                          Guifftes giuen and deliuered at sundrie
                          tymes in maner and fourme Following
                                            Viz

78.421   Sir Cormak
          First given and Delyuered the xxix^th of May Ao Regni Regine
          Elizabeth xix^no to Sir Cormak an Irissh gent a Cheyne of golde
          of our store of the charge of John Asteley Esquir Mr and Treausoror
          of our Juelles and plate / and parcell of Fyve hundreth one poundes
          xxiij di qrt by vs appoynted to by golde for like purposes . . xxij oz di di qrt
          golde
78.422   Themperors Ambassador
          Itm moare given and delyuered the xix^th of June Ao pred to Baron
          John Prayner Ambassador sent from the Emperor of Alman one
          cheyne of golde of the charge of the said John Asteley and parcell
          of the said Some &c. . . . . Liiij oz di qrt vj gr golde
78.423   The Vicount of Gaunt
          Itm given and delyuered the 6th of July Ao pd to vicount of gawnte
          sent from the States of the Loue country acheyne of golde poiz—

                                         244

Lxviij ounces di qrt of the charge of John Asteley / and parcell of
the said some . . . . Lxvij oz di qrt golde

78.424 Mounsieur Labopine

Itm given and delyuered the xvj^th^ of November Ao pred to mounsieur
lobopyne a messanger sent from the Frenche king acheyne of golde
poz—xxxiij oz iij qrt of the charge of the said John Asteley and
parcell of the said Some. . . . . xxxiij oz iij qrt golde

78.425 Mounsieur Gastell

Itm more given and delyuered the xj^th^ of December Ao xx° Regine to
Mounsieur Gastell sent from Senior Don John Daustria gouernor of
the Lowe countrie / a cup with acouer guilte poz—Lxxviij oz qtr Acup
of Siluer and guilte poiz—Liij oz Di / acup of Siluer and guilte poz—
Lj oz di di qrt / Acup of Siluer and guilte poz—xlj oz iij qrt / and one
cup of Siluer and guilte poz—xxxviij oz di qrt / all being of the charge
of the said John Asteley / and parcel of iiij^m^ ounces &c . . . .
. . . . CClxiij oz qt Siluer

78.426 Marques Hauering

Itm moare given by her said Matie and Delyuered the xvj^th^ day of
December Ao xxo pred to the marques Havering sent from the state
of the Lowe countrie of Flaunders / a Bason and aleyer of Siluer and
guilte poiz—Cxlvij oz / A peir of potts of Siluer and guilte poz—
CCxix oz qrt / Apeir of Flagonnes of Siluer and guilte poz—
CCxxxvij oz di / Thre guilte Booles with acouer poz—Cxxiij oz qrt /
and one Salte of Siluer and guilte poz—Liiij oz di qrt / all being of
the charge of the said John Asteley and parcell of the said iiij^m^
ounces in toto. . . . . vij^C^ iiij^xx^ j oz di qrt Siluer

78.427 Monsieur Adolf Medilkyrk

Itm moare given by her Matie and Delyuered the said xvj^th^ of December
Ao pred to Mounsieur Adolf Medilkyrk a gentilman of the said
Marquesse apeir of small pottes of Siluer and guilte poz—lxxiiij
oz di and one Boole of Siluer and guilte poz—xxx oz qrt bought of
Hugh Keele one of our goldesmythes in toto . . . . Ciiij oz iij qrt Siluer

78.428 Doctor Bewtrick

Itm more geven by her saide Maiestie and Deliuerid the secunde of
Marche Anno xx° pred to Doctor Bewtrick sent from Duke
Cashamere a Chaine of golde bought of Robt Brandon and Hugh
Keall our Goldmithes poz . . . . xxxiij oz j d ob wait golde

Elizabeth R
[sign manual]

J Astley
Bristow
Pigeon
Ste Fulwell
Richard Asteley

Anno Regni
Regine Eliz xxj

Newyers Guiftes giuen to the Quenes
maiestie at her highnes Manor of Richmond
by thise persones whose names hereafter do
ensue the First of January the yere abouesaid

Elizabeth R
[sign manual]

79.1   By the Lady Margrett Countes of Darby a Trayne Gowne of Tawny vellat
                                    dd to Rauff Hope yoman of the Roobes
79.2   By the Sir Nicholas Bacon Knight Lorde Keper of the greate Seale of
       Inglande in golde and Siluer . . . . xiij li vj s viij d
79.3   By the Lorde Burley Lorde high Treausoror of Inglande in gold . . . . xx li
79.4   By the Lorde Marques of winchester in golde . . . . xx li
                                    dd to henry Sackford grome

Earles

79.5   By therle of Leycetor Mr of the horses averey feyer Juell of golde being a
       Clocke garnesshed fully with Diamondes and Rubyes with apendant of
       Diamondes and Rubyes / and an Appile of golde ennamuled grene and
       Russet
                                    dd to the Lady hawarde
79.6   By therle of Arondell in golde. . . . . xxx li
79.7   By therle of Shrewesbury in golde . . . . xx li
79.8   By Therle of Darby in golde . . . . xx li
79.9   By Therle of Sussex Lorde Chamberleyn in golde . . . . xx li
79.10 By Therle of Lincoln Lorde Admirall of Inglande in golde. . . . . x li
                                    dd to the foresaid H Sackford
79.11 By Therle of Warwyck a Juell of golde being agreat Tophas set in golde
       ennamuled with viij perles pendant
                                    dd to the Lady hawarde
79.12 By Therle of Bedforde in golde. . . . . xx li
                                    dd to the foresaid H Sackford
79.13 By therle of Oxforde afeyer Juell of golde wherein is ahelmet of golde and
       small Diamondes furnesshed and vnder the same v Rubyes one bigger
       then threst / and all threst of the same Juell furnesshed with small
       Diamondes
                                    dd to the Lady hawarde
79.14 By Therle of Rutlande in golde. . . . . x li
79.15 By Therle of Huntingdon in golde . . . . x li
79.16 By Therle of Penbroke in golde. . . . . xx li
79.17 By Therle of Northumberlande in golde . . . . x li

79.18   By Therle of Southampton in golde . . . . xx li
                                         dd to the foresaid H Sackford

79.19   By Therle of hertford a small peyer of writing Tabilles with agreshopper
      all of golde ennamuled grene on the backsyde / and a small pynne of
      golde hauyng asmall perle at thende thereof

79.20   By Therle of Ormonde a feyer Juell of golde wherin ar thre Large
      Emeraldes set in Roses white & red one bigger then thother two / all
      threst garnesshed with Roses and Flowers ennamuled all threst
      furnesshed with very smale Dyamondes & Rubys

79.21   By Therle of Surr[ey] agyrdill of Tawny vellat enbrawdred with sede perle
      the buckyll and pendant of golde
                                        dd to the Lady hawarde

Vicont

79.22   By the vicounte Mountague in golde . . . . x li
                                      dd to the foresaid H Sackford

Duchesses Marquisses & Countesses

79.23   By the Duches of Suffolke alylly pot of Agathe alylly Flower going owte
      of it garnesshed with Roses of Rubyes and Diamondes hanging at two
      small Cheynes of golde
                                 dd to the said Lady Hawarde

79.24   By the Duches of Somerset in golde and Siluer . . . . xviij li vj s viij d

79.25   By the Lady Marques of winchester in golde. . . . . x li
                                      dd to the foresaid h Sackford

79.26   By the Lady Marques of Northampton a Gyrdill of golde with Buckelles
      and pendantes of golde garnesshed with Sparkes of Rubyes and
      Diamondes and also ten perles set in Collettes of golde
                                 dd to the said Lady hawarde

79.27   By the Countes of Shrewesbury a Mantyll of Tawny Satten enbrawdred
      with aborder of venice golde and Siluer lyned with white Taphata / and
      faced with white Satten

79.28   By the Countes of Warwyk a Cap of black vellatt with xiij buttons of
      golde in euery of them eyther a Ruby or Diamonde / and aknot of small
      perle with agarter & abyrde vpon the same / and aperle pendant
                                 dd to the foresaid Rauf Hoope

79.29   By the Countes of Sussex in golde . . . . x li
                                      dd to foresaid H Sackford

79.30   By the Countes of Bedford a foreparte of white Satten enbrawdred with
      black sylke and golde with two feyer borders of venice golde and sede
      perle embrawdred
                                   dd to the foresaid Rauf hoope

79.31   By the Countes of Lincoln a Jug of Marbill garnesshed with golde
      poiz. . . . . xviij oz di qtr
                   Remaynyng with John Astley Mr of the Juelles

79.32   By the Countes of Huntington in golde . . . . viij li
                                            dd to the foresaid henry Sackford
79.33   By the Countes of Oxford a foreparte of a kyrtyll of white Satten
        enbrawdred with Flowers of Siluer and two borders of golde and sede
        perle enbrawdred vpon Black vellat
                                            dd to the foresaid Rauf hoope
79.34   By the Countes of Penbroke Doager in golde . . . . xij li
79.35   By the Countes of Penbroke Junior in golde . . . . x li
79.36   By the Countes of Northumberlande in golde . . . . x li
79.37   By the Countes of Southampton in golde . . . . x li
                                            dd to the foresaid h Sackford
79.38   By the Countes of Essex agreate cheyne of Amber slightly garnesshed
        with golde and small perle
                                            dd to the Lady hawarde
79.39   By the Countes of Rutlande in golde . . . . x li
                                            dd to the foresaid henry Sackford
79.40   By the Countes of Kent Doager a mufler of purple vellat Enbrawdred with
        venice and Damaske golde & perle
                                            dd to Mrs Elizabeth Knowlles
79.41   By the Countes of Kent Junior a forparte of akyrtyll network floresshed
        with golde and tuftes of sundry colored sylke
                                            dd to the foresaid Rauf hoope

Vicountes

79.42   By the Vicecountes Mountague in golde. . . . . x li
                                            dd to the foresaid H Sackford

Busshops

79.43   By Thearchbusshop of Yorke in golde . . . . xxx li
79.44   By the Busshop of Ely in golde. . . . . xxx li
79.45   By the Busshop of Dureham in golde. . . . . xxx li
79.46   By the Busshop of London in golde . . . . xx li
79.47   By the Busshop of winchester in golde. . . . . xx li
79.48   By the Busshop of Salisbury in golde. . . . . xx li
79.49   By the Busshop of Lincoln in golde . . . . xx li
79.50   By the Busshop of Norwiche in golde . . . . xx li
79.51   By the Busshop of worcetor in golde . . . . xx li
79.52   By the Busshop of Lichfelde in golde and Siluer . . . . xiij li vj s viij d
79.53   By the Busshop of Hereford in golde . . . . x li
79.54   By the Busshop of Seint Dauid in golde. . . . . x li
79.55   By the Busshop of Karlyle in golde . . . . x li
79.56   By the Busshop of Bathe in golde. . . . . x li
79.57   By the Busshop of Peterburgh in golde . . . . x li
79.58   By the Busshop of Glocetor in golde . . . . x li
79.59   By the Busshop of Chichester in golde. . . . . x li
79.60   By the Busshop of Rochester in golde . . . . x li

Lordes

79.61   By the Lorde of Burgevenny in golde . . . . v li

                                    dd to the forsaid h Sackford

79.62   By the Lorde Hayward alock of golde black ennamuled garnesshed with
      xvj small Diamondes

                                    dd the Lady Hawarde

79.63   By the Lorde Russell acawle of Here garnesshed with Buttons of golde
      within ennamuled and set with ragged perle

                              dd to Mrs Elizabeth Knowlles

79.64   By the Lorde Ryche in golde . . . . x li
79.65   By the Lorde Darcy of Chytte in golde. . . . . x li
79.66   By the Lorde Shandowes in golde and Siluer . . . . vj li xiij s iiij d
79.67   By the Lorde Bokehurst in golde . . . . v li
79.68   By the Lorde North in golde. . . . . x li
79.69   By the Lorde Paget in golde . . . . x li
79.70   By the Lorde Stafford in golde . . . . x li
79.71   By the Lorde Compton in golde . . . . x li
79.72   By the Lorde Norrys of Rycote in golde. . . . . x li
79.73   By the Lorde Lumley in golde. . . . . x li
79.74   By the Lorde Wharton in golde . . . . x li
79.75   By the Lorde Morley in golde . . . . x li

                                    dd to the foresaid h Sakford

79.76   By the Lorde Cobham a Dublet of white Satten lyned with murry white
      sercenet leyed with apasmane of gold & sylke

                                  dd to the foresaid Rauf Hope

79.77   By the Lorde Henry hawarde a Juell of golde being adedtre with mystiltow
      set at the rote with Sparkes of Diamondes & Rubyes

Baronesses

79.78   By the Lady Baronesse Burleigh xxxvj buttons of golde one broken

                                    dd to the Lady haward

79.79   By the Lady Barones howarde Dowager in golde. . . . . x li

                                    dd to the forsaid h Sackford

79.80   By the Lady Barones howard Junior a Juell of golde garnesshed with
      Rubyes and Diamondes and thre perles pendant

                                  dd to the same La Hawarde

79.87   By the Lady Barones Cobham a petticote of Crymsen rewed with Siluer
79.82   By the Lady Barones Dacres agowne of wrought vellat

                                    dd to the forsaid Rauf hope

79.83   By the Lady Barones Taylboyes in golde . . . . x li

                                    dd to the forsaid H Sackford

79.84   By the Lady Barones Shandowes Douger a feyer skarf of grene sersenet
      enbrawdred with Byrdes and Flowers of sylke and golde of sundry
      collors frenged with venice golde and Lyned with murry Sarceonet

79.85   By the Lady Barones Shandowes Junior a vale of black networke flurresshed
     with flowers of Siluer & a small bonelace
                                    dd to Mrs Elizabeth Knowlles

79.86   By the Lady Barones Seint John Bletzelow in golde. x li
                                      dd to the forsaid h Sackford

79.87   By the Lady Barones Paget the Lordes wyf a petty cote of cloth of
     golde stayned black and white with abone lace of golde and Spangilles
     Leyed Lyke waves of the See
                                      dd to the foresaid Rauf hope

79.88   By the Barones Paget Caree asmall cheyne of golde with a luer of gold
     hanging at it on thone syde a white Dove and on thother syde a hawke
     with a Button white ennamuled

79.89   By the Lady Barones Cheyny a carcanet of golde cont viij peces with Byrdes
     and frute ennamuled
                                      dd to the foresaid La haward

79.90   By the Lady Barones Awdeley aforeparte of a kyrtill of Orenge collored
     Satten
                                      dd to the forsaid Rauf hope

79.91   By the Lady Barones Barkeley in golde . . . . x li

79.92   By the Lady Barones Bookehurst in golde . . . . v li

79.93   By the Lady Barones Norris in golde . . . . x li
                                      dd to the forsaid h Sackford

79.94   By the Lady Barones Sheffelde a kyrtill of purple Satten with roses of
     white Lawne enbrawdred with golde vnlined
                                      dd to the forsaid Rauf hope

79.95   By the Lady Vere Mr Bartewes wyf a vale of open worke with golde and
     Spangilles
                                      dd to Mrs Elizabeth Knowlles

79.96   By the Lady Barones Morley apettycote of white Satten alouer enbrawdred
     with Roses of golde and iij gardes likewyse enbrawdred / Lyned with
     white Satten and fringed with sylke and golde
                                      dd to the forsaid Rauf hope

79.97   By the Lady Barrones Wharton a Juell of golde wherein is aparret hanging
     garnesshed with small Diamondes and acluster of perle pendaunt lacking
     aFyshe on thonesyde
                                      dd to the forsaid La haward

Ladies

79.98   By the Lady Mary Sydney a Smock and two pillowbyres of Cameryk feyer
     wrought with black worke and edged with abrode bonelace of black
     Sylke
                                      dd to Mrs Skydmore

79.99   By the Lady Mary Semer wif to Mr Rogers A Touthe pike of golde made
     gonne fation
                                      dd to the foresaid La haward

79.100 By the Lady Elizabeth Semer alis Knightley A kyrtell of Oring Tawnye
Satten edged with a passamayne of Siluer

dd to the forsaid Rauf hope

79.101 By the Lady Stafforde a Juell of golde being an Agath sett about with
Sparkes of Rubyes & Diamondes with a smale perle pendaunt

dd to the forsaid Lady haward

79.102 By the Lady Carowe A Cusshen clothe Camereke blake worke and frenged
with venice golde

dd to Mrs Skydmore

79.103 By the Lady Cheeke A fore parte of golde and siluer networke

dd to the forsaid Rauf hope

79.104 By the Lady Butler in golde . . . . vj li

dd to the foresaid h Sackford

79.105 By the Lady Heniaige A pomaunder garn with golde and xij sparkes of
Rubies & perles pendaunt poz

dd to the foresaid Lady haward

79.106 By the Lady Waulsingham iiij paire of gloves set with buttons of golde

dd to the Mrs Elizabeth Knowlles

79.107 By the Lady Drury Afore parte of Clothe of siluer alouer enbrawdrid with
Clothe of golde

dd to the foresaid Rauf hope

79.108 By the Lady Pawlet in golde . . . . v li

dd to the forsaid h Sackford

79.109 By the Lady Willoby, Sir Fraunces wif two pillowberes of Camerike
wroughte allouer withe Carnatyon silke

dd to Mrs Skydmore

79.110 By the Lady Gresham in golde . . . . x li

79.111 By the Lady Cromwell Sir Henryes wif in golde . . . . v li

dd to the forsaid h Sackford

79.112 By the Lady Ratclyf a vale of white worke with spangles and a smale bone
lace of Siluer a swete bag beinge of Chaungeable silke with a smale bone
lace of golde

The vale dd to Mrs Elizabeth Knowlles
and the Bag to Mrs Skydmore

79.113 By the Lady Frogmorton a large bag to put a pillowe in of morre Satten
allouer enbrawderid with golde siluer & silke of sondry collores with iiij
Tasselles of grene silke and golde / And a Cusshen clothe of Networke
florisshed ouer with flowers of golde siluer & silke of sondry colloures
lyned with white Satten

dd to Mrs Skydmore

79.114 By the Lady Cromwell Lorde Cromwelles wyf iij sutes of Ruffes of white
cuteworke edged withe a passamayne of white

dd to Mrs Jane Bresilles

79.115 By the Lady Wilforde thre peces of Lawne wroughte with white and
florisshed with golde

dd to Mrs Skydmore

79.116 By the Lady Marven a paire of Sleaves of oringecolor Satten

dd to forsaid Rauf hope

79.117 By the Lady Croftes a peticote of Carnation Satten embrawderid with
flowers of silke of sondry Colors

dd to same Rauf hope

79.118 By the Lady Souche thre peces of Sipers Cutworke florisshed with golde

dd to Mrs. Skydmore

Knightes

79.119 By Sir Fraunces Knowles Treasoror of our Householde in Angelles. . . . . . . x li
79.120 By Sir James Croftes Comptrolor of the same in Di. soueraignes. . . . . x li

dd to the forsaid H Sackford

79.121 By Sir Chrystopher Hatton vice Chamberlen a Carket and a border for
the hed of golde cont vij red Roses of golde in euery of them very smale
Dyamondes & in the Top a garnet and viij Troches of mene perle iiij in
euery Troche & xiiij pearles pendaunte being lose &c

dd to the Lady haward

79.122 By Sir Fraunces Waulsingham pryncipall Secretary a night Gowne of
Tawney Satten allouer enbraderid faced with Satten like heare collor

dd to the forsaid Rauf hope

79.123 By Mr Thomas wilson Esquire also Secretary a Cup of Agath with a
couer and garnisshment of golde enamvled / the same Agath crased
in Dyvers places poz . . . . .xvij oz qtr

dd to Mr Asteley Mr & Threausoror of the Juelles

79.124 By Sir Rauf Sadler Chauncellor of the Duchey. . . . . xv li
79.125 By Sir Waulter Mildemay Chauncellor of the Exchequer in Angelles. . . . . . x li
79.126 By Sir William Cordell Mr of the Rolles in golde . . . . x li

dd to the forsaid H Sackford

79.127 By Sir Henry Sydney Lorde Deputie of Irelande afeyer Juell of golde with a
Dyana in fully garnisshed wythe Dyamondes &c

dd to the Lady hawarde

79.128 By Sir William Damsell Recevor of the Corte of wardes. . . . . x li
79.129 By Sir Owine Hopton Livetenant of the Tower . . . . x li

dd to the forsaid h Sackford

79.130 By Sir Thomas Hennaige Treasoror of the Chamber A proper Ringe of
golde ennamulled in the Top thereof an white Rubye without a foyle
with a grahounde in it

79.131 By Sir Edward Horsey Captayne of Thile of wight a Touthe picke of golde
the top beinge garneshid with a faire emeraude a Dyamond & Ruby &
other smale Dyamondes and Rubies with ij perles pendaunt

dd to the Lady hawarde

79.132 By Sir Guilbarte Dethicke alis Garter principall kinge at Armes / a booke
at Armes

[blank]

79.133 By Sir Christopher Haydon in golde. . . . . x li

79.134 By Sir Henry Cromwell in golde . . . . x li
dd to the forsaid h Sackford

79.135 By Sir Gawine Carowe a Smoke of Cameryke wrought with blake worke &
    edged with bone lace of golde
dd to Mrs Skydmore

79.136 By Sir Thomas Gresham in golde . . . . x li

79.137 By Sir John Thynne in golde . . . . v li
dd to the forsaid h Sackford

79.138 By Sir Henry Lee a Juell of golde beinge afaire Emeraude cut lozanged
    Hartwise
dd to the La hawarde

79.139 By Sir William Drury a paire of myttons of blake vellat enbraudered withe
    Damaske golde and Lyned with vnshorne vellat carnation
dd to Mrs Elizabeth Knowlles

79.140 By Sir Amyas Pawlet a pece of Tyssue of Carnation golde & siluer cont
. . . . xviij yerdes qtr
dd to the forsaid Rauf hope

79.141 By Sir Edwarde Clere in golde. . . . . x li
dd to the forsaid h Sackford

Gentilwomen

79.142 By Mrs Blanche Parry apeir of Braslettes of Cornelion heddes two small
    perles betwixt euery hed garn with golde
dd to the Lady haward

79.143 By Mrs Fraunces Howarde two sute of Ruffes of Stitched clothe florisshed
    at the sides thone withe golde thother with siluer with spangles
dd to Mrs Jane Bressilles

79.144 By Mrs Elizabethe Knowles afayre Cap of blacke vellat garnished] with
    longe Agettes of gold enamvled
dd to the forsaid Rauf hope

79.145 By Mrs Edmondes iij peces of Networke with spangles and threddes of golde
dd to Mrs Skydmore

79.146 By Mrs Skydmore aforeparte with bodyes and Sleaves of Satten ginger
    color cut lyned with mvrre Taphata withe ij laces of golde and siluer
    and frenged with like golde and siluer
dd to the forsaid Rauf hope

79.147 By Mrs Snowe Six handkercheues faire wrought and edged with abrode
    passamayne of golde
dd to Mrs Skydmore

79.148 By Mrs Bapteste A lace of Russet silke and sede perle
dd to Mrs Elizabeth Knowlles

79.149 By Mrs Chaworthe two handkercheues of hollande wroughte with blacke
    worke and edged with a smale bone Lace of golde and siluer and an
    Asse of golde enamvled
The handekerchers with Mrs Skydmore
and the Asse with the La haward

79.150   By Mrs Weste a faire Scarfe of grene Networke florisshed with gold and
siluer and edged at bothe endes with a brode bone lace and at the sides
with a narrowe passamane of gold and siluer and lyned with morre
serceonete

dd to Mrs Elizabeth Knowlles

79.151   By Mrs Katherin Newton a foreparte of a kirtill of Tawny Satten
enbroderid with gardes of golde and siluer lyned with white serceonet

dd to the foresaid Rauf hope

79.152   By Mrs Marbery Six handekerchers of Cameryke faire wroughte with
blacke silke edged with a smale bone lace of golde and siluer

79.153   By Mrs Digby vj faire handkerchers of Camerike of blake spanishe worke
edged with a brode bone lace of gold & siluer

dd to Mrs Skydmore

79.154   By Mrs Jane Brissels a partelet and Ruffes of lawne wrought with white
worke with a blake sipers vpon yt garn wythe bewgles

dd to Mrs Jane Brisselles

79.155   By Mrs Townesend A Cheyne of Amber Jeate and mouther of pearll

dd to the Lady Hawarde

79.156   By Mrs Cave two pillowberes of hollande wroughte with blacke silke &
edged with a pasamane of blacke silke

79.157   By Mrs Lichefelde A fare lokinge glasse set in a case of purple Taphata
allouer fare enbraudered with seade perle and Damaske golde

79.158   By Mrs Sackefourde a paire of Sleaves of lawne wrought with knitworke
striped with golde and siluer and edged with a bone lace of golde and
siluer

dd to Mrs Skydmore

79.159   By Mrs Elizabethe Howarde a vale of Networke florisshed with gold and
spangles of gold & a smale bone Lace of golde

dd to Mrs Elizabeth Knoweles

79.160   By Mrs Wingefeld a cheyne and a border of Bewegels and seed perles very
smale

dd to the Lady haward

79.161   By Mrs Hermon a faire Smoke the Sleves wroughte with blake silke and
edged with gold

79.162   By Mrs Taylor A Coif and a forehead clothe of blake edged with a smale
bone lace of gold & roses of gold and silke

dd to the Mrs Skydmore

79.163   By Mrs Twiste Six Towthclothes wroughte with blake silke and edged with
golde and a Sute off Ruffes of lawne wroughte with spanisshe worke

The toth clothes dd to Mrs Skydmore /
and the Ruffes dd to Mrs Jane Brissells

79.164   By Mrs Note sixe handkerchers of Camerike edgid with bone lace of gold
and siluer

79.165   By Mrs Barley six handekechers lykewyse edged with venice golde

dd to Mrs Skydmore

79.166   By Mrs Mountague a pertelet of fyne Camerycke wroughte with flowers of
          blake silke
                                                          dd to Mrs Jane Bressells
79.167   By Mrs Dane thre peces of lawne
                                                          dd to Mrs Blanche Parry
79.168   By Mrs Crokson a night coyf of white Sipers florisshed ouer with siluer
79.169   By Mrs Huggaynes iiij handekercheres faire wroughte with spanyshe
          worke
79.170   By Mrs Amye Shelton sixe handkercheves edged with black worke with a
          passamaine of gold & siluer
                                                          dd to Mrs Skydmore
79.171   By Mrs Julio a Dublet of Crymsen Satten cut & laide with a passamayne
          of siluer
79.172   By Mrs Dale a Dublate and a foreparte of clothe of gold garnisshed with
          passamayne of golde
                                                          dd to the forsaid Raul hope
79.173   By Mrs Allen a fayre Cawle of Damaske golde withe pypes and Flowers
          garnished with smale seade perle
                                                          dd to Mrs Skydmore

Chaplyns

79.174   By Archedeacon Carewe in golde . . . . x li
                                                          dd to the forsaid h Sackford
79.175   By Absolyn Clerc of the closet aboke couered with cloth of Tyssue
          garnesshed with Siluer and guilte
                                                          with her Matie by Mr Sackford

Gentilmen

79.176   By Mr Phillip Sydney awast cote of white Sarceonet quylted and
          enbrawdred with gold Siluer and Silke of Diuers collors with apasmane
          lace of golde and Siluer rownde abought yt
                                                          dd to Mrs Skydmore
79.177   By Mr Rauffe Bowes A Hat of Tawny Taphata enbrauderid with scorpions
          of venice golde and a border garnisshed with sede perle
                                                          dd to the forsaid Rauf hope
79.178   By Mr John Harington a Bole of Christall without a couer grased garn
          with gold enamuled about the mouth & fote poz . . . . iiij oz iij qtr di
                                                          with Mr Asteley Mr of the Juelles
79.179   By Mr Edward Basshe in golde. . . . . x li
                                                          dd to h Sackford
79.180   By Mr Dyer aforeparte of white Satten with a brode garde of purple
          Satten enbraudered withe Venice golde siluer and sede perle vnlyned
79.181   By Mr Stanhope a Dublate of Oringe Tawnie Satten with a brode
          passamayne of siluer and buttens of the same
                                                          dd to the forsaid Ra Hope

79.182 By Mr Foulke Grevill a smale Juell being a Lam[b]e of mother of perle
garnisshed with two smale Dyamondes two smale Rubies and three
perles pendante

dd to the La hawarde

79.183 By Mr Smythe Coustomer two boultes of Cameryck

dd to Mrs Blanch Pary

79.184 By Mr Beinodicke Spenolle a foreparte of white & tawnie Satten alouer
faire enbrauderid with golde and siluer and two fannes of Strawe
wrought with silke of sondry collores

The forparte with R Hope
the Fannes with Mrs Eliz Knowlles

79.185 By Mr Wolly a forke of agathe garnisshed with golde

dd to the Lady hawarde

79.186 By Mr Lychefeld a very fayre Lute the backeside and necke of mother of
perle the Case of crymsen vellat enbrawdered with flowers & the inside
grene vellate

with her Matie by Charles Smyth

79.187 By Mr Newton a paire of Sleves of Satten ginger collor enbrauderid
with borders of gold & siluer lined with white serceonet

dd to the foresaid Ra hope

79.188 By Mr Doctor Hewicke two pottes of Oringe flowers and Cande Jenger
79.189 By Doctor Master two lyke pottes
79.190 By Doctor Julio two lyke pottes
79.191 By John Hemingeway A potticary Sittornes preservid
79.192 By John Ryche apotticary Abrycox ij boxes & ij glasses of peare
plomes

dd to Mrs Skydmore

79.193 By John Smythesone alis Taylor Mr Cooke a fayre marche pane with a
casttell in myddes

79.194 By John Dudley Sargeaunte of the Pastry a fayre pye of Quinces

[blank]

79.195 By William Huggans a fere grete swete bag of serceonet enbraudered
[and] xvj smale swete bagges

dd to Mrs Skydmore

79.196 By Mr Edwarde Stafforde two Laces of golde and siluer

dd to Mrs Eliz Knowlles

79.197 By Mr Thomas Layton Captayne of garnesey a gowne of blacke vellat
with bodyes & sleaves cut Lyned with white sarceonet & sett with longe
aglettes of golde white enamvled

dd to the forsaid Ra hope

79.198 By Marke Anthony Gaiardell iiij venyse glasses
79.199 By Ambroso Lupo a box of Lute strynges
79.200 By Petricho a boke of Italion with pictures of the lyfe & metomorpheses
of Oved

dd to Mr Baptest

79.201 By Charles Smythe a smale Juell beinge a Sallamaunder a smale Ruby
    ij smale Dyamondes and iij smale perles pendaunte
                                      dd to the La hawarde

79.202 By Peter Wolfe v songe bookes
                             with her Matie by Mr Knevet

79.203 By Anthonias Phenotus a smale booke in Italion meter
                                   dd to Mr Baptest

79.204 By Mr Henry Bronker a pese of stitched clothe wroughte with gold
    cont . . . . xv yerdes di
                                      dd to Ra hope

79.205 By William Russell a paire of gloves garnisshed with gold and sede perle
                              dd to Mrs Eliza Knowlles

79.206 By Guylham Sketes a Dyall Noctornalla Di once of Copper and guylte
                             with her Matie by Mr Knevet

79.207 By Morrys Watkins xviij larkes in a Cage
                                 dd to Mrs Blanch Parry

Summa totalis of all the / money giuen to her / Majestie and deliuered in maner
and fourme aboue declared . . . . .iv^{C} iiij^{xx} xvij li xiij s iiij d

Elizabeth R
[sign manual]

                                     J Asteley
                       Exa[mina]t[io] per Bristow
                                 J Pigeon
                                 Ste Fulwell
                           Richard Asteley

                      Anno Regni
              Regine Elizabeth xxj

      Newyers Guiftes giuen by the Quenes
   maiestie at her highnes Manor of Richmond
    to thise persons whose names hereafter ensue
      the First of January the yere abouesaid

Elizabeth R
[sign manual]

79.208 To the Lady Margret Countes of Darby in guilte plate Brandon . . . . L oz di
79.209 To Sir Nicholas Bacon Knight Lorde keper of the greate Seale of
    Inglande in guilte plate Brandon. . . . . xxv oz di di qtr
79.210 To Lorde Burley Lorde high Threausoror of Inglande in guilte plate keele . xl oz
79.211 To the Lorde Marques of winchester in guilte plate of our store . . . . .xxx oz

Earles

79.212   To Therll of Leycetor Mr of our horses in guilte plate Keele . . . . C oz

79.213   To therll of Arondell in guilte plate Brandon . . . . L oz iij qtr di

79.214   To therll of Shrewesburye a guilt bolle with a couer Keele poz . . . . .xxx oz

79.215   To therll of Darbye a guilt Cup with a Couer Brandon poz . . . . xxx oz di di qtr

79.216   To therle of Sussex lord Chambeleyn a bole with a Couer Keall
        poz . . . . .xxxv oz qtr

79.217   To therle of warwicke A Bason & Ewer Brandon poz . . . . Cvij oz di

79.218   To therle of Lincolne Lord Admerall in guilt plate Keale . . . . xxij oz

79.219   To therle of Oxfourde A Bason & Ewer of our store poz—Lxxij oz di
        qtr And a payre of Pottes Brandon poz—Cxx oz iij qtr in toto
        . . . . .C iiij xx xij oz iij qtr di

79.220   To therle of Rutlande a guilte bole with a Couer Brandon poz . . . . xx oz di

79.221   To therle of Huntingedon A guilt bole with a Couer Keell poz . . . . . .xx oz iij qtr

79.222   To therle of Bedfourde in guilt plate Keele poz . . . . xxxj oz di

79.223   To therle of Penbroke a guilte bolle with a Couer Keall poz . . . . xxix oz di

79.224   To therle of Northumberland a guilt pott Keall poz . . . . xix oz iij qtr di

79.225   To therle of Herfourd A Haunse potte guilt Brandon poz . . . . .xx oz iij qtr

79.226   To therle of Sowthampton a guilt Cup with a couer Brandon poz
        . . . . .xxx oz iij qtr

79.227   To therle of Ormewoode a peyre of guilt flagons Kealle poz . . . . Cxliiij oz

79.228   To therle of Surr[ey] a guilte bolle with a couer Brandon poz . . . . xxiiij oz di

79.229   To the vicounte Mountegue A Hans potte Keale poz . . . . xx oz

Duchesses Marquises & Countises

79.230   To the Duches of Suffolke in guilte plate Brandon poz . . . . .xl oz

79.231   To the Duches of Somersett a guilte bole Keale poz . . . . xxiiij oz iij qtr di

79.232   To the Lady Marquies of Northampton in guilte plate Keale poz . . . . . . .xlij oz

79.233   To the Lady Marquies of Winchester Dowager a guilte bole Keale
        poz . . . . xxxix oz iij qtr di

79.234   To the Countes of Shrewesburie a guilte bole withe a couer Brandon
        poz . . . . .xxx oz iij qtr

79.235   To the Countes of Huntingdon a guilte bole with a couer Keele poz
        . . . . .xxxv oz di di qtr

79.236   To the Countes of Sussex a guilte cup with a couer Keall poz . . . . xxij oz

79.237   To the Countes of Bedforde in guilt plate Kealle poz . . . . L oz di

79.238   To the Countes of Lincolne A guilte Cup with a Couer poz . . . . L oz

79.239   To the Countes of Warwicke A Doble Cup with a couer Keale poz . . . . L oz

79.240   To the Countes of Oxforde a guilt bole with a couer Keele poz . . . . . . xx oz qtr

79.241   To the Countes of Pembroke Dowager a guilt cup with a couer Brandon
        poz . . . . .xxv oz qtr di

79.242   To the Countes of Penbroke a guilt pott Keale poz . . . . xxiij oz iij qtr di

79.243 To the Countes of Northumberland A guilt pot Kele poz......... xix oz iij qtr

79.244 To the Countes of Sowthampton A guilte bolle with a Couer Brandon
poz .... xx oz qtr di

79.245 To the Countes of Essex a guilt Cup with a Couer Brandon poz
....xxviij oz di di qtr

79.246 To the Countes of Rutlande a guilt bole with a couer Brandon poz
.... xx oz qtr di

79.247 To the Countes of Kente Doager a guilte bole with a couer Brandon
poz ....xx oz qtr

79.248 To the Countes of Kent a guilte bole with a couer Brandon poz.... xx oz qtr di

Vicountes

79.249 To the vicountes Montague in guilte plate Keele poz........... xix oz di di qtr

Busshoppes

79.250 To thearchebusshop of yorke in guilte plate Keele poz .... xxxvj oz

79.251 To the Busshop of Eley in guilt plate A bole Keale poz............ xxxvj oz

79.252 To the Bushop of Durham a Doble bole guilte of the store poz
.... xxxij oz di di qtr

79.253 To the Bushop of London a guilte Salte Keale poz .... xxix oz

79.254 To the Bushop of winchester a guilt bolle with a couer Brandon poz
.... xxx oz iij oz di

79.255 To the Bushop of Salisbury a Saulte with a couer Keale poz........... xxix oz

79.256 To the Bushop of lyncolne in guilte plate Brandon poz............... xxxj oz

79.257 To the Bushop of Norwich a guilt bole Brandon poz .... xxiiij oz iij qtr

79.258 To the Bushop of Worsester a guilt bole Keale poz .... xxiij oz iij qtr

79.259 To the Bushop of Lychefeld a guilt pot Brandon poz .... xx oz iij qr di

79.260 To the Bushop of Herfourd a guilt pot Keale poz .... xvj oz qtr

79.261 To the Bushop of St Davies A guilt Tankerd of the store poz ...... xvj oz di qtr

79.262 To the Bushop of Carlell a guilt bole with a couer Keale poz .... xv oz iij qtr di

79.263 To the Bushop of Bathe a guilt cup with a couer of the store .... xvj oz iij qtr di

79.264 To the Bushop of Peterborowe a guilt bole with a couer Kealle poz
....xv oz iij qtr

79.265 To the Bushop of Gloster a guilt Tankerd Brandon poz .... xix oz

79.266 To the Bushop of Chitchester a guilt Tankerd Keale poz .... xvj oz di qtr

79.267 To the Bushop of Rochester A guilt pot of the store ....xv oz qtr

Lordes

79.268 To the Lorde Hawarde in guilte plate of the store—xij oz of Brandon
—xxxj oz qtr di & of Ke—lxj oz di qtr in tot................... Ciiij oz di

79.269 To the Lorde Russell in guilte plate Brandon .... xviij [oz] qtr di

79.270 To the Lorde of Burgevenny in guilte plate of the Store poz........ x oz qtr di

79.271 To the Lorde Riche in guilte plate Keele poz .... xix oz iij qtr di

79.272 To the Lorde Darcy of Chittye in guilte plate Keele .... xix oz di di qtr

79.273	To the Lorde Shandowes in guilte plate Brandon poiz.	xiij oz qtr
79.274	To the Lorde of Bokehurst in guilte plate of the store poz	xj oz iij qtr
79.275	To the Lorde Northe in guilte plate	xxj oz di di qtr
79.276	To the Lorde Paget in guilte plate Keele poiz	xix oz di di qtr
79.277	To the Lorde Stafforde in guilte plate Keele poz	xix oz iij qtr
79.278	To the Lorde Compton in guilte plate Keele poz	xix oz iij qtr di
79.279	To the Lorde Norrys of Rycot in guilte plate Keele poz	xix oz di di qtr
79.280	To the Lorde Cobham in guilte plate Keele poz.	xxj oz
79.281	To the Lorde Lumley in guilte plate Keele poz.	xix oz iij qtr
79.282	To the Lorde Wharton in guilte plate Keele poz.	xx oz
79.283	To the Lorde Morley in guilte plate Keele poz	xix oz iij qtr di
79.284	To the Lorde Henry Hawarde in guilte plate Keele poz	viij oz di

Baronesses

79.285	To the Lady Barones Burligh in guilte plate Keele poiz	xxiiij oz qtr
79.286	To the Lady Barownes Howarde Dowager a guilt cup with a couer of the store poz.	xxj oz
79.287	To the Lady Barownes Howard Junior a guilt bole with a couer Brandon poiz.	xxiiij oz di
79.288	To the Lady Cobham in guilt plate Keale poz	L oz
79.289	To the Lady Dakers A guilt pott Keale poz	xvij oz iij qtr
79.290	To the Barronesse Talboyes a bole with a couer Keall poz.	xxj oz
79.291	To the Barrownesse Shandowes Dowager in guilt plate Brandon poz. . . .	xvj oz di
79.292	To the Barrownesse Shandowes Junior a Castinge bottle guilt Keale poz	xj oz qtr
79.293	To the Barrownesse Ste John Bletzo a guilt bole with a couer Brandon poz	xix oz qtr
79.294	To the Barownesse Pagett the Lordes wif a guilt bole with a couer of the store poz.	xxxj oz di
79.295	To the Barrownesse Paget Care a guilt bole with a couer Keale poz	xxv [oz] di qtr
79.296	To the Barrownesse Chanie a guilt cup with a couer Brandon poz	xl oz qtr
79.297	To the Barronesse Awdley a guilt bole with a couer Brandon poz.	xij oz di
79.298	To the Barrownesse Barckeley a guilt Tankerd Brandon poz.	xix oz
79.299	To the Barrownesse Buckehurst a guilt bole of the store poz	xj oz di qtr
79.300	To the Barrownesse Norrys a guilt bole Brandon poz	xx oz di di qtr
79.301	To the Barrownesse Sheffeld in guilt plate Brandon poz	xvj oz qtr
79.302	To the Lady Mary Bartewe a guilt bole Brandon poz	xvj oz di qtr
79.303	To the Barrownesse Morley a guilt pot Brandon poz.	xx oz di qtr
79.304	To the Barownesse Wharton a guilt pot of the store poz	xxij oz qtr
79.305	To the Barrownesse Crumell a guilt Tankerde Brandon poz	xij oz qtr

Ladies

79.306	To the Lady Mary Sydney iij guilt Bolles with a couer of our store poz	xxx oz
79.307	To the Lady Mary Semer wyf to Mr Rogers a guilt bole Keale poz	xiij oz

79.308	To the Lady Elizabeth Semer alis Knightley a guilt bole with a couer
	Keale po . . . . xiiij oz iij qtr
79.309	To the Lady Stafforde a guilt bole with a couer Keall poz . . . . .xxx oz qtr
79.310	To the Lady Carowe in guilt plate of the store poz . . . . .xxxv oz
79.311	To the Lady Cheake a guilt cup Keall poz . . . . xxiiij oz qtr
79.312	To the Lady Butler a guilt Sault Keall poz . . . . xvj oz
79.313	To the Lady Hennage in guilt plate Keall poz . . . . xxij oz di qtr
79.314	To the Lady Wallsingham in guilt plate Brandon poz . . . . xvj oz di di qtr
79.315	To the Lady Drury viij guilt spones Keale poz . . . . xvj oz
79.316	To the Lady Pawlett a guilte bolle with a couer of the store poz . . . . . . xvj oz qtr
79.317	To the Lady Willowby Sir Fraunses wif a guilt boll with a couer Kelle
	poz . . . . xij oz
79.318	To the Lady Gressham a guilt bolle with a couer Keall poz . . . . . . xix oz iij qtr di
79.319	To the Lady Crumwell Sir Henryes wyf a guilt bole with a couer of the
	store poz . . . . xj oz qtr
79.320	To the Lady Ratlyef a guilt bole with a couer brandon poz . . . . xiiij oz di qtr
79.321	To the Lady Frogmorton a guilt bole with acouer brandon poz
	. . . . xxij oz iij qtr di
79.322	To the Lady Wilfourd a guilt pott Keall poz . . . . xix oz di di qtr
79.323	To the Lady Marven a guilt bole Keale poz . . . . xiiij oz
79.324	To the Lady Croftes a guilt bole Keale poz . . . . xx oz
79.325	To the Lady Souche a guilt bole of the store poz . . . . xiij oz

Knightes

79.326	To Sir Fraunces Knowlles Threausoror of the Housholde in guilt plate
	Keele. . . . . .xxx oz
79.327	To Sir James Croftes Comtroler of the same a guilt boll with a couer
	Keale poz . . . . xxiiij oz iij qtr
79.328	To Sir Christofer Hatton vicechamberlen in guilt plate Keale poz . . . .CCCC oz
79.329	To Sir Fraunces Walsingham pryncipall secretary iij bolles with a couer
	Keale poz . . . . .Lix oz iij qtr
79.330	To Mr Thomas Wylson esquire also secretary a guilt bole with a couer
	Keale poz . . . . .xxv oz iij qtr
79.331	To Sir Rauf Sadler Chauncellor of the Duchie a guilt bole with a couer
	Keale poz . . . . xxix oz di
79.332	To Sir Waulter Myldmay Chauncellor of the excheaquier a guilt bole with
	a couer of our store poz . . . . xxvij oz di di qtr
79.333	To Sir William Cordoll Mr of the Rolles A guilt pot Keale poz . . . . xx oz
79.334	To Sir Henry Sydney in guilt plate Keale poz . . . . .Cxxxiij oz qtr di
79.335	To Sir William Damsell Recevor of the Courte of Wardes in guilt plate
	Kele poz . . . . xix oz iij qtr
79.336	To Sir Owine Hopton Livetenante of the Tower a guilte bole Keale poz
	. . . . xxij oz
79.337	To Sir Thomas Hennage threasoror of the Chamber in guilt plate Kele
	poz . . . . xlviij oz

79.338	To Sir Edwarde Horsey Captayne of the Ile of Wighte a guilt bole with a couer Keale poz . . . . xxxj oz qtr
79.339	To Sir Guilbert Dethicke principall knight at armes a guilt Tankerd Brandon poz . . . . xij oz
79.340	To Sir Chrystopher Heydone a guilt bole with a couer of the store poz . . . xxj oz
79.341	To Sir Henry Cromwell A guilt Tankerd Kele poz . . . . xx oz qtr di
79.342	To Sir Gawine Carowe in guilte plate of our store—xxiij oz di qtr / vj spones Keale—xij oz / in toto . . . . xxxv oz di qtr
79.343	To Sir Thomas Gresham a guilt Tankerd Kell poz . . . . xx oz di di qtr
79.344	To Sir John Thynne a guilt Saulte of the store . . . . xij oz di qtr
79.345	To Sir Henry Lee a Doble bolle Brandon poz . . . . .xxxvij oz
79.346	To Sir William Drury guilte plate of the store—xij oz di qtr and ij spones Keale—iiij oz / in toto . . . . xvj oz di qtr
79.347	To Sir Amyas Pawlet in guilt plate of the store poz . . . . xxx oz iij qtr di
79.348	To Sir Edwarde Clere a guilt tankerd Keale poz. . . . . .xviij oz di

Gentilwomen

79.349	To Mrs Blanche Parry in guilte plate Keele poz . . . . xviij oz qtr
79.350	To Mrs Fraunces Howard a guilt bole Keale poz. xv oz
79.351	To Mrs Elizabeth Knowles a guilt bole of the store poz . . . . .xv oz iij qtr
79.352	To Mrs Edmondes in guilt plate Brandon poz . . . . xv oz
79.353	To Mrs Skydmore in guilt plate Keale poz . . . . xvij oz iij qtr di
79.354	To Mrs Snowe A guilt Tankerd Brandon poz. . . . . .xiij oz qtr di
79.355	To Mrs Baptest in guilt plate Keale poz . . . . xvj oz
79.356	To Mrs Chaworthe a guilt Saulte with a couer of the store poz. . xiiij oz di di qtr
79.357	To Mrs Weste a guilt bole with a couer Keale poz . . . . xiiij oz iij qtr di
79.358	To Mrs Katheryn Paston alis Newton in guilt plate Keale poz . . . . . xv oz di qtr
79.359	To Mrs Marbury vj guilt spones Keale poz . . . . xiiij oz di qtr
79.360	To Mrs Dygby a guilt bole with a couer Keale poz . . . . xvj oz di di qtr
79.361	To Mrs Jane Bryssells a guilt bole of the store poz . . . . xv oz di qtr
79.362	To Mrs Townnsende a guilt boule with a couer Kealle poz . . . . . xxv oz iij qtr di
79.363	To Mrs Cave A Tankerd Keale poz. . . . . xv oz
79.364	To Mrs Lychefeld a guilt Tankerd of the store poz . . . . xvj oz qtr di
79.365	To Mrs Sackeford in guilt plate Keale poz . . . . xxij oz
79.366	To Mrs Elizabethe Howarde a guilt bole with a couer Kele poz . xiiij oz iij qtr di
79.367	To Mrs Wingefeld A guilt Tankerd Brandon poz. . . . . xij oz di qtr
79.368	To Mrs Harmon A peper boxe guilt Brandon poz. . . . . viij oz di di qtr
79.369	To Mrs Smythsone in guilte plate Brandon poz. vij oz
79.370	To Mrs Twiste in guilt plate Keale poz . . . . v oz
79.371	To Mrs Note A guilt Tankerd Brandon poz. . . . . .xiij oz
79.372	To Mrs Barley A guilt bolle with a couer Keale poz . . . . xij oz di
79.373	To Mrs Mountegue a guilt bole with a couer Keale poz . . . . xiij oz di qtr
79.374	To Mrs Dane A guilt pot Keale poz . . . . xx oz di di qtr
79.375	To Mrs Croxson iiij^{or} guilt spones Keale poz . . . . viij oz
79.376	To Mrs Hugganes a guilt bole with a couer Brandon poz . . . . xix oz qtr
79.377	To Mrs Amy Shelton A guilt cup Keale poz. . . . . .xj oz di

79.378	To Mrs Dale a guilt bole with a Couer Keale poz	xxiiij oz iij qtr di
79.379	To Mrs Julio a guilt cup with a couer Keale poz	x oz iij qtr di
79.380	To Mrs Allen a guilt boulle with a couer Keale poz	xij oz di qtr

Fre guiftes to Maydes of honor

79.381	To Mrs Mary Ratclyf in guilte plate Keele poz	ix oz di di qtr
79.382	To Mrs Ellyn Bridges in guilte plate Keele poz	x oz
79.383	To Mrs Katheryn Hawarde in guilte plate Keele poz	x oz
79.384	To Mrs Elizabeth Garret in guilte plate Keele poz	x oz di qtr
79.385	To Mrs Fraunces vaughan in guilte plate Brandon poz	x oz di qtr
79.386	To Mrs Hyde mother of the maydes in guilte plate Keele poz	xij oz iij qtr

Chaplyns

79.387	To ArchDeacon Carow Deane of the chappell in guilte plate Brandon poz	xxij oz di qtr
79.388	To Absolon clerc of the Closet in guilt plate Keele poz	iij oz iij qtr

Gentilmen

79.389	To Mr Phillip Sydney in guilte plate Brandon poz	xx oz di di qtr
79.390	To Mr Raulf Bowles a guilt pot Key poz	xxj oz qtr di
79.391	To Mr John Harringeton in guilt plate Keale poz	xl oz
79.392	To Mr Edward Basshe a guilt boule with a couer Brandon poz	xx oz
79.393	To Mr Dyer a guilte Tankerd of the store poz	xv oz iij qtr
79.394	To Mr Stanhoppe a guilt pott Keale poz	xxj oz qtr di
79.395	To Mr Foulke Grevell a guilt boule of the store poz	xj oz qtr
79.396	To Mr Smythe Customer in guilte plate Brandon poz	xv oz
79.397	To Mr Benodicke Spenolla a paire of guilt pottes Keall poz	iiij^{xx} oz di
79.398	To Mr Wollye a guilt Cup with a couer Brandon poz	xxiiij oz qtr
79.399	To Mr Lechefeld a guilt bole with a couer Brandon poz	xxv oz di di qtr
79.400	To Mr Newton guilt plate Keale poz	xv oz
79.401	To Mr Doctor Hewicke a guilt bole of the store poz	xiiij oz iij qtr
79.402	To Mr Doctor Masteres a Tankerd Brandon poz	xiiij oz iij qtr
79.403	To Mr Doctor Julio a guilt boule Brandon poz	xiiij oz di di qtr
79.404	To John Hemingeway Pottecary in guilt plate Keale poz	vij oz di
79.405	To John Ryche Pottecary guilt plate Keale poz	vij oz di
79.406	To John Smythsone alis Taylor Mr Cooke guilt plate Brandon poz	viij oz
79.407	To John Dudley Sergeant of the Pastry two guilt spones Keale poz	v oz di qtr
79.408	To Williams Huggans a guilt bole of the store poz	xxxj oz qtr di
79.409	To Mr Edwarde Stafforde a guilt cup Keale poz	x [oz] qtr di
79.410	To Mr Thomas Layton in guilt plate Keale poz	Lx oz qtr di
79.411	To Marke Anthony in guilt plate Keele poz	v oz di
79.412	To Ambroso Lupo in guilt plate Kealle poz	v oz di
79.413	To Petruchio ij guilt sponnes Keele poz	v oz qtr
79.414	To Charles Smythe a guilt boule Brandon poz	xx oz di
79.415	To Peter Woulf in guilt plate Keale poz	v oz
79.416	To Anthonius Phinotus a bolle without a couer brandon poz	vij oz di

79.417 To Mr Henry Bronker a guilt Tankerd Keale poz . . . . xvj oz di qtr
79.418 To William Russell a guilt cup with a couer Keale poz . . . . xj oz di di qtr
79.419 To Gylham Skeates A guilt boule Brandon poz . . . . x oz qtr di

Fre Guiftes

79.420 To Sir George Hawarde gent vssher of the privey chamber in guilt plate
        Keele poz . . . . xij oz di
79.421 To Mr John Asteley Mr & treasoror of her Maiesties Juelles & plate a guilt
        bole Keale poz . . . . xviij oz iij qtr di
79.422 To Mr Thomas Asteley grome of the saide pryvy Chamber a guilt cup
        Keale poz . . . . ix oz
79.423 To Mr Edward Care also grome of the said pryvy Chamber a guilt cup
        Keale poz . . . . ix oz
79.424 To Mr Henry Sackforde grome also in lyke guilte plate Keale poz . . . . ix oz
79.425 To Mr John Baptest grome also in guilte plate Keale poz . . . . ix oz
79.426 To Mr Henry Mydlemor grome also in guilt plate Keale poz . . . . ix oz
79.427 To Mr Thomas Knevet grome also in guilte plate Keale poz . . . . ix oz
79.428 To Mr Thomas Gorge grome also in guilt plate Keale poz . . . . ix oz
79.429 To Mr William Kyllygrewe grome also in guilt plate Keale poz . . . . ix oz
79.430 To Raufe Hope yeoman of the Robes in guilt plate Brandon poz
        . . . . xij oz iij qtr di
79.431 To Nicholas Bristow Clerke of the Juelhouse a guilt cruse Keale poz
        . . . . x oz iij qtr di
79.432 To John Pigeon yeoman of the saide office a guilt Casting bottle poz
        . . . . x oz iij qtr di
79.433 To Steven Fulwell also yeoman of the same office a guilt Cruse Brandon
        poz . . . . x oz iij qtr di
79.434 To Richarde Asheley grome also of the said office guilte plate Brandon
        poz . . . . x oz iij qtr di
79.435 Delyvered too the Queene by Mr. Knevet a guilt boule with a couer
        Keale poz . . . . xv oz di di qtr

        Summa totalis / of all the plate giuen
        in maner & forme aforesaid. . . . . v^m vij^C xxxiiij oz iij qtr

A Rewarde

79.436 Paid by the Threausoror of the chamber to Morrys watkyns in Rewarde
        for xviij Larkes in acage. . . . . xx s

Guiftes giuen by her Maiestie
and deliuered at sundry times in maner and
fourme following / that is to say

79.437 Mr Norrys
  First given by her Matie and Delyuered the xxvj^th of March Ao xxo
    Regni Sui at the cristenyng of Mr Norrys childe a Doble cup of siluer
    and guilte of the store of iiij^m ounces / it is moare then ordinary her
    pleauser reported by the Lo Chamberleyn . . . . xxxvij oz di

79.438 Mr Rogers
  Item geven by her saide Matie & delivered the iiij^th of Apriell anno
    pred to the Christeninge of Mr Rogers child who maryed the Lady
    Mary Seamer one guilt bolle with a couer of the afforesaid iiij^m oz
    poz . . . . xxiiij oz di qtr

79.439 Mouns[ieu]r Gounde
  Item geven by her saide Matie & delivered the viij^th of May Anno pd
    to Mounsieur Goundie Ambassator sent from the french Kinge a
    chayne of gould poz – xl oz iij qtr of our store of the charge of the
    said John Asteley beinge xxij carats one grayne . . . . xl oz iij qtr   golde

79.440 Capten Furbussher
  Item geven by her said Matie & delivered the xxj^th of Maye to
    Captayne Forbussher at his departure in his viage a chaine of
    gould borowed of Mr Rogers poz – xxiiij oz qtr of the goodnes of
    xxij karretes . . . . xxiiij oz qtr   golde

79.441 A Gentilman of the countie of Emdon
  Item more geven by her said Matie & delivered the xxij^th of the saide
    monethe of Maye to a gentleman of the Country of Emdens a chayne
    of goulde poz - vj oz iij qtr iiij penywayte & vj graynes beinge of the
    goodnes of xxij Carrettes iij qtr of a grayne
    . . . . vj oz iij qtr iiij d wayte and vj graynes   gold

79.442 A Gentilman of Duke Cashamere
  Itm more geven by her Matie & delivered the xxv^th of May to a
    gentleman sent from Duke Cashamere A Chayne of gould poz—
    xiij oz iij qtr j d wayte beinge of the goodnes of xxij Carettes
    . . . . xiij oz iij qtr j d wayte   golde

79.443 To Mounsieur Vray
  Itm more geven by her said Matie & delivered the xix^th of June to
    Monsieur Vray a gentleman sent from the french Kinge a chayne of
    gould poz – xxvij oz qtr beinge of the goodnes of xxij Carrettes iij
    qtr of a grayne and of the charge of the saide John Assteley
    . . . . .xxvij oz qtr   golde

79.444 Mr Wotton
  Itm geven by her Matie & delivered the seconde of July at the
    Christeninge of Mr Edward Wottones Sonne a cup of siluer guilt
    of the charge of the office & the parcell of the saide iiij^m oz poz
    . . . . xxxix oz qtr di

79.445 La Marques
  Item geven by her Matie & delivered the vij^th of August To the La
    Marques of Northampton a doble boule of siluer gilt parcell of
    the iiij^m oz poz . . . . .xxxv oz

79.446   To Mounsieur Remboilet

Itm geven by her Matie & delivered by the vijth of september anno
pred to Monsieur Remboillet ambassador from the french Kinge a
Bason & Ewer guilt poz—iiij^{xx} xiiij oz di di qtr a payre of guilt
pottes poz—Cxviij oz di qtr & a pare of guilt flagons poz—Clxxix
oz di All beinge of the iiij^m oz aforesaid in toto . . . . .CCCiiij^{xx} xij oz qrt

79.447   Monsieur plasses

Item geven by her Matie and delivered at Norwiche in the progresse
Anno xx^{mo} pred a Chayne of gould borowed of Mr Edwarde
Stafforde gent pentioner to Monsieur Plasses a frenche gent poz
. . . . .xvij oz di qtr   golde

79.448   Mounsieur Cussie

Item geven by her Matie & delivered the xth of september anno pred
to Monsieur Cussi a frenche gent A Chayne off gould of the Charge
of thoffice beinge of the goodnes of xxij Carettes iij qtr of a grayn
poz . . . . xxij oz xiiij d wayte   golde

79.449   Monsieur Sauernij Torsack & Ninsoniann

Item more geven by her Matie & delivered the said xth of semptember
to thre gent more that came with Mounsieur Bacueuile viz Monsieur
Savernij Torsacke & Ninsonann / two of the sayde Chaynes being of
paris worke garn with sede perles & enamvled poz together—vij oz
viij d wayte & xviij graynes a Lv s the once for the gould—xx li ix s
ob qtr & for the fassion of them—vj li & thother chayne beinge of
gould wyer worke poz—iiij oz iij qtr iiij d wayte at like pryce for the
gold—xiij li vij s iij d & for fassion of it—iiij li x s in tot
. . . . xij oz qtr ij d wayie & xviij graynes golde

79.450   To Thabbott of Dunfermlyng

Item geven by her said Matie & delyvered the 4th of Auguste to the
Abott of Dunferinglinge sent Ambassator out of Skotland a Chayne
of gould beinge of iij peces bought of Thomas Covell of london
Gouldsmythe & beinge parcell of the charge of the sayde John
Assteley poz . . . . xxxiiij oz iiij d wayte di   golde

79.451   To Dr Junuis

Item geven by her sayde Matie & delivered the xvijth of October to
Doctor Junius Ambassator sent from Duke Cassamere a Chayne of
gould poz – xvij oz j di ob wayte beinge of xxij Caretes iij qrt le gr of
the charge of the said [John Asteley]. . . . . xvij oz jd ob wayte golde

79.452   Duk Casshamer

Item gevon by her said Matie and Deliuered the xijth of Februarij To
Duke Casshamere A Coller of golde of Thorder with knottes and
red Rooses cont xliiij peces poz – xxx oz di And a George of golde
enameled with collors poz -- iij oz di All being of the Chardge of the
said John Asteley in toto . . . . xxxvij oz allouer   golde

Item more gevon vnto hym and Deliuered the saide Daye Two Cuppes
or bolles of golde with Couers and Lions in the toppe of them
holding her Mates Armes enamelid the golde being of xxij karrettes

and haulf a graine fine the same golde bought of Alderman Marten

poz . . . . CCj oz qtr   golde

79.453   Lorde Audley

Item geven by her said Matie and deliuerid the vj^th of Februarij pred

at the Christeing of the Lorde Audlies Childe A guilt bolle with a

Couer bought of Robt Brandon poz. . . . . xxviij oz iij qtr

79.454   The Portingale Ambassator

Item gevon by her said Majestie and Deliuered the xxvij^th of Marche

Anno pred to Le signoir Gerauldy Ambassator Leger from the late

King of Portingale at his Departure A Basone and Laire guilt poz—

Clxiiij oz di / A paire of guilt pottes poz—CCxvij oz iij qtr di / A

paire of guilt Flagones poz—CCxlvij oz di qtr / A guilt bolle with

a Couer poz—xxxj oz qtr di /A guilt bolle with a couer poz—xxxj

oz di qtr / and two guilt Saultes with a Couer poz—iiij^xx viij oz

di qtr All being of the store and parcell of the foresaid iiij^m oz in

toto . . . . DCCiiij^xx oz di qtr

79.455   mounsieur St marie

Item more gevon by her saide Matie and Deliuered the last of Marche

Anno pred to Mounsieur Saincte Marie a Frenche gent sent from

Mounsieur A Chaine of golde of Paine worke enamelid poz—ix oz

qtr of the chardge of the saide John Asteley. . . . . ix oz qtr

79.456   Sir Thomas Laiton

Item more gevon by her said Matie and Deliuered the xth day of May

Anno pred at the Marriage of Sir Thom Laitone Knighte A guilt

Cup with a Couer with plates enamelid with tharmes of the Sinque

Portes and in the top of the couer a Lion holding her Maties Armes

enamelid of the chardge of the saide John Asteley poz . . .lxvij oz di allouer

Elizabeth R

[sign manual]

J Astley

Ex[aminatio] per Ed Pigeon

J. Pigeon

Ste. Fulwell

Richard Asteley

Anno 23rd Elizabethae Reginae, Juelles given to her Majestie
at Newyer's tyde, 1581
Anno Regni Regine Elizabeth vicesimo tercio

Newyersguiftes giuen to her Matie
at her Palloice of westminster by thise
persons whose names do hereafter
ensue the First day of January
the yere aforesaid

81.1 By Sir Thomas Bromley Knight Lorde Chauncellor of Inglande in
golde. . . . . xiij li vj s viij d
81.2 By the Lorde Burleigh Lorde high Treausuror of Inglande in golde . . . . xx li
81.3 By the Lorde Marques of Winchester in golde. . . . . xx li
dd to henry Sackford grome of the privey Chamber

Earles

81.4 By therle of Leycestor Mr of the Horses a Gyrdill of golde made like vnto
apeir of Beedes cont eight Longe peces fully garnesshed with small
Diamondes and Foure score and one small peces fully garnesshed with
lyke Diamondes / with alitle cros of golde also garnesshed with Lyke
Diamondes / hanging thereat arownde Clocke of golde fully garnisshed
with lyke Diamondes and apendant of golde lykewyse garnesshed with
Diamondes
dd to the Lady Haward
81.5 By therle of Arondell a Bodkyn of golde with apendant being aCradill
garnesshed with small Diamondes
dd to the said Lady Haward
81.6 By therle of Shrewesbury in golde . . . . xx li
81.7 By therle of Darby in golde. . . . . xx li
81.8 By therle of Sussex Lorde Chamberlyn in golde . . . . xx li
81.9 By therle of Lincoln Lord Admyrall in golde. . . . . x li
81.10 By therle of Bedford in golde . . . . xx li
dd to the said Sackford
81.11 By therle of Warwyck thre score Buttons of golde set with Amatastes &
ragged perle one perle in apece
dd to the foresaid Lady Howard
81.12 By therle of Oxford afeyer Juell of golde being abeeste of Ophalles with
afeyer Lozenged Diamonde thre perlles pendant / and fully garnesshed
with small Rubys Diamondes & small perlles one horne Lackyng
dd to the foresaid Lady Haward
81.13 By therle of Rutlande in golde . . . . x li
81.14 By therle of Huntingdon in golde. . . . . x li

81.15 By therle of Bathe in golde . . . . x li
           dd to the foresaid Sackford

81.16 By therle of Penbroke a Cabonet of marqtre standing vpon acase of grene
  vellat with lockes & garnettes guilte
        dd to Thomas Knevet keper of the palloyce of Westmer

81.17 By therle of Northumberland in golde . . . . x li
          dd to the foresaide Sackford

81.18 By therle of Hereford too Large Ruffes and two peier of Cuffes edged with
  abrode pasmane Lace thone of golde and thother of Syluer
        dd to Mrs Jane Brisselles chamberer

81.19 By the viscount Mountague in golde . . . . x li

Duchesses Marquesses & Countesses

81.20 By the Duches of Somerset in golde . . . . xiij li vj s viij d
          dd to the said Sackford

81.21 By the Lady marques of Northampton a cheyne of mother of perle and
  other small sede perles Cornelions and other stones / and a nother
  Cheyne of black Bewgilles
        dd to the foresaid Lady hawarde

81.22 By the Lady Marques of winchester in golde . . . . x li
          dd to the foresaid Sackford

81.23 By the Countes of Shrewesbury A Gowne of white Satten the Sleaves of
  Asshcollored Satten cut and Embrodered with Venice golde and Tawny
  sylke the gowne garn with passamayne of golde
        dd to Rauf Hope yoman of the Roobes

81.24 By the Countes of Huntingdon in golde . . . . viij li
          dd to the foresaid Sackford

81.25 By the Countes of Oxforde xxiiij Buttons of golde enamvled with one
  perle in every Button
        dd to the foresaid Lady Hawarde

81.26 By the Counties of Lincolne A Rounde Kyrtelle of Clothe of Siluer prynted
  with a passamayne of flate [sic] golde vnlyned
        dd to the foresaid Rauf Hoope

81.27 By the Counties of Warwicke fyve Dosen buttens of golde set with smale
  Rubies and perles
        dd to the foresaid Lady Hawarde

81.28 By the Counties of Sussex in golde . . . . x li

81.29 By the Counties of Penbroke douger in golde . . . . xij li
          dd to the foresaid Sackford

81.30 By the Counties of Pembroke Junior A Mantle of Lawne networke garn
  and florisshed ouer with Golde and Spangels
        dd to the foresaid Ra Hoope

81.31 By the Counties of Bedforde Afaire longe cusshion Embradored with
  verbum Dei and pictetures lined with purple Tynsell and her Maties
  owne picteture
        dd to the foresaid Mr Knevet

81.32 By the Countes of Northumberland in golde . . . . x li
81.33 By the Countes of Sowthampton in golde . . . . x li
81.34 By the Countes of Rutlande in golde . . . . x li
                                                            dd to the foresaid Sackford
81.35 By the Countes of Kente Dowager A Kyrtill of Asshecollored satten
        striped with a brode passamayne of golde & buttons of the same
81.36 By the Countes Lennex A Kyrtle of Orraynge Tawny Satten cut and lyned
        with white serseonet, laide all ouer with passamayne of Sylver
                                                            dd to the foresaid Ra Hoope

Vicountisses

81.37 By the viscountes Mountague in golde . . . . x li
                                                            dd to the foresaid Sackford

Busshops

81.38 By the Arche Busshopp of yorke in golde . . . . xxx li
81.39 By the Busshoppe of Elye in golde . . . . xxx li
81.40 By the Busshopp of Durham in golde . . . . xxx li
81.41 By the Busshopp of wynchester in golde . . . . xx li
81.42 By the Busshopp of London in golde . . . . xx li
81.43 By the Busshop of Salisbury in golde . . . . xx li
81.44 By the Busshoppe of Lincolne in golde . . . . xx li
81.45 By the Busshoppe of Norwiche in golde . . . . xx li
81.46 By the Busshoppe of Worster in golde . . . . xx li
81.47 By the Busshopp of St Davies in golde . . . . x li
81.48 By the Busshopp of Herforde in golde . . . . x li
81.49 By the Busshopp of Carlell in golde . . . . x li
81.50 By the Busshopp of Lychefelde in golde . . . . viij li vj s viij d
81.51 By the Busshop of Peterborowgh in golde . . . . x li
81.52 By the Busshop of Bathe in gold . . . . x li
81.53 By the Busshop of Exeter in golde . . . . x li
81.54 By the Busshop of Chitchester in golde . . . . x li
81.55 By the Busshop of Chester in golde . . . . x li
81.56 By the Busshopp of Rochester in golde . . . . x li

Lordes

81.57 By the Lorde Burgaveny in golde . . . . v li
                                                            dd to the foresaid Sackford
81.58 By the Lorde Hunsdon A foreparte of A kyrtill of lawne all ouer enbraudered
        with golde
                                                            dd to the foresaid Ra Hoope
81.59 By the Lorde Howarde two Bodkyns of golde havinge pendauntes
        gar with smale Dyamondes and eyther of them an Emeraulde
        without foyle
                                                            dd to the La Hawarde
81.60 By the Lorde Ryche in golde . . . . x li

81.61 By the Lorde Darsy in golde . . . . x li
　　　　　　　　　　　　　　　　　　　　dd to the foresaid Sackford
81.62 By the Lorde Russell A wache set in Mother of pearle with iij pendauntes
　　　　of golde garnished] with sparckes of Rubyes, and an Opall in euery of
　　　　them and iij small perlles pendaunt
　　　　　　　　　　　　　　　　　　　　dd to the foresaid La Haward
81.63 By the Lorde Cobham in golde . . . . v li
81.64 By the Lorde Shandowes in golde . . . . v li xiij s iiij d
81.65 By the Lorde Northe in golde . . . . x li
81.66 By the Lorde Pagett in golde . . . . x li
81.67 By the Lorde Stafforde in golde . . . . x li
81.68 By the Lorde Compton in golde . . . . x li
81.69 By the Lorde Norrys in golde . . . . x li
81.70 By the Lorde Dudley in golde . . . . x li
　　　　　　　　　　　　　　　　　　　　dd to the foresaid Sackford
81.71 By the Lorde Winsor A Dublate of Carnation Satten with waves of sylver
　　　　lace, & spangells Layde betwixte
　　　　　　　　　　　　　　　　　　　　dd to the foresaid Ra Hoope
81.72 By the Lorde Lumley in golde . . . . x li
81.73 By the Lorde Wharton in [golde] . . . . x li
　　　　　　　　　　　　　　　　　　　　dd to the foresaid Sackford

Baronesses

81.74 By the Barronesse Burley A Dublate of white Satten with tuftes of Carnation or
　　　　Tawny silke
81.75 By the Barronesse Dakers A petticote of Clothe of siluer with iij gardes
81.76 By the Barronesse Cobham a Rounde Kyrtle of yellowe and white Satten
　　　　payned & Cut, layde with A Lase of Tawnye silke and siluer & lyned
　　　　with Tawny serceonett
　　　　　　　　　　　　　　　　　　　　dd to the foresaid Ra Hope
81.77 By the Barronesse Howarde Dowager in golde . . . . x li
　　　　　　　　　　　　　　　　　　　　dd to the foresaid Sackford
81.78 By the Barronesse Howarde A bodkyn of golde with a flower at the ende
　　　　garn with smale Dyamondes And a pendaunt beinge a sonne with v
　　　　Table dyamondes and two meane perlls pendaunte
　　　　　　　　　　　　　　　　　　　　dd to the foresaid La hawarde
81.79 By the Barronesse Honsdon in golde . . . . x li
　　　　　　　　　　　　　　　　　　　　dd to the foresaid Sackford
81.80 By the Barronesse Shandowes Dowager a paire of Slippers of Carnation
　　　　vellate enbraudered with a border of perle and hands and Eyes
　　　　enbraydered
　　　　　　　　　　　　　　　　　　　　dd to the Roabes by Charles Smythe
81.81 By the Barronesse Shandowes Junior in golde . . . . vj li xiij s iiij d
81.82 By the Barronesse St John Bletsoe in golde . . . . x li
　　　　　　　　　　　　　　　　　　　　dd to the foresaid Sackforde

81.83   By the Barronesse Paggett Cary a Deske plated with siluer parsell gylte,
        being a Callender of the xij Monethes, lyned with purple Satten & the
        back parte quilted with like satten

                                            dd to the Lady Stafford

81.84   By the Barronesse Cheyney A Chayne of pomaunders and Ambers and
        beades of perles

                                            dd to Lady Hawarde

81.85   By the Barronesse Barckeley in golde . . . . x li
81.86   By the Barronesse Tailboyes in golde . . . . x li
81.87   By the Barronesse Norres in golde . . . . x li

                                            dd to the foresaid Sackford

81.88   By the Barronesse Dudley a Cusshenclothe of lawne wroughte with openworke
        of blacke silke & syluer

                                            dd to Ms Skydmore

81.89   By the Barronesse Sheffeild a Juell of golde with thre white Doves one
        bygger then the reste with a Rocke Ruby in her brest & garni with very
        smale Rubyes & dyamondes with iij mene perles pendaunte

                                            Geuen by the quenes Matie to Mrs An West
                                            by the reporte of Mr Sackford

81.90   By the Barronesse Morley A Doblate of Carnation Satten allouer
        enbradored with hoopes and Flowers of Golde and garn withe seede
        perles

81.91   By the Barronesse Wharton a kyrtle of Clothe of siluer with boddyes of
        the same vaved with wattched silke And buttons of Venice golde, & lase
        of the same golde with spangles on eytherside

                                            dd to the foresaid Ra hoope

81.92   By the Barronesse Ritche A Bodkyn of golde with a pendaunt of golde
        being a wrethe sett with smale perle and a Harte in the myddeste being a
        [blank] And two handkerchers of lawne wrought withe hartes of sondry
        collored sylke

                                            dd to the Lady Haward the bodkyn
                                            and the handkyrchers dd to Mrs Skydmore

81.93   By the Barronesse Wylloby the Lordes wyfe a foreparte of white Satten
        enbradored with pescoddes frogges & strabury flowers with a border of
        Strawecollored satten enbradored with golde lyned with strawcollored
        Taphata

                                            dd to the foresaid Ra Hoope

Ladies

81.94   By the Lady Mary Sydney a foreparte of a kyrtle of Carnation Taphata
        enbradored with flowers of Silke and siluer

                                            dd to the foresaid Ra Hoope

81.95   By the Lady Mary Seymer wyfe to Mr Rogers a Caule of pypes of golde
        and smale perle

                                            dd to Mrs Chaworth

81.96   By the Lady Elizabeth Seymer als Knightley a Cusshion Clothe of
       Networke florisshed ouer with golde Sylver and sylke of sondry
       collors & edged with bone lase of golde & buttens of the same
dd to Mrs Skydmore

81.97   By the Lady Stafforde a bodkin of golde with a pendawnte of Mother
       of perle like a white Rose & garnished] withe Sparkes of Rubyes and
       a Jasente pendawnte & a meane Emeraulde
dd to the Lady haward

81.98   By the Lady Wallsingeham thre peeses of fyne Launde florisshed with gold
       and siluer and a fann offethers of sundrye Collors withe a Cristall Handle
dd to Mrs Jane Brisselles
and the fan to Rafe hope

81.99   By the Lady Drury A Rounde kyrtle of Strawcollored Taphata with a
       border embradored with a Cordante of Blacke Sylke
dd to the foresaid R hope

81.100   By the Lady Carowe a Cusshion clothe of Camerycke wrought with
       Acornnes of black silke & frenged with venice golde

81.101   By the Lady Laighton a wastecote of Stytched Clothe all ouer florysshed
       with golde and Spangels
dd to Mrs Skydmore

81.102   By the Lady Cheake a Vale or Mantle of Networke grene and yellowe
       silke

81.103   By the Lady Croftes a foreparte and apayre of sleaves of Orringe collored
       Satten with a border of enbrawdery wythe Flowers of silke
dd to the foresaid Ra Hoope

81.104   By the Lady Hennage a Stole of the wood of seder of Lybanus Covered
       with blacke vellat enbradored with too borders of golde sylke and siluer
       with beastes and wormes & frenged with a deap fringe of golde & silke
dd to Mr Knevet keper of westminster pallayce

81.105   By the Lady Pawlett in golde. . . . . v li
dd to the foresaid Sackford

81.106   By the Lady Fyzwarren a fan of fethers of sondry Collors of the birde of
       paradice with a Lase of caule worke in a Case of paper paynted
dd to Mrs Brisselles

81.107   By the Lady wylloby Sir Fraunses wife thre peces of Lawne white worke
[blank]

81.108   By the Lady Gresham in golde . . . . x li

81.109   By the Lady Cromwell Sir Henryes wyfe in golde . . . . v li

81.110   By the Lady Ratlyfe in golde. . . . . v li
dd to the forsaid Sackford

81.111   By the Lady Froegemerton too smockes of Camerycke black worke
dd to Mrs Skydmore

81.112   By the Lady An Askewe on Ancker of golde garnisshed with smale
       sparckes of Dyamondes hanginge at a Bodkin of golde enamvled
       with a smale perle pendaunte
dd to the Lady Haward

81.113   By the Lady Marven a kirtle of white wroughte Satten wroughte with
Oring Colored sylke and wyth a passamayne of Blacke silke and golde
and spangles on eyther side lyned with blacke serceonet

dd to the Roobes by Charles Smyth

81.114   By the Lady Souche a smocke of Camerycke the boddyes and sleaves
wroughte with blacke silke and Edged wyth a passamayne of golde

dd to Mrs Skydmore

81.115   By the Lady Katheryn Constable a bodken of golde enamvled with a Rose
beinge Rubies wyth a greate perle in the myddeste

dd to the Lady Haward

Knights

81.116   By Sir Fraunces Knowles Threasoror of your Householde in golde . . . . x li
81.117   By Sir James Croftes Comptroler of the same in golde . . . . x li

dd to the foresaid Sackford

81.118   By Sir Christofer Hatton vice Chamberlyne A paire of Braselettes of
golde with xij Esses of smale Dyamondes and xxiiij perles / A Juell of
golde garn with Dyamondes and iij meane perlles To hange at yt / And a
Carcanet or a Tyer for the hed of golde cont xxxiiij peces fully garnysshed
withe smale Dyamondes, at euery seconde pece A perlle pendaunte

dd to the Lady Haward

81.119   By Sir Fraunces Walsingham principall secretory A Gowne of Russet
Clothe of Siluer stryped wythe golde and a border of Feathers

dd to the foresaid Ra hoope

81.120   By Sir Raufe Sadler Chauncellor of the Duchie in golde. . . . . xv li
81.121   By Sir Walter Mildemaye Chauncellor of thexchequire in golde . . . . x li

dd to the foresaid Sackford

81.122   By Thomas Willson esquire also Secretary A folde Table of wod vernisshed
and paynted with Antyckes of golde And a longe Cusshion of purple
Satten enbradored with golde silver and silke of Sondry collers the
backeside purple Satten and iiij Tassels of venice golde and silke / A
Braselet of Taffata garn with flyes of golde and a Trayle of perlles

The Table & Cushion dd to Mr Knevet
and the Braslette dd to the La haward

81.123   By Sir Thomas Henage Threasorer of the Chamber a folde Table of Ceder
of Lybanus and a Carpet of blacke vellat enbradored with a fayre brode
border of beastes and wormes & foules wrought with Golde silke and
siluer of sondry collors lyned with grene Taphata & frenged with golde
and silke

dd to foresaid Mr Knevet

81.124   By Sir William Cordall Mr of the Rolles in golde . . . . x li
81.125   By Sir William Damsell Receuor of the Courte of wardes in golde . . . . x li
81.126   By Sir Owen Hopton Levetenante of the Tower xxxj Counters of golde
with the Quenes Armes one the one side and a Sonne on the other side
poz . . . . iiij oz qrt di

dd to the foresaid Sackford

81.127 By Sir Edwarde Horsey Captayne of the Ile of wighte A layre of Christall
garn with golde with A Bounche of Roses in the top Cont v Roses with
sparckes of dyamondes the eare vnmoved and lose

                              In charge of Mr Asteley Mr of the Juelles

81.128 By Sir Gylberte Dethicke principall kinge of Armes a Booke of Armes
of the Earles in The tyme of Kinge John and Kinge Henry the thirde

                              dd to the foresaid Mr Knevet

81.129 By Sir Gawyn Carow A Smocke of camerycke the sleaves fayre wroughte
and edged with smale bone lase of golde

                              dd to Mrs Skydmore

81.130 By Sir Henry Cromwell in golde . . . . x li

                              dd to the foresaide Sackford

81.131 By Sir Henry Lee alawnce stafe of golde set with sparkes of Rubies and
Dyamondes

                              dd to the Lady Haward

81.132 By Sir William Drury a paire of hose of watched silke garn in the top
with golde and siluer apaire of garters of yellowe serceonet gar at the
endes with golde & siluer & a skarfe of watched sipers florisshed with
frogges

                              The hoste [sic] and garters dd to Mrs Skydmore
                              and the skarf to Mrs Chaworth

81.133 By Sir Edwarde Clere in golde . . . . x li

                              dd to the foresaide Sackford

81.134 By Sir Edwarde Vmpton a payre of Braselettes of golde cont xvj peeces in
euery of them a smale Rubye garnished withe smale perle

                              dd to the La haward

81.135 By Sir Thomas Laighton a smale Cup of Christall ye foote garnished with
gold & smale Rubies with a Couer in the Top thereof a flower of white
Roses and set with iij smale Rubies

                              In charge of Mr Asteley Mr of the Juelles

Gentlewomen

81.136 By Mrs Blaunche Parry a Juell of golde beinge a Crane with a meane perle
pendante

                              dd to the Lady haward

81.137 By Mrs Fraunces Howard a vayle of Networke with a border of flowers
of Siluer & florished ouer with siluer and spangels

                              dd to Mrs Chaworth

81.138 By Mrs Dale a doblate and a gathered foreparte of Orrenge collored
golde prented

81.139 By Mrs Skydmor a doblate of white Satten stryped with golde lyned with
yellowe serseonett

                              dd to the foresaid Ra Hoope

81.140 By Mrs Edmondes a Gyrdle or a skarfe of lawne florished with golde
siluer and silke

                              dd to Mrs Chaworth

81.141   By Mrs Snowe xij handkerches of Camerycke edged with a pasamayn of
    golde
                          dd to Mrs Skydmore

81.142   By Mrs Bapteste a Ruffe a paire of Cuffes a Shadowe & a paire of laces
    garn with sede perle in a box

81.143   By Mrs Weste a Ruffe of Lawne spangled with smale Rubies
                          dd to Mrs Jane Briselles

81.144   By Mrs Chaworthe a rownde Kyrtle of white wrought satten vnlyned with
    iij passamaynes of golde & blacke silke
                          dd to Ra hoope

81.145   By Mrs Newton a Mantle of mvrry sypers edged with a smale bone lase
    of golde in a box
                          dd to the foresaid Ra hoope

81.146   By Mrs Marbury a paire of sleaves of white & yellowe satten laid with
    siluer lace lined with yellowe Taphata
                          dd to the roobes by Charles Smyth

81.147   By Mrs Digby a smocke of Cameryke wroughte with blacke worke & edged
    with a pasamayne of blacke silke
                          dd to Mrs Skydmore

81.148   By Mrs Jane Bryssels a Ruffe and Cuffes of Cutworke and a lase of
    golde networke
                The ruffes & Cuffes dd to herself and
                the Lace dd to Mrs Chaworth

81.149   By Mrs Townesende A Bodkin of golde enamvled grene with a pendaunte
    with ij white birdes of Mother of perle and smale sparkes of Rubies &
    dyamondes with a pendaunte stone being a Jacent hartwies
                          dd to the La howard

81.150   By Mrs Morgayn A Birde beinge a Stare
                          with her Matie

81.151   By Mrs Cave Six handkerchers wroughte with blacke silke and golde

81.152   By Mrs Sackeforde a faire Smocke of Cameryke alouer wrought with
    blacke & edged with Bugels
                          dd to Mrs Skydmore

81.153   By Mrs Elizabethe Hawarde A Snufkin of purple satten enbradored with
    flowers of gold and siluer & A Masse of smale seade perle
                          dd to Mrs Chaworth

81.154   By Mrs Wingfelde ij paire of Snvffers of Siluer gilte poz. . . . . v oz
                with Mr Asteley Mr of the Juelles

81.155   By Mrs Cromer iij peces of Lawne wrough[t] with white worke & florisshed
    with golde
                          dd to Mrs Jane Brisselles

81.156   By Mrs Smythsonne A Coyfe of lawne garnished with golde

81.157   By Mrs Twyste a waystcoate of fauell wrought slytelie with blacke silke
    edged with a bonelase of golde
                          dd to Mrs Skydmore

81.158   By Mrs Note Six handkercheres of Camerycke edged with venice golde

81.159   By Mrs Barley Six handkerchers edged with venice golde

dd to the said Mrs Skydmore

81.160   By Mrs Assouer a Snusekyn of Clothe of siluer enbradored with sondry
Byrdes Flowers and Trees with a border of ye same

dd to Mrs Chaworth

81.161   By Mrs Mowntague a payre of hose of Carnation silke enbradored vppon
the top and apaire of garters of Carnation Taphata serceonet, with a
brode passamayne of golde and siluer

81.162   By Mrs Croxson a nightcoyfe of sipers garn with pypes and Spangles of
siluer with too longe pendantes of the same Stuffe

81.163   By Mrs Hugganes a fan of silke of sondry collered flowers with leaues of
golde & a handle of siluer and guilte

81.164   By Mrs Othomer of Coventry a long Bodkyn of Crystall for the Quenes
heare, beinge a Ragged Staffe withe iij Barres of golde enamvled with a
picture of her Matie

81.165   By Mrs Allen vj handkerchers of Camerick wroughte with Cutworke

81.166   By Mrs Haynese a Smocke of Cameryke Blacke worke with Roses and
flowers

dd to Mrs Skydmore

81.167   By Mrs Tommyseende the Dwarfe a fan of fethers with a glasse in the
myddeste

dd to Mrs Chaworth

Chaplyns

81.168   By Archedeacon Carow deane of the Chappell in gold . . . . x li

dd to the foresaid Sackford

81.169   By Absolon Clerke of the closet, the Byble in iiij Tomes being in latten
couerid with Crymson vellat

81.170   By Brydges Deane of Salesbury a Testament in Engelissh of old wrytten
hand couerd with purple vellate and garn and Clapsed with golde

dd to Mr Knevet

Gentlemen

81.171   By Mr Philip Sydney a Juell golde being a whippe garnisshed with smale
Dyamondes in iiij^{or} Rowes and Cordes of smale sede perlle

dd to the La Haward

81.172   By Mr John Harrington a Skimskyn of grene vellate alouer enbradored
with sede perle

dd to Mrs Chaworth

81.173   By Mr Thomas Knevett a chare, too longe Cussions & too shorte
Cusshions and a wrytinge borde All Covered with purple fygured
vellatt

remaining with hymself in Westmr pallayce

81.174   By Mr Packington a Juell of golde beinge an Anker fullye garn with smalle
dyamondes & ameane perle pendaunte

dd to the La haward

81.175   By Mr William Cornwallis a foreparte of blacke vellate wroughte with
braunches of Russet vellate vnshorne and garnisshed with smale seede
perle

> dd to the foresaid Ra hoope

81.176   By Mr Edwarde Stafforde a small cup of Christall with a couer slytelie
garn with golde & a clocke within A Christall garn with gold with
sparckes of smale dyamondes sparckes of Rubies & sparckes of
Emeraldes, And Furnisshed on the backside with other dyamomondes
[sic] Rubyes & other stones of smale vallue

> The cup with Mr Asteley Mr of the Juelles
> and the clock with the La haward

81.177   By Mr Wolley a foreparte of a kyrtle a paire of sleaves a partelett a greate
Ruffe a paire of Cuffes of Lawne edged with a passamayne of golde and
Spangles in a box

> The foreparte partlett & Sleaves with Mrs Skydmore
> and the ruffes and cuffes with Mrs Brisselles

81.178   By Mr Stanhoppe a Cusshion Clothe of white networke florisshed with
siluer

81.179   By Mr Foulke Grevell a wastecote of white Taphata quilted with
Cordauntes of Sylke bands of venice golde

81.180   By Mr Dyer a wastecote of white serceonet enbradored alouer with
Carnation silke

> dd to Mrs Skydmore

81.181   By Mr Raffe Bowes a partelet & sleves of lawne striped with plates of
gold and silver

> dd to Mrs Jane Brisselles

81.182   By Mr Gyfforde A pece of Tawny striped Saten Cont . . . . xix yerdes di
xix ydes di dd to Ra hoope

81.183   By Mr Hobbye a smocke of Camerike of blacke worke edged with asmale
bone lase of golde and siluer

> dd to Mrs Skydmour

81.184   By Mr Edward Basshe in golde . . . . x li
dd to the foresaid Sackford

81.185   By Mr Lichfelde a fayr Instrument beinge a Bandoro

> dd too Mathius

81.186   By Mr Newton two necke laces of Networke florisshed with gold and
siluer

> dd to Mrs Chaworth

81.187   By Mr Docter Master a pott of Candeginger & a pot of Sithen flowers

81.188   By Mr Docter Julio a pott of Cande Ginger and oringes Candit

87.189   By John Hemyngwaye a pott of Condit peares

81.190   By Docter Baylye a pott of Candy Ginger and orringes flowers

81.191   By John Riche potycary plommes of Jeneva Abracockes dry and peares drye

> dd to Mrs Skydmore

81.192   By John Smytheson als Taylor Mr Cooke A marchepayne Lyke a Cheste borde

81.193   By John Dudley Sergeaunt of the Pastery a faire Pye of Quinses

81.194 By William Huggaynes afaire swete badge of white sercenet with a Rose of
        perle fayer embradored and xviij smale Sweate Bagges

                                                    dd to Mrs Skydmore

81.195 By Ambroso Lupo two smale Bottels of glasse with water in them

                                            dd to the same Mrs Skydmore

81.196 By Petro Lupo a payre of sweate gloves

                                given by her majestie to the La Cobham

81.197 By Charles Smythe a pettycoate of chaungeable Taphata serceonett alouer
        enbradored with a twiste of watched silke and siluer

                                                        dd to Raf hoope

81.198 By Petrucio Vbaldino An Italian Booke of a phisition towching mans
        Complextion and physike

                                                        dd to Mr Baptest

81.199 By Marke Antonio two drynking glasses of venis making, and a smalle
        glas of sweate water

                                    the swete water dd to Mr Baptest

81.200 By Mr Hewes ij peces of Lawne

                                            dd to Mrs Blanche Parry

81.201 By Bassanowes the musitians a Fan of fethers paynted within a Case with
        a glasse in the mydeste

                                                    dd to Mrs Chaworth

81.202 By Christofer Barker the Quenes prynter a Byble in Inglishe couered with
        crymson vellate enbradored

                                                        dd to Mr Knevet

81.203 By Gowre her Maties paynter a fayre Table paynted beinge a Lylly pott
                                            dd to the same Mr Knevet

81.204 By Chater ij paire of swete gloves

                                                    dd to Mrs Chaworth

81.205 By Gylham Byliard a proper dadge guilt and well wroughte
                                In the charge of the saide John Asteley

81.206 By Customary Smythe a Bolte of Camerycke

                                            dd to Mrs Blanche Parry

        Summa totalis of all the money / giuen to her maiestie &
        Deliuered vt supra . . . . ix C xiij li vj s viij d

81.207 Over and besides xxxj Counters of golde presented by the liutenant of the
        Tower poz. . . . . iij oz qrt di
                                                    all dd to H Sackford

        Elizabeth R
        [sign manual]

                                                            J Astley
                                                    ex[aminatio] per
                                                            Bristow
                                                            J Pigeon
                                                        Ste Fulwell

Anno Regni Regine
Elizabeth xxiij

Newyeres giftes giuen by her Matie
at her pallayce of Westmr to thise
persons whose names do hereafter
ensue the First day of January
the year aforesaid

81.208	To Sir Thomas Bromley knighte Lord Chauncellor of Englande in guilt plate Brandon & Keyle poz . . . . xxxiiij oz di
81.209	To the Lorde Burley Lorde high Threasoror of England in guilte plate Brandon & Keyle poz . . . . xl oz qrt di
81.210	To the Lorde Marquies of wynchester in guilte plate Brandon & Keyle poz . . . . .xxx oz

Earles

81.211	To Therle of Lecestor Mr of the horses in guilte plate Brandon & Keyle poz . . . . Cxxxij oz
81.212	To Therle of Arrundell in guilt plate Brandon & Keyle poz . . . . xxiiij oz di
81.213	To Therle of Shrewesbury in guilte plate Brandon & Keyle poz . . . . . . xxx oz di
81.214	To Therle of Darbie in guilt plate Brandon & Keyle poz. . . . . xxix di di qrt
81.215	To Therle of Sussex Lorde Chamberlyn in guilt plate Brandon & Keyle poz . . . . .xxxv oz
81.216	To Therle of Lyncolne Lorde Admyrall in guilte plate Brandon & Keyle poz . . . . xix oz iij qrt
81.217	To Therle of Oxforde in guilte plate Brandon & Keyle poz . . . Ciiij^{xx} ix oz qrt di
81.218	To Therle of Warwicke in guilt plate Brandon & Keyle poz . . . . iiij^{xx} xix oz di di qrt
81.219	To Therle of Rutlande in guilte plate Brandon & Keyle poz . . . . xx oz
81.220	To Therle of Bedforde in guilt plate Brandon & Keyle poz . . . . .xxxj oz di
81.221	To Therle of Huntingdon in guilt plate Brandon & Keyle poz . . . . . xx oz di qrt
81.222	To Therle of Penbroke in guilt plate Brandon and Keyle poz . . . . . xxxj oz di qrt
81.223	To Therle of Northumberlande in guilt plate Brandon and Keyle poz . . . . xx oz
81.224	To Therle of Bathe in guilt plate Brandon and Keyle poz . . . . xx oz
81.225	To Therle of Herforde in guilt plate Brandon and Keyle poz . . . . xx oz

Vicount

| 81.226 | To Viscounte Mountague in guilte plate Brandon and Keyle poz . . . xix oz iij qrt |

Duchesses Marquesses & Countesses

| 81.227 | To The Duches of Somerset in guilte plate Brandon and Keyle poz . . . . xxiiij oz di qrt |
| 81.228 | To The Lady Marquies of Northampton in guilte plate Brandon and Keyle poz . . . . .xl oz |

81.229 To The Lady Marquies of Wynchester in guilte plate Brandon and Keyle
        poz . . . . xix oz di qrt
81.230 To The Countes of Shrewesburye in guilte plate Brandon and Keyle
        poz . . . . .xxx oz
81.231 To The Countes of Huntingdon in guilt plate Brandon and Keyle
        poz . . . . .xxxiiij oz qrt
81.232 To The Countes of Oxford in guilte plate Brandon and Keyle poz . . . . xx oz
81.233 To The Countes of Lyncoln in guilt plate Brandon and Keyle poz . . . L oz di qrt
81.234 To The Countes of Warwycke in guilt plate Brandon and Keyle
        poz . . . . Lvij oz qrt di
81.235 To The Countes of Sussex in guilte plate Brandon and Keyle . . . xxiij oz di di qrt
81.236 To The Countes of Penbroke dowager in guilte plate Brandon and
        Keyle poz . . . . xxiiij oz qrt
81.237 To The Countes of Penbroke junior in guilt plate Brandon and Keyle
        poz . . . . .xxiij oz
81.238 To The Countes of Bedforde in guilt plate Brandon and Keyle poz . . . . . L oz di
81.239 To The Countes of Northumberlande in guilte plate Brandon and Keyle
        poz . . . . xx oz di qrt
81.240 To The Countes of Southampton in guilte plate Brandon and Keyle
        poz . . . . xix oz di di qrt
81.241 To The Countes of Rutlande in guilte plate Brandon and Keyle poz . . . . . xx oz
81.242 To The Countes of Kentt Dowager in guilt plate Brandon and Keyle
        poz . . . . xix oz iij qrt di
81.243 To The Countes of Linnex in guilte plate Brandon and Keyle poz
        . . . . xviij oz qrt di

Vicountes

81.244 To The Viscountes Mountague in guilte plate Brandon and Keyle
        poz . . . . xix [oz] iij qrt

Busshops

81.245 To The Arche Busshopp of Yorke in guilte plate Brandon and Keyle
        poz . . . . xxxvij oz di di qrt
81.246 To The Busshopp of Elye in guilt plate Brandon and Keyle poz . . . . xxxvj oz qrt
81.247 To The Busshopp of Durham in guilt plate Brandon and Keyle poz
        . . . . .xxxv oz qrt
81.248 To The Busshop of London in guilt plate Brandon and Keyle poz . . . xxix oz qrt
81.249 To The Busshopp of Salesbury in guilte plate Brandon and Keyle
        poz . . . . xxix oz iij qrt di
81.250 To The Busshopp of Winchester in guilte plate Brandon and Keyle
        poz . . . . xxx oz iij qrt di
81.251 To The Busshopp of Lyncolne in guilt plate Brandon and Keyle
        poz . . . . xxxj oz

81.252 To The Busshopp of Norwich in guilt plate Brandon and Keyle poz
. . . . xxvij oz di di qrt
81.253 To The Busshopp of Worster in guilt plate Brandon and Keyle poz . . . . . . .xxx oz
81.254 To the Busshopp of St Davys in guilte plate Brandon and Keyle poz
. . . . xv oz iij qrt di
81.255 To the Bushopp of Carlell in guilte plate Brandon and Keyle poz . . . . xvj oz qrt
81.256 To the Bushopp of Hereforde in guilte plate Brandon and Keyle poz
. . . . xv oz di
81.257 To the Bushopp of Bathe in guilt plate Br and K poz . . . . xvj oz iij qrt
81.258 To the Bushopp of Peterborow in guilt plate Br. and K poz . . . . .xv oz iij qrt
81.259 To the Bushopp of Chitchester in guilte plate Br and K poz . . . . . . .xv oz iij qrt
81.260 To the Bushop of Chester in guilte plate Br and K poz . . . . xv oz di di qrt
81.261 To the Bushopp of Rochester in guilte plate Br. and K poz. . . . . xv oz
81.262 To the Bushopp of Exetor in guilte plate Br and K poz. . . . . .xv oz iij qrt
81.263 To the Bushopp of Lychefeld in guilte plate Br and K poz . . . . . . xix oz iij qrt di

Lordes

81.264 To The Lorde Burgaveni in guilte plate Brand and K poz . . . . ix oz iij qrt
81.265 To The Lorde Hunsedon in guilte plate Br and K poz. . . . . .xxx oz di qrt
81.266 To The Lorde Howard in guilte plate Br and K poz. . . . . C oz di di qrt
81.267 To The Lorde Ryche in plate Br and K poz . . . . xix oz iij qrt di
81.268 To The Lorde Darsy in guilte plate Br and K poz . . . . xix oz
81.269 To The Lorde Russell in guilt plate Br and K poz . . . . .xviij oz di di qrt
81.270 To The Lorde Cobham in guilte plate Br and K poz . . . . xv oz
81.271 To The Lorde Shandowes in guilt plate Br and K poz . . . . xij oz iij qrt di
81.272 To the Lorde Northe in guilte plate Br and Keyle poz . . . . xx oz
81.273 To the Lorde Paget in guilte plate Br and K poz . . . . xix oz di di qrt
81.274 To the Lorde Stafford in guilt plate Br and K poz . . . . xix oz iij qrt
81.275 To the Lorde Compton in guilte plate Br and K poz . . . . xix oz iij qrt
81.276 To the Lorde Norrys in guilte plate Br and K poz . . . . xix oz di
81.277 To the Lorde Dudley in guilt plate Br and K poz. . . . . xix oz iij qrt
81.278 To the Lorde Wynsor in guilte plate Br and K poz . . . . xviij oz qrt
81.279 To the Lorde Lumley in guilt plate Br and K poz . . . . xix oz iij qrt di
81.280 To the Lord Wharton in guilte plate Br and K poz . . . . xix oz iij qrt di

Baronesses

81.281 To the Baronesse Burley in guilt plate Br and K poz . . . . xxiiij oz di qrt
81.282 To the Baronesse Dakers in guilt plate Br and K poz. . . . . .xviij oz di
81.283 To the Baronesse Cobham in guilte plate Br and Ke poz. . . . . L oz
81.284 To the Baronesse Talboyes in guilt plate Br and K poz . . . . xx oz
81.285 To the Baronesse Howard Dowager in guilt plate Br and K poz . . . . . . .xx oz qrt
81.286 To the Baronesse Howard Junior in guilte plate Br and K poz . . . xxviij oz qrt di
81.287 To the Baronesse Hunsedon in guilt plate Br and K poz . . . . .xxx oz qrt
81.288 To the Baronesse Shandowes Junior in guilt plate Br and K poz. . . . . xj oz iij qrt
81.289 To the Baronesse Shandowes Dowager in guilt plate Br and K poz . . . . . . xv oz
81.290 To the Baronesse St John Bletzo in guilte plate Br and K poz. . . . . xx oz

81.291	To the Baronesse Pagett Care in guilte plate Br and K poz	xxv oz
81.292	To the Baronesse Chayney in guilt plate Br and K poz	xxxj oz di qrt
81.293	To the Baronesse Barkeley in guilt plate Br and K poz	xx oz di qrt
81.294	To the Baronesse Norres in guilt plate Br and K poz	xx oz
81.295	To the Baronesse Dudley in guilt plate Br and K poz	xj oz
81.296	To the Baronesse Sheffeld in guilt plate Br and K poz	xvj oz
81.297	To the Baronesse Morley in guilte plate Br and K poz	xix [oz] di di qrt
81.298	To the Baronesse Wharton in guilt plate Br and K poz	xxij oz qrt di
81.299	To the Baronesse Riche in guilt plate Br and K poz	xvij oz iij qrt di
81.300	To The Barronesse Wylloby in guilt plate Br and K poz	xvij oz di

Ladies

81.301	To The Lady Mary Sydney in guilte plate Br and K poz	xxx oz qrt di
81.302	To the Lady Mary Semer in guilt plate Br and K poz	xiij oz iij qrt di
81.303	To the Lady Elizabeth Semer als Knightlie in guilte plate Br and K poz	xij oz iij qrt
81.304	To the Lady Stafford in guilt plate Br and K poz	xxx oz
81.305	To the Lady Walsingham in guilt plate Br and K poz	xviij oz qrt di
81.306	To the Lady Drury in guilt plate Br and K poz poz [sic]	xvij oz iij qrt
81.307	To the Lady Carowe in guilt plate Br and K poz	xxxv oz qrt di
81.308	To the Lady Cheeke in guilt plate Br and K poz	xxiiij oz
81.309	To the Lady Hennage in guilt plate Br and K poz	xxij oz
81.310	To the Lady Laighton in guilt plate Br and K poz	xviij oz di qrt
81.311	To the Lady Pawlett in guilt plate Br and K poz	x oz iij qrt di
81.312	To the Lady Croftes in guilt plate Br and K poz	xx oz qrt
81.313	To the Lady Wylloby in guilt plate Br and K poz	xj oz iij qrt di
81.314	To the Lady Gresham in guilte plate Br and K poz	xviij oz qrt di
81.315	To the Lady Cromwell Sir Henryes wyfe in guilte plate Br and K poz	xj oz
81.316	To the Lady Ratclyffe in guilt plate Br and K poz	xj oz iij qrt di
81.317	To the Lady Frodmorton in guilt plate Br and K poz	xx oz iij qrt
81.318	To the Lady Anne Askewe in guilte plate Br and K poz	xv oz
81.319	To the Lady Fyzewarren guillt plate Br and K poz	vij oz
81.320	To the Lady Marven in guilte plate Br and K poz	xv oz
81.321	To the Lady Souche in guilt plate Br and K poz	xiiij oz
81.322	To the Lady Katheryn Constable in guilte plate Br and K poz	xij oz qrt di

Knightes

81.323	To Sir Fraunces Knowles Threasor of the householde in guilt plate Br and K poz	xxv oz
81.324	To Sir James Croftes Comtroler of the same in guilt plate Br and K poz	xxiiij oz iij qrt
81.325	To Sir Christover Hatton vicechamberlyn in guilte plate B and K poz	CCCC oz
81.326	To Sir Fraunces Wallsingeham principall Secrytory in guilt plate Br and K poz	Lxij oz di
	To Sir Thomas Wilson also Secretory in guilt plate Br and K poz	xxiiij oz di qrt

81.328	To Sir Thomas Hennage Threasoror of the Chamber in guilte plate Br and K poz .... xlviij oz
81.329	To Sir Raufe Sadler Chauncellor of the Duchie in guilte plate Br and K poz .... xxviij oz qrt
81.330	To Sir Walter Mildmaye Chauncellor of the Exchequire in guilte plate Br and K poz .... xxvij oz di
81.331	To Sir William Cordalle Mr of the Rolles in guilt plate Br and K poz .... xx oz qrt
81.332	To Sir William Damsell Recevor of the Courte of Wardes in guilt plate Br and K poz .... xviij oz qrt
81.333	To Sir Owen Hopton Levetenante of the Tower in guilt plate Br and K poz .... xxii oz qrt di
81.334	To Sir Edward Horssey Captayne of thile of wight in guilt plate Br and K poz .... xxix oz di di qrt
81.335	To Sir Gylberte Dethick pryncipall king of Harroldes in guilt plate Br and K poz .... xiiij oz iij qrt di
81.336	To Sir Henry Cromwell in guilte plate Br and K poz.................. xx oz
81.337	To Sir Gawyn Carow in guilt plate Br and K poz................ xxxv oz di
81.338	To Sir Henry Lee in guilt plate Br and K poz......................... xl oz
81.339	To Sir William Drury in guilte plate Br and K poz .... xvj oz qrt di
81.340	To Sir Edward Cleere in guilt plate Br and K poz .... xx oz di
81.341	To Sir Edward Vmpton in guilt plate Br and K poz............ xxij oz qrt di
81.342	To Sir Thomas Layton in guilt plate Br an K poz .... xxxj oz iij qrt

Gentilwomen

81.343	To Mrs Blaunche Parry in guilt plate Br and K poz............. xviij oz iij qrt
81.344	To Mrs Fraunces Howarde in guilte plate Br and K poz .... xvj oz di di qrt
81.345	To Mrs Dale in guilt plate Br and K poz .... xxiij oz iij qrt
81.346	To Mrs Edmondes in guilte plate Br and K poz..................... xv oz
81.347	To Mrs Skydmore in guilt plate Br and K poz .... xvj oz di di qrt
81.348	To Mrs Snowe in guilte plate Br and Ke poz .... xvij oz iij qrt di
81.349	To Mrs Bapteste in guilt plate Br and Ke poz...................... xv oz
81.350	To Mrs Weste in guilt plate Br and Ke poz.....................xv oz qrt
81.351	To Mrs Katharyn Paston in guilte plate Br and Ke poz................ xv oz
81.352	To Mrs Chaworthe in guilt plate Br and Ke poz.................... xv oz
81.353	To Mrs Marbury in guilte plate Br and Ke poz .... xv oz
81.354	To Mrs Digbye in guilte plate Br and Ke poz..................... xvj oz
81.355	To Mrs Jane Bryssels in guilt plate Br and Ke poz................. xv oz
81.356	To Mrs Townesende in guilt plate Br and Ke poz............... xxij oz di
81.357	To Mrs Cave in guilte plate Br and Ke poz...................... xv oz
81.358	To Mrs Sackforde in guilt plate Br and Ke poz .... xxij oz
81.359	To Mrs Elizabethe Howarde in guilt plate Br and Ke poz .... xv oz iij qrt di
81.360	To Mrs Winkefelde in guilt plate Br and Ke poz poz [sic] .... vij oz iij qrt di
81.361	To Mrs Cromer in guilte plate Br and Ke poz ....x oz qrt
81.362	To Mrs Smytheson in guilte plate Br and Ke poz................ vij oz di qrt
81.363	To Mrs Twiste in guilt plate Br and Ke poz .... vj oz iij qrt

81.364	To Mrs Noote in guilte plate Br and Ke poz	xij oz iij qrt di
81.365	To Mrs Barley in guilt plate Br and Ke poz	xiij oz
81.366	To Mrs Assoner in guilt plate Br and Ke poz	x oz qrt
81.367	To Mrs Mountague in guilte plate Br and Ke poz	xij oz
81.368	To Mrs Croxson in guilt plate Br and Ke poz	vj oz di
81.369	To Mrs Hyggaynes in guilt plate Br and Ke poz	xxj oz di
81.370	To Mrs Otham of Coventry in guilt plate Br and Ke poz	xj oz di di qrt
81.371	To Mrs Allen in guilte plate Br and Ke poz	xij oz di di qrt
81.372	To Mrs Haynnes in guilte plate Br and Ke poz	xiiij oz
81.373	To Mrs Tomasyn in guilt plate Br and K poz	v oz
81.374	To Mrs Morgayne in guilt plate Br and Ke poz	vij oz

Maydes of Honor

81.375	To Mrs Marye Ratlyffe in guilte plate Br and Ke poz	x oz qrt
81.376	To Mrs Ellen Brydges in guilte plate Br and Ke poz	x oz qrt di
81.377	To Mrs Katheryn Howarde in guilte plate Br and Ke poz	x oz
81.378	To Mrs Elizabethe Garrett in guilte plate Br and Ke poz	x oz di qrt
81.379	To Mrs Mackewillyams in guilte plate Br and Ke poz	ix oz iij qrt di
81.380	To Mrs Vaviser in guilte plate Brandon and Keyle poz	ix oz iij qrt di
81.381	To Mrs Hide Mother of the Maydes in guilte plate Brandon and Keyle poz	xij oz di di qrt

Chaplyns

81.382	To Archedeacon Carow in guilte plate Brandon and Keyle poz	xxij oz
81.383	To Absalon Clerke of the Clossett in guilt plate Brandon and Keyle poz	vij oz di
81.384	To Brygges Deane of Salysbury in guilt plate Brandon and Keyle poz	xv oz di

Gentilmen

81.385	To Mr Philip Sydney in guilt plate Br and Ke poz	xx oz iij qrt di
81.386	To Mr John Harington in guilt plate Br and Ke poz	xl oz
81.387	To Mr Thomas Knevett in guilt plate Br and Ke poz	xx oz
81.388	To Mr Dyer in guilte plate Brandon and Ke poz	xvj oz di qrt
81.389	To Mr Raffe Bowes in guilte plate Brandon and Keyle poz	xvj oz di di qrt
81.390	To Mr Foulke Grevill in guilt plate Brandon and Keyle poz	xj oz iij qrt di
81.391	To Mr Packyngton in guilte plate Brandon and Ke poz	xvj oz di qrt
81.392	To Mr Wollye in guilte plate Brandon and Keyle poz	xxiiij oz qrt
81.393	To Mr Hobby in guilte plate Brandon and Keyle poz	viij oz iij qrt di
81.394	To Mr Edward Stafforde in guilte plate Br and K poz	xx oz iij qrt di
81.395	To Mr Gyfforde in guilte plate Br and Keyle poz	xxiij oz iij qrt
81.396	To Mr Stanhoppe in guilte plate Br and Keyle poz	xv oz di qrt
81.397	To Mr Lichfeld in guilt plate Br and Ke poz	xviij oz di qrt
81.398	To Mr Edward Basshe in guilte plate Brandon and Keyle poz	xx oz iij qrt di
81.399	To Mr Smythe Customer in guilt plate Brandon and Keyle poz	xiiij oz iij qrt di
81.400	To Mr Newton in guilte plate Brandon and Keyle poz	xiiij oz iij qrt di

81.401	To Mr Docter Masters in guilte plate Br and Keyle poz . . . . xiiij oz iij qrt
81.402	To Mr Docter Julio in guilte plate Brandon and Keyle poz . . . . xiiij oz iij qrt
81.403	To Mr Docter Baylye in guilt plate Brandon and Keyle poz . . . . xiij oz iij qrt
81.404	To John Hemyngway in guilte plate Brandon and Keyle poz . . . . vj oz iij qrt
81.405	To John Riche in guilt plate Br and Ke poz . . . . vij oz qrt

81.406   To John Smytheson al Taylor Mr Cooke in guilt plate Br and Keyle
poz . . . . viij oz di

81.407   To John Dudley Sergiaunt of the Pastry in guilte plate Br and Keyle
poz . . . . v oz di

81.408	To William Huggaynes in guilte plate Br and Keyle poz . . . . xxviij oz qrt
81.409	To William Cornewallys in guilte plate Brandon and Keyle poz . . . x oz iij qrt di
81.410	To Marke Anthony in guilte plate Brandon and Keyle poz. . . . . v oz di
81.411	To Petrucho Vbaldino in guilte plate Brandon and Keyle poz. . . . . v oz di
81.412	To Ambroso Lupo in guilte plate Br and Keyle poz. . . . . v oz di
81.413	To Chawrles Smythe in guilte plate Br and Keyle poz . . . . xviij oz
81.414	To Petruchio Lupo in guilte plate Br and Ke poz. . . . . v oz di
81.415	To Hewes in guilte plate Brandon and Keyle poz. . . . . xij oz iij qrt di
81.416	To Bassanoes the Brethren in guilte plate Br and K poz . . . . iij oz

81.417   To Chrystofer Barker the Quenes prynter in guilte plate Br and Keyle
poz . . . . vij oz di qrt

| 81.418 | To Gouer Oone Chater in guilte plate Brandon and Keyle poz. . . . . iij oz |
| 81.419 | To Guilham Byllyard in guilt plate Brandon and Keyle poz . . . . vij oz |

Fre Guiftes

81.420   To Mr Astely Mr and Threasoror of the Juelles in guilte plate Brandon
and Keyle poz . . . . xviij oz iij qrt di

81.421   To Mr Thomas Astely grome of the prevy Chamber in guilt plate Brandon and
Ke poz . . . . ix oz

81.422   To Mr Edwarde Cary grome of the prevy chamber in guilt plate Br and
Ke poz . . . . ix oz

81.423	To Mr Knevett in guilte plate Brandon and Keyle poz . . . . ix oz
81.424	To Mr Henry Sackforde also grome in guilt plate Br and Ke poz . . . . ix oz
81.425	To Mr Myddlemore in guilt plate Br and Ke poz. . . . . ix oz
81.426	To Mr Goorges another grome in guilt plate Brandon and Keele poz . . . . . ix oz
81.427	To Mr Babteste grome also in guilte plate Br and Kele poz. . . . . ix oz
81.428	To Mr Kyllygrayve grome also in guilt plate also Br and Kele poz . . . . ix oz

81.429   To Rawffe Hope yoman of the Robes in guilt plate Br and Kee poz
. . . . xij oz iij qrt di

81.430   To Nicholas Bristow Clerke of her Maties Juelles and plate in guilt
plate Br and Kee poz. . . . . x oz iij qrt di

81.431   To John Pygeon on of the yeomen of her Maties Juelles and plate in
guilte plate Br & Kee poz. . . . . x oz iij qrt di

81.432   To Steaven Fulwell an other yeoman of the same office in guilt plate Br
and Ke poz. . . . . x oz iij qrt di

81.433   To Richarde Astely grome of same office in guilte plate Br and Kee
poz . . . . x oz iij qrt di

Summa totalis of all the plate / giuen awey as aforesaid . . . . v^m Clxxv oz di

Guiftes giuen and deliuered at sundry
tymes in maner and fourme folloing
that is to say

81.434   Mounsieur La Bourge a frenche Ambassadour
       Item geven by her Matie the xviij of Marche to Mounsier La Bourge
       a frenche gentleman by the Reporte of Mr Edwarde Stafforde A
       Cheyne of golde bought of Alderman Martyn poz . . . . . . xxix oz di   golde

81.435   Therle of Penbrokes childe
       Item geven by her Matie the xxv Daye of Aperell at the Crystenynge of
       Therle of penbrokes Sonne one Bason and a Layre of Syluer and
       guilte poz—Ciiij oz di and one Duble Almayne Cup of Syluer and
       guilte poz—xliij oz bought of Richarde Martin esquire & the same
       plate presented by Mr Boyer . . . . Cxlviij oz di

81.436   Mounsieur Devre Mounsieur Setretary [sic]
       Item more geven by her Matie Anno xxij^mo the xvj of Maye to
       Mounsieur Devre Mounsiers Secritory on Chayne of golde smale
       lynkes bought of Alderman Martyn poz – xxxiij oz di di qtr presented
       by Edwarde Stafforde. . . . . xxxiij oz di di qrt   golde

81.437   The Lorde Morlys childe
       Item geven by her Matie Anno xxij^mo the vij of August at the
       Christeninge of the lorde morles daughter & Delyver to Mr Boyer
       A Doble Bole guilte boughte of Hugh Keale poz. . . . . xl oz iij qtr di

81.438   Mr Verney Mr vicechamberleyns serunt
       Item geven to Mr Verney serunt to Mr vicechamberleyne the xviij
       Day of Septembere Maties reward a Cheyne of golde of the value
       of xix li x s teste Sir Thomas Huneage & Mr Henry Sackeforde
       . . . . xix li x s   golde

81.439   Count montroyall
       Item geven by her Matie Anno xxij^mo the xvij of Januarij to
       Countmont Royall A Chayne of golde smale Lynkes poz
       . . . . lxj oz qrt   golde

81.440   Ambassador for the king of Portingale
       Item geven more by her Matie vnto Con [sic i.e. Don] Joau Buger
       dasousa Imbasitor for king Anthony of portingale A Chayne of
       golde brought of Alderman Martyn poz – xxxij oz di of xxij Carettes
       or better signifyed by therl of Lecetor. . . . . .xxxij oz di   golde

81.441   Mr Ed Stafford childe
       Item more geven by her Matie at the Christeninge of Mr Edwarde
       Staffordes Child on duble Boole boughte of Alderman Martyn poz
       —L oz qtr signifyed by the lorde chamberlyne & delyvered to Mr
       perse pennante . . . . L oz qrt

81.442   Mr Darcy

Item given by her said Matie and Delyuered the last Day of July Ao
xxj^{mo} Regine at the mariage of Mr Thomas Asteleys Daughter
maried to Mr Edward Darcy a Tancard of Siluer guilt fayerly
embossed and set on the syde with Camewes heddes of the charge
of John astely Mr of the Juelles and parcell of such plate as serued
her Matie in her prevy chamber poz . . . . xxxj oz qrt di

81.443   From the king of Denmark

Item given by her said Matie and Delyuered the xxixth of Nouember to George
Swooke a gent sent from the kinge of Denmarke acheyne of
golde bought of Alderman Martyn poz – xx oz xiiij d weite being of
xxij kar qrt le grayne fyne . . . . xx oz L xiiij dweite   golde

81.444   Lord Willobye

Item gevon by her saide Matie and Delyuered the vth of Marche Ao
xxiijtie pred at the Christening of the Lorde willobyes Childe A
bolle of siluer guilt with a Couer bought of the said Alderman
Marten poz . . . . xl oz

81.445   The Prince Dolphen

Item gevon by her saide Matie and deliueied the xiijth of June Ao pred
To the prince Dolphen sent out of Fraunce as a Comissioner to her
said Matie A bolle of golde with a Couer bought of Alderman
Marten poz. . . . . Ciiij oz   golde

Item more gevon vnto him and Deliuerid the same tyme a paire of
Flagons of siluer guilt poz—CClij oz qrt di / A paire of pottes guilt
poz—CCClix oz / a nest of bolles with a Couer guilt poz—Cxliiij
oz iij qrt / A Basone and Ewer guilt poz—CCij oz di / A bason and
Ewer guilt poz—Cvij oz di di qrt / another basone and Ewer guilt
poz—Cxxxviij oz di qtr / A paire of Flagones guilt poz—Clv oz iij
qrt / two bolles with two Couers guilt poz—Lxv oz qrt / a paire of
vases or Laues guilt per oz iiij^{xx} j oz iij [qrt] di / a paire of Saultes
guilt with a couer poz—Lxxij oz iij qrt / And two Candelstikes guilt
poz—iiij^{xx} xij oz / All bought of the said Alderman
. . . . MDClxij oz qrt   siluer

81.446   Monsieur de Cosse

Item more gevon and Deliuered the same tyme to Monsieur Marshall
De Cosse oone other of the said comissioners A basone and Ewer
guilt poz—Ciiij^{xx} xij oz iij qrt / Another bason and Ewer guilt poz
—Clix oz qrt / another bason & Ewer guilt poz—iiij^{xx} vij oz iij qrt
di / A paire of Flagons guilt poz—CCv oz / a paire of pottes guilt
poz—CCxliij oz qrt / another paire of guilt pottes poz Clx oz / a
nest of bolles with a couer guilt—Cxxiij oz / a bolle with a couer
guilt—Lxij oz qrt / A bolle with a couer guilt—xl oz qrt/ A bolle
with cristall in it—lxvj oz qrt di / two Cupes with couers guilt—
Cxij oz foure Frutedisshes guilt—iiij^{xx} ix oz di / thre Chaundellors
guilt poz—Cxxxvj oz qrt / a Sault with a couer with cristall stone
and pearle in it poz—iiij^{xx} xvij oz di di qrt / And a guilt Saulte

with a couer with like stone and pearl in it poz—xlviij oz iij qrt di all
bought of the said Alderman . . . . MDCCCxxxiiij oz qrt   siluer

81.447   Monsieer Lansacke

Item more gevon and Deliuerid the said Day to Monsieur Lansacke
oone other of saide Comissioners A Basone and Ewer guilt poz—
Cxlv oz di / A basone and Ewer guilt poz—Cv oz iij qrt di / Another
basone and Ewer guilt poz—iiij^{xx} xij oz / A paire of guilt pottes
poz—Cxxxvj oz qrt / Another paire of guilt pottes poz—iiij^{xx} xiij
oz di qrt / A paire of guilt Flagones poz—Ciiij^{xx} xj oz / Thre guilt
bolles with a Couer poz – Cxix oz iij qrt / thre other guilt bolles
with a Couer poz—Lxix oz di qrt / two Frenche bolles with Couers
poz—iiij^{xx} ix oz di di qrt / two bolles with two Couers poz—Lxix
oz di di qrt / a bolle with a Couer guilt poz—xxiiij oz di qrt / a guilt
Spiceplate poz—xxiiij oz / three frute bolles guilt poz—Lxxvj oz iij
qrt di / two Can[dle]stickes guilt poz—iiij^{xx} xiij oz di di qrt / two
Saultes guilt poz—Lj oz And a guilt bolle with a Couer poz—Lij
oz All bought of the said Alderman in toto . . . . MCCCCxxxij oz di   siluer

81.448   Monsieur Caruge

Item more gevon and Deliuerid the same Day to Monsieur Caruge oone
other of the saide Comissioners a basone and Ewer guilt poz—Cl oz
di / another Basone and Ewer guilt poz—iiij^{xx} j oz qrt / A paire of
guilt pottes poz—Ciiij^{xx} viij oz di qrt / a paire of guilt pottes poz—
iiijxx ij oz iij qrt di / a nest of guilt bolles with a Couer poz—iiij^{xx} xviij
oz iij qrt / thre guilt bolles with a Couer poz—Lxxij oz qrt / a bolle
with a Couer guilt poz—xxxj oz qrt di / a standing Cup with a couer
guilt poz—Lxj oz iij qrt di / a standing Cup with Cristall in it poz—
iiij^{xx} xvij oz iij qrt di / two Cuppes with Couers poz—Lj oz qrt /
two Laires guilt poz – Lxix oz di qrt / two Chaundellors guilt poz
—iiij^{xx} xiiij oz di di qrt / two Saultes with a Couer poz—Lxj oz qrt
di / And A Spice box guilt poz—xxxij oz qrt di All bought of said
Alderman in toto . . . . MClxxiij oz di di qrt   siluer

81.449   Monsieur la Mote

Item more gevon and Deliuerid vt supra to Monsieur La Mote A
Basone and Ewer guilt poz—C oz di qrt / a paire of guilt pottes
poz—Clxxij oz / a paire of guilt pottes poz—Lxxix oz / a nest of
guilt bolles poz—Cxix oz / two guilt bolles with Couers poz—Lxxvij
oz iij qrt di / a paire of guilt Flagones poz—Cvj oz / two Standing
Cuppes with couers guilt poz—Lxxvij oz di qrt / a Spoute potte guilt
poz—xxix oz iij qrt / two Chaundellors guilt poz—Lxiij oz iij qrt di /
And a guilt Saulte with a Couer poz—xlvj oz di All bought as
aforesaide in toto . . . . viij^c lxxj oz qrt   siluer

81.450   Monseur Le President Busson

Item more gevon and Deliuerid as aforesaide to Monsieur Le president
Busson a Basone and Ewer guilt poz—iiij^{xx} xix oz iij qrt / a paire of
guilt pottes poz—Cxix oz / a paire of guilt Flagones poz—Clxxvij
oz / A nest of guilt bolles with a Couer poz—iiij^{xx} xiiij oz / two guilt

bolles with Couers poz—Lxj oz qrt / a guilt Cup with a Couer poz
—xxxij oz di di qrt / two guilt Chaundellors poz—xlj oz qrt / and a
paire of Saultes guilt poz—xxxviij oz All bought of the said
Alderman Marten in toto . . . . DClxiij oz   Siluer

81.451   Monsieur Pinart

Item more gevon and Deliuerid the same tyme To Monsieru Pinart a
Basone and Ewer guilt poz—Cxj oz di di qrt / another basone and
Ewer guilt poz—Lxiij oz di qrt / a paire of pottes guilt poz—Cxx
oz di qrt / another paire of pottes guilt poz—Lxxij oz qrt / Thre
bolles with a Couer guilt poz—Lxv oz di / two bolles with Couers
guilt poz—Lxxiij oz / two guilt Chaundellors poz—Lxvij oz qrt di /
thre guilt chaundellors poz—Lxj oz iij qrt / a Cup with a Couer guilt
poz—xxxiij oz qrt / And a paire of guilt Saultes poz—xxxiij oz di
qrt All bought as aforesaid in toto . . . . DCCj oz di qrt   Siluer

81.452   Monsieur Vray

Item more gevon and Deliuerid as aforesaid to Monsieur Vray oone
Basone and Ewer guilt poz—iiij^{xx} ix oz iij qrt / a paire of pottes
guilte poz—Lxxiij oz iij qrt / another paire of guilt pottes poz—xlix
oz qrt di / Thre guilt bolles poz—Lxviij oz di / Thre guilt bolles with
a Couer poz—Lxj oz di qrt / Two Candelstikes guilt poz—xl oz qrt
di / A Spoutpott guilt poz—xxix oz qrt / And a belle Saulte with a
Couer guilt poz—xx oz di qrt All bought as aforesaid in to to
. . . . CCCCxxxij oz qrt   Siluer

Elizabeth R
[sign manual]

J Astley
ex[aminatio] per
Bristow
J Pigeon
Ste Fulwell

Anno Regne Regine
Elizabethe xxiiij

Newyeres Guiftes geuen to the Quenis Maiestie
at her pallice at wesminster by theise persones whose
names hearafter ensue the First of January the yeare
abouesaid

[Primary]

By the Lady Margret Countes of Darbe

82.1 By mouns[ieur] the Frenche kinges brother a Juell being a Ship of golde
alouer with sparkes of Diamondes & Rubies all the sailes spred with a
worde enamelid on them / A flower of gold with a faire whit rose & iiij
small in the greate rose a smale blewe Sapher, & iiij smale Rubies and in
the top a colored Dasye with a smale lozenged Diamonde in it a butterflye
onder the same garn with small sparkes of Rubies / A flower of golde
garn alover with sperkes of Rubies & Diamondes & a hinde sitting
vpon it with ij smale perles pendante
Item a shakell of golde with theise wordes *Serviet eternum dulcis quem
torquet Eliza*, And a locke of golde hanging at it with a litell chaine of
golde poz . . . . vj oz di qrt

82.2 By Sir Thomas Brumley Lordchaunciler of England. . . . . . . ~~xx li~~ xiiij li vj s viij d
82.3 By the Lord Burly Lord high Threasoror of Englande in new Angelles . . . . xx li
82.4 By the Lorde Marques of winchester in golde . . . . xx li
dd to Mr Sackeford
Summa pag – liij li vj s viij d
By Sir Thomas Bromley Lorde

Earles

By the Earle of

82.5 Lecestor Mr of the horse A Chaine of golde cont sertaigne peces of golde
enamelid two of them garn with Ragged staues of smale sperkes of
Diamondes and in iiij of them two smale Diamondes a pece and two
smale sperkes of Rubies xvj lesser peces in eury of golde in euery of
them a smale Diamonde also xxiiij peces of golde in euery of them iiij
pearles with a litell ring of golde to hang it by And also a booke of golde
enamelid furnisshid with small Diamondes and Rubies bothe ch claspes
and all

82.6 Aarundell a peir of Braselettes of golde cont viij peces euery of them an
Amatest / and viij othr peces in euery of them a ~~feyer~~ perle

82.7 Sherewesbery in golde . . . . xx li

291

82.8	Darby in golde	xx li
82.9	Sussex Lord Chamberlen.	xx li

dd to the said Sackeford

82.10   Warwicke a faire Cloth of Estate of cloth of Siluer with the Quenis Armes
enbr therevpon Diuers stones and sede pearles and also sertaigne Trees
richely embraw and a faire border likewise set rounde about enbrauderid /
And a Coller of like clothe of siluer the Sonne therein likewise enbrauderd
with venice golde & iij vallaunces of like stuf likewise enbrauderd with
golde silke and siluer / and a Depe frenge to the same of venice golde
and grene silke

            dd to Mr Thomas Knevet keper of her Maties pallice of westminster

82.11   Lincolne Lorde Admerall in golde . . . . x li

dd to the said Sackeford

Summa – lxx li

yeat Earles

By the Earle of

82.12	Bedford in golde	xx li

X Oxford

82.13	Rutlande in golde.	x li
82.14	Huntingdon in golde	x li
82.15	Bathe in golde	xx li
82.16	Penbrouke in golde	xx li
82.17	Northumberland in golde	x li

dd to the said Sackeford

Summa – iiij^{xx} x li

yeat Earles

By the Earle of

82.18   Herforde A Bodken of golde garn at thende with iiij smale table Diamondes
a smale Rubye and a Crowne of Opalles and a smale pearle pendaunt
peare fation

            dd to the Lady Howard

X Ormowod

82.19   Vicount Mountegue in golde. . . . . x li

dd to the said Sackeford

Summa – x li

Duchesses Marquesses

By the

82.20   Duches of Sumerset in golde. . . . . xiij li vj s viij d

dd to the said Sackeford

82.21   Lady Marques of Northampton a fore part of a kirtell of whit Satten with
a brode border and flowers enbrauderid frenged with venice gold and whit
silke

            dd to Rauf hoope

82.22 Lady Marques of winchester Doger in golde . . . . x li

                                                    dd to the said Sackeford

82.23 Countes of Shrewesbery a tra gowne of whit clothe of siluer lynde with
    yelo & imbrodered with pillares & esse ac firmae [essefirmes]

                                                    dd to Rauf hoope

82.24 Huntingdon in golde . . . . viij li

                                                    dd to the said Sackeford

82.25 Oxforde A Juell of golde being a Serpent having two ~~faire~~ Emeraudes and
    the rest garn with smale Diamondes and Rubies, and a smale pearle
    pendant

                                        dd to the said La howard

                                        Summa – xxxj li vj s viij d

yeat Countesses

By the Countes of

82.26 Lincolne a knif a Spone and a Forke thaftes of Chrestall garn with golde
    and sperkes of garnettes

        ~~dd in chardge to John Asteley esquier Mr of the Juelhouse~~ La howard

82.27 Sussex in golde . . . . x li

                                                    dd to the said Sackeford

82.28 Warwick a faire Chaire of clothe of siluer enbrauderd with trees and
    beastes of venice gold and silke and frenged with a Depe frenge of venice
    gold and grene silke with two pommelles of Siluer / A long cusshion of
    like clothe of siluer with likeworke the backe side of grene satten and
    iiij tasselles of venice gold and grene silke / And ij short coussihons to sit
    vpon of like stuf and likewise furnisshed thone longer then thother, and a
    fotstowl of like stuf in euery degre

                                        dd to the said Mr Knevet

~~Sussex in golde~~

82.29 Penbrouke Douger in golde . . . . xij li

82.30 Penbrouke in golde . . . . x li

                                        dd to the said Sackeford

    Summa – xxxij li

yeat Countesses

By the Countes of

82.31 Bedforde A faire Chaire of Crimsen Carnation Satten enbrauderd with the
    picture of her Matie and Dyvers other personages and allouer enbr with
    venice gold and silke and lyke wise fringed with like gold and silke and
    in the Seate a lion embrauderd

                                  dd to ~~Tod~~ the said Mr Knevet

82.32 Northumberlande in golde . . . . x li

82.33 Southampton in golde . . . . x li

82.34 Rutland in golde . . . . x li

                                        dd to the said sackeford

82.35   Kent Douger a rounde kirtell of strawcolorid Satten rewid with siluer
edged with a passamane of siluer

dd to Ra hoope

X Lennex

82.36   Vicountes [Montagu] in golde . . . . x li

dd to the said sackeford

Summa – xl li

Busshoppes

By the

82.37   Arche Busshoppe of Canterbery in gold . . . . CC li
82.38   Arche Busshoppe of yorke in golde . . . . xxx li

X Elye

82.39   Durhum in gold of sundery Coines . . . . xxx li
82.40   Winchester in golde . . . . xx li
82.41   London in golde . . . . xx li
82.42   Salesbery in golde . . . . xx li

dd to the said sackeford

Summa – CCC xx li

yeat Busshopes

By the Busshoppes

82.43   Lincolne in golde . . . . xx li
82.44   Norwege in golde . . . . xx li
82.45   Worcester in golde . . . . xx li

X ~~St Davies~~

82.46   Harford in golde . . . . x li
82.47   Carleyle in golde . . . . x li
82.48   Lichfeld in golde and siluer . . . . xiij li vj s viij d

X Bathe

dd to the said sackeford

Summa – iiij^{xx} xiij li vj s viij d

yeat Busshoppes

By the Busshope of

82.49   Peterborowe in golde . . . . x li
82.50   Exetoure in golde . . . . x li
82.51   Chethestour in golde . . . . x li
82.52   Chester in golde . . . . x li
82.53   Rochester in golde . . . . x li
82.54   Gloster in golde . . . . x li

dd to the said Sackeford

Summ – lx li

Lordes

By the

82.55 Burgany in golde . . . . v li

dd to the said Sackeford

82.56 Hunsdon ~~iiij~~ oone faire longe Carpettes of Turquiworke cont ~~thone being Longe and iij shorte~~ in length [blank] and in bredth [blank]

dd to the said Knevet

82.57 Hawoord A chaine of golde with pillors & pomaunders garnisshid with smale pearle in xxxvj peces garn with x ragged pearles the pece xij pomaunders garnished with sede pearles and xlviij other peces of golde betwene them poz all . . . . xiij oz di

dd to the said La howard

Riche

82.58 Darsie in golde. . . . . x li

dd to the said Sackeford

X Russell

82.59 Cobhame in golde . . . . v li

dd to the said Sackeford

Summa – ~~xl li~~ xx li

Lordes

By the Lorde

82.60 Shandoys A Remnent of Crimsen clothe of golde with braunches of greene cont . . . . v yerdes iij qrt

dd to the said hoope

Northe in golde . . . . x li

82.61 Paget in golde. . . . . x li

82.62 Stafforde in golde. . . . . x li

82.63 Coumton in golde . . . . x li

82.64 Norres in golde . . . . x li

82.65 X Dudley

dd to the said Sackeford

82.66 Windsor A bolster and a paire of Pillowberes of Camrike enbrauderd with leaves of venice golde with a brode bone lace of like venice golde and either of them iiij buttons of Damaske golde ^Mr Darce^

dd to Mrs Skidmor

Summa – L li

yeat Lordes

By the

82.67 Lumley in golde. . . . . x li

82.68 Wharton in golde. . . . . x li

dd to the said Sackeford

82.69 Thomas Haward a Juell of golde being the personage of awoman a Ruby
       in her belly and threst of it garnesshid with small Rubyes and Diamondes
       and a small perle pendant

                                                     dd to the said La howard

82.70 Taulbot A wastcoate of Camrike faire wrought with brode blake flowers
       wrought with golde silke and siluer with a smale bonelace of golde

                                                     dd to Mrs Skidmor

       Summa – xx li

Baronesses

       By the Lady Baronesse

82.71 Burley a paire of brasselettes cont xxij peces of golde in x be Agath heades
       and xij in euery of them a garnet and ij smale pearles

                                                     dd to the said La howard

82.72 Dakers a Rounde kertell of yellowe clothe of Siluer edged with two
       passamanes of siluer ~~lined~~ ^{Rauf hoope}

82.73 Cobham A rounde kirtell of white Tincell wrought with blewe and yellowe
       flowers and edged with a passamaine of blacke silke and siluer

                                                     dd to Rauf Hoope

       X ~~Haward Duger~~

82.74 Haward A Juell of golde being a Catt and mise plaieng with her garnisshid
       with small Diamondes and smale pearles poz

                                                     dd to Mr Sackford

82.75 Hunsdone Thre smale Carpettes of turquey making thone being longer
       then thother two

                                                     dd to the said knevet

       Fizwarren

yeat Baronesses

       By the Lady Baronesses

       ~~Shandowes Douger a remnant of Crimsen clothe of Tincell gold with branches~~
       ~~of greene cont . . . . v yerdes iij qrt~~

82.76 Shandowes Doger a peticoate of Carnation Taphata Sercenet quilted with
       v borders enbrauderid with grene silke and venice golde ^{Killegraw}

                                                     dd to Rauf Hoope

82.77 St John Bletzo a Swete bagge enbrauderd with Damaske golde vj
       handkercheues and two smale swete bagges ^{Cardle yeo}

                                                     dd to Mrs Skidmor

82.78 Paget Care a forepart of a kirtell of whit ~~Tincell~~ clothe of siluer allouer
       spotted with bees and a border being a honecome of venice golde
       fringed with venice gold and blacke silke ^{Mr Gorges}

                                                     dd to Rauf hoope

82.79 Chanye vij dosson of buttons ^{lacking j button} of golde thone a pearle in
       it thother a smale emeraude

                              Mrs Skidmor retd to hir Matie by Mr Kyllegrave

82.80 Wharton a faire large glasse of peachecolorid Satten allouer enbrauderid
with venice golde and sede pearle

dd to Mr Thomas knevet

~~Willoby the Lord willolbys wif a partelet a paire of Sleves and a scarf florisshed with gold and siluer~~ ^{Mrs paston}

Mrs Newton

yeat Baronesses

By the Lady Baronesses
82.81 Barcley in golde . . . . x li
82.82 Taibbois in golde . . . . x li
82.83 Norres . . . . x li

dd to the said sackeford

Dudley
82.84 Sheffelde two Cusshenclothes and a night raile of Camrike wrought allouer
with golde silke and siluer of sundry collors edged with a bonelace of
golde and siluer

dd to Mrs Skidmor

82.85 Taulbout a foreparte of networke florisshid with siluer

dd to Mrs Skidmor

Summ – xxx li

yeat Baronesses

By the Lady Baronsses
82.86 Morle a Doublet of Lawne garn[ished] with plate lace and spangles

~~dd to Tod~~ to said Ra Hoope

82.87 Ryche Doger A foreparte of networke florisshed with golde Lined with
murre Serceonet and a Swetebage of morre Taphata ^{Gane}

dd to Rauf hoope

82.88 Willobye A partlet and a paire of Sleues of Lawne florisshed with siluer
whit worke And a Scarf of Sipers florisshed with a wod binde of siluer
^{Chaworth}

82.89 Riche junior a Dressing for a hed of networke florisshed with golde and
siluer ^{Chaworthe}

dd to Mrs Skidmor

Lades

By the Lady
Mary Sydney
82.90 Mary Semer wif to Mr Rogers a paire of Sleues of cutworke florisshed
with golde
82.91 Eliz Se[m]er alias Knitley a partlett and a paire of Sleves of ~~Lawne v~~
networke vnmade florisshed with golde and spangles

dd to Tod
dd to Mrs Skidmor

297

82.92   Staffvrde a Deske wrought with nedleworke, a paire of gloves and a
        cushion cloth

                                                                    knevet
                                               ~~with herself the bag~~
                                                                  chaworth

82.93   Walsingham a Snusken of blake vellat allouer enbrauderd with ostrige
        fethers of venice golde and siluer and furrid throwe with Sables / Thre
        handkercheuers of Camrike with a faire border of silke and golde of
        sundry collors with Turquey worke edged with a bonelace of golde and
        siluer / and iiij paire of Swete gloves with small buttones of golde in euery
        of them a smale pearle And a paire of pantophelles of blake vellet
        enbrauderd with a border of venice golde ^{Chaworth}

                                                     The handker Mrs Skidmore
                                                     ~~The snuskin Mr Sackeford~~
                                                          j paire with the Quene
                                                                     Chaworth
                                                     pantophelles Raf hoope

82.94   Drury iij peces of Lawne Cutworke florisshid with golde ^{Skidmor}

                                                            dd to Mrs Skidmor

        ~~Henry Cobham a Cage of golde with a hoope in it~~

82.95   Carowe a Cusshen clothe of Camrike wrought with blacke silke and fringed
        with a Depe fringe of venice golde

                                                            dd to Mrs Skidmor

yeat Ladyes

        By the Lady
82.96   Laiton a ~~Vaile~~ mantell of morrye sipers striped with siluer

                                                            dd to Water Trimnell
                                                            dd to Rauf hoope

82.97   Cheeke a vaile of whit Lawne

                                                            dd to Rauf hoope

82.98   Croftes a Forepar of Carnation Satten couerid with whit cutworke with
        braunches florished with siluer ^{Mr Gorges}

                                                            dd to Rauf hoope

82.99   Henige a Coming clothe with a Ruff and a paire of couffes wrought with
        Flowers and beastes of sundry collors silke and golde ^{with Raf Mr Killegrew}

                                                            dd to Mrs Skidmor

82.100 Pawlat in golde. . . . . v li

                                                            dd to Sackford

82.101 Fizwarren A paire of sleues of herecolorid and carnation Satten Chequerid
        laid betwene with siluer lace And a Sauegarde couering for a gowne of
        wrought blake sipers for bodie and skertes bounde with a passamen of
        blake silke and siluer ^{Tod}

                                                            dd to Rauf hoope

        Summa – v li

298

yeat Ladyes

By the Lady

82.102   Willoby Sir Fraunces wif a Cusshen clothe of networke florisshed with
blake silke and edged with a passamayne ^{Mrs Skidmore}

                                               Mrs Skidmore

82.103   Greshm in golde . . . . x li

82.104   Cromvell in golde . . . . v li

                                         dd to h Sackford

82.105   Ratlif two Swete bagges being large of Serceonet and vj handkercheues
wrought with silke of sundry collors spanishe worke ^{Killegrew}

                           The bagges Mrs Chaworth
                           handkerches Mrs Skidmor

82.106   Frogmorton Six handkercheues and two paire of gloues

                                             chaworthe

82.107   Anne Askewe A round Kertell of Peachecolorid Satten striped Downe with
borders of siluer and spangles

                                     dd to Rauf hoope

  Summa – xv li

yeat Lades

By the Lady

82.108   Maruen A Doublet of Carnation couerid with white laune cutworke and
set with spangles edged with a smale passamen of golde in a box ^{rauf hoope}

                                     dd to Rauf hoope

Souche

82.109   Katerine Counstable a vaile of hearecolorid Sipers in a box ^{whinyard}

Knightes

By Sir

82.110   1 Fraunces knowles Treasoror of the houshold . . . . x li

82.111   2 Jomes Croftes Comptrolor of the same in gold. . . . . x li

                                         dd to h Sackford

82.112   Walsingham prencipall Secretary ~~Christopher Hattone vicechamberlin a~~
~~paire of~~ Brasselettes of golde cont xvj peces enamelid in viij of the said
peces two smale sparkes of Diamondes and a small rubie / and in thother
viij iiij pearles a pece poz

                                         mr Sackeford

82.113   ~~Fraunces Walsingam prencipall Secretary~~ xpor hatton vicechamberlaine
A Juelle of golde with a buckell and a pendaunt of golde garn and
furnisshed with Rubies and Diamondes / vj peces of golde enamelid
fulli furnisshed with smale Rubies, betwixt euery of the same peces are
iiij^{xx} meane pearles hanging vnto the same peces of gold and pearles
are xiij pendauntes of garnished] with small rubies and smale
Diamondes thone pend[ant] is a ~~fower~~ flower of very small rubies and

thother very smale Diamondes oone pearle broken of[f] & more Seven
score & 4 buttones pescod fassyon of gould & grene enamelid halfe of
them

N pigion
dd to the said La howard

82.114   Thomas Henniage ~~a greate white ruby~~ A Juell of golde set with a greate
whit Rubye stone cut lozanged and borderid rounde with smale Rubies
and Diamondes with a pendaunt being a marmeset

dd to the said La howard

82.115   Rauf Sadler Chauncelor of the Duchey in golde . . . . xv li
82.116   Waulter Mildmay Chancellor of the Exchequer in golde . . . . x li
82.117   Gilbert Gerrard Mr of the Roolles in golde . . . . xx li

dd to h Sackford

Summa – Lxv li

yeat knightes

By Sir
~~William Cardall Mr of the Rolles~~

82.118   William Dansell Receuor of the Court of wardes in golde . . . . x li
82.119   Owne Hopten Leaueftenant of the Touor . . . . x li

dd to h Sackford

82.120   Edward Horsey Captine of the thill of wight a faire paire of smale
virgenelles couerid with grene vellat enbrauderid with sede [pearl] and a
band of venice golde and sede pearles in a case of greene wodde

La Stafford
dd to the said Knevet

82.121   Guilbart Dethicke prencipall Kinge at Armes a Booke of Armes of
noble personages of Englande in the time of King Edward the first
and Kinge Ed the seconde couerid with crimsen vellat

with the Quene by mr Sackford

82.122   Gauin Carowe a Smoke of Camrike wrought with blake silke
82.123   Henry Croumell in golde . . . . x li

dd to h Sakford

Summa – xxx li

yeat Knightes

By Sir
~~Henry Kneuet~~

82.124   Henry Cobham a Cage of golde with a hoope in it

La howard

82.125   Henry Lee a Cofer for Juelles of Crymsen Satten with passamen of golde
lined with glasse And more two sarpentes of golde knit together and
with iij very small pearles hanging at it

Gevon by her Matie to mounsier
The Juell h La howard

82.126 William Drury A Juell of golde being a pomaunder garn with speckes of
Diamondes Rubies and pearle ^Tod

La howarde

82.127 Edwarde Cleare in golde in a paper ^Sackeford . . . . x li

dd to h Sackford

Edwarde Vmptone

88.128 Thomas Laitone a Kirtell of cloth of siluer with carnation floweres and
edged with a passamaine of golde and siluer

~~dd to Mrs Skidmor~~ Rauf hoope

82.129 John Souche A partlet and a paire of Sleues of Lawne garnisshed with
rewes of flat golde and spanglees ^Mrs Skidmor

Mrs Skidmor

Summa – x li

Gentelwomen

By Mrs

82.130 Blaunche Parrye in golde. . . . . v li

82.131 Fraunces Haward a nitecoif of Sipers garn with venice golde with spangles
and two labelles of the same stuf with two other smale peces

Mrs Skidmor

82.132 Dale a pet Doublet and a Forepart of clothe of siluer printed with a
passamaine of golde ^La Stafford

dd to Rauf hoope

82.133 Skydmor A peticoate of Carnation Taphata quilted allouer with a cordant
of siluer with iij passamaine laces of siluer

Retor[ned] to her self

82.134 Edomondes a Smoke ~~of Camrike~~ holland the Sleves and body coller
wrought with flowers of blake silke and edged with a bonelace of
venice golde

82.135 Snowe xij handkercheues of holland edged with a passamaine of golde

Mrs Skidmor

82.136 Bredeman iij paire of Sweete gloves

dd ~~to Tod~~ Mrs Chaworth

~~Bapst~~
~~Bapteste~~
Summa – v li

yeat Gentelwomen

By Mrs

82.137 West a foreparte of networke florisshed allouer with venice golde with a
corde rounde about of like venice golde

dd to Rauf hoope

82.138 Chaworth a box of siluer guilt to put in swete meates poz—v oz iij qrt di
and two forehedclothes of lawne wrought with black . . . . v oz iij qrt di

Retor[ned] to her by Mr Middelmor

82.139 Newtone a Cusshencloth of Camrike with a border of Cut whitworke and
        edged with a bonelace of venice golde and iiij smale buttons of Damaske
        golde
                                              dd to Tod Mrs Skidmor

82.140 Marbery Six handkercheues of Camrike spanisheworke with a smale
        bonelace of siluer and golde ᴹʳˢ ᴺᵉʷᵗᵒⁿ

82.141 Digby a Smoke thupper parte of the body and sleues wrought with blacke
        silke and golde and edged with a bonelace of gold
                                               Mrs Skidmor

82.142 Jane Brisselles two bandes and two paire of Cuffes of Camrike Cutworke
                              dd to ~~whineyard~~ her self

82.143 Elizabeth Brouke a Sute of Ruffes of Lawne wrought with blake silke and
        florisshed with gold and siluer cont iij peces
                                                  dd to Gane

82.144 Tounsende a Cusshenclothe of Lawne Cutworke florisshed allouer with
        siluer and edged with a brode bonelace of siluer
                                           Mrs Skidmor

82.145 Morgayne v boxes of preseruid plomes, and two glasses
                              dd to Mrs Blaunche by Nich Pigeon

yeat Gentelwomen

82.146 By Mrs
        Caue A night raile of Camebr[ick] wrought with blacke silke

82.147   Mrs Skidmor
        Sackefourde A short Cloke of Cloth ~~of golde~~ Tincell the grounde russet
        enbrauderid allouer with venice golde with a border enbrauderid with
        smale pearle garn with longe buttons of Damaske golde with a
        passamaine Lase of Damaske golde

82.148   ~~dd to Mr Sackeford~~ dd to Rauf hoope
        Eliz Hawarde a Scarf of networke garn with spangles and florisshed with
        siluer with a smale bonelace of siluer

82.149   chaworth
        ~~Penipole~~ Philadelepa Care a vaile for the heade of white tufte silke netted
        betwene with siluer with a wire in the toppe

82.150   Mrs Skidmor
        Wingfelde a part bande and a paire of Ruffes of Lawne florisshed with
        flowers and beastes of blake silke ᵀʳⁱᵐᵐᵉˡˡ

82.151   Geane
        Cromer a paire of pillowbeares of Camrike all ouer wrought with brode
        flowers of blacke silke and golde

82.152   dd to Mrs Skidmor
        Smithsone allis Tailor a Coif of Lawne florisshed with blacke silke and
        edged with a bonelace of venice golde and vj totheclothes of holland
        wrought with spanishworke

82.153 Twist A paire of Sleves of Camrike wrought with blacke silk and vj
touthclothes

Mrs Skidmor

cate

82.154 Noote vj handkerchers of Cameryk edged with alace of venice golde
stoleworke

82.155 Barly vj handkerchers of Cameryk edged with alace of venice gold and
Siluer stoleworke

dd to Mrs Skydmor

yeat Gentelwomen

By

82.156 ~~Asson~~

82.157 Cromsone ~~a nite coif of Sipers~~ with a Dresseng of a hed of white Sipers ^{Sackeford}

dd to Arter Middelton

Mrs Skidmor

82.158 Hugganes A greate Swete bag of purple Ser Taphata enbrauderid with a
Tree and a phenix in the top and xx smale bages of Serceonet

dd to Mrs Skidmor

Othome[r] of Couentry

82.159 Li[ch]filde Six handkercheues wrought with silke of sundry collors and
edged with a passa bonelace of golde and siluer ^{killegrew}

dd to Mrs Skidmor

82.160 Allen A paire of Pantophelles of blake vellat with a border enbrauderid
with sede pearle

dd to Rauf Hoope

82.161 Haynes Six handkercheues of of [sic] Camrike wrought with blacke silke
spanishe worke edged with a bonelace of venice gold and siluer

dd to Mrs Skidmor

82.162 Fraunces Drury Sir willims Daughter a smale forke of Corrall slitly garn
with golde

dd to the La howard

82.163 Tomisen the Dwarf A faire handekercheue wrought with a brode border
of venice golde and silke of sundry collors ^{Skidmor}

dd to Mrs Skidmor

~~Mountegue~~

82.164 Dives a garlande of wodbindes of silke of sundry collors

Mrs Skidmor

The maydes

~~Mary Ratlife~~
~~Katteren Haward~~

303

G

Chaplaines

By

82.165 Arche Deacon Carowe Deane of the Chappell. . . . . x li

dd to h Sakf

82.166 Absalon Clerke of the Closet a smale booke in latten of Busshop Fisshers
Salmes couerid with crimsen vellat faire enbrauderid

with the Quene by ~~dd to~~ mr Waulter Trimmell

~~Bridges~~
Summa – x li

Gentelmen

~~Phillip Sidny~~

82.167 4 John Harington A Fanne of purple Satten enbrauderid allouer with a
lillie pott of Sede pearle thandell likwiese garn bothe sides being like

82.168 2 Wolley a forepart of a kirtell of Sipers wrought allouer with blake silke
and siluer with flowerdeluces of the said stuf and Lined with murre
Serceonet

dd to Rauf hoope

82.169 7 Lichfeld A Sute of Ruffes ~~and a paire of sleves~~ of Lawne cutworke edged
with a brode bone lace made like Crownes / A partlet and a paire of
Sleues of open networke florisshed allouer with golde

~~dd to Mr Sackeford~~

82.170 3 Peckington A boke of golde set with xiiij Amatastes

dd to Mrs Skidmor

82.171 6 Stafford a foreparte of a kertell of Lawne cutworke florisshed with siluer
with tuftes and siluer spangles

dd to Rauf hoope

~~Thomas Knevet~~

82.172 5 Edward Basshe in golde . . . . x li

dd to Mr Sackeford

82.173 8 Guifford A foreparte partlet and Sleues of Lawne cut florisshid with golde

dd to Mrs Skidmor

Summa – x li
Summa total 879 li

Gentelmen

~~Dyer~~

~~Forteskewe Mr of the wardrobe a Traie of Agathe garn with golde a bout~~
~~the foote and a smale bottole of Agathe garn slitly with golde in iij smale~~
~~chaines of golde~~

with the Quene by Mrs Skidmor not gevon for a Newyeresguift
~~Rauf Bowes~~

82.174 10 Stanhope a bagge of wadget Taphate enbrauderid all ouer with siluer
and golde Lined with oring color taphata with laces and buttons of oring
color silke and siluer the same to pet [sic] her Maties nitegere in

82.175 Skidmor a waste coate of white Taphate enbrauderid all ouer with siluer and
golde and set with spangles linde edged with a passamaine lase of gold

Mrs Skidmor dd to Tod

Foulkgreuell

82.177 12 Smyth Coustomer Two boltes of Camrike

Mrs Blaunche

Hobbye

82.178 20 Mountegue a paire of Stockinges of Strawcollored silke knit and a
paire of garters of whit striped sipers edged with a brode bonelace of
siluer spaingled

the garters dd to Mrs Skidmor

82.179 13 Brounker a Night gowne of Crymsen Satten laide about with a brode
passamaine of golde and siluer with long buttons of the same Faced
with whit Satten rased

dd to hickeson dd to Ra hoope

82.180 1 Mr Diar a blacke veluet hat with a whitt fether in a band of goulde of
[blacke bead] & sede parle

dd to Ra hoope

82.181 9 Newton a Doublet of cloth of Siluer with buttons of venice golde and
carnation silke and smale sede pearle

dd to Ra hoope

82.182 16 Doctor Masters a pott of Orange flowers and a pott of ginger Condite

82.183 19 John Edward Hemingway a box of Lozanges and *manus Christie* and a
pot of Abricockes

82.184 18 Doctor Bayle two pottes of the like

dd to Mrs Skydmor

82.185 17 Doctor Lopus a paire of gloves and two boxes

dd to Mrs Chewerth

82.186 18 John Ryche poticary a box of Abricokes condite and Siterns

dd to Mrs Skydmor

82.187 21 John Smithson alis Tailor Mr Coke A marchepane with her Mates
Armes faire guilded

82.188 22 John Dudlye Sergaunt of the pastrey a pie of Oranges made Castell
fation

82.189 23 William Huggans vj handkercheues of Camrike wrought with blacke
silke edged with a p bonelace of gold and siluer and a Rye eare of venice
golde Cotton

Mrs Skidmor

Packington

82.190 William Cornewallys a Cusshen cloth of C holland wrought with blake and
gold and edged with a bonelace of gold and a swete bagg of wadget
taphata ^{Mrs Paston}

with Mrs Newton dd to Mrs Skidmor

305

82.191 26 Ambroso Lupo a painted box with iij glasses of swete water

dd to Mr Baptest

82.192 27 Petrolupo a paire Swete gloves

with to mr knevet

82.193 15 Charles Smithe a small Juell of golde with a whit hare in it and garn
with xij small rubies and vij small pea[r]le ^{Mrs Newton}

with Mrs Newton gevon to Mrs Fraunces Drury by Mrs Newtons report

82.194 25 Petrucho vbaldino a booke of the liues of two greke Orators

dd to Mr Baptest

82.195 24 Marke Anthony galiardo a basket with a glasse of Swetewater in it

dd to Mr Baptest

82.196 28 Hewes Two peces of Lawne

Mrs Blaunche

82.197 29 Bassonowes the musitians A Drinking glasse with a couer
~~Christopher Barker~~

~~Gower her Ma^{ries} paynter~~

82.198 32 Thomas Leueroge Crosbowe Maker a faire crosbowe
~~Chater~~

82.199 Parker page A Lute of Ivory a Bandore and a Sittern

The bandor & Cithern dd to Mr Parke

Reported by Mr Baptest the Lute to Mathias

~~Guilhm Bilyard~~

82.200 30 Dunstone Anes a ~~besaunt bessart~~ stone pedra bazar

dd to Mrs Skidmore

82.201 31 Guilhm Skeetes a paire of faire bellowes lined with Satten with an
Antique heade strange Armes

~~dd to Tod~~ dd to Mr Knevet

In Angelles.. viijC xix li
In Di Soueragnes .... CClxlvj li x s
In Frenche Crownes.. xlij s
In a Ducket ....vj s viij d
Itm in Siluer.. xlj s iiij d
Summa – M li lxx li
[£1120]

Anno Regni Regine
Elizabeth &c xxiiij

Newyeres Guiftes geven by the Quenis Maiestie
at her Magisties pallice at Wesmister to theise persones
whose Mames [sic] hear after ensue the first of January the
yeare aboue said

[Primary]

X To the Lady margret Countes of Darbe

82.202 To Sir Thomas Brumley Lord Chanciler of England A guilte bolle with a
        couer Marton poz . . . . ~~xxx oz~~ xxxiij oz
        dd Char Smith

82.203 2 To the Lord Burly Lord Highe Threasoror of England A guilt bolle
        with a couer Mart poz . . . . xxxix oz qrt
        dd Mr Lichfeld

82.204 [ms torn] To the Lord Marques of Winchester A guilt bolle with a couer
        Keall poz . . . . xxix oz qrt
        Mr Pennant

        Summa total – Cj oz di [ms torn]

        ... orquet thi ... [ms torn]

Earles

To the Earle

82.205 1 Lecester Mr of the horse A guilt bolle with a couer m poz—xlix oz di
        di qrt A basone and Ewer Keall poz—L oz di and in g plate Martin
        —xxxj oz iij qrt di in to to . . . . Cxxxij oz
        dd to Mr killegrew

82.206 2 Arundell A guilt Cup with a couer Keall poz . . . . xxiij oz
        Dd to Mr baptest

82.207 3 Shrewisbery A guilt bolle with a couer Keall poz . . . . xxix oz di
        ~~dd to Brouke~~ Mr Bristow

82.208 4 Darby A guilt bolle with a couer marten poz . . . . xxix oz
        ~~dd to Mr Bristowe~~ Mr Brooke

82.209 5 Sussex Lord Chamberlen A guilt bolle with a couer Marten poz
        . . . . .xxxv oz iij qrt
        dd to Mr Middelmore

82.210 6 Lincolne Lord Admirall A guilt bolle with a couer Marten poz . . . . x[x oz]
        dd [...]

        X Oxforde

82.211 7 [W]ar[wick A bason]e and Ewer guilt K[eall poz] . . . . [Cxiiij oz iij] qrt
        [Mr] Astley

        375 . 1
        2

Yeat Earles

To the Earle of

82.212 8 Rutland A guilt Cup with a couer Keall poz . . . . xx oz qrt di
        dd to Lingard

82.213 9 Bedforde in guilt plate Keall poz . . . . xxxj oz di
        dd to St Fulwell

82.214 10 Huntingdon A guilt bolle with a couer Marten poz . . . . .xx oz qrt
        dd to Mr gorges

82.215 11 Pembrocke A guilt bolle with a couer Marten poz . . . . xxix oz
                                                                    dd to Mr Sackf[ord]
82.216 12 Northumberlande A guilt bolle with a couer Keall . . . . xx oz di
                                                                    dd to Mr wingfeld
82.217 13 Bathe thre guilt bolles with a couer Keall poz . . . . xxviij oz di
                                                                    dd to Art Middelton
82.218 14 Herforde A guilt Stope Marten poz . . . . xx xix oz iij qrt
                                                                    dd to James
82.219 15 Vicount mountague A guilt bolle with a couer Marten . . . . ix oz di
                                                                    dd to bigerstaf

        Summa – C iiij^xx ~~viij~~ ix oz qrt di
        188 . 1 . 2 [189 . 1 . 2]
        3

Duchesses / marquesses / and Countesses

To the
82.220 1 Duches of Sumerset A guilt bolle with a couer marten poz . . . . xxiiij oz di qrt
                                                                    dd to Mr brakenbury
82.221 2 Lady Marques of Northamptone ~~A guilt bolle with a couer keall poz~~
        A g[uilt] pott Marten poz—xxj oz qrt Di And a g[uilt] bolle marten poz
        —xviij oz di di qrt . . . . xl oz
                                                                    Willm Gaskin
82.222 3 Lady Marques Winchester douger A guilt bolle with a couer ^ Keall
        ~~marten~~ poz . . . . xviij oz di di qrt
                                                                    dd to Mr Marten
82.223 4 Countes of Shrewisbery in guilt plate marten . . . . xxx oz di di qrt
                                                                    per marten
82.224 5 Huntingdon A guilt bolle with a couer Marten poz . . . . xxxij oz di qrt
        Summa—Cxlv oz di
        145 . 2
        4

Yeat Countesses

To Countes of
82.225 6 Oxford A Double bolle Sault guilt marton poz . . . . xx oz qrt di
                                                                    John Fluellen
82.226 7 Lincolne A guilt Cup with a couer marten poz—xxxvj oz qrt Di / a
        guilt bolle marten—x oz qrt , and iii Spones Keall poz—iij oz qrt
        Di Sum . . . . L oz
                                                                    collyer
82.227 8 Warwick A guilt bolle with a Couer Marten poz . . . . Lj oz di di qrt
                                                                    dd Ric Asteley
82.228 9 Sussex A guilt bolle with a couer Keall poz . . . . xxiij oz qrt
                                                                    dd to Mr Morgan Sewer

82.229   10 Pembroucke douger a guilt bolle with a couer ~~marten~~ keall . . . . xxiij oz qrt di
dd to Jo Bistowe

82.230   11 Pembroucke A guilt bolle with a couer Marten poz . . . . xxiij oz qrt di
Mr kneuit by Cardill

82.231   12 Bedforde A guilt bolle with a couer Keall poz . . . . L oz di
Horsman

Summa – CCxliij oz
243
5

Yeat Countesses

To the Countes of

82.232   13 Northumberlande A guilt bolle with a couer keall . . . . xix oz
Gene

82.233   14 Southampton A Doble bolle Sault guilt marten poz . . . . xviij oz iij qrt di
dd to Reade grome

82.234   15 Rutlande A guilt bolle Keall poz . . . . xix oz di di qrt
dd to Ducke

82.235   16 Kente Douger A g bolle with a couer Keall . . . . xix oz di di qrt
dd to Goldwell

~~Lincon~~
~~Faizwarrin~~

82.236   17 Vicountes Mountegue A guilt bolle with a couer marten poz . . . . xix oz iij qrt
Robe Atkins

Summa – iiij^{xx} xvj oz iij qrt di
96 . 3 . 2
6

Busshoppes

To the

82.237   1 Arche Busshop of Caunterbury A Basone & Ewer guilt marten poz—
Cxiiij oz iij qrt di & a paire of guilt pottes poz – iiij^{xx} iiij oz qrt in to
to . . . . Ciiij^{xx} xviij oz iij qrt di
Mr Bowyer gent vssher

82.238   2 Arche Busshope of yeorke in guilt plate Kea mar poz . . . . xxxviij oz
Jo Pigeon

~~Elye~~

82.239   3 Durhum A guilt Cup with a couer marten poz . . . . xxxiiij oz iij qrt di
Mr Bristo

82.240   4 London A guilt Cup with a couer marten poz . . . . xxix oz qrt
dd

82.241   5 Salsbury A guilt bolle with a couer Keall poz . . . . .xxx oz
dd to Leeche

82.242   6 Wynchester A guilt bolle with a couer marten poz . . . . .xxx oz qrt

dd to J pigeon

      Summa – CCClxj oz qrt

361 . 1

7

yeat Busshoppes

To the Busshopes

82.243   7 Lincolne A guilt bolle with a couer marten poz . . . . xxxj oz

per Marten

82.244   8 Norwiche A guilt bolle with a couer ~~Keall~~ poz . . . . xxviij oz iij qrt

dd to hatton page

82.245   9 Worcester A guilt bolle with a couer marten poz. . . . . .xxx oz

per marten Jo burcholl

~~St Dauies~~

82.246   10 Carlell A guilt bolle with a couer Keall poz. . . . . xv oz qrt di

82.247   11 Hereforde A guilt Tankerd Keall poz. . . . . xv oz di

dd to Conway

      Summa – Cxx oz di di qrt

120 . 2 . 2

8

yeat Busshoppes

To the Busshope of

~~Bathe~~

82.248   12 Peterborowe a guilt Tankerd marten poz. . . . . xv oz di

dd to hickeson

82.249   13 Chichester A guilt bolle with a couer marten poz . . . . xvj oz

dd to mekens

82.250   14 Chester A guilt bolle with a couer marten poz . . . . .xv oz qrt

dd to prince Ewery

82.251   15 Rochester A guilt Cup bolle with a couer ~~keall~~ mar poz

. . . . .xvj oz ~~iij qr~~ qrt ~~di~~ 6 . 1 .

dd to the mr by haull Scowlery

82.252   16 Exetor A Double belle Sault marten poz. xv oz di qrt

Ja. wolton

82.253   17 Lichefeld a guilt pott marten poz. . . . . .xix oz di

dd to Powell buttry

82.254   18 Gloster A guilt Pott marten poz. . . . . xv oz qrt di

dd to xtopoer mannington

      Summa – Cxiij oz

113

9

Lordes

To the Lord

82.255 1 Burgayney A guilt Cup with a couer Keall ~~mar~~ poz . . . . ix oz qrt
dd to Birde

82.256 2 Hunsdon A guilt bolle with a couer marten poz . . . . .xxx oz qrt di
dd to Skeetes

82.257 3 Howard Two Cruettes mar poz—xxx oz iij qrt, two Saltes—xxxiiij
oz iij qrt / A Tankerd marten poz—xix oz qrt Di / and a g tankerd
Keall—xx oz . . . . Ciiij oz iij qrt di
Step Fulwell

~~4 Ryche~~

82.258 5 Darcye A guilt Sault with a couer Keall poz . . . . xviij oz iij qrt
dd to Mr Cotton

~~Russell~~

82.259 6 Cobhm A ~~guilt bolle with a couer Keall~~ Double belle Salt marten poz
xvj oz di qrt therof for his guift . . . . ~~xij oz xvj oz qrt~~ xij oz di qrt
dd to wat Trimnell

82.260 7 Shandeyes A guilt bolle K poz . . . . xiiij oz qrt di
miller Seller

Summa—Ciiij^xx ix oz iij qrt
189 . 3
10

yeat Lordes

To the Lorde

82.261 7 Northe ~~in guilt plate~~ a guilt Cup Keall poz . . . . xx oz xix oz iij qrt
dd to Henry wodde

82.262 8 Paget a guilt bolle with a couer Keall poz . . . . xix oz di di qrt
dd to Jo Ceely

82.263 9 Stafforde A barrell pott guilt marten poz . . . . xx oz
dd to Todde

82.264 10 Coumpton A guilt bolle marten poz . . . . xix oz qrt
dd to Rutter

82.265 11 Norres in guilt plate Keall poz . . . . xx oz
per Keall Goddeyere

X Dudley

82.266 12 Windsor A guilt bolle with a couer marten poz . . . . xviij oz di di qrt
Summa – Cxvj oz iij qrt
116 . 3
11

yeat Lordes

To the Lorde

82.267 13 Lumley a ~~Doble bolle Salt~~ bolle marten poz . . . . xviij oz ~~di di qrt~~ qrt di
Burde buttry

311

82.268	14 Wharton A guilt Cup with a couer Keall poz . . . . xix oz iij qrt
	dd to Tho Atkins
82.269	15 ~~Henry~~ Thomas Howard A guilt Stope marten poz . . . . xx oz di
82.270	16 Taulbot A guilt Cup marten poz . . . . xv oz di
	mr Page harbinger

Summa – lxxiij oz di di qrt

73 . 2 . 2

12

Baronesses

To the Lady Baronesse

82.271	1 Burley A guilt bolle with a couer marten poz . . . . xxiiij oz qrt di
82.272	2 Dakers A guilt bolle with a couer marten poz . . . . xviij oz di di qrt
	dd to vnderhill
	iiij oz bated because my Lo had iiij oz to muche
82.273	3 Cobham in guilt plate Keall poz – xlvj oz And part of a guilt Salt marten poz
	– xvj oz di qrt there of – iiij oz in to to . . . . ~~L oz xlvj oz~~ L oz
	per Keall John whinyerd
82.274	4 Talboyes A guilt Cup Mar poz . . . . .xx oz qrt
	dd by mr marten Alderman

~~Howard Douger~~

82.275	5 Howard a guilt bolle with a couer keall poz . . . . .xxxv oz di qrt
	dd to Thoms Laward [sic]
82.276	6 Hunsdon A guilt bolle with Stoope a couer marten poz . . . . xxviij oz di
	dd to killivite [sic, i.e. killigrew]

Summa – Clxvj oz qrt di

166 . 1 . 2

yeat Baronesses

To the Lady Baronesse

	~~7 Shandowes A guilt bolle with a couer keall poz . . . . xiiij oz qrt di~~
82.277	8 Shandowes Douger A guilt bolle with a couer K poz . . . . xv oz di di qrt
	dd to Ailworth
82.278	9 St John Bletzo a guilt bolle with a couer marten . . . . xx oz di qrt
	dd to Carter grome
82.279	10 Paget Care A guilt bolle with a couer K poz . . . . xxv oz di
	dd to mr Stanton
82.280	11 Chaney A ~~guilt~~ Doble ~~bolle marten~~ guilt bolle with a couer marten
	poz . . . . xxxiiij oz di
	dd to mr Bristowe Junior
82.281	12 Wharton A guilt Stope Keall marten poz . . . . xix oz iij qrt di
	dd to Tho Atkins

Summa – Cxv oz di di qrt

115 . 2 . 2

14

Yeat Baronesses

To the Lady Baronesse
82.282 13 Barcley A guilt potte Keall poz . . . . xx oz
82.283 14 Norris in guilt plate Keall poz . . . . xx oz
per Keall

~~Dudliy~~
82.284 15 Sheffelde parte of a guilt Chaundeller mar poz—xx oz qrt there of
. . . . xvj oz qrt
dd to Frier
82.285 16 Talbot A Doble belle Saulte marten poz . . . . xiiij oz di
dd to Page Scullery
82.286 17 Moreley A guilt bolle with a couer Keall poz . . . . xix oz iij qrt di
dd to Reme Sellar

18 ~~Barones wharton~~
82.287 19 Ryche Doger A guilt Double belle sault guilt marten poz . . . . xvj oz qrt di
82.288 20 Wylloby A rounde guilt Sault with a couer Mar . . . . xvij oz di di qrt
water Freman
82.289 21 Riche Junior A g bolle mar poz . . . . xj oz di di qrt
Summa—Cxxxvj oz qrt
136 . 1
15

Ladyes

To the Lady
X Mary Sydney . . . .
82.290 1 Mary Semer wif to Mr Rogers A guilt Sault with a couer Keall
poz . . . . xij oz di di qrt
dd to Ed Jinkens
82.291 2 Eliz Se[m]er alis Knitly A guilt bolle with a couer Mar poz . . . . xiij oz qrt
~~dd to Ed Jinkens~~
dd to Peter Gray
82.292 3 Stafford A guilt bolle with a couer mar poz . . . . xxx oz qrt di
dd to Clarke
82.293 4 Walsanghm A guilt bolle with a couer Keall . . . . xviij oz di qrt
82.294 5 Drury A guilt bolle with a couer Keall poz . . . . xvij oz iij qrt di
dd to haidon cart
82.295 6 Carowe A guilt Cup K poz . . . . xxx oz di
Summa – Cxxvij oz iij qrt
127 . 3
16

Ladyes

To the Lady

82.296   7 Cheeke A guilt bolle with a couer mar poz . . . . ~~xxiiij oz qrt di~~ xxvij oz

                                                   Garret

82.297   8 Heniage A guilt Stope mar xvij oz iij qrt and a g bolle mar—x oz di di

     qrt therof iiij oz qrt . . . . xxij oz

                                         dd Bar. Knarsboroue

82.298   9 Laiton A guilt Tankerd Keall poz . . . . xviij oz di

                                                     dd

82.299   10 Pawlat A guilt Cup with a couer K poz . . . . xj oz di di qrt

                                       dd to Perse Griffin

82.300   11 Croughtes A Doble belle Salt mar poz. . . . . xx oz di di qrt

                                             dd to Friher

      Summa – iiij^xx xix oz iij qrt

    99 . 3

    17

yeat Ladyes

To the Lady

82.301   12 Willoby Sir Fra[nces wife] A g bolle with a couer K poz. . . . . xij oz

                                               ~~dd to Freman~~

                                               Morgan grome

82.302   13 Greshum A g bolle K poz. . . . . xviij oz di

                                                    dd to Smith

82.303   14 Cromvell Sir Henrys wife A g Cup As[...] K . . . . ~~xj oz di di qrt~~ xij oz di

                                                    Sno[w]

82.304   15 Ratclif A guilt Cup K poz . . . . xij oz di

                                              Thoms humfrey

82.305   16 Frogmorton A barrell potte K poz. . . . . xx oz

                                          dd to Sex [sic Cox]

    ~~Anne Askewe~~ Anne Askewe ~~A round kirtell of Peachecolorid Satten striped~~

      ~~Downe with j borders of siluer and spamgelles~~

                                              Mrs Skidmor

82.306   17 ~~Fizwarren~~ Fizwarren A guilt Salt k poz. . . . . ix oz iij qrt di

                                           ~~binges~~ Tho Astey

82.307   20 Anne Askewe A guilt Cupe K poz . . . . xvi oz iij qrt

                                             dd to byby

      Summa – Cij oz di qrt

    102 . . 2

    18

yeat Ladyes

To the Lady

82.308   18 Maruen A guilt bolle mar poz . . . . xv oz qrt

                                              dd to Sherman

~~Souche~~

82.309 19 Katerin Counstable A guilt bolle K poz. . . . . xij oz

 dd to lekavile

Summa – xxvij oz qrt

27 . 1

19

Knightes

To Sir

82.310 1 Fraunces Knowles Threasoror of the housholde A guilt bolle with a

 couer Keall poz . . . . xxiiij oz iij qrt

 dd to Cox pantry

82.311 2 James Croftes Comptrolor of the same A g bolle with a couer Mar

 poz—xxv oz iij qrt thereof . . . . xxiiij oz iij qrt

 dd to ware

82.312 3 Christophor Hattone vicechamberlin in guilt pate Keall poz . . . . CCCC oz

 per Keall Rich Asteley

82.313 4 Fraunces Walsinghm prencipall Secretary A basone and a Laire guilt

 Keall poz . . . . lxiij oz

 Fra Gorges

~~Thomas Wilsone esquier alsquire also Secetary~~

82.314 5 Thomas Henige A guilt bolle with a couer K poz—xlj oz di and parte of a

 guilt bolle mar poz—x oz di di qrt ther of vj oz qrt di Sm. . . . xlvij oz iij qrt di

 dd Goodman

82.315 6 Rauf Sadler Chauncellor of the Duchey a guilt Bolle with a couer

 Marten poz . . . . xxviij oz qrt di

 dd nicho pigeon

82.316 7 Wavlter Mildmay Chauncellor of the Exchequor A guilt bolle with a

 couer marten poz. . . . . xxvj oz di qrt

 dd to Lilley

Summa—vj^c xiiij oz iij qrt di

614 . 3 . 2

20

yeat Knightes

To [Sir]

82.317 8 Guilbart Jared a Double bolle guilt K poz . . . . xxxiiij oz iij qrt di

82.318 7 William Dansell Receuor of the Court of wardes A g bolle with a couer

 K poz . . . . xviij oz di di qrt

 dd to Tho Garton

82.319 10 Owine Hoptone Lweftenant of the Touer A g bolle K poz. . . . . . xxj oz iij qrt

82.320 11 Edwarde Horsey A g Cup K poz . . . . xxxj oz di

 James Eaton

82.321 12 Guilbart Dethicke prencipall Kinge [of] Armes A guilt Boll mar

 poz . . . . xiiij oz

 Flud Ewery

82.322	13 Henry Cromell A Tankerd K poz.. xx oz
82.323	14 Gawine Caro A guilt Cup Keall poz .... xxxiij oz
	Summa – Clxxiij oz iij qrt
	173 . 3
	21

yeat Knightes

To Sir

82.324	15 Henre Lee in guilt plate K poz.................................. xl oz
	per Keall
82.325	16 Willyam Drury A guilt bolle K poz .... xv oz iij qrt di
	dd to mekens chaundry
82.326	17 Edward Clere A guilte Salt K poz .... xix oz iij qrt
	dd Stone grome
82.327	Henry Cobhm in guilt plate marten poz............................xxx oz
	per Marten
	~~Edward Vmpton~~
82.328	18 Sir Thomas Laitone A guilt Cup Mar ....xxx oz qrt di
	~~dd to S~~
82.329	19 John Souche A guilt bolle K mar........................... xij oz qrt di
	dd to bartlet
	Summa – Cxlviij oz qrt di
	148 . 1 . 2
	22

Gentel Women

To Mrs

	1 Blaunche Parrye x guilt Spones K poz—xij oz qrt di and a Casting
82.330	bottell K poz—v oz iij qrt Di in toto .... xviij oz qrt
	2 Fraunces Howarde A guilt bolle mar poz .... xvj oz qrt
82.331	dd to marshall
	3 Dale A guilt ~~Sault K~~ bolle Mar poz
82.332	.... ~~xxiij oz di di qrt xxiiij oz qrt di~~ xxij oz iij qrt di
	dd to Eaton
	4 Edmoundes in guilt plate K poz................................ xv oz
82.333	per Keall
	5 Skydmor xij guilt Spones K poz........................... xvj oz di qrt
82.334	dd to her self Browne
	Snowe A guilt bolle with a couer Mar poz .... xvij oz di di qrt
82.335	To Griff
	~~Snowe~~
	6 Bridman A Casting bottell g K poz......................... vj oz iij qrt
82.336	dd to Alderton Coke
	~~Baptest~~

Summa – ~~Cxiij oz di di qrt~~ Cxij oz iij qrt di

113 . 2 . 2

23

Yeat Gentelwomen

To Mrs

82.337	7 West A guilt bolle mar poz............................... xv oz di di qrt	
	dd to Roger Lowe	
82.338	8 Chaworthe ~~A~~ in guilt ~~Cup~~ plate with a couer K poz................. xv oz	
	dd to her self	
	per Keall Broune	
82.339	9 Katerine Paston alis Newton ~~A Salt mar poz—xvij oz iij qrt di thereof~~	
	~~for her guift~~ parte of g Cup mar poz—xxxj oz therof .... xv oz	
	dd to her self	
82.340	10 Marbery A ~~guit~~ guilt bolle mar poz..................... xiiij oz iij qrt di	
	dd to her housband	
82.341	11 Digby A guilt bolle mar poz................................. xvj oz	
	dd to Battye	
82.342	12 Jane Brissells a boll K ix oz iij qrt and iiij Spones K poz	
	.... ~~vj oz therof~~ v oz qrt xv oz	
	dd to herself	
82.343	13 Eliz Browke A guilt bolle mar poz......................... xiiij oz qrt	
	xpor Estwodde	
82.344	14 Thomisende A guilt ~~bolle~~ Salt K poz........................ xxj oz qrt	
	dd to Parker page	
82.345	15 Morgan A guilt Casting bottell K poz........................... vij oz	
	Edward Jones	

Summa – Cxxxiiij oz

134

24

Yeat Gentelwomen

To Mrs

82.346	16 Caue A guilt Tankerd mar poz.......................... xiiij oz iij qrt	
	dd to Burges Sculery	
82.347	17 Sackefourde A guilt bolle mar poz...................... xxiiij oz di	
	dd to Gent	
82.348	18 Eliz Howarde A guilt bolle mar poz...................... xv oz di di qrt	
	dd to [blank]	
82.349	33 Philodelpha Caue A g bolle mar poz...................... xiiij oz di qrt	
	Rich becher	
82.350	19 Wingfelde A ~~Casting bottell~~ bolle without a couer guilt K poz	
	.... ~~vij oz iij qrt di~~ viij oz qrt di	
	dd to Greete	
82.351	20 Cromer a guilt bolle mar poz.......................... xiiij oz iij qrt	
	dd to the mr by haull	

82.352   21 Smithsone parte of a bolle with out a couer K poz – xiij oz thereof . . . vij oz
                                                                                        dd to Hewes
            ~~22 Twist in guilt plate mar poz~~ . . . . ~~xiiij oz~~
82.353   22 Twist A g Salt K poz – ~~ij~~ ij oz qrt di And ij Spones K poz – iiij oz di qrt . vj oz
            di
82.354   23 Noote in guilt plate ~~mar K~~ marten poz . . . . xiij oz
                                                            ~~per marten per Keall~~ per marten
82.355   24 Barley in guilt plate ~~marten~~ K poz . . . . xiij oz
                                                            ~~per marten~~ per Keall

~~Asson~~
     Summa – Cxxxj oz di di qrt
     131 . 2 . 2
     25

Yeat Gentelwomen

To Mrs
~~Mountegrie~~
82.356   25 Cromsone iij guilt Spones K poz . . . . vj oz di qrt
         Children of the haul place
82.357   26 Hugganes a guilt Tankerd K poz . . . . xx oz di di qrt
~~Othmer of Coventrye~~
82.358   27 La[ch]felde A ~~Casting bottell~~ Doble Cup g K poz . . . . . ~~v oz qrt di~~ ix oz di qrt
                                                                                        Browne Lardar
82.359   28 Allen A guilt bolle mar poz . . . . xij oz iij qrt di
                                                                                        dd to Oldhm grome
82.360   29 Haines A guilt Tankerd Ke poz . . . . xiiij oz di di qrt
                                                                                        dd to Clement
82.361   30 Tomisen the Dwarf A Sallte K poz—j oz di di qrt and two Spones
            K—iij oz di . . . . v oz di qrt
                                                                                        dd to Mrs Skidmer
         Chaworth
82.362   31 Duves two guilt Spones K poz . . . . iiij oz
                                                                                        dd to Mrs Skidmor
            32 ~~Morgaine iij guilt Spones K poz~~ . . . . ~~v oz di qrt~~
            Summa – lxxij oz di di qrt
            72 . 2 . 2
            26

The maides

Mrs
82.363   1 Mary Ratclif A g bolle Keall poz . . . . x oz qrt di
                                                                                        dd to Baudwine
~~Ellen Bridges~~
82.364   2 Katterne howarde A bolle K poz . . . . x oz di qrt
                                                                                        dd to Pucket

82.365   3 Eliz Garrat A g bolle mar poz . . . . x oz di di qrt
                                                                                    dd to Laurence Cook

82.366   4 Mackewillms A guilt bolle K ~~Cup K~~ poz. . . . . ~~ix oz di qrt~~ x oz qrt di
                                                                                    dd to Robt Louche

82.367   5 ~~hawces~~ Eliz Trentam A guilt Cup K poz . . . . ix oz di qrt
                                                                                    dd to Powell

82.368   6 Edgecome A guilt bolle mar poz . . . . x oz di qrt
                                                                                    dd to Anwilde

82.369   7 Mrs Baptest mother A guilt bolle mar poz . . . . xij oz di qrt
                                                                                    dd to Owine grome

          Summa – lxxiij oz qrt di
          73 . 1. 2
          27

Chaplaines

82.370   Arche Deacone Caro in guilt plate mar . . . . xxij oz
                                                                                    per marte est Lawnd

82.371   Absolon ~~iij guilt Spones mar poz~~ parte of a guilt bolle K—viij oz di qrt
          d therof . . . . vj oz ~~iij qrt di~~ qrt di

Gentelmen

          Mr
          1 X ~~Phillip Sidney~~

82.372   2 John Harington in guilt plate Keall poz. . . . . .xl oz
                                                                                    per Keall

82.373   j oz Di bated of this guift that he owed the last yere
          Wolle A guilt Salt ~~wolle marten poz bolle marten poz~~ Salt K— ~~xxviij~~
              ~~oz qrt di there of for his guift~~ . . . . xxv oz di qrt
              . . . . ~~xxiiij oz qrt di, xxiiij oz qrt di, xxiij oz di di qrt~~
              ~~Lichefeld a guilt Chaundellor mar poz~~. ~~xx oz di qrt~~

82.374   4 Lichefelde a guilt bolle mar poz. . . . . xviij oz di qrt
                                                                                    dd to himself

82.375   5 Stafforde A guilt Chaundlor mar poz . . . . xx oz di qrt
                                                                                    Rogers

82.376   1 Pakington A guilt potte mar poz . . . . .xxj oz di di qrt
                                                                                    Dd to Jo Wheler

82.377   6 Edward Basshe A guilt bolle mar poz . . . . xxj oz di qrt
                                                                                    Griff Seller

82.378   32 Guifforde A guilt bolle with a couer mar poz . . . . xxiij oz qrt di
                                                                                    dd to Cox cartaker

          Summa – Ciiij^xx xvj oz ^ ~~iij qrt~~ di qrt
          196 . . 2
          28

82.379   7 Stanhope A gult [sic] Cup mar poz . . . . xiiij oz di di qrt
                                                                                    Longe

82.380   8 Skidmor A guilt bolle mar poz............................ xvj oz qrt
                                dd to Mathew pantry

82.381   9 Smith Costomer A guilt parte of a g Cup K poz – xl oz qrt therof ..... xlv oz
                                dd

82.382   10 Mountecute A g bolle K poz .... xij oz qrt

82.383   11 Brounker A guilt bolle with a couer mar poz.................xx oz iij qrt
                                  Brite

82.384   12 Newton A guilt bolle with a couer mar poz—xij oz di qrt and ~~parte of~~
       ~~a salt mar poz—xvij oz iij qrt di ther of—ij oz iij qrt Di~~ parte of a g
       bolle mar poz—xxxj oz ther of Summa .... xvj oz

82.385   13 Doctor Mr A g bolle mar poz .... xiiij oz di di qrt
                                  dd to him self

82.386   14 Doctor Bailye A guilt Tankerde K poz – xvj oz iij qrt di there of ..... xiiij oz
                                  dd to himself

82.387   15 Doctor Lopas A guilt Cup K poz—xv oz therof.................. xiiij oz
                                  dd to Mrs Chaworth

82.388   Dier in guilt plate marten poz................................... xvj oz qrt
                                  per Marten

         Summa – Cliij oz iij qrt
         153 . 3
         29

82.389   16 John Rige potecary in guilt plate K poz....................... viij oz di
                                  per Keall

82.390   17 Ed Hemingway in guilt plate Keall............................. vij oz

82.391   18 John Smithson Mr Cooke parte of a boll p k poz—xiij oz there of vj
       oz and a small Salt K poz di in to to .... vij oz di

82.392   19 John Dudley Sergant of the pastry in guilt plate Keall poz.......... vj oz di
                                  poz Keall

82.393   20 Willm Huggans A g Cup Keall poz .... xxix oz qrt di

82.394   21 Willm Cornewalles A guilt boll mar poz ....xiij oz di di qrt
                           dd to Goodman Grigore Larder

82.395   22 Ambroso Lupo in guilt plate Keall .... v oz di
                                  per Keall

82.396   23 Petricho Lupo in guilt plate K poz........................... v oz di
                                  per Keall

82.397   24 Charles Smith in guilt plate mar poz .... xv oz
                                  per marten

         Summa – iiij^{xx} xvj oz di
         95
         30

82.398   25 Petricho vbaldino in guilt plate K poz........................ v oz di
                                  per Keall

82.399   26 Marke Anthony galiardo in guilt plate K poz .... v oz di
                                  per Keall

82.400   27 Hewes Lennen Draper A guilt bolle Mar................... xiij oz iij qrt
                                 ~~dd to Reyes Ce te~~

82.401	28 Bassanos the brethen in guilt plate Keall . . . . iij oz	
		per Keall
82.402	29 Thoms Leuerege Crosbomaker . . . . vj oz	
82.403	Parker page A guilt bolle marten . . . . xij oz iij qrt	
		dd to himself
82.404	30 Dunstone Anes A guilt Tankerd K poz . . . . .xx oz iij qrt	
		dd to him self
82.405	31 Guilham Skeetes ij guilt Spones mar poz. . . . . v oz iij qrt di	

Summa – ~~lxvij oz di qrt~~ Lxxiij oz di qrt

31

Fre guiftes

82.406	To John Asteley esquire Mr and Threasoror of her Mates Juelles ~~in vij g~~
	~~Sponis marten = xiij oz iij qrt di and v oz in moniy marten~~ . . . xviij oz iij qrt di
	~~marten~~ Keall
82.407	To Mr Thoms Gorges grome of her highnes previe Chamber A Doble
	Salt guilt mar poz—xvj oz qrt di therof . . . . ix oz
	dd to himself
82.408	To Mr Thoms Asteley also grome &c in guilt plate Keall poz . . . . ix oz
	per Keall
82.409	To Mr henry Sackeforde in guilt plate Keall poz . . . . ix oz
	per Keall
82.410	To Mr Baptest also grome in guilt plate marten poz . . . . ix oz
	per ~~marten~~ Keall
82.411	To Mr Middelmor also grome &c in guilt plate K poz. . . . . ix oz
	per Keall
82.412	To Mr Killegrew also grome in guilt plate Keall poz . . . . ix oz
	per Keall
82.413	To Mr Ed Care also grome &c in g plate marten poz. . . . . ix oz
	per marten
82.414	To Mr Tho Kneuet grome also in g plate marten poz . . . . ix oz
	per ~~marten~~ Keall
82.415	To Rauf Hoope yeoman of the Roobes in guilt plate marten poz . xij oz iij qrt di
	per marten
82.416	To Nicholas Bristowe Clerke of the Juelhouse in guilt plate Keall . x oz iij qrt di
	Keall
82.417	To John Pigeon yeoman of the same office in guilt plate Keall . . . . x oz iij qrt di
	Keall
82.418	To Stephan Fulwell oone other of the yeoman of the same Office in guilt
	plate Keall . . . . x oz iij qrt di
	Keall
82.419	To Richard Asteley grome of the same Office in guilt plate. . . . . . . x oz iij qrt di
	Keall

Summa – Cxlviij oz qrt

523 . 3 Summa to 5030 . . 2

32

Rewardes vppon Newye|re|s day

The Q: maties servants
Fyrst Paid to the Harroldes at Armes.............................. xj lb

Marquesses and Earles

82.420	Item paid to the Lo: Chauncellor serunt	xxvj s viii d
82.421	Itm pd to the Marquesse of Winchestre serunt	xx s
82.422	Itm pd to Therle of Arrundell serunt	xx s
82.423	Itm pd to Therle of darbye serunt................................	xx s
82.424	Itm pd to Therle of Shrewisburie serunt...........................	xx s
82.425	Itm pd to Therle of Sussex serunt..............................	xx s
82.426	Itm pd to Therle of Bedfordes serunt	xx s
82.427	Itm pd to Therle of Huntington serunt	xx s
82.428	Itm pd to Therle of Warwick serunt..............................	xx s
82.429	Itm pd to Therle of Leicestre serunt	xx s
82.430	Itm pd to Therle of Pendbroke serunt	xx s
82.431	Itm pd to Therle of Rutland serunt	xx s
82.432	Itm pd to Therle of Hertford serunt	xx s
82.433	Itm pd To Therle of Lincoln serunt	xx s
82.434	Itm pd to the Viscount Mountague serunt	xx s
82.435	Itm pd Therle of Northumberland serunt	xx s
82.436	Itm pd to Therle of Bathe serunt	xx s

17—6—8 exam et oner

Busshopps

82.437	Itm pd to the Archebusshop of canterbury serunt..................	Liij s iiij d
82.438	Itm pd to the Arche busshop of Yorke serunt	Liij s iiij d
82.439	Itm pd to the Busshop of durham serunt...........................	xl s
82.440	Itm pd to the B: of winchestre serunt................................	xl s
82.441	Itm pd to the B: of London serunt	xx s
82.442	Itm pd to the B: of Excestre serunt................................	xx s
82.443	Itm pd to the B: of Lichefeld serunt	xx s
82.444	Itm pd to the B: of hereford serunt...............................	xx s
82.445	Itm pd to the B: of Peterborrow serunt	xx s
82.446	Itm pd to the B: of Sarum serunt	xx s
82.447	Itm pd to the B: of Lincoln serunt	xx s
82.448	Itm pd to the B: of Chichestr serunt..............................	xx s
82.449	Itm pd to the B: of norwich serunt	xx s
82.450	Itm pd to the B: of Carlile serunt	xx s
82.451	Itm pd to the B: of Chester serunt	xx s
82.452	Itm pd to the B: of Rochester serunt	xx s
82.453	Itm pd to the B: of Glocester serunt..............................	xx s

82.454	Itm pd to the B: of worcester serunt . . . . .xx s	

23—6 exam et oner

Barrons and Lordes

82.455	Itm pd to the Lo: Darcye of the Sowth serunt . . . . .xx s
82.456	Itm pd to the Lord Burgany serunt. . . . . .xx s
82.457	Itm pd to the Lo: Northe serunt . . . . .xx s
82.458	Itm pd to the Lord Rich serunt. . . . . .xx s
82.459	Itm pd to the Lo: Hundson serunt . . . . .xx s
82.460	Itm pd to the Lo: Shandoyes serunt . . . . .xx s
82.461	Itm pd to the Lo: pagget serunt . . . . .xx s
82.462	Itm pd to the Lo: Stafford serunt . . . . .xx s
82.463	Itm pd to the Lo: Burghley serunt . . . . .xx s
82.464	Itm pd to the Lo: Compton serunt . . . . .xx s
82.465	Itm pd to the Lo: Norris servant. . . . . .xx s
82.466	Itm pd to the Lo: Lumley serunt. . . . . .xx s
82.467	Itm pd to the Lo: Howard serunt . . . . .xx s
82.468	Itm pd to the Lo: Cobham serunt. . . . . .xx s
82.469	Itm pd to the Lo: wharton serunt . . . . .xx s
82.470	Itm pd to the Lo: Russell serunt . . . . .xx s
82.471	Itm pd to the Lo: windsor serunt . . . . .xx s
82.472	Itm pd to the Lo: Thoms Howard serunt . . . . .xx s
82.473	Itm pd to the Lo: Talbott serunt. . . . . .xx s

19 exam et oner

duchesses and Countesses

82.474	Itm pd to the Duches of Somerset serunt. . . . . .liij s iij d
82.475	Itm pd to the marquess of winchestr dowger serunt . . . . .xx s
82.476	Itm pd to the Marquesse of northampton serunt. . . . . .xx s
82.477	Itm pd to the Countesse of Sussex serunt. . . . . .xx s
82.478	Itm pd to the Countesse of Huntington serunt . . . . .xx s
82.479	Itm pd to the Countes of shrewesbury serunt. . . . . .xx s
82.480	Itm pd to the Countes of Bedd[ford] serunt . . . . .xx s
82.481	Itm pd to the Countes of warwick serunt. . . . . .xx s
82.482	Itm pd to the yonge Countes of Penbrook serunt . . . . .xx s
82.483	Itm pd to the La: Mary Sydney serunt . . . . .xx s
82.484	Itm pd to the La: vicountes Mountague serunt . . . . .xx s
82.485	Itm pd to the Countes of Sowthampton serunt . . . . .xx s
82.486	Itm pd to the Countes of Lincoln serunt . . . . .xx s
82.487	Itm pd to the Countes of Oxford serunt. . . . . .xx s
82.488	Itm pd to the Countes of Rutland serunt . . . . .xx s
82.489	Itm pd to the Countes of Kent Dowger serunt. . . . . .xx s
82.490	Itm pd to the Countes of Northombrl[and] serunt . . . . .xx s
82.491	Itm pd to the old Countes of pendbrowk serunt . . . . .xx s
82.492	Itm pd to the Countes of Lynox serunt . . . . xx s

20—13—4 exam et oner

Barronesses

82.493	Itm pd to the Lady Bartley serunt.	xx s
82.494	Itm pd to the La: Dakers serunt	xx s
82.495	Itm pd to the La: Howard serunt	xx s
82.496	Itm pd to the La: Hunsdon serunt	xx s
82.497	Itm pd to the La: Chandoys dowger serunt	xx s
82.498	Itm pd to the La: willinghby serunt	xx s
82.499	Itm pd to the La Pagett Cary serunt	xx s
82.500	Itm pd to the La: Burghley serunt.	xx s
82.501	Itm pd to the La: St John of Bletso serunt	xx s
82.502	Item paid to the La: Tailboys serunt.	xx s
82.503	Itm pd to the La: norris serunt	xx s
82.504	Itm payd To the Lady Howard serunt.	xx s
82.505	Itm payd To the yonge La: Shandyes serunt	xx s
82.506	Itm pd to the La: Cobham serunt	xx s
82.507	Itm pd to the La: Sheffeld serunt	xx s
82.508	Itm pd to the La: Cromwell serunt	xx s
82.509	Itm pd to the La: wharton serunt	xx s
82.510	Itm pd to the La: dudley servunt	xx s
82.511	Itm pd to the La: Anne Ascughe serunt	xx s
82.512	Itm paid to the La: Riche dowger serunt	xx s
82.513	Itm pd to the La: Fitzwarren serunt	xx s
82.514	Itm pd to the La: Mary Rogers serunt	xx s
82.515	Itm pd to the La: Catherin Cunstable serunt	xx s
82.516	Itm pd to the La: Elisabeth Knightley serunt	xx s
82.517	Itm pd to the La: Chenye serunt	xx s
82.518	Itm pd to the La: Russell serunt	xx s
82.519	Itm pd to the La: Morley serunt	xx s
82.520	Itm pd to the La: Riche serunt	xx s

28 / 0 / 0 exam et oner

Knightes

82.521	Itm pd to Sir Frauncis Knolles knight Threasurer of her Maties howshold serunt-	xx s
82.522	Itm pd to Sir James Croftes Comptrollor of her Maties howshold serunt	xx s
82.523	Itm pd to Sir Thomas Henneage knight Threasurer of Her Maties Chamber serunt.	xx s
82.524	Itm pd to Sir Fraunces walsingham serunt	xx s xiij s iiij d
82.525	Itm pd to Sir Xtopher Hatton serunt	xiij s iiij d
82.526	Itm pd to Sir Raphe Sadler serunt	xiij s iiij d
82.527	Itm pd to Sir walter Myldmay serunt	xiij s iiij d
82.528	Itm pd to Sir Gilber Jarret serunt	xiij s iiij d
82.529	Itm pd to Sir william Damsell serunt	xiij s iiij d
82.530	Itm pd to the Dean of the Chapple serunt	xiij s iiij d

82.531	Itm pd to Sir Henry Cromewell serunt	xiij s iiij d
82.532	Itm pd to Sir Gilbert dethick serunt	xiij s iiij d
82.533	Itm pd to Sir Gawyn Caro serunt	xiij s iiij d
82.534	Itm pd to Sir Owyn Hopton serunt	xiij s iiij d
82.535	Itm pd to Sir Henry Leighe serunt	xiij s iiij d
82.536	Itm pd to Sir wm Drewry serunt	xiij s iiij d
82.537	Itm pd to Sir Edward Clere serunt	xiij s iiij d
82.538	Itm pd to Sir Edward Horsey serunt	xiij s iiij d
82.539	Itm pd to Sir Thomas Layton serunt	xiij s iiij d
82.540	Itm pd to Sir Edward Vmpton serunt	xiij s iiij d
82.541	Itm pd to Sir John Sowche serunt	xiij s iiij d
82.542	Itm pd to Sir Henry Cobham serunt	xiij s iiij d

15—13—4 exam et oner

Knightes Wyves

82.543	Itm pd to La: hughe Pawlet serunt	xiij s iiij d
82.544	Itm pd to La: Henneage serunt	xiij s iiij d
82.545	Itm pd to La: walsingham serunt	xiij s iiij d
82.546	Itm pd to La: Gresham serunt	xiij s iiij d
82.547	Itm pd to La: Caro serunt	xiij s iiij d
82.548	Itm pd to La: Stafford serunt	xiij s iiij d
82.549	Itm pd to La: Ratclif serunt	xiij s iiij d
82.550	Itm pd to La: Cheeke serunt	xiij s iiij d
82.551	Itm pd to La: Cromwell serunt	xiij s iiij d
82.552	Itm pd to La: Throkmortin serunt	xiij s iiij d
82.553	Itm pd to La: Marvin serunt	xiij s iiij d
82.554	Itm pd to La: willinghby serunt	xiij s iiij d
82.555	Itm pd to La: Drewry serunt	xiij s iiij d
82.556	Itm pd to La: Layton serunt	xiij s iiij d
82.557	Itm pd to La: Croft serunt	xiij s iiij d

10 *li exam et oner*

gentleman

82.558	Itm payd To Mr doctor Master serunt	x s
82.559	Itm pd to Mr Doctor Balye serunt	x s
82.560	Itm pd to Mr Doctor Lopus serunt	x s
82.561	Itm pd to the Master Cook serunt	vj s viij d
82.562	Itm pd to Mr Basshe serunt	vj s viij d
82.563	Itm pd to Mr Customer Smith serunt	vj s viij d
82.564	Itm pd to Mr Huggins serunt	vj s viij d
82.565	Itm pd to Mr Marke Anthony serunt	vj s viij d
82.567	Itm pd to Mr Ambrose Lupo serunt	vj s viij d
82.568	Itm pd to Mr Riche serunt	vj s viij d
82.569	Itm pd to the Sergeant of the pastry serunt	vj s viij d
82.570	Itm pd to Mr petrucio vbaldino serunt	vj s viij d
82.571	Itm pd to Mr Stanhop serunt	vj s viij d

82.572	Itm pd to Mr Harrington serunt	.vj s viij d
82.573	Itm pd to Mr Edward Stafford serunt	.vj s viij d
82.574	Itm pd to Mr Charles Smithe serunt	.vj s viij d
82.575	Itm pd to Mr Henry Newton serunt	.vj s viij d
82.576	Itm pd to Mr Absolon serunt	.vj s viij d
82.577	Itm pd to Mr wolley serunt	.vj s viij d
82.578	Itm pd to Mr Lichfeld serunt	.vj s viij d
82.578	Itm pd to Mr Peter Lupo serunt	.vj s viij d
82.579	Itm pd to Mr pagington serunt	.vj s viij d
82.580	Itm pd to Mr william Cornewallis serunt	.vj s viij d
82.581	Itm pd to Mr Hewghes serunt	.vj s viij d
82.582	Itm pd to Mr Jefford serunt	.vj s viij d
82.583	Itm pd to Mr Dyer serunt	.vj s viij d
82.584	Itm pd to the bretherin Bassano serunts	.vj s viij d
82.585	Itm pd to Mr Mountague serunt	.vj s viij d
82.586	Itm pd to Mr Skydmore serunt	.vj s viij d
82.587	Itm pd to Mr Hemyningway serunt	.vj s viij d
82.588	Itm pd to Mr Broukhorne serunt	.vj s viij d
82.589	Itm pd to Mr Dunston Anus serunt	.vj s viij d

11—3—4 exam et oner

Gentlewomen

82.590	Itm pd to Mrs Blanshe Apparry serunt	.vj s viij d
82.591	Itm pd to Mrs Cave serunt	.vj s viij d
82.592	Itm pd to Mrs Edmondes serunt	.vj s viij d
82.593	Itm pd to Mrs Twyst serunt	.vj s viij d
82.594	Itm pd to Mrs Huggins serunt	.vj s viij d
82.595	Itm pd to Mrs Barly serunt	.vj s viij d
82.596	Itm pd to Mrs Snowe serunt	.vj s viij d
82.597	Itm pd to Mrs Fraunces Howard serunt	.vj s viij d
82.598	Itm pd to Mrs Elsabeth Howard serunt	.vj s viij d
82.599	Itm pd to Mrs Wingfeld serunt	.vj s viij d
82.600	Itm pd to Mrs Mary Skydmore serunt	.vj s viij d
82.601	Itm pd to Mrs Crockston serunt	.vj s viij d
82.602	Itm pd to Mrs Note serunt	.vj s viij d
82.603	Itm pd to Mrs Marbery serunt	.vj s viij d
82.604	Itm pd to Mrs Cromer serunt	.vj s viij d
82.605	Itm pd to Mrs Newton serunt	.vj s viij d
82.606	Itm pd to Mrs West serunt	.vj s viij d
82.607	Itm pd to Mrs Tayller serunt	.vj s viij d
82.608	Itm pd to Mrs Jane Brusselles serunt	.vj s viij d
82.609	Itm pd to Mrs Digbie serunt	.vj s viij d
82.610	Itm pd to Mrs Dale serunt	.vj s viij d
82.611	Itm pd to Mrs Sackforde serunt	.vj s viij d
82.612	Itm pd to Mrs Allen serunt	.vj s viij d
82.613	Itm pd to Mrs Chaworthe serunt	.vj s viij d

82.614	Itm pd to Mrs Townesend serunt . . . . .vj s viij d
82.615	Itm pd to Mrs Haynes serunt . . . . .vj s viij d
82.616	Itm pd to Mrs Elsabeth Brooke serunt . . . . .vj s viij d
82.617	Itm pd to Mrs Bryddeman serunt . . . . .vj s viij d
82.618	Itm pd to Mrs Morgan serunt . . . . .vj s viij d
82.619	Itm pd to Mrs penelope Carewe [sic, i.e. Philadelphia Carey] serunt. . . .vj s viij d
82.620	Itm pd to Mrs Lichefeld serunt . . . . .vj s viij d
82.621	Itm pd to Mrs Dyve serunt . . . . .vj s viij d
82.622	Itm pd to the Q:s Maties dwarf serunt . . . . .vj s viij d

11—0—0 exam et oner

279—3—4 exam et oner

Newyersguiftes giuen to Her Maiestie at Her
Paloyce of Westminster by thise persons
Whose names doo hereafter ensue
the First day of January
the yere aforesaid

Elizabeth R
[sign manual]

84.1 By Sir Thomas Bromley knight Lorde Chauncellor of Inglande in golde
and Siluer . . . . xiij li xj s viij d
84.2 By Sir William Cicell knight Lorde Burligh Lorde high Threausoror of
Inglande in golde . . . . xx li
84.3 By the Lorde Marques of winchester in golde . . . . xx li
dd to Henry Sekford

Earles

84.4 By Therle of Leycetor Mr of the horses A fayer Cheyne of golde cont
xxiiij knottes lyke Bowsers knottes / xij Mattrevers knottes / and xij
litle Synkefoyles, on thone syde all garnesshed with smawle diamondes
/ and akey of golde hanginge at it garnysshed on thonesyde with lyke
Diamondes / and also one poranger of blodestone garnesshed with
thre fete and two handilles of golde being Snakes
dd to the Lady Hawarde the juell,
the porringer dd to John Astley Esquier
Mr of the Juelles & plate
84.5 By therle of Shrewesbury in golde . . . . xx li
84.6 By therle of Darby in golde. . . . . xx li
84.7 By therle of Sussex in golde . . . . x li
84.8 By therle of Lincoln in golde . . . . x li
dd to the said Mr Sekford
84.9 By therle of Warwyk a Juell of golde beinge a cheyne of Fysshes cont
xxiiij Fysshes in xij of them are iij smaule garnettes on thone syde /
and thother xij ennamuled and vj knottes in euery knott on thone
syde a sparke of a Diamonde / and xij knottes in euery of them aperle
on thone syde / and v knottes garnesshed with opaules on thone syde
dd to the foresaid Lady Hawarde
84.10 By therle of Bedford in golde . . . . xx li
84.11 By therle of Penbroke in golde . . . . xx li
84.12 By therle of Rutlande in golde . . . . x li
84.13 By therle of Huntingdon in golde. . . . . x li

84.14 By therle of Bathe in golde . . . . xx li
                dd to the foresaid Mr Sekford

84.15 By therle of Essex acase for a dublet and aforeparte of Lawnde cutworke
 floresshed with Sylver and Spangilles

84.16 By therle of Hertford a pettycote of pechecollored Satten enbrawdered
 alouer verey Feyer with Flowers of venice golde Sylver and Sylke of
 diuers collors
            dd to Rauf Hope yoman of the robes

84.17 By the vicecount Montague in golde. . . . . x li
                dd to the forsaid Mr Sekford

84.18 By the vicecount Byndhin apece of purple clothe of golde with workes
 cont . . . . xxij yardes di
                dd to the forsaid R Hope

Duchesses and Countesses

84.19 By the Duches of Somerset in golde and Siluer . . . . xiij li vj s viij d
                dd to the forsaid Mr Sekford

84.20 By the Lady Marques of Northampton arounde kyrtill of white Satten
 cut alouer set with knottes of carnacon Silke and Spangilles and bounde
 abought with abrode plate lace of venice golde and carnacion Sylke
              dd to the forsaid Rauf Hope

84.21 By the Lady Marques of Winchester in golde . . . . x li
                dd to the foresaid Mr Sekford

84.22 By the Countes of Shrewesbury a french gowne with high boddies of
 black Tufte Taphata striped with golde and syluer Layd abought with
 apasmene of venice golde lyned with white Taphata or Serceonet
              dd to the forsaid Rauf Hope

84.23 By the Countes of Huntingdon in golde. . . . . viij li
                dd to the forsaid Mr Sekford

84.24 By the Countes of Oxforde a Juell of golde being an Anker garnisshed
 with smaule Rubys and Diamondes on thone syde and three smaule
 perles pendaunt
              dd to the forsaid La Hawarde

84.25 By the Countes of Lincoln a rounde kyrtill of Siluer Chamlet striped in
 sundry places with asmaule plate lace of venice golde / and bounde
 abought with alike plate lace
              dd to the forsaid Rauf Hope

84.26 By the Countes of Warwyck a knot of mother of perle garnesshed on
 thone syde with sparckes of Rubys / ij pendant Opalles and apendant
 with a Diamonde on thone syde therof with a smaule perle thereat
              dd as aforsaid to the La Haward

84.27 By the Countes of Sussex in golde . . . . x li

84.28 By the Countes of Penbroke Dowager in golde . . . . xij li

84.29 By the Countes of Penbroke Junior in golde . . . . x li
                dd to the forsaid Mr Sekford

84.30	By the Countes of Bedford a foreparte of a kirtill of cloth of Siluer enbrawdered alouer with Damaske golde purle dd to the forsaid Rauf Hope
84.31	By the Countes of Southampton in golde . . . . x li
84.32	By the Countes of Rutlande in golde . . . . x li
84.33	By the vicecountess Mountague in golde . . . . x li

dd to the forsaid Mr Sekford

Busshopps

84.34	By the Archbusshop of Caunterbury in golde . . . . .xl li
84.35	By the Archbusshop of yorke in golde . . . . xxx li
84.36	By the Busshop of Durham in golde . . . . xxx li
84.37	By the Busshop of London in golde. . . . . xx li
84.38	By the Busshop of Salisburye in golde . . . . xx li
84.39	By the Busshop of Winchester in golde . . . . xx li
84.40	By the Busshop of Lyncolne in golde . . . . xx li
84.41	By the Busshop of Norwich in golde . . . . xx li
84.42	By the Busshop of Carlell in golde . . . . x li
84.43	By the Busshop of Hereforde in golde . . . . x li
84.44	By the Busshop of Peterborow in golde . . . . x li
84.45	By the Busshop of Chester in golde . . . . x li
84.46	By the Busshop of Rochester in golde . . . . x li
84.47	By the Busshop of Exeter in golde . . . . x li
84.48	By the Busshop of Lychefelde in golde. . . . . xiij li vj s viij d
84.49	By the Busshop of St Davis in golde. . . . . x li
84.50	By the Busshop of Gloster in golde . . . . x li

dd to the forsaid Mr Sekford

Lordes

84.51	By the Lorde of Burgavenny in golde . . . . v li

dd to the forsaid Mr Sekford

84.52	By the Lorde of Hunsdon parte of a Nightgowne of Carnacion Satten Raced alover furred thowrow with mynyuer and edged Rounde aboute with powdered Armors

dd to the forsaid Rauf Hope

84.53	By the Lorde Howarde Lo. Chamberlen A Juell of gold beinge the personage of a woman of mother of perle garnisshed on the on side with smale Dyamondes and Rubies and ij pendant Rubyes and one Emeraulde pendante with a Lozenged emerald in the Top

dd to the forsaid La Haward

84.54	By the Lorde Cobham in golde. . . . . v li

dd to the foresaid Mr Sekford

84.55	By the Lorde Taulbott a foreparte of a kertle of white Satten alouer embr with great braunches of venys golde siluer and Sylke of sondry Collers

with a fayre border of the same Stuffe with a smale Frynge of venis golde & syluer

dd to the forsaid Rauf Hope

84.56   By the Lorde Darcye in golde . . . . x li
84.57   By the Lorde Shandoyes in golde and Silver . . . . vj li xij s iiij d
84.58   By the Lorde Northe in golde . . . . x li
84.59   By the Lorde Coumpton in golde . . . . x li
84.60   By the Lorde Norrys in golde . . . . x li

dd to the foresaid Mr Sekford

84.61   By the Lorde Wynsor A Coueringe for a frenche gowne of blacke sylke sylver and gold networke wyth Spangles

dd to the foresaid Rauf Hope

84.62   By the Lorde Loumleye in golde . . . . x li
84.63   By the Lorde Wharton in golde . . . . x li

dd to the forsaid Sakford

84.64   By the Lorde Ryche A Dublet of pechecollored Satten enbradored alouer with venys gold & sylke
84.65   By the Lorde Russell A foreparte of networke garn with silver spangles

dd to the foresaid Rauf Hope

Barronesses

84.66   By the Barronesse Bourley A Saulte of golde with a couer with two personages naked with a Lyon in the Topp of the Couer poz . . . . vij oz di

In charge of Jo Astley Esquier Mr and Treasorer of the Juelles

84.67   By the Barronesse Dakers A pettycote of sadd Carnation satten enbradered alouer with a Twiste of gold venice and sylver with iij brode borders of venys golde and sylver
84.68   By the Barrones Cobham a Duche Cloke of white Satten alouer enbradored with venis gold with iij borders enbradored lyke fryers knottes lyned with strawcollored and blewe changeable Taphata
84.69   By the Barronesse Hunsedon parte of a Nyte goune of Carnation Satten rased furred thorowe out with mynyver, and edged rownde aboute withe powdered Armyons

dd to the foresaid Rauf Hope

84.70   By the Barronesse Howarde a Juell of golde beinge a Dolfyne fully garnyshed with sparckes of Rubyes wythe a personage vppon his backe havinge a Lute in his hande

dd to the same La Hawarde

84.71   By the Barronesse Loumley a Mantle of white striped Lavne set with tuftes & spangles of blacke sylke
84.72   By the Barronesse Shaundoyes Dowager a Coveringe for afrenche gowne of blacke styched Cloth enbradored with venys golde edged with a passamayne of venys golde

dd to the forsaid Rauf Hope

84.73   By the Barronesse Shandowes Junior in golde and syluer . . . . vj li xiij s iiij d

dd to the foresaid Mr Sekford

84.74   By the Barronesse St John Bletzo widdow in golde . . . . x li
and a swete badge of Crymson satten enbradored

> The golde dd to Mr Sekford and
> the swete bagge to Mrs Skidmore

84.75   By the Barronesse Pagett Cary a lose gowne of blacke Satten stryped with
golde / bounde aboute with A Byllymente Lace of car silke and silver
faced with stryped Laune & lyned with Carnatyon Taffata

> dd to the foresaid Ra Hope

84.76   By the Barronesse Chayney a paire of Brasellettes of golde cont xvj peces,
viij withe Emeraudes and viij withe one perle the peace

> dd to the forsaid La Howarde

84.77   By the Barronesse Wharton in golde . . . . x li
84.78   By the Barronesse Barcley in golde. . . . . x li

> dd to the forsaid h Sakford

84.79   By the Barronesse Russell a vaylle / a partlett and a paire of sleaves of
Networke garn with sylver spangles

> dd the vayle to Mrs Skydmore & threst to Mrs Chaworth

84.80   By the Barronesse Norres in golde . . . . x li

> dd to the foresaid h Sakford

84.81   By the Barronesse Morley a Mantle of lawne florisshed with golde &
spangles & edged with a passemayne of golde

> dd to the foresaid Ra hope

84.82   By the Barronesse Ryche Dowager a smocke of Camerycke / the sleaves
and Collor wrought with balack [sic] sylke, and iiij Handkerchers
wrought with blacke silke & edged with passamayne of golde and
silver

84.83   By the Barrones Wylloby A foreparte of cutworke florysshed with silver
and Spangles

> dd to Mrs Skydmore

Ladies

84.84   By the Lady Mary Seymer wyfe to Mr Rogers a Ruffe of lavne with ij
borders of Cutworke

> dd to Jane Brisselles

84.85   By the Ladye Sydney a wastecoate of white Taffata serceonet enbr alouer
with venys golde spangels and blacke sylke

84.86   By the Lady Elizabethe Seymer wyfe of Mr Knyghtley a Rayle a Coyfe
and a Forehedclothe of Lawne wroughte with silke of sondry Collors

> dd to the forsaid Mrs Skydmore

84.87   By the Lady Stafforde A Square Table of walnutre & a Carpet of
Carnacon vellat enbradored wythe venys golde lyke esseFirmes

> dd Mr Thomas Knevet Keper of Westminster paloyse

84.88   By the Lady Walsingham a Shaddo of smale sede pe[r]les Leves and
Ladycowes Enamyled

> dd to the foresaid Mrs Skydmore

84.89 By the Lady Arrondell a nyghtgowne of Toufte Taffata tawny and blacke
striped layde with a Lace of blacke sylke and golde furred thorowe with
greye spotted Coney

dd to the foresaid Rauf Hope

84.90 By the Lady Drurye A Cusshionclothe of lawne wroughte alouer with
silke of sundry Collers florisshed withe gold and syluer and bownde
about with a bone Lace of lyke silke and syluer

84.91 By the Lady Carow a Cusshionclothe of Camberycke wroughte with blacke
silke

dd to the foresaid Mrs Skydmore

84.92 By the Lady Cheake a foreparte of Knytworke florysshed with sylver
plate

dd to the foresaid Rauf Hope

84.93 By the Lady Hennage a Juell of golde beinge agate garnysshed with
smale sparckes of rubyes and a smale perle pendante hanginge at a
bodkyn of golde

dd to the foresaid Lady Haward

84.94 By the Lady Layton a Cusshion Clothe of lawne alouer wrought with silke
and golde of sondry collors edged with a brode passamayne of Lace of
golde and syluer

dd to the foresaid Mrs Skydmore

84.95 By the Lady Pawlatt in golde. . . . . v li

dd to the foresaid h Sakford

84.96 By the Lady Jarrade a vale of lawne Cut out with Roses and Oken
leaves

84.97 By the Lady Wylloby Sir Fraunses wyfe a payre of sleaves of lawne
Cutworke wrought with syluer and blacke sylke

dd to the forsaid Mrs Skydmore

84.98 By the Lady Gressam in golde . . . . x li

84.99 By the Lady Cromewell in golde . . . . v li

dd to the said h Sakford

84.100 By the Lady Barkeley the Wydowe a Smocke of Camericke the sleaves
wrought with blacke silke and edged with a smale Lace of venys golde

84.101 By the Lady Ratlyffe ij large sweate Baddges of Serseonett and vj
handkercheaves wrought with blacke silke and edged withe golde

84.102 By the Lady Croftes a Cusshion clothe of lawne wrought alouer with
venys golde sylver and silke of sundry Collors with grapes and vyne
leaves with a faire passamayne about yt of gold and siluer with
spangles

84.103 By the Lady Frogmerton ij Pyllowberes of Camerycke wrought with gold
siluer & silke of sundry colers

dd to the foresaid Mrs Skidmore

84.104 By the Lady Fyez Warren a foreparte & avale of lawne Cut alouer and
florysshed with syluer

dd the foreparte to R hope &
the vale to Mrs Brisselles

84.105 By the Lady Catheryn Constable a kyrtle of Oringtawny gold Chamlet
bound with a silver lace
84.106 By the Lady Thyn a hat of Carnation Taffata Covered alouer wythe
Flowers and greshoppers of Damaske golde and syluer

> dd to the foresaid R hope

Knyghtes & A Chaplyn

84.107 By Sir Fraunses Knowles Threasoror of the household in golde. . . . . x li
84.108 By Sir James Acroftes Comptroller of the same in golde. . . . . x li
dd to the foresaid Sakford
84.109 By Sir Christofer Hatton knight vice cham an Attyre for the hed cont vij
peces of golde, iij of them beinge crownes of golde enperyal garn with
smale Dyamondes Rubyes perles and Opalles on the one syde and the
other iiij being Victoryes garn with Dyamondes Rubyes perles and
opalles on the on syde

> dd to the foresaid Lady howarde

84.110 By Sir Fraunses Walsingham knight principall secretory a frenche gowne
of oringe tawny satten stryped with siluer garded with a very brode
garde of Tawny Satten cut enbradored with venice golde syluer Damaske
golde purll and spangles

> dd to the foresaid Rauf hope

84.111 By Sir Raffe Sadler knighte Chauncellor of the Duchy in golde . . . . xv li
84.112 By Sir Walter Myldemaye knight Chauncellor of thexchequier in golde
. . . . x li

> dd to the foresaid Sekford

84.113 By Sir Thomas Hennage knight threasoror of the Chamber a Juell being
a bodkyn of golde with A Flower thereat garn with smale Rubyes and
Opalles on the on syde

> dd to the foresaid La howarde

84.114 By Sir Gylbarte Jarrade Knighte master of the Rolles in golde. . . . . xx li
84.115 By Sir Owyn Hopton knighte levetenaunte of the Tower in golde . . . . x li

> dd to the foresaid Sakford

84.116 By Sir Gylbarte Dethycke knight espetiall kinge of Armes a booke of
Armes conteynynge the Armes of the noble men of Inglande in the
tyme of Kinge Richarde the seconde

> dd to Mrs Blanche Parry

84.117 By Sir Henrye Cromwell knighte in golde . . . . x li

> dd as aforesaid to h Sekford

84.118 By Sir Gawen Carowe knighte a Smocke wroughte in the sleaves and collor
with blacke sylke

> dd to Mrs Skydmore

84.119 By Sir Henrye Lee knighte a smale Bottle of aggattes garn with gold and
smale sparkes of Rubyes and Dyamondes hanginge by a smale Chayne
of golde lykewise garn

> dd to the La howarde

84.120 By Sir William Drury knighte a Juell of golde being ij snakes wounde to
 gether garn with sparckes of Ruby and smale Dyamondes and on smale
 Emerod on the on syde

 dd to the said La howarde

84.121 By Sir Edwarde Cleare knighte in golde . . . . x li

 dd to the foresaid Sakford

84.122 By Sir Thomas Layton knight a Nightgowne of Russett Satten stryped
 with golde lyned with vnshorne vellat spotted white and blacke

 [blank]

84.123 By Sir John Souche knighte a Case for a Doblett of white sipers garn
 with Damaske gold & heare collored sylke

84.124 By Sir Phillipp Sydney knight a paire of Slippers of blacke vellatt alouer
 enbradored with venys golde perle and smale garnettes with a border
 in the Top of seconde sede perle and smale garnettes in Collyttes of
 golde

 dd to the foresaid R hope

84.125 By Absalon a booke entytuled explicacio orationis domine couered with
 blacke vellatt enbradored with venys golde

 dd to Mrs Blanche Parry

84.126 Also ij payre of longe aglettes of gold alouer garnyshed with Rubyes and
 smale perle and eche of them a smale perle / no report made who gave
 them poz. . . . . iij oz di di qtr

84.127 More xviij payre longe aglettes of golde enamvled / no report made who
 gave them poz . . . . xiiij oz di di qtr

 dd to the foresaid Lady haward

Gentlewomen

84.128 By Mrs Blaunche Parrye A payre of Braslettes of golde poz. . . . . oz qtr

 dd to the La Haward

84.129 By Mrs Fraunces Howarde senior a Dublate of lawne Cutworke slytely
 florisshed with siluer and spangels edged withe a smale Sylver Lace
 vnlyned

84.130 By Mrs Dale a Dublate / and a foreparte of purple Clothe of golde striped
 with golde and siluer & edged with passamayne of golde

84.131 By Mrs Edmondes a Case for a dublate of lawne Cut garnysshed with gold
 and spangles

84.132 By Mrs Southewell a forparte of a kyrtle of laune cut dyamond wyse
 wythe Tuftes of Carnatyon sylke And spangles of gold cut with Lawne
 betwene

84.133 By Mrs Skydmore a gowne of blacke Taffata with a border of ij plate
 laces of venys golde and syluer

 dd to the foresaid R hope

84.134 By Mrs Weste a vale of white stryped lawne striped with syluer with
 wrethes of the same stuf

 dd to Mrs Skydmore

84.135 By Mrs Chaworthe a Rownde Kyrtle of Ashecollored and white Damaske
    bownde aboute with a passamayne of venys golde and Carnation silke
                       dd to Ra hope

84.136 By Mrs Myddelmore too Comes of Ivery in a Case of whatchett vellatt
    enbradored with venys golde and perle
                   dd to Mrs Chaworth

84.137 By Mrs Elizabethe Browke a Ruf of lawne of whyte cut worke vnmade
                  dd to Jane Brisselles

84.138 By Mrs Gyfforde parte of the Couering of a gowne of gold plate with
    Tuftes of pechecollored silke

84.139 By Mrs Dygby a Doblett of lawne alouer wrought with blacke silke and
    golde bownde about withe A smale passamayne of golde
                        dd to R hope

84.140 By Mrs Jane Brysselles a wastecoate of white satten striped with golde
    lyned with strawcolored Sersesonet
                  dd to Mrs Skydmore

84.141 By Mrs Townesend a Bodkyn of golde the pendante a coney opall
    standing vppon a Rocke of Opall garnysshed with very smale sparckes
    of rubyes and one smale perle pendante
                 dd to the La haward

84.142 By Mrs Scrowpe a Cusshyn Clothe of lawne Cutworke florysshed with
    syluer & a passamayne lace of like siluer

84.143 By Mrs Snowe xij handkerchers of Cameryricke edged with a passamayne
    of venys golde

84.144 By Mrs Cave vj handkerchers wrought with blacke silke and edged with a
    passamayne of gold & syluer
                  dd to Mrs Skydmore

84.145 By Mrs Sackeforde a Screne of walnuttre with a clothe of purple clothe of
    golde garn with lace of venys golde and frenged with a frynge of golde and
    syluer
            dd in charge to Mr Knevet at Westminster

84.146 By Mrs Winckefelde a Ruf of lawne wrought with Cut worke
                  dd to Jane Bresselles

84.147 By Mrs Cromer a nyght Rayle of Camerycke wrought alouer with blacke
    sylke and powdered with venyse golde

84.148 By Mrs Smythson A Shaddowe and A handekercher

84.149 By Mrs Twyste too pyllobers of Assaye of hollande wrought alouer on the
    on syde with blacke silke

84.150 By Mrs Note vj handkerchers of Cameryke edged with a passamayne of
    golde and syluer
                  dd to Mrs Skydmore

84.151 By Mrs Marbury A Ruf of lawne cutworke vnmade
                  dd to Jane Brisselles

84.152 By Mrs Newton a doblat of Carnation satten cut and layde Chevernewise
    with siluer plate lace
                        dd to R hope

84.153 By Mrs Croxson a Cusshion clothe of hollande with a border of Cutworke
edged with a passamayne of golde and syluer

dd to Mrs Skydmor

84.154 By Mrs Fraunces Howarde the yonger a scarfe of white Networke and
a foreparte of networke Florysshed wih syluer and spangles

the scarf with Mrs Chaworth

threst with R hope

84.155 By Mrs Huggaynes vj handkerchers wrought with blacke silke and edged
with gold and syluer & xxiiij smale sweate bagges of Serceonett

84.156 By Mrs Lyfelde vj handkerchers of Camerycke with Cut worke and a bone
Lace

84.157 By Mrs Haynes a Cusshinclothe of lawne wrought with blacke silke &
edged with a pasamayne of gold & siluer

84.158 By Mrs Tomysend the Dwarfe a fare handkercher of Camerycke wroughte
with blacke sylke

dd to Mrs Skydmore

84.159 By Mrs Gylham a large Ruffe and apayre of Cuffes set with knottes

dd to Jane Briselles

Gentlemen

84.160 By Mr Wolley a pettycote of Plunkett Satten alouer enbradored with a
smale Twiste of venys golde and iij borders about yt of lyke enbradere
and frenged with golde and syluer

84.161 By Mr Dyer a pettycote of mvrre satten wrought with golde and iij brode
borders of white satten enbradored with venyce gold syluer and purle

dd to Ra hope

84.162 By Mr Stanhop a pece of networke floryshed with venys gold and Copper
plate

84.163 By Mr Southewell a partelet and a payre of Sleaves of lawne cut
dyamondewise

dd to Mrs Skydmore

84.164 By Mr Newton a foreparte of a kyrtell of carnasion satten Cut and layd
chevernewyse with a A [sic] plate lase of Syluer

dd to forsaid Ra hope

84.165 By Mr Myddlemore a payre of parfumed gloves the Cuffes enbradored
with venys gold and perle

dd to Mrs Chaworth

84.166 By Mr Foulke Grevell a fan of feathers Carnation and white set in golde
with a handle of Christall

dd to Ra hope

84.167 By Mr Lychefelde a spannysshe Gyttorne lute in a Case of blewe vellat
edged with a passamayne of golde

with her Matie by Mr Darcy grome

84.168 By Mr Raulfe Bolse a Ruff and a paire of Cuffes of lawne Cut worke
with ij borders

dd to Jane Bresselles

84.169   By Mr Bronker a foreparte and a paire of boddyes of Nettworke
florrysshed with blacke sylke and Syluer Lyned with Carnation
Tafata

dd to Ra hope

84.170   By Mr Basshe in gold . . . . x li

dd to henry Sakford

84.171   By Mr Skydmore iij peces of lawne Cut worke for a partelet and sleaves
floryshed ouer with siluer and set with spangles

dd to Mrs Skydmore

84.172   By Mr Care Rawley a foreparte of purple Tafata enbradored alouer
ritcheley with venys golde siluer purle and perle

dd to Ra hope

84.173   By Mr Thomas Wodhouse a Juell of golde beinge a Ton garnysshed with
dyamondes Rubyes and emeralles on the syde, and a safar pendante
without foyle with a naked boy in the Top & a flying horse above yt

84.174   By Mr Nowell a smale Juell of gold being a spade the showe thereof
mother of perle garnysshed wythe Dyamondes on the on syde yt is to
ware vppon a Ruffe

with her Majestie by Mrs Skydmore

84.175   By Mr Smythe Customar a Bolte of camericke
84.176   By Mr Hughes lynon Draper a pece of Lawne

dd to Mrs Blaunch Parry

84.177   By Mr William Cornwallys a Bodken of golde with a ploughe garnyshed
with smale dyamondes on thone syde

dd to the La Haward

84.178   By Mr Mowntague a night rayle of Camericke wrought alouer with blacke
sylke

84.179   By Mr Docter Masters ij Boxes of Concerves
84.180   By Mr Docter Balye ij Boxes of Concerves
84.181   By Mr Docter Lopus iij Brusshes the handels enbradered

dd to Mrs Skydmore
the Brusshes dd Mrs Chaworth

84.182   By Mr Morgayne a pothecarye ij pottes of preserved things and on Box
84.183   By Mr Hemyngeway a pothecary ij boxes thone manus Christi theother
Qinces preserved

dd to Mrs Skydmore

84.184   By Mr Charles Smythe a wastecote of oringecollored taffata Cut alouer
layde with a smale plate Lace of golde and siluer lyned with white siluer
tyncell

dd to the La haward

84.185   By Mr Gyfforde parte of the Couering of a gowne of golde plate with
tuftes of peache cullored sylke

dd to Ra hope

84.186   By Mr Huggins a longe sweate bagge of whyte satten alouer enbradored on
thone syde with venys golde Damaske golde and silke of sondrye collors

dd to Mrs Skydmore

84.187   By John Smytheson a Marchepayne with a castle in yt

84.188   By John Dudley Sergiant of the pasterie a pie of Qinces made in to letters.
      E. and R.

                                                      [blank]

84.189   By Christofer Barker prynter a large Byble in englysshe couered with
      crymson vellat alouer enbradered wythe venys golde and seade perle
                                          dd to Mrs Blanch

84.190   By Nicholas Hyllyarde a faire Table being pyctures Conteyninge the
      history of the fyve wise virgins and the fyve follysshe virgins
                          dd to Mr Tho Knevet at Westminster pallace

84.191   By Ambroso lupo iij glasses of swete waters
                                       dd to Mrs Chaworth

84.192   By the fyve Bretheren a Drynkinge glasse with a Cover

84.193   By Petro Lupo a payre of perfumed gloves
                                       dd to Mrs Chaworth

84.194   By Petuchio Vbaldino a Booke couered with vellam
                                 dd to Mrs Blanch Parry

84.195   By Marke Antonyo a smale glasse of swete water and a Drinkinge glasse
      with a couer
                                       dd to Mrs Chaworth

84.196   By Dunstone Anes a Beserde stone
                                      dd to the La haward

84.197   By Syppio gentilis a booke of latten verses couered with Crymson
      vellatt

84.198   By Ogerius Bellehachius a Booke of latten verses couered with vellam
                               dd to Mrs Blanch Parry

Summa totalis of all the / money giuen to her
Matie & delivered ut supra . . . . viij^{C} xxxviij li vij s

Elizabeth R
[sign manual]

                                          John Asteley
                                    Ex[aminatio] per
                                    Bristow senior
                                    Bristow Junior
                                    J Pigeon
                                    Ste. Fulwell
                                    N Pigeon

Anno Regni Regine
Elizabeth xxvj^{to}

Newe yeares guiftes giuen by her Matie at her pallayce of Westminster
whose names hereafter ensueth the First
Day of January the yere aforesaid

Elizabeth R
[sign manual]

84.199	To Sir Thomas Bromley knight Lorde Chauncellor of Inglande in guilte plate Martyn . . . . xxxj oz di di qrt	
84.200	To the Lorde Burligh Lorde high Threasoror of Inglande in gylte plate Martyn . . . . xlj oz qrt	
84.201	To the Lorde Marques of winchester in guilt plate Martyn . . . . .xxx oz di qrt	

Earles

84.202	To therle of Leycetor Mr of the horses in guilte plate Kell poz—xl oz di and in guilt plate Martyn—iiij^{xx} xj oz di Summa . . . . Cxxxij oz
84.203	To therle of Shrewesbury in guilt plat Kell . . . . .xxx oz
84.204	To therle of Darby in guilte plate K . . . . xxix oz di di qrt
84.205	To therle of Sussex in guilte plate Kell . . . . xix oz iij qrt di
84.206	To therle of Lyncolne in guilte plate Martyn . . . . xx oz qrt di
84.207	To therle of Warwicke in guilte plate Kell . . . . Ciiij oz qrt di
84.208	To therle of Rutlande in guilte plate martyn . . . . xx oz di di qrt
84.209	To therle of Bedforde in guilte plate Kell . . . . xxxj oz di
84.210	To therle of Huntingdon in guilt plate martyn . . . . .xx oz iij qrt
84.211	To therle of Pembroke in guilte plate martyn . . . . xxxj oz qrt
84.212	To therle of Essex in guilte plate martyn . . . . xx oz di
84.213	To therle of Bathe in guilt plate Kell . . . . .xxvij oz iij qrt
84.214	To therle of Hertforde in guilte plate Kell . . . . xxv oz iij qrt di
84.215	To the Vicounte Mountigue in guilte plate Martyn . . . . xx oz qrt di
84.216	To the Vicounte Byndam in guilte plate martyn . . . . .xxij oz qrt

Duchesses and Countesses

84.217	To the Duches of Somersett in guilt plate Kell . . . . xxv oz iij qrt di
84.218	To the Lady Marques of Northamton in guilt plate Kell . . . . .xl oz
84.219	To the Lady Marques of winchester in guilt plate Martin . . . . .xx oz qrt
84.220	To the Counties of Shrewesburye in guilt plate Kell . . . . xxxij oz di qrt
84.221	To the Countes of Huntington in gilte plate Martyn . . . . xxxj oz qrt
84.222	To the Countes of Oxforde in guilt plate Martyn . . . . .xx oz qrt
84.223	To the Countes of Lyncolne in guilt plate Martyn and Kell . . . . L oz qrt
84.224	To the Countes of Warwycke in guilt plate Martyn and Kell . . . . . . .Lj oz qrt di
84.225	To the Countes of Sussex in guilte plate Kell . . . . xviij oz qrt di
84.226	To the Countes of Penbroke Doager in guilte plate Martyn . . . . xxij oz
84.227	To the Countes of Penbroke Junior in guilt plate martyn . . . . xxij oz

84.228 To the Countes of Bedford in guilt plate Kell . . . . L oz di
84.229 To the Countes of Southampton in guilte plate Martyn . . . . xix oz di
84.230 To the Countes of Rutlande in guilte plate Kell . . . . xix oz qrt
84.231 To the Vicountes Mountigue in guilte plate Kell . . . . xix oz qrt

Busshopps

84.232 To the Arche Busshop of Canterburye in guilt plate Keele . . . . xlj oz iij qrt
84.233 To the Arche Busshop of Yorke in guilte plate Martyn . . . . xxxviij oz qrt
84.234 To the Busshop of Durham in guilt plate martyn . . . . xxxvj oz qrt di
84.235 To the Busshop of London in guilt plate martyn . . . . xxxj oz
84.236 To the Busshop of Salesburye in guilte plate Kell . . . . xxx oz iij qrt di
84.237 To the Busshop of Winchester in guilte plate Martyn . . . . .xx oz iij qrt
84.238 To the Busshop of Lyncolne in guilte plate Martyn . . . . .xxx oz
84.239 To the Busshop of Norwiche in guilte plate martyn . . . . xxxj oz
84.240 To the Busshop of Carlell in guilt plate Keyll . . . . xvj oz di
84.241 To the Busshop of Hereforde in plate martyn . . . . xiiij oz di
84.242 To the Busshop of Peterborow in guilt plate martyn . . . . xvj oz di
84.243 To the Busshop of Chester in guilt plate Kele . . . . .xv oz iij qrt
84.244 To the Busshop of Rochester in guilt plate Kell . . . . .xv oz qrt
84.245 To the Busshop of Exeter in guilte plate Kell . . . . xv oz di
84.246 To the Busshop of Lichefelde and Coventry in guilt plate martyn . . xx oz di qrt
84.247 To the Busshop of St Davys in guilt plate Kell . . . . xiiij oz iij qrt di
84.248 To the Busshop of Gloster in guilte plate Kell . . . . xv oz

Lordes

84.249 To the Lorde of Hunesdon in guilte plate Martyn poz . . . . .xxx oz
84.250 To the Lorde of Burgaveny in guilte plate Martyn . . . . xj oz qrt
84.251 To the Lorde Howarde of Effyngam in guilte plate Martyn and Kell
. . . . Ciij oz qrt di
84.252 To the Lorde Cobham in guilte plate Martyn & Kell . . . . xj oz di di qrt
84.253 To the Lorde Talbott in guilte Martyn . . . . .xviij oz di
84.254 To the Lorde Shandowes in guilte plate Martyn . . . . xij oz di
84.255 To the Lorde Northe in guilte plate Martin . . . . .xx oz iij qrt
84.256 To the Lorde Compton in guilte plate Martin . . . . xx oz qrt di
84.257 To the Lorde Wynsor in guilt plate .K. . . . . xx oz di
84.258 To the Lorde Loumley in guilt plate Mar . . . . xx oz di
84.259 To the Lorde Wharton in guilte plate Kell . . . . .xx oz iij qrt
84.260 To the Lorde Riche in guilte plate Kell . . . . xxj oz qrt
84.261 To the Lorde Russell in guilt plate Kell . . . . .xx oz qrt
84.262 To the Lorde Darsy in gilt plate Martin . . . . xviij oz iij qrt di
84.263 To the Lorde Norris in gilt plate Martin . . . . .xx oz qrt

Baronesses

84.264 To the Barronesse Burligh in guilt plate Martin . . . . xxxij oz di di qrt
84.265 To the Barronesse Dakers in guilt plate Martin . . . . xviij oz di

84.266	To the Barronesse Cobham in guilte plate Martin . . . . lij oz
84.267	To the Barronesse Howarde in guilt plate Martyn . . . . .xx oz iij qrt
84.268	To the Barronesse Hunesedon in gilt plate Martin. . . . . xxvij [oz] iij qrt di
84.269	To the Barronesse Lomley in gillte plate Keyle mr. . . . . xx oz di
84.270	To the Barronesse Shandowes Dowager in guilt plate mr . . . . .xvj oz
84.271	To the Barronesse Shandowes Junior in gilt plate mr. . . . . .xv oz qrt
84.272	To St John Bletzo in gilt plate Martin. . . . . xx oz di di qrt
84.273	To the Barronesse Paget Cary in gilt plate Martin . . . . .xxv oz qrt
84.274	To the Barronesse Chayney in gilt plate Martin . . . . xxxviij oz qrt di
84.275	To the Barronesse Wharton in gilte plate Martin. . . . . xxj oz
84.276	To the Barronesse Barkeley in gilt plate Kele . . . . xx oz qrt di
84.277	To the Barronesse Russell in gilte plate Kele. . . . . xvij oz iij qrt di
84.278	To the Barronesse Norres in gilte plate Kele. . . . . .xx oz qrt
84.279	To the Barronesse Morley in gilt plate Kele . . . . .xx oz iij qrt
84.280	To the Barronesse Ryche Dowager in gilt plate Martin . . . . xix oz
84.281	To the Barronesse Wylloby in gilte plate martyn . . . . xix oz di qrt

Lades

84.282	To the Lady Marie Seymer wyfe to Mr Rogers in gilt plate martin xij oz iij qrt di
84.283	To the Lady Sydney in gilte plate Martin . . . . xxxj oz iij qrt di
84.284	To the Lady Elizabeth Semer als Knightley in gilt plate Martin . . . . xxiiij oz
84.285	To the Lady Stafforde in gilt plate Kele . . . . xxix oz di
84.286	To the Lady waalsingham [sic] in gilte plate Martin. . . . . xx oz
84.287	To the Lady Arrondell in gilte plate Martin . . . . xv oz iij qrt di
84.288	To the Lady Drury in gilte plate martin . . . . xvij oz
84.289	To the Lady Carowe in gilt plate Kele. . . . . .xxxv oz
84.290	To the Lady Cheake in gilte plate Kele . . . . xxvij oz di qrt
84.291	To the Lady Hennage in gilte plate Kele. . . . . xxij oz
84.292	To the Lady Layton in gilte plate Martin . . . . xvij oz iij qrt
84.293	To the Lady Pawlett in gilte plate martin . . . . .xj oz qrt
84.294	To the Lady Jarrad in gilt plate Keyle. . . . . .xvj oz di
84.295	To the Lady Croftes in gilte plate Martin . . . . xx oz
84.296	To the Lady Wyllowby in gilte plate martin . . . . xiiij oz di qrt
84.297	To the Lady Gressham in gilt plate martin . . . . xix oz
84.298	To the Lady Cromwell in gilt plate Kele . . . . x oz di
84.299	To the Lady Ratclyff in gilt plate martin . . . . xij oz qrt
84.300	To the Lady Frogmorton in gilt plate Keele . . . . xx oz di di qrt
84.301	To the Lady Fyzwarren in gilt plate Keele . . . . xix [oz] iij qrt
84.302	To the Lady Catheryn Constable in gilte plate martin . . . . xv oz qrt di
84.303	To the Lady Barkeley in gilt plate Kele. . . . . xv oz di di qrt
84.304	To the Lady Thyn in gilt plate Keele. . . . . xj oz di di qrt

Knyghtes and Chaplynes

84.305	To Sir Fraunses Knowles Treasoror of the householde in gilt plate Keele xxiiij oz
84.306	To Sir James Croftes knight Comptroler in gilt plate Martin. . . . . xxiiij oz
84.307	To Sir Christofer Hatton vice Chamberlen in guilt plate Keele . . . . CCCC oz

84.308	To Sir Fraunses Walsingham pryncipall Secretory in gilt plate Keele.	Lxij oz qrt
84.309	To Sir Raufe Sadler Chauncellor of the Duchye in gilt plate Keele	xxvij oz di
84.310	To Sir Walter Mildemaye Chauncellor of Thexchequier in gilt plate Martin	xxvj oz iij qrt
84.311	To Sir Thomas Hennage Threasoror of the Chamber in gilte plate Keele.	xlviij oz
84.312	To Sir Gylberte Jarratt Mr of the Rolles in guilt plate Martin	xxxiiij oz di qrt
84.313	To Sir Owyn Hopton Levetenante of the Tower in guilt plate martin	xxiij oz
84.314	To Sir Gylberte Dethicke principall kinge of Armes in gilte plate Martin	xij oz iij qrt di
84.315	To Sir Henry Cromwell in gilte plate Martin	xx oz
84.316	To Sir Gawyn Carow in gilt plate Kele	xxxv oz di qrt
84.317	To Sir Henry Lee in gilt plate Martin	xxxviij oz qrt
84.318	To Sir William Drury in guilt plate martin	xv oz di
84.319	To Sir Edward Cleare in gilt plate martin	xix oz
84.320	To Sir Thomas Layton in gilte plate martin	xxxij oz iij qrt
84.321	To Sir John Souche in gilte plate Kele.	xiij oz di
84.322	To Sir Philipp Sydney in gilte plate Kele.	xxij oz di qrt
84.323	To Absolon Clerke of the closet in gilte plate Martin	vij oz di

Gentlewomen

84.324	To Mrs Blanche Parry in gilte plate Martin	xviij oz
84.325	To Mrs Fraunses Howarde senior in gilte plate Martin	xvj oz
84.326	To Mrs Dale in gilte plate Kele	xxij oz qrt
84.327	To Mrs Edmondes in gilt plate Kele	xv oz
84.328	To Mrs Skydmour in giltte plate Kele.	xvj oz iij qrt
84.329	To Mrs Southwell in gilt plate Martin	xv oz di di qrt
84.330	To Mrs Snowe in gilte plate martin	xvij oz iij qrt di
84.331	To Mrs Gyfforde in gilt plate Kele	xvj oz iij qrt di
84.332	To Mrs Weste in gilte plate martin	xv oz qrt di
84.333	To Mrs Chaworthe in gilte plate Kele	xv oz
84.334	To Mrs Myddlemore in gilte plate Kele	viij oz iij qrt
84.335	To Mrs Fraunses Howarde Junior in gilt plate Martin.	xv oz qrt
84.336	To Mrs Digbye in gilte plate Kele	xvj oz iij qrt di
84.337	To Mrs Jane Brysselles in gilte plate Martin.	xv oz
84.338	To Mrs Browke in gilt plate Martin	xv oz
84.339	To Mrs Townesend in gilt plate Kele.	xvj oz di di qrt
84.340	To Mrs Scroope in gilte plate Kele	xiiij oz iij qrt
84.341	To Mrs Cave in gilte plate Kele	xiiij oz qrt
84.342	To Mrs Sackeforde in gilte plate Kele	xxiiij oz
84.343	To Mrs Winckefeld in gilt plate Kele.	x oz qrt di
84.344	To Mrs Cromer in gilt plate Kele	xv oz iij qrt di
84.345	To Mrs Smythson in gilte plate Keele	vij oz
84.346	To Mrs Twyste in gilt plate martin	vij oz
84.347	To Mrs Noote in gilt plate Kele	x oz

84.348	To Mrs Howggaynes in gilt plate Kele	xx oz
84.349	To Mrs Lyfelde in gilt plate Martyn	x oz
84.350	To Mrs Haynes in gilt plate Kele................................	xv oz qrt
84.351	To Mrs Tomysen the Dwarffe in gilte plate Kele	ij oz qrt
84.352	To Mrs Marbury in gilte plate Kele	xiiij oz qrt
84.353	To Mrs Newton in gilt plate Martin	xv oz
84.354	To Mrs Croxson in gilte plate Keele	vj oz iij qrt

Maides

84.355	To Mrs Mary Ratclyff in gilt plate Martin....................	x oz di di qrt
84.356	To Mrs Katheryn Howard in gilt plate Martin.....................	xj oz
84.357	To Elizabethe Garrett in gilt plate Martin	xj oz qrt
84.358	To Mrs Mackewylliams in gilte plate Kele	x oz qrt
84.359	To Mrs Elizabethe Trentham in gilt plate Martyn	x oz di di qrt
84.360	To Mrs Eggecom in gilte plate Keele	x oz qrt
84.361	To Mrs Baptiste mother of the maydes in gilte plate Keele	xij oz di

Gentlemen

84.362	To Mr Wolley in gilte plate Martin	xxvj oz
84.363	To Mr Dyer in gilt plate Kele	xvj oz qrt di
84.364	To Mr Stanhope in gilt plate Kele.............................	xiij oz
84.365	To Mr Southwell in gilt plate Kell............................	xij oz
84.366	To Mr Myddlemore in gilt plate Martin......................	xij oz di di qrt
84.367	To Mr William Cornewallys in gilt plate Kele	xiij oz di di qrt
84.368	To Mr Fowlke Grevill in gilte plate Martin	xiij oz di qrt
84.369	To Mr Skydmore in gilte plate Kele	xvij oz di qrt
84.370	To Mr Gyfforde in gilt plate Kele	xxij oz
84.371	To Mr Newton in gilt plate Martin...........................	xvj oz qrt
84.372	To Mr Nowell in gilt plate Martin	xv oz qrt
84.373	To Mr Care Raweley in gilt plate Martin	xxj oz
84.374	To Mr Thomas Woodhouse in guilt plate Keele................	xx oz
84.375	To Mr Basshe in gilt plate Martin............................	xx oz di
84.376	To Mr Raufe Bowes in gilt plate Martin......................	xj oz di
84.377	To Mr Smythe Customar in gilt plat Kele......................	xv oz
84.378	To Mr Charles Smyth in gilt plate Martin	xvj oz
84.379	To Mr Hughes lynen draper in gilt plate Martin	xiij oz di qrt
84.380	To Mr Mowntague in gilt plate Martin........................	xij oz qrt di
84.381	To Mr Barker prynter in gilt plate Martin	xj oz di qrt
84.382	To Mr Huggins in gilte plate Kele............................	xxx oz
84.383	To Mr Docter Master in gilt plate Kele	xiiij oz iij qrt
84.384	To Mr Docter Bayly in gilte plate Kele	xiiij oz iij qrt
84.385	To Mr Docter Lopus in gilte plate Kele	xiiij oz di di qrt
84.386	To Morgayne pottycarye in gilte plate Kele	vij oz qrt
84.387	To Hemawaye pottycary in gilt plate Kele	vij oz
84.388	To John Smytheson Mr cooke in gilt plate Kele..............	viij oz
84.389	To John Dudley Sergiant of the pastry in gilt plate Martin	vj oz

84.390	To Ambroso Lvpo in gilt plate Kele	v oz di
84.391	To Mr Petrusio Lupo in gilte plate Kele	v oz di
84.392	To Petrusio Vbaldino in gilte plate Kele	v oz di
84.393	To Marke Antony gallyardo in gilte plate Kele.	v oz di
84.394	To Dunstone Anes in gilt plate Martin	xviij oz di di qrt
84.395	To Mr Lychefeld in gilte plate Martin.	xvij oz qrt
84.396	To Mr Brounker in gilte plate Kelle	xix oz di

Free Gifts

84.397   To John Asteley Mr and Threasoror of the Juelles and plate in gilte plate
Kele . . . . xviij oz iij qrt di

84.398   To Thomas Asteley grome of the prevye Chamber in gilte plate Martin
. . . . ix oz

84.399   To Edward Carey grome of the sayde chamber in gilt plate Martin . . . . ix oz

84.400   To Thomas Knevett an other grome of the sayde Chamber in gilt plate
Martin . . . . ix oz

84.401   To Henry Sackeforde also grom of the saide Chamber in gilte plate Kele. . . ix oz

84.402   To William [sic Henry] Myddlemore grom of the saide Chamber in gilt
plate Martin . . . . ix oz

84.403   To Thomas Gorge also grome in gilte plate Kele . . . . ix oz

84.404   To John Baptiste grome also of the sayde Chamber in gilte plate Kele . . . . . ix oz

84.405   To William Kyllygrave grome of the sayde Chamber in gilte plate Kele . . . . ix oz

84.406   To Edwarde Darsey an other grome in gilte plate Martin . . . . ix oz

84.407   To Edward Denny also grome there in gilte plate martin . . . . ix oz

84.408   To Raufe Hope yomaman [sic] of the Robes in gilte plate martin
. . . . xij oz iij qrt di

84.409   To Nicholas Bristow Clerke of the Juelles and plate in gilte plate
Martin . . . . x oz iij qrt di

84.410   To John Pigeon on of the yomen of her Maties Juelles and plate in
gilt plate Martin. . . . . x oz iij qrt di

84.411   To Steven Fulwell an other yoman of the same office in gilt plate
Martin . . . . x oz iij qrt di

84.412   To Richarde Asteley grome of the same office in gilte plate martin
. . . . x oz iij qrt di

Summa totalis of all the plate
Giuen awey as aforesaid . . . . mmmm viij^C xxj oz qrt

Guiftes giuen and deliuered at sundry tymes
in maner & fourme folloing that is to say

84.413   Firste geven by her Matie and delivered the xxiij^th of Maye Anno xxv^to
to Davy Lynsye A preacher sente to her Matie from the Kinge of
Skottes iij gilt bolles with a couer bought of Alderman Martin poz . . . lxxj oz

84.414   Item more geven and Delyvered the same Daye and yere to Mr George
Yonge Clerke of the Cownsell to the said Kinge of Skottes iij gilte
bolles with a couer bought of the said Alderman Martyn poz
. . . . lxviij oz iij qrt di

84.415   Item Delivered to her sayd Matie by the handes of the Lady Stafforde
the xx^th of July Anno predicto A gilte Cup with a couer boughte of
the said Alderman Martin poz . . . . xxiiij oz iij qrt di

84.416   Item geven by her said Matie & delivered the xix of october Anno pred
to John George Henrycke, a messenger sent from the Kinge of
Denmarke a gilt bole with a couer bought of the sayd Alderman Martin
poz . . . . lxij oz di

84.417   Item geven by her sayde Matie and delivered the xxvij of November Anno
xxvjto to Erycon County of wesynburg Ambassitor sent from the Kinge
of swethelande a chayne of golde bought of martin being of the goodnes
of xxij carrets fyne poz . . . . lxix oz iij qrt

84.418   Item geven by her sayde Matie and delyvered the same tyme to Nichlas
Rasshe secretory to the saide Kinge A Chayne of golde bought of the
sayde Alderman Martin beinge of the lyke goodnes poz . . . . xxij oz iij qrt

84.419   Item more geven by her sayde Matie and delyvered the same tyme to
Erycon Johnson a gentleman also sent from the saide kinge. A chayne
of golde bought as aforesayd beinge of the lyke goodnes poz . . . . xiij oz iij qrt

84.420   Item geven by her sayde Matie and Delyvered the xviij of December
Anno pred at the Cristenynge of Mr Care Rawles Childe A gilte Cup
with A Couer boughte of the saide Alderman martin poz. . . . . xxxvj oz

84.421   Item more geven by her Matie and delyvered the sayde daye and yere to
Androwe Kethe a gent sent from the sayde kinge of Swethelande a
Chayne of gold bought of the sayd Alderman martin of the like
goodnes poz. . . . . xl oz xviij d wayte

84.422   Item geaven by her Matie and Delyvered the xxix^th of Apryll Anno pred
To Mathaes Budde a gent from the Kinge of Denmark a Chayne of
golde bought of Alderman marten being of goodnes of xxj Carrenttes
iij Graynes iij qrt poz. . . . . xliij oz di

Elizabeth R
[sign manual]

John Asteley
Ex[aminatio] per
Bristow thelder
Bristow younger
J Pigeon
Ste Fulwell
N Pigeon

Anno Regni
Regine Elizabeth xxvij^{mo}

Neweyearsguiftes gyuen
to her Matie at her Mannor
of Grenewich by these
persones whose names doe
hereafter ensue the Fyrste
daye of January the
yeare aforesaide

Elizabeth R
[sign manual]

85.1 By Sir Thomas Brovmley Knight Lord Chavnsoler of Ingland in gold and
Sylver . . . . xiij li vj s viij d
85.2 By the Lorde Bourghley Lord high Threasorer of Ingland in gold . . . . xx li
85.3 By the Lord Marques of Winchester in gold . . . . xx li
dd to henry Sekford groum of the pryuey Chaumber

Earles & Vicounte

85.4 By the Erlle of Lecetor Lorde Steuard of the Houssehold A Nytegoune of
Tavny wrought vellat one the oute syde the Insyde being Carnation
vnshornne vellat bound A bovte with A Byllimentt Lace and Buttenes
and Louppes of venis gold and plate Lace
dd Raulfe hope yeoman of the Robes
By the said Erlle geven morre A Sable Skynne the hed and fourre featte of
gold fully fournyshed with Dyamondes and Rubyes of Sundery sorttes
85.5 By the Erlle of Arrundell A Carkyonett of golde Conteyning seven peses of
golde Syx truloves of smaull Sparckes of Dyamondes and many perlles of
sondery bygnes and smavll sparkes of Rubyes
dd the Lady howard
85.6 By the Erlle of Shrewesbury in gold . . . . xx li
85.7 By the Erlle of Darby in gold . . . . xx li
85.8 By the Erlle of Sussex in gold . . . . x li
85.9 By the Erlle of of Lyncolne in gold . . . . x li
dd the forseid henry Sekford
85.10 By the Erlle of Warwycke ACarkyonett of golde Conteyning Syxtenne
peses eyght sett with thre smal Rubyes A pece and eyght sett with
smaull perlles Lyke knottes
dd the forseid Barrones howard
85.11 By the Erlle of Rutland in golde . . . . x li
85.12 By the Erlle of Bedford in golde . . . . xx li
85.13 By the Erlle of Huntington in gold . . . . x li
dd the forseid Sakford

85.14   By the Erlle of Penbroke A forparte of white Satten enbraudred with
       Eglentyne flowers and other Leves
                                    dd the forseid Raulfe hope

85.15   By the Erlle of Bathe in golde . . . . xx li
                                    dd the forsaid Henry Sackford

85.16   By the Erlle of Coumberland A Juell of gold being A Ovlle garnished one
       the brest and Eyes with Opalles and Emeroddes
                                   dd in chardge to Mrs Blaunce Parye

85.17   By the Erlle of Hertff[ord] A Doblett of pechcolored satten enbravdered
       with Roses of venis golde and Sylke
                                   dd the forseid Raufe hope

85.18   By the vicount Mountighu in gold . . . . x li

Duchesses Marquesses & Countesses

85.19   By the Duches of Soumersett in gold . . . . xiij oz vij s
                                   dd the forsaid Sakford

85.20   By the Lady Marques of Northampton A Mantle of Lawne Covtworke with
       Roses and Okenleves with Lyttle blacke Sylke in yt
                                   dd to forseid Raulfe hope

85.21   By the Lady Marques of winchester Dowger in gold . . . . x li
                                   dd the forseid Sackford

85.22   By the Countis of Oxford A Juell being A Carkyonett of golde Conteyning
       xij peces garnished with eyghte smaull sparckes of Rubyes and this worde
       Durabo of smaull perlles and knottes of Truloves of smaull perlle
                                   dd the forseid Barrones howard

85.23   By the Countis of Shrewesbury A goune of Tavny wrought vellatt satten
       ground bound A boute with plate Lace of venis gold and Sylver Fased
       with Ashecolored and Orring tavny Fringed Sylke spotted with Buttens
       and Loppes of venis golde and Sylver
                                   dd Raulfe Hope

85.24   By the Countis of Hountingdon in gold . . . . viij li
                                   dd to the forseid Sackeford

85.25   By the Countis of Lyncolnne A Round kertle of Cloth of Sylver with
       workes of Carnation Sylke with buttens and Lopes Doune before of
       venis golde
                                   dd the forseid Raulfe hope

85.26   By the Countis of Warwicke thre Dosen of Buttens of golde eyghtene of
       them sett with smaull sparkes of Dyamondes the other eyghtene sett with
       Truloves of smaull perlles
                                   dd the Barrones Howard

85.27   By the Countis of Penbroke Dowger in golde . . . . xij li
                                   dd Mr Sackford

85.28   By the Countis of Penbroke Junior A Covering of A goune of Lavnne
       Covtworke floryshed with venis gold
                                   dd Raulfe hope

85.29	By the Countis of Sussex Dowger in gold . . . . x li	
	dd Mr Sackeford	
85.30	By the Countis of Bedford A Kertle of white Satten all over Embravdered with Mvrry satten sett with sede perlles and bygger perlles	
	dd to Raufe hope	
85.31	By the Countis of Coumberland A Mantle of lavnne Covtworke floryshed with Sylver	
	dd Raulfe hope	
85.32	By the Countis of Sowthampton in gold . . . . x li	
85.33	By the Countis of Rutland in gold . . . . x li	
	dd henry Sekeford	
85.34	By the Countis of Bathe A forparte of A kertle of whyte Satten vnmade embravdered all ouer with flowers and Leves of venis gold and Damaske purlle wrethed garn with sundery perlles in the Myddest of the Flowers	
	dd Raulfe hope	
85.35	By the Countis of Sussex Junior in gold. . . . . x li	
85.36	By the vicountis of Mountighu in gold. . . . . x li	

Busshoppes

85.37	By the Arche Busshop of Caunterbury in golde. . . . . .xl li	
85.38	By the Arche Busshop of Yorke in golde . . . . xxx li	
85.39	By the Busshop of Durham in golde . . . . xxx li	
85.40	By the Busshop of Lovndon in golde . . . . xx li	
85.41	By the Busshop of Sarum in golde . . . . xx li	
85.42	By the Busshop of Winchester in gold . . . . xx li	
85.43	By the Busshop of Lyncolne in golde. . . . . xx li	
85.44	By the Busshop of Wourster in golde. . . . . xx li	
85.45	By the Busshop of Bathe and Welles in gold . . . . xx li	
85.46	By the Busshop of Carlell in golde . . . . x li	
85.47	By the Busshop of Herreforde in golde . . . . x li	
85.48	By the Busshop of Peterborow in golde . . . . x li	
85.49	By the Busshop of Chester in golde . . . . x li	
85.50	By the Busshop of Rochester in gold . . . . x li	
85.51	By the Busshop of Exetor in golde . . . . x li	
85.52	By the Busshop of Lychfelde in golde . . . . xiij li vj s viij d	
85.53	By the Busshop of St Davyes in gold . . . . x li	
85.54	By the Busshop of Gloster in golde . . . . x li	

Lordes

85.55	By the Lord of Bourgaveny in golde. . . . . v li	
	dd the forseid Sekford	
85.56	By the Lord Howard Lord Chaumberlen A Juell of golde being A payre of Brasselettes of fyve Rowes of perlles & foure perlles in eache Space forty eyght smaull Dyamondes and forty eyght smaull Rubyes	
	dd the forseid Barrones Howard	

85.57 By the Lorde of Hounsdon parte of A Forparte of A kertle of Satten of
sundery Colores Imbraudered with the Twelve Synnes of venis golde
Sylver & Sylke of sundery Colores vnmade

85.58 By the Lorde Cobham A Round Kertle of white Satten cut & Ruft vp with
A smaull passamayn of venis golde and Sylke

dd the forseid Raulfe hope

85.59 By the Lorde Darcy of Chytchey in golde . . . . x li

85.60 By the Lorde Shandoyes in golde and Sylver . . . . vj li xiij s iiij d

85.61 By the Lorde Northe in golde . . . . x li

85.62 By the Lorde Coumpton in golde . . . . x li

85.63 By the Lorde Norres in golde . . . . x li

dd the forseid Sakeford

85.64 By the Lorde Wynsovr A Juell of golde Fasshioned lyke A Syckle and A
wheate sheaffe the Syckle garnished one the one syde with verry smaull
sparkes of Rubyes and Dyamondes

dd the forseid Barrones howard

85.65 By the Lorde Loumley in golde. . . . . x li

85.66 By the Lorde Wharton in golde . . . . x li

dd the forseid Sekford

85.67 By the Lorde Rych A Forparte of A Kertle of whyte Satten Rychly
Imbraudered

dd the forseid Raufe hope

85.68 By the Lorde Taulbott one Coup of Cristaull with A Couer garn with
golde & sett with Smaull Rubyes and Opalles the Cristaull being Canted
Long wayes poz . . . . xiij oz qrt di

dd John Astley esquire Mr the Juells and plate

Baronesses

85.69 By the Barrones Bourghley A Juell of golde Lyke a cravne the boddy garn
with Opalles standing vppon thre smaull Rubyes and too smaull
Dyamondes And A verry smaull perlle pendantt

85.70 By the Barrones Howard A wast gerdle of blacke vellatt with Buckles
Studdes and pendantes of golde garn with too Senckefoyll of smaull
Dyamondes & too sparkes of Dyamondes A pece att the ende of the
pendanttes

dd the Barrones howard

85.71 By the Barrones Cobham A Doblett of white satten Cout ruft Vp &
stryped ouer Twhart with A smaull passamayn lace of venis gold and
Sylke

85.72 By the Barrones Hounsdon parte of A forparte of A Kertle of Satten of
Dyvers Colores embravdered with the twelve synnes with golde Sylver &
Sylke of Dyvers Colores vnmade

85.73 By the Barrones Dakers A Kertle of white Satten Cout all ouer & stryped
ouer Twhart with A plate Lace of venis golde and Lyned with blacke
Taffatay

85.74   By the Barrones Loumley A Doblett of white Satten slytely enbraudered
      with sundery flowers And Draune oute with Lavune
                                    dd the forseid Raulfe hope

85.75   By the Barrones Shandoyes Dowger too pillowbers of Camberycke wrought
      all ouer with blacke Sylke and tooe swete bagges of Carnation Taffatay
                                       dd Mrs Scudmoure

85.76   By the Barrones Shandoyes Junior in golde and Sylver . . . . vj li xiij s iiij d

85.77   By the Barrones St John Blettzo in golde . . . . x li
                                       dd the said Sackforde

85.78   By the Barrones Paggett Cary A nyght goune of pechcolored Satten
      prynted and Rased lyke havlfe mounes edged with A smaull plate
      Lasse of venis golde and Sylver Furred with myniver and Fased with
      Orringcolored sylke Fryng
                                       dd the forseid Raulfe hope

85.79   By the Barrones Chany A bodkyn of golde with A pendantt of golde garn
      with meane Rubyes and thre meane perlles pendantt
                                dd the forseid Barrones howard

85.80   By the Barrones Wharton A skimskyn of Lether enbraudered all ouer &
      Furred with Sables
                                           dd Mrs Carre

85.81   By the Barrones Barkele in golde . . . . x li

85.82   By the Barrones Norres in golde. . . . . x li
                                       dd the forseid Sekeforde

85.83   By the Barrones Morley A Cusshion Cloth & A Forparte of Lavune
      Covtworke with An Edgge of Boune Lace of white Thredde
                                    dd to Mrs Skydmoure

85.84   By the Barrones Rych Dowger in gold . . . . x li
                                       dd the forseid Sekeford

85.85   By the Barrones Bourrowes Junior A Lapcote the oune syde here Coler
      the other syde Ashe Coler Frynged sylke edged with A plate Lasse of
      venis gold and Sylver & foure buttens of Lyke gold and Sylver
                                         dd Ralfe hope

85.86   By the Barrones Howard wyfe to the Lord Thomas A Pettycoate of
      Carnation Cloth of Tynsell prynted with A brode Border of Crymson
      Satten embraudered with sundery devises
                                       dd the forseid Raulfe hope

85.87   By the Barrones Croumwell A Shadowe of Sylke and Sede perlles
                                       dd Mrs Skydmore

85.88   By the Barrones Taulbott vidow A Mantle or Valle of Lavune Coutworke
      Lyke haulfe mounes
                                       dd the forseid Raulfe hope

Ladies

85.89   By the Lady Mary Seymer A Shadow of venis golde and sede perlles

85.90   By the Lady Elizabeth Seymer foure handkerchers of holland wrought with
      sylke of sundery Colers

85.91   By the Lady Sydney A wastcoate or Dublett of Laune wrought with
Dyvers Flowers and Leves of blacke sylke venis golde and Sylver

85.92   By the Lady Catheryn Counstable too Smokes of Fynne Holland wrought
with Blacke sylke

dd the forseid Mrs Skydmore

85.93   By the Lady Stafford A payre of Brasselettes of golde Conteyning eyght
peses of Aggatt and eyght peses of Mother of perlles

dd the Barrones Howard

85.94   By the Lady Waullsingham An attyre of white Lavune with A Shaddow
garn with sede perlles

dd Mrs Skydmore

85.95   By the Lady Drury A Doublett of Cloth of Sylver Imbraudered with Oken
Leves of blacke Sypers

dd to Raulfe hope

85.96   By the Lady Carow A payre of Pyllowberes of Fynne Holland wrought
with blacke Sylke

dd to Mrs Skydmore

85.97   By the Lady Hennage A Hat of Tauny Bever with A bande of venis golde
& A white Fether

dd to Ravlfe hope

85.98   By the Lady Cheake A Skarffe of blacke sylke knyt worke cut open &
floryshed with venis golde

dd to Mrs Carr

85.99   By the Lady Layton A Skimskyn of Murray vellatt enbraudered with
Peskodes and Flowers of venis golde & Sylver Lyned with Frynge of
Orring Colored Sylke / More too payre of writing Tables covered with
vellatt with too Clapses of Sylver Allso a Fanne of Dyvers Colored fethers
And too fannes of paper

dd all to Mrs Carr saving the fanne of fethers
& that delivered to Raulf hope

85.100 By the Lady Pavlett in golde . . . . v li

dd to the forsaid henry Sekeford

85.101 By the Lady Jarrett A Fan of Fethers white and Carnation with A handle
of golde

dd to Rauf hope

85.102 By the Lady Willowbye A Skarffe of white Coutworke

dd to Mrs Carr

85.103 By the Lady Gressam in golde . . . . x li

dd to henry Sekeford

85.104 By the Lady Souche A Skarffe of white Laune Coutworke

dd to Mrs Carr

85.105 By the Lady Barkeley A Smoke of Fynne holland wrought with blacke Sylke

dd Mrs Skydmore

85.106 By the Lady Ratcleffe A Skarffe of Laune Coutworke floryshed with
Sylver edged with Sylke

dd Mrs Carr

85.107   By the Lady Frogmorton two Cusshions of Crymson Cloth of golde lyned
with Crymson Satten Frynged and buttened with Crymson sylke and
golde
dd to Robert Cotton yeoman of the Guardrop

Knightes

85.108   By Sir Fraunses Knolles knight Threasorer of the Housseholde in golde . . . x li
85.109   By Sir Jaymes A Croftes knight Comptroler of the Same in golde . . . . x li
dd henry Sekeford

85.110   By Sir Xpofer Hatton knight vice chaumberlen An vpper and Nether
Abyllementtes of golde the vpper Abylyment Conteyning A Leven
peses syx of them Lyke harttes the other fyve Crounes Imperiall garn
with sparkes of Rubies Dyamondes & perles / The Nether Conteyning
seventene peses eyght of them Synckes of perlles and too sparkes of
Dyamondes the other nynne peses sett with Roses of sparkes of
Dyamondes And smaull Rubies in the Myddest of ether of them
dd the Barr[ones] howard

85.111   By Sir Fraunses Waullsingham knight prynsaipall Secritory A French
goune of Russett Satten Floryshed with Leves of Sylver bound A boute
with A passamayn of venis golde with pendante Sleves Lyned with
Cloth of Sylver & A payre of wering Sleves of Cloth of Sylver Cutt in
Risinges paynnes of Cloth of golde and Sylver
dd to Raulfe hope

85.112   By Sir Ravlfe Sadler knight Chavnseler of the Duchy in golde . . . . xv li
85.113   By Sir Waulter Myldmay knight Chaunseler of the Exchequer in golde. . . . . x li
dd the forseid Sekeford

85.114   By Sir Thomas Hennag knight Threasorer of the Chavmber A bodkyn of
golde with A pendantt Lyke A brode Arrow hed garn with smaull
Sparckes of Dyamondes and A verry meane perlle pendantt
dd the Barr[ones] howard

85.115   By Sir Gylbertt Jarrett knight Mr of the Rolles in golde . . . . xx li
85.116   By Sir Owyn Hopton knight Lyvetenaunte of the Tower in golde . . . . x li
dd to the said Sekeford

85.117   By Sir Henry Lee knight A bodkyn of golde with A pendantt being A
Hunters hornne And A Bucke in the Myddest of yt / garn with
sparckes of Dyamondes & Opalles one the one syde with A verry Lyttle
mene perlle pendantt
dd to the Barr[ones] howard

85.118   By Sir Wylliam Drury Knight A payre of sleves of Camberycke vnmade
wrought with blacke Sylke & venis golde with vine Leves roses &
pomidgarnettes
dd to Mrs Skydmore

85.119   By Sir Edward Clere knight in golde. . . . . x li
dd to henry Sekeford

85.120   By Sir Thomas Layton knight A french goune of Herecolored Cloth of
Sylver with workes edged with A plate Lace of venis golde the Sleves

Lyned with Cloth of Sylver prynted with A payre of sleves of Cloth of Golde Cut in Rysing paynnes

> dd to Raf hope

85.121   By Sir Henry Croumwell knight in golde . . . . x li

> dd the said Sackeford

85.122   By Master Absalon Clerke of the Clossett A boke of Cristian exersyes covered with Crymsonn vellatt embraundered with venis golde and Sylver

> dd Mrs Blanch parry

Gentlewomen

85.123   By Mrs Blanche A Parry A wast Gerdle of blacke vellatt buckles pendant and Studdes golde thirty one buttens of golde and verry Smaull perlles betwene

> dd to the Barrones howard

85.124   By Mrs Fraunses Howard thelder A Forparte of A Kertle of Laune Coutworke Floryshed with golde

85.125   By Mrs Fraunses Howard Junior A Covering of A Doblett of white Lavnne Coutworke

85.126   By Mrs Southwell A Forparte of A kertle of Lavne Cout worke floryshed with plate and Spangles of Sylver

> dd to Rauf hope

85.127   By Mrs Skroupe A Nyte Coyffe & Forhedcloth of Camberycke wrought with venis golde and blacke Sylke More A Cusshioncloth of Lavnne Cout worke

> dd to Mrs Skydmore

85.128   By Mrs Broucke A Skarffe of Laune Coutworke with plates of Sylver and Owes

> dd to Mrs Carr

85.129   By Mrs West A Doblett of blacke Satten enbraudered with Fethers of golde and Sylver and smaull sede perlles

> dd to Rauf hope

85.130   By Mrs Edmoundes A Skarffe of white knytworke Floryshed with venis Sylver and Spangles

> dd to Mrs Carr

85.131   By Mrs Skydmour A Goune of blacke Tufte Taffataye edged Round A boute with A lace buttens and Louppes of venis gold and blacke Sylke

85.132   By Mrs Dalle A Dublett and Forparte of A kertle of cloth of Sylver with a passamayn of golde Lace

85.133   By Mrs woulley A Savegard of blacke wrought vellatt the ground Sylver garnished A Fore with buttens and Loppes of Venis Sylver

85.134   By Mrs Carre A Round Kertle of white satten prynted with Skallop Shelles & bag pyppes edged with too plate Lases of venis golde

> dd to Rauf hope

85.135　By Mrs Gyfford A handkercher of Laune wrought with gold and sylke of
　　　　sundery Colers and more A swette bagge of white Satten enbravdered
　　　　with venis golde sylver and sylke of sundery Colers

85.136　By Mrs Lyfelde syx handkerchers edged with coutworke & A smaull bag
　　　　of Carnation Taffatay
　　　　　　　　　　　　　　　　　　　　　　　　　　　　dd to Mrs Skydmor

85.137　By Mrs Dygby A Forparte of Laune Coutworke
　　　　　　　　　　　　　　　　　　　　　　　　　　　　dd to Rauf hope

85.138　By Mrs Jhonnes A ruff vnmade of Laune Coutworke
　　　　　　　　　　　　　　　　　　　　　　　　　　　dd Mrs Janne Bryselles

85.139　By Mrs Tovnnesend A Skarffe of Lavnne Coutworke Lyned with
　　　　Carnation Sersseonett and edged with A brode passamayn Lace of venis
　　　　Sylver
　　　　　　　　　　　　　　　　　　　　　　　　　　　　dd Mrs Carr

85.140　By Mrs Snowe Twelve Handkerchers of Camberycke edged with A bone
　　　　Lace of venis golde and Sylver

85.141　By Mrs Cave A Nyte Raylle of Camberyke wrought with black sylke

85.142　By Mrs Elizabeth Frogmorton A nytecoyfe and A Nyte Raylle of fynne
　　　　holland wrought with blacke Sylke
　　　　　　　　　　　　　　　　　　　　　　　　　　　　dd to Mrs Skydmor

85.143　By Mrs Sackeford A bodkyn of golde with A pendant Emerod with A
　　　　smaull perlle ther att
　　　　　　　　　　　　　　　　　　　　　　　　　　dd to the Bar[ones] Howard

85.144　By Mrs Winkefeld A Nytecoyffe of Camberycke Floryshed with Sylver
　　　　and blacke Sylke and smaull buttens of golde and sede perles one the
　　　　Endes

85.145　By Mrs Cromer A payre of pyllowberes of Camberycke fayre wrought with
　　　　venis golde sylver & Sylke

85.146　By Mrs Noote syx hankerchers of Camberycke edged with A passamayn of
　　　　golde and Sylver
　　　　　　　　　　　　　　　　　　　　　　　　　　　　dd to Mrs Skydmor

85.147　By Mrs Newton A Forparte of Orringcolored Satten Coutt white stryped
　　　　ouer wharte with a smaull Lace of venis Sylver

85.148　By Mrs Janne Brysselles A Doblett of white Satten Cout bound Aboute
　　　　with A Sylver Lace
　　　　　　　　　　　　　　　　　　　　　　　　　　　　dd to Rauf hope

85.149　By Mrs Crouxson A valle and A Shadow of white Nettworke

85.150　By Mrs Huggaynnes Six Handkerchers of Camberycke wrought with
　　　　blacke Sylke edged with A passamayn of venis golde and Sylver

85.151　By Mrs Haynnes too Pyllowberes of Laune wrought with Flowers of
　　　　blacke sylke

85.152　By Mrs Tomysen the Dwarffe A Fayre handkercher of Lavnne bordred
　　　　Aboute with Coutt worke of sundery sylke

85.153　By Mrs Smythsonn A Nytecoyffe of Lavnne wrought with blacke sylke
　　　　and Syluer

85.154　By Mrs Twyst A payre of sleves of Camberycke wrought with blacke Sylke

85.155   By Mrs Morgayne too boxses the one of Abrycockes the other Sytheron
          Ryndes Condyte
85.156   By [blank] Gyllam the Frow A Quayfe and A Forhed Cloth of Lavnne
          Coutworke
                                                            dd to Mrs Skydmore
85.157   By Mrs Allen A Cusshien box Couored with Carnation vellat
                                                            dd to Mrs Carr

Gentlemen

85.158   By Mr Wolley A Duche Cloke of blacke wrought vellatt the ground Sylver
          Doune the Armes with buttens and Loppes of venis Sylver
                                                            dd to Ravf hope
85.159   By Mr Lychfelde too suttes of Ruffes
                                                      dd to Mrs Janne Brysselles
85.160   By Mr Southwell A Skarfe of whitt knytworke stryped with plate of Sylver
          and tvftes of blacke Sylke
                                                            dd to Mrs Carr
85.161   By Mr Dyer A pettycoate of watched Satten Imbraudered all over with
          Knottes of Lace of venis Sylver with tuftes of sylke of Colers
85.162   By Mr John Norris A Doblet of white Satten Imbraudered all over byas
          with Flowers of venis gold Sylver and Sylke
                                                            dd to Ravf hope
85.163   By Mr Basshe in gold . . . . x li
                                                            dd to Henry Sekeford
85.164   By Mr Frogmorton A skimsskyn of Cloth of Sylver Imbraudered all ouer
          with venis golde Sylver and sylke of sundery Colers Furred with Swannes
          Doune
                                                            dd to Mrs Carr
85.165   By Mr Stanhop A Cloke of Peache Colored vellatt Layd with thre brode
          Lases of venis Sylver buttens and Louppes of Lyke Sylver and Lyned
          with Carnation vnshornne vellatt spotted with white
85.166   By Mr Foulke Grevell A Covering for A French goune of Lavnne
          Imbraudered with Fountaynnes Snakes and Swordes all over
85.167   By Mr Skydmour A Forparte of white Knytworke Floryshed thicke with
          Spangles
85.168   By Mr Gyfford A Mantle of blacke knytworke floryshed with Sylver and
          stryped with Lyke lace
85.169   By Mr Bruncker A Savegard of Russett Cloth of Sylver wrought with
          Pomigarnettes and Roses with Buttens and Louppes of venis gold
          and plate Lace
85.170   By Mr Newton A payre of sleves of Orring Colored Satten Cout white
          Stryped ouer wharte with A smaull Lace of venis Sylver
                                                            dd to Ravf hope

82.171   By Mr Smyth Coustomer A boulte of Camberycke More A pece of watched
         Satten floryshed with flowers of Sylver Conteyning in Len[g]th twenty too
         yardes and A havllf

                                        dd Mrs Blaunche Appary the Cambricke
                                                      the Satten to Rafe hope

85.172   By Mr Docter Masters too pottes one grenne Gynger the other Orring
         Flowers

85.173   By Mr Docter Bayly too pottes one grenne Gynger the other Orring
         Flowers

85.174   By Mr Docter Lopus A box of peches and ploumes of Janua

85.175   By Mr Morgaynne A pottycary too boxses the onne of peches genuay the
         other grenne Gynger Canded

85.176   By Mr Hemyngway an other Apottycary A box of lozenges & A pott of
         Conservues

85.177   By Mr Houggaynes A large swette bagge of white Satten Inbraudered
         with Roses of venis golde and grenne Sylke and foure and Twenty
         smaull swette bagges

                                                          dd to Mrs Skydmore

85.178   By Mr Charlles Smyth A smavll Juell of golde being a Hartte Nypped
         with A payre of tongges

                                 gevon by her Matie to Lady Laytons daughter

85.179   By Mr Hues A holle pece of Laune

                                                          dd Mrs Blaunch Parry

85.180   By Mr Carnarvan A Largge Lokyng glasse Sett in wod & Mother of
         perlle paynted

                                                          dd Mrs Skydmor

85.181   By John Smythsonn Mr Cooke A Fayre Marthepaynne with An Oulle in
         the Myddest garn with smaull byrddes aboute yt

                                                                    [blank]

85.182   By John Doudley Sergiant of the Pastery A fayre Pye Orringed

                                                                    [blank]

85.183   By Ambroso Lupo A glas of swette water

                                           with her Matie by Mr Darsey

85.184   By Petruchio Lupo A payre of perfumed gloves

                                                          dd Mrs Carr

85.185   By Petruchio Vbaldino A Pettygrye

                                                          dd Mrs Blanch Parry

85.186   By Marke Antonio Bassino A glas of swette water

                                                          dd Mrs Carr

85.187   By Fraunsisco A box of lutte strynges

                                           with her Matie by Mr Darsey

85.188   By Dunstanne Anes A besert stonne

85.189   By Dethicke Allis Yorke A boke of Armes of the knightes of the Noble
         order of the Garter made sence her Majestyes Reignne

                                                          dd Mrs Blanche Aparre

85.190 By Mountiggue A Smocke all wrought sleves and bodyes with blacke sylke
                                                              dd Mrs Skydmore

85.191 By Marke Antonio A glas of swete water
                                                    with her Matie by Mr Darsey

Summa totalis of all the money gyuen to her
Matie & deliuered vt supra . . . . viij^C xxviij li vij s

Elizabeth R
[sign manual]

                                                              J Ashley
                                                        Examinat[i]o per
                                                              Bristowe
                                                              J Pigeon
                                                              S Fulwell
                                                              N Pigeon

                              Anno Regni
                        Regine Elizabeth xxvij^mo

                        Neweyeares guiftes gyuen by
                        her Matie at her Mannor of
                        Grenewich to these persones
                        whose names hereafter ensue
                        the Fyrste daye of January
                        the Yeare aforesaide

Elizabeth R
[sign manual]

85.192 Too Sir Thomas Broumley knight Lorde Chaunsioler of Ingland in guilt
            plate Marten . . . . xxx oz iij qrt di
85.193 Too the Lorde Burghlygh Lord high Threasorer of Ingland in guilt plate
            Kelle. . . . . xlj oz di qrt
85.194 Too the Lorde Marques of winchester in guilt plate Marten . . . . . . .xxx oz di qrt

Earles

85.195 Too the Erlle of Lecetor Lorde Stuard in guilt plate Mr . . . . Cxxxij oz
85.196 Too the Erlle of Arrundell in guilt plate Mr. . . . . xxx oz di di qrt
85.197 Too the Erlle of Shrewesbury in guilt plate Kelle. . . . . .xxx oz
85.198 Too the Erlle of Darby in guilt plate Mr . . . . xxx oz di di qrt
85.199 Too the Erlle of Sussex in guilt plate K . . . . .xx oz qrt
85.200 Too the Erlle of Lyncolne in guilt plate K . . . . .xx oz iij qrt

85.201	Too the Erlle of Warwicke in guilt plate Mr....................Cvj oz qrt di
85.202	Too the Erlle of Rutland in guilt plate K .... xx oz di qrt
85.203	Too the Erlle of Bedford in guilt plate K ....xxxj oz di
85.204	Too the Erlle of Huntingdonne in guilt plate Mr..................xx oz iij qrt
85.205	Too the Erlle of Penbroke in guilt plate K ....xxx oz qrt
85.206	Too the Erlle of Bathe in guilt plate K .... xxix oz di
85.207	Too the Erlle of Hertff[ord] in guilt plate K .... xxiiij oz di
85.208	Too the Erlle of Coumberland in guilt plate K............... xxx oz iij qrt di
85.209	Too the vicount Mountighu in guilt plate K.................... xix oz di di qrt

Duchesses Marquesses & Countesses

85.210	Too the Duches of Sumersett in guilt plate Mr ....xxv oz
85.211	Too the Lady Marques of Northamton in guilt plate K ....xl oz
85.212	Too the Lady Marques of Wynchester in guilt plate K .... xix oz iij qrt
85.213	Too the countis of Shrewesbury in guilt plate K .... xxxj oz di
85.214	Too the countis of Oxford in guilt plate Mr......................... xx oz
85.215	Too the countis of Huntingtonn in guilt plate Mr .... xxix oz qrt di
85.216	Too the countis of Lincolnne in guilt plate Mr ....l oz di di qrt
85.217	Too the countis of Warwicke in guilt plate Mr.................. lj oz di di qrt
85.218	Too the countis of Sussex Dowger in guilt plate K ....xxiij oz di di qrt
85.219	Too the countis of Sussex Junior in guilt plate K...................... xx oz
85.220	Too the countis of Penbroke Dowger in guilt plate Mr .... xxij oz qrt di
85.221	Too the countis of Penbroke Junior in guilt plate K .... xxij oz
85.222	Too the countis of Bedford in guilt plate K ....l oz di
85.223	Too the countis of Southampton in guilt plate Mr .... xix oz di di qrt
85.224	Too the countis of Coumberland in guilt plate Mr .... xx oz di di qrt
85.225	Too the countes of Rutland in guilt plate K...................... xix oz qrt
85.226	Too the countes of Bathe in guilt plate K......................... xxvij oz
85.227	Too the Vicountis of Mountighu in guilt plate K............... xx oz di di qrt

Busshoppes

85.228	Too the Arche Busshop of Caunterbury in guilt plate K............... xlv oz
85.229	Too the Arche Busshop of Yorke in guilt plate Mr ....xxxviij oz
85.230	Too the Busshop of Durham in guilt plate Mr...............xxxv oz iij qrt di
85.231	Too the Busshop of Loundon in guilte plate K .... xxviij oz iij qrt
85.232	Too the Busshop of Salesbury in guilt plate K.......................xxx oz
85.233	Too the Busshop of winchester in guilt plate Mr .... xix oz
85.234	Too the Busshop of Lyncolne in guilt plate Mr ....xxx oz
85.235	Too the Busshop of Wourster in guilt plate K .... xxix oz iij qrt di
85.236	Too the Busshop of Carlell in guilt plate K ....xv oz iij qrt
85.237	Too the Busshop of Herreforde in guilt plate K..................... xv oz
85.238	Too the Busshop of Peterborow in guilt plate K .... xvj oz di qrt
85.239	Too the Busshop of Chester in guilt plate K .... xv oz
85.240	Too the Busshop of Exetor in guilt plate K .... xv oz di di qrt
85.241	Too the Busshop of Rochester in guilt plate K....................... xv oz

85.242	Too the Busshop of Lychfeld and Couentry in guilt plate mr	xx oz qrt di
85.243	Too the Busshop of St Davyes in guilt plate K	xv oz di qrt
85.244	Too the Busshop of Gloster in guilt plate Mr.	xv oz di qrt
85.245	Too the Busshop of Bathe in guilt plate Mr	xxx oz

Lordes

85.246	Too the Lord of Bourgaveny in guilt plate mr	xj oz qrt di
85.247	Too the Lorde Howard Lord Chavmberlyn in guilt plate Mr & K	Ciij oz qrt di
85.248	Too the Lord of Cobham in guilt plate mr	xj oz
85.249	Too the Lorde Hounsdonn in guilt plate mr	xxx oz
85.250	Too the Lorde Darssy in guilt plate mr	xix oz di di qrt
85.251	Too the Lorde Chandoyes in guilt plate K	xiij oz iij qrt di
85.252	Too the Lorde Northe in guilt plate mr	xx oz di qrt
85.253	Too the Lorde Compton in guilt plate mr.	xviij oz iij qrt di
85.254	Too the Lorde Norres in guilt plate mr	xviij [oz] iij qrt di
85.255	Too the Lorde Winsour in guilt plate mr	xx oz iij qrt di
85.256	Too the Lorde Lovmley in guilt plate K	xx oz di
85.257	Too the Lorde Wharton in guilt plate mr	xx oz di
85.258	Too the Lorde Ryche in guilt plate K	xx oz di di qrt
85.259	Too the Lord Tavlbotte in guilt plat mr poz	xxviij oz iij qrt di

Baronesses

85.260	Too the Barrones Burghlay, in guilt plate mr	xxxij oz
85.261	Too the Barrones Dakers in guilt plate mr	xix oz
85.262	Too the Barrones Cobham in guilt plate mr	lij oz
85.263	Too the Barrones Howard in guilt plate mr	xxv oz
85.264	Too the Barrones Hunsdonn in guilt plate mr	xxx oz di qrt
85.265	Too the Barrones Lovmley in guilt plate mr	xix oz di
85.266	Too the Barrones Shandoyes thelder in guilt plate K	xvj oz qrt di
85.267	Too the Barrones Shandoyes Junior in guilt plate Martyn	xv oz di qrt
85.268	Too the Barrones St John Bletzsow in guilt plate mr	xx oz qrt
85.269	Too the Barrones Paggett Cary in guilt plate K	xxiiij oz di di qrt
85.270	Too the Barrones Chayny in guilt plate mr	xxxv oz iij qrt di
85.271	Too the Barrones Whartonn in guilt plate K	xxj oz
85.272	Too the Barrones Barckeley in guilt plate K	xx oz
85.273	Too the Barrones Tavlbott thelder in guilt plate K	xiiij oz di qrt
85.274	Too the Barrones Norres in guilt plate mr	xix oz di qrt
85.275	Too the Barrones Morley in guilt plate mr	xx oz iij qrt
85.276	Too the Barrones Ryche thelder in guilt plate mr	xix oz di qrt
85.277	Too the Barrones Crovmwell in guilt plate K	xiij oz di di qrt
85.278	Too the Barrones Howard the Lord Thomases wyffe in guilt plate mr	xxij oz
85.279	Too the Barrones Burrowes Junior in guilt plate K	xv oz di

Ladyes

85.280	Too the Lady Mary Seymor wyfe to Mr Rogers in guilt plate K	xij oz qrt
85.281	Too the Lady Eliz Seymor wyfe to Mr Knightley in guilt plate K	xiiij oz qrt
85.282	Too the Lady Catheryn Counstable in guilt plate K	xv oz qrt
85.283	Too the Lady Sydney in guilt plate mr	xxx oz
85.284	Too the Lady Fyezwarren in guilt plate	nill
85.285	Too the Lady Waulsingham in guilt plate mr	xx oz di di qrt
85.286	Too the Lady Stafford in guilt plate K	xxx oz
85.287	Too the Lady Drury in guilt plate K	xvij oz
85.288	Too the Lady Hennage in guilt plate K	xxij oz
85.289	Too the Lady Laytonne in guilt plate mr	xvij oz iij qrt
85.290	Too the Lady Willowby in guilt plate mr	xij oz iij qrt di
85.291	Too the Lady Carowe in guilt plate mr	xxxv oz qrt
85.292	Too the Lady Cheake in guilt plate mr	xxvij oz di qrt
85.293	Too the Lady Pavlett in guilt plate mr	xj oz di
85.294	Too the Lady Jarratt in guilt plate K	xv oz iij qrt di
85.295	Too the Lady Barkeley in guilt plate K	xx oz iij qrt di
85.296	Too the Lady Ratclyeff in guilt plate mr	xij oz di qrt
85.297	Too the Lady Gressam in guilt plate mr	xix oz qrt
85.298	Too the Lady Frogmorton in guilt plate mr	xxj oz
85.299	Too the Lady Souche in guilt plate mr	xij oz di

Knightes

85.300	Too Sir Xpofer Hatton Knight vice chaumberlen in guilt plate K	CCCC oz
85.301	Too Sir Fraunses Knolles Knight Threasorer of the Housseholde in guilt plate	xxiiij oz
85.302	Too Sir Jaymes A Croftes knight Comptroller of the Housseholde in guilt plate K	xxiiij oz di qrt
85.303	Too Sir Fraunses Waulsingham knight principaull Secritory in guilt plate mr	lxiiij oz di
85.304	Too Sir Raulfe Sadler knight Chaunseler of the Duchy in guilt plate K	xxvij oz
85.305	Too Sir Waulter Myldmay knight Chavnseler of thexchaquer in guilt plate K	xxvij oz qrt
85.306	Too Sir Thomas Hennage knight Threasorer of the Chamber in guilt plate K	xlviij oz
85.307	Too Sir Gylbert Jarret knight Mr of the Rolles in guilt plate mr	xxxiiij oz di
85.308	Too Sir Owyn Hoptone knight Lyvetennaunt of the Tower in guilt plate K	xxiij oz iij qrt di
85.309	Too Sir Henry Lee knight in guilt plate K	xxxiiij oz
85.310	Too Sir Wylliam Drury knight in guilt plate mr	xv oz di
85.311	Too Sir Thomas Layton knight in guilt plate K	xxxij oz qrt
85.312	Too Sir Edward Clere knight in guilt plate mr	xx oz qrt
85.313	Too Sir Henry Croumwell knight in guilt plate K	xix oz qrt di

Gentlewomen

85.314	Too Mrs Blanch Parry in guilt plate K	xviij oz
85.315	Too Mrs Franses Howard thelder in guilt plate mr	xvj oz di di qrt
85.316	Too Mrs Fraunses Howard the younger in guilt plate K	xiiij oz iij qrt di
85.317	Too Mrs Skroupe in guilt plate mr	xvj oz
85.318	Too Mrs Southwell in guilt plate mr	xv oz iij qrt
85.319	Too Mrs Broucke in guilt plate K	xv oz di qrt
85.320	Too Mrs Lyfeld in guilt plate mr	x oz
85.321	Too Mrs West in guilt plate mr	xv oz di di qrt
85.322	Too Mrs Dalle in guilt plate K	xxij oz iij qrt di
85.323	Too Mrs Woulley in guilt plate K	xxj oz qrt di
85.324	Too Mrs Edmondes in guilt plate mr	xv oz
85.325	Too Mrs Skydmour in guilt plate K	xvij oz iij qrt di
85.326	Too Mrs Snowe in guilt plate mr	xvij oz
85.327	Too Mrs Gyfforde in guilt plate mr	xvj oz qrt di
85.328	Too Mrs Carre in guilt plate mr	xv oz
85.329	Too Mrs Newton in guilt plate K	xv oz qrt
85.330	Too Mrs Dygby in guilt plate mr	xvj oz qrt di
85.331	Too Townesend in guilt plate K	xvj oz di qrt
85.332	Too Mrs Allen in guilt plate mr	xiiij oz
85.333	Too Mrs Cave in guilt plate K	xiiij oz iij qrt di
85.334	Too Mrs Sackeford in guilt plate K	xxiiij oz
85.335	Too Mrs Winkefelde in guilt plate mr	x oz qrt
85.336	Too Mrs Cromer in guilt plate K	xv oz di
85.337	Too Mrs Jhonnes in guilt plate K	xij oz qrt di
85.338	Too Mrs Frogmorton in guilt plate mr	xv oz qrt di
85.339	Too Mrs Haynnes in guilt plate K	xiiij oz iij qrt
85.340	Too Mrs Havckes all Bryselles in guilt plate mr	xv oz di
85.341	Too Mrs Notte in guilt plate K	x oz iij qrt
85.342	Too Mrs Twyst in guilt plate mr	vij oz
85.343	Too Mrs Houggaynes in guilt plate K	xix oz di qrt
85.344	Too Mrs Tomysen the Dwarfe in guilt plate K	ij oz
85.345	Too Mrs Smythson in guilt plate mr	vij oz
85.346	Too Mrs Crouxsonn in guilt plate K	vj oz
85.347	Too Mrs Morgayn in guilt plate mr	v oz di qrt
85.348	Too Gyllames wyffe the Starcher in guilt plate mr	v oz di qrt

Maydes of honnor

85.349	Too Mrs Catheryn Howard in guilt plate K	x oz iij qrt
85.350	Too Mrs Mary Ratclyeffe in guilt plate mr	x oz iij qrt
85.351	Too Mrs Mackewilliams in guilt plate K	x oz di di qrt
85.352	Too Mrs Trentham in guilt plate mr	x oz di di qrt
85.353	Too Mrs Edgecoum in guilt plate K	x oz iij qrt

| 85.354 | Too Mrs Babtest Mother of the Maydes in guilt plate | xij oz di qrt |
| 85.355 | To Mrs Hopton in guilt plate K | x oz |

85.356

Gentlemen

85.357	Too Mr Absalon Clerke of the Closett in guilt plate K	vij oz di
85.358	Too Mr Woulley in guilt plate mr	xxiiij oz iij qrt di
85.359	Too Mr Southwell in guilt plate mr	xij oz iij qrt
85.360	Too Mr Dyer in guilt plate K	xvj oz qrt
85.361	Too Mr John Norris in guilt plate mr	xxiij qrt
85.362	Too Mr Lychffelde in guilt plate K	xvij oz iij qrt di
85.363	Too Mr Basshe in guilt plate K	xix oz di qrt
85.364	Too Mr Frogmorton in guilt plate K	xij oz di qrt
85.365	Too Mr Gyfford in guilt plate K	xvij oz di qrt
85.366	Too Mr Stanhop in guilt plate K	xvj oz di qrt
85.367	Too Mr Foulke Gryvell in guilt plate K	xxiij oz iij qrt
85.368	Too Mr Skydmour in guilt plate K	xvij oz
85.369	Too Mr Bruncker in guilt plate mr	xx di di qrt
85.370	Too Mr Newton in guilt plate K	xvj oz
85.371	Too Mr Smythe Coustomer in guilt plate K	xv oz
85.372	Too Mr Docter Masters in guilt plate mr	xiiij oz iij qrt di
85.373	Too Mr Docter Bayly in guilt plate mr	xiiij oz
85.374	Too Mr Docter Lopus in guilt plate mr	xiij oz iij qrt
85.375	Too Mr Morgaynne A pottycary in guilt plate mr	vij oz qrt
85.376	Too Mr Hemyngway An other Apottycary in guilt plate K	vij oz
85.377	Too Mr Houggaynnes in guilt plate K	xxx oz di di qrt
85.378	Too Mr Charlles Smyth in guilt plate mr	xvj oz
85.379	Too Mr Huges in guilt plate mr	xiij oz di
85.380	Too Mr Carmarden in guilt plate K	xj oz
85.381	Too Mountighu in guilt plate K	xiij oz
85.382	Too John Smythsonn in guilt plate mr	viij oz
85.383	Too John Dudley in guilt plate mr	vj oz
85.384	Too Dunstone Anes in guilt plate mr	xvj oz iij qrt di
85.385	Too Dethicke all Garter in guilt plate mr	ix oz di qrt
85.386	Too Ambroso Lupo in guilt plate K	v oz di
85.387	Too Petruchio Lupo in guilt plate K	v oz di
85.388	Too Marke Antonio Basino in guilt plate K	v oz di
85.389	Too Petruchio vbaldino in guilt plate K	v oz di
	Too Fraunsisco in guilt plate K	v oz di

Free giftes

| 85.390 | Too John Astelly esquire Mr and Threasorer of the Juelles and plate in guilt plate mr | xviij oz iij qrt di |

85.391 Too Thomas Astelly one of the groumes of the pryvy Chaumber in guilt
plate mr . . . . ix oz

85.392 Too Thomas Knevett an other groume of the same Chavmber in gult
plate mr . . . . ix oz

85.393 Too Edward Cary Lykewyes groum of the same Chavmber in guilt plate
mr. . . . . ix oz

85.394 Too Henry Sackeforde an other groum ther in guilt plate K . . . . ix oz

85.395 Too Wylliam [sic Henry] Myddlemoure Lykewyes groum ther in guilt
plate mr . . . . ix oz

85.396 Too Thomas Goorges Allso groum ther in guilt plate mr . . . . ix oz

85.397 Too John Babtest An other groum ther in guilt plate K . . . . ix oz

85.398 Too Edward Denny Lykewyes groum ther in guilt plate mr. . . . . ix oz

85.399 Too Wylliam Kyllygray An other groume ther in guilt plate K . . . . ix oz

85.400 Too Ravlfe hope yeoman of the Robbes in guilt plate mr . . . . xij oz iij qrt di

85.401 Too Nicholas Bristow Clerke of the Juelles and plate in guilt plate
mr. . . . . x oz qrt di

85.402 Too John Pygeon one of the yeoman of the Juelles and plate in guilt
plate mr . . . . x oz iij qrt di

85.403 Too Steven Fulwell an other yeoman of the saide offyce in guilt plate
. . . . x oz iij qrt di

85.404 Too Nicholas Pygeon groume of the same offyce in guilt plate . . . . x oz iij qrt di

85.405 To Mr Darssy one other groume of the pryvy Chaumber for his gyftes
in Annos xxiiijto xxv^{to} et nvncke xxvij Dicte Regine Eliz in guilt plate
mr poz . . . . xxvij oz

Summa totalis of
all the plate gyuen
as aforesaide. . . . . .iiij^m viij^C ix oz di di qrt

Gyftes gyuen and Delyuered
at Sundry tymes in mannor
and forme followinge
that is to Saye

85.406 First geven by her Majesty and Delyvered the xviij Daye of Aperell 1584
at the Cristening of the Earle of Covmberlandes Childe A Bason and
Eewer gylt bought of Allderman Marten poz . . . . .Cxl oz

85.407 Item geven by her said Matie and Delivered the xxv of Aperell Anno pred
at the Cristening of Mr Southwelles Childe A guilte Covp with A couer
bought of the said Allderman poz . . . . xliij oz qtr

85.408 Item geven by her Matie and Delivered the xxix of Aperell Anno pred
too Mathias Budde A gent sent from Kyng of Denmarke A chaynne of
golde poz—xliij oz di bought of Allderman Marten being of the goodnes
of xxj kar iij graynes iij qtr . . . . xliij oz di golde

85.409 Item geven by her Matie and Delivered the xx of Jhune Anno pred to
John Everard A gent off Allmayn A chayne of golde being of the
goodnes of xxj carats iij graynes bought of Allderman Marten poz
. . . . xj oz ij d wayte golde

85.410 Item geuen by her Matie and Delivered the xj^{th} of August by spetiall
warant at the Cristening of the Lord Thomas Howard of Audly ende
his Childe A guilt bolle with A couer bought of Allderman Marten
poz . . . . xxxvj oz qtr

85.411 Item geven by her Matie and Delivered the xiiij of August by spetiall
warrent at the Cristening of Mr Skroppe his Childe guilt plate bought
of Allderman Marten poz . . . . xlj oz di

85.412 Item geven by her Matie and Delivered the fourth of September to
Guilham Sotherman A gent sent from the Admirall of the Stattes A
chaynne of gold bought of Allderman Marten being of the goodnes
of xxj kar qtr Le graynne. . . . . x oz qtr di

85.413 Item geven by her Matie and and Delivered the xxiiij of December at
the Cristning of the Lord Talbottes Childe A guilt Coup with A
Couer bought of Mr Alderman Marten poz . . . . .xxvij oz iij qrt

85.414 Item geuen by her Matie and Delivered the xxvij of December at the
marriage of Sir Henry Nevelles son and Mr Henry Kyllygreves
Daughter A guilt Coup with A Cover bought of Allderman Marten
poz . . . . xxvj oz iij qtr di

85.415 Item geuen by her Matie and Delivered xxviij of December to the Lorde
of Greyes Ambassator sent from the Kyng of Skottes in guilt plate
bought of Allderman Marten . . . . Cxxxvij oz

85.416 Item geuen by her Matie and Delivered the xxiij Daye of Januarij Anno
pred to Robert Cooke all Clarentious Kyng of Armes by hym to be
carryed and presented as her highnes gyfte too her dere Brother [blank]
French Kyng one wes Chaynne of golde with A George with in A Garter
garn with thre smaull dyamondes and a smaull Ruby hanging at yt
bought of Mr Alderman Marten . . . . viij oz

85.417 Item more geven by her said Matie and Delivered the second of Januarij at
the Cristening of Sir Amias Pavlett his Childe A guilt Bolle with A Cover
bought of the same Allderman Marten poz . . . . xx oz di di qtr

85.418 Item mor geven by her Matie and Delivered the xxvij of Marche at the
Cristeninge of Mr Dygby his Childe A guilt saulte with A Cover
bought of Alderman Marten poz . . . . xx oz di qtr

85.419 Item Mor geven by her Matie and Delivered the vij^th of Maye to An
Imbassitor out of Skotlan Cauled the Justes Clerke in guilt plate of
sundery kyndes bought off Alderman Marten poz . . . . v^c xlv oz

Elizabeth R
[sign manual]

Asteley
Bristow
J Pigeone
Ste Fulwell
N Pigeone
Ex[aminatio] per

Anno Regni Regine Elizabeth
Tricesimo

Newyeares guifts geuen to
her Matie at her heighnes
mannor of Greenewich
by thies persons whose
names do heareafter ensue
the First daie of January
the yeare aforesaide

Elizabeth R
[sign manual]

88.1   By Sir Christopher Hatton knighte Lorde Chauncellour of Englande
one Necklace Conteyning Three fayre Juells of golde like Starres garn
with Dyamondes and Rubies of Sondrie Bignesses wheareof Two
Dyamonds and Two Rubyes bigger then the rest having xxix Rubyes
pendaunt without foyle with Eight triangled peeces of golde garnished
with Sparkes of Rubyes / And having Foure other peeces of goldsmithes
wourke in ech Foure small dyamonds betwene them Two Roses of small
Rubyes with three pendaunts hanging at one of the three fayre Juells
garn with Seaven Rubyes one bigger then the residue and sparkes of
Dyamondes about two of them, and one Bigger Dyamonde in the
middest of the three pendaunts, And CCCiiij^{xx} middle sysed perlls
whereof Seaven pendaunts. And Two Eringes having two garnets
without foyle, and three pearles pendaunt a peace, Also a paire of
Braselettes of lape Lazella pomaundore and small pearles

dd to Mrs Ratcliffe

88.2   By the Lorde Burghleigh lorde heigh Treasor of Englande in golde . . . . xx li
88.3   By the Lorde marques of Wynchester in golde. . . . . xx li
dd to Mr Sackforde one of the groomes of the privie chamber

Earles

88.4   By the Earle of Leycester Lorde Stewarde of her Matie howseholde A
Carkyonett of golde conteyninge xix peeces of letters and Ragged
staves garnished with Dyamondes with one broade peece in the middest
like a Sonne, the Beames garnished with Sparkes of Dyamondes with a
Rubye in the midst theareof cut with her Maties picture, And a Beare
with a Ragged staffe garnished with Sparkes of Dyamondes and Rubyes
hanging theareat
88.5   By the Earl of Essex maister of her Maties horses a Bodkyn of golde with
a fayre flower of golde hanging at it fullie garnished with Dyamondes

having a naked man thearein with Two pendauntes of Dyamondes and
one pearle pendaunt

dd to the saide Mrs Ratcliffe

88.6   By the Earle of Shrewsburye in golde . . . . xx li

88.7   By the Earle of Darbye in golde . . . . xx li

88.8   By the Earle of Sussex in golde. . . . . x li

dd to the said Mr Sackforde

88.9   By the Earle of Warwicke Five Bodkyns of golde garnished at the endes
with small Rubyes and opaulles

dd to the said Mrs Ratlyff

88.10 By the Earle of Huntington in golde . . . . x li

88.11 By the Earle of Rutlande in golde. . . . . x li

dd to the said Mr Sackforde

88.12 By the Earle of Ormound parte of a foreparte of a kertle of white Satten
Imbrothered all over with venus golde and flowers of sonderie sortes

dd to Sir Thomas Gorges

88.13 By the Earle of Bathe in golde . . . . xx li

88.14 By the Earle of Hertff[ord] in golde . . . . x li

dd to the said Mr Sackforde

88.15 By the Earle of Northumberlande a Juell of golde like an Eaelle Speare
through a Harte garnished one the one syde with Sparkes of Dyamondes
and two small pearles pendaunt

dd to her Maties owne hande

88.16 By the Earle of Lincolne in golde . . . . x li

88.17 By the Earle of Pembroke in golde . . . . x li

dd to the said Mr Sackforde

Viscount

88.18 By the viscount Mountague in golde . . . . x li

dd to the said Mr Sackforde

[Marquesses, Countesses]

88.19 By the Lady marques of Northampton one sprigge of Five Toppes all
garnished with pearles of sonderie sortes and Bignesses three of them
set with Sparkes of Rubies with a flower vnderneathe of like pearles
likewies garnisshed with Sparkes of Rubyes

dd to the said Mrs Ratcliffe

88.20 By the Countys of Shrewsburye a gowne of blacke satten prynted faced
and garded rounde aboute with three gardes of Oringe colloured Flushe
and three passamane Laces of venus silver

dd to the said Sir Thomas Gorges

88.21 By the Countys of Huntington in golde . . . . viij li

dd to the said Mr Sackforde

88.22 By the Countys of Oxforde a Bodkyn with a pendaunt of three Opaulles,
Foure Rubyes and two litle Dyamondes triangled pendaunt and one litle
Dyamonde in the middest

368

88.23 By the Countys of Warwicke Two pendauntes of golde for the Eares garn
with Opaulles and Rubyes and one litle Flower of golde like a Starre
garnished with nyne litle Rubyes, Eight small Opaulles Two litle pearles
and one Ragged pearle pendaunt

dd to the said Mrs Ratcliff

88.24 By the Countys of Lincolne widdowe A Peticoate of Sea water greene Satten
Inbrothered all over with Floweres in lillye pottes of venus golde silver and
silke

dd to the said Sir Thomas Gorges

88.25 By the Countys of Lincolne in golde . . . . x li
88.26 By the Countys of Sussex Dowager in golde . . . . x li
88.27 By the Countys of Sussex Iunior in golde. . . . . x li
88.28 By the Countys of Pembroke widdowe in golde. . . . . xij li
88.29 By the Countys of Pembroke junior in golde . . . . x li

dd to the said Mr Sackforde

88.30 By the Countes of Bedforde A peticoate of haerecolloured Satten
Imbrothered all over with leaves of venus golde silver and silke with a
Brode Border Imbrothered with Floweres Byrdes and a fewe pearles
88.31 By the Countys of Cumberlande a peaticote of Carnation Satten
Imbrothered all over with venes golde and silver with a narrowe Border
likewise Imbrothered

dd to the said Sir Tho: Gorges

88.32 By the Countys of Southampton in golde . . . . x li
88.33 By the Countys of Rutlande in golde . . . . x li
88.34 By the Countys of Hertff[ord] in golde. . . . . x li

dd to the said Mr Sackford

88.35 By the Countys of Ormound parte of a foreparte of white Satten
Imbrothered all overwith venus golde and Floweres of sondrie sortes

dd to the said Sir Tho: Gorges

Viscountisse

88.36 By the vicecountes Montague in golde . . . . x li

dd to the said Mr Sackford

Bisshops

88.37 By the Archbisshop of Canterburye in golde . . . . xl li
88.38 By the Archbisshop of Yorke in golde . . . . xxx li
88.39 By the Bisshop of London in golde . . . . xx li
88.40 By the Bisshop of Salisburye in golde. . . . . xx li
88.41 By the Bisshop of Winchester in golde . . . . xx li
88.42 By the Bisshop of Lyncolne in golde . . . . xx li
88.43 By the Bisshop of Worcester in golde . . . . xx li
88.44 By the Bisshop of Bathe in golde . . . . xx li
88.45 By the Bisshop of Norwiche in golde . . . . xx li
88.46 By the Bisshop of Lichfield and Coventrie in golde and silver . . . xiij li vj s viij d
88.47 By the Bisshop of Carlyle in golde . . . . x li

88.48   By the Bisshop of Peterborowe in golde.............................. x li
88.49   By the Bisshop of Chester in golde................................. x li
88.50   By the Bisshop of Excetor in golde................................. x li
88.51   By the Bisshop of Rochester in golde............................... x li
88.52   By the Bisshop of St Davies in golde .... x li
88.53   By the Bisshop of Chichester in golde .... x li
88.54   By the Bisshop of Glocester in golde .... x li
88.55   By the Bisshop of Herreford in golde............................... x li
dd to the said Mr Sackforde

Lords

88.56   By the Lorde Hounsdon Lorde Chamberlein parte of a valle of Lawne
      pynched up Striped with a small passament of venus golde and Owes
      of golde
dd to the saide Sir Tho: Gorges

88.57   By the Lorde Howarde Lorde Admirall a Sea Capp of black velvett
      Imbrothered all over with Shippes and Ankers of ragged pearle of
      sondrie sortes, with a Flower of aggatt with three Rowes of Dyamondes,
      one Rubye in the middest in the Top Foure Dyamondes and a pendaunt
      of a Rundell of a Crosse of small Dyamondes
dd to the saide Mrs Ratcliffe

88.58   By the Lorde Cobham in golde..................................... x li
dd to the said Mr Sackford

88.59   By the Lorde Talbott a foreparte of white satten Imbrothered all over with
      venus golde silver and Carnation silke in Squarres
dd to the said Sir Tho: Gorges

88.60   By the Lorde Darcye in golde .... x li
88.61   By the Lorde Shandoyes in golde .... x li
88.62   By the Lorde Compton in golde .... x li
88.63   By the Lorde Norres in golde .... x li
88.64   By the Lorde Lumley in golde...................................... x li
88.65   By the Lorde Wharton in golde .... x li
88.66   By the Lorde Ryche in golde .... x li
88.67   By the Lorde Buckhurst in golde .... v li
88.68   By the Lorde Northe in golde .... x li
88.69   By the Lorde Windsour in golde.................................... x li
dd to the said Mr Sackforde

88.70   By the Lorde Seymer one Fether of Five sprigges of small pearles and
      blewe bugles with a small Brooche of Lape Lazella
dd to the said Mrs Ratclif

Baronesses

88.71   By the Baronesse Burley one Juell of golde like a Camelion garn with
      Opaulls on bothe sides and with Six litle Rubyes three little pearles
      pendaunt and one pendaunt of three sparkes of Dyamonds
Geven by her Matie to Mr Henry Brooke

88.72　By the Baronesse Hunsdon parte of a valle of Lawne pynched vp striped
　　　　with a small lace of venus golde and Owes

dd to the said Sir Tho: Gorges

88.73　By the Baronesse Howarde one Juell of golde like an Eryingg garnished with
　　　　Sparkes of Dyamondes and Two verie litle pearles pendaunt

dd to the said Mrs Ratcliffe

88.74　By the Baronesse Cobham a Rounde kertill of Carnation Satten striped with
　　　　golde and bounde aboute with a lace of silver

88.75　By the Baronesse Dakers a Peticoate of white and Oringtawny Flusshe
　　　　striped with lace of venus silver over thwarte

88.76　By the Baronesse Lumley a Dublett of Carnation Satten Imbrothered with
　　　　venies golde, silver and silke of Divers cullours

dd to the said Sir Tho: Gorges

88.77　By the Baronesse Shandoyes Knolles one Cheare of wood, the seate, Back
　　　　and Elbowes covered with purple vellatt Imbrothered with Flowers with
　　　　Compartiments with a Foote stoole of the same wourke

dd to Robert Cotton
yeoman of her Maties standinge wardrobe of beddes

88.78　By the Baronesse Shandoyes in golde . . . . x li

88.79　By the Baronesse St John Blettzo vydow in golde . . . . x li

dd to the said Mr Sackforde

88.80　By the Baronesse Paggett Care one peaticoate of Carnation Taffata
　　　　Imbrothered all over with Twists of venus silver and a Dublett of white
　　　　satten cut all over in leaves and lyned with Carnation Flusshe

88.81　By the Baronesse Dudley one Dublett of white Satten cut lyned with
　　　　Carnation plushe

dd to the said Sir Tho: Gorges

88.82　By the Baronesse Chanye a litle juell of golde like a Slynge garnished with
　　　　Sparkes of Rubyes and Dyamondes with two litle pearles pendaunt and a
　　　　small Rubye pendaunt without foyle

dd to the said Mrs Ratcliffe

88.83　By the Baronesse Wharton A Smock of hollande wrought with Blacke
　　　　silke

dd to Mrs Skydmore

88.84　By the Baronesse Buckhurst in golde . . . . v li

88.85　By the Baronesse Barkeley in golde . . . . x li

dd to the said Mr Sackforde

　　　　By the Baronesse Talbot junior one Dublett vnmade of white satten

88.86　Imbrothered all over with venus Golde, Silver and Carnation silke
　　　　in Squares

dd to the said Sir Tho: Gorges

88.87　By the Baronesse Norres in golde . . . . x li

dd to the said Mr Sackforde

88.88　By the Baronesse Rich Junior a foreparte of white clothe of silver prynted
　　　　Imbrothered all over very Fayre with Fourkage

371

88.89 By the Baronesse Talbot vidowe a Cloake of blacke silke netwourke
flourisshed with golde and silver lyned with Strawe colloured Taffata
and Carnation flushe

dd to the said Sir Tho: Gorges

88.90 By the Baronesse Burrowe Two fayre Ruffes of Lawne Cutwourke

dd to Mrs Brysselles

88.91 By the Baronesse Rich vidowe One valle of white cutwourke flourisshed
with silver plate and Foure handkerchers wrought with Blacke silke

dd the vale to Mrs Carr and
dd the handkerchers to Mrs Skydmour

Ladies

88.92 By the Lady Mary Seymer wife to Mr Rogers a faire Bagge of nedlewourke
of silke of Esses of venus silver and a paire of perfumed gloves

dd to the said Mrs Skydmore

88.93 By the Lady Elizabeth Seymer wyfe to Sir Richarde Knighteslie a Skarfe of
Russet silke of networke flourisshed with golde and silver and lyned with
peachecolloured Sarsenet

dd to the said Mrs Carre

88.94 By the Ladye Katherin Counstable a foreparte and a paire of Sleeves of
lawne cutworke flourisshed with silver spangles and Owes

dd to the said Sir Tho: Gorges

88.95 By the Ladye Stafforde a paire of Braselettes of golde conteyning Twelve
peeces with amatestes and Twelve peeces with two pearles in a peece

dd to the said Mrs Ratcliffe

88.96 By the Ladye Walsingham a peticoate of Carnation satten Imbrothered
all over with a plate and purles of golde and a broade Border fayre
Imbrothered

dd to the said Sir Tho: Gorges

88.97 By the Ladye Hennage a waist girdell of Blacke vellat with Buckles and
Studdes of golde garnished with Two Emerodes and foure sparkes of
Rubyes and xxxv small Buttons of golde with one small pearle in a peace

dd to the said Mrs Ratcliffe

88.98 By the Lady Carewe a smocke of Cambricke wrought with blacke silke

dd to the said Mrs Skydmore

88.99 By the Ladye Cheake a valle clothe of lawne Cutworke with silver plates
and Owes

dd to the said Mrs Carre

88.100 By the Ladye Druerye one paire of writing Tables the one side mother of
pearle slightlye garnished with silver and guilt, the other side being a
glasse with a Cutworke over it of like silver and guilt

dd to the said Mrs Ratcliff

88.101 By the Ladye Layton a paire of Sleeves A Basse and a Stomacher of white
Sarsonett Imbrothered with Esse Firmys of venis golde and blacke silke

dd to the said Mrs Skydmore

88.102 By the Ladye Southwell a foreparte of lawne Cutworke with Tuftes of
murrye silke and a [blank] of lawne Cutworke flourisshed with
Silver

dd to the said Mrs Brysselles

88.103 By the Ladye Paulatt in golde . . . . v li

88.104 By the Ladye Jarrad in golde. . . . . x li

dd to the said Mr Sackforde

88.105 By the Ladye Digbye a longe Quisshin of needlewourke coverued with silke
of divers cullours Fringed Buttoned and Tasselled with venus golde and
silver Backed with crymsen satten

dd to Robert Cotton

88.106 By the Ladye Willowbye Sir Fraunces his wife a Quisshin clothe of lawne
Cutwourke flourisshed with venus golde and blacke silke

dd to the said Mrs Skydmore

88.107 By the Ladye Gressham in golde. . . . . x li

dd to the said Mr Sackforde

88.108 By the Ladye Ratcliffe a Covering of a Dublett of lawne Cutwourke with
Tuftes of Carnation silke

dd to the said Sir Tho: Gorges

88.109 By the Ladye Souch a paire of pillowbeares of Cambrick wrought all over
with Blacke silke

dd to the said Mrs Skydamore

88.110 By the Ladye West a foreparte of Carnation Satton

dd to the said Sir Tho: Gorges

88.111 By the Ladye Longe a peticoate of Carnation Taffata Imbrothered with a
broade Border of venus golde silver and silke and all over with a Twist
of like golde

88.112 By the Ladye Harrington one peece of heare colloured vellat Cut
Curryously conteyning . . . . xx yeards

dd to the said Sir Tho: Gorges

88.113 By the Ladye Stafforde vidowe Sir Roberts wife one sweete Bagge of
Satten Imbrothered, one paire of perfumed gloves and one glasse of
sweet water

the Bag delivered to Mrs Skydamore and
the gloves & sweetewater dd to Mrs Carre

Knight

88.114 By Sir Frauncis Knolles Treasoror of the householde in golde . . . . x li

88.115 By Sir James Croftes Comptroller of the same in golde. . . . . x li

dd to the said Mr Sackforde

88.116 By Sir Frauncis Walsingham principall secretarye one pouche of Blacke
vellat garnished with golde on bothe sydes, the one side fullie furnisshed
with Sparkes of Dyamondes Rubyes and Opaulls with a course pearle
pendaunt theareat

88.117   By Sir Thomas Hennage vicechamberlein one pouche of Blacke vellat
garnished on the oneside with Cutwourke like Knotts set with Sparkes of
Rubyes, and in Five places Dyamondes of sondry Bignesses

dd to the said Mrs Ratcliffe

88.118   By Sir Walter Myldmaye Chauncellour of the Exchequior in golde . . . . x li
88.119   By Sir Gilbert Jarrad Mr of the Rolles in golde . . . . xx li
88.120   By Sir Owen Hopton Levetenaunt of the Tower in golde . . . . x li

dd to the said Mr Sackforde

88.121   By Sir Thomas Layton Capitayne of Garnesey one peticoate of white
Sarsonet Imbrothered all over with a Cordaunt of venus golde, and
three narrowe Borders likewise Imbrothered with venus golde and some
blewe silke like flowres

dd to the said Sir Tho: Gorges

88.122   By Sir Henrye Cromwell in golde . . . . x li
88.123   By Sir Edwarde Cleare in golde. . . . . x li

dd to the said Mr Sackforde

88.124   By Sir Thomas Cicill a fayre chayne of Smavllsysed pearles of sundery
bignesses waying with the lace xv oz di di qrt conteyning xxj Rowes each
Rowe conteyning by estimacon . . . . one yeardes poz

With her Matie by Mrs Carr

Chaplyn

88.125   By John Thorneborowe Clerke of the Closset a small Booke covered with
Carnation vellat being Intituled Speculum virtutis

[blank]

Gentlewomen

88.126   By Mrs Blanche Parrye a longe Quisshin of murry clothe of golde Fringed
Buttoned and tasselled with Golde Backed with murry taffata

dd to Robert Cotton

88.127   By Mrs Ratclyffe two Ruffes of lawne Cutwourke
88.128   By Mrs Frauncis Howarde one Rabatue made and an other vnmade of lawne
Cutworke

dd to the said Jane Brisselles

88.129   By Mrs Elizabeth Brooke a skarffe of knitwourke florrisshed

dd to the said Mrs Carre

88.130   By Mrs Edmondes a quisshin clothe of lawne Cutwourke with Tuftes of
Carnation silke

dd to the said Mrs Skydmore

88.131   By Mrs Scudemore parte of a gowne of blacke Tufte Taffata Imbrothered
all over with Owes
88.132   By Mrs Wolley a foreparte of a kertill of blacke stitch clothe Imbrothered all
over with a twist of venus golde and silver layde vppon Tynsell and lyned
with Carnation Taffata

dd to the said Sir Thomas Gorges

88.133 By Mrs Elizabeth Throgmorton a sprigg & pendaunt of venus golde and
          sede pearles
                                                    dd to the said Mrs Ratclif
88.134 By Mrs Newton a Ruffe vnmade of Lawne Cutwourke
                                                    dd to the said Mrs Brissells
88.135 By Mrs Cave a nightrayle of hollande wrought with blacke silke
                                                    dd to the said Mrs Skydmore
88.136 By Mrs Allen a Rabatue Ruffe of lawne Cutwourke
                                                    dd to the said Mrs Brissells
88.137 By Mrs Townesende a Covering for a Dublett of lawne striped with silver
          plate puffed like Rolles
                                                    dd to the said Sir Tho: Gorges
88.138 By Mrs Dalle one foreparte of clothe of silver laide about with a passamaye
          lace of venis gold
                                                    dd to the said Sir Tho: Gorges
88.139 By Mrs Sackforde a Ruffe vnmade of lawne Cutwourke with small Buttons
          of thred
                                                    dd to the said Mrs Brysselles
88.140 By Mrs Wingfielde one Ruffe vnmade of Lawne with sede pearles on the
          edge and a wourke like Waves of blacke silke
                                                    dd to the said Mrs Skydmore
88.141 By Mrs Carre Two staves of Brassell to beate a bed, the endes garnished
          with silver and guilt
88.142 By Mrs Jane Brysselles a longe Cusshin of blacke vellat Imbrothered with
          sondrie Flowres of silke nedlewourke, fringed buttoned and tasselled
          with silke, Backed with purple Taffata
                                                    dd to the said Robert Cotton
88.143 By Mrs Adrian Shelton a small cofer of mother of pearle garnished with
          silver white
                                                    dd to the said Mrs Ratclife
88.144 By Mrs Smithson Two handkerchers and two toothclothes
                                                    dd to the said Mrs Skydmore
88.145 By Mrs Twest a paire of sleeves of lawne wrought with blacke silke and a
          sweete Bagge of Taffata Imbrothered
88.146 By Mrs Cromer a Smocke of holland wrought with blacke silke
88.147 By Mrs Lyfielde Six handkerchers of Cambricke and a sweete bagge
          Imbrothered in some places
                                                    dd to the said Mrs Skydmore
88.148 By Mrs Over a Fan of nedlewourke flowers of sondrie sortes
                                                    dd to the said Mrs Carre
88.149 By Mrs Robynson an Attyre for the hed of Lawne flourisshed with silver
          and Spangels
                                                    dd to the said Mrs Skydmore
88.150 By Mrs Jones Six handkerchers of holland clothe wrought with blacke
          silke
88.151 By Mrs Barley Six handkerchers

88.152 By Mrs Morgayne A Box of Aberycocke
88.153 By Mrs Thomysen a faire handkercher
88.154 By Mrs Katherine West one paire of pillowbeares of Assaye of lawne
        wrought with blacke silke

                                        dd to the said Mrs Skydmore
88.155 By Mrs Guilham als Boune a Ruffe of lawne Cutwourke with a silver plate

                                        dd to the said Mrs Bryssells

Gentlemen

88.156 By Mr Wolley one of her Majesties Secretaries a Peticoate of Sea water
        greene satten Imbrothered all over with knottes and Trees like holly
        Busshes of venus golde silver and silke
88.157 By Mr Dyer one peticoate of white watched and Carnation plushe cut in
        tryangles lozenges / And a Boune lace betweene them of venis golde and
        silver having six broade bone laces on the border of like golde and silver

                                        dd to the said Sir Tho: Gorges
88.158 By Mr Bruncker one nightgowne of hayre collour vellat laced aboute with
        a passamayn lace of Venice golde and silver faced and edged round aboute
        with Carnation plusshe

                                        dd to the said Sir Tho: Gorges
88.159 By Mr Smith Customer one Cofer of vellat Imbrothered with Seade
        pearles

                                        dd to the said Mrs Ratcliffe
88.160 By Mr Garter kinge of Armes a Booke covered with purple vellatt
88.161 By Mr Chidley one Juell of golde with a hande out of Clouds garnished
        with Opaulls and a pen thearein garnisshed with Sparkes of Dyamondes
        and three litle pearles pendaunt

                                        dd to the said Mrs Ratclif
88.162 By Mr Newton a Foreparte of murrye Lawne netwourke Flourisshed all
        over with Venis golde and silver lyned with Strawe collour and white
        Sarsonett

                                        dd to the said Sir Tho: Gorges
88.163 By Mr Stanhoppe a foreparte of a kertle of Lawne Cutwourke striped with
        silver plate and puffed up like Rolls
88.164 By Mr Scudamore parte of a nightgowne of Blacke Tufte Taffata set with
        Owes

                                        dd to the said Sir Tho: Gorges
88.165 By Mr Doctor Masters one pott of greane ginger and an other of Oringe
        Flowres
88.166 By Mr Doctor Baily one pot of greane ginger and and an other of Oringe
        Flowres
88.167 By Mr Doctor Lopus a paire of sweete gloves

                    dd to the said Mrs Skydmore and the gloves to the said Mrs Carre
88.168 By Mr William Broucke a Ball of Awmber wraught over with golde
        Inameled white with a small Emerod pendant without foyle

                                        dd to the said Mrs Ratcliffe

88.169   By Mr Carmardenn a Bodkyn of silver and guilt with a pendaunt of a
       Sallamander of mother of pearlls

                                   Given by her Matie to Mrs Ratcliffe

88.170   By Mr Broucke one longe Robe like a cloke of Ashe colloured satten striped
       with golde lyned with strawe coloured Taffata tufte

                                   dd to the said Sir Tho: Gorges

88.171   By Mr Montague Silkman a smocke of fyne hollande wrought with Blacke
       silke

                                   dd to the said Mrs Skydmore

88.172   By Mr James Huishe lynnen Draper a whole peece of Lawne

                                   dd to the said Mrs Brysselles

88.173   By Mr Morgan Apothycarye one Box of Canded gynger, an other of
       Brunolyon plomes and peaches of Janna

                                   dd to the said Mrs Skidmore

88.174   By Mr John Smithson Mr Cooke a faire marchpayne vppon Foure pynacles

                                       [blank]

88.175   By Mr John Dudley Sargeaunt of the Paystrye a faire Pye Oringed

88.176   By Mr Dunstane Anes a Besert stone

88.177   By Mr Jacomyn xxx glasses for wyne and Beare

                                 dd in to the privey chamber

88.178   By Mr Ambrose two glasses of sweete water

88.179   By Mr Petruchio two Bookes of Italian

                                 dd to Mr Babtest

88.180   By Mr Frauncisco one Box of lute strings

88.181   By Mr Innocent Comy one Box of lute strings

                                 dd to Mathathina

88.182   By Mr Petro Lupo a paire of perfumed gloves

88.183   By Mr Caesar Galiardo a paire of perfumed gloves

                                 dd to the said Mrs Carr

88.184   By Mr Jeremye Bassano two drinking glasses

                                 dd to the said Mr Babtest

88.185   By Mr Hemingway A pott of Peares preserved and A Box of manoscriste
       & Lozenges

                                 dd to the said Mrs Skydamore

J Astley
   Ex[aminatio] per

                                      Bristow
                                      Jh Pigeon
                                 Steven Fulwell
                                      N Pigeon

Anno Regni Regine Elizabeth
Tricesimo—xxx[no]

Newyeares guifts giuen by her
Ma[tie] at her heighnes mannor
of Greenwich To thies persones
whose names do hereafter
ensue the first of January
the yeare aforesaid

Elizabeth R
[sign manual]

88.186 To Sir Christopher Hatton Knight Lorde Chauncellor of Englande in guilt
plate Martin & Kaylle . . . . CCCC oz iij qtr

88.187 To the Lorde Burghley Lorde heigh Treasoror of Englande in guilt plate
M . . . . xl oz

88.188 To the Lorde Marques of Wynchester in guilt plate K . . . . xxix oz iij qtr di

Earles

88.189 To the Earle of Leycestor Lorde Stewarde of her Ma[ties] householde
M . . . . Cxxxij oz

88.190 To the Earle of Essex Mr of the Horses in guilt plate K . . . . .xxx oz qrt di

88.191 To the Earle of Shrewsburye in guilt plate M . . . . xxix oz iij qtr

88.192 To the Earle of Darbye in guilt plate M . . . . xxix oz qrt di

88.193 To the Earle of Sussex in guilt plate K . . . . .xx oz iij qtr

88.194 To the Earle of warwick in guilt plate K . . . . .Cj oz qtr di

88.195 To the Earle of huntington in guilt plate K . . . . xx oz qtr di

88.196 To the Earle of Rutlande in guilt plate M . . . . xix oz iij qtr di

88.197 To the Earle of Bathe in guilt plate K . . . . xxix oz iij qtr

88.198 To the Earle of Hertforde in guilt plate M . . . . xxij oz iij qtr

88.199 To the Earle of northumberland in guilt plate K . . . . xix oz iij qtr

88.200 To the Earle of Lyncolne in guilt plate M . . . . xx oz

88.201 To the Earle of Penbrooke in guilt plate M . . . . .xxx oz

88.202 To the Earle of Ormount in guilt plate M & K . . . . Cxl oz dd qtr

Vicounte

88.203 To the vicount Mountague in guilt plate M . . . . xix oz iij qtr di

Marquesses Countesses

88.204 To the Lady marques of northampton in guilt plate M . . . . xliij oz qtr

88.205 To the Countis of Shrewsburye in guilt plate K . . . . .xxx oz

88.206 To the Countis of huntington in guilt plate K . . . . xxix oz iij qtr

88.207 To the Countis of Oxforde in guilt plate K . . . . xix oz iij qtr

88.208 To the Countis of warwicke in guilt plate m and K . . . . Lv oz di

88.209 To the Countis of Lyncolne vidow in guilt plate K . . . . L oz di qtr

88.210	To the Countis of Lyncolne Junior in guilt plate M	xix oz iij qrt
88.211	To the Countis of Sussex Junior in guilt plate K	xix oz di
88.212	To the Countis of Sussex vidow in guilt plate K	xxj oz
88.213	To the Countis of Penbroke vidow in guilt plate K	xxij oz
88.214	To the Countis of Penbroke Junior in guilt plate M	xx oz
88.215	To the Countys of Bedforde in guilt plate K	L oz di
88.216	To the Countys of Comberlande in guilt plate K	xx oz di
88.217	To the Countys of Southampton in guilt plate K	xix oz qtr
88.218	To the Countys of Rutland in guilt plate K	xx oz qtr di
88.219	To the Countys of Hertforde in guilt plate K	xx oz qtr
88.220	To the Countis of Ormount in guilt plate K	xviij oz di qtr

Vicountes

| 88.221 | To the vicountis mountague in guilt plate M | xix oz di di qtr |

Bysshoppes

88.222	To the Archbisshop of Canterburye in guilt plate M	xliiij oz iij qtr di
88.223	To the Archbisshop of Yorke in guilt plate K	xxxviij oz
88.224	To the Bisshop of london in guilt plate K	xxx oz di di qtr
88.225	To the Bisshop of Salesbury in guilt plate K	xxx oz di
88.226	To the Bisshop of Wynchester in guilt plate K	xxx oz
88.227	To the Bisshop of Lyncolne in guilt plate K	xxx oz
88.228	To the Bisshop of Wourster in guilt plate K	xxix oz di di qtr
88.229	To the Bisshop of Bathe in guilt plate K	xxx oz
88.230	To the Bisshop of norwiche in guilt plate M	xxx oz
88.231	To the Bisshop of Lichfielde and Coventrie in guilt plate M	xxj oz di di qtr
88.232	To the Bisshop of Carlell in guilt plate M	xv oz
88.233	To the Bisshop of Peterborowe in guilt plate M	xv oz
88.234	To the Bisshop of Chester in guilt plate K	xv oz di di qtr
88.235	To the Bisshop of Rochester in guilt plate K	xv oz iij qtr di
88.236	To the Bisshop of Excetor in guilt plate K	xv oz qtr
88.237	To the Bisshop of Saint Davies in guilt plate M	xiiij oz iij qtr
88.238	To the Bisshop of Chichester in guilt plate M	xiiij oz iij qtr
88.239	To the Bisshop of Glocester in guilt plate M	xiiij oz iij qtr
88.240	To the Bisshop of Hereforde in guilt plate K	xiiij oz iij qtr

Lordes

88.241	To the Lorde Hunsdon Lorde Chamberleyn in guilt plate M	xxx oz qtr
88.242	To the Lorde Howard Lorde Admyrall in guilt plate M	Cvj oz
88.243	To the Lorde Cobham in guilt plate K	xxiiij oz
88.244	To the Lorde Talbott in guilt plate K	xx oz di qtr
88.245	To the Lorde Darcye in guilt plate M	xx oz qtr
88.246	To the Lorde Shandoyes in guilt plate M	xviij oz
88.247	To the Lorde Coumpton in guilt plate M	xx oz
88.248	To the Lorde Norres in guilt plate M	xix oz iij qtr di

88.249	To the Lorde Loumley in guilt plate M.....................	xx oz iij qtr di
88.250	To the Lorde wharton in guilt plate K	xviij oz iij qtr
88.251	To the Lorde Rych in guilt plate K	xx oz di qtr
88.252	To the Lorde Northe in guilt plate K	xx oz
88.253	To the Lorde Buckhurst in guilt plate M	xij oz
88.254	To the Lorde windsour in guilt plate M	xix oz di qtr
88.255	To the Lorde Henrye Seymor in guilt plate M	ix oz qtr

Baronesses

88.256	To the Baronesse Burghley in guilt plate K.................	xxx oz
88.257	To the Baronesse Hounsdon in guilt plate M	xxx oz
88.258	To the Baronesse Howarde in guilt plate M	xxv oz
88.259	To the Baronesse Cobham in guilt plate M.................	Lj oz
88.260	To the Baronesse Dakers in guilt plate M..................	xx oz
88.261	To the Baronesse Loumley in guilt plate M	xix oz iij qtr
88.262	To the Baronesse Shandovis Knolles in guilt plate K.......	xviij oz di di qtr
88.263	To the Baronesse Shandoyes in guilt plate K	xviij oz qtr
88.264	To the Baronesse St John Bletzo in guilt plate K	xix oz
88.265	To the Baronesse Pagett Carie in guilt plate K	xxv oz di di qtr
88.266	To the Baronesse Chanye in guilt plate K.................	xxxv oz
88.267	To the Baronesse Dudley in guilt plate M..................	xvij oz di di qtr
88.268	To the Baronesse wharton in guilt plate K	xviij oz di
88.269	To the Baronesse Buckhurst in guilt plate M	xj oz iij qtr
88.270	To the Baronesse Barkeley in guilt plate K................	xx oz di di qtr
88.271	To the Baronesse Talbott in guilt plate M.................	xij oz di di qtr
88.272	To the Baronesse Norres in guilt plate M	xix oz iij qtr
88.273	To the Baronesse Rych vidow in guilt plate K	xx oz
88.274	To the Baronesse Rych Junior in guilt plate M.............	xvij oz iij qtr
88.275	To the Baronesse Burrowe Junior in guilt plate K	xx oz qtr
88.276	To the Baronesse Talbott vidow in guilt plate K	xv oz di di qtr

Ladyes

88.277	To the Lady Mary Seymer wyfe to Mr Rogers in guilt plate M	xiij oz qtr
88.278	To the Lady Elizabeth Seymer wife to Mr Richard Knightly in guilt plate K	xij oz iij qtr di
88.279	To the Lady Catherin Counstable in guilt plate K	xiij oz di di qtr
88.280	To the Lady Stafforde in guilt plate M	xxx oz qtr
88.281	To the Lady walsingham in guilt plate M.....................	xx oz iij qtr di
88.282	To the Lady Carewe in guilt plate M.........................	xxxvj oz di
88.283	To the Lady Cheake in guilt plate M..........................	xxvj oz iij qtr
88.284	To the Lady Druerye in guilt plate M	xvij oz iij qtr
88.285	To the Lady Leighton in guilt plate M	xix oz di qtr
88.286	To the Lady Southwell in guilt plate M	xvj oz di
88.287	To the Lady Paulett in guilt plate M..........................	xj oz di di qtr
88.288	To the Lady Jarrat in guilt plate M	xx oz iij qrt di
88.289	To the Lady Digbye in guilt plate K	xvj oz di

88.290	To the Lady willowbie Sir Frauncis his wife in guilt plate K . . . . xiij oz di
88.291	To the Lady Gressham in guilt plate M . . . . xvij oz di di qtr
88.292	To the Lady Ratcliffe in guilt plate M . . . . xiij oz iij qtr
88.293	To the Lady Souche in guilt plate K . . . . x oz
88.294	To the Lady Longe in guilt plate K . . . . xiiij oz iij qtr di
88.295	To the Lady harrington in guilt plate M . . . . xix oz
88.296	To the Lady West in guilt plate M . . . . xvij oz
88.297	To the Lady Stafforde in guilt plate M . . . . xij oz di qtr

Knights

88.298	To Sir Frauncis Knolles Treasurer of householde in guilt plate K . xxiiij oz iij qtr
88.299	To Sir James Crofte Comptroller of the same in guilt plate K . . . . xxiiij oz
88.300	To Sir Thomas Hennage vicechamberlein in guilt plate K . . . . L oz iij qtr di
88.301	To Sir Frauncis Walsingham principall secretarye in guilt plate K . . . Lxx oz qtr
88.302	To Sir Walter Mildmaye Chauncellour of Eschequer in guilt plate M . . . . xxvij oz di di qtr
88.303	To Sir Gilbert Jarrat Mr of the Rolles in guilt plate K . . . . xxx oz
88.304	To Sir Owyn Hopton Levetenaunt of the Tower in guilt plate K . . . . . . xxij oz qtr
88.305	To Sir Thomas Layton Capitaine of Gavrnsey in guilt plate M . . xxxj oz iij qtr di
88.306	To Sir Henrye Cromwell in guilt plate K . . . . xx oz di
88.307	To Sir Edward Cleare in guilt plate K . . . . xx oz qtr
88.308	To Sir Thomas Cicill in guilt plate M . . . . xxx oz di qtr
88.309	To John Thornneborowe Clarke of the Closset in guilt plate K and M . . . . . vj oz

Gentlewomen

88.310	To Blaunch Parry in guilt plate m and K . . . . xviij oz qtr di
88.311	To Mrs Marye Ratclyffe in guilt plate M . . . . xvj oz di qtr
88.312	To Mrs Frauncis Howarde in guilt plate M . . . . xvj oz
88.313	To Mrs Elizabeth Brooke in guilt plate K . . . . xvj oz iij qtr
88.314	To Mrs Edmondes in guilt plate M . . . . xv oz di qtr
88.315	To Mrs Scudamore in guilt plate K . . . . xvij oz di qtr
88.316	To Mrs wolley in guilt plate M . . . . xx oz di qtr
88.317	To Mrs Elizabeth Throgmorton in guilt plate K . . . . xiiij oz iij qtr
88.318	To Mrs Newton in guilt plate M . . . . xvj oz
88.319	To Mrs Cave in guilt plate K . . . . xiij oz di di qtr
88.320	To Mrs Allen in guilt plate K . . . . xiiij oz qtr di
88.321	To Mrs Townesende in guilt plate M . . . . xvj oz di qtr
88.322	To Mrs Dalle in guilt plate M . . . . xxij oz
88.323	To Mrs Sackford in guilt plate M . . . . xxj oz iij qtr di
88.324	To Mrs wingfielde in guilt plate K . . . . x oz di di qtr
88.325	To Mrs Car in guilt plate K . . . . xiiij oz iij qtr
88.326	To Mrs Jane Brusselles in guilt plate K . . . . xv oz qtr di
88.327	To Mrs Adryan Shelton in guilt plate M . . . . xv oz
88.328	To Mrs Smithson in guilt plate K . . . . vij oz
88.329	To Mrs Twyst in guilt plate K . . . . vij oz qtr di
88.330	To Mrs Cromer in guilt plate M . . . . xv oz di

88.331	To Mrs Ly[c]hfielde in guilt plate K	xj oz iij qtr
88.332	To Mrs Tomysen in guilt plate K	j oz di di qtr
88.333	To Mrs Over in guilt plate K	x oz qtr
88.334	To Mrs Robysen in guilt plate M	iiij oz iij qtr di
88.335	To Mrs Jones in guilt plate K	xij oz iij qtr
88.336	To Mrs Barley in guilt plate K	xiij oz qtr
88.337	To Mrs Morgan in guilt plate M	v oz
88.338	To Mrs Gylham als Boune in guilt plate K	v oz di
88.339	To Mrs Katherin West in guilt plate K	x oz di qtr

Maydes of honor

88.340	To Mrs Katherin Howarde in guilt plate K	x oz di qtr
88.341	To Mrs Margaret Mackewilliams in guilt plate K	x oz
88.342	To Mrs Elizabeth Trentham in guilt plate M	x oz di qtr
88.343	To Mrs Anne Hopton in guilt plate M	x oz qtr
88.344	To Mrs Anne [sic, i.e. Elizabeth] Southwell in guilt plate K	x oz
88.345	To Mrs Elizabeth Candyshe in guilt plate K	x oz iij qtr di
88.346	To Mrs Babtest mother in guilt plate M	xij oz di

Gentilmen

88.347	To Mr Wolley one of her Maties Secretaries in guilt plate M	xxv oz
88.348	To Mr Dyer in guilt plate K	xxj oz iij qtr
88.349	To Mr Bruncker in guilt plate M	xx oz di qtr
88.350	To Mr Smithe Customer in guilt plate K	xv oz di
88.351	To Mr Garter king of Armes in guilt plate K	ix oz iij qtr
88.352	To Mr Chidley in guilt plate M	xix oz qtr
88.353	To Mr Newton in guilt plate M	xv oz qtr
88.354	To Mr Stanhoppe in guilt plate M	xiiij oz iij qtr di
88.355	To Mr Scudamour in guilt plate M	xviij oz di qtr
88.356	To Mr Doctor Masters in guilt plate K	xiiij oz di qtr
88.357	To Mr Doctor Bailie in guilt plate K	xiiij oz qtr di
88.358	To Mr Doctor Lopus in guilt plate K	xiiij oz di qrt
88.359	To Mr Carmarden in guilt plate M	xiiij oz iij qtr di
88.360	To Mr Henry Brooke in guilt plate M	xix oz di di qrt
88.361	To Mr Willyam Brouke in guilt plate M	xvij oz iij qtr
88.362	To Mr Mountague the silkman in guilt plate M	xiij oz
88.363	To Mr James Huishe lynnen draper in guilt plate M	xiij oz qtr
88.364	To Mr Morgane apoticarye in guilt plate M	vij oz
88.365	To Mr Edward Hemingway in guilt plate M	vij oz di
88.366	To Mr John Smithson in guilt plate K	vij oz iij qtr di
88.367	To Mr John Dudley Sargeaunt of the Pastry in guilt plate K	vj oz
88.368	To Mr Dunstane Añes in guilt plate K	xvj oz di
88.369	To Mr Jacomo in guilt plate K	x oz iij qtr
88.370	To Mr Ambrose Lupo in guilt plate K	v oz di
88.371	To Mr Innocent Comy in guilt plate M	v oz di
88.372	To Mr Caesar Galiardo in guilt plate M	v oz di

88.373	To Mr Petruchio Vbaldyno in guilt plate K	v oz di
88.374	To Mr Frauncisco Comis in guilt plate K	v oz di
88.375	To Mr Petro Lupo in guilt plate M	v oz di
88.376	To Mr Jeremye Bassano in guilt plate K	v oz di

Fre guiftes

88.377 To Mr John Astely Mr and Threasoror of her Maties Juelles and plate in guilt plate K . . . . xviij oz iij qtr di

88.378 To Sir Thomas Gorges Groome of her highnes privie Chamber in guilt plate K . . . . ix oz

88.379 To Mr Thomas Astely an other groome etc in guilt plate M . . . . ix oz

88.380 To Mr Henry Sackforde also groome, in guilt plate K . . . . ix oz

88.381 To Mr John Babtest also groome in guilt plate K . . . . ix oz

88.382 To Mr Henry Middlemour in guilt plate M . . . . ix oz

88.383 To Mr William Killygrey in guilt plate K . . . . ix oz

88.384 To Edward Carye in guilt plate M . . . . ix oz

88.385 To Thomas Knevett in guilt plate K . . . . ix oz

88.386 To Edward Darssey in guilt plate K . . . . ix oz

88.387 To Edward Denny in guilt plate K . . . . ix oz

88.388 To Michael Stanhope in guilt plate K . . . . ix oz

88.389 To Ferdynando Richardson in guilt plate K . . . . xij oz di

88.390 To Humfrey Adderly yeoman of the Robes in guilt plate K . . . . . . x oz iij qtr di

88.391 To Nicholas Bristow Clerke of the Jueles in guilt plate M . . . . x oz iij qtr di

88.392 To John Pigeon yeoman of the same in guilt plate M . . . . x oz iij qtr di

88.393 To Steven Fulwell an other yeoman of the same office in guilt plate M . . . . x oz iij qtr di

88.394 To Nicholas Pigeon groome of the saide office in guilt plate K . . . . x oz iij qtr di

Summa total of all the plate / geuen awaye as aforesaide. . .iiij^m vij^C xiiij oz di qtr

Guyftes geuen and deliuered at
sundrie times in manner and
fourme following. That
is to saye

88.395 A Gent of the Duke of Bullenes . . . .
Item A Chayne of Gold borrowed of the lady Cobham and geuen by her Matie to a gentleman of the Duke of Bullens Valued in gold and fation Threscore Poundes . . . . lx li

88.396 Colixtus Sken
Item geuen by her said Matie and deliuered the Fourtenth of June Anno pred to a gent Named Calextus Skene one chaine of golde boute being of the goodnes of xxij kar j gr di poz . . . . xiiij oz ij dwait

88.397   Mounseur Freeman
    Item more geuen by her said Matie and Deliuered the same time to
        Mounseur Freeman one chaine of Golde poz – xj oz d waite being
        of the said Goodnes of xxij kar j gr di bought of the said M
        . . . . xj oz j dwait

88.398   Mr Burgraill
    Item more geuen by her said Matie and Deliuered the xxj^th of June Anno
        pred to a gent of the lowe countrie named Mr Burgraill a chaine of Golde
        poz – xviij oz di ix di thereof being of xxij kar j gr iij qrt and thother ix
        being of xxj kar iij gr di all bought of M . . . . xviij oz di

88.399   Junius
    Item more geuen by her said Matie and Deliuered the first of December
        to a gent of Duke Cassameres named Junius a chaine of golde poz
        xxij oz vj dwaite and Six graines being xxij kar----- bought of the said
        Alderman Martin. . . . . xxij oz vj d vj gr

88.400   Mr Bapteste Daughter
    Item geuen by her said Matie and Deliuered the iiij^th of December at
        the marriage of Mr Baptist groome of the privy chamber his Daughter
        one Bason and Lauer guilt bought of M . . . . iiij^xx v oz di

88.401   To the Lorde Chauncellor
    Item more geuen by her said Matie and Deliuered the iiij^th of January
        Anno pred to Sir Christofer hatton knight lord Chauncellor of
        England One Boll of gold with a couer of the charge of John Astley
        esquire Mr and Threasoror of her highnes Juelles and plate. The same
        geuen to her sayde Matie by Sir Thomas Rivett in progress poz
        . . . . xxxiij oz iij qtr   allouer golde

88.402   To Madam Breuele
    Item more geuen by her said Matie and Deliuered the viijth of January
        aforesaid to Madam Brevell a French lady a Bason and laue guilt
        bought of the said Alderman Martin . . . . Cxxxj oz iij qrt di

88.403   To the Lorde St John Pallat his Childe
    Item more geuen by her said Matie and Deliuered the xxj of January
        Anno pred at the Christning of the lord St John Pallat his childe one
        cup with a couer of siluer and guilt bought of the saide Alderman
        Martin poz . . . . xxvij oz

88.404   To Mr Harington his Childe
    Item more geven by her said Matie and Deliuered the xxij of January
        aforesaide at the christning of Mr Harringtons childe a guilt boll
        with a couer bought of the said Ald M. .xxx oz qtr di

88.405   Sent beyond the Seaes
    Item sent by her said Matie xxj of February Anno pred too Sir Wylliam
        Russell Knighte Lorde gouerner of Vlysshing by hym to be Dyssposed
        According too oure Express Commavndement signyfyed vnto hym by
        oure Letters in thatt behavllfe Fore Chaynes of golde of sundery
        goodnesses bought of the saide Avlderman Marten poz together
        . . . . lxvij oz iij qrt iiij dwayte xx graynes

88.406   A Gentleman off Denmarke
      Item geuen by her said Matie too A gentleman sent from the Kynge
        of Denmark one Chayne of golde bought of the saide Avlderman
        Martin poz . . . . .xlj oz qtr iij dwait

88.407   To a messenger From duke Charles
      Item geuen by her said Matie to a messenger sent from Duke Charles
        brother to the Kyng of Denmarke onne Chayne of golde bought of
        the said Avlderman Martin being of the goodnes of xx caret ij graynes
        d poz xvj oz vij d wayte vj gr . . . . xvj oz vij dwait vj gr

Neweyeares giftes gyuen to the Queenes
Majestie at her highnes Mannour of Richmond
by these personnes whose names doe hereafter
ensue the Firste daye of January the Yeare aforesaide

Elizabeth R
[sign manual]

89.1   By Sir Christofer Hatton Knighte L. Chauncellor of England A Coller of
gold Conteyninge xj peeces whereof iiij made like Scallop shells garn
round aboute with small Diamondes and Rubyes, one pearle pendaunt
and two Rubyes pendaunt without foyle Sixe other longer peeces eche
garnished with vij pearles, v Rubyes of two sortes, sparkes of Diamondes
and two Rubyes pendaunt without foyle, having a bigger peece in the
middest like A scallopp shell, garn with Diamondes and Rubyes of
sundry bignesses, one pearle in the topp, one Rocke Ruby in the middest
having iij fishes pendaunt garn on tho'ne side with sparkes of Diamondes
and two Rubyes pendaunt, without foile And with one peece at eche end
of them garn with two small Rubyes and one pearle / And a paire of
bracelettes of gold Cont xij peeces vj like knottes garn with sparkes of
Diamondes, and vj like knottes garn with sparkes of Rubyes, And two
pearles in a peece and two pearles betwene eche peece

dd to Mrs Ratcliffe

89.2   By the Lorde Burleigh Lord high Treasorer of England in gold . . . . xx li
89.3   By the Lorde marques of winchester in gold . . . . xx li

dd to Mr henry Sackford one of
the groomes of her Majesties pryvie Chamber

Earles

89.4   By the Earle of Shrewsbury in gold . . . . xx li
89.5   By the Earle of Darby in gold. . . . . xx li
89.6   By the Earle of Sussex in gold. . . . . x li
89.7   By the Earle of huntington in gold. . . . . x li
89.8   By the Earle of Bath in gold . . . . xx li

dd to the said Mr Sackford

89.9   By the Earle of Warwick A Carconett of gold Cont xv peeces vij sett with
foure Rubyes and one small Diamond in the middest, the other viij sett
with nyne pearles in a peece sett in gold having a Rowe of small pearles
on thupside, and pendauntes of sparkes of Rubyes oppalls and Ragged
pearles

dd to the said Mrs Ratcliff

89.10   By the Earle of Hertford in golde . . . . x li
89.11   By the Earle of Lincoln in golde . . . . x li
89.12   By the Earle of Southampton in golde . . . . xx li

dd to the said Mr Sackford

89.13   By the Earle of Ormound parte of a petticote of carnation satten
      embrodered with a broade garde or border of Antyques of flowers and
      fyshes of venis gold silver and silke and all over with a twist of venis
      gold

dd to the Robes

89.14   By the Earle of Northumberland One Jewell of gold like a Lampe garnished
      with sparkes of Diamonds and one Oppall
89.15   By the Earle of Cumberland A Jewell of gold like A sacrifice

dd to the said Mrs Ratclife

Vicounte

89.16   By the vicounte Mountague in gold . . . . x li

dd to the said Mr Sackford

Marquesses & Countesses

89.17   By the Lady Marquesse of Northampton A peire of Bracelettes of gold
      Cont xvj peeces iiij enamuled white sett with one pearle in a peece and
      iiij sparkes of Rubyes a peece, the other foure sett with one Dasy and a
      small Ruby in the middest thereof and iij small pearles and viij longe
      peeces betwene them ech sett with one small Diamond and two sparks of
      Rubyes

dd to the said Mrs Ratclife

89.18   By the Countesse of Shrewsbury A safegard with a Jhup or gaskyn Coate
      of haire Cullored satten like flames of fire of gold and garn with buttons
      loupes and lace of venis siluer

dd to the Robes

89.19   By the Countesse of Huntington in gold . . . . .viij li

dd to the said Mr Sackford

89.20   By the Countesse of Warwick A Chayne Conteyning xxij Aggettes slytely
      garnished with gold and xxij bawles of Jheat slytely garn over with seede
      pearels

dd to the said Mrs Ratclife

89.21   By the Countesse of Lyncoln widdowe A longe cloake of murry velvett
      with a border round aboute of a small Cheyne lace of venis siluer and
      two rowes of buttons and lowpes of like siluer furred thorough with
      mynnyover and calloper like myll pykes

dd to the Robes

89.22   By the Countesse of Sussex widdowe in gold . . . . x li
89.23   By the Countesse of Sussex in gold. . . . . x li
89.24   By the Countesse of Penbrok in gold . . . . x li

dd to the said Mr Sackford

89.25 By the Countesse of Bedford two large Candlestickes of Cristall garn with
siluer gilt paynted poz altogether . . . . iiij^{xx} xj oz
Charged upon John Astelly Esq Master of our Juells and Plate

89.26 By the Countesse of Cumberland A peire of braselettes Cont eight peeces
of gold sette with sparkes of Diamondes and Rubyes and knottes or
Rundells of small pearles betwene them threded
dd to the said Mrs Ratclife

89.27 By the Countesse of Southampton in gold. . . . . x li
89.28 By the Countesse of Rutland in gold . . . . x li
89.29 By the Countesse of Hertford in gold. . . . . x li
dd to the said Mr Sackford

89.30 By the Countesse of Ormounte parte of a petticote of Carnacon satten
ymbrodered with a broade garde or border of Antickes of flowers and
fishes of vienis gold siluer and all over with a twist of venis gold
dd to the Robes

89.31 By the Countesse of Bath A Fanne of Swanne Downe with a maze of
greene velvett ymbrodered with seed pearles and a very small Chayne
of siluer gilte and in the middest a border on both sides of seed pearles
sparks of Rubyes and Emerodes and therein a monster of gold the head
and breaste of mother of pearles, And a skarfe of white stitchte Cloth
florished with venis gold siluer and Carnation silke
dd the fanne to the Robes and the skarfe to Mrs Carr

Vicountesse

89.32 By the vicountesse Mountagu in gold. . . . . x li
dd to the said Mr Sackford

Busshopps

89.33 By the Archbusshopp of Caunterbury in gold . . . . .xl li
89.34 By the Busshopp of London in gold. . . . . xx li
89.35 By the Busshopp of Salisbury in gold. . . . . xx li
89.36 By the Busshopp of Winchester in gold . . . . xx li
89.37 By the Busshopp of Lincoln in gold . . . . xx li
89.38 By the Busshopp of Worcester in gold . . . . xx li
89.39 By the Busshopp of Bathe in gold . . . . xx li
89.40 By the Busshopp of Norwich in gold . . . . xx li
89.41 By the Busshopp of Lichfeild and Coventry in gold and siluer . . . xiij li vj s viij d
89.42 By the Busshopp of Carleill in gold . . . . x li
89.43 By the Busshopp of Peterburrowe in gold . . . . .ix li xvij s vj d
89.44 By the Busshopp of Chester in gold . . . . x li
89.45 By the Busshopp of Rochester in gold . . . . x li
89.46 By the Busshopp of Exceter in gold . . . . x li
89.47 By the Busshopp of Ste Davies in gold. . . . . x li
89.48 By the Busshopp of Chichester in gold. . . . . x li
89.49 By the Busshopp of Gloucester in gold . . . . x li

89.50   By the Busshopp of Herreford in gold .... x li
                                                    dd to the said Mr Sackford

Lordes

89.51   By the Lord Hunsdon Lord Chamberleyne the nether skertes of the
            Coveringe of a gowne black stitcht cloth florished with gold and some
            Owes
                                                        dd to the Robes
89.52   By the Lord Howard Lord Admirall a Carconett of gold Cont fyve peeces
            garn with sparkes of Diamoundes foure whereof each a Ruby, foure lesse
            peeces like knottes garn with sparkes of Diamounds viij litle pendauntes
            of Diamoundes without foile, and ix small pearles pendaunt
                                                Delivered to the said Mrs Ratcliff
89.53   By the Lord Cobham in gold .... x li
89.54   By the Lord Darcy of Chichche in gold ....ix li xvij s vj d
89.55   By the Lord Shandoys in gold...................................... x li
89.56   By the Lord Compton in gold...................................... x li
89.57   By the Lord Norris in gold .... x li
89.58   By the Lord Lumley in gold .... x li
89.59   By the Lord Wharton in gold .... x li
89.60   By the Lord Ritch in gold .... x li
89.61   By the Lord Buckhurst in gold .... v li
89.62   By the Lord North in gold .... x li
                                                    dd to the said Mr Sackford
89.63   By the Lord Seymer A Comfett box of mother of pearles garn with gold
            and sett with small sparkes of Rubies
                                                    dd to the said Mrs Ratcliff

Barronesses

89.64   By the Barronesse Burghley a porringer of gold with a cover per oz. .... xxiiij oz
                                                Charged upon John Asteley Esq
89.65   By the Barrones Hunsdon a peire of bodies for the covering of a gowne of
            black sticht cloth florished with gold and some owes
89.66   By the Barronesse Howard a covering of a gowne of black nettwork faire
            florished over with venis gold
89.67   By the Barrones Cobham a petticote of haire cullored Caffa laid with vj
            laces of venis siluer with plate
89.68   By the Barrones Dakers a petticote of white Chamlett striped with siluer
            printed with a border of vj broade bone laces of venis gold and siluer
            plate and striped all over with broade arrowehed wyse with a lesse lace
            of like venis gold and siluer plate
                                                        dd to the Robes
89.69   By the Barrones Lumley a wastecoate of white taffety imbrodered all over
            with a twist of flowers of venis gold siluer and some black silke
                                                        dd to Mrs Skidmore

89.70   By the Barrones Shandowes Knolls a stoole of wood paynted the seate
covered with murry velvet ymbrodered all over with pillers arched of
venis gold siluer and silke
                   Charged upon Roberte Cotton Yeoman of the Wardrobe of bedds

89.71   By the Barrones Shandoyes in gold. . . . . x li

89.72   By the Barronesse Saint John Bletzowe in gold . . . . x li

89.73   By the Barronesse Pagett Cary in gold . . . . x li
                                dd to the said Mr Sackford

89.74   By the Barronesse Dudley two ruffes with rabatines of lawne cut-worke and
one ruff of lawne cutt-work unmade
                                dd to the said Mrs Bonne

89.75   By the Barronesse Cheney a small jewell of gold sett wyth fyve diamounds
of sundry cutts without foyle and three small pearles pendaunt
                             dd to the said Mrs Ratcliffe

89.76   By the Barronesse Wharton in gold . . . . x li

89.77   By the Barronesse Buckhurst in gold . . . . v li

89.78   By the Barronesse Barkeley in gold. . . . . x li

89.79   By the Barronesse Norris in gold . . . . x li

89.80   By the Barronesse Ritch [widow] in gold . . . . x li
                                dd to the said Mr Sackford

89.81   By the Barronesse Sheffield one saddle cloth of black velvett ymbrodered
all over with venis gold with all the furniture belonginge for a saddle
                                   dd to the Stable

89.82   By the Barronesse Rich a fore parte of white nettworke like rundells and
buttons florished with venis gold and owes layde upon purple satten
lined with white sarsonet

89.83   By the Barronesse Talbot widdowe a mantle black stitch cloth florished
and seamed with venis siluer
                                    dd to the Robes

Ladyes

89.84   By the Lady Mary Seymer wife to Mr Rogers A Standitch of wood
Covered with silke needlework garnished with a fewe seede pearles
                                dd to the said Mrs Skidmore

89.85   By the Lady Elizabeth Seymer wife to Sir Richard Knightley A skarfe of
black nettwork florished with siluer and lyned with haire Cullored sarsenett
                                dd to the said Mrs Carre

89.86   By the Lady Katheryn Constable one longe Cushion of black velvett
ymbrodered all over with flowers of silke needleworke of sundry Cullors
and sortes and backed with watchett Damaske
                                dd to the Robert Cotton

89.87   By the Lady Stafford a peire of braselettes of gold Conteyninge xvj peeces
whereof viij enamuled white iiij very small sparkes of Rubyes in a peece
and one Ragged pearle in a peece of eche the other viij enamuled with v
Ragged pearles in a peece
                                dd to the said Mrs Ratcliff

89.88   By the Lady Walsingham one Skimskyn of Cloth of siluer ymbrodered all
         over very faire with beastes fowles and trees of venis gold siluer silke and
         small seed pearles with fyve buttons of seede pearles lyned with Carnation
         plushe a peire of perfumed gloves the covffes ymbrodered with seed pearle
         and lyned with Carnation velvett

                                        dd to the said Mrs Carre

89.89   By the Lady Hennage one shorte Cloke of black Cloth of siluer layde
         round about with A Passamayne before with buttons and lowpes of
         like lace of venis gold and siluer lyned with white plushe

                                            dd to the Robes

89.90   By the Lady Carow one smock of fyne holland about wroughte with black
         silke

                             Delivered to the said Mrs Skidmore

89.91   By the Lady Cheake A foreparte of white nettworke florished with venis
         gold siluer and Carnation silke layde vpon white satten

                                            dd to the Robes

89.92   By the Lady Drewry A Skimskyn of black Cipres florished with venis golde
         and small seed pearles with a border or Rowe of seed pearles with viij
         buttons of gold ech of them iiij small Ragged pearles with a garnet in
         eche of them

                                        dd to the said Mrs Carre

89.93   By the Lady Leyton A wastecote of white sarsnett ymbrodered round
         about with a border of eglantyne flowers and ymbrodered all over with
         a twist of venis gold

                                dd to the said Mrs Skidmore

89.94   By the Lady Southwell A Dooblett of lawne Cutworke florished with
         squares of siluer owes

                                            dd to the Robes

89.95   By the Lady Pawlett in gold . . . . v li

89.96   By the Lady Jarrett in gold . . . . x li

                                      dd to the said Mr Sackford

89.97   By the Lady Digby one Cloke of black silke stitched Cloth florished with
         siluer striped layd vpon haire Cullored taffety lyned with white plushe

89.98   By the Lady Willoughby A foreparte of lawne Cuttwork florished with
         siluer and spangles

                                            dd to the Robes

89.99   By the Lady Scroope a vaile of white knittwork striped with Rowles and
         siluer plate

                                        dd to the said Mrs Carre

89.100   By the Lady Gresham in gold . . . . .ix li xvij s vj d

                                      dd to the said Mr Sackford

89.101   By the Lady Ratcliff A vaile of white stitch Cloth striped florished with
         venis gold siluer & some Owes

                                      dd to the said Mrs Carre

89.102   By the Lady Souche A smock of fyne holland wrought with black silke

                                  dd to the said Mrs Skidmore

89.103   By the Lady weste A Skimskyn of watched satten ymbrodered with knottes
         of venis gold and lyned with Carnation Flushe

89.104   By the Lady Longe A Skimskyn of Cloth of siluer ymbrodered all ouer
         with beastes and Flowers and a woman in the middest lyned with
         Carnation Flushe
                                                         dd to the said Mrs Carre

89.105   By the Lady Harrington A wastecote of lawne faire wroughte with venis
         gold & black silke
                                                         dd to the said Mrs Skidmore

89.106   By the Lady Townesende one large Ruffe of lawne cuttworke Vnmade
                                                         dd to the said Mrs Bonne

Knights

89.107   By Sir Fraunces Knowles Treasorer of the houshold in gold. . . . . x li
89.108   By Sir James Croftes Comptroller of the same in gold . . . . x li
                                                         dd to the said Mr Sackford

89.109   By Sir Frauncis Walsingham principall Secretary A Cloke and A Savegard
         of haire Cullored velvett laide Round aboute and striped Downe Eighte
         and lowpes in the fore qrters of a broade passamayn lace of venis gold
         and siluer plate the Cloke lyned with printed cloth of silver and the
         Savegard lyned with white sarsenett, and a Dooblett of white satten
         cutt ymbrodered all over with Owes of venis gold and striped ouer
         whart [sic] with a passamayn of venis golde and plate
                                                         dd to the Robes

89.110   By Sir Thomas Hennage one Jewell of gold like an Alpha and Omega with
         sparkes of Diamoundes
                                                         dd to the said Mrs Ratcliff

89.111   By Sir Walter Mildemay Chauncellor of thexchequer in gold . . . . x li
89.112   By Sir Gilberte Jarrett Master of the Rowles in gold . . . . xx li
89.113   By Sir Owen Hopton Lievtenaunte of the Tower in gold. . . . . x li
                                                         dd to the said Mr Sackford

89.114   By Sir Thomas Layton Capteine of Garnsey A petticote of white sarsnett
         Imbrodered round about with a broade border like Eglantyne flowers
         and all over ymbrodered with a twist of venis gold and powderings of
         Carnation silke

89.115   By Sir Robert Sydney A Dooblett of white satten embrodered all over
         like Cloudes very faire of Scallopp fashion with flowers and fruites of
         venis gold siluer and silke betwene them
                                                         dd to the Robes

89.116   By Sir Henry Cromwell in gold . . . . x li
89.117   By Sir Edwarde Cleare in gold . . . . x li
                                                         dd to the said Mr Sackford

89.118   By Sir Thomas Cecil A French gowne of black silke nettworke of twoo
         sortes florished with venis gold and lyned with white Chamlett

89.119   By Sir Roberte Southwell A foreparte of lawne Cutwork florished with squares
       with owes

dd to the Robes

89.120   By Sir John Parrett one very small salte of Aggett with a Cover and foote
       gold enamyled garnished with small sparkes of Rubyes and oppalls the
       foote garn with like Rubyes poiz – j oz iij quarters, And two Irishe mantles
       the one murry th'other Russet the one laced with siluer lace and freindge the
       other with gold lace and freindge

the salte Charged upon the said John Asteley Esquire
and the mantles Deliuered to John Whinyard

89.121   By Sir Oratio Pavlavizino one bodkyn of siluer gilte havinge a pendaunt
       Jewell of gold like A shipp garnished with Opaulls sparkes of Diamondes
       and iij small pearles pendaunt

dd to the said Mrs Ratcliff

89.122   By Sir George Cary A Doblett of Copper Damaske siluer turned freindge
       lace wroughte with purle and edged with a passamayn of siluer

dd to the Robes

Chaplyn

89.123   John Thorneborow Clarck of the Closett one small cupp the bowle foote
       and parte of the cover of Aggath garn with gold and sett with small
       Rubyes pearles and litle Oppalls poiz all. . . . . v oz di qtr

Charged on the said John Asteley

Gentlewomen

89.124   By Mrs Blaunch Aparry one long Cushion of tawny cloth of gold backed
       with tawny taffety

dd to the said Mr Robert Cotton

89.125   By Mrs Mary Ratcliff A Jewell of gold sett with a stone without a foyle
       Called Icentabella

dd to her owne hande

89.126   By Mrs Fraunces Howard A skarf of black stitch cloth florished with
       venis gold and siluer

dd to the said Mrs Carre

89.127   By Mrs Elisabeth Brooke A skarf of white sticht cloth striped with black
       silke and silver and florished with silver

dd to the said Mrs Carre

89.128   By Mrs Elisabeth Throgmorton two Ruffes of lawne Cutworke made

dd to the said Mrs Bonne

89.129   By Mrs Edmoundes A Cushencloth of lawne Cutwork like leaves and a
       fewe owes of siluer

dd to the said Mrs Skideamore

89.130   By Mrs Skudeamore parte of a loose gowne of black taffety with a border
       ymbrodered with A Chayne lace of venis gold and tuftes of white silke

89.131   By Mrs Wolley A Doblett of black sticht cloth of two sortes florished with
          venis gold & siluer
                                                                    dd to the Robes

89.132   By Mrs Newton A skarf of black silke network florished with venis gold
          and silver and lyned with haire Cullored sarsenett and two peire of
          wrytinge tables the one Couered with needleworke the other with
          Crimson velvett
                                                            dd to the said Mrs Carre

89.133   By Mrs Allein A Ruff of lawne Cuttwork vnmade
                                                            dd to the said Mrs Bonne

89.134   By Mrs Dale A savegard of Russett satten florished with gold and silver
          with buttons and lowpes Downe before of venis gold and silver and
          bound about with a lace of like gold and silver

89.135   By Mrs Sackford one peece of Carnation grogreyne florished with gold
          Cont nyne yerdes
                                                                    dd to the Robes

89.136   By Mrs Wyngfield a Nighte Raile of Camberick wroughte all over with
          black silke

89.137   By Mrs Carre one sheete of fyne Camberick wroughte all over with
          sundry fowles beastes and wormes of silke of sundry Cullers
                                                         dd to the said Mrs Skidmore

89.138   By Mrs Jane Brizelles A Ruff of Lawne Cuttwork with lilies of like
          Cuttwork sett with very small seed pearles
                                                            dd to the said Mrs Bonne

89.139   By Mrs Vaughan one peire of silke stockinges and a peire of garters of
          white Sypres
                                                         dd to the said Mrs Skidmore

89.140   By Mrs Smithson two handkerchers of holland wroughte with black
          silke

89.141   By Mrs Twist a peire of sleeves of Camberyck wroughte with black
          silke

89.142   By Mrs Cromer A smock of fyne holland and the bodyes and sleeves
          wroughte all over with black silke

89.143   By Mrs Lyfield a sweete bagge all over ymbrodered and vj handkerchers

89.144   By Mrs Huggens xxiiij small sweete bagges of sarsenett of sundry Cullors
          and vj handkerchers of Camberick wroughte with black silke and edged
          with a passamayn of gold
                                                         dd to the said Mrs Skidmore

89.145   By Mrs Over a gerdle of white sipres Imbrodered at both endes with leaves
          of haire Cullored silk of needleworke friendged with venis gold silver and
          silke
                                                            dd to the said Mrs Carre

89.146   By Mrs Jones six handkerchers of Cambrick wroughte with black silke

89.147   By Mrs Robinson a quoyfe and a forehead cloth florished with gold and
          silver

89.148   By Mrs Barley vj handkerchers of Cambrick wroughte with black silke

89.149 By Mrs Morgan two boxes of wood one Cherryes th'other Aberycockes
89.150 By Mrs Tomasen one Handekercher of Cambrick wroughte with black
       silke
89.151 By Mrs West one Attyre of stitched Cloth and haire wroughte in rysing
       puffes

dd to the said Mrs Skidmore

89.152 By Mrs Bowne one ruffe of lawne Cuttwork made vpp

dd to her Maties own hands

Gentlemen

89.153 By Mr Wolley one of her Majesties Secretaries A Round Cloke of black
       Cloth of gold with buttons and lowpes on thinside of venis gold and
       black silke
89.154 By Mr Dyer A petticote of white satten quilted all over with venis gold
       and silver with some plates with iiij borders embrodered with gillyflowers
       and Roses of venis gold and lyned with white sarsenett
89.155 By Mr Bruncker one shorte Cloke of white stitcht Cloth florished all over
       with venis gold siluer and some Carnation silke layde vpon white taffety
       and lyned with white plushe And a skarf of white stitch Cloth and striped
       with venis silver

dd to the Robes saving the Skarfe to Mrs Carre

89.156 By Mr Smith Customer one boult of Camberick and a whole peece of
       lawne
89.157 By Mr Garter king of Armes A booke of Armes of the noble men in
       Henry the Fiftes tyme
89.158 By Mr Newton a bodkyn of siluer gilte with a pendaunt like a Sonne
       enamuled Redd and A moone therein garn with sparkes of Diamoundes
       and iiij very small pearles pendaunt

dd to Mrs Ratcliffe

89.159 By Mr Henry Brooke a petticote of Carnation Capha florished with siluer
       with fyve broade passamayn laces of gold silver and watched silke
89.160 By a Gentleman vnknowne A Fanne of sundry Cullored Fethers with A
       handle of Aggeth garn with silver gilte

dd to the Robes

89.161 By Mr John Stanhop A large bagg of white satten Ymbrodered all over
       with flowers beastes and burdes of venis gold silver and silke

dd to the said Mrs Skidmore

89.162 By Mr Skudamour parte of a loose gowne of black taffety with a border
       Imbrodered with A Chaine lace of venis gold and tuftes of white silke

dd to the Robes

89.163 By Mr Doctor Bayly A pott of greene gynger and a pott of the Ryndes
       of lemons
89.164 By Mr Doctor Gyfford A pott of greene gynger and a pott of the Ryndes
       of lemons

dd to the said Mrs Skidmore

89.165   By Mr Doctor Lopus A peire of perfumed gloves and a peece of white
silke Sypres

dd the gloves to Mrs Carre / the sipres to Mrs Ratcliffe

89.166   By Mr Fynes a longe Cushion of purple satten ymbrodered all over with
Damaske gold plate venis gold and seed pearles of sundry sortes with
Justice in the myddest backed with yellow satten frenged buttoned &
tasselld with venis gold and purple silke

dd to the said Robert Cotton

89.167   By Mr Spillman A small peire of wrytinge tables of glasse garn with siluer
gilte

dd to Mrs Ratliff

89.168   By Mr William Huggens A large sweete bagg of white satten ymbrodered
all over with venis gold silver and silke of sundry Cullors

dd to the said Mrs Skidmore

89.169   By Mr Carr iiij stomachers of velvett trymmed with a passamayn of venis
gold on the toppes And two bells of Jett the clappers aggettes

dd the stomacher to Mrs Skidmore
/the bells to Mrs Ratcliff

89.170   By Mr Mountighu one smock of fyne holland Cloth faire wroughte with
black silke

dd to the said Mrs Skidmore

89.171   By Mr Capteine Crosse A faire large looking glasse sett in a frame Couered
with Crimsen velvett bound with a passamayn lace of venis gold

The glass broken

89.172   By Mr Huishe one whole peece of Lawne

89.173   By Mr Dunston Anys A Beserte stone

dd to the said Mrs Skidmore

89.174   By John Smithson Mr Cooke one faire Marchpayne with Ste George in
the Middest

89.175   By John Dudley Sargeante of the Pastry one faire pye of quinces orringed

[blank]

Summa totalis of the money
gyuen to her Majestie amounteth to . . . . vij^C iiij^{xx} xv li xix s ij d

Elizabeth R
[sign manual]

J Asteley
N Bristowe
J Pigeon
St Fullwell
N Pigeon

[note—A separate piece of vellum was reversed when glued to the main roll.
This piece contains gifts from and to ten 'Gentlemen' participants omitted
from the main roll.]

Anno xxxj Reginae Elizabethae &c

89.176 By Morgan the Apothecary A box of wood with Prunolynn
89.177 By Hemyngewaye the Apothecary A pott of preserved peares and a box of
manus Christi

dd to Mrs Skidmore

89.178 By Jacomy xxiiij Drinkinge glasses
89.179 By Petruchio Vbaldino a booke Covered with vellam of Italian

dd to Mr Baptiste

89.180 By Ambrosio Lupo A glasse of sweete water

dd to Mrs Carre

89.181 By Innocent Comy A boxe of Lute stringes

dd to Mr Richardson

89.182 By Jeromy Bassano two drinkinge glasses

dd to Mr Baptiste

89.183 By Petro Lupo A peire of sweete gloves
89.184 By Josepho Lupo A peire of sweete gloves
89.185 By Caesar Galiardo a peire of sweete gloves

dd to Mrs Carre

J Asteley
ex[aminatio] per
Bristow
Jh Pigeon
Ste Fulwell
N Pigeon

Elizabeth R
[sign manual]

Anno Regni Regine Elizabeth nunc Tricesimo Primo 1588

Neweyeares [Gifts] gyuen by her Majestie at her
Highnes Mannor of Richmond to these
Parsons whose names doe hereafter
ensue the Fyrste of January
the yeare aforesaide

89.186 To Sir Xpofer Hatton knighte Lord Chauncellor of England in gilte plate
Martyn. . . . . .iiij^C oz iij qtr
89.187 To the Lord Burghley Lord High Treasoror of England in gilte plate M . . . xl oz
89.188 To the Lord marques of Wynchester in gilte plate Keele . . . . .xxx oz iij qtr

Earles

89.189	To the Earle of Shrewsbury in guilt plate K	xxx oz di di qtr
89.190	To the Earle of Darby in guilte plate K	xxx oz iij qtr
89.191	To the Earle of Sussex in gilte plate M	xx oz iij qtr
89.192	To the Earle of Huntington in gilte plate M	xx oz iij qtr
89.193	To the Earle of Bath in gilte plate M	xxix oz
89.194	To the Earle of Warwick in guilte plate M	Cij oz qtr
89.195	To the Earle of Hereff in gilte plate K	xx oz di di qtr
89.196	To the Earle of Lincoln in gilte plate K	xx oz iij qtr di
89.197	To the Earle of Penbrok in guilte plate K	xxx oz
89.198	To the Earle of Ormound in guilte plate M and K	Cxl oz di
89.199	To the Earle of Northumberland in gilte plate K	xxix oz di di qtr
89.200	To the Earle of Cumberland in gilte plate M	xxij oz di di qtr

Vicounte

89.201	To the vicounte Mountaghu in gilte plate K	xxj oz qtr

Marquesse and Countesses

89.202	To the Lady Marquesse of Northampton guilte plate M and K	xlij oz
89.203	To the Countesse of Shrewsbury in gilte plate K	xxxj oz
89.204	To the Countesse of Huntington in gilte plate M	xxix oz iij qtr
89.205	To the Countesse of Warwick in gilte plate K	Lvj oz iij qtr
89.206	To the Countesse of Lincoln widdowe in gilte plate M	L oz qtr
89.207	To the Countesse of Sussex [widow] in gilte plate K	xix oz qtr
89.208	To the Countesse of Sussex in gilte plate K	xix oz di di qtr
89.209	To the Countesse of Penbrok in guilte plate K	xix oz iij qtr
89.210	To the Countesse of Bedford in gilte plate K	L oz
89.211	To the Countesse of Cumberland in gilte plate K	xix oz iij qtr
89.212	To the Countesse of Southampton in gilte plate K	xx oz
89.213	To the Countesse of Rutland in gilte plate K	xix oz iij qtr di
89.214	To the Countesse of Hertf[ord] in gilte plate K	xix oz iij qtr di
89.215	To the Countesse of Ormount in gilte plate K	xviij oz iij qtr
89.216	To the Countesse of Bath in gilte plate K	xxv oz qtr

Vicountesse

89.217	To the vicountesse Mountaghu in gilte plate M	xix oz di di qtr

Busshhopps

89.218	To the Archbushopp of Caunterbury in gilte plate M	xlv oz
89.219	To the Bushopp of London in guilte plate K	xxix oz
89.220	To the Bushopp of Salisbury in gilte plate K	xxx oz
89.221	To the Bushopp of Winchester in gilte plate M	xxx oz
89.222	To the Bushopp of Lincoln in gilte plate M	xxx oz
89.223	To the Bushopp of Worcester in gilte plate M and K	xxx oz iij qtr di

89.224	To the Bushopp of Bathe in gilte plate K	xxix oz
89.225	To the Bushopp of Norwich in gilte plate M	xxx oz
89.226	To the Bushopp of Lichfield and Coventry in gilte plate K	xx oz di qtr
89.227	To the Bushopp of Carleill in gilte plate M	xiiij oz iij qtr
89.228	To the Bushopp of Peterborow in gilte plate M	xv oz di di qtr
89.229	To the Bushopp of Chester in gilte plate M	xiiij oz di qtr
89.230	To the Bushopp of Rochester in gilte plate K	xv oz
89.231	To the Bushopp of Exeter in gilte plate M	xiiij oz iij qtr di
89.232	To the Bushopp of Ste Davies in gilte plate M	xiiij oz iij qtr
89.233	To the Bushopp of Chichester in gilte plate M	xiiij oz iij qtr di
89.234	To the Bushopp of Glocester in gilte plate K	xiiij oz qtr
89.235	To the Bushopp of Hereford in gilte plate K	xv oz

Lordes

89.236	To the Lord Hunsdon Lord Chamberleyne in gilte plate K	xxx oz
89.237	To the Lorde Hawarde Lorde Admirall in gilte plate M and K	Ciiij oz iij qtr di
89.238	To the Lord Cobham in guilte plate K	xxiij oz di qtr
89.239	To the Lord Darcey in gilte plate M	xx oz qtr
89.240	To the Lorde Shandoyes in gilte plate M	xx oz qtr
89.241	To the Lord Compton in gilte plate M	xix oz di di qtr
89.242	To the Lord Norris in guilte plate M	xix oz iij qrt di
89.243	To the Lord Lumley in guilte plate K	xix oz
89.244	To the Lord Wharton in guilte plate K	xix oz iij qtr
89.245	To the Lord Rich in gilte plate K	xx oz di qtr
89.246	To the Lord Buckhurste in gilte plate K	xiij oz
89.247	To the Lorde North in gilte plate K	xx oz di
89.248	To the Lorde Seymer in gilte plate M	xxij oz iij qtr

Barronesses

89.249	To the Barrones Burghley in gilte plate K	xxxij oz
89.250	To the Barronesse Hunsdon in gilte plate M and K	xxix oz iij qtr di
89.251	To the Barronesse Howarde in gilte plate M and K	xxv oz qtr di
89.252	To the Barronesse Cobham in gilte plate M	Lij oz
89.253	To the Barronesse Dakers in gilte plate M	xx oz iij qtr
89.254	To the Barronesse Lumley in gilte plate K	xx oz di qtr
89.255	To the Barronesse Shandoyes Knolls in gilte plate K	xviij oz qtr di
89.256	To the Barronesse Shandoys in gilte plate K	xviij oz di di qtr
89.257	To the Barronesse Ste John Bletzo in gilt plate K	xix oz
89.258	To the Barronesse Pagett Cary in gilte plate K	xxiij oz di di qtr
89.259	To the Barronesse Dudley in guilte plate K	xvij oz qtr
89.260	To the Barronesse Cheyny in guilte plate M	xxxv oz iij qtr
89.261	To the Barronesse Wharton in gilte plate K	xx oz
89.262	To the Barrones Buckhurste in gilte plate K	xj oz qtr
89.263	To the Barrones Barkeley in guilte plate K	xx oz qtr di
89.264	To the Barrones Talbott widdow in gilte plate M	xv oz qtr

89.265	To the Barrones Norris in gilte plate M . . . . .xx oz qtr
89.266	To the Barrones Rich widdowe in gilte plate K . . . . xx oz di qtr
89.267	To the Barrones Rich in gilte plate K . . . . xvj oz
89.268	To the Barrones Sheffeild in gilte plate M. . . . . .xxj oz di

Ladies

89.269	To the Lady Mary Seymer wife to Mr Rogers in gilte plate K . . . . xij oz di
89.270	To the Lady Elizabeth Seymer wife to Sir Richard Knightely in gilte
	plate M. . . . . .xiij oz di
89.271	To the Lady Katheryn Constable in guilte plate K . . . . xiiij oz iij qtr
89.272	To the Lady Stafford in gilte plate M . . . . .xxx oz qtr
89.273	To the Lady Walsingham in guilt plate K . . . . xx oz
89.274	To the Lady Hennage in guilt plate M . . . . xxij oz di qtr
89.275	To the Lady Carowe in guilt plate M and K . . . . xxxiiij oz
89.276	To the Lady Cheake in guilte plate K . . . . xxvij oz
89.277	To the Lady Drury in guilte plate M. . . . . xvij oz iij qtr di
89.278	To the Lady Leyton in guilt plate K . . . . xx oz
89.279	To the Lady Southwell in gilte plate M. . . . . xvj oz di
89.280	To the Lady Pawlett in guilt plate K . . . . .xj oz iij qtr
89.281	To the Lady Jarrett in guilt plate K. . . . . xix oz
89.282	To the Lady Digby in guilt plate K . . . . xv oz iij qtr di
89.283	To the Lady Willoughby Sir Frauncis his wife in gilt plate K . . . . .xiij oz
89.284	To the Lady Scroupe in gilte plate K. . . . . xvj oz
89.285	To the Lady Gresham in gilte plate M . . . . xviij oz iij qtr di
89.286	To the Lady Ratcliff in gilte plate K . . . . xiiij oz di di qtr
89.287	To the Lady Souche in gilte plate K . . . . x oz
89.288	To the Lady West in guilt plate M. . . . . xvij oz di di qtr
89.289	To the Lady Longe in guilt plate M . . . . xv oz
89.290	To the Lady Harrington in guilt plate M . . . . xx oz
89.291	To the Lady Townesend in guilt plate M. . . . . xvj oz di qtr

Knightes

89.292	To Sir Frauncis Knolles Threasorer of the Houshold in guilte plate
	K . . . . xxiiij oz di di qtr
89.293	To Sir James Crofte Comptroller of the same in guilt plate K. . . . . xxiiij oz
89.294	To Sir Frauncis Walsingham principall Secretary in guilt plate K . . . Lx oz di qtr
89.295	To Sir Thomas Hennage vicechamberlayne in guilte plate M . . . . L oz di
89.296	To Sir Walter Mildemay Chauncellor of thexchequier in guilt plate K . . xxviij oz
89.297	To Sir Gilberte Jarrett master of the Rowles in guilt plate K. . . . . xxix oz di
89.298	To Sir Owen Hopton Levtennte of the tower in guilt plate M. . . . . xxiij oz
89.299	To Sir Thomas Leyton Capteine of Garnesey in guilt plate K. . . . . xxx oz di
89.300	To Sir Henry Crumwell in guilt plate M. . . . . xx oz
89.301	To Sir Edward Cleare in guilt plate M . . . . xix oz iij qtr di
89.302	To Sir Thomas Cecill in guilt plate M. . . . . .xxx oz qtr di
89.303	To Sir George Cary in guilte plate M . . . . xxviij oz iij qtr di

89.304   To Sir Robert Southwell in guilt plate K. . . . . xv oz di
89.305   To Sir John Parrett in gilte plate M. . . . . xx oz di di qtr
89.306   To Sir Roberte Sydney in guilt plate K . . . . xxiij oz qtr
89.307   To Sir Oratio Paula vizino in guilte plate K . . . . xxiij oz di di qtr
89.308   To John Thorneburrowe Clarck of the Clossett in guilte plate M . . xvij oz di qtr

Gentlewomen

89.309   To Mrs Blanch Aparry in guilte plate M . . . . xvij oz di
89.310   To Mrs Mary Ratcliff in guilte plate M . . . . xviij oz di
89.311   To Mrs Frauncis Howard in guilt plate K . . . . xv oz di qtr
89.312   To Mrs Elizabeth Brooke in guilte plate K . . . . xvj oz di qtr
89.313   To Mrs Elizabeth Throgmorton in guilt plate K. . . . . .xv oz iij qtr
89.314   To Mrs Edmoundes in guilt plate K . . . . xv oz
89.315   To Mrs Scudeamour in guilt plate K . . . . xvij oz di qtr
89.316   To Mrs Wolley in guilt plate M. . . . . xix oz iij qtr di
89.317   To Mrs Newton in guilt plate K . . . . xvj oz
89.318   To Mrs Allein in guilte plate K . . . . xiiij oz iij qtr di
89.319   To Mrs Dale in guilt plate M. . . . . xxij oz
89.320   To Mrs Sackford in guilte plate K. . . . . xxij oz
89.321   To Mrs Winckfield in guilt plate M. . . . . x oz
89.322   To Mrs Carre in guilt plate K . . . . xv oz
89.323   To Mrs Jane Brissells in guilt plate K . . . . xv oz di di qtr
89.324   To Mrs Vaughan in guilt plate K . . . . xiiij oz iij qtr
89.325   To Mrs Smithson in guilt plate M. . . . . vij oz
89.326   To Mrs Twist in guilt plate K . . . . vij oz di
89.327   To Mrs Cromer in guilt plate K . . . . xv oz di qtr
89.328   To Mrs Lyfeyld in guilt plate M . . . . x oz
89.329   To Mrs Huggens in guilt plate K. . . . . xv oz
89.330   To Mrs Over in guilt plate M . . . . ix oz iij qtr
89.331   To Mrs Jones in guilt plate K . . . . x oz
89.332   To Mrs Robinson in guilt plate K . . . . iiij oz di di qtr
89.333   To Mrs Barley in guilt plate M . . . . xij oz
89.334   To Mrs Morgan in guilt plate K . . . . v oz
89.335   To Mrs Tomyson in guilt plate K . . . . iij oz
89.336   To Mrs West in guilt plate K . . . . x oz
89.337   To Mrs Bonne in guilt plate K . . . . v oz iij qtr di

Maides of Honor

89.338   To Mrs Katheryn Howard in guilt plate K. .x oz qtr
89.339   To Mrs Anne Hopton in guilt plate K . . . . x oz qtr di
89.340   To Mrs Trentham in guilt plate M . . . . .x oz qtr
89.341   To Mrs Elizabeth Mackwilliams in guilt plate K . . . . x oz di qtr
89.342   To Mrs Southwell in guilt plate K. . . . . x oz di qtr

| 89.343 | To Mrs Cavendishe in guilte plate K | x oz |
| 89.344 | To Mrs Jones mother of the maides in guilte plate K | xij oz |

Gentlemen

89.345	To Mr Wolley one of her Majesty's secretaries in guilt plate M	xxv oz di qtr
89.346	To Mr Dyer in guilte plate M	xix oz di
89.347	To Mr Bruncker in gilte plate M	xix oz iij qtr di
89.348	To Mr Smith Customer in guilte plate M	xiiij oz di di qtr
89.349	To Mr Garter king of Armes in guilt plate K	ix oz qtr
89.350	To Mr Newton in guilte plate K	xv oz qtr
89.351	To Mr Henry Brooke in guilte plate K	xx oz di
89.352	To A gentleman unknown in gilt plate M	xij oz di
89.353	To Mr Stanhopp in gilte plate M	xiij oz qtr di
89.354	To Mr Skudeamour in guilte plate K	xviij oz qtr
89.355	To Mr Doctor Baylif in gilte plate K	xiiij oz iij qtr
89.356	To Mr Doctor Gyfford in gilte plate M	xiiij oz qtr
89.357	To Mr Doctor Lopus in gilte plate M	xviij oz di di qtr
89.358	To Mr William Huggens in guilte plate K	xv oz
89.359	To Mr Fynes in gilte plate M	xxj oz di
89.360	To Mr Spillman in gilte plate M	x oz qtr
89.361	To Mr Mountaghu in gilte plate K	xiiij oz
89.362	To Mr Huishe in guilte plate M	xiij oz
89.363	To Mr Capteine Crosse in guilte plate M	xviij oz di di qtr
89.364	To Mr Dunston Anis in gilte plate M	xvi oz
89.365	To Mr Carr in gilte plate M	xiiij oz qrt di
89.366	To Mr [blank] Smithson in gilte plate M	viij oz
89.367	To Mr [blank] Dudley in gilte plate M	vj oz

[note—A separate piece of vellum was reversed when glued to the main roll. This piece contains gifts from and to ten 'Gentlemen' participants omitted from the main roll.]

Anno 31st Elizabethae Reginae &c.

89.368	To Morgan the apothecary in gilte plate K	vj oz di
89.369	To Hemingwaye the Apothecary in gilte plate M	vij oz
89.370	To Jacomyn in gilte plate K	v oz di qrt
89.371	To Petruchio Vbaldino in gilte plate K	v oz di
89.372	To Ambrosio Lupo in gilte plate K	v oz di
89.373	To Innocente Comy in gilte plate K	v oz di
89.374	To Jeromy Bassano in gilte plate K	v oz di
89.375	To Petro Lupo in gilte plate K	v oz di

| 89.376 | To Josepho Lupo in gilte plate K . . . . v oz di |
| 89.377 | To Caesar Galiardo in gilte plate K . . . . v oz di |

Elizabeth R
[sign manual]

J Asteley
ex[aminatio] per
Bristow
Jh Pigeon
Ste Fulwell
N Pigeon
[sign manual]

Free Guifts

89.378	To Mr John Asteley Esquier Master and Treasorer of her Majesties Jewells and plate in guilte plate M. . . . . xviij oz iij qtr di
89.379	To Sir Thomas Gorges one of the groomes of her Highnes privie Chamber in gilte plate M. . . . . ix oz
89.380	To Mr Thomas Asteley Esquier also groome of the said Chamber in gilte plate M. . . . . ix oz
89.381	To Mr Henry Sackford also groome in gilte plate K . . . . ix oz
89.382	To Mr Baptest also groome in gilte plate M . . . . ix oz
89.383	To Mr Edward Cary also groome in gilte plate M . . . . ix oz
89.384	To Mr Middlemour also groome in gilte plate M. . . . . ix oz
89.385	To Mr Killygrey also groome in gilte plate K . . . . ix oz
89.386	To Mr Knevett also groome in gilte plate K. . . . . ix oz
89.387	To Mr Darsey also groome in gilte plate M . . . . ix oz
89.388	To Mr Edward Denny also groome in gilte plate M. ix oz
89.389	To Mr Stanhopp also groome in gilte plate M . . . . ix oz
89.390	To Mr Ferdynando Richardson also groome in gilte plate M . . . . ix oz
89.391	To Humfrey Adderley Yeoman of the Roabes in gilte plate M . . . . xij oz
89.392	To Nicholas Bristowe Clerck of the Jewells in gilte plate M . . . . . . x oz iij qtr di
89.393	To John Pigeon Yeoman of the same office in gilte plate M . . . . . . x oz iij qtr di
89.394	To Stephen Fulwell an other Yeoman of the same office in guilte plate M. . . . . x oz iij qtr di
89.395	To Nicholas Pigeon groome of the said office in guilte plate M and K . . . . x oz iij qtr di

Summa totalis of all the plate gyven
away as aforesaid amounteth to . . . . .iiij^m v^C xlj oz iij qtr di
Summa totalis of the plate
gyven as aforesaide cometh to . . . . lxij oz di qrts

Guiftes gyuen by Her Matie and delyuered at
sundry tymes in mannor & Forme followinge
that is to saye

Earle of Ormound

89.396   Gyuen by her said Matie the xxiijth of Aprill Ao xxx^{mo} Regine
Elizabeth &c vnto the Earle of Ormound One George of gold
enamuled white sett with foure Rubyes and sixe opalles of the
Chardge of John Asttley Esquier mr and Treasorer of her highnes
Juells and plate poz . . . . j oz vij d wzt allouer

Item more gyven to the said Earle the Daye and yeare aforesaid One
garter enamuled white havinge ouer the buckell vj Diamondes and
foure Rubyes and on the pendaunte foure Diamoundes and two
Rubyes of the Chardge of the said John Asteley poz
. . . . iij oz iij d wzt allouer

Earle of Essex

89.397   Item gyven by her said Matie the Daye and yeare above written vnto the
Earle of Essex one garter enamuled redd and white having one Rock
Ruby with a pearle pendaunt and vij small Rubyes betwene the lettres
of the Chardge of the said John Asteley poz . . . . iij oz di allouer

Lorde Chauncellor

89.398   Item gyven by her said Matie the said xxiijth of Aprill Ao predco vnto
Sir Xpofer Hatton Knighte Lord Chauncellor of England One George
of gold enamuled white of the chardge as afore poz . . . j oz vj d wzt allouer

Item more to him one garter of gold enamuled white having ouer the
buckell foure Diamondes and one Diamond ouer the pendaunte of the
Chardge of the said John Asteley poz . . . . iij oz ij d wzt allouer

Sir Martyn Shynke

89.399   Item gyven by her said Matie the thurd of June Ao predco vnto Sir
martyn Shinke Knighte parte of A Chaine of gold Rec of Mr Willm
Killegrew of the goodnes of xxj karr two graynes qrt of the said
Chardge poz . . . . Cx oz iij qtr allouer

Mr George

89.400   Item gyven by her said Matie the xjth of June Ao predco vnto Mr
George [blank] servunte to the Kinge of Denmark parte of a Chaine
of gold Rec of mr Thomas Knyvett of the goodnes of xxj karr iij
graynes of the Chardge of the said John Asteley poz . . . . x oz allouer

Sir Richard Knightley his sonne

89.401   Item gyven by her said Matie the xxvth of Septembr Ao predco at
the Christening of Sir Richard Knighteley his sonne one Cupp of
siluer gilte boughte of mr Alderman Martyn poz . . . . xxiij oz iij qtr

89.402 La: Digby

Item gyven by her said Matie the xxj^th of October at the marriadge of the La Digby to Mr Edward Cordall one gilte Cupp with a cover bought of the said Alderman poz . . . . Lx oz di qtr

89.403 The Earle of Ormound his Daughter

Item gyven by her said Matie the xxvij^th of October Ao xxx° predct at the Christeninge of the Earle of Ormound his Daughter one Bason and Ewer gilte poz—Cxix oz iij qtr di and one peire of gilte stoopes poz—Cxxxvj oz qtr boughte of the said Alderman martyn poz all . . . . CCLvj oz di qtr

89.404 Lorde Riche his Childe

Item gyven by her said Matie the xxvj^th of november Ao xxxj^mo Regine Elizabeth at the Christning of the Lord Rich his Childe One Bowle with a Couer of siluer gilte boughte of the said Alderman Martyn poz . . . . Lj oz iij qtr

89.405 Mr Jacob Rastrop

Item gyven by her said Matie the thurd of December Ao predicto vnto Mr Jacob Rastropp of Juteland sent from the Kinge of Denmark parte of a Chaine of gold Rec of the said Thoms Knyvett of the chardg aforesaid poz . . . . xxxiiij oz allouer

89.406 Musshac Keyes [sic Reyz]

Item more gyven by her said Matie and Deliuered the thurd of March Ao predco One Chaine of gold vnto musshac Keyes [sic Reyz] Ambassator from the King of Fesse boughte of the said Alderman poz . . . . xlv oz qtr   j d wzt & vj gr

89.407 John Spillman

Item Deliuered by her Maties Comaundment signified by the La Cobhm vnto John Spilman Jeweller by him to be made into buttons for her Maties [vse to] Chaynes of Esses and knottes of golde with two greate Roses enamuled in the middest of them being of the chardge of said John Asteley poz altogether . . . . lxvj oz iij qtr allouer

Elizabeth R
[sign manual]

Anno Regni Regine
Elizabeth Tricesimo
Sexto 1593

Neweyeares guiftes gyuen to the
Queenes Maiesty at her highnes
honor of Hampton Courte by
These persons Whose Names doe here-
after Ensewe, the Fyrste Daye of
January the yeare abouesayde

94.1 By Sir John Puckering Knighte Lord Keeper of the greate Seale of
Englande One Bodkyn of golde, with a fayre Large Juell att it, Lyke
an halfe Moone, Garnished with Dyamondes, And a Border of
Diamondes of sundrey Cutts aboute it A Table Ruby in the Mydeste,
And a Small pearle Pendante

dd to Mrs Radclyffes

94.2 By the Lord Burghley Lorde Threasorer of Englande in Golde . . . . xx li
94.3 By the Lorde Marques of winchester in Golde . . . . xx li

Earles

94.4 By the Earle of Shrewesbury in golde . . . . xx li
94.5 By the Earle of Darby in golde . . . . xx li
94.6 By the Earle of Sussex in golde . . . . x li
94.7 By the Earle of Huntington in golde . . . . x li
94.8 By the Earle of Bathe in golde . . . . x li
94.9 By the Earle of Hertforde in golde . . . . x li
94.10 By the Earle of Penbroke in golde . . . . xx li

dd to Mr Sackeford

94.11 By the Earle of Northumberland One Bodkyn of gold with a Juell at it
Lyke An *E*. Garnished with small Dyamondes within A Serkle of
Dyamondes and Fover small Rubyes and one small Dyamonde pendant
withoute foyle
94.12 By the Earle of Essex Maister of the Horsses Three Bodkyns of golde with
pendantes of golde, sett one with A Table Ballas Ruby thother Twoe with
Twoe Rocke Ruby Ballaces And sett aboute with Sparkes of Dyamondes
and each havinge one pearle pendante

dd to Mrs Ratclyffes

94.13 By the Earle of Bedforde in golde . . . . xx li

dd to Mr Sackeford

94.14 By the Earle of wourster parte of A Girdle of Golde Conteyninge
Threescore and Tenn peces sett with Small Rubyes Dyamondes and
pearles in Twoes whereof Six peeces without stone

dd to Mrs Ratclyffes

Marquesses and Countesses

94.15 By the Lady Marques of Northampton One Mantle of Blacke Nettworke
florished with venis Sylver in waves Dyamondewise

dd to the Robbes

94.16 By the Countis of Kente A Bagg of Tauny Satten thoneside Ymbravdwred
all ouer with A Red Rose in the mideste and Twoe Quiltes within the
same

dd to Mrs Radclyffes

94.17 By the Countis of Oxenford One Loose gowne of white Satten printed
ymbravderd all ouer with a plate of golde and Owes

dd to the Robbes

94.18 By the Countis of Shrewesbury Widdow in golde . . . . .xl li

dd to Mr Sackeford

94.19 By the Countis of Shrewesbury One peece of Raysed Heare Collor
Mossewoorke Embravderd all ouer with Leaves pommgarnettes and
men, Conteyninge Seaven yardes

dd to the Robbes

94.20 By the Countis of Huntingdon in golde . . . . .viij li

dd to Mr Sackeforde

94.21 By the Countis of Warwicke One Gerdle of Golde Conteyninge Three
score and Eleaven peeces Garnished with small Rubyes and pearles, And
Three Bodkynnes of Golde with pendantes of golde made Lyke Hartes
Garnished with Sparkes of Rubyes and one Dyamonde in the middell and
Small Pearles

dd to Mrs Ratclyffes

94.22 By the Countis of Penbroke in golde . . . . x li
94.23 By the Countis of Darby Junir in golde . . . . x li

dd to Mr Sackeforde

94.24 By the Countis of Bedforde One Rounde goune of Cloth of Sylver prynted
bounde aboute with a plate Lace of Venis golde

dd to the Robbes

94.25 By the Countis of Sovthampton Widdowe in golde. x li
94.26 By the Countis of Rutland Widdowe in golde . . . . x li
94.27 By the Countis of Hertford in golde. . . . . x li
94.28 By the Countis of Bathe in golde . . . . x li

dd to Mr Sackeforde

94.29 By the Countis of Cumberlande One Pettycoate of Heare Collored Taffata
ymbroderd all ouer with a Twiste of venis Sylver and Roses with a Twiste
of venis golde and somme owes

dd to the Robbes

94.30 By the Countis of Wourster perte of A Girdle of Golde Conteyninge
Threescore and Tenne peeces sett with small Rubyes Dyamondes and
pearles in Twoes whereof Six peeces without stones

dd to Mrs Ratclyffes

94.31 By the Countis of Sussex in Gold . . . . x li

Vicountesse

94.32   By the vicountis Mountaghu in golde . . . . x li

Bushoppes

94.33   By the Arche Bushopp of Caunterbury in gold . . . . xl li
94.34   By the Bushopp of yorke in golde . . . . xxx li
94.35   By the Bushopp of Durham in golde . . . . xxx li
94.36   By the Bushopp of Saulsbury in golde . . . . xx li
94.37   By the Bushopp of Londonn in golde . . . . xx li
94.38   By the Bushopp of Winchester in golde . . . . xx li
94.39   By the Bushopp of Norwiche in golde . . . . xx li
94.40   By the Bushopp of Lyncolnn in golde . . . . xx li
94.41   By the Bushopp of Wourcester in golde . . . . xx li
94.42   By the Bushopp of Lychefeilde and Coventry in golde and Sylver
        . . . . xiij li vj s viij d
94.43   By the Bushopp of Carlyll in golde . . . . x li
94.44   By the Bushopp of Rochester in golde . . . . x li
94.45   By the Bushopp of Checester in golde . . . . x li
94.46   By the Bushopp of Chester in golde . . . . x li
94.47   By the Bushopp of Peterborow in golde . . . . x li
94.48   By the Bushopp of Glocester in golde . . . . x li
94.49   By the Bushopp of Herreforde in golde . . . . x li
94.50   By the Bushopp of Exetor in golde . . . . x li
94.51   By the Bushopp of Bathe and Welles in golde . . . . xx li
                                                    dd to Mr Sackeforde

Lordes

94.52   By the Lorde of Hunsdon Lorde Chamberlen parte of A Carkyonett
        Conteyninge Fyve peeces of golde garnished with Sparkes of Dyamondes
        and Rubyes and pearles Threided and pearles pendaunt
94.53   By the Lorde Howard Lord Admyrall, One Attyer for the hedde Conteyning
        Seaven peeces of golde Lyke peramyodes vnder them Syfers garnished
        with Dyamondes and Rubyes of sonndery Bygnesses with Thirtene pearles
        and her Maiesties pycture Cutt vppon A Safyor in the Middest
                                      Delivered to Mrs Ratclyffes
94.54   By the Lorde Cobham in golde . . . . x li
94.55   By the Lorde Buckehurste in golde . . . . v li
94.56   By the Lorde Northe in golde . . . . x li
94.57   By the Lorde Shandoyes in golde . . . . x li
                                                      dd to Mr Sackeford
94.58   By the Lorde Coumpton A Payre of Braselettes of gold Conteyninge
        Sixtene peeces. Eighte garnished with Sparkes of Dyamondes and
        Rubyes and ffover pearles Theother Eighte with Lyke Rubyes and one
        pearle in the middeste
                                      dd to Mrs Ratclyffes

94.59 By the Lorde Lomley in golde. . . . . x li
94.60 By the Lorde Norris in golde . . . . x li
94.61 By the Lorde Wharton in golde . . . . x li
94.62 By the Lorde Riche in golde . . . . x li
94.63 By the Lorde Burrowes One Carkyonett Conteyninge Fyve peeces of golde
      Lyke Gloobes Enamyolede. Garnished with Sparkes of Dyamondes A
      Rowe of pearles Threded and Eleaven small pearles pendant
                                dd to Mrs Radclyffes
94.64 By the Lorde Darcey in gold. . . . . x li
                             dd to the said Mr Sackeforde

Barronesses

94.65 By the Barrones Hunsdon parte of A Carkyonett of golde Conteyninge
      Fyve peeces Garnished with Sparkes of Dyamondes and Rubyes and
      pearles Threded and pearles pendante
94.66 By the Barrones Howarde One Carkyonett of golde Conteyninge Seaven
      peces Lyke Knottes and Havlfe Moones garnished with small Diamondes
      and pearles with a bigg Opavll in the mideste with Eighte pearles pendante
      And a bigger in the mideste
                                dd to Mrs Radclyffes
94.67 By the Barrones Paggett Cary One Rounde Gowne of Lawne Cutt and
      Snypte with small Sylver plates in paynes vppon Sylver Chamblett
                                dd to the Robbes
94.68 By the Barrones Shandoyes Knolles One Longe Cushion of sylke
      Needleworke the Grounde White Backed with Carnation Satten.
      Fringed Buttoned and Tasseled with Venis golde and Sylver Conteyninge
      in Length One yarde in Breadth halfe a yarde
                     dd to John Whynneyarde of the warderobe
94.69 By the Barrones Shandoyes in golde. . . . . x li
                                dd to Mr Sackeforde
94.70 By the Barrones Dacers A Mantle of Blacke Styched Cloth florished allouer
      Dyamond wyse with A Threede of venis golde and Stares and Owes in the
      middeste
                                dd to the Robes
94.71 By the Barrones Lumley One Rounde Kertle of Blacke Cloth of golde
      Stryped and Raysed with Sylver
                                dd to the Robbes
94.72 By the Barrones Scroupe one Juell of golde made Cumpas Garnished with
      Sparkes of Dyamondes Rubyes and Fover small Opavlles in the mideste
                                dd to Mrs Radclyffes
94.73 By the Barrones Arbella One Muffler Case of Silke Needlewoorke the
      grownde Golde. and Twoe payer of Cuffes of Cambrycke Richly
      wroughte with golde sylver and Silke needlewoorke
                           dd The Case to Mrs Hyde
                     The Couffes to the Lady Skudamor

94.74   By the Barrones Cheney One Payer of Blaselettes [sic] of golde Conteyninge
Sixtene peeces, Eighte sett with Sparkes of Rubyes Dyamondes and
pearles and Eighte with Sparkes of Rubyes and one pearle in the
Mideste

94.75   By the Barrones Burrowes Seaven Small Juells of gold Inamyoled Lyke
Fernne Brakes Garnished with Sparkes of Rubyes and Dyamondes
                                                  dd to Mrs Ratclyffes

94.76   By the Barrones Sheffeilde Stafforde One Skarfe of Ashecolored Knitworke
florished with A Threede of Venis Sylver, somme Heare Cullored Sylke
and Sylver Owes
                                                     dd to Mrs Hyde

94.77   By the Barronesse Buckhurste in golde . . . . v li

94.78   By the Barronesse Barkeley in golde . . . . x li

94.79   By the Barronesse Norris in gold . . . . x li
                                                    dd to Mr Sackeforde

94.80   By the Barronesse Dudley One Purse mother of pearle On boath sides
Slytely Garnished with golde and sett with verry small Rubyes and
pearles
                                                  dd to Mrs Radclyffes

Ladyes

94.81   By the Lady Mary Seymer wiefe to Mr Rogers A Smocke of Fyne holland
Cloth the Sleves wroughte with Blacke Sylke
                                            dd to the Lady Skudamor

94.82   By the Lady Elizabeth Seymer Wife to Sir Richarde Knightley One Skarfe
of Asshecolored Knittewoorke, floryshed with A Threed of venis golde
and Sylver some Carnacon Sylke and Sylver owes

94.83   By the Lady Elizabeth Veare One Skimskyn of Heare Collored velvett Cutt
and vncutt, Imbrodred with venis sylver Lyned with white plushe

94.84   By the Lady Bridgett Manners A Skarfe of Flamecolored Netwoorke
florished with A Threde of venis Sylver and some Owes Lyned with white
Serssionett
                                                     dd to Mrs Hyde

94.85   By the Lady Stafforde A Shorte Carkyonett with Rowes of Seede pearles One
pece in the midest with Small Rubyes and Dyamondes
                                                  dd to Mrs Ratclyffes

94.86   By the Lady Southwell One Hede Attyer with Labells of white Stytched Cloth
Stripen
                                                   dd to Mrs Norton

94.87   By the Lady Cheeke A small Juell of golde Lyke a flowerdeluce Garnished
with small Sparkes of Dyamondes and a Serkle Aboute itt and a Smale
pearle pendant
                                                  dd to Mrs Radclyffes

94.88   By the Lady Leighton One wastcoate of white Sersionett Slytely imbrodered
         all ouer with A Twyste of venis Sylver and Carnation Sylke, and Certayne
         Flyes and wormes in Divers places
                                                            dd to the Lady Skudamor

94.89   By the Lady Scott One Skimskyn of Cloth of Sylver Improdered [sic] all
         ouer with Starres of venis golde seede pearles and Bugles with Fover
         Buttons of golde sett with Sparkes of Rubyes and pearles, and Lyned
         with Carnation plush
                                                                      dd to Mrs Hyde

94.90   By the Lady Carowe Twoe pillowbeares of Fyne holland Cloth wrought
         with Sylke of Dyuers Collors one thone side
                                                            dd to the Lady Skudamor

94.91   By the Lady Radclyff A Ruffe with a Rabata of Laune with Cuttworke
                                                                    dd to Mrs Boone

94.92   By the Lady Weste One wastcoate of White Sarsionett Ymbrodered all ouer
         with awoorke of Venis golde the moste of Greene and Carnacon Sylke
                                                            dd to the Lady Skudamor

94.93   By the Lady Dygby One Cloake of Knittwoorke florished with a Threde of
         Venis Golde Lyned with white Plushe
                                                                    dd to the Robbes

94.94   By the Lady Jarrett in golde . . . . x li
94.95   By the Lady Gressam in golde . . . . x li
                                                                 dd to Mr Sackeforde

94.96   By the Lady Willouwby Sir Fraunces his wife A Cushion Cloth of white
         Cuttwoorke

94.97   By the Lady Longe Twoe payer of Sylke Knytt Hose and One payer of White
         Sypers Garters Imbraudered in thendes

94.98   By the Lady Souch one Ruffe of Cambricke Cuttwoorke vnmade

94.99   By the Lady Harrington one wastcoate of white Sarsionett fayrely Ymbrodred
         all ouer with venis Sylver and purle
                                                              dd to Lady Skudamor

94.100   By the Lady Tounesend One Skimskyn of Cloth of Sylver Ymbrodered All
         ouer with venis golde Lyned with white plushe
                                                                      dd to Mrs Hyde

94.101   By the Lady Cecill Sir Roberte his wife one payer of Braselettes of golde
         Conteyninge Sixtene peeces. Eighte with Sparkes of Dyamondes and
         Rubyes and Eighte with Three pearles A peece
                                                                dd to Mrs Radclyffes

94.102   By the Lady Scudamor parte of A Lose gowne of Heare Colored Taffata
         the sleves and Border Abovte Imbrodred with owes and Dravne out with
         Laune
                                                                    dd to the Robbes

94.103   By the Lady Wolley One Cannopy the Heade Couered with Carnation
         Cloth of Sylver with Curteynes of Carnation and white Caffa

94.104   By the Lady Edmounde One Square Stoole of Sylver paynted the Seate Couered
with Sylke Needlewoorke Lyke Honysuckells
dd to Whynyard yeoman of The Guardrob

94.105   By the Lady Newtonn One Carkyonett Conteyninge Six peeces of Golde
garnished with Sparkes of Rubyes and Rowes of pearles Threded and
Tenne small pendantes with one Sparke of A Ruby and Fover Little
pearles in Eache

94.106   By the Lady Cary Sir George Knighte Marshall his Wife One Small
Carkyonett Conteyninge Nyne Peeces of golde Lyke Knottes and
Mullettes and A Flowerdeluce in the Mydeste

94.107   By the Lady Hawkynes One Juell of golde Lyke a pecockes Tayle made
Rounde garnished with Small Rubyes Dyamondes Opavlls and Three
Pearles pendant
dd to Mrs Radclyffes

94.108   By the Lady Waullsingham One Loosse gowne of white Satten the Sleves
Snipte and Cutt
dd to the Robes

94.109   By the Lady Paulavizino One Cumfett Boxe of Golde Inamyoled Lyke A
Roose, the one syde sett with smavle Dyamondes and Rubyes
dd to Mrs Radclyffes

Knights

94.110   By Sir Fraunces Knolles Threasorer of her Maiesties houshold in gold . . . . . x li
dd to Mr Sackeforde

94.111   By Sir Thomas Hennage Vice Chaumberlen One Juell of golde Lyke A
Crosse and a halfe Moone vnder itt Garnished with Dyamondes of
Sundrey Bignesses and Three pearles one Biger then thother Twoe,

94.112   By Sir Thomas Leyghton One Tablett of golde made Ovall fashion
Enamyoled bothe sides A Lyke and a Lyttle pearle pendante
dd to Mrs Radclyffes

94.113   By Sir Henry Croumwell in golde . . . . x li

94.114   By Sir Edwarde Cleere in golde . . . . x li
dd to Mr Sackeforde

94.115   By Sir Thomas Cecyll A Tooth picker Case of golde Garnished with Sparkes
of Dyamondes and Rubyes Three pearles pendant One Bigger then the
Residue, and a Small Chayne of golde to hange itt by

94.116   By Sir Roberte Cecyll A Shorte Carkyonett of golde with Three Rowes of
pearles Threeded and Fyve small peeces of golde Garnished with Sparkes
of Dyamondes and A Checker of Dyamondes with a small pearle
pendant

94.117   By Sir William Russell Tenne Eies of golde Inamyoled Each havinge Three
verry Small pendantes garnished with one Sparke of A Dyamonde in Eache

94.118   By Sir Edwarde Stafforde One Armyolett of golde Conteyninge Twenty
peeces whereof Tenne with Cammeves and Fover pearles in Apeece. And
Tenne with Three pearles in apeece beinge all Corosse pearles
dd to Mrs Radclyffes

94.119   By Sir John Sckudeamor parte of A Loose Gowne of Heare Collored
         Taffata The Sleves and Border Abovte Imbrawdered with Owes and Drawne
         out with Lawne

                                                            dd to the Robbes
94.120   By Sir Henry Newton Seaven pendantes of golde Fover garnished with
         sparkes of Rubyes and one pearle in the Mydest And Three with sparkes
         of Dyamondes and either havinge Three small pearles pendant
94.121   By Sir Edwarde Hobby Seaven pendantes of golde Garnished with small
         Sparkes of Dyamondes and Rubyes and Each Havinge Three small
         pearles pendante

                                                          dd to Mrs Radclyffes
94.122   By Sir Thomas Garrett A Skimskyn of Cloth of Sylver Ymbrodered all ouer
         with venis Golde Sylver and sylke of Sondrey Collors and some pearle
         Lyned with white plushe

                                                             dd to Mrs Hyde
94.123   By Sir John Fortescue Chauncellor of Thexcheaquer in golde . . . . x li
                                                           dd to Mr Sackeforde
94.124   By Sir John Wolley Secretary For the Lattyn Tonge One Lapp Mantle of
         Blacke Clothe of golde Layde abovte with Twoe plate Laces of Venis
         golde Lyned with white plushe

                                                            dd to the Robbes
94.125   By Sir Oratio Pavlavizino One payer of writinge Tables Couered with golde
         Enamyoled One Boath sydes with A Favlcon and a Septer garnished with
         small Sparkes of Rubyes Lyke Roosses
94.126   By Sir Charlles Blounte Seaven Pendantes of golde garnished with Sparkes of
         Dyamondes and Rubyes and Eache havinge Three Smalle pearles pendante
                                                          dd to Mrs Ratclyffes

Gentlewoemen

94.127   By Mrs Mary Ratclyff One Skimskyn of Purpell velvett Imbraudered all
         ouer with venis golde and Sylver plate and a knott of Purle in the Middeste
         Lyned with white plushe
94.128   By Mrs Elizabethe Bridges A valle of white Nettwoorke floryshed with A
         Twiste of Sylver and Sylver Spanges [sic]

                                                             dd to Mrs Hyde
94.129   By Mrs Car Twoe pyllowes with Pyllowbeares of fyne hollande Clothe
         wroughte on the one syde with Blacke Sylke

                                                            dd to Whinyarde
94.130   By Mrs Hennage Mr William his wife One Smocke of fyne Holland Cloth
         wroughte with Blacke Sylke on the sleeves

                                                          dd to the La: Skudamor
94.131   By Mrs Luce Hyde One Capp of Lavne Imbrodred with Owes the Bande
         sett with Flowers of Woemans woorke

                                                            dd to the Robbes

94.132   By Mrs Anne Norton An Attyer for the Head Lyke A Crowne garnished
with Sypers and Venis Sylver with Labells of Lyke Sypers

dd to Mrs Norton

94.133   By Mrs Twiste Twoe Pyllowebeares of Assay of Holland Cloth wrought
with Blacke Sylke

dd to the La: Skudamor

94.134   By Mrs Wallsingham A pettycoate of white Sersyonett Imbrodred all ouer with
venis golde and Sylke Lyke Roses

dd to the Robbes

94.135   By Mrs Cromer A Smocke of fyne Hollande Cloth The Sleeves wrought with
Blacke Sylke

dd to the La: Skudamor

94.136   By Mrs Huggens widdowe A Large Sweetebagge of white Sersyonett
Imbraudered all ouer with A Sphre in the Midest, And Sixe small
Sweetebagges

94.137   By Mrs Fraunces Huggens, Six handkerchers wrought with Blacke Sylke

94.138   By Mrs Thommason One Nighte Coyfe and a forhead Clothe wroughte
with Blacke Sylke

94.139   By Mrs Barley Six handkerchers of fyne Cambrick Edged with Bonne Lace
of Venis Venis golde

94.140   By Mrs Bonne als Gillham One Ruffe with a Rabata of Laune Cuttwoork

94.141   By Mrs wynckefeilde A Nighte Rayle of Fyne Holland wroughte with
Blacke Sylke

dd to the said Mrs Bonne

Gentlemen

94.142   By Mr Henry Brooke One Jhupp of Orrynge Collor velvett Cutt and vncutt
The Sleeves Donne before garnished with a lace of Venis sylver Lyke Esse
firmes and Layde Aboute with Twoe plate Laces of Lyke sylver

dd to the Robbes

94.143   By Mr John Stanhope One small Juell of golde with An Amataste and An
Arrowe through the same / And a small Garnett pendante

dd to Mrs Ratclyffes

94.144   By Mr Ralphe Bousse One Skimskyn of Cloth of Sylver Imbraudered all
ouer Lyke Paunces of Venis golde and some Seede pearles

dd to Mrs Hyde

94.145   By Mr Henry Bruncker One Cappe of Blacke Velvett Sett all ouer with
fover and Twenty Buttons of golde Eache havinge one small Ruby and
Fover small pearles and one flower of golde Garnished with Sparkes of
Dyamondes and Rubyes and A Sallamander in the Mideste

dd to the Robbes

94.146   By Mr Garter Kinge of Armes One Booke of Armes Couered with Black
Vellvett

dd to Mr Darcey

94.147 By Mr Foulke Gryvell Three Longe Cushiones of flame Collor Cloth of
Sylver Backed with Lyke Collored Satten Frynged Buttoned and Tasceled
with Venis Sylver

dd to Jo: Winyarde

94.148 By Mr Edwarde Dyer A Rownde Kirtell of Cloth of Syluer with Grapes
Vines and Vyne Leaves of Dyvers Collored Sylkes

dd to the Robbes

94.149 By Mr Car One Square Stoole of Tymber paynted The Seate of Silke
Needellwoorke Lyke Paunces and a Border of Clothe of Sylver with
Lyke Flowers

dd to Jo: Whinyarde

94.150 By Mr William Cornewallis One wastecoate of Cambricke wroughtw all
ouer with venis golde and Blacke Sylke Lyke fyshes and other Devices

dd to La: Skudamor

94.151 By Mr Thomas Woodhouse One payer of Gloves of perfumed Lether Cutt
Imbraudered with A Twiste of Sylver the Covffes Sylke Woemans Woorke
lyned with Orringe Collored plussh

dd to Mrs Hyde

94.152 By Mr Mountague One Smocke of fyne Hollande The Sleeves and Coller
wroughte with Blacke Silke

94.153 By Mr Symeon Boyer One wastecoate of white Sersyonett Ymbraudered all
ouer Lyke Knottes and Starres of Carnaconn Sylke in them

94.154 By Mr Carmarden One fayre Rayle of Cambricke wroughte with Black Sylke
and Syxe partriges

dd to the La: Skudamor

94.155 By Mr Spyllman One Large Opavll within a Lyttle grasp of golde

dd to Mrs Radclyffes

94.156 By Mr Docter Smith A pott of Greene Ginger an other of Orringe
flowers

94.157 By Mr Docter Gyfford A pott of Greene Ginger an other of Orringe
flowers

94.158 By Mr Docter Lopus Twoe Handkerchers

94.159 By Mr Hughe Morgayne Appottycary One pott of Greene Ginger and a
pott of Orringe flowers

94.160 By Mr William weston A Box of Peaches preserued and A pott of Orringe
Flowers

94.161 By Mr Ewarde Hemingewaye Appotticary One pott of Peaches preserved
and a Box of Lozenges and manus Christe

dd to the La: Skudamor

94.162 By Mr Dunstone Annes A Besers Stone

dd to Mrs Radclyffes

94.163 By Mr Busshopp Stationer Twelve Bookes of Latten poettes Couered with
vellam

dd to Mr Knevett

94.164 By Mr Jacomy Vezalmo Twenty Drinckinge Glasses with Covers

dd into the privy Chamber

94.165　By Mr John Braddyshe Lynnen Draper One Whole peece of Lawne
　　　　　　　　　　　　　　　　　　　　　　　　dd to Mrs Radclyffes

94.166　By Mr William Cordall Mr Cooke A fayer Marchpaynne

94.167　By Mr Ralphe Bate Sergaunte of the Pastrey One pye Orringed
　　　　　　　　　　　　　　　　　　　　　　　　　　　[dd to blank]

94.168　By Mr Robynson Six Stomachers of white Cuttwoorke

94.169　By Mr Petro Lupo A glasse of Sweete water
　　　　　　　　　　　　　　　　　　　　　　　dd to La: Skudamor

94.170　By Mr William Clarke A booke of Ceasears Dealogges Couered with Vellam
　　　　　　　　　　　　　　　　　　　　　　　　dd to Mr Knevett

94.171　By Mr Josofe Lupo A payer of perfwmed Gloves

94.172　By Mr Thomas Lupo A payer of perfwmed Gloves

94.173　By Mr Jerolimo Bassano A payer of perfwmed Gloves

94.174　By Mr Cesar Galliardello A payer of perfwmed Gloves
　　　　　　　　　　　　　　　　　　　　　　　　dd to Mrs Hyde

94.175　By Mr Innosent Comye A Box of Lute stringes
　　　　　　　　　　　　　　　　　　　　　　　dd to Mr Richardson

94.176　By Mr Arthur Bassano A payre of perfumed Gloves

94.177　By Mr Andrew Bassano A payer of perfumed Gloves
　　　　　　　　　　　　　　　　　　　　　　　　dd to Mrs Hyde

94.178　By Mr Petruchio Vballdino A Booke Couered with Vellam in Italian
　　　　　　　　　　　　　　　　　　　　　　　　dd to Mr Knevett

94.179　By Mr Thomas Middleton A Bolte of fyne Cambricke and Halfe A peece
　　　　of Laune
　　　　　　　　　　　　　　　　　　　　　　　dd to Mrs Radclyffes

94.180　By Mr Winter One Wastecoate of Cambrick wroughte all ouer with Sylke
　　　　of Sonndery Collors and some peramyodes
　　　　　　　　　　　　　　　　　　　　　　　dd to La: Skudamor

94.181　By Mr Warberton One pettycoate of Carnaconn Satten Ymbraudered all
　　　　ouer with a woorke Lyke Roses and other Flowers
　　　　　　　　　　　　　　　　　　　　　　　　dd to the Robbes

94.182　By Mr Baker One Juell of golde with a Safyer without foyle Garnished with
　　　　Opavlles Rounde aboute and Three small pearlles pendante
　　　　　　　　　　　　　　　　　　　　　　　　with her Matie

94.183　By Gyllham Skeatte A payer of Virgynalles of waynskotte
　　　　　　　　　　　　　　　　　　　　　　dd into the privy Chamber

94.184　By Mr Willmm Huggens one Hatt of siluer chamblett enbr with venice
　　　　siluer and siluer owes
　　　　　　　　　　　　　　　　　　　　　　　　dd to the Robes

Summa totalis of the money
giuen to her Majestye as . . . . viij^c j li vj s viij d
aforesaide Amounteth unto

Anno Regni Regine Elizabeth
Tricesimo Sexto 1593

Neweyeares guiftes giuen by the Quenes
Matie at her heighnes honor of Hampton
Courte To those persons whose Names Doe here-
after ensewe The Fyrste daye of January the yeare aforesaide

Elizabeth R
[sign manual]

94.185	To Sir John Puckeringe Knighte Lord Keeper of the Greate Sealle of Englande in guilte plate	xlj oz qtr
94.186	To the Lorde Burghley Lord Threasoror of Englande in guilte plate	xlj oz di qtr
94.187	To the Lord Marques of Winchester in guilte plate	xxix oz qtr

Earles

94.188	To the Earle of Shrewesbury in guilte plate	xxxj oz iij qtr
94.189	To the Earle of Darby in guilte plate	xxxj oz iij qtr di
94.190	To the Earle of Sussex in guilte plate	xx oz di qtr
94.191	To the Earle of Huntingeton in guilte plate	xx oz di qtr
94.192	To the Earle of Bathe in guilte plate	xx oz di di qtr
94.193	To the Earle of Hertffes in guilte plate	xxj oz iij qtr
94.194	To the Earle of Penbroke in guilte plate	xxxj oz iij qtr
94.195	To the Earle of Northumberlande in guilte plate	xx oz di di qtr
94.196	To the Earle of Essex Maister of her Maties Horsses in guilte plate	CCCCCx oz qtr di
94.197	To the Earle of Worchester in guilte plate	xxxiiij oz di qtr
94.198	To the Earle of Bedforde in guilte plate	xxx oz di

Marquesses & Countesses

94.199	To the Lady Marques of Northampton guilte plate	xliiij oz iij qtr di
94.200	To the Countis of Kente in guilte plate	xix oz iij qtr
94.201	To the Countis of Oxenford in guilte plate	xxxiiij oz di
94.202	To the Countis of Shrewesbury widdowe in guilte plate	xxxij oz iij qtr
94.203	To the Countis of Shrewesbury in guilte plate	xx oz
94.204	To the Countis of Huntington in guilte plate	xxix oz di qtr
94.205	To the Countis of Bedforde in guilte plate	L oz di
94.206	To the Countis of Warwicke in guilte plate	Lvj oz
94.207	To the Countis of Penbroke in guilte plate	xix oz qtr di
94.208	To the Countis of Southhampton widdow in guilte plate	xx oz qtr
94.209	To the Countis of Rutlande widdowe in guilte plate	xxj oz
94.210	To the Countis of Hertford in guilte plate	xxj oz di
94.211	To the Countis of Bathe in guilte plate	xxij oz iij qtr di
94.212	To the Countis of Cumberland in guilte plate	xx oz qtr di
94.213	To the Countis of Sussex in guilte plate	xx oz di qtr

94.214 To the Countis of wourster in guilte plate .... xix oz qtr di
94.215 To the Countis of Darby the younger in guilte plate .... xxj oz di

Vicountis

94.216 To the Vicountis Mountighu in guilte plate .... xviij oz di qtr

Busshhopps

94.217 To the Arche bushopp of Caunterbury in guilte plate .... xliiij oz iij qtr
94.218 To the Archbushop of Yorke in guilte plate .... xxxviij oz
94.219 To the Busshopp of Durhamm in guilte plate .... xxxv oz
94.220 To the Busshopp of Salisbury in guilte plate .... xxxj oz
94.221 To the Bushopp of London in guilte plate .... xxix oz iij qtr di
94.222 To the Busshopp of winchester in guilte plate .... xxx oz qtr di
94.223 To the Busshopp of Norwich in guilte plate..................... xxx oz di
94.224 To the Busshopp of Lyncolne in guilte plate .... xxx oz
94.225 To the Busshopp of Lychfeilde and Coventry in guilte plate .... xxij oz
94.226 To the Busshopp of Carlyll in guilte plate .... xv oz qtr di
94.227 To the Busshopp of Rochester in guilte plate..................... xv oz
94.228 To the Busshopp of Chechester in guilte plate ....xv oz qtr
94.229 To the Busshopp of Chester in guilte plate..................... xv oz di qtr
94.230 To the Busshopp of Peterborow in guilte plate.............. xv oz di di qtr
94.231 To the Busshopp of Glosester in guilte plate .... xv oz
94.232 To the Busshopp of Hereford in guilte plate................. xv oz di di qtr
94.233 To the Busshopp of Exeter in guilte plate..................... xv oz di qtr
94.234 To the Busshopp of Worcester Amner in guilte plate................. xxix oz
94.235 To the Busshopp of Bathe in guilte plate .... xxix oz iij qtr di

Lordes

94.236 To the Lord Hunsdon in guilte plate............................xxx oz
94.237 To the Lord Hawarde in guilte plate .... Ciiij oz
94.238 To the Lord Cobham in guilte plate .... xxiiij oz qtr
94.239 To the Lord Buckehurste in guilte plate .... xxij oz qtr di
94.240 To the Lord Northe in guilte plate .... xij oz qtr di
94.241 To the Lord Shandoyes in guilte plate.........................xxj oz
94.242 To the Lord Compton in guilte plate .... xx oz qtr di
94.243 To the Lord Lumley in guilte plate ....xxj oz di
94.244 To the Lord Norris in guilte plate............................. xx oz
94.245 To the Lord Wharton in guilte plate....................... xix oz iij qtr di
94.246 To the Lord Riche in guilte plate ....xx oz qtr
94.247 To the Lord Burrowes in guilte plate....................... xxij oz iij qtr di
94.248 To the Lord Darsey of Chiche in guilte plate.................... xix oz iij qtr

Barronesses

94.249 To the Barrones Hounsdon in guilte plate ....xxx oz
94.250 To the Barrones Howarde in guilte plate .... xx oz
94.251 To the Barrones Paggett Cary in guilte plate .... xxix oz iij qtr

94.252	To the Barrones Shandoyes Knolles in guilte plate	xx oz z
94.253	To the Barrones Shandoyes in guilte plate	xx oz di qtr
94.254	To the Barrones Dacers in guilte plate	xx oz
94.255	To the Barrones Loumley in guilte plate.....................	xix oz di di qtr
94.256	To the Barrones Skroupe in guilte plate	xx oz di qtr
94.257	To the Barrones Arabella in guilte plate	xix oz qtr di
94.258	To the Barrones Cheny in guilte plate.........................	xxx oz
94.259	To the Barrones Burrowes in guilte plate	xx oz di di qtr
94.260	To the Barrones Dudley in guilte plate	xvj oz di di qtr
94.261	To the Barrones Sheffeilde in guilte plate	xx oz qtr di
94.262	To the Barrones Buckehurste in gilte plate	xj oz
94.263	To the Barrones Barkeley in guilte plate	xxj oz iij qtr
94.264	To the Barrones Norris in guilte plate........................	xx oz

Ladies

94.265	To the Lady Mary Seymer wife to Mr Rogers in guilte plate..........	xij oz di
94.266	To the Lady Elizabeth Seymer wife to Sir Richarde Knightely in guilte plate	xiij oz
94.267	To the Lady Elizabeth Veare in guilte plate	xvij oz di di qtr
94.268	To the Lady Bridgett Manners in guilte plate................	xvij oz di di qtr
94.269	To the Lady Stafford in guilte plate	xxix oz
94.270	To the Lady Southwell in guilte plate	xvij oz di qtr
94.271	To the Lady Cheake in guilte plate	xxviij oz qtr
94.272	To the Lady Leyghton in guilte plate	xx oz di
94.273	To the Lady Skott in guilte plate..........................	xv oz di di qtr
94.274	To the Lady Carow in guilte plate...........................	xxx oz di qtr
94.275	To the Lady Radeclyff in guilte plate	xvj oz
94.276	To the Lady Weste in guilte plate	xvj oz di
94.277	To the Lady Digby in guilte plate	xvj oz di qtr
94.278	To the Lady Jarrett in guilte plate.........................	xx oz
94.279	To the Lady Gressham in guilte plate	xix oz di
94.280	To the Lady Willowby in guilte plate	xij oz di
94.281	To the Lady Souche in guilte plate	xiij oz qtr
94.282	To the Lady Longe in guilte plate..........................	xxij oz di
94.283	To the Lady Harrington in guilte plate......................	xx oz qtr
94.284	To the Lady Tounsende in guilte plate	xvj oz di qtr
94.285	To the Lady Cicell Sir Roberte his Wiefe in guilte plate..........	xvij oz iij qtr
94.286	To the Lady Scudeamor in guilte plate	xvij oz di
94.287	To the Lady Wolle in guilte plate	xx oz di di qtr
94.288	To the Lady Edmoundes in guilte plate	xvj oz di
94.289	To the Lady Newton in guilte plate..........................	xvj oz qtr di
94.290	To the Lady Cary Sir George Knighte Marshall his wife in guilte plate ..	xviij oz
94.291	To the Lady Hawkynes in guilte plate........................	xviij oz qtr
94.292	To the Lady Wallsingeham in guilte plate	xxj oz qtr
94.293	To the Lady Paulavizino in guilte plate.....................	xviij oz iij qtr di

Knightes

94.294 To Sir Fraunces Knolles Threasorer of the Househoulde in guilte
plate . . . . xxiiij oz di qtr

94.295 To Sir Thomas Hennage Vice Chamberlayne in guilte plate . . . . Lij oz

94.296 To Sir John Forteskeaue Chauncelor of Thexcheaquer in guilte plate
. . . . xix oz iij qtr

94.297 To Sir John Wolley Secritory for the Latten tounge in guilte plate . . . . . . xxvj oz

94.298 To Sir Thomas Cecill in guilte plate . . . . xxxj oz di di qtr

94.299 To Sir Roberte Cecill in guilte plate . . . . .xxx oz

94.300 To Sir William Russell in guilte plate . . . . xxiiij oz

94.301 To Sir Charlles Blunte in guilte plate . . . . xxvj oz di qtr

94.302 To Sir Edwarde Stafforde in guilte plate . . . . xix oz di

94.303 To Sir Thomas Layton in guilte plate . . . . xxxj oz

94.304 To Sir John Skuedamor in guilte plate . . . . xviij oz iij qtr

94.305 To Sir Henry Newton in guilte plate . . . . xvij oz di di qtr

94.306 To Sir Edwarde Hobby in guilte plate . . . . xix oz qtr

94.307 To Sir Thomas Jarrett in guilte plate . . . . .xxv oz di qtr

94.308 To Sir Oratio Paulavizino in guilt plate . . . . .xxv oz di qtr

94.309 To Sir Henry Croumwell in guilte plate . . . . xx oz di di qtr

94.310 To Sir Edwarde Cleere in guilte plate . . . . xix oz

Maydes of Honnor

94.311 To Mrs Mary Twitchett the Lorde Audley his Daughter in guilte plate K
. . . . x oz di qtr

94.312 To Mrs Southwell in guilte plate K . . . . x oz

94.313 To Mrs Cristian Anneslowe in guilte plate Mar . . . . x oz di di qtr

94.314 To Mrs Fraunces Drury in guilte plate Mar . . . . x oz di

94.315 To Mrs Elizabeth Vernon in guilt plate Mar . . . . x oz iij qtr

94.316 To Mrs Margarett Radclyff in guilte plate K . . . . x oz di qtr

94.317 To Mrs Bromefeilde Mother of the Maydes in guilte plate Mar . . . . xij oz di qtr

Gentlewoemen

94.318 To Mrs Mary Ratclyff in guilte plate . . . . xviij oz qtr

94.319 To Mrs Elizabeth Brydges in guilte plate . . . . xvj oz qtr di

94.320 To Mrs Carre in guilte plate . . . . xv oz

94.321 To Mrs Hennage Mr William his wife in guilte plate . . . . xv oz di qtr

94.322 To Mrs Wallsinghamm in guilte plate . . . . xvj oz di di qtr

94.323 To Mrs Luce Hyde in guilte plate . . . . xv oz qtr di

94.324 To Mrs Anne Norton in guilte plate . . . . xiiij oz

94.325 To Mrs Twiste in guilte plate . . . . vij oz di

94.326 To Mrs Cromer in guilte plate . . . . xvj oz qtr di

94.327 To Mrs Winckefeilde in guilte plate . . . . xviij oz iij qtr di

94.328 To Mrs Huggens in guilte plate . . . . xix oz

94.329 To Mrs Fraunces Huggens in guilte plate . . . . xij oz qtr

94.330 To Mrs Thomasen in guilte plate . . . . vij oz iij qtr

94.331	To Mrs Barley in guilte plate	xij oz
94.332	To Mrs Bone in guilte plate	v oz

Gentlemen

94.333	To Mr Henry Brooke in guilte plate	xix oz iij qtr di
94.334	To Mr John Stanhope in guilte plate	xvj oz di di qtr
94.335	To Mr Ralph Boulles in gilte plate	xvij oz
94.336	To Mr Henry Brounker in guilte plate	xix oz iij qtr
94.337	To Mr Foulke Gryvell in guilt plate	xxij oz di di qtr
94.338	To Mr Edwarde Dyer in guilte plate	xix oz di di qtr
94.339	To Mr Carre in guilte plate	xv oz
94.340	To Mr William Cornewallis in guilte plate	xviij oz iij qtr
94.341	To Mr Symon Boyer in guilte plate	xiij oz iij qtr di
94.342	To Mr Thomas Woodhouse in guilte plate	xix oz qtr
94.343	To Mr Winter in guilte plate	xxij oz di
94.344	To Mr Warberton in guilte plate	xx oz iij qtr di
94.345	To Mr Garter Kinge att Armes in guilte plate	viij oz
94.346	To Mr Mountaghue in guilte plate	xvj oz
94.347	To Mr Carmarden in guilte plate	xvj oz
94.348	To Mr John Spyllman in guilte plate	xvij oz iij qtr
94.349	To Mr William Huggens in guilte plate	xxij oz
94.350	To Mr Docter Gyfforde in guilte plate	xiiij oz iij qtr
94.351	To Mr Docter Smyth in guilte plate	xiiij oz iij qtr
94.352	To Mr Docter Lopus in guilte plate	xiiij oz di di qtr
94.353	To Mr Hughe Morgayn in guilte plate	vij oz di
94.354	To Mr Edwarde Hemingewaye in guilte plate	vij oz qtr di
94.355	To Mr William Weston in guilte plate	viij oz di di qtr
94.356	To Mr Dunstone Anes in guilte plate	xiij oz di di qtr
94.357	To Mr Baker in guilte plate	xviij oz di
94.358	To Mr Busshoppe Stationer in guilte plate	xiiij oz
94.359	To Mr Jacome Vezelino in guilte plate	xj oz di di qtr
94.360	To Mr William Clerke in guilte plate	vj oz
94.361	To Mr John Braddishe Lynnen Draper in guilte plate	xij oz qrt
94.362	To Mr William Cordall Mr Cooke in guilte plate	ix oz iij di
94.363	To Mr Ralphe Batte Sargaunte of the Pastery in guilte plate	vj oz
94.364	To Mr John Robynson in guilte plate	v oz
94.365	To Mr Petro Lupo in guilte plate	v oz
94.366	To Mr Joseffe Lupo in guilte plate	v oz
94.367	To Mr Thomas Lupo in guilte plate	v oz
94.368	To Mr Jerolimo Bassano in guilte plate	v oz
94.369	To Mr Andrewe Bassano in guilte plate	v oz
94.370	To Mr Arthur Bassano in guilte plate	v oz
94.371	To Mr Sesar Galliardo in guilte plate	v oz
94.372	To Mr Innosent Comy in guilte plate	v oz
94.373	To Mr Petruchio Vbaldino in guilte plate	v ozd
94.374	To Mr Thomas Myddleton in guilte plate	xiij oz di qtr

94.375   To Mr Gylham Skeattes in guilte plate . . . . viij oz iij qtr di

Free Guiftes

94.376   To Mr John Astley Esquier Master and Threasorer of her Maties Juelles
         and plate in guilte plate . . . . xviij oz iij qtr di

94.377   To Sir Thomas Gorges Knight one of the Gromes of the pryvy Chamber
         in guilte plate . . . . ix oz

94.378   To Sir Edwarde Denny Knight one other Grome of the saide Chamber in
         guilte plate . . . . ix oz

94.379   To Mr Thomas Astley One other grome in guilt plate . . . . ix oz

94.380   To Mr Henry Sackeforde One other grome in guilte plate . . . . ix oz

94.381   To Mr Edwarde Cary One other grome in guilte plate . . . . ix oz di qtr

94.382   To Mr William Kylliogrewe One other Grome in guilte plate . . . . ix oz

94.383   To Mr Knyvett One other grome in guilte plate . . . . ix oz

94.384   To Mr Edwarde Darsey One other grome in guilte plate . . . . ix oz

94.385   To Mr Michaell Stanhopp One other grome in guilte plate . . . . ix oz

94.386   To Mr Bapteste one other grome in guilte plate . . . . ix oz

94.387   To Mr Ferdinando Richardsonn One other grome in guilte plate . . . . ix oz

94.388   To Humfrey Adderley Yeoman of the Roabes in guilte plate. . . . . xij oz di qtr

94.389   To Nicholas Bristowe Clarke of the Juelles and plate in guilte plate   x oz iij qtr di

94.390   To Nicholas Pygeon Yeoman of the Juelles and plate in guilte plate   x oz iij qtr di

94.391   To Roberte Cranmer grome of the saide office in guilte plate . . . . .   x oz iij qtr di

Somma totalis of all the Plate giuen
awaye as aforesaide Amounteth to . . . . iiij^M v^C ij oz di

Guiftes gyuen by her saide Matie to Sundry
parsons att Sundry tymes as followeth
viz

94.392   Sir Roberte Meluell
         Gyuen by her Heighnes the xx^th Daye of July Anno xxxv^to Regine
         Elizabeth &c vnto Sir Roberte Meluell Knighte Ambassador oute of
         Scotlande One Cheyne of golde of the goodnes of xxj karrettes iij gr
         qtr. Boughte of Sir Richarde Marten Knighte poz . . . . . xxxiiij oz qtr vij d wzt

94.393   Mounsieur Vidam De Chartois
         Item gyven by her saide heighnes the xx^th of September Anno predicto
         vnto Mounsieur Vidam Chartois One Bason and one Layer of sylver
         guilte poz – Cxxxviij oz. One payer of guilte vases poz – CCxv oz. One
         payer of Haunce Pottes guilte poz – Clxvij oz. One Neste of Three guilte
         Boulles with a Couer poz – Lxxiij oz qtr. One guilte Boule with a Couer
         poz – xxx oz di di qtr. And one guilte Boule with a Couer poz – xxxiij oz
         qtr. All Boughte of the saide Sir Richarde Marten. In Toto poz
         . . . . vj^C Lvij oz di qtr

94.394   Mounsieur Gedeneere [La Verenne]
Item gyven by her saide heighnes The Thirde of December Anno xxxvj^{to}
Regine Elizabeth &c vnto Mounsieur Gedeneere One Cheyne of golde
of goodnes of xxj Karrettes iij graines Boughte of the saide Sir Richard
Martin poz. . . . . xx oz   xij gr

Elizabeth R
[sign manual]

ex[amina]to per
Bristow
N Pigeon
Robert Cranmer

Anno regni regine Elizabeth
Tricesimo nona Anno dmi: 1596

New yerres guiftes giuen to the
Queenes Maiestie at her highnes
Pallase of westminster by those
parsons whose names heareafter
doe ensue the first of January in
the yeare abouewritten

97.1   By Sir Thomas Egerton knight Lord keeper of the great Seale of
Englande in golde . . . . xiij li vj s viij d
97.2   By the Lord Burghley Lord highe Threasorer of Englande in gold. . . . . xx li
97.3   By the Lord Marques of Winchester in golde . . . . xx li
dd to Mr Sackford grome of her Maties privey Chamber

Earles

97.4   By the Earle of Shrewsbury one doublet of siluer Chamlet imbrothered and
raised vp with white satten
Delivered to the Robes
97.5   By the Earle of Darby in golde . . . . x li
97.6   By the Earle of Sussex in golde . . . . x li
97.7   By the Earle of Bath in golde . . . . x li
97.8   By the Earle of Hartford in gold. . . . . x li
97.9   By the Earle of Huntington in golde . . . . x li
97.10 By the Earle of Penbrooke in golde . . . . xx li
97.11 By the Earle of Bedford in golde. . . . . xx li
97.12 By the Earle of Lincolne in golde . . . . x li
dd to Mr Sackford vt supra
97.13 By the Earle of Northumberlande one Jewell of gold like a Rainebowe
& the Sonne ouer yt garnished with Sparkes of Dyamondes
97.14 By the Earle of Southampton one Pendante of gold garnished with five
small dyamondes, one longe dyamonde and a triangled Dyamond and
three small pearles pendant
97.15 By the Earle of Essex one fayre paire of Brasselettes conteyninge xiiij
peeces of golde whereof six made like Bowsers knotted and sett with
small Dyamondes and eight peeces like Letters garnished with fower
small dyamondes and one small Ruby in the middest and lxviij pearles
in the same Brasselettes
97.16 By the Earle of Cumberlande two pendantes of gold each garnished with
vij small Dyamondes and one Rocke ruby in the middest, and one small
pearle pendant
Delivered to Mrs Ratcliffe

97.17 By the Vicount Mountigue . . . . .nil
97.18 By the Vicount Byndoun. . . . . .nil

Marques and Counntes

97.19 By the Lady Marques of Northampton a payre of Brasselettes
          conteyninge vj peeces of gold garnished with sparkes of Rubies and
          small Dyamondes in the middest and three rowes of small pearles
          threeded
                                                      Delivered to Mrs Ratcliffe
97.20 By the Countes of Kent fower handkerchers imbrothered in whit
          Cuttworke
                                                      dd to the La: Scudamore
97.21 By the Countes of Oxenford one rounde kertle of Cloth of siluer with
          braunches of golde
                                                      dd to the Robes
97.22 By the Countes of Shrewsbury widdowe in golde . . . . x li
                                                      dd to Mr Sackforde
97.23 By the Countes of Shrewesbury one rounde Kertle with a trayne of cloth
          of siluer with a border downe before of whit satten imbrodered
                                                      dd to the Robes
97.24 By the Countes of Lincolne in golde . . . . x li
97.25 By the Countes of Sussex in golde . . . . x li
97.26 By the Countes of Huntington Widdowe in golde. . . . . .viij li
                                                      dd to Mr Sackford
97.27 By the Countes of Huntington Junior in golde . . . . .viij li
97.28 By the Countes of Penbrooke in golde . . . . x li
97.29 By the Countes of Hartford in golde . . . . x li
                                                      Delivered to Mr Sackford
97.30 By the Countes of Darby Junior one rounde kertle of Tabyne cloth of
          siluer wrought with slips of Venis golde siluer & carnation silke
                                                      Delivered to the Robes
97.31 By the Countes of Warwicke a payre of Brasselettes conteyninge xij
          peeces of gold like knottes, sett with Sparkes of Rubies and a Sparke
          of a Dyamonde in the middest of eache peece and xij halfe pearles and
          xlviij little pearles
                                                      dd to Mrs Ratcliffe
97.32 By the Countes of Darby widow one kirtle of Tabyne cloth of siluer cutt
          Billett wise vpon murrey silke with flames of Venis golde betweene
                                                      dd to the Robes
97.33 By the Countes of Bath in golde. . . . . x li
                                                      dd to Mr Sackford
97.34 By the Countes of Bedford Junior one doublett of white satten cut &
          imbrodered all ouer like knottes and roses tufted ouer with Lawne
97.35 By the Countes of Southampton a loose gowne of white Lawne networke
          imbrodered all ouer with venis golde and siluer like flowers
                                                      dd to the Robes

97.36 By the Countes of Cumberlande two ringes of golde set with Sparkes and
       Dyamondes & iiij^or ringes of small perles to hange them by
                                                    Delivered to Mrs Ratcliffe
97.37 By the Countes of Keldare one Lose gowne of hayrecoulored Nettework
       florished with venis siluer
97.38 By the Countes of Northumberlande one Peticoate of oringe coulored
       satten painted set with Sifers of siluer plate
                                                            dd to the Robes
97.39 By the Vicountes Mountigue Widow in gold . . . . x li
                                                    Delivered to Mr Sackford
97.40 By the Countes of Bedforde widow one gowne of siluer Chamblet couered
       with a Couer of Cobwebb Lawne florished with venis Siluer like
       parimedds
                                                            dd to the Robes

Bushopes

97.41 By the Archebushop of Canterbury in golde . . . . xl li
97.42 By the Archebushop of yorke in gold . . . . xxx li
97.43 By the Bushop of Durham in gold . . . . xxx li
97.44 By the Bushop of Worcester in golde . . . . xx li
97.45 By the Bushop of Norwiche in gold . . . . xx li
97.46 By the Bushop of Lincolne in golde . . . . xx li
97.47 By the Bushop of Lincolne Lichefeild and Couentry in gold and siluer
       . . . . xiij li vj s viij d
97.48 By the Bushop of Carlile in gold. . . . . x li
97.49 By the Bushop of Rochester in golde . . . . x li
97.50 By the Bushop of Chichester Amner in golde . . . . x li
97.51 By the Bushop of Peterborrow in golde . . . . x li
97.52 By the Bushop of Glocester in golde . . . . x li
97.53 By the Bushop of Hereford in gold. . . . . x li
97.54 By the Bushop of Bath and Wells in gold . . . . xx li
97.55 By the Bushop of St Davies in gold . . . . x li
97.56 By the Bushop of Excetor in golde . . . . x li
                                                    dd to Mr Sackford vt supra

Lordes

97.57 By the Lorde Cobham Lord Chamberlayne in golde . . . . x li
                                                            dd to Mr Sacford
97.58 By the Lord Haward Lord Admirall one karkyonet conteyninge ix peeces
       of golde whereof the biggest peace is in the middest iiij^or of thother like
       knottes
                                                            dd to Mrs Ratcliffe
97.59 By the Lord Shandoys in gold. . . . . x li
97.60 By the Lord Buckehurst in gold . . . . v li
97.61 By the Lord Norres in gold. . . . . x li
97.62 By the Lord Northe in gold. . . . . x li

97.63	By the Lord Barkeley in golde. . . . . x li
97.64	By the Lord Wharton in golde . . . . x li
97.65	By the Lord Lomley in golde . . . . x li
97.66	By the Lord Rych in golde. . . . . x li

dd to Mr Sackford

97.67 By the Lord Compton a lose gowne of blacke Networke florished all ouer
with sparkes workes of golde and siluer in a parchement & bone lace of
gold & siluer

Delivered to the Robes

97.68 By the Lord Darcy of Chichey in golde . . . . x li

dd to Mr Sackford

97.69 By the Lord Broughe parte of one Karkionet of gold conteyninge five
peeces set with small Dyamondes and Rubies with a rowe of small
pearles threeded

dd to Mrs Ratcliffe

97.70 By the Lord Thomas Haward a Rounde kertle of white Tiffenie tissued
with golde

dd to the Robes

97.71 By the Lord Mountjoy one wastcoat of Cambericke imbrordered all ouer
with venis siluer owes and some Carnation silke

dd to the Lady Scudamore

97.72 By the Lord Stafford in golde . . . . x li

dd to Mr Sackford

97.73 By the Lorde Hunsdoun one pinpillow of gold garnished with Dyamondes
Rubies and six pearles, and a Needlecase of golde garnished with like
small Dyomondes Rubyes and two small pearles

Delivered to Mrs Ratcliffe

Baronesses

97.74 By the Barronnes Howard one paire of Brasselettes of gold conteyninge
xviij peeces garnished with small sparkes of Rubies or garnettes

dd to Mrs Ratcliffe

97.75 By the Baronnes Paget Cary one Peticoate of white satten fayre
imbrordered all ouer with a runninge Worke of Roses, and three
broad borders likewise imbrodered with flowers of sundry kindes

dd to the Robes

97.76 By the Barones of Hunsdon widow one Canapy of Straw coloured China
worke trimmed vp with Silke

dd to Mr Knevet keper of her Maties pallace at Westminster

97.77 By the Baronnes Shandoys knolles one longe Cushion of Crimson veluet
inbrodered all ouer with a Cutt of cloth of golde and five Rundles
likewise imbrodered with deuises havinge a backe of Caffa Damaske

dd to John Cotten keper of her Maties
standing warderobe at westminster

97.78 By the Barones Lombley one mantle of siluer printed, bound about with a
parchment Lace of siluer

427

97.79 By the Baronnes Willoby one peece of whit knit worke set with siluer owes
conteyninge fyue yeardes and a half

dd to the La Skudamore

97.80 By the Baronnes Skroupe one Mantle and a heade vale of siluer striped
Tinsell

dd to the Robes

97.81 By the Baronnes Dallaware one Skrenne of watched clothe of golde
imbroadered vpon with a threed of venis golde and Lyned with Oringe
coloured Taffata

dd to Mr Knevett ut supra

97.82 By the Baronnes Hunsdon one Case of gold garnished with Dyomondes
Rubies and three small pearles pendant with Sisers and tooth Pikes
therin

dd to Mrs Ratcliffe

97.83 By the Baronnes Arbella one dublet of white satten imbrodered vpon with
Leaues and garlandes of silke Needleworke

dd to the Robes

97.84 By the Baronnes Ryche one Pendant of gold like a fountaine garnished with
Dyomondes and three small pearles pendant

dd to Mrs Ratcliffe

97.85 By the Baronnes Howard Lord Thomas his wyef one doublet of white
Tiffenie tissued with golde

97.86 By the Baronnes Sheffeeld Stafford one Round kertle of Mayden blush of
siluer Chamlett

dd to the Robes

97.87 By the Baronnes of Buckehurst in golde. . . . . v li

97.88 By the Baronnes Norres in golde . . . . x li

97.89 By the Baronnes of St John Bletzo in golde . . . . x li

dd to Mr Sackford

97.90 By the Baronnes Dudley one Needle case of gold Percia worke garnished
with small garnettes and a pendant at the end thereof Likewise
garnished

dd to Mrs Ratcliffe

Ladyes

97.91 By the Lady Mary Seymer wyfe to Mr Rogers one Snuskynne of blacke
Veluet imbrodered all ouer with flowers of Venis gold Siluer and Silke
and some small seed pearles Lyned with Carnation Plushe

97.92 By the Lady Elizabeth Seymer Wyef to Sir Rychard Knightley one
Snuskinne of white Siluer Chamblett imbroadered vpon with Venis gold
and siluer and Lyned with white Plushe

dd to Mrs Hide

97.93 By the Lady Eliz: Somerset wief to Sir Henry Gilford parte of a round
kertle of cloth of siluer with workes of Bever colored silke

dd to the Robes

97.94 By the Lady Stafford one paire of Brasselettes of golde conteyninge xvj
    peeces whereof viij sett with fower garnettes and one pearle in the middest
    thother viij sett with fower pearles and one Ruby in the middest

97.95 By the Lady Cheake one paire of Braselettes conteyninge xvj peeces of
    golde sett with Spyders, Waspes and Frogges and xvj meane pearles
                      dd to Mrs Ratclyffe

97.96 By the Lady Leighton one Wastcoat of white Sarcenett imbrodered all
    ouer with a twist of Venis siluer & Carnation twiste
                      dd to the Lady Skidamore

97.97 By the Lady Scott a Lose gowne of white networke florished ouer with
    threeds of gold and tuftes of Oringe coloured silke
                      dd to the Robes

97.98 By the Lady Digby seven Pendantes of gold garnished with sparkes of
    Dyamondes Rubies & small pearles pendant
                      dd to Mrs Ratclyffe

97.99 By the Lady Jarrat in gold . . . . v li
                      dd to Mr Sackeford

97.100 By the Lady Cecil Sir Robert his wyef one Jewell of gold made like a hart
    garnished with Sparkes of Diamondes Rubies with a Ruby pendant
    without a foyle in the middest and smale Rubies Pendant about the
    Same
                      dd to Mrs Ratclyffe

97.101 By the Lady Scudamore parte of a lose gowne of Mayden Blushe Taffata
    Cut

97.102 By the Lady Wolley one lose gowne of White Stitched Satten inbrodered all
    ouer with owes and bordered rounde about with plate and owes sett like
    paramides of Venis golde
                      dd to the Robes

97.103 By the Lady Edmondes one Vale of white knitworke florished with a twist of
    Venis siluer
                      dd to the La: Skudamore

97.104 By the Lady Newton one Crosbowe of gold garnished with small sparkes
    of Rubyes and Dyamondes
                      dd to Mrs Ratclyffe

97.105 By the Lady Walsingham one straite bodyed gowne of clay colored
    Taffata wrought with Braunches of siluer bound aboute with a broade
    bone Lace of Venis golde
                      dd to the Robes

97.106 By the Lady Hawkins one paire of Braselettes of gold sett with x small
    Rubyes and xl Ragged pearles
                      dd to Mrs Ratclyffe

97.107 By the Lady Zouche one smocke of Holland cloth the sleues wrought with
    blacke silke drawne worke

97.108 By the Lady Longe parte of a Mantle of Knitworke Cut and Tucked Vp in
    Tuftes
                      dd to the La: Skudamore

97.109   By the Lady Harrington one Peticoat of White Satten imbroadered all ouer with Leaves and flowers of Venis gold and silk and three borders likewise imbroadered

dd to the Robes

97.110   By the Lady Townesend one skarfe of Whit knitworke florished with Venis siluer and owes

dd to the said Mrs Hide

97.111   By the Lady Hobby one Mantle of Ashcolored sipers striped with siluer and tuftes of like coloured silke

dd to the Robes

97.112   By the Lady Puckeringe in golde. . . . . x li

dd to Mr Sackford

97.113   By the Lady Palavizino one peece of White Tiffenie conteyninge threescore yeardes

97.114   By the Lady Southwell one Mantle of white knitworke florished with siluer plate

dd to the Robes

97.115   By the Lady Willoughby one Lawne Ruffe with a Rabata

dd to the La: Skudamore

Knightes

97.116   By Sir William Knolles Comptroller of her Maties Householde one Round kirtle of cloth of siluer wrought with braunches of Silke of soundry Colors

Delivered to the Robes

97.117   By Sir John Forteskew Chauncellor of the Exchequor in golde. . . . . x li

to Mr Sackforde

97.118   By Sir Robert Cicell Principall Secritory to her Matie three Pendantes of gold each garnished with small Dyomondes one Ruby ouer them and eache havinge three smalle pearles pendant

97.119   By Sir Thomas Cicell two pendantes of gold sett with small Rubies and fower small pearles

dd to Mrs Ratclif

97.120   By Sir Thomas Leighton Captaine of Garnesey one Peticoat of white Sarcenet imbroathered all ouer with a runninge worke of venis siluer and Carnation silke twistes with a broad border likewise imbroadered

Delivered to the Robes

97.121   By Sir Henry Cromwell in golde. . . . . x li
97.122   By Sir Edward Cleare in golde . . . . x li

dd to Mr Sackford

97.123   By Sir William Brooke one Castinge Bottle of Aggot garnished with golde

dd to Mrs Ratcliffe

97.124   By Sir Edward Stafford one paire of Braselettes conteyninge xxvj Letters garnished with sparkes of Rubyes and small pearles betweene them

430

97.125 By Sir William Russell Lord Deputie of Ireland two pendantes of gold
Cutworke garnished with smalle Dyomonds and Rubies and two little
smalle Pearles pendant

                dd to Mrs Ratcliffe

97.126 By Sir John Scudamore parte of a lose gowne of Pincked colored Taffata
called Maiden Blushe

              dd to the Roabes vt supra

97.127 By Sir Henry Newton one karkyonet conteyninge fyue peeces of gold sett
with small Rubyes & smaule pendant pearles

                dd to Mrs Ratcliffe

97.128 By Sir Edward Hobby one Peticoate of white Sarsionet imbrodered all ouer
with gold watched and Carnation silke with thre borders likewise
imbroadered

               Delivered to the Robes

97.129 By Sir Thomas Jarrat one Snuskyn of Veluet imbroadered with soundry
pictures havinge the picture of a Queene in the middest

               Delivered to Mrs Hide

97.130 By Sir Horatio Palavizino ij Pendantes of gold Like Layers garnished with
small Dyomondes

97.131 By Sir John Standhop Threasorer of her Maties chamber one paire of
Braselettes conteyninge xvj peeces of gold, viij of essefirmes and viij Roses
with Sparkes of Rubies or garnettes in them and fower Rowes of smaule
pearles threeded between them

               Delivered to Mrs Ratclife

97.132 By Sir Edward Dyer Chauncellor of the garter one peticoate pincked
colored satten imbrodered all ouer with venis golde havinge thre borders
of Venis golde

               Delivered to the Robes

97.133 By Sir Robert Sydney . . . . .nil

97.134 By Sir Willyam Hatton one karkionet conteyninge thre peces of golde like
Bowsers Knotts garnished with small Rubies five small Dyomondes in
the middest crosse wise two small peeces of gold garnished with gold
one Dyomonde and & two Rubies a peece one pendant in the middest
garnished with one Ruby and fower Dyomondes and peece pendant and
fower pendantes more

               dd to Mrs Ratclif

97.135 By Sir William Cornewallis one cloke thovtside Clay colored Cloth of
siluer printed the Inside peache colored Plushe wrought with Venis
golde and siluer

97.136 By Sir Robert Crosse one Lap Mantle of watched cloth of siluer with thre
bone Laces of venis gold Lyned with Crimson Plushe

97.137 By Sir Henry Gilford parte of a round Kertle of cloth of Siluer with workes
of hayre coloured & bever colored silke

               dd to the Robes

97.138   By my Skimskine for my pantables one Sknuskyn of blacke veluet imbroadered all ouer like bee hives and bees of seede pearles

dd to Mrs Hyde

Gentlewomen

97.139   By Mrs Mary Ratclyf one Kertle of white satten Cutt and tufte and striped with siluer

97.140   By Mrs Elizabeth Bridges one Mantle of white Tiffenie striped with siluer

97.141   By Mrs Carre one cap of Tawny Taffata imbrodered with seed pearles and Venis golde

97.142   By Mrs Lydy Lucy Hide one Cap of Sipers tuft vp and sett with siluer spangles and ten smale buttons of gold eache sett with fower pearles apeece and a garnett in the middest

Delivered to Mrs Hide the Robes

97.143   By Mrs Walsingham one head Vale of Lawne cutworke florished with venis gold and a broad parchment lase of like worke

97.144   By Mrs Coppyn one Ruffe of knitworke with a Rebata

97.145   By Mrs Twist one paire of Sleeues of Cambericke wrought with blacke silke drawne Worke

97.146   By Mrs Cromer one smocke of Holland cloth the sleeues wrought with blacke silke and edged with Venis gold

97.147   By Mrs Huggins one Large Sweet bagg faire imbroadered all ouer with a devise in the middest

97.148   By Mrs Frauncis Huggins six handkerchers wrought with blacke silke edged with venis golde

97.149   By Mrs Thomasin one handkercher wrought with white worke

97.150   By Mrs Barley six handkerchers with a passamayne Lace of gold

97.151   By Mrs Elizabeth Greane one Ruffe of knitworke with a Rebata

97.152   By Mrs Wincfeeld one night rayle of Camericke vnmade wrought with blacke silke

97.153   By Mrs Bromfeld Mother of the Maides one shoulder cloake of white Caffa striped with golde

97.154   By Mrs Elizabeth Russell one attyre for the heade of striped Tiffanie

97.155   By Mrs Alley one Nyght attyre of Camericke wrought with black silke and gold with a Lawne ouer yt

Delivered to the La: Skudamore

97.156   By Mrs Griffeth one Peticote of Carnation silke knitworke florished with venis gold siluer and silke

Delivered to the Robes

97.157   By Mrs Britten one attyre for the heade

dd to the La: Skudamore

Gentlemen

97.158   By Mr Henry Brouke one Peece of cloth of siluer tisshued with venis gold like flames conteyninge x yeardes and a qrter

dd to the Robes

97.159 By Mr Foulke Gryvell one karkyonet conteyninge ix peeces of gold sett
with great and small sparkes of Rubies or garnettes fower Rowes of small
pearles threeded and nyne small Pearles pendant

dd to Mrs Ratclif

97.160 By Mr Ralphe Bowes one Snoskynne of Haire colored Veluet laid all ouer
with silke womans worke Spheres or Globes and flowers of silke
needleworke Lyned with murrey Plushe

Delivered to Mrs Hyde

97.161 By Mr Henry Brouncker one Bodkin of golde with a Pendant of golde
sett with eight smalle dyomondes one little Ruby in the middest

Delivered to Mrs Ratclif

97.162 By Mr Carre one round kertle of white Taffata Striped with golde

Delivered to the Robes

97.163 By Mr Mountague one Smocke of Camericke wrought with blacke silke

dd to the La: Skudamore

97.164 By Mr Garter Kinge of Armes one booke couered with blewe veluett of
the knightes of thorder of the garter that haue benn elected sithens her
Maties comminge to the crowne vntill this yeare

dd to Mrs Ratclif

97.165 By Mr Simon Boyer parte of a mantle of Knitworke cut and tacked vp in
Tuftes

dd to the Robes

97.166 By Mr Carmarden one faire Night raile of Cambericke wrought all ouer
with black silke and gold Drawen worke

dd to the La: Skudamore

97.167 By Mr John Spilman one Pendant of three doublettes without foyle and a
knott of pearles

dd to Mrs Ratclife

97.168 By Mr Doctor James two Pottes one of greene ginger thother of Oringe
flowers

97.169 By Mr Doctor Gifford ij Pottes one of greene ginger thother of Oringe
flowers

97.170 By Mr Doctor Smithe two Pottes one of greene ginger thother of Oringe
flowers

97.171 By Mr Morgan Apothecary a pott of greene ginger and a pott of oringe
flowers

97.172 By Mr Hemingway Apothecary a pott of preserved Peares and box of
Lozenges and manescriste

97.173 By Mr Weston three of [sic] boxes of Plums preserved

dd to the La: Skudamore

97.174 By Mr Bushop a Stacioner one faire Bible in latine of the vulgure
Translation

Delivered to Mr Knevet vt supra

97.175 By Mr William Cordall Mr Cooke for her Matie one faire Pye oringed

97.176 By Mr George Lee Mr Cooke of the Householde one Marchepane beinge
Justice and Charitie on each side of yt

97.177   By Mr Thomas Frenche Serjaunte of the pastery one fayre Pye
        Oringed
97.178   By Mr Ralph Batty Serjaunt of the pastery one faire pye oringed
97.179   By Mr Abraham Speckarke a smocke of Holland wrought with black
        silke Drawne Worke

Delivered to the La: Skudamore

97.180   By Mr Petro Lupo six bottles of sweet water
97.181   By Mr Josephe Lupo a payre of perfumed gloues
97.182   By Mr Thomas Lupo one Paire of perfumed gloues
97.183   By Mr William Warren one Paire of perfumed gloues
97.184   By Mr Peter Guye ij flutes
97.185   By Mr Jeronimo Bassano one paire of perfumed gloues
97.186   By Mr Arthur Bassano one paire of perfumed gloues
97.187   By Mr Edward Bassano a paire of perfumed gloues
97.188   By Mr Andrew Bassano a paire of perfumed gloues
97.189   By Mr Caesar Galliardo one paire of perfumed gloues
97.190   By Mr Innocent Comy one paire of perfumed gloues

dd to Mrs Hide

97.191   By Mr Petruchio Vbaldino one Booke of Italian Couered with in vellam
        of the florentine meletiany [i.e. militia]

Delivered to Mr Knevet

97.192   By Mr William Huggens one little Coffer couered with cloth of siluer
        wrought with golde

dd to the La: Skudamore

97.193   By Mr Warberton one cloke of blacke knitworke florished with venis
        golde siluer and some owes Lyned with cloth of siluer printed and one
        Doublet of siluer Chamlett Layd vpon with a knitworke of Venis golde
        wrought with white Lawne puffed and tufte with Carnation silke

dd to the Robes

97.194   By Mr Billingsley two half peeces of Lawne

Delivered to Mrs Ratclife

97.195   By Mr Henry Sackford one longe Cushion of white Taffata imbrodered
        with Chyna worke backed with carnation satten

dd to the said John Cotten vt supra

97.196   By Mr Fraunces Bacon a Cloake of blacke veluett the grounde gold with a
        flatte lace of venis golde siluer about yt Lyned with Ashecolored Plushe

dd to the Robes

97.197   By Mr Goodderige one glasse of Jellie made of hartes horne
97.198   By Mr Baker one glasse of Precious water for the teath

dd to the La: Skudamore

97.199   By Mr Thomas Middleton half a peece of Lawne and half a bolt of
        Cambericke

dd to Mrs Ratclife

97.200   By Mr Frauncis Woolley one Mantle of white Striped tiffany bound about
        with a Lace of venis siluer and orenge colored silke tuftes

dd to the Robes

Summa totalis of all the money

Geuon to her highnes this yere . . . . vij^c xxij li xiij s iiij d

Elizabeth R
[sign manual]

Edwarde Carye
N Bristow
N Pigeon
Robert Cranmer
Nicholas Hottofte

New yeeres guiftes giuen by
the Queenes Maiesty at her
highnes pallace at westminster
to those parsons whose names
heareafter ensue the first day
of January in the year abouesaid

Elizabeth R
[sign manual]

97.201	To Sir Thomas Egerton knight Lord Keeper of the great Seale of England in gilte plate M . . . . xxxij oz iij qrters di
97.202	To the Lord Burghley Lord Highe Threasorer of England in gilte plate M . . . . xlv oz di
97.203	To the Lord Marques of Winchester in gilt plate K . . . . xxix oz qrter di

Earles

97.204	To the Earle of Shrewsbury in gilt plat K . . . . xxxj oz
97.205	To the Earle of Darby in gilt plate K . . . . xx oz di di qrter
97.206	To the Earle of Sussex in gilte plate K . . . . xx oz iij qrters di
97.207	To the Earle of Bath in gilt plate M . . . . xx oz iij qrters di
97.208	To the Earle of Hartford in gilt plate K . . . . xx oz iij qrters
97.209	To the Earle of Pembrooke in gilt plate K . . . . xxx oz qrter
97.210	To the Earle of Northumberland in gilt plate M . . . . xxvj oz di
97.211	To the Earle of Huntington in gilt plate M . . . . xx oz qrter
97.212	To the Earle of Essex in gilt plate M . . . . Cxlj oz di
97.213	To the Earle of Bedford in gilte plate K . . . . xxx oz qrter di
97.214	To the Earle of Southampton in gilt plate M . . . . xxx oz qrter
97.215	To the Earle of Lincolne in gilt plate K . . . . xx oz iij qrters
97.216	To the Earle of Cumberland in gilt plate K . . . . xxxj oz

Marques & Counteses

97.217	To the Lady Marques of Northampton in gilte plate K	xliiij oz
97.218	To the Countes of Kent in gilte plate K	xx oz qtr
97.219	To the Countes of Oxenford in gilt plate K	xxxvj oz
97.220	To the Countes of Shrewsbury widow in gilt plate K	xl oz di qrter
97.221	To the Countes of Shrewsbury in gilt plate K	xxj oz di
97.222	To the Countes of Darby widow in gilt plate M	xxj oz iij qrters di
97.223	To the Countes of Darby Junior in gilt plate K	xxiiij oz qrter di
97.224	To the Countes of Huntington widdow in gilt plate K	xxxj oz
97.225	To the Countes of Bedford in gilt plate K	xxv oz qrter di
97.226	To the Countes of Southampton in gilt plate M	xxj oz iij qrters di
97.227	To the Countes of Penbroke in gilt plate M	xxj oz di qrter
97.228	To the Countis of Hartford in gilt plate K	xxj oz qtr di
97.229	To the Countes of Lincolne in gilte plate K	ix oz iij qrters di
97.230	To the Countes of Bath in gilt plate K	xx oz qrter di
97.231	To the Countes of Bedford widow in gilte plate M	xlix oz di
97.232	To the Countes of Cumberland in gilte plate K	xx oz di qrter
97.233	To the Countes of Huntington in gilt plate K	xviij oz iij qrters
97.234	To the Countes of Sussex in gilte plate K	xx oz iij qrters di
97.235	To the Countes of Warwicke in gilte plate K M	liiij oz iij qrters di
97.236	To the Countes of Northumberland in gilt plate M	xxj oz di
97.237	To the Countes of Kildare in gilte plate M	xxv oz iij qrters
97.238	To the Viscountis Mountague widowe in gilte plate K	xx oz

Bushopes

97.239	To the Archebushop of Canterbury in gilt plate K	xlv oz
97.240	To the Archebushop of Yorke in gilt plate K	xxxvij oz di
97.241	To the Bushop of Durisme in gilt plate M	xxxv oz qrter
97.242	To the Bushop of Norwich in gilt plate K	xxx oz qrter di
97.243	To the Bushop of Lincolne in gilt plate K	xxx oz qrter di
97.244	To the Bushop of Worcester in gilte plate M	xxx oz di
97.245	To the Bushop of Lichefeeld and Couventry in gilte plate K	xx oz di qrter
97.246	To the Bushop of Carlile in gilt plate M	xv oz qrter
97.247	To the Bushop of Rochester in gilte plate K	xv oz di
97.248	To the Bushop of Exetor in gilt plate K	xvj oz di qrter
97.249	To the Bushop of Chichester in gilt plate M	xv oz di di qrter
97.250	To the Bushop of Peterborowe in gilt plate M	xv oz
97.251	To the Bushop of Glocester in gilt plate K	xv oz iij qrters
97.252	To the Bushop of Hereford in gilte plate K	xiiij oz di di qtr
97.253	To the Bushop of Bathe and Wells in guilte plate K	xxx oz iij qrters
97.254	To the Bushop of St Davies in guilt plate K	xv oz qrter di

Lordes

97.255 To the Lord Cobham Lord Chamberleyne in gilte plate K . . . . xxv oz qrter
97.256 To the Lord Howard Lo Admirall in gilt plate M . . . . Cviij oz
97.257 To the Lord Buckhurst in gilt plate M . . . . .xij oz qrter di
97.258 To the Lord North Threasorer of the Household in gilt plate M
. . . . xx oz iij qrters di
97.259 To the Lord Hunsdon in gilt plate M . . . . xxvij oz di qrter
97.260 To the Lord Shandoys in gilt plate M . . . . xx oz iij qrters di
97.261 To the Lord Compton in gilt plate K . . . . xxj oz di qrter
97.262 To the Lord Lomley in gilte plate K . . . . xx oz di di qrter
97.263 To the Lord Burroughe in gilt plate K . . . . xxiij oz qrter
97.264 To the Lord Norres in gilte plate M . . . . xix oz di qrter
97.265 To the Lord Wharton in gilt plate M . . . . xx oz di
97.266 To the Lord Riche in gilt plate K . . . . .xix oz iij qrters di
97.267 To the Lorde Stafford in gilt plate K. . . . . xxv oz qrter
97.268 To the Lord Darcey of Chichey in gilt plate K. . . . . .xx oz di di qrter
97.269 To the Lord Thomas Howard in gilt plate K . . . . .xxj oz di
97.270 To the Lord Mountjoy in gilt plate M. . . . . .xxxj oz
97.271 To the Lord Barkley in gilte plate M. . . . . xix oz qrter di

Baronesses

97.272 To the Baronnes Howard in gilte plate M. . . . . xx oz di
97.273 To the Baronnes Pagett Cary in gilt plate M. . . . . .xxxv oz
97.274 To the Baronnes Shandoys knolles in gilt plate M . . . . xx oz iij qrters di
97.275 To the Baronnes Hunsdon widow in gilt plate K . . . . xxx oz iij qrters
97.276 To the Baronnes Lombley in gilt plate K . . . . xx oz di
97.277 To the Baronnes Hunsdon in gilt plate K . . . . xix oz di di qrter
97.278 To the Baronnes Willoby in gilte plate M . . . . .xxij oz qrter di
97.279 To the Baronnes Scroup in gilte plate M. . . . . xx oz iij qrters di
97.280 To the Baronnes Arbella in gilt plate K . . . . xxj oz qrter
97.281 To the Baronnes Sheffeeld Stafford in gilt plate M. . . . . xx oz
97.282 To the Baronnes Riche in gilte plate M. . . . . xx oz qrter di
97.283 To the Baronnes Boroughe in gilt plate M . . . . .xxj oz iij qrters di
97.284 To the Baronnes Dudley in gilt plate M . . . . .xvj oz iij qrters di
97.285 To the Baronnes St John Bletzo in gilt plate M . . . . .xix oz iij qrters di
97.286 To the Baronnes Buckhurst in gilt plate K . . . . .xj oz iij qrters
97.287 To the Baronnes Howard Lo: Thomas his wief in gilt plate K. . . . . .xxj oz
97.288 To the Baronnes Norres in gilt plate M. . . . . xx oz di
97.289 To the Baronnes Delaware in gilt plate K . . . . xx oz iij qrters

Ladyes

97.290 To the Lady Mary Seymer Mr Rogers his wiefe in gilte plate K . . . . xij oz di

437

97.291	To the Lady Elizabeth Seymer Sir Richard Knightley his wief in gilte Plate M.	xiij oz iij qrters
97.292	To the Lady Elizabeth Somerset Sir Henry Gilford his wief in guilt Plate K	xvij oz iij qrters di
97.293	To the Lady Stafford in gilt plate K	xxxij oz di qrter
97.294	To the Lady Cheeke in gilte plate M	xxxj oz di qrter
97.295	To the Lady Leighton in gilt plate M	xvij oz qrter di
97.296	To the Lady Scott in gilt plate M	xvij oz iij qrters
97.297	To the Lady Southwell in gilt Plate M	xviij oz di qrter
97.298	To the Lady Cecill Robert his wiefe in gilt plate K	xvij oz iij qrters
97.299	To the Lady Skudamore in gilte Plate K	xvij oz di di qrter
97.300	To the Lady Wolley in gilte plate K	xvij oz iij qrters
97.301	To the Lady Edmondes in gilt plate K	xvj oz qrter
97.302	To the Lady Newton in gilt Plate K	xvij oz
97.303	To the Lady Hawkins in gilte plate K	xvij oz di qrter
97.304	To the Lady Hobby in gilt plate K	xvij oz iij qrters di
97.305	To the Lady Digby in guilt plate K	xvj oz iij qrters di
97.306	To the Lady Jarrat in guilt plate K	xix oz di
97.307	To the Lady Walsingham in gilt plate K	xxv oz
97.308	To the Lady Zouche in guilt Plate K	xiiij oz iij qrters
97.309	To the Lady Longe in gilt plate M	xvij oz qrter
97.310	To the Lady Harrington in gilte Plate K	xix oz iij qrters
97.311	To the Lady Townsende in gilt plate K	xvij oz iij qrters
97.312	To the Lady Puckeringe in gilt plate M	xix oz iij qrters
97.313	To the Lady Palavizino in gilt plate M	xxj oz iij qrters
97.314	To the Lady Willoughby in gilt plate K	xv oz qrter di

Knightes

97.315	To Sir William Knolles Comptroller of her Maties Householde in gilt plate M	xxiiij oz di
97.316	To Sir John Fortescue Chauncellor of the Exchequor in gilt plate K	xxiij oz di qrter
97.317	To Sir Robert Cicill principall secretary to her Matie in gilte plate K	xxxj oz qrter
97.318	To Sir Thomas Cicill in gilte plate K	xxxj oz iij qrters di
97.319	To Sir William Russell Deputy of Irelande in gilte plate K	xxx oz
97.320	To Sir Thomas Layton Captaine of Garnsey in gilt plate M K	xxxiiij oz di di qrter
97.321	To Sir John Stanhop in gilt plate K	xxiiij oz di di qrter
97.322	To Sir Edward Stafford in gilte plate M	xx oz
97.323	To Sir John Skudamore in gilte plate M K	xix [oz] iij qrters di
97.324	To Sir Edward Hobby in gilte plate M	xx oz qrter di
97.325	To Sir Henry Newton in gilt plate K	xviij oz
97.326	To Sir Edward Dyer Chauncellor of the garter in gilt plate M	xx oz

97.327 To Sir Horatio Palavizino in gilt Plate M . . . . .xxiiij oz qrter di

97.328 To Sir Thomas Jarrett in gilt plate M . . . . xxv oz iij qrters di

97.329 To Sir William Cornewallis in gilt plate K . . . . xix oz di qrter

97.330 To Sir Henry Cromwell in gilt plate K . . . . xix oz di di qrter

97.331 To Sir William Hatton in gilt Plate M. . . . . .xxx oz

97.332 To Sir Edward Cleare in gilt plate M . . . . .xix oz iij qrters

97.333 To Sir Robert Crosse in gilt plate K . . . . .xxiij oz iij qrters di

97.334 To my Skunskyne for my Pantaples in gilte Plate K . . . . xx oz qrter di

97.335 To Sir William Brooke in guilt plate K . . . . .xxj oz iij qrters di

97.336 To Sir Henry Gilforde in gilt plate K . . . . xx oz

Maidens of Honor

97.337 To Mrs Elizabeth Vernon in gilt plate K. . . . . .x oz di di qrter

97.338 To Mrs Margaret Ratclife in gilt plate M .ix oz iij qrters

97.339 To Mrs Mary Fitton in gilt plate M . . . . .x oz qrter di

97.340 To Mrs Anne Russell in gilte plate K . . . . x oz qrter

Gentlewomen

97.341 To Mrs Mary Ratclyf in guilt plate K. . . . . xviij oz qrter di

97.342 To Mrs Elizabeth Bridges in gilt plate M . . . . xvij oz di qrter

97.343 To Mrs Carr in gilt plate K . . . . xvj oz di qrter

97.344 To Mrs Lucy Hide in gilt plate M . . . . xvij oz qrter di

97.345 To Mrs Coppyn in gilte plate K . . . . xvj oz

97.346 To Mrs Twist in gilt plate K . . . . .viij oz iij qrters di

97.347 To Mrs Walsingham in gilt plate K. . . . . xvij oz qrter

97.348 To Mrs Alley in gilt plate M . . . . vij oz

97.349 To Mrs Cromer in gilt plate M . . . . .xvij oz di di qrter

97.350 To Mrs Huggins in gilte plate K . . . . xvj oz

97.351 To Mrs Fraunces Huggins in gilt plate M. . . . . .xiiij oz qrter di

97.352 To Mrs Britten in gilt plate K . . . . vj oz

97.353 To Mrs Thomasyne Huggins [sic] in gilt plate M . . . . viij oz di

97.354 To Mrs Barley in gilte plate K. . . . . xij oz

97.355 To Mrs Greene in gilt plate M. . . . . iiij oz iij qrters di

97.356 To Mrs Winckefeild in gilt plate K . . . . xvij oz qrter di

97.357 To Mrs Elizabeth Russell in guilt plate M. xvij oz di

97.358 To Mrs Gryffen in gilt plate M . . . . xix oz qrter di

97.359 To Mrs Brumfeild Mother of the Maides in guilt plate K . . . . .xxj oz di

Gentlemen

97.360 To Mr Henry Brooke in gilt plate K . . . . xxij oz di di a qrter

97.361 To Mr Foulke Grivell in gilt plate M. . . . . .xxiiij oz iij qrters

97.362 To Mr Ralf Bowes in gilt plate K . . . . xvij oz a qrter di

97.363	To Mr Henry Brouncker in gilt plate M	xxj oz iij a qrters di
97.364	To Mr Henry Sackford in gilt plate K	xx oz di
97.365	To Mr Carre in gilt plate M	xx oz di a qrter
97.366	To Mr Garter kinge at Armes in gilt plate M	viij oz
97.367	To Mr Mountague in gilt plate K	xvj oz iij a qrters
97.368	To Mr Symon Boyer in guilt plate M	xix oz a qrter
97.369	To Mr Carmarden in gilt plate K	xix oz a qrter di
97.370	To Mr John Spillman in gilt plate K	xviij oz iij a qrters
97.371	To Mr Doctor Gyfford in gilte plate M	xiiij oz iij a qrters di
97.372	To Mr Doctor Smith in gilt plate M	xiiij oz iij a qrters di
97.373	To Mr Docter James in gilt plate K	xiiij [oz] iij a qrters
97.374	To Mr Morgan Apothecary in gilt plate M	vij oz
97.375	To Mr Hemmingway in gilt plate M	viij oz di
97.376	To Mr Weston Apothecary in gilt plate M	ix oz di
97.377	To Mr William Cordall Mr Cooke in gilte plate M	vj oz iij a qrters di
97.378	To Mr George Lee Mr Cooke of the Householde in gilt plate K	vj oz di
97.379	To Mr Thomas French Serjaunt of the Pastery in gilt plate M	vj oz
97.380	To Mr Ralfe Battey Serjeant of the Pastry in gilt plate M	v oz iij a qrters di
97.381	To Mr Abraham Speckard in gilt plate K	viij oz
97.382	To Mr Petro Lupo in gilt plate K	v oz
97.383	To Mr Josephe Lupo in gilt plate M	v oz
97.384	To Mr Thomas Lupo in gilte plate M	v oz
97.385	To Mr William Warren in gilt plate K	v oz
97.386	To Mr Jeronimo Bassano in gilt plate K	v oz
97.387	To Mr Arthur Bassano in gilt plate K	v oz
97.388	To Mr Andrewe Bassano in gilt plate K	v oz
97.389	To Mr Edward Bassano in gilte plate K	v oz
97.390	To Mr Cesar Galliardo in gilte plate M	v oz
97.391	To Mr Innocent Comy in gilt plate M	v oz
97.392	To Mr Petrucio Vbaldino in gilt plate K	v oz
97.393	To Mr Peeter Guye in gilte plate M	v oz
97.394	To Mr William Huggens in guilte plate M	xxiij oz
97.395	To Mr Frauncis Bacon in gilt plate M	xxxij oz di a qrter
97.396	To Mr Billingsley in gilt plate M	xxij oz
97.397	To Mr Thomas Middleton in guilt plate K	xv oz di qrt
97.398	To Mr Warberton in gilte plate K	xxv oz a qrter
97.399	To Mr Bushop in gilt plate M	xvij oz di di a qrter
97.400	To Mr Baker in guilt plate M	xviij oz di di a qrter
97.401	To Mr Frauncis Woolley in gilt plate K	xviij oz a qrter
97.402	To Mr William Goodderige in gilt plate K	xiij oz a qrter

Freguiftes

97.403	To Sir Edward Cary Mr and Treasorer of her Maties Jewells and plate in gilte plate m	xviij oz iij a qrters di

97.404	To Sir Thomas Gorges in guilt plate K	x oz
97.405	To Sir Edward Denny in guilt plate K	x oz
97.406	To Mr Henry Sackeford in gilt plate K	x oz
97.407	To Mr John Baptist in gilte plate K	x oz
97.408	To Mr William Killigraue in gilte plate K	x oz
97.409	To Mr Thomas Knyvett in gilte plate m	x oz iij a qrters di
97.410	To Mr Michaell Stanhop in gilt plate m	x oz
97.411	To Mr Edward Darcy in gilte plate K	x oz
97.412	To Sir Edward Cary groome in gilt Plate m	x oz di
97.413	To Mr Ferdinando Richardson in gilt plate m	x oz
97.414	To Mr Humphrey Adderley yeoman of the Robes in gilte plate K	xij oz
97.415	To Mr Nicholas Bristow in gilte Plate m	x oz iij a qrters di
97.416	To Mr Nicholas Pigeon in gilt plate K	x oz iij a qrters di
97.417	To Mr Robert Cranmer in gilt plate m	x oz iij a qrters di
97.418	To Mr Nicholas Hattoft in gilt plate K	x oz iij a qrters di

Summa Total of all the plate

Geuon by her highnes this yere . . . . iiij^m viij^C xviij oz

Guiftes giuen by her Matie to Soundry
persons and deliuered at sondry tymes
as followeth

97.419   Earle of Northumberlande

First given by her highnes the third of July Anno xxxviij Regni Reginae
Elizabethae &c To the Christeninge of the Earle of Northumberlande
his Childe one payre of guilte Flagons poiz—Cxliiij oz di and one guilt
Bole with a Cover guilte poz—xxiiij oz qrter bought of Richard Martin
Goldsmith in toto . . . . .Clxviij oz iij qrters

97.420   Landsgraue van Hest:

Item given by her saide highnes the vjth of July Anno pred To the
Christeninge of the Landsgraue van Hest his child one paire of
guilt Pottes poiz—vij^C xx oz iij qrters Item one paire of guilt Flagons
poiz—viij^C lij oz / Item one nest of thre guilt pottes with a couer
poz—CClij oz / all beinge the charge of Edward Cary Esquier Mr
and Thresorer of her Maties Jewells and Plate And more one Bason
and a Layer guilt poiz—ij^C iiij oz bought of the said Richard Martin
in toto . . . . mm iiij^{xx} viij oz iij qrters

97.421   Sir Edwarde Winter

Item given by her saide highnes the xvjth of July Anno pred To the
Christeninge of Sir Edwarde Winter knight his childe twoe guilt
Bolles with Couers bought of the saide Richarde Martin poiz . . . . . lxiiij oz

97.422   **Earle of Sussex**

Item given by her said highnes the xijth of August Anno pred To the
Christeninge of the Earle of Sussex his sonne one paire of guilt
Pottes poiz—lxxvj oz iij qrters di and one guilt Bole with a Cover
poiz—lxv oz qrter di bought of the saide Richarde Martin in toto
. . . . Cxlij oz qrter

97.423   **Duke of Bullion**

Item given by her sayd highnes the second of September Anno predicto
To the Duke of Bullion one Bason and a Layer guilt poz—Cxlij oz
qrter, Item one Bason and a Layer guilt poz—Ciij oz di qrter, Item
one Bason and a Layer guilte poz—Cj oz , Item one paire of Pottes
guilte poz—Ciiij^{xx} xviij oz di, Item one paire of guilt pottes poz—
Cliiij oz di qrter, Item one paire of Pottes guilte poz—Cix oz iij qrters,
Item one paire of Stoapes guilte poz—Cix oz iij qrters, Item paire of
guilte Stoapes poz—iiijxx oz, Item one paire of guilte Flagons poz
—CCxxxv oz di di qrter, Item one paire of guilte Flagons poz—
CCxiij oz iij qrters, Item one paire of guilte Flagons poz—Cxxix
oz di qrter, Item one Nest of three guilte Bolles with a Couer poz
—iiij^{xx} viij oz iij qrters di, Item one Peare Cup with a Couer guilte
poz—iiij^{xx} xj oz di di qrter, Item one peare Cup with a Couer guilte
poz—lxij oz qrter, Item one peare Cup with a Couer guilt poz—lv
oz di di qrter, Item one peare Cup with a Couer guilt poz—xliij oz
di qrter, Item one guilt Cup with a Couer poz—iiij^{xx} ix oz, Item one
guilt Cup and a Cover poz—lxxvij oz qrter di, Item one guilte Bole
with a Cover poz—lxvj oz qrter di, Item one guilte Bole with a Cover
poz—lx oz, Item one guilte Bole with a cover poz—lvj oz qrter, Item
one guilt Bole with a cover poiz—xlj oz di qrter, Item one guilte Bole
with a couer poiz—xxx oz qrter, Item iij guilte Chaundellors poz—
CCviij oz qrter, Item one guilte Standishe poz—xliij oz qrter, Item
one Christall Spice box with a salte havinge a Spoone white and a
little pepperbox guilte therein guilt poz—xl oz qrter di, Item two guilt
Saltes with out Couer poiz—C iiij^{xx} xviij oz, Item two guilte Saltes
with one Couer poz—iiij^{xx} xvj oz, Item one guilt Spout pott poz—
xxxix oz, Item one guilt Spout Pott poz—xxxiij oz qrter in toto mm
ix^C iiijxx xviij oz all bought of the saide Richard Martin, Item one nest
of three guilte Boles with a Cover poz – iiij^{xx} xv oz iij qrters di bought
of Hughe Kayle goldsmith in toto . . . . .mmm iiij^{xx} xiij oz iij qrters di

97.424   **French king**

Item given by her saide highnes the vijth of September Anno pred at the
enstallinge of the Frenche Kynge one Collar of golde of the order of
the garter Conteyninge xxij peeces enamuled with roses within the
garter and xxij peeces with knottes of the Charge of the saide
Edwarde Cary Esquier poz . . . . xxxiiij oz iij qrters   golde

Item given by her said highnes to the said French Kinge one George of
gold garnished with iiij^or Table Dyomondes and smaller Dyomondes
of soundry Cuttes poz all iij oz di di qrter and one Garter of Purple
velatt imbroadered with Letters of gold garnished with small
Dyomondes and Rubyes with Buckle and pendant of like gold
garnished likewise with Dyomondes and Rubies poz all iiij oz di
bought of Abraham harderett Jeweller in toto poz . . . . viij oz di qrter

97.425   Item given by her said highnes the xxx^th of October Anno predicto to
a french youth one Chayne bought of the goodnes of xxij karates
bought of the sayd Richarde Martin poz . . . . .xviij oz iiij dwait   golde

97.426 Mr Barkley

Item geven by her saide highnes the xxx^th of December Anno xxxix
R Reginae Elizabethae To the chistening of Mr Barkeley his childe
one Bason and a Layer guilte bought of the saide Richarde Martin
poz . . . . Lxix oz iij qrters

Elizabeth R
[sign manual]

Edwarde Carye
N Bristow
N Pigeon
Robert Cranmer
Nicholas Hottofte

443

Anno Regni Regine Elizabetha
Quadragilimo Anno Dm 1597

New Yeares giftes giuen to the Queenes
maiesty at her highnes pallace at Westmister
By these persones whose names hearrafter
ensue the first day of January in the yere
abovesaide viz

Elizabeth R
[sign manual]

98.1   By Sir Thomas Egerton Knight Lord Keeper of the great Seale of
England in golde . . . . xiij li vj s viij d

98.2   By the Lord Burghley Lord highe Threasorer of England in a purse of
siluer in golde. . . . . xx li

98.3   By the Lord Marques of Wincester in golde . . . . xx li
        delivered to Henry Sakford esquir one of the gromes of the Privie Chamber

Earles

98.4   By the Earle of Essex Mr of her Maties horses Mr of the Ordinaunces
and Earle marshall of Englande one short armlet conteyninge vijty
peeces whereof the middle peece is biggest garnished with dyamondes
Rubies and pearles of sondry sortes vj payre of Aglettes of golde
garnished three square with smalle Rubyes and smale pearles and a knot
in the top with a dyamonde and six opaulls and one Braselett of gold
conteyninge Cxij perlles with a lock of gold garnished with smale
dyamondes
                  delivered to Mrs Ratclyf

98.5   By the Earle of Nottingham Lord Admirall one attyre of pearle for the
heade with xv smalle pearle pendant garnished with Rubies and
dyamondes and six smalle pendantes being tryangled dyamondes and
eache a smalle pearle pendant
                  dd to Mrs Ratclyf

98.6   By the Earle of Darby in golde. . . . . x li
98.7   By the Earle of Sussex in golde. . . . . x li
98.8   By the Earle of Bathe in golde . . . . x li
98.9   By the Earle of Hertford in golde. . . . . x li
98.10 By the Earle of Huntingdon in golde . . . . x li
98.11 By the Earle of Penbroke in golde . . . . xx li
98.12 By the Earle of Bedford in golde. . . . . xx li
                  delivered to Mr Sackford

98.13 By the Earle of Northumberland one Cup with a Couer of Elitropia
garnished with golde

> Charged upon Sir Edwarde Carey Knight
> & treas of her Maties Juells and plate

98.14 By the Earle of Shrewsbury in golde. . . . . xx li
98.15 By the Earle of Rutland in golde . . . . x li

> delivered to Mr Sackford

98.16 By the Earle of Southampton one Kartionet of golde conteyninge ix
peeces of chein havinge a Ruby and viij with every of them a pearle one
smale pendant of golde with a Spinell and three small pearles and viij
smale pearles pendant and eight smale Rubies pendant without a foyle

> delivered to Mastris Ratclyf

Marquesses and Countesses

98.17 By the Lady Marques of Northampton two knottes of golde garnished with
smale Rubies and iij smale pearles pendant to either knot

> delivered to Mystris Ratclyf

98.18 By the Countes of Kent one Quosion clothe of Cambricke imbrodered
all ouer with venis golde siluer and silke of sondry coulors

> delivered to the La Skudamore

98.19 By the Countes of Oxenford one Rounde Kertle of cloth of Siluer printed
downe before and round about like pannades

> delivered to the Robes

98.20 By the Countes of Shrewesbury widowe in golde. . . . . .xl li
98.21 By the Countes of Shrewesbury junior in golde . . . . x li
98.22 By the Countes of Sussex in golde . . . . x li
98.23 By the Countes of Huntingdon widow. . . . . .viij li
98.24 By the Countes of Huntington junior. . . . . .viij li

> delivered to Mr Sackford

98.25 By the Countes of Notingham one short Armelet of golde garnisshed
with Smale rubies and diamondes and one bigger dyamond & one Opall
with xiij pearles pendant and one bigger pearle

> delivered to Mrs Ratclyf

98.26 By the Countes of Penbroke in golde . . . . x li
98.27 By the Countes of Hertford in golde . . . . x li

> delivered to Mr Sackford

98.28 By the Countes of Darby widow one vale of siluer Knitworke

> delivered to the Robes

98.29 By the Countes of Warwicke a paire of brasseletts of golde conteyninge
xvj peeces viij longe and viij shorter fully garnished with smale Rubyes
and halfe pearles and viij bigger Rubies and viij sparkes of dyamondes
about each of them

> delivered to Mrs Ratclyf

98.30 By the Countes of Darby junior one peticoate of white satton embrodered
all ouer with venis golde siluer and silke of soundry collours and workes
beinge Slippes of Roses and Paunses

Delivered to the Robes

98.31 By the Countes of Bathe in golde . . . . x li

delivered to Mr Sackford

98.32 By the Countes of Bedford widowe one garde of golde conteyninge xviij
peeces like esses garnished with smale Rubies and two smale pearles a
peece and xviij smale peeces garnished with one smale dyamonde and ij
smale perles

delivered to Mistris Ratclyf

98.33 By the Countes of Bedford junior one rounde Kirtle of clothe chamblet
like droppes and starres

delivered to the Robes

98.34 By the Countes of Southampton widow one mantle cut and florished with
venis siluer and owes

delivered to the Robes

98.35 By the Countes of Cumberland a paire of brasseletts of golde conteyninge
xxiiij peeces garnished with smale sparkes of dyamondes and Rubies
Lyned with mother of pearle

delivered to Mrs Ratclyf

98.36 By the Countes of Kildare one Karkyonet of golde conteyning fyve
peeces garnished with smale dyamondes and rubies and every peece
havinge a small pearle pendant

delivered to Mistris Ratclyf

98.37 By the Countes of Northumberland one fanne of white Feathers with a
handle of Christall slightly garnished with golde and some pearles

delivered to Mistris Ratclyf

98.38 By the Viscountess Montague widow in golde . . . . x li

delivered to Mr Sackford

Bishops

98.39 By the Archbushop of Canterbury in golde . . . . xl li
98.40 By the Archbushop of Yorke in golde. . . . . xxx li
98.41 By the Bushop of London in golde. . . . . xx li
98.42 By the Bushop of Durham in golde . . . . xxx li
98.43 By the Bushop of Norwiche in golde . . . . xx li
98.44 By the Bushop of Lincolne in golde . . . . xx li
98.45 By the Bushop of Lichfield & Couventry in golde . . . . xiij li vj s viij d
98.46 By the Bushop of Carlile in golde. . . . . x li
98.47 By the Bushop of Rochester in golde . . . . x li
98.48 By the Bushop of Winchester in golde . . . . x li
98.49 By the Bushop of Chichester in golde. . . . . xxx li
98.50 By the Bushop of Worcester in golde . . . . x li
98.51 By the Bushop of Peterborow in golde. . . . . x li
98.52 By the Bushop of Glocester in golde . . . . x li

98.53	By the Bushop of Hereford in golde	x li
98.54	By the Bushop of Bath and Wells in golde	xx li
98.55	By the Bushop of St Davyes in golde	x li
98.56	By the Bushop of Chester in golde	x li

delivered to Mr Sackford

Lordes

98.57 By the Lord Hunsdon, Lord Chamberlain one Karkyonet hayinge a Row
of pearles conteyninge xxij pearles threeded with five peeces of golde

delivered to Mrs Ratclyf

98.58	By the Lord North in golde	x li
98.59	By the Lord Buckhurst in golde	v li
98.60	By the Lord Norris in golde	x li
98.61	By the Lord Barckley in golde	x li
98.62	By the Lord Wharton in golde	x li
98.63	By the Lord Lombley in golde	x li
98.64	By the Lord Ryche in golde	x li

delivered to Mr Sackford

98.65 By the Lord Compton on cloake of siluer chamblet florished with slippes
of flowers of gold and silke of sundry colors lined with maidesblush
printed Sarcenet

delivered to the Robes

98.66 By the Lord Darcy of Chiche in golde . . . . x li

delivered to Mr Sackford

98.67 By the Lord Thomas Howard parte of a ronde kertle of cloth of siluer
striped with venis golde like clawes and corded betweene

delivered to the Robes

98.68 By the Lord Sheffelde one rounde kertle of white satten imbrodered all
ouer with slips of flowers with a brocade border rounde about and
before like pillowes wounde about with grapes

delivered to the Robes

98.69 By the Lord Mountjoy a paire of brasseletts of gold conteyninge xiiij
peeces whereof viij bigger than the rest and vj lesser granished with
smale Rubies and smalle pearles threeded between them

delivered to Mrs Ratclyf

98.70 By the Lord Stafford in golde . . . . x li

delivered to Mr Sackford

98.71 By the Lord Cobham one ronde kertle of cloth of siluer with golde

delivered to the Robes

98.72 By the Lord Willoby one wastcoate of taffata faire imbrodered all ouer
with venise golde and siluer and silke of sundry coulors

delivered to the said Lady Skudamore

Baronesses

98.73 By the Baronnes Paget-Carey in golde . . . . L li

deliverered to Sackford

447

98.74   By the Baronnes Hunsdon widow one snufkin purple imbrodered all ouer
        like grapes Lined with white plush

                                                delivered to Mistris Hyde
98.75   By the Baronnes Hunsdon junior one Mantle of white Networke with a
        net of venis siluer

                                                delivered to the Robes
98.76   By the Baronnes Shandoys Knolles one lounge Qushion of clothe of
        siluer imbrodered all ouer with venis siluer and golde

                                        delivered to Henry [Thomas] Knyvett
98.77   By the Baroness Lombley one peticoate of white Sarcenett imbrodered all
        ouer with Sunnes and Sonnebeames and a broad border rounde about
        with venis golde and silke of sondry colors

                                                delivered to the Robes
98.78   By the Baronnes Sheffeeld Junior parte of a round kertle of white satten
        imbrothered all ouer with slippes of flowers with a border [downe]
        before as p[illers] & wound aboute with grapes

                                                delivered to the Robes
98.79   By the Baronnes Scrope one vale or mantle of tawney striped networke
        flourisshed with siluer
98.80   By the Baronnes Delloware one Sheete of fine holland imbrothered all ouer
        with venise siluer and carnation silke fringed with venis golde
98.81   By the Baronnes Arabella one ronde kertle of lawne imbrothered all ouer
        like Waves of the Sea and fethers of siluer and silke

                                                delivered to the Robes
98.82   By the Baronnes Ryche one pendant of golde with a faire white Ruby and
        ij smale pearles & one small pendant

                                                delivered to Mistris Ratclyf
98.83   By the Baronnes Howard Lord Thomas his wife parte of a ronde kertle of
        cloth of siluer striped with venis golde like cheynes and corded between

                                                delivered to the Robes
98.84   By the Baronnes Sheffield ij pendants of gold havinge a star of smalle
        dyamondes in the middest and iij smalle pearlles pendant in every of
        them

                                                delivered to Mrs Ratclyf
98.85   By the Baronnes Buckhurst in golde. . . . . v li
98.86   By the Baronnes Norris in golde. . . . . x li
98.87   By the Baronnes St John Bletzo in golde . . . . x li

                                                Deliverered to Mr Sackford
98.88   By the Baronnes of Dudley one small Juell of golde like a hunteres horne
        of Amatistes and without foyle

                                                Delivered to Mistris Ratclyf
98.89   By the Baronnes of Boroughe one lose gowne of black silke and siluer
        stitchedcloth garnished with Roses of venice siluer
98.90   By the Baronnes of Ephingham one doublet of white satten cutt Compasse
        imbroidered upon with peramids

                                                Delivered to the Robes

Ladyes

98.91   By the Lady Mary Seamer wief to Mr Rogers ij pilloberes wrought with
        black silke
                                          Delivered to the La Skudmor
98.92   By the Lady Elizabeth Seymer wief to Sir Richard Knightley one snuffkyn
        of haircolored satten imbrodered all ouer with venis golde and siluer and
        lyned with white plush
                                              Delivered to Mistris Hide
98.93   By the Lady Elizabeth Somerset wyef to Sir Henry Gulforde parte of a
        rounde kertle of claycolored taffata lyned with Lawne cutworke florished
        with venis siluer like flowers
                                                Delivered to the Robes
98.94   By the Lady Stafford one paire of brasseletts conteyninge xij peeces vj
        beinge lapis lasule and vj aggetes and xij smale peeces of golde sett
        with ij perles
98.95   By the Lady Cheke vj pendants of golde each havinge vj smale Rubyes and
        ij smale pearles pendant
                                          Delivered to the Mistris Ratclyff
98.96   By the Lady Lighton one cabonet of purple vellat imbrothered all over
        with venis gold and siluer
                                             Delivered to Mr Knevet
98.97   By the Lady Cornwallis one Rounde kertle of plain cloth of siluer
                                                     To the Robes
98.98   By the Lady Digby one fann or Skryne of Caffa Damaske and one
        wastcoate of ashcolored stitched cloth
                                   Delivered the fanne to Mr Knevet and
                                   the wastcoate delivered to Lady Skudamore
98.99   By the Lady Jarret in golde . . . . x li
                                             Delivered to Mr Sackford
98.100 By the Lady Skudamore parte of a loose gowne Bezer colored Taffata
        imbrodered with a faire border of siluertwiste & plate
98.101 By the Lady Egerton one gowne of white tufte taffata the ground siluer
        florished with oues the sleves of white satten cutt and enbrothered with
        venis golde and siluer owes
                                                Delivered to the Robes
98.102 By the Lady Edmonds one couerpane of camericke wrought in divers
        places with venis golde siluer & silke of sundry colours
                                           Delivered to Guarderobe of Robes
98.103 By the Lady Newton ix smale pendants of golde garnished with sparckes
        of rubies and one of them a smalle diamonde and smale perle pendaunte
                                              Delivered to Mistriss Ratliff
98.104 By the Lady Hatton xviij Sprigges of golde garnished with rubies and
        pearles and xxtie little starres of golde with twenty perles in them all
                                              Delivered to Mistriss Ratliff

98.105 By the Lady Walsingham one petticoate of clay colored satten rased with
        a broade border of venis siluer place like a perramides
98.106 By the Lady Walsingham widow one round gowne of white Tabyune
        striped with siluer the sleves edged and border garnisshed and spangled
                                                    Delivered to the Robes
98.107 By the Lady Hawkins one short carkeknett of golde garnished with smale
        rubies and pearles
                                Given by her Matie to Mrs Lighton the same day
98.108 By the Lady Zouche one paire of Faire pilloberes wrought with silke and
        golde
                                            Delivered to the Lady Scudamore
98.109 By the Lady Longe one quosion clothe of fine camericke wrought all over
        with black silke and golde
98.110 By the Lady Harrington one wastcoat of cambricke wrought all over with
        venis siluer and silke
                                            Delivered to the Lady Scudamore
98.111 By the Lady Townesend one skarfe of white knitworke florished with a
        thread of venis golde & topped with carnation silke
                                                    Delivered to Mrs Hyde
98.112 By the Lady Hobby one doublett of siluer chambett striped ouerthwarte
        with a siluer plate lace & lawne cuff in strippes & siluer spangles
                                                    Delivered to the Robes
98.113 By the Lady Puckering in golde . . . . x li
                                                    Delivered to Mr Sackford
98.114 By the Lady Palavazino one doublett of lawne imbrothered with golde
        and siluer with worke like parimides & grapes
98.115 By the Lady Southwell one peticoate of gold chamblett imbrothered in a
        brode border of parimides and flowers between them
                                                    Delivered to the Robes
98.116 By the Lady Willoby one paire of pilloberes of Fyne Hollande wrought
        with silk of sundry colors
                                                    Delivered to Mr Knyvet

Knights

98.117 By Sir William Knolles Comptroller of her Maties Householde one
        peticoate of maidenblush satten imbrodered all ouer with flowers and
        Deuises of venis golde and siluer
                                                    Delivered to the Robes
98.118 By Sir James Fortescue Chancellor of the Exchequer in golde . . . . x li
                                                    Delivered to Mr Sackford
98.119 By Sir Robert Cicell Principall Secreatory one Sprigg of golde conteyninge
        five pearles & one garnet in yt foote
                                                    Delivered to Mistriss Ratclyf
98.120 By Sir Thomas Cicell one Square Canapy of Tawny and white Damaske
        Laced and buttoned in sundry places with a Lace of venis golde and

viij plumes of Oringe coloured featheres and three longe Quishions of
like stuff

> Delivered to Mr Knyvet

98.121 By Sir Thomas Leighton one peticoate of white Serceonet imbrothered
all ouer with Carnation siluer and golde

> Delivered to the Robes

98.122 By Sir Henry Cromwell in golde . . . . x li
98.123 By Sir Edward Cleare in golde . . . . x li

> Delivered to Mr Sackford

98.124 By Sir Edward Stafford one paire of brasseletts of gold conteyninge viij
peeces like Esses garnished with smale Rubyes and eight other peeces
eache with iiij^or pearles and one Ruby in the middest

> Delivered to Mistris Ratclyff

98.125 By Sir William Russell one Sprigg of golde garnished with smale Rubies
and pearles and one pearle pendant

> Delivered to Mistris Ratclyff

98.126 By Sir John Scudamore parte of a loose gowne of Beser coloured taffata
imbrodered with a faire border of siluer twiste & plate

> Delivered to the Robes

98.127 By Sir Henry Newton ij smale pendants of golde garnished with Rubyes
and Opalls eache havinge one pearle pendant

> Delivered to Mistris Ratclyff

98.128 By Sir Edward Hobby one peticoate of white tuft taphata the ground
siluer with three braud laces of venis golde and siluer sett upon carnation
silke

> Delivered to Lady Scudamore

98.129 By Sir John Stanhope one wastcoate of Cambericke wrought with venis
gold siluer and silke of sundry colours

> Delivered to the Robes

98.130 By Sir Edward Dyer one rounde kertle of white satten plushe imbrothered
all ouer with sundry wormes and flyes with a border like parimides
couerid about and downe before

> Delivered to the Robes

98.131 By Sir William Cornwallis a bottle of Aggat hanginge at a smale cheyne of
gold with a steple of golde

> Delivered to Mistris Ratclyff

98.132 By Sir Robert Crosse iij longe cushiones of Oringe coloured cloth of
gold fringed with siluer and oringcoloured silke and backed with
Oringe coloured Satten

> Delivered to the Guarderobe of Robes

98.133 By Sir Henry Gilford parte of a Rounde kertle of clay coloured taffata
Lined upon with Lawne knitworke flourished with venis siluer like flowers

> Delivered to the Robes

98.134 By Sir Horatio Palavizino One Rounde kertle of Lawne embrothered with
golde and siluer with a worke like parimides and grapes

> Delivered to the Robes

98.135   By Sir Henry Billingsley one peece of Lawne

Delivered to Mistriss Hyde

98.136   By Sir Henry Broucker one wastcoate of fine holland imbrothered all ouer
with venis gold silluer and silke of sundry colours

Delivered to the Robes

Gentlewomen

98.137   By Mistres Mary Ratclyff one Snufkynne of white satten stripped laide with
siluer lace & lined with white plush

Delivered to Mistris Hyde

98.138   By Mistres Elizabeth Bridges one doublet of siluer chamblett striped and
laide upon with lined of black Networke flourished with siluer Rives and
flowers of Knitworke

Delivered to the Robes

98.139   By Mistres Carre one Stoole the seat couered with cloth of siluer Wrought
with nedleworke of silke of sundry colours

Delivered to Mr Knyvet

98.140   By Mistres Lucy Hyde ij Skarfes thone lawne garnished at both ends with
venis golde thother of Striped stitchedcloth tufted with peachecoloured
and claye coloured silke

98.141   By Mistres Choppinye one Snufkynne of cloth of siluer cuffed with golde
like birdes and white eares of venis golde siluer & silke

Delivered to Mistriss Hyde

98.142   By Mistres Twiste one nightcoyfe of cambericke wrought with blacke silke
and siluer and a paire of pillowberes of Assay

98.143   By Mistres Cromer one smocke of finne hollande wrought with blacke silke

Delivered to the Lady Scudamore

98.144   By Mistres Huggins one large swete bagg imbrothered like An Eglontine
tree of venis siluer and silke and xij smalle sweet bagges of sarcenett

98.145   By Mistres Frauncis Huggins vi handkercheves of camericke wrought with
blacke silke drawen worke

98.146   By Mistres Tomasyne A faire handkercheve of camericke wrought with
black silke

98.147   By Mistres Barley six handkercheves wrought with black silke and edged
with venis golde

98.148   By Mistres Greene als Gilham vj pynneres one of networke

98.149   By Mistres Winkfield Mother of the Maides one handkerchefe of
camericke wrought with blacke silke and golde

Delivered to the Lady Scudamore

98.150   By Mistres Elizabeth Russell one Skarfe of white sarcenet imbrothered
all ouer with sundry formes and flowers of venis golde siluer and silke
of sundry colours

Delivered to Mrs Hyde

98.151   By Mistres Alley a Ruff of white worke unmade and ij handkercheves of
like worke

Delivered to the Lady Scudamore

98.152 By Mistres Griffin one skarfe of white knitworke florished with suns and
moones of venis golde and siluer and one fanne of Indeaworke and one
Snufkine of hairecoloured vellatt and one paire of perfumed gloves
Delivered to Mistris Hyde

98.153 By Mistres Elizabeth Leighton one handkercheve of cambericke wrought
with venis golde and blacke silke and one paire of writing tables couered
with needleworke of Vens golde and siluer

98.154 By Mistres Sackforde ij Ruffes with a Rebata of fine lawne cutworke
garnisshed with flowers of venice siluer

98.155 By Mistres Elizabeth Norton one paire of inner sleeves of fine holland
clothe wrought with blacke silke

98.156 By Mistres Frances Kerckham parte of a wastcoate of cambericke wrought
and Florished with venis golde and blacke silke

98.157 By Mistres Dorothy Speckeard Thre handkercheves of holland clothe
wrought with black silke
Delivered to the Lady Scudamore

Gentlemen

98.158 By Fulke Greveille one doublet of white satten cutt and stripped downe
richly with venis golde and siluer
Delivered to the Robes

98.159 By Ralph Bowes one bagg for sables of cloth of siluer imbrothered all ouer
with venis golde pearle and Peacockes feathers Lyned with watched
sarcenett
Delivered to the Robes

98.160 By Mr Carre one paire of perfumed gloves
Delivered to Mrs Hyde

98.161 By Mr Montague a smocke of fine hollandcloth wrought with blacke
silke drawneworke
Delivered to the Lady Scudamore

98.162 By Mr Garter King of Armes one Booke Couered with Crimson vellat
conteyninge the Arms of the Noblemen attending on her Matie at the
last parliament in Anno 1597
Delivered to Mr Darcy

98.163 By Mr Carmarden one night raile of cambericke wrought with blacke
silke imbrothered
Delivered to the Lady Scudamore

98.164 By Mr John Spillman Two of rings of golde set with very smale sparkes
of Rubies each a smale pearle pendant
Delivered to Mistris Ratclyf

98.165 By Mr Doctor James one pot of greene gynger and one pot of pomecitrons

98.166 By Mr Doctor Smith one pot of greene gynger and one pot of pomecitrons

98.167 By Mr Doctor Browne one pot of greene gynger and one pot of
pomecitrons

98.168 By Mr Morgan apothecary one pot of pomecitrons

98.169 By Mr Hemmingway apothecary one pot of Pere condita and one box of
       of manus Christi and Lozenges
98.170 By Mr Weston Apothecary three boxes of preserved plums
                          Delivered to the Lady Scudamore
98.171 By Mr Bushop a Stationer one booke of Eclesiasticall histories in frenche
                          Delivered to the Chappell
98.172 By Mr William Cordall Master Cooke A marchepane
98.173 By Mr Daniel Clerke Mr Cook of the Household a fayre marchepane
98.174 By Mr Thomas French Sargeaunt of the Paystrye a pye of Oringeado
98.175 By Mr Ralfe Batty Sargeaunt of the Paystrye a pye of Oringado
98.176 By Mr George [sic Thomas] Ducke sereant of the cellar two bottells of
       Ippocresse
                                    [blank]
98.177 By Mr Abraham Speckard one Ruffe of Lawne cutwork with deuises of
       silkwoman work vpon yt
98.178 By Mr Peter Lupo vj bottels of sweet water
98.179 By Mr Joseph Lupo a Payre of perfumed gloves
98.180 By Mr Thomas Lupo a paire of perfumed gloves
98.181 By Mr William Warren a paire of perfumed gloves
98.182 By Mr Peter Guy ij mute cornetts
98.183 By Mr Jeronimo Bassano a paire of perfumed gloves
98.184 By Mr Arthur Bassano a paire of perfumed gloves
98.185 By Mr Edward Bassano a paire of perfumed gloves
98.186 By Mr Andrew Bassano a paire of perfumed gloves
98.187 By Mr Casar Galliardo a paire of perfumed gloves
98.188 By Mr Trochius a paire of perfumed gloves
                          Delivered to Mrs Hyde
98.189 By Mr Innocent Comy a box of lutestrings
                          Delivered to Mathias
98.190 By Mr Peter Vbaldino one Booke of Italian couered with vellam
                                    [blank]
98.191 By Mr William Huggins one Attyre of Venis siluer garnished with
       Spangles
                          Delivered Mrs Norton
98.192 By Mr Warburton one paire of Brasseletts conteyninge xxj peeces of gold
       garnished with Rubies and smale pearles
                        Delivered to Mistres Ratclyff
98.193 By Mr Fraunces Bacon ij pendants of golde garnished with Rubies and
       dyamonds and iij pearles pendant in eache
                        Delivered to Mistres Ratclyff
98.194 By Mr William Guddericke one glasse of Jellie of hartes horne
98.195 By Mr George Baker one glasse of precious water for the teeth
                        Delivered to the Lady Scudamore
98.196 By Mr Thomas Middleton half a bolte of camericke and haulfe a peece
       of Lawne
                        Delivered to Mrs Ratclif

98.197   By Mr Fraunces Wolley one Skrene with a frame of Caffa Branched with
         siluer and one smale skrene of the same stuff
                                             Delivered to the Lady Skydmore
98.198   By Mr Hughe Miller two pillowbres of holland wrought with black silke
         and golde unmade
                                             Delivered to the Lady Skydmore
98.199   By Mr George Kerckham parte of a wastcoate of cambericke faire
         wrought and imbossed with venis golde and black silke
                                             Deliverd to the Lady Skudamor
98.200   By Mr William Johanes a mantle of carnation Taffata furred through with
         white fox powdered with blacke
                                             Delivered to the Robes
98.201   By Mr William Skeates one catt of Stone
                                             [dd blank]

Summa Totalis of the money given
to her Maiestie this yeare. . . . . vj^C iiij^{xx} ij li xiij s iiij d

Elizabeth R
[sign manual]

Anno Regni Regine Elizabetha
Quadragilimo Anno Dm 1597

New Yeares giftes giuen by the
Queenes Matie at her highnes
pallace at Westmister the first
day of January in the yere
abovesaide to those personnes
whose names hearafter ensue viz :

Elizabeth R
[sign manual]

98.202   To Sir Thomas Egerton knight Lord Keeper of the great Seale of
         Englande in guilte plate K . . . . xxxj oz iij qrter di
98.203   To the Lorde Burghley Lord highe Threasorer of Englande in guilte
         plate K . . . . xix oz di
98.204   To the Lorde Marquis of Winchester in guilte plate K . . . . .xxx oz

Earles and Viscounts

98.205   To the Earle of Essex Master of her Maties horses Master of
         Thordinaunces and Earle Marshall of England in gilt plate K & M
         . . . . Ciiij oz qrter

98.206 To the Earle of Nottingham Lord Admirall in gilte plate K and Martin
.... Cvij oz iij qrter di
98.207 To the Earle of Shrewsbury in gilt plate M..................... xxx oz qrter
98.208 To the Earle of Darby in guilte plate K .... xx oz di
98.209 To the Earle of Sussex in gilt plate K .... xx oz di
98.210 To the Earle of Bathe in gilte plate M......................... xx oz qrter
98.211 To the Earle of Hartford in guilte plate K .... xx oz iij qrter di
98.212 To the Earle of Penbroke in gilt plate K .... xxx oz iij qrter di
98.213 To the Earle of Northumberland in gilte plate M .... xxvij oz di di qrter
98.214 To the Earle of Huntingdon in gilte plate K..................... xxj oz di
98.215 To the Earle of Bedford in gilte plate M................... xxix oz di di qrter
98.216 To the Earle of Southampton in gilte plate K .... xxx oz iij qrter
98.217 To the Earle of Rutland in gilte plate K .... xxij oz iij qrter

Marquesses and Countesses

98.218 To the Lady Marques of Northampton in gilte plate K and M... xlij oz qrter di
98.219 To the Countesse of Kent in gilte plate K......................... xx oz
98.220 To the Countes of Oxford in gilte plate K .... xxxvij oz qrter
98.221 To the Countes of Shrewsbury in gilte plate M .... xij oz
98.222 To the Countes of Notingham in gilte plate K............... xx oz iij qrter di
98.223 To the Countes of Shrewsbury junior in gilt plate M........... xxj oz qrter di
98.224 To the Countes of Darby widow in gilte plate K .... xx oz di di qrter
98.225 To the Countes of Darby junior in gilte plate K................. xx oz qrter
98.226 To the Countes of Huntingdon widow in gilte plate K .... xxvij oz
98.227 To the Countes of Huntingdon Junior in gilte plate K .... xv oz iij qrter di
98.228 To the Countes of Bedford widow in gilte plate K.................. xlix oz
98.229 To the Countes of Southampton in gilte plate K .... xxij oz
98.230 To the Countes of Penbroke in gilte plate K................. xxj oz qrter di
98.231 To the Countes of Hertford in gilte plate K .... xxj oz di qrter
98.232 To the Countes of Bath in gilte plate M .... xx oz di qrter
98.233 To the Countes of Bedford Junior in gilte plate K .... xxiiij oz qrter
98.234 To the Countes of Cumberland in gilte plate K .... xxj oz di qrter
98.235 To the Countes of Northumberland in gilt plat M................. xx oz di
98.236 To the Countes of Sussex in gilte plate K .... xxj oz
98.237 To the Countes of Warwick in gilt plate K .... Lv oz di qrter
98.238 To the Countes of Kildare in gilte plate K .... xxvj oz iij qrter
98.239 To the Viscountis Montague in guilte plate M .... xx oz di

Busshopps

98.240 To the Archbushop of Canterbury in gilte plate K .... xlv oz
98.241 To the Archbushop of Yorke in gilte plate K .... xxxviij oz
98.242 To the Bushop of London in gilte plate K .... xxx oz di qrter
98.243 To the Bushop of Durham in gilte plate K .... xxx oz di di qrter

98.244	To the Bushop of Norwich in gilt plate K	xxx oz qrter
98.245	To the Bushop of Lincolne in gilt plate K	xxx oz
98.246	To the Bushop of Worcester in gilt plate M	xx oz di qrter
98.247	To the Bushop of Lichfield and Coventry in gilt plate K	xx oz di
98.248	To the Bushop of Carlisle in gilte plate M	xv oz iij qrter di
98.249	To the Bushop of Rochester in gilte plate K	xv oz
98.250	To the Bushop of Chester in gilt plate M	xvj oz
98.251	To the Bushop of Chichester B. Amner in gilt plate K	xiij oz
98.252	To the Bushop of Winchester in gilte plate K	xx oz di qrter
98.253	To the Bushop of Peterborough in gilte plate M	x oz qrter di
98.254	To the Bushop of Gloucester in gilt plate M	xij oz di
98.255	To the Bushop of Hereford in gilt plate K	xv oz iij qrt di
98.256	To the Bushop of Bath in gilt plate K	xxx oz di qtr
98.257	To the Bushop of St Davies in gilt plate K	xv oz iij qrt di

Lords

98.258	To the Lorde Hunsdon Lord Chamberleyne in gilte plate K	xxx oz
98.259	To the Lorde Northe in gilte plate M	xx oz di di qrter
98.260	To the Lord Buckhurste in gilte plate K	xj oz iij qrter di
98.261	To the Lord Compton in gilte plate K	xx oz di qrter
98.262	To the Lord Lombley in gilte plate K	xx oz iij qrter di
98.263	To the Lord Cobham in gilte plate K	xxix oz qrt di
98.264	To the Lord Norris in gilte plate M	xix oz di qrt
98.265	To the Lord Willoby of Earsby in gilte plate M	xix oz di di qrt
98.266	To the Lord Wharton in gilte plate K	xx oz
98.267	To the Lord Riche in gilte plate K	xx oz di qrt
98.268	To the Lord Stafford in gilte plate K	xxvij oz di di qrter
98.269	To the Lord Darcy of Chichey in gilte plate K	xx oz di qrt
98.270	To the Lord Thomas Howard in gilte plate K	xx oz di
98.271	To the Lord Sheffeeld in gilte plate M	xx oz qrt
98.272	To the Lord Mountjoy in gilte plate K	xxx oz
98.273	To the Lord Barkeley in gilte plate K	xxx oz

Baronesses

98.274	To the Baronnes Paget Cary in gilt plate K	xxvij oz
98.275	To the Baronnes Chandos Knolles in guilt plate M	xx oz
98.276	To the Baronnes Lomley in gilt plate K	xx oz iij qrt di
98.277	To the Baronnes Hunsdon widow in gilte plate M	xxxiij oz di qrt
98.278	To the Baronnes Hunsdon junior in gilt plate K	xxx oz
98.279	To the Baronnes Arabella in gilte plate K	xxj oz iij qrt
98.280	To the Baronnes Delaware in gilte plate K	xxj oz qrt
98.281	To the Baronnes Sheffeeld Stafford in gilt plate M	xix oz di qrt
98.282	To the Baronnes Riche in gilte plate M	xx oz

98.283	To the Baronnes Borough in gilt plate K	xxj oz di qrt
98.284	To the Baronnes Dudley in gilte plate M	xviij oz qrt di
98.285	To the Baronnes St John Beltzo in gilte plate K	xix oz di
98.286	To the Baronnes of Buckhurst in gilte plate K	xij oz di qrt
98.287	To the Baronnes Howard Lord Thomas his wief in guilt plate K	xxj oz qrt
98.288	To the Baronnes Norris in guilte plate M	xix oz
98.289	To the Baronnes Ephingham in guilte plate K	xix oz iij qrt di
98.290	To the Baronnes Sheffeeld in gilte plate K	xxj oz qrter
98.291	To the Baronnes Scroope in gilte plate K	xx oz

Ladyes

98.292	To the Lady Mary Seymer Mr Rogers his wief in gilte plate K	xij oz iij qrter di
98.293	To the Lady Elizabeth Seymer Sir Richard Knightley his wief in gilte plate K	xij oz iij qrter di
98.294	To the Lady Elizabeth Somersett Sir Henry Gilford his wief in gilte plate K	xvij oz iij qrter di
98.295	To the Lady Kathrin Cornewallis in guilt plate K	xiij oz iij qrter di
98.296	To the Lady Stafford in guilte plate K	xxxi oz qrt
98.297	To the Lady Cheke in guilte plate M	xxxj oz qrt
98.298	To the Lady Leighton in guilte plate M	xvij oz di di qrt
98.299	To the Lady Southwell in guilte plate M	xvij oz qrt di
98.300	To the Lady Scudamore in guilte plate K	xvij oz iij qrter
98.301	To the Lady Egerton in gilte plate K	xvij oz qrter di
98.302	To the Lady Edmonds in guilt plate K	xvj oz di
98.303	To the Lady Newton in guilte plate M	xvij oz iij qrt di
98.304	To the Lady Hawkins in guilte plate K	xvij oz
98.305	To the Lady Hobby in guilte plate K	xvij oz iij qrter di
98.306	To the Lady Walsingham widow in guilte plate K	xxv oz iij [qrter] di
98.307	To the Lady Digby in gilte plate K	xvij oz qrter
98.308	To the Lady Jarret in gilt plate K	xx oz
98.309	To the Lady Walsingham in gilt plate K	xvij oz qrter di
98.310	To the Lady Longe in guilte plate K	xvij oz iij qrter di
98.311	To the Lady Harrington in guilte plate K	xx oz
98.312	To the Lady Townsende in guilte plate K	xviij oz iij qrter di
98.313	To the Lady Puckering in guilt plate K	xix oz qrter
98.314	To the Lady Palavizino in guilt plate M	xviij oz iij qrter di
98.315	To the Lady Hatton in gilte plate M	xxx oz qrter di
98.316	To the Lady Zouche in guilt plate K	xvj oz
98.317	To the Lady Willoby in guilt plat K	xv oz

Knights

98.318	To Sir William Knolles Comptroller of her Matie househoulde in gilte plate M	xxiiij oz

458

98.319	To Sir John Fortescue Chauncellor of the Exchequer in guilte plate M . . xxiij oz
98.320	To Sir Robert Cicell Principall Secretary in guilte plate M . . . xxix oz iij qrter di
98.321	To Sir Thomas Cicell in guilte plate K . . . . xxx oz iij qrter di
98.322	To Sir William Russell in guilte plate M . . . . xxix oz iij qrter di
98.323	To Sir Thomas Leighton in guilte plate M . . . . .xxxiiij oz qrt
98.324	To Sir John Standhopp in guilte plate K . . . . xxiiij oz iij qrt di
98.325	To Sir Edward Stafford in guilte plate K . . . . xx oz iij qrter di
98.326	To Sir John Scudamore in guilte plate K . . . . xx oz
98.327	To Sir Henry Newton in guilte plate M . . . . xviij oz iij qrter di
98.328	To Sir Edward Hobby in guilte plate K . . . . xx oz iij qrter di
98.329	To Sir Edward Dyer in guilte plate K . . . . xx oz di
98.330	To Sir Horatio Palavizino in guilte plate M . . . . xxij oz
98.331	To Sir William Cornwallis in guilte plate M . . . . xx oz qrter
98.332	To Sir Henry Cromwell in guilte plate K . . . . xx oz qrter
98.333	To Sir Edward Cleare in guilte plate M . . . . xviij oz di di qrter
98.334	To Sir Robert Crosse in guilte plate M . . . . xxv oz qrter
98.335	To Sir Henry Gilford in gilt plate K . . . . xx oz di
98.336	To Sir Henry Billingsly in guilte plate M . . . . xx oz di
98.337	To Sir Henry Brounker in gilt plate M . . . . xxv oz di di qrter

Maydes

98.338	To Mrs Elizabeth Vernon in guilte plate M . . . . xx oz iij qrter di
98.339	To Mrs Anne Russell in guilte plate M . . . . xx oz iij qrter di
98.340	To Mrs Margaret Ratclife in guilte plate M . . . . xx oz iij qrter di
98.341	To Mrs Mary Fitton in guilte plate M . . . . x oz di
98.342	To Mrs Anne Cary in gilte plate M . . . . xx oz iij qrter di
98.343	To Mrs Cordall Annesley in gilte plate M . . . . xx oz iij qrter di

Gentlewomen

98.344	To Mrs Mary Ratcliffe in guilte plate K . . . . xviij oz
98.345	To Mrs Carre in guilte plate M . . . . xvij oz
98.346	To Mrs Lucy Hyde in guilte plate K . . . . xvij oz qrter
98.347	To Mrs Coppyn in guilt plate M . . . . xvij oz
98.348	To Mrs Twist in guilte plate K . . . . vij oz
98.349	To Mrs Alley in guilt plate K . . . . vij oz di
98.350	To Mrs Cromer in gilt plate M . . . . xvij oz qrter
98.351	To Mrs Huggins in guilt plate M . . . . xvj oz qrter di
98.352	To Mrs Frauncis Huggins in guilte plate M . . . . xiiij oz di
98.353	To Mrs Elizabeth Bridges in guilt plate K . . . . xvij oz di qrter
98.354	To Mrs Thomazine in guilte plate K . . . . viij oz iij qrter di
98.355	To Mrs Barley in guilte plate . . . . xij oz
98.356	To Mrs Elizabeth Greene in guilte plate M . . . . iiij oz di
98.357	To Mrs Sackford in guilte plate K . . . . xx oz di
98.358	To Mrs Elizabeth Russell in guilte plate K . . . . xx oz iij qrter di

98.359	To Mrs Griffin in guilte plate K	xviij oz iij qrter di
98.360	To Mrs Wingfeelde Mother of the Maides in guilt plate M	xvj oz qrter
98.361	To Mrs Elizabeth Leighton in guilte plate K	xiij oz qrt di
98.362	To Mrs Frauncis Kirckam in guilte plate K	xvj oz iij qrters
98.363	To Mrs Norton in guilte plate M	viij oz
98.364	To Mrs Dorothy Speckard in guilte plate M	vj oz

Gentlemen

98.365	To Mr Fulke Greville in guilte plate M	xxv oz iij qrter di
98.366	To Mr Ralfe Bowes in guilte plate K	xxij oz qrt
98.367	To Mr Garter kinge at Armes in guilt plate K	viij oz di qrt
98.368	To Mr Carre in guilte plate M	xix oz di
98.369	To Mr Montague in guilte plate K	xv oz iij qrter di
98.370	To Mr Carmarden in guilte plate K	xxj oz qrter
98.371	To Mr John Spilman in guilte plate K	xviij oz iij qrter di
98.372	To Mr Doctor Browne in guilte plate K	xiiij oz iij qrter di
98.373	To Mr Doctor Smithe in guilte plate M	xiiij oz di di qrter
98.374	To Mr Doctor James in guilte plate K	xiiij oz iij qrter di
98.375	To Mr Morgan Apothecary in guilte plate Keale	viij oz di qrter
98.376	To Mr Hemmingway Apothecary in guilte plate K	viij oz
98.377	To Mr Weston Apothecary in guilte plate K	x oz di qrter
98.378	To Mr William Cordell Mr Cooke in guilte plate K	viij oz di di qrter
98.379	To Mr Daniel Clark Mr Cooke of the Household in guilte plate K	vj oz qrter
98.380	To Mr Thomas Frenche Serjeaunt of the Pastry in guilt plate K	vj oz
98.381	To Mr Ralphe Batty one other Serjeant of the Pastry in guilte plate K	vj oz
98.382	To Mr Abraham Speckard in guilte plate M	vij oz iij qrter di
98.383	To Mr Petro Lupo in guilte plate	v oz
98.384	To Mr Josephe Lupo in guilte plate	v oz
98.385	To Mr Thomas Lupo in guilte plate M	v oz
98.386	To Mr William Warren in guilte plate	v oz
98.387	To Mr Jerolimo Bassano in guilte plate K	v oz
98.388	To Mr Arthur Bassano in guilte plate K	v oz
98.389	To Mr Andrew Bassano in guilte plate K	v oz
98.390	To Mr Edward Bassano in guilte plate K	v oz
98.391	To Mr Cesar Galiardo in guilte plate	v oz
98.392	To Mr Innocent Comy in guilte plate	v oz
98.393	To Mr Petruchio Ubaldino in guilte plate M	v oz
98.394	To Mr Trochiuo in guilte plate	v oz
98.395	To Mr Peter Guye in guilte plate	v oz
98.396	To Mr William Huggens in guilte plate	xxiij oz
98.397	To Mr Frauncis Bacon in guilte plate K	xxxiij oz di qrter
98.398	To Mr Thomas Middleton in guilte plate K	xv oz qrter
98.399	To Mr Warburton in guilte plate K	xxvj oz qrter
98.400	To Mr Bushop alias stationary in guilte plate K	xvij oz

98.401	To Mr Henry Miller in guilte plate K	vij oz di di qrter
98.402	To Mr Baker in guilte plate K	xiiij oz di di qrter
98.403	To Mr Frauncis Wolley in guilte plate K	xiij oz
98.404	To Mr William Godderd in guilte plate K	xvj oz
98.405	To Mr George Kirckham in guilte plate K	xvj oz
98.406	To Mr William Johns in guilte plate M	xviij oz di qrter
98.407	To Mr Thomas Ducke Serieant in guilte plate K	ix oz di di qrter
98.408	To Mr Gillam Skeath in guilte plate	x oz di qrter

Free Gifts

98.409	To Sir Edward Cary knight Mr and Treasorer of her Maties Juwells and plate in guilte plate K	xviij oz iij qrt di
98.410	To Sir Thomas Gorges knight in guilte plate	x oz qrt
98.411	To Sir Edward Denny knight in guilte plate	x oz
98.412	To Mr Henry Sackford in guilte plate K	x oz
98.413	To Mr John Baptiste in guilte plate K	x oz
98.414	To Mr William Killegrew in guilte plate K	x oz
98.415	To Mr Thomas Knevet in guilte plate K	x oz iij qrt di
98.416	To Mr Edwarde Darcy in guilt plate K	x oz qrter di
98.417	To Mr Mychaell Standhopp in guilte plate K	x oz
98.418	To Sir Edward Carey one other groome xtra in guilt plate K	x oz
98.419	To Mr Ferdinardo Richardson in guilte plate K	x oz
98.420	To Humfrey Adderley in guilte plate M	x oz iij qrt di
98.421	To Nicholas Bristow in guilte plate	x oz iij qrt di
98.422	To Nicholas Pigeon yeoman in guilte plate	x oz iij qrt di
98.423	To Robert Cranmer yeoman in guilte plate	x oz iij qrt di
98.424	To Nicholas Hattofte Groome in guilte plate	x oz iij qrt di

Summa totall of all the plate given im manner and forme aforesaid	m m m m viij^C lxxvj oz

Giftes giuen by her Matie to sundry persones
and delivered at sundry tymes as followeth viz:

98.425 Mounsieur Huitfilde

Item primius given by her highnes the xxvijth of September Anno xxxix° Regni Regine Elizabethe And delivered to Mounsieur Huifilde Chancellor of the Kinge of Denmarke one Basen and yewer gilte poz —Cxlj oz di ; Item one paire of guilte Flagens Clxij oz qrter ; Item one paire of guilte Flagons poiz—Clxxiij oz qrter ; Item one guilte Bole with a couer poiz—Lxxiij oz qrter di ; Item one Bolle with a couer poiz—Lxiij oz di qrter ; Item one guilt Bole with a couer poiz —Lxi oz qrter ; Item one payre of guilte Saultes with a couer poiz

—iiij^{xx} xj oz qrter ; Item one guilte Bolle with a couer—iiij^{xx} xj oz di ; Item one guilte bole with a couer—Lxxviij oz di di qrter ; Item one peere cup guilte with a couer—xxxij oz di ; Item one peere cupp guilt with a couer—xxxj oz iij qrt fayre bought of Keyle Goldsmith in toto. . . . . mx oz Di

98.426 Christian Barra

Item given by her saide Matie the day and yeere aforesaide To Christian Barra Ambassador sent from the kinge of Denmarke one bason and yewer guilte poiz—Ciij oz ; Item one paire of guilte pottes poiz— clxvij oz ; Item one paire of guilt pots poiz—cl oz iij qrters ; Item one guilte Bolle and a couer poiz—lxi oz iij qrter ; Item one guilte Bole with a couer poiz—xxvij oz di ; Item one paire of guilte Saultes with a couer poiz - lxvij oz di qrter ; Item one peare cupp with a couer guilte poiz—xxvij oz qrter ; Item one double Allmaine Cupp guilte poiz—lxxvj oz di ; Item one Portingell Cupp with a couer guilte poiz —lxij oz qrter all bought of the saide Hugh Kayle in toto . . . . .DCCxxxviij oz qrt di

98.427 Haunce Newcam

Item giuen by her Matie the daie and yeere abovesaide to Haunce Newcam a gentleman sent by the kinge of Denmarke one chaine of golde of the goodnes of xxj karrettes iij graines boughte of the said Hughe Kayle . . . . [xij oz]

98.428 William Peetre

Item giuen by her saide Matie the vj of October Anno predicto to the Christening of Mr William Peetre his Childe with a couer poiz— Lj oz qrter and one other guilte Bole with a couer poiz—xxxij oz di Kayle in toto . . . . lxxxiiij oz iij qrter

98.429 Adam Viman

Item giuen by her saide Matie the xixth of January Anno xl Regine Elizabethae to Adam Viman a gentleman sent from the Duke of Wetemberge one chaine of golde of the goodnes of xx karrettes iij graines bought of the saide Kayle. . . . . .xxj oz di

98.430 [no heading in left margin]

Item giuen by her said Matie the xxxth of January Anno predicto to the Christening of the Lord Windsor his child A Cup with a couer guilte bought of the said Hughe Kayle . . . . Liiij oz di

Anno Regni Regine Elizabethe
Quadragesimo primo Anno Dni
1598

New yeares giftes giuen to the Queenes
maiestie at her Highnes pallace at Westminster
by these parsones whose names heareafter
ensue the firste day of January in the yeare
abouesaide viz

99.1 By Sir Thomas Egerton knight Lord Keeper of the greate Seale of Englande
one Karkionett Conteyninge xj peeces of golde lyke halfe Moones and
two half peeces garnyshed with sparkes of Rubyes iiij pendantes with
foures of pearle in a peece vj pendantes with threds of pearle one
pendante in the myddest with a ruby or garnett sett in golde pendante
andfyve pearles about yt one of them pendante & pearles thryded betwene
Delyvered to Mrs Ratclyfe

Earles

99.2 By the Earle of Nottingham Lord Admyrall one Armelett or Karkeonett
of golde conteyninge vj peeces lyke halfe Moones garnyshed with small
rubyes pearles and Opalles pendante and a large Opall pendante of golde in
the myddest garnyshed with opalles and a Ruby therin and a large Ophall
wherein is a claspe pendante
dd to Mrs Ratclyfe

99.3 By the Earle of Shrewesburye in golde . . . . xx li
99.4 By the Earle of Darby in golde . . . . x li
99.5 By the Earle of Pembroke in golde . . . . xx li
99.6 By the Earle of Rutlande in golde . . . . x li
99.7 By the Earle of Sussex in golde . . . . x li
99.8 By the Earle of Bathe in golde . . . . x li
99.9 By the Earle of Hartforde in golde . . . . x li
99.10 By the Earle of Huntington in golde . . . . x li
99.11 By the Earle of Bedforde in golde . . . . xx li
dd to Henry Sackforde Esquire
one of the gromes of her Majesties privye Chamber

99.12 By the Earle of Northumberlande One gowne with a Trayne of pynke
Colored taffeta florished all over with lawne Cutworke lyke roses and
leaves florished with venys sylver
dd to the Robes

Marques and Counteses

99.13 By the Lady Marquess of Northampton two pendantes of golde lyke knottes
garnished with sparkes of Rubyes and eche havinge fower pearles pendante
dd to Mrs Ratclyfe

463

99.14   By the Countes of Kente three handkercheves of fyne Camricke wrought
with white Cutworke

                                 dd to the La: Scudamore

99.15   By the Countes of Oxonford a Louse gowne of white Tabyne with A lace
of venys silver and spangles

                                 dd to the Robes

99.16   By the Countes of Shrewesbury widowe in golde . . . . x li

99.17   By the Counteis of Shrewesbury Junior in golde . . . . x li

99.18   By the Counteis of Sussex in golde . . . . x li

                                   dd to Mr Sackford

99.19   By the Counteis of Nottingham one shorte Karkionett Conteyninge xvij
ballas rubies set in golde xvij pendantes in eche two sparkes of Dyamondes
and xxxiij pearles pendante of sondry bignesses

                                   dd to Mrs Ratclyfe

99.20   By the Counteis of Huntington widowe in golde . . . . viij li

99.21   By the Counteis of Huntington Junior in golde . . . . viij li

99.22   By the Counteis of Pembroke in golde . . . . x li

                                   dd to Mr Sackforde

99.23   By the Counteis of Darby widowe one rounde Kirtell of silver knytworke
with sylver plates

                                   dd to the Robes

99.24   By the Counteis of Darby Junior one rounde Kirtell of peache colored
Clothe of silver with workes of peache Colored frynge lyke esses

                                   dd to the Robes

99.25   By the Counteis of Warwicke one Karkionett conteyninge xxviij small
peeces of golde set with small table rubyes xiij halfe pearles set in golde
xiij pearles pendante one ruby set in golde tryangle wyse with a pearle on
eche syde

                                   dd to Mrs Ratclyfe

99.26   By the Counteis of Bathe in golde . . . . x li

                                   dd to Mr Sackforde

99.27   By the Counteis of Bedforde widowe one paire of Bracelettes conteyninge
xxiiij peeces of golde set with sparkes of Rubyes and half pearles

                                   dd to Mrs Ratclyfe

99.28   By the Counteis of Cumberlande two pendantes of golde Cutworke set
with sparkes of Rubyes eche with foure pearle and one small pearle
pendante

                                   dd to Mrs Ratclyfe

99.29   By the Counteis of Southampton widowe one Pettycote of white satten
embrodered all over with trayles of golde twysts and garlandes of
Colored silke and golde with a faire border ymbrothered lyke frutage

                                   dd to the Robes

99.30   By the Counteis of Northumberland one Louse gowne of Cutworke
lawne florished all over with silver like Leaves and Flagon worke

                                   dd to the Robes

99.31 By the Counteis of Kildare one shorte Karkionett conteyninge Nyne peeces
of golde garnyshed with sparkes of Dyamondes rubyes and pearles with
an Amytist pendante without foile

dd to Mrs Ratclyf

99.32 By the Vicounteis Mountague in golde............................... x li

dd to Mr Sackford

Byshoppes

99.33 By the Archbyshoppe of Canterbury in golde ....xl li
99.34 By the Archbyshopp of Yorke in golde........................... xxx li
99.35 By the Byshop of London in golde................................ xx li
99.36 By the Byshop of Durham in golde .... xxx li
99.37 By the Byshop of Norwiche in golde .... xx li
99.38 By the Byshop of Lyncolne in golde............................. xx li
99.39 By the Byshop of Lychefeild and Coventry in golde ....xiij li vj s vij d
99.40 By the Byshop of Carlyle in golde .... x li
99.41 By the Byshop of Rochester in golde .... x li
99.42 By the Byshop of Wynchester in golde........................... xxx li
99.43 By the Byshop of Chichester in golde........................... x li
99.44 By the Byshop of Worcester in golde .... xx li
99.45 By the Byshop of Peterboroughe in golde .... x li
99.46 By the Byshop of Glocester in golde .... x li
99.47 By the Byshop of Hereforde in golde .... x li
99.48 By the Byshop of Bathe and Welles in golde .... xx li
99.49 By the Byshop of St Davyes in golde .... x li
99.50 By the Byshop of Chester in golde .... x li
99.51 By the Byshop of Exeter in golde .... x li
99.52 By the Byshop of Salesbury in golde .... xx li

dd to Mr Sackford

Lordes

99.53 By the Lorde Hunsdon Lord Chamberlayne one Trayne gowne of pynk
colored Tabyne imbrothered all over with sunnes half Moones and
flowers

dd to the Robes

99.54 By the Lord North Thresorer of her Majesties Houshoulde in golde .... x li
99.55 By the Lord Buckhurste in golde .... v li
99.56 By the Lord Norreis in golde .... x li
99.57 By the Lord Barkeley in golde................................. x li
99.58 By the Lord Wharton in golde .... x li
99.59 By the Lord Lomeley in golde................................. x li
99.60 By the Lord Riche in golde .... x li
99.61 By the Lord Darcy of Chichey in golde .... x li

dd to Mr Sackford

99.62   By the Lord Compton two longe pendantes of golde Cutworke enamelled
        lyke leaves and Snaykes garnyshed with sparkes of Dyamondes and
        rubyes and two small pearles pendante
                                                          dd to Mrs Ratclyf

99.63   By the Lord Henry Howarde one Mantle of Tyffanye stryped with sylver
                                                          dd to the Robes

99.64   By the Lord Audeley parte of A Jupe of peache colored Tuftaffeta the
        grounde Cloth of silver with knotted buttones of venyce golde
                                                          dd to the Robes

99.65   By the Lord Burghley one Jewell beinge a Ruby ballace without foile with
        a Rymme of golde and viij graspes set with sparkes of dyamondes and a
        small pearle pendante
                                                          dd to Mrs Ratclyf

99.66   By the Lord Mountjoy one paire of Bracelettes conteyninge vj rounde
        peeces of golde enamuled white with flowers in them set with sparkes
        of rubyes and vj peeces of golde set lyke roses havinge sparkes of rubies
        in them and one sparke of a Dyamonde in eche
                                                          dd to Mrs Ratclyfe

99.67   By the Lord Cobham one strayte bodyed gowne of Ashe colored Clothe
        of silver with a faire border downe before embrothered with venice
        silver
                                                          dd to the Robes

99.68   By the Lord Willowby of Earseby Governor of Barwicke one Karkionett
        conteyninge fyve bigger and fowre lesser peeces of golde garnished with
        small Opalles pearles pendante and pearles threeded
                                                          dd to Mrs Ratcliff

Baronesses

99.69   By the Barrones Paget Carye one Mantell of blacke networke stryped with
        silver the seames tufted with venys sylver and spangles
                                                          dd to the Robes

99.70   By the Barones Hunsdon widowe one waste Coate of Sarcyonett
        embrothered with venyce golde and Carnacyon sylke
                                                          dd to the La: Scudamore

99.71   By the Barones Hunsdon Junior one Cloake of Taffata with braunches
        & flowers lyned with white plushe
                                                          dd to the Robes

99.72   By the Baronnes Chandoys Knowles one square stoole of wood painted
        & guilt the seate covered with Clothe of siluer imbrothered in squares
        with venyce golde & roses & strawberries of silke womans worke
                                                  dd Mr Thomas Knevett esquyer
                                          Keeper of her Majesties Pallace at westminster

99.73   By the Baronnes Lomley one Kirtell of peache colored Tabyne with
        knotted buttones of venyce silver
                                                          dd to the Robes

99.74 By the Baronnes Scroope one paire of Bracelettes conteyninge foure bigger
      & foure lesser peeces of golde garnyshed with sparkes of Rubyes & three
      Rowes of small pearle threded betwene
dd to Mrs Ratclyf

99.75 By the Baronnes Deleware one Louse gowne of blacke Networke florished
      all over with braunches like roses of venyce silver and owes
dd to the Robes

99.76 By the Baronnes Arbella A lose gowne of lawne florished all over with
      golde & siluer lyned with silver tyffanye
dd to the Robes

99.77 By the Baronnes Riche one Doblett of Networke floryshed all over with
      silver & silver spangles
dd to the Robes

99.78 By the Baronnes Audeley parte of a Jupe of peache colored tuftaffeta
      the grounde Cloth of silver with knotted buttons of venyce golde
dd to the Robes

99.79 By the Baronnes Shefeilde Stafford one wastecote of peach colored
      sarcenett embrothered all over like leaves of venyce golde sylver &
      owes
dd to the La: Scudamore

99.80 By the Baronnes Buckhurste in golde . . . . v li
99.81 By the Baronnes Norreis in golde . . . . x li
99.82 By the Baronnes St John Bletzo in golde . . . . x li
dd to Mr Sackford

99.83 By the Baronnes Dudley one Carcanet conteyninge xvij peeces of golde
      garnyshed with sparkes of rubies pearles & pearles pendante and a
      Rowe of pearles threeded
dd to Mrs Ratclyf

99.84 By the Baronnes Boroughe one Doublet of siluer chamblett embrothered
      vpon like leaves of like syluer chamblett with owes and spangles
dd to the Robes

99.85 By the Baronnes Ephingham one wastCoate of knytworke florished with
      venis golde and small tuftes of carnacion silke
dd to the La: Scudamore

99.86 By the Baronnes Barkeley one Lose gowne razed all over faced & edged
      with white plushe
dd to the Robes

99.87 By the Baronnes Katheryn Cornewalles one pettycote of pyncke
      Colored sarcenet embrothered all over with a Twiste of venyce golde
dd to the Robes

Ladyes

99.88 By Lady Mary Seamer wyefe to Mr Rogers one Attire for the heade
      wrought with venyce silver with Labelles of Lawne
dd to Mrs Norton

99.89   By Lady Elizabeth Seymer wyefe to Sir Richard Knightley one snouskyn
of blacke cloth of gold with Needle worke of golde and silver lyned with
peache colored plushe

dd to Mrs Hide

99.90   By Lady Elizabeth Somerset wiefe to Sir Henry Gilford parte of a Pettycote
of Clay colored satten embrothered all over with branches of owes & three
brode borders of venyce silver

dd to the Robes

99.91   By Lady Stafford one pare of Bracelettes conteininge xvj peeces of golde
set with pearle & garnettes

dd to Mrs Ratclyf

99.92   By Lady Cheeke one shorte Carcanet conteyninge fyve peeces of golde
garnished with sparkes of rubyes and one Dyamonde in the myddest
& three rowes of pearle thryded

dd to Mrs Ratclyf

99.93   By Lady Leighton one Mantell of tyffany stryped with silke & golde with
small tuftes of venyce golde and spangles downe the seames

dd to the Robes

99.94   By Lady Digbye two square quosions of silke needleworke cheverne wise
of two sortes thone backed with Crymsen satten and thother with orenge
colored leather

dd to Mr Knevet

99.95   By Lady Jarratt in golde . . . . x li
99.96   By Lady Puckeringe in golde. . . . . x li

dd to Mr Sackforde

99.97   By Lady Scudamore parte of an Ashe colored wrought vellet gowne the
grounde silver faced and edged with powdered Armens furred throughe
with pure

dd to the Robes

99.98   By Lady Egerton one Cannopey the top thereof cloth of silver chekared
the valance of Clowdye colored sarcenet one seate with thre large
quosiones of Cloth of silver chekared backed with changable colored
satten frynged and tasselled with peache colored silke and siluer

dd to Mr Knevet

99.99   By Lady Edmondes one Ruffe of Camericke Cutworke vnmade

dd to the La: Scudamore

99.100   By Lady Southwell A rounde kirtell of Cloth of siluer with branches &
flowers of silke of sondry Colors

dd to the Robes

99.101   By Lady Newton fyve small pendantes of gold garnished with sparkes of
rubyes emerodes & small pearle

dd to Mrs Ratclyf

99.102   By Lady Walsingham widowe one pettycote of Carnacyon embrothered
all over like Clowdes hoopes and peramydes

dd to the Robes

99.103 By Lady Walsingham Junior parte of a pettycote of white satten
      embrothered all over with venyce golde with a brode border of venyce
      golde and silke

                                          dd to the Robes

99.104 By Lady Hawkyns one Mantell of tyfanny striped with golde and white
      silke with small tuftes of Orenge colored silke

                                          dd to the Robes

99.105 By Lady Zouche one night rayle of fine Camricke wroughte with blacke
      silke drawne worke

                                    dd to the La: Scudamore

99.106 By Lady Longe one smocke of fine Hollande cloth the sleves wrought
      with black silke drawne worke

                                    dd to the La: Scudamore

99.107 By Lady Willowby one smocke of fine Camerick the sleves wrought with
      blacke silke drawne worke

                                    dd to the La: Scudamore

99.108 By Lady Harington one pettycote of white satten cut & tufted embrothered
      all over like starres of golde owes & Carnacon silke tuftes

                                          dd to the Robes

99.109 By Lady Hobbye one Mantell of tyfany tufted with peache colored silke

                                          dd to the Robes

99.110 By Lady Palavizino one rounde Jewell of golde like a Whele with three
      sprigges garnished with rubyes or garnettes and some small pearles
      about the whele

                                      dd to Mrs Ratclyf

Knights

99.111 By Sir William Knolles Comptroller of her Majesties Housholde one rounde
      kyrtell of orenge colored cloth of siluer like Droppes and braunches with
      knotted buttons of venyce silver downe before

                                          dd to the Robes

99.112 By Sir John Fortescue Chauncellor of the Exchequer in golde . . . . x li

                                      dd to Mr Sackford

99.113 By Sir Roberte Cecill princypall Secretary one Carcanet conteyninge xiij
      peeces of golde set with rubyes xiiij pearles laced by twoes, one half
      Moone pendante garnished with sparkes of Dyamondes one greate
      Ameteste without foile thre pendantes with sparkes of rubyes & three
      sparkes of Dyamondes pendante

                                      dd to Mrs Ratclyf

99.114 By Sir Thomas Leighton one rounde kirtell of white satten embrothered
      all over with single braunches like owes

                                      dd to the Robes

99.115 By Sir Henry Cromwell in golde . . . . x li

99.116 By Sir Edwarde Cleare in golde. . . . . x li

                                      dd to Mr Sackford

99.117   By Sir Edwarde Stafford a short Carcanet conteyninge vij peeces like half
     Moones garnished with sparkes of Rubyes and small Dyamondes
dd to Mrs Ratclyf

99.118   By Sir John Scudamore parte of an ashe colored wrought veluet gowne
     the grounde silver faced & edged with powdered Armens and furred
     throughe with pure
dd to the Robes

99.119   By Sir Henry Newton one Carcanet conteyninge vij peeces of golde
     garnished with sparkes of rubyes perles pendante and pearles threeded
dd to Mrs Ratclyf

99.120   By Sir Edward Hobby one cloke of peache colored cloth of silver lyned
     with Ashecolored vnshorne Veluett
dd to the Robes

99.121   By Sir John Stanhop one paire of Bracelettes conteyninge viij peeces of
     golde like snakes garnished with sparkes of rubyes & two pearles in a
     peece & viij peeces of golde set with fower perles & a sparke of a
     dyamonde in the myddest
dd to Mrs Ratclyf

99.122   By Sir Edward Dyer one rounde kirtell of white satten embrothered all
     over like flames with a brode border imbrothered like Roses
dd to the Robes

99.123   By Sir William Cornewallis one pendant of golde make like a harte with a
     ruby or garnet in the myddest & three small rubyes or garnettes without
     foile pendante
dd to Mrs Ratclyf

99.124   By Sir Robert Crosse one lap Mantell of siluer tabyne razed with carnacon
     tuftaffeta like fethers on braunches
dd to the Robes

99.125   By Sir Henry Gilforde parte of a Pettycoate of Clay colored satten
     embrothered with branches & owes
dd to the Robes

99.126   By Sir Henry Bronker one lap Mantell thoneside of orenge color
     vnshorne Veluett with a brode silver lace the otherside Ashecolor
     vnshorne Veluet with a brode golde lace rounde about
dd to the Robes

99.127   By Sir Henry Billingesley twoe half peeces of fyne Lawne
dd to Mrs Ratclyf

99.128   By Sir Oracio Palavizino one Carcanet conteyninge Nyne peeces of golde
     set with small rubyes pearles pendante and Dyamondes pendante
dd to Mrs Ratclyf

99.129   By Sir Thomas Walsingham parte of A pettycote of white satten
     embrothered all over with venyce golde with a broade border of venyce
     golde and silke
dd to the Robes

99.130 By Sir Thomas Jarratt the Netherskirtes of a Pettycote of white satten
embrothered all over like fountaynes and flowers with a broade border
likewise embrothered

dd to the Robes

99.131 By Sir Robert Cydney one snouskyn of clothe of silver like Mosseworke
embrodered all over very faire lyke grapes & other frute of razed worke
of venyce golde silver & silke lyned with white plushe

dd to Mrs Hide

Gentlewomen

99.132 By Mrs Mary Ratclyff one tablet of Eletropia cut hartwise with a rymme
of golde about yt enameled & a perle pendaunte

dd to Mrs Ratclyf

99.133 By Mrs Knevett one square stoole with a backe couered all over with
orenge colored cloth of silver

dd to John Winneyard
yoman of the removing wardrobe of beddes

99.134 By Mrs Carre parte of a paire of Bracelettes conteyninge xij peeces of
golde garnisshed with Ametestes & pearles

dd to Mrs Ratclyff

99.135 By Mrs Luce Hide two shoulder clothes of flannell wrought with silke of
sondry colores and two forehead clothes of Camericke

dd to Mrs Hide

99.136 By Mrs Coppyn thre handkerchers of Cambrick wrought with blacke silke
and golde

dd to the La: Scudamore

99.137 By Mrs Twyste one paire of inner sleeves of fine hollande clothe wrought
with blake silke

dd to the La: Scudamore

99.138 By Mrs Cromer one smocke of fyne holland clothe wrought with black
silke

dd to the La: Scudamore

99.139 By Mrs Huggyns widow one faire sweet bagge of hare colored satten
embrothered on thone side with hoopes pillers and roses with garlandes
of venyce golde & silver and xij small sweet bagges of sarceonett

dd to the La: Scudamore

99.140 By Mrs Francis Huggins six hankerchers of Camerick wrought with blacke
silke & edged with venyce golde

dd to the La: Scudamore

99.141 By Mrs Thomazine one paire of gloves perfumed

dd to Mrs Hide

99.142 By Mrs Barley six hankerchers of Camerick edged about with a lace of
venyce golde

dd to the La: Scudamore

99.143 By Mrs Elizabeth Grene alias Gilham one Ruff of Lawne Cutworke

dd to the La: Scudamore

99.144   By Mrs Wingfield Mother of the Maids one nyght rayle of Lawne wrought with black silke

dd to the La Scudamore

99.145   By Mrs Elizabeth Russell one Cappe of Tyffany wrought with Lawne and Spangeles

dd to the La Scudamore

99.146   By Mrs Verney Alley one paire of Ruffes of Lawne cutworke

dd to the La: Scudamore

99.147   By Mrs Gryffyn one Mantell of Tyffany

dd to the Robes

99.148   By Mrs Sackforde one couerpane of Lawne fayre wrought all over with sondry devises and in the myddest a Swarme of Bees

[blank]

99.149   By Mrs Elizabeth Norton one paire of inner sleeves of fine holland clothe wrought with black silke

dd to the La: Scudamore

99.150   By Mrs Francis Kirkeham one large hankercher of Camerick edged rounde about with a broade border of Lawne cutworke

dd to the La: Scudamore

99.151   By Mrs Dorothye Speckarde one Fanne of white boane wrought with venyce silver

dd to Mrs Carre

99.152   By Mrs Huggyns Mr William his wief a scarfe of Lawne thendes embrothered with silke of sondry colores

dd to Mrs Hide

Gentlemen

99.153   By Mr Foulke Gryvell one shorte Carcanett conteyninge fyftene peeces of golde xij set with rubyes and three with Dyamondes havinge xxxij pearles placed thre perles set in golde & foure small Dyamondes pendante & thre perles pendante

dd to Mrs Ratclyf

99.154   By Mr Carre parte of a paire of Braceletts conteyninge xij peeces of golde garnished with Amiteste and pearle

dd to Mrs Ratclyf

99.155   By Mr Mountague one smocke of fyne hollan clothe the sleves wrought with blacke silke drawne worke

dd to the La: Scudamore

99.156   By Mr Garter kinge at Armes one Booke of Armes Covered with Crymsen veluett

dd to the Lo: Admyrall

99.157   By Mr Carmarden one Mantell of white tyffany stryped with siluer with tuftes on the seames of Venice siluer and spangles

dd to the Robes

99.158   By Mr John Spilman two pendantes being two Amatestes without foyle
      eche havinge thre perles a pece pendante
          dd to Mrs Ratclyf

99.159   By Mr Doctor James one pott of grene gynger and one pott of pome
      Citrones

99.160   By Mr Doctor Smyth one pott of grene gynger and one pott of pome
      Citrones

99.161   By Mr Doctor Browne one pott of grene gynger and one pott of pome
      Citrones

99.162   By Mr Morgan a Potycary one pot of grene gynger & one pott of pome
      Citrones

99.163   By Mr Hemyngway A pottycary one pot of grene gynger and one pot of
      pome Citrones

99.164   By Mr Weston Apothycary one box of Manus Christi and one pott of
      pome Citrones
          dd to the La: Scudamore

99.165   By Mr Byshop A Stacyoner twoe Bookes of Plynnies workes in Frenche
          Delivered to Mr Knevett

99.166   By Mr William Cordall Mr Cooke one Marchepane with the Queenes
      Armes in the Myddest

99.167   By Mr Danyell Clarke Mr Cooke of the houshoulde one faire Marchepane
      lyke a shippe of suger plate

99.168   By Mr Thomas Frenche Serjante of the Pastrye one Pye of Quynces

99.169   By Mr Raphe Batty one other Serjante one Pye of Orengado
          [blank]

99.170   By Mr Frauncys Bacon two pendants of golde garnished with sparkes of
      Opalls ande eche havinge three Opalls pendante
          dd to Mrs Ratclyf

99.171   By Mr Warberton A pettycote of silver tabyne with workes of purple
      tuftaffeta in braunches
          dd to the Robes

99.172   By Mr Frauncys Wolley one large skrene of Clowdy colored sarcenett &
      one lyttle rounde skrene of lyke stuffe
          dd to Mr Knevett

99.173   By Mr Thomas Myddleton one peece of Lawne and one boulte of
      Camericke
          dd to Mrs Ratclyf

99.174   By Mr Thomas Ducke Sergeant of the Sceller two bottells of Ippocras
      thone white thother red

99.175   By Mr Abraham Speckard three paire of Chynne Ruffes of Lawne
          dd to Mrs Carre

99.176   By Mr Peter Lupo fower bottells of sweete water

99.177   By Mr Josephe Lupo one paire of perfumed gloves

99.178   By Mr Thomas Lupo one paire of perfumed gloves

99.179   By Mr William Warren one paire of perfumed gloves

99.180   By Mr Peter Guye one paire of perfumed gloves

99.181   By Mr Jerrolymo Bassano one paire of perfumed gloves
99.182   By Mr Arthure Bassano one paire of perfumed gloves
99.183   By Mr Edwarde Bassano one paire of sweete gloves
99.184   By Mr Andrewe Bassano one paire of sweete gloves
99.185   By Mr Cesar Gallyardo one paire of perfumed gloves
99.186   By Mr Trochius one paire of perfumed gloves

dd to Mrs Hide

99.187   By Mr Innocent Comye one Boxe of Lute Strynges

[blank]

99.188   By Mr Petruchio Vbaldyno A Table with a picture and a Booke in Italian

dd to Mr Knevett

99.189   By Mr Richarde Graves one paire of perfumed gloves

dd to Mrs Hide

99.190   By Mr William Huggyns one Attyre for the heade with silke of sondry Colors

dd to Mrs Norton

99.191   By Mr William Goodres one glasse of Jelly made of harteshorne

dd to the La: Scudamore

99.192   By Mr George Baker one Glasse of water for the Teeth

dd to the La: Scudamore

99.193   By Mr George Kirkeham twoe sutes of ruffes of Lawne Cutworke vnmade

dd to the La: Scudamore

99.195   By Mr Gilham Skeates one lytel rounde Lampe of silver white with a
      glasse

dd to himself

99.195   By Mr Ferris a Merchant one guilte Cuppe with a Cover stayned with
      sondry colors & some siluer leaves poiz . . . . xj oz iij qtrs di

charged vpon Sir Edward Carye knight
Mr and Thresurer of her Maties Jewelles and plate

Elizabeth R
[sign manual]

Summa totalis of all the money
gyven to her highnes this yeare . . . . vij^C xxix li vj s viij d

Edwarde Carye
Ex[aminatio] per
N Bristowe
N Pigeon
Robert Cranmer
Nicholas Hottofte

Anno Regni Regine Elizabethe
Quadragesimo primo Anno Dei 1598

Newyeares giftes gyuen by the
Queenes Matie at her highnes pallace
at Westmister the first daye of January
in the yeare aboveaide to those persones
whose names heareafter ensue viz :

Elizabeth R
[sign manual]

99.196 To Sir Thomas Egerton knight Lord Keeper of the greate Seale of England
in guilt plate K & M . . . . xxxiij oz di qtr

Earles

99.197 To the Earle of Nottingham Lorde Admyrall in guylte plate K . . . . . . Cvij oz di
99.198 To the Earle of Shrewesbury in guylte plate K . . . . xxix oz iij qtrs
99.199 To the Earle of Darby in guylte plate K .xxij oz iij qtrs di
99.200 To the Earle of Sussex in guylte plate M . . . . xxj oz qtr
99.201 To the Earle of Bathe in guylte plate K . . . . xxj oz iij qtrs
99.202 To the Earle of Hartforde in guylte plate K . . . . xviij oz iij qtrs di
99.203 To the Earle of Pembroke in guylte plate K . . . . xxxj oz di qtr
99.204 To the Earle of Northumberlande in guylte plate K . . . . xxix oz qtr
99.205 To the Earle of Huntington in guylte plate K. . . . . xx oz di qtr
99.206 To the Earle of Bedforde in guylte plate M . . . . .xxxj oz di
99.207 To the Earle of Rutlande in guylte plate K. xx oz qtr di
354.1.2

Marques and Counteses

99.208 To the Lady Marquess of Northampton in guylte plate M . . . . . . xliiij oz iij qtrs
99.209 To the Counteis of Kente in guylte plate K . . . . xxj oz iij qtrs di
99.210 To the Counteis of Oxeford in guylte plate K. . . . . .xxxvij oz
99.211 To the Counteis of Shrewesbury widowe in guylte plate K . . . . . xlj oz di di qtr
99.212 To the Counteis of Shrewesbury Junior in guylte plate K . . . . xix oz di di qtr
99.213 To the Counteis of Nottingham in guylte plate K . . . . xxvj oz
99.214 To the Counteis of Darbye widowe in guylte plate M . . . . xxj oz di
99.215 To the Counteis of Darbye Junior in guylte plate M . . . . .xxv oz
99.216 To the Counteis of Huntington wydowe in guylte plate K. . . . . . xxix oz di di qtr
99.217 To the Counteis of Huntington Junior in guylte plate K . . . . xix oz iij qtrs di
99.218 To the Counteis of Bedforde widowe in guylte plate K and M . . . . L oz
99.219 To the Counteis of Southampton widowe in guylte plate M . . . . xxij oz di di qtr
99.220 To the Counteis of Pembrooke in guylte plate K . . . . .xx oz qtr
99.221 To the Counteis of Bathe in guylte plate M . . . . xix oz
99.222 To the Counteis of Cumberlande in guylte plate K . . . . xxj oz
99.223 To the Counteis of Northumberlande in guylte plate M . . . . xx oz

99.224	To the Counteis of Sussex in guylte plate M	xx oz di di qtr
99.225	To the Counteis of Warwicke in guylte plate K and M	Lvj oz
99.226	To the Counteis of Kildare in guylte plate M	xxvj oz
99.227	To the Vicounteis Mountague in guylte plate K	xxj oz iij qtrs

564.0.2

Byshoppes

99.228	To the Archbyshoppe of Canterbury in guylte plate M	xlv oz qtr
99.229	To the Archbyshopp of Yorke in guylte plate M	xxxviij oz di
99.230	To the Byshopp of London in guylte plate K	xxx oz qrter di
99.231	To the Byshoppe of Durham in guylte plate M	xxxvij oz iij qrtrs
99.232	To the Byshopp of Norwiche in guylte plate M	xxx oz qrter di
99.233	To the Byshoppe of Lyncolne in guylte plate K	xxxij oz
99.234	To the Byshoppe of Worcester in guylte plate K	xxx oz iij qrters
99.235	To the Byshoppe of Salesbury in guylte plate M	xxx oz iij qrtrs di
99.236	To the Byshoppe of Lychefeilde & Coventry in guylte plate M	xx oz
99.237	To the Bushoppe of Carlyle in guylte plate K	xviij oz di di qrter
99.238	To the Byshoppe of Rochester in guylte plate K	xv oz di
99.239	To the Byshoppe of Chester in guylte plate K	xvj oz iij qrtrs
99.240	To the Byshopp of Wynchester in guylte plate K	xxxv oz iij qrtrs
99.241	To the Byshoppe of Chichester Amner in guylte plate M	xix oz qtr di
99.242	To the Byshoppe of Peterboroughe in guylte plate K	xviij oz qrter
99.243	To the Byshopp of Glocester in guylte plate M	xvj oz di qrter
99.244	To the Byshopp of Hereforde in guylte plate K	xvj oz di di qrter
99.245	To the Byshoppe of Bathe and Welles in guylte plate K	xxx oz
99.246	To the Byshoppe of St Davyes in guylte plate M	xvj oz qrter di
99.247	To the Byshopp of Exeter in guylte plate K	xv oz di

514.1.0

Lordes

99.248	To the Lord Hunsdon Lorde Chamberlayne in guylte plate M	xxxij oz di
99.249	To the Lorde Northe in guylte plate M	xxj oz di qrt
99.250	To the Lord Buckhurste in guylte plate M	xij oz qrt
99.251	To the Lord Compton in guylte plate M	xx oz di
99.252	To the Lorde Lomeley in guylte plate K	xx oz di qrt
99.253	To the Lorde Cobham in guylte plate M	xxx oz
99.254	To the Lorde Norreys in guylte plate K	xix oz di
99.255	To the Lorde Willowby in guylte plate K	xx oz
99.256	To the Lorde Wharton in guylte plate M	xx oz iij qrts
99.257	To the Lorde Ryche in guylte plate K	xx oz qrt
99.258	To the Lorde Burghley in guylte plate M	xxx oz iij qrt
99.259	To the Lorde Darcye of Chichey in guylte plate K	xxj oz qrt
99.260	To the Lorde Audeley in guylte plate K	xxij oz iij qrters
99.261	To the Lorde Mountjoye in guylte plate K	xxxj oz

99.262	To the Lorde Barkeley in guylte plate K	xix oz iij qrters di
99.263	To the Lorde Henry Howarde in guylte plate K	xxiij oz iij qrters
		366. 2.2

Baronesses

99.264	To the Baronnes Paget Cary in guylte plate M	xxxvj oz iij qrters di
99.265	To the Baronnes Shandoyes Knowles in guylte plate M	xx oz di
99.266	To the Baronnes Lomley in guylte plate K	xx oz
99.267	To the Baronnes Hunsdon wydowe in guylte plate M	xxxij oz iij qrters di
99.268	To the Baronnes Hunsdon Junior in guylte plate M	xxxj oz
99.269	To the Baronnes Scroupe in guylte plate K	xx oz di
99.270	To the Baronnes Audeley in guylte plate K and M	xxij oz iij qrters
99.271	To the Baronness Arbella in guylte plate M	xx oz qrt di
99.272	To the Baronnes Delleware in guylte plate M	xx oz di qrt
99.273	To the Baronnes Sheifeilde Stafforde in guylte plate M	xx oz di di qrt
99.274	To the Baronnes Riche in guylte plate K	xx oz di qrt
99.275	To the Baronnes Broughe in guylte plate K	xxiij oz
99.276	To the Barronnes Dudley in guylte plate K	xix oz iij qrters
99.277	To the Baronnes St John of Bletzo in guylte plate K	xxij oz qrt di
99.278	To the Baronnes Buckhurste in guylte plate K	xij oz
99.279	To the Baronnes Norreis in guylte plate K	xix oz iij qrters di
99.280	To the Baronnes Ephingham in guylte plate K	xx oz qrt di
99.281	To the Baronnes Barkeley in guylte plate K	xx oz di
99.282	To the Baronnes Katheryn Cornwalles in guylte plate K	xix oz qrt
		422.3.2

Ladies

99.283	To the Lady Mary Seymer Mr Rogers his wyef in guylte plate M	xij oz iij qrters
99.284	To the Lady Elizabeth Seymer Sir Richard Knightley his wyef in guylte plate K	xiij oz qrt
99.285	To the Lady Elizabeth Somersett Sir Henry Gylfordes wyef in guylte plate M	xvij oz di
99.286	To the Lady Stafforde in guylte plate K	xxxj oz qrt
99.287	To the Lady Cheeke in guylte plate K	xxx oz iij qrters di
99.288	To the Lady Leyghton in guylte plate M	xvij oz iij qrters di
99.289	To the Lady Southwell in guylte plate K	xviij oz di di qrter
99.290	To the Lady Scudamore in guylte plate K	xvij oz iij qrters
99.291	To the Lady Zouche in guylte plate K	xvj oz
99.292	To the Lady Egerton in guylte plate M	xviij oz di qrt
99.293	To the Lady Edmondes in guylte plate K	xvij oz di qrt
99.294	To the Lady Newton in guylte plate M	xvij oz di di qrt
99.295	To the Lady Hawkyns in guylte plate K	xix oz
99.296	To the Lady Hobby in guylte plate K	xix oz di qrt
99.297	To the Lady Walsingham widowe in guylte plate K	xxvj oz iij qrters di
99.298	To the Lady Walsingham Junior in guylte plate M and K	xvij oz qrt

99.299	To the Lady Dygbye in guylte plate M and K .... xvij oz di
99.300	To the Lady Jarrett in guylte plate K .... xix oz qrt
99.301	To the Lady Longe in guylte plate M .... xix oz
99.302	To the Lady Harrington in guylte plate K .... xix oz di qrt
99.303	To the Lady Puckaringe in guylte plate K .... xix oz di qrt
99.304	To the Lady Willowby in guylte plate K .... xv oz
99.305	To the Lady Palavizino in guylte plate K .... xviij oz di qrt

438.0.2

Knights

99.306	To Sir William Knowles Comptroller of her Majesties Housholde in guylte plate M... xxiiij oz
99.307	To Sir John Fortescue Chauncellor of the Exchequor in guylte plate M .... xxiiij oz
99.308	To Sir Roberte Cycell pryncypall Secretary in guylte plate M ... xxxj oz di di qtr
99.309	To Sir Thomas Leighton in guylte plate M.................... xxxiij oz qtr
99.310	To Sir John Stanhoppe in guylte plate M and K .... xxv oz di qtr
99.311	To Sir Edwarde Stafforde in guylte plate M .... xx oz di
99.312	To Sir John Scudamore in guylte plate K and M .... xx oz di qtr
99.313	To Sir Henry Newton in guylte plate K .... xx oz qtr di
99.314	To Sir Edwarde Dyer in guylte plate K...................... xxij oz qtr di
99.315	To Sir Edwarde Hobby in guylte plate K .... xxij oz di di qtr
99.316	To Sir Thomas Jarrett in guylte plate M................xxiiij oz iij qtrs di
99.317	To Sir William Cornewalles in guylte plate M .... xviij oz iij qtrs
99.318	To Sir Henry Cromwell in guylte plate M...................... xx oz qtr
99.319	To Sir Edwarde Cleare in guylte plate M .... xx oz di di qtr
99.320	To Sir Henry Gylforde in guylte plate M .... xx oz qtr
99.321	To Sir Roberte Scydney in guylte plate M.................. xx oz qtr di
99.322	To Sir Henry Bronker in guylte plate K .... xxv oz iij qters di
99.323	To Sir Roberte Crosse in guylte plate K .... xxiiij oz di qtr
99.324	To Sir Henry Byllingesley in guylte plate M...................... xviij oz
99.325	To Sir Oracyo Palavizino in guylte plate K.................. xxij oz iij qters
99.326	To Sir Thomas Walsingham in guylte plate K and M .... xx oz qtr

480.0.2

Maydes

99.327	To Mrs Anne Russell one parcell guilte Trencher plate K poiz—ix oz di di qtr and two guylte spones K poiz .... ij oz di
99.328	To Mrs Margaret Ratclyffe one parcell guilte Trencher plate K poiz— ix oz iij qters di and twoe guylte spones K poiz .... ij oz di di qtr
99.329	To Mrs Marye Fytten one parcell guilte Trencher plate K poiz—ix oz and two guylte spoones K poiz .... iij oz
99.330	To Mrs Anne Carye one parcell guilte Trencher plate K poiz—x oz di di qtr and twoe guylte spones K poiz .... ij oz di
99.331	To Mrs Cordall Ansley one parcell guilte Trencher plate K poiz—ix oz di di qtr and two guylte spones K poiz .... ij oz di

99.332   To the Lady Dorathy Hastinges one parcell guilte Trencher plate K poiz—
x oz and twoe guylte spones K poiz . . . . ij oz di di qtr
15.3.0

Gentlewomen

99.333   To Mrs Marye Ratclyff in guylte plate M . . . . xviij oz di qtr
99.334   To Mrs Luce Hyde in guylte plate K . . . . xvij oz
99.335   To Mrs Knevett in guylte plate K . . . . .xxx oz qtr
99.336   To Mrs Twyste in guylte plate K . . . . viij oz iij qters di
99.337   To Mrs Alley in guylte plate K . . . . vij oz di
99.338   To Mrs Cromer in guylte plate K . . . . xvj oz di di qtr
99.339   To Mrs Huggyns widowe in guylte plate K. xvj oz qtr
99.340   To Mrs Fraunces Huggyns in guylte plate K . . . . xvj oz qtr
99.341   To Mrs Thomazine in guylte plate M . . . . vij oz di di qtr
99.342   To Mrs Barley in guylte plate M . . . . xij oz
99.343   To Mrs Greene in guylte plate K. . . . . iiij oz qtr di
99.344   To Mrs Sackforde in guylte plate K . . . . xx oz di qtr
99.345   To Mrs Elizabeth Russell in guylte plate K. . . . . xvij oz di
99.346   To Mrs Gryffyn in guylte plate M. . . . . xix oz di
99.347   To Mrs Wyngfield mother of the Maydes in guylte plate K. . . . . xx oz
99.348   To Mrs Huggyns Mr William his wyef in guylte plate . . . . .xv oz iij qters di
99.349   To Mrs Fraunces Kirkeham in guylt plate K . . . . xvij oz
99.350   To Mrs Elizabeth Norton in guylte plate M . . . . .xiiij oz iij qtrs
99.351   To Mrs Dorathye Speckarde in guylte plate K . . . . viij oz qtr
99.352   To Mrs Carre in guylte plate M and K . . . . xvij oz qtr di
99.353   To Mrs Coppin in guylte plate M . . . . xvij oz
322.1.0

Gentlemen

99.354   To Mr Foulke Gryvell in guylte plate M. . . . . xxvj oz
99.355   To Mr Garter kinge at Armes in guylte plate K .viij oz
99.356   To Mr Carre in guylte plate M . . . . .xx oz iij qtrs
99.357   To Mr Mountague in guylte plate M . . . . xvj oz di qtr
99.358   To Mr Carmarden in guylte plate K . . . . .xxij oz qtr
99.359   To Mr John Spilman in guylte plate K . . . . xviij oz qtr di
99.360   To Mr Docter James in guylte plate M and K . . . . xv oz qtr di
99.361   To Mr Docter Smythe in guilte plate K . . . . xv oz
99.362   To Mr Docter Browne in guilte plate K . . . . xv oz
99.363   To Mr Morgan a Pottycary in guylte plate M. . . . . viij oz di qtr
99.364   To Mr Hemyngway a Pottycary in guilte plate K . . . . viij oz qtr
99.365   To Mr Weston A Pottycary in guilte plate M . . . . ix oz iij qtrs
99.366   To Mr william Cordall Mr Cooke in guilte plate M. . . . . .viij oz di di qtr
99.367   To Mr Danyell Clarke Mr Cooke of the housholde in guilte plate K . . viij oz qtr
99.368   To Mr Thomas Frenche Serjante of the Pastery in guilte plate K . . . . . . viij oz di
99.369   To Mr Raphe Battye one other Serjant in guylte plate K. . . . . viij oz qtr
99.370   To Mr Frauncys Bacon in guylte plate M. xxxiij oz di qtr

99.371	To Mr Warberton in guylte plate K	xxvj oz qtr di
99.372	To Mr Frauncys Wolley in guylte plate K.	xxj oz
99.373	To Mr Abraham Speckarde in guylte plate K	viij oz di
99.374	To Mr Peter Lupo in guylte plate M.	v oz
99.375	To Mr Josephe Lupo in guylte plate M.	v oz
99.376	To Mr Thomas Lupo in guylte plate M	v oz
99.377	To Mr William Warren in guylte plate M	v oz
99.378	To Mr Jerolymo Bassano in guylte plate M	v oz
99.379	To Mr Arthure Bassano in guylte plate M	v oz
99.380	To Mr Andrewe Bassano in guylte plate M	v oz
99.381	To Mr Edwarde Bassano in guylte plate M	v oz
99.382	To Mr Richarde Greves in guylte plate M	v oz
99.383	To Mr Cesar Gallyardo in guylte plate M.	v oz
99.384	To Mr Innocent Comye in guylte plate M	v oz
99.385	To Mr Petruchio Vbaldyno in guylte plate M.	v oz
99.386	To Mr Trochius in guylte plate M.	v oz
99.387	To Mr Peter Guye in guylte plate M.	v oz
99.388	To Mr William Huggyns in guylte plate K.	xv oz
99.389	To Mr Thomas Myddleton in guylte plate K	xvj oz di
99.390	To Mr Byshoppe a Stacyoner in guylte plate K	xvj oz qtr di
99.391	To Mr William [sic George] Baker in guylte plate K	xvij oz di qtr
99.392	To Mr William Goodres Serjeant Surgeon in guilte plate M	xiiij oz iij qtrs di
99.393	To Mr George Kirkeham in guylte plate K.	xviij oz iij qtrs di
99.394	To Mr Thomas Ducke in guylte plate M	x oz qtr di
99.395	To Mr Gylham Skeates in guylte plate M.	viij oz
99.396	To Mr Ferrys in guylte plate K	xiij oz iij qrters
		1500.1.0

Free Gifts

99.397	To Sir Edwarde Carey knighte Mr & Threasorer of her Majesties Jewells & Plate in guylte plate M.	xviij oz iij qters di
99.398	To Sir Thomas Gorge in guylte plate M	x oz
99.399	To Sir Edwarde Dennye knighte in guylte plate M.	x oz
99.400	To Mr Henrye Sackforde in guylte plate K.	x oz
99.401	To Mr Thomas Knevett in guylte plate M	x oz
99.402	To Mr William Killegrew in guylte plate K	x oz
99.403	To Mr Edwarde Darcye in guylte plate K.	x oz
99.404	To Mr Michaell Stanhoppe in guylte plate K.	x oz
99.405	To Sir Edwarde Carye one other Groome &c in gilte plate M	x oz
99.406	To Mr Fardynando Richardson in guylte plate K	x oz
99.407	To Mr Richarde Nightingale yoman of the Robes in guylte plate M	xij oz qtr di
99.408	To Mr Nicholas Brystowe Clarke of her Majesties Jewells & Plate in gilte plate M.	x oz iij qters di
99.409	To Mr Nicholas Pigeon yoman of her Majesties Jewells & Plate in guylte plate K.	x oz iij qters di

99.410 To Mr Robert Crammer one other yoman in guylte plate K . . . . . . x oz iij qtrr di
99.411 To Mr Nicholas Hottoste Groome in guylte plate M . . . . x oz iij qtrr di

164.3

4182.1.2

Sume totallis of all the guilte plate giuen
in manner and forme abouesaide . . . . iiij^m Ciiij^{xx} ij oz qtr di
and in Parcell guylte Plate . . . . Lviij oz iij qtrs

Giftes gyuen by her Majestie to sundrye persones
and delyvered at sondrye tymes as followeth viz

99.412 Sir Henry Guldforde
        Firste gyven by her highnes and delyvered the xxijth of Maye Anno
           xl^{to} Regni Regine Elizabethe &c. at the Christenynge of Sir Henry
           Guilforde knight his Childe One Bason and Ewer gilte poiz—iiij^{xx}
           xiiij oz iij qtrs and one guylte Stope poiz—xiiij oz bought of the
           saide Hughe Kayll In toto . . . . Cviij oz iij qtr
99.413 Mr Roberte Dygbye
        Item gyven by her saide hignes and delyvered the ixth of June Anno
           pre dicto At the Maradge of Mr Robert Dygbye to Mrs Lettis Garrett
           One guylte Bolle with a Couer bought of the saide Hughe Kayll poiz
           . . . . lxj oz iij qtrs di
99.414 Mr Nicholas Cragius
        Item gyven by her sayde Hignes and delyvered the xxiiijth of April
           Anno xlj^{mo} Regne Regine Elizabethe &c unto Nicholas Cragius
           gentleman sent from the kinge of Denmarke One Chayne of golde
           of the goodnes of xxijtie karrettes one grayne bought of the sayde
           Hughe Kayll poiz . . . . xxx oz qtr di
99.415 Johannes Nicholai
        Item gyven by her sayde Hignes and delyvered the xviijth of Maye
           Anno predicto To Johannes Nicholai gentleman sent from Duke
           Charles of Swethlande One Cheyne of golde of the goodnes of xxj^{tie}
           karretts iij graynes & a qtr bought of the sayde Hughe Kayll poiz
           . . . . xvij oz
99.416 James Hill
        Item gyven by her sayde hignes and delyvered the daye and yeare
           abouesaide to James Hill gentleman sent from the saide Duke Charles
           One Cheyne of golde of the goodnes of xxj karretts ij graynes & a
           qtr boughte of Richarde Martyn goldesmyth poiz . . . . xxiiij oz

        Edwarde Carye
        Ex[aminatio] per
        N Bristowe
        N Pigeon
        Robert Cranmer
        Nicholas Hottofte

Anno Regni Regine Elizabethe
Quadragesimo secundo Anno Dei
1599

Newyeares Guyftes gyven to the Queens Matie
Att her highnes Mannor of Richmonde the Fyrst
daye of Januarie in the Yeare abouesayde by these
personnes whose names hereafter ensue. viz.

00.1 By Sir Thomas Egerton Knight Lorde Keeper of the greate Seale of
Englande one Armylet of golde garnished with sparkes of Rubyes pearle
and halfe pearle

dd to Mrs Ratclyf

00.2 By the Lorde Buckhurste Lorde high Treasorer of Englande in golde . . . . . . x li
00.3 By the Lorde Marques of Wintchester in golde . . . . xx li

dd to henry Sackforde
Esquier one of the Groomes of her Maties privy Chamber

Earles

00.4 By the Earle of Nottingham Lord Admyrall one Karcanett conteyninge
xix peeces of golde whereof nyne bigger peeces and tenne lesser xviij
pendantes like mullettes likewyse garnished with small rubyes and pearle
with a rounde Jewell pendant in the myddest garnished with one white
Topas & a pearle pendante and ix small rubyes

dd Mrs Ratclyf

00.5 By the Earle of Darbye in golde . . . . x li
00.6 By the Earle of Sussex in golde. . . . . x li
00.7 By the Earle of Bathe in golde . . . . x li
00.8 By the Earle of Hartforde in golde . . . . x li
00.9 By the Earle of Huntington in golde . . . . x li
00.10 By the Earle of Pembrooke in golde. . . . . xx li
00.11 By the Earle of Bedforde in golde. . . . . x li

dd to Mr Sackford

00.12 By the Earle of Northumberland one Carcanett of golde conteyninge v
square peeces iiij pendantes like mullettes and half Moones garn with
sparkes of Dyamondes rubyes and pearles threeded betwene

dd Mrs Ratclyf

00.13 By the Earle of Shrewesbury parte of a Doublett of white satten
embrothered all over lyke snakes wounde together of venyce sylver
richlie wroughte and puffes of lawne embrothered with venyce silver
lyke wheate Eares

dd to the Robes

00.14 By the Earle of Cumberland one Pettycote of white sarcenett embrothered all
over with venyce silver plate and some Carnaconn silke like Colombines

dd to the Robes

482

00.15 By the Earle of Rutlande in golde. . . . . x li
                                                     dd to Mr Sackforde

00.16 By the Earle of Worcester one Hatt of Tiffany garnished with xxviij
    buttons of golde of one sorte and xiiij buttons of another sorte about
    the bande and upp the feather
                                                 dd to the Robes

Marquesses and Counteses

00.17 By the Lady Marques of Northampton two knottes of golde garnished
    with sparkes of rubyes & pearles pendantes
                                                 dd Mrs Ratclyf

00.18 By the Lady Marques of Winchester wydowe one sprigge of golde garn
    with sparkes of rubyes one small Dyamonde and pearles of sondry
    sortes and bignesses
                                                 dd Mrs Ratclyf

00.19 By the Countes of Kente vj hankerchers of Cambricke wrought with
    blacke silke & edged about with gold lace
                              Delivered to the Lady Scudamore

00.20 By the Countesse of Oxenforde one rounde kyrtell of silver tabynne with
    slyppes of white sylke like vellat and tuftes of Carnaconn silke with
    some golde
                                                 dd to the Robes

00.21 By the Countes of Shrewesbury wydowe in golde . . . . .xl li
                                                dd Mr Sackforde

00.22 By the Countes of Shrewesbury Junior parte of a Doublet vnmade of
    white satten embrothered all over like snakes wounde together of venyce
    silver richely wrought & puffes of lawne embrothered with venice silver
    like wheate Eares
                                                 dd to the Robes

00.23 By the Countesse of Sussex in golde. . . . . x li
                                                dd to Mr Sackforde

00.24 By the Countesse of Nottingham one Carcanett of golde garnished with
    xv peeces of golde set with sparkes of Rubyes and A small Dyamond in
    the myddest of every of them and vij peeces lyke mullettes with pearles
    with a Ruby in the myddest of eche of them and perles threeded betwene
    them
                                                 dd Mrs Ratclyf

00.25 By the Countesse of Huntington Widowe in golde .viij li
00.26 By the Countesse of Huntington Junior in golde. .viij li
00.27 By the Countesse of Pembroke in golde. . . . . x li
00.28 By the Countesse of Rutland in golde . . . . x li
                                                dd Mr Sackforde

00.29 By the Counteis of Darby Wydowe one pettycote without bodyes of silver
    tynsell wrought in squares with A border of trees of grene sylke
    needleworke
                                                 dd to the Robes

00.30   By the Counteis of Darby Junior one Doblett of Taffeta embrothered all
over with a twyste of venyce silver and spangles with flowers of silke
Womans Worke

dd to the Robes

00.31   By the Counteis of Warwicke fyve sprigges of golde garnished with
sparkes of Rubies & perles pendantes & v half perle

dd to Mrs Ratclyf

00.32   By the Counteis of Bathe in golde . . . . x li

00.33   By the Counteis of Bedford in golde. . . . . x li

dd to Mr Sackford

00.34   By the Countes of Bedford widowe vij sprigges of golde garn with sparkes
of Rubies & perle and vij pearles pendant iij bigger and iiij lesser

dd to Mrs Ratclyf

00.35   By the Counteis of Comberland one paire of Bracelettes of golde
conteyninge viij peeces like knottes and viij rounde peeces garnished
with small sparkes of Rubyes pearle and half perles

dd to Mrs Ratclyf

00.36   By the Counteis of Southampton senior one vale or mantell of white
knytworke florished with silver

dd to the Robes

00.37   By the Counteis of Northumberland one Jewell of golde set with a longe
white Topas and one longe pearle pendante

dd to Mrs Ratclyf

00.38   By the Counteis of Kildare xij buttons of golde of two sortes garnished
with sparkes of rubyes & pearle

dd to Mrs Ratclyf

00.39   By the Counteis of Worcester one Ruffe of Lawne Cutworke set with xx
small knottes of golde like mullettes garn with small sparkes of Rubyes
and pearle

dd to Lady Scudamore

00.40   By the Viscounteis Mountagewe widowe in golde . . . . x li

dd Mr Sackforde

Byshoppes

00.41   By the Archbyshoppe of Canterbury in golde . . . . .xl li

00.42   By the Archbyshopp of Yorke in golde. . . . . xxx li

00.43   By the Byshopp of Durham in golde . . . . xxx li

00.44   By the Byshopp of Winchester in golde . . . . xxx li

00.45   By the Byshopp of London in golde. . . . . xx li

00.46   By the Byshopp of Salisbury in golde. . . . . xx li

00.47   By the Byshopp of Bathe & Welles in golde . . . . xx li

00.48   By the Byshoppe of Norwich in golde . . . . xx li

00.49   By the Byshoppe of Lyncolne in golde. . . . . xx li

00.50   By the Byshopp of Worcester in golde . . . . xx li

00.51   By the Byshopp of Lytchfelde & Coventry in golde. . . . . viij li xj s viij d

00.52   By the Byshopp of Carlyle in golde . . . . x li

00.53   By the Byshopp of Rochester in golde . . . . x li
00.54   By the Byshopp of Chichester in golde. . . . . x li
00.55   By the Byshopp of Peterborowe in golde . . . . x li
00.56   By the Byshoppe of Glocester in golde. . . . . x li
00.57   By the Byshopp of Heryforde in golde . . . . x li
00.58   By the Byshopp of St Davyes in golde . . . . x li
00.59   By the Byshoppe of Chester in golde . . . . x li
00.60   By the Byshoppe of Exeter in golde . . . . x li
dd Mr Sackforde

Lordes

00.61   By the Lorde Hunsdon Lord Chamberlyne tenne large buttons of golde
       garnished with small rubyes and greate Ragged pearle
dd Mrs Ratclyf
00.62   By the Lord North Threasurer of her Majesties howsholde in golde . . . . x li
00.63   By the Lorde Norres in golde . . . . x li
00.64   By the Lorde Barkeley in golde. . . . . x li
00.65   By the Lord Wharton in golde . . . . x li
00.66   By the Lord Lomley in golde . . . . x li
00.67   By the Lord Ryche in golde. . . . . x li
dd Mr Sackford
00.68   By the Lord Henry Howard one Pettycote of white tynsell stryped with
       three brode laces of golde with tuftes of watchet and Carnacionn silke
dd to the Robes
00.69   By the Lorde Darcy of Chichey in golde . . . . x li
00.70   By the Lord Delaware in golde . . . . x li
dd to Mr Sackforde
00.71   By the Lorde Audeley parte of a rounde kyrtell of white Clothe of silver
       bounde about with a Lace of venice golde and vij buttons lyke the
       birdes of Arabia
dd to the Robes
00.72   By the Lorde Burghley one Jewell of golde with a long table sapher
       without foile havinge eight small Dyamones about yt and one pearle
       pendant
dd to Mrs Ratclyf
00.73   By the Lord Mountjoy one paire of Bracelettes of golde conteyninge xvj
       peeces garnished with opalles and small rubyes whereof viij of those
       peeces are lyke snakes
dd to Mrs Ratclyf
00.74   By the Lord Cobham one rounde kyrtell of silver tabyne with starres &
       droppes of gold tyssued
00.75   By the Lord Willoby of Earesby Governor of Barwicke one Mantell of
       Networke
dd to the Robes

Barronneses

00.76   By the Barronnes Pagett Cary one lapp Mantell of Ashe colored &
heare colored vnshorne veluett lozengwise lyned with Crymson
vnshorne veluett thone side with abrode passamyne lace of golde and
thother with silver lace

dd to the Robes

00.77   By the Barronnes of Hunsdon Wydowe one Loose gowne blacke of
networke florished all over with venyce golde and silver lyke feathers

dd to the Robes

00.78   By the Barronnes Hundson Junior one Doublet of white satten
embrothered and razed vppon like flyes and leaves of venyce silver
and garnished with white knyttworke

dd to the Robes

00.79   By the Barronnes Shandoes Knowlys one Pettycote of white sarcenett
embrothered all over with venice gold silver & silke of Dyverse colores
like peramydes with three borders likewise embrothered

dd to the Robes

00.80   By the Barronnes Lomley one round kyrtell of silver tynsell stryped with
golde and knotted buttons

00.81   By the Barronnes Scroope one loose Gowne of blacke tyffany stryped
with siluer & lined with sarcenet

dd to the Robes

00.82   By the Barronnes Delaware in golde . . . . x li

dd to Mr Sackforde

00.83   By the Barronnes Arbella one skarfe or heade Vaile of Lawne Cutworke
florished with silver & silke of sondrye Colores

dd to Mrs Luce Hide

00.84   By the Barronnes Ryche one Rounde White kirtell of tabyne in squares
of silver & white tuftes

dd to the Robes

00.85   By the Barronnes Chandoes widowe one Round kyrtell of silver Chamlett
or Tabyne with flowers of golde silver and silke of sondrye Colores

dd to the Robes

00.86   By the Barronnes Audeley parte of a Rounde kyrtell of white cloth of
siluer bound about with a lace of Venyce golde & vij buttons like birds
dd to the Robes

00.87   By the Barronnes Sheiffeilde Stafforde one Pettycote without bodyes of
sarcenet embrothered all over with a twyste of venyce silver and owes

dd to the Robes

00.88   By the Barronnes Buckhurst in golde . . . . x li
00.89   By the Barronnes St John of Bletzo in golde . . . . x li

dd to Mr Sackforde

00.90   By the Barronnes Burghley one Wastecote of white sarcenett embrothered
with flowers of silke of sondry Colors

dd to the Lady Scudamore

00.91 By the Barronnes Barkeley one Mantell of Lawne Cut and florished with
      silver plate
dd to the Robes

00.92 By the Barronnes Katheryn Cornwalleis one Pettycote of Ashe colored
      China Taffeta embrothered all over like Oaken leaves & ackhornes and
      slyppes of venyce golde silver and silke
dd to the Robes

Ladyes

00.93 By the Lady Mary Seamer wyfe to Mr Rogers one Quosyen Cloth of fine
      Cambricke wrought all over with venyce golde and silke
dd to the Lady Scudamore

00.94 By the Lady Elizabeth Seamer wyfe to Sir Richard Knyghtley one snoskyn
      of Crymson satten laide vppon with perfumed leather Cutt embrothered
      with venyce golde silver and silke
dd to Mrs Hide

00.95 By the Lady Guylforde parte of a Rounde kyrtell of orenge color Tabyne
      with slippes & lozenges of ashe color silke
dd to the Robes

00.96 By the Lady Stafforde one paire of Braceletts of golde cont xij peeces
      whereof vj bigger & vj lesser garnished with pearle and garnettes
dd to Mrs Ratclyf

00.97 By the Lady Cheeke one Jewell of golde lyke a starre garnished with
      sparkes of Dyamones of sondry Cuttes and one small pearle pendante
dd to Mrs Ratclyf

00.98 By the Lady Leighton one kyrtell of white knyttworke tufted all over with
      pincke colored silke
dd to the Robes

00.99 By the Lady Digbye Twoe square Cushions thone silke needleworke
      chevernewise backed with orenge colored satten thother redde leather
      embrothered with flowers of silke
dd to Stephen Peerce keeper of the
standinge wardrope att Rychmond

00.100 By the Lady Puckeringe in golde. . . . . x li
00.101 By the Lady Jarrett in golde . . . . x li
dd to Mr Sackforde

00.102 By the Lady Scudamore parte of a Loose Gowne of ashe colored taffeta
      the sleves coller and border embrothered with leaves of venyce golde
dd to the Robes

00.103 By the Lady Egerton one rounde kyrtell of white satten Cutt and
      embrothered all over like esses of venyce golde and a border
      embrothered like peramydes and one Doublet of silver Chamlett
      embrothered with puffes lyke leaves florished with silver
dd to the Robes

00.104   By the Lady Southwell one Loose Gowne of Tiffany florished with venyce
      silver and small tuftes of golde with spangles att the ende
dd to the Robes

00.105   By the Lady Edmondes one Rufe of Lawne vnmade
dd to the Lady Scudamore

00.106   By the Lady Newton one Doublet and a kyrtell of black stryped Tynsell
      with a brode border Downe afore and the bodyes Cutt & tacked vpp
      garnished with venyce golde
dd to the Robes

00.107   By the Lady Wallsingham widowe one Pettycote of white satten
      embrothered all over with flyes & branches with a broade border
dd to the Robes

00.108   By the Lady Hawkyns one snoskyn of Clothe of silver embrothered all over
      with flowers & braunches of venyce golde silver and silke of sondry Colores
dd to Mrs Hide

00.109   By the Lady Zouche one paire of pillowbeares of fine hollan clothe
      wrought with blacke silke Drawneworke

00.110   By the Lady Longe one smocke of fine hollan the sleves wrought with
      blacke silke

00.111   By the Lady Willoby one Quosion cloth of lawne cutworke florished with
      blacke silke and golde
dd to Lady Scudamore

00.112   By the Lady Hobby one Snoskyn of clothe of silver embrothered all over
      with flowers of venyce golde silver and silke of sondry colors
dd to Mrs Hide

00.113   By the Lady Harrington one Rounde kyrtell of Lawne cut in Workes like
      flowers and frutage laide vppon blacke Cypres tufted
dd to the Robes

00.114   By the Lady Walsingham Junior parte of a Pettycote of clay color satten
      embrothered all ouer with branches of siluer
dd to the Robes

Knightes

00.115   By Sir Willyam Knowlys Comptroller of her Maties howsholde one rounde
      Kirtell of ashe colored clothe of silver lyke slyppes of trees of orenge
      color silke with viij buttons embrothered like Coronettes
dd to the Robes

00.116   By Sir Robert Cecill pryncipall Secretory vij sprigges of golde garnished
      with sparkes of rubies Dyamondes and perles pendante And A Jewell
      of golde lyke a honters horne with a stone called a [Topas] garnished
      with small rubyes and a small pearle pendante
dd to Mrs Ratclyf

00.117   By Sir John Fortescue Chauncelor of Thexchequor in golde. . . . . x li
00.118   By Sir John Popham Lorde Cheif Justyce in golde . . . . x li
dd to Mr Sackforde

00.119   By Sir Thomas Leighton one Cloke of blacke networke florished with
      venyce golde bounde with a lace of venice silver

dd to the Robes

00.120   By Sir Henry Cromwell in golde . . . . x li

00.121   By Sir Edwarde Cleare in golde. . . . . x li

dd to Mr Sackforde

00.122   By Sir Edwarde Stafforde one Jewell of golde garnished with two spynnelles
      and sparkes of Dyamondes about yt and iij small pendantes with like
      sparks of dyamones

dd to Mrs Ratclyf

00.123   By Sir John Scudamore part of A Louse Gowne of ashe color taffeta
      embrothered with leves of venice gold

dd to the Robes

00.124   By Sir Edward Hobbye one Doublet of white satten Cutt & snypped
      embrothered with owes of venyce golde

dd to the Robes

00.125   By Sir John Stanhoppe twoe pendantes of golde like gates garnished
      with sparkes of Rubyes and eche with iiij small pearles pendante

dd to Mrs Ratclyf

00.126   By Sir Edward Dyer one Pettycote of white satten embrothered all over
      like grapes and pyne apples and a very broade border likewyse
      embrothered

dd to the Robes

00.127   By Sir William Cornwallies one pere of pillowberes of fyne Cambricke
      wrought all over with venice golde & silke

dd to the Ladye Scudamore

00.128   By Sir Henry Gyllforde parte of a Rounde kyrtell of Orenge color Tabyne
      with slyppes & lozenges of ashe color silke with a border Downe before
      like hollybery leaves

dd to the Robes

00.129   By Sir Henry Bronker one Pettycote of Taffeta scarcenet quilted all over
      with A border imbrothered with golde & carnaconn silke with poyntes

dd to the Robes

00.130   By Sir Thomas Wallsingham parte of A Pettycote of cley color satten
      embr all ouer with branches of silver

dd to the Robes

00.131   By Sir Thomas Jarrett One loose Gowne of orenge colored Tuftetafeta
      the grounde golde Tabyne with slyppes of ashe colored silke

dd to the Robes

00.132   By Sir Henry Billingsley one whole peece of Lawne

dd to Mrs Ratclyf

Gentlewomen

00.133   By Mistris Mary Ratclyffe one rounde kyrtell of white china damaske
      bound about with passamyne lace

dd to the Robes

00.134 By Mrs Knevett one longe Quoshion of clothe of silver with branches of flowers with silkwomans worke of venyce golde silver and silke of sondry Colores

dd to Mr Thomas Knevet keeper of Westminster Pallace

00.135 By Mrs Carre one pendante of golde cutworke garnished with small sparkes of garnettes and one small pearle pendante

dd to Mrs Ratclyf

00.136 By Mrs Luce Hyde one hatt and a feather of White tyffany imbrothered all over

dd to the Robes

00.137 By Mrs Coppyn one snoskyn of blacke velvet faire embrothered with venice silver & gold & lyned with white plushe

dd to Mrs Hide

00.138 By Mrs Twyste one paire of Inner sleves of hollan cloth the sleves wrought with blacke silke

00.139 By Mrs Cromer one smocke of fyne hollan cloth the sleves wrought blacke silke

00.140 By Mrs Huggyns Widowe one large swete bagge of sarcenett embrothered on thone side

00.141 By Mrs Frauncys Huggyns vj handkercheres of fine hollan cloth wrought with blacke silke

00.142 By Mrs Thomazine one handkercheve of fyne Camericke faire wrought with a venyce golde & silke

00.143 By Mrs Barley vj handkercheres of fyne hollan clothe wrought with black silke & edged venice golde & siluer

00.144 By Mrs Elizabeth Grene one Ruffe of Lawne Cutworke florished with a Wreath of venice silver knotted

dd to the Lady Scudamore

00.145 By Mrs Wingfeilde Mother of the Maydes iiij ruffes of Lawne and a Fanne

dd Lady Scudamore the ruffes and the Fanne to Mistris Hyde

00.146 By Mrs Elizabeth Russell one skarfe of white Cypres embrothered all over with flowers and leaves of silke of sondry colors

dd to Mrs Hyde

00.147 By Mrs Verney Alley one sute of Ruffes of fine Lawne Cutworke

dd to the Lady Scudamore

00.148 By Mrs Gryffyn one Vaile of white Tyffanye stryped with silke

dd to the Robes

00.149 By Mrs Sackforde one Loose gowne of blacke Networke stryped with silver and edged with silver lace

dd to the Robes

00.150 By Mrs Norton one Cappe of Cypres florished with silver plate and spangles

dd to Herself

00.151 By Mrs Frauncys Kirkham one Ruff of Lawne Cutworke and a paire of Ruffes

dd to the Lady Scudamore

00.152   By Mrs Dorathy Speckard parte of a heade Vaile of stryped Networke
         florished with carnaconn silke & some Owes

                                                           dd to the Robes

00.153   By Mrs Huggyns Mr William hys wyef one Ruffe of Lawne Cutworke

                                                    dd to the Lady Scudamore

00.154   By Mrs Elizabeth Brydges one Doublett of Networke Lawne Cutt and
         tufted vpp with white knytworke floryshed with silver

                                                           dd to the Robes

Gentlemen

00.155   By Mr Foulke Gryvell One Cloke and one snoskyn of sylver Tabyne tufted
         with ashe color silke and lyned with white plushe

                                                           dd to the Robes
                                                   snoskyn dd to Mrs Hide

00.156   By Mr Carre One pendant of golde Cutworke garnished with small
         sparkes of Garnettes and one small pearle pendante

                                                           dd to Mrs Ratclyf

00.157   By Mr Mountagewe one smocke of fine hollan with sleves wrought with
         blacke silke

                                                    dd to the Lady Scudamore

00.158   By Mr Garter Kinge Att Armes one booke of Heraldry of the Knightes
         of thorder this yere

                                                           dd to Mrs Ratclyf

00.159   By Mr Carmarden Two Boultes of Camericke

                                                           dd to Mrs Ratclyf

00.160   By Mr John Spillman one lyttell Garlande of silver curyously wrought
         with flowers enamelled

                                                           dd to Mrs Ratclyf

00.161   By Mr Docter James one Pott of grene Gynger and a Pott of Orenge
         flowers

00.162   By Mr Docter Browne One pott of grene gynger and A pott of orenge
         flowers

00.163   By Mr Morgan A Potycary one pott of grene gynger and a pott of orenge
         flowers

00.164   By Mr Hemingway a potycary one boxe of Manus i and a Pott of preserved
         peares

00.165   By Mr Weston A Pottcary Three boxes of preservatiues

                                                    dd to the Lady Scudamore

00.166   By Mr Byshop A Stacyoner two bookes of Titus Lyvius in Frenche

                                                    dd to Mr Thomas Knevett

00.167   By Mr William Cordall Maister Cooke One Marchpaine
00.168   By Mr Danyell Clarke Mr Cooke of the Housholde one Marchpane
00.169   By Mr Thomas Frenche Serjant of the Pastery one Pye of Orengado
00.170   By Mr Raphe Batty one other Serjant of the Pastery one Pye of Orengado

                                                                   [blank]

00.171 By Mr Fraunces Bacon one Pettycote of white satten embrothered all
over lyke feathers & billetts with thre brode borders faire embrothered
with snakes and frutage

dd to the Robes

00.172 By Mr Fraunces Wolley one Mantell of Pinke colored stryped Cobwebbe
lawne striped with sylver

dd to the Robes

00.173 By Mr Thomas Myddleton one half peece of Lawne and half A peece
of Camericke

dd to Mrs Ratclyf

00.174 By Mr Thomas Ducke serjant of the Sceller Two Botteles of ypocras

[blank]

00.175 By Mr Abraham Speckard parte of A heade Vale of stryped Networke
florished with carnaconn silke and some owes

dd to the Robes

00.176 By Mr Peter Lupo vj bottles of sweete Water
00.177 By Mr Josephe Lupo one paire of perfumed gloves
00.178 By Mr Thomas Lupo Josephe his sonne one paire of perfumed gloves
00.179 By Mr William Warren one paire of perfumed gloves
00.180 By Mr Peeter Guye one paire of perfumed gloves
00.181 By Mr Jerolimo Bassano one paire of perfumed gloves
00.182 By Mr Arthure Bassano one paire of perfumed gloves
00.183 By Mr Edwarde Bassano one paire of perfumed gloves
00.184 By Mr Andrewe Bassano one paire of perfumed gloves
00.185 By Mr Casar Gallyardo one paire of perfumed gloves
00.186 By Mr Trochius one paire of perfumed gloves
00.187 By Mr Innocent Comye one paire of perfumed gloves
00.188 By Mr Richard Graves one paire of perfumed gloves

dd to Mrs Hide

00.189 By Mr William Huggyns one large swete bagge of ashe color satten
embrothered all over very faire with a branch of Eglentyne Tree

dd to the Lady Scudamore

00.190 By Mr William Goodres two glasses of pretyous Water
00.191 By Mr George Baker one glasse of precyous Water

dd to the Lady Scudamore

00.192 By Mr Walter Pearce one paire of perfumed gloves
00.193 By Mr Robert Hales one paire of perfumed gloves
00.194 By Mr Thomas Lupo Peter Lupo his sonne one paire of perfumed gloves

dd to Mrs Hide

00.195 By Mr Randall Bull one Very lyttle locke made in A garnett

dd to Mr Ferdynandoe

00.196 By Mr Robert Lane one Rounde boxe of golde with dyverse drawinge
boxes in yt the outside enamelled

dd to Mrs Ratclyf

00.197 By Mr Richarde Frenche one mantell of white curled Cypres with tuftes
of silver Downe the seames

dd to the Robes

Elizabeth R
[sign manual]

Summa totalis of all the money gyuen to her highnes this yeare
. . . . vij^c lix li vj s viij d

Edwa: Carye
Ex[aminatio] per
Bristow
N Pigeon
Robert Cranmer
Nicholas Hottofte

Anno Regni Regine Elizabethe
Quadragesimo Secundo Anno Dei
1599

New yeares Guyftes geven by the Quenes
Matie: Att her highness Mannor of Rychmonde the
Firste day of Januarie in the yeare abouesayde to
these persones whose names hereafter ensue: viz

Elizabeth R
[sign manual]

00.198 To Sir Thomas Egerton knight lord Keeper of the Greate Seale of
Englande in guilt plate K . . . . xxxiiij oz di qrter
00.199 To the Lorde Buckhurste Lord highe Threasorer of England in guilte
plate M . . . . xxiij oz di di qrter
00.200 To the Lorde Marques of winton in guilte plate K . . . . xxix oz iij qrters di
87.2.2.

Earles

00.201 To the Earle of Nottingham Lorde Admyrall in guilte plate M & K
. . . . Cvj oz qrter
00.202 To the Earle of Shrewesbury in guilte plate M . . . . xxxj oz di
00.203 To the Earle of Darby in guilte plate K . . . . xxxj oz di
00.204 To the Earle of Sussex in guilte plate K . . . . xx oz qrter di
00.205 To the Earle of Comberlande in guilte plate M . . . . xxij oz
00.206 To the Earle of Bathe in gilte plate M . . . . xx oz di di qrter
00.207 To the Earle of Hartforde in gilte plate M . . . . xxj oz di di qrter

00.208	To the Earle of Pembrooke in guylte plate M..................... xxxj oz
00.209	To the Earle of Northumberland in guilte plate M .... xxix oz qrter di
00.210	To the Earle of Huntington in guilte plate M...................... xx oz
00.211	To the Earle of Worcester in guilte plate M ....xxv oz
00.212	To the Earle of Bedforde in gilte plate K .... xix oz di di qrter
00.213	To the Earle of Rutlande in gilte plate K ....xxj oz di

300.1.2

Marquesses and Counteses

00.214	To the Lady Marques of Northampton in guilte plate K & M
	....xliiij oz iij qrters
00.215	To the Lady Marques of winton Wydowe in guilte plate M ....xxx oz
00.216	To the Countes of Oxenforde in guilte plate K and M............. xxxiiij oz
00.217	To the Countes of Kente in guilte plate K ....xix oz iij qrters
00.218	To the Counteis of Shrewesbury wydowe in guilte plate M ....xlj oz qrter di
00.219	To the Counteis of Shrewesbury Junior in guilte plate M .... xix oz di
00.220	To the Counteis of Nottingham in guilte plate K............... xxvj oz qrter
00.221	To the Counteis of Darby Wydowe in guilte plate K .... xxj oz di di qrter
00.222	To the Counteis of Darby Junior in guilte plate K....................xxiij oz
00.223	To the Counteis of Huntington Widowe in guilte plate K ...... xxix oz qrter di
00.224	To the Counteis of Huntington Junior in guilte plate K .... xix oz qrter
00.225	To the Counteis of Bedforde Widowe in guilte plate M...................Lj oz
00.226	To the Counteis of Southampton Senior in guilte plate M .... xxij oz qrter
00.227	To the Counteis of Pembrooke in guilte plate M .... xix oz qrter
00.228	To the Counteis of Worcester in guilte plate K.................... xix oz di
00.229	To the Counteis of Bathe in guilte plate M.................. xix oz di di qrter
00.230	To the Counteis of Bedforde Junior in guilte plate K.......... xix oz di di qrter
00.231	To the Counteis of Comberlande in guilte plate M ....xxj oz iij qrters
00.232	To the Counteis of Northumberlande in guilte plate K .... xxiij oz qrter
00.233	To the Counteis of Kildare in guilte plate M .... xxiij oz qrter
00.234	To the Counteis of Sussex in guilte plate K .... xix oz
00.235	To the Counteis of warwicke in guilte plate K and M .... Liiij oz qrter di
00.236	To the Counteis of Rutlande in guilte plate M.................... xxij oz di
00.237	To the viscounteis Mountagewe widowe in guilte plate K ..... xix oz di di qrter

643.3.2

Bysshoppes

00.238	To the Archbyshoppe of Canterbury in guilte plate K................. xlv oz
00.239	To the Archbyshoppe of Yorke in guilte plate M .... xxxviij oz
00.240	To the Byshoppe of London in guilte plate M .... xxx oz qrter di
00.241	To the Byshopp of Durham in guilte plate M .... xxxviij oz
00.242	To the Byshoppe of Norwiche in guilte plate M................. xxx oz qrter
00.243	To the Byshopp of Lyncolne in guilte plate K .... xxx o
00.244	To the Byshopp of Worcester in guilte plate K......................xxx oz
00.245	To the Byshoppe of Salesbury in guilte plate K .... xxxj oz di di qrter
00.246	To the Byshoppe of Lytchfelde in guilte plate K .... xix oz

00.247	To the Byshoppe of Carlyle in guilte plate K . . . . xvij oz di di qtr
00.248	To the Byshoppe of Rochester in guilte plate K . . . . xv oz di
00.249	To the Byshoppe of Chester in guilte plate K . . . . xvij [oz] di
00.250	To the Byshoppe of Wynchester in guilte plate M . . . . .xxxvj oz iij qrters
00.251	To the Byshoppe of Chycester Aulmer in guilte plate K . . . . . . xix oz di di qrter
00.252	To the Byshoppe of Peterboroughe in guilte plate M. . . . . xv oz qrter
00.253	To the Byshopp of Glocester in guilte plate M. . . . . xv oz qrter
00.254	To the Byshoppe of Hereforde in guilte plate M . . . . .xv oz di di qrter
00.255	To the Byshoppe of Bathe & Welles in guilte plate K. . . . . xxx oz qrter
00.256	To the Byshoppe of St Davyes in guilte plate M . . . . xvij oz iij qrters di
00.257	To the Byshoppe of Exeter in guilte plate K. . . . . xvj oz di di qrter
	510.0.2

Lordes

00.258	To the Lorde of Hunsdon Lorde Chamberleyne in guylte plate K & M
	. . . . .xxxij oz di qrter
00.259	To the Lorde Northe in guilte plate K . . . . .xxj oz iij qrters
00.260	To the Lorde Lomeley in guilte plate K . . . . xx oz qrter
00.261	To the Lorde Cobham in guilte plate K . . . . .xxx oz
00.262	To the Lorde Norreis in guilte plate K . . . . xx oz di qrter
00.263	To the Lorde Willoby in guilte plate K. . . . . xxj oz qrter
00.264	To the Lorde Wharton in guilte plate M. . . . . xx oz qrter
00.265	To the Lorde Ryche in guilte plate M . . . . xx oz di qrter
00.266	To the Lorde Burghley in guilte plate M. xxx oz qrter
00.267	To the Lorde Darcy in guilte plate K . . . . xx oz qrter
00.268	To the Lorde Audeley in guilte plate K. .xxij oz qrter
00.269	To the Lorde Mountjoye in guilte plate K . . . . .xxx oz qrter di
00.270	To the Lorde Barkeley in guilte plate M . . . . xx oz qrter
00.271	To the Lorde Henry Howarde in guilte plate M . . . . xxv oz di
00.272	To the Lorde Delaware in guilte plate K. . . . . xxiiij oz iij qrters di
	350.2.2

Barronnesses

00.273	To the Barronnesse Pagett Cary in guilte plate K. . . . . .xxxvj oz iij qrters di
00.274	To the Barronnesse Chandoes Knowlys in guilte plate M and K
	. . . . xxj oz di qrter
00.275	To the Barronnes Lumley in guilte plate K. . . . . xx oz di qrter
00.276	To the Barronnes Hunsdon Wydowe in guilte plate K . . . . xxxij oz di qrter
00.277	To the Barronnes Hundson Junior in guilte plate M . . . . xxxj oz di qrter
00.278	To the Barronnes Scroupe in guilte plate K . . . . xvij oz iij qrters
00.279	To the Barronnes Audeley in guylte plate K. . . . . xx oz
00.280	To the Barronnes Arbella in guylte plate M . . . . .xix oz iij qrters di
00.281	To the Barronnes Delaware in guilte plate K . . . . xix oz
00.282	To the Barronnes Sheiffelde Stafforde in guylte plate M . . . . xx oz
00.283	To the Barronnes Ryche in guilte plate M. . . . . xxj oz di qrter
00.284	To the Barronnes Burghley in guilte plate M . . . . xxv oz iij qrters

00.285	To the Barronnes St John of Bletzo in guilte plate K . . . . .xix oz iij qrters di
00.286	To the Barronnes Chandowis Widowe in guilte plate K . . . . xxij oz qrter
00.287	To the Barronnes Buckhurste in guylte plate M . . . . xxj oz qrter
00.288	To the Barronness Barkeley in guilte plate M . . . . xix oz qrter di
00.289	To the Barronnes Katheryne Cornewalleis in guylte plate M. . . . . xx oz

387.2.2

Ladyes

00.290	To the Lady Mary Seamer Mr Rogers his Wyef in guylte plate M
	. . . . xij oz qrter
00.291	To the Lady Elizabeth Seamer Sir Richarde Knyghtley his Wyef in guilte
	plate K . . . . xiij oz qrter di
00.292	To the Lady Guylforde in guylte plate M . . . . xvij oz di di qrter
00.293	To the Lady Stafforde in guilte plate K and M. . . . . xxxj oz
00.294	To the Lady Cheeke in guilt plate K . . . . xxx oz di qrter
00.295	To the Lady Leyghton in guylt plate K. . . . . xvij oz di
00.296	To the Lady Southwell in guilte plate K . . . . xvij oz qrter di
00.297	To the Lady Scudamore in guilte plate K . . . . xvij oz iij qrters
00.298	To the Lady Zouche in guilte plate M. . . . . xvj oz di
00.299	To the Lady Egerton in guylte plate K . . . . xvij oz iij qrters di
00.300	To the Ladye Edmondes in guilte plate K. . . . . xvij oz iij qrters
00.301	To the Ladye Newton in guilte plate K. . . . . xvij oz iij qrters di
00.302	To the Lady Hawkyns in guylte plate M. . . . . .xviij oz di
00.303	To the Lady Hobby in guilte plate K . . . . xviij oz di qrter
00.304	To the Lady Wallsingham Wydowe in guilte plate M. . . . . xxvij oz di
00.305	To the Lady Walsingham Junior in guilte plate K . . . . .xvj oz iij qrters di
00.306	To the Lady Dygbye in guilte plate K . . . . xvij oz qrter di
00.307	To the Lady Jarrett widowe in guilte plate M . . . . xviij oz qrter
00.308	To the Lady Longe in guilte plate K . . . . xviij oz di qrter
00.309	To the Lady Harrington in guilte plate K. . . . . xix oz qrter di
00.310	To the Lady Puckeringe in guilte plate M. . . . . .xviij oz
00.311	To the Lady Willoby in guilte plate M . . . . xv oz iij qrters

445.3.3

Knightes

00.312	To Sir Willam Knowlys Comptroller of her Ma[ties] housholde in guilte
	plate M. . . . . .xxvj oz di
00.313	To Sir John Popham Cheif Justice in guilte plate M . . . . .xxiij oz di
00.314	To Sir John Fortescue Chauncelor of Thexchequor in guilte plate M . . . xxiiij oz
00.315	To Sir Robert Cicell Principall Secretory in guilte plate M . . . . .xxxj oz di
00.316	To Sir Thomas Leyghton in guylte plate K and M. . . . . .xxxij oz di di qrter
00.317	To Sir John Stanhoppe in guilte plate M . . . . .xxv oz di di qrter
00.318	To Sir Edwarde Stafford in guylte plate M . . . . xx oz
00.319	To Sir John Scudamore in guilte plate M . . . . xx oz
00.320	To Sir Edward Dyer in guilte plate M. . . . . xxiij oz di di qrter
00.321	To Sir Edward Hobby in guilte plate M . . . . .xxiij oz iij qrters

00.322	To Sir Thomas Jarrett in guilte plate M	xxij oz iij qrters
00.323	To Sir William Cornewalleis in guilte plate K	xvij oz di qrter
00.324	To Sir Henry Cromwell in guilte plate M	xix oz qrter di
00.325	To Sir Edward Cleare in guilte plate K and M	xix oz iij qrters di
00.326	To Sir Henry Gyllford in guilte plate K	xxj oz qrter
00.327	To Sir Henry Bronker in guilte plate M	xxiiij oz qrter
00.328	To Sir Thomas Wallsingham in guylte plate K	xxj oz qrter
00.329	To Sir Henry Billingesley in guilte plate K	xxj oz di

443.2

Fregiftes

00.330	To Mistris Anne Russell in guylte plate K	xj oz
00.331	To the Lady Dorothy Hastinges in guilte plate K	x oz qrter
00.332	To Mrs Marye Fytten in guilte plate K	ix oz iij qrters di
00.333	To Mrs Anne Carye in guylte plate K	x oz qrter
00.334	To Mrs Cordall Anslowe in guilte plate M	ix oz di di qrter

51

Gentlewomen

00.335	To Mistris Mary Ratclyffe in guylte plate K	xviij oz qrter di
00.336	To Mrs Knevett in guylte plate K	xxxij oz
00.337	To Mrs Carre in guylte plate K	xvij oz qrter di
00.338	To Mrs Luce Hide in guylte plate M	xvij oz
00.339	To Mrs Elizabeth Brydges in guylte plate K and M	xvij oz di di qrter
00.340	To Mrs Coppyn in guylte plate K	xvij oz qrter
00.341	To Mrs Twyste in guylte plate M	viij oz qrter di
00.342	To Mrs Alley in guylte plate K	vj oz di di qrter
00.343	To Mrs Cromer in guylte plate M	xvj oz di di qrter
00.344	To Mrs Huggyns widowe in guylte plate K	xvj oz
00.345	To Mrs Fraunces Huggyns in guylte plate M	xvj oz
00.346	To Mrs Huggyns Mr William his wyef in guylte plate K	xvj oz
00.347	To Mrs Thomazine in guylte plate K	vj oz iij qrters
00.348	To Mrs Barley in guylte plate K	xij oz
00.349	To Mrs Grene in guylte plate K	v oz
00.350	To Mrs Sackforde in guylte plate M	xx oz
00.351	To Mrs Elizabeth Russell in guylte plate K	xvij oz iij qrters di
00.352	To Mrs Gryffen in guylte plate M	xxj oz iij qrters
00.353	To Mrs Winckfeilde Mother of the Maydes in guylte plate M	xx oz qrter di
00.354	To Mrs Fraunces Kyrkham in guylte plate K	xvij oz di qrter
00.355	To Mrs Elizabeth Norton in guylte plate K	xvj oz di di qrter
00.356	To Mrs Dorathy Speckarde in guylte plate K	viij oz di qrter

344.3.2

Gentlemen

| 00.357 | To Mr Foulke Gryvell in guylte plate M | xxv oz qrter |
| 00.358 | To Mr Garter Kinge at Armes in guylte plate K | viij oz |

00.359	To Mr Carre in guylte plate K. . . . . xix oz di di qrter
00.360	To Mr Mountague in guylte plate M . . . . xiiij oz
00.361	To Mr Carmarden in guylte plate K. . . . . xvij oz
00.362	To Mr John Spillman in guylt plate M . . . . xvij oz di qrter
00.363	To Mr Docter James in guylte plate K . . . . xiiij oz iij qrters di
00.364	To Mr Docter Browne in guylte plate K . . . . iiij oz iij qrters di
00.365	To Mr Morgan a Pottycary in guylt plate M . . . . viij oz di qrter
00.366	To Mr Hemyngwaye a Potycary in guylt plate K . . . . viij oz di qrter
00.367	To Mr Weston a Potycary in guylte plate K . . . . viij oz qrter di
00.368	To Mr William Cordall Mr Cooke in guilte plate K. . . . . vij oz di di qrter
00.369	To Mr Dannyell Clarke Mr Cooke of the housholde in guylte plate K . . . . vij oz qrter
00.370	To Mr Thomas Frenche Serjant of the Pastery in guilte plate K . . . . viij oz qrter
00.371	To Mr Raphe Batty one other Serjant of the Pastery in guilte plate K . . . . viij oz
00.372	To Mr Frauncis Baconn in guylte plate M . . . . xxxiij oz
00.373	To Mr Frauncis Wolley in guylte plate K . . . . xxij oz
00.374	To Mr Abraham Speckard in guylte plate K . . . . viij oz
00.375	To Mr Peter Lupo in guylte plate K . . . . v oz
00.376	To Mr Joseph Lupo in guylte plate K. . . . . v oz
00.377	To Mr Thomas Lupo sonne to Joseph Lupo in guylte plate K . . . . v oz
00.378	To Mr Thomas Lupo sonne to Peter Lupo in guilte plate M. . . . . v oz
00.379	To Mr William Warren in guylte plate K . . . . v oz
00.380	To Mr Jerolymo Bassano in guylte plate M . . . . v oz
00.381	To Mr Arthure Bassano in guylte plate K . . . . v oz
00.382	To Mr Andrewe Bassano in guylte plate M . . . . v oz
00.383	To Mr Edward Bassano in guylte plate K . . . . v oz
00.384	To Mr Richard Greves in guylte plate M . . . . v oz
00.385	To Mr Casar Gallyardoe in guylte plate K . . . . v oz
00.386	To Mr Innocent Comye in guylte plate M . . . . v oz
00.387	To Mr Walter Peerce in guylte plate K . . . . v oz
00.388	To Mr Roberte Hales in guylte plate M . . . . v oz
00.389	To Mr Trochius in guilte plate K. . . . . v oz
00.390	To Mr Peter Guye in guylte plate M . . . . v oz
00.391	To Mr William Huggyns in guilte plate K . . . . xviij oz
00.392	To Mr Thomas Myddleton in guilte plate K . . . . xv oz di qrter
00.393	To Mr Byshoppe A stacyoner in guylte plate K . . . . xvj oz qrter
00.394	To Mr William Goodres in guilte plate M . . . . xiiij oz qrter di
00.395	To Mr George Baker in guylte plate K . . . . xiiij oz di
00.396	To Mr Thomas Ducke Sergeant of the Sceller in guilte plate M . ix oz di di qrter
00.397	To Mr Roberte Lane in guilte plate K. . . . . xxx oz
00.398	To Mr Randall Bull in guylte plate M. . . . . x oz
00.399	To Mr Richarde Frenche in guylte plate K . . . . xj oz qrter
	468.2.1

Fregiftes

00.400	To Sir Edwarde Carye Mr and Threasorer of her Ma[ties] Jewelles and Plate in guylte plate M. . . . . xviij oz iij qrters di

00.401	To Sir Thomas Gorges in guylte plate M	x oz
00.402	To Sir Edwarde Dennye in guylte plate M	x oz
00.403	To Mr Henry Sackforde in guylte plate M	x oz
00.404	To Mr Thomas Knevett in guylte plate K.	x oz
00.405	To Mr Edwarde Darcye in guylte plate M	x oz
00.406	To Mr William Kyllegrewe in guylte plate K	x oz
00.407	To Mr Michaell Stanhoppe in guylte plate K.	x oz
00.408	To Sir Edwarde Carye one other Grome &c in guylte plate M	x oz
00.409	To Mr Ferdinando Richardsonne in guylte plate M	x oz
00.410	To Mr Richarde Nightingale Yoman of the Robes in guilte plate K	xij oz

00.411 To Mr Nicholas Brystowe Clerke of her Maties Jewelles and Plate in
      guylte plate K. . . . . x oz iij qrters di
00.412 To Mr Nicholas Pygeon Yoman of her Maties Jewelles and Plate in
      guylte plate K. . . . . x oz iij qrters di
00.413 To Mr Roberte Cranmer one other Yoman in guilte plate K . . . . x oz iij qrters di
00.414 To Mr Nicholas Hottofte Groome in guylte plate K . . . . x oz iij qrters di
                                                     164.1.2

Some totall of all the Plate gyuen
in manner and forme abouesayd . . . . iiij^m CCxxxvj oz di qrter

Guyftes gyuen by her Majestie to sondrye personnes
and Delyvered at sonndry tymes as followethe / viz /

00.415 Marye hemynham
    Fryste gyven by her highnes and delyvered the xxiiij^{th} daye of June Anno
        xlj^{mo} regni Regine Elizabethe &c Att the Marryage of Mistris Marye
        Hemyngham One guylte Boule with a Cover bought of Richarde
        Martyn goldsmythe poiz . . . . xlij oz di
00.416 Mr Attorney
    Item gyven by her sayde highnes and Delyvered the xij^{th} of Auguste
        Anno pred at the Christeninge of Mr Cooke Attorney generall to her
        Majesty his Childe one guylte Boule with a Cover boughte of the
        sayde Richard Martyn poiz . . . . xlj oz di di qrter
00.417 Mounser Caron
    Item gyven by her sayde highnes and Delyvered the xv^{th} of October
        Anno pred To Mounser Caron Agent for Flaunders at his Departure
        out of England Parte of one Cheyne of golde bought of Hughe
        Kaylle poiz—xxxv oz qrter of the goodnes of xxjtie karrettes di graine
        and parte of one other Cheyne bought of the sayde Richard Martyn
        poiz—xxxiij oz qrter iij d weyt vj graynes of the goodnes of xxijtie
        karrettes di graine. In toto . . . . lxviij oz di iij d weyt vj granes

Edward Carye
Ex[aminatio] per
N Pigeon
Robert Cranmer
Nicholas Hottofte

Anno regni Regine Elizabethe
Quadragesimo Quinto Annoque
Domini. 1602.

Newyeres guiftes giuen to the
Queenes Matie at her highnes Pallace
at westminster by these persones whose names
hereafter ensue, the firste daye of January
in the yere abouesaide. viz.

James R
[sign manual]

03.1   By Sir Thomas Egerton Knighte Lorde Keeper of the greate Seale of
Englande, One Jewell of Golde fashioned Like a Feather, and garnished
with Dyamondes and Rubyes
Delivered to Mrs Mary Ratcliff
one of the gentlewomen of the Privey Chamber
03.2   By the Lorde Buckhurste Lorde highe Thresorer of Englande, in golde . . . . . x li
Delivered to Henry Sackford
one of the gromes of her Maties privie chamber
03.3   By the Lorde marques of Wynchester . . . . nihil

Earles

03.4   By the Earle of Nottingham Lorde highe Admirall of Englande Seaven
peeces of Golde, All garnished with Dyamondes Rubyes & pearles the
midle peece bigger then the reste having three Opalles in it, and a Shipp
over them
03.5   By the Earle of Worcester Mr of her Majesties Horses One paire of
Bracelettes of Golde, conteyning Sixteene peeces, whereof Fower
garnished with three smalle Dyamondes, fower of them with two
smale Rubyes, & the other eighte with two half Pearle a peece
Delivered to the saide Mrs Ratcliffe
03.6   By the Earle of Shrewsburye, in Golde . . . . xx li
Delivered to the said Henry Sackford
03.7   By the Earle of Darbye One mantell of white Silke Cypres, Imbrodered
all over with Beastes Byrdes Flyes of Silke of sondrye Collors
Delivered into thoffice of her majesties wardrobe of Robes
03.8   By the Earle of Huntingdon in golde . . . . x li
03.9   By the Earle of Sussex in golde . . . . x li
03.10 By the Earle of Bathe in golde . . . . x li
[Delivered to the said Henry Sackford]

03.11 By the Earle of Cumberlande, One Loose Gowne of Spanishe Taffata,
florished with golde and silver like Piramides and peces of Silke of
sondrye Colors
Delivered into the saide wardrobe of Robes

03.12 By the Earle of Northumberlande, One loose gowne of Brasell Cullor
Tabyne, garnished with Buttons and Loopes of Vennys silver Clowde
lace
Delivered into the saide wardrobes of Robes

03.13 By the Earle of Hartford, in golde . . . . x li
03.14 By the Earle of Pembroke in golde . . . . xx li
03.15 By the Earle of Bedforde in golde. . . . . x li
03.16 By the Earle of Rutlande in golde. . . . . x li
Delivered to the said Henry Sackford

03.17 By the Earle of Klenrickett One kyrtle of Clothe of Silver like Clowdes,
with a brode Border ymbrodered downe before of Venys sylver and silke
in Cullors

03.18 By the Vycounte Byndonn One gowne of Networke or stitched Clothe
Florished all over with Vennys silver golde and silke of diverse Cullors
like Pyramydes and garlandes
Delivered into the saide wardrobe of Robes

Marqueses & Countesses

03.19 By the Marquesse of Northamptonn One paire of Bracelettes of Golde
conteyning twelve peces, in each one half Pearle and foure Sparkes of
Rubyes
Delivered to the said Mrs Ratcliffe

03.20 By the Countesse of Kente widowe one very fayre quishion Clothe of
Lawne wroughte all over with vennys golde Silver and silke of sondry
Cullors with the borders indented
Delivered to the Lady Scudamore
one of the gentlewomen of the Privey Chamber

03.21 By the Countesse of Oxforde one Mantle of white Lawne, florished with
Flowers of Silke of sondry Cullors, Lyned with Lawne striped with
silver
Delivered into the said wardrobe of Robes

03.22 By the Countesse of Shrewsbury widowe, in golde . . . . xl li
03.23 By the Countesse of Shrewsbury Junior in golde. x li
03.24 By the Countesse of Sussex in golde. . . . . x li
03.25 By the Countesse of Bedforde in golde. . . . . x li
03.26 By the Countesse of Huntingtonn widowe, in golde . . . . viij li
03.27 By the Countesse of Huntingtonn Junior in golde. . . . . viij li
03.28 By the Countesse of Pembroke widowe in golde . . . . x li
03.29 By the Countesse of Hartforde in golde . . . . x li
03.30 By the Countesse of Bathe in Golde. . . . . x li
Delivered to the said Henry Sackford

03.31 By the Countesse of Darbye Egertonn one rounde kertle of Brasell Collor
 Tabyne, the ground silver
Delivered into the said wardrobe of Robes

03.32 By the Countesse of Warwicke one Jewell of golde like a Feather, garnished
 with smale Rubyes, Pearle, Pearle Pendante, Opalles pendante, with a
 sunne in the middle garnished with sparkes of Rubyes, One smale
 Diamond in the midest & a Jacynte pendant Cut like a Harte
Delivered to the said Mrs Ratcliff

03.33 By the Countesse of Darby Junior one Rounde kertle of white nett in
 workes, ymbrodered all ouer like Calteroppe knottes of vennys golde &
 Plates, and Orrenge tuffes all over
Delivered into the said wardrobe of Robes

03.34 By the Countesse of Rutlande in golde. . . . . x li
[Delivered to the said Henry Sackford]

03.35 By the Countesse of Comberlande, One Pendante of golde conteyning
 two ballaces, the one Rocke the other table and one Pearle pendante
Delivered to the said Mrs Ratcliff

03.36 By the Countesse of Northumberlande, One pettycote of white Sattenn,
 ymbrodered all over with a thredd of Carnation silke & golde like
 knottes, and a very broade border richelye ymbrodered with sondrye
 Fowles
Delivered into the said wardrobe of Robes

03.37 By the Countesse of Nottingham, One Armelett of golde Conteyning
 seaven peeces garnished with dyamondes Rubies & pearle, with six
 pendantes in the mydle pece, being a gordyan knotte like wise garnished,
 and three pendantes of smale dyamondes & pearle, & one Rubye with
 out a foyle pendante

03.38 By the Countesse of Kildare, One paire of Bracelettes of golde Conteyning
 xvj peeces garnished with smale Rubyes and halfe pearle
Delivered to the said Mrs Ratcliffe

03.39 By the Countesse of Worcester, three flatt bodkyns of golde with three
 pendantes, eache pendant garnished with one Sparke of a diamonde,
 one smale table ruby & three smale pearle pendant
Delivered to the said Mrs Ratcliffe

03.40 By the Countesse of Southamptonn senior one round kertle of maiden
 blushe Collor knyttworke florished with Vennys silver byrdes & fishes
 of silke of sondry Cullors

03.41 By the Countesse of Essex one Petticote withoute bodyes of Ashe Cullored
 Satten ymbrodered all over with a fayre worke of Branches and Foules of
 vennys golde silver and silke
Delivered into the said wardrobe of Robes

03.42 By the Vicountesse Mountagewe in golde. . . . . x li
Delivered to the said Henry Sackford

Bishoppes

03.43 By the Arche Bishop of Canterbury in gold . . . . xl li
03.44 By the Arche Bishopp of Yorke in golde . . . . xxx li
03.45 By the Bishopp of Durham in golde . . . . xxx li
03.46 By the Bishopp of Eley in golde . . . . xxx li
03.47 By the Bishopp of Wynchester in golde . . . . xxx li
03.48 By the Bishopp of Londonn in golde . . . . xx li
03.49 By the Bishopp of Salisburye in golde . . . . xx li
03.50 By the Bishopp of Lyncolne in Golde . . . . xx li
03.51 By the Bishopp of Bathe & Welles in golde . . . . xx li
03.52 By the Bishopp of Worcester in golde . . . . xx li
03.53 By the Bishopp of Litchfeild & Coventrey in golde . . . . xiij li vj s viij d
03.54 By the Bishopp of Rochester in golde . . . . x li
03.55 By the Bishopp of Chichester in golde . . . . x li
03.56 By the Bishopp of Chester in golde . . . . x li
03.57 By the Bishopp of Glocester in golde . . . . x li
03.58 By the Bishopp of Exeter in golde . . . . x li
03.59 By the Bishopp of Peterboroughe . . . . x li
03.60 By the Bishopp of Carlile in golde . . . . x li
03.61 By the Bishopp of St Davyes in golde . . . . x li

Delivered to the said Henry Sackford

Lordes

03.62 By the Lorde Hunsdon Lorde Chamberlenn one Jewell of golde like a
branche garnished with Dyamondes of sondrie bignesses and cuttes

Delivered to the said Mrs Ratcliff

03.63 By the Lorde Cobham one Pettycote of Carnaconn Sattenn ymbrodered
all over with Flowers of Vennys golde and silke with a broad border
ymbrodered like Piramides

Delivered into the said wardrobe of Robes

03.64 By the Lorde Lomley in golde . . . . x li
03.65 By the Lorde Norrys in golde . . . . x li
03.66 By the Lorde Whartonn in golde . . . . x li
03.67 By the Lorde Riche in golde . . . . x li

Delivered to the said Henry Sackford

03.68 By the Lorde Comptonn one Jewell of golde like a paire of Bellowes,
garnished with Diamondes and smale Rubyes and two smale Pearle
pendante

Delivered to the said Mrs Ratcliff

03.69 By the Lord Darcye of Chichley in golde . . . . x li

[Delivered to the said Henry Sackford]

03.70 By the Lorde montjoye One pettycote of white satten with oute bodyes
ymbrodered all over with Sonnes Cloudes and Raynbowes

03.71   By the Lorde Thomas Howard parte of a Frenche gowne of Tawney
knyttworke florished with golde with a border downe before, and upon
the sleeves of lawne ymbrodered with silver owes

Delivered into the said wardrobe of Robes

03.72   By the Lorde Burghley two Pendantes of golde garnished with rubyes &
Diamondes with oute Foyle, eache one haveing three pearle pendante

Delivered to the said Mrs Ratcliff

03.73   By the Lorde Barkeley in golde. . . . . x li

[Delivered to the said Henry Sackford]

03.74   By the Lorde Henry Howarde one Cloke of Orrange Cullor velvett
imbrodered with silver like maces

Delivered into the said wardrobe of Robes

03.75   By the Lorde Stafford in golde . . . . x li

Delivered to the said Henry Sackford

Baronnesses

03.76   By the Barronnesse Hundson Junior one Petticote of Dove Cullored
Sattenn ymbrodered all over with slipps of Flowers & a broad border
rounde aboute ymbrodered like fountaines

Delivered into the said wardrobe of Robes

03.77   By the Barrones Pagett Carye one short Carcanet conteyning seaven peces
of golde with seaven smale rubyes & Pearles betweene with six Pendantes
like half moones, garnished with sparkes of Dyamondes & rubyes

Delivered to the said Mrs Ratcliff

03.78   By the Baronnesse Chandos Knowles one Dublett of white satten Cutt
vp like leaves ymbrodered vponn with Carnaconn silke & owes

03.79   By the Baronnes Chandos widowe one straight boddied gowne of Silver
Chamlett striped ymbrodered all over like Rockes & Birdes

03.80   By the Baronnes Lomley one round kertle of white silver Tabyne like
Clowdes, with Loopes Downe before of Vennys gold & silver

03.81   By the Baronnes Scroope One Mantle of Tiffeney Cullor de Roy striped
with gold

Delivered into the said wardrobe of Robes

03.82   By the Baronnes Shefeild Stafford, One wastcoate of white sarcenett
ymbrodered with leaves of gold & billettes of Carnaconn silke

Delivered to the said Lady Scudamore

03.83   By the Baronnes Arbella One rounde kertle of white Sattenn ymbrodered
all over with sondrye Devices with a border of Rockes

03.84   By the Baronnes Howard Lord Thomas his wief parte of a Frenche gowne
of tawny knytt worke florished with gold with a border Downe before, &
uponn the sleeves of lawne ymbrodered with silver Owes

Delivered into the said wardrobe of Robes

03.85   By the Baronnes De La Ware, one Large Bagge of Changeable Taffata
ymbrodered all over with vennice golde, to Carry Sables in

Delivered to the said Lady Scudamore

03.86   By the Baronnes Barkley one loose gowne of white Sattenn rased like
      peramides the sleeves and faceing garnished with Orange Cullored
      Taffata like half Moones

Delivered into the said wardrobe of Robes

03.87   By the Baronnes Broughe, two paire of perfumed gloves, the Cuffes sett
      with some smale ragged Pearle

Delivered to Mrs Hide one of her Majesties chamberers

03.88   By the Baronnes Katherin Cornwallys the foreparte and sleeves for a gowne
      of white Clothe of Silver lyned with Orrange Cullored sarcenett

03.89   By the Barrones Elizabeth Graye One Mantle of Networke withoute a
      trayne sett all over with Roses and LadyCowes

Delivered to the said wardrobe of Robes

03.90   By the Baronnes Hunsdonn widowe in gold. . . . . x li

03.91   By the Barones Buckhurste in golde. . . . . x li

03.92   By the Barronnes St John of Bletsoe widowe in golde . . . . x li

Delivered to the saide Henry Sackforde

Ladyes

03.93   By Lady Anne Harbert one Dublett of Lawne Cut vp & ymbrodered with
      Vennys silver and Owes

03.94   By Lady Bridgett Manners Tyrwhitt One rounde kertle of white knytt worke
      florished with vennys golde & silver with billettes of heare collered taffata
      ravelled

03.95   By Lady Suzan Vere One Mantell of Collor De Roye Tiffeney striped with
      silver

Delivered to the said wardrobe of Robes

03.96   By Lady Mary Semer Rogers One Smocke of Camericke wrought with
      black silke Drawne worke

Delivered to the said Lady Scudamore

03.97   By Lady Gilford One attyre for the head of white knytt worke

Delivered to Mrs Rainsforde

03.98   By Lady Southwell one Lose gowne of Tawny knytt worke florished like
      leaves foure square of Venyce golde & silver

Delivered to the Robes

03.99   By Lady Stafford one paire of Bracelettes of gold conteyning xvj peeces
      whereof viijt set with foure perles foure smale garnettes in a peece, &
      eight with two Pearles and one smale Rubye

Delivered to the said Mrs Ratcliff

03.100   By Lady Cheeke two pendantes of gold garnished with rubyes Opalles &
      each with three pearles pendante

03.101   By Lady Leightonn One bodkynn of silver gylte with a pendant of
      Christall Cutt in Squares with an Amatiste pendante over it a cyrcle of
      pearle, & a Cluster of smale Pearle pendante

Delivered to the said Mrs Ratcliff

03.102   By Lady Scudamore parte of a Loose gowne of white silver Tabyne lyned
      with orange Collored Sarcenett & faced with Orrange Cullored satten

03.103   By Lady Walsingham parte of a Loose gowne of Claye Cullored sattenn
rased & pynckt with buttons & Loopes of Vennys silver
Delivered into the said wardrobe of Robes

03.104   By Lady Digby two square quosions of silke needle worke Cheverne wise
backed with watchett sattenn, frynged buttoned & tasselled with Vennys
silk & silver
Delivered to Sir Thomas Knevett
keeper of her majesties pallace at Westminster

03.105   By Lady Newtonn one pair of bracelettes of gold conteyning xiiijene
peces, whereof viij are sett with sparkes of rubyes & ij smale pearle a
peece & the other viijt are sett with two smale pearle in a peece filled
with Pommaunder
Delivered to the said Mrs Ratcliff

03.106   By Lady Jarratt in golde . . . . x li

03.107   By Lady Puckering in golde . . . . x li
Delivered to the said Henry Sackford

03.108   By Lady Edmondes one sute of ruffes of Lawne Layde worke
Delivered to the said Lady Scudamore

03.109   By Ladye Hawkyns fyve pendantes of gold eache garnished with Opalles
rubyes three smale pearle pendante in a peece
Delivered to the said Mrs Ratcliff

03.110   By Lady Hobby parte of a rounde kertle of white golde Chamlett with a
border downe before of Owes vpon white taffata parte like piramides
Delivered into the said wardrobe of Robes

03.111   By Ladye Harrington one paire of bracelettes of gold conteyning xvjtene
peeces whereof viijt of them are sett with iiijor perle a peece & a smale
Diamond in the midest, & the other viijt peeces sett with two half pearle
a pece and one smale rubye in the mydest all the peeces garnished with
sparkes of rubyes
Delivered to the said Mrs Ratcliff

03.112   By Ladye Knyvett one Chaire of wood painted the seate backe & elbowes
of Clothe of silver embrodered with flowers of silke needleworke
Delivered to the said Thomas Knevett

03.113   By Ladye Kateryne Peter one Jewell of gold being a Pendante, conteyning
twoe peeces one above an other, thone haveing a litle white rubye with
in a garland thother a hard Topas bothe with oute foyle and three Pearle
Pendante
Delivered to the said Mrs Ratcliff

03.114   By Lady Hatton Cooke one Dublett of white silver Chamlett raised vpon
with white satten like Flyes and leaves with Silver and silke of divers Cullors

03.115   By the Ladye Elizabeth Gorges, two paire of perfumed gloves with foure
buttons of golde in either glove sett with one smale pearle a peece
Delivered to the said Mrs Hyde

03.116   By the Lady Longe one smocke of Fyne Holland wrought with blacke
silke Drawne worke
Delivered to the said Lady Scudamore

Knightes

03.117   By Sir William Knowles Threasurer of her Majesties houshold One
            Pettycote of Clay Collored Satten ymbrodered all over with Trees
            Piramides Pillers & feathers
                                         Delivered to the said wardrobe of Robes

03.118   By Sir Edward Wotton Comptroller of her Majesties houshold One Jewell
            of gold like a feather garnished with Dyamondes Rubyes & pendantes of
            Rubyes and a rocke rubye cutt in the middest Fawcettwise
                                         Delivered to the said Mrs Ratcliff

03.119   By Sir Roberte Cicill Principalle Secretary one Jewell of gold like Mercury
            his staff garnished with Sparkes of Rubyes & Dyamondes two pendantes
            with Dyamondes without Foyle & two smale rubyes, two pearles
            pendante a peece, more two pendantes with one Table Rubye & one
            pearle pendant in a peece / One rocke Ballace withoute Foyle & a pearle
            in the topp thereof
                                         Delivered to the said Mrs Ratcliff

03.120   By Sir John Fortescue Chauncellor of the Exchequere in gold . . . . x li
03.121   By Sir John Popham Lord Cheef Justice of England in golde. . . . . x li
03.122   By Sir Henry Cromwell in golde . . . . x li
                                         Delivered to the said Henry Sackford

03.123   By Sir John Stanhop Vicechamberlen one kertle of Clothe of Silver Cullor
            de Roye with a border downe before ymbrodered like Lyllyes
                                         Delivered into the said wardrobe of Robes

03.124   By Sir Thomas Leighton, one paire of bracelettes of gold conteyning xiiij
            peces garnished with smale Dyamondes rubyes & pearle
                                         Delivered to the said Mrs Ratcliff

03.125   By Sir John Scudamore parte of a loose gowne of white Silver Tabyne
            lyned with Orange cullored sarcenett & faced with Orange Cullor
            Sattenn

03.126   By Sir Edward Dyer one Pettycote of Carnaconn taffata sarcenett
            ymbrodered all over with Venice golde & some silver in the Border,
            & workes about the border like peramides
                                         Delivered to the said wardrobe of Robes

03.127   By Sir Edward Stafford, xviijen sprigges of golde garnished with smale
            Rubyes & Pearle & one bigger sprigge garnished with diamondes rubyes
            & pearle & a Cinque of small dyamondes in the middest
                                         Delivered to the said Mrs Ratcliffe

03.128   By Sir Henry Gilford one mantle or lose gowne of silver Tiffeny sett vpon
            with floures of Silke womans worke

03.129   By Sir Thomas Jarrat, one Lapp mantell of silver Tabyne lyned with white
            Plush

03.130   By Sir Edwarde Hobbye parte of a rounde kertle of white golde Chamlett
            with a border downe before of Owes vpon white taffata parte like
            Piramides
                                         Delivered to the said wardrobe of Robes

03.131   By Sir Edward Cleare in golde . . . . x li
Delivered to the said Henry Sackford

03.132   By Sir Thomas Walsingham parte of a loose gowne of Claye Cullored
Sattenn rased & Pincked with buttons and Loopes of Vennice Silver
Delivered into the said wardrobe of Robes

03.133   By Sir William Cornwallys fyve long peeces of golde like beames, whereof
foure of them are sett with two garnettes a peece the fifte with three
garnettes all enamelled greene and garnished with smale pearle & pearle
pendant
Delivered to the said wardrobe of Robes

03.134   By Sir Henry Bronker one kertle of Russett silver Tabyne with a brode
border ymbrodered like Leaves vpon Lawne with silver Owes
Delivered to the said wardrobe of Robes

03.135   By Sir Edward Radcliffe one Jewell of golde Piramides fashon being a
pendant garnished with two Diamondes two Rubies & one Pearle
Pendant

03.136   By Sir Walter Rawley one Jewell of golde like a Spade garnished with
Sparkes of Diamondes & Rubyes, and a Snake wyndeing rounde
aboute it with one Dyamonde in the head & a Rubye pendante
withoute foyle
Delivered to the said Mrs Ratcliff

Gentlewomen

03.137   By Mistres Mary Ratcliffe one kertle of white Tiffeney striped with silver

03.138   By Mrs Elizabeth Bridges one mantell of blacke Tiffeney striped with silver
Delivered into the said wardrobe of Robes

03.139   By Mrs Carre one Fanne of India horne & three litle botelles of blew
glasse with sweet powder
Delivered to the said Mrs Hide

03.140   By Mrs Lucye Hyde One Capp of pincked Collor Taffata embroidered all
over with venis gold silver & Silke
Delivered to the said wardrobe of Robes

03.141   By Mrs Anne Vavasor one Nightraile of Cambrick wrought with black
silk drawn worke
Delivered to the said Lady Scudamore

03.142   By Mrs Sackford one Snoskyn of purple veluet embroidered all over with
Leaues and Flowers sett with Seed Pearle
Delivered to the said Mrs Hide

03.143   By Mrs Griffyn of Dingley one Dublet of knitworke florished with silver
& byrdes of silke of sondry Cullors with two paire of Aglettes of Seed
pearle on the Sleeves

03.144   By Mrs Coppyn one Mantell of white nett striped with silver
Delivered into the said wardrobe of Robes

03.145   By Mrs Raynsford one Snoskyn of lawne ymbrodered with owes & lyned
with Carnaconn plush
Delivered to the said Mrs Hide

03.146   By Mrs Burtonn one Nightraile of Cambricke wrought with black silk
      Drawn work

03.147   By Mrs Alley Blunt four forhead Clothes whereof ij are Cambrick wrought
      with black silke Drawn work & thother two of Lawne pufte vp with
      silver & Spangles

03.148   By Mrs Twiste one sute of ruffes of lawn Cutworke & one handkercher of
      Camricke wroughte with black silke Drawne worke

03.149   By Mrs Huggyns widdowe, one large sweet bagg of white satten
      ymbrodered with Venice golde Silver & Silk

03.150   By Mrs Huggyns Williams wief, one sute of Ruffes of Lawn Cutwork

03.151   By Mrs Barley six handkerchers of Cambrick edged aboute with Venice
      gold & silver

03.152   By Mrs Bone als Gilham, One ruff of Lawne Cutworke

03.153   By Mrs Frances Kerkham one sute of ruffes of Lawn Cutworke vnmade

03.154   By Mrs Thomasine one paire of white silke hose embrodered in the
      Clockes

                                Delivered to the said Lady Scudamore

03.155   By Mrs Elizabeth Wake one square quosion of Silke Nedleworke
      Chevernwise, frynged buttoned & tasselled with Venice golde & silke,
      backed with crymsonn Satten

                                Delivered to the said Sir Thomas Knevett

03.156   By Mrs Dorothie Speckard one Lardge handkercher of Cambrick with a
      brode work of Cutworke

                                Delivered to the said Lady Scudamore

03.157   By Mrs Anne Leighton one Fanne of white bone India worke with a
      floure at the end & a Smale Jewell

                                Delivered to the said Mrs Hide

03.158   By Mrs Strangwaies one Jewell of gold being a knott haveing three
      pendantes being Amatistes without Foile

                                Delivered to the said Mrs Ratcliff

03.159   By Mrs Frances Huggyns six Handkerchers of Cambrick wrought with
      black silke Drawn worke

                                Delivered to the said Lady Scudamore

Gentlemen

03.160   By Mr Foulke Grevile one white Satten Dublett rased and Cutt in snippes
      embrodered with gold Twiste and Owes

                                Delivered to the said wardrobe of Robes

03.161   By Mr Carre three bodkyns of gold with three pendantes garnished with
      smale Diamondes rubies & three smale Pearles Pendant

                                Delivered to the said Mrs Ratcliffe

03.162   By Mr Carmardenn one Mantle of Beser Cullor knytworke florished with
      silver like Copwebbs & Flyes

03.163   By Mr Frances Baconn, One Dublett of white satten rased & pufte vpp
      billett wise

                                Delivered to the said wardrobe of Robes

03.164   By Mr Garter king at Armes One booke Couered with Purple vellett, of the
         knightes of the garter this present yere
                                Delivered to the said Mrs Ratcliff

03.165   By Mr Francis Wolley One Cloke of Spanish Taffata Florished all over
         with Venice golde and Silver like Piramides and Panses of Cullored silke
                                Delivered to the said wardrobe of robes

03.166   By Mr Mountague one smocke of Cambrick wrought with black silke
         Drawn worke
                                Delivered to the said Lady Scudamore

03.167   By Mr Thomas Midletonn one bolte of Cambricke & half a peece of
         Lawne

03.168   By Mr Frances Cherrye One Tippett of Sables lyned with purple vellett
         ymbrodered with Arches and Piramides of Pearle of sondry sizes
                                Delivered to the said Mrs Ratcliffe

03.169   By Mr John Spilman one Pendant of Foure peeces one being an
         Aquamarina, and another Amatiste and Two Topasses withoute Foyle
         sleightly sett in golde & Fyve pearle pendant
                                Delivered to the said Mrs Ratcliff

03.170   By Mr Doctor Browne one Pott of greene ginger and a Pott of Orange
         Floures

03.171   By Mr Doctor Gilberte one Pott of Orange Floures & an other of greene
         ginger

03.172   By Mr Doctor Marbecke one Pott of green ginger and an other of Orange
         Floures
                                Delivered to the said Lady Scudamore

03.173   By Mr Doctor Padye one Fanne of white Feathers the handle Christall
         garnished with gold like a Crowne
                                Delivered into the said wardrobe of Robes

03.174   By Mr Morgan Apothecary one Pott of greene ginger and an other of
         Orange Floures

03.175   By Mr Weston Apothecary three boxes of Peaches of Janna & suche Like
         Confeccons

03.176   By Mr Hemyngway Apothecary one boxe of Manus Christi & a pott of
         preserved Peares
                                Delivered to the said Lady Scudamore

03.177   By Mr Barker her Majesties Prynter one bible of a large volume faier
         bounde
                                Delivered into the Privie Chamber

03.178   By Mr William Goodroes Sergeante Surgeon one glasse of precious
         Water

03.179   By Mr George Baker one other Surgeon one glasse of precious Water
                                Delivered to the said Mrs Hide

03.180   By Mr William Cordall Mr Cooke one Marchpane

03.181   By Mr Daniell Clarke Mr Cooke of the houshold one marchpane

03.182   By Mr Raphe Battye Sergeant of the Pastery one Pye of Orangado

03.183 By Mr Thomas Frenche an other Sergeante of the Pastery one pie of
Orangeado

[blank]

03.184 By Mr William Huggins three pair of perfumed gloves the one pair the
Cuffes lyned with Orange Cullor Vellett & Layed with three bone
Laces of Venice silver

Delivered to the said Mrs Hide

03.185 By Mr Thomas Ducke Sergeaunte of the Celler Two bottelles of Ippocrase
thone white thother red

[blank]

03.186 By Mr Peter Lupo sixe Bottelles of Rose Water
03.187 By Mr Thomas Lupo his sonne one paire of perfumed gloves
03.188 By Mr Joseph Lupo one paire of perfumed gloves
03.189 By Mr Thomas Lupo his sonne one paire of perfumed gloves
03.190 By Mr Walter Pearce one paire of perfumed gloves
03.191 By Mr Jerolimo Bassano one paire of perfumed gloves
03.192 By Mr Arthur Bassano one pair of perfumed gloves
03.193 By Mr Edward Bassano one paire of perfumed gloves
03.194 By Mr Andrew Bassano one paire of perfumed gloves
03.195 By Mr Roberte Hales one pair of perfumed gloves
03.196 By Mr Cesar Galliardo one paire of perfumed gloves
03.197 By Mr John Lanere one paire of perfumed gloves
03.198 By Mr Innocent Comye one paire of perfumed gloves
03.199 By Mr William Warrenn one paire of perfumed gloves
03.200 By Mr Henry Trochius one paire of perfumed gloves
03.201 By Mr Peter Edneye one paire of perfumed gloves
03.202 By Mr Robert Baker one pair of perfumed gloves
03.203 By Mr Samuell Gashe one paire of perfumed gloves
03.204 By Mr Peter Guye one paire of perfumed gloves
03.205 By Mr James Harden one paire of perfumed gloves
03.206 By Mr Guilliam Burshewe one paire of perfumed gloves

Delivered to the said Mrs Hide

03.207 By Mr More Aldermann foure paire of plaine spanishe gloves & one
Jewell of golde like a peramides garnished with Diamondes & three
Pearle

The Jewell delivered to Mrs Ratcliff the gloves to Mrs Hide

03.208 By Mr John Baker Vpholster one paire of fustian blankettes brode ij
yerdes di & in length three yardes

Delivered to the Removing wardrobe

03.209 By Mr Ferrys Lynnon Draper half a peece of Lawne

Delivered to the said Mrs Ratcliffe

03.210 By Mr Saltonstall two half peeces of Lawne & one Bolte of Cambricke

Delivered to the said Mrs Ratcliffe

03.211 By Mr Richard Frenche one Dublett of Black Tiffeney striped with silver
pufte vp

Delivered into the said wardrobe of Robes

03.212   By Mr Thomas Woodhouse two pair of Silke hose thone a Carnaconn
         thother Ashcoller, the Clockes of bothe imbrodered with Venice golde
         & Owes

                                        Delivered to the said Lady Scudamore

03.213   By Mr Sharpe imbroderer one girdle of Scumm Scipres imbrodered at
         both endes with Paunsies Peramides & sonne beames of golde silver
         & Silke

                                        Delivered to the said Mrs Hide

Summa totalis of all the money
geuen to her highnes this yeare . . . . vij^C lix li vj s. viij d.

                                                        Edwa: Carye
                                                        Ex[aminatio] per
                                                            Bristowe
                                                            N Pigeon
                                                        Robert Cranmer

                        Anno regni Regine Elizabethe
                        Quadragesimo Quinto Annoque
                               Domini, 1602

                        Newyeres guiftes giuen to the
                        Queenes Majestie at her highnes Pallace
                        at Westmr by these persones whose names
                        hereafter ensue, the firste daye of January
                               in the yere abovesaide viz

03.214   To Sir Thomas Egerton Knight Lorde Keeper of the great Seale of
         England in guilt Plate K . . . . xxxvj oz
03.215   To the Lorde Buckhurste Lorde High Thresuror of England in guilte
         Plate K . . . . xxiiij oz quarter
03.216   To the Lorde Marquesse of Wynchester in guilte Plate . . . . nihil

Earles

03.217   To the Earle of Nottingham Lorde highe Admirall of England in guilt
         Plate K & W. . . . . Cvij oz qrter di
03.218   To the Earle of Worcester in guilte Plate K . . . . xxxj oz iij qrter
03.219   To the Earle of Shrewsbury in guilt Plate K . . . . xxx oz iij qrter
03.220   To the Earle of Darbye in guilt Plate W . . . . xx oz qrter
03.221   To the Earle of Huntingdonn in guilte Plate W . . . . xx oz iij qrter di

03.222	To the Earle of Sussex in guilte Plate K	xx oz qrter
03.223	To the Earle of Bathe in guilt Plate K	xx oz di
03.224	To the Earle of Cumberlande in guilt Plate K	xxiij oz di qrter
03.225	To the Earle of Northumberlande in guilt Plate W	xxx oz
03.226	To the Earle of Hertforde in guilte Plate K	xxij oz
03.227	To the Earle of Pembrooke in guilte Plate K	xxx oz qrter
03.228	To the Earle of Bedforde in guilte Plate K	xxx oz di qrter
03.229	To the Earle of Rutlande in guilte Plate K	xx oz di qrter
03.330	To the Earle of Klenrickett in guilte Plate W	xxx oz iij qrter di
03.331	To the Vycount Byndon in guilte Plate W	xxj oz di di qrter

Marquises & Countesses

03.232	To the Marquesse of Northampton in guilte Plate K & W	xliiij oz qrter di
03.233	To the Countesse of Kente in guilte Plate K	xxij oz
03.234	To the Countis of Oxforde in guilte Plate K	xxxiiij oz
03.235	To the Countis of Shrewsbury widowe in guilte Plate W	xlj oz di di qrter
03.236	To the Counteis of Shrewsbury Junior in guilte Plate K	xx oz iij qrter
03.237	To the Counteis of Sussex in guilt Plate K	xx oz di qrter
03.238	To the Counteis of Bedforde in guilte Plate W	xix oz iij qrter di
03.239	To the Counteis of Huntingdon widow in guilte Plate K	xxx oz
03.240	To the Counteis of Huntingdon junior in guilte Plate K	xx oz iij qrter di
03.241	To the Counteis of Pembroke widow in guilte Plate K	xix oz iij qrter di
03.242	To the Counteis of Hartford in guilte Plate K	Liiij oz di di qrter
03.243	To the Counteis of Bathe in guilte Plate K	xxiij oz
03.244	To the Counteis of Warwick in guilte Plate K & W	liij oz di di qrter
03.245	To the Counties of Darbye Egerton in guilt Plate K	xxiij oz
03.246	To the Counteis of Darbye Junior in guilte Plate K	xxvj oz iij qrter di
03.247	To the Counteis of Rutland in guilte Plate K	xix oz di di qrter
03.248	To the Counteis of Comberlande in guilte Plate W	xxj oz
03.249	To the Counteis of Northumberland in guilt Plate K and W	xxiij oz di
03.250	To the Counteis of Southamptonn senior in guilt Plate K	xx oz iij qrter
03.251	To the Counteis of Nottingham in guilte Plate K	xxj oz qrter di
03.252	To the Counteis of Kildare in guilte Plate W	xxv oz iij qrter
03.253	To the Counteis of Worcester in guilte Plate K	xx oz iij qrter
03.254	To the Counteis of Essex in guilte Plate K	xxxj oz qrter
03.255	To the Vicounteis Mountagew in guilte Plate W	xx oz

Bishops

03.256	To the Arch Bishoppe of Canterbury in guilt Plate K	xlv oz
03.257	To the Arch Bishoppe of Yorke in guilte Plate K	xxxviij oz di
03.258	To the Bishopp of Durham in guilte Plate K	xxxviij oz qrter
03.259	To the Bishopp of Eley in guilte Plate W	xxxiiij oz di di qrter
03.260	To the Bishoppe of Wynchester in guilte Plate K	xxxviij oz

03.261	To the Bishoppe of London in guilte Plate W	xxxj oz
03.262	To the Bishoppe of Salisburye in guilte Plate K	xxxj oz di qrtr
03.263	To the Bishopp of Lyncolne in guilte Plate K	xxxj oz di qrter
03.264	To the Bishopp of Bathe and Welles in guilte Plate W	xxxj oz
03.265	To the Bishopp of Worcester in guilte Plate K	xxxj oz
03.266	To the Bishopp of Litchfield and Coventrey in guilte Plate K	xix oz qrter di
03.267	To the Bishopp of Rochester in guilte Plate W	xvj oz qrter
03.268	To the Bishoppe of Chichester in guilte Plate K	xviij oz qrter
03.269	To the Bishoppe of Chester in guilt Plate K	xiiij oz iij qrter di
03.270	To the Bishoppe of Gloster in guilt Plate W	xv oz di di qrter
03.271	To the Bishoppe of Exeter in guilte Plate K	xv oz di di qrter
03.272	To the Bishoppe of Peterborrough in guilt Plate K	xvj oz iij qrters di
03.273	To the Bishoppe of Carlile in guilte Plate K	xvj oz iij qrters di
03.274	To the Bishoppe of St Davyes in guilte Plate K	xv oz di qrter

Lordes

03.275	To the Lorde Hunsdon Lorde Chamberleyn in guilt Plate K	xxxij oz
03.276	To the Lorde Cobham in guilte Plate K	xxix oz di
03.277	To the Lorde Lomley in guilte Plate K	xx oz qrter di
03.278	To the Lorde Norryes in guilte Plate W	xix oz di
03.279	To the Lorde Wharton in guilte Plate W	xx oz qrter di
03.280	To the Lorde Riche in guilte Plate K	xix oz di qrter
03.281	To the Lorde Comptonn in guilte Plate K	xxj oz
03.282	To the Lorde Darcye of Chichley in guilt Plate K	xx oz di qrter
03.283	To the Lorde Mountjoye in guilte Plate K	xxvij oz
03.284	To the Lorde Thomas Howard in guilt Plate W	xxij oz iij qrter
03.285	To the Lorde Burghley in guilte Plate K	xxx oz qrter di
03.286	To the Lorde Barkley in guilte Plate W	xx oz
03.287	To the Lorde Henry Howarde in guilte Plate W	xxv oz qrter di
03.288	To the Lorde Stafforde in guilte Plate W	xx oz di

Baronesses

03.289	To the Barrones Hunsdonn Junior in guilte Plate W	xxxj oz di
03.290	To the Barrones Hunsdon senior in guilte Plate K	xxxij oz qrter
03.291	To the Baronnes Pagett Carey in guilte Plate K	xxxvj oz
03.292	To the Barronnes Chandos Knowles in guilte Plate K	xxj oz qrter
03.293	To the Baronnes Chandos widowe in guilte Plate K	xx oz iij qrter
03.294	To the Baronnes Lomley in guilte Plate K	xx oz qrter
03.295	To the Baronnes Scroope in guilte Plate K	xx oz qrter di
03.296	To the Baronnes Buckhurste in guilte Plate K	xx oz di
03.297	To the Baronnes Sheffield Stafforde in guilte Plate W	xxj oz di qrter
03.298	To the Baronnes Howard lord Thomas his wief in guilte Plate W & K	xxj oz qrter

03.299	To the Baronnes Arbella in guilte Plate K	xx oz di
03.300	To the Baronnes De La Ware in guilte Plate K	xx oz
03.301	To the Baronnes Barkley in guilte Plate K	xx oz qrter
03.302	To the Baronnes St John of Bletsoe in guilte Plate W	xx oz di
03.303	To the Baronnes Borough in guilte Plate W	xxiiij oz di
03.304	To the Baronnes Katherin Cornwallys in guilte Plate K	xxij oz
03.305	To the Baronnes Bridgett Manners Tirwitt in guilte Plate K	xx oz qrter
03.306	To the Baronnes Elizabeth Graye in guilte Plate W	xvij oz iij qrter
03.307	To the Barronnes Anne Harbert in guilte Plate W	xviij oz di

Ladies

03.308	To Ladye Mary Seymer Rogers in guilt Plate W	xj oz qrter
03.309	To Ladye Gilforde in guilte Plate K	xix oz di qrt
03.310	To Ladye Southwell in guilt Plate W	xviij oz di
03.311	To Ladye Stafforde in guilt Plate W	xxx oz qrt
03.312	To Ladye Cheek in guilt Plate W	xxx oz iij qrt di
03.313	To Ladye Suzan Vere in guilte Plate K	xvij oz iij qrter
03.314	To Ladye Leighton in guilt Plate K	xvij oz iij qrter
03.315	To Ladye Scudamore in guilte Plate K	xvij oz iij qrter
03.316	To Ladye Katherine Peter in guilt Plate W	xvij oz di
03.317	To Ladye Elizabeth Gorges in guilt Plate K	xviij oz di di qrter
03.318	To Ladye Digby in guilte Plate W	xvij oz qrter
03.319	To Ladye Walsingham in guilt Plate W	xvij oz iij qrters
03.320	To Ladye Jarratt in guilt Plate K	xx oz iij qrter
03.321	To Ladye Puckering in guilte Plate W	xx oz di qrter
03.322	To Ladye Edmondes in guilte Plate W	xvij oz iij qrters
03.323	To Ladye Hawkins in guilte Plate W	xviij oz qrter di
03.324	To Ladye Hobbye in guilte Plate W	xix oz di
03.325	To Ladye Harrington in guilte Plate W	xix oz iij qrters di
03.326	To Ladye Hattonn in guilte Plate K	xxv oz iij qrters
03.327	To Ladye Longe in guilte Plate W	xx oz di qrter
03.328	To Ladye Knevytt in guilte Plate K	xxx oz iij qrters
03.329	To Ladye Newtonn in guilte Plate K	xviij oz

Knightes

03.330	To Sir William Knowles Thresurer of her majesties Houshold in guilt Plate W	xxvj oz iij qrters
03.331	To Sir Edward Wottonn Comptroller of her majesties Houshold in guilt Plate K	xxxj oz di qrt
03.332	To Sir Robert Cecyll Principall Secretary in guilt Plate K	xxj oz qrt
03.333	To Sir John Stanhopp Vicechamberlenn in guilt Plate W	xxxj oz iij qrts
03.334	To Sir John Fortescue Chaunncellor of thexchetquer in guilt Plate K	xxiiij oz qrt

03.335   To Sir John Popham Lord Cheefe Justice of England in guilte Plate K
.... xxiij oz qrt
03.336   To Sir Thomas Leightonn in guilt Plate K ....xxxiiij oz qrt
03.337   To Sir John Scudamore x x x x [sic] in guilt Plate...................xx oz qrt
03.338   To Sir Edward Dyer in guilte Plate K .... xxij oz
03.339   To Sir Edward Stafforde in guilte Plate W .... xx oz di di qrt
03.340   To Sir Henry Gilforde in guilte Plate W ....xx oz iij qrt
03.341   To Sir Henry Cromwell in guilte Plate K ....xx oz iij qrts
03.342   To Sir Edward Hobby in guilte Plate K .... xix oz qrt
03.343   To Sir Edward Cleere in guilt Plate W ....xx oz iij qrts
03.344   To Sir Thomas Jarratt in guilte Plate K ....xxiij oz
03.345   To Sir Thomas Walsinghamm in guilte Plate K ....xx oz qrt
03.346   To Sir William Cornwallys in Guilt Plate K .... xix oz iij qrts
03.347   To Sir Henry Bronker in guilte Plate K........................ xxiij oz iij qrt
03.348   To Sir Walter Rawley in guilt Plate K .... xxiij oz iij qrts
03.349   To Sir Edward Ratcliffe in guilt Plate K ....xxj oz

Gentlewomen

03.350   To Mrs Mary Ratcliffe in guilte Plate W..................xviij oz iij qrters di
03.351   To Mrs Elizabeth Bridges in guilt Plate K .... xvij oz qrter
03.352   To Mrs Carr in guilte Plate K .... xvij oz qrter di
03.353   To Mrs Lucye Hide in guilte Plate K .... xvij oz qrter
03.354   To Mrs Sackforde in guilte Plate W .... xx oz
03.355   To Mrs Griffyn of Dingley in guilte Plate W ....xxj oz iij qrters
03.356   To Mrs Ann Vavasor in guilte Plate K .... xvij oz qrter
03.357   To Mrs Raynsforde in guilt Plate K .... vij oz iij qrters
03.358   To Mrs Coppyn in guilte Plate W ....xvij oz di qrter
03.359   To Mrs Alley Blunte in guilte Plate W ....vj oz iij qrters
03.360   To Mrs Twiste in guilte Plate W ....vj oz iij qrters
03.361   To Mrs Burtonn in guilte Plate W............................ xvij oz qrter
03.362   To Mrs Huggyns Widowe in guilte Plate W .... xvij oz iij qrter
03.363   To Mrs Huggins William His Wief in guilte Plate K .... xvij oz di
03.364   To Mrs Frauncis Huggins in guilte Plate W .... xvj oz
03.365   To Mrs Barley in guilte Plate W .... xij oz
03.366   To Mrs Bone Alias Gilham in guilte Plate K .... vij oz di di qrter
03.367   To Mrs Frances Kerkham in guilte Plate W .... xviij oz qrter
03.368   To Mrs Thomasine in guilte Plate K............................v oz di qrter
03.369   To Mrs Elizabeth Wake in guilte Plate W .... xvij oz iij qrters
03.370   To Mrs Anne Leightonn in guilte Plate W ....xj oz di
03.371   To Mrs Dorothie Speckarde in guilte Plate K .... ix oz qrter
03.372   To Mrs Strangwayes in guilte Plate K.......................xiiij oz di di qrter

Maids of Honor

03.373	To Lady Dorothie Hastings in guilte Plate K	x oz di di qrter
03.374	To Mrs Mary Wharton in guilte Plate K	x oz
03.375	To Mrs Cordall Anslowe in guilte Plate K	x oz
03.376	To Mrs Elizabeth Southwell in guilte Plate K.	x oz di
03.377	To Mrs Mary Nevell in guilte Plate K.	x oz di
03.378	To Mrs Gresham Thynne in guilt Plate K.	x oz qrter
03.379	To Mrs Bridges Mother of the Maydes in guilt Plate K.	xiij oz

Gentlemen

03.380	To Mr Fulke Grevile in guilte Plate K	xxv oz iij qrters
03.381	To Mr Carre in guilt Plate W & K	xx oz di di qrter
03.382	To Mr Carmarden in guilte Plate W	xiiij oz iij qrters
03.383	To Mr Frances Baconn in guilte Plate K	xxxij oz
03.384	To Mr Moore Aldermann in guilte Plate W	xv oz iij qrters
03.385	To Mr Garter king at armes in guilte Plate K.	viij oz qrter
03.386	To Mr Mountagew in guilt Plate K.	xiiij oz qrter
03.387	To Mr Fraunces Wolley in guilt Plate W.	xvij oz iij qrters
03.388	To Mr Thomas Midleton in guilt Plate K.	xiij oz di qrter
03.389	To Mr Fraunces Cherrey in guilt Plate K	xl oz di
03.390	To Mr Johnn Spilmann in guilt Plate K	xix oz iij qrters di
03.391	To Mr Doctor Browne in guilt Plate K.	xiiij oz iij qrters
03.392	To Mr Doctor Gilberte in guilt Plate W	xiiij oz iij qrters
03.393	To Mr Doctor Marbecke in guilt Plate W	xv oz di di qrter
03.394	To Mr Doctor Paddye in guilt Plate K	xv oz iij qrters
03.395	To Mr Morgann Appothecary in guilt Plate K.	vij oz di
03.396	To Mr Hemingwaye Appothecary in guilt Plate W	viij oz qrter di
03.397	To Mr Weston Appothecary in guilt Plate W	x oz iij qrters di
03.398	To Mr Barker her majesties Prynter in guilte Plate K	xviij oz di
03.399	To Mr William Goodroes the Sergeant Surgeonn in guilt plate K.	xv oz
03.400	To Mr George Baker in guilt Plate K	xiiij oz qrter di
03.401	To Mr Willam Cordall Mr Cooke for the Queene in guilt Plate K	viij oz
03.402	To Mr Daniell Clarke Mr Cooke of the Houshold in guilte Plate K.	viij oz qrter di
03.403	To Mr Raphe Battye Sergeant of the Pastery in guilt Plate	viij oz
03.404	To Mr Thomas Frenche one other sergeant of the Pastery in guilt Plate W.	viij oz di
03.405	To Mr Richard Frenche in guilt Plate W	xiiij oz di qrter
03.406	To Mr William Huggyns in guilte Plate K	xvij oz di
03.407	To Mr Thomas Duck Sergeant of the Celler in guilt Plate K	viij oz di qrter
03.408	To Mr Peter Lupo in guilt Plate	v oz
03.409	To Mr Thomas Lupo his sonne in guilte Plate K	v oz
03.410	To Mr Joseph Lupo in guilt Plate K	v oz

03.411	To Mr Thomas Lupo his sonne in guilt Plate K	v oz
03.412	To Mr Walter Pearce in guilte Plate W	v oz
03.413	To Mr William Warren in guilte Plate	v oz
03.414	To Mr Peter Guye in guilt Plate W	v oz
03.415	To Mr Jerolimo Bassano in guilte Plate W	v oz
03.416	To Mr Samuell Saltonstall in guilte Plate W	xvj oz iij qrters
03.417	To Mr Arthur Bassano in guilte Plate W	v oz
03.418	To Mr Andrew Bassano in guilte Plate W	v oz
03.419	To Mr Edward Bassano in guilte Plate W	v oz
03.420	To Mr Robert Hales in guilte Plate K	v oz di qrter
03.421	To Mr John Lanere in guilt Plate W	v oz
03.422	To Mr Cesar Galliardo in guilt Plate	v oz
03.423	To Mr Innocent Comye in guilt Plate W	v oz
03.424	To Mr Samuell Garshe in guilt Plate W	v oz
03.425	To Mr Henry Trochius in guilte Plate K	v oz
03.426	To Mr Robert Baker in guilt Plate W	v oz
03.427	To Mr Peter Edney in guilte Plate W	v oz
03.428	To Mr James Hardenn in guilte Plate W	v oz
03.429	To Mr Thomas Woodhouse in guilt Plate K	xxiiij oz iij qrters
03.430	To Mr Guilliam Burshe in guilt Plate K	iij oz iij qrters
03.431	To Mr John Baker Vpholster in guilt Plate K	vj oz iij qrters di
03.432	To Mr Shawe ymbroderer in guilt Plate W	vij oz di di qrter

Free Gifts

03.433	To Sir Edwarde Cary Knight Mr & Thresurer of her Majesties Jewelles & Plate in guilt Plate K	xx oz
03.434	To Sir Thomas Gorges in guilt Plate K	x oz
03.435	To Sir Thomas Knevett in guilte Plate K	x oz
03.436	To Mr Henry Sackford in guilte Plate W	x oz
03.437	To Mr Edward Darcye in guilte Plate W	x oz qrter
03.438	To Mr William Killygrewe in guilte Plate K	x oz
03.349	To Mr Michaell Stanhopp in guilte Plate W	x oz
03.440	To Mr [sic] Edward Cary one other grome of her Majesties Privie Chamber in guilt plate w	x oz di
03.441	To Mr Ferdinando Richardsonn in guilt Plate W	x oz
03.442	To Mr Robert Pamphalynn yeoman of the Robes in guilt Plate W	xiij oz qrter
03.443	To Mr Nicholas Bristowe Clerk of her Majesties Jewelles & plate, in guilt plate	xij oz
03.444	To Mr Nicholas Pigeon yeomann in guilt Plate	xij oz
03.445	To Mr Robert Cranmer one other yeomann in guilte Plate	xij oz
03.446	To Mr Nicholas Hottofte grome in guilte Plate K	xij oz

Edwa: Carye]
 Ex[aminatio] per

Bristowe
N Pigeon
Robert Cranmer
Nicholas Hottofte

Summa of all the plate geuen / in manner and forme abovesaide
. . . . iiij^m li iiij^C Lxxvij oz di

Guiftes geuen by her said Majestie to sondry persons and
deliuered at sondrie tymes as followeth

03.447 Earle of Northummberland
 Fyrste geven by her saide Majestie & delivered the xiiijth of October
  Anno xliiijo regni Regine Elizabethe etc. To the Christening of the
  Earle of Northumberland his sonne One Bowle with a Cover of silver
  guilte poz lxxxix oz of the Charge of Sir Edward Carye Knight Mr &
  Thresurer of her Majesties Jewelles & plate / More one Bason & a
  layer of Silver guilte poiz lxij oz iij qrters / And one paire of guilte
  Pottes poiz lxxxxviij oz bought of Hugh Kayle goldsmith in toto
  . . . . CCxlix oz iij qrters
03.448 Anne Bennet
 Item geven by her said Majestie & delivered the xiiijth of October
  Anno Predicto, To Anne Bennet wief to Anthony Bennett one of
  her Majesties Footmenn one boule of Silver guilte bought of the
  said Hughe Kayle poz . . . . xix oz qrter
03.449 Counte de Beaumonte
 Item geven by her said Majestie & delivered the viijth of December
  Anno xlvo regni Regine Elizabethe etc. to the Christening of
  Mounseur La Counte de Beaumont leiger Ambassador out of France
  One fayre bason and a layer guilte poiz Cxxxij oz One paire of guilt
  Stopes poiz Cxxxv oz quarter / And One guilt Bowle with a Cover
  poz lxvij oz di boughte of the said Hugh Kayle in toto CCCxxxiiij oz qrter
03.450 Lo: Effingham
 Item geven by her said Majestie and deliuered the vijth of February
  Anno predicto At the Christening of the Lord Effingham his Childe
  One Basonn and a layer of silver guilte bought of John Williams
  Goldsmith poz . . . . lxxix oz di di qrter

James I
[sign manual]

Edwarde Carye
Nicholas Bristowe
Nicholas Pigeon
Robert Cranmer
Nicholas Hottofte

Bibliography

Adams, S., ed., *Household Accounts and Disbursement Books of Robert Dudley, Earl of Leicester, 1558–1561, 1584–1586*, Royal Historical Society Camden Fifth Series, vol. 6 (Cambridge, 1995).

Allgemeines Künstlerlexikon: Bio-Bibliographischer Index A-Z = The Artists of the World: Bio-Bibliographical Index A-Z ([67] vols, München, 1999-[2020]).

Alsop, J., 'Nicholas Brigham (d. 1558), Scholar, Antiquary, and Crown Servant', *Sixteenth Century Journal*, 12 (1981), pp. 49–67.

Ames-Lewis, F., ed., *Sir Thomas Gresham and Gresham College: Studies in the Intellectual History of London in the Sixteenth and Seventeenth Centuries* (Aldershot, Hampshire, 1999).

Andrews, K. R., *English Privateering Voyages to the West Indies,1588–1595* (Cambridge, 1959).

Anglo, S., *The Great Tournament Roll of Westminster: A Collotype Reproduction of the Manuscript* (Oxford, 1968).

——, *Spectacle, Pageantry, and Early Tudor Policy* (Oxford, 1969).

Archer, I., 'City and Court Connected: The Material Dimensions of Royal Ceremonial, ca. 1480–1625', *Huntington Library Quarterly*, 71 (2008), pp. 157–79.

Archer, J. E., E. Goldring, and S. Knight, ed., *The Progresses, Pageants, and Entertainments of Queen Elizabeth I* (Oxford, 2007).

Arkwright, G. E. P., 'Sebastian Westcote', *The Musical Antiquary*, 4 (1912–13), pp. 187–9.

Armitage, S., ed., *Sir Gawain and the Green Knight: A New Verse Translation* (New York, 2007).

Arnold, J., *A Handbook of Costume* (London, 1973).

——, 'Lost from Her Majesties Back', *Costume,* Extra Series 7 (1980), pp. 1–95.

——, *Queen Elizabeth's Wardrobe Unlock'd* (Leeds, 1988).

Ashbee, A, ed., *Records of English Church Music* (9 vols, Aldershot, 1987–96).

——, and D. Lasocki, ed., *A Biographical Dictionary of English Court Musicians, 1485–1714* (2 vols, Aldershot, 1998).

Ashelford, J., *A Visual History of Costume* (London, 1983).

——, *Dress in the Age of Elizabeth I* (London, 1988).

Auerbach, E., 'Portraits of Elizabeth I', *The Burlington Magazine*, 95 (1953), pp. 196–205.

——, *Tudor Artists; A Study of Painters in the Royal Service and of Portraiture on Illuminated Documents from the Accession of Henry VIII to the Death of Elizabeth I* (London, 1954).

Austen, G., *George Gascoigne* (Woodbridge, 2008).

Aylmer, G. E., *The King's Servants: the Civil Service of Charles I* (New York, 1961).

Backhouse, J., 'Sir Robert Cotton's Record of a Royal Bookshelf', *British Library Journal*, 18 (1992), pp. 44–51.

Baldwin, D., *The Chapel Royal, Ancient and Modern* (London, 1990).

Bayer, P., 'Lady Margaret Clifford's Alchemical Receipt Book and the John Dee Circle', *Ambix*, 52 (2005), pp. 271–84.

Beaven, A. W., *The Aldermen of the City of London, temp. Henry III - 1908* (2 vols, London, 1908–13).

Benham, W. G., 'New Year Presents in Queen Elizabeth's Court', *The Essex Review*, 44 (1935), p. 106.

Bergmans, S., 'The Miniatures of Levina Teerling', *The Burlington Magazine for Connoisseurs*, 64 (1934), pp. 232–3, 235–6.

Berlatsky, J., 'A Reformation Survivor: the Case of Archbishop Nicholas Heath, Lord Chancellor of England, and the Rule of Women', *The Historian*, 65 (2003), pp. 1147–64.

Berton, C., *Dictionnaire des Cardinaux* (Paris, 1857).

Biddle, M., 'Nicholas B. of Modena, An Italian artificer at the Courts of François I and Henry VIII', *Journal of the British Archaeological Association*, 29 (1966), pp. 106–21.

Bindoff, S. T., ed., *The House of Commons, 1509–1558* (3 vols, London, 1982).

Binns, J. W., *Intellectual Culture in Elizabethan and Jacobean England: The Latin Writings of the Age* (Leeds, 1990).

Birrell, T. A. C., *English Monarchs and Their Books: From Henry VII to Charles II* (London, 1987).

Black, J., 'Sir John Harrington and the Book as Gift', *The Library*, 3 (1987), pp. 424–5.

Blackmore, H. L., *A Dictionary of London Gunmakers 1350–1850* (Oxford, 1986).

Blair, C., ed., *The Crown Jewels: The History of the Coronation Regalia in the Jewel House of the Tower of London* (London, 1998).

Blake, W., *William Maitland of Lethington, 1528–1573: A Study of the Policy of Moderation in the Sixteenth-Century Scottish Reformation* (Lewiston, NY, 1990).

Blezzard, J., 'The Lumley Books', *The Musical Times*, 112 (1971), pp. 128–30.

Borman, T., *Elizabeth's Women: Friends, Rivals and Foes Who Shaped the Virgin Queen* (London, 2009).

Bourne, H. R. F., *English Merchants: Memoirs in Illustration of the Progress of British Commerce* (London, 1866).

Bowler, H., ed., *Recusant Roll No. 2 (1593–1594): An Abstract in English* (London, 1965).

Braddock, R. C., *The Royal Household, 1540–1560* (Chicago, 1971).

Bradford, C. A., *Blanche Parry: Queen Elizabeth's Gentlewoman* (London, 1934).

——, *Helena, Marchioness of Northampton* (London, 1936).

——, *Nicasius Yetsweirt, Secretary for the French Tongue* (London, 1934).

——, *Rowland Vaughan, an Unknown Elizabethan: also Elizabeth Voss, a Legend of Boverton Castle* (London, 1937).

Bricka, C. F., ed., *Dansk Biografisk Leksikon* (27 vols, København, 1933–44).

Briggs, A. and G. N. S. Clark, *A History of the Royal College of Physicians of London* (Oxford, 2005).

Briley, J. R., *A Biography of William Herbert Third Earl of Pembroke, 1580–1630* (Birmingham, 1961).

Brimacombe, P., *All the Queen's Men: The World of Elizabeth I* (New York, 2000).

Briscoe, A. D., *A Tudor Worthy: Thomas Seckford of Woodbridge* (Ipswich, 1979).

Britton, J. and E. W. Brayley, *Memoirs of the Tower of London* (London, 1830).

Brook, V. J. K., *Whitgift and the English Church* (London, 1957).

——, *A Life of Archbishop Parker* (Oxford, 1962).

Brooks, A. A., *The Woman Who Defied Kings: The Life and Times of Doña Gracia Nasi--A Jewish Leader During the Renaissance* (St Paul, MN, 2002).

Brooks, E. S. J., *Sir Christopher Hatton: Queen Elizabeth's Favourite* (London, 1947).

Buettner, B., 'Past Presents: New Year's Gifts at the Valois Courts, ca. 1400', *Art Bulletin*, 84 (2001), pp. 598–625.

Burke, A. M., ed., *Memorials of St. Margaret's Church, Westminster, Comprising the Parish Registers, 1539–1660, and Other Churchwardens' Accounts, 1460–1603* (London, 1914).

Burrow, J. A., ed., *Sir Gawain and the Green Knight* (Harmondsworth, 1972).

Byrne, M. S. C., *Elizabethan Life in Town and Country* (London, 1961).

——, ed., *The Lisle Letters* (6 vols, Chicago, 1981).

Calendar of Inquisitions Post Mortem and other Analogous Documents Preserved in the Public Record Office (26 vols, London, 1904–2004).

Calendar of the Patent Rolls Preserved in the Public Record Office: Elizabeth I, 1558–1582 (9 vols, London, 1939–1986).

Calendar of State Papers, Domestic, of the Reigns of Edward VI, Mary, Elizabeth, James I (12 vols, London, 1856–72).

Calendar of State Papers, Foreign Series, of the Reign of Elizabeth; Preserved in the State Paper Department of Her Majesty's Public Record Office (23 vols, London, 1863–1950).

Calendar of State Papers Relating to Ireland, of the Reigns of Henry VIII, Edward VI, Mary, and Elizabeth (11 vols, London, 1860–1912).

Calendar of the State Papers Relating to Scotland and Mary, Queen of Scots, 1547–1603: Preserved in the Public Record Office, the British Museum, and Elsewhere in England (13 vols, London, 1898–1969).

Calendar of Letters and State Papers Relating to English Affairs: Preserved Principally in the Archives of Simancas: Elizabeth, 1558–[1603] (4 vols, London, 1892–99).

Calendar of State Papers, Relating to English Affairs, Preserved Principally at Rome, in the Vatican Archives and Library (2 vols, London, 1916–26).

Campbell, J. C. and J. L. Cockcroft, *The Lives of the Chief Justices of England: From the Norman Conquest till the Death of Lord Tenterden* (5 vols, Northport, 1894–9).

Campling, A., *The History of the Family of Drury in the Counties of Suffolk and Norfolk: From the Conquest* (London, 1937).

Campos, E. V., 'Jews, Spaniards, and Portingales: Ambiguous Identities of Portuguese Marranos in Elizabethan England', *English Literary History*, 69 (2002), pp. 599–616.

Cappelli, A., *Lexicon Abbreviaturarum: Dizionario Di Abbreviature Latine Ed Italiane* (Milan, 1929, repr. 1990).

Carley, J. P., *The Books of King Henry VIII and his Wives* (London, 2004).

——, *The Libraries of King Henry VIII* (London, 2000).

—— and C. G. C. Tite, ed., *Books and Collectors, 1200–1700* (London, 1997).

Carmichael, W. L., ed., *Callaway Textile Dictionary* (LaGrange, GA, 1947).

Chalmers, P., *Historical and Statistical Account of Dunfermline* (Edinburgh & London, 1844).

Challis, C. E., *The Tudor Coinage* (Manchester, 1978).

Chambers, E. K., *The Elizabethan Stage* (4 vols, Oxford, 1923).

Chapman, C. R., *How Heavy, How Much, and How Long?: Weights, Money and Other Measures Used By Our Ancestors* (Dursley, 1995).

Clifford, H., *The Life of Jane Dormer, Duchess of Feria,* ed. E. E. Estcourt and J. Stevenson (London, 1887).

Cocke, Z., 'A Queen's Christmas Gifts', *St Nicholas*, 30 (1902–3), pp. 236–7.

Coignet, C., *A Gentleman of the Olden Time: François de Scepeaux, Sire de Vielleville 1509–1571* (London, 1887).

Cokayne, G. E., *Complete Peerage of England, Scotland, Ireland, Great Britain and the United Kingdom* (13 vols in 6, Stroud, Gloucestershire, first published 1910–40, repr. 1982, 2000).

Collins, A., *Collins' Peerage of England; Genealogical, Biographical, and Historical* (9 vols, London, 1812).

Collins, A. J., *Jewels and Plate of Queen Elizabeth I: The Inventory of 1574* (London, 1955).

Collinson, P., *Archbishop Grindal 1519–1583: The Struggle for a Reformed Church* (London, 1979).

Crum, M., *English and American Autographs in the Bodmeriana* (Cologny-Geneve, 1977).

Davies, J., *The Poems of Sir John Davies,* ed. R. Krueger (Oxford, 1975).

Davis, N. Z., 'Beyond the Market: Books as Gifts in Sixteenth-Century France', *Transactions of the Royal Historical Society,* 33 (1983), pp. 69–88.

De Lisle, L., *The Sisters Who Would be Queen: Mary, Katherine, & Lady Jane Grey, A Tudor Tragedy* (New York, 2008).

Demers, P., 'The Seymour Sisters: Elegizing Female Attachment', *Sixteenth Century Journal,* 30 (1999), pp. 343–55.

Dennys, R., *Heraldry and the Heralds* (London, 1982).

Dent, C. M., *Protestant Reformers in Elizabethan Oxford* (London, 1983).

Donald, M. B., *Elizabethan Monopolies: the History of the Company of Mineral and Battery Works from 1565 to 1604* (Edinburgh, 1961).

Donawerth, J., 'Women's Poetry and the Tudor-Stuart System of Gift Exchange', in M. Burke, J. Donawerth, L. L. Dove, and K. Nelson, ed., *Women, Writing, and the Reproduction of Culture in Tudor and Stuart Britain* (Syracuse, NY, 2000), pp. 3–18.

Doran, S., *Elizabeth I and Religion, 1558–1603* (London, 1994).

—— and N. Jones, ed., *The Elizabethan World* (London, 2011).

Dovey, Z. M., *An Elizabethan Progress: The Queen's Journey into East Anglia, 1578* (Stroud, 1996).

Draper, M. C. M., 'The New Year's Gifts of Queen Elizabeth', *National Review,* 108 (1937), pp. 76–81.

Dumas, A., *The Two Dianas* (London, 1857).

Dunlop, I., *Palaces & Progresses of Elizabeth I* (London, 1962).

Dunning, R.W. and J. Bickersteth, *Clerks of the Closet in the Royal Household: Five Hundred Years of Service to the Crown* (Stroud, 1991).

Durant, D. N., *Bess of Hardwick: Portrait of an Elizabethan Dynasty* (London, 1977).

Eccles, M., 'Brief Lives: Tudor and Stuart Authors', *Studies in Philology,* 79 (1982), pp. 1–135.

Edward VI, *Literary Remains of King Edward the Sixth* , ed. J. G. Nichols (London, 1857).

Elizabeth I, *Elizabeth I: Collected Works,* ed. L. S. Marcus, J. Mueller, and M. B. Rose (Chicago, 2000).

——, *Queen Elizabeth I: Selected Works,* ed. S. W. May (New York, 2004).

Emmison, F. G., *Tudor Secretary: Sir William Petre at Court and Home* (London, 1961).

——, *Elizabethan Life: Disorder* (Chelmsford, 1970).

——, *Elizabethan Life: Home, Work & Land: From Essex Wills and Sessions and Manorial Records* (Chelmsford, 1976).

——, *Elizabethan Life: Wills of Essex Gentry & Yeomen Preserved in the Essex Record Office* (Chelmsford, 1980).

——, *Wills of Essex Gentry & Merchants, Proved in the Prerogative Court of Canterbury* (Chelmsford, 1978).

Farrer, W. and J. S. Curwen, *Records Relating to the Barony of Kendale* (4 vols, Kendal, 1998).

Fénelon, B. d. S., *Correspondance Diplomatique* (7 vols, Paris, 1838–40).

Ferrières, J. d., *Vie de J. de F., Vidame de Chartres, Seigneur de Maligny* (Auxerre, 1858).

Ffoulkes, C. J., *The Armourer and His Craft* (London, 1912).

Ficaro, B., 'Canterbury's First Dean', *Sixteenth Century Journal,* 8 (1987), pp. 343–6.

Fischer, T. A., *The Scots in Sweden* (Edinburgh, 1907).

Fletcher, G., *Russia at the Close of the Sixteenth Century. Comprising, the Treatise 'Of the Russe Common Wealth', by G. Fletcher and the Travels of Sir J. Horsey* ed. E.A. Bond (London, 1856).

Foster, J. A., "Cesar' de Jacques Grevin: Edition Critique Avec Introduction et des Notes', unpubl. PhD thesis (Rice University, 1968).

Foxe, J., *The New and Complete Book of Martyrs* (London, 1784).

Freedman, S., *Poor Penelope: Lady Penelope Rich an Elizabethan Woman* (Bourne End, 1983).

Friedman, A. T., *House and Household in Elizabethan England: Wollaton Hall and the Willoughby Family* (Chicago, 1989).

Fumerton, P. 'Exchanging Gifts: The Elizabethan Currency of Children and Poetry', *English Literary History*, 53 (1986), pp. 241–78.

Furdell, E. L., *The Royal Doctors, 1485–1714: Medical Personnel at the Tudor and Stuart Courts* (Rochester, NY, 2001).

Gascoigne, G., *The Complete Works of George Gascoigne*, ed. J. W. Cunliffe (2 vols, New York, 1969).

Gater, G. H. and E. P. Wheeler, *Survey of London* (45 vols, London, 1935).

Glasheen, J., *The Secret People of the Palaces: The Royal Household from the Plantagenets to Queen Victoria* (London, 1998).

Godelier, M., *The Enigma of the Gift* (Cambridge, 1999).

Goldsmith, V. F., *A Short Title Catalogue of French Books, 1601–1700, in the Library of the British Museum* (7 vols, Folkestone, 1969–73).

Goldwyn, M. H., 'Notes on the Biography of Thomas Churchyard', *Review of English Studies*, 17 (1966), pp. 1–15.

Great Britain. Royal Commission on Historical Manuscripts, *Calendar of the Manuscripts of the Most Honourable the Marquess of Salisbury* (24 vols, London, 1883–1976).

——, *The Manuscripts of his Grace the Duke of Rutland* (4 vols, London, 1888).

——, *Report on the Manuscripts of the Late Reginald Rawdon Hastings* (4 vols, London, 1528–47).

——, *Report on the Manuscripts of Lord De L'Isle and Dudley* (4 vols, London, 1925–42).

Gunn, S. J., *Charles Brandon, Duke of Suffolk, c.1484–1545* (Oxford, 1988).

Guy, J. A., ed., *The Reign of Elizabeth I: Court and Culture in the Last Decade* (Cambridge, 1995).

Hammer, P. E. J., *The Polarisation of Elizabethan Politics: The Political Career of Robert Devereux, 2nd Earl of Essex, 1585–1597* (Cambridge, 1999).

Hammond, N. G. L. and H. H. Scullard, ed., *The Oxford Classical Dictionary*, 2nd edition (Oxford, 1970).

Hannay, D., *A Short History of the Royal Navy* (London, 1898).

Hannay, M. P., ed., *Silent But for the Word: Tudor Women as Patrons, Translators, and Writers of Religious Works* (Kent, OH, 1985).

——, *Philip's Phoenix: Mary Sidney, Countess of Pembroke* (Oxford, 1990).

Harder, J., 'Calixtus Schein', in A. Bruns, ed., *Lübecker Lebensläufe* (Neumünster, 1993), pp. 336–9.

Harrison, G. B., *The Elizabethan Journals, Being a Record of Those Things Most Talked About During the Years 1591–1603* (London, 1938).

Harvey, S., 'The Cooke Sisters: A Study of Tudor Gentlewomen', unpubl. PhD thesis (Indiana University, 1981).

Hasler, P. W., ed., *The House of Commons, 1558–1603* (3 vols, London, 1981).

Hasted, E., *The History and Topographical Survey of the County of Kent* (4 vols, Canterbury, 1778–99).

Haydn, J., *The Book of Dignities* (London, 1851).

Hayward, J. F., *The Huguenot Gunmakers of London* (London, 1968).

Hayward, M. A., *Dress at the Court of King Henry VIII* (Leeds, 2007).

——, 'Gift Giving at the Court of Henry VIII: The 1539 New Year's Gift Roll in Context', *The Antiquaries Journal*, 85 (2006), pp. 125–75.

Heal, F., *Of Prelates and Princes: A Study of the Economic and Social Position of the Tudor Episcopate* (Cambridge, 1980).

Hicks, C., *The King's Glass: A Story of Tudor Power and Secret Art* (London, 2007).

Hilliard, N., *Nicholas Hilliard's Art of Limning*, ed. A. F. Kinney (Boston, 1983).

Hirschbiegel, J., *Étrennes: Untersuchungen zum Hofischen Geschenkverkehr im Spatmittelalterlichen Frankreich der Zeit König Karls VI (1380–1422)* (Munchen, 2003).

Hoak, D. E., *The King's Council in the Reign of Edward VI* (Cambridge, 1976).

Hoby, M., *The Private Life of an Elizabethan Lady: The Diary of Lady Margaret Hoby, 1599–1605,* ed. J. Moody (Stroud, Gloucestershire, 1998).

Holman, P., *Four and Twenty Fiddlers: The Violin at the English Court 1540–1690* (Oxford, 1993).

Holt, M. P., *The French Wars of Religion, 1562–1629* (Cambridge, 2005).

Hooper, W., 'Tudor Sumptuary Laws', *English Historical Review*, 30 (1915), pp. 433–49.

Horton-Smith, L. G. H., *Dr. Walter Baily (or Bayley), c.1529–1592: Physician to Queen Elizabeth* (St Albans, 1952).

Hotson, L., *The First Night of Twelfth Night* (London, 1964).

Hughes, P. L. and J. F. Larkin, ed., *Tudor Royal Proclamations* (3 vols, New Haven, CT, 1964–9).

Index to Administrations in the Prerogative Court of Canterbury and Now Preserved in the Principal Probate Registry, Somerset House, London (10 vols, London, 1944–86).

Jackson, C. J., *English Goldsmiths and Their Marks; A History of the Goldsmiths and Plate Workers of England, Scotland, and Ireland* (London, 1949).

Jagger, C., *Royal Clocks: The British Monarchy and Its Timekeepers 1300–1900* (London, 1983).

James, S. E., *The Feminine Dynamic in English Art, 1485–1603* (Farnham, 2008).

——, *Kateryn Parr: The Making of a Queen* (Aldershot, 1999).

Jensen, D. J., 'French Diplomacy and the Wars of Religion', *Sixteenth Century Journal*, 5 (1974), pp. 23–6.

Joy, F. W., 'Queen Elizabeth's New Year's Gifts', *Notes and Queries*, 6th Ser, 9 (1884), pp. 241–2.

Katz, D., *History of the Jews in England 1485–1850* (Oxford, 1994).

Keene, D. and V. Harding, ed., *Historical Gazetteer of London Before the Great Fire* (57 microfiches, Cambridge, 1987).

Kenny, R. W., *Elizabeth's Admiral: The Political Career of Charles Howard, Earl of Nottingham, 1536–1624* (Baltimore, 1970).

Kettering, S., 'Gift-Giving and Patronage in Early Modern France', *French History*, 2 (1988), pp. 131–51.

King, D. and S. Levey, *The Victoria and Albert Museum's Textile Collection: Embroidery in Britain from 1200 to 1750* (London, 1993).

King, J. N., *Tudor Royal Iconography: Literature and Art in an Age of Religious Crisis* (Princeton, NJ, 1989).

Kinney, A. F., *Titled Elizabethans: A Directory of Elizabethan State and Church Officers and Knights with Peers of England, Scotland, and Ireland, 1558–1603* (Hamden, CT, 1973).

Klein, L. M., 'Your Humble Handmaid: Elizabethan Gifts of Needlework', *Renaissance Quarterly,* 50 (1997), pp. 459–93.

Kocher, P. H., 'Paracelsan Medicine : The First Thirty Years (ca.1570–1600)', *Journal of the History of Medicine and Allied Science*, 2 (1947), pp. 451–80.

Kompter, A., 'Gifts and Social Relations: The Mechanisms of Reciprocity', *International Sociology*, 22 (2007), pp. 93–107.

Laffleur de Kermaingant, P. P., *L'Ambassade de France en Angleterre Sous Henri IV: Mission de Christophe de Harlay, Comte de Beaumont (1602–1605)* (Paris, 1895).

Lamb, M. E., 'Patronage and Class in Aemilia Lanyer's *Salve Deus Rex Judaeorum*', in M. Burke, J. Donawerth, L. L. Dove, and K. Nelson, ed., *Women, Writing, and the Reproduction of Culture in Tudor and Stuart Britain* (Syracuse, NY, 2000), pp. 38–57.

Lambley, K. V., *The Teaching and Cultivation of the French Language in England During Tudor and Stuart Times* (Manchester, 1920).

Lang, R. G., *Two Tudor Subsidy Assessment Rolls for the City of London: 1541 and 1582* (London, 1993).

Lasocki, D. and R. Prior, *The Bassanos: Venetian Musicians and Instrument Makers in England, 1531–1665* (Aldershot, 1995).

Lawson, J. A., 'Gift Books for Queen Elizabeth I: Court Ceremony vs. the Printing House', *Proceedings of the International Colloquium: Book Gifts and Cultural Networks from the 14ᵗʰ to the 16ᵗʰ Century* (Munster, 2011) in press.

——, 'Rainbow for a Reign: The Colours of a Queen's Wardrobe', *Costume,* 41 (2007), pp. 26–44.

——, 'This Remembrance of the New Year: Books Given to Queen Elizabeth as New Year's Gifts', in P. Beal and G. Ioppolo, ed., *Elizabeth I and the Culture of Writing* (London, 2007), pp. 133–71.

Lehmberg, S. E., *Sir Walter Mildmay and Tudor Government* (Austin, TX, 1964).

Leimon, G. P., 'Treason and Plot in Elizabethan Diplomacy', *English Historical Review*, 111 (1996), pp. 1134–58.

Levey, S. M., *Elizabethan Treasures: The Hardwick Hall Textiles* (London, 1998).

——, *Lace: A History* (London, 1983).

Lévi-Strauss, C., 'The Principle of Reciprocity', in A. Kompter, ed., *The Gift: An Interdisciplinary Perspective* (Amsterdam, 1996), pp. 18–26.

Lewalski, K. F., 'Sigismond I of Poland, Renaissance King and Patron', *Studies in the Renaissance*, 14 (1967) pp. 49–72.

Linthicum, M. C., *Costume in the Drama of Shakespeare and His Contemporaries* (Oxford, 1936).

Litzenberger, C., 'Richard Cheyney, Bishop of Gloucester: An Infidel in Religion?', *Sixteenth Century Journal*, 25 (1994), pp. 567–84.

Lloyd, J. E. and R.T. Jenkins, ed., *The Dictionary of Welsh Biography Down to 1940* (Oxford, 1959).

Loades, D. L., *The Tudor Court* (London, 1986).

Lockhart, P. D., *Frederik II and the Protestant Cause: Denmark's Role in the Wars of Religion, 1559–1596* (Leiden, 2004).

Loftie, W. J., *Memorials of the Savoy* (London, 1878).

Lumley, J. L., *The Lumley Library; The Catalogue of 1609*, ed. A. Alcock, S. Jayne and F. R. Johnson (London, 1956).

Lyttelton, C., 'Account of New Years Gifts Presented to Queen Elizabeth 1584–5', *Archaeologia*, 1 (1770), pp. 9–11.

McCracken, G., 'The Exchange of Children in Tudor England: An Anthropological Phenomenon in Historical Perspective', *Journal of Family History*, 8 (1983), pp. 303–13.

——, 'Dress Colour at the Court Of Elizabeth I: An Essay in Historical Anthropology', *Canadian Review of Sociology and Anthropology-Revue Canadienne de Sociologie et de Anthropologie*, 22 (1985), pp. 515–33.

McCutcheon, E. 'Life and Letters of Elizabeth Wolley', *Quiddatas,* 20 (1999), pp. 31–53.

McFarlane, I. D., *A Literary History of France* (New York, 1974).

Machyn, H., *The Diary of Henry Machyn: Citizen and Merchant-Taylor of London from A.D. 1550 to A.D. 1563*, ed. J. G. Nichols (London, 1848).

McIntosh, M. K., *The Cooke Family of Gidea Hall* (Boston, 1967).

——, 'Sir Anthony Cooke: Tudor Humanist, Educator and Religious Reformer', *Proceedings of the American Philological Society*, 119 (1975), pp. 233–50.

Macleod, J., *Dynasty: The Stuarts, 1560–1807* (London, 1999).

MacNalty, A., 'Medicine in the Time of Queen Elizabeth', *British Medical Journal*, 1 (1953), pp. 1179–84.

Madariaga, I. de, *Ivan the Terrible: First Tsar of Russia* (New Haven, 2005).

Madden, F., ed., *Privy Purse Expenses of the Princess Mary, Daughter of King Henry the Eighth, Afterwards Queen Mary: With a Memoir of the Princess, and Notes* (London, 1831).

Marlet, L., *Comte de Montgomery* (Paris, 1890).

Marlow, R., 'Sir Ferdinando Heyborne alias Richardson', *Musical Times*, 115 (1974), pp. 736–79.

Martin, C. T., *The Record Interpreter: A Collection of Abbreviations, Latin Words and Names Used in English Historical Manuscripts and Records* (London, 1949).

Mason, T., ed., *A Register of Baptisms, Marriages, and Burials in the Parish of St. Martin in the Fields: In the County of Middlesex, from 1550 to 1619* (London, 1898).

Matthews, L. G., 'Royal Apothecaries of the Tudor period', *Medical History,* 8 (1964), pp. 170–80.

——, *The Royal Apothecaries* (London, 1967).

Mauss, M., *The Gift: The Form and Reason for Exchange in Archaic Societies* (New York, 1967).

May, S. W., *The Elizabethan Courtier Poets: The Poems and Their Contexts* (Columbia, 1991).

——, *Sir Walter Ralegh* (Boston, 1989).

—— and W. A. Ringler, ed., *Elizabethan Poetry: A Bibliography and First-Line Index of English Verse, 1559–1603* (3 vols, London, 2004).

Mentzer, R. A. and A. Spicer, *Society and Culture in the Huguenot World, 1559–1685* (Cambridge, 2002).

Merton, C. I., 'The Women Who Served Queen Mary and Queen Elizabeth: Ladies, Gentlewomen and Maids of the Privy Chamber, 1553–1603', unpubl. PhD thesis (Cambridge University, 1992).

Naylor, K., *Richard Smith, MD, the Founder of Christ's Hospital, Lincoln* (London, 1951).

Nef, J. U., 'Richard Carmarden's 'A Caveat for the Quene' (1570)', *Journal of Political Economy*, 41 (1933), pp. 33–41.

Nelson, A. H., *Monstrous Adversary: The Life of Edward de Vere, 17th Earl of Oxford* (Liverpool, 2003).

Nevinson, J. L. 'New Year's Gifts to Queen Elizabeth I, 1584', *Costume,* 9 (1975), pp. 27–31.

Newman, H., *An Illustrated Dictionary of Jewelry* (New York, 1981).

Nichols, J., *The Progresses and Public Processions of Queen Elizabeth* (3 vols, London, 1823).

——, *The Progresses, Processions, and Magnificent Festivities, of King James the First, His Royal Consort, Family, and Court* (4 vols, London, 1828).

Nicolas, N. H., ed., *Privy Purse Expenses of Elizabeth of York* (London, 1830).

——, *Privy Purse Expenses of Henry VIII* (London, 1827).

Nolan, J. S., *Sir John Norreys and the Elizabethan Military World* (Exeter, 1997).

Noorthouck, J., *A New History of London, Including Westminster and Southwark* (2 vols, London, 1773).

Norris, M., *Monumental Brasses: The Portfolio Plates of the Monumental Brass Society, 1894–1984* (Woodbridge, 1988).

O'Connor, R., *A Historical and Genealogical Memoir of the O'Connors, Kings of Connaught and Their Descendants* (Dublin, 1861).

Paris, M., *Matthæi Parisiensis, Monachi Sancti Albani, Chronica Majora*, H. R. Luard, ed. (7 vols, London, 1876).

Patry, R., *Philippe du Plessis-Mornay: un Huguenot Homme d'État (1549–1623)* (Paris, 1933).

Paul, J. B., *The Scots' Peerage* (Edinburgh, 1905).

Pearsall, E. S., 'Tudor Court Musicians, 1485–1547: Their Number, Status and Function', unpubl. PhD thesis (New York University, 1986).

Pellegrini, G., *Un Fiorentino alla Corte d'Inghilterra nel Cinque-cento, Petruccio Ubaldini* (Turin, 1967).

Percy, H., *The Household Papers of Henry Percy, Ninth Earl of Northumberland, 1564–1632*, ed. G.R. Batho (London, 1962).

Perrenot, F., *Memoires de Frederic Perrenot, Sieur de Champagney, 1573–1590* (Bruxelles, 1860).

Phillimore, W. P. W., *Some Account of the Family of Middlemore, of Warwickshire and Worcestershire* (London, 1891).

Pollard, A. F., 'New Year's Day and Leap Year in English History', *English Historical Review*, 55 (1940), pp. 177–93.

Power, D., 'Some Notes on Edmund Harman, King's Barber, 1509(?) to 1576', *Proceedings of the Royal Society of Medicine*, 9 (1916), pp. 67–88.

Powicke, F. B. and E. B. Fryde, ed., *Handbook of British Chronology* (London, 1961).

Price, W. H., *The English Patents of Monopoly* (New York, 1906).

Prior, R., 'Jewish Musicians at the Tudor Court', *Musical Quarterly*, 69 (1983), pp. 253–65.

Prud'Homme van Reine, R. B. and E. W. van der Oest, *Kapers op de Kust: Nederlandse Kaapvaart en Piraterij 1500–1800* (Vlissingen, 1991).

Rabb, T. K., *Jacobean Gentleman: Sir Edwin Sandys, 1561–1629* (Princeton, NJ, 1998).

Read, C., *Mr. Secretary Walsingham and the Policy of Queen Elizabeth* (3 vols, Oxford, 1925).

——, *Lord Burghley and Queen Elizabeth* (London, 1960).

Read, E., *Catherine, Duchess of Suffolk* (London, 1962).

Richardson, R., *Mistress Blanche: Queen Elizabeth's Confidante* (Woonton, 2007).

Rickman, J., *Love, Lust, and License in Early Modern England: Illicit Sex and the Nobility* (Aldershot, 2008).

Rimbault, E. F., ed., *The Old Cheque-book, or Book of Remembrance, of the Chapel Royal, 1561–1744* (London, 1872).

Rouse, W. H. D., *A History of Rugby School* (London, 1898).

Sainty, J. C., ed., *Office Holders in Modern Britain* (12 vols, London, 1972–98).

Salmonsens Konversations Leksikon (26 vols, Copenhagen, 1915–1930)

Scott, A. V., *Selfish Gifts: The Politics of Exchange and English Courtly Literature, 1580–1628* (Madison, NJ, 2006).

Scott, G. G., *Gleanings from Westminster Abbey* (London, 1863).

Shaw, W. A., *The Knights of England* (2 vols, London, 1906).

Shorter, A. H., *Paper Mills and Paper Makers in England 1495–1800* (Hilversum, 1957).

Sicca, C. M., 'Consumption and Trade of Art Between Italy and England in the First Half of the Sixteenth Century: The London House of the Bardi and Cavalcanti Company', *Renaissance Studies*, 16 (2002), pp. 163–201.

Siddons, M. P., *The Heraldry of Foreigners in England 1400–1700*, Harleian Society, new series vol. 19 (London, 2010).

Sitwell, H. D. W., 'The Jewel House and the Royal Goldsmiths', *The Archaeological Journal*, 117 (1960), pp. 131–55.

Skovgaard-Petersen, K., *Historiography at the Court of Christian IV (1588–1648)* (Copenhagen, 2002).

Slavin, A. J., *Politics and Profit: A Study of Ralph Sadler, 1507–1547* (Cambridge, 1966).

Smith, R. L., *Ahmad al-Mansur: Islamic Visionary* (New York, 2006).

Stanley, A. P., *Historical Memorials of Westminster Abbey*, 4th edition (London, 1876).

Starkey, D., *Elizabeth: The Exhibition at the National Maritime Museum,* ed. S. Doran (London, 2003).

——, *Elizabeth: The Struggle for the Throne* (London, 2000).

——, ed., *Henry VIII: A European Court in England* (London, 1991).

——, ed., *The Inventory of King Henry VIII: Society of Antiquaries MS 129 and British Library MS Harley 1419* (London, 1998).

——, *Rivals in Power: Lives of the Great Tudor Dynasties* (London, 1990).

Stone, L., *An Elizabethan: Sir Horatio Palavicino* (Oxford, 1956).

Stopes, C. C., *Shakespeare's Environment* (London, 1918).

——, *William Hunnis and the Revels of the Chapel Royal* (Louvain, 1910).

Stow, J., *A Survey of London*, ed. C. L. Kingsford (2 vols, Oxford, 1971).

Strangford, P. E. F. W. S., ed., 'Household Expenses of the Princess Elizabeth During her Residence at Hatfield October 1, 1551 to September 30, 1552', in *Camden Miscellany Volume the Second* (London, 1853).

Streitberger, W., "Last of the Poore Flock of Hatfield': Sir Thomas Benger's Biography'', *Review of English Studies*, ns vol 55 (2004), pp. 662–89.

Strickland, A., *Lives of the Queens of England* (8 vols, London, 1851–2).

Strype, J., *Ecclesiastical Memorials* (3 vols, London, 1721).

——, *Historical Collections of the Life and Acts of the Right Reverend Father in God, John Aylmer, Lord Bishop of London in the Reign of Queen Elizabeth* (Oxford, 1821).

——, *The Life and Acts of Matthew Parker* (London, 1711).

Swain, M. H., *Figures on Fabric: Embroidery Design Sources and Their Application* (London, 1980).

——, 'A New Year's Gift from the Princess Elizabeth', *Connoisseur*, 183 (1973) pp. 258–66.

Thornbury, G. W. and E. Walford, *Old and New London* (6 vols, London, 1878).

Tighe, W., 'The Gentlemen Pensioners in Elizabethan Politics and Government', unpubl. PhD thesis (Cambridge University, 1983).

Turner, G. L. E. and K. v. Cleempoel, 'A Tudor Astrolabe by Thomas Gemini and its Relationship to an Astrological Disc by Gerard Mercator of 1551', *The Antiquaries Journal,* 81 (2001), pp. 400–9.

Varlow, S., 'Sir Francis Knollys's Latin Dictionary: New Evidence for Katherine Carey', *Historical Research*, 80 (2007), pp. 315–3.

Wagner, A., *Heralds of England: A History of the Office and College of Arms* (London, 1967).

Weaver, F. J., 'Anglo-French Diplomatic Relations, 1558–1603', *Bulletin of the Institute of Historical Research*, 4 (1926), pp. 73–86; 5 (1927), pp. 13–22; 6 (1928), pp. 1–9; 7 (1929), pp. 13–26.

Weinreb, B. and C. Hibbert, ed., *The London Encyclopaedia* (London, 1984).

Westlake, H. F., ed., *The Register of St. Margaret's, Westminster, London, 1660* (London, 1935).

White, F. O., *Lives of the Elizabethan Bishops of the Anglican Church* (London, 1898).

White, M., 'A Biographical Sketch of Dorcas Martin: Elizabethan Translator, Stationer, and Godly Matron', *Sixteenth Century Journal*, 30 (1999), pp. 775–92.

Widmore, R., *A History of the Church of St Peter, Westminster* (London, 1751).

Williams, F. B., *Index of Dedications and Commendatory Verses in English Books Before 1641* (London, 1962).

Ziegler, G., ed., *Elizabeth I: Then and Now* (Washington, DC, 2003).

——, 'More Than Feminine Boldness: The Gift Books of Esther Inglis', in M. Burke, J. Donawerth, L. L. Dove, and K. Nelson, ed., *Women, Writing, and the Reproduction of Culture in Tudor and Stuart Britain* (Syracuse, NY, 2000), pp. 19–37.

Appendix 1
Gift Descriptions and Motifs

See Editorial Procedures for an explanation of this Appendix.

Accidence of Arms 63.169

acorn 77.35, 77.168, 81.100, 00.92

adedtre see tree, dead

Aeneid 59.190

agate 67.5, 67.96, 67.122, 67.147, 71.151, 75.27, 75.116, 76.37, 76.89, 76.105, 76.171, 76.172, 77.44, 77.80, 77.136, 78.1, 78.104, 78.126, 79.23, 79.101, 79.123, 79.185, 82.71, 82.174, 84.93, 84.119, 85.93, 88.57, 89.20, 89.120, 89.123, 89.160, 89.169, 97.123, 98.94, 98.131

Agememnon 64.131

aglet 71.162, 76.2, 77.95, 79.144, 79.197, 84.126, 98.4, 03.143; see also points

Ahasuerus see Assuerus

alabaster 62.61, 63.2, 71.96, 75.85; see also stone

alcorse 59.195

Alexander the Great 71.151

Almain 77.423, 78.422, 81.435, 85.409, 98.426

Alpha and Omega 89.110

Ambassador 62.378, 62.380, 62.391–394, 63.363–364, 64.218–219, 64.224, 64.227, 67.359, 68.347–348, 71.362, 75.250, 76.413, 76.418–419, 76.422–423, 77.419, 77.423, 78.422, 79.439, 79.446, 79.450, 79.451, 79.454, 81.434, 84.417, 85.415, 85.419, 89.406, 94.392, 98.426, 03.449

amber 79.38, 79.155, 81.84, 88.168; see also stone

amethyst 77.34, 81.11, 82.6, 82.170, 88.95, 94.143, 98.88, 99.31, 99.113, 99.134, 99.154, 99.158, 03.101, 03.158, 03.169; see also stone

anchor 81.112, 81.174, 84.24, 88.57

andiron 59.206

angel (motif) 71.119, 71.322, 77.184

Angel (money) 59.5–6, 59.14, 59.26, 59.36–37, 59.41–42, 59.45, 59.47, 59.53, 59.56, 59.65, 59.71, 59.77, 59.81, 59.86–88, 59.94, 59.97, 59.103, 59.111–112, 59.115, 59.122, 59.135, 59.161, 59.192, 62.3, 62.5, 62.8, 62.10–11, 62.14, 62.19–21, 62.29, 62.31–33, 62.35–36, 62.39, 62.46–47, 62.51, 62.57, 62.65, 62.70, 62.75, 62.77, 62.82, 62.93, 62.101, 62.108, 62.110, 62.113–114, 62.123, 62.146, 63.8, 63.11–12, 63.18, 63.24, 63.43, 63.48, 63.55, 63.57, 63.60, 63.66, 63.76–77, 63.80, 63.84, 63.90, 63.95, 63.103, 63.106–108, 63.111–112, 63.121, 63.136, 63.146, 64.8, 64.18, 64.33, 64.40–41, 64.48, 64.58, 64.72, 64.83, 64.89–90, 64.97, 64.99, 64.102, 64.104, 65.20, 65.33, 65.37–39, 67.7, 67.10, 67.19, 67.31, 67.39–40, 67.44, 67.66, 67.81, 67.89, 67.105, 67.108, 67.111, 67.151, 68.13, 68.17, 68.27, 68.34, 68.37, 68.39–41, 68.46, 68.50–52, 68.56, 68.69–70, 68.85, 68.87, 68.90, 68.148–149, 71.15, 71.19–20, 71.34, 71.39, 71.49, 71.53, 71.59, 71.76, 71.85, 71.104, 71.149–150, 76.4–5, 76.7, 76.10, 76.15–17, 76.21, 76.24, 76.27–28, 76.32–33, 76.35, 76.43, 76.45, 76.47, 76.49, 76.55, 76.59, 76.61, 76.64, 76.68–69, 76.72, 76.74, 76.80, 76.82, 76.84–85, 76.88, 76.114–115, 76.117, 76.128, 76.169, 76.179, 79.119, 79.125, 82.3, 82.201; includes dimy, good and bad, Flemish, half, new, old; see also money

antic, antique 81.122, 82.201, 89.13, 89.30

Antwerp 76.425

541

partlet), 84.137 (ruff), 84.151 (ruff), 85.34 (forepart of kirtle), 85.57 (forepart of kirtle), 85.72 (forepart of kirtle), 85.118 (sleeves), 85.138 (ruff), 88.86 (doublet), 88.128 (rebato), 88.134 (ruff), 88.139 (ruff), 88.140 (ruff), 89.74 (ruff), 89.106 (ruff), 89.133 (ruff), 97.152 (night rail), 98.151 (ruff), 98.198 (pillow bere), 99.99 (ruff), 99. 193 (ruff), 00.22 (doublet), 00.105 (ruff), 03.153 (ruff); see also costume

upside   89.9

valance   67.139, 99.98
varnished   81.122
vase   94.393
veil   71.77, 71.154, 75.88, 77.28, 77.41, 77.90, 77.140, 78.142, 79.85, 79.95, 79.112, 79.159, 81.102, 81.137, 82.97, 82.109, 82.149, 84.79, 84.96, 84.134, 84.151, 85.88, 88.56, 88.72, 88.91, 88.99, 89.99, 89.101, 94.128, 97.80, 97.103, 97.143, 98.21, 98.79, 99.175, 00.36, 00.83, 00.148, 00.152, 00.175; see also costume, mantle
vellum   84.192, 84.196, 89.179, 94.163, 94.170, 94.178, 98.190
velvet   *passim*; 62.132 (unshorn), 67.116 (unshorn), 76.14 (unshorn), 76.23 (unshorn), 79.139 (unshorn), 81.173 (unshorn) (figured), 81.175 (unshorn), 84.122 (unshorn), 85.4 (unshorn), 85.165 (unshorn), 94.83, 94.127, 94.142, 94.145–146, 99.120 (unshorn), 99.126 (unshorn), 00.76 (unshorn); see also fabric
Venice, Venetian   *passim*, 65.95 (lute), 71.165 (soap), 81.99 (making)
Venus   63.61
verbum Dei   81.31
verse   59.167, 59.190, 62.157, 71.5, 77.197, 84.197, 84.198
vetus   76.195
Victories   84.109
vine   84.102, 85.118, 94.148; see also flower, woodvine
viol   78.191; see also musical instrument
violin   59.216, 59.440, 65.91, 68.160, 71.165, 75.226, 75.227, 76.192, 76.193; see also musical instrument

virgins   84.190
virginals, a pair of   59.204, 77.195, 82.120, 94.183; see also musical instrument
Virtute   78.198
Vita Plutarchi   65.34
vizard   59.178; see also costume
Vlysshing   see Flushing

wainscot   94.183
waistcoat   63.86, 63.160, 65.4, 75.36, 75.93, 77.141, 79.176, 81.101, 81.157, 81.179, 81.180, 82.70, 82.176, 84.85, 84.140, 84.184, 85.91, 85.123, 89.69, 89.93, 89.105, 94.88, 94.92, 94.99, 94.150, 94.153, 94.180, 97.71, 97.96, 98.72, 98.98, 98.110, 98.129, 98.136, 98.156, 98.199, 99.70, 99.79, 99.85, 00.90, 03.82; see also costume
waistgirdle   75.14, 85.70, 88.97; see also costume
walnut   62.157, 75.85, 78.137, 84.87; see also wood
warden   59.182, 71.161, 78.186, 78.189; see also apple, fruit
warming ball   62.80; see also plate
warrant, special   76.413, 85.411
wasp   97.95; see also insect
watch   81.62
watchet   76.99, 76.134, 78.181, 81.91, 81.132, 81.197, 82.175, 82.190, 84.136, 85.161, 85.171, 88.157, 89.86, 89.103, 89.159, 97.81, 97.128, 97.136, 98.159, 00.68, 03.104; see also colour
water   59.176, 59.216, 63.85, 67.167, 71.165, 71.168, 81.195, 81.199, 82.191, 82.195, 84.191, 84.195, 85.183, 85.186, 85.191, 88.24, 88.113, 88.156, 88.178, 89.180, 94.169, 97.180, 97.198, 98.178, 98.195, 99.176, 99.192, 00.176, 00.190–191, 03.178–179, 03.186; includes orange water, musk water, precious water, rosewater, seawater green, sweetwater
wave   77.83, 78.84, 79.87, 81.71, 81.91, 88.140, 94.15, 98.81
weapon   see crossbow, dag, gaffle, lance staff, mace, sword
wedge   68.93; see also plate
wheat   85.64, 00.13, 00.22

Appendix 2
Glossary

See Editorial Procedures for an explanation of this Appendix.

&c   abbreviation for *et cetera;* etc.

abiliment   variant of habiliment

abracock, aberycocke   variant of apricot; 79.192

acatery   household office under the Lord Steward, responsible for the reception and storage of meat for the royal tables

agate   a variety of chalcedony or quartz that has a varigated colour in parallel stripes or bands, or blended in clouds, and often with curious markings; 67.5

aglet   a point; an ornament consisting of a gold or silver tag or pendent attached to a fringe or worn on the dress; 71.162

alabaster   a fine translucent variety of carbonate or sulfate of lime, especially the pure white variety used for vases and ornaments; 62.61

alcorse   cork sole, from Spanish *alcorque*, probably from Arabic *al-qurq*; see also pantofle; 59.195

alias   otherwise called or named; used in reference to any other surname, including married, unmarried, and foreign surnames as well as offices; 62.145

Almain   German; 77.423

almoner   an official of the royal house-hold, usually a chaplain, who distributed alms and said grace before meals; 59.135

almonry   this office distributed charity at palace gates

alpha and omega   Greek letters signifyng the beginning and the end; 89.110

amner   variant of almoner

Angel   an English gold coin, properly an Angel-Noble; originally a new issue of the Noble, with the device of the archangel Michael standing upon and piercing the dragon; 59.5

ansa, anse   see hanse

antic, antique   grotesque, in composition or shape; grouped or figured with fantastic incongruity; bizarre; uncouthly ludicrous; 81.122

ao   abbreviation for *anno* [year]

Arion   Greek poet, known for the myth of his kidnapping by pirates and miraculous rescue by dolphins; 84.70

armyone   variant of ermine

armyns   variant of ermine

armlet   an ornament or band worn round the arm; 98.4

arras   a rich tapestry fabric, in which figures and scenes are woven in colours; 68.33

assay cup   a vessel for tasting drink, as a test for poison or as a ceremonial act, before it was consumed; see also say as a fabric; 59.454

ash-colour   a grayish-pink colour; 77.40

Assuerus   Greek name for Xerxes, King of Persia, in the biblical books of Esther, Ezra and Daniel; 59.212

attire   a woman's headdress; 76.160

avery, avernary   household office under the Master of the Horses; the avener was a chief officer of the stable, who had charge of the provender for the horses

b.   born

B, Br, Bra   abbreviation used by scribes to designate the goldsmith, Robert Brandon

balas   a delicate rose-red variety of the spinel ruby; 65.42

bandore   a musical instrument resembling a guitar or lute, with three, four, or six wire strings, used as a bass to the cittern; later corrupted to banjo; 81.185

barberry   a shrub with small yellow flowers and red berries; the bark yields a bright yellow dye; 75.119

base   a pleated skirt of cloth, velvet, or rich brocade, appended to the doublet, and reaching from the waist to the knee; the skirt of a woman's outer petticoat or robe; 88.101

bat   a lump, piece, bit; 75.24

baudekin   a rich embroidered silk fabric woven with gold thread, derived from the Italian form of Bagdad; 59.140; see also bodkin

bear with a ragged staff   crest of the Dudley family, Earls of Leicester and Warwick; 81.164

beasts   ornamental designs of animals, not specified; 67.51

beaver   a shade of brown resembling the fur of a beaver, similar to hair-colour; 85.97

bell salt   silver or gilt plate in an overall bell-like profile, usually comprised of two containers and a pepper shaker; 81.451

bere   variant of pillow-bere, pillowcase

beryl   a precious stone in colours of pale green, light-blue, yellow, and white; called an aquamarine when of pale bluish-green colour; 63.156

bezoar-colour   a colour usually associated with semi-precious stones, most probably a shade of soft brown or beige; 98.100

bezoar stone   a stone found in the gastrointestinal system of certain ruminant animals, especially the wild goat of Persia; supposed to be an antidote to poison; taken internally in powdered form or worn as an amulet, sometimes mounted in gold or silver decorated with silver-gilt overlaid openwork; 82.200

billament   variant of habiliment

billet-wise   a rectangular shape placed on end, variously conjectured to represent a folded letter, a brick, or a bar of gold; 97.32

bird of Arabia   variant of phoenix

bloodstone   variant of heliotrope

bodices   the upper part of a woman's dress, usually appearing as a pair of bodices; 71.1

bodkin   a long pin made of gold or silver and richly decorated with gemstones, used to fasten up the hair; 81.5; see also baudekin

bolt   a roll of fabric, generally forty yards in length; 59.185

bone lace   lace made with bobbins, of gold, silver, silk and linen threads; 63.83

Bra   see B

brake   fern, bracken; 94.73

Brazil   a reddish brown colour, the hard brownish-red wood of the Sappan tree from which dyers obtain a red colour; 03.12

Bruner   see Brunolyon

Brunolyon   plum grown in Lyon, France; see plum; 88.173

bugle   a tube-shaped glass bead, usually black, used to ornament wearing apparel; 75.135

buttery   household office under the Lord Steward, which stored and delivered liquors other than wine; the cellar was the household office for storing and delivery wine

c.   *circa*, about

caduceus   the wand carried by Mercury as the messenger of the gods; usually represented with two serpents twined round it; 82.125

caffa   a rich silk cloth, similar to damask; 89.67

calaber   a kind of fur, apparently obtained from some foreign species of squirrel; see also miniver; 89.21

cambric   a kind of fine white linen, originally made at Cambray in Flanders; 59.90

camlet   a beautiful and costly eastern fabric, originally made by a mixture of silk and camel's hair; it is now made with wool and silk; 84.25

canopy   a covering or hangings suspended over a throne, couch, bed, etc., or held over a person walking in procession; 67.93

car   variant of carat or carnation

carn   variant of carnation

carat   A measure of weight used for diamonds and other precious stones, A proportional measure of one twenty-fourth used in stating the fineness of gold; see also dwait; 79.439

carcanet   an ornamental collar or necklace, usually of gold or set with jewels; 77.34

carnation   the colour of raw flesh or skin, also a light rosy pink or a deeper crimson colour; 63.24

carpet   a thick fabric, commonly of wool, used to cover tables and beds; 62.84

carte   a chart, map, plan, diagram; 75.103

casket   a small box or closed compartment, contained within or forming part of a larger box, chest, or cabinet; used for keeping valuables, documents, etc., more safely; see also coffer; 62.174

caul   a kind of close-fitting cap, a net for the hair; a netted cap or head-dress, often richly ornamented; 59.7

caulsidon   see chalcedony

cedar of Lebanon   evergreen conifer named for its early locality; 81.104

chain-lace   lace made with chain-stitch, type of braid; 89.21

chalcedony   a semi-precious stone, a variety of quartz that is usually pale blue or grey; 71.91

chameleon   small lizard-like creature, with a prehensile tail, long tongue, eyes moving independently, and by the power to change their skin colour, varying through different shades of yellow, red, gray, brown, and dull inky blue; a contraction of camel and lion; 88.71

chamlett   variant of camlet

changeable   showing different colours under different aspects; shot silk, the warp and weft of different colours; 63.121

cherry-bag   a kind of purse for holding gold, similar to but distinct from a purse; 62.39

chevron   a zig-zag pattern; 62.84

cinnamon   a spice from the dried inner bark of an East Indian tree; 59.181

cinque   from the number five; cinque-petal, a flower with five petals; 85.110

cinquefoil   an ornamental design resembling a flower with five petals; 84.4

cipher   a symbolic character, a hiero-glyph; an astrological sign or figure; 97.38

cithern   an instrument of the guitar kind, strung with wire and played with a plectrum or quill, also called cither or zither; 62.160

citron   citrus fruit with a pale yellow rind, including lemon, and perhaps, lime; 65.81

clapper   the tongue of a bell, which strikes it on the inside and causes it to sound; 77.152

clock   1) an instrument for the measure-ment of time; 59.208; 2) an ornamental pattern in silk thread worked on the side of a stocking; 03.154

cloth of estate   a cloth spread over a throne or other seat of dignity; a canopy; 82.10

cloudy-colour   a shade of gray, not transparent or clear; 99.98

cobweb   a fine, almost transparent material made of linen; 97.140

coffer   a box, chest: *esp.* a strong box in which money or valuables are kept, see also casket; 59.51

coif   a close-fitting cap covering the top, back, and sides of the head; 63.130

collar   an ornamental band or chain worn round the neck for ornament, a necklace; 59.109

collar of esses   a badge of office or livery; 62.383

collet   the neckband of a garment, a collar or band worn round the neck; a necklet; see also collar; a circular band of metal in which a gemstone is set; 75.14

colliander   variant of coriander

collog   variant of collet

colour-de-roy   king's colour, a bright tawny colour; 03.81

combing cloth   a cloth placed over the shoulders while the hair is dressed and combed; 82.99

comfit a sweetmeat made of some fruit or root, preserved with sugar; now usually a small round or oval mass of sugar enclosing a caraway seed, almond, etc; see also condite; 59.163

compass round, circular, curved; artifice, skillful or crafty device; 94.72

conceit a fancy article; a fanciful, ingenious, or witty notion or expression; 78.195

condite a preserve or pickle; a conserve, electuary; see also comfit and warden's condite; 62.158

confection a preparation of fruit, spices, sugar, or the like, used as a relish or dainty; a preserve, sweetmeat, comfit; 03.175

conserve a medicinal or confectionary preparation of some part of a plant preserved with sugar; confections, preserves; 63.149

cont variant of containing

cony, coney a rabbit; 77.104

cord, cordant a string composed of several strands twisted or woven together; in ordinary popular use, now restricted to small ropes, and thick or stout strings; 75.88

cordial a medicine, food, or beverage which invigorates the heart and stimulates the circulation; a comforting or exhilarating drink; see also manus Christi; 65.86

coriander an herb seed with a mild, distinctive taste similar to a blend of lemon and sage, the leaves are known as cilantro 65.86

cornelian a variety of chalcedony, a semi-transparent quartz, of a deep dull red, flesh, or reddish white colour; 79.142

cornet a wind instrument with a trumpet-type mouthpiece and fingering like a recorder, with a sound like a mellow trumpet; 98.192

coronet a fillet or wreath worn as an ornament encircling the head, a small crown; 62.383

Corsili variant of Corsica, also known as Corfu; 67.163

counter a piece of metal, ivory, or other material, formerly used in performing arithmetical operations; also, applied to the 'pieces' or 'men' used in playing shovelboard, chess, draughts and other games; 62.102

cover-pane a cover cloth, a counterpane, probably more or less ornamental, woven in a raised pattern, quilted, or made of patchwork; 71.138

crane a long legged wading bird characterized by very long legs, neck, and bill; 71.61

crazed broken, cracked, flawed; having the surface or glaze covered with minute cracks; 71.57

crepine a net or caul for the hair, of gold or silver thread, silk lace; 78.114

crewel a thin worsted yarn, used for tapestry and embroidery; also formerly for making fringes, laces, vestments, and hosiery

crippin variant of crepine

crown a name for various coins; originally one bearing the imprint of a crown; 59.82

crown of the rose gold pieces coined by Henry VIII in 1526; 67.65

crusado a Portuguese coin bearing the figure of a cross, originally of gold, but also of silver; 59.51

crystal of the mountain rock crystal, natural quartz, usually transparent, that can be carved or faceted; 63.173

curiously with careful art, skillfully, elaborately, cunningly; 67.362

cushion cloth a cushion case or covering; 59.90

cutwork in embroidery, elaborately cut-out edges, a kind of openwork embroidery or lace; in gold, work produced by cutting or carving; 76.93

cypress a name of several textile fabrics originally imported from or through Cyprus; a cloth of gold or other valuable material; a valuable quality of satin, called more fully satin of Cypress; a light transparent material resembling cobweb lawn or crepe; 62.79

cypress wood   hard durable wood from a coniferous tree, a native of Persia and the Levant

d.   died

d   abbreviation for penny, from the Latin *denairus*

d **weight**   variation of pennyweight

dag, dagg   a small pistol with a wheel-lock mechanism which could be easily concealed and could be loaded and primed in advance; often ornate and lavishly ornamented; 81.205

Dame Flora   goddess of flowers in the garden among the Romans, symbolizes perpetual youth; 75.101

damask, damaskeen   1) from the city of Damascus; 59.159. 2) a rich silk fabric woven with elaborate designs and figures, often of a variety of colours; 63.155. 3) to ornament (metal-work, steel) with designs incised in the surface and filled in with gold or silver; 62.167

dd   abbreviation for delivered

demi   half; half-sovereign equals ten shillings; 59.9

device   a fancifully conceived shape or figure; something artistically devised or framed; 59.158

di   demi, half, (½)

di di qtr   half plus half of a quarter, (3/8)

di qtr   half of a quarter, (5/8); see also qtr di (3/8)

dial   a sun-dial; a timepiece or chronometer of any kind; a clock or watch; 62.115

dial nocturnal   a dial which shows the time by means of the moon's shadow; 79.206

Diana   Roman goddess of the hunt and chastity, counterpart of the Greek goddess Artemis; 63.61

diaper   a linen fabric woven with a small and simple pattern, formed by different directions of the thread; 63.135

die, dice   a small cube of ivory, bone or other material, having its faces marked with spots numbering from one to six, used in games of chance; ornamental pattern of cubes or squares; 75.32

docket   see pocket

doublet   a close-fitting upper body-garment, with or without sleeves; 75.5

dowager   a woman whose husband is dead and who is in the enjoyment of some title or some property that has come to her from him, a widow; 59.42

dove-colour   a warm grey with a tone of pink or purple; 03.76

ducat, ducket   a European gold coin of valued at 4s. 6d. in 1525 and at 6s. 4d. in 1554; 59.55

Durabo   from the Latin, *durare*, to endure; I will endure; 85.22

dwait   variation of pennyweight

earpick   an instrument for clearing the ear of wax; 75.74

ebony   a hard black wood; 65.56

eel spear   a forked or pronged instrument for catching eels as they lie in the mud; 88.15

eglantine   eglantine rose, sweet-briar, or honeysuckle; 85.14

elbow   an arm of a chair, made to support the elbow; 88.77

elitrope   see heliotrope

embr, enbr   variant of embroidered

ermine   a weasel, a stoat, whose fur is reddish brown in summer, but in winter wholly white, except the tip of the tail, which is always black; trimmings, or garments, made of this fur; 67.77

esses   the letter 's', nineteenth letter of the alphabet; the shape of an object, having the shape of this letter, often combined as collar of esses ; 62.383

essefirme   a combination of shapes in the form of the letter 's'; 82.23

étrenne   a New Year's gift; a gift or present (expressive of good wishes) at the beginning of a New Year; French from the Latin *strena*; the English equivalent is handsel

ewer   a pitcher with a wide spout, used to bring water for washing the hands; see also lave or lair; 59.454

ewery   household office under the Lord Steward, responsible for the provision and storage of linen and for serving water in ewers after a meal

ex et oner   abbreviation for *examinari et onerare*, auditor's mark to examine and weigh, meaning the item was inspected and passed on to the collection, referring to the disposition of an item; 59.4

ex per   variant of *examinatio per*;

examinatio per   examined by; auditor's term for the receipt and verification of amounts of money to certify their accuracy

facet   one of the sides of a body that has numerous faces; one of the small cut and polished faces of a diamond or other gem ; 03.118

fallow, favel   pale brownish or reddish yellow colour, as withered grass or leaves or exposed soil; 62.127

figured   adorned or ornamented with patterns or designs; 81.173

fl.   flourished during this period, for persons of unknown dates of birth and death

flagon   a large bottle for holding wine or other liquors; 66.266

flannel   an open woollen stuff, of various degrees of fineness, usually without a nap; 76.140

fleur-de-lis   heraldic lily representing a lily flower or iris, the royal arms of France; 82.168

flower   the blossom of a plant; 62.140; a jewel; 64.217; a confection; 59.216

flower-de-luce   variant of *fleur-de-lis*

flush   variant of plush

fly   a winged insect; often in combination with black-fly, dragon-fly, or butter-fly; 75.86

foil   a thin leaf of some metal placed under a precious stone to increase its brilliancy; the setting of a jewel; metal hammered or rolled into a thin layer; 59.221

footsheet   a sheet used to sit upon while dressing or undressing; also, a narrow sheet spread across the foot of a bed

forehead cloth   a triangular piece of material to tie over the hair above the forehead, usually with a matching coif; 62.139

forepart   the front part of any piece of dress as the forepart of a sleeve or the forepart of a kirtle; when used alone it usually refers to the detachable, inverted V-shaped panel worn to fill in the open front of the gown between waist and hem; 59.159

friars knots   knots made in imitation of the knotted cords of the Franciscans, a term used in goldsmith's work; 84.68

frutage   a decorative arrangement of fruits; a representation of this in embroidery or painting; 99.29

furred   see pure

fustian   the name of a suburb of Cairo where cloth was manufactured; a kind of coarse cloth made of cotton and flax; a blanket made of this material; 03.208

g   variation of gilt

gaffle   a steel lever for bending the cross-bow; 62.172

gar, garn   variant of garnished

garter   a band worn round the leg, either above or below the knee, to keep the stocking from falling down; the Garter, the badge of the highest order of English chivalry; hence, membership in this order; 64.226

Gascon   pertaining to Gascony, a province in south-western France

Genoa   a city state in Italy; 75.126

George-noble   a gold coin with the image of St George slaying the dragon, valued at 6*s* 8*d*, in 1543; see also noble; 63.76

gillyflower   applied to native plants having flowers scented like a clove, esp. to the clove-scented pink; 89.154

gilt   gilt plate, gold-plated, overlaid with a thin coating of gold; gold or silver vessels and utensils, see also plate; 59.1

ginger   a rhizome, remarkable for its hot spicy taste; used in cookery and as a medicine; also preserved in syrup or candied as a sweetmeat; 59.181

ginger-colour   a light sandy colour resembling the spicy root of the same name; 76.96

girdle   a belt worn round the waist, hanging down two or more feet; also employed as a means of carrying light articles, such as fans, girdle books, purses, needlecases, scissors, pomanders and pendants; also called waist girdle; 71.24

gittern   a quill-plucked, gut strung instrument; also called cithern or zither; faded in popularity to the larger lute and guitar; 59.202

Gordian knot   an intricate knot tied by Gordius, king of Gordium in Phrygia. The oracle declared that whoever should loosen it should rule Asia. Alexander the Great overcame the difficulty by cutting through the knot with his sword; 03.37

gourd   the large fleshy fruit of a trailing or climbing plant, which when dried and hollowed out is used as a vessel; 64.130

gown, French   a gown with a square neckline, close-fitting bodice and full skirt sweeping the ground at the back; 84.22

granator   one who has charge of a granary or grange; usually coupled with purveyor, as in 'purveyor and granitor of the stables'

grased   variant of crazed

grasp   a type of gemstone setting; 94.155

grosgrain   a coarse fabric of silk, of mohair and wool, or of these mixed with silk; often stiffened with gum; 89.136

ground   the bottom, the lowest part or downward limit of anything; 64.92

guard   an ornamental border or trimming on a garment; the original notion may have been that of a binding to keep the edge of the cloth from fraying; see also safeguard; 71.1

guilt   variant of gilt

habiliment   outfit, accoutrement, attire, array, dress, anything worn as an ornament, also spelled biliment or abiliment; 84.75

hair-colour   a pale grey or beige, also called maidenhair colour; 79.122

haft   a handle of a dagger or knife; 59.220

handsel   see *étrenne*

hanse-pot   a handled vessel with a cover, similar to a tankard, but lacking the tapering body, with two horizontal ribs or bars. The name, thought to derive from hanse for Hanseatic, has its roots in the Latin *ansa*, or French *anse* for handle; see also tankard; 59.99

hartshorn jelly   a nutritive jelly made formerly from the shavings of harts' (deer) horns, now from those of calves' bones; 97.197

haunce pott   see hanse-pot

hawthorn   a thorny shrub or small tree, extensively used for forming hedges; the blossoms are white, red, or pink and the fruit, the haw, is a small, round, dark-red berry; 65.67

heliotrope   a green variety of quartz, with spots or veins of red jasper; also called bloodstone; 71.114

hippocras   a cordial drink made of wine flavoured with spices, of varied colours including white and red; 64.144

history, story   a relation of incidents, either true or imaginary; a narrative, tale, story; 59.453

Holland   a linen cloth from the Netherlands; 64.140

Holofernes   see Judith and Holofernes

honeysuckle   woodbine, eglantine rose, or sweet briar; 77.129

hoste   variant of hose

hound   a drinking cup of gilt plate; 65.73

hyacinth   a precious stone of a strong blue colour, probably sapphire; a plant in the lily family, with bell-shaped six parted flowers, of various colours, arranged in a loose, upright spike; see also jacinth bell; 81.97

ibonett   variant of ivory

icentabella   variant of hyacinth or jacinth bell

Icarus   son of Dædalus, who attempted to fly by means of artificial wings constructed of feathers and wax. He ignored instructions not to fly too close to the sun, and the melting wax caused him to fall to his death; 78.116

iheat   variant of wheat; 85.64

iij qtr   three quarters, (¾)

iij qtr di   three quarters plus half of a quarter, (3/8)

iiij^c   four hundred

iiij^m   four thousand

iiij^{xx}   eighty

imperial crown   a diadem or covering for the head, made of or adorned with precious metals and jewels, worn by a monarch as a mark or symbol of sovereignty; 84.109

India horn   probably ivory from India; 03.139

India-work   porcelain, a translucent ceramic material made from china clay or kaolin; originating in China, hence called china-ware, and shipped through India, hence called India-work; 98.152

inner sleeve   a sleeve of light material, worn beneath another; 98.155

Irish mantle   a kind of blanket or plaid worn until the seventeenth century by the rustic Irish, often as their only covering; 89.120

Iugum necessitatis   necessary yoke, a reference to the myth of Agamemnon agreeing to sacrifice his daughter to appease the goddess Diana/Artemis; 64.131

ivory   the tusks of elephant, hippopotamus, walrus, narwhal, and other mammal used for ornamentation; ivory-colour; 59.85

jacinth bell   variant of hyacinth, also spelled icentabella

Janna, Jennewey   variant of Genoa

jet   a compact, velvet-black substance that is a variety of coal or lignite, formed by pressure, heat and chemical action on ancient driftwood; 79.155

jewel   an article of value used for personal adornment; a costly ornament, esp. one made of gold, silver, or precious stones; a thing of great worth or highly prized, regalia; a 'treasure'.

jewel-house   a repository of treasures and regalia

Job   name of an ancient patriarch, whose story forms a book of the Old Testament; used in proverbial phrases as a type of destitution or of patience; 59.453

Judgement of Paris   in Greek mythology, Paris was appointed by Zeus to select the most beautiful goddess among Venus, Athena, and Juno; 63.61

Judith and Holofernes   in the apocryphal Book of Judith; Judith uses her charm to become an intimate friend of Holofernes, then she beheads him allowing Israel to counter-attack the Assyrians. Judith is an example of the courage of local people against tyrannical rule; 78.193

Jula and Sectra   Julia Domna, Empress, and Lucius Septimus Severus, Roman Emperor from 191 to 211. Julia collected about her a large coterie of learned men and was among the most important women ever to exercise power behind the throne in the Roman Empire; 78.193

Juno   Roman queen of the gods, wife of Jupiter, counterpart of the Greek goddess Hera; 63.61

jupe   a woman's jacket, kirtle, or bodice; 89.18

K, Ka, Ke   abbreviation used by scribes to designate the goldsmith, Hugh Keall

karat   see carat

KB   abbreviation for Knight of the Bath

Ke   see K

KG   abbreviation for Knight of the Garter

kirtle   a short jacket or blouse; a woman's gown; a skirt or outer petticoat; 59.159

knitwork   a knitted fabric; 62.83

knot   intertwined cords in the form of slackened, symmetrical knots were particularly effective as badges; knots described in the gift lists include truelove, caltrop, gordion knot, bowen knot, bourchier knot, friars knot, maltravers knot; 65.53

kntd.   abbreviation for knighted

KT   abbreviation for Knight of the Thistle

label   a narrow band or strip of linen, cloth, etc.; a fillet, ribbon, tassel; 82.131

lady-cow   a small beetle, also called a lady-bird and a lady-bug; used as an embroidery motif; often associated with the Virgin Mary, as in 'Lady Mary's bug' and good luck, as in 'God's little cow ; 84.88

laid   to embroider with gold thread or the like laid flat on the surface; 59.169

lair   A pitcher with a wide spout, used to bring water for washing the hands; see also ewer and laver; 59.22

lapis lazuli   a gemstone of bright blue colour; 88.1

lave, laver   a vessel, basin, or water-jug, usually of metal; see also ewer and lair; 81.445

lawn   a kind of fine linen, resembling cambric; an article of dress made of lawn; 59.159

li   abbreviation for pound, £, from Latin *libre*, currency symbol for pound

liam   a leash or lead for hounds; 59.109

lily-pot   a flower-pot with a lily growing in it; a representation of this, commonly occurring as a symbolic accessory in pictures of the Annunciation, and hence frequent as a religious emblem; 78.63

loose gown   overgown, hanging loosely from the shoulders, not fitting tightly to the body; 84.75

lure   an apparatus used by falconers, to recall their hawks, constructed of a bunch of feathers, to which is attached a long cord or thong and from the interstices of which, during its training, the hawk is fed; 79.88

lye pot   an ornamental vessel to hold lye for use as a hair wash; 59.39

M, Ma, Mar   abbreviation used by scribes to designate the goldsmith, Richard Martin

mace   a sceptre or staff of office, resembling in shape the weapon of war; 03.74

mademoiselle   title of respect applied also to married women whose husbands were below the rank of knighthood; 76.42

magdalen   a gilt cup with a cover; a type of covered beaker; 59.297

maidenblush   a rosy colour or glow, a very delicate pink; 97.86

maidenhair   see hair-colour

mantle   a loose, sleeveless cloak of varying length; see also Irish mantle; 79.27

manus Christi   hand of Christ; a confection made from a mixture of sugar, rose water and egg whites flavored by spices; 62.168

mar   married

marchpane   variant of marzipan

marmalade   a preserve or confection made from fruits such as quinces or oranges; 68.156

marmoset   a New World monkey; 82.114

marquetry   wooden inlaid work, as used for the decoration of furniture; 59.205

marzipan   a kind of confectionery composed of a paste of pounded almonds, sugar, etc., made up into small cakes or moulded into ornamental forms; 59.152

Matie   abbreviation for majesty; form of address to the sovereign; 62.16

mill-pick   an iron tool for producing a corrugated surface on a millstone, used in heraldry as a representation of a mill-pick ; 89.21

miniver   a squirrel fur used as a lining and trimming in costume; from the *petit-gris*, a variety of the common squirrel or the white fur of the Siberian squirrel; 84.52

moss-work   embroidery or fabric decoration resembling moss; 99.131

mount   a spherical box; 59.6

MP   abbreviation for Member of Parliament

ms, mss   abbreviation for manuscript(s)

muffler   a scarf or kerchief to cover part of the face and neck; 79.40

murrey   mulberry colour; dull purplish red or blood colour; 68.19

Muses   nine Greek goddesses who embody the arts and inspire the creation process; they are Calliope (epic poetry),

Clio (history), Erato (love/erotic poetry), Euterpe (lyric poetry), Melpomene (tragedy), Polyhymnia (sacred poetry), Terpsichore (choral dance and song), Thalia (comedy), and Urania (astronomy); 75.85

musk-cat   a small, lithe-bodied, mostly arboreal mammal native to the tropics of Africa and Asia, ranking in size and appearance between the fox and the weasel; the strong-smelling secretion from this animal highly was valued as a fragrance and stabilizing agent for perfume; also called civet; 59.109

musk water   water flavoured or perfumed with musk; 59.176

nail   a measure of length for cloth; 2¼ inches, or the sixteenth part of a yard; 76.1

née   originally called, see also alias; term not used until 1700s

Neptune   Roman god of the sea, corresponding to the Greek Poseidon; 77.870

net, network   a piece of fine mesh-work used as a part of dress; 62.137

nether   designating the lower or bottom part of a thing; 85.110

newmaking   to make again or anew; 59.455

night coif   see coif

nightgear   nightclothes; 77.2

night gown   long over-gown, worn for warmth both indoors and out; 77.3

night-rail   a loose wrap, dressing-jacket, or dressing-gown; see also rail; 63.124

noble   a gold coin, first minted by Edward III; an old noble or Henry noble was valued at 10*s* in 1543 while a George noble was worth 6*s* 8*d*. In 1584 two new noble coins were minted, the single rose noble at 15*s* and the double noble at 30*s*; 63.76

nosegay   a bunch of flowers or herbs, especially sweet smelling flowers; 76.110

nvncke   variant of nunc, meaning now at the present time; 85.405

ob   abbreviation of the Latin word *obolus*, a coin worth half a *denarius*; one half penny, ½*d*

offethers   combined word, of feathers

orangeado   candied orange-peel; 98.174

Orpheus   the famous mythical musician and singer of Thrace, who was said to charm beasts and to move rocks and trees by the strains of his lyre; 67.51

ouch   a clasp, buckle, fibula, or brooch, for holding together the two sides of a garment, sometimes set with precious stones; 59.165

overthwart   passing or lying across; 85.71

ovlle, ouelle   variant of owl

ower, ore   precious metal; 59.6

owes   anything round, as the letter 'o', a circle, or orb; small circular spangles used to decorate clothing; 85.128

oz   abbreviation for ounce

P, Par   abbreviation used by scribes to designate the goldsmith, Affabel Partrige

pane   a piece, width, or strip of cloth, of which several were joined together side by side, so as to make one cloth, curtain, or garment; see also cover-pane; strips made by cutting or slashing a garment longitudinally for ornamental purposes, to show the fine stuff with which it was lined, or of which an undergarment was composed; 81.76

panade   a kind of sword or dagger; 98.19

pannier   a wicker basket of considerable size for carrying of provisions, fish or other commodities; 98.148

pantler   the household officer who supplied the bread and had charge of the pantry; one of several ceremonial positionas at the coronation of the monarch; 59.453

pantofle   in-door slippers or loose shoes; also spelled pantable; see also cork; 77.183

Par   see P

parchment lace   a kind of lace, braid, or cord, the core of which was parchment; 97.78

Paris   in Greek mythology, Paris (Roman counterpart is Alexander) was appointed by Zeus (Jupiter) to select the most beautiful goddess among Aphrodite (Venus), Athena (Diana), and Hera (Juno); see also Judgement of Paris; 63.61

partlet   a small yoke piece to cover a low neckline, often richly decorated and usually in the same material as the gown; 59.21

partigal   variant of Portuguese; also called portingale

pasmane lace   gold or silver lace of silk or other material, for decorative trimming, also spelled passamain; 59.101

pear fashion   a gilt cup shaped like a pear; 63.62

pearl, ragged   pearls of irregular form; 71.5

pearl, Scottish   freshwater pearl from Scottish rivers; 71.153

peasecod   the pod of the pea-plant; a pea-pod; 81.93

penknife   a small knife, used originally for making and mending quill pens; 59.220

pennyweight   a unit of weight equal to twenty-four grams; 77.417

pepper-box   a small box with a perforated lid, used for sprinkling powdered pepper; 59.402

pescod   variant of peasecod

petticoat   a garment worn by women, girls, and young children; a skirt, worn either externally, or beneath the gown or frock as part of the costume, and trimmed or ornamented; an outer, upper, or show petticoat; 62.99

petra   from Greek and Latin, denoting stone as a material; 82.200

phoenix   the bird of Arabia, a mythical bird and a type of Christ; of gorgeous plumage, fabled to be the only one of its kind, and to live five or six hundred years in the Arabian desert, after which it burnt itself to ashes on a funeral pile of aromatic twigs ignited by the sun and fanned by its own wings, but only to

emerge from its ashes with renewed youth, to live through another cycle of years; 76.150

physic   medicine; the knowledge of the human body; the art or practice of healing; 81.198

physiognomy   a representation of a face, a portrait; 71.118

piece   a length of cloth, generally twelve yards, longer than a remnant; 59.96

pied marble   a mottled or dappled marble; 71.125

pillow-bere   the case or covering over a pillow, pillow-case; 62.151

pinched up   gathered, pleated; 88.56

pineapple   the fruit of the pine tree; a pine cone; 00.126

pinked   a technique of making small cuts on the fabric surface, giving a decorative pattern; similar to slashed; 74.41

pipe   small rolls of gold and silver used as trim; 59.144

pirl   variant of purl

pistolet   a Spanish gold coin worth 5*s* 10*d* in 1560; 59.23

placard   an article of dress, sometimes richly embroidered worn beneath an open coat or gown; 68.24

plate   gilt plate; gold or silver vessels and utensils, see also gilt; 59.1, 62.102

plum   a fruit, also called a prune, damson for Damascus and Prunolyon for Lyon plum; 75.126

plunket   a grey or light blue colour, a woollen fabric of varying texture; 84.158

plush   a kind of cloth, of silk, cotton, wool, or other material, having a nap longer and softer than that of velvet; used for rich garments; also written as flush; 88.20

pocket   a sack or bag, sometimes used as a measure of quantity; originally, any small bag or pouch worn on the person; 65.24

point   see aglet

poiz   variant of poz

pomander   a mixture of aromatic substances rolled into a ball; the open-work metal containers used to hold the scented ball; 62.1

pomecitron   a fruit of the apple kind or resembling an apple plus citron; an ovate acid juicy tree-fruit with a pale yellow rind; 98.165

pomegranate   literally 'grained apple'; a large roundish many-celled berry, with many seeds, each enveloped in a pleasantly acid, juicy, reddish pulp, enclosed in a tough leathery rind of a golden or orange colour tinged with red; indigenous to Iran and Turkey, introduced into Spain by the Moors; 59.183

pommel   a ball, a round boss, knob or button; 82.28

porringer   a small basin or similar vessel of gilt plate, metal, earthenware, or wood; 78.182

portague   Portuguese gold coin, also called a crusado; its value ranged between £3 5*s* and £4 10*s*; 59.132

portingale   Portuguese; 59.218

poultry   household office under the Lord Steward which provided fruit, greens, butter, eggs and other dairy products

powdering   decoration with spots or small figures disposed as if sprinkled over a surface; the spots on a heraldic fur scattered over the field; 67.77

poz   definite or specified weight; the amount that a thing weighs; a measure or standard of weight; 59.39

Praxithea   Greek mythological figure; see *Sapient Victrix*

precious water   a medicinal mixture as a preventative against sickness; 81.195

pred   abbreviation for *predicto*, aforesaid

printed   impressed, stamped, marked, moulded; to stamp or mark a textile fabric, as silk, satin and velvet, with a pattern or decorative design using hot irons; 68.16

puffed, puft   blown up, inflated; distended by inflation; stuffed or padded so as to swell out; gathered in so as to produce a soft swelling mass; 03.147

pull, pulling   to draw the lining out through slashes in a sleeve or garment so as to display it; 65.2

pure   of fur, trimmed or cut down so as to show one colour only; the grey fur of the back of the squirrel in winter, without any of the white of the belly; the white belly part of these furs, with the dark or grey sides trimmed off; half-pured miniver, in which a narrow strip of the grey colour was left at the edges; 99.97

purl   thread or cord made of twisted gold or silver wire, used for bordering and embroidering; a series or chain of ornamental, minute loops or twists; 63.79

purled   ornamented with or as with an edging of minute twisted loops; to pleat or frill like a ruff; to frill the edge of; 59.144

Pyramus and Thisbe   a love story narrated in verse in Ovid's *Metamorphoses*; 68.169

qtr   abbreviation for quarter, one fourth (¼)

qtr di   abbreviation for half of a quarter, (3/8); see also di qtr (5/8)

quill   a hollow stem or stalk; the tube or barrel of a feather; the feather of a large bird formed into a pen by pointing and slitting the lower end of the barrel; a toothpick made of a quill; 71.86

quilted   padded with some soft substance held in position by being sewn as in a quilt, composed of several layers sewn together, usually by stitches arranged in some regular or decorative pattern; 75.92

quoshon   see cushion

quoyfe   variant of coif

rabatine   a low collar; 89.74

ragged pearl   see pearl, ragged

ragged staff   an untrimmed stick with projecting stumps used for the badge or crest of the Dudley family including the Earls of Warwick and Leicester; 81.164

rail   a garment, dress, mantle, cloak; a piece of linen or other cloth formerly worn about the neck by women; a neckerchief; see also night-rail; 63.71

raised   pattern given to the surface of satin or velvet pile by scraping it with a sharp knife in such a manner as to leave a raised pattern; 65.35

rasp   a twilled material, similar to saye or grosgrain, made in both silk and wool; a ribbed band, a raised ridge in a knitted cloth, characterized by a distinct cord or ridge; 64.146

real   variant of royal

rebato   a kind of stiff collar worn by both sexes from about 1590 to 1630; a collar of this kind used to support a ruff, or a frame of wire serving the same purpose; 88.128

remt   abbreviation for remnant

remnant   a length of cloth, generally five to ten yards, shorter than a piece; 59.66

rewed, rowed   things set or arranged in a straight line; in knitting, one line of stitches; 78.173

rial   variant of royal

rive   a stream or rill, the seashore; 98.138

roll   a round cushion or pad of hair or other material, forming part of a woman's head-dress; a support for a gown or petticoat, used instead of a farthingale; 88.137

roots of Spain   see pomegranates

rosewater   water with the essence of roses; used as a perfume; 03.186

rowed   variant of rewed

royal   a gold coin valued at 14*s*. 6*d*. in 1549; variant spellings include rial, real, ryal; 59.65

roundel   a circle; a circular form, appearance, or arrangement; a circular wooden trencher; 68.71

russet   a brown color with a reddish tinge, similar to copper and ginger; 59.121

ryal   variant of royal

s.   abbreviation for shilling, from the Latin *solidus*; twenty shillings equal one pound or one sovereign; 59.3

sable   a small mammal with highly valued light or mid-brown fur related to the marten; native to Russia; 82.93

sackbut   a musical instrument of the Renaissance; a bass trumpet with a slide like that of a trombone for altering the pitch; a player on the sackbut, also spelled sagbut; 59.178

sackcloth   a material for dresses probably similar to canvas, made from hemp or linen, in various weights; used for doublets and for linings; 68.81

sacrifice   implies an 'altar' on which the victim is placed; figurative uses are often associated with references to a metaphorical altar; 89.15

safeguard   an outer protective skirt or petticoat, guards other clothes from soiling, see also guard; 65.10

sagbut   variant of sackbut

salamander   an amphibian similar to a lizard, supposedly able to resist flame for a time, but not able to live in or quench the fire; 77.171

salt   a vessel used for holding salt, usually gilt plate, sometimes with a cover; 59.67

Sapient Victrix   a wise female victor; a reference to Greek mythological figure, Praxithea, the wife of Erectheus, King of Athens. She was willing to sacrifice her own daughter before the battle to assure victory for the city of Athens; 75.63

sarceonet   a very fine and soft silk material made both plain and twilled, in various colours; 62.99

say   a cloth of fine texture resembling serge; sometimes partly of silk, subsequently entirely of wool; 75.112

sea-water green   a shade of green, aquamarine; 88.24

sergeant   titles of certain officers of the Royal Household; the name of a specified department, as sergeant of the cellar, sergeant of the pastry, sergeant-surgeon; 59.214

Sectra   Lucius Septimius Severus, Roman Emperor, 192-211, married Julia Domna, spent time in Britain in 208, and died at York in 211; 78.193

Seigneur   from the French *Signiour* and the Italian *Signore*, both from the Latin

Senior, an elder, a title of respect; 79.454

serton variant of certain

sewer server, household servant who superintended the arrangement of the table, the seating of the guests, and the tasting and serving of the dishes

shadow a woman's headdress, or a portion of a headdress, projecting forward so as to shade the face; 81.142

shank the narrow part of a spoon-handle; 63.161

sheaf a large bundle of reaped cereal plants, usually wheat or rye; 85.64

shilling a unit of currency, valued at twelve pence, from the Latin *solidus*, abbreviated as *s.*; twenty shillings equals one pound or one sovereign; 59.3

ship a vessel, utensil, ornament, shaped like a ship; an incense boat; 59.459

shoe footwear; 77.183; a spade-like implement for digging; 84.174

show see shoe

sickle an agricultural implement with a curved or crescent form and a serrated cutting edge; an ornamental design in metal-work or embroidery; 85.64

Sidon a city in Lebanon, known in Phoenician times for its production of glass and purple dye, a city of Phoenicia known for its filth; 67.162

Signiour, *Signore* variant of Seigneur

sinkfoil variant of cinquefoil

sipers variant of cypress

sithrus variant of citron

sirrop variant of syrup

skewed set obliquely or aslant, possibly fabric on a bias; 71.40

skimskin a muff, a covering of a cylindrical shape into which both hands may be thrust from opposite ends to keep them warm, of embroidered fabric, leather or fur; see also snufkin/snoskin; 81.172

sleeve the part of a garment which covers the arm, a separate article of dress; 59.21

sleeve-silk silk thread capable of being separated into smaller filaments for use in embroidery; 67.73

slip a needlework design, usually applique, representing a cutting of a plant with flowers, leaves and stems; 97.30

smock a woman's undergarment; a shift or chemise; 59.38

smoke variant of smock

snuffer an instrument used for snuffing out, candles, usually in pairs; 59.201

snufskin/snoskin a muff, a covering of a cylindrical shape into which both hands may be thrust from opposite ends to keep them warm, of embroidered fabric, leather or fur; see also skimskin; 76.23

soope variant of soap; 71.165

sound of the belly the front bulging surface of a violin or other stringed instrument; 67.164

sovereign a gold coin minted in England from the time of Henry VII, one sovereign equals one pound or twenty shillings; 59.2

spade a tool for digging; 84.174

spark a small diamond, ruby, or other precious stone; 64.131

Speculum Virtutis Mirror of Virtue; 88.125

spinel a gem or precious stone of a red or scarlet colour, closely resembling the true ruby; 98.16

sprig an ornament in the form of a sprig or spray, especially one made of diamonds; 88.19

square the term for the square neckline of a smock, or, in the case of a high necked smock, the area of the chest revealed by the square neckline of the gown worn over it; 62.132

staff, stave a stick carried in the hand as an aid in walking or climbing or as a weapon; 76.26

standish a stand containing ink, pens and other writing materials and accessories; an inkstand; also, an inkpot; 59.220

starcher a servant of the bedchamber who starched linen and other fabrics

stare a bird of the genus *sturmus*; a starling; 85.150

steel a steel rod, fitted with a handle, used for sharpening knives; 59.138

steyer variant of stair

stitched embroidered, worked with ornamental stitches; 79.143

stomacher an ornamental covering for the chest, often covered with jewels, worn under the lacing of the bodice; 88.101

stole, stowle variant of stool; 59.150

stone a reference to a semi-precious or precious gemstone; see also heliotrope, touchstone, bezoar stone, cloudstone, bugle, bugle, crystal, spark, diamond; 62.115

stop, stoup a pail or bucket; a holy-water stoup; a pitcher, flagon, tankard; 62.296

strainer a utensil or device for straining, filtering, or sifting; 59.453

strena gifts exchanged at New Year's as well as the ritual of the exchange; *étrenne* in French and handsel in English

stuff 'of like stuff', constructed of similar material; 75.32; stuffing or padding; 76.22; also fabric not yet made up into garments

succade fruit preserved in sugar, either candied or in syrup; sweetmeats of candied fruit or vegetable products; also spelled sucket; 62.88

sugar loaf a moulded conical mass of hard sugar made by passing syrup through already refined sugar in a sugar pot; 59.183

suit a set of garments intended to be worn together at the same time; 75.115

Susanna apocryphal addition to the Old Testament Book of Daniel, known as Susanna and the Elders; Susanna is falsely accused of promiscuity by the Elders who observe her bathing. She is saved from execution when they disagree upon the type of tree under which the lovers supposedly met; 71.138

swan's-down the down or soft under-plumage of the swan, used for dress-trimmings, powder-puffs; 85.166

sweetbag a small bag or sachet filled with a scented or aromatic substance, used for perfuming the air or clothes; 59.83

sweet-briar see eglantine rose or honeysuckle

sweet water a sweet-smelling liquid preparation; a liquid perfume or scent, such as rose water; 59.216

synamond variant of cinnamon

syrup juice of Syria, a thick sweet liquid, consisting of a concentration of sugar in water or fruit juice, sometimes used as a medium for medication; 59.162

tabine watered silk, a thin silk of taphata weave, given a watered or moire finish, with a slight nap, sometimes enriched with silver or gilt thread; 97.30

taffeta a finely woven silk fabric mainly used for linings; sometimes woven with raised stripes which could be cut and left like the pile of velvet; see also tuft taffeta; 59.7

tag, tagged variant of aglet; an ornament consisting of a gold or silver tag or pendent attached to a fringe or worn on the dress; 71.162

tankard a drinking-vessel, formerly made of wooden staves and hooped; now a tall one-handled jug or mug, of silver or gold gilt, now of pewter, with a lid, a tapering body and two horizontal ribs or bars, see also hanse pot; 59.336

taphata variant of taffeta

tapnet a basket made of rushes, in which figs are imported; also a conventional measure of quantity, twenty pounds; 67.161

Tartarian of or pertaining to Tartary in Asia or the Tartars; 62.386

tawny the colour of a lion, a rusty reddish tan; 62.38

thwart variant of overthwart, passsing across; 85.71

tie an ornamental knot or bow of ribbon, head-tie, a head-band or scarf worn by women, that with which anything is tied; 71.154

tiffany a fine, transparent silk fabric, richly coloured and decorated; also a sheer fabric or fine gauze, cobweb lawn or any woven fabric of fine quality; 97.70

tills   a small box, casket, or closed compartment, contained within or forming part of a larger box, chest, or cabinet; used for safe keeping of valuables and documents; 62.174

tinsel   silk woven with metal threads, silver or gold; see baudekin; 62.122

tippet   A garment, usually of fur or wool, covering the shoulders, or the neck and shoulders; a cape or short cloak, often with hanging ends; 03.168

tissue   a rich kind of cloth, often interwoven with gold or silver; 69.2

tot   variant spelling of total

ton   variant of tun

touchstone   a very smooth, fine-grained, black or dark-coloured variety of quartz or jasper, used for testing the quality of gold and silver alloys by the colour of the streak produced by rubbing them upon it; 68.144

train   an elongated part of a robe or skirt trailing behind on the ground; 64.125

trencher   a flat piece of wood, square or circular, on which meat was served and cut up; a plate or platter of wood, metal, or earthenware; 59.453

troche   a cluster of three or more tines at the summit of a deer's horn; distinguished from a *fourche* (fork) of two tines; an ornamental button consisting of or set with three or more jewels in a bunch; 68.73

true-love knot   the whorl of four leaves with the single flower or berry in the midst suggesting the figure of a true-love knot, a name for the herb Paris; see also knot; 85.5

tuft taffeta   a kind of taffeta with a pile or nap arranged in tufts, see also taffeta; 71.18

tun   a large cask or barrel for wine, ale, or beer; 84.173

turkey   designating workmanship or manufacture from a foreign land (possibly, but not limited to Turkey), something from far away, not English or European; 63.152

twelve signs of Zodiac   certain constellations that are supposed to resemble living creatures and are twelve in number, viz. Aries the ram, Taurus the bull, Gemini the twins, Cancer the crab, Leo the lion, Virgo the virgin, Scorpio the scorpion, Sagittarius the archer, Capricorn the horned goat, Aquarius the water bearer, and Pisces the two fishes; 85.57

twist   thread or cord composed of two or more fibres or filaments of hemp, silk, wool, cotton, or the like, wound round one another; often with a defining word, such as silk, woollen, cotton, gold or silver twist; 78.115

unshorn   not shorn, cut, or cropped; unshorn velvet; usually understood to mean velvet with the looped side uncut, but perhaps cut velvet with a fairly long pile which had not been shorn to make it even; 62.132

upside   the upper side or surface of a thing; the upper half or part; 89.9

valance   draped edging of a specified material; 67.139

vane   variant of fan

varnished   coated with varnish, painted; 81.122

vaved   variant of waved

veil   a thin, lightweight fabric of mesh, net, or similar material cloth or a silk head covering worn by women, also used to describe a loose mantle or gown with sleeves, when made of very light material; 71.77

vellat   variant of velvet

vellum   a kind of parchment prepared from the skin of calves, lambs or kids and used especially for writing, painting, or binding; 84.192

velvet   a textile fabric of silk having a short, dense, and smooth piled surface; also with defining terms as cut, raised, and stamped velvet; 59.1

Venice gold   gold or silver-gilt thread manufactured by the Venetians and imported from Venice; 59.51

Venice silver   silver-gilt thread manufactured by the Venetians and imported from Venice; 64.2

Venus   the Roman goddess of beauty and love, counterpart of the Greek goddess Aphrodite; 63.61

vetus   Latin for old, ancient, antiquity, having been in existence for a long time; 76.195

Victory   the Roman goddess representing or typifying victory; counterpart of the Greek goddess Nike; 75.63

Victrix   see *Sapient Victrix*

vidame   formerly in France, the one who held lands from a bishop as his representative and defender in temporal matters; 71.363

virgins   parable of the ten virgins, found in Matthew 25:1-13, tells the story of the five wise virgins who are prepared for the bridegroom's arrival and are rewarded contrasted with the foolish five who are not prepared and are excluded; 84.190

virginals   a keyed musical instrument resembling a spinet, but set in a box or case without legs, referred to as a pair of virginals, applied to a single instrument; 59.204

Virtute   valor, virtue; see woman of valor; 78.198

viscount   a member of the British peerage, ranking between an earl and a lord; in Continental usage, the son or younger brother of a count; 59.23

viscountess   a member of the British peerage, ranking between a countess and a baroness; the wife of a viscount; 59.51

vizard   a mask, visor; 59.178

wainscot   a superior quality of oak boarding imported from Russia, Germany, and Holland, used for fine panel-work; 94.183

waistcoat   a short garment, often elaborate and costly, worn by women about the upper part of the body; 63.86

waist girdle   see girdle

warden   an old variety of baking pear; 59.182

wardens condite   a pear-shaped sweet-meat, usually flavoured with jargonelle-pear essence; also called wardens gilt; see also condite; 78.186

watchet   light blue or greenish blue colour; 76.99

water   with various qualifying words, denoting kinds of water distinguished by their properties; gift lists include musk-water, precious water, rose-water, sea-water, and sweetwater; 59.176

waved   an undulating line or streak of colour; 81.91

wedge   an ingot of gold, silver, other precious metal; 68.93

wicker   a pliant twig or small rod, usually of willow, used for making baskets and other objects; 62.166

wire   pieces of fine coiled wire covered with silk and gold used for embroidery; 78.15

wch   variant of which

wt, wth   variants of with

woman of valor   a reference to Proverbs 31, a woman called *Virtute*; 78.198

woodbine   see honeysuckle

woodvine   common types are English ivy, trumpet creeper, and wintercreeper; 82.88

wreath   something wound or coiled into a circular shape or form; a twisted band or fillet; 81.92

writhen   twisted out of regular shape or form; 59.453

writing board   a board on which to rest the paper while writing; 68.166

ybanes   variant of ebony

ypocras   variant of hippocras

Appendix 3
Offices and Occupations

See Editorial Procedures for an explanation of this Appendix.

Part 1 – State and Household

Principal Officers of State
>Lord Chancellor
>Lord Keeper of the Great Seal (an alternate title for the Lord Chancellor)
>Lord Treasurer
>Lord Privy Seal
>Privy Councillors
>Principal Secretary
>Chancellor of the Exchequer
>Chancellor of the Duchy of Lancaster
>Lord High Admiral
>Treasurer of the Navy

Officers of Law
>Attorney General
>Solicitor General
>Lord Chief Justice of the Queen's Bench
>Lord Chief Justice of the Common Pleas
>Master of the Court of Wards
>Receiver of the Court of Wardss
>Master of Requests

Officers and Divisions of the Royal Household
>**Lord Chamberlain**—responsible for the sovereign's ceremonies, entertainments, and social life; household above stairs
>>[The Chamber: composed of the Privy, Great, Presence, and Bed Chambers]
>Vice-Chamberlain
>Treasurer of the Chamber
>Departments and Offices
>>**Apothecaries** see under Physicians
>>**Arms** Sergeants at Arms Kings of Arms: Garter, Clarenceux, Norroy Heralds: Chester, Lancaster, Richmond, Somerset, Windsor, York Pursuivants: Bluemantle, Portcullis, Rouge Croix, Rouge Dragon
>>**Artificer** Arrow-Head Maker, Bowyer, Buckle Maker, Clock-Keeper, Clockmaker, Coffer-Maker, Crossbow Maker, Cutler, Distiller of Waters, Embroiderer, Featherbed Dresser, Fletcher, Glazier, Gunmaker, Herber, Librarian, Locksmith, Moletaker, Pinner, Planter of Trees, Printer, Ratcatcher, Sergeant Painter, Shipwright, Silkwoman, Skinner, Stationer, Strewer of Herbs, Watchmaker, Weaver, Wheelwright

Astronomers   see under Physicians
Barges and Boats   Master of the Barges, Watermen
Chapel Royal   Dean, Sub-Dean, Gentlemen, Master of the Children,
  Children of the Chapel
Chaplain   Clerk of the Closet, Keeper of the Oratory, Almoner
Dancing Master
Queen's Dwarf
Queen's Fool
Gentlemen Pensioners   Captain, Lieutenant, Standard Bearer, Clerk of the
  Check, Gentlemen Pensioners, Harbinger
Great Chamber   Doorkeeper, Groom, Groom Porter, Harbinger, Messenger,
  Page, Yeomen
Harbinger
Henchmen   Members, Schoolmaster, Page
Heralds
Jewels and Plate   Master of the Jewel House, Clerk, Grooms, Yeomen
Keeper of the Swans
Musician   Bagpipes, Drummer, Flute Player, Harp, Instrument Maker,
  Lutenist, Minstrel, Organmaker, Rebeck, Sackbut, Sergeant, Trumpet,
  Violin, Viol, Virginal Player
Nurse   Nurse, Midwife, Rocker, Wetnurse
Physician   Physicians, Surgeons, Apothecaries, Astronomers
Posts   Master of the Posts
Outer Chamber   Carver, Cupbearer, Esquires for the Body, Gentlemen Usher,
  Grooms of the Chamber, Groom Porter, Page of the Chamber, Sewer,
  Surveyor of the Dresser, Yeomen Messenger, Yeomen of the Guard, Yeomen
  Usher
Guard   Captain of the Guard, Standard Bearer, Clerk of the Cheque,
  Messenger
Presence Chamber   Gentlemen Waiter, Maids of Honour, Sewer for the
  Body, Page
Privy Chamber   Chief Gentlewoman of the Privy Chamber, Gentlewomen
  and Ladies, Gentlemen, Gentlemen Usher, Grooms, Keeper of Queen's Jewels
  Joiner of the Privy Chamber, Laundress for the Body, Pages of Honour,
  Sewer of the Chamber, Sewer for the Queen, Starcher, Yeomen
Bedchamber   Chamberer/Gentlewoman of the Bedchamber
Requests   Master of Requests
Robes, Wardrobe of   Master of the Robes, Brusher, Clerk Comptroller,
  Furrier, Groom, Messenger, Page, Tailor, Yeomen
Schoolmaster
Secretariat   Secretary for French, Secretary for Latin, Clerk of the Signet,
  Clerk of the Privy Council
Surgeons   see under Physicians
Surveyor of Ways
Wardrobe of Beds   Master, Clerk, Groom, Yeomen
Wardrobe, Removing   Clerk, Groom, Keeper of the Removing Wardrobe,
  Keeper of Standing Wardrobe, Yeomen, Page

Lord Steward—responsible for functioning of the household, culinary and domestic needs of sovereign; household below stairs (formerly Lord Great Master of the Household)

Treasurer of the Household

Comptroller of the Household

Cofferer

Clerks of the Board of Greencloth

Clerk Comptrollers

(The Board of Greencloth is comprised of the preceding six officials)

Departments and Personnel

    Acatery Clerk, Gentleman, Sergeant, Groom, Yeomen, Purveyor

    Almonry Children, Groom, Sub-Almoner, Yeoman

    Bakehouse Sergeant, Clerk, Groom, Yeomen, Yeoman Purveyor

    Boiling House Groom, Yeomen

    Buttery Gentleman, Groom, Yeomen, Purveyor, Page

    Cellar Sergeant, Gentleman, Groom, Yeomen, Page

    Chandlery Sergeant, Groom, Yeomen, Yeoman Purveyor, Page

    Counting House Sergeant, Groom, Yeomen, Messenger, Cofferer's Clerk

    Confectionery Sergeant, Groom, Yeomen, Page

    Ewery Sergeant, Groom, Yeomen, Page

    Gate Sergeant Porter, Yeoman Porter At Gate, Groom Porter at Gate

    The Hall Marshal of the Hall, Server, Surveyor, Gilder, Bellringer, Wine Porter, Children

    Harbinger Gentlemen, Groom

    Kitchen, Privy Chief Clerk, Clerk, Groom, Queen's Master Cook, Doorkeeper, Porter, Scourer, Soil-Carrier, Yeomen

    Kitchen, Household Cook, Clerk, Groom, Yeoman, Children, Doorkeeper, Porter, Scourer, Soil-Carrier, Yeomen

    Larder Sergeant, Gentleman, Groom, Page, Yeomen, Children

    Laundry Groom, Page, Yeomen

    Pantry Sergeant, Bread-Bearer, Groom, Yeomen, Children

    Pastry Sergeant, Clerk, Groom, Yeomen, Children

    Pitcher House Groom, Page, Yeomen

    Porter Groom, Sergeant Porter, Yeomen

    Poultry Clerk, Groom, Purveyor, Sergeant, Yeomen

    Scalding House Groom, Page, Yeomen, Children

    Scullery Clerk, Sergeant, Groom, Page, Scourer, Yeomen, Children

    Spicery Clerk, Grocer, Yeomen

    Wafery Groom, Yeomen

    Woodyard Sergeant, Groom, Woodbearer, Page, Yeomen, Children

Master of the Horse—Responsible for stables, races, breeds of horses, transportation and all outside activities

    Bears and Mastiffs Master, Sergeant, Groom, Yeomen, Children

    Carts Clerk, Groom, Yeomen

    Coachmen

    Crossbows Master, Sergeant, Groom, Yeomen, Children

    Equerries

    Falconer Master, Sergeant, Groom, Keeper, Yeomen, Children

    Footmen

Harbinger
The Hawks   Master, Sergeant, Groom, Keeper, Taker, Yeomen, Children
Hunting: Harriers and Hart Hounds   Master, Sergeant, Groom, Keeper, Yeomen, Children
Hunting: Buckhounds   Master, Sergeant, Groom, Keeper, Yeoman, Children
Hunting: Otter Hounds   Master
Littermen
Pages of Honour
Riders
Stables   Armourer, Bitmaker, Clerk, Under Clerk, Clerk of the Avery, Clerk of the Stables, Stable Keeper, Purveyor and Granator, Farrier, Surveyor, Porter, Groom of the Stable, Page
Waymaker

Standing Offices—Household-related departments, each under its own Master; officers were members of the Household, subject to the supervision of the Lord Chamberlain

Armoury   Master, Clerk, Groom, Yeomen
Mint   Master, Clerk, Groom, Yeomen
Ordnance   Master, Clerk, Groom, Yeomen
Revels   Master of the Revels, Clerk, Groom, Yeomen
Tents   Master, Comptroller, Clerk, Groom, Yeomen
Toils   Master, Groom, Yeoman, Officer of the Leash, Children of the Leash
Wardrobe, Great   Master, Arrasmaker, Clerk, Deputy Master, Embroiderer, Groom, Porter, Tailor, Tradesman, Yeomen
Works   Surveyor, Master, Clerk, Comptroller, Paymaster, Purveyor Artisan, Bricklayer, Glazier, Joiner, Laborer, Master Carpenter, Mason, Plasterer, Sergeant Plumber, Surveyor of the Mines

Part 2: Alphabetical Listing of Offices and Positions held by Gift Exchange Participants (This listing does not include office holders and individuals who did not participate in the Gift Exchanges)

Alderman of London   William Dane, John More, Richard Martin, Thomas Rivett
Ambassador/Envoy:
  From England To France
    Thomas Hoby, Henry Killigrew, Henry Neville, Henry Norris, Roger North, Amias Paulet, Thomas Smith, Edward Stafford, Nicholas Throckmorton, Francis Walsingham

  From England To Russia
    Francis Cherry

  To England From Duke John Casimir, Count Palatine
    Peter Beutterich

  To England From Denmark
    Christian Barnikou, Mathias Budde, Nicholas Cragius, Arild Huitfeldt, Hans Neukom, Jacob Rastrup, George Schuavenius

  To England From Emperor
    John Preyner, Philippe de Maldeghem

To England From France
> Monsieur du Bourg, Arthur de Cossé, Bertrand de Salignac Fénelon, Jean de Ferrières, Prégent de la Fin, Guillaume Fouquet de la Varenne, Paul de Foix, George Fremin, Nicolas des Gallars, Hiéronime Gondi, Christoph de Harlay, Charles de la Chatre, Charles de L'Aubespine, Nicholas Martel, Michel de Castelnau Mauvissière, Monsieur de Ninsonan, Beriginer Portall, Phillippe du Plessis-Mornay, Pierre Clausse, Charles Angennes de Rambouillet, Monsieur de Saverne, François de Scepeaux, Michel de Seurre, Charles de Teligny, Monsieur de Torsac, Jacques de Vray

To England From Low Countries
> Jean Boischet, Noel Caron, François Halewyn, Frederic Perrenot, Ludwig Stolberg, William Suderman

To England From Morocco
> Mushac Reyz

To England From King of Navarre
> Paul Choart de Buzenval

To England From Portugal
> Don Juan Rodriguez de Souza, Francesco Giraldi

To England From Russia
> Ivan Grigorievich, alias Andrei Grigorievich Savin

To England From Duke of Savoy
> Count Montreal, Rupertino Solari de Moretta

To England From Scotland
> Lewis Bellenden, Patrick Gray, William Maitland, Robert Melville, Robert Pitcairn, George Young

To England From Spain
> Bernardino de Mendoza, Gomez Suarez de Figueroa Count of Feria

To England From Sweden
> Dionysius Burreus, Nils Göransson Gyllenstierna, James Hill, Ericson Johnson, Andrew Keith, Johannes Nicholai, Nicholas Rasche

To England From Duke of Wurttemberg
> Adam Viman

Archdeacon   George Carew
Armourer   Alan Bawdenson, Lewis Byllyard, William Byllyard, Thomas Laverock
Attorney-General   Edward Coke, Thomas Egerton, Gilbert Gerard, John Popham
Bitmaker   Thomas Doughty
Buttery   Bird, Powell
Captain of the Guard   Edward Rogers, Francis Knollys, Christopher Hatton, Walter Ralegh
Captain/Governor of Guernsey   Francis Chamberlain, Thomas Leighton
a captain of Ireland   Brian McPhelim O'Neill
Captain of the Isle of Wight   Edward Horsey, George Carey
Caretaker   Cox
Cellar   Miller, Reme, Piers Griffin
Chamberer   see Bedchamber, Gentlewomen of the
Chancellor of the Duchy of Lancaster   Ambrose Cave, Robert Cecil, John Fortescue, Thomas Heneage, Ralph Sadler, Francis Walsingham

Chancellor of the Exchequer   John Fortescue, Walter Mildmay
Chester Herald   Robert Cooke
Chief Almoner at Coronation   Edward Braye
Chief Butler at Coronation   Thomas Leigh
Chief Gentlewoman of the Privy Chamber   Catherine Astley, Blanche Parry
  (Mary Radcliffe performed function, never received title)
Chief Pantler at Coronation   Ambrose Dudley
Children of the Hall Place   unnamed
Clarenceux King of Arms   Robert Cooke
Clerk of the Closet   William Absolon, John Thornborough
Clerk of the Jewels and Plate   Nicholas [I] Bristow, Nicholas [II] Bristow
Clerk of the Privy Council   Edmund Tremayne
Clerk of the Spicery   Henry Trafford
Clockmaker   Randall/Randolph Bull, Nicholas Urseau
Coffermaker   John Greene
Comptroller of the Household   Thomas Parry, Edward Rogers, James Croft,
  William Knollys, Edward Wotton
Cook   Thomas Alderton, John Bartlett, Lawrence
Crossbowmaker   Alan Bawdenson, Lewis Byllyard, William Byllyard, Thomas
  Laverock
Customer of London   Thomas Smith
Cutler   Richard Matthew, Christopher Giles
Dancing Master   Thomas Cardell
Dean of Canterbury   Nicholas Wotton
Dean of the Chapel Royal   George Carew
Dean of Salisbury   Peter Vannes, John Bridges
Dean of Westminster   William Bill
Dean of Winchester   Francis Newton
Dean of Windsor   George Carew
Earl Marshal of England   Thomas Howard, George Talbot, Robert Devereux
Ewery   Prince
Farmer (of Customs)   George Mantell
Footman   Anthony Bennett, Thomas Duck, Richard Hughes, Hugh Miller, John
  Read, George Stone
Fruiterer   Nicholas Harris
Garter King of Arms   Gilbert Dethick, Robert Cooke (acting, not appointed),
  William Dethick
Gentleman of the Black Rod   Simon Bowyer, Anthony Wingfield
Gentleman of the Privy Chamber   John Astley, George Bridgeman, Alfonso
  Ferrabosco, Christopher Hatton, Thomas Heneage, Thomas Leighton, John
  Stanhope
Gentleman of the Robes   Thomas Gorges
Gentlemen Usher   Simon Bowyer, John Frankwell, Robert King, Anthony Light,
  Robert Newport, Piers Pennant, Anthony Wingfield
Gentlemen Usher of the Privy Chamber   Dru Drury, George Howard
Gentlewomen of the Bedchamber   Catherine Astley, Elizabeth Berkeley, Jane
  Brussells, Dorothy Broadbelt, Elizabeth Brooke, Frances Brooke, Elizabeth
  Carew, Elizabeth Drury, Margaret Hawkins, Lucy Hyde, Catherine [I] Knollys,
  Elizabeth Marbury, Catherine Newton, Anne Norton (Coppyn), Elizabeth
  Norton (Raynsford), Catherine Paget, Nazareth Paget, Blanche Parry, Mary

Scudamore, Dorothy Stafford, Anne [II] Vavasour, Audrey Walsingham, Elizabeth Wingfield

Gentlewomen of the Privy Chamber   Anne Askew, Catherine Astley, Catherine [I] Berkeley, Mary Bertie, Elizabeth Brooke, Jane Brussells, Elizabeth Brydges, Mary Brydges, Anne [I] Carey, Bridget Carr, Bridget Cave, Elizabeth Cavendish, Mary Cheke, Catherine Clark, Lettice Devereux, Dorothy Edmonds, Elizabeth Fiennes, Elizabeth [II] Grey, Elizabeth Guildford, Isabella Harington, Elizabeth Haynes, Anne Heneage, Anne [II] Herbert, Catherine [I] Howard, Frances [II] Howard, Margaret [I] Howard, Margaret [II] Howard, Catherine [I] Knollys, Elizabeth Leighton, Catherine Paget, Bridget [II] Manners, Amy Marvyn, Anne Parry, Blanche Parry, Mary Radcliffe, Margaret Russell, Philadelphia Scrope, Elizabeth Shelton, Mary Sidney, Mary Sutton, Elizabeth Throckmorton, Elizabeth Vere, Susan Vere, Audrey Walsingham, Elizabeth Wolley, Margaret York

Glazier   James Nicholson

Goldsmith   Robert Brandon, Randall/Randolph Bull, William Cater, Thomas Conell, John Everard, Everard Everdice, Abraham Harderet, Hugh Keall, John Keyne, John Lonison, Richard Martin, Thomas Middleton, Affabel Partridge, J.P. (John Penford or John Pilkening), Robert Raynes, Ralph Robinson, John Spilman, John Williams

Grocer   Dunston Añes, Lawrence Sheriff, William Smallwood

Groom of the Chamber   John Bybee, James Eaton, John Llewelyn, Peter Pamlyn, John Read, William Stone, Walter Trimmell

Groom of the Jewels and Plate   Richard Astley, Stephen Fulwell, Nicholas Huttofte, John Pigeon, Nicholas Pigeon

Groom of the Privy Chamber   John Astley, Thomas Astley, George Bridgeman, Edward Carey, John Baptist Castilion, Edward Darcy, Edward Denny, Dru Drury, Thomas Gorges, William Killigrew, Thomas Knyvett, Thomas Lichfield, Henry Middlemore, Ferdinando Richardson alias Heyborne, Henry Seckford, Michael Stanhope, John Tamworth

Gunmaker   Alan Bawdenson, Lewis Byllyard, William Byllyard, Thomas Laverock

Haberdasher   Thomas Allen, Henry Billingsley, Richard Graves, Thomas Smith

Harbinger   Page

Ironmonger   William Dane

Jeweller   Abraham Harderet, John Spilman

Keeper of Great Wardrobe   Edward Waldegrave, John Fortescue

Keeper of Hampton Court   John Frankwell

Keeper of the Privy Purse   Henry Seckford, John Tamworth

Keeper of Queen's Jewels   Blanche Parry, Catherine Carey, Mary Radcliffe

Keeper of Records at Whitehall   John James

Keeper of the Standing Wardrobe of Beds   John Wynyard, John Cotton

Keeper of Standing Wardrobe at Hampton Court   David Vincent, Richard Todd

Keeper of Wardrobe at Richmond   James Harman, Stephen Pearce

Keeper of Westminster Palace   George Bridgeman, Thomas Knyvett

Keeper of the Wildfowl of the River   John Roose

Knight Marshal of the Household   George Carey, Thomas Gerard

Larder   Browne, John Gregory

Laundry   Martin

Lieutenant of the Ordnance   William Bromfield

Lieutenant of the Tower   Edward Warner, Francis Jobson, Owen Hopton
Linen Draper   John Bradish, William Dane, William Ferrers, James Hughes
Locksmith   John Keyne
Lord High Admiral   Edward Clinton, Charles Howard
Lord Chamberlain   William Brooke, George Carey, Henry Carey, Charles
    Howard, William Howard, Thomas Radcliffe
Lord Chief Justice of the Queen's Bench   John Popham
Lord Chancellor   Thomas Bromley, Christopher Hatton
Lord Deputy of Ireland   Charles Blount, Thomas Burgh, Thomas Radcliffe,
    William Russell, Henry Sidney
Lord Justice Clerk of Scotland   Lewis Bellenden
Lord Keeper of the Great Seal   Nicholas Bacon, Thomas Egerton, John
    Puckering
Lord Lieutenant of Ireland   Robert Devereux, Thomas Radcliffe
Lord Mayor of London   Thomas Leigh, Richard Martin, Henry Billingsley
Lord Steward   Edward Clinton, Robert Dudley, Henry FitzAlan, William Herbert,
    Charles Howard, Henry Stanley
Lord Treasurer   William Paulet, William Cecil, Thomas Sackville,
Lutenist   Thomas Cardell, Mathias Mason
Maids of Honour   Christian Annesley, Cordelia Annesley, Susan Bourchier,
    Dorothy Brooke, Elizabeth Brooke, Eleanor Brydges, Mary Burgh, Frances
    Burgh, Anne [II] Carey, Elizabeth Cavendish, Catherine Cooke, Lettice
    Copinger, Abigail Digby, Frances Drury, Margaret Edgecombe, Mary Fitton,
    Elizabeth FitzGerald, Lettice FitzGerald, Catherine Grey, Elizabeth
    Guildford, Dorothy [II] Hastings, Anne Hopton, Catherine [II] Howard,
    Martha Howard, Mary Howard, Margaret Mackwilliam, Isabel Manners,
    Mary Mansell, Frances Mewtas, Jane Neville, Mary Neville, Catherine Paget,
    Margaret Radcliffe, Mary Radcliffe, Anne [II] Russell, Jane Seymour, Douglas
    Sheffield, Catherine Somerset, Elizabeth [II] Somerset, Elizabeth [I]
    Southwell, Elizabeth [II] Southwell, Gresham Thynne, Maria Tuchet,
    Elizabeth Vere, Anne [I] Vavasour, Elizabeth Vernon, Margaret Wharton,
    Anne [I] Windsor
Master Cook   William Cordell, Daniel Clark, Francis Pigott, John Smithson,
    George Webster
Master of the Court of Wards   Robert Cecil, William Cecil, Thomas Parry
Master of the Guild of Merchants   John Aylworth
Master of the Horse   Robert Devereux, Robert Dudley, Edward Somerset
Master of the Jewels and Plate   John Astley, Edward Carey
Master of the Mint   John Lonison, Richard Martin, Thomas Stanley
Master of the Ordnance   Robert Devereux, Ambrose Dudley, Richard Southwell
Master of Requests   Edmund Guest, John Mason, Thomas Wilson
Master of the Revels   Thomas Benger
Master of the Rolls   William Cordell, Thomas Egerton, Gilbert Gerard
Master of the Posts   John Mason, John Stanhope
Master of the Savoy   William Absolon, John Thornborough
Mercer   Ralph Burnell, William Ferris, Thomas Gresham, Thomas Leigh
Merchant   Thomas Allen, William Watson, John White
Mother of the Maids of Honour   Mary/Anne Aglionby, Catherine Bromfield,
    Mistress Brydges, Margaret Castilion, Elizabeth Hyde, Elizabeth Jones,
    Mistress Harvey, Anne Morice, Elizabeth Wingfield

Musician   Nicholas Andrew, Robert Baker, Andrea Bassano, Anthony Bassano, Arthur Bassano, Augustine Bassano, Baptista Bassano, Edward Bassano, Jasper Bassano, Jeronimo Bassano, John Bassano, Ludovico Bassano, Mark Anthony Bassano, Thomas Browne, George Comy, Innocent Comy, Anthony Conti, William Damon, Alphonso Ferrabosco, Caesar Galliardello, Mark Anthony Galliardello, Paul Galliardello, Samuel Garshe, Peter [I] Guy, Peter [II] Guy, Robert Hales, James Harden, William Hunnis, Albert Kellim, Frances Kellim, Thomas Kent, John Lanier, Thomas Lichfield Ambrose Lupo, Joseph Lupo, Peter Lupo, Thomas [I] Lupo, Thomas [II] Lupo, Mathias Mason, Anthony Mary Peacock, Edward Peacock, Devise Peacock, John Peacock, Walter Pierce, Ferdinando Richardson alias Heyborne, Edmund Schetts, William Treasurer, William Warren

Nurse to King Edward VI   Sibell Penne

Page of the Chamber   Thomas Goodyear, Randall Hatton, Thomas Kent, Arthur Middleton, John Parker, Edward Schetts

Page of the Wardrobe of Beds   Thomas Garton

Painter/Artist   Nicholas Belin, George Gower, Nicholas Lizard, Levina Teerlinc

Pantry   Francis Cox, Matthew

Physician   Jean Antoine Fenot, Jacques Grevin, Thomas Phaer

Principal Secretary   Robert Cecil, William Cecil, Thomas Smith, Francis Walsingham, Thomas Wilson

Printer   Christopher Barker, Robert Barker, George Bishop, John Cawood, Thomas Gemini, Richard Jugge, Edward Whitchurch, Reyner Wolfe

Privy Councillor   Nicholas Bacon, Thomas Bromley, William Brooke, George Carey, Henry Carey, Ambrose Cave, Robert Cecil, William Cecil, Edward Clinton, James Croft, Robert Devereux, Ambrose Dudley, Robert Dudley, Thomas Egerton, Henry FitzAlan, John Fortescue, Christopher Hatton, Nicholas Heath, Thomas Heneage, William Herbert, Thomas Howard, William Howard, Francis Knollys, William Knollys, John Mason, Walter Mildmay, Roger North, William Parr, Thomas Parry, Amias Paulet, William Paulet, John Perrot, William Petre, Thomas Radcliffe, Edward Rogers, Francis Russell, Richard Sackville, Thomas Sackville, Ralph Sadler, Henry Sidney, Edward Somerset, John Stanhope, Edward Stanley, Henry Stanley, Francis Talbot, George Talbot, Gilbert Talbot, Francis Walsingham, John Whitgift, Thomas Wilson, John Wolley, Edward Wotton, Nicholas Wotton

Queen's Almoner   Edmund Guest, Richard Fletcher, Edmund Freake, Anthony Watson

Queen's Apothecary   Edward Hemingway, John Hemingway, Hugh Morgan, John Rich, John Soda, William Weston

Queen's Champion at Coronation   Robert Dymoke

Queen's Chaplain   William Bill, George Carew, Peter Vannes, Nicholas Wotton, Francis Newton, William Dorrell, William Absolon, John Bridges, Thomas Dove

Queen's Dwarf   Ipolyta the Tartarian, Thomasine de Paris

Queen's Fool   Patch (Henry VIII's fool), Stone the fool (subjects of gifts, not participants)

Queens's Laundress   Agnes Byllyard, Elizabeth Smithson, Anne Twist

Queen's Physician   Walter Bayley, William Bill, Guilio Borgarucci, Lancelot Browne, Roger Gifford, William Gilbert, Robert Huicke, John James, Roderigo Lopez, Roger Marbeck, William Master, William Paddy, Richard Smith, Thomas Wendy

Queen's servant (otherwise unidentified) William Anwick, Aylworth, William Baldwin, Richard Beacher, Anthony Bickerstaff, Bright, John Bristow, Brown, Clark, Clement, Edward FitzGerald, Freer, Ganes, William Gaskin, Gent, Goodman, Heydon, Thomas Hixon, Thomas Humphrey, James, Edward Jenkins, Edward Jones, Bartholomew Knasborough, Lawrence, Leake, Lekaville, Lilly, Lingard, Long, Robert Louche, Roger Lowe, Christopher Mannington, Marshall, Morgan, Oldham, Owen, Powell, Prince, Pucket, Reme, Rogers, Rutter, Sherman, John Wheeler, Henry Wood, James Woolton

Receiver of the Court of Wards William Damsell

Schoolmaster to the Henchmen Clement Adams, Petruccio Ubaldini

Schoolmaster to King Edward VI Jean Belmaine

Scullery Burges, John Cely, John Hall, John Page

Sergeant of the Bears John Parker

Sergeant of the Cellar Robert Gardiner, Thomas Duck

Sergeant of the Pantry Robert Newport, John Ware

Sergeant of the Pastry John Betts, John Dudley, Thomas French, Ralph Batty

Sergeant of the Scullery William Smith

Sergeant Painter George Gower, Nicholas Lizard

Sewer Nicholas Brooke, Richard Holford, John White, Morgan

Silkman/Silkwoman Roger Montague, Alice Montague, Abraham Speckard, Dorothy Speckard

Skinner Roger Montague, Thomas Smith

Stationer George Bishop

Surgeon George Baker, William Goodrouse

Surveyor of the Works Lawrence Bradshaw, John Revell, Lewis Stockett

Treasurer of the Chamber John Mason, Francis Knollys, Thomas Heneage, John Stanhope

Treasurer of the Household Francis Knollys, William Knollys, Roger North, Thomas Parry

Treasurer of the Navy Fulke Greville

Vice Chamberlain of the Household Christopher Hatton, Thomas Heneage, Francis Knollys, Edward Rogers, John Stanhope

Victualler of the Navy Edward Bashe

Yeoman of the Chamber Richard Hicks, Thomas Kent, John Parker

Yeoman of the Confectionery John Bartlett

Yeoman of the Crossbows Robert Childers, Giles Churchill

Yeoman of the Jewels and Plate Robert Cranmer, John Kirkby, Richard Nightingale, Edmund Pigeon, John Pigeon, Nicholas Pigeon

Yeoman of the Kitchen Thomas Alderton, Walter Freeman

Yeoman of the Leash John Cox

Yeoman of Pitcherhouse John Cely

Yeoman of the Posts Richard Nightingale

Yeoman of the Privy Chamber Richard Hicks

Yeoman of the Removing Wardrobe of Beds Robert Cotton, John Wynyard

Yeoman of the Robes Humphrey Adderley, Ralph Hope, Richard Nightingale, Robert Pamplyn, Robert Robotham, John Roynon

Yeoman of the Stable Alexander Zinzano

Yeoman Purveyor of Wine Edward Atkinson

Yeoman Usher Thomas Conway

Appendix 4
Custodians of Gifts

See Editorial Procedures for an explanation of this Appendix.

Custody of Gifts to Household Offices, no individual named:

Office	One/Multiple Gift(s)
With the Queen	multiple
To the Chapel	one
To the Groom of the Privy Chamber	four
To Hampton Court Gallery	one
To the Leash	one
To the Office of Jewels and Plate	four
To the Privy Chamber	multiple
To the Removing Wardrobe of Beds	one
To the Robes	multiple
To the Stable	four
To the Wardrobe of Robes	multiple
unknown custody,	thirty-nine

Custody of Gifts to Household Officers:

Individual	Position	Qty Gift(s)
Thomas Alderton	Yeoman Cook	one
Dunstan Añes	Grocer	one
William Anwick	Queen's servant	one
John Astley	Master of Jewels and Plate	multiple
Richard Astley	Groom of the Jewels and Plate	two
Thomas Astley	Groom of the Privy Chamber	multiple
Robert Atkins	Groom of the Poultry	one
William Baldwin	Queen's servant	one
John Bartlett	Sergeant of the Pastry	one
Ralph Batty	Sergeant of the Pastry	one
Walter Bayley	Physician	one
Richard Beacher	Queen's servant	one
Anthony Bickerstaff	Queen's servant	one
John Birchall	Clerk of the Closet	one
Bird	Buttery	two
Cecilia Bone	Starcher	ten
Simon Bowyer	Gentleman Usher	one
Stephen Brackenbury	Gentleman Usher	one
George Bridgeman	Keeper of Westminster Palace	multiple
Bright	Queen's servant	one
John Bristow	Queen's servant	one

Nicholas Bristow	Clerk of the Jewels	two
Dorothy Broadbelt	Gentlewoman of the Bedchamber	multiple
Frances Brooke	Gentlewoman, Privy Chamber & Bedchamber	multiple
Nicholas Brooke	Sewer of the Chamber	one
Browne	Larder	one
Jane Brussells	Gentlewoman of the Bedchamber	multiple
Burges	Scullery	one
John Bybye	Groom of the Chamber	one
Thomas Cardell	Lutenist, Dancing master	one
Edward Carey	Groom of the Privy Chamber	multiple
John Baptist Castilion	Groom of the Privy Chamber	multiple
William Cecil	Principal Secretary	one
John Cely	Yeoman of the Pitcherhouse	two
Bridget Carr	Gentlewoman of the Privy Chamber	multiple
Robert Childers	Yeoman of the Crossbow	one
Children of the Hall Place	Queen's servant	one
Giles Churchill	Yeoman of the Crossbow	one
Clark	Queen's servant	one
Clement	Queen's servant	one
Elizabeth [I] Clinton	Countess of Lincoln	one
John Collier	Queen's servant	one
Thomas Conell	Queen's servant	one
Thomas Conway	Yeoman Usher	one
John Cotton	Keeper of the Standing Wardrobe, Westminster	two
Robert Cotton	Yeoman, Removing Wardrobe of Beds	multiple
John Cox	Yeoman, Removing Wardrobe of Beds	one
Cox	Caretaker	one
Cox	Pantry	one
Edward Darcy	Groom of the Privy Chamber	one
Elizabeth Drury	Gentlewoman of the Bedchamber	multiple
Thomas Duck	Sergeant of the Cellar	one
Robert Dudley	Master of the Horse	one
Christopher Eastwood	Queen's servant	one
James Eaton	Groom of the Chamber	two
Walter Fish	Tailor	one
Edward FitzGerald	Queen's servant	one
William/Richard Fludd	Queen's servant	one
John Frankwell	Keeper of Hampton Court, Gentleman Usher	two
Walter Freeman	Queen's servant	one
Freer	Queen's servant	one
Stephen Fulwell	Yeoman of the Jewels and Plate	one
Thomas Garton	Queen's servant	one
William Gaskin	Queen's servant	one
Goldwell	Queen's servant	one
Goodman	Queen's servant	one
Thomas Goodyear	Queen's servant	one
Francis Gorges	Queen's servant	one
Thomas Gorges	Groom of the Privy Chamber	multiple
John Grete	Queen's servant	one

Peter Grey	Queen's servant	one
Piers Griffin	Cellar	one
Gregory	Larder	one
Hall	Scullery	one
James Harman	Keeper of the Standing Wardrobe, Westminster	two
Randall Hatton	Page of the Chamber	one
Thomas Heneage	Treasurer of the Chamber	one
Heydon	Carts	one
Hickson	Queen's servant	one
Ralph Hope	Yeoman of the Robes	multiple
Horsman	Queen's servant	one
Catherine [I] Howard	Gentlewoman of the Privy Chamber	multiple
Charles Howard	Lord Admiral	one
Richard Hughes	Footman	one
Thomas Humphrey	Queen's servant	one
Lucy Hyde	Gentlewoman of the Bed Chamber	multiple
James	Queen's servant	one
Edward Jenkins	Queen's servant	one
Edward Jones	Queen's servant	one
William Killigrew	Groom of the Privy Chamber	multiple
Bartholomew Knasbrough	Queen's servant	one
Catherine Knollys	Gentlewoman of the Privy Chamber	one
Thomas Knyvett	Keeper of Westminster Palace	multiple
Lawrence	Cook	one
Leake	Queen's servant	one
Elizabeth Leighton	Gentlewoman of the Privy Chamber	multiple
Lekaville	Queen's servant	one
Thomas Lichfield	Groom of the Privy Chamber	multiple
Anthony Light	Gentleman Usher	one
Lilly	Queen's servant	one
Lingard	Queen's servant	one
John Llewellyn	Queen's servant	one
Long	Queen's servant	one
Robert Louche	Queen's servant	one
Roger Lowe	Queen's servant	one
Christopher Mannington	Queen's servant	one
Elizabeth Marbury	Gentlewoman of the Privy Chamber	multiple
Thomas Marbury	Sergeant of the Pantry	one
Martin	Laundry	one
Mathias Mason	Lutenist	four
Richard Master	Physician	one
Edward Mathew	Pantry	one
Robert Meekins	Chandry	one
Henry Middlemore	Groom of the Privy Chamber	four
Arthur Middleton	Page of the Chamber	two
Miller	Cellar	one
Master Morgan	Sewer	one
Morgan	Groom	one
William Norris	Servant of the Countess of Lincoln	one
Anne Norton	Gentlewoman of the Privy Chamber	one

Elizabeth Norton	Gentlewoman of the Privy Chamber	three
Oldham	Groom	one
Owen	Groom	one
John Page	Scullery	one
Mr Page	Harbinger	one
John Parker	Page, Yeoman of Chamber	three
Blanche Parry	Chief Gentlewoman of the Privy Chamber	multiple
Piers Pennant	Gentleman Usher	one
Steven Pierce	Keeper of Standing Wardrobe at Richmond	one
Powell	Buttery	one
Prince	Ewery	one
Pucket	Queen's servant	one
Mary Radcliffe	Gentlewoman of the Privy Chamber	multiple
John Read	Groom of the Chamber, Footman	one
Reme	Cellar	one
Ferdinando Richardson	Groom of the Privy Chamber	one
Rogers	Queen's servant	one
John Roynon	Yeoman of the Robes	multiple
John Russell	Clerk of the Closet	one
Rutter	Queen's servant	one
Mary Scudamore	Gentlewoman of the Bedchamber	multiple
Henry Seckford	Groom of the Privy Chamber	multiple
Sherman	Queen's servant	one
Charles Smith	Groom of the Chamber, Page of the Robes	multiple
William Smith	Sergeant of the Scullery	one
Dorothy Stafford	Gentlewoman of the Privy Chamber	multiple
William Stone	Groom of the Chamber	one
John Tamworth	Groom of the Privy Chamber	multiple
Walter Trimmell	Groom of the Chamber	two
Richard Todd	Keeper of Standing Wardrobe, Hampton Court	multiple
David Vincent	Keeper of Standing Wardrobe, Hampton Court	one
John Ware	Sergeant of the Pantry	one
John Wheeler	Queen's servant	one
Anthony Wingfield	Gentleman Usher	one
James Woolton	Queen's servant	one
John Wynyard	Yeoman, Removing Wardrobe of Beds	seven

Appendix 5
Biographical Sketches

See Editorial Procedures for an explanation of this Appendix.

Abergavenny, Lord/Baroness—see Elizabeth Neville, née Darrell, c.1577-c.1602; Frances Neville, née Manners, 1556–1576; Henry [I] Neville, 6th, 1535–1587

Abington, Dorothy—see Dorothy Broadbelt

Absolon, William (d.1586) Chaplain to the Queen, Master of the Savoy, Clerk of the Closet. Mar Jane Appleby. *CPR, 1572–1575, 1575–1578, 1578–1580*; *Index to Privy Bills*; *VCH, Bedfordshire*; PRO LC 4/59; Loftie.
Chaplain: 78.172, 78.380, 79.175, 79.388, 81.169, 81.383, 82.166, 82.371, 84.125, 84.323, 85.122, 85.356
Gentleman: 82.575

Acroft—see Croft

Adams, Clement (c.1519–1588) Schoolmaster to the Henchmen, Map Engraver. *ODNB*; *CPR, 1569–72.*
Gentleman: 62.170, 62.357, 63.159, 63.338, 64.140, 64.200, 65.98, 67.168, 67.344, 68.163

Adderley, Humphrey (1512–1598) Yeoman and Groom of the Wardrobe of Robes under Henry VIII, Edward VI, Mary I, and Elizabeth. Son of Thomas Adderley and Joan Thirkill; mar 1st 1571 Anne North, 2nd 1581 Elizabeth Capel. *ODNB*; *Index to Privy Bills*; PRO LC 5/33, 5/34; will PCC 64, 65 Lewyn.
Free Gift: 88.391, 89.391, 94.388, 97.414, 98.420

Admiral of France—see Gaspard de Coligny

Admiral of the Dutch States General—see William Blois van Treslong

Aglionby, Mary/Anne [née?] (d.aft.1568) Mother of the Maids, Mistress Eglonby. Mar Edward Aglionby. PRO SP 12/166, f.32; Bindoff under husband.
Maid of Honour: 62.338, 63.321, 64.189, 67.322, 68.313

Ahmad—see al-Mansur

Albert de Venice—see Albert Kellim

Alberti, Antonio Maria—see Galliardello, Mark Anthony

Alderton, Thomas (fl.1580s–1590s) Yeoman of the Kitchen, Cook. PRO E 115.
Custody of Gift: 82.336

A Lee—see also Lee, Leigh

Alee, John—see John Leigh

Alençon—see François, Duc d'Anjou

Alexander—see Zinzano

Alington, Sir Giles (c.1500–1586) Treasurer of Lyon's Inn, kntd 1530, MP. Son of Giles Alington and Mary Gardner; mar 1st 1515 Ursula Drury, 2nd 1524 Alice Middleton, 3rd 1564 Margaret Tolkarne; grandfather of Mary Alington*. Bindoff; *Visitations, Cambridge*; *Visitations, Lincolnshire*; will PCC 49 Windsor.
Sundry Gift: 59.457 (Coronation Fees)

Alington, Mary (c.1552–1635) Mistress Savage. Niece of William Cordell*, granddaughter of Sir Giles Alington*; mar 1576 John Savage*. *Visitations, Cambridge*; *Visitations, Lincolnshire*.
  Sundry Gift: 77.415 (Marriage Gift)
Allen/Alen—see Alan Bawdenson
Allen, Joan, née Woodgate (fl.1570s–1580s) Mistress Allen. Daughter of Edward Woodgate, mar 1564 Thomas Allen*. Husband's will PCC 1 Watson.
  Gentlewoman: 76.157, 76.345, 77.158, 77.355, 79.173, 79.380, 81.165, 81.371, 82.160, 82.359, 82.612, 85.157, 85.332, 88.136, 88.320, 89.133, 89.318
Allen, Thomas (c.1524–1583) Merchant, Citizen and Haberdasher of London. Mar 1st Eleanor Harris, 2nd 1564 Joan Woodgate (Allen*). Will PCC 1 Watson; *CPR, 1575–78*; *CSP Domestic, 1547–80*.
  Gentleman: 63.171, 63.350, 65.090, 67.160, 67.336, 68.153, 68.325, 76.182, 76.384
Alley, Lucy, née Twist (c.1570–1612) Mistress Alley, Mistress Blount. Daughter of Thomas Twist and Anne Twist*; mar 1st Verney Alley, 2nd John Blount. *Index to Privy Bills*.
  Gentlewoman: 97.155, 97.348, 98.151, 98.349, 99.146, 99.337, 00.147, 00.342, 03.147, 03.359
Alley, Verney—see Lucy Alley
Alley, William (c.1510–1570) Bishop of Exeter 1560–1570. *ODNB*; will PCC 10 Lyon.
  Bishop: 62.33, 62.213, 63.32, 63.204, 64.31, 65.133, 67.33, 67.203, 68.48, 68.217
Almaliach—see Lupo
al-Mansur, Ahmad (1549–1603) King of Fez, Emperor of Morocco, King of Barbary, alias Muley Hamet. Gift to his envoy Mushac Reyz*. Smith; *CSP Foreign, 1589*.
  Sundry Gift: 89.406 (Sovereign sending Envoy to England)
Alphonsus—see Alfonso Ferrabosco
Andrew, Nicholas (d.1564) Musician, Sackbut. *BDECM*; *RECM*; LP Henry VIII.
  Gentleman: 59.178, 59.402
Añes, Dunstan (c.1520–1594) Purveyor and Merchant of Queen's household, Grocers' Company. Formerly Gonsalvo Añes, alias Gonzalo Jorge. Son of Jorge Añes and Elizabeth Rodrigues; mar 1549 Constance Ruiz; father-in-law of Roderigo Lopez*. *ODNB*; *Visitations, London*; Siddons.
  Gentleman: 67.169, 67.345, 82.200, 82.404, 82.589, 84.196, 84.394, 85.188, 85.383, 88.176, 88.368, 89.173, 89.364, 94.162, 94.356
  Custody of Gift: 82.404 (delivered to himself)
Anjou, Duke of—see François, Duc d'Anjou
Annesley, Christian (d.1605) Maid of Honour. Daughter of Brian Annesley and Audrey Tyrrell; mar 1595 William Lord Sandys. Cokayne under husband.
  Maid of Honour: 94.313
Annesley, Cordelia (c.1566–1636) Maid of Honour. Daughter of Brian Annesley and Audrey Tyrrell; mar 1608 Sir William Harvey. *ODNB* and Hasler under husband.
  Maid of Honour: 98.343, 99.331, 00.334, 03.375
Anthony, Anthony (d.1563) Groom of the Chamber 1530, Surveyor General of Ordnance 1553, Brewer. Son of William Anthony, mar 1st 1517 Anne Roy, 2nd c.1559 Alice [née?] Norton. *ODNB*; will PCC 32 Chayre; BL Additional MS 22407.
  Gentleman: 59.192, 59.417, 62.174, 62.361, 63.161, 63.340
Anthony of Milan—see Anthony Donato
Anthony, Signor—see Anthony Conti
Anthony, Mark/Mary—see Mark Anthony Galliardello; Anthony Maria Peacock; Mark Anthony Bassano; Mark Anthony Erizo

Dom António of Portugal (1531–1595) King Anthony of Portugal, Jun-Aug 1580, Claimant to the Portuguese throne. Great-grandson of Ferdinand II of Aragon and Isabella of Castile; 1ˢᵗ cousin of Sebastian of Portugal. Gift to his envoy Juan Rodriguez de Souza*. *CSP Spanish, 1580–86* ; *CSP Foreign, 1579–80, 1581–82, 1583–84, 1586–88*.

Sundry Gift: 81.440 (Sovereign sending Envoy to England)

Anwick, William (fl.1580s) Queen's servant, possible identification. PRO E 115.

Custody of Gift: 82.368

Aparry—see Parry

Arbella—see Arbella Stuart

Arco, Oliver d' (fl.1560s) Count d'Arco, alias Olivero d'Arco. Envoy from Maximilian*, Holy Roman Emperor and King of Bohemia, visited England on private business. HMC 70 Pepys MSS; BL Cotton MS Titus B VII.

Sundry Gift: 64.217, 67.364 (Gift to Envoy)

Arundel, Earl—see Henry FitzAlan, 12ᵗʰ, 1544–1580; Philip Howard, 13ᵗʰ, 1580–1589

Arundell, Margaret, née Willoughby (1544–1584) Mistress Arundell, Lady Arundell, Gentlewoman of the Privy Chamber to Mary I and Elizabeth. Daughter of Henry Willoughby and Anne Grey; mar 1559 Sir Matthew Arundell. Hasler; BL Sloane MS 814.

Gentlewoman: 62.140, 62.320, 65.58, 65.224, 67.127, 67.297

Lady: 77.116, 77.313, 78.116, 78.317, 84.89, 84.287

Ascough—see Askew

Askew, Lady Anne, née Clinton (1546–1585) Lady Anne Askew, Lady of the Privy Chamber. Daughter of Edward Clinton*, Earl of Lincoln and Ursula Stourton; sister of Henry Clinton* and Frances Brydges*; mar 1563 William Askew, niece by marriage to Anne Askew, Protestant martyr. *Visitations, Lincolnshire.*

Lady: 81.112, 81.318, 82.107, 82.307, 82.522

Assoner, Mistress (fl.1580s) unidentified. possible variant spelling of Othomer*.

Gentlewoman: 81.160, 81.366

Astley, Andrew (b.1562) son of Thomas Astley* and Mary Denny (Astley*); brother of Elizabeth Astley*.

Sundry Gift: 63.365 (Christening Gift)

Astley, Catherine, née Champernowne (d.1565) Mistress Astley, Governess to Princess Elizabeth, Gentlewoman of the Bedchamber, Chief Gentlewoman of the Privy Chamber. Daughter of Sir Philip Champernowne and Catherine Carew; sister-in-law of Arthur Denny* and Catherine [I] Blount*; mar c.1545 John Astley*; aunt of Sir Carew Ralegh*, Sir Walter Ralegh*, Douglas Dyve*, Edward Denny*, and Mary Astley*. *ODNB*; Merton; Collins, *Jewels*; Richardson.

Gentlewoman: 59.137, 59.356, 62.131, 62.311, 63.124, 63.297, 64.116, 64.170, 65.53, 65.220

Astley, Elizabeth (fl.1560s–1580s) Daughter of Thomas Astley* and Mary Denny (Astley*); sister of Andrew Astley*; mar 1579 Edward Darcy*; Hasler under husband.

Sundry Gift: 81.442 (Marriage Gift)

Astley, John (c.1507–1596) Master of the Jewels and Plate 1558, Gentleman of the Privy Chamber 1558, MP. Son of Thomas Astley and Anne Wood; brother of Richard Astley*; half-brother of Thomas Astley*; mar 1ˢᵗ c.1545 Catherine Champernowne*, 2ⁿᵈ 1565 Margaret Grey alias Lenton. *ODNB*; Collins, *Jewels*; Hasler; Bindoff.

Gentleman: 59.155, 59.380, 62.152, 62.339, 63.143, 63.322, 64.130, 64.190, 65.75, 67.347, 68.144, 68.316

Free Gift :71.348, 75.235, 76.399, 77.401, 78.407, 79.421, 81.420, 82.406, 84.397, 85.390, 88.376, 89.378, 94.376

Custody of Gift: 62.61, 62.106, 62.188, 62.197, 63.2, 63.62, 63.78, 63.104, 63.161, 63.165, 63.271, 64.1, 64.68, 64.217, 64.220–221, 64.227, 65.19, 65.73, 65.77, 67.15, 67.96, 67.148, 67.362, 68.144, 68.162, 71.57, 71.91, 71.100, 71.113, 71.125, 71.127, 71.164, 71.166, 75.15, 75.24, 76.104, 76.147–148, 77.79, 77.169, 77.204, 77.417, 77.419–423, 78.202, 78.421–426, 79.31, 79.123, 79.178, 79.439, 79.443, 79.450–452, 79.455–456, 81.127, 81.135, 81.154, 81.176, 81.205, 81.442, 82.211, 84.4, 84.66, 85.68, 88.401, 89.25, 89.64, 89.120, 89.123, 89.396–398, 89.400, 89.407

Regifted: 62.152 (Queen re-gifted his gift to William Herbert*)

Astley, Mary (b.c.1543) Mistress Astley. Daughter of Anthony Denny and Joan Champernowne; sister of Edward Denny* and Douglas Dyve*; niece and sister-in-law of Catherine Astley*; sister-in-law of John Astley*; mar 1561 Thomas Astley*; mother of Andrew Astley* and Elizabeth Astley*. *Visitations, Bedfordshire.*

Sundry Gift: 63.365 (Christening Gift for her child)

Astley, Richard (d.1601) Groom of the Jewels and Plate. Son of Thomas Astley and Anne Wood; brother of John Astley*; half-brother of Thomas Astley*; mar 1567 Margaret Stanford. Will PCC 31 Woodhall.

Free Gift: 75.248, 76.412, 77.414, 78.420, 79.434, 81.433, 82.419, 84.412

Custody of Gift: 82.227, 82.312

Astley, Thomas (1516–1595) Groom of the Privy Chamber, Gentleman Pensioner 1539–1554. Son of Thomas Astley and Anne Cruse; half-brother of John Astley* and Richard Astley*; mar c.1561 Mary Denny (Astley*); father of Andrew Astley* and Elizabeth Astley*. PRO LC 5/49, C 43/6/69.

Free Gift: 59.445, 62.369, 63.353, 64.207, 67.348, 68.335, 71.349, 75.236, 76.400, 77.402, 78.408, 79.422, 81.421, 82.408, 84.398, 85.391, 88.379, 89.380, 94.379

Sundry Gift: 63.365 (Christening Gift for his child)

Custody of Gift: 62.158–59, 62.168–69, 82.306

Atkins, Robert (fl.1580s) Groom of the Poultry. Longleat House MS DU/vol. III, 1559–1601; PRO E 115.

Custody of Gift: 82.236

Atkinson, Edward (fl.1550s–1560s) Yeoman Purveyor of Wine. PRO E 115; *Visitations, London.*

Gentleman: 59.207, 59.431

Audley, Lord/Baroness—see Lucy Tuchet, née Mervyn, c.1578–1610; George Tuchet, 11th, 1563–1616

Audley of Walden, Baroness—see Lady Elizabeth Audley, née Grey, 1538–1561

Audley, Lady Elizabeth, née Grey (c.1510–1564) Baroness Audley of Walden. Daughter of Thomas Grey, Marquess of Dorset and Margaret Wotton; mar 1st 1538 Thomas, Lord Audley, 2nd George Norton; sister-in-law of Lady Anne Grey*; mother of Margaret Howard*. GEC, *Peerage.*

Baroness: 59.80, 59.300

Audley, Margaret—see Margaret Howard

Aylmer, John (1521–1594) Bishop of London 1577–1594. *ODNB*; PCC 81 Dixy.

Bishop: 78.48, 78.249, 79.46, 79.253, 81.42, 81.248, 82.41, 82.240, 82.441, 84.37, 84.235, 85.40, 85.231, 88.39, 88.224, 89.34, 89.219, 94.37, 94.221

Aylworth, John (c.1515–1575) Master of Guild of Merchants. Related by marriage to Walter Bayley*. Hasler; Bindoff; will PCC 4 Carew.

Gentleman: 59.174, 59.397

Aylworth, unidentified (fl.1580s) Queen's servant.

Custody of Gift: 82.277

Babington, Gervase (1550–1610) Bishop of Llandaff 1591–1597, Bishop of Exeter 1597–1598, Bishop of Worcester 1598–1610. *ODNB*.
    Bishop: 97.56, 97.248, 98.50, 98.246, 99.44, 99.234, 00.50, 00.244, 03.52, 03.265

Bacon, Sir Francis (1561–1626) Essayist, Lawyer, Philosopher, later Lord Chancellor, kntd 1603. Son of Sir Nicholas Bacon* and Anne Cooke; grandson of Sir Anthony Cooke* and Anne Fitzwilliam and of Robert Bacon and Isabel Cage (Bacon*). *ODNB*; Hasler; BL Sloane MS 3078.
    Gentleman: 97.196, 97.395, 98.193, 98.397, 99.170, 99.370, 00.171, 00.372, 03.163, 03.383

Bacon, Isabel, née Cage (fl.1550s–1560s) Mistress Bacon of Northhall. Daughter of John Cage and Margaret Tawyer; mar 1504 Robert Bacon; mother of Sir Nicholas Bacon*, grandmother of Sir Francis Bacon*. *Visitations, Suffolk*. probable identification.
    Gentlewoman: 59.147, 59.363

Bacon, Sir Nicholas (1510–1579) Lord Keeper of the Great Seal 1558, Privy Councillor 1558, courtier poet, kntd 1558. Son of Robert Bacon and Isabel Cage (Bacon*); brother-in-law of Sir Thomas Gresham* and Sir William Cecil*; mar 1st c.1540 Jane Fernley, 2nd c.1553 Anne Cooke; father of Sir Francis Bacon*. *ODNB*; Hasler; Bindoff; PCC 1 Bakon; May, *Elizabethan Courtier*.
    Lord: 59.53, 59.274, 62.51, 62.231, 63.52, 63.224, 64.52, 65.153
    Primary: 67.2, 67.172, 68.3, 68.172, 71.3, 71.172, 75.2, 76.3, 76.198, 77.4, 77.201, 78.4, 78.204, 79.2, 79.209

Bacqueville, Monsieur de—see Nicholas Martel

Badenson—see Bawdenson

Bailey—see Bayley

Bailhache—see Bellehachius

Baker, Cecily—see Cecily Sackville

Baker, George (1540–1612) Surgeon. *ODNB*; will PCC 114 Fenner.
    Gentleman: 94.182, 94.357, 97.198, 97.399, 98.195, 98.402, 99.192, 99.391, 00.191, 00.395, 03.179, 03.400

Baker, John (fl.1600s) Upholsterer. PRO LC 2/4 (4).
    Gentleman: 03.208, 03.431

Baker, Robert (d.1637) Musician, Recorder. *BDECM*; *RECM*.
    Gentleman: 03.202, 03.426

Baldry, Elizabeth—see Elizabeth Rich

Baldwin, William (fl.1580s) Queen's servant, possible identification. PRO E 115.
    Custody of Gift: 82.363

Ball, Lawrence (1505–1561) Silkman. will PCC 34 Loftes.
    Gentleman: 59.186, 59.410

Bancroft, Richard (1544–1610) Bishop of London 1597–1604, Archbishop of Canterbury 1604–1610. *ODNB*; will PCC 96 Wingfield.
    Bishop: 98.41, 98.242, 99.35, 99.230, 00.45, 00.240, 03.48, 03.261

Baldini—see Petruccio Ubaldini

Baptist—see Castilion

Barker, Christopher (c.1529–1599) Queen's Printer. Father of Robert Barker*. *ODNB*.
    Gentleman: 81.202, 81.417, 84.189, 84.381

Barker, Robert (c.1568–1646) Queen's/King's Printer. Son of Christopher Barker*. *ODNB* under father and Authorized Version of the Bible, Translators of the.
    Gentleman: 03.177, 03.398

Barkley—see Berkeley

Barley, Elizabeth—see Elizabeth Hardwick

Barley, Lucy—see Lucy Penne

Barlow, William (c.1490s–1568) Bishop of Chichester 1559–1568. Father-in-law of Tobie Matthew*, Herbert Westfaling*, William Day*, William Overton*, and William Wickham*. *ODNB*; will PCC 17 Babington.
Bishop: 62.26, 62.206, 63.25, 63.197, 64.27, 65.129, 67.29, 67.199, 68.44, 68.213

Barnaby, Frances—see Frances Bourchier

Barnekow, Christian (1566–1612) Christian Barra or Barnikou, Danish nobleman, extensive traveller, and diplomat. Ambassador from Christian IV*, King of Denmark. Accompanied Arild Huitfeldt* to England. *Salmonsens*.
Sundry Gift: 98.426 (Gift to Envoy)

Barnes, Richard (1532–1587) Bishop of Carlisle 1570–1577, Bishop of Durham 1577–1587. Brother-in-law of Roger Gifford*. *ODNB*.
Bishop: 78.47, 78.248, 79.45, 79.252, 81.40, 81.247, 82.39, 82.239, 82.439, 84.36, 84.234, 85.40, 85.231

Baronville—see Nicholas Martel

Barra, Christian—see Christian Barnekow

Barrett, Joyce—see Joyce Wilford

Bartlett, John (fl.1580s) Yeoman of Confectionery, Sergeant of the Pastry. PRO E 315/1954, E 115.
Custody of Gift: 82.329

Bartew—see Bertie

Bashe, Edward (1507–1587) Victualler of the Navy. Son of Alexander Bashe and Anne Barley; mar 1st Thomaine Baker, 2nd Jane Sadler; son-in-law of Sir Ralph Sadler*. *ODNB*; Hasler; Bindoff.
Gentleman: 62.155, 62.342, 63.146, 63.325, 64.132, 64.193, 67.151, 67.327, 68.148, 68.320, 71.149, 71.327, 75.118, 75.215, 76.179, 76.379, 77.177, 77.379, 78.177, 78.385, 79.179, 79.392, 81.184, 81.398, 82.172, 82.377, 82.562, 84.170, 84.375, 85.163, 85.362

Bassano, the brethren—first generation (Alvise Bassano, Anthony Bassano, Baptista Bassano, Jasper Bassano and John Bassano); second generation (Augustine Bassano, Andrea Bassano, Arthur Bassano, Edward Bassano, Jeronimo Bassano, Ludovico Bassano, and Mark Anthony); *ODNB*; *BDCEM*, Siddons.

Bassano, Andrea (1554–1626) Musician, Sackbut. Son of Anthony Bassano*, brother of Arthur Bassano*, Edward Bassano*, Jeronimo Bassano*, and Mark Anthony Bassano*. *BDECM*; Lasocki; Siddons.
Gentleman: 75.233, 81.201, 81.416, 82.197, 82.401, 82.584, 84.192, 94.177, 94.369, 97.187, 97.387, 98.186, 98.389, 99.184, 99.380, 00.184, 00.382, 03.194, 03.419

Bassano, Anthony (c.1520–1574) Musician, Recorder. Son of Jeronimo Bassano, brother of Batista Bassano*, Jasper Bassano* and John Bassano*, father of Andrea Bassano*, Arthur Bassano*, Edward Bassano*, Jeronimo Bassano*, and Mark Anthony Bassano*. *BDECM*; Lasocki; Siddons.
Gentleman: 59.176, 59.399

Bassano, Arthur (1547–1624) Musician, Recorder. Son of Anthony Bassano*, brother of Andrea Bassano*, Edward Bassano*, Jeronimo Bassano*, and Mark Anthony Bassano*. *BDECM*; Lasocki; Siddons.
Gentleman: 75.233, 81.201, 81.416, 82.197, 82.401, 82.584, 84.192, 94.176, 94.370, 97.185, 97.386, 98.184, 98.388, 99.182, 99.379, 00.182, 00.381, 03.192, 03.418

Bassano, Augustine (1535–1604) Musician, Recorder. Son of Alvise Bassano, grandson of Jeronimo Bassano, brother of Ludovico Bassano*, father-in-law of Thomas [I] Lupo*. *ODNB*; *BDECM*; Lasocki.
Gentleman: 59.176, 59.399, 75.233, 81.201, 81.416, 82.164, 84.192

Bassano, Baptista (d.1576) Musician, Recorder. Alias John Baptist Bassano. Son of Jeronimo Bassano, brother of Anthony Bassano*, Jasper Bassano*, and John Bassano*. *ODNB*; *BDECM*; Lasocki.
Gentleman: 59.176, 59.399, 68.167

Bassano, Edward (1551–1615) Musician, Recorder. Son of Anthony Bassano*, brother of Andrea Bassano*, Arthur Bassano*, Jeronimo Bassano*, and Mark Anthony Bassano*. *BDECM*; Lasocki; Siddons.
Gentleman: 75.233, 97.186, 97.388, 98.185, 98.390, 99.183, 99.381, 00.183, 00.383, 03.193, 03.420

Bassano, Jasper (c.1520–1577) Musician, Recorder, Sackbut. Son of Jeronimo Bassano, brother of Anthony Bassano*, Baptista Bassano* and John Bassano*. *BDECM*; Lasocki.
Gentleman: 59.176, 59.399

Bassano, Jeronimo (1559–1635) Musician, Recorder. Son of Anthony Bassano*, brother of Andrea Bassano*, Arthur Bassano*, Edward Bassano*, and Mark Anthony Bassano*. *ODNB*; *BDECM*; Lasocki; Siddons.
Gentleman: 75.233, 81.201, 81.416, 82.197, 82.401, 82.584, 84.192, 88.184, 88.376, 89.182, 89.373, 94.173, 94.368, 97.184, 97.385, 98.183, 98.387, 99.181, 99.378, 00.181, 00.380, 03.191, 03.416

Bassano, Ludovico (c.1520–1593) Musician, Recorder. Son of Alvise Bassano*, grandson of Jeronimo Bassano, brother of Augustine Bassano*; mar Elizabeth Damon; son-in-law of William Daman*. *ODNB*; *BDECM*; Lasocki.
Gentleman: 75.233, 81.201, 81.416, 82.197, 82.401, 82.584, 84.192

Bassano, Mark Anthony (1546–1599) Musician, Sackbut. Son of Anthony Bassano*, brother of Andrea Bassano*, Edward Bassano*, Jeronimo Bassano*, and Arthur Bassano*. *BDECM*; Lasocki; Siddons.
Gentleman: 75.233, 81.201, 81.416, 82.197, 82.401, 82.584, 84.192, 85.186, 85.387

Bath, Earl/Countess—see Elizabeth Bourchier, née Russell, 1583–1605; John Bourchier, 2nd, 1539–1561; Margaret Bourchier, née Donnington, 1548–1561; William Bourchier, 3rd, 1561–1623

Bath and Wells, Bishop—see Gilbert Bourne, 1554–1560; Gilbert Berkeley, 1560–1581; Thomas Godwin, 1584–1590; John Still, 1594–1608

Batty, Ralph (1532–1603) Sergeant of the Pastry. Adams; PRO SP 46/39, E 115; Bodleian MS Rawlinson A 331.
Gentleman: 94.167, 94.363, 97.178, 97.380, 98.175, 98.381, 99.169, 99.369, 00.170, 00.371, 03.182, 03.403
Custody of Gift: 82.341

Bawdenson, Alan (d.1564) Gunmaker and Crossbow maker, King's Armourer, Keeper of the Armouries at Whitehall, Clockmaker. PRO E115; Blackmore; Ffoulkes.
Gentleman: 59.211, 59.434, 63.167, 63.346

Bayard, William (fl.1550s–1560s) Painter. PRO C 142/160/54, E115.
Gentleman: 59.215, 59.439

Bayley, Walter (1529–1592) Royal Physician. Son of Henry Bayley; mar c.1566 Anne Evans. *ODNB*; *CPR, 1580–82*; will PCC 24 Harrington; Horton-Smith.
Gentleman: 81.190, 81.403, 82.184, 82.386, 82.559, 84.180, 84.384, 85.173, 85.372, 88.166, 88.357, 89.163, 89.355
Custody of Gift: 82.386 (delivered to himself)

Baynes, Ralph (d.1559) Bishop of Lichfield and Coventry 1554–1559 (deprived). *ODNB*.
Bishop: 59.28, 59.248

Beacher, Richard (fl.1580s) Queen's servant, possible identification. PRO E 115.
Custody of Gift: 82.349

Beaufort, Charlotte Mademoiselle, née Montgomery (fl.1570s) Mademoiselle Beaufort. Daughter of Gabriel Montgomery and Isabel de la Touche, Countess Montgomery*; mar 1545 Christophe de Chateaubriand, Seigneur de Beaufort. Marlet.
Countess: 76.42, 76.237

Beaumont—see Harlay

Beauvoir la Nocle—see Jean de la Fin

Bedford, Earl/Countess—see Bridget Russell, née Hussey, 1566–1601; Edward Russell, 3rd, 1585–1627; Francis Russell, 2nd, 1555–1585; Lucy Russell, née Harington, 1594–1627; Margaret Russell, née St John, 1555–1562

Bedingfield, Alice—see Alice Seckford

Belin, Nicholas (c.1490–1569) Nicholas Belin de Modeno, Painter, Sculptor, Miniature Painter, Stucco Worker, Servant of Henry VIII, Edward VI, Mary I, and Elizabeth. Gift was picture of Patch the fool*. *CPR, 1558–60*; *LP Henry VIII, 1539–40*; Biddle.
Gentleman: 62.177, 62.364

Bellehache, Oger (fl.1580s) alias Ogerius Bellehachius, Bailhache, Huguenot from Caen. Author, *Ogerii Bellehachii Sacrosancta Bucolica* (1583), STC 1846.
Gentleman: 84.198

Bellenden, Lewis (c.1552–1591) Lord Justice Clerk of Scotland, Special Ambassador from James VI*, King of Scotland. Paul; BL Additional MS 32657.
Sundry Gift: 85.419 (Gift to Envoy)

Bellot, Jacques (d.1590) Poet, Huguenot from Caen, France. author: *Le Jardin de Vertu* (1581), STC 1854; BL Sloane MS 3316; Lambley.
Gentleman: 68.168

Belmaine, Jean (d.c.1582) Schoolmaster to Edward VI, French tutor. Mar Jane Alington; nephew by marriage to Sir John Cheke and Sir William Cecil*. *ODNB*; *Visitations, Lincolnshire;* Siddons.
Gentleman: 59.179, 59.404

Benger, Thomas (d.1572) Master of the Revels, Auditor to Princess Elizabeth, kntd 1553, MP. Son of Robert Benger and Agnes Vavasour; mar 1st Agnes Seycolle, 2nd Dorothy Raynsford. Hasler; Streitberger; will PCC 11 Daughtry; BL Sloane MS 814.
Knight: 59.133, 59.352, 62.119, 62.298, 63.115, 63.288, 64.108, 64.162, 65.42, 65.209, 67.115, 67.285, 68.113, 68.282, 71.113, 71.283

Bennett, Anne [née?] (fl.1600s) mar 1st Anthony Bennett*, 2nd John Llewellyn*. Collins, *Jewels*.
Sundry Gift: 03.448 (Gift from the Queen)

Bennett, Anthony (fl.1580s–1600s) One of Queen's eight Footmen, by 1585. Mar Anne [née?] Bennett*. Collins, *Jewels*.
Sundry Gift: 03.448 (Gift from the Queen to his wife, Anne)

Benninck, Levina—see Levina Teerlinc

Bentham, Thomas (1514–1579) Bishop of Lichfield and Coventry 1560–1579. *ODNB*.
Bishop: 62.29, 62.209, 63.28, 63.200, 64.26, 65.128, 67.28, 67,198, 68.43, 68.212, 71.42, 71.212, 75.50, 75.158, 76.53, 76.248, 77.53, 77.250, 78.54, 78.255, 79.52, 79.259

Berkeley, Lord/Baroness—see Catherine [I] Berkeley, née Howard, 1554–1596; Henry Berkeley, 7th, 1534–1613; Jane Berkeley, née Stanhope, 1598–1618

Berkeley, Catherine [I], née Blount (c.1518–1560) Lady Berkeley, Sir Maurice's wife, Governess to Princess Elizabeth, Extraordinary Lady of the Privy Chamber. Daughter of William Blount, Lord Mountjoy and Alice Keble; sister-in-law of Catherine Astley*; aunt of James Blount*, Lord Mountjoy; mar 1st John Champernowne, 2nd 1545 Sir Maurice Berkeley* MP. Hasler and Bindoff under husband.
Lady: 59.87, 59.307

Berkeley, Catherine [II], née Howard, Baroness Berkeley (1538–1596) Daughter of Henry Howard, Earl of Surrey and Frances Vere (Howard*); sister of Thomas [I] Howard*, Henry [I] Howard*, and Jane Neville*; mar 1554 Henry, Lord Berkeley*; mother of Thomas Berkeley* and unidentified child, 2nd cousin of Queen Elizabeth. GEC, *Peerage*; Hasler.

Lady: 59.100, 59.319, 62.74, 62.256, 63.73, 63.245, 64.71, 65.3, 65.170, 67.70, 67.240, 68.69, 68.238, 71.97, 71.267

Baroness: 75.78, 75.186, 76.80, 76.284, 77.85, 77.282, 78.89, 78.299, 79.91, 79.299, 81.85, 81.293, 82.81, 82.282, 82.493, 84.78, 84.276, 85.81, 85.272, 88.85, 88.270, 89.78, 89.263, 94.78, 94.263

Sundry Gift: 62.385 (Christening Gift for her child), 76.416 (Christening Gift for her child)

Berkeley, Elizabeth [I], née Sandys (c.1532–1585) Mistress Elizabeth Sandys, Lady Berkeley, Gentlewoman to Princess Elizabeth, Gentlewoman of the Chamber. Daughter of Anthony Sandys and Anne Mann; mar c.1561 Sir Maurice Berkeley* MP, mother of Robert Berkeley*. Merton; Hasler and Bindoff under husband; will PCC 33 Brudenell.

Gentlewoman: 62.138, 62.318

Lady: 84.100, 84.303, 85.105, 85.295

Sundry Gift: 64.223 (Christening Gift for her child)

Berkeley, Elizabeth [II], née Carey (1576–1635) Daughter of George Carey* and Elizabeth Spencer (Carey*); mar 1596 Thomas Berkeley; mother of Theophila Berkeley*.

Sundry Gift: 77.416 (Christening Gift), 97.426 (Christening Gift for her child)

Berkeley, Gilbert (1501–1581) Bishop of Bath and Wells, 1560–1581. *ODNB*; will PCC 43 Darcy.

Bishop: 62.32, 62.212, 63.31, 63.203, 64.30, 65.132, 67.32, 67.202, 68.47, 68.216, 71.45, 71.215, 75.54, 75.162, 76.57, 76.252, 77.58, 77.254, 78.59, 78.260, 79.56, 79.263, 81.52, 81.257, after 82.38

Berkeley, Henry (1534–1613) Lord Berkeley, KB 1553. Mar 1st 1554 Lady Catherine Howard (Berkeley*), 2nd 1598 Jane Stanhope (Townsend*); father of Thomas Berkeley*. GEC, *Peerage*.

Lord: 59.64, 59.285, 62.62, 62.243, 63.63, 63.234, 64.57, 65.158, 67.58, 67.228, 68.56, 68.225, 71.54, 71.224, 75.60, 75.168, 97.63, 97.271, 98.61, 98.273, 99.57, 99.262, 00.64, 00.270, 03.73, 03.286

Sundry Gift: 62.385 (Christening Gift for his child), 76.416 (Christening Gift for his child)

Berkeley, Jane—see Jane Townsend

Berkeley, Sir Maurice (c.1513–1581) Gentleman Usher to Henry VIII, kntd 1544, MP. Mar 1st c.1545 Catherine Blount*, 2nd c.1561 Elizabeth [I] Sandys (Berkeley*); father of Robert Berkeley*. Hasler; Bindoff; will PCC 40 Darcy.

Sundry Gift: 64.223 (Christening Gift for his child)

Berkeley, Robert (1563–1614) Son of Sir Maurice Berkeley* and Elizabeth [I] Sandys (Berkeley*).

Sundry Gift: 64.223 (Christening Gift)

Berkeley, Theophila (1596–1643) Daughter of Thomas Berkeley* and Elizabeth [II] Carey (Berkeley*).

Sundry Gift: 97.426 (Christening Gift)

Berkeley, Thomas (1575–1611) Son of Henry, Lord Berkeley* and Catherine Howard (Berkeley*), mar 1596 Elizabeth [II] Carey (Berkeley*). Hasler.

Sundry Gift: 76.416 (Christening Gift), 97.426 (Christening Gift to his child)

Berkeley, infant (b.1561) Child of Henry, Lord Berkeley* and Catherine Howard (Berkeley*).
    Sundry Gift: 62.385 (Christening Gift)

Bertie, Catherine—see Catherine Brandon

Bertie, infant [Elizabeth?] (1581–1584) child of Peregrine Bertie* and Lady Mary Vere (Bertie*). GEC, *Peerage*.
    Sundry Gift: 81.444 (Christening Gift)

Bertie, Lady Mary, née Vere, Baroness Willoughby de Eresby (c1554–1624) Lady of the Privy Chamber. Daughter of John de Vere*, Earl of Oxford and Margery Golding (Vere*); sister of Edward de Vere*; mar 1st 1578 Peregrine Bertie*, Lord Willoughby de Eresby, 2nd 1605 Eustace Hart; mother of infant Bertie*. GEC, *Peerage*; BL Sloane MS 814.
    Lady: 76.103, 76.298, 77.100, 77.298, 78.99, 78.300, 79.95, 79.302
    Baroness: 81.93, 81.300, 82.88, 82.288, 82.498, 84.83, 84.281, 94.16, 94.200, 97.79, 97.278
    Sundry Gift: 81.444 (Christening Gift for her child)

Bertie, Peregrine, Lord Willoughby de Eresby (1555–1601) Military Commander, Governor of Berwick, kntd 1587. Son of Richard Bertie and Catherine Willoughby (Brandon*), Duchess of Suffolk; brother of Susan Bertie*; mar 1578 Lady Mary Vere (Bertie*); father of infant Bertie*. will PCC 58 Whitehall.
    Lord: 98.72, 98.265, 99.68, 99.255, 00.75, 00.263
    Sundry Gift: 81.444 (Christening Gift his child)

Bertie, Susan—see Susan Grey

Betts, John (c.1534-c.1588) Sergeant of the Pastry. Son of Robert Betts; mar 1559 Godly Videan. Will Archdeaconry of Rochester; PRO LC 2/4(3).
    Gentleman: 59.214, 59.438, 62.180, 62.367, 63.164, 63.343, 64.143, 64.203, 65.89, 67.166, 67.342, 68.165, 68.333

Beutterich, Peter (1545–1587) 'Doctor Beutrich'. Counsellor to and Envoy from John Casimir*, Duke of Bavaria. *CSP Foreign, 1577–78, 1582*.
    Sundry Gift: 78.428 (Gift to Envoy)

Bickerstaff, Anthony (fl.1580s) Queen's servant. Mar Catherine Hayward. PRO E 115; *CSP Domestic, 1581–1590*; *VCH, Surrey*.
    Custody of Gift: 82.219

Bickley, Thomas (d.1596) Bishop of Chichester 1586–1596. *ODNB*.
    Bishop: 88.53, 88.238, 89.48, 89.233, 94.46, 94.229

Bill, William (d.1561) Dean of Westminster. Physician to Henry VIII and Edward VI, Chaplain to Edward VI, Chief Almoner under Edward VI and Queen Elizabeth. *ODNB*.
    Chaplain: 59.135, 59.354

Billiard—see Byllyard

Billingsley, Sir Henry (c.1535–1606) Lord Mayor of London 1597, Haberdasher, kntd 1597. Son of William Billingsley and Elizabeth Harlow, married five times. *ODNB*; will PCC 91 Stafford.
    Knight: 97.194, 97.396, 98.135, 98.336, 99.127, 99.324, 00.132, 00.329

Bilson, Thomas (1547–1616) Bishop of Worcester 1596–1597, Bishop of Winchester 1597–1616. *ODNB*.
    Bishop: 97.44, 97.244, 98.48, 98.252, 99.42, 99.240, 00.44, 00.250, 03.47, 03.260

Birchall, John (fl.1580s) Clerk of the Closet.
    Custody of Gift: 82.245

Bird, Helen—see Helen Seckford

Bissells—see Brussells

Bishop, George (c.1536–1610) Stationer, Queen's Deputy Printer, Alderman of London. Son-in-law of John Cawood*; mar c.1556 Mary Cawood. Will PCC 2 Wood.
Gentleman: 94.163, 94.358, 97.174, 97.399, 98.171, 98.400, 99.165, 99.390, 00.166, 00.393

Bloomfield—see Bromfield

Blount, Alley—see Lucy Alley

Blount, Catherine, née Leigh, Baroness Mountjoy (d.1576) Daughter of Thomas Leigh and Elizabeth Rolleston, mar 1558 James Blount*, Lord Mountjoy, mother of Charles Blount* and William Blount*. GEC, *Peerage*; *ODNB* under husband.
Baroness: 59.104, 59.323, 62.75, 62.257, 63.74, 63.246, 64.74, 65.6, 65.173, 67.73, 67.243, 76.102, 76.297
Sundry Gift: 62.388 (Christening Gift for her child)

Blount, Catherine—see Catherine Berkeley, Catherine Croft

Blount, Charles, Lord Mountjoy (c.1562–1606) Lord Deputy of Ireland, kntd 1587, KG 1597. Son of James Blount*, Lord Mountjoy and Catherine Leigh (Blount*); brother of William Blount*; mar 1605 Penelope Devereux*, Lady Rich. *ODNB*; GEC, *Peerage*; Hasler.
Knight: 94.126, 94.301
Lord: 97.71, 97.270, 98.69, 98.272, 99.66, 99.261, 00.73, 00.269, 03.70, 03.283

Blount, Elizabeth—see Elizabeth Paulet

Blount, James (1533–1581) Lord Mountjoy. Son of Charles Blount, Lord Mountjoy and Anne Willoughby; nephew of Catherine [I] Berkeley*; mar 1558 Catherine Leigh (Blount*); father of William Blount* and Charles Blount*, Lord Mountjoy. *ODNB*; GEC, *Peerage*.
Lord: 59.68, 59.289, 62.63, 62.244, 63.64, 63.237, 64.60, 65.162
Sundry Gift: 62.388 (Christening Gift for his child)

Blount, William (1561–1594) Son of James Blount*, Lord Mountjoy, and Catherine Leigh (Blount*); brother of Charles Blount*. GEC, *Peerage*; *ODNB* under father and brother.
Sundry Gift: 62.388 (Christening Gift)

Boischot, Jean de (fl.1570s) Ambassador from Flanders, representing Don John of Austria*. *CSP Foreign, 1580.*
Sundry Gift: 76.418 (Gift to Envoy)

Boleyn, Sir James (1480–1561) kntd 1520, MP. Son of William Boleyn and Margaret Butler; uncle of Queen Anne Boleyn; great-uncle of Queen Elizabeth; mar c.1518 Elizabeth Wood. Bindoff; *Visitations, Norfolk*; will PCC 35 Loftes.
Knight: 59.131, 59.350

Bolse—see Bowes

Bone, Cecilia, [née?] (d.aft 1617) Mistress Bone alias Guilliam, Gyllam the Frau, Starcher. Mar Guilliam Bone; mother of Elizabeth Green*. husband's will PCC 52 Weldon; Stow.
Gentlewoman: 84.159, 85.156, 85.348, 88.155, 88.338, 89.152, 89.337, 94.140, 94.332, 03.152, 03.366;
Custody of Gift: 89.74, 89.106, 89.128, 89.133, 89.138, 94.136–141,

Bone, Elizabeth—see Elizabeth Green

Borgarucci, Eleanor, [née?] (d.1581) alias Mistress Julio. Mar 1st unidentified Cooper, 2nd c.1576 Guilio Borgarucci*. *ODNB* under husband.
Gentlewoman: 78.170, 78.370, 79.171, 79.379

Borgarucci, Guilio (d.1581) Physician, alias Doctor Julio. Son of Carlo Borgarucci and Caliope [née?]; mar 1st Alice Nosworthy, 2nd c.1576 Eleanor Cooper (Borgarucci*). *ODNB*; *CSP Domestic, 1547–1580; CPR, 1580–82*; Siddons.
    Gentleman: 75.124, 75.220, 76.187, 76.389, 78.185, 78.394, 79.190, 79.403, 81.188, 81.402

Borona, Lucretia—see Lucretia Swigo

Borough—see Burgh

Boteler—see Butler

Boughser—see Bourchier

Bouillon—see de la Tour d'Auvergne

Bourchier, Elizabeth, née Russell, Countess of Bath (1555–1605) Daughter of Francis Russell*, Earl of Bedford and Margaret St John (Russell*); sister of Anne Dudley*, John [I] Russell*, Margaret Clifford*, and William Russell*; aunt of Elizabeth [II] Russell*; mar 1583 William Bourchier*, Earl of Bath. *ODNB*; GEC, *Peerage*.
    Countess: 85.34, 85.226, 89.31, 89.216, 94.28, 94.211, 97.33, 97.230, 98.31, 98.232, 99.26, 99.221, 00.32, 00.229, 03.30, 03.243

Bourchier, Frances, née Kitson (d.1586) Lady FitzWarin. Daughter of Thomas Kitson and Margaret Donnington (Bourchier*); half-sister of Lady Susan Bourchier*; mar 1st 1547 John Bourchier, Lord FitzWarin, 2nd 1558 William Barnaby; mother of William Bourchier*, Earl of Bath. GEC, *Peerage*, will PCC 21 Windsor.
    Lady: 81.106, 81.319, 82.101, 82.306, 82.513, 84.104, 84.301, 85.284

Bourchier, John, Earl of Bath (1500–1561) Son of John Bourchier, Earl of Bath and Cecilia Daubney; mar 1st c.1521 Elizabeth Hungerford, 2nd 1528 Eleanor Manners, 3rd 1548 Margaret Donnington (Bourchier*); father of Lady Susan Bourchier*; grandfather of William Bourchier*. GEC, *Peerage*; will PCC 12 Loftes.
    Earl: 59.17, 59.238

Bourchier, Margaret, née Donnington, Countess of Bath (c.1510–1561) Daughter of John Donnington and Elizabeth Pye; mar 1st 1520 Thomas Kitson, 2nd 1541 Richard Long, 3rd 1548 John Bourchier*, Earl of Bath; mother of Frances Bourchier* and Lady Susan Bourchier*. GEC, *Peerage*; will PCC 5 Streat.
    Countess: 59.49, 59.270

Bourchier, Martha—see Martha Howard

Bourchier, Lady Susan (b.c.1549) Maid of Honour. Daughter of John Bourchier*, Earl of Bath and Margaret Donnington (Bourchier*); half-sister of Frances Bourchier*; aunt of William Bourchier*, Earl of Bath; probably unmarried. *Visitations, Suffolk*.
    Maid of Honour: 71.316, 75.202, 76.365, 77.368, 78.372

Bourchier, William, Earl of Bath (1557–1623) Son of John Bourchier*, Earl of Bath and Frances Kitson (Bourchier*); nephew of Lady Susan Bourchier*; brother-in-law to William Cornwallis*; mar 1st Mary Cornwallis (annulled), 2nd 1583 Elizabeth Russell (Bourchier*). *ODNB*; GEC, *Peerage*; will PCC 53 Skynner.
    Earl: 81.15, 81.224, 82.15, 82.217, 82.436, 84.14, 84.213, 85.15, 85.206, 88.13, 88.197, 89.8, 89.193, 94.8, 94.192, 97.7, 97.207, 98.8, 98.210, 99.8, 99.201, 00.7, 00.206, 03.10, 03.223

Bourg, Monsieur du (fl.1580s) Captain Bourg, Mounsieur La Bourge, Envoy from France. *CSP Foreign, 1579–80*; Fénelon.
    Sundry Gift: 81.434 (Gift to Envoy)

Bourke, Frances—see Frances Sidney

Bourke, Richard, Earl of Clanricarde (c.1572–1635) Son of Ulick Bourke (de Burgh), Earl of Clanricarde and Grace O'Carroll; mar 1603 Frances Walsingham (Sidney*), Countess of Essex. *ODNB*; GEC, *Peerage*.

Earl: 03.17, 03.230

Bourne, Gilbert (c.1510–1569) Bishop of Bath and Wells 1554–1559 (deprived). *ODNB*.
Bishop: 59.31, 59.252

Bowes, Abigail—see Abigail Digby

Bowes, Ralph (d.1598) Gentleman Pensioner. Son of John Bowes and Anne Huddleston; mar aft.1591 Abigail Heveningham (Digby*). Tighe; will PCC 47 Lewyn 1598.
Gentleman: 78.174, 78.382, 79.177, 79.390, 81.181, 81.389, 84.168, 84.376, 94.144, 94.335, 97.160, 97.362, 98.159, 98.366

Bowser—see Bourchier

Bowyer, Simon (d.1606) Gentleman Usher, Gentleman of the Black Rod. Mar Barbara Carne. *Visitations, Hampshire*; PRO E 115; *CSP Domestic, 1598–1601*.
Gentleman: 94.153, 94.341, 97.165, 97.368
Custody of Gift: 81.435, 81.437, 82.237

Brackenbury, Stephen (fl.1580s) Gentleman Usher. Dovey; PRO E 115.
Custody of Gift: 82.220

Bradbridge, William (1507–1578) Bishop of Exeter 1571–1578. *ODNB*.
Bishop: 75.53, 75.161, 76.56, 76.251, 77.57, 77.253, 78.58, 78.259

Bradish, John (d.1594) Linen draper, Mercer. mar Elizabeth Denham. Will PCC 21 Dixy; PRO E115.
Gentleman: 94.165, 94.261

Bradshaw, Lawrence (d.1581) Surveyor of the Works, Carpenter. PRO E 115, E 351/3326.
Gentleman: 59.188, 59.413

Brandon, Catherine, née Willoughby, Duchess of Suffolk (1519–1580) Baroness Willoughby de Eresby. Daughter of William Willoughby and Mary de Salinas; mar 1st 1534 Charles Brandon, 2nd 1552 Richard Bertie; mother of Peregrine Bertie* and Lady Susan Grey*. *ODNB*; HMC Ancaster; will PCC 38 Dixy; Read.
Duchess: 63.37, 63.209, 64.37, 65.137, 67.37, 67.207, 68.19, 68.188, 71.17, 71.187, 75.20, 76.22, 76.217, 77.26, 77.223, 78.23, 78.224, 79.23, 79.230

Brandon, Lady Frances - see Lady Frances Grey

Brandon, Rebecca—see Rebecca Seckford

Brandon, Robert (d.1591) Goldsmith, alias 'B', 'Br', or 'Bra'. Mar 1st 1548 Catherine Barber, 2nd aft 1574 Elizabeth Osborne; father of Rebecca Seckford*; father-in-law of Henry Seckford* and Nicholas Hilliard*; related by marriage to Richard Martin*. will PCC 43 Sainberbe; Sitwell.
Goldsmith: *passim* 1559–1579

Bray, Dorothy—Dorothy Brydges

Bray, Sir Edward (c.1519–1581) Shared office of Chief Almoner at Coronation with John Neville Lord Latimer and Sir John Gascoigne MP. Son of Edward Bray and Beatrice Shirley; mar 1st c.1542 Mary Elrington, 2nd 1547 Elizabeth Roper, 3rd 1560 Mary Cotton who mar 2nd Edmund Tilney. Hasler; will PCC 22 Darcy.
Sundry Gift: 59.459 (Coronation Fees)

Bray, Elizabeth—see Elizabeth Catesby

Bray, Frances—see Frances Lyfield

Brereton, Margaret (d.bef.1599) Gentlewoman, Mistress Britten. possible identification. Daughter of John Savage and Elizabeth Manners; mar William Brereton MP; sister of John Savage*. Hasler under husband.
Gentlewoman: 97.157, 97.352

Breville, Mariette, née Bizet (b.c.1551) Madame Brevell, Breuel and Brevele ,'a French lady', from Caen, France, mar Seigneur Michel de Breville. possible identification.
Sundry Gift: 88.402 (Gift from the Queen)

Bridgeman, Edith, née Brocas (fl.1550s–1580s) Mistress Bridgeman, Gentlewoman of the Bedchamber to Mary I. Daughter of John Brocas; mar 1556 George Bridgeman*. *Visitations, Bedfordshire*; PRO LC 5/49, *CPR, 1557–58*.

Gentlewoman: 82.136, 82.336, 82.617

Bridgeman, George (d.1580) Gentleman and Groom of the Privy Chamber, Keeper of Westminster Palace. Mar 1556 Edith Brocas (Bridgeman*). *CPR, 1557–58*; BL Additional MS 5751A, Stowe MS 142.

Custody of Gift: 59.6, 59.72, 59.160, 59.167, 59.174, 59.178, 59.180, 59.189, 59.206, 59.212, 59.215, 62.157, 62.177, 63.61, 63.102, 65.56, 65.94, 65.98, 68.169

Bridges—see also Brydges

Bridges, John (1535–1618) Chaplain, Dean of Salisbury, later Bishop of Oxford 1604. *ODNB*.

Chaplain: 81.170, 81.384

Brigham, Margaret—see Margaret Hunnis

Bright, unidentified (fl.1580s) Queen's servant.

Custody of Gift: 82.383

Brissells—see Brussells

Brisson, Barnabé (fl.1580s) Sieur de Gravelle, President of the Parliament of Paris, French Commissioner for marriage settlement between Elizabeth and the Duke of Anjou*. *CSP Foreign, 1581–82, 1583–84*; BL Cotton MS Galba E VI, Cotton MS Caligula E XII.

Sundry Gift: 81.450 (Gift to Envoy)

Bristow, John (fl.1580s) Son of Nicholas [I] Bristow* and Lucy Barley, brother of Nicholas [II] Bristow*.

Custody of Gift: 82.229

Bristow, Nicholas [I] (c.1494–1584) Clerk to the Wardrobe of the Robes and Beds, Keeper of the Little Wardrobe of the Beds at the Tower, Clerk of the Jewels. Mar c.1535 Lucy Barley; father of Nicholas [II] Bristow* and John Bristow*. Will PCC 20 Watson; *CPR, 1558–60, 1563–66, 1566–69; 1569–72*.

Free Gift: 59.448, 62.374, 63.358, 64.212, 67.354, 68.341, 71.356

Bristow, Nicholas [II] (1537–1616) Clerk of the Jewels, Clerk of the Wardrobe of the Robes and Beds. Son of Nicholas [I] Bristow* and Lucy Barley; brother of John Bristow*; mar c.1562 Margaret Butler. *CPR, 1569–72*.

Free Gift 75.245, 76.409, 77.411, 78.417, 79.431, 81.430, 82.416, 84.409, 85.401, 88.391, 89.392, 94.389, 97.414, 98.421, 99.408, 00.411, 03.443

Custody of Gift: 82.207, 82.239

Britton—see Brereton

Broadbelt, Dorothy (fl.1560s–1570s) Mistress Broadbelt, Mistress Abington, Gentlewoman of the Bedchamber. Mar 1567 John Abington. *Visitations, Gloucester*; *Visitations, Worcester*; *VCH, Worcester*; *VCH, Yorkshire*; PRO E 134/35 Eliz/Trin 2.

Gentlewoman: 62.137, 62.317, 63.129, 63.302, 64.120, 64.174, 65.60, 65.226, 67.129, 67.299, 68.126, 68.294, 71.129, 71.299, 75.92, 76.140, 76.333, 77.141, 77.338

Custody of Gift: 59.153, 63.50, 63.67, 63.71, 63.83, 63.87–88, 63.92, 63.94, 63.97, 63.116, 63.124–126, 63.128–129, 63.134, 63.138–142, 63.152–153, 63.166, 64.50, 64.88, 64.109, 64.116–118, 64.120–122, 64.124, 64.126–127, 64.129, 64.140, 64.146, 65.2, 65.4, 65.12–13, 65.22–23, 65.25, 65.43, 65.55, 65.58–60, 65.62–63, 65.65, 65.67–72, 65.74, 65.82, 65.84, 67.1, 67.53, 67.83, 67.85, 67.87, 67.90–93, 67.95, 67.97, 67.113, 67.117, 67.124–134, 67.136–146, 67.154–156, 67.161–163, 67.169, 68.2, 68.15, 68.67, 68.75, 68.80, 68.82–83, 68.88, 68.91–92, 68.94–95, 68.96–97, 68.112, 68.115, 68.120–122, 68.124–132, 68.134, 68.136, 68.138–140, 68.150–151, 68.154–157, 68.160, 68.163, 68.167, 71.69,

71.71, 71.74–75, 71.79–81, 71.86, 71.92, 71.96, 71.120–121, 71.126, 71.129, 71.133, 71.138, 71.142, 71.156–159, 75.36, 77.28, 77.41, 77.90, 77.102, 77.140

Brocas, Edith—see Edith Bridgeman

Bromfield, Catherine, née Fromond (d.1597) Mistress Bromfield, Mother of the Maids. Daughter of Bartholomew Fromond and Elizabeth Mynd; sister-in-law of John Dee; mar William Bromfield; succeeded by Elizabeth Wingfield*. Will PCC 2 Cobham; husband's will PCC 7 Rowe; *Visitations, Surrey*.

Gentlewoman: 94.317, 97.153, 97.359 [designated as 'Mother of the Maids', although listed with Gentlewomen]

Bromfield, William (d.c.1564) Lieutenant of the Ordnance. Father of William Bromfield, Gentleman Pensioner; father-in-law of Catherine Bromfield*. *CSP Foreign, 1561–62*; Tighe; will PCC 20 Stevenson.

Gentleman: 62.167, 62.348

Bromley, Sir Thomas (1530–1587) Lord Chancellor 1579, Privy Councillor 1579, kntd 1579, MP. Son of George Bromley and Jane Lacon; mar c.1560 Margaret Fortescue. *ODNB*; Hasler; Bindoff; will PCC 18 Spencer.

Primary: 81.1, 81.208, 82.2, 82.202, 82.420, 84.1, 84.199, 85.1, 85.192.

Brooke, Dorothy (c.1550–1622) Maid of Honour to Mary I and Elizabeth. Daughter of William [I] Brooke,* Lord Cobham and Dorothy Neville; half-sister of Henry [II] Brooke*, Lord Cobham, William [II] Brooke*, Lord Cobham, and Elizabeth Brooke*; mar Thomas Parry, daughter-in-law of Sir Thomas Parry*. *ODNB* under husband.

Maid of Honour: 67.321, 68.311

Brooke, Elizabeth (1562–1597) Mistress Brooke, Lady Cecil, Gentlewoman of the Privy Chamber and of the Bedchamber. Daughter of William [I] Brooke,* Lord Cobham and Frances Brooke* née Newton; sister of Henry Brooke*, Lord Cobham, and Sir William [II] Brooke*; half-sister of Dorothy Brooke*; mar 1589 Sir Robert Cecil*. *ODNB* under husband.

Maid of Honour: 71.322

Gentlewoman: 82.143, 82.343, 82.616, 84.137, 84.338, 85.128, 85.319, 88.129, 88.313, 89.127, 89.312

Lady: 94.101, 94.285, 97.100, 97.298

Regifted: 71.119, 71.322 (Queen gave gift from Blanch Parry* to her)

Brooke, Elizabeth—see Elizabeth Parr

Brooke, Frances, née Newton, Baroness Cobham (c.1532–1592) Mistress Newton, Lady of the Bedchamber. Daughter of John Newton and Margaret Poyntz; sister of Henry Newton*; Jane Newton* and Francis Newton*; mar 1560 William [I] Brooke*, Lord Cobham; mother of Elizabeth Brooke*, Henry Brooke*, and William [II] Brooke*. Mertens; *ODNB*; Hasler under husband; GEC, *Peerage* under husband.

Baroness: 62.79, 62.254, 63.78, 63.250, 64.73, 65.28, 65.195, 67.77, 67.247, 68.71, 68.240, 71.70, 71.240, 75.188, 76.92, 76.276, 77.83, 77.280, 78.84, 78.284, 79.81, 79.288, 81.76, 81.283, 82.73, 82.273, 82.506, 84.68, 84.266, 85.71, 85.262, 88.74, 88.259, 89.67, 89.252

Custody of Gift: 59.21, 59.38–39, 59.70, 59.81, 59.83, 59.85, 59.89–90, 59.92–93, 59.98, 59.101–102, 59.139, 59.142, 59.144, 59.149, 59.156–157, 59.159, 59.169, 59.175–176, 59.185–186, 59.188, 59.194, 62.15, 62.49, 62.72, 62.81, 62.83, 62.86, 62.89–91, 62.94–97, 62.100, 62.131, 62.133–142, 62.145, 62.148, 62.150–151, 62.154, 62.161, 62.163–164, 62.166, 62.170–171, 63.1, 63.37, 63.85–86, 63.89, 63.91–93, 63.96–98, 63.127, 63.131, 63.133, 63.139, 63.145, 63.151–152, 63.154, 63.159, 64.2, 64.14, 64.70, 64.77, 64.81, 64.84, 64.92, 64.119, 64.123, 64.128, 64.136, 81.96, 88.395, 89.407

Brooke, Frances - see Frances [II] Howard

Brooke, Henry, Lord Cobham (1564–1619) KG 1599, MP. Son of William [I] Brooke* and Frances Newton (Brooke*); brother of Elizabeth Brooke* and Sir William [II] Brooke*; half-brother of Dorothy Brooke*; mar 1601 Frances [II] Howard*. *ODNB*; Hasler; GEC, *Peerage*.
  Gentleman: 88.170, 88.360, 89.159, 89.351, 94.142, 94.333, 97.158, 97.360
  Lord: 98.71, 98.263, 99.67, 99.253, 00.74, 00.261, 03.63, 03.276
Brooke, Henry—see Henry Cobham
Brooke, Nicholas (fl.1580s) Sewer of the Chamber, Queen's servant, probable identification. father-in-law of Thomas Lisle and Edmund Lisle, also sewers. PRO E 115; will PCC 27 Dixy.
  Custody of Gift: 82.208
Brooke, William [I], Lord Cobham (1527–1597) Privy Councillor, Lord Warden of the Cinque Ports 1558, Lord Chamberlain 1597, kntd 1548, KG 1585, MP. Son of George Brooke and Anne Bray; brother of Sir Henry Cobham* and Elizabeth Parr*; mar 1st 1545 Dorothy Neville, 2nd 1560 Frances Newton (Brooke*); father of Henry Brooke* Lord Cobham, Sir William [II] Brooke*, Dorothy Brooke*, and Elizabeth Brooke*. *ODNB*; GEC, *Peerage*; Bindoff.
  Lord: 71.57, 71.227, 75.75, 75.183, 76.77, 76.260, 77.76, 77.273, 78.77, 78.277, 79.76, 79.280, 81.63, 81.270, 82.59, 82.259, 82.468, 84.54, 84.252, 85.58, 85.248, 88.58, 88.243, 89.53, 89.238, 94.54, 94.238, 97.57, 97.255
  Free Gift/Regifted: 71.119, 71.322 (Queen gave gift from Blanch Parry to his daughter)
Brooke, Sir William [II] (1565–1597) Keeper of Eltham Park, kntd 1591, MP, killed in duel. Son of William [I] Brooke* and Frances Newton (Brooke*); brother of Henry Brooke*, Lord Cobham and Elizabeth Brooke*; half-brother of Dorothy Brooke*; unmarried. *ODNB* under father; Hasler; will PCC 10 Cobham.
  Gentleman: 88.168, 88.361
  Knight: 97.123, 97.335
Brouncker, Sir Henry (1550–1607) Lord President of Munster, kntd 1597, MP. Son of Henry Brouncker and Ursula Yate; mar Anne Parker. Hasler.
  Gentleman: 79.204, 79.417, 82.179, 82.383, 82.588, 84.169, 84.396, 85.169, 85.368, 88.158, 88.349, 89.155, 89.347, 94.145, 94.336, 97.161, 97.363
  Knight: 98.136, 98.337, 99.126, 99.322, 00.129, 00.327, 03.134, 03.347
Broughton, Dorothy—see Dorothy Brooke
Browne, Anthony (1528–1592) Viscount Montagu, kntd 1547, KG 1555, MP. Son of Anthony Browne and Alice Gage; mar 1st c.1551 Jane Radcliffe, 2nd 1558 Magdalen Dacre (Browne*); father of Elizabeth Browne*; grandfather of Anthony Maria Browne*, Viscount Montagu. *ODNB*; GEC, *Peerage*; Bindoff; will PCC 22 Nevell.
  Viscount: 59.23, 59.244, 62.16, 62.196, 63.15, 63.187, 64.15, 65.116, 67.16, 67.186, 68.18, 68.187, 71.16, 71.186, 75.19, 76.21, 76.216, 77.24, 77.221, 78.22, 78.223, 79.22, 79.229, 81.19, 81.226, 82.19, 82.219 82.434, 84.17, 84.215, 85.18, 85.209, 88.18, 88.203, 89.16, 89.201
  Sundry Gift: 62.381 (Christening Gift for his child)
Browne, Anthony Maria (1574–1637) Viscount Montagu. Son of Anthony Browne and Mary Dormer; grandson of Anthony Browne*, Viscount Montagu; godson of Queen Elizabeth; mar 1591 Jane Sackville. GEC, *Peerage*.
  Viscount: 97.17 (gave 'nil')
Browne, Edmund (d.1606) Gentleman of Chapel Royal. Probable identification. *BDECM*.
  Custody of Gift: 82.334, 82.338
Browne, Elizabeth (1561–1631) Daughter of Anthony Browne*, Viscount Montagu, and Magdalen Dacre (Browne*); mar 1572 Sir Robert Dormer. Collins, *Peerage*.

Sundry Gift: 62.381 (Christening Gift)

Browne, Elizabeth—see Elizabeth Fitzgerald, Elizabeth Somerset

Browne, Lancelot (c.1552–1605) Physician. *ODNB*; *CSP Domestic, 1581–90, 1595–97,1598–1600, 1603–10.*

    Gentleman: 98.167, 98.372, 99.161, 99.362, 00.162, 00.364, 03.170, 03.391

Browne, Magdalen, née Dacre, Viscountess Montagu (1538–1608) Daughter of William Dacre and Elizabeth Talbot; sister of Anne Dacre* and Thomas Dacre*; mar 1558 Anthony Browne*, Viscount Montagu; mother of Elizabeth Browne*. GEC, *Peerage*.

    Viscountess: 59.52, 59.273, 62.50, 62.230, 63.51, 63.223, 64.51, 65.152, 67.52, 67.223, 68.31, 68.200, 71.31, 71.201, 75.39, 75.147, 76.43, 76.238, 77.45, 77.242, 78.44, 78.245, 79.42, 79.249, 81.37, 81.244, 82.36, 82.236, 82.484, 84.33, 84.231, 85.36, 85.227, 88.36, 88.221, 89.32, 89.217, 94.32, 94.216, 97.39, 97.238, 98.38, 98.239, 99.32, 99.227, 00.40, 00.237, 03.42, 03.255

    Sundry Gift: 62.381 (Christening Gift for her child)

Browne, Mary—see Mary Grey, Mary Wriothesley

Browne, Thomas (d.1582) Musician, Singer, served Edward VI, Mary I, and Elizabeth. *BDECM*; *RECM*.

    Gentleman: 59.184, 59.408

Browne, unidentified (fl.1580s) of the Larder, Queen's Servant. Son of Lionel Browne.

    Custody of Gift: 82.358

Brussells, Jane, née Hawk (c.1543–1596) Mistress Brussells, Mistress Heneage, Gentlewoman of the Privy Chamber, Gentlewoman of the Bedchamber, of Flanders. Daughter of Francis Hawk and Barbara [née?] Hawk, both parents served Mary I; cousin by marriage to Thomas Heneage*; mar 1st by 1566 unidentified Brussells, 2nd aft.1589 William Heneage. Tighe; PRO E 179/266/13, E 35/542, LC 5/49; BL Lansdowne MSS 30, 34, Harleian MS 1644.

    Gentlewoman: 76.143, 76.337, 77.151, 77.348, 78.152, 78.353, 79.154, 79.361, 81.148, 81.355, 82.142, 82.342, 82.608, 84.140, 84.337, 85.148, 85.340, 88.142, 88.326, 89.138, 89.323, 94.130, 94.321

    Custody of Gift: 77.98, 77.103, 77.114, 77.177, 78.34, 78.152, 78.155, 78.157, 78.176, 79.114, 79.143, 79.154, 79.163, 79.166, 81.18, 81.98, 81.106, 81.148, 81.155, 81.177, 81.181, 82.142, 82.342, 84.84, 84.104, 84.137, 84.146, 84.151, 84.159, 84.168, 85.138, 85.159, 88.90, 88.102, 88.128, 88.134, 88.136, 88.139, 88.155, 88.172

Brydges, Mistress [née?] (fl.1600s) Mother of the Maids. unidentified.

    Maid of Honour: 03.379

Brydges, Dorothy, née Bray, Baroness Chandos (c.1530–1605) Baroness Chandos Knollys. Daughter of Edmund, Lord Bray and Jane Halywell; sister of Elizabeth Catesby* and Frances Lyfield*; 1st cousin of Sir Edward Bray*; mar 1st c.1548 Edmund Brydges*, Lord Chandos, 2nd c.1578 Sir William Knollys*, later Earl of Banbury. *ODNB*; GEC, *Peerage*.

    Baroness: 59.81, 59.301, 62.83, 62.263, 68.75, 68.245, 71.74, 71.244, 75.193, 76.90, 76.282, 77.89, 77.286, 78.93, 78.288, 79.84, 79.291, 81.80, 81.289, 82.76, 82.277, 82.497, 84.72, 84.270, 85.75, 85.266, 88.77, 88.262, 89.70, 89.255, 94.68, 94.252, 97.77, 97.274, 98.76, 98.275, 99.72, 99.265, 00.79, 00.274, 03.78, 03.292

Brydges, Edmund (d.1573) Lord Chandos, KG (1572). Son of John Brydges, Lord Chandos and Elizabeth Grey; mar c.1548 Dorothy Bray (Brydges*); father of Giles Brydges*, Lord Chandos, William Brydges*, and Eleanor Brydges*. *ODNB*; GEC, *Peerage*; Hasler; will PCC 20 Peter.

    Lord: 59.71, 59.292, 62.70, 62.250, 68.62, 68.233, 71.59, 71.229

Brydges, Eleanor (fl.1570s–1580s) Maid of Honour, Mistress Gifford, Gentlewoman of the Privy Chamber. Daughter of Edmund Brydges*, Lord Chandos and Dorothy Bray (Brydges*); sister of William Brydges*; mar 1581 Sir George Gifford*. Name listed, but struck through, as Maid for 1582. Hasler.
  Maid of Honour: 75.204, 76.367, 77.370, 78.375, 79.382, 81.376
  Gentlewoman: 84.138, 84.331, 85.135, 85.327
Brydges, Elizabeth (1578–1617) Mistress Brydges, Gentlewoman of the Privy Chamber. Daughter of Giles Brydges*, Lord Chandos and Frances Clinton (Brydges*); mar 1603 John Kennedy. GEC, *Peerage* and Hasler under father; May, *Elizabethan Courtier*; Davies.
  Gentlewoman: 94.128, 94.319, 97.140, 97.342, 98.138, 98.353, 00.154, 00.339, 03.138, 03.351
Brydges, Elizabeth—see Elizabeth Fane, Elizabeth Grey
Brydges, Lady Frances, née Clinton, Baroness Chandos (1542–1623) Daughter of Edward Clinton*, Earl of Lincoln and Ursula Stourton; sister of Lady Anne Askew* and Henry Clinton*; mar 1573 Giles Brydges*, Lord Chandos; mother of Elizabeth Brydges*. GEC, *Peerage*; will PCC 12 Dixy.
  Baroness: 75.199, 76.85, 76.283, 77.90, 77.287, 78.94, 78.289, 79.85, 79.292, 81.81, 81.288, 82.505, 84.73, 84.271, 85.76, 85.267, 88.78, 88.263, 89.71, 89.256, 94.69, 94.253, 00.85, 00.286, 03.79, 03.293
  Sundry Gift: 75.251 (Christening Gift for her child)
Brydges, Giles, Lord Chandos (1548–1594) Son of Edmund Brydges*, Lord Chandos and Dorothy Bray (Brydges*); brother of William Brydges* and Eleanor Brydges*; mar c.1573 Frances Clinton (Brydges*); father of Elizabeth Brydges*. GEC, *Peerage*; will PCC 12 Dixy.
  Lord: 75.64, 75.172, 76.67, 76.269, 77.69, 77.266, 78.68, 78.270, 79.66, 79.273, 81.64, 81.271, 82.60, 82.260, 82.460, 84.57, 84.254, 85.60, 85.251, 88.61, 88.246, 89.55, 89.240, 94.57, 94.241
  Sundry Gift: 75.251 (Christening Gift for his child)
Brydges, Mary, née Hopton, Baroness Chandos (d.1624) Gentlewoman of the Privy Chamber. Daughter of Sir Owen Hopton* and Anne Ichingham; sister of Anne Hopton (Brydges*); mar 1575 William Brydges*, Lord Chandos. GEC, *Peerage*.
  Gentlewoman: 76.144, 76.338
  Sundry Gift: 77.421 (Christening Gift for her child)
Brydges, son (b.1576) Son of William Brydges* and Mary Hopton (Brydges*).
  Sundry Gift: 77.421 (Christening Gift)
Brydges, daughter (b.1575) Daughter of Giles Brydges* and Frances Clinton (Brydges*).
  Sundry Gift: 75.251 (Christening Gift)
Brydges, William (1548–1602) Lord Chandos. Son of Edmund Brydges* and Dorothy Bray (Brydges*); brother of Giles Brydges*; mar c.1575 Mary Hopton (Brydges*). GEC, *Peerage*.
  Lord: 97.59, 97.260
  Sundry Gift: 77.421 (Christening Gift for his child)
Brydges, Winifred—see Winifred Paulet
Brydges—see also Bridges
Buckhurst, Lord/Baroness—see Cecily Sackville, née Baker, 1567–1615; Thomas Sackville, 1567–1608
Buckler, Catherine, née Denys (c.1512-c.1584) Lady Buckler. Daughter of Sir William Denys and Anne Berkeley; sister of Sir Walter Denys and Sir Maurice Denys*; mar 1st

1522 Edmund Tame, 2nd Sir Walter Buckler, 3rd Roger Lygon. *CSP Mary, 1554* ; PRO C 1/1267/44–45.

Lady: 59.95, 59.315

Budde, Mathias (c.1553–1591) Special Ambassador from Frederick II*, King of Denmark, Royal Governor of Arensburg on Ösel, 1584–1587, several times special ambassador from Denmark. *CSP Foreign, 1581–82*; Lackhart.

Sundry Gift: 84.422, 85.408 (Gift to Envoy)

Buillon—see Henri de la Tour d'Auvergne

Bull, Randall/Randolph (d.1617) Goldsmith, Queen's Clockmaker. PRO C 2/Eliz/B11/17; will PCC 123 Weldon; *CSP Domestic, 1591–1594*.

Gentleman: 00.195, 00.398

Bullen—see Boleyn

Bullingham, John (1534–1598) Bishop of Gloucester 1581–1598. *ODNB*.

Bishop: 82.54, 82.254, 82.453, 84.50, 84.248, 85.54, 85.244, 88.54, 88.239, 89.49, 89.234, 94.48, 94.231, 97.52, 97.251, 98.52, 98.254

Bullingham, Nicholas (c.1511–1576) Bishop of Lincoln 1560–1571, Bishop of Worcester 1571–1576. *ODNB*; Hasler under son, Francis Bullingham.

Bishop: 62.25, 62.205, 63.24, 63.196, 64.23, 65.125, 67.25, 67.195, 68.40, 68.209, 71.39, 71.209, 75.48, 75.156, 76.51, 76.246

Bullion, Duke of—see Henri de la Tour d'Auvergne

Burd, Helen—see Helen Seckford

Burges, Isaac (fl.1580s) of the Scullery, Gentleman of the Chamber. PRO E 115; *CSP Domestic, 1598–1601*; Bowler.

Custody of Gift: 82.346

Burgh, Lord/Baroness –Frances Burgh, née Vaughan, c.1580–1647; Thomas Burgh, 5th, 1584–1597

Burgh—see also Bourke

Burgh, Frances, née Vaughan, Baroness Burgh (c.1562–1647) Maid of Honour. Daughter of John Vaughan and Anne Pickering; great-niece of Blanche Parry*; mar 1580 Thomas, Lord Burgh*. GEC, *Peerage*.

Maid of Honour: 79.385

Baroness: 85.85, 85.279, 88.90, 88.275, 94.75, 94.259, 97.283, 98.89, 98.283, 99.84, 99.275, 03.87, 03.303

Burgh, Mary (fl.1570s) Maid of Honour. Daughter of William, Lord Burgh and Lady Catherine Clinton; sister of Thomas, Lord Burgh*; mar 1577 Sir Richard Bulkeley. GEC, *Peerage*.

Maid of Honour: 75.207, 76.370, 77.373

Burgh, Thomas, Lord Burgh (1558–1597) Lord Deputy of Ireland, Gentleman Pensioner, KG (1593). Son of William, Lord Burgh and Lady Catherine Clinton; brother of Mary Burgh*; mar 1580 Frances Vaughan (Burgh*). GEC, *Peerage*; will PCC sentence 57 Lewyn; Tighe.

Lord: 94.63, 94.247, 97.69, 97.263

Burghley, Lord/Baroness—see Dorothy Cecil, née Neville, 1598–1609; Mildred Cecil née Cooke, 1571–1589; Thomas Cecil, 2nd, 1598–1605; William Cecil, 1st, 1571–1598

Burgrail—see Burgrave

Burgrave, Daniel (c.1555-aft.1609) Procureur-General of Flanders, formerly Earl of Leicester's secretary in the Low Countries, alias Burgrail, Burchgrave. *CSP Foreign, 1584–85, 1596–87, 1588*; Nichols, *Progresses James*; BL Additional MSS 48084, 48149.

Sundry Gift: 88.398 (Gift to Envoy)

Burke—see Bourke

Burrell, Henry (d.1562) Sergeant at Arms to the Queen. will PCC 24 Streat.
Gentleman: 59.205, 59.429

Burreus, Dionysius (fl.1560s) Mounsieur Dennys. Resident Ambassador from Gustav* and Eric XIV*, Kings of Sweden, 1558–1561. *CSP Foreign, 1558–59*.
Sundry Gift: 62.380 (Gift to Envoy upon his departure from England)

Burroughs, Burrowes—see Burgh

Bursch, William (fl.1600s) unidentified.
Gentleman: 03.206, 03.430

Burton, Anne (fl.1600s) Possible identification, daughter of Catherine Cromer*, alias Anne Vinton, related to Barnard Burton. Mother's will PCC 25 Montague.
Gentlewoman: 03.146, 03.361

Burton, Catherine—see Catherine Cromer

Busson—see Brisson

Butler, Elizabeth [I], née Sheffield, Countess of Ormond (1561–1600) Gentlewoman of the Privy Chamber. Daughter of John Sheffield* and Douglas Howard (Sheffield*); sister of Edmund, Lord Sheffield*; 2nd cousin of Queen Elizabeth; mar 1582 Thomas Butler*, Earl of Ormond; mother of Elizabeth [II] Butler*. *ODNB*; GEC, *Peerage*.
Countess: 88.35, 88.220, 89.30, 89.215
Sundry Gift: 62.389 (Christening Gift), 89.403 (Christening Gift for her child)

Butler, Elizabeth [II] (1588–1628) Daughter of Thomas Butler*, Earl of Ormond and Elizabeth [I] Sheffield (Butler*); granddaughter of John Sheffield* and Douglas Howard (Sheffield*); mar 1st Theobald Butler, 2nd Richard Preston. *ODNB*; GEC, *Peerage*.
Sundry Gift: 89.403 (Christening Gift)

Butler, Griselda, née Roche (1516–1581) Lady Butler. Daughter of Brian Roche and Elizabeth Carew; 1st cousin of Anne Carew*; mar c.1528 Sir John Butler MP; 1st cousin of Anne Throckmorton*; 1st cousin once removed of Arthur Throckmorton* and Elizabeth Throckmorton*. *CSP Domestic, 1547–1580*; Bindoff and Hasler under husband; *VCH, Hertfordshire*.
Lady: 59.82, 59.302, 62.85, 62.267, 63.82, 63.261, 64.86, 65.17, 65.184, 67.88, 67.258, 68.84, 68.253, 71.83, 71.253, 76.109, 76.304, 77.109, 77.306, 78.106, 78.307, 79.104, 79.312

Butler, Thomas, Earl of Ormond (1532–1614) KG 1588. Son of James Butler and Joan Fitzgerald; mar 1st c.1559 Elizabeth Berkeley, 2nd 1582 Elizabeth Sheffield (Butler*), 3rd 1601 Helen Barry; father of Elizabeth [II] Butler*. Name listed with 'X' and no participation for 1582. *ODNB*; GEC, *Peerage*; BL Sloane MS 814.
Earl: 67.15, 67.185, 68.16, 68.185, 77.22, 77.220, 78.21, 78.222, 79.20, 79.227, 88.12, 88.202, 89.13, 89.198
Sundry Gift: 89.396 (installed KG), 89.403 (Christening Gift for his child)
Regifted: 67.20–26, 67.29, 67.30, 67.32–36 (Queen gave him a silver and gilt cup plus £220 from gifts she received from bishops)

Bybye, John (fl.1580s) Groom of the Chamber. Mar 1554 Helena Lawrence. PRO LC 5/33, E 115.
Custody of Gift: 82.307

Byllyard, Agnes, née Hilton (fl.1550s–1560s) Mistress Byllyard. Laundress to Queen Elizabeth. probable relative of Joan Hilton, also Laundress to Queen Elizabeth; mar c.1548 Lewis Byllyard*. Madden; Mertens.
Gentlewoman: 59.154, 59.372

Byllyard, Lewis (d.1590) Crossbow-maker and Handgun-maker to the Queen. Mar by 1548 Agnes Hilton (Byllyard*), master/adopted father of William Byllyard*. Blackmore; *CPR, 1565*.

Gentleman: 63.168, 63.347

Byllyard, William (fl.1580s) Crossbowmaker to the Queen. Apprentice/adopted son of Lewis Byllyard*, alias William Wood. Blackmore; *CPR, 1565,*
Gentleman: 81.205, 81.420

Cage, Isabel—see Isabel Bacon

Calveley, John (d.1559) Gentleman Pensioner, Ranger of Delamere Forest in Cheshire. Tighe; *CPR, 1558–60*; *Visitations, Cheshire*; will PCC 34 Chaynay; PRO C 1/1111/11.
Gentleman: 59.191, 59.416

Campagni—see Compagni

Canterbury, Archbishop—see Matthew Parker, 1559–1575; Edmund Grindal, 1576–1583; John Whitgift, 1583–1604

Cardell, Thomas (d.1621) Lutenist, Dancing master. *BDECM.*
Custody of Gift: 82.77, 82.230

Carew—see also Carey

Carew, Sir Lauren's wife—see Elizabeth Carew

Carew, Anne—see Anne Throckmorton

Carew, Elizabeth, née Norwich (fl.1560s–1580s) Lady Carew, Lady of the Bedchamber, alias Sir Lauren's wife (scribal error for Gawain, 1564). Daughter of John Norwich and Susan [née?]; mar bef 1562 Sir Gawain Carew*. Hasler under husband; Mertens.
Lady: 62.96, 62.265, 63.93, 63.254, 64.81, 65.13, 65.179, 67.85, 67.255, 68.82, 68.251, 71.82, 71.252, 76.106, 76.301, 77.105, 77.302, 78.103, 78.304, 79.102, 79.310, 81.100, 81.307, 82.95, 82.295, 82.547, 84.91, 84.289, 85.96, 85.291, 88.98, 88.282, 89.90, 89.275, 94.90, 94.274,

Carew, Sir Gawain (1503–1585) Gentleman Pensioner 1539–1547, kntd 1545, MP. Son of Edmund Carew and Catherine Huddlesfield; brother of George Carew*; mar 1st 1531 Anne Brandon, 2nd Mary Wotton, 3rd 1562 Elizabeth Norwich (Carew*). Hasler; *ODNB* under brother; Tighe.
Knight: 59.132, 59.351, 62.120, 62.299, 63.116, 63.289, 64.109, 64.163, 65.43, 65.210, 67.113, 67.283, 68.112, 68.281, 71.112, 71.282, 76.131, 76.321, 77.129, 77.326, 78.135, 78.334, 79.135, 79.342, 81.129, 81.337, 82.122, 82.323, 82.533, 84.116, 84.316

Carew, George (c.1498–1588) Dean of the Chapel Royal 1558, Dean of Exeter, Archdeacon, Chaplain to Henry VIII, Edward VI, and Elizabeth. Son of Edmund Carew and Catherine Huddlesfield; brother of Gawain Carew*; mar c.1552 Anne Harvey. *ODNB*; will PCC 40 Rowe.
Chaplain: 59.134, 59.353, 62.128, 62.308, 63.121, 63.294, 64.114, 64.168, 65.51, 65.218, 67.120, 67.290, 68.141, 68.314, 71.145, 71.323, 75.114, 75.200, 76.169, 76.364, 77.170, 77.367, 78.171, 78.379, 79.174, 79.387, 81.168, 81.382, 82.165, 82.370, 82.530

Carew, Margaret—see Margaret Lady Tailboys

Carew, Penelope—see Philadelphia Scrope

Carew, Peter (1514–1575) Gentleman Pensioner, kntd 1545, MP. Son of William Carew and Jane Courtenay; mar 1547 Margaret Tailboys (Carew*). Hasler; *ODNB*; will PCC 1 Carew.
Knight: 62.121, 62.300, 63.117, 63.290, 64.110, 64.164, 65.44, 65.211, 67.110, 67.280, 68.107, 68.275, 71.107, 71.277

Carey—see also Carew

Carey, Anne [I], née Morgan, Baroness Hunsdon (c.1530–1607) Lady of the Privy Chamber. Daughter of Thomas Morgan and Anne Whitney; mar 1545 Henry Carey*; mother of George Carey*, Catherine Berkeley*, Margaret Hoby*, and Philadelphia Scrope*; grandmother of Anne [II] Carey*. *ODNB*; GEC, *Peerage.*

Baroness: 59.107, 59.326, 62.77, 62.252, 63.76, 63.244, 64.76, 65.8, 65.175, 67.75, 67.245, 68.76, 68.246, 75.189, 76.81, 76.277, 77.84, 77.281, 78.81, 78.285, 81.79, 81.287, 82.75, 82.276, 82.496, 84.69, 84.268, 85.72, 85.264, 88.72, 88.257, 89.65, 89.250, 94.65, 94.249, 97.76, 97.275, 98.74, 98.277, 99.70, 99.267, 00.77, 00.276, 03.90, 03.290

  Sundry Gift: 63.366 (Christening Gift for her child, Philadelphia)

Carey, Anne [II] (1580-c.1617) Maid of Honour. Daughter of John, Lord Carey and Mary Hyde; granddaughter of Henry Carey* and Anne Morgan (Carey*); mar 1601 Francis Lovell. *Visitations, Norfolk*; Merton.

  Maid of Honour: 98.342, 99.330, 00.333

Carey, Catherine—see Catherine Knollys, Catherine Howard, Catherine Paget Carey

Carey, Edward (c.1540–1618) Groom of the Privy Chamber, Master of the Jewels and Plate, kntd 1596, MP. Son of John Carey and Joyce Denny; half-brother of Francis Walsingham*; 1st cousin of Henry Carey*; brother-in-law to John Tamworth* and Walter Mildmay*; mar 1575 Catherine [I] Knyvett*. Hasler; will PCC 75 Meade.

  Gentleman: 77.174

  Free Gift: 62.372, 63.356, 64.210, 67.352, 68.339, 71.352, 75.239, 76.401, 77.403, 78.409, 79.423, 81.422, 82.413, 84.399, 85.393, 88.384, 89.383, 94.381, 97.403, 97.412, 98.409, 98.418, 99.397, 99.405, 00.400, 00.408, 03.433, 03.440

  Custody of Gift: 62.158–59, 62.168–69, 97.420, 97.424, 98.13, 99.195, 03.447

Carey, Elizabeth, née Spencer, Baroness Hunsdon (1547–1618) Daughter of Sir John Spencer and Catherine Kitson; sister of Alice Stanley*; mar 1st 1574 George Carey*, Lord Hunsdon, 2nd 1613 Ralph, Lord Eure; mother of Elizabeth [II] Berkeley*. *ODNB*; GEC, *Peerage*.

  Baroness: 97.82, 97.277, 98.75, 98.278, 99.71, 99.268, 00.78, 00.277, 03.76, 03.289

  Lady: 94.106, 94.290

  Sundry Gift: 77.416 (Christening Gift for her child)

Carey, George, Lord Hunsdon (1547–1603) Gentleman Pensioner 1573, Knight Marshal of the Household 1578, Captain of the Isle of Wight 1583, Captain of the Gentlemen Pensioners 1596, Lord Chamberlain 1597, Privy Councillor 1597, kntd 1570, KG 1597. Son of Henry Carey* and Anne Morgan (Carey*); brother of Catherine Berkeley*, Margaret Hoby*, and Philadelphia Scrope*; 1st cousin once removed to Queen Elizabeth; mar 1574 Elizabeth Spencer (Carey*); father of Elizabeth Berkeley*. *ODNB*; GEC, *Peerage*.

  Knight: 89.122, 89.303

  Lord: 97.73, 97.259, 98.57, 98.258, 99.53, 99.248, 00.61, 00.258, 03.62, 03.275

  Sundry Gift: 77.416 (Christening Gift for his child)

Carey, Henry, Lord Hunsdon (c.1524–1596) Captain of the Gentlemen Pensioners 1564, Privy Councillor 1577, Lord Chamberlain 1585, KG 1561. Son of William Carey and Mary Boleyn; 1st cousin of Queen Elizabeth and Edward Carey*; mar 1545 Anne Morgan (Carey*); father of George Carey*, Catherine Berkeley*, Margaret Hoby*, and Philadelphia Scrope*; grandfather of Anne [II] Carey* and Elizabeth [II] Berkeley*. *ODNB*; GEC, *Peerage*; will PCC 54 Drake.

  Lord: 62.66, 62.233, 63.67, 63.226, 64.67, 65.167, 67.65, 67.235, 68.65, 68.234, 71.61, 71.231, 75.65, 75.173, 76.66, 76.263, 77.64, 77.261, 78.63, 78.264, 81.58, 81.265, 82.56, 82.256, 82.459, 84.52, 84.250, 85.57, 85.249, 88.56, 88.241, 89.51, 89.236, 94.52, 94.236

  Sundry Gift: 63.366 (Christening Gift for his child, Philadelphia)

Carey, Margaret—see Margaret Hoby

Carey, Philadelphia—see Philadelphia Scrope

Carlell—see Carlisle

Carlisle, Bishop—see Owen Oglethorpe, 1556–1559; Richard Barnes, 1570–1577; John May, 1577–1598; Henry Robinson, 1598–1618

Carmarvan—see Carmarden

Carmarden, Richard (c.1535–1604) Surveyor of Customs. Mar 1ˢᵗ 1564 Alice More, 2ⁿᵈ Mary Alington; related to Elizabeth Wolley*. Nef; *CSP Domestic, 1547–1580, 1591–94, 1595–97, 1598–1601.*

> **Gentleman**: 85.180, 85.379, 88.169, 88.359, 94.154, 94.347, 97.166, 97.369, 98.163, 98.370, 99.157, 99.358, 00.159, 00.361, 03.162, 03.382

Carmichael, Hugh (d.1572) Mar Jane Newton*; brother-in-law of Frances Brooke*, Henry Newton*, Nazareth Paget*, and Francis Newton*.

> **Sundry Gift**: 71.361 (Marriage Gift)

Caron, Noel (c.1530–1624) Agent for Flanders, Lord of Schoonewalle, resident Dutch Agent 1591–1624. Son of Jacques Caron van Schonewalle, unmarried. *ODNB*; will PCC 74 Barrington; Siddons.

> **Sundry Gift**: 00.417 (Gift to Envoy)

Carovacant—see Cavalcanti

Carr, Bridget, née Chaworth (1548–1621) Gentlewoman of Privy Chamber, Mistress Chaworth, Mistress Carr. Daughter of John Chaworth and Mary Paston; mar 1584 William Carr*; mother of Bridget Carr; 3ʳᵈ cousin of Queen Elizabeth. *Visitations, Lincolnshire*; Arnold, *QE Wardrobe.*

> **Gentlewoman**: 79.149, 79.356, 81.144, 81.352, 82.138, 82.338, 82.613, 84.135, 84.333, 85.134, 85.328, 88.141, 88.325, 89.137, 89.322, 94.129, 94.320, 97.141, 97.343, 98.139, 98.345, 99.134, 99.352, 00.135, 00.337, 03.139, 03.352

> **Custody of Gift**: 81.95, 81.132, 81.137, 81.140, 81.148, 81.153, 81.160, 81.167, 81.172, 81.186, 81.201, 82.88–89, 82.92, 82.387, 82.93, 82.105, 82.387, 84.79, 84.136, 84.154, 84.165, 84.181, 84.191–193, 84.195, 85.98–99, 85.102, 85.104, 85.106, 85.128, 85.130, 85.139, 85.157, 85.160, 85.164, 85.184, 85.186, 88.91, 88.93, 88.99, 88.113, 88.124, 88.129, 88.148, 88.167, 88.182–183, 89.85, 89.88, 89.92, 89.99, 89.101, 89.103–104, 89.126–127, 89.132, 89.145, 89.155, 99.151, 99.175

Carr, William (1551–1608) Esquire for the Body. Son of Robert Carr and Elizabeth Cawthorne; mar 1584 Bridget Chaworth (Carr*). *Visitations, Lincolnshire.*

> **Gentleman**: 89.169, 89.365, 94.149, 94.339, 97.162, 97.365, 98.160, 98.368, 99.154, 99.356, 00.156, 00.359, 03.161, 03.381

Carrouges—see Veneur

Casimir, Johann (1543–1592) Count Palatine of the Rhine, Duke of Bavaria, KG 1579. Gifts to his envoys: Peter Beutterich* and Joannes Junius*. *CSP Foreign, 1577–78*; PRO E 351/2215.

> **Sundry Gift**: 78.428, 79.442, 79.451 (Sovereign sending Envoy to England)

Casimir, Gent from (fl.1570s) Gentleman representing Johann Casimir, Duke of Bavaria.

> **Sundry Gift**: 79.442 (Gift to Envoy)

Castelnau, Michel de Mauvissière—see Mauvissière, Michel Castelnau de

Castiglione—see Castilion

Castilion, Elizabeth (d.1599) Daughter of John Baptist Castilion* and Margaret Campagni (Castilion*); granddaughter of Bartholomew Campagni*, mar Peter Leigh*. Burke.

> **Sundry Gift**: 88.400 (Marriage Gift)

Castilion, John Baptist (c.1515–1598) Italian tutor to Princess Elizabeth, Groom of the Privy Chamber, courtier poet, alias Master Baptist, Giovanni Battista Castiglione. Son of Piero Castiglione; grandson of Baldassare Castiglione; mar 1558 Margaret Compagni (Castilion*); father of Elizabeth Castilion*. *CPR 1563–66, 1566–69; 1569–72*; *Visitations, Berkshire*; Acontius, J.: *Vna Essortatione al Timor di Dio; Con alcune rime Italiane nouamente messe in luce.* ed. Giovanni Battista Castiglioni (1580), STC 92; Hasler under son Francis Castilion; Siddons; Lawson, *Gift Books.*

Free Gift: 59.447, 62.158–59, 62.168–69, 62.371, 63.355, 64.209, 67.351, 68.338, 71.351, 75.238, 76.403, 77.405, 78.411, 79.425, 81.427, 84.404, 85.397, 88.381, 89.382, 94.386, 97.407, 98.413

Custody of Gift: 59.143, 59.200, 62.173, 65.46, 76.150, 76.168, 76.194, 77.194, 78.191, 78.193, 79.198–200, 79.203, 81.198–199, 82.199, 82.410, 89.178–179, 89.381

Sundry Gift: 88.400 (Marriage Gift to his daughter)

Castilion, Margaret, née Compagni (c.1535-c.1622) Mistress Baptist, Gentlewoman of the Privy Chamber, Mother of the Maids. Daughter of Bartholomew Compagni*, mar 1ˢᵗ Lazarus Allen, 2ⁿᵈ by 1558 John Baptist Castilion* MP; mother of Elizabeth Castilion*. Father's will PCC 24 Loftes; Hasler under husband.

Gentlewoman: 62.142, 62.322, 63.133, 63.306, 65.71, 65.236, 67.144, 67.314, 68.129, 68.297, 71.135, 71.305, 75.96, 76.146, 76.349, 77.145, 77.342, 78.147, 78.348, 79.148, 79.355, 81.142, 81.349

Maid of Honour: 82.369, 84.361, 85.354, 88.346 (Mother of Maids)

Cater, William (c.1530-aft.1581) Goldsmith. *Visitations, Berkshire*; PRO C 1/1293/18–22, E 115.

Gentleman: 81.204, 81.418

Goldsmith: 67.313, 67.330

Catesby, Elizabeth, née Bray (d.1573) Lady Catesby. Daughter of Edmund, Lord Bray and Jane Halywell; sister of Frances Lyfield* and Dorothy Brydges*; 1ˢᵗ cousin of Edward Bray*; mar 1ˢᵗ 1528 Ralph Verney, 2ⁿᵈ 1548 Sir Richard Catesby, 3ʳᵈ William Clarke, 4ᵗʰ Henry Phillips. GEC, *Peerage*.

Lady: 59.86, 59.306

Cavalcanti, Stiatta (1527–1560s) Venetian Merchant, alias Carovacant. Son of Giovanni (John) di Lorenzo Cavalcanti and Monna Ginevra; mar 1563 Ipolyta Castiglione; probably related by marriage to John Baptist Castilion*; connected with Guido Cavalcanti, envoy from France. *CSP Domestic, 1547–1580*; Sicca; Siddons.

Sundry Gift: 64.225 (Gift from Queen)

Cave, Sir Ambrose (c.1503–1568) Privy Councillor 1558, Chancellor of the Duchy of Lancaster 1558, kntd 1525. Son of Richard Cave and Margaret Saxby; uncle of Anne Hampden*; brother-in-law of Bridget Cave*; mar c.1546 Margaret Willington; father of Margaret Knollys*. *ODNB*; Hasler; BL Royal MS 18 D III.

Knight: 59.113, 59.332, 62.104, 62.284, 63.102, 63.275, 64.96, 64.150, 65.32, 65.199, 67.102, 67.272, 68.101, 68.270

Cave, Anne—see Anne Hampden

Cave, Bridget, née Skipwith (d.1587) Gentlewoman of the Privy Chamber. Daughter of William Skipwith and Alice Dymoke; sister of Henry Skipwith* and Margaret Tailboys*; sister-in-law of Sir Ambrose Cave*; mar c.1566 Brian Cave. Merten.

Gentlewoman: 62.133, 62.313, 63.126, 63.299, 64.118, 64.172, 65.55, 65.222, 67.125, 67.295, 68.122, 68.290, 71.123, 71.293, 75.90, 76.145, 76.339, 77.153, 77.350, 78.154, 78.355, 79.156, 79.363, 81.151, 81.357, 82.146, 82.346, 82.591, 84.144, 84.341, 85.141, 85.333, 88.135, 88.319

Cave, Margaret—see Margaret Knollys

Cavendish, Elizabeth (fl.1580s) Maid of Honour. Daughter of William Cavendish and Mary Wentworth. HMC Salisbury, vol 4, p. 153.

Maid of Honour: 88.345, 89.343

Cavendish, Elizabeth—see Elizabeth Hardwick, Elizabeth Snowe, Elizabeth Stuart

Cavendish, Mary—see Mary Talbot

Caverley—see Calveley

Cawood, John (1514–1572) Royal Printer, shared position with Richard Jugge*. father-in-law of George Bishop*; mar 1st unidentified, 2nd 1569 Agnes Keyne. *ODNB*.
Gentleman: 59.199, 59.423

Cecil, Anne—see Anne Vere

Cecil, Dorothy, née Neville, Baroness Burghley (1548–1609) Daughter of John Neville and Lucy Somerset (Neville*); mar 1564 Thomas Cecil*, later Lord Burghley. *ODNB*; GEC, *Peerage*.
Baroness: 00.90, 00.284

Cecil, Elizabeth (1564–1583) Daughter of William Cecil* and Mildred Cooke (Cecil*); sister of Robert Cecil* and Anne Vere*; half-sister of Thomas Cecil*; godchild of Queen Elizabeth; aunt of Elizabeth Hatton*; mar 1582 William Wentworth. *ODNB* under father.
Sundry Gift: 64.230 (Christening Gift)

Cecil, Elizabeth—see Elizabeth Brooke, Elizabeth Hatton

Cecil, Lucy—see Lucy Paulet

Cecil, Mildred, née Cooke, Baroness Burghley (1526–1589) Lady Cecil. Daughter of Anthony Cooke* and Anne FitzWilliam; sister of Catherine Cooke* and Elizabeth Russell*; mar 1545 William Cecil*; mother of Anne Vere*, Elizabeth Cecil*, William [II] Cecil and Robert Cecil*. *ODNB*; Harvey.
Lady: 59.94, 59.314, 62.89, 62.266, 63.86, 63.259, 64.78, 65.11, 65.178, 67.83, 67.253, 68.80, 68.249, 71.80, 71.250
Baroness: 75.196, 76.94, 76.275, 77.80, 77.277, 78.80, 78.281, 79.78, 79.285, 81.74, 81.281, 82.71, 82.271, 82.500, 84.66, 84.264, 85.69, 85.260, 88.71, 88.256, 89.64, 89.249
Sundry Gift: 62.379, 64.230 (Christening Gift for her child), 64.231 (Gift to her daughter)

Cecil, Robert (1563–1612) Privy Councillor 1591, Chancellor of the Duchy of Lancaster 1597, Principal Secretary 1598, later Lord Cecil 1603, later Earl of Salisbury 1605, kntd 1591. Son of William Cecil* and Mildred Cooke (Cecil*), brother of Elizabeth Cecil* and Anne Vere*, half-brother of Thomas Cecil*, mar 1589 Elizabeth Brooke* (Cecil). *ODNB*; Hasler; GEC, *Peerage*.
Knight: 94.116, 94.299, 97.118, 97.317, 98.119, 98.320, 99.113, 99.308, 00.116, 00.315, 03.119, 03.332

Cecil, Thomas (1542–1623) Lord Burghley 1598, kntd 1575, KG 1601; cr. Earl of Exeter 1605. Son of William Cecil* and Mary Cheke; half-brother of Robert Cecil*; mar 1st 1564 Dorothy Neville (Cecil*), 2nd 1610 Frances Brydges; father of Elizabeth Hatton*. *ODNB*; Hasler; GEC, *Peerage*.
Knight: 88.124, 88.308, 89.118, 89.302, 94.115, 94.298, 97.119, 97.318, 98.120, 98.321, 99.65, 99.258, 00.72, 00.266, 03.72, 03.285

Cecil, Sir William [I] (1521–1598) Privy Councillor 1558, Principal Secretary 1558, Lord Burghley cr.1571, Lord Treasurer 1572, courtier poet, kntd 1551, KG 1572, MP. Son of Robert Cecil and Jane Heckington; mar 1st 1541 Mary Cheke, 2nd 1545 Mildred Cooke (Cecil*); father of Thomas Cecil*, Anne Vere*, Elizabeth Cecil*, William [II] Cecil* and Robert Cecil*. *ODNB*; GEC, *Peerage*; Hasler; Kinney.
Knight: 59.111, 59.330, 62.102, 62.282, 63.100, 63.273, 64.95, 64.148, 65.30, 65.198, 67.101, 67.271, 68.100, 68.269, 71.100, 71.270
Primary: 75.3, 76.4, 76.199, 77.5, 77.202, 78.5, 78.206, 79.3, 79.210, 81.2, 81.209, 82.3, 82.203, 82.456, 84.2, 84.200, 85.2, 85.193, 88.2, 88.187, 89.2, 89.187, 94.2, 94.186, 97.2, 97.202, 98.2, 98.203
Sundry Gift: 62.379 (Christening Gift for his child), 64.230 (Christening Gift for his child), 64.231 (Gift to his daughter)
Custody of Gift: 62.126

Cecil, William [II] (1561–1562) Son of William [I] Cecil* and Mildred Cooke (Cecil*); brother of Anne Vere* and Elizabeth Cecil*; godchild of Queen Elizabeth.
Sundry Gift: 62.379 (Christening Gift)

Cecilia, Princess of Sweden (1540–1627) visited England 1565–66. Daughter of Gustav I*, King of Sweden; sister of Eric XIV*, King of Sweden, John III*, King of Sweden, and Charles IX*, King of Sweden; mar 1564 Christoph, Margrave of Baden-Rodemachern. *CSP Domestic, 1547–1580*; *CSP Foreign, 1566–68*; Corpus Christi, Cambridge, Parker MS 105 (Christening Gift for her son 1565).
Sundry Gift: 67.358 (Gift upon her departure from England)

Cely, John (fl.1580's) Yeoman of the Pitcherhouse, Yeoman of the Scullery. *CPR, 1580–82*; draft CPR, 1586–87.
Custody of Gift: 82.262

Chaderton, William (1540–1608) Bishop of Chester 1579–1595, Bishop of Lincoln 1595–1608. *ODNB*; will PCC 47 Windebanck.
Bishop: 81.55, 81.260, 82.52, 82.250, 82.451, 84.45, 84.243, 85.49, 85.239, 88.49, 88.234, 89.44, 89.229, 94.45, 94.228, 97.46, 97.243, 98.44, 98.245, 99.38, 99.233, 00.49, 00.243, 03.50, 03.263

Chalonges, Monsieur de (fl.1580s) Envoy from the Duke of Bouillon, François de la Tour d'Auvergne*. *CSP Foreign, 1586–88*.
Sundry Gift: 88.395 (Gift to Envoy)

Chamberlain, Cecilia—see Cecilia Stonor

Chamberlain, Dorothy, née Newdigate (b.c.1521) Lady Chamberlain. Daughter of Thomas Newdigate; mar Sir Leonard Chamberlain; mother of Francis Chamberlain* and Cecilia Stonor*. *ODNB* under husband; husband's will PCC 28 Loftes.
Lady: 59.102, 59.321

Chamberlain, Francis (fl.1560s) Captain (Governor) of Guernsey, Lieutenant of Woodstock. Son of Leonard Chamberlain and Dorothy Newdigate (Chamberlain*); brother of Cecilia Stonor*. *Visitations, Oxford*.
Gentleman: 62.171, 62.358, 63.160, 63.339, 67.150, 67.326, 68.147, 68.319

Chamberlain, Joan, née Luddington (c.1524–c.1567) Daughter of Henry Luddington and Joan Kirkby; mar 1st John Machell, 2nd Thomas Chamberlain*, mother of Theophila Chamberlain*. *ODNB* and Hasler under 2nd husband.
Sundry Gift: 63.368 (Christening Gift)

Chamberlain, Theophila (b.1563) Daughter of Thomas Chamberlain and Joan Luddington (Chamberlain*); mar Dr. Hughes.
Sundry Gift: 63.368 (Christening Gift)

Chamberlain, Sir Thomas (1504–1580) Groom of the Bedchamber to Henry VIII, Ambassador to Spain 1560–1562, kntd 1542, MP. Son of William Chamberlain and Elizabeth Fleming; mar 1st 1550 Anne VanderZeny, 2nd 1558 Joan Luddington (Chamberlain*), 3rd 1567 Anne Monk, father of Theophila Chamberlain*. *ODNB*; Hasler; Bell; will PCC 45 Arundell.
Sundry Gift: 63.368 (Christening Gift for his child)

Chambers, Elizabeth—see Elizabeth St John

Champernowne, Catherine—see Catherine Astley

Chandos, Lord/Baroness—see Dorothy Brydges, née Bray, 1557–1605; Edmund Brydges, 2nd, 1557–1573; Giles Brydges, 3rd, 1573–1594; William Brydges, 4th, 1594–1602; Frances Brydges, née Clinton, 1573–1623; Mary Brydges, née Hopton, 1594–1624

Chappell, Alice [née?] (fl.1550s) Gentlewoman. Mar Thomas Chappell, London upholsterer and bedmaker to Mary I. PRO PROB 11/41 1558.
Gentlewoman: 59.141, 59.368

Charles IX of France (1550–1574) King of France, KG 1564. Gifts to his envoys: Nicolas des Gallars*, Michel de Seurre*, François de Scepeaux*, Artus de Cossé*, and Paul de Foix*. Son of Henry II of France and Catherine de Medici; brother of Henry III*, François II, and François*, Duc de Anjou*; mar Elisabeth of Austria.

> **Sundry Gift**: 62.378, 62.392, 63.364, 64.226, 64.227, 67.359, (Sovereign sending Envoy to England); 64.226 (Installation as Knight of the Garter)

Charles IX of Sweden (1550–1611) Duke Charles, King of Sweden. Gifts to his envoys: James Hill*, George Schuavenius*, and Johannes Nicholai*. Son of Gustav I*, King of Sweden; brother of Princess Cecilia* of Sweden and John III*, King of Sweden and Poland; half-brother of Eric XIV*, King of Sweden; uncle of Sigismund, King of Poland and Sweden.

> **Sundry Gift**: 88.407, 99.415, 99.416 (Sovereign sending Envoy to England)

Charles Emmanuel (1562–1630) Duke of Savoy. Gift to his envoy Count Montreal. Son of Emmanuel Philibert, Duke of Savoy and Margaret of France.

> **Sundry Gift**: 81.439 (Sovereign sending Envoy to England)

Charlton, Elizabeth—see Elizabeth [I] Manners

Chartres, Vidam de—see Jean de la Fin Beauvoir la Nocle, Jean de la Fin, Jean de Ferrières

Chastre—see La Chastre

Chater—see Cater

Châtre—see La Châtre

Chaworth, Bridget—see Bridget Carr

Cheke, Mary, née Hill (c.1530–1616) Lady Cheke, Extraordinary Lady of the Privy Chamber, courtier poet. Daughter of Richard Hill and Elizabeth Isley (Hill*); step-daughter of Sir John Mason*; mar 1st 1547 John Cheke, 2nd 1558 Henry Mackwilliam*, mother of Margaret Mackwilliam* and Elizabeth Mackwilliam*. *ODNB* under 1st husband; BL Sloane MS 814; May, *Elizabethan Courtier*.

> **Lady**: 59.91, 59.311, 62.92, 62.273, 63.89, 63.255, 65.25, 65.192, 67.91, 67.261, 68.89, 68.258, 71.87, 71.257, 76.108, 76.303, 77.108, 77.305, 78.105, 78.306, 79.103, 79.311, 81.102, 81.308, 82.97, 82.296, 82.550, 84.92, 84.290, 85.98, 85.292, 88.99, 88.283, 89.91, 89.276, 94.87, 94.271, 97.95, 97.294, 98.95, 98.297, 99.92, 99.287, 00.97, 00.294, 03.100, 03.312
>
> **Sundry Gift**: 64.229 (Christening Gift for her child)

Cherry, Francis (1552–1605) Ambassador to Russia 1598–99. Son of John Cherry; mar Margaret Hayward; brother-in-law of Elizabeth Knyvett*. Bell; will PCC 35 Hayes; BL Additional MS 12503; *ODNB* under sons-in-law, William Russell and John Merrick.

> **Gentleman**: 03.168, 03.389

Chester, Bishop—see Cuthbert Scott, 1556–1559; William Downham, 1561–1577; William Chaderton, 1579–1595; Richard Vaughan, 1597–1604

Chevall, Lucy—see Lucy Penne

Cheyne, Lord/Baroness—see Henry Cheyne, 1572–1587; Jane Cheyne, née Wentworth, 1572–1614

Cheyne, Henry (1540–1587) kntd 1563, Lord Cheyne cr. 1572, MP. Son of Sir Thomas Cheyne and Anne Broughton; mar 1560 Jane Wentworth (Cheyne*). GEC, *Peerage*; Hasler; *ODNB*.

> **Lord**: 78.79, 78.280

Cheyne, Jane, née Wentworth, Baroness Cheyne (d.1614) Daughter of Thomas Wentworth and Margaret Fortescue; sister of Margery Wentworth (Williams*); mar 1560 Sir Henry Cheyne*, later Lord Cheyne. GEC, *Peerage*.

Lady: 65.27, 65.194, 67.94, 67.264, 68.92, 68.261, 71.90, 71.260; Baroness: 75.198, 76.95, 76.287, 77.94, 77.291, 78.90, 78.293, 79.89, 79.296, 81.84, 81.292, 82.7, 82.280, 82.517, 84.76, 84.274, 85.79, 85.270, 88.82, 88.266, 89.75, 89.260, 94.74, 94.258

Cheyne, Jane—see Jane Wriothesley

Cheyney, Richard (1513–1579) Bishop of Gloucester 1562–1579, Bishop of Bristol *in commendam* 1562–1579. *ODNB*; Litzenberger.

    Bishop: 63.35, 63.207, 64.34, 65.136, 67.36, 67.206, 68.51, 68.220, 71.48, 71.218, 75.57, 75.165, 76.60, 76.255, 77.61, 77.257, 78.61, 78.262, 79.58, 79.265

Chichester, Bishop—see William Barlow, 1559–1569; Richard Curteys, 1570–1582; Thomas Bickley, 1586–1596; Anthony Watson, 1596–1605

Chidley, John - see John Chudleigh

Childers, Robert (fl.1560s) Yeoman of the Crossbow.

    Custody of Gift: 63.167, 63.168

Children of the Hall Place. Office of the Lord Steward's department.

    Custody of Gift: 82.356

Cholmley, Catherine—see Catherine Scrope

Chontus—see Conti

Chowne, Jane—see Jane Puckering

Christian IV of Denmark (1577–1648) King of Denmark. Gifts to his envoys: George Schuavenius*, Jacob Rostrup*, Arild Huitfeldt*, Christian Barnikow*, Hance Newcom*, and Niels Krag*. Son of Frederick II of Denmark and Sophie Mecklenburg, brother of Anne of Denmark*, brother-in-law of James VI*.

    Sundry Gift: 89.400, 89.405, 98.425, 98.426, 98.427, 99.414 (Sovereign sending Envoys to England)

Chudleigh, John (1564–1589) Privateer, Adventurer, MP, probable identification as 'unknown Gentleman'* 1589. Son of Christopher Chudleigh and Christian Strechley, mar 1581 Elizabeth Speak. Hasler; *CSP Domestic, Addenda 1580–1625*; Andrews.

    Gentleman: 88.161, 88.352, (probable 89.160, 89.352)

Churchill, Giles (fl.1550s) Yeoman of the Crossbows.

    Custody of Gift: 59.211

Churchyard, Thomas (c.1520–1604) Soldier and poet. *ODNB*; May, *Elizabethan Courtier*; Goldwyn.

    Gentleman: 75.130, 75.234

Clanricarde, Earl/Countess—see Richard Bourke, 4th, 1601–1635; Frances Sidney Devereux Bourke, née Walsingham, 1603–1632

Clarke, Amy—see Amy Marvyn

Clarke, Catherine (fl.1550s) Lady Clarke, Extraordinary Lady of the Privy Chamber. Daughter of Thomas Le Strange and Anne Vaux; sister-in-law of Amy Clarke (Marvyn*); aunt of Lucy Marvyn (Tuchet*); mar Sir Roland Clarke. possible identification. *Visitations, Norfolk*.

    Lady: 59.108, 59.327

Clarke, Daniel (fl.1590s–1600s) Master Cook. PRO E 115.

    Gentleman: 98.173, 98.379, 99.167, 99.367, 00.168, 00.369, 03.181, 03.402

Clarke, unidentified (fl.1580s) Queen's servant.

    Custody of Gift: 82.292

Clarke, William (d.1625) Son of Nicholas Clarke and Elizabeth Ramsey, mar Elizabeth Bourne, kntd 1594. *CSP, Domestic, 1601–1603; VCH, Buckinghamshire*.

    Gentleman: 94.170, 94.360

Clement, unidentified (fl.1580s) Queen's servant.

    Custody of Gift: 82.360

Clenton—see Clinton

Clere, Edward (1539–1606) Kntd 1578, MP. Son of John Clere and Anne Tyrrell; mar 1st 1554 Frances Fulmerston; 2nd 1580 Agnes Crane, widow of Christopher Heydon*; 2nd cousin of Queen Elizabeth. Hasler; Bindoff; *Visitations, Norfolk*.
 Gentleman: 75.212, 76.173, 76.378, 77.175, 77.378, 78.175, 78.383
 Knight: 79.141, 79.348, 81.133, 81.340, 82.127, 82.326, 82.537, 84.121, 84.319, 85.119, 85.312, 88.123, 88.307, 89.117, 89.301, 94.114, 94.310, 97.122, 97.332, 98.123, 98.333, 99.116, 99.319, 00.121, 00.325, 03.131, 03.343

Clerke—see Clarke

Clifford, Anne, née Dacre, Countess of Cumberland (c.1535–1581) Daughter of William Dacre and Elizabeth Talbot; sister of Magdalen Browne* and Thomas Dacre*; mar 1554 Henry Clifford*, Earl of Cumberland; mother of Frances Wharton* and George Clifford*. GEC, *Peerage*.
 Countess: 78.43, 78.244

Clifford, Catherine—see Catherine Scrope

Clifford, Frances—see Frances Wharton

Clifford, Francis (1584–1589) Styled Lord Clifford. Son of George Clifford*, Earl of Cumberland and Margaret Russell (Clifford*); godchild of Queen Elizabeth. GEC, *Peerage*; *ODNB* under father.
 Sundry Gift: 85.406 (Christening Gift)

Clifford, George, Earl of Cumberland (1558–1605) KG 1592, courtier poet. Son of Henry Clifford*, Earl of Cumberland and Anne Dacre (Clifford*); brother of Frances Wharton*; mar 1577 Margaret Russell (Clifford*); father of Francis Clifford*. *ODNB*; GEC, *Peerage*.
 Earl: 85.16, 85.208, 89.15, 89.200, 97.16, 97.216, 00.14, 00.205, 03.11, 03.224
 Sundry Gift: 85.406 (Christening Gift for his child)

Clifford, Henry (1517–1570) Earl of Cumberland. Son of Henry Clifford, Earl of Cumberland and Margaret Percy; mar 1st 1537 Eleanor Brandon, 2nd 1554 Anne Dacre (Clifford*); father of Frances Wharton* and George Clifford*. *ODNB*; GEC, *Peerage*.
 Earl: 59.20, 59.241, 65.110

Clifford, Margaret—see Margaret Stanley

Clifford, Margaret, née Russell, Countess of Cumberland (1560–1616) Daughter of Francis Russell*, Earl of Bedford and Margaret St John (Russell*); sister of Anne Dudley*, Elizabeth Bourchier*, John [I] Russell* and William Russell*; mar 1577 George Clifford*, Earl of Cumberland; mother of Francis Clifford*. *ODNB*; Bayer.
 Countess: 85.31, 85.224, 88.31, 88.216, 89.26, 89.211, 94.29, 94.212, 97.36, 97.232, 98.35, 98.234, 99.28, 99.222, 00.35, 00.231, 03.35, 03.248
 Sundry Gift: 85.406 (Christening Gift for her child)

Clinton—see also Fiennes

Clinton, Lady Anne—see Lady Anne Askew

Clinton, Catherine, née Hastings, Countess of Lincoln (1542–c.1585) Lady Clinton. Daughter of Francis Hastings*, Earl of Huntingdon and Catherine Pole (Hastings*); sister of Henry Hastings*, George Hastings*, Frances Compton*, and Elizabeth [II] Somerset*; mar 1567 Henry Clinton*; mother of Elizabeth [I] Gorges*. GEC, *Peerage*; *ODNB* under father; BL Sloane MS 814.
 Lady: 1572

Clinton, Edward (1512–1585) Lord Clinton, Privy Councillor 1550, Lord Admiral 1550. KG 1551, Earl of Lincoln cr.1572. Son of Thomas, Lord Clinton and Jane Poynings; mar 1st 1534 Elizabeth Blount, 2nd 1541 Ursula Stourton, 3rd 1552 Elizabeth FitzGerald (Clinton*); father of Henry Clinton*, Lady Frances Brydges* and Lady Anne Askew*. *ODNB*; GEC, *Peerage*; will PCC 26 Brudenell.

Lord: 59.56, 59.277, 62.54, 62.235, 63.55, 63.227, 64.55, 65.156, 67.56, 67.226, 68.54, 68.223, 71.52, 71.222

Earl: 75.11, 76.11, 76.206, 77.13, 77.210, 78.10, 78.211, 79.10, 79.218, 81.9, 81.216, 82.11, 82.210, 82.433, 84.8, 84.206, 85.9, 85.200

Clinton, Elizabeth [I], née FitzGerald, Countess of Lincoln (c.1528–1590) Lady Geraldine, Lady of the Privy Chamber. Daughter of Gerald FitzGerald, Earl of Kildare and Elizabeth Grey; sister of Gerald Fitzgerald*, aunt of Elizabeth [II] FitzGerald*; mar 1st 1542 Anthony Browne, 2nd 1552 Edward Fiennes*, Lord Clinton. *ODNB*; GEC, *Peerage*; BL Sloane MS 814.

Baroness: 59.78, 59.298, 62.72, 62.253, 63.71, 63.243, 64.70, 65.2, 65.169, 67.68, 67.238, 68.67, 68.236, 71.67, 71.237

Countess: 75.35, 75.142, 76.37, 76.232, 77.34, 77.230, 78.29, 78.230, 79.31, 79.238, 81.26, 81.233, 82.26, 82.226, 82.486, 84.25, 84.223, 85.26, 85.216, 88.24, 88.209, 89.21, 89.206

Custody of Gift: 76.99

Clinton, Elizabeth [II], née Morrison, Countess of Lincoln (d.1611) Daughter of Richard Morrison and Bridget Hussey (Morrison*); mar 1st c.1577 William [I] Norris*, 2nd 1586 Henry Clinton*, Earl of Lincoln; mother of Francis Norris*. GEC, *Peerage*; *ODNB* under son.

Countess: 88.25, 88.210, 97.24, 97.229

Sundry Gift: 79.437 (Christening Gift for her child)

Clinton, Elizabeth—see Elizabeth Gorges, Elizabeth Fitzgerald

Clinton, Lady Frances - see Lady Frances Brydges

Clinton, Henry (1541–1616) Earl of Lincoln, KB 1553, MP. Son of Edward Clinton* and Ursula Stourton (Clinton*); brother of Anne Askew* and Frances Brydges*; mar 1st 1567 Catherine Hastings*, 2nd 1586 Elizabeth Morrison*; father of Elizabeth [I] Gorges*. Hasler; GEC, *Peerage*.

Earl: 88.16, 88.200, 89.11, 89.196, 97.12, 97.215

Cobham, Lord/Baroness—see Frances Brooke, née Newton, 1560–1592; Henry Brooke, 11th, 1597–1603 (forfeited); William Brooke, 10th, 1558–1597; Frances [II] Seymour, née Howard, 1601–1628

Cobham, Sir Henry (1538–1592) Gentleman Pensioner, Ambassador to France 1579–1583, kntd 1575, MP. Son of George Brooke and Anne Bray; brother of Elizabeth Parr* and William [I] Brooke*, Lord Cobham; mar c.1566 Anne Sutton. Hasler; Tighe; BL Sloane MS 814.

Knight: 82.124, 82.327, 82.542

Coke, Edward (1552–1634) Solicitor-General 1592, Speaker of the House of Commons 1593, Attorney General 1594–1613, kntd 1603, MP. Son of Robert Coke and Winifred Knightley; mar 1st 1582 Bridget Paston, 2nd 1598 Elizabeth Cecil (Hatton*), Lady Hatton; father of Elizabeth Coke*. *ODNB*; Hasler.

Sundry Gift: 00.416 (Christening Gift for his child)

Coke, Elizabeth—see Elizabeth Hatton

Coke, Elizabeth (1599–1623) Daughter of Edward Coke* and Elizabeth Cecil (Hatton*); godchild of Queen Elizabeth.

Sundry Gift: 00.416 (Christening Gift)

Coldwell, John (1531–1596) Dean of Rochester, Bishop of Salisbury, 1591–1596. ODNB.

Bishop: 94.36, 94.220

Coligny, Gaspard de (c.1517–1572) Admiral of France. Gift to his messenger and son-in-law Charles de Teligny*. father-in-law of William of Orange*. *CSP Foreign, 1563.*

Sundry Gift: 64.219 (Official sending Envoy to England)

Collier, Elizabeth—see Elizabeth Randall alias Smallpage

Collier, John (fl.1580s) possible identification. PRO E 115.
> **Custody of Gift**: 82.226

Comey, George (c.1525–1587) Musician, Violin. brother of Innocent Comey*. *BDECM*; Holman; will PCC 22 Daughtry.
> **Gentleman**: 59.200, 59.424

Comey, Innocent (c.1530–1603) Musician, Violin. brother of George Comey*. *BDECM*.
> **Gentleman**: 59.216, 59.440, 88.181, 88.371, 89.181, 89.373, 94.175, 94.372, 97.190, 97.391, 98.189, 98.392, 99.187, 99.384, 00.187, 00.386, 03.198, 03.423

Compagni, Bartholomew (1503–1561) King's Merchant to Henry VIII and Edward VI. father of Margaret Compagni (Castilion*), father-in-law of John Baptist Castilion*. *LP Henry VIII, 1543, CSP Domestic, 1557–58*; will PCC 24 Loftes; Machyn; Siddons.
> **Gentleman**: 59.160, 59.384

Compagni, Margaret—see Margaret Castilion

Compton, Lord/Baroness—see Frances Compton, née Hastings, 1572–1574, Henry Compton, 1st, 1572–1589; William Compton, 2nd, 1589–1618

Compton, Frances, née Hastings (d.1574) Lady Compton. Daughter of Francis Hastings*, Earl of Huntingdon and Catherine Pole (Hastings*); sister of Henry Hastings*, George Hastings*, Catherine Clinton*, and Elizabeth [II] Somerset*; mar 1567 Henry Lord Compton*; mother of William Lord Compton*. GEC, *Peerage*; *ODNB* under father.
> **Lady**: 71.94, 71.264

Compton, Henry (1538–1589) Kntd 1567, Lord Compton cr. 1572, MP. Son of Peter Compton and Anne Talbot; mar 1st 1567 Frances Hastings (Compton*), 2nd 1581 Anne Spencer; father of William Lord Compton*. GEC, *Peerage*; Hasler; will PCC 88 Leicester.
> **Lord**: 75.71, 75.179, 76.73, 76.264, 77.74, 77.271, 78.73, 78.275, 79.71, 79.278, 81.68, 81.275, 82.64, 82.264, 84.464, 84.59, 84.256, 85.62, 85.253, 88.62, 88.247, 89.56, 89.241

Compton, William (1568–1630) Lord Compton, Master of the Leash, later Earl of Northampton. Son of Henry Lord Compton* and Frances Hastings (Compton*), mar 1599 Elizabeth Spencer. GEC, *Peerage*.
> **Lord**: 94.58, 94.242, 97.67, 97.261, 98.65, 98.261, 99.62, 99.251, 03.68, 03.281

Conell, Thomas (fl.1570s) Goldsmith. Jackson.
> **Custody of Gift**: 79.450

Constable, Lady Catherine, née Neville (b.c.1541) Lady Neville. Daughter of Henry [II] Neville*, Earl of Westmorland, and Anne Manners; sister of Charles Neville*; mar c.1564 John Constable. Hasler under husband; will PCC 47 Sainberbe.
> **Lady**: 81.115, 81.322, 82.109, 82.309, 82.515, 84.105, 84.302, 85.92, 85.282, 88.94, 88.279, 89.86, 89.271.

Conti, Anthony (d.1579) Musician, Lute Player. Mar 1567 Lucretia de Tedeschi (Conti*). *BDECM*; *RECM*; Prior.
> **Gentleman**: 71.168, 71.346
> **Sundry Gift**: 68.345 (Gift from Queen)

Conti, Lucretia de, née Tedeschi (d.1577) alias Chontus. Mar 1st Antonio Pagano, 2nd 1567 Anthony Conti*. BL Harleian MS 1644; *BDECM*; *RECM*; *CSP Domestic, 1547–80*; Prior.
> **Gentlewoman**: 65.69, 65.240, 71.144, 71.314, 76.167, 76.361, 77.168, 77.365

Conway, Thomas (d.1607) Yeoman Usher. *Index to Privy Bills*; Will PCC 91 Huddlestone.
> **Custody of Gift**: 82.247

Conyers, Lucy—see Lucy Griffin

Cooke, Catherine (c.1547–1583) Maid of Honour. Daughter of Anthony Cooke* and Anne FitzWilliam; sister of Mildred Cecil* and Elizabeth [I] Russell*; mar 1565 Henry Killigrew*, mother of Anne Killigrew*. *ODNB*; Harvey.
   Maid of Honour: 64.188
Cooke, Elizabeth—see Elizabeth [I] Russell
Cooke, Mildred—see Mildred Cecil
Cooke, Robert (d.1593) Chester Herald 1562, Clarenceux King of Arms 1567, Acting Garter King of Arms 1584–1586. *ODNB*; Wagner.
   Gentleman: 63.170, 63.349, 65.96, 67.170, 67.346, 85.416
Cooper, Eleanor—see Eleanor Borgarucci
Cooper, Thomas (c.1517–1594) Bishop of Lincoln 1571–1584, Bishop of Winchester 1584–1594. *ODNB*; will PCC 44 Dixy.
   Bishop: 75.47, 75.155, 76.50, 76.245, 77.51, 77.248, 78.51, 78.252, 79.49, 79.256, 81.44, 81.251, 82.43, 82.243, 82.447, 84.40, 84.238, 85.42, 85.233, 88.41, 88.226, 89.36, 89.221, 94.38. 94.822
Copinger, Lettice, née FitzGerald (fl.1590s–1600s) Mistress Copinger, Maid of Honour. Daughter of Edward FitzGerald and Anne Leigh; niece of Gerald Fitzgerald* and Mabel Browne; 1st cousin of Lettice FitzGerald*; mar 1st 1584 Ambrose Copinger, 2nd 1606 Sir John Morice alias Poyntz. Tighe.
   Gentlewoman: 97.144, 97.345, 98.141, 98.347, 99.136, 99.353, 00.137, 00.340, 03.144, 03.358
Copley, Catherine, née Luttrell (fl.1550s–1560s) Gentlewoman of the Privy Chamber to Mary I. Daughter of Sir John Luttrell; mar 1558 Thomas Copley*; mother of Henry Copley*. *ODNB* under husband.
   Sundry Gift: 62.382 (Christening Gift for her child)
Copley, Catherine—see Catherine Lane
Copley, Henry (1561–1580) Son of Thomas Copley* and Catherine Luttrell (Copley*); godchild of Queen Elizabeth. *ODNB* under father.
   Sundry Gift: 62.382 (Christening Gift)
Copley, Thomas (1532–1584) Landowner and Roman Catholic exile, MP, kntd by French king, ennobled by Philip II. Son of Sir Roger Copley and Elizabeth Shelley; brother of Catherine Lane*; mar 1558 Catherine Luttrell (Copley*); father of Henry Copley*; 2nd cousin twice removed to Queen Elizabeth. *ODNB*; Hasler; will PCC 13 Brudenell.
   Sundry Gift: 62.382 (Christening Gift for his child)
Cordell, Abigail—see Abigail Digby
Cordell, Edward (d.1590) Clerk of Chancery. Son of John Cordell and Emma Webb; brother of William [I] Cordell*; mar 1st Elizabeth Harrison, 2nd 1589 Abigail Digby (Cordell*). Hasler; will PCC 4 Sainberbe.
   Sundry Gift: 89.402 (Marriage Gift)
Cordell, Sir William [I] (1522–1581) Master of the Rolls, kntd 1558, MP. Son of John Cordell and Emma Webb; brother of Edward Cordell*; uncle of Mary Alington*; related to William [II] Cordell* Master Cook; mar Mary Clopton. *ODNB*; Hasler; Bindoff; will PCC 42 Darcy.
   Knight: 59.126, 59.345, 62.113, 62.293, 63.111, 63.284, 64.104, 64.158, 65.39, 65.206, 67.105, 67.275, 68.104, 68.273, 71.104, 71.274, 76.123, 76.318, 77.125, 77.322, 78.128, 78.330, 79.126, 79.333, 81.124, 81.331
Cordell, William [II] (d.1611) Master Cook to Elizabeth and James I. Son of John Cordell; relative of William [I] Cordell* Master of the Rolls. PRO E 179/70/107, E 315/1974; will PCC 17 Wood; *Index to Privy Bills*; *Visitations, London*; *Visitations, Middlesex*.
   Gentleman: 94.166, 94.362, 97.175, 97.377, 98.172, 98.378, 99.166, 99.366, 00.167, 00.368, 03.180, 03.401

Cormack—see Cormack MacTeig MacCarty

Cornwallis, Lady Catherine, née Wriothesley (d.1632) Baroness Catherine Cornwallis, Lady of the Privy Chamber. Daughter of Thomas Wriothesley, Earl of Southampton and Jane Cheyne (Wriothesley*); sister of Lady Mary Lister* and Henry [I] Wriothesley*, Earl of Southampton; aunt of Henry [II] Wriothesley*, Earl of Southampton; mar Thomas Cornwallis, Groom Porter. Tighe; husband's will PCC 56 Cobham; HMC Salisbury, 8; Price.

Lady 98.97, 98.295

Baroness: 99.87, 99.282, 00.92, 00.289, 03.88, 03.304

Cornwallis, Sir William (1549–1611) Kntd 1594, MP. Son of Thomas Cornwallis and Anne Jerningham; related by marriage to Lady Catherine Cornwallis*; brother-in-law to William Bourchier*, Earl of Bath; mar 1st c.1566 Lucy Neville, 2nd 1608 Jane Mewtas. Hasler; will PCC 93 Wood.

Gentleman: 81.175, 81.409, 82.190, 82.394, 82.580, 84.177, 84.367

Knight: 97.135, 97.329, 98.131, 98.331, 99.123, 99.317, 00.127, 00.323, 03.133, 03.346

Cossé, Artus de, Sieur de Gonor (1512–1582) Special Ambassador from Charles IX* of France, French Commissioner for marriage settlement between Elizabeth and the Duke of Anjou*. Holt; *CSP Domestic, 1547–1580*; Fénelon; PRO E 30/1145.

Sundry Gift: 64.227, 79.439, 81.446 (Gift to Envoy)

Cotton, Henry (1545–1615) Bishop of Salisbury 1598–1615, Chaplain. Son of Richard Cotton and Jane Onley; uncle of Mary Stanley*; godchild of Princess Elizabeth; no known relationship to William Cotton*. *ODNB*.

Bishop: 99.52, 99.235, 00.46, 00.245, 03.49, 03.262

Cotton, John (fl.1590s) Keeper of the Standing Wardrobe at Westminster. Possible relative of Robert Cotton*. *CSP Domestic, 1598–1601*.

Custody of Gift: 97.77, 97.195

Cotton, Mary—see Mary Stanley

Cotton, Robert (d.1591) Yeoman of Removing Wardrobe of Beds. possible relative of John Cotton*. Will PCC 73 Sainberbe, 40 Harrington; BL Additional MS 39794; PRO LC 5/49.

Custody of Gift: 82.189, 85.107, 88.77, 88.105, 88.126, 88.142, 89.70, 89.86, 89.124, 89.166

Cotton, William (d.1621) Bishop of Exeter 1598–1621. no known relationship to Henry Cotton*. *ODNB*.

Bishop: 99.51, 99.247, 00.60, 00.257, 03.58, 03.271

Countie Ferre—see Figueroa

County Arco—see Oliver Count d'Arco

Cox, Francis (fl.1580s) Yeoman of the Pantry. Draft CPR, 1586–87.

Custody of Gift: 82.310

Cox, John (fl.1560s–1580s) Yeoman of the Leash, Caretaker. *CPR, 1580–82*.

Custody of Gift: 62.127

Cox, unidentified (fl.1580s) Caretaker.

Custody of Gift: 82.378

Cox, Richard (1500–1581) Bishop of Ely 1559, Tutor to Edward VI and Elizabeth, Chaplain to Henry VIII. Name listed on 1582 roll with 'X'; died before 1582 exchange. *ODNB*.

Bishop: 62.20, 62.199, 63.19, 63.191, 64.19, 65.120, 67.20, 67.190, 68.35, 68.204, 71.35, 71.205, 75.43, 75.151, 76.46, 76.241, 77.47, 77.244, 78.46, 78.247, 79.44, 79.251, 81.39, 81.246

Cragius, Nicholas—see Niels Krag

Cranmer, Robert (fl.1590s–1600s) Yeoman of the Jewels and Plate.

Free Gift: 94.391, 97.417, 98.423, 99.410, 00.413, 03.445

Crockson—see Cruxson

Croft, Catherine, née Blount (d.1606) Lady Croft. Daughter of Edward Blount and Margaret Garneys; mar 1573 Sir James Croft*. *ODNB* and Hasler under husband; will PCC 37 Stafforde.

> **Lady**: 78.119, 78.320, 79.117, 79.324, 81.103, 81.312, 82.98, 82.300, 82.557, 84.102, 84.295

Croft, Sir James (1518–1590) Comptroller of the Household, Privy Councillor 1570, kntd 1547, MP. Son of Richard Croft and Catherine Herbert; mar 1st c.1540 Alice Warnecombe, 2nd c.1573 Catherine Blount (Croft*); father of James Croft; father-in-law of John Scudamore* and Margery Williams*. *ODNB*; Hasler; Bindoff.

> **Knight**: 71.99, 71.269, 76.118, 76.313, 77.120, 77.317, 78.122, 78.323, 79.120, 79.327, 81.117, 81.324, 82.111, 82.311, 82.522, 84.108, 84.306, 85.109, 85.302, 88.115, 88.299, 89.108, 89.293

Croft, Margery—Williams, Margery

Cromer, Catherine [née?] (d.1602) Mar 1st Burton, 2nd c.1580 William Cromer MP; possibly mother of Anne Burton*. Hasler under husband; will PCC 25 Montague.

> **Gentlewoman**: 81.155, 81.361, 82.151, 82.351, 82.604, 84.147, 84.344, 85.145, 85.336, 88.146, 88.330, 89.142, 89.327, 94.135, 94.326, 97.146, 97.349, 98.143, 98.350, 99.138, 99.338, 00.139, 00.343

Cromwell, Lord/Baroness—see Mary Cromwell, c.1560–1592

Cromwell, Henry (c.1537–1604) alias Williams, kntd 1564, MP. Son of Richard Cromwell alias Williams and Frances Murfyn; great-grandson of Thomas Cromwell; 1st cousin once removed to Henry, Lord Cromwell; mar 1st Joan Warren (Cromwell*), 2nd c.1584 Susan Weeks; grandfather of Oliver Cromwell. Hasler.

> **Knight**: 65.50, 65.217, 67.106, 67.276, 68.110, 68.279, 71.110, 71.280, 76.126, 76.322, 77.128, 77.325, 78.131, 78.333, 79.134, 79.341, 81.130, 81.336, 82.123, 82.322, 82.531, 84.117, 84.315, 85.121, 85.313, 88.122, 88.306, 89.116, 89.300, 94.113, 94.309, 97.121, 97.330, 98.122, 98.332, 99.115, 99.318, 00.120, 00.324, 03.122, 03.341

Cromwell, Joan, née Warren (c.1540–1584) Lady Cromwell. Daughter of Ralph Warren and Joan Trelake; mar Sir Henry Cromwell*. Hasler.

> **Lady**: 71.95, 71.265, 76.115, 76.307, 77.113, 77.310, 78.109, 78.314, 79.111, 79.319, 81.109, 81.315, 82.104, 82.303, 82.551, 84.99, 84.298

Cromwell, Mary, née Paulet (d.1592) Lady Cromwell. Daughter of John Paulet*, Marquess of Winchester and Elizabeth Willoughby; sister of William [II] Paulet*; mar Henry, Lord Cromwell. GEC, *Peerage*.

> **Baroness**: 67.78, 67.248, 68.73, 68.242, 76.100, 76.292, 77.98, 77.295, 79.114, 79.305, 82.508, 85.87, 85.277

Crosse, Robert (d.1611) Sea Captain, sailed with Sir Francis Drake, kntd 1596, MP. Son of William Crosse and Grace [née?]; unmarried. Hasler; *Visitations, Somerset*; will PCC 94 Wood.

> **Gentleman**: 89.171, 89.363
>
> **Knight**: 97.136, 97.333, 98.132, 98.334, 99.124, 99.323

Croy, Charles Philip de, Marquis de Havrech (fl.1570s) Special Ambassador with Adolf van Meetkerk* from the States of the Low Countries. Son of Philip de Croy; brother of Alexandre Duke d'Arschot. *CSP Foreign, 1577–78*.

> **Sundry Gift**: 78.426 (Gift to Envoy)

Cruxson, Catherine [née?] (d.1586) Mar Simon Cruxson. Will PCC 37 Windsor; husband's will PCC 7 Watson; Keene.

Gentlewoman: 75.109, 76.160, 76.353, 77.165, 77.362, 78.166, 78.371, 79.168, 79.375, 81.162, 81.368, 82.157, 82.356, 82.601, 84.153, 84.354, 85.149, 85.346

Cumberland, Earl/Countess—see Anne Clifford, née Dacre, 1554–1581; George Clifford, 3ʳᵈ, 1570–1605; Henry Clifford, 2ⁿᵈ, 1542–1570; Margaret Clifford, née Russell, 1570–1616

Curteys, Richard (c.1532–1582) Bishop of Chichester 1570–1582. *ODNB*.
    Bishop: 71.49, 71.219, 75.58, 75.166, 76.61, 76.256, 77.62, 77.258, 78.62, 78.263, 79.59, 79.266, 81.54, 81.259, 82.51, 82.249, 82.448

Cuson—see Mark Anthony Galliardello

Cussi—see Quissé

Cycell—see Cecil

Cydney—see Sidney

Dacre of the North, Lord/Baroness—see Thomas Dacre, 4ᵗʰ, 1563–1566; Elizabeth Dacre, née Leybourne, d.1567

Dacre of the South, Lord/Baroness—see Anne Sackville, née Fiennes, 1558–1595

Dacre, Anne—see Anne Clifford

Dacre, Elizabeth, née Leybourne, Baroness Dacre of the North (d.1567) Duchess of Norfolk. Daughter of James Leybourne and Helen Preston; mar 1ˢᵗ 1556 Thomas, Lord Dacre*, 2ⁿᵈ 1567 Thomas [II] Howard*, Duke of Norfolk. GEC, *Peerage*.
    Baroness: 65.5, 65.172, 67.71, 67.241

Dacre, Magdalen—see Magdalen Browne

Dacre, Thomas, Lord Dacre of the North (c.1527–1566) MP. Son of William, Lord Dacre and Elizabeth Talbot; brother of Anne Dacre* and Magdalen Dacre*; mar 1ˢᵗ Elizabeth Neville, 2ⁿᵈ 1556 Elizabeth Leybourne*. GEC, *Peerage*; Bindoff.
    Lord: 65.159

Dakers—see Dacre of the North, Dacre of the South

Dale, Elizabeth, née Scherer (1531–1590) Mistress Dale. Daughter of Lawrence Scherer, mar 1ˢᵗ unidentified Froth, 2ⁿᵈ c.1557 Valentine Dale, Ambassador to France. *ODNB*, Hasler and Bindoff under husband.
    Gentlewoman: 77.169, 77.366, 78.169, 78.359, 79.172, 79.378, 81.138, 81.345, 82.132, 82.332, 82.610, 84.130, 84.326, 85.132, 85.322, 88.138, 88.322, 89.134, 89.319

Daman, William (c.1540–1591) Musician, Recorder. also known as Guillelmo Damano. Mar Anne Derifield. *ODNB*; *BDECM*.
    Gentleman: 82.197, 82.401, 82.584

Damsell, Sir William (c.1521–1582) Receiver of the Court of Wards, kntd 1553, MP. Mar Margaret Berney. Hasler; will PCC 34 Tirwhite.
    Knight: 59.128, 59.347, 62.118, 62.297, 63.114, 63.287, 64.107, 64.161, 65.41, 65.208, 67.109, 67.279, 68.108, 68.276, 71.108, 71.278, 76.125, 76.320, 77.127, 77.324, 78.130, 78.332, 79.128, 79.335, 81.125, 81.332, 82.118, 82.318, 82.529

Dane, Margaret, née Kempe (1521–1579) Mistress Dane. Daughter of Edmund Kempe and Bridget Styles; mar 1540 William Dane*. Will PCC 42 Bakon; Adams.
    Gentlewoman: 62.144, 62.324, 63.135, 63.307, 65.68, 65.234, 67.139, 67.309, 68.133, 68.304, 71.138, 71.308, 75.101, 76.158, 76.341, 77.164, 77.361, 78.165, 78.367, 79.167, 79.374

Dane, William (1517–1573) Linen Draper, Alderman of London, Ironmonger. Mar 1540 Margaret Kempe (Dane*). Will PCC 29 Peter; Beaven; PRO LC 5/34, f.14.
    Gentleman: 59.169

Daniel, Mary—see Mary Fortescue

Darby—see Derby

d'Arco—see Arco

Darcy of Chiche, Lord/Baroness—see John Darcy, 2nd, 1558–1581; Thomas Darcy, 3rd, 1581–1639

Darcy, Edward (1543–1612) Groom of Privy Chamber, MP. Son of Arthur Darcy and Mary Carew; son-in-law of Thomas Astley*; mar 1579 Elizabeth Astley*. Hasler; *CSP Foreign, 1583*; *Visitations, Yorkshire*.
  Free Gift: 84.406, 85.405, 88.386, 89.387, 94.384, 97.411, 98.416, 99.403, 00.405, 03.437
  Sundry Gift: 81.442 (Marriage Gift)
  Custory of Gift: 94.146

Darcy, Elizabeth—see Elizabeth Darcy, Elizabeth Lumley

Darcy, John, Lord Darcy of Chiche (1532–1581) KB 1559. Son of Thomas Darcy and Elizabeth Vere; brother-in-law of Roger, Lord North* and Robert [I] Rich*; mar 1564 Frances Rich; father of Thomas, Lord Darcy of Chiche*, and Elizabeth Lumley*. *ODNB*; GEC, *Peerage*; will PCC 1 Darcy.
  Lord: 62.68, 62.248, 63.69, 63.241, 64.64, 65.165, 67.63, 67.233, 68.61, 68.230, 71.58, 71.228, 75.62, 75.170, 76.64, 76.268, 77.68, 77.265, 78.67, 78.268, 79.65, 79.272, 81.61, 81.268

Darcy, Thomas (1565–1639) Lord Darcy of Chiche. Son of John Darcy* and Frances Rich; brother of Elizabeth Lumley*; mar 1583 Elizabeth Kitson. GEC, *Peerage*; BL Additional MS 5751A.
  Lord: 82.58, 82.258, 82.455, 84.56, 84.262, 85.59, 85.250, 88.60, 88.245, 89.54, 89.239, 94.64, 94.248, 97.68, 97.268, 98.66, 98.269, 99.61, 99.259, 00.69, 00.267, 03.69, 03.282

Darrell, Anne—see Anne Leighton

Darrell, Elizabeth—see Elizabeth Neville

Darrell, Lady—see Mary Fortescue

Darell, William (d.c. 1580) Clergyman, Lichfield Cathedral prebendary. Lichfield Record Office MS D30/12/10; ODNB.
  Chaplain: 68.143

Daustria, John—see John of Austria

Davies, Richard (c.1501–1581) Bishop of St David's 1561–1581. *ODNB*; will PCC 45 Darcy. Name listed on 1582 roll with 'X'; died before 1582 exchange.
  Bishop: 62.31, 62.211, 63.30, 63.202, 64.29, 65.131, 67.31, 67.201, 68.46, 68.215, 71.44, 71.214, 75.52, 75.160, 76.55, 76.250, 77.56, 77.252, 78.56, 78.257, 79.54, 79.261, 81.47, 81.254

de Burgh—see Bourke

de Conti—see Conti

de Tedeschi—see Tedeschi

de la Touche, Isabel—see Isabel Montgomery

de la Tour d'Auvergne, François, Duke of Bouillon (d.1588) Vicomte de Turenne. Gift to his envoy M. de Chalonges*. father of Henri de la Tour d'Auvergne*. *CSP Foreign, 1587*.
  Sundry Gift: 88.395 (Official sending Envoy to England)

de la Tour d'Auvergne, Henri, Duke of Bouillon (1555–1623) Vicomte de Turenne, visited England in 1590, 1596. Son of François de la Tour d'Auvergne*; son-in-law of William of Orange*; mar 1st Charlotte de La Marck, 2nd Elizabeth of Nassau (godchild of Queen Elizabeth). *CSP Domestic, 1602*; *CSP Foreign, 1588*.
  Sundry Gift: 97.423 (Gift from Queen)

de la Warr, Lord/Baroness—see Anne West, née Knollys, 1595–1603; Thomas West, 2nd, 1595–1602

Denmark, Gentleman of (fl.1580s) Gentleman representing Duke Charles (later Charles IX* of Denmark).
  Sundry Gift: 88.406 (Envoy from Duke Charles)

Denny, Douglas—see Douglas Dyve

Denny, Sir Edward (1547–1600) Groom of the Privy Chamber, MP, kntd 1589. Son of Anthony Denny and Joan Champernowne; brother of Douglas Dyve* and Mary Astley*; nephew of Catherine Astley*; mar 1585 Margaret Edgecombe*. *ODNB*; Hasler.

Free Gift: 84.407, 85.398, 88.387, 89.388, 94.378, 97.405, 98.411, 99.399, 00.402

Denny, Mary—see Mary Astley

Dennys—see Dionysius Burreus

Denys, Catherine—see Catherine Buckler

Denys, Sir Maurice (c.1502–1563) Treasurer of Calais under Mary I, kntd 1547, MP. Son of William Denys and Anne Berkeley; brother of Catherine Buckler* and Sir Walter Denys; mar Elizabeth Holwood; stepfather of Elizabeth Randall alias Smallpage*. Bindoff; *Visitations, Gloucester.*

Knight: 62.115, 62.305

Derby, Earl/Countess—see Alice Stanley, née Spencer, 1593–1637; Edward Stanley, 3rd, 1521–1572; Elizabeth Stanley, née Vere, 1595–1627; Ferdinando Stanley, 5th, 1593–1594; Henry Stanley, 4th, 1572–1593; Margaret Stanley, née Clifford, 1572–1596; Mary Stanley, née Cotton, 1562–1575; William Stanley, 6th, 1594–1642; see also Strange, Lord/Baroness

de Seurre—see Seurre

de Sousa—see Sousa

Dethick, Alice, née Peterson (d.1572) Lady Dethick. Daughter of Leonard Peterson; mar Gilbert Dethick*; mother of William Dethick* and Robert Dethick*. *ODNB* under husband; *Visitations, Buckinghamshire.*

Sundry Gift: 62.387 (Christening Gift for her child)

Dethick, Sir Gilbert (c.1500–1584) Garter King of Arms, kntd 1551. Listed (incorrectly) as Clarenceux on 1575 roll. Mar 1st c.1541 Alice Peterson (Dethick*), 2nd Jane Duncombe; father of William Dethick* and Robert Dethick*. *ODNB*; Wagner; Siddons; BL Stowe MS 684; Yale Beinecke MS 97; Yale Hazen MS 2551; Royal Collection RCIN 1047442, RCIN 1047443.

Knight: 62.124, 62.303, 63.120, 63.293, 64.113, 64.167, 65.46, 65.213, 67.118, 67.288, 68.117, 68.286, 71.116, 71.286, 75.83, 75.230, 76.132, 76.327, 77.133, 77.330, 78.136, 78.338, 79.132, 79.339, 81.128, 81.335, 82.121, 82.321, 82.532, 82.113, 84.116, 84.314

Sundry Gift: 62.387 (Christening Gift for his child)

Dethick, Robert (b.1561) Son of Sir Gilbert Dethick* and Alice Peterson (Dethick*); godchild of Queen Elizabeth.

Sundry Gift: 62.387 (Christening Gift)

Dethick, William (1542–1612) York Herald, Garter King of Arms, kntd 1603. Son of Sir Gilbert Dethick* and Alice Peterson (Dethick*). *ODNB*; Wagner.

Gentleman: 85.189, 85.384, 88.160, 88.351, 89.157, 89.349, 94.146, 94.345, 97.164, 97.366, 98.162, 98.367, 99.156, 99.355, 00.158, 00.358, 03.164, 03.385

De Vere—see Vere

Devereux, Dorothy—see Dorothy Percy

Devereux, Frances—see Frances Walsingham

Devereux, Lettice, née Knollys, Countess of Essex (1543–1634) Viscountess Hereford, Countess of Leicester. Gentlewoman of the Privy Chamber. Daughter of Sir Francis Knollys* and Catherine Carey (Knollys*); sister of William Knollys*, Henry Knollys*, Elizabeth Leighton*, Anne West* and Catherine Knollys*; 1st cousin once removed to Queen Elizabeth; mar 1st 1560 Walter Devereux*, Earl of Essex, 2nd 1578 Robert Dudley*, Earl of Leicester, 3rd 1589 Christopher Blount; mother of Robert Devereux*, Earl of Essex, Penelope Rich* and Dorothy Percy*. *ODNB*; Hasler; Varlow.

Viscountess: 64.50, 67.53, 67.222

Countess: 75.36, 75.143, 76.38, 76.233, 77.40, 77.238, 78.34, 78.235, 79.38, 79.245;

Sundry Gift: 63.367 (Christening Gift for her child)

Devereux, Margaret, née Garnish, Viscountess of Hereford (1513–1599) Lord Willoughby's wife. Daughter of Robert Garnish and Anne Bacon; mar 1st c.1538 Walter Devereux, Viscount Hereford, 2nd 1559 William, Lord Willoughby. GEC, *Peerage*; will PCC 2 Wallop; 2nd husband's will PCC 25 Martyn.

Viscountess: 59.51, 59.272, 62.49, 62.229, 63.50, 63.222

Devereux, Penelope—see Penelope Rich

Devereux, Robert, Earl of Essex (1565–1601) Master of the Horse 1587, Master of the Ordnance, Earl Marshal, KG 1588, courtier poet, Privy Councillor 1593, Lord Lieutenant of Ireland 1599, executed for high treason 1601. Son of Walter Devereux*, Earl of Essex and Lettice Knollys (Devereux*); stepson of Robert Dudley*, Earl of Leicester; brother of Dorothy Percy* and Penelope Rich*; 1st cousin twice removed to Queen Elizabeth; mar 1590 Frances Sidney (Devereux*). *ODNB*; GEC, *Peerage*.

Earl: 84.15, 84.214, 88.5, 88.190, 94.12, 94.196, 97.15, 97.212, 98.4, 98.205

Sundry Gift: 89.397 (Installation as KG)

Devereux, Walter, Earl of Essex (1539–1576) Viscount Hereford, KG, cr Earl of Essex, 1572. Son of Richard Devereux and Dorothy Hastings; mar 1560 Lettice Knollys (Devereux*); father of Dorothy Percy*, Penelope Rich*, and Robert Devereux*. *ODNB*; GEC, *Peerage*.

Earl: 76.20, 76.215

Sundry Gift: 63.367 (Christening Gift for his child)

Devre—see Jacques du Vray

Digby, Abigail, née Heveningham (c.1552–1611) Maid of Honour, Gentlewoman of the Privy Chamber, Mistress Digby, Lady Digby. Daughter of Arthur Heveningham and Mary Shelton (Heveningham*); mar 1st c.1571 Sir George Digby*, 2nd 1589 Edward Cordell*, 3rd 1591 Ralph Bowes*; mother of Robert Digby* and Elizabeth Digby*. Hasler under 1st and 2nd husbands.

Maid of Honour: 68.312, 71.318

Gentlewoman: 76.153, 76.342, 77.149, 77.346, 78.151, 78.352, 79.153, 79.360, 81.147, 81.354, 82.141, 82.341, 82.609, 84.139, 84.336, 85.137, 85.330

Lady: 88.105, 88.289, 89.97, 89.282, 94.93, 94.277, 97.98, 97.305, 98.98, 98.307, 99.94, 99.299, 00.99, 00.306, 03.104, 03.318

Sundry Gift: 85.418 (Christening Gift for her child), 89.402 (Marriage Gift)

Digby, Elizabeth (b.1585) Daughter of Sir George Digby* and Abigail Heveningham (Digby*); mar 1600 Baldwin Wake.

Sundry Gift: 85.418 (Christening Gift)

Digby, George (c.1550–1587) Kntd 1586, MP. Son of John Digby and Anne Throckmorton; mar c.1571 Abigail Heveningham*; father of Elizabeth Digby* and Robert Digby*; brother of Robert Digby*. Hasler; *ODNB* under son; will PCC 31 Spencer.

Sundry Gift: 85.418 (Christening Gift for his child)

Digby, Lettice—see Lettice FitzGerald

Digby, Robert (1574–1618) Son of George Digby* and Abigail Heveningham (Digby*); brother of Elizabeth Digby*; mar 1598 Lettice [II] FitzGerald*. GEC, *Peerage*.

Sundry Gift: 99.413 (Marriage Gift)

Dive—see Dyve

Donato, Anthony (fl.1560s) alias Anthony of Milan, Merchant of Venice. Will PCC 38 Lyon; *CSP Domestic, 1547–1580*.

Gentleman: 63.166, 63.345

Donnington, Margaret—see Margaret Bourchier

Dorrell, William—see Darell, William
    Chaplain: 68.143

Doughtie, Thomas (fl.1550s–1560s) Bitmaker. PRO LC 5/33.
    Gentleman: 59.196, 59.421

Douglas, Lady Margaret—see Margaret Stuart, Countess of Lennox

Dove, Thomas (1555–1630) Royal Chaplain, Bishop of Peterborough 1601–1630. *ODNB*.
    Bishop: 03.59, 03.272

Downham, William (1511–1577) Chaplain to Elizabeth as Princess and Queen, Bishop of Chester 1561–1577. *ODNB*.
    Bishop: 62.35, 62.215, 63.34, 63.206, 64.33, 65.135, 67.35, 67.205, 68.50, 68.219, 71.46, 71.216, 75.55, 75.163, 76.58, 76.253, 77.59, 77.255

Drury, Dru (1531–1617) Gentleman Usher of the Privy Chamber at Coronation, Groom of the Privy Chamber, Lieutenant of the Tower 1596, kntd 1579, MP. Son of Robert Drury and Elizabeth Brudenell; brother of William [I] Drury*; mar 1st 1565 Elizabeth Calthorpe, 2nd 1582 Catherine Finch. *ODNB*; Hasler.
    Free Gift: 59.443

Drury, Elizabeth, née Stafford (c.1556–1600) Mistress Elizabeth Stafford, Mistress Drury, Lady Drury, Lady Scott, Gentlewoman of the Bedchamber. Daughter of William Stafford and Dorothy Stafford*; sister of Edward [II] Stafford*, mar 1st 1573 Sir William [II] Drury*, 2nd 1590 Sir John Scott; mother of Robert Drury* and Frances Drury*. *ODNB*; Merton; 1st husband's will PCC 40 Scott; BL Harleian MS 6986, BL Sloane MS 814.
    Gentlewoman: 71.131, 71.301, 75.94, 76.138, 76.335
    Lady: 77.110, 77.307, 78.110, 78.310, 79.107, 79.315, 81.99, 81.306, 82.94, 82.294, 82.555, 84.90, 84.288, 85.95, 85.287, 88.100, 88.284, 89.92, 89.277, 94.89, 94.273, 97.97, 97.296
    Sundry Gift: 75.252 (Christening Gift for her child)
    Custody of Gift: 71.82, 71.86, 71.93, 71.112, 71.123–124, 71.131–137, 71.139, 71.141, 71.143–144, 71.163, 76.159, 77.107

Drury, Frances (1576–1642) Mistress Drury. Daughter of Sir William [II] Drury* and Elizabeth Stafford (Drury*); sister of Robert Drury*; mar c.1594 1st Sir Nicholas Clifford MP, 2nd 1599 Sir William Wray MP. Hasler under husbands.
    Gentlewoman: 82.162
    Maid of Honour: 94.314
    Regifted 82.193 (Queen gave gift from Charles Smith to her)

Drury, Margery—Margery Williams

Drury, Robert (1575–1615) Son of William [II] Drury* and Elizabeth Stafford (Drury*); mar 1592 Anne Bacon. *ODNB*; will PCC 98 Rudd, sentence 22 Cope.
    Sundry Gift: 75.252 (Christening Gift)

Drury, William [I] (1527–1579) Lord Chief Justice of Ireland, MP, kntd 1570. Son of Robert Drury and Elizabeth Brudenell; brother of Dru Drury*; mar 1560 Margery Wentworth (Williams*). *ODNB*; Hasler.
    Gentleman: 67.153, 67.329

Drury, William [II] (1550–1590) Sheriff of Suffolk, Marshal of Berwick, kntd 1576. Son of Robert Drury and Audrey Rich; mar 1573 Elizabeth Stafford (Drury*); father of Robert Drury* and Frances Drury*. *ODNB*; will PCC 40 Scott.
    Gentleman: 75.214, 76.177
    Knight: 77.135, 77.332, 78.139, 78.340, 79.139, 79.346, 81.132, 81.339, 82.126, 82.325, 82.536, 84.120, 84.318, 85.118, 85.310

Sundry Gift: 75.252 (Christening Gift for his child)

Drury Scott, Elizabeth—see Elizabeth Drury

Duck, Thomas (d.1609) Sergeant of the Cellar, Footman. Mar Susan [née?] Anslow. PRO LC 5/33; Collins, *Jewels*; will PCC 63 Dorset.
   Gentleman: 98.407, 99.174, 99.394, 00.174, 00.396, 03.185, 03.407
   Custody of Gift: 82.234

Dudley (or Sutton), Lord/Baroness—see Mary Sutton, née Howard, 1571–1600; Elizabeth Dudley; Edward Dudley, 4th, 1553–1586

Dudley, Ambrose (c.1528–1590) Lord Ambrose Dudley, Earl of Warwick 1561, Chief Pantler at Coronation, Master of the Ordnance, Privy Councillor 1573, kntd 1549, KG 1563. Son of John Dudley, Duke of Northumberland and Jane Guildford; brother of Robert Dudley* Earl of Leicester, Lady Catherine [II] Hastings* and Lady Mary Sidney*; mar 1st 1545 Anne Whorwood, 2nd 1553 Elizabeth Tailboys*, 3rd 1565 Anne Russell (Dudley*). *ODNB*; GEC, *Peerage*; BL Sloane MS 814.
   Lord: 59.66, 59.287
   Earl: 62.15, 62.190, 64.14, 65.115, 67.14, 67.184, 68.15, 68.184, 71.11, 71.181, 75.14, 76.14, 76.209, 77.14, 77.211, 78.15, 78.212, 79.11, 79.217, 81.11, 81.216, 82.10, 82.211, 82.428, 84.9, 84.207, 85.10, 85.201, 88.9, 88.194, 89.9, 89.194
   Sundry Gift: 59.453 (Coronation Fees)

Dudley, Anne, née Russell, Countess of Warwick (1548–1604) Daughter of Francis Russell*, Earl of Bedford, and Margaret St John (Russell*); sister of John [I] Russell*, William Russell*, Elizabeth Bourchier*, and Margaret Clifford*; aunt of Anne Russell*; mar 1565 Ambrose Dudley*, Earl of Warwick. *ODNB*; GEC, *Peerage*; BL Sloane MS 814.
   Countess: 67.51, 67.221, 68.30, 68.199, 71.24, 71.194, 1572, 1573, 1574, 75.27, 75.134, 76.30, 76.225, 77.35, 77.231, 78.30, 78.231, 79.28, 79.239, 81.27, 81.234, 82.28, 82.227, 82.481, 84.26, 84.224, 85.26, 85.217, 88.23, 88.208, 89.20, 89.205, 94.21, 94.206, 97.31, 97.235, 98.29, 98.237, 99.25, 99.225, 00.31, 00.235, 03.32, 03.244

Dudley, Lady Catherine—see Lady Catherine Hastings

Dudley, Douglas—see Douglas Sheffield

Dudley, Edward—see Edward Sutton

Dudley, Elizabeth, née Tailboys, Baroness Dudley (1520–1563) Baroness Tailboys. Daughter of Gilbert Tailboys and Elizabeth Blount; sister-in-law of Margaret Tailboys*; mar 1st by 1552 Thomas Wimbish, 2nd 1553 Ambrose Lord Dudley*. *ODNB* under 2nd husband.
   Baroness: 59.92, 59.312

Dudley, Elizabeth—see Elizabeth Southwell

Dudley, John (1526–1593) Sergeant of the Pastry. succeeded John Betts*; related to Robert Dudley*, Earl of Leicester, and Ambrose Dudley*, Earl of Warwick; mar 1st 1562 Alice Colley, 2nd 1574 Elizabeth Gardiner, 3rd 1583 Agnes [née?] Mortimer. will PCC 17 Dixy.
   Gentleman: 71.161, 71.340, 75.129, 75.225, 76.191, 76.394, 77.190, 77.391, 78.189, 78.398, 79.194, 79.407, 81.193, 81.407, 82.188, 82.392, 82.568, 84.188, 84.389, 85.182, 85.382, 88.175, 88.367, 89.175, 89.367

Dudley, Mary—see Mary Sidney, Mary Sutton

Dudley, Robert, Earl of Leicester (1532–1588) Lord Robert Dudley, Master of the Horse 1559, KG 1559, Privy Councillor 1562, cr. Earl of Leicester 1564. Son of John Dudley, Duke of Northumberland and Jane Guildford; brother of Ambrose Dudley*, Earl of Warwick, Lady Catherine [II] Hastings*, and Lady Mary Sidney*; mar 1st 1550 Amy Robsart, 2nd 1573 (alleged) Douglas Howard (Sheffield*), 3rd 1578 Lettice Knollys

(Devereux*); 3rd cousin of Edward Sutton*, Lord Dudley. *ODNB*; GEC, *Peerage*; *CSP Foreign*; BL Sloane MS 814.

Lord: 59.74, 59.294, 64.225, 64.226

Earl 75.5, 76.6, 76.201, 77.7, 77.204, 78.7, 78.208, 79.5, 79.212, 81.4, 81.211, 82.5, 82.205, 82.449, 84.4, 84.202, 85.4, 85.195, 88.4, 88.189

Custody of Gift: 62.167

Regifted: 59.120, 59.294 (Gift received from Henry Jerningham*)

Dunfermline, Abbot of—see Robert Pitcairn

Dwarf, Queen's—see Thomasine de Paris

Durham, Bishop—see Cuthbert Tunstall, 1559; James Pilkington, 1561–1576; Richard Barnes, 1577–1587; Matthew Hutton, 1589–1595; Tobie Matthew, 1595–1606

Dyer, Sir Edward (1543–1607) Chancellor of the Garter, courtier poet, kntd 1596, MP. Son of Thomas Dyer and Frances Dyer; unmarried. *ODNB*; Hasler; May, *Elizabethan Courtier*.

Gentleman: 71.152, 71.330, 78.178, 78.386, 79.180, 79.393, 81.180, 81.388, 82.180, 82.388, 82.583, 84.161, 84.363, 85.161, 85.359, 88.157, 88.348, 89.154, 89.346, 94.148, 94.338

Knight: 97.132, 97.326, 98.130, 98.329, 99.122, 99.314, 00.126, 00.320, 03.126, 03.338

Dymoke, Robert (c.1508–1567) Hereditary Champion of England at coronations. Son of Sir Edward Dymoke and Anne Tailboys; mar Bridget Clinton. *ODNB*.

Sundry Gift : 59.455 (Coronation Fees)

Dyve, Douglas, née Denny (c.1545–1598) Mistress Dyve. Daughter of Anthony Denny and Joan Champernowne; sister of Edward Denny* and Mary Astley*; niece of Catherine Astley*; mar John Dyve. *Visitations, Bedfordshire*.

Gentlewoman: 82.164, 82.362, 82.621

Eastwood, Christopher (fl.1580s) Queen's servant. PRO E 115.

Custody of Gift: 82.343

Eaton, James (fl.1580s) Groom of the Chamber. BL Stowe MS 155; PRO LC 5/34, E 115.

Custody of Gift: 82.320, 82.332

Edgecombe, Margaret (1565–1613) Maid of Honour, Gentlewoman of the Privy Chamber. Daughter of Peter Edgecombe and Margaret Luttrell; mar 1585 Sir Edward Denny* MP. *ODNB* and Hasler under husband; BL Additional MS 64079.

Maid of Honour: 82.368, 84.360, 85.353

Edmonds, Dorothy, née Lidcott (1545–1615) Mistress Edmonds, Gentlewoman of the Privy Chamber. Daughter of Christopher Lidcott and Catherine Cheyne; mar c.1554 Christopher Edmonds. *Visitations, Buckinghamshire*; Hasler; Tighe.

Gentlewoman: 67.132, 67.302, 68.124, 68.292, 71.127, 71.297, 75.91, 76.137, 76.332, 77.140, 77.337, 78.144, 78.345, 79.145, 79.352, 81.140, 81.346, 82.134, 82.333, 82.592, 84.131, 84.327, 85.130, 85.324, 88.130, 88.314, 89.129, 89.314

Lady: 94.104, 94.288, 97.103, 97.301, 98.102, 98.302, 99.99, 99.293, 00.105, 00.300, 03.108, 03.322

Edney, Peter (fl.1600s) mar 1st 1590 Catherine Stowe, 2nd 1598 Alice Garthorne. PRO E 179/146/372, PRO E 179/146/399; Parish Records, St Botolph, Aldgate, London and Saint Olave Hart Street, London.

Gentleman: 03.201, 03.427

Edzard II (1532–1599) Count of Emden, Count of East Frisia. Son-in-law of Gustav I* of Sweden, mar Catarina Vasa. *CSP Foreign, 1586–88*.

Sundry Gift: 79.441 (Noble sending Envoy to England)

Effingham (Howard of Effingham), Lord/Baroness—see Catherine [I] Howard, née Carey, 1573–1597; Charles Howard, 2nd, 1573–1597; Margaret Howard, née Gamage, 1554–1573, dowager 1573–1581; William [I] Howard, 1st, 1554–1573

Egerton, Alice—see Alice Stanley

Egerton, Elizabeth—see Elizabeth Wolley

Egerton, Sir Thomas (1540–1617) Lord Keeper of the Great Seal, Master of the Rolls, Privy Councillor 1596, Attorney General 1592, kntd 1594, MP. Son of Richard Egerton and Alice Sparke; mar 1st by 1573 Elizabeth Ravenscroft, 2nd 1598 Elizabeth More (Wolley*), 3rd 1600 Alice Spencer (Stanley*), Countess of Derby. *ODNB*; GEC, *Peerage*; Hasler; will PCC 22 Weldon.
   Primary: 97.1, 97.201, 98.1, 98.202, 99.1, 99.196, 00.1, 00.198, 03.1, 03.214

Eglonby—see Aglionby

Ellen, Frau—see Helena Gorges

Ely, Bishop—see Richard Cox, 1559–1581; vacant, 1582–1600; Martin Heton, 1600–1609

Emden—see Edzard

Emden, Gent from (fl.1570s) Envoy from Edzard II*, Count of Emden.
   Sundry Gift: 79.441 (Gift to Envoy)

Emmanuel Philibert (1528–1580) Duke of Savoy, KG 1554. Gift to his envoy, Rupertino/Bertino Solari de Moretta*. Mar Margaret of France; father of Charles Emmanuel*.
   Sundry Gift: 62.391 (Noble sending Envoy to England)

Enrique of Portugal—see Henrique of Portugal

Englefield, Sir Francis (1534–1596) Master of the Court of Wards under Mary I, lived abroad from 1559, kntd 1547, MP. Son of Thomas Englefield and Margaret Throckmorton; mar 1554 Catherine Fettiplace. *ODNB*; Bindoff.
   Knight: 59.118, 59.337

Eric XIV of Sweden (1533–1568) King of Sweden*. Gifts to his envoys: Dionysius Burreus* and Nils Göransson Gyllenstierna*. Son of Gustav I of Sweden and Catarina von Sachsen-Laurenburg; half-brother of Cecilia* of Sweden, John III*, King of Sweden, and Charles IX*, King of Sweden; mar Karin Mansdotter.
   Sundry Gift: 62.380, 62.393 (Sovereign sending Envoy to England), 67.358 (Gift to his sister)

Ericson—see Ericson Johnson; Ericson Wissenburg

Erizo, Mark Anthony (fl.1540s–1560s) Merchant, also known as Anthony Errizius. Son of Domenco Erizo. *CSP Foreign, 1561–62*; PRO SP 46/27, E 178/1390; Collins, *Jewels*; *CPR, 1560–62, 1563–66*.
   Gentleman: 59.166, 59.391, 62.173, 62.360, 63.165, 63.344, 67.164, 67.340, 68.164

Essex, Earl/Countess—see Robert Devereux, 2nd, 1576–1601; Walter Devereux, 1st, 1572–1576; Lettice Devereux, née Knollys, 1572–1578; Frances Devereux, née Walsingham, 1590–1603

Eure, Lord/Baroness—see Elizabeth Carey, née Spencer, 1613–1618

Eure, Elizabeth—see Elizabeth Carey

Everard, John (d.1598) Goldsmith of London, 'a gent of Germany'. Mar Judith [née?]. will PCC 44 Lewyn; *CSP Ireland, 1600*.
   Sundry Gift: 85.409 (Gift from Queen)

Everdice, Everard (d.1565) Goldsmith from Antwerp, alias Everard. Mar Anna Varden Velde. Will PCC 13 Morrison, 19 Crymes.
   Gentleman: 59.221, 59.442
   Goldsmith: 64.226

Exeter, Bishop—see William Alley, 1560–1570; William Bradbridge, 1571–1578; John Woolton, 1579–1594; Gervase Babington, 1595–1597; William Cotton, 1598–1621

Eynns, Elizabeth—see Elizabeth Haynes

Fainine/Famars—see Charles de Lieven

Fane, Elizabeth, née Brydges (d.1568) Lady Fane, Lady of Privy Chamber. Daughter of Roland Brydges MP and Margery [née?]; mar c.1540 Sir Ralph Fane MP. *ODNB*; Bindoff under father and husband.
  Lady: 68.97, 68.266

Fawkenstone, Margaret [née?] (fl.1550s) unidentified.
  Gentlewoman: 59.152

Fénelon, Bertrand de Salignac, Seigneur de la Mothe Fénelon (1523–1589) Ambassador from France 1568–1575, Commissioner for marriage settlement between Elizabeth and the Duke of Anjou*. Holt; Fénelon; *CSP Foreign, 1579–80, 1585–86, 1586–88*; BL Cotton MSS Caligula E VI, Caligula C III.
  Sundry Gift: 76.419, 76.422, 81.449 (Gift to Envoy)

Fenot, Jean Antoine (b.c.1540) Physician, Alchemist, also known as Joannes Antonius Phenotus or John Anthony Fenotus. author: *Alexipharmacum* (Basil, 1575); Strype, *Historical*; BL Lansdowne MS 27; *CSP Foreign, 1578–79*; Kocher.
  Gentleman: 79.203, 79.416

Feria, Count of—see Figueroa

Fernley, Anne—see Anne Gresham

Ferrabosco, Alfonso (1543–1588) Musician, Composer, Lutenist, Gentleman of the Privy Chamber. *BDECM*; *RECM*; *ODNB*; *CPR, 1575–78*.
  Gentleman: 76.183, 76.385, 77.180, 77.393

Ferre , Count of—see Figueroa

Ferrers, Thomas (fl.1590s–1600s) London merchant, Governor of Merchant Adventurers, Esquire for the Body to James I. Son of John Ferrers and Barbara Cokayne; brother of Humphrey Ferrers. BL Stowe MS 150; Folger MS L.e.514.
  Gentleman: 99.195, 99.396

Ferrers, William (fl.1600s) Linen Draper, Mercer, Alderman of London. Beaven; *Visitations, London*.
  Gentleman: 03.209

Ferrières, Elizabeth (1570) Daughter of Jean de Ferrières, born and died July 1570.
  Sundry Gift: 71.363 (Christening Gift)

Ferrières, Jean de (c.1521–1586) Vidame de Chartres, Seigneur de Maligny, Huguenot refugee. father of Elizabeth Ferrières*, uncle of Prégent de la Fin* Beauvoir la Nocle. BL Cotton MS Caligula E VI.
  Sundry Gift: 71.363 (Christening Gift for his child)

Fesse—see Muley Hamet, King of Fez

Fiennes—see also Clinton

Fiennes, Anne, née Sackville, Baroness Dacre of the South (c.1540–1595) Daughter of Richard Sackville* and Winifred Brydges (Sackville*); sister of Thomas Sackville*, Lord Buckhurst; 2ⁿᵈ cousin of Queen Elizabeth; mar by 1558 Gregory Fiennes, Lord Dacre of the South. GEC, *Peerage*; Hasler; will PCC 41 Scott; husband's will 64 Dixy.
  Baroness: 62.80, 62.259, 63.79, 63.251, 64.72, 65.4, 65.171, 67.72, 67.242, 68.70, 68.239, 71.69, 71.239, 75.80, 75.187, 76.91, 76.285, 77.86, 77.283, 78.92, 78.286, 79.82, 79.289, 81.75, 81.282, 82.72, 82.272, 82.494, 84.67, 84.265, 85.73, 85.261, 88.75, 88.260, 89.68, 89.253, 94.70, 94.254

Fiennes, Master (fl.1580s) unidentified.
  Gentleman: 89.166, 89.359

Figueroa, Gómez Suárez de, Count de Feria (1520–1571) Spanish Ambassador 1558–1559. Mar Jane Dormer. *ODNB*; Clifford; Siddons.
Earl: 59.22, 59.243

Fin, Prégent de la (d. 1624) Vidam de Chartres, Seigneur Beauvoir la Nocle. French Ambassador, son of Jean de la Fin, nephew of Jean de Ferrières* Vidam de Chartres. CSP Foreign, CSP Domestic.
Sundry Gift: 94.393 (Gift to Envoy)

Finch, William—see William Barlow

Fish, Walter (c.1522–1585) Merchant Tailor, Queen's Tailor. succeeded by William Jones*. Arnold, *QE Wardrobe*; BL Additional MS 35328; will PCC 53 Brudenell.
Custody of Gift: 71.70

Fitton, Mary (1578–1647) Maid of Honour. Daughter of Edward Fitton and Alice Holcroft; liaison with William [II] Herbert*, Earl of Pembroke, and Richard Leveson; mar 1st 1606 William Polwhele, 2nd 1612 John Lougher. *ODNB*; *CSP Domestic, 1601*; will PRO PROB 11/201.
Maid of Honour: 97.339, 98.341, 99.329, 00.332

FitzAlan, Henry, Earl of Arundel (1512–1580) Privy Councillor 1558, Lord Steward 1558, KG 1544. Son of William FitzAlan and Anne Percy; mar 1st 1535 Catherine Grey, 2nd 1545 Mary Arundell; father of Jane FitzAlan (Lumley*) and Mary FitzAlan; father-in-law of Thomas [II] Howard*; grandfather of Philip Howard*. *ODNB*; GEC, *Peerage*.
Earl: 59.7, 59.228, 62.5, 62.185, 63.6, 63.178, 64.6, 65.105, 68.8, 68.177, 71.6, 71.176, 75.6, 76.7, 76.202, 77.8, 77.205, 78.8, 78.209, 79.6, 79.213

FitzAlan, Jane—see Jane Lumley

FitzGerald, Catherine—see Catherine Knollys

FitzGerald, Edward (fl.1580s) Queen's servant. PRO E 115.
Custody of Gift: 82.296

FitzGerald, Elizabeth (c.1560–1617) Daughter of Gerald Fitzgerald* and Mabel Browne (FitzGerald*); niece of Elizabeth [I] Clinton*, mar 1585 Donough O'Brien. GEC, *Peerage* under husband; Collins, *Peerage*.
Maid of Honour: 75.206, 76.369, 77.372, 78.376, 79.384, 81.378, 82.365, 84.357

FitzGerald, Elizabeth—see Elizabeth Fiennes

FitzGerald, Gerald, Earl of Kildare (1525–1585) Son of Gerald FitzGerald and Elizabeth Grey; brother of Edward FitzGerald* and Elizabeth [I] Clinton*; father-in-law of Catherine Knollys* and Frances [II] Howard*; uncle of Lettice Copinger*; grandfather of Lettice FitzGerald*; mar 1554 Mabel Browne; father of Elizabeth [II] FitzGerald*. *ODNB*; GEC, *Peerage*.
Earl: 77.16, 77.213

FitzGerald, Frances—see Frances [II] Howard

FitzGerald, Lettice (c.1579–1658) Maid of Honour. Daughter of Gerald FitzGerald and Catherine Knollys; granddaughter of Gerald Fitzgerald* and Mabel Browne; 1st cousin of Lettice Copinger*; mar 1598 Robert Digby*. GEC, *Peerage*; Birmingham City Archives MS 3888/A 934, MS 3888/A 928/1.
Sundry Gift: 99.413 (Marriage Gift)

FitzGerald, Lettice—see Lettice Copinger

FitzJames, Jane—see Jane Newton

FitzWarin, Frances—see Frances Bourchier

FitzWilliam, Jane, née Roberts (fl.1530s–1560s) Lady FitzWilliam. Daughter of John Roberts and Mary Sackville; 1st cousin of Richard Sackville*; mar 1539 Sir William Fitzwilliam. *ODNB* under husband; *Visitations, Kent*.
Lady: 62.99, 62.279, 65.23, 65.190

FitzWilliam, John (1526–1568) Gentleman. Son of William FitzWilliam and Anne Sapcote; mar 1548 Elizabeth Clifford. Hasler.
   Gentleman: 63.173
Fletcher, Richard (1545–1596) Queen's Almoner, Bishop of Worcester 1593–1595, Bishop of London 1595–1596. *ONDB*.
   Bishop: 94.41, 94.234
Fludd (Lloyd), Richard (fl.1580s) of the Ewery. PRO E 115.
   Custody of Gift: 82.321
Fluellen—see Llewellyn
Foix, Paul de (1528–1584) Resident Ambassador from Charles IX* of France 1562–1566. Jensen; Fénelon.
   Sundry Gift: 67.359 (Gift to Envoy on his departure)
Folemy, Brian Mack—Brian McPhelim O'Neill
Fortescue, John (1533–1607) Household of Princess Elizabeth, Keeper of the Great Wardrobe 1559, Privy Councillor 1588, Chancellor of the Exchequer 1589, kntd 1592, Chancellor of the Duchy of Lancaster 1601, MP. Son of Adrian Fortescue and Anne Read; step-son of Thomas Parry*; mar 1st Cecily Ashfield, 2nd Alice Smith. *ODNB*; Hasler.
   Knight: 82.174, 94.123, 94.296, 97.117, 97.316, 98.118, 98.319, 99.112, 99.307, 00.117, 00.314, 03.120, 03.334
Fortescue, Mary (fl.1550s) styled Lady Darrell. Daughter of James Daniel, mar 1st (or liaison with) Edward Darrell, 2nd Philip Mansell, 3rd Henry Fortescue. Hasler under son William Fortescue and husband Henry Fortescue; *CPR, 1550–53*.
   Lady: 59.89, 59.309
Fouquet de la Varenne, Guillaume (1560–1616) Envoy from Henry IV* of France, Groom and Chef to French king, créateur de la Poste aux lettres.
   Sundry Gift: 94.394 (gift to envoy)
Fowkes, Elizabeth—see Elizabeth Middlemore
Francisco de Venice—see Francis Kellim
François, Duc d'Anjou (1555–1584) Monsieur, Duc d'Alençon, Suitor to Queen Elizabeth, visited England 1579, 1581–2. Son of Henry II of France and Catherine de Medici; brother of François II, Henri III*, and Charles IX*; unmarried. *CSP Domestic, 1547–80*; *CSP Foreign, 1572–74, 1579–80, 1582*; Holt.
   Primary: 82.1
   Regifted: 82.125 (Queen regifted gift from Sir Henry Lee)
   'unknown person' (possible identification): 78.199–202
François de Bourbon (1539–1592) Prince Dauphin, French Commissioner for marriage settlement between Elizabeth and the Duke of Anjou*. Son of the Duc de Montpensier. *CSP Domestic, Addenda 1580–1625; CSP Foreign, 1586–88*; BL Cotton MS Galba E VI.; Cotton MS Caligula E XII.
   Sundry Gift: 81.445 (Gift from the Queen)
Frankwell, John (d.1560) Keeper of Hampton Court, Gentleman Usher. Mar 1st Millicent [née?] (Frankwell*), 2nd 1560 Alice Downe. PRO LC 2/1; BL Sloane MS 3194; will PCC 5 Loftes.
   Gentleman: 59.171, 59.393
   Custody of Gift: 59.109
Frankwell, Millicent, [née?] (d.1560) Mistress Frankwell. Mar 1st George Alesbury, 2nd John Frankwell*. BL Sloane MS 3194; husband's will PCC 5 Loftes.
   Gentlewoman: 59.151, 59.359

Freake, Edmund (1516–1591) Bishop of Rochester 1572–1575, Bishop of Norwich 1575–1584, Bishop of Worcester 1584–1591, Queen's Almoner. *ODNB*.
  Bishop: 75.49, 75.157, 76.52, 76.247, 77.52, 77.249, 78.52, 78.253, 79.50, 79.257, 81.45, 81.252, 82.44, 82.244, 82.449, 84.41, 84.239, 85.44, 85.235, 88.43, 88.228, 89.38, 89.223
Frederick II of Denmark (1534–1588) King of Denmark, KG 1578. Gifts to his envoys: George Swooke*, John George Henrick*, George Schuavenius*, and Mathias Budde*; son of Christian III of Denmark; father of Anne of Denmark; mar Sophie Mecklenburg.
  Sundry Gift: 81.443, 84.416, 84.422, 85.408, 88.406, (Sovereign sending Envoy to England)
Freeman, M.—see George Fremin
Freeman, Walter (fl.1580s) Yeoman of the Kitchen. *CPR, 1575–78*; PRO E 115.
  Custody of Gift: 82.287, 82.288
Freer, unidentified (fl.1580s) Queen's servant.
  Custody of Gift: 82.284, 82.300
Fremin, George (fl.1580s) Colonel of a French company, later governor of Safting. Envoy from France.
  Sundry Gift: 88.397 (gift to envoy)
French, Richard (fl.1600s) Merchant Taylor
  Gentleman: 00.197, 00.399, 03.211, 03.405
French, Thomas (fl.1590s–1600s) Sergeant of the Pastry.
  Gentleman: 97.177, 97.379, 98.174, 98.380, 99.168, 99.368, 00.169, 00.370, 03.183, 03.404
French youth (fl.1590s) Unidentified, Frenchman accompanying Colonel Baldi, a Swiss 1596.
  Sundry Gift: 97.425 (Gift to Envoy)
Friedrich I, Duke of Wurttemberg (1557–1608) Gift to his envoy Adam Viman*. grandson of Philip I of Hesse; first cousin of Maurice of Hesse*.
  Sundry Gift: 98.429 (Sovereign sending Envoy to England)
Frobisher, Martin (c.1535–1594) Captain, Adventurer, Privateer, Explorer. Son of Bernard Frobisher and Margaret York; nephew of John York*; mar 1st 1559 Isobel [née?] Rigatt, 2nd 1591 Dorothy Wentworth. *ODNB*; BL Additional MS 39852.
  Sundry Gift: 79.440 (Departure Gift, voyage to 'Friesland')
Frogmerton—see Throckmorton
Fromond, Catherine—see Catherine Bromfield
Frow, Ellen—see Helena Gorges
Frow, Gyllam—see Cecilia Bone
Fulnetby, Elizabeth—Elizabeth Master
Fulwell, Stephen (d.1593) Yeoman and Groom of the Office of Jewels and Plate. Will PCC 67 Nevell; *CSP Domestic, Addenda 1580–1625*.
  Free Gift: 62.377, 63.361, 64.215, 67.357, 68.344, 71.359, 75.247, 76.411, 77.413, 78.419, 79.433, 81.432, 82.418, 84.411, 85.403, 88.393, 89.394
  Custody of Gift: 82.213
Furbussher, Captain—see Martin Frobisher
Fyshe—see Fish
Gallars, Nicolas des (c.1520–1581) Monsieur de Saulte, Special Ambassador from Charles IX* of France, Seigneur de Saules, Reformed minister. *ODNB*.
  Sundry Gift: 62.378 (Gift to Envoy)
Galliardello, Caesar (1568–1627) Musician, Violin. Son of Mark Anthony Galliardello*, brother-in-law of Henry Troches* and John Lanier*. *BDECM*; *ODNB*.

Gentleman: 88.183, 88.372, 89.185, 89.377, 94.174, 94.371, 97.189, 97.390, 98.187, 98.391, 99.185, 99.383, 00.185, 00.385, 03.196, 03.422

Galliardello, Mark Anthony (d.1585) Musician, Violin. father of Caesar Galliardello*; father-in-law of Henry Troches* and John Lanier*; also known as Mark Antonio Alberti, 'de Venice', Cuson and Gershom; sometimes confused with Mark Antonio Erizo*. *ODNB*; *BDECM*; *RECM*; Siddons.

Gentleman: 59.216, 59.440, 65.91 71.163, 68.162, 68.332, 71.340, 75.127, 75.226, 76.195, 76.395, 77.193, 77.395, 78.192, 78.401, 79.197, 79.411, 81.198, 81.410, 82.195, 82.399, 82.565, 84.195, 84.393, 85.191

Galliardello, Paul (d.1563) Musician, Violin. *BDECM*; will PCC 5 Stevenson.

Gentleman: 59.216, 59.440

Gamage, Margaret—see Margaret Howard

Gane/Gean, unidentified (fl.1580s) Queen's servant.

Custody of Gift: 82.87, 82.143, 82.150, 82.232

Gardiner, Robert (d.1571) Sergeant of the Cellar. *CSP Domestic, 1547–80*; Collins, *Jewels*; will PCC 4 Daper 1571.

Gentleman: 64.144

Garneys—see Garnish

Garnish, Margaret—see Margaret Devereux

Garrett—see FitzGerald

Garshe, Samuel (d.c.1628) Musician, Sackbut. *BDECM*; *RECM*.

Gentleman: 03.203, 03.424

Garton, Thomas (fl.1580s) Page of Wardrobe of Beds. PRO E 115; *LP Henry VIII*.

Custody of Gift: 82.318

Gaskin, William (fl.1580s) Queen's servant.

Custody of Gift: 82.221

Gastel, Jean Marinier (fl.1570s) Sieur de Gastel, Envoy from Don John of Austria. *CSP Foreign, 1575–77, 1578–79*; Collins, *Jewels*.

Sundry Gift: 77.422, 78.425 (Gift to Envoy)

Gaunt, Viscount - see Robert de Melun

Gean—see Gane

Gemini, Thomas (c.1510–1562) Engraver, Printer, Musical and Surgical Instrument Maker. alias Thomas Lambert/Lambritt. *ODNB*; Will PCC 14 Streat; BL Additional MS 10398.

Gentleman: 59.203, 59.427

Gent[leman], unidentified (fl.1580s) Queen's servant.

Custody of Gift: 82.347

Gentili, Scipione (1563–1616) Poet and Professor of Law, Protestant refugee. brother of Alberico Gentili, dedicated works to Sir Philip Sidney* and Queen Elizabeth. Binns; *ODNB* under brother.

Gentleman: 84.197

George, John—see John George Henrick

George, Master—see John George H, George Schuavenius, George Swoke

Gerard, Anne, née Radcliffe (b.c.1535) Lady Gerard. Daughter of Thomas Radcliffe and Alice Redman; mar 1555 Sir Gilbert Gerard*; mother of Thomas Gerard*. *ODNB* and Hasler under husband.

Lady: 84.96, 84.294, 85.101, 85.294, 88.104, 88.288, 89.96, 89.281, 94.94, 94.278, 97.99, 97.306, 98.99, 98.308, 03.106, 03.320

Gerard, Gilbert (d.1593) Master of the Rolls 1581, Attorney General 1559–1581, kntd 1579, MP. Mar 1555 Anne Radcliffe (Gerard*); father of Thomas Gerard*. *ODNB*; Hasler; will PCC 30 Nevell.
   Knight: 82.117, 82.317, 82.582, 84.114, 84.312, 85.115, 85.307, 88.119, 88.303, 89.112, 89.297

Gerard, Thomas (1564–1618) Knight Marshal of the Household 1597, Knight Marshal at Queen's Funeral 1603, kntd 1591, MP. Son of Gilbert Gerard* and Anne Radcliffe (Gerard*); related by marriage to Christopher Heydon*; mar 1ˢᵗ Alice Rivett, 2ⁿᵈ c.1613 Elizabeth Woodford, 3ʳᵈ Mary Dormer. Hasler; will PCC 46 Meade.
   Knight: 94.122, 94.307, 97.129, 97.328, 99.130, 99.316, 00.131, 00.322, 03.129, 03.344

Geraulty—see Giraldi

Gershom—see Mark Anthony Galliardello

Ghent, Viscount—see Charles L'Aubespine; Robert de Melun

Gifford, Eleanor—see Eleanor Brydges

Gifford, George (1553–1613) Gentleman Pensioner, kntd 1596, MP. Son of John Gifford and Elizabeth Throckmorton; mar c.1583 Eleanor Brydges*. Hasler; Tighe.
   Gentleman: 81.182, 81.395, 82.173, 82.378, 82.582, 84.185, 84.370, 85.168, 85.364

Gifford, Roger (1538–1597) Physician, Doctor Gifford. brother-in-law of Richard Barnes*. *ODNB*; Hasler; will PCC 77 Cobham, 2 Pynnyng.
   Gentleman: 89.164, 89.356, 94.157, 94.350, 97.169, 97.371

Gilbert, William (c.1544–1603) Physician, author. Son of Jerome Gilbert and Elizabeth Coggeshall; unmarried. *ODNB*; Furdell.
   Gentleman: 03.171, 03.392

Giles, Christopher (fl.1570s) Cutler.
   Gentleman: 78.195, 78.405

Giraldi, Francesco (fl.1570s) Chevalier Giraldi. Ambassador from Henrique* of Portugal. PRO SP 46/29/fo 229; BL Additional MS 34329, Egerton MS 1694, Cotton MS Nero, B I, Cotton MS Titus B VII.
   Sundry Gift: 79.454 (Gift to Envoy upon his departure from England)

Gittens, Henry (d.1598) Tailor of London, Lambert alias Gittens, possible identification. Will PRO PCC 70 Lewyn.
   Gentleman: 77.197, 77.399

Gloucester, Bishop—see Richard Cheyney, 1562–1579; John Bullingham, 1581–1598; Godfrey Goldsborough, 1598–1604

Goddard, Anne—see Mistress [Anne?] Huggins

Godwin, Thomas (1517–1590) Bishop of Bath and Wells 1584–1590. *ODNB*.
   Bishop: 85.45, 85.245, 88.44, 88.227, 89.39, 89.224

Golding, Margery—see Margery Vere

Goldsborough, Godfrey (1548–1604) Bishop of Gloucester 1598–1604. *ODNB*.
   Bishop: 99.46, 99.243, 00.56, 00.253, 03.57, 03.270

Goldwell, George (fl.1570s–80s) Groom of the Chamber. PRO LC 5/34
   Custody of Gift: 82.235

Gondi, Jeronimo (fl.1570s) Messenger, Special Ambassador from Henry III* of France; associate of Charles de L'Aubespine*. Fénelon.
   Sundry Gift: 78.424 (Gift to Envoy)

Gonor, Monsieur—see Artus de Cossé

Gooderus, William (d.1613) Surgeon. *ODNB* under George Baker; Furdell; will PCC 120 Capell.
   Gentleman: 97.197, 97.402, 98.194, 98.404, 99.191, 99.392, 00.190, 00.394, 03.178, 03.399

Goodman, unidentified (fl.1580s) Queen's servant.
   Custody of Gift: 82.315
Goodyear, Thomas (fl.1570s–1580s) Page of the Chamber. PRO LC 5/35.
   Custody of Gift: 76.94
Gorges, Lady Elizabeth [I], née Clinton (1573–1659) Lady Gorges. Daughter of Henry
   Clinton*, Earl of Lincoln, and Catherine Hastings (Clinton*); niece by marriage to
   Helena Gorges*; mar 1597 Arthur Gorges; mother-in-law of Robert Lane*. will PRO
   PROB 11/292, *ODNB* under husband.
   Lady: 03.115, 03.317
Gorges, Elizabeth [II] (1578–1659) daughter of Thomas Gorges* and Helena Snakenborg
   (Gorges*); mar Hugh Smith. *Visitations, Somerset*.
   Sundry Gift: 79.445 (Christening Gift)
Gorges, Elizabeth—see Elizabeth Wake
Gorges, Francis (fl.1580s) Queen's servant, probably related to Sir Thomas Gorges*. PRO
   E 115.
   Custody of Gift: 82.78, 82.98, 82.214, 82.313
Gorges, Helena, née Snakenborg, Lady Marquess of Northampton (1548–1635) Mistress/
   Frau Ellen, Maid of Honour to Princess Cecilia*, Chief Mourner at Elizabeth's funeral;
   daughter of Ulf Henriksson Snakenborg and Agnetta Knutsdotter; mar 1st 1571
   William Parr*, Marquess of Northampton, 2nd 1576 Thomas Gorges*; mother of
   Elizabeth [II] Gorges*, aunt of Elizabeth [I] Gorges*. *ODNB*; GEC, *Peerage*; BL Sloane
   MS 814.
   Gentlewoman: 67.145, 67.315, 68.128, 68.296, 71.133, 71.303
   Lady Marquess: 1573, 75.21, 77.28, 77.225, 78.25, 78.226, 79.26, 79.232, 81.21, 81.228,
   82.21, 82.221, 82.476, 84.20, 84.218, 85.20, 85.211, 88.19, 88.204, 89.17, 89.202, 94.15,
   94.199, 97.19, 97.217, 98.17, 98.218, 99.13, 99.208, 00.17, 00.214, 03.19, 03.232
   Sundry Gift: 79.445 (Christening Gift for her daughter)
Gorges, Jane—see Jane Hawke, Jane Stafford
Gorges, Sir Thomas (1536–1610) Groom of the Privy Chamber, Gentleman of the Robes,
   kntd 1586, MP. Son of Edward Gorges and Mary Poyntz; brother of Elizabeth Wake*
   and Jane Stafford*; mar 1576 Helena Snakenborg (Gorges*), Lady Marquess of
   Northampton; father of Elizabeth [II] Gorges*. *ODNB*; Hasler; will PCC 64
   Wingfield.
   Free Gift: 75.242, 76.406, 77.408, 78.414, 79.428, 81.426, 82.407, 84.403, 85.396, 88.378,
   89.379, 94.377, 97.404, 98.410, 99.398, 00.401, 03.434
   Custody: 82.214, 82.407, 88.12, 88.20, 88.24, 88.31, 88.35, 88.56, 88.59, 88.72, 88.76,
   88.81, 88.86, 88.88–89, 88.94, 88.96, 88.108, 88.110–112, 88.121, 88.131–132, 88.137–
   138, 88.156–158, 88.162, 88.164, 88.170
   Sundry Gift: 79.445 (Christening Gift for his daughter)
Goring, Mary—see Mary Neville
Gormanston, Viscount—see Christopher Preston, 4th, 1560–1600
Gounde, Mounsieur - see Artus de Cossé, Sieur de Gonor
Gower, George (c.1540–1596) Sergeant Painter. Mar 1st Catherine Cotton, 2nd Grace
   Hughson. *ODNB*; will PCC 1597 50 Cobham.
   Gentleman: 81.203, 81.418
Graves, Richard (1572–1626) Citizen and Haberdasher of London. will PRO PROB 11/149
   1626.
   Gentleman: 99.189, 99.382, 00.188, 00.384
Gray, Patrick (c.1559–1611) Master of Gray, later Lord Gray, Special Ambassador from
   James VI* of Scotland. GEC, *Peerage*.

Sundry Gift: 85.415 (Gift to Envoy)

Green, Elizabeth, née Bone (fl.1590s–1600s) Mistress Green alias Guilliam. Daughter of Guilliam Bone, coachman, and Cecilia [née?] Bone*; mar 1596 Francis Green, Queen's servant. Father's will PCC 52 Weldon.
Gentlewoman: 97.151, 97.355, 98.148, 98.356, 99.143, 99.343, 00.144, 00.349

Green, John (d.c.1567) Coffermaker to Mary I and Elizabeth; father, brothers and son were also Royal Coffermakers. PRO LC 5/49; Nichols, *Privy*; Madden.
Gentleman: 59.187, 59.411

Gregory, John (fl.1580s) of the Larder, Queen's servant.
Custody of Gift: 82.394

Gresham, Anne, née Fernley (d.1596) Lady Gresham. Daughter of William Fernley; mar 1st William Read, 2nd 1544 Thomas Gresham*; sister-in-law of Sir Nicholas Bacon*. *ODNB* under 2nd husband.
Lady: 62.100, 62.280, 63.96, 63.269, 64.91, 65.22, 65.189, 67.92, 67.262, 68.90, 68.259, 71.88, 71.258, 76.116, 76.306, 77.112, 77.309, 78.108, 78.313, 79.110. 79.318, 81.108, 81.314, 82.103, 82.302, 82.546, 84.98, 84.297, 85.103, 85.297, 88.107, 88.191, 89.100, 89.285, 94.95, 94.279

Gresham, Elizabeth - see Elizabeth Wingfield

Gresham, Sir Thomas (1519–1579) Mercer, Founder of the Royal Exchange and Gresham College, Queen's principal financial agent, kntd 1559. Son of Richard Gresham; brother-in-law to Sir Nicholas Bacon*; mar 1544 Anne Fernley (Gresham*). *ODNB*.
Knight: 62.123, 62.302, 63.119, 63.292, 64.112, 64.166, 65.45, 65.212, 67.116, 67.286, 68.114, 68.283, 71.117, 71.287, 76.127, 76.324, 77.130, 77.327, 78.132, 78.335, 79.136, 79.343

Grete, John (fl.1580s) Queen's servant, possible identification. PRO E 115.
Custody of Gift: 82.350

Greville, Anne, née Neville, Baroness Willoughby de Broke (1533–1580) Lady Willoughby of Warwick. Daughter of Ralph Neville and Catherine Stafford; mar c.1553 Fulke Greville; mother of Fulke Greville*. GEC, *Peerage*; *Visitations, Warwickshire*; *ODNB* under son.
Baroness: 76.101, 76.296, 77.101, 77.297

Greville, Fulke (1554–1628) Treasurer of Navy, courtier poet, later Lord Brooke of Beauchamps Court. Son of Fulke Greville, Lord Willoughby de Broke and Anne Neville (Geville*); unmarried. *ODNB*; May, *Elizabethan Courtier*.
Gentleman: 76.180, 77.183, 77.398, 78.180, 78.388, 79.182, 79.395, 81.179, 81.390, 84.166, 84.368, 85.166, 85.366, 94.147, 94.337, 97.159, 97.361, 98.158, 98.365, 99.153, 99.354, 00.155, 00.357, 03.160, 03.380

Grevin, Jacques (c.1538–1570) French Dramatist and Poet, Physician, Huguenot protestant. McFarlane; Foster; *ODNB* under Thomas Gemini*; Sambucus, J. *Les emblemes*, translated by J. Grevin (Antwerp, 1567).
Gentleman: 68.161

Grey of Wilton, Lord/Baroness—see William Grey, 13th, c.1521–1562

Grey, Anne—see Anne Windsor

Grey, Anne, née Jerningham (d.1559) Lady Anne Grey, Gentlewoman to Mary Tudor, Anne of Cleves and Mary I. Daughter of Edward Jerningham and Margaret Bedingfield; mar 1st c.1516 Edward, Lord Grey, 2nd unidentified Barkeley, 3rd Henry Barley MP, 4th Sir Robert Drury MP, 5th 1543 Sir Edmund Walsingham; daughter-in-law of Thomas Grey, Marquess of Dorset; sister-in-law of Lady Elizabeth Audley* and Lady Mary [I] Grey*. Bindoff under 3rd, 4th, and 5th husbands; BL Additional MS 38136; *Visitations, Suffolk*.
Lady: 59.79, 59.299

Grey, Lady Catherine, Countess of Hertford (1540–1568) Maid of Honour. Daughter of Henry Grey, Duke of Suffolk and Frances Brandon (Grey*), Duchess of Suffolk, sister of Lady Jane Grey and Lady Mary [II] Grey*, granddaughter of Charles Brandon, Duke of Suffolk and Mary Tudor, Queen of France; 1st cousin once removed to Queen Elizabeth; mar 1st 1553 Henry Herbert*, Earl of Pembroke, 2nd 1560 Edward Seymour*, Earl of Hertford. GEC, *Peerage*; *ODNB*; De Lisle.
  Maid of Honour: 59.373

Grey, Elizabeth—see Elizabeth Audley

Grey, Elizabeth [I] (1574–1614) Daughter of Sir Henry Grey*, later Lord Grey of Groby and Anne [I] Windsor (Grey*); granddaughter of Lord John Grey* of Pyrgo and Mary Browne (Grey*) and of Thomas Windsor and Dorothy Dacre; probably unmarried, not named in father's will.
  Sundry Gift: 75.249 (Christening Gift)

Grey, Lady Elizabeth [II], née Talbot (1582–1651) Lady of the Privy Chamber, later Countess of Kent. Daughter of Gilbert Talbot*, Earl of Shrewsbury and Mary Cavendish (Talbot*); sister of Alethea Talbot*; mar 1601 Henry Grey, later Earl of Kent. GEC, *Peerage*.
  Baroness: 03.89, 03.306

Grey, Lady Frances, née Brandon, Duchess of Suffolk (1517–1559) Daughter of Charles Brandon, Duke of Suffolk and Mary Tudor, Queen of France; granddaughter of Henry VII and Elizabeth of York; mar 1st 1533 Henry Grey, Duke of Suffolk, 2nd 1555 Adrian Stokes; mother of Lady Jane Grey, Lady Catherine Grey* and Lady Mary [II] Grey*; 1st cousin of Queen Elizabeth. *ODNB*; Hasler; GEC, *Peerage*; De Lisle.
  Primary: 59.1, 59.222

Grey, Henry (1547–1614) Gentleman Pensioner, Lieutenant of the Gentleman Pensioners c.1589, kntd 1587, later Lord Grey of Groby. Son of John Grey* and Mary Browne (Grey*); mar 1572 Anne [I] Windsor (Grey*); father of Elizabeth [I] Grey*. GEC, *Peerage*; Tighe.
  Sundry Gift: 75.249 (Christening Gift for his child)

Grey, Lord John (1527–1564) Son of Thomas Grey, Marquess of Dorset and Margaret Wotton; mar c.1547 Mary Browne (Grey*); father of Henry Grey*; grandfather of Elizabeth [I] Grey*. GEC, *Peerage*; *ODNB*.
  Lord: 59.62, 59.283, 62.61, 62.242, 63.62, 63.236, 64.68

Grey, Mary [I] (c.1527–c.1578) Lady Grey of Pyrgo. Daughter of Sir Anthony Browne and Anne Gage; mar 1st Lord John Grey*, 2nd c.1572 Henry Capel; daughter-in-law of Thomas Grey., Marquess of Dorset; sister-in-law of Lady Elizabeth Audley* and Lady Anne Grey*. mother of Henry Grey*, grandmother of Elizabeth [I] Grey*. *ODNB*; GEC, *Peerage*.
  Baroness: 64.92, 76.97, 76.294

Grey, Lady Mary [II] (1545–1578) Daughter of Henry Grey, Duke of Suffolk and Frances Brandon (Grey*), Duchess of Suffolk; sister of Lady Catherine Grey* and Lady Jane Grey; granddaughter of Charles Brandon, Duke of Suffolk and Mary Tudor, Queen of France; 1st cousin once removed to Queen Elizabeth; mar 1565 Thomas Keyes. *ODNB*; BL Sloane MS 814; De Lisle.
  Lady: 63.1, 64.1, 65.101, 76.1, 76.196, 77.2, 77.199, 78.2, 78.203

Grey, Peter (fl.1580s) Queen's servant. *CPR, 1575–78.*
  Custody of Gift: 82.291

Grey, Lady Susan, née Bertie, Countess of Kent (1554–aft.1611) Daughter of Richard Bertie and Catherine Willoughby (Brandon*); sister of Peregrine Bertie*; mar 1st 1571 Reginald Grey, Earl of Kent, 2nd 1581 Sir John Wingfield. GEC, *Peerage*.

Countess: 75.38, 75.145, 76.40, 76.235, 77.42, 77.241, 78.42, 78.242, 79.40, 79.247, 81.35, 81.242, 82.35, 82.235, 82.489, 97.20, 97.218, 98.18, 98.219, 99.14, 99.209, 00.19, 00.217, 03.20, 03.233

Grey, William, Lord Grey of Wilton (c.1510–1562) KG 1557. Son of Edmund, Lord Grey and Florence Hastings; mar c.1535 Mary Somerset. GEC, *Peerage*.
  Lord: 59.73

Griffin, Lucy, née Conyers (fl.1590s–1600s) Mistress Griffin of Dingley. Daughter of Reginald Conyers and Elizabeth Chambers(St John*); stepdaughter of Oliver, Lord St John*; mar c.1569 Edward Griffin. *VCH, Rutland*; *VCH, Leicestershire*.
  Gentlewoman: 97.156, 97.358, 98.152, 98.359, 99.147, 99.359, 00.148, 00.352, 03.143, 03.355

Griffin, Mary—see Mary Markham

Griffin, Piers (fl.1580s) of the Cellar, Queen's servant.
  Custody of Gift: 82.299, 82.335, 82.377

Grigorievich, Ivan - see Andrei Grigorievich Savin

Grigorey, Euan—see Andrei Grigorievich Savin

Grindal, Edmund (1519–1583) Bishop of London 1559–1570, Archbishop of York 1570–1576, Archbishop of Canterbury 1576–1583. *ODNB*.
  Bishop: 59.27, 59.245, 62.22, 62.202, 63.21, 63.193, 64.21, 65.121, 67.21, 67.191, 68.36, 68.205, 71.33, 71.203, 75.41, 75.149, 76.44, 76.239, 77.46, 77.243, 82.37, 82.237, 82.437

Guest, Edmund (1514–1577) Bishop of Rochester 1560–1571, Bishop of Salisbury 1571–1577, Almoner, Master of Requests. *ODNB*.
  Bishop: 62.30, 62.210, 63.29, 63.201, 64.25, 65.127, 67.27, 67.197, 68.42, 68.211, 71.41, 71.211, 75.46, 75.154, 76.49, 76.244, 77.50, 77.247

Guildenstern, Nicholas—see Nils Göransson Gyllenstierna

Guildford, Edward (b.1598) Son of Henry Guildford* and Lady Elizabeth Somerset (Guildford*).
  Sundry Gift: 99.412 (Christening Gift)

Guildford, Lady Elizabeth (1572–1621) Lady Guildford, Lady of the Privy Chamber. Daughter of Edward Somerset*, Earl of Worcester, and Lady Elizabeth Hastings (Somerset*); sister of Lady Anne Winter* and Lady Catherine Petre*; mar 1596 Sir Henry Guildford*. PRO LC 5/37.
  Lady: 97.93, 97.292, 98.93, 98.294, 99.90, 99.285, 00.95, 00.292, 03.97, 03.309
  Sundry Gift: 99.412 (Christening Gift for her child)

Guildford, Henry (c.1556–1646) kntd 1591. Son of Thomas Guildford and Elizabeth Shelley; mar 1596 Lady Elizabeth Somerset (Guildford*); father of Edward Guildford*. PRO AO 3/128.
  Knight: 97.137, 97.336, 98.133, 98.335, 99.125, 99.320, 00.128, 00.326, 03.128, 03.340;
  Sundry Gift: 99.412 (Christening Gift for his child)

Guillam—see Bone

Gustav of Sweden (1496–1560) King of Sweden, Gustav Eriksson, Gustav Vasa. Gifts to his envoys: Dionysius Burreus* and Nils Göransson Gyllenstierna*. Mar 1st Catarina von Sachsen-Laurenburg, 2nd Margaret Leijonhufvud; father of Eric XIV*, John III*, Cecilia*, and Charles IX*.
  Sundry Gift: 62.380 (Gift to his Envoy)

Guy, Peter [I] (d.1606) Musician. father of Peter [II] Guy*. *BDECM*; PRO E101/430/15; BL Harleian MS 1644.
  Gentleman: 97.184, 97.393, 98.182, 98.395, 99.180, 99.387, 00.180, 00.390

Guy, Peter [II] (d.1649) Musician. Son of Peter [I] Guy*. *BDECM*.
  Gentleman: 03.204, 03.414

Gyllenstierna, Nils Göransson (1526–1601) alias Gildenstern. Chancellor of Sweden, Ambassador from Gustav* and Eric XIV*, Kings of Sweden. *CSP Domestic, 1547–1580*; *CSP Foreign, 1561–62*.
  Sundry Gift: 62.393 (Gift to Envoy upon his departure from England)
Habingdon, Mary—see Mary Parker
Habingdon, Dorothy—see Dorothy Broadbelt
Haec/Hake—see Jane Brussells
Hales, Robert (d.1615) Musician, Lute Player, Singer. *BDECM*; will PCC 99 Rudd.
  Gentleman: 00.193, 00.388, 03.195, 03.420
Halewyn, François (fl.1560s) Seigneur de Sweveghem/Zueveghem, Special Ambassador from Margaret Duchess of Parma*, Regent of the Low Countries. *CSP Foreign, 1575–77, 1581–82, 1583*.
  Sundry Gift: 64.224 (Gift to Envoy)
Hall, unidentified (fl.1580s) of the Scullery. Queen's servant.
  Custody of Gift: 82.251, 82.351
Hamet, Muley—see Ahmad al-Mansur
Hampden, Anne, née Cave (1545–1593) Mistress Hampden. Daughter of Anthony Cave and Elizabeth Lovett*; sister of Mary Cave; niece by marriage to Sibell Penne*; cousin of Margaret Knollys*; mar 1565 Griffith Hampden MP. Hasler under husband and son; *Visitations, Buckinghamshire* : *Visitations, Leicestershire*.
  Gentlewoman: 75.113, 76.154, 76.347
Hampden, Sibell—see Sibell Penne
Harbert—see Herbert
Harden, James (d.1626) Musician, Flute. *BDECM*; *RECM*.
  Gentleman: 03.205, 03.428
Hardaret, Abraham (fl.1590s) Goldsmith, later Jeweller to King James. CSP Domestic, 1603–10.
  Sundry Gift: 97.424 (Goldsmith)
Hardwick, Elizabeth (1527–1608) Lady St Loe, Countess of Shrewsbury, 'Bess of Hardwick'. Daughter of John Hardwick and Elizabeth Leake; half-sister of Elizabeth Wingfield*; mar 1st c.1543 Robert Barley, 2nd 1548 William Cavendish, 3rd 1559 William St. Loe, 4th 1568 George Talbot*, Earl of Shrewsbury; mother of Elizabeth Stuart* and Mary Talbot*. *ODNB*; GEC, *Peerage*.
  Lady: 62.94, 62.275, 63.91, 63.267
  Countess: 68.24, 68.193, 71.20, 71.190, 75.24, 75.131, 76.26, 76.221, 77.31, 77.228, 78.31, 78.232, 79.27, 79.234, 81.23, 81.230, 82.23, 82.223, 82.479, 84.22, 84.220, 85.23, 85.213, 88.20, 88.205, 89.18, 89.203, 94.18, 94.202, 97.22, 97.220, 98.20, 98.221, 99.16, 99.211, 00.21, 00.218, 03.22, 03.235
Harington, Anne, née Kelway (c.1554–1620) Lady Harington. Daughter of Robert Kelway and Cecily Bulstrode; mar bef 1580 Sir John Harington of Exton; mother of Lucy Harington*. *ODNB* and GEC, *Peerage* under husband.
  Lady: 88.112, 88.295, 89.105, 89.290, 94.99, 94.283, 97.109, 97.310, 98.110, 98.311, 99.108, 99.302, 00.113, 00.309, 03.111, 03.325
Harington, Isabella, née Markham (d.1579) Mistress Harington, alias Elizabeth, Maid of the Privy Chamber at the Coronation, Gentlewoman of the Privy Chamber. Daughter of John Markham and Anne Strelley; sister of Thomas Markham*; mar 1559 John [I] Harington*, mother of John [II] Harington*. *Visitations, Nottinghamshire*.
  Gentlewoman: 62.135, 62.315, 63.127, 63.300
Harington, John [I] (1517–1582) Treasurer of Camps and Buildings to Henry VIII, courtier poet, MP. Son of Alexander Harington; mar 1st 1547 Audrey Malte, 2nd 1553 Isabella

Markham (Harington*); father of John [II] Harington*. *ODNB*; Hasler; BL Sloane MS 814.

Gentleman: 62.154, 62.341, 63.145, 63.324, 65.77, 67.148, 67.324, 68.146, 68.318, 71.148, 71.326, 76.172, 76.377, 77.173, 77.377, 78.173, 78.381, 79.178, 79.391, 81.172, 81.386, 82.167, 82.372, 82.571

Harington, John [II] (1560–1612) Courtier poet, Translator, kntd 1599. Son of John [I] Harington* and Isabella Markham (Harington*); godson of Queen Elizabeth; mar 1583 Mary Rogers (Harington*); father of infant Harington*. *ODNB*.

Sundry Gift : 88.404 (Christening Gift for his child)

Harington, Lucy—see Lucy Russell

Harington, Mary, née Rogers (d.1634) Mistress Harington. Daughter of George Rogers and Jane Winter; granddaughter of Sir Edward Rogers*; mar 1583 John [II] Harington*; mother of infant Harington*. *ODNB* under husband.

Sundry Gift: 88.404 (Christening Gift for her child)

Harington, unidentified (b.1588) Infant child of John [II] Harington* and Mary Rogers*.

Sundry Gift : 88.404 (Christening Gift)

Harlay, Christoph de (fl.1600s) Comte de Beaumont, Resident Ambassador from Henry IV* of France 1600–1605. Son of Achille de Harlay and Catherine de Thou. BL Stowe MS 157–158; Laffleur.

Sundry Gift: 03.449 (Christening Gift)

Harman, Mistress [née?] (fl.1570s) Unidentified, possible relative of James Harman*, Edmund Harman, Barber-Surgeon to Henry VIII, and John Harman, Gentleman Usher to Henry VIII.

Gentlewoman : 77.157, 77.354, 78.159, 78.361, 79.161, 79.368

Harman, James (d.1581) Keeper of the Standing Wardrobe at Westminster, mar Elizabeth [née?]; relative of Edmund Harman, Barber-Surgeon to Henry VIII. PRO E 115; *Visitations, Surrey*.

Custody of Gift: 59.140, 59.141, 65.53

Harris, Nicholas (fl.1550s) Fruiterer. Edward VI, *Literary Remains*.

Gentleman: 59.182, 59.406

Hartford—see Hertford

Harvey, Cordelia—see Cordelia Annesley

Harvey, Elizabeth (b.1569) Daughter of Henry Harvey* and Jane Thomas (Harvey*).

Sundry Gift: 71.360 (Christening Gift)

Harvey, Henry (d.1589) Gentleman Pensioner, Sergeant of the Buckhounds. Son of Nicholas Harvey and Bridget Wiltshire; 1st cousin of Isabel Radcliffe*; mar 1560 Jane Thomas (Harvey*); father of Elizabeth Harvey*. Tighe; *Visitations, Suffolk*; PRO C 142/232/50; *ODNB* under son.

Sundry Gift: 71.360 (Christening Gift for his child)

Harvey, Isabel—see Isabel Radcliffe

Harvey, Jane, née Thomas (fl.1570s) Daughter of James Thomas and Jane Vanne, mar 1560 Henry Harvey*; mother of Elizabeth Harvey* and William Harvey MP; mother-in-law of Mary Wriothesley* and Cordelia Annesley*. *ODNB* and Hasler under son.

Sundry Gift: 71.360 (Christening Gift to her child)

Harvey, Mrs [née?] (d.c.1573) Mistress Harvey, Mother of the Maids, unidentified, possible Mother of the Maids who died suddenly at Greenwich. Strickland; Thornbury.

Maid of Honour: 71.321 (Mother of the Maids)

Harvey, Mary—see Mary Wriothesley

Hastings, Catherine [I], née Pole, Countess of Huntingdon (d.1576) Daughter of Henry Pole and Jane Neville; mar 1532 Francis Hastings*, Earl of Huntingdon; mother of

Henry Hastings*, George Hastings*, Frances Compton*, Catherine Clinton*, and Elizabeth Somerset*; 3rd cousin of Queen Elizabeth. GEC, *Peerage*; *ODNB* under husband.

Countess: 59.46, 59.267, 62.45, 62.225, 63.48, 63.220, 64.48, 65.149, 67.48, 67.219, 68.26, 68.195, 71.22, 71.192, 75.25, 75.132, 76.27, 76.222

Hastings, Lady Catherine [II], née Dudley, Countess of Huntingdon (c.1537–1620) Daughter of John Dudley, Duke of Northumberland and Jane Guildford; sister of Robert Dudley*, Earl of Leicester, Ambrose Dudley*, Earl of Warwick, and Lady Mary Sidney*; mar 1553 Henry Hastings*, Earl of Huntingdon. *ODNB*; GEC, *Peerage*; BL Sloane MS 814.

Countess: 62.46, 62.226, 63.47, 63.219, 64.47, 65.150, 67.49, 67.219, 68.27, 68.196, 71.23, 71.193, 75.26, 75.133, 76.28, 76.223, 77.33, 77.233, 78.32, 78.233, 79.32, 79.235, 81.24, 81.231, 82.24, 82.224, 82.478, 84.23, 84.221, 85.24, 85.215, 88.21, 88.206, 89.19, 89.204, 94.21, 94.204, 97.26, 97.224, 98.23, 98.226, 99.20, 99.216, 00.25, 00.223, 03.26, 03.239

Hastings, Dorothy [I], née Port, Countess of Huntingdon (c.1542–1607) Daughter of John Port and Elizabeth Gifford; mar 1557 George Hastings*, Earl of Huntingdon; mother of Dorothy [II] Hastings*. GEC, *Peerage*.

Countess: 97.233, 98.24, 98.227, 99.21, 99.217, 00.26, 00.224, 03.27, 03.240

Hastings, Lady Dorothy [II] (1579–1622) Maid of Honour. Daughter of George Hastings*, Earl of Huntingdon and Dorothy Port (Hastings*); mar 1st 1603 James Stuart, 2nd 1609 Robert Dillon. GEC, *Peerage*.

Maid of Honour: 99.332, 00.331, 03.373

Hastings, Edward, Lord Hastings of Loughborough (c.1520–1573) Master of the Horse to Mary I, KG 1555, MP. Son of George Hastings, Earl of Huntington and Anne Stafford; brother of Francis Hastings*, Earl of Huntingdon; mar Joan Harington. GEC, *Peerage*; *ODNB*; Bindoff.

Lord: 59.59, 59.280, 62.58, 62.239, 63.59, 63.232, 64.67, 65.166, 67.64, 67.234, 68.63, 68.231, 71.60, 71.230

Hastings, Lady Elizabeth—see Lady Elizabeth [II] Somerset

Hastings, Lady Frances—see Lady Frances Compton

Hastings, Francis, Earl of Huntingdon (1514–1560) KG 1549, Privy Councillor 1550. Son of George Hastings, Earl of Huntingdon and Anne Stafford, mar 1532 Catherine Pole (Hastings*), father of Elizabeth [II] Somerset*, Henry Hastings*, Catherine Clinton*, Frances Compton*, and George Hastings*, brother of Edward Hastings*. GEC, *Peerage*; *ODNB*.

Earl: 59.10, 59.231

Hastings, George, Earl of Huntingdon (1540–1604) Son of Francis Hastings*, Earl of Huntingdon and Catherine Pole (Hastings*); brother of Henry Hastings*; Frances Hastings*, and Elizabeth [II] Somerset*; mar 1557 Dorothy Port (Hastings*); father of Dorothy Hastings*. GEC, *Peerage*.

Earl: 97.9, 97.211, 98.10, 98.214, 99.10, 99.205, 00.9, 00.210, 03.8, 03.221

Hastings, Henry, Earl of Huntingdon (1535–1595) Lord Hastings, KG 1570. Son of Francis Hastings*, Earl of Huntington, and Catherine Pole (Hastings*); brother of Henry Hastings*, Catherine Clinton*, Frances Compton*, George Hastings*, and Elizabeth [II] Somerset*, mar 1553 Catherine Dudley (Hastings*). GEC, *Peerage*; *ODNB*.

Lord: 59.72, 59.293

Earl: 62.11, 62.192, 63.12, 63.184, 64.11, 65.112, 67.11, 67.181, 68.13, 68.182, 71.10, 71.180, 75.13, 76.13, 76.208, 77.18, 77.215, 78.14, 78.216, 79.15, 79.221, 81.14, 81.221,

82.14, 82.214, 82.427, 84.13, 84.210, 85.13, 85.204, 88.10, 88.195, 89.7, 89.192, 94.7, 94.191

Hatton, Sir Christopher (c.1540–1591) Gentleman Pensioner 1564, Captain of the Guard 1572, Privy Councillor 1577, Vice Chamberlain 1577, Lord Chancellor 1587, courtier poet, kntd 1577, KG 1588. Son of William Hatton and Anne Saunders; unmarried. *ODNB*; Kinney; Folger MS L.d.880; BL Sloane MS 814; Tighe.

Gentleman: 71.153, 71.331, 75.117, 75.209, 76.170, 76.372, 77.172, 77.375

Knight: 78.123, 78.324, 79.121, 79.328, 81.118, 81.325, 82.113, 82.312, 82.525, 84.109, 84.307, 85.110, 85.300

Primary: 88.1, 88.186, 89.1, 89.186

Sundry Gift: 89.398 (Installation as KG); 88.401 (Gift to Queen from Thomas Rivett)

Regifted: 88.401 (Gift to Queen from Thomas Rivett)

Hatton, Elizabeth, née Cecil (1578–1646) Lady Hatton, Lady Hatton Coke. Daughter of Thomas Cecil* and Dorothy Neville (Cecil*); granddaughter of William Cecil* and Mildred Cooke (Cecil*) and of John Neville and Lucy Somerset (Neville*); niece of Elizabeth [I] Cecil*; mar 1ˢᵗ William Hatton*, 2ⁿᵈ 1598 Edward Coke*; mother of Elizabeth Coke*. *ODNB*.

Lady: 98.104, 98.315, 03.114, 03.326

Sundry Gift: 00.416 (Christening Gift for her child)

Hatton, Randall (d.1587) Page of the Chamber. *CSP Domestic, 1582–83*.

Custody of Gift: 82.244

Hatton, William (c.1565–1597) Formerly William Newport, kntd 1586, MP. Son of John Newport and Dorothy Hatton; nephew of Christopher Hatton*; mar 1ˢᵗ 1589 Elizabeth Gawdy, 2ⁿᵈ Elizabeth Cecil (Hatton*). Hasler; will PCC 8, 41 Cobham; PRO E315/1954.

Knight: 97.134, 97.331

Havrech/Havering, Marquis—see Charles Philip de Croy

Haward—see Howard

Hawk, Jane—see Jane Brussells

Hawkins, Margaret, née Vaughan (d.1619) Lady Hawkins, Gentlewoman of the Bedchamber. Daughter of Charles Vaughan and Margaret Vaughan; relative of Blanche Parry*; mar 1591 Sir John Hawkins. BL Additional MS 35831; *ODNB* under husband.

Gentlewoman: 89.139, 89.324

Lady: 94.107, 94.291, 97.106, 97.303, 98.107, 98.304, 99.104, 99.295, 00.108, 00.302, 03.109, 03.323

Regifted: 98.107 (Queen regifted her gift to Elizabeth Leighton*)

Haynes, Elizabeth, née Neville (c.1527–1585) Mistress Haynes (Eynns). Extraordinary Gentlewoman of the Privy Chamber. Daughter of Edward Neville and Eleanor Windsor; mar Thomas Haynes (Eynns). Norris.

Gentlewoman: 59.142, 59.369, 67.142, 67.312, 81.166, 81.372, 82.161, 82.360, 82.615, 84.157, 84.350, 85.151, 85.339

Hayward, Elizabeth—see Elizabeth Knyvett

Heath, Nicholas (c.1501–1579) Archbishop of York 1555–1559 (deprived), Lord Chancellor, Privy Councillor, Almoner to Mary I, Privy Councillor. *ODNB*; Berlatsky.

Bishop: 59.24, 59.245

Hemingway, Edward (fl.1580s–1600s) Apothecary to Queen Elizabeth. Probable nephew of John Hemingway*. *CSP Domestic, 1599*; PRO LC 2/4/4; Matthews.

Gentleman: 82.183, 82.390, 82.587, 84.183, 84.387, 85.176, 85.375, 88.185, 88.365, 89.177, 89.369, 94.161, 94.354, 97.172, 97.375, 98.169, 98.376, 99.163, 99.364, 00.164, 00.366, 03.176, 03.396

Hemingway, John (fl.1540s–1580s) Apothecary to Henry VIII, Edward VI and Elizabeth. Probable uncle of Edward Hemingway*. PRO E 41/106, E 41/167, E 134/30 Eliz/Hil20; Strype, *Ecclesiastical*.
> **Gentleman**: 62.168, 62.355, 63.157, 63.336, 64.139, 64.199, 65.86, 67.162, 67.338, 68.156, 68.328, 71.158, 71.336, 75.125, 75.221, 76.188, 76.390, 77.187, 77.388, 78.186, 78.395, 79.191, 79.404, 81.189, 81.404

Heneage, Anne, née Poyntz (c.1530–1593) Mistress Heneage, Lady Heneage, Gentlewoman of the Privy Chamber. Daughter of Nicholas Poyntz and Joan Berkeley; sister-in-law of Anne Poyntz*; mar 1554 Sir Thomas Heneage* MP. *ODNB* and Hasler under husband.
> **Gentlewoman**: 59.144, 59.358, 62.136, 62.316, 63.128, 63.301, 64.119, 64.173, 65.57, 65.223, 67.126, 67.296, 68.123, 68.291, 71.125, 71.295, 75.89, 76.136, 76.331, 77.137, 77.334
> **Lady**: 78.111, 78.308, 79.105, 79.313, 81.104, 81.309, 82.99, 82.297, 82.544, 84.93, 84.291, 85.97, 85.288, 88.97, 89.89, 89.274

Heneage, Jane—see Jane Brussells

Heneage, Mary—see Mary Wriothesley

Henninham—see Heveningham

Heneage, Thomas (c.1532–1595) Gentleman of the Privy Chamber 1559, Treasurer of the Chamber 1570, Chancellor of the Duchy of Lancaster 1590, courtier poet, kntd 1577, MP. Son of Robert Heneage and Lucy Buckton; mar 1st 1554 Anne Poyntz (Heneage*), 2nd 1594 Mary Browne (Wriothesley*), Countess of Southampton. *ODNB*; Hasler; will PCC 70 Scott.
> **Gentleman**: 59.157, 62.153, 62.340, 63.144, 63.323, 64.131, 64.191, 65.76, 67.147, 67.323, 68.145, 68.317, 71.147, 71.325, 75.116, 75.210, 76.171, 76.373, 77.171, 77.376
> **Knight**: 78.138, 78.329, 79.130, 79.337, 81.123, 81.328, 82.114, 82.314, 82.523, 84.113, 84.311, 85.114, 85.306, 88.117, 88.300, 89.110, 89.295, 94.111, 94.295
> **Custody of Gift**: 81.438

Henningham—see Heveningham

Henrick, John George (fl.1580s) Messenger from Frederick II* of Denmark. *CSP Foreign, 1583–84*.
> **Sundry Gift**: 84.416 (Gift to Envoy)

Henrique of Portugal (1512–1580) King of Portugal 1578–1580, known as the Cardinal King, Gift to his Ambassador, Francesco Giraldi*. Son of King Manoal I of Portugal; brother of Prince John of Portugal; uncle of Sebastian I.
> **Sundry Gift**: 79.454 (Sovereign sending Envoy to England, gift on departure)

Henry III of France (1551–1589) KG 1575. Gift to his envoys: Claude de la Chatre*, Bertrand de Salignac* de la Mothe Fénelon, Gilles de Noailles*, Charles de L'Aubespine*, and Jeronimo Gondi*. Son of Henry II of France and Catherine de Medici; brother of François II, Charles IX*, and François, Duke of Anjou*; mar Louise de Lorraine.
> **Sundry Gift**: 76.413, 76, 419, 76.422, 76.423, 77.417, 78.424 (Sovereign sending Envoy to England), 85.416 (Installation as Knight of the Garter)

Henry IV of France (1553–1610) King Henry III of Navarre, KG 1590. Gifts to his envoys: Charles Angennes de Rambouillet*, Phillippe du Plessis Mornay*, Henri de la Tour d'Auvergne*, Guillaume Fouquet de la Varenne*, Jean de la Fin Beauvoir la Nocle* and Christoph de Harlay*. Son of Antoine de Bourbon, King of Navarre and Jeanne of Navarre; mar 1st Margaret of France, 2nd Marie de Medici.
> **Sundry Gift**: 79.446, 79.447, 03.449 (Sovereign sending Envoy to England); 97.424 (Garter Installation)

Herbert, Anne [I], née Talbot, Countess of Pembroke (c.1515–1588) Daughter of George Talbot and Elizabeth Walden (Talbot*); half-sister of Francis Talbot*; mar 1st 1537 Peter Compton, 2nd c.1552 William [I] Herbert*, Earl of Pembroke; mother of Henry Compton*. *ODNB*; GEC, *Peerage*; will PCC 54 Rutland.
  Countess: 59.41, 59.262, 62.39, 62.219, 63.49, 63.221, 64.49, 65.151, 67.50, 67.220, 68.28, 68.197, 71.25, 71.195, 75.30, 75.136, 76.33, 76.227, 77.43, 77.235, 78.35, 78.236, 79.34, 79.241, 81.29, 81.236, 82.29, 82.229, 82.491, 84.28, 84.226, 85.27, 85.220, 88.28, 88.213

Herbert, Lady Anne [II] (b.1582) Lady of the Privy Chamber. Daughter of Henry Herbert*, Earl of Pembroke, and Mary Sidney (Herbert*). BL Stowe MS 749; Collins, *Peerage*.
  Lady: 03.93, 03.307

Herbert, Anne—see Anne Talbot

Herbert, Catherine, née Talbot, Countess of Pembroke (d.1576) Daughter of George Talbot* and Gertrude Manners (Tablot*); sister of Francis [II] Talbot* and Gilbert Talbot*; mar 1563 Henry Herbert*, Earl of Pembroke. GEC, *Peerage; ODNB* under husband and father.
  Countess: 71.26, 71.196, 75.31, 75.138, 76.32, 76.228

Herbert, Catherine—see Catherine Grey

Herbert, Henry, Earl of Pembroke (1539–1601) KG 1574. Son of William [I] Herbert and Anne Parr; brother of Anne [I] Herbert*; mar 1st 1553 Lady Catherine Grey, 2nd 1563 Catherine Talbot (Herbert*), 3rd 1577 Mary Sidney (Herbert*); father of William [II] Herbert* and Lady Anne [II] Herbert*. *ODNB*; GEC, *Peerage*.
  Earl: 71.13, 71.183, 75.16, 76.16, 76.211, 77.19, 77.216, 78.17, 78.218, 79.16, 79.223, 81.16, 81.222, 82.16, 82.215, 82.430, 84.11, 84.211, 85.14, 85.205, 88.17, 88.201, 89.197, 97.10, 97.209, 98.11, 98.212, 99.5, 99.203, 00.10, 00.208
  Sundry Gift: 81.435 (Christening Gift for his child)

Herbert, Mary, née Sidney, Countess of Pembroke (1561–1621) Courtier poet. Daughter of Sir Henry Sidney* and Mary Dudley (Sidney*); sister of Philip Sidney* and Robert Sidney*; mar 1577 Henry Herbert*, Earl of Pembroke; mother of William [II] Herbert*, Earl of Pembroke and Anne [II] Herbert*. *ODNB*.
  Gentlewoman: 76.163, 76.348, 77.150, 77.347
  Countess: 78.36, 78.237, 79.35, 79.242, 81.30, 81.237, 82.30, 82.230, 82.482, 84.29, 84.227, 85.28, 85.221, 88.29, 88.214, 89.24, 89.209, 94.22, 94.207, 97.28, 97.227, 98.26, 98.230, 99.22, 99.220, 00.27, 00.227, 03.28, 03.241
  Sundry Gift: 81.435 (Christening Gift for her child)

Herbert, Susan—see Lady Susan Vere

Herbert, William [I], Earl of Pembroke (1506/7–1570) Privy Councillor, Lord Steward of Household, KG 1549. Son of Richard Herbert and Margaret Craddock; brother-in-law to Queen Catherine Parr; mar 1st 1538 Anne Parr, 2nd 1552 Anne [I] Talbot (Herbert*); father of Henry Herbert* and Anne Talbot*; grandfather of William [II] Herbert*. GEC, *Peerage; ODNB*.
  Earl: 59.14, 59.235, 62.8, 62.188, 63.14, 63.186, 64.13, 65.114, 67.13, 67.183, 68.7, 68.176
  Regifted: 62.152 (Queen regifted gift from John Astley*)

Herbert [II], William [II], Earl of Pembroke (1580–1630) Son of Henry Herbert* and Mary Sidney (Herbert*); grandson of William [I] Herbert*; godchild of Queen Elizabeth; liaison with Mary Fitton*; mar 1604 Mary Talbot. GEC, *Peerage*.
  Earl: 94.10, 94.194, 03.14, 03.227
  Sundry Gift: 81.435 (Christening Gift)

Hereford, Bishop—see John Scory, 1559–1585; Herbert Westfaling, 1586–1602

Hereford, Viscount/Viscountess—see Lettice Devereux, 1582–1601; Margaret Devereux, 1550–1600; Robert Devereux, 3rd, 1576–1601; Walter Devereux, 2nd, 1572–1576

Hertford, Earl/Countess—see Lady Catherine Grey, 1560–1568; Edward Seymour, 1559–1621; Frances [I] Seymour, née Howard, 1585–1598; Frances [II] Seymour, née Howard, 1601–1621

Hervey—see Harvey

Hesse, Agnes von, née von Solns-Laubach (1578–1602) Duchess of Hesse. Mar Moritz von Hesse*; mother of Elizabeth von Hesse*.
  Sundry Gift: 97.420 (Christening Gift for her child)

Hesse, Elizabeth von (1596–1625) Daughter of Moritz von Hesse* and Agnes von Solns-Laubach*.
  Sundry Gift: 97.420 (Christening Gift)

Hesse, Moritz von (1572–1632) Landgrave of Hesse. Son of William IV von Hesse-Kassel and Sabine von Württemberg; mar Agnes von Solns-Laubach*; father of Elizabeth von Hesse*.
  Sundry Gift: 97.420 (Christening Gift for his child)

Hest—see Hesse

Heton, Martin (1554–1609) Bishop of Ely 1600–1609. *ODNB*.
  Bishop: 03.46, 03.259

Heveningham, Abigail—see Abigail Digby

Heveningham, Mary [I], née Shelton (c.1512–1571) Lady Heveningham. Daughter of Sir John Shelton and Anne Boleyn (aunt of Queen Anne Boleyn); sister of Margaret Wodehouse*; aunt of Mary Scudamore*; 1st cousin to Queen Anne Boleyn, 1st cousin once removed to Queen Elizabeth; mar 1st c.1535 Sir Anthony Heveningham, 2nd c.1557 Philip Appleyard; mother of Abigail Digby*; grandmother of Mary [II] Heveningham*. *ODNB*.
  Lady: 59.90, 59.310, 62.91, 62.272, 63.88, 63.263, 64.87, 65.18, 65.185, 67.89, 67.259, 68.85, 68.254, 71.84, 71.254

Heveningham, Mary [II] (fl.1600s) Daughter of Arthur Heveningham and Catherine Calthorpe; niece of Abigail Digby*; granddaughter of Mary [I] Heveningham*; mar 1599 James Pitts*.
  Sundry Gift: 00.415 (Marriage Gift)

Hewick—see Huicke

Heybourne, Ferdinando—see Ferdinando Richardson

Heydon, Christopher (1519–1579) Kntd 1549. Son of Christopher Heydon and Anne Heveningham; related by marriage to Thomas Gerard* and Anne Bird*; mar 1st 1539 Anne Drury, 2nd c.1563 Temperance Carew; 3rd c.1578 Agnes Crane.
  Knight: 59.117, 59.336, 62.110, 62.290, 63.108, 63.281, 64.102, 64.156, 65.37, 65.204, 67.107, 67.277, 68.105, 68.274, 71.105, 71.275, 76.124, 76.319, 77.126, 77.323, 78.129, 78.331, 79.133, 79.340.

Heydon, unidentified (fl.1580s) of the Carts, Queen's servant.
  Custody of Gift: 82.293, 82.294

Heynes—see Elizabeth Haynes

Heyward—see Hayward

Hicks, Richard (fl.1560s) Yeoman of the Privy Chamber.
  Gentleman: 62.176, 62.363

Hickson, Thomas (fl.1580s) Page of the Wardrobe of Beds. PRO E 115; draft CPR, 1586–87.
  Custody of Gift: 82.248

Hildyard, Elizabeth—see Elizabeth Willoughby

Hill, Elizabeth—see Elizabeth Isley

Hill, James (fl.1590s) Special Ambassador from Duke Charles of Sweden, later Charles IX*, King of Sweden.
  Sundry Gift: 99.416 (Gift to Envoy)

Hill, Mary—see Lady Mary Cheke

Hilliard, Nicholas (1547–1619) Artist, Miniature Painter, Goldsmith. Son of Richard Hilliard and Laurence Wall; mar 1576 Alice Brandon. *ODNB*.
  Gentleman: 84.190

Hilton, Agnes—see Agnes Byllyard

Hixon—see Hickson

Hoby, Edward (1560–1617) Courtier poet, later Gentleman of the Privy Chamber to James I, kntd 1582. Son of Thomas Hoby* and Elizabeth [I] Russell (Hoby*); brother of Thomas Posthumous Hoby*; mar 1st 1582 Margaret Carey*, 2nd c.1613 Cecily Unton. *ODNB*; will PCC 24 Weldon.
  Gentleman: 81.183, 81.393
  Knight: 94.121, 94.306, 97.128, 97.324, 98.128, 98.328, 99.120, 99.315, 00.124, 00.321, 03.130, 03.342

Hoby, Elizabeth—see Elizabeth Russell

Hoby, Margaret, née Carey (1564–1605) Lady Hoby. Daughter of Henry Carey* and Anne Morgan*, sister of George Carey*, Catherine [I] Howard*, and Philadelphia Scrope*, 1st cousin once removed to Queen Elizabeth, mar 1582 Sir Edward Hoby*. *ODNB*; Harvey.
  Lady: 97.111, 97.304, 98.112, 98.305, 99.109, 99.296, 00.112, 00.303, 03.110, 03.324

Hoby, Thomas (1530–1566) Translator, Ambassador to France 1566, kntd 1566, MP. Son of William Hoby and Catherine Forden; mar 1558 Elizabeth [I] Cooke*; father of Edward Hoby* and Thomas Posthumous Hoby*. Hasler; *ODNB*.
  Gentleman: 59.158, 59.382
  Sundry Gift: 67.361 (Christening Gift for his child)

Hoby, Thomas Posthumous (1566–1640) Son of Thomas Hoby* and Elizabeth [I] Russell (Hoby*); brother of Sir Edward Hoby*; mar 1596 Margaret Dakins. *ODNB*.
  Sundry Gift: 67.361 (Christening Gift)

Hogan—see Huggins/Hogan

Holcroft, Isabel—see Isabel Manners

Holford, Richard (b.c.1520) Sewer of the Chamber to Henry VIII. PRO E 115, C 1/1434/56–57, C 1/1437/43–49.
  Gentleman: 59.194, 59.419

Hooftman, Anna—see Anna Palavicino

Hope, Ralph (fl.1550s–1580s) Yeoman of the Robes, served in household of Princess Elizabeth. Mar 1556 Mary Pigeon. *Visitations, Middlesex*; *CPR, 1575–78*; Strangford.
  Gentleman: 63.357, 64.211, 67.353, 68.340, 71.355, 75.244, 76.408, 77.410, 78.416, 79.430, 81.429, 82.415, 84.408, 85.400
  Custody of Gift: 62.99, 63.79, 63.144, 64.39, 65.10–11, 65.27–28, 65.47, 67.38, 67.46, 67.77–79, 67.84, 67.94, 67.116, 67.126, 67.131, 67.157, 68.16, 68.19, 68.24, 68.71, 68.73, 68.81, 68.116, 68.123, 71.1–2, 71.21, 71.27, 71.67, 71.70, 71.90, 71.115, 71.148, 71.154, 71.162, 71.169, 75.27–28, 75.35, 75.92, 76.2, 76.14, 76.20, 76.26, 76.30, 76.77, 76.91–93, 76.95–98, 76.111, 76.135–138, 76.140, 76.144, 76.149, 76.174, 76.176–178, 77.1, 77.26, 77.31, 77.36, 77.40, 77.63–64, 77.66, 77.76, 77.82–83, 77.86, 77.89, 77.93–95, 77.99, 77.104, 77.106, 77.110, 77.116, 77.118, 77.122, 77.134–135, 77.139, 77.142–143, 77.146,

77.149, 77.158, 77.179, 77.182, 77.196, 78.3, 78.15, 78.25, 78.29–31, 78.33, 78.36, 78.37, 78.41, 78.64, 78.77, 78.79–80, 78.84, 78.90–93, 78.95, 78.99, 78.102, 78.105, 78.110, 78.115, 78.125, 78.138–139, 78.143–145, 78.149, 78.153, 78.169, 78.178, 78.181, 79.1, 79.27–28, 79.30, 79.33, 79.41, 79.76, 79.81–82, 79.87, 79.90, 79.94, 79.96, 79.100, 79.103, 79.107, 79.116–117, 79.122, 79.140, 79.144, 79.146, 79.151, 79.172, 79.177, 79.181, 79.184, 79.187, 79.197, 79.204, 81.23, 81.26, 81.30, 81.35–36, 81.58, 81.71, 81.74–76, 81.90–91, 81.93–94, 81.98–99, 81.102–103, 81.119, 81.138–139, 81.144–145, 81.175, 81.182, 81.197, 82.21, 82.23, 82.35, 82.72–73, 82.76, 82.78, 82.86–87, 82.96–98, 82.101, 82.107–108, 82.128, 82.132, 82.137, 82.147, 82.160, 82.167–168, 82.171, 82.179–181, 84.15–16, 84.18, 84.20, 84.22, 84.25, 84.30, 84.52, 84.55, 84.61, 84.64–65, 84.67–69, 84.71–72, 84.75, 84.81, 84.89, 84.92, 84.104–106, 84.110, 84.123–124, 84.129–133, 84.135, 84.139, 84.152, 84.154, 84.160–161, 84.164, 84.166, 84.169, 84.172, 84.185, 85.4, 85.14, 85.17, 85.20, 85.23, 85.25, 85.28, 85.30–31, 85.34, 85.57–58, 85.67, 85.71–74, 85.78, 85.85–86, 85.88, 85.95, 85.97, 85.99, 85.101, 85.111, 85.120, 85.124, 85.125–126, 85.129, 85.131–134, 85.137, 85.147–148, 85.158, 85.161–162, 85.165–171

Hopton, Anne (d.1625) Daughter of Owen Hopton* and Anne Ichingham; sister of Mary Hopton*; mar 1st 1589 Henry Lord Wentworth, 2nd 1595 William Pope. GEC, *Peerage*.
Maid of Honour: 85.355, 88.343, 89.339

Hopton, Mary—see Mary Brydges

Hopton, Owen (c.1524–1595) Lieutenant of the Tower, kntd 1561. Son of Arthur Hopton and Anne Owen; mar 1542 Anne Ichingham; father of Mary Brydges* and Anne Hopton*. *ODNB*; Hasler; BL Sloane MS 814.
Knight: 71.118, 71.288, 75.81, 76.128, 76.325, 77.131, 77.328, 78.133, 78.336, 79.129, 79.336, 81.126, 81.207, 81.119, 82.319, 82.534, 82.115, 84.115, 84.313, 85.116, 85.308, 88.120, 88.304, 89.113, 89.298

Horne, Robert (c.1515–1579) Bishop of Winchester 1561–1579. *ODNB*.
Bishop: 62.21, 62.201, 63.20, 63.192, 64.20, 65.122, 67.22, 67.192, 68.37, 68.206, 71.37, 71.207, 75.45, 75.153, 76.48, 76.243, 77.49, 77.246, 78.49, 78.250, 79.47, 79.254

Horsey, Edward (d.1583) Captain of the Isle of Wight 1565, kntd 1576. Mar c.1556 Madame [née?] Horsey*. *ODNB*; BL Sloane MS 814.
Gentleman: 71.151, 71.329
Knight: 76.174, 76.381, 78.140, 78.341, 79.131, 79.338, 81.127, 81.334, 82.120, 82.320, 82.538

Horsey, Madame [née?] (fl.1560s) Unnamed French woman, mar c.1556 Edward Horsey* kntd 1576. *ODNB* under husband.
Lady: 67.98, 67.268

Horsman, Thomas (fl.1580s) Gentleman Sewer, Queen's servant.
Custody of Gift: 82.231

Hottoft—see Huttofte

Howard of Bindon, Viscount/Viscountess—see Henry [II] Howard, 2nd, 1582–1590; Thomas [I] Howard, 1st, 1559–1582; Thomas [III] Howard, 3rd, 1590–1611; Frances Howard, née Mewtas, 1566–1582, dowager, 1582-c.1595

Howard of Effingham—see Effingham

Howard de Walden, Lord/ Baroness—see Catherine [III] Howard, née Knyvett, 1581–1626; Thomas [IV] Howard, 1st, 1597–1626

Howard, Anne, née St John, Baroness Howard of Effingham (d.1638) Daughter of John, Lord St John of Bletsoe and Catherine Dormer; granddaughter of Oliver, Lord St John* of Bletsoe; mother of Elizabeth [II] Howard*; mar 1597 William [II], Lord Howard* of Effingham. GEC, *Peerage*; Hasler.
Baroness: 98.90, 98.289

Sundry Gift: 03.450 (Christening Gift for her child)

Howard, Anne/Agnes—see Anne/Agnes Paulet

Howard, Catherine—see Catherine [II] Berkeley

Howard, Catherine [I], née Carey, Countess of Nottingham (c.1548–1603) Gentlewoman of the Privy Chamber, Baroness Howard of Effingham, Keeper of the Queen's Jewels. Daughter of Henry Carey*, Lord Hunsdon, and Anne Morgan (Carey*); sister of George Carey*, Margaret Hoby*, and Philadelphia Scrope*; 1st cousin once removed to Queen Elizabeth; niece of Catherine [I] Knollys*; mar 1563 Charles Howard* MP; mother of Elizabeth Southwell*, Frances [I] Howard*, and William [I] Howard*. *ODNB*; GEC, *Peerage*; Hasler; BL Sloane MS 814.

Gentlewoman: 62.141, 62.321, 63.131, 63.304, 64.121, 65.56, 67.123, 67.293, 68.120, 68.289, 71.120, 71.290

Baroness: 75.192, 76.89, 76.279, 77.82, 77.279, 78.91, 78.283, 79.80, 79.287, 81.78, 81.286, 82.74, 82.275, 82.495, 84.70, 84.267, 85.70, 85.263, 88.73, 88.258, 89.66, 89.251, 94.66, 94.250, 97.74, 97.272

Countess: 98.25, 98.222, 99.19, 99.213, 00.24, 00.220, 03.37, 03.251

Sundry Gift: 64.228 (Christening Gift for her child)

Custody of Gift: 75.5, 75.7, 75.14, 75.63, 75.79, 75.86, 75.89, 75.110, 75.116–117, 76.6, 76.34, 76.37, 76.65–66, 76.78, 76.89, 76.105, 76.120, 76.130, 76.133–134, 76.163, 76.170–172, 76.184, 76.193, 77. 7, 77.10, 77.14–16, 77.21–22, 77.25, 77.34–35, 77.44, 77.80, 77.108, 77.136–137, 77.144, 77.147, 77.152, 77.171–172, 77.176, 77.184, 78.1, 78.7, 78.20–21, 78.63, 78.78, 78.96, 78.111, 78.116, 78.123, 78.137, 78.140–141, 78.179, 78.194, 78.198–201, 79.5, 79.11, 79.13, 79.19–21, 79.23, 79.26, 79.38, 79.62, 79.77–78, 79.80, 79.88–89, 79.97, 79.99, 79.101, 79.105, 79.121, 79.127, 79.130–131, 79.138, 79.142, 79.149, 79.155, 79.160, 79.182, 79.185, 79.201, 81.4–5, 81.11–12, 81.21, 81.25, 81.27, 81.59, 81.62, 81.78, 81.84, 81.92, 81.97, 81.112, 81.115, 81.118, 81.122, 81.131, 81.134, 81.136, 81.149, 81.171, 81.174, 81.176, 82.1, 82.18, 82.25–26, 82.57, 82.69, 82.71, 82.113–114, 82.124–126, 82.162, 84.4, 84.9, 84.24, 84.26, 84.53, 84.70, 84.76, 84.93, 84.109, 84.113, 84.119–120, 84.127–128, 84.141, 84.177, 84.184, 84.196, 85.4–5, 85.10, 85.22, 85.26, 85.56, 85.64, 85.69–70, 85.79, 85.93, 85.110, 85.114, 85.117, 85.123, 85.143

Howard, Catherine [II] (c.1560–1599) Mistress Howard, Maid of Honour. Daughter of William [I], Lord Howard* and Margaret Gamage*; sister of Charles, Lord Howard*, Douglas Sheffield*, Frances [I] Seymour*, and Mary Sutton*; half-sister of Anne/Agnes Paulet*; unmarried; 1st cousin once removed to Queen Elizabeth. Collins, *Peerage*.

Maid of Honour: 75.205, 76.368, 77.369, 78.374, 79.383, 81.377, 82.364, 84.356, 85.349, 88.340, 89.338

Howard, Catherine [III], née Knyvett, Baroness Howard de Walden (1564-c.1626) Countess of Suffolk 1603, succeeded Mary Radcliffe* as Keeper of Queen's Jewels for Queen Anne of Denmark. Daughter of Henry Knyvett and Elizabeth Stumpe; niece of Catherine Paget* and Thomas Knyvett*; mar 1st Richard Rich, 2nd c.1581 Lord Thomas Howard*; mother of Theophilus Howard*. *ODNB*; GEC, *Peerage*.

Baroness: 82.504, 85.86, 85.278, 97.85, 97.287, 98.83, 98.287, 03.84, 03.298

Sundry Gift: 85.410 (Christening Gift for her child)

Howard, Charles (1536–1624) Lord Admiral, Lord Howard of Effingham, Earl of Nottingham 1597, KG 1575. Son of William [I], Lord Howard* and Margaret Gamage*; brother of Douglas Sheffield*, Mary Sutton*, Frances [I] Seymour*, and Catherine [II] Howard*; half-brother of Anne/Agnes Paulet*; 1st cousin once removed to Queen Elizabeth mar 1st 1563 Catherine [II] Carey (Howard*), 2nd 1603 Margaret Stuart; father of Elizabeth Southwell*, Frances [I] Seymour*, and William [II] Howard*. GEC, *Peerage*; *ODNB*; BL Sloane MS 814.

Lord: 75.63, 75.171, 76.65, 76.258, 77.63, 77.260, 78.64, 78.265, 79.62, 79.268, 81.59, 81.266, 82.57, 82.257, 82.467, 84.53, 84.251, 85.56, 85.247, 88.57, 88.242, 89.52, 89.237, 94.53, 94.237, 97.58, 97.256

Earl: 98.5, 98.206, 99.2, 99.197, 00.4, 00.201, 03.4, 03.217

Sundry Gift: 64.228 (Christening Gift for his child)

Custody of Gift: 99.156

Howard, Douglas—see Douglas Sheffield

Howard, Elizabeth [I] (1564–1646) Mistress Howard, Mistress Southwell, Lady Southwell. Daughter of Charles Howard* and Catherine [II] Carey (Howard*); mar 1st 1583 Robert Southwell, 2nd 1604 John Stuart; mother of Anne Southwell* and Elizabeth [II] Southwell*; 2nd cousin of Queen Elizabeth. Collins, *Peerage*.

Gentlewoman: 78.157, 78.358, 79.159, 79.366, 81.153, 81.359, 82.148, 82.348, 82.598, 84.132, 84.329, 85.126, 85.318

Lady: 94.86, 94.270, 88.102, 88.286, 89.94, 89.279, 97.114, 97.297, 98.115, 98.299, 99.100, 99.289, 00.104, 00.296

Sundry Gift: 64.228 (Christening Gift); 85.407 (Christening Gift for her child)

Howard, Elizabeth [II] (1603–1671) Daughter of William [II], Lord Howard* of Effingham and Anne St John (Howard*); mar 1620 John Mordaunt; 2nd cousin of Queen Elizabeth. GEC, *Peerage*.

Sundry Gift: 03.450 (Christening Gift)

Howard, Elizabeth—see Elizabeth Leybourne

Howard, Frances [I], née Vere, Countess of Surrey (1517–1577) Lady Steyning. Daughter of John de Vere, Earl of Oxford and Elizabeth Trussell; sister of John de Vere*, Earl of Oxford; aunt of Edward de Vere*, Earl of Oxford; mar 1st 1532 Thomas Howard, 2nd 1553 Thomas Steyning; mother of Thomas Howard*, Catherine [II] Berkeley*, Henry [I] Howard*, and Jane Neville*. GEC, *Peerage*.

Countess: 59.40, 59.261, 62.38, 62.218, 63.40, 63.212, 64.40, 65.140, 67.39, 67.209, 68.21, 68.190, 71.19, 71.189, 75.23, 76.25, 76.220, 77.30, 77.227

Howard, Frances [II], Countess of Kildare (1564–1628) Gentlewoman of the Privy Chamber. Daughter of Charles Howard* and Catherine [II] Carey (Howard*), sister of Elizabeth [I] Howard* and William [II] Howard*; mar 1st 1590 Henry FitzGerald, Earl of Kildare, 2nd 1601 Henry [II] Brooke*, Lord Cobham; 2nd cousin of Queen Elizabeth. *ODNB*; GEC, *Peerage*.

Gentlewoman: 84.154, 84.335, 85.125, 85.316, 88.128, 88.312, 89.126, 89.311

Countess: 97.37, 97.237, 98.36, 98.238, 99.31, 99.226, 00.38, 00.233, 03.38, 03.252

Howard, Frances—see Frances [I] Seymour; Frances [II] Seymour; Frances Mewtas; Frances Vere

Howard, Sir George (c.1523-c.1580) Master of the Armoury, Gentleman Usher of the Privy Chamber, kntd 1547, MP. Son of Edmund Howard and Joyce Culpepper; brother of Queen Catherine Howard; 1st cousin once removed to Queen Elizabeth; unmarried. *ODNB*; Hasler.

Knight: 59.129, 59.348, 62.126, 62.307

Free Gift: 76.398, 77.400, 78.406, 79.420

Howard, Henry [I] (1540–1614) Lord Henry Howard, later Earl of Northampton. Son of Henry Howard, Earl of Surrey and Lady Frances Vere (Howard*); brother of Thomas [I] Howard*, Catherine [II] Berkeley*, and Jane Neville*; 2nd cousin of Queen Elizabeth; unmarried. *ODNB*; GEC, *Peerage*; Folger MS L.d.880.

Lord: 77.66, 77.263, 79.77, 79.284, 99.63, 99.263, 00.68, 00.271, 03.74, 03.287

Howard, Henry [II], Viscount Howard of Bindon (1542–1591) Son of Thomas [I] Howard*, Viscount Howard of Bindon and Elizabeth Marney; brother of Thomas [III] Howard*, Viscount Howard of Bindon; half-brother of Frances [II] Howard*; mar 1566 Frances Mewtas (Howard*); 2nd cousin of Queen Elizabeth. GEC, *Peerage*.
Viscount: 84.18, 84.216

Howard, Jane—see Jane Neville

Howard, Margaret [I], née Gamage, Baroness Howard of Effingham (1515–1581) Lady of the Privy Chamber. Daughter of Sir Thomas Gamage and Margaret St John; mar 1536 William [I], Lord Howard* of Effingham; mother of Douglas Sheffield*, Frances [I] Seymour*, Charles Howard*, Mary Sutton*, and Martha Howard*. Name listed and struck through on 1582 roll; died before 1582 exchange. GEC, *Peerage*; *ODNB* and Hasler under husband and sons.
Baroness: 59.77, 59.297, 62.71, 62.251, 63.70, 63.242, 64.75, 65.7, 65.174, 67.74, 67.244, 68.74, 68.244, 71.73, 71.243, 75.79, 75.191, 76.82, 76.278, 77.88, 77.285, 78.82, 78.282, 79.79, 79.286, 81.77, 81.285

Howard, Margaret [II], née Audley, Duchess of Norfolk (1540–1564) Lady of the Privy Chamber. Daughter of Thomas, Lord Audley and Elizabeth Grey (Audley*); mar 1st 1553 Henry Dudley, 2nd 1558 Thomas [II] Howard*, Duke of Norfolk; mother of Lord Thomas [IV] Howard*; sister-in-law of Robert Dudley*, Earl of Leicester and Ambrose Dudley*, Earl of Warwick. GEC, *Peerage*; *ODNB* under husbands.
Duchess: 59.37, 59.258, 62.36, 62.216, 63.36, 63.208, 64.36

Howard, Margaret—see Margaret Scrope

Howard, Martha (c.1552–1598) Maid of Honour. Daughter of William [I], Lord Howard* and Margaret Gamage (Howard*); sister of Charles Howard*, Mary Sutton*, Douglas Sheffield*, Frances [I] Howard*, and Catherine [II] Howard*; half-sister of Anne/Agnes Howard*; mar 1578 Sir George Bourchier. GEC, *Peerage* under son, Henry Bourchier, Earl of Bath; PRO SP 15/25/71.
Maid of Honour: 78.377

Howard, Mary—see Mary Sutton

Howard, Philip (1557–1595) Earl of Surrey, Earl of Arundel, courtier poet. attainted 1589, imprisoned until his death, canonised 1970. Son of Thomas [II] Howard*, Duke of Norfolk and Lady Mary FitzAlan; grandson of Henry Howard, Earl of Surrey and Lady Frances [I] Howard* and of Henry FitzAlan*, Earl of Arundel and Lady Catherine Grey; nephew of John, Lord Lumley*; second cousin once removed to Queen Elizabeth; mar 1571 Anne Dacre. *ODNB*; GEC, *Peerage*; Folger MS L.d.880.
Earl: 76.12, 77.10, 77.207, 79.21, 79.228, 81.5, 81.212, 82.6, 82.206, 82.422, 85.5, 85.196

Howard, Theophilus (1584–1640) Son of Thomas [IV] Howard* and Catherine Knyvett (Howard*). GEC, *Peerage*.
Sundry Gift: 85.410 (Christening Gift)

Howard, Thomas [I], Viscount Howard of Bindon (c.1520–1582) Son of Thomas Howard and Elizabeth Stafford; mar 1st c.1542 Elizabeth Marney, 2nd 1564 Gertrude Lyte, 3rd 1576 Mabel Burton, 4th Margaret Manning; father of Henry [II] Howard*, Thomas [III] Howard*, and Frances [II] Howard*. GEC, *Peerage*.
Lord: 59.67, 59.288

Howard, Thomas [II], Duke of Norfolk (1537–1572) Privy Councillor 1562, KG 1559, executed for high treason 1572. Son of Henry Howard and Frances Vere (Howard*); brother of Catherine [II] Berkeley*, Henry [I] Howard* and Jane Neville*; 2nd cousin of Queen Elizabeth; mar 1st 1555 Mary FitzAlan, 2nd 1558 Margaret Audley (Howard*),

3rd Elizabeth Leybourne (Howard*); father of Thomas [IV] Howard*. *ODNB*; GEC, *Peerage*.

Primary: 59.4, 59.225, 62.2, 62.182, 63.3, 63.175, 64.3, 65.102, 67.3, 67.173, 68.4, 68.173

Howard, Thomas [III], Viscount Howard of Bindon (1544–1611) KG 1597. Son of Thomas [I] Howard* and Elizabeth Marney; brother of Henry [II] Howard*, Viscount Howard of Bindon; half-brother of Frances [II] Howard*; mar 1580 Grace Duffield. GEC, *Peerage*.

Viscount: 97.18, 03.18, 03.231

Howard, Thomas [IV] Lord Howard de Walden (1561–1626) Son of Thomas [II] Howard and Margaret Audley (Howard*); mar 1st 1577 Mary Dacre, 2nd c.1581 Catherine [III] Knyvett (Howard*); father of Theophilus Howard*. *ODNB*; GEC, *Peerage*.

Lord: 82.69, 82.269, 82.472, 97.70, 97.269, 98.67, 98.270, 03.71, 03.284

Sundry Gift: 85.410 (Christening Gift for his child)

Howard, William [I] (c.1510–1573) Lord Howard of Effingham, Privy Councillor 1554, Lord Chamberlain, Lord Privy Seal, KG 1554. Son of Thomas Howard and Agnes Tilney; uncle of Queen Catherine Howard; great-uncle of Queen Elizabeth; mar 1st 1531 Catherine Broughton, 2nd 1536 Margaret Gamage (Howard*); father of Anne/Agnes Paulet*, Douglas Sheffield*, Frances [I] Seymour*, Charles Howard*, Mary Sutton*, and Martha Howard*. GEC, *Peerage*; *ODNB*.

Lord: 59.55, 59.276, 62.52, 62.232, 63.53, 63.225, 64.53, 65.154, 67.54, 67.224, 68.52, 68.221, 71.50, 71.220

Howard, William [II] (1577–1615) Lord Howard of Effingham, MP. Son of Charles Howard* and Catherine [II] Carey (Howard*); mar 1597 Anne St John (Howard*); father of Elizabeth [II] Howard*. GEC, *Peerage*; Hasler; will PCC 74 Sainberbe.

Sundry Gift: 03.450 (Christening Gift for his child)

Howland, Richard (1540–1600) Bishop of Peterborough 1585–1600. *ODNB*.

Bishop: 88.48, 88.233, 89.43, 89.228, 94.47, 94.230, 97.51, 97.250, 98.51, 98.253, 99.45, 99.242, 00.55, 00.252

Huggins/Hogan, Anne (d. 1609) Mistress Huggins/Hogan. Mar William [II] Huggins/Hogan*; mother of Charles* Huggins/Hogan. HMC Hatfield; CSP Domestic.

Gentlewoman: 99.152, 99.34, 00.153, 00.346, 03.150, 03.363

Huggins/Hogan, Elizabeth [née?] (fl.1560s–1600s) Gentlewoman of the Privy Chamber, of Hampton Court. Mar William [I] Huggins/Hogan; possible mother of William [II] Huggins/Hogan*.

Gentlewoman: 62.151, 62.328, 63.141, 63.314, 64.128, 64.180, 65.67, 65.233, 67.138, 67.308, 68.130, 68.298, 71.137, 71.307, 75.99, 76.164, 76.359, 77.167, 77.363, 78.168, 78.368, 79.169, 79.376, 81.163, 81.369, 82.158, 82.357, 82.594, 84.155, 84.348, 85.150, 85.343, 89.144, 89.329, 94.136, 94.328, 97.147, 97.350, 98.144, 98.351, 99.139, 99.339, 00.140, 00.344, 03.149, 03.362

Huggins/Hogan, Frances (fl.1590s–1600s) unidentified. Probable relative of William [I] Huggins/Hogan* and William [II] Huggins/Hogan*.

Gentlewoman: 94.137, 94.329, 97.148, 97.351, 98.145, 98.352, 99.140, 99.340, 00.141, 00.345, 03.159, 03.364

Huggins/Hogan, Mary (d.1580) Mistress Huggins/Hogan, Gentlewoman of Norfolk. Daughter of Thorne, sister-in-law of William [I] Huggins/Hogan* and Thomas Huggins/Hogan, niece of Edward Aglionby, mar Robert Hogan/Huggins. Will PCC 17 Arundell; *CPR, 1575–78*.

Gentlewoman: 67.141, 67.311, 68.131, 68.299

Huggins, Thomasine—see Thomasine de Paris (scribal error)

Huggins/Hogan, William [I] (c.1524–1588) Keeper of the Gardens at Hampton Court. Son of Robert Huggins/Hogan and Bridget Fowler (Huggins/Hogan*); mar Elizabeth [née?]*; brother-in-law of Mary Thorne (Huggins/Hogan*); possible father of William [II] Huggins/Hogan*. Bindoff; Adams; HMC Hatfield; CSP Domestic.

    Gentleman: 62.160, 62.347, 63.151, 63.330, 64.146, 64.205, 65.84, 67.154, 67.330, 68.150, 68.322, 71.163, 71.338, 75.119, 75.216, 76.195, 76.392, 77.191, 77.392, 78.190, 78.399, 79.195, 79.408, 81.194, 81.408, 82.189, 82.393, 82.564, 84.186, 84.382, 85.177, 85.376

Huggins/Hogan, William [II] (d.aft.1611) Keeper of the Gardens at Hampton Court for Elizabeth and James I, Esquire for the body at Elizabeth's funeral. Possible son of William [I] Huggins/Hogan* and Elizabeth [née?] (Huggins/Hogan*); mar Anne [née?]*; father of Charles Huggins/Hogan). HMC Hatfield; CSP Domestic; PRO LC 2/4 (4).

    Gentleman: 89.168, 89.358, 94.184, 94.349, 97.192, 97.394, 98.191, 98.396, 99.190, 99.388, 00.189, 00.391, 03.184, 03.406

Hughes, James (fl.1580s) Linen Draper of London.

    Gentleman: 81.200, 81.415, 82.196, 82.400, 82.581, 84.176, 84.379, 85.179, 85.378, 88.172, 88.363, 89.172, 89.362

Hughes, Richard (fl1580s–1600s) Footman, Queen's servant.

    Custody of Gift: 82.352

Huicke, Atalanta (b.1563) Daughter of Robert Huicke* and Elizabeth [née?]; mar 1ˢᵗ William Chetwynd, 2ⁿᵈ Mark Steward. *ODNB* under father.

    Sundry Gift: 64.216 (Christening Gift)

Huicke, Robert (c.1510–1580) Physician to Henry VIII, Catherine Parr, Edward VI, and Elizabeth. Mar 1ˢᵗ Elizabeth [née?], 2ⁿᵈ 1575 Mary Woodcock; father of Atalanta Huicke*. *ODNB*; Hasler; will PCC 13 Darcy 1581.

    Gentleman: 62.159, 62.346, 63.150, 63.329, 64.135, 64.195, 65.80, 67.155, 67.331, 68.154, 68.326, 71.156, 71.334, 75.122, 75.218, 76.185, 76.387, 77.185, 77.386, 78.183, 78.392, 79.188, 79.401

    Sundry Gift: 64.216 (Christening Gift for his child)

Huitfeldt, Arild (1546–1609) Chancellor of Denmark, alias Arnold Witfeldt or Arnold de Wittie, Special Ambassador from Christian IV* of Denmark, Danish historian. Came to England with Christian Barnekow*. *CSP Foreign, 1588; Dansk Biografisk Leksikon*.

    Sundry Gift: 98.425 (Gift to Envoy)

Humphrey, Thomas (fl.1580s) Queen's servant. PRO E 115.

    Custody of Gift: 82.304

Hunnis, Margaret, née Warner (d.1559) Mistress Hunnis. Daughter of Richard Warner; mar 1ˢᵗ Nicholas Brigham, 2ⁿᵈ 1558 William Hunnis*. *ODNB* under husbands; will PCC 46 Chaynay; Alsop.

    Gentlewoman: 59.153, 59.366

Hunnis, William (d.1597) Musician, Gentleman of the Chapel Royal, Master of the Children of the Chapel. Mar 1ˢᵗ 1558 Margaret Warner (Hunnis*), 2ⁿᵈ c.1560 Agnes Blagge. Stopes; *ODNB*; *BDECM*.

    Gentleman: 59.220, 59.412

Hunsdon, Lord/Baroness—see George Carey, 2ⁿᵈ, 1596–1603; Henry Carey, 1ˢᵗ, 1559–1596; Anne Carey, née Morgan, 1559–1607; Elizabeth Carey née Spencer, 1596–1612

Huntingdon, Earl/Countess—see Catherine [I] Hastings, née Pole, 1544–1576; Catherine [II] Hastings, née Dudley, 1560–1620; Francis Hastings, 2ⁿᵈ, 1544–1560; George Hastings, 4ᵗʰ, 1595–1604; Henry Hastings, 3ʳᵈ, 1560–1595; Dorothy Hastings, née Port, 1595–1607

Hussey, Bridget—see Bridget [I] Manners

Huttofte, Nicholas (d. 1603) Groom of the Jewels and Plate. Son of Thomas Huttofte, mar Margaret [née?]. Will PCC 75 Bodlein; uncle's will PCC 3 Brudenell.
Free Gift: 97.415, 98.424, 99.411, 00.414, 03.446

Hutton, Matthew (c.1529–1606) Archbishop of York 1595–1606. *ODNB*.
Bishop: 94.35, 94.219, 97.42, 97.240, 98.40, 98.241, 99.34, 99.229, 00.42, 00.239, 03.44, 03.257

Hyde, Elizabeth, née Shipman (b.c.1529) Mistress Hyde, Mother of the Maids. Daughter of unidentified Shipman; mother of Lucy Hyde*; mar c.1550 William Hyde. Husband's will PCC 29 Drury 1590.
Maid of Honour: 75.208, 76.371, 77.374, 78.378, 79.386, 81.381 (Mother of Maids)

Hyde, Lucy (fl.1590s–1600s) Gentlewoman of the Bedchamber. Daughter of William Hyde and Elizabeth Shipman (Hyde*); related to Lawrence Hyde and Anne Sibell (Hyde). PRO LC 5/37, LC 5/49.
Gentlewoman: 94.131, 94.323, 97.142, 97.344, 98.140, 98.346, 99.135, 99.334, 00.136, 00.338, 03.140, 03.353
Custody of Gift: 94.73, 94.76, 94.82–84, 94.89, 94.100, 94.122, 94.127–128, 94.144, 94.151, 94.171–174, 94.176–177, 97.138, 97.160, 97.180–190, 98.74, 98.92, 98.111, 98.135, 98.137, 98.140–141, 98.150, 98.152, 98.160, 98.177–188, 99.89, 99.131, 99.135, 99.141, 99.152, 99.176–186, 99.189, 00.83, 00.94, 00.108, 00.112, 00.137, 00.145–146, 00.155, 00.176–188, 00.192–194, 03.87, 03.114–115, 03.139, 03.142, 03.145, 03.157, 03.178–179, 03.184, 03.186–207, 03.213

Ipolyta the Tartarian (d.c.1576) Gentlewoman. Mertens; Arnold, *QE Wardrobe*; Stopes, *Shakespeare's*; PRO LC 2/2, LC 5/33, LC 5/49; BL Egerton MS 2806.
Gentlewoman: 63.142, 67.140, 67.310, 68.138, 68.306, 76.165, 76.363
Sundry Gift: 62.386 (Christening Gift at her Conversion)

Isaac, Anne—see Anne Morice

Isley, Elizabeth—see Elizabeth Mason

Ivan IV (1530–1584) Emperor of Russia, Grand Duke of Moscow, Ivan the Terrible. Gift to his envoy: Ivan Grigorievich Savin*.
Sundry Gift: 71.362 (Sovereign sending Envoy to England)

Jacomo—see Jacomo Manucci

James VI (1566–1625) King of Scotland, later James I, King of England, KG 1590. Gifts to his envoys: Robert Pitcairn*, David Lindsay*, George Young*, Patrick Gray*, Robert Melville* and Lewis Bellenden*. Son of Henry Darnley and Mary Queen of Scots, 1st cousin twice removed to Queen Elizabeth, mar 1589 Anne of Denmark.
Sundry Gift: 67.362 (Christening Gift), 79.450, 84.413, 84.414, 85.415, 85.419 (Sovereign sending Envoy to England)

James, unidentified (fl.1580s) Queen's servant.
Custody of Gift: 82.218

James, John (d.1601) Royal Physician, Record-keeper, MP. Mar 1570 Elizabeth Caplin. *ODNB*; Hasler.
Gentleman: 97.168, 97.373, 98.165, 98.374, 99.159, 99.360, 00.161, 00.363

Jarrat—see Gerard

Jenkins, Edward (fl.1580s) Queen's servant.
Custody of Gift: 82.290

Jerningham, Anne—see Anne Grey, Anne [I] Russell

Jerningham, Sir Henry [I] (1509–1572) Vice Chamberlain under Henry VIII, Master of the Horse to Mary I, kntd 1553. Son of Edward Jerningham and Mary Scrope; half-brother of Margaret St Loe*; mar Frances Baynham; father of Henry [II] Jerningham*. *ODNB*; *Visitations, Suffolk*.

Knight: 59.120, 59.339, 62.111, 62.291, 63.109, 63.282, 65.49, 65.216, 67.112, 67.282, 68.106, 68.278, 71.106, 71.276

Jerningham, Henry [II] (1533–1619) Son of Henry [I] Jerningham* and Frances Baynham; mar 1561 Eleanor Dacre. *Visitations, Suffolk*.
Gentleman: 77.179, 77.382

Jewel, John (1522–1571) Bishop of Salisbury 1560–1571. *ODNB*.
Bishop: 62.23 62.203, 63.22, 63.194, 64.35, 65.123, 67.23, 67.193, 68.38, 68.207, 71.38, 71.208

Jobson, Elizabeth, née Plantagenet (b.c.1516) Lady Jobson. Daughter of Arthur Plantagenet, Lord Lisle and Elizabeth Grey, Lady Lisle; step-daughter of Honor Grenville, Lady Lisle; mar c.1536 Sir Francis Jobson* MP. *ODNB*; Hasler; Bindoff; Byrne.
Lady: 62.97, 62.277, 63.94, 63.257, 64.83, 65.14, 65.181, 67.87, 67.257, 68.83, 68.252

Jobson, Sir Francis (c.1509–1573) Lieutenant of the Tower, kntd c.1550, MP. Mar 1536 Elizabeth Plantagenet*; son-in-law of Arthur Plantagenet, Lord Lisle and Elizabeth Grey. *ODNB*; Bindoff; Hasler.
Knight: 65.48, 65.215, 67.111, 67.281, 68.109, 68.277, 71.109, 71.279

John of Austria (1547–1578) Governor of the Low Countries, Don Juan of Austria. Gifts to his envoy: Jean Marinier Gastel*. Son of Charles V, half-brother of Philip II* of Spain and Margaret*, Duchess of Parma.
Sundry Gift: 76.418, 77.422, 78.425 (Sovereign sending Envoy to England)

John III of Sweden (1537–1592) Duke of Finland, King of Sweden. Gifts to his envoys: Nicholas Rasche*, Ericson Johnson*, Ericson Wissenburg*, and Andrew Keith*. Son of Gustav I, King of Sweden; half-brother of Eric XIV*, King of Sweden, brother of Princess Cecilia* of Sweden and Charles IX*, King of Sweden.
Sundry Gift: 84.417, 84.418, 84.419, 84.421 (Sovereign sending Envoy to England)

Johnson, Ericson (fl. 1580s) Envoy from John III* of Sweden, accompanied Nicholas Rasche* to England. *CSP Foreign, 1583–84*.
Sundry Gift: 84.419 (Gift to Envoy)

Jones, Edward (fl1580s) Queen's servant.
Custody of Gift: 82.345

Jones, Elizabeth, née Wodehouse (d.1608) Mother of the Maids, Mistress Jones. Daughter of Thomas Wodehouse and Margaret Shelton*; sister of Thomas [I] Wodehouse*; great-aunt of Thomas [II] Wodehouse*; 2nd cousin twice removed to Queen Elizabeth; mar 1588 Thomas Jones. BL Additional MS 22924; *Visitations, Norfolk*; will PCC 110 Windebanck.
Maid of Honour: 89.344
Gentlewoman: 85.138, 85.337, 88.150, 88.335, 89.146, 89.331

Jones, William (d.c.1613) Citizen and Merchant Tailor, succeeded Walter Fish* as Queen's Tailor, 1582–1603. Arnold, *QE Wardrobe*; PRO LC 5/37; BL Egerton MS 2806.
Gentleman: 98.200, 98.406

Josselyn, Thomas (1506–1562) Kntd 1547. Son of John Josselyn and Philippa Bradbury; mar 1524 Dorothy Gates.
Knight: 59.124, 59.343, 62.116, 62.295

Jugge, Richard (d.1577) Royal Printer, shared position with John Cawood*. *ODNB*.
Gentleman: 59.180, 59.403

Julio—see Eleanor Borgarucci; Guilio Borgarucci

Junius, Joannes (fl.1560s–1580s) Dr. Junius. Envoy from Duke John Casimir*. *CSP Foreign, 1569–71, 1578–79*; PRO E 351/2215.
Sundry Gift: 79.451, 88.399 (Gift to Envoy).

Justice Clerk—see Lewis Bellenden

Karvile—see Kervill

Kayle, Hugh—see Hugh Keall

Keall, Hugh (fl.1570s–1600s) Goldsmith. alias 'K' or 'Ke'. Collins, *Jewels*; Jackson; Sitwell.
> **Goldsmith**: *passim* 1574–1603

Kelway, Anne—see Anne Harington

Keith, Andrew (c.1550-c.1599) Lord Dingwall, Scottish Envoy from John III* of Sweden. GEC, *Peerage*; *CSP Foreign, 1583–84*; Fischer.
> **Sundry Gift**: 84.421 (Gift to Envoy)

Kellim, Albert (d.1559) Musician, Violin. Albert de Venice. probable father of Frances Kellim*. *BDECM*; Holman; *RECM*.
> **Gentleman**: 59.216, 59.440

Kellim, Francis (d.1588) Musician, Violin. Francisco de Venice. probable son of Albert Kellim*. *BDECM*; Holman; *RECM*.
> **Gentleman**: 59.216, 59.440, 85.187, 85.389, 88.180, 88.374

Kempe, Margaret—see Margaret Dane

Kent, Countess—see Susan Grey, née Bertie, 1572-aft.1611; Mary Grey, née Cotton, 1575–1580

Kent, Thomas (1525–1590) Musician, Singer, Page, Yeoman of the Chamber, served Henry VIII, Edward VI, Mary I, and Elizabeth. Ashbee; will PCC 55 Drury 1590.
> **Gentleman**: 59.177, 59.401

Kervill, Alice—see Alice Seckford

Keyes, Musshac—see Mushac Reyz

Keyne, John (fl.1550s–1560s) Locksmith, Goldsmith. Arnold, *QE Wardrobe*.
> **Gentleman**: 59.206, 59.430

Kildare, Earl/Countess—see Gerald FitzGerald, 11th, 1569–1585; Frances [II] FitzGerald, née Howard, 1590–1597, dowager 1597–1628

Killigrew, Anne (c.1567–1632) Daughter of Henry Killigrew* and Catherine Cooke*; mar 1584 Henry [IV] Neville*. Harvey; *ODNB* under husband.
> **Sundry Gift**: 85.414 (Marriage Gift)

Killigrew, Sir Henry (1528–1603) Special Ambassador to France and elsewhere. Son of John Killigrew and Elizabeth Trewenard; brother of William Killigrew*, brother-in-law of William Cecil*, Nicholas Bacon*, Thomas Hoby*, and John Russell*; mar 1st 1565 Catherine Cooke*, 2nd 1590 Jaél de Peigne; father of Anne Killigrew*. *ODNB*; Hasler; will PCC 26 Bolein.
> **Gentleman**: 65.97
> **Sundry Gift**: 85.414 (Marriage Gift for his daughter)

Killigrew, William (d.1622) Groom of the Privy Chamber. Son of John Killigrew and Elizabeth Trewenard; brother of Henry Killigrew*; mar 1580 Margaret Saunders. *ODNB* under son.
> **Free Gift**: 75.243, 76.407, 77.409, 78.415, 79.429, 81.428, 82.412, 84.405, 85.399, 88.383, 89.385, 94.382, 97.408, 98.414, 99.402, 00.406, 03.438
> **Custody of Gift**: 77.180, 78.200, 82.79, 82.205, 82.276, 89.399

King, Robert (fl.1550s–1580s) Gentleman usher under Mary I and Elizabeth. *VCH, Somerset*; *CPR, 1558–60*.
> **Gentleman**: 59.198, 59.422

Kingston, Margaret—see Margaret St Loe

Kingston, Robert (fl.1550s) Queen's servant. Possible relative of Margaret St Loe*, gave gift jointly with George Rotheham/Rotheridge*.

Gentleman: 59.218

Kirby, John (fl.1540s–1550s) Yeoman of the Jewels and Plate under Henry VIII and Edward VI. *LP Henry VIII, 1540*; *CPR, 1549*.
Free Gift: 59.449

Kirkham, Frances [née?] (fl.1590s–1600s) Mar George Kirkham*.
Gentlewoman: 98.156, 98.362, 99.150, 99.349, 00.151, 00.354, 03.153, 03.367

Kirkham, George (d.1613) Mar Frances [née?] Kirkham*. PRO E 115; *CPR, 1575–78*; *Visitations, London*.
Gentleman: 98.199, 98.405, 99.193, 99.393

Kitson, Frances—see Frances Bourchier

Kitson, Margaret—see Margaret Bourchier

Klenrickett—see Bourke

Knasbrough, Bartholomew (fl.1580's) Queen's servant.
Custody of Gift: 82.297

Knightley, Elizabeth—see Lady Elizabeth Seymour

Knightley, Richard (1533–1615) Son of Valentine Knightley and Anne Ferrers; mar 1ˢᵗ Mary Fermor, 2ⁿᵈ 1578 Lady Elizabeth Seymour*. Hasler.
Sundry Gift: 89.401 (Christening Gift for his child)

Knightley, unidentified (b.1588) son of Richard Knightley* and Lady Elizabeth Seymour*.
Sundry Gift: 89.401 (Christening Gift)

Knollys, Anne—see Anne West

Knollys, Catherine [I], née Carey (1525–1569) Lady of the Privy Chamber and of the Bedchamber, Lady Knollys. Daughter of William Carey and Mary Boleyn; sister of Henry Carey*; aunt of Catherine [I] Howard*; 1ˢᵗ cousin of Queen Elizabeth; mar c.1539 Sir Francis Knollys; mother of Lettice Devereux*, Elizabeth Leighton*, Anne West*, William Knollys*, and Catherine Knollys*. *ODNB*; GEC, *Peerage*; Varlow.
Lady: 59.98, 62.84, 62.264, 63.81, 63.253, 64.77, 65.10, 65.177, 67.80, 67.250, 68.78, 68.247
Sundry Gift: 63.362 (Christening Gift for her child)
Custody of Gift: 67.73

Knollys, Catherine [II] (1559–1632) Lady Fitzgerald, daughter of Francis Knollys* and Catherine Carey (Knollys*); mar 1ˢᵗ 1578 Gerald FitzGerald, Lord Gerald, 2ⁿᵈ 1580 Sir Philip Butler. GEC, *Peerage*; Varlow.
Sundry Gift: 63.362 (Christening Gift)

Knollys, Elizabeth (b.1576) Daughter of Henry Knollys* and Margaret Cave (Knollys*), granddaughter of Sir Francis Knollys* and Catherine Carey (Knollys*) and of Ambrose Cave* and Margaret Willington; mar Henry Willoughby.
Sundry Gift: 77.420 (Christening Gift)

Knollys, Elizabeth—see Elizabeth Leighton

Knollys, Sir Francis (1512–1596) Captain of the Guard 1565, Treasurer of the Household, Treasurer of the Chamber, Privy Councillor, kntd 1547, KG 1593, MP. Son of Robert Knollys and Lettice Peniston; mar 1539 Catherine Carey (Knollys*); father of William Knollys*, Henry Knollys*, Lettice Devereux*, Elizabeth Leighton*, and Anne West*. *ODNB*; Hasler; Bindoff; Varlow.
Knight: 62.103, 62.283, 63.101, 63.274, 64.94, 64.149, 65.31, 65.197, 67.100, 67.270, 68.99, 68.268, 71.98, 71.268, 76.117, 76.312, 77.119, 77.316, 78.121, 78.322, 79.119, 79.326, 81.116, 81.323, 82.110, 82.310, 82.521, 84.107, 84.305, 85.108, 85.301, 88.114, 88.298, 89.107, 89.292, 94.110, 94.294
Sundry Gift: 63.362 (Christening Gift for his child)

Knollys, Henry (1541–1582) Esquire for the Body. Son of Sir Francis Knollys* and Catherine Carey (Knollys*); brother of William Knollys*, Lettice Devereux*, Elizabeth Leighton*, Anne West*, and Catherine Knollys*; mar 1565 Margaret Cave (Knollys*); father of Elizabeth Knollys*. Hasler; will PCC 27 Rowe; Varlow.

> **Sundry Gift**: 77.420 (Christening Gift for his child)

Knollys, Lettice - see Lettice Devereux

Knollys, Margaret, née Cave (1548–1606) Mistress Knollys. Daughter of Sir Ambrose Cave* and Margaret Willington; mother of Elizabeth Knollys*; cousin of Anne Hampden*; mar 1565 Henry Knollys* MP. Hasler under husband; *Visitations, Warwickshire.*

> **Sundry Gift**: 77.420 (Christening Gift for her child)

Knollys, William (1545–1632) Treasurer of the Household, Comptroller of the Household, Privy Councillor, Gentleman Pensioner, kntd 1586, MP. Son of Francis Knollys* and Catherine Carey (Knollys*); brother of Lettice Devereux*, Henry Knollys*, Elizabeth Leighton*, and Anne West*; 1st cousin once removed to Queen Elizabeth; mar 1st c.1578 Dorothy Bray (Brydges*), 2nd 1605 Elizabeth Howard. *ODNB*; Hasler; Tighe; Varlow.

> **Knight**: 97.116, 97.315, 98.117, 98.318, 99.111, 99.306, 00.115, 00.312, 03.117, 03.330

Knyvett, Catherine—see Catherine Paget, Catherine [III] Howard

Knyvett, Elizabeth, née Hayward (d.1622) Mistress Knyvett, Lady Knyvett, later Governess to daughters of James I. Daughter of Rowland Hayward and Joan Tillsworth; sister-in-law of Francis Cherry*; mar 1st Richard Warren, 2nd 1597 Sir Thomas Knyvett*. GEC, *Peerage*; Hasler; *ODNB* under husband.

> **Gentlewoman**: 99.133, 99.335, 00.134, 00.336
> **Lady**: 03.112, 03.328

Knyvett, Thomas (c.1545–1622) Keeper of Westminster Palace, Groom of the Privy Chamber, later Lord Knyvett, kntd 1601, MP. Son of Henry Knyvett and Anne Pickering; brother of Catherine [III] Howard*; 2nd cousin once removed to Queen Elizabeth; mar 1597 Elizabeth Hayward (Knyvett*). *ODNB*; GEC, *Peerage*; Hasler; will PCC 78 Savile.

> **Gentleman**: 81.173, 81.387
> **Free Gift**: 71.353, 75.240, 76.405, 77.407, 78.413, 79.427, 81.423, 82.414, 84.400, 85.392, 88.385, 89.386, 94.383, 97.409, 98.415, 99.401, 00.404, 03.435
> **Custody of Gift**: 71.5, 77.192, 79.202, 79.206, 79.435, 81.16, 81.31, 81.104, 81.122–123, 81.128, 81.170, 81.202–203, 82.28, 82.31, 82.56, 82.75, 82.80, 82.92, 82.120, 82.192, 82.201, 84.87, 84.145, 84.190, 89.400, 89.405, 94.163, 94.170, 94.178, 97.76, 97.81, 97.174, 97.191, 98.76, 98.96, 98.98, 98.116, 98.120, 98.139, 99.72, 99.94, 99.98, 99.165, 99.172, 99.188, 00.134, 00.166, 03.104, 03.112, 03.155

Krag, Niels (1546–1602) Special Ambassador from Christian IV* of Denmark, alias Nicholas Cragius. author of *De Republica Lacedæmoniorum libri IIII,* 1593; Skovgaard-Petersen; BL Cotton MS Nero B. iii, Cotton MS Nero B. iv.

> **Sundry Gift**: 99.414. (Gift to Envoy)

Labopine, M.—see Charles L'Aubespine

La Chatre, Claude de (fl.1570s–1580s) La Châtre, La Chastre, La Shattera, Special Ambassador from Henry III* of France. *CSP Foreign, 1575–77, 1577–78, 1586–87*; Fénelon.

> **Sundry Gift**: 76.413 (Gift to Envoy)

Laiton—see Leighton

Lambert, Thomas—see Thomas Gemini; Henry Gittens

la Mothe Fénelon—see Bertrand de Salignac Fénelon

Lane, Catherine, née Copley (fl.1550s–1560s) Lady Lane. Daughter of Sir Roger Copley and Elizabeth Shelley; sister of Sir Thomas Copley*; 2nd cousin twice removed to Queen Elizabeth; mar c.1550 Sir Robert Lane MP. Hasler and Bindoff under husband.
Lady: 59.88, 59.308, 62.90, 62.271, 63.87, 63.262

Lane, Robert (d.1624) Son of Robert Lane and Catherine Copley (Lane*); mar Dudley Gorges; 1st cousin twice removed to Catherine Parr.
Gentleman: 00.196, 00.397

Lanier, John (d.1616) Musician. Mar 1583 Frances Galliardello; son-in-law of Mark Antony Galliardello*, brother-in-law of Henry Troches* and Caesar Galliardello*. *BDECM*.
Gentleman: 03.197, 03.421

Lanison—see Lonison

Lansac—see Lusignan

La Shattera—see La Chastre

Latimer, Baroness; Latimer, Lady—see Lucy Neville, née Somerset, 1545–1583

L'Aubespine, Charles de (fl.1570s) Son of Claude L'Aubespine. Envoy from Henry III* of France, French Secretary of Finance; associate of Jerenomo Gondi*. *CSP Foreign, 1586–88*; Fénelon.
Sundry Gift: 78.424 (Gift to Envoy)

Laverock, Thomas (d.1621) Crossbowmaker, Gunmaker, Maker of Handguns in the Tower of London, Armourers Company. Blackmore; *CSP Domestic, 1598–1601*; BL Additional MS 5752.
Gentleman: 82.198, 82.402

Lawrence, unidentified (fl.1580s) Cook, Queen's servant.
Custody of Gift: 82.365

Layton—see Leighton

Leake, Elizabeth—see Elizabeth Wingfield

Leake, unidentified (fl.1580s) Queen's servant.
Custody of Gift: 82.241

Lee, George (fl.1570s–1590s) Master Cook of the Household, Master Cook of the Privy Kitchen. PRO SP 12/166.
Gentleman: 97.176, 97.378

Lee, Sir Henry (1533–1611) Master of the Armoury, Leading Participant in Accession Day Tilts, courtier poet, kntd 1553, KG 1597. Son of Anthony Lee and Margaret Wyatt; mar bef 1554 Anne Paget; liaison with Anne [I] Vavasour*. *ODNB*; Hasler; will PCC 41 Wood.
Knight: 75.84, 76.130, 76.323, 77.134, 77.331, 78.137, 78.339, 79.138, 79.345, 81.131, 81.338, 82.125, 82.324, 82.535, 84.119, 84.317, 85.117, 85.309

Lee, Sir Richard (c.1501–1575) Surveyor of the King's Works, kntd 1544. Son of Richard Lee and Elizabeth Hall; mar 1537 Margaret Grenville. *ODNB*; Bindoff.
Knight: 75.85

Leicester, Earl—see Robert Dudley, 1564–1588

Leigh, Catherine—see Catherine Blount

Leigh, Sir John (d.1565) kntd 1553. Mar Jane [née?]. PRO C 1/138/18; *CSP Spanish, 1558–67*; will PCC 3 Crymes.
Knight: 62.125, 62.304

Leigh, Peter (d.1614) Son of Sir Richard Leigh and Clemence Holcroft; son-in-law of John Baptist Castilion* and Margaret Campagni (Castilion*); mar 1587 Elizabeth Castilion*. Burke.
Sundry Gift: 88.400 (Marriage Gift)

Leigh, Sir Thomas (d.1571) Lord Mayor of London 1558–1559, Mercer, Butler at Coronation. *ODNB*; will PCC 48 Holney; *Visitations, London*.
> **Sundry Gift**: 59.456 (Coronation Fees)

Leighton, Anne [I], née Darrell (b.c.1530) Lady Leighton. Daughter of Paul Darrell and Frances Saunders; sister-in-law of Thomas Leighton* and Elizabeth [I] Leighton*; mar 1553 Sir Edward Leighton; grandmother of Anne [II] Leighton*. Hasler under husband.
> **Lady**: 98.96, 98.298

Leighton, Anne [II] (b.c.1591) Gentlewoman. Daughter of Thomas Leighton and Elizabeth Gerrard; granddaughter of Anne [I] Leighton*; great-niece of Thomas Leighton*; mar George Greaves.
> **Gentlewoman**: 03.157, 03.370

Leighton, Elizabeth [I], née Knollys (c.1546–1626) Mistress Knollys, Lady Leighton. Gentlewoman of the Privy Chamber. Daughter of Sir Francis Knollys* and Catherine Carey*; sister of William Knollys*, Henry Knollys*, Lettice Devereux*, and Anne West*; 1st cousin once removed to Queen Elizabeth; mar 1579 Thomas Leighton*; mother of Elizabeth [II] Leighton*. *ODNB*; Hasler; Rimbault; *Index to Privy Bills*.
> **Gentlewoman** 65.59, 65.225, 67.124, 67.294, 68.121, 71.122, 71.292, 75.88, 76.134, 76.330, 77.139, 77.336, 78.143, 78.343, 79.144, 79.351
> **Lady**: 81.101, 81.310, 82.96, 82.298, 82.556, 84.94, 84.292, 85.99, 85.289, 88.101, 88.285, 89.93, 89.278, 94.88, 94.272, 97.96, 97.295, 98.153, 98.361, 99.93, 99.288, 00.98, 00.295, 03.101, 03.314
> **Custody of Gift**: 67.135, 71.77, 71.84, 71.86, 71.96, 71.154, 71.165, 71.168, 75.94, 75.100, 75.107, 76.42, 76.150, 77.117, 77.138, 77.174, 78.2, 78.34, 78.42, 78.97, 78.100, 78.142, 78.155, 79.40, 79.63, 79.85, 79.95, 79.106, 79.112, 79.139, 79.148, 79.150, 79.159, 79.184, 79.196, 79.205
> **Sundry Gift**: 79.456 (Marriage Gift)
> **Regifted**: 65.54 (Queen regifted gift from Blanche Parry*)

Leighton, Elizabeth [II] (b.1582) Daughter of Thomas Leighton* and Elizabeth Knollys (Leighton*); mar Sharington Talbot. BL Additional MS 5751A, Harleian MS 1644.
> **Regifted**: 85.178 (Gift given to Queen by Charles Smith), 98.107 (Gift given to Queen by Margaret Hawkins*)

Leighton, Thomas (1535–1610) Gentleman of the Privy Chamber, Captain of Guernsey, kntd 1579, MP. Son of John Leighton and Joyce Sutton; mar 1579 Elizabeth Knollys (Leighton*); father of Elizabeth [II] Leighton*. *ODNB*; Hasler.
> **Gentleman**: 75.223, 76.175, 76.380, 77.176, 77.380, 79.197, 79.410
> **Knight**: 81.135, 81.342, 82.128, 82.328, 82.539, 84.122, 84.320, 85.120, 85.311, 88.121, 88.305, 89.114, 89.299, 94.112, 94.303, 97.120, 97.320, 98.121, 98.323, 99.114, 99.309, 00.119, 00.316, 03.124, 03.336
> **Sundry Gift**: 79.456 (Marriage Gift)

Lekaville, unidentified (fl.1580s) Queen's servant.
> **Custody of Gift**: 82.309

Lennox, Earl/Countess—see Elizabeth Stuart, née Cavendish, 1574–1582; Margaret Stuart, née Douglas, 1544–1578; Matthew Stuart, 13th, 1526–1571

Lethington—see Maitland

Leverege—see Laverock

Leybourne, Elizabeth—see Elizabeth Dacre

Lichfield and Coventry, Bishop—see Ralph Baynes, 1554–1559; Thomas Bentham, 1560–1579; William Overton, 1580–1609

Lichfield, Margaret, née Pakington (b.c.1558) Mistress Lichfield. Daughter of Thomas Pakington and Dorothy Kitson; granddaughter of Margaret Bourchier*; sister of John Pakington*; 2nd cousin of John Scudamore*; mar 1573 Thomas Lichfield*. Hasler under husband; *Visitations, Buckinghamshire*.
Gentlewoman: 75.107, 76.151, 76.346, 77.154, 77.351, 78.155, 78.356, 79.157, 79.364, 82.159, 82.358, 82.620

Lichfield, Thomas (d.1586) Lute Maker, Musician, Groom of the Privy Chamber, MP. Mar 1573 Margaret Pakington (Lichfield*). *BDECM*; *Hasler*; *Visitations, Buckinghamshire*.
Gentleman: 79.186, 79.399, 81.185, 81.397, 82.169, 82.374, 82.577, 84.167, 84.395, 85.159, 85.361
Custody of Gift: 59.177, 59.184, 59.202, 65.95, 67.164, 76.18, 82.203

Lidcott, Dorothy—see Dorothy Edmonds

Lieven, Charles de (fl.1570s) Seigneur de Famars, Envoy from William* of Orange. *CSP Foreign, 1589*.
Sundry Gift : 77.424 (Gift to Envoy)

Light, Anthony (fl. 1570s) Gentleman Usher. PRO E115
Custody of Gift: 71.360

Lilly, unidentified (fl.1580s) Queen's servant.
Custody of Gift: 82.316

Lincoln, Bishop—see Thomas Watson, 1556–1559; Nicholas Bullingham, 1560–1571; Thomas Cooper, 1571–1584; William Wickham, 1584–1595; William Chaderton, 1595–1608

Lincoln, Earl/Countess—see Edward Clinton, 1st, 1572–1585; Elizabeth [I] Clinton , née FitzGerald, 1572–1590; Elizabeth [II] Clinton, née Morrison, 1585–1611; Henry Clinton, 2nd, 1585–1616

Lindsay, David (1541–1613) Preacher, Bishop of Ross. Envoy from James VI* of Scotland. *ODNB*.
Sundry Gift: 84.413 (Gift to Envoy)

Lingard, unidentified (fl.1580s) Queen's servant.
Custody of Gift: 82.212

Lister, Lady Mary, née Wriothesley (b.1537) Lady Lister. Daughter of Thomas Wriothesley, Earl of Southampton and Jane Cheyne (Wriothesley*); sister of Catherine Cornwallis* and Henry [I] Wriothesley; aunt of Henry [II] Wriothesley*, Earl of Southampton; mar 1st William Shelley, 2nd Richard Lister. Collins, *Peerage*.
Lady: 59.101, 59.320

Lizard, Nicholas (d.1571) Sergeant Painter to Henry VIII, Edward VI, Mary I, and Elizabeth. Mar Margaret Woodnet. *ODNB*; will PCC 18 Holney.
Gentleman: 59.212, 59.435

Llewellyn (Fluellen), John (fl.1570–80s) Groom of the Chamber. Mar 1574 Anne [née?] Bennett. BL MS Stowe 155; *CPR, 1575–78*.
Custody of Gift: 82.225

Lloyd—see Fludd

Loe—see St Loe

London, Bishop—see Edmund Grindal, 1559–1570; Edmund Sandys, 1570–1577; John Aylmer, 1577–1594; Richard Bancroft, 1597–1604

Long, unidentified (fl.1580s) Queen's servant.
Custody of Gift: 82.379

Long, Catherine, née Thynne (d.1613) Maid of Honour, Lady Long, of the Privy Chamber. Daughter of Sir John Thynne* and Dorothy Wroughton (Long*); sister of Gresham

Thynne*; mar 1ˢᵗ 1584 Sir Walter Long MP, 2ⁿᵈ 1611 Edward Fox. *Visitations, Wiltshire*; Hasler under husband.

Lady: 88.111, 88.294, 89.104, 89.289, 94.97, 94.282, 97.108, 97.309, 98.109, 98.310, 99.106, 99.301, 00.110, 00.308, 03.116, 03.327

Long, Margaret—see Margaret Bourchier

Lonison, John (fl.1570s) Master of the Mint, Goldsmith. Son of William van Pontsendall alias Lonison, mar Mary Colt. BL Lansdowne MS 34, Sloane MS 814; Jackson; will PCC 45 Tirwhite; Siddons.

Gentleman: 76.184, 76.386, 77.184, 77.385

Lopez, Roderigo (c.1517–1594) Queen's Physician. Son of Antonio Lopez, son-in-law of Dunstan Añes*, mar 1563 Sara Añes. *ODNB*.

Gentleman: 82.185, 82.387, 82.560, 84.181, 84.385, 85.174, 85.373, 88.166, 88.358, 89.165, 89.357, 94.158, 94.352

Louche, Robert (fl.1580s) Queen's servant.

Custody of Gift: 82.366

Lovell, Anne—see Anne Carey

Lovett, Elizabeth—see Elizabeth Weston

Lowe, Dorothy [née?] (b.c.1547) Mistress Lowe. Mar 1562 Jasper Lowe. PRO E 115.

Gentlewoman: 68.139

Lowe, Roger (fl.1580s) Queen's servant, possible identification. PRO E 115.

Custody of Gift: 82.337

Lucretia—see Lucretia di Conti

Luddington, Joan—see Joan Chamberlain

Ludington—see Maitland

Lumley, Lord/Baroness—see Elizabeth Lumley, née Darcy, 1582–1617; John Lumley, 1547–1609

Lumley, Elizabeth, Baroness Lumley (c.1566–1617) Daughter of John Darcy* and Frances Rich; sister of Thomas, Lord Darcy* of Chiche; mar 1582 John, Lord Lumley*. *ODNB*; GEC, *Peerage*; BL Additional MS 12506; will PCC 13 Weldon, 34 Dorset.

Baroness : 84.71, 84.269, 85.74, 85.265, 88.76, 88.261, 89.69, 89.254, 94.71, 94.255, 97.78, 97.276, 98.77, 98.276, 99.73, 99.266, 00.80, 00.275, 03.80, 03.294

Lumley, John, Lord Lumley (1533–1609) Son-in-law of Henry FitzAlan*; cousin of Lucy Conyers*; mar 1ˢᵗ 1552 Jane FitzAlan, 2ⁿᵈ 1582 Elizabeth Darcy (Lumley*). *ODNB*; GEC, *Peerage*; will PCC 34 Dorset.

Lord: 59.75, 59.295, 62.57, 62.238, 63.58, 63.231, 64.59, 65.161, 67.60, 67.230, 68.58, 68.227, 71.55, 71.225, 75.73, 75.181, 76.70, 76.259, 77.77, 77.276, 78.75, 78.278, 79.73, 79.281, 81.72, 81.279, 82.67, 82.267, 82.466, 84.62, 84.258, 85.65, 85.256, 88.64, 88.249, 89.58, 89.243, 94.59, 94.243, 97.65, 97.262, 98.63, 98.262, 99.59, 99.252, 00.66, 00.260, 03.64, 03.277

Lupo, Ambrose (1505–1591) Musician, Violin. Son of Gian-Battista Lupo, mar Lucia [née?]; father of Joseph Lupo* and Peter Lupo*. *BDECM*; Siddons.

Gentleman: 59.216, 59.440, 68.160, 71.165, 71.342, 75.227, 76.192, 76.396, 77.193, 77.395, 78.192, 78.402, 79.199, 79.412, 81.195, 81.412, 82.191, 82.395, 82.566, 84.191, 84.390, 85.183, 85.385, 88.178, 88.370, 89.180, 89.372

Lupo, Joseph (c.1536–1616) Musician, Violin. Son of Ambrose Lupo*; brother of Peter Lupo*; mar Laura Bassano. *BDECM*; *ODNB*; Siddons.

Gentleman: 89.184, 89.376, 94.171, 94.366, 97.181, 97.383, 98.179, 98.384, 99.177, 99.375, 00.177, 00.376, 03.188, 03.410

Lupo, Peter (1534–1608) Musician, Violin, alias Peter Wolfe. Son of Ambrose Lupo*; brother of Joseph Lupo*; mar 1st 1567 unidentified Koven, 2nd 1575 Katherine Wickers. *BDECM*; *ODNB*; Siddons.
Gentleman: 79.202, 79.415, 81.196, 81.414, 82.192, 82.396, 82.578, 84.193, 84.391, 85.184, 85.386, 88.182, 88.375, 89.183, 89.375, 94.169, 94.365, 97.180, 97.382, 98.178, 98.383, 99.176, 99.374, 00.176, 00.375, 03.186, 03.408

Lupo, Thomas [I] (1571–1628) Musician, Violin. Son of Joseph Lupo* and Laura Bassano; mar Lydia [née?]. *BDECM*.
Gentleman: 94.172, 94.367, 97.182, 97.384, 98.180, 98.385, 99.178, 99.376, 00.178, 00.377, 03.189, 03.411

Lupo, Thomas [II] (1577-aft 1647) Musician, Violin. Son of Peter Lupo*; mar 1599 Joanne Smithson. *BDECM*; *ODNB*.
Gentleman: 00.378, 03.187, 03.409

Lusignan de St Gelais, Louis de (1513–1589) Sieur de Lansac, French Commissioner for marriage settlement between Elizabeth and the Duke of Anjou*. Holt; *CSP Foreign, 1581*.
Sundry Gift: 81.447 (Gift to Envoy)

Luttrell, Catherine—see Catherine Copley

Luxemburg, Louis de (fl.1560s) formerly French hostage, Count de Roussy, Special Ambassador from Charles IX* of France. *CSP Foreign, 1559–60*.
Sundry Gift: 62.394 (Gift to Envoy)

Luzard—see Lizard

Lyfield, Frances, née Bray (c1535–1597) Mistress Lyfield. Daughter of Edmund, Lord Bray and Jane Halywell; sister of Elizabeth Catesby* and Dorothy Brydges*; 1st cousin of Edward Bray*; mar c.1562 Thomas Lyfield. GEC, *Peerage*.
Gentlewoman: 84.156, 84.349, 85.136, 85.320, 88.147, 88.331, 89.143, 89.328

Lygon, Catherine—see Denys, Catherine

Lyster—see Lister

Lyttleton, Elizabeth—see Elizabeth Willoughby

MacCarty, Sir Cormack MacTeig (d.1583) Lord of Muskerry (S). Mar Joan Butler. Will Diocese of Cork. *CSP Ireland, 1596–97, 1600*.
Sundry Gift: 78.421 (Gift on his visit to England)

MacPhelim—see O'Neill

Mackwilliam, Elizabeth (b.1563) Maid of Honour. Daughter of Henry Mackwilliam* and Lady Mary Cheke*; sister of Margaret Mackwilliam*; godchild of Queen Elizabeth.
Maid of Honour: 89.341

Mackwilliam, Henry (d.1586) Gentleman Pensioner, Keeper of Colchester Castle. Son of Henry Mackwilliam and Elizabeth Leyes; mar 1558 Lady Mary Cheke*; father of Margaret Mackwilliam* and Elizabeth Mackwilliam*. Hasler; Tighe; will PCC 26 Spencer.
Sundry Gift: 64.229 (Christening Gift for his child)

Mackwilliam, Margaret (c1564–1640) Maid of Honour, later Baroness Stanhope. Daughter of Henry Mackwilliam* and Lady Mary Cheke*; sister of Elizabeth Mackwilliam*; mar 1589 John Stanhope* later Lord Stanhope. GEC, *Peerage* under husband.
Maid of Honour: 81.379, 82.366, 84.358, 85.351, 88.341
Sundry Gift: 64.229 (Christening Gift)

Mackwilliam, Mary—see Mary Cheke

Mainwaring, Philip (1530–1573) son of John Mainwaring and Catherine Hanford; mar Anne Leycester. *Visitations, Cheshire*.
Gentleman: 59.172, 59.394

Maitland, William (1525–1573) Ambassador from Mary Stuart* of Scotland, Laird of Lethington. *ODNB*; Blake.
  Sundry Gift: 63.363, 64.218 (Gift to Envoy)
Maldeghem, Philippe de (1547–1611) Ambassador from Margaret*, Duchess of Parma, Regent of the Low Countries, accompanied by Ludwig Stolberg* from the Emperor.
  Sundry gift: 68.348 (Gift to Envoy)
Mandeghene—see Maldeghem
Manners, Bridget [I], née Husssey, Countess of Bedford (d.1601) Countess of Rutland. Daughter of John, Lord Hussey and Lady Anne Grey; mar 1ˢᵗ 1546 Richard Morrison, 2ⁿᵈ 1560 Henry Manners*, Earl of Rutland, 3rd 1566 Francis Russell*, Earl of Bedford; mother of Elizabeth [II] Clinton*. GEC, *Peerage*; BL Sloane MS 814.
  Countess: 62.48, 62.228, 63.43, 63.218, 64.46, 65.147, 67.46, 67.216, 68.29, 68.198, 71.27, 71.197, 75.32, 75.139, 76.34, 76.229, 77.36, 77.232, 78.37, 78.238, 79.30, 79.237, 81.31, 81.238, 82.31, 82.231, 82.480, 84.30, 84.228, 85.30, 85.222, 88.30, 88.215, 89.25, 89.210, 94.24, 94.205, 97.40, 97.231, 98.32, 98.228, 99.27, 99.218, 00.34, 00.225
Manners, Bridget [II] (c.1576–1604) Lady of the Privy Chamber, Lady of the Bedchamber, 'Lady Manners Tyrwhitt'. Daughter of John Manners*, Earl of Rutland, and Elizabeth Charleton*; mar 1594 Robert Tyrwhitt. *HMC Rutland*; GEC, *Peerage* under Philip Wharton.
  Lady: 94.84, 94.268, 03.94
  Baroness: 03.305
Manners, Edward (1549–1587) Lord Ros, Earl of Rutland, KG 1584. Son of Henry Manners*, Earl of Rutland, and Margaret Neville (Manners*); brother of John Manners*, Earl of Rutland; mar 1573 Isabel Holcroft (Manners*); father of Elizabeth [II] Manners*. GEC, *Peerage*.
  Earl: 71.15, 71.185, 75.12, 76.207, 77.17, 77.214, 78.16, 78.217, 79.14, 79.220, 81.13, 81.219, 82.13, 82.212, 82.431, 84.12, 84.208, 85.11, 85.202
  Sundry Gift: 76.421 (Christening Gift for his child)
Manners, Elizabeth [I], née Charlton, Countess of Rutland (d.1595) Daughter of Francis Charlton and Cecily Fitton, mother of Roger Manners* and Bridget [II] Manners*, mar 1575 John Manners*. GEC, *Peerage*; *HMC Rutland*.
  Countess: 88.33. 88.218, 89.28, 89.213, 94.26, 94.209
Manners, Elizabeth [II] (1576–1591) Baroness Ros 1587. Daughter of Edward Manners*, Earl of Rutland and Isabel Holcroft (Manners*); mar 1589 William Cecil, later Earl of Exeter; daughter-in-law of Thomas Cecil*, Lord Burghley. GEC, *Peerage*; Hasler.
  Sundry Gift: 76.421 (Christening Gift)
Manners, Elizabeth [III], née Sidney, Countess of Rutland (1585–1612) Daughter of Sir Philip Sidney* and Frances Walsingham (Sidney*); step-daughter of Robert Devereux*, Earl of Essex; granddaughter of Sir Francis Walsingham* and Ursula St Barbe (Walsingham*) and of Sir Henry Sidney* and Mary Dudley (Sidney*); mar 1599 Roger Manners*, Earl of Rutland. GEC, *Peerage*; *ODNB* under husband.
  Countess: 00.28, 00.236, 03.34, 03.247
Manners, Frances—see Frances Neville
Manners, Gertrude—see Gertrude Talbot
Manners, Henry, Earl of Rutland (1526–1563) KG 1559. Son of Thomas Manners and Eleanor Paston; brother of Gertrude Talbot* and Frances Neville*; mar 1ˢᵗ 1536 Margaret Neville*, 2ⁿᵈ 1560 Bridget [II] Hussey*. GEC, *Peerage*; *ODNB*.
  Earl: 59.13, 59.234, 62.10, 62.191, 63.11, 63.183

Manners, Isabel, née Holcroft, Countess of Rutland (1562–1606) Maid of Honour. Daughter of Thomas Holcroft and Juliana Jennings; mar 1573 Edward Manners*, Earl of Rutland; mother of Elizabeth [II] Manners*. GEC, *Peerage*.
Maid of Honour: 71.320
Countess: 75.37, 75.144, 76.39, 76.234, 77.39, 77.239, 78.40, 78.241, 79.39, 79.246, 81.34, 81.241, 82.34, 82.234, 82.488, 84.32, 84.230, 85.33, 85.225
Sundry Gift: 76.421 (Christening Gift for her child)
Manners, John, Earl of Rutland (1552–1588) Son of Henry Manners*, Earl of Rutland, and Margaret Neville (Manners*); brother of Edward Manners*; mar 1575 Elizabeth [I] Charleton (Manners*); father of Roger Manners* and Bridget [II] Manners*. GEC, *Peerage*; *HMC Rutland*; will PCC 1, 29 Rutland.
Earl: 88.11, 88.196
Manners, Margaret, née Neville, Countess of Rutland (c.1530–1559) Daughter of Ralph Neville and Catherine Stafford; sister of Henry [II] Neville*; mar 1536 Henry Manners*, mother of Edward Manners* and John Manners*. GEC, *Peerage*.
Countess: 59.48, 59.269
Manners, Roger, Earl of Rutland (1576–1612) Son of John Manners*, Earl of Rutland, and Elizabeth [I] Charleton (Manners*); mar 1599 Elizabeth [II] Sidney (Manners*). GEC, *Peerage*; *ODNB*.
Earl: 98.15, 98.217, 99.6, 99.207, 00.15, 00.213, 03.16, 03.229
Mannington, Christopher (fl.1580's) Queen's servant.
Custody of Gift: 82.254
Mansell, Mary (1548-c.1564) Maid of Honour. Daughter of Rhys Mansell and Cecily Dabridgecourt; mar 1563 Thomas Southwell*. PRO C 3/38; Hasler under husband.
Maid of Honour: 59.378, 62.333, 63.317
Mantell, George (fl.1560s) Queen's Farmer [of Customs]. PRO E 134.
Gentleman: 62.164, 62.352, 63.154, 63.333
Manucci, Jacomo (fl.1580s) Merchant from Venice, aliasVezelmo, Agent of Sir Francis Walsingham*. PRO SP 46/125/, SP 85/1; BL Lansdowne MS 31, Lansdowne MS 67; Leimon.
Gentleman: 88.177, 88.369, 89.178, 89.370, 94.64, 94.359
Manxell—see Mansell
Marbeck, Roger (1536–1605) Physician, Calligrapher, admitted to Gray's Inn. Son of John Marbeck; uncle-in-law of Thomas Middleton*; mar c.1566 Anne Williams. *ODNB*.
Gentleman: 03.172, 03.393
Marbury, Elizabeth, née Marbury (d.aft.1591) Gentlewoman of the Bedchamber, served Princess Elizabeth. Daughter of Thomas Marbury and Agnes Lynne; mar Thomas Marbury*; mother of John Marbury*. Husband's will PCC 14 Lewyn; *Visitations, London*; *CPR, 1558–60*.
Gentlewoman: 62.139, 62.319, 63,130, 63.303, 64.122, 64.175, 65.61, 65.227, 67.130, 67.300, 68.127, 68.295, 71.130, 71.300, 75.112, 76.142, 76.343, 77.150, 77.345, 78.150, 78.351, 79.152, 79.359, 81.146, 81.353, 82.140, 82.340, 82.603, 84.151, 84.347
Custody of Gift: 59.151, 59.171, 62.143, 62.162, 63.130, 64.117, 64.131, 64.137, 67.158, 68.158
Marbury, John (b.c.1557) Son of Thomas Marbury* and Elizabeth Marbury*; godson of Queen Elizabeth; mar 1576 Dorothy Medigert.
Sundry Gift: 76.424 (Marriage Gift)
Marbury, Thomas (d.1598) Sergeant of the Pantry. Mar 1st Alice Marbury, 2nd Elizabeth Marbury*; father of John Marbury*. Will PCC 14 Lewyn; *Visitations, London*; *CPR, 1558–60*.

Custody of Gift: 82.340

Margaret, Duchess of Parma (1522–1586) Margaret of Austria, Regent of the Low Countries. Gifts to her envoys François Halewyn* and Philippe de Maldeghem*. Daughter of Charles V; half-sister of Philip II* of Spain and Don John* of Austria; mar Ottavio Farnese, Duke of Parma.

    Sundry Gift: 64.224, 68.348 (Sovereign sending Envoy to England)

Markham, Mary, née Griffin (fl.1560s) Daughter of Rice Griffin and Anne Roos, mar 1564 Thomas Markham*; mother of Griffin Markham*. Hasler and Bindoff under husband; Tighe.

    Sundry Gift: 67.363 (Christening Gift for her child)

Markham, Griffin (b.1566) Son of Thomas Markham* and Mary Griffin (Markham*); cousin of John [I] Harington*, nephew of Isabella Harington*.

    Sundry Gift: 67.363 (Christening Gift)

Markham, Isabella—see Isabella Harington

Markham, Thomas (c.1538–1607) Gentleman Pensioner, MP. Son of Sir John Markham and Anne Strelley; brother of Isabella Harington*; mar 1564 Mary Griffin (Markham*); father of Griffin Markham*. Tighe; Hasler; Bindoff.

    Sundry Gift: 67.363 (Christening Gift for his child)

Marrow, Thomas (1516–1561) Mar bef 1541 Alice Young. Will PCC 37 Loftes; *VCH, Warwick*.

    Gentleman: 59.165, 59.389

    Regifted: 59.164 (Queen regifted gift from William Watson*)

Marshall, unidentified (fl.1580s) Queen's servant.

    Custody of Gift: 82.330, 82.331

Martel, Nicholas (fl.1570s) Monsieur de Bacqueville, Envoy from Duke of Anjou*, Household Officer to the Duke of Anjou, at court with three others: Monsieur de Saverne*, Monsieur de Torsac*, and Monsieur de Ninsonan*. Nichols; *CSP Foreign, 1583–84*; Dovey.

    Sundry Gift: 79.449 (Gift to Envoy)

Martin, Richard (1534–1617) Goldsmith, Master of the Mint, Alderman of London, Lord Mayor of London 1589 and 1594, alias 'M' or 'Mar'. Mar 1ˢᵗ c.1559 Dorcas Eccleston, 2ⁿᵈ c.1616 Elizabeth Cottesford. *ODNB*; White, *Biographical*.

    Goldsmith: 67.362, 79.452, 81.434–436, 81.440–441, 81.443–81.452, *passim* 1582–1600

Martin, unidentified (fl.1580s) of the Laundry, Queen's servant.

    Custody of Gift: 82.327, 82.370

Marvyn, Amy, née Clarke (d.c.1590) Mistress Marvyn, Lady Marvyn. Daughter of Valentine Clarke and Elizabeth Brydges; mar 1ˢᵗ Edmund Horne, 2ⁿᵈ by 1559 Thomas Marvyn, MP; mother of Lucy Tuchet*. *Visitations, Oxford*; Hasler under husband.

    Gentlewoman: 59.143, 59.370, 62.134, 62.314, 67.133, 67.303, 68.125, 68.293, 71.128, 71.298

    Lady: 76.114, 76.311, 77.118, 77.315, 78.118, 78.319, 79.116, 79.323, 81.113, 81.320, 82.108, 82.308, 82.553

Marvyn, Lucy—see Lucy Tuchet

Mary, Anthony—see Mark Anthony Galliardello; Mark Anthony Erizo

Mary Queen of Scots—see Mary Stuart

Mason, Sir John (c.1503–1566) Treasurer of the Chamber, Master of the Posts, Master of Requests, Privy Councillor 1551, kntd 1547, MP. Mar 1540 Elizabeth Isley; stepfather of Lady Mary Cheke*. *ODNB*; Hasler; Bindoff; will PCC 2 Stonard.

    Knight: 59.115, 59.334, 62.106, 62.286, 63.104, 63.277, 64.98, 64.152, 65.34, 65. 201

Mason, Elizabeth, née Isley (d.1594) Lady Mason. Daughter of Thomas Isley and Elizabeth Guildford; mar 1ˢᵗ Richard Hill, 2ⁿᵈ 1540 Sir John Mason* MP; mother of Lady Mary Cheke*. *ODNB*; Hasler and Bindoff under husband.
  Lady: 59.84, 59.304, 62.87, 62.269, 63.84, 63.260, 64.85, 65.16, 65.183
Mason, Mathias (d.1609) Musician, Lute. *BDECM*; *RECM*; will PCC 113 Dorset 1609.
  Custody of Gift: 81.185, 82.199, 88.180, 88.181, 98.189
Master, Elizabeth, née Fulnetby (fl.1560s) Mistress Master. Daughter of John Fulnetby, mar Richard Master*; mother of Henry Master*. ODNB under husband.
  Sundry Gift: 64.220 (Christening Gift for her child)
Master, Henry (1564–1631) Son of Richard Master* and Elizabeth Fulnetby.
  Sundry Gift: 64.220 (Christening Gift)
Master, Richard (c.1515–1588) Queen's Physician. Mar Elizabeth Fulnetby (Master*), father of Henry Master*. *ODNB*; will PCC 34 Rutland.
  Gentleman: 59.163, 59.387, 62.158, 62.345, 63.149, 63.328, 64.134, 64.194, 65.81, 67.156, 67.332, 68.155, 68.327, 71.157, 71.335, 75.123, 75.219, 76.186, 76.388, 77.186, 77.387, 78.184, 78.393, 79.189, 79.402, 81.187, 81.401, 82.182, 82.385, 82.558, 84.179, 84.383, 85.172, 85.371, 88.165, 88.356
  Sundry Gift: 64.220 (Christening Gift for his child)
  Custody of Gift: 82.385 (delivered to himself)
Matthew, unknown (fl.1580s) of the Pantry, Queen's servant.
  Custody of Gift: 82.380
Matthew, Richard (fl.1560s) Cutler. Possible relative of Nathaniel Matthew, Cutler under James I. PRO LC 5/49
  Gentleman: 62.178, 62.365, 63.172, 63.351
Matthew, Tobie (1544–1628) Bishop of Durham 1595–1606, later Archbishop of York 1606–1628, Chaplain to Queen Elizabeth. Son-in-law of William Barlow*; brother-in-law of Herbert Westfaling*, William Day*, William Overton*, and William Wickham*. *ODNB*.
  Bishop: 97.43, 97.241, 98.42, 98.243, 99.36, 99.231, 00.43, 00.241, 03.45, 03.258
Mauvissière, Michel Castelnau de (c.1520–1592) Sieur de Mauvissiere, Special French Ambassador 1564, Resident Ambassador 1575–1585. *CSP Foreign, 1581–82*; *CSP Spanish, 1580–86*; Fénelon; Corpus Christi, Cambridge, Parker MS 105.
  Sundry Gift: 64.222 (Gift to Envoy), 77.423 (Christening Gift for his child, Robert)
Maximilian II (1527–1576) Holy Roman Emperor, King of Bohemia, KG 1567. Nephew of Charles V; uncle of Philip II* of Spain; Don John* of Austria, and Margaret*, Duchess of Parma. Gift to his envoys: Oliver d'Arco* and Ludwig Stolberg*; envoy of Rudolf II*, John Preyner* who returned Garter insignia upon death of Maximilian.
  Sundry Gift: 64.217, 68.347, 68.348 (Sovereign sending Envoy to England); 78.22 (return of Garter insignia).
May, John (d.1598) Bishop of Carlisle 1577–1598. *ODNB*.
  Bishop: 78.57, 78.258, 79.55, 79.262, 81.49, 81.255, 82.47, 82.246, 82.450, 84.42, 84.240, 85.46, 85.236, 88.47, 88.232, 89.42, 89.227, 94.43, 94.226, 97.48, 97.246, 98.46, 98.248
Mayor of London—see Thomas Leigh
Medilkyrk—see Meetkerk
Meekins, Robert (fl.1580s) of the Chandry. probable identification. PRO E 115.
  Custody of Gift: 82.249, 82.325
Meetkerk, Adolf van (1528–1591) President of Flanders, Envoy from the States of the Low Countries, came to England with Charles Philip de Croy*, Marquis of Havrech. *CSP Foreign, 1587*.
  Sundry Gift: 78.427 (Gift to Envoy)

Melun, Robert de (fl.1570s) Vicomte de Ghent, Ambassador from Don John* of Austria. *CSP Foreign, 1578–79, 1583–84*.
    Sundry Gift; 78.423 (Official sending Envoy to England)
Melville, James (c.1535–1617) Envoy from Mary Stuart* of Scotland. Son of John Melville and Helen Napier; brother of Robert Melville*. *ODNB*.
    Sundry Gift: 67.360 (Gift to Envoy)
Melville, Robert (c.1527–1621) Ambassador from Mary Stuart* and James VI* of Scotland, later Lord Melville. Son of John Melville and Helen Napier; brother of James Melville*. GEC, *Peerage* : *ODNB*.
    Sundry Gift: 68.346 (Gift to Envoy), 94.392 (Gift toe Envoy)
Mendoza, Bernardino de (c.1540–1604) Special Ambassador from Low Countries 1574, Resident Spanish Ambassador 1578–1584 from Philip II*, expelled from England, Ambassador to France, 1584–1590. *CSP Spanish, 1569–79* ; *CSP Domestic,1547–80* .
    Sundry Gift: 75.250 (Gift to Envoy)
Mewtas, Frances (c.1548-c.1595) Maid of Honour, Viscountess Howard of Bindon. Daughter of Peter Mewtas and Jane Astley; mar 1st 1566 Henry Howard*, Viscount Howard of Bindon, 2nd c.1591 Edward Stanhope. GEC, *Peerage*; *CSP Domestic, 1595*.
    Maid of Honour: 62.337, 63.320, 64.187
Middlemore, Elizabeth [née?] (fl.1580s) Mistress Middlemore. Mar 1st c.1578 Henry Middlemore*, 2nd c.1594 Vincent Skinner. Possible identification. Evans.
    Gentlewoman: 84.136, 84.334
Middlemore, Henry (1535–1592/3) Groom of the Privy Chamber. Son of William Middlemore and Margery Gatacre; cousin of Nicholas Throckmorton*; mar c.1578 Elizabeth Fowkes*. Scribal error of William for Henry in several rolls. Collins, Jewels; *CSP Foreign, 1560–61, 1562, 1569–71, 1579–80*; *CPR, 1575–78*; *Index to Privy Bills*.
    Gentleman: 84.165, 84.366
    Free Gift: 71.354, 75.241, 76.404, 77.406, 78.412, 79.426, 81.425, 82.411, 84.402, 85.395, 88.382, 89.384
    Custody of Gift: 71.89, 71.119, 78.148, 82.138, 82.209
Middlemore, William—scribal error for Henry Middlemore
Middleton, Arthur (fl.1580s) Page of the Chamber, Ranger of the Forest of Dean, Gloucestershire. *CPR, 1580–82*.
    Custody of Gift: 82.157, 82.217
Middleton, Marmaduke (d.1593) Bishop of St David's 1582–1592 (deprived). *ODNB*.
    Bishop: 84.49, 84.247, 85.53, 85.243, 88.52, 88.237, 89.47, 89.232
Middleton, Thomas—see Thomas Myddelton
Milan—see Anthony Donato, Ambrose Lupo
Mildmay, Walter (c.1523–1589) Chancellor of the Exchequer 1559, Privy Councillor 1566, founder of Emmanuel College Cambridge, courtier poet, kntd 1547, MP. Son Thomas Mildway and Agnes Read; brother-in-law of Francis Walsingham*; mar 1546 Mary Walsingham. *ODNB*; Hasler; Bindoff; May, *Elizabethan Courtier*; will PCC 51 Leicester.
    Knight: 59.116, 59.335, 62.108, 62.288, 63.106, 63.279, 64.100, 64.154, 65.36, 65.203, 67.104, 67.274, 68.103, 68.272, 71.103, 71.273, 76.122, 76.317, 77.124, 77.321, 78.127, 78.327, 79.125, 79.332, 81.121, 81.330, 82.116, 82.316, 82.527, 84.112, 84.310, 85.113, 85.305, 88.118, 88.302, 89.111, 89.296
Miller, unidentified (fl.1580s) Cellar, Queen's servant.
    Custody of Gift: 82.260
Miller, Hugh (d.1616) Footman, Keeper of Eltham Little Park, Kent. BL Harleian MS 1644, Lansdowne MS 59.
    Gentleman: 98.198, 98.401

Modeno, Nicholas Belin de—see Nicholas Belin

Monge, William—see William Mugge

Monmouth, Anne—see Anne Payne

Montagu, Viscount/Viscountess—see Anthony Browne, 1st, 1554–1592; Anthony Maria Browne, 2nd, 1592–1682; Magdalen Browne, née Dacre, 1558–1608

Montague, Alice, née Smith (d.1582) Mistress Montague, Silkwoman. Mar 1562 Roger Montague*. BL Additional MS 35328; Arnold, *QE Wardrobe*; Archer.
  Gentlewoman: 71.142, 71.312, 75.105, 76.159, 76.340, 77.163, 77.360, 78.164, 78.366, 79.166, 79.373, 81.161, 81.367

Montague, Roger (d.1619) Silkman, Master of Skinners Company. Son of Edward Montague and Eleanor Roper; mar 1562 Alice Smith (Montague*). Will PCC 38 Parker; Archer.
  Gentleman: 82.178, 82.382, 82.585, 84.178, 84.380, 85.190, 85.380, 88.171, 88.362, 89.170, 89.361, 94.152, 94.346, 97.163, 97.367, 98.161, 98.369, 99.155, 99.357, 00.157, 00.360, 03.166, 03.386

Monteagle, *de jure* Baroness—see Elizabeth Parker, née Stanley, 4th, 1581–1585

Montgomery, Charlotte—see Charlotte Beaufort

Montgomery, Isabel [née?] (fl.1570s) Countess of Montgomery, Huguenot refugee. Mar Gabriel Montgomery Seigneur de Lorges who was executed 1574; mother of Charlotte Beaufort*. Marlet; Dumas.
  Countess: 75.146, 76.41, 76.236

Montreal, Count of (fl.1580s) Special Ambassador from Charles Emmanuel*, Duke of Savoy. *CSP Foreign, 1583–84.*
  Sundry Gift: 81.439 (Gift to Envoy)

More, Elizabeth—see Elizabeth Wolley

More, John (d.1603) Alderman of London. Will PCC 26 Bolein.
  Gentleman: 03.207, 03.384

Moretta, Rupertino/Bertino Solari di (fl.1560s) Envoy from Emmanuel Philibert*, Duke of Savoy to England and Scotland, Mounsieur Morett. *CSP Foreign,1561–62*; *CSP Spain, 1558–67*; *CSP Venice, 1558–80.*
  Sundry Gift: 62.391 (Gift to Envoy)

Morgan, Anne—see Anne Carey

Morgan, Henry (1500–1559) Bishop of St David's 1554–1559 (deprived). *ODNB.*
  Bishop: 59.35, 59.254

Morgan, Hugh (c.1510–1613) Apothecary. Mar Lucy Sibell (Morgan*). *ODNB*; Matthews.
  Gentleman: 78.196, 78.400, 84.182, 84.386, 85.175, 85.374, 88.173, 88.364, 89.176, 89.368, 94.159, 94.353, 97.171, 97.374, 98.168, 98.375, 99.162, 99.363, 00.163, 00.365, 03.174, 03.395

Morgan, Lucy, née Sibell (d.1606) Mistress Morgan. Daughter of Nicholas Sibell and Joan Sommer; sister of Anne Hyde; mar Hugh Morgan*. *ODNB* under husband.
  Gentlewoman: 81.150, 81.374, 82.145, 82.345, 82.618, 85.155, 85.347, 88.152, 88.337, 89.149, 89.334

Morgan, unidentified (fl.1580s) Master Morgan, Sewer, Queen's servant.
  Custody of Gift: 82.228

Morgan, unidentified (fl.1580s) Groom, Queen's servant.
  Custody of Gift: 82.301

Morice, Anne, née Isaac (fl.1550s) Mistress Morice, Mother of the Maids. Daughter of [unidentified] Isaac and Margery Wroth; step-daughter of Thomas Wyatt; mar c.1526

William Morice MP. *Visitations, Essex*; Bindoff under husband; mother's will PCC 24 Hogen, 9 Alenger.

Maid of Honour: 59.379

Morley, Lord/Baroness—see Edward Parker, 12th, 1577–1618; Elizabeth Parker, née Stanley, 1577–1585

Mornay, Phillippe du Plessis (1549–1623) Seigneur du Plessis Marly, Ambassador from Henry of Navarre (later Henry IV* of France). Mar Charlotte Arbaleste. Patry.

Sundry Gift: 79.447 (Gift while on Progress, given at Norwich at his departure)

Morrison, Bridget—see Bridget Radcliffe

Morrison, Elizabeth—see Elizabeth Clinton

Mothe Fénelon, Bertrand de la– see Bertrand de Salignac Fénelon

Mountjoy, Lord/Baroness—see Catherine Blount, née Leigh, 1558–1576, Charles Blount, 8th, 1594–1606; James Blount, 6th, 1544–1581; Penelope Blount, née Devereux, 1605–1607; William Blount, 7th, 1581–1594

Mountroyal—see Montreal

Mugge, William (d.c.1581) Merchant.

Gentleman: 63.169, 63.348

Myddelton, Thomas (1550–1631) Goldsmith, Merchant, Surveyor of Customs, Lord Mayor of London 1613, kntd 1613, MP. Son of Richard Myddleton and Jane Dryhurst; related to Thomas Middleton, playwright; mar 1st c.1585 Hester Saltonstall, 2nd 1587 Elizabeth Danvers, 3rd Elizabeth Brooke, 4th Anne Vanacker. *ODNB*; Hasler; Beaven.

Gentleman: 94.179, 94.374, 97.199, 97.397, 98.196, 98.398, 99.173, 99.389, 00.173, 00.392, 03.167, 03.388

Neukom, Hans (fl.1590s) Envoy from Christian IV* of Denmark.

Sundry Gift: 98.427 (Gift to Envoy)

Neville, Anne—see Anne Greville

Neville, Catherine—see Lady Catherine Constable, Catherine Percy

Neville, Charles (1543–1601) Earl of Westmorland, lived in exile from 1570. Son of Henry [II] Neville* and Anne Manners; mar 1564 Jane Howard (Neville*). GEC, *Peerage*.

Earl: 65.107, 67.7, 67.177, 68.10, 68.179

Neville, Dorothy—see Dorothy Cecil

Neville, Lady Eleanor (1547–1574) Lady Neville. Daughter of Henry [II] Neville*, Earl of Westmorland, and Anne Manners; sister of Ladu Catherine Constable* and Charles Neville*; mar c.1565 William Pelham.

Lady: 63.271

Neville, Elizabeth, née Darrell, Baroness Abergavenny (d.c.1602) Daughter of Stephen Darrell and Philippa Weldon; mar 1st 1576 Henry [I] Neville*, Lord Abergavenny, 2nd c.1588 Sir William Sedley. GEC, *Peerage*.

Baroness: 77.81, 77.278

Neville, Elizabeth—see Elizabeth Haynes

Neville, Frances, née Manners, Baroness Abergavenny (c.1537–1576) Daughter of Thomas Manners and Eleanor Paston; sister of Gertrude Manners* and Henry Manners*; mar bef 1554 Henry [I] Neville*. GEC, *Peerage*.

Baroness: 59.105, 59.324, 62.76, 62.258, 63.75, 63.247, 64.69, 65.1, 65.168, 67.69, 67.239, 68.68, 68.237, 71.68, 71.238, 75.185, 76.79, 76.274

Neville, Henry [I], Lord Abergavenny (c.1527–1587) Son of George Neville and Mary Stafford; mar 1st bef 1554 Frances Manners (Neville)*, 2nd 1576 Elizabeth Darrell (Neville)*; uncle of Eulalia St Leger*; 2nd cousin once removed to Elizabeth. GEC, *Peerage*.

Lord: 59.69, 59.290, 62.64, 62.245, 63.65, 63.238, 64.54, 65.155, 67.55, 67.225, 68.53, 68.225, 71.51, 71.221, 75.59, 75.167, 76.62, 76.257, 77.65, 77.262, 78.65, 78.266, 79.61, 79.270, 81.57, 81.264, 82.55, 82.255, 82.456, 84.51, 84.250, 85.55, 85.246

Neville, Henry [II], Earl of Westmorland (c.1525–1564) KG 1552. Son of Ralph Neville and Catherine Stafford; mar 1st 1536 Anne Manners, 2nd c.1549 Jane Cholmley, 3rd 1560 Margaret Cholmley; father of Lady Catherine Constable*, Charles Neville*, and Lady Eleanor Neville*. *ODNB*; GEC, *Peerage*.

Earl: 59.011, 59.232, 62.12, 62.193, 63.8, 63.180, 64.8

Neville, Sir Henry [III] (1520–1593) Son of Edward Neville and Eleanor Windsor; mar 1st c.1560 Eleanor Gresham, 2nd c.1573 Eleanor Bacon; father of Henry [IV] Neville*. *ODNB*.

Sundry Gift: 85.414 (Marriage Gift to his son)

Neville, Sir Henry [IV] (1564–1615) MP, Ambassador to France 1599–1601. Son of Sir Henry [III] Neville* and Elizabeth Gresham; mar 1584 Anne Killigrew*; 1st cousin once removed to Mary Neville*. *ODNB*; Hasler.

Sundry Gift: 85.414 (Marriage Gift)

Neville, Jane, née Howard, Countess of Westmorland (1542–1593) Maid of Honour, Lady Jane Howard. Daughter of Henry Howard, Earl of Surrey and Lady Frances Vere (Howard*); sister of Thomas [I] Howard*, Viscount Howard of Bindon, Henry Howard [I]*, and Lady Catherine Berkeley [II]*; mar 1564 Charles Neville, Earl of Westmorland; 2nd cousin of Queen Elizabeth. GEC, *Peerage*.

Maid of Honour: 59.275

Countess: 65.143, 67.42, 67.212

Neville, Lucy, née Somerset (c.1527–1583) Lady Latimer. Daughter of Henry Somerset, Earl of Worcester and Elizabeth Browne (Somerset*), mar 1545 John Neville; mother of Catherine Percy* and Dorothy Cecil*. GEC, *Peerage*; will PCC 16 Rowe.

Baroness: 59.103, 59.322, 77.102, 77.299

Neville, Margaret—see Margaret Manners

Neville, Mary (c.1585–1648) Maid of Honour. Daughter of Edward Neville, Lord Abergavenny and Rachel Lennard; mar c.1608 George Goring, later Earl of Norwich; 1st cousin once removed to Henry [IV] Neville*; related by marriage to Edward Denny*, Douglas Dyve*, and Mary Astley*. Collins, *Peerage*; *ODNB* and Cokayne under husband; PRO E 179/70/115, LC 2/4 (4); *CSPD*.

Maid of Honour: 03.377

Newdigate, Anne—see Anne Seymour

Newdigate, Dorothy—see Dorothy Chamberlain

Newport, Robert (fl.1550s) Gentleman Usher, Sergeant of Pantry. PRO E115, C 4/111/113, C 4/121/96.

Gentleman: 59.209

Newport, William—see William Hatton

Newton, Catherine, née Paston (b.c.1547) Mistress Paston, Mistress Newton, Lady Newton. Gentlewoman of the Bedchamber. Daughter of Thomas Paston and Agnes Leigh; mar 1578 Henry Newton*; mother of Frances Strangeways*; sister-in-law of Frances Brooke*, Jane Newton*, and Francis Newton*. Hasler under husband; Merten.

Gentlewoman: 75.100, 76.141, 76.336, 77.147, 77.344, 78.149, 78.351, 79.151, 79.358, 81.145, 81.351, 82.139, 82.339, 82.605, 84.152, 84.353, 85.147, 85.329, 88.134, 88.318, 89.132, 89.317

Lady: 94.105, 94.289, 97.104, 97.302, 98.103, 98.303, 99.101, 99.294, 00.106, 00.301, 03.105, 03.329

Newton, Francis (d.1572) Chaplain, Dean of Winchester. Son of John Newton and Margaret Poyntz; brother of Frances Brooke*, Jane Newton*, Nazareth Paget*, and Henry Newton*; unmarried. *ODNB*.
   Chaplain: 67.121, 67.291, 68.141, 68.315, 71.146, 71.324
Newton, Frances—see Frances Brooke, Frances Strangeways
Newton, Henry (c.1531–1599) kntd 1592. Son of John Newton and Margaret Poyntz; brother of Frances Brooke*, Jane Newton*, Nazareth Paget*, and Francis Newton*; mar 1578 Catherine Paston (Newton*); father of Frances Strangeways*. Hasler; will PCC 49 Kidd; Collins, *Jewels*.
   Gentleman: 79.187, 79.400, 81.186, 81.400, 82.181, 82.384, 82.574, 84.164, 84.371, 85.170, 85.369, 88.162, 88.353, 89.158, 89.350, 94.120, 94.305
   Knight: 97.127, 97.325, 98.127, 98.327, 99.119, 99.313
Newton, Jane (fl.1570s) Daughter of John Newton and Margaret Poyntz; sister of Frances Brooke*, Henry Newton*, Nazareth Paget*, and Francis Newton*; mar 1st 1570 Hugh Carmichael*, 2nd 1574 James FitzJames. *Visitations, Gloucestershire*.
   Sundry Gift: 71.361 (Marriage Gift)
Newton, Nazareth—see Nazareth Paget
Nicholson, Peter (d.c.1568) Royal Glazier, from Flanders, served under Henry VIII and Elizabeth. Possible son or relative of James Nicholson. Hicks; *LP Henry VIII, 1540*.
   Gentleman: 59.189, 59.414
Nicolai, Johannes (fl.1590s) Envoy from Duke Charles, later Charles IX*, King of Sweden, also called Jehan Nicolay. *CSP Foreign, 1585–86*.
   Sundry Gift: 99.415 (Gift to Envoy)
Nicolay, Jehan—see Johannes Nicolai
Nightingale, Richard (fl.1590s–1600s) Yeoman of the Post, Groom of the Robes, Yeoman of the Robes. Arnold, *QE Wardrobe*; PRO LC 5/49, 84, C 142/266/83; BL Egerton MS 2806.
   Free Gift: 99.407, 00.410
Ninsonan, Monsieur de (fl.1570s) Gentleman with Nicholas Martel*, Monsieur de Bacqueville from the Duke of Anjou*, with Monsieur de Saverne* and Monsieur de Torsac*. Nichols, *Progresses*; Dovey.
   Sundry Gift: 79.449 (Gift to Envoy)
Noailles, Gilles de (1524–1600) Ambassador from Henry III* of France, Monsieur de la Porte. *CSP Foreign, 1575–77*.
   Sundry Gift: 76.423, 77.417 (Gift to Envoy)
Nocle, Beauvoir la—see Fin, Prégent de la
Noel, Henry (1553–1597) Courtier poet. Son of Andrew Noel and Elizabeth Hopton; brother of Andrew Noel; unmarried. *ODNB*; Hasler; May, *Elizabethan Courtier*; BL Harleian MS 4698, BL Sloane MS 814.
   Gentleman: 84.174, 84.372
Norfolk, Duke/Duchess—see Margaret Howard, née Audley, 1558–1564; Thomas Howard, 4th, 1554–1572
Norreys—see Norris
Norris, Lord/Baroness—see Francis Norris, 2nd, 1601–1623; Henry Norris, 1st, 1572–1601; Margery Norris, née Williams, 1572–1599
Norris, Catherine—see Catherine Paulet
Norris, Elizabeth—see Elizabeth Clinton
Norris, Francis (1579–1623) Lord Norris of Rycote, later Earl of Berkshire. Son of William [I] Norris* and Elizabeth Morrison*; grandson of Henry, Lord Norris* and Margery Williams*; mar c.1599 Lady Bridget Vere. GEC, *Peerage*; *ODNB*; BL Additional MS 5751A.

Lord: 03.65, 03.278

Sundry Gift: 79.437 (Christening Gift)

Norris, Henry (1525–1601) Lord Norris of Rycote, Ambassador to France. Son of Henry Norris and Mary Fiennes; mar c.1544 Margery Williams*; father of William [I] Norris*, John Norris*, Catherine Paulet*, Henry Norris*, and Maximilian Norris*; grandfather of Francis Norris* and Elizabeth Paulet*. GEC, *Peerage*; *ODNB*; Hasler; will PCC 51 Woodhall.

    Lord: 75.72, 75.180, 76.75, 76.272, 77.75, 77.272, 78.74, 78.276, 79.72, 79.279, 81.69, 81.276, 82.65, 82.265, 82.465, 84.60, 84.263, 85.63, 85.254, 88.63, 88.248, 89.57, 89.242, 94.60, 94.244, 97.61, 97.264, 98.60, 98.264, 99.56, 99.254, 00.63, 00.262

    Sundry Gift: 68.349 (Christening Gift for his child)

Norris, John (1547–1597) Son of Henry Norris* and Margery Williams Norris*, brother of Henry Norris, William [I] Norris*, Francis Norris*, Thomas Norris, Edward Norris, Maximilian Norris*, and Catherine Norris*, unmarried. *ODNB*; Nolan.

    Gentleman: 85.162, 85.360

Norris, Margery, née Williams, Baroness Norris of Rycote (d.1599) Lady Norris. Daughter of John Williams* and Elizabeth Bletsoe; mar 1544 Henry, Lord Norris*; mother of William [I] Norris*, John Norris*, Maximilian Norris*, and Catherine Paulet* grand-mother of Francis Norris* and Elizabeth Paulet*. GEC, *Peerage*; will PCC 51 Woodhall; BL Sloane MS 4108; Strangford.

    Lady: 68.96, 68.265

    Baroness: 71.96, 71.266, 76.86, 76.291, 77.97, 77.294, 78.88, 78.297, 79.93, 79.300, 81.87, 81.294, 82.83, 82.283, 82.503, 84.80, 84.278, 85.82, 85.274, 88.87, 88.272, 89.79, 89.265, 94.79, 94.264, 97.88, 97.288, 98.86, 98.288, 99.81, 99.279

    Sundry Gift: 68.349 (Christening Gift for her child)

Norris, Maximilian (1567–1591) Son of Henry Norris* and Margery Williams Norris*, brother of William [I] Norris*, Thomas Norris, Henry Norris, Catherine Norris*, John Norris*, and Edward Norris, unmarried. *ODNB* under father and brother. Nolan.

    Sundry Gift: 68.349 (Christening Gift)

Norris, William [I] (c.1545–1579) Son of Henry, Lord Norris* and Margery Williams Norris*; brother of John Norris*, Henry Norris*, Catherine Norris*, and Maximilian Norris*; mar c.1577 Elizabeth Morrison*; father of Francis Norris*. Hasler; GEC, *Peerage*; *ODNB*.

    Sundry Gift: 79.437 (Christening Gift for his child)

Norris, William [II] (fl.1570s) Servant of the Countess of Lincoln. Related to Henry, Lord Norris*.

    Custody of Gift: 76.98

North, Lord—see Edward North, 1st, 1554–1564; Roger North, 2nd, 1564–1600

North, Edward, Lord North (1496–1564) Son of Roger North and Christina Warcop; mar 1st c.1528 Alice Squire, 2nd c.1561 Margaret Butler; father of Roger, Lord North*. GEC, *Peerage*.

    Lord: 59.63, 59.284, 62.56, 62.237, 63.57, 63.230, 64.65

North, Roger, Lord North (1531–1600) Treasurer of the Household 1596, Privy Councillor 1596, Knight of the Bath 1559. Son of Edward North* and Alice Squire; mar c.1550 Winifred Rich; brother-in-law of Robert [I] Rich* and John Darcy*. GEC, *Peerage*; *ODNB*; BL Stowe MS 774.

    Gentleman: 59.156, 59.381

    Knight: 62.122, 62.301, 63.118, 63.291, 64.111, 64.165

    Lord: 67.66, 67.236, 71.63, 71.233, 75.68, 75.176, 76.70, 76.262, 77.71, 77.268, 78.68, 78.272, 79.68, 79.275, 81.65, 81.272, 82.61, 82.261, 82.457, 84.58, 84.255, 85.61, 85.252,

88.68, 88.252, 89.62, 89.247, 94.56, 94.240, 97.62, 97.258, 98.58, 98.259, 99.54, 99.249, 00.62, 00.259

Northampton, Marquess/Lady Marquess—see Helena Parr, née Snakenborg, later Gorges 1571–1635; Elizabeth Parr, 1548–1565, née Brooke; William Parr, 1547–1552, 1559–1571

Northampton, Earl—see William Compton, 1618–1630; Henry Howard, 1604–1614

Northumberland, Earl/Countess—see Anne Percy, née 1558–1572; Catherine Percy, née Neville, 1572–1585, dowager 1585–1596; Dorothy Percy, née Devereux, 1594–1619; Henry [I] Percy, 8th, 1572–1585; Henry [II] Percy, 9th, 1585–1632; Thomas Percy, 7th, 1557–1572

Norton, Anne (b.c.1578) Gentlewoman of the Privy Chamber. Daughter of Thomas Norton and Alice Cranmer; great-niece of Archbishop Thomas Cranmer, sister of Elizabeth Norton*; mar 1st c.1596 George Coppyn. *ODNB* under father; Hasler under husband.
Gentlewoman: 94.132, 94.324
Custody of Gift: 94.86

Norton, Elizabeth (b.c.1577) Gentlewoman of the Privy Chamber. Daughter of Thomas Norton and Alice Cranmer; great-niece of Archbishop Thomas Cranmer, sister of Anne Norton*; mar 1st c.1600 Miles Rainsford, 2nd c.1604 Simon Bassell. *ODNB* under father.
Gentlewoman: 98.155, 98.363, 99.149, 99.350, 00.150, 00.355, 03.145, 03.357
Custody of Gift: 98.191, 99.88, 99.190, 00.150, 03.97

Norwich, Bishop—see Richard Cox, 1559; John Parkhurst, 1560–1575; Edmund Freake, 1575–1584; Edmund Scambler, 1585–1595; William Redman, 1595–1602

Norwich, Elizabeth—see Elizabeth Carew

Nott, Elizabeth, née Smith (d.1587) Mistress Nott, Gentlewoman of the Privy Chamber. Daughter of unidentified Smith, mar William Nott. will PCC 36 Spencer; husband's will PCC 40 Carew, 22 Bakon.
Gentlewoman: 75.111, 76.162, 76.357, 77.161, 77.358, 78.162, 78.364, 79.164, 79.371, 81.158, 81.364, 82.154, 82.354, 82.602, 84.150, 84.347, 85.146, 85.341

Nottingham, Earl/Countess—see Catherine [I] Howard, née 1597–1603; Charles Howard, 1st, 1597–1624

O'Brien, Elizabeth—see Elizabeth FitzGerald

O'Connor Sligo, Sir Donald, Sir (fl.1560s) Irish knight. Mar Eleanor Butler who was widow of Gerald FitzJames, Earl of Desmond. O'Connor; GEC, *Peerage* under wife's first husband.
Sundry Gift: 68.351 (Gift on his visit to England)

Odell, Mary—see Mary Seymour

Odonerle—see O'Donnell

O'Donnell, Calvagh (d.1566) Lord O'Donnell, Irish Chieftain called Chief of Tyrconnell, Lord Odonerle. GEC, *Peerage*; *CSP Ireland,1571–75* ; HMC D'Lisle.
Sundry Gift: 62.384 (The patent for this Earldom was never recorded, but the collar and coronet of the appointment were delivered.)

Oglethorpe, Owen (1510–1559) Bishop of Carlisle 1556–1559 (deprived). Will PCC 29 Mellershe; *ODNB*.
Bishop: 59.34, 59.256

Oldham, unidentified (fl.1580s) Groom, Queen's servant.
Custody of Gift: 82.359

O'Neill, Brian McPhelim (1540–1575) alias Brian Mack Folemy, a Captain of Ireland. Son of Phelim Baccach O'Neil, father of Shane McBrian O'Neill. *CSP Domestic, 1547–80*; *CSP Ireland, 1509–1573*.
  Sundry Gift: 71.364 (Gift on visit to England)
Oraily—see O'Reilly
O'Reilly, Malachias (d.1565) Irish Chieftain called Chief of O'Reilly, Lord Oraily. GEC, *Peerage*; *CSP Ireland, 1509–73*; HMC D'Lisle.
  Sundry Gift: 62.383 (The patent for this Earldom was never recorded, but the collar and coronet of the appointment were delivered.)
Ormond, Earl/Countess—see Thomas Butler, 10th, 1546–1614; Elizabeth Butler, née Sheffield, 1582–1600
Othomer, Mistress (fl.1580s) of Coventry. unidentified, possible connection with Earls of Leicester or Warwick; gift includes ragged staff motif. Variant spelling of Assoner*
  Gentlewoman: 81.164, 81.370
Oursiau, Nicholas—see Urseau, Nicholas
Over, Mistress (fl.1580s) unidentified.
  Gentlewoman: 88.148, 88.333, 89.145, 89.330
Overton, William (1525–1609) Bishop of Lichfield and Coventry 1580–1609. Son-in-law of William Barlow*; brother-in-law of Tobie Matthew*, Herbert Westfaling*, William Day*, and William Wickham*. *ODNB*.
  Bishop: 81.50, 81.263, 82.48, 82.253, 82.443, 84.48, 84.246, 85.52, 85.242, 88.231, 89.41, 89.226, 94.42, 94.225, 97.47, 97.245, 98.45, 98.247, 99.39, 99.236, 00.51, 00.246, 03.53, 03.266
Owen, unidentified (fl.1580s) Groom, Queen's servant.
  Custody of Gift: 82.369
Oxford, Bishop—does not participant in any extant New Year's gift exchange
Oxford, Earl/Countess—see Anne Vere, née Cecil, 1571–1588; Edward de Vere, 17th, 1562–1604; Elizabeth Vere, née Trentham, 1591–1613; John de Vere, 16th, 1540–1562; Margery Vere, née Golding, 1548–1568
P, J (fl.1550–1570s) London Goldsmith, possible identity: John Penford or John Pikening. Jackson.
  Goldsmith: 75.164
Paddy, Sir William (1554–1634) Royal Physician, kntd 1603. *ODNB*.
  Gentleman: 03.173, 03.394
Pagano—see Elizabeth de Tedeschi, Lucretia de Conti
Page, John (d.1597) Yeoman of the Scullery. Collins, *Jewels*; PRO E 315/1954, PROB 11/89; will PCC 16 Cobham.
  Custody of Gift: 82.285 (delivered to himself)
Page, unidentified (fl.1580's) Harbinger, Queen's servant.
  Custody of Gift: 82.270
Paget, Earl/Baroness—see Anne Paget, née Preston, 1549–1587; Catherine Paget, née Knyvett, 1567–1622; Nazareth Paget, née Newton, 1571–1583; Henry Paget, 2nd, 1563–1568; Thomas Paget, 4th, 1570–1590; William Paget, 1st, 1549–1563
Paget, Anne, Baroness Paget (d.1587) Lady Paget. Daughter of Henry Preston; mar c.1534 William, Lord Paget*; mother of Henry Paget* and Thomas Paget*. ODNB under husband; GEC, *Peerage*; PCC 32 Rutland.
  Baroness: 59.76, 59.296, 62.74, 62.255, 63.72, 63.248
Paget, Catherine, Baroness Paget (c.1547–1622) Maid of Honour, alias Baroness Paget Carey, Lady of the Privy Chamber. Daughter of Henry Knyvett and Anne Pickering;

sister of Thomas Knyvett*; aunt of Catherine Knyvett* and Anne [I] Vavasour*; 2nd cousin once removed to Queen Elizabeth; mar 1st 1567 Henry, Lord Paget*, 2nd 1575 Sir Edward Carey*. GEC, *Peerage*; BL Sloane MS 814.

Maid of Honour: 62.334, 63.318, 64.185, 67.319

Baroness: 68.77, 68.243, 71.77, 71.247, 75.195, 76.84, 76.280, 77.92, 77.289, 78.96, 78.292, 79.88, 79.295, 81.83, 81.291, 82.78, 82.279, 82.499, 84.75, 84.273, 85.78, 85.269, 88.80, 88.265, 89.73, 89.258, 94.67, 94.251, 97.75, 97.273, 98.73, 98.274, 99.69, 99.264, 00.76, 00.273, 03.77, 03.291

Paget, Henry, Lord Paget (1537–1568) Son of William, Lord Paget* and Anne Preston*; brother of Thomas Paget*; mar 1567 Catherine Knyvett*. Hasler; GEC, *Peerage*; will PCC 11 Sheffield.

Lord: 64.63, 67.67, 67.237, 68.64, 68.232

Paget, Nazareth (d.1583) Gentlewoman of the Bedchamber, Mistress Newton, Mistress Southwell, Baroness Paget. Daughter of John Newton and Margaret Poyntz; sister of Henry Newton*, Frances Brooke*, Jane Newton*, and Francis Newton*; mar 1st 1565 Thomas Southwell*, 2nd 1571 Thomas, Lord Paget*; mother of Elizabeth [I] Southwell*. *ODNB* and GEC, *Peerage* under 2nd husband; PRO LC 5/49; BL Sloane MS 814.

Gentlewoman: 65.62, 65.228, 67.131, 67.301, 71.124, 71.294

Baroness: 75.197, 76.93, 76.281, 77.93, 77.290, 78.95, 78.291, 79.87, 79.294

Sundry Gift: 68.350 (Christening Gift for her child)

Paget, Thomas, Lord Paget (1544–1590) Son of William Paget* and Anne Preston (Paget*); brother of Henry Paget*; mar 1571 Nazareth Newton (Paget*). *ODNB*; GEC, *Peerage*.

Lord: 71.64, 71.234, 75.69, 75.177, 76.72, 76.265, 77.72, 77.269, 78.71, 78.273, 79.69, 79.276, 81.66, 81.273, 82.62, 82.262, 82.461

Paget, William, Lord Paget (1506–1563) KG 1547. Son of William Paget; mar c.1534 Anne Preston (Paget*); father of Henry Paget* and Thomas Paget*. *ODNB*; GEC, *Peerage*.

Lord: 59.54, 59.275, 62.53, 62.234, 63.54, 63.228

Pakington, John (1549–1625) kntd 1587. Son of Thomas Pakington and Dorothy Kitson; grandson of Margaret Bourchier*; brother of Margaret Lichfield*; 2nd cousin of John Scudamore*; mar 1598 Dorothy Smith. *ODNB*.

Knight: 81.174, 81.391, 82.170, 82.376, 82.579

Pakington, Margaret—see Margaret Lichfield

Palavicino, Anna, née Hooftman (d.1626) Lady Palavicino. Daughter of Gieles van Eychelberg, alias Hooftman; mar 1st 1591 Horatio Palavicino*, 2nd 1601 Sir Oliver Cromwell MP uncle of the Protector. *ODNB* and Hasler under husband; Siddons; Stone.

Lady: 94.109, 94.293, 97.113, 97.313, 98.114, 98.314, 99.110, 99.305

Palavicino, Horatio (c.1540–1600) Merchant, Special Ambassador, kntd 1587. Son of Tobias Palavicino and Bettina Spinola; related to Benedict Spinola*; mar 1st unidentified, 2nd 1591 Anna Eychelber (Hooftman*). *ODNB*; Stone; will PCC 64 Wallop; Siddons.

Knight: 89.121, 89.307, 94.125, 94.308, 97.130, 97.327, 98.134, 98.330, 99.128, 99.325

Pallat—see Paulet

Pamplyn, Robert (fl.1570s–1600s) Gentleman of the Chamber, Yeoman of the Robes, Brusher of the Robes. Arnold, *QE Wardrobe*; PRO LC 5/34–37; BL Egerton MS 2806.

Free Gift: 03.442

'Pantables, my skimskin for my'—see Robert Sidney

Paris, Thomasine de—see Thomasine de Paris

Parker, Edward, Lord Morley (1550–1618) Son of Henry Parker, Lord Morley and Elizabeth Stanley; mar 1ˢᵗ c.1574 Elizabeth Stanley (Parker*), 2ⁿᵈ Gertrude Denis; father of Mary Parker*. *ODNB*; GEC, *Peerage*.
   Lord: 79.75, 79.283
   Sundry Gift: 81.437 (Christening Gift for his child).
Parker, Elizabeth, née Stanley, Baroness Morley (c.1556–1585) Baroness Monteagle *de jure*. Daughter of William Stanley, Lord Monteagle and Anne Leybourne; mar c.1574 Edward Parker*, Lord Morley; mother of Mary Parker*. GEC, *Peerage*.
   Baroness: 79.96, 79.303, 81.90, 81.297, 82.86, 82.286, 82.519, 84.81, 84.279, 85.83, 85.275
   Sundry Gift: 81.437 (Christening Gift for her child)
Parker, John (fl.1580s) Page, Yeoman of the Chamber, Sergeant of the Bears. *CSP Domestic, 1603*.
   Gentleman: 82.199, 82.403
   Custody of Gift: 82.199, 82.344, 82.403
Parker, Mary (1580-aft.1656) Daughter of Edward Parker*, Lord Morley and Elizabeth Stanley (Parker*); goddaughter of Queen Elizabeth; mar c.1595 Thomas Habington. *ODNB* under husband.
   Sundry Gift: 81.437 (Christening Gift)
Parker, Matthew (1504–1575) Archbishop of Canterbury, 1559–1575. *ODNB*; White, *Lives*.
   Bishop: 62.17, 62.197, 63.16, 63.188, 64.16, 65.117, 67.17, 67.187, 68.32, 68.201, 71.32, 71.202, 75.40, 75.148
Parkhurst, John (1511–1575) Bishop of Norwich 1560–1575. *ODNB*; will PCC 10 Daughtry.
   Bishop: 62.27, 62.207, 63.26, 63.198, 64.24, 65.126, 67.26, 67.196, 68.41, 68.210, 71.40, 71.210
Parr, Elizabeth, née Brooke, Lady Marquess of Northampton (1526–1565) Daughter of Sir George Brooke and Anne Bray; sister of William [I] Brooke*, Lord Cobham, and Sir Henry Cobham*; sister-in-law of Frances Brooke*; mar 1547 William Parr*, Marquess of Northampton. GEC, *Peerage*; *ODNB* under husband.
   Lady Marquess: 59.39, 59.260, 63.39, 63.211, 64.39, 65.139
   Custody of Gift: 64.231
Parr, Helena—see Helena Gorges
Parr, William, Marquess of Northampton (1513–1571) Privy Councillor, KG 1543, degraded 1553, re-elected 1559. Son of Thomas Parr and Maude Greene; brother of Catherine Parr; mar 1ˢᵗ 1526 Anne Bourchier, 2ⁿᵈ 1547 Elizabeth Brooke (Parr*), 3ʳᵈ 1571 Helena Snakenburg (Gorges*). *ODNB*; GEC, *Peerage*.
   Primary: 59.6, 59.227, 67.5, 67.175, 68.6, 68.175, 71.5, 71.174
   Marquess: 62.4, 62.183, 63.4, 63.176, 64.4, 65.104
Parry, Anne, née Read (d.1585) Lady Parry, Lady of the Privy Chamber. Daughter of William Read; mar 1ˢᵗ Giles Greville, 2ⁿᵈ Adrian Fortescue, 3ʳᵈ c. 1540 Thomas Parry*; mother-in-law of Thomas Bromley* and Dorothy Brooke*.
   Lady: 59.99, 59.318, 65.24, 65.191
Parry, Blanche (c.1507–1590) Chief Gentlewoman of the Privy Chamber, Keeper of the Queen's Jewels, served in household of Princess Elizabeth. Daughter of Henry Parry and Alice Milbourne; unmarried; aunt of Margaret Hawkins* and Frances Burgh*. *ODNB*; will PCC 16 Drury 1590; Bradford, *Blanche Parry*; Richardson; BL Sloane MS 814, MS Royal AP 68.

Gentlewoman: 59.148, 59.357, 62.132, 62.312, 63.125, 63.298, 64.117, 64.171, 65.54, 65.221, 67.122, 67.292, 68.119, 68.288, 71.119, 71.289, 75.86, 76.133, 76.328, 77.136, 77.333, 78.141, 78.342, 79.142, 79.349, 81.136, 81.343, 82.130, 82.330, 82.590, 84.128, 84.324, 85.123, 85.314, 88.126, 88.310, 89.124, 89.309

Regifted: 71.322 (Queen gave gift from her to Elizabeth Brooke*)

Custody of Gift: 59.102, 59.145–147, 59.172–173, 59.179, 59.191, 59.193, 59.197–199, 59.207–208, 59.219, 62.120, 62.124–125, 62.144, 62.149, 62.160, 62.165, 63.104, 63.135, 63.155, 63.169, 63.171–172, 64.25, 64.138, 64.145, 65.34, 65.42, 65.85, 65.88–92, 67.14, 67.51, 67.68, 67.86, 67.98, 67.114–115, 67.118, 67.147, 67.159–160, 68.15–16, 68.20, 68.29–30, 68.67, 68.113, 68.115, 68.117–119, 68.133, 68.135, 68.137, 68.143, 68.145–146, 68.152–153, 68.161, 68.164, 68.166, 71.11, 71.23–24, 71.61, 71.66, 71.87, 71.114, 71.116, 71.138, 71.140, 71.147, 71.151–153, 71.155, 75.83, 75.101, 75.120, 76.132, 77.133, 77.164, 77.181, 78.136, 78.165, 78.197, 79.167, 79.183, 79.207, 81.200, 81.206, 82.145, 82.177, 82.196, 84.116, 84.125, 84.175, 84.176, 84.189, 84.194, 84.197–198, 85.16, 85.122, 85.179, 85.185, 85.189

Parry, Dorothy—see Dorothy Brooke

Parry, Thomas (c.1510–1560) Cofferer to Princess Elizabeth, Treasurer of the Household 1558, Comptroller, Privy Councillor, Master of the Court of Wards, kntd 1558, MP. Son of Henry Vaughan and Gwenlian ap Grene; mar c.1540 Anne Read (Parry*); step-father of John Fortescue*, father-in-law of Dorothy Brooke*. *ODNB*; Hasler.
>   **Knight**: 59.109, 59.328

Partridge, Affabel (fl.1500s-fl.1590s) Royal Goldsmith, alias 'P' or 'Par'. Sitwell.
>   **Gentleman**: 59.201, 59.425
>   **Goldsmith**: *passim* 1559–1576

Paston, Catherine—see Catherine Newton

Patch the fool (fl.1530s) Nicholas Belin* gave picture of Patch, Henry VIII's fool, as gift. Farrer.
>   **Gentleman**: 62.177

Pates, Richard (c.1504–1565) Bishop of Worcester 1555–1559. *ODNB*.
>   **Bishop**: 59.29, 59.250

Paulet, Sir Amias (c.1533–1588) Ambassador to France 1576–1579, Privy Councillor 1585, Keeper of Mary, Queen of Scots, Chancellor of the Garter, kntd 1575. Son of Hugh Paulet and Phillipa Pollard; mar 1555 Margaret Harvey; father of Elizabeth Paulet*. *ODNB*; Hasler; will PCC 27 Leicester.
>   **Knight**: 79.140, 79.347
>   **Sundry Gift**: 77.419 (Mentioned in gift to Arthur Throckmorton* upon their departure for France)

Paulet, Anne, née Howard, Lady Marquess of Winchester (c.1542–1601) Daughter of William Howard* and Catherine Broughton; half-sister of Charles Howard*, Catherine [II] Howard*, Mary Sutton*, Douglas Sheffield*, Martha Howard*, and Frances [I] Howard*; mar by 1548 William [II] Paulet*, Marquess of Winchester; 1st cousin once removed to Queen Elizabeth. GEC, *Peerage*; *ODNB* under husband.
>   **Lady Marquess**: 78.27, 78.228, 00.18, 00.215

Paulet, Anthony (1562–1600) Governor of Jersey. Son of Sir Amias Paulet* and Margaret Harvey; mar 1583 Catherine Norris (Paulet*); father of Elizabeth [II] Paulet*. Scribal error of Sir Amias for Anthony. *ODNB*; PRO E 351/542.
>   **Sundry Gift**: 85.417 (Christening Gift for his child)

Paulet, Catherine, née Norris (c.1560–1602) Mistress Paulet. Daughter of Henry, Lord Norris* and Margery Norris (Williams*); mar 1583 Anthony Paulet*; mother of Elizabeth [II] Paulet*. *ODNB*.

Sundry Gift: 85.417 (Christening Gift for her child)

Paulet, Elizabeth [I], née Blount (c.1517–1593) Lady Paulet. Daughter of Walter Blount and Margaret Sutton; mar 1ˢᵗ Anthony Beresford, 2ⁿᵈ 1541 Sir Thomas Pope, 3rd 1560 Sir Hugh Paulet. *ODNB* under husbands; will PCC 15 Dixy.

    Lady: 62.93, 62.274, 63.90, 63.266, 64.90, 65.21, 65.188, 67.82, 67.252, 68.87, 68.256, 71.85, 71.255, 76.110, 76.305, 77.111, 77.308, 78.107, 78.311, 79.108, 79.316, 81.105, 81.311, 82.100, 82.299, 82.543, 84.95, 84.293, 85.100, 85.293, 88.103, 88.287, 89.95, 89.280

Paulet, Elizabeth [II] (b.1584) Daughter of Anthony Paulet* and Catherine Norris (Paulet*); granddaughter of Henry, Lord Norris* and Margery Norris (Williams*). Scribal error of Sir Amias for Anthony. PRO E 351/542.

    Sundry Gift: 85.417 (Christening Gift)

Paulet, John, Marquess of Winchester (c.1510–1576) Lord St John, kntd 1544. Son of William [I] Paulet* and Elizabeth Capel; mar 1ˢᵗ c.1528 Elizabeth Willoughby, 2ⁿᵈ 1554 Elizabeth Seymour, 3ʳᵈ 1568 Winifred Brydges (Paulet*); father of William [II] Paulet* and Mary Cromwell*. GEC, *Peerage*; will PCC 48 Daughtry.

    Primary: 75.4, 76.5, 76.200

Paulet, Lucy, née Cecil, Lady St John (1568–1614) Lady Marquess of Winchester. Daughter of Thomas Cecil* and Dorothy Neville (Cecil*); granddaughter of William Cecil* and Mildred Cooke (Cecil*) and of John Neville and Lucy Somerset (Neville*); mar 1587 William [III] Paulet*; mother of William [IV] Paulet*. GEC, *Peerage*.

    Sundry Gift: 88.403 (Christening Gift for her child)

Paulet, Mary—see Mary Cromwell

Paulet, William [I], Marquess of Winchester (c.1475–1572) Lord St John, Privy Councillor 1542, Lord Treasurer of England, kntd 1525, KG 1543. Son of John Paulet and Alice Paulet; mar c.1509 Elizabeth Capel; father of John Paulet*. *ODNB*; GEC, *Peerage*; will PCC 12 Pickering.

    Primary: 59.5, 59.226, 62.3, 62.183, 63.5, 63.176, 64.5, 65.103, 67.4, 67.174, 68.5, 68.174, 71.4, 71.173

Paulet, William [II], Marquess of Winchester (1532–1598) Lord St John, KB 1553. Son of John Paulet* and Elizabeth Willoughby; brother of Mary Cromwell*; mar c.1548 Anne/Agnes Howard (Paulet*); father of William [III] Paulet*. *ODNB*; GEC, *Peerage*; Hasler.

    Primary: 77.6, 77.203, 78.6, 78.207, 79.4, 79.211, 81.3, 81.210, 82.4, 82.204, 82.421, 84.3, 84.201, 85.3, 85.194, 88.3, 88.188, 89.3, 89.188, 94.3, 94.187, 97.3, 97.203, 98.3, 98.204

Paulet, William [III], Marquess of Winchester (1550–1629) Lord St John. Son of William [II] Paulet* and Anne/Agnes Howard (Paulet*), mar 1587 Lucy Cecil (Paulet*), father of William [IV] Paulet*. GEC, *Peerage*.

    Primary: 00.03, 00.200, 03.3, 03.216

    Sundry Gift: 88.403 (Christening Gift for his child)

Paulet, William [IV] (1588–1621) Lord St John. Son of William [III] Paulet* and Lucy Cecil (Paulet*); mar 1615 Mary Browne. GEC, *Peerage*.

    Sundry Gift: 88.403 (Christening Gift)

Paulet, Winifred, née Brydges, Lady Marquess of Winchester (d.1586) Lady Sackville. Daughter of Sir John Brydges and Agnes Ayloffe; mar 1ˢᵗ c.1536 Sir Richard Sackville*, 2ⁿᵈ c.1568 John Paulet*, Marquess of Winchester. *ODNB*; GEC, *Peerage*; will PCC 32 Windsor.

Lady: 62.98, 62.278, 63.95, 63.265, 64.89, 65.20, 65.187, 67.81, 67.251, 68.86, 68.255, **Lady Marquess**: 75.22, 76.24, 76.219, 77.29, 77.226, 78.27, 78.227, 79.25, 79.233, 81.22, 81.229, 82.22, 82.222, 82.475, 84.21, 84.219, 85.21, 85.212

Payne, Anne, née Monmouth (fl.1550s) Mistress Payne. Daughter of John Monmouth and Alice Stalbrook; mar William Payne. *Visitations, Essex*; husband's will PCC 20 Sheffeld; PRO E 101/483/12, C 1/389/35, C 241/281/118.
  Gentlewoman: 59.140, 59.367

Peacock, Anthony Maria (fl.1550s) Musician, Sackbut. *BDECM*.
  Gentleman: 59.178, 59.402

Peacock, Devise (fl.1550s) Musician, Sackbut. *BDECM*.
  Gentleman: 59.178, 59.402

Peacock, Edward (fl.1550s) Musician, Sackbut. *BDECM*.
  Gentleman: 59.178, 59.402

Peacock, John (d.1565) Musician, Sackbut. *BDECM*.
  Gentleman: 59.178, 59.402

Peckham, Sir Edmund (c.1495–1564) Treasurer of the Mint, kntd 1542. Mar 1516 Anne Cheney. *ODNB*; will PCC 28 Stevenson.
  Knight: 59.121, 59.340, 62.109, 62.289, 63.107, 63.280, 64.101, 64.155

Pembroke, Earl/Countess—see Anne Herbert, née Talbot, 1552–1588; Catherine Herbert, née Talbot, 1570–1576; Henry Herbert, 2nd, 1570–1601; Mary Herbert, née Sidney, 1577–1621; William [I] Herbert, 1st, 1551–1570; William [II] Herbert, 3rd, 1601–1630

Pennant, Piers (c.1533–1590) Gentleman Usher. PRO E 115, PROB 11/76
  Custody of Gift: 81.441, 82.204

Penne, Lucy, née Chevall (fl.1540s–1600s) Mistress Penne, alias Mistress Barley. Daughter of Edmund Chevall; mar 1st 1545 John Penne; 2nd 1560 Henry Barley. *Visitations, Bedfordshire*; PRO C 4/19/45; *VCH, Hertfordshire*.
  Gentlewoman: 59.139, 59.365, 62.145, 62.325, 63.134, 63.308, 64.124, 64.176, 65.63, 65.229, 67.146, 67.316, 68.140, 68.307, 71.143, 71.313, 75.106, 76.161, 76.358, 77.162, 77.359, 78.163, 78.365, 79.165, 79.372, 81.159, 81.365, 82.155, 82.355, 82.595, 88.151, 88.336, 89.150, 89.333, 94.139, 94.331, 97.150, 97.354, 98.147, 98.355, 00.143, 00.348, 03.151, 03.365

Penne, Sibell, née Hampden (d.1562) Mistress Penne, Nurse to Prince Edward. Daughter of Edmund Hampden and Elizabeth Hampden; aunt by marriage to Anne Hampden*; mar David Penne. *CPR, 1575–78*; *LP Henry VIII, 1540–41*; *Visitations, Buckinghamshire*; *VCH, Middlesex*.
  Gentlewoman: 59.146, 59.362, 62.143, 62.323

Percy, Algernon (1602–1668) Son of Henry [II] Percy*, Earl of Northumberland, and Dorothy Devereux*; brother of Henry [III] Percy*. *ODNB* under father.
  Sundry Gift: 03.447 (Christening Gift)

Percy, Anne, née Somerset, Countess of Northumberland (1538–1591) Daughter of Henry Somerset, Earl of Worcester and Elizabeth Browne (Somerset*); great-aunt of Lady Anne Winter*; mar 1558 Thomas Percy*, Earl of Northumberland. *ODNB*; GEC, *Peerage*.
  Countess: 62.47, 62.227, 63.42, 63.214, 64.42, 65.142, 67.41, 67.211, 68.23, 68.192

Percy, Catherine, née Neville, Countess of Northumberland (c.1545–1596) Daughter of John Neville and Lucy Somerset (Neville*); mar 1st bef 1562 Henry [I] Percy, later Earl of Northumberland, 2nd Francis Fitton; mother of Henry [II] Percy*. GEC, *Peerage*; *ODNB*.
  Countess: 75.33, 75.140, 76.35, 76.230, 77.37, 77.236, 78.38, 78.239, 79.36, 79.243, 81.32, 81.239, 82.32, 82.232, 82.490

Percy, Dorothy, née Devereux, Countess of Northumberland (1564–1619) Lady Perrott, Countess of Northumberland. Daughter of Walter Devereux*, Earl of Essex, and Lettice Knollys (Devereux*); stepdaughter of Robert Dudley*, Earl of Leicester; sister of Penelope Rich* and Robert Devereux*, Earl of Essex; 1st cousin twice removed to Queen Elizabeth; mar 1st 1583 Sir Thomas Perrott, 2nd 1594 Henry [II] Percy*, Earl of Northumberland; mother of Henry [III] Percy* and Algernon Percy*. GEC, *Peerage*; BL Lansdowne MS 39; *ODNB* under husbands.
Countess: 97.38, 97.236, 98.37, 98.235, 99.30, 99.223, 00.37, 00.232, 03.36, 03.249;
Sundry Gift: 97.419 (Christening Gift for her child), 03.447 (Christening Gift for her child)

Percy, Henry [I], Earl of Northumberland (c.1532–1585) Son of Thomas Percy and Eleanor Harbottle; mar c.1562 Catherine [I] Neville*; father of Henry [II] Percy*; brother of Thomas Percy*. GEC, *Peerage*; *ODNB*.
Earl: 75.17, 76.17, 76.212, 77.20, 77.217, 78.18, 78.219, 79.17, 79.224, 81.17, 81.223, 82.17, 82.216, 82.435

Percy, Henry [II], Earl of Northumberland (1564–1632) KG 1593. Son of Henry [I] Percy*, Earl of Northumberland and Catherine [I] Neville*; mar 1594 Dorothy Devereux*; father of Henry [III] Percy* and Algernon Percy*. *ODNB*; GEC, *Peerage*.
Earl: 88.15, 88.199, 89.14, 89.199, 94.11, 94.195, 97.13, 97.210, 98.13, 98.213, 99.12, 99.204, 00.12, 00.209, 03.12, 03.225
Sundry Gift: 97.419, 03.447 (Christening Gifts for his children)

Percy, Henry [III] (1596–1597) Son of Henry [II] Percy* and Dorothy Devereux (Percy*); brother of Algernon Percy*. *ODNB* under father.
Sundry Gift: 97.419 (Christening Gift)

Percy, Thomas, Earl of Northumberland (1528–1572) KG 1563. Son of Thomas Percy and Elizabeth Harbottle; brother of Henry [I] Percy*; mar 1558 Anne Somerset (Percy*). *ODNB*; GEC, *Peerage*.
Earl: 59.19, 59.240, 62.14, 62.195, 63.7, 63.179, 64.7, 65.106, 67.6, 67.176, 68.9, 68.178

Perrenot, Frederic (1536–c.1601) Sieur de Champagny, Governor of Antwerp. brother of Cardinal Granvelle. Perrenot.
Sundry Gift: 76.425 (Gift from Queen in March 1576)

Perrott, Sir John (1527–1592) Lord Deputy of Ireland, Privy Councillor 1589, kntd 1549. Son of Thomas Perrott and Mary Berkeley; mar 1st Anne Cheney, 2nd Jane Prust; father of Thomas Perrott; father-in-law of Dorothy Devereux (Percy*). *ODNB*; Collins, *Jewels*.
Knight: 89.120, 89.305

Peterborough, Bishop—see David Pole, 1557–1559; Edmund Scambler, 1561–1585; Richard Howland, 1585–1600; Thomas Dove, 1601–1630

Petre, Lady Catherine, née Somerset (1574–1624) Maid of Honour, Lady Petre. Daughter of Edward Somerset*, Earl of Worcester and Elizabeth Hastings (Somerset*); sister of Lady Anne Winter* and Lady Elizabeth Guildford*; mar 1596 William Petre; mother of Elizabeth Petre*.
Lady: 03.113, 03.316
Sundry Gift: 98.428 (Christening Gift for her child)

Petre, Elizabeth (b.1597) daughter of William Petre* and Lady Catherine Somerset (Petre*).
Sundry Gift: 98.428 (Christening Gift)

Petre, Sir William (1506–1572) Chancellor of the Order of the Garter, Privy Councillor, kntd 1544, MP. Son of John Petre and Anne Colling; mar 1st c.1533 Gertrude Tyrrell,

2nd 1542 Anne Browne; grandfather of William Petre*; great-grandfather of Elizabeth Petre*. *ODNB*; Hasler.

Knight: 59.112, 59.331, 62.107, 62.287, 63.105, 63.278, 64.99, 64.153, 65.35, 65.202, 67.103, 67.273, 68.102, 68.271, 71.102, 71.272

Petre, William (1575–1637) Son of John Petre and Mary Waldegrave; mar Lady Catherine Somerset (Petre*); father of Elizabeth Petre*.

Sundry Gift: 98.428 (Christening Gift for his child)

Petruccio—see Petruccio Ubaldini

Phaer, Thomas (c.1510–1560) Lawyer, Physician, Poet, Translator. *ODNB*; Hasler; Bindoff; will PCC 23 Loftes.

Gentleman: 59.190, 59.415

Phenotus, Anthonias—see Anthony Fenotus

Philip II (1527–1598) King of Spain, KG 1554. Son of Charles V and Isabella of Portugal, half-brother of Don John* of Austria and Margaret* Duchess of Parma, brother-in-law of Queen Elizabeth; mar 1st Maria Manuela of Portugal, 2nd Mary I of England, 3rd Elizabeth of Valois, 4th Anna of Austria. Gift to his envoy Bernardino de Mendoza*.

Sundry Gift: 75.250 (Sovereign sending Envoy to England)

Pickering, Hester—see Hester Wotton

Pickering, Sir William (1516–1575) kntd 1547, MP. Son of William Pickering and Eleanor Fairfax; unmarried; father of Hester Wotton*; father-in-law of Edward Wotton*. *ODNB*; Bindoff; will PCC 1 Pickering.

Knight: 67.114, 67.284, 68.116, 68.285, 71.115, 71.285

Pierce, Stephen (fl.1600s) Keeper of Standing Wardrobe at Richmond.

Custody of Gift: 00.99

Pierce, Walter (d.1604) Musician, Lute Player. *RECM*; *BDECM*.

Gentleman: 00.192, 00.387, 03.190, 03.412

Piers, John (1523–1594) Almoner, Bishop of Rochester 1576, Bishop of Salisbury 1577–1589, Archbishop of York 1589–1594. *ODNB*.

Bishop: 77.54, 77.259, 78.50, 78.251, 79.48, 79.255, 81.43, 81.249, 82.42, 82.241, 82.446, 84.38, 84.236, 85.41, 85.232, 88.40, 88.225, 89.35, 89.220, 94.34, 94.218

Pigeon, Edmund (d.1573) Yeoman of the Jewels and Plate. Son of John Pigeon and Isabel Webb; mar 1st Alice Bristow, 2nd Joan Fowler; father of John Pigeon* and Nicholas Pigeon*. will PCC 39 Peter; *VCH, Middlesex*.

Free Gift: 59.450, 62.375, 63.359, 64.213, 67.355, 67.363, 68.342, 71.357

Pigeon, John (d.1579) Groom and Yeoman of the Jewels and Plate. Son of Edmund Pigeon* and Joan Fowler; half-brother of Nicholas Pigeon*. will PCC 39, 40 Peter; *VCH, Middlesex*.

Free Gift: 59.451, 62.376, 63.360, 64.214, 67.356, 68.343, 71.358, 75.246, 76.410, 77.412, 78.418, 79.432, 81.431, 82.417, 84.410, 85.402, 88.392, 89.393

Pigeon, Nicholas (d.1619) Groom and Yeoman of the Jewels and Plate. Son of Edmund Pigeon* and Alice Bristow; half-brother of John Pigeon*. Collins, *Jewels*; *VCH, Middlesex*.

Free Gift: 85.404, 88.393, 89.395, 94..390, 97.415, 98.422, 99.409, 00.412, 03.444

Pigott, Francis (fl. 1550s) Master Cook, Queen's servant. PRO E 115, LC 2/4(3).

Gentleman: 59.213, 59.437

Pilkington, James (1520–1576) Bishop of Durham 1561–1576. *ODNB*.

Bishop: 62.19, 62.200, 63.18, 63.190, 64.18, 65.119, 67.19, 67.189, 68.34, 68.203, 71.34, 71.204, 75.42, 75.150, 76.45, 76.240

Pinart, Claude (d.1605) Sieur de Cramailles, French Commissioner for marriage settlement between Elizabeth and the Duke of Anjou*, one of four principal secretaries of state. *CSP Foreign, 1581–82*.
    Sundry Gift: 81.451 (Gift to Envoy)
Pitcairn, Robert (c.1520–1584) Abbot of Dunfermline, Ambassador from James VI* of Scotland. *ODNB*; Chalmers.
    Sundry Gift: 79.450 (Gift to Envoy)
Pitts, James (fl.1600s) Member of the Inner Temple. Mar 1599 Mary Heveningham*.
    Sundry Gift: 00.415 (Marriage Gift)
Plantagenet, Elizabeth—see Elizabeth Jobson
Plasse—see Phillippe du Plessis Mornay
Pole, Catherine—see Catherine Hastings
Pole, David (1505–1568) Bishop of Peterborough 1557–1559. *ODNB*; will PCC 14 Babington.
    Bishop: 59.32, 59.253
Pole, Ursula—see Ursula Stafford
Polsted, Elizabeth—see Elizabeth More
Popham, Sir John (c.1532–1607) Speaker of House of Commons 1581, Attorney General 1581–1592, Lord Chief Justice of the Queen's Bench 1592, kntd 1592, MP. Son of Alexander Popham and Joan Stradling; mar Amy Adams. *ODNB*; Hasler; will PCC 58 Windebanck.
    Knight: 00.118, 00.313, 03.121, 03.335
Port, Dorothy—see Dorothy [I] Hastings
Portall, Beriginer (d.1588) General Portall, Councillor to Henry III* of France, later refugee in England. *CSP Scotland, 1587*; *CSP Foreign, 1585–86*; will PCC 20 Drury.
    Sundry Gift: 77.417 (Gift to Envoy)
Portingale (Portuguese) Ambassador—see Francesco Giraldi
Pound, Honor—see Honor Radcliffe
Powell, unidentified (fl.1582) of the Buttery, Queen's servant.
    Custody of Gift: 82.367
Poyntz, Anne—see Anne Heneage
Poyntz, Anne, née Verney (b.c.1518) Lady Poyntz. Daughter of Ralph Verney and Margaret Iwardby, sister-in-law of Anne Heneage*, mar 1555 Sir Nicholas Poyntz, MP. Merten; Hasler under husband.
    Lady: 59.106, 59.325
Preston, Anne - see Anne Paget
Preston, Christopher, Viscount Gormanston (1537–1600) Son of Jenrico Preston and Catherine Fitzgerald; mar c.1582 Catherine Fitzwilliam. GEC, *Peerage*.
    Viscount: 77.25, 77.222
Preyner, John (fl.1570s) Baron Preyner. Special Ambassador from Rudolf II* to return Garter insignia of Emperor Maximilian II*, deceased.
    Sundry Gift: 78.422 (Gift to Envoy)
Prince, unidentified (fl.1582) of the Ewery, Queen's servant.
    Custody of Gift: 82.250
Puckering, Jane, née Chowne (d.1611) Lady Puckering. Daughter of Nicholas Chowne and Elizabeth Scott; mar 1ˢᵗ 1569 John Puckering* MP, kntd 1592, 2ⁿᵈ William Combe. *ODNB* and Hasler under 1ˢᵗ husband; *Visitations, Hertfordshire*.
    Lady: 97.112, 97.312, 98.113, 98.313, 99.96, 99.303, 00.100, 00.310, 03.107, 03.321

Puckering, John (1544–1596) Speaker of the House of Commons, Privy Councillor, Lord Keeper of the Great Seal 1592, kntd 1592. Son of William Puckering and Anne Ashton, mar Jane Chowne (Puckering*). *ODNB*; Hasler; *Visitations, Hertfordshire*.
  Primary: 94.1, 94.185
Pucket, unidentified (fl.1582) Queen's servant.
  Custody of Gift: 82.364
Pyrgo—see Grey of Pyrgo
Quissé, Monsieur de (fl.1570s) Envoy from the Duke of Anjou*, alias M. Cussi. *CSP Foreign, 1578–79*.
  Sundry Gift: 79.448 (Gift to Envoy)
Radcliffe, Anne—see Anne Gerard
Radcliffe, Bridget, née Morrison, Countess of Sussex (1575–1623) Daughter of Charles Morrison and Dorothy Clark; mar 1592 Robert Radcliffe*, Earl of Sussex; mother of Henry [II] Radcliffe*. *ODNB* under husband; GEC, *Peerage*.
  Countess: 94.31, 94.213, 97.25, 97.234, 98.22, 98.236, 99.18, 99.224, 00.23, 00.234, 03.24, 03.237
  Sundry Gift: 97.422 (Christening Gift for her child)
Radcliffe, Sir Edward (c.1559–1643) kntd 1594. Son of Sir Humphrey Radcliffe and Isabel Harvey (Radcliffe*); brother of Mary Radcliffe*; mar 1st c.1582 Elizabeth Petre, 2nd 1594 Jane Hine, 3rd 1634 Eleanor Whortley. GEC, *Peerage*.
  Knight: 03.135, 03.349
Radcliffe, Frances, née Sidney, Countess of Sussex (1531–1589) Founder of Sidney Sussex College Cambridge. Daughter of William Sidney and Anne Pakington; sister of Henry Sidney*; aunt of Philip Sidney*, Mary Herbert*, and Robert Sidney*; mar 1555 Thomas Radcliffe*, Earl of Sussex. GEC, *Peerage*.
  Countess: 59.47, 59.268, 65.148, 67.47, 67.217, 71.30, 71.200, 75.29, 75.137, 76.31, 76.226, 77.32, 77.229, 78.28, 78.229, 79.29, 79.236, 81.28, 81.235, 82.27, 82.228, 82.477, 84.27, 84.225, 85.29, 85.218, 88.26, 88.212, 89.22, 89.207
Radcliffe, Henry [I], Earl of Sussex (c.1532–1593) kntd 1553, KG 1589. Son of Henry Radcliffe, Earl of Sussex and Elizabeth Howard; brother of Thomas Radcliffe*; mar 1549 Honor Pound (Radcliffe*); father of Robert Radcliffe*, Earl of Sussex; grandfather of Henry [II] Radcliffe*; uncle of Mary Radcliffe*. GEC, *Peerage*; Bindoff.
  Earl: 84.7, 84.205, 85.8, 85.199, 88.8, 88.193, 89.6, 89.191
Radcliffe, Henry [II] (1596–1620) Lord Fitzwalter. Son of Robert Radcliffe*, Earl of Sussex, and Bridget Morrison (Radcliffe*); grandson of Henry [I] Radcliffe* and Honor Pound (Radcliffe*); mar 1613 Jane Stanhope. GEC, *Peerage*.
  Sundry Gift: 97.421 (Christening Gift)
Radcliffe, Honor, née Pound, Countess of Sussex (d.1593) Daughter of Anthony Pound and Anne Wingfield; mar Henry [I] Radcliffe*, Earl of Sussex; mother of Robert Radcliffe*. GEC, *Peerage*; *HMC Salisbury*.
  Countess: 85.35, 85.219, 88.27, 88.211, 89.23, 89.208
Radcliffe, Isabel, née Harvey (1515–1594) Lady Radcliffe. Daughter of Edmund Harvey and Margaret Wentworth; aunt of Thomas Radcliffe*; 1st cousin of Henry Harvey*; mar 1530 Sir Humphrey Radcliffe MP; mother of Edward Radcliffe* and Mary Radcliffe*. Hasler under husband.
  Lady: 59.83, 59.303, 62.86, 62.268, 63.83, 63.264, 64.88, 65.19, 65.186, 67.90, 67.260, 68.88, 68.257, 71.86, 71.256, 76.107, 76.308, 77.114, 77.311, 78.114, 78.315, 79.112, 79.320, 81.110, 81.316, 82.105, 82.304, 82.549, 84.101, 84.299, 85.106 85.296, 88.108, 88.292, 89.101, 89.286, 94.91, 94.275

Radcliffe, Margaret (1573–1599) Maid of Honour. Daughter of John Radcliffe and Anne Asshawe; twin sister of Alexander Radcliffe who was killed in Ireland 1599; unmarried. Harrison.
Maid of Honour: 94.316, 97.338, 98.340, 99.328

Radcliffe, Mary (c.1548–1618) Maid of Honour, Gentlewoman of the Privy Chamber, Keeper of Queen's Jewels. Daughter of Sir Humphrey Radcliffe and Isabel Harvey (Radcliffe*); sister of Thomas Radcliffe; niece of Thomas Radcliffe* and Henry [I] Radcliffe*, 1st cousin of Robert Radcliffe* and Henry Radcliffe*; unmarried. *ODNB*; will 76 Meade; BL Royal MS Appendix 68, Additional MS 5751A.
Maid of Honour: 62.336, 63.319, 64.186, 67.320, 68.310, 71.319, 75.203, 76.366, 77.371, 78.373, 79.381, 81.375, 82.363, 84.355, 85.350
Gentlewoman: 88.127, 88.311, 89.125, 89.310, 94.127, 94.318, 97.139, 97.341, 98.137, 98.344, 99.132, 99.333, 00.133, 00.335, 03.137, 03.350
Custody of Gift: 88.1, 88.4–5, 88.9, 88.19, 88.22–23, 88.57, 88.70, 88.73, 88.82, 88.95, 88.97, 88.100, 88.116–117, 88.133, 88.143, 88.159–161, 88.168–169, 89.1, 89.9, 89.14–15, 89.17, 89.20, 89.26, 89.52, 89.63, 89.75, 89.87, 89.110, 89.121, 89.125, 89.156–158, 89.165, 89.167, 89.169, 94.1, 94.11–12, 94.14, 94.16, 94.21, 94.30, 94.52–53, 94.58, 94.63, 94.65–66, 94.72, 94.74–75, 94.80, 94.85, 94.87, 94.101, 94.105–107, 94.109, 94.111–112, 94.115–118, 94.120–121, 94.125–126, 94.143, 94.155, 94.162, 94.165, 94.179, 97.13–16, 97.19, 97.31, 97.36, 97.58, 97.69, 97.73–74, 97.82, 97.84, 97.90, 97.94–95, 97.98, 97.100, 97.104, 97.106, 97.118–119, 97.123–125, 97.127, 97.130–131, 97.134, 97.159, 97.161, 97.164, 97.167, 97.194, 97.199, 98.4–5, 98.16–17, 98.25, 98.29, 98.32, 98.35–37, 98.57, 98.69, 98.82, 98.84, 98.88, 98.94–95, 98.103–104, 98.119, 98.124–125, 98.127, 98.131, 98.164, 98.192–193, 98.196, 99.1–2, 99.13, 99.19, 99.25, 99.27–28, 99.31, 99.62, 99.65–66, 99.68, 99.74, 99.83, 99.91–92, 99.101, 99.110, 99.113, 99.117, 99.119, 99.121, 99.123, 99.127, 99.132, 99.134, 99.153–154, 99.158, 99.170, 99.173, 00.1, 00.4, 00.17–18, 00.24, 00.31, 00.34–35, 00.37–38, 00.61, 00.72–73, 00.96–97, 00.116, 00.122, 00.125, 00.132, 00.135, 00.156, 00.158–160, 00.173, 00.196, 03.1, 03.4–5, 03.19, 03.32, 03.35, 03.37–39, 03.62, 03.68, 03.72, 03.77, 03.99, 03.101, 03.105, 03.109, 03.111, 03.113, 03.118–119, 03.124, 03.127, 03.135–136, 03.158, 03.161, 03.164, 03.167–169, 03.209–210

Radcliffe, Robert, Earl of Sussex (1573–1629) kntd 1596, KG 1599. Son of Henry [I] Radcliffe* and Honor Pound*; mar 1st 1592 Bridget Morrison (Radcliffe*), 2nd 1623 Frances Mewtas. *ODNB*; GEC, *Peerage*.
Earl: 94.6, 94.190, 97.6, 97.206, 98.7, 98.209, 99.7, 99.200, 00.6, 00.204, 03.9, 03.222
Sundry Gift: 97.422 (Christening Gift for his child)

Radcliffe, Thomas, Earl of Sussex (1525–1583) Privy Councillor 1570, Lord Chamberlain, kntd 1544, KG 1558, MP. Son of Henry Radcliffe and Elizabeth Howard; brother of Henry [I] Radcliffe*; 1st cousin of Mary Radcliffe*; mar 1st 1545 Elizabeth Wriothesley, 2nd 1555 Frances Sidney (Racliffe)*. *ODNB*; Hasler; Bindoff; will PCC 52 Brudenell.
Earl: 59.18, 59.239, 65.111, 67.10, 67.180, 71.9, 71.179, 75.10, 76.10, 76.205, 77.9, 77.206, 78.9, 78.210, 79.9, 79.216, 81.8, 81.215, 82.9, 82.209, 82.425

Raines—see Raynes

Ralegh, Carew (c.1550–1625) kntd 1601, MP. Son of Walter Ralegh and Catherine Champernowne; brother of Sir Walter Ralegh*; nephew of Catherine Astley*; mar c.1580 Dorothy Wroughton (Thynne*); father of infant daughter Ralegh*. *ODNB* under brother and son; Hasler.
Gentleman: 84.172, 84.373
Sundry Gift: 84.420 (Christening Gift for his child)

Ralegh, unidentified (b.1583) Daughter of Carew Ralegh* and Dorothy Wroughton (Thynne*).

Sundry Gift: 84.420 (Christening Gift)

Ralegh, Dorothy—see Dorothy Thynne

Ralegh, Elizabeth—see Elizabeth Throckmorton

Ralegh, Walter (1554–1618) Captain of the Guard 1591, courtier poet, kntd 1585. Son of Walter Ralegh and Catherine Champernowne; brother of Carew Ralegh*; nephew of Catherine Astley*; mar 1591 Elizabeth Throckmorton*. *ODNB*; Hasler; Kinney; May, *Elizabethan Courtier*; May, *Ralegh*.

    Knight: 03.136, 03.348

Rambouillet, Charles Angennes de (1530–1587) Special Ambassador from King Henry III* of France, Agent of the Duke of Anjou*. Berton; Corpus Christi College, Cambridge, Parker MS 105.

    Sundry Gift: 79.446 (Gift to Envoy)

Randall alias Smallpage, Elizabeth, née Collier (d.1580) Mistress Randall alias Smallpage. Daughter of Robert Collier and Elizabeth Holwood; stepdaughter of Maurice Denys*; mar 1st unidentified Smallpage, 2nd Vincent Randall. Will PCC 32 Arundell; Hasted; *Visitations, London*.

    Gentlewoman: 62.150, 62.327, 63.140, 63.313

Rasche, Nicholas (fl.1580s) Ambassador from Sweden, Secretary to John III*, King of Sweden, accompanied Ericson Johnson*. *CSP Foreign, 1583–84*.

    Sundry Gift: 84.418 (Gift to Envoy)

Rastorp—see Rostrup

Raynsford, Elizabeth—see Elizabeth Norton

Raynes, Robert (fl.1550s–1560s) Royal Goldsmith under Mary I and Elizabeth. *CSP Mary, 1553–58*; *CPR, 1557–58*; PRO SP 38/1; Sitwell.

    Goldsmith: *passim* 1559

Read, Anne—see Anne Parry

Read, John (fl.1582) Groom, Footman. BL Harleian MS 1644.

    Custody of Gift: 82.233

Redman, William (1540–1602) Bishop of Norwich 1595–1602. *ODNB*.

    Bishop: 97.45, 97.242, 98.43, 98.244, 99.37, 99.232, 00.48, 00.242

Remboillet—see Rambouillet

Reme, unidentified (fl.1580s) of the Cellar, Queen's servant.

    Custody of Gift: 82.286

Revell, John (d.1564) Surveyor of the Works. PRO E 351/3200, E 351/3201; will PCC 20 Stevenson; Collins, *Jewels*.

    Gentleman: 62.163, 62.351

Reyz, Mushac (fl.1580s) Ambassador from Ahmad al-Mansur*, King of Fez, King of Barbary, and Emperor of Morocco, alias Muley Hamet. *CSP Foreign, 1589*, Smith.

    Sundry Gift: 89.406 (Envoy to England)

Rich, Lord/Baroness—Elizabeth Rich, née Baldry, 1567–1591; Penelope Rich, née Devereux, 1581–1605; Richard Rich, 1st, 1547–1567; Robert [I] Rich, 2nd, 1567–1581; Robert [II] Rich, 3rd, 1581–1618

Rich, Catherine—see Catherine [III] Howard

Rich, Elizabeth, née Baldry (1537–1591) Baroness Rich. Daughter of George Baldry; mar c.1554 Robert [I], Lord Rich*. GEC, *Peerage*.

    Baroness: 81.92, 81.299, 82.87, 82.287, 82.512, 84.82, 84.280, 85.84, 85.276, 88.91, 88.273, 89.80, 89.266

Rich, John (d.1593) Royal Apothecary. Matthews; Furdell; E179/266/13.

    Gentleman: 59.175, 59.398, 75.126, 75.222, 76.189, 76.391, 77.188, 77.389, 78.187, 78.396, 79.192, 79.405, 81.191, 81.405, 82.186, 82.389, 82.567

Rich, Mary (b.1588) Daughter of Robert Rich* and Penelope Devereux (Rich*); died in infancy.
   Sundry Gift: 89.404 (Christening Gift)
Rich, Penelope, née Devereux, Baroness Rich (1563–1607) Daughter of Walter Devereux*, Earl of Essex and Lettice Knollys; stepdaughter of Robert Dudley*, Earl of Leicester; sister of Dorothy Percy* and Robert Devereux*, Earl of Essex; 1st cousin twice removed to Queen Elizabeth; mar 1st 1581 Robert [II], Lord Rich* (div 1605); 2nd 1605 Charles Blount*, Lord Mountjoy; mother of Robert [III] Rich*. *ODNB*; GEC, *Peerage*.
   Baroness: 82.89, 82.289, 82.520, 88.88, 88.274, 89.82, 89.267, 97.84, 97.282, 98.82, 98.282, 99.77, 99.274, 00.84, 00.283
   Sundry Gift: 63.367 (Christening Gift), 89.404 (Christening Gift for her child)
Rich, Richard, Lord Rich (1496–1567) kntd 1536, MP. Son of Richard, Lord Rich and Joan Dingley; mar 1525 Elizabeth Jenks; father of Robert [I], Lord Rich*. *ODNB*; Bindoff; GEC, *Peerage*; will PCC 12 Babington.
   Lord: 59.58, 59.279, 62.55, 62.236, 63.56, 63.229, 64.62, 65.164, 67.62, 67.232
Rich, Robert [I], Lord Rich (c.1537–1581) Knight of the Bath 1559. Son of Richard, Lord Rich* and Elizabeth Jenks; mar c.1554 Elizabeth Baldry (Rich*); father of Robert [II] Rich*; brother-in-law of Roger, Lord North* and John Darcy*, Lord Darcy of Chiche. Name listed but no participation for 1582 exchange. *ODNB*; GEC, *Peerage*; Hasler; will PCC 21 Drury.
   Lord: 68.60, 68.229, 71.56, 71.225, 75.61, 75.169, 76.63, 76.261, 77.67, 77.264, 78.66, 78.267, 79.64, 79.271, 81.60, 81.267
Rich, Robert [II], Lord Rich (1560–1619) MP. Son of Robert [I] Rich* and Elizabeth Baldry (Rich*); mar 1st 1581 Penelope Devereux (Rich*) (div 1605), 2nd 1616 Frances Wray; father of Robert [III], Lord Rich*. *ODNB*; GEC, *Peerage*; Hasler; will PCC 51 Soame.
   Lord: 82.458, 84.64, 84.260, 85.67, 85.258, 88.66, 88.251, 89.60, 89.245, 94.62, 94.246, 97.66, 97.266, 98.64, 98.267, 99.60, 99.257, 00.67, 00.265, 03.67, 03.280
   Sundry Gift: 89.404 (Christening Gift for his child)
Rich, Robert [III] (1588–1658) Lord Rich, later Earl of Warwick. Son of Robert [II], Lord Rich* and Penelope Devereux (Rich*); mar 1st Frances Hatton, 2nd Susan Rowe, 3rd Eleanor Whortley. GEC, *Peerage*.
   Sundry Gift: 89.404 (Christening Gift)
Richardson, Ferdinando (c.1558–1618) Groom of the Privy Chamber, Musician, alias Ferdinando Heybourne. Mar 1st 1592 Anne Chandler, 2nd 1616 Elizabeth Moore. BL Additional MS 30485; *BDECM*; Marlow.
   Free Gift: 88.389, 89.390, 94.387, 97.413, 98.419, 99.406, 00.409, 03.441
   Custody of Gift: 94.175
Ricote—see Norris of Rycote
Rivett, Anne—see Anne Windsor
Rivett, Thomas (d.1582) Alderman of London, Merchant Adventurer. Mar Griselda Paget; son-in-law of William Paget* and Anne Preston (Paget*); father of Anne Windsor*, Alice Gerard, and Mirabel Heydon; father-in-law of Henry, Lord Windsor* and Sir Thomas Gerard*. Gave gift to Queen in Cambridgeshire during 1578 Progress. Beaven; Collins, *Jewels*.
   Sundry Gift: 88.401 (Queen regifted his gift to Sir Christopher Hatton)
Roberts, Jane—see Jane FitzWilliam
Robinson, Catherine, née Cruxson (fl.1580s) Daughter of Simon Cruxson and Catherine [née?] Cruxson*, mar John Robinson*. PRO LC 2/4/3; Mertens.
   Gentlewoman: 88.149, 88.334, 89.147, 89.332

Robinson, Henry (1551–1616) Bishop of Carlisle 1598–1616. *ODNB*.
  Bishop: 99.40, 99.237, 00.52, 00.247, 03.60, 03.273
Robinson, John (d.1604) merchant, tailor. mar Catherine [née?] (Robinson*). Will PCC 41 Harte.
  Gentleman: 94.168, 94.364,
Robinson, Ralph (1520–1577) Goldsmith, Master of the Mint, Translator. *ODNB*.
  Gentleman: 76.178, 76.376
Robotham, Robert (c.1522–1571) Yeoman of the Robes, served in household of Edward VI, MP. Son-in-law of William Paget* and Anne Preston (Paget*); mar 1551 Grace Paget. Bindoff; Hasler; will PCC 47 Holney.
  Gentleman: 59.170, 59.436, 62.162, 62.350, 63.153, 63.332, 64.137, 64.197, 65.83, 67.158, 67.334, 68.158, 68.330
Roche, Griselda—see Griselda Butler
Rochester, Bishop—see Edmund Guest, 1560–1571; Edmund Freake, 1572–1575; John Piers, 1576–1577; John Young, 1578–1605
Rogers, Andrew (c.1547-c.1600) MP. Son of Richard Rogers and Cecilia Luttrell; mar 1st c.1571 Elizabeth Poynings, 2nd 1577 Lady Mary Seymour*. Hasler.
  Sundry Gift: 79.438 (Christening Gift for his child)
Rogers, son (b.1578) Son of Andrew Rogers* and Lady Mary Seymour*, died in infancy.
  Sundry Gift: 79.438 (Christening Gift)
Rogers, Sir Edward (c.1500–1568) Vice Chamberlain 1558, Captain of the Guard 1558, Privy Councillor 1558, Comptroller of the Household 1560, kntd 1547, MP. Son of George Rogers and Elizabeth [née?]; mar Mary Lisle; grandfather of Mary Harington*. *ODNB*; Hasler; Bindoff; will PCC 11 Babington.
  Knight: 59.110, 59.329, 62.101, 62.281, 63.99, 63.272, 64.93, 64.147, 65.29, 65.196, 67.99, 67.269, 68.98, 68.267
Rogers, Mary—see Mary Harington
Rogers, unidentified (fl. 1580s) Queen's servant.
  Custody of Gift: 82.375
Roose, John (fl.1550s) Keeper of the Wildfowl of the River. *CPR, 1560*.
  Gentleman: 59.202, 59.426
Rostrup, Jacob (fl.1580s) Ambassador from Denmark. Nobleman. See also George Schuavenius* who received another piece of the chain given. *Dansk*; Collins, *Jewels*.
  Sundry Gift: 89.395
Rotheham/Rotheridge, George (fl.1550s) Portingale (Portuguese), Queen's servant, unidentified. Gave gift jointly with Robert Kingston*.
  Gentleman: 59.218
Roussy, Count de—see Louis de Luxemburg
Roynon, John (d.c.1582) Yeoman of the Robes, served in household of Princess Elizabeth. *Visitations, Somerset*; PRO LC 5/49, LC 5/33–35.
  Free Gift: 59.444, 62.373
  Custody of Gift: 59.66, 59.96, 59.159, 62.99
Rudd, Anthony (1549–1615) Bishop of Saint David's 1594–1615. *ODNB*.
  Bishop: 97.55, 97.254, 98.55, 98.257, 99.49, 99.246, 00.58, 00.256, 03.61, 03.274
Rudolf II (1552–1612) Holy Roman Emperor, KG 1578, Gift to his envoy John Preyner*. Grandson of Charles V*; nephew of Philip II*; unmarried.
  Sundry Gift: 78.422 (Sovereign sending Envoy to England)
Russell, Anne [I], née Sapcote, Countess of Bedford (d.1559) Daughter of Guy Sapcote and Margaret Wolston; mar 1st John Broughton, 2nd c.1519 Richard Jerningham, 3rd 1526 John Russell, later Earl of Bedford; mother of Francis Russell*. GEC, *Peerage*.

Countess: 59.42, 59.263

Russell, Anne [II] (1578–1639) Maid of Honour, later Countess of Worcester. Daughter of John Russell* and Elizabeth [I] Cooke (Russell*); sister of Elizabeth [II] Russell*, niece of Anne Dudley*; mar 1600 Henry Somerset, later Marquess of Worcester. GEC, *Peerage*; Harvey.

    Maid of Honour: 97.340, 98.339, 99.327, 00.330

Russell, Anne—see Anne Dudley

Russell, Bridget - see Bridget Manners

Russell, Edward, Earl of Bedford (1572–1627) Son of Francis Russell and Juliana Foster; grandson of Francis Russell*, Earl of Bedford and Margaret St John (Russell*); mar 1594 Lucy Harington (Russell*). GEC, *Peerage*; *ODNB* under grandfather.

    Earl: 94.13, 94.198, 97.11, 97.213, 98.12, 98.215, 99.11, 99.206, 00.11, 00.212, 03.15, 03.228

Russell, Elizabeth [I], née Cooke (c.1540–1609) Lady Hoby, Baroness Russell, courtier poet. Daughter of Anthony Cooke* and Anne FitzWilliam; sister of Catherine Cooke* and Mildred Cecil*; mar 1st 1558 Thomas Hoby*, 2nd 1574 John [I] Russell*; mother of Thomas Posthumous Hoby*, Sir Edward Hoby*, Elizabeth [III] Russell*, and Anne [II] Russell*. *ODNB*; Harvey; May, *Elizabethan Courtier*.

    Baroness: 76.98, 76.295, 82.518, 84.79, 84.277

    Sundry Gift: 67.361 (Christening Gift for her child), 76.420 (Christening Gift for her child)

Russell, Elizabeth [II] (1575–1600) Gentlewoman of the Privy Chamber. Daughter of John Russell* and Elizabeth [I] Cooke (Russell*); sister of Anne [II] Russell; niece of Elizabeth Bourchier*; unmarried. Harvey.

    Gentlewoman: 97.154, 97.357, 98.150, 98.358, 99.145, 99.345, 00.146, 00.351

    Sundry Gift: 76.420 (Christening Gift)

Russell, Elizabeth—see Elizabeth Bourchier, Elizabeth Shelton

Russell, Francis, Earl of Bedford (1527–1585) Privy Councillor, kntd 1547, KG 1564, MP. Son of John Russell and Anne Sapcote (Russell*(; mar 1st c.1546 Margaret St John (Russell*), 2nd 1566 Bridget Hussey (Russell*); father of John [I] Russell*, William Russell*, Elizabeth Bourchier*, Anne Dudley*, and Margaret Clifford*; grandfather of Edward Russell*. *ODNB*; Hasler; Bindoff.

    Earl: 59.16, 59.237, 62.9, 62.189, 63.13, 63.185, 64.12, 65.113, 67.12, 67.182, 68.14, 68.183, 71.12, 71.182, 75.15, 76.15, 76.210, 77.15, 77.212, 78.11, 78.213, 79.12, 79.222, 81.10, 81.220, 82.12, 82.213, 82.426, 84.10, 84.208, 85.12, 85.203

Russell, John [I], Lord Russell (1550–1585) Son of Francis Russell*, Earl of Bedford and Margaret St John (Russell*); brother of Anne Dudley, Elizabeth Bourchier*, Margaret Clifford*, and William Russell*; mar 1574 Elizabeth Cooke*; father of Elizabeth [II] Russell* and Anne [II] Russell*. Name listed with 'X', but no gift recorded for 1582, Somerset MS DD\MI/19/1; although his servant received a reward, BL MS Harleian 1644. *ODNB*; GEC, *Peerage*.

    Lord: 78.78, 78.269, 79.63, 79.269, 81.62, 81.269, 82.470, 84.65, 84.261

    Sundry Gift: 76.420 (Christening Gift for his child)

Russell, John [II] (fl.1570s) Clerk of the Closet. PRO SP 12/126/6, SP 12/166; LP Henry VIII.

    Custody: 78.172

Russell, Lucy, née Harington, Countess of Bedford (1581–1628) Daughter of Sir John Harington of Exton and Anne Kelway (Harington*); mar 1594 Edward Russell*, Earl of Bedford. *ODNB*; GEC, *Peerage*; BL Additional MS 5751.

    Countess: 97.34, 97.225, 98.33, 98.233, 00.33, 00.230, 03.25, 03.238

Russell, Margaret—see Margaret Clifford

Russell, Margaret, née St John, Countess of Bedford (c.1524–1562) Lady of the Privy Chamber. Daughter of Sir John St John and Margaret Waldegrave; mar 1st c.1539 William Gostwick, 2nd c.1546 Francis Russell*, Earl of Bedford; mother of John [I] Russell*, William Russell*, Elizabeth Bourchier*, Anne Dudley* and Margaret Clifford*; grandmother of Edward Russell*, Earl of Bedford. *ODNB*; GEC, *Peerage*; Hasler under husband.

Countess: 59.43, 59.264, 62.40, 62.220

Russell, William (c.1553–1613) Lord Deputy of Ireland, Governor of Flushing, later Lord Russell of Thornhaugh, Gentleman Pensioner, kntd 1581. Son of Francis Russell*, Earl of Bedford and Margaret St John (Russell*); brother of Anne Dudley*, Elizabeth Bourchier*, John Russell*, and Margaret Clifford*; mar 1585 Elizabeth Long. *ODNB*; GEC, *Peerage*; Tighe; will PCC 86 Capell.

Gentleman: 79.205, 79.418

Knight: 94.117, 94.300, 97.125, 97.319, 98.125, 98.322

Sundry Gift: 88.405 (Gift on his Appointment at Flushing and Departure for the Low Countries)

Russey—see Roussy

Rutland, Earl/Countess—see Bridget Manners, née Hussey, 1560–1566; Edward Manners, 3rd, 1563–1587; Elizabeth [I] Manners, née Charlton, 1587–1595; Elizabeth [III] Manners, née Sidney, 1599–1612; Henry Manners, 2nd, 1543–1563; Isabel Manners, née Holcroft 1573–1587, dowager, 1587–1606; John Manners, 4th, 1587–1588; Margaret Manners, née Neville, 1536–1559; Rogers Manners, 5th, 1588–1612

Rutter, unidentified (fl.1580s) Queen's servant.

Custody: 82.264

Rycote, Rycott—see Norris of Rycote

Sackbuts—see Nicholas Andrew, Anthony Maria Peacock, Devise Peacock, Edward Peacock, John Peacock

Sackford—see Seckford

Sackville, Anne—see Anne Fiennes, Anne Spencer

Sackville, Cecily, née Baker, Baroness Buckhurst (c.1535–1615) Mistress Sackville, later Countess of Dorset. Daughter of John Baker and Elizabeth Dingeley; mar 1554 Thomas Sackville*, Lord Buckhurst; mother of Robert Sackville*. *ODNB*; GEC, *Peerage*; Hasler under husband; will PCC 9 Cope.

Baroness: 71.78, 71.248, 76.86, 76.290, 77.96, 77.293, 78.87, 78.296, 79.92, 79.299, 88.84, 88.269, 89.77, 89.262, 94.77, 94.262, 97.87, 97.286, 98.85, 98.286, 99.80, 99.278, 00.88, 00.287, 03.91, 03.296

Sundry Gift: 62.390 (Christening Gift for her child)

Sackville, Dorothy—see Dorothy Lowe

Sackville, Richard (1507–1566) Under Treasurer of the Exchequer, Privy Councillor, kntd 1549, MP. Son of John Sackville and Margaret Boleyn; mar by 1536 Winifred Brydges (Sackville*); father of Anne Fiennes* and Thomas Sackville*; 1st cousin once removed of Queen Elizabeth. Hasler; Bindoff; will PCC 14 Crymes.

Knight: 59.114, 59.333, 62.105, 62.285, 63.103, 63.276, 64.97, 64.151, 65.33, 65.200

Sackville, Robert (1561–1609) later Earl of Dorset. Son of Thomas Sackville* and Cecily Baker (Sackville*); 2nd cousin once removed to Queen Elizabeth; mar 1st 1580 Margaret Howard, 2nd 1592 Anne Spencer. GEC, *Peerage*.

Sundry Gift: 62.390 (Christening Gift)

Sackville, Thomas (1536–1608) Lord High Treasurer 1599, Privy Councillor, Lord Buckhurst 1567, courtier poet, kntd 1567, KG 1589, MP. Son of Richard Sackville* and Winifred Brydges (Sackville*); brother of Anne Fiennes*; 2nd cousin of Queen Elizabeth; mar 1554 Cecily Baker (Sackville*); father of Robert Sackville*. *ODNB*; Hasler; Bindoff; GEC, *Peerage*; will PCC 1 Dorset.

Gentleman: 67.149, 67.325

Lord: 68.66, 68.235, 71.62, 71.232, 75.67, 75.175, 76.69, 76.270, 77.70, 77.267, 78.69, 78.271, 79.67, 79.274, 88.67, 88.253, 89.61, 89.246, 94.55, 94.239, 97.60, 97.257, 98.59, 98.260, 99.55, 99.250, 00.2, 00.199, 03.2, 03.215

Sundry Gift: 62.390 (Christening Gift for his child)

Sackville, Winifred—see Winifred Paulet

Sadler, Sir Ralph (1507–1587) Privy Councillor 1558, Chancellor of the Duchy of Lancaster 1568, kntd by 1540, MP. Son of Henry Sadler; father-in-law of Edward Bashe*; mar 1535 Ellen Mitchell. *ODNB*; Hasler; Slavin; will PCC 23 Spencer.

Knight: 71.101, 71.271, 76.121, 76.316, 77.123, 77.320, 78.124, 78.325, 79.124, 79.331, 81.120, 81.329, 82.115, 82.315, 82.526, 84.111, 84.309, 85.112, 85.304

Sagbutt—see Sackbut

St Barbe, Ursula—see Ursula Walsingham

St Barbe, William (d.1562) Groom of the Privy Chamber to Edward VI. Son of Richard St Barbe and Margery Grey; uncle of Ursula Walsingham*; mar 1st Mary Little, 2nd Elizabeth. Will PCC 62 Chayre.

Gentleman: 59.210, 59.433, 62.172, 62.359

St David's, Bishop—see Henry Morgan, 1555–1559; Thomas Young, 1559–1561; Richard Davies, 1561–1581; Marmaduke Middleton, 1582–1592; Anthony Rudd, 1594–1615

St John of Bletsoe, Lord/Baroness—see Elizabeth St John, née Chambers, 1572–1603; Oliver St John, 1st, 1559–1582

St John, Anne—see Anne Howard

St John, Elizabeth, née Chambers, Baroness St John of Bletsoe (d.1603) Daughter of Geoffrey Chambers; mar 1st Reginald Conyers, 2nd 1559 Edward Griffin, 3rd 1560 Francis Stonor, 4th c.1572 Oliver St John, Lord St John of Bletsoe; mother of Lucy Griffin*. GEC, *Peerage*; *CSP Domestic, 1595–96.*

Baroness: 75.194, 76.83, 76.288, 77.91, 77.288, 78.85, 78.290, 79.86, 79.293, 81.82, 81.290, 82.77, 82.278, 82.501, 84.74, 84.272, 85.77, 85.268, 88.79, 88.264, 89.72, 89.257, 97.89, 97.285, 98.87, 98.285, 99.82, 99.277, 00.89, 00.285, 03.92, 03.302

St John, Margaret—see Margaret Russell

St John, Oliver, Lord St John of Bletsoe (c.1522–1582) Son of Sir John St John and Margaret Waldegrave; mar 1st 1543 Agnes Fisher, 2nd 1572 Elizabeth Chambers; grandfather of Anne Howard*. GEC, *Peerage*; Bindoff.

Lord: 59.65, 59.286

St Leger, Eulalia—see Eulalia Tremayne

St Loe, Elizabeth—see Elizabeth Hardwick

St Loe, Margaret, née Kingston (fl.1560s) Lady St Loe. Gentlewoman of the Privy Chamber. Daughter of William Kingston MP and Mary Scrope; mar Sir John St Loe MP; halfsister of Henry [I] Jerningham*; mother of William St Loe. Bindoff under husband and father; Hasler under husband and sons, William and Edward; *Visitations, Wiltshire*.

Lady: 67.95, 67.265

St Marie, Nicholas (c.1520–1591) Sieur D'Aigneaux, Envoy from Duke of Anjou*. *CSP Foreign, 1562–63, 1569–71.*

Sundry Gift: 79.455 (Gift to Envoy)

Salignac de la Mothe Fénelon, Bertrand de—see Bertrand de Salignac Fénelon

Salisbury, Bishop—see John Jewel, 1560–1571; Edmund Guest, 1571–1577; John Piers, 1577–1589; John Coldwell, 1591–1596; Henry Cotton, 1598–1615

Saltonstall, Samuel (d.1640) son of Richard Saltonstall, Lord Mayor of London, and Susanna Poyntz; mar 1585 Anne Ramsden. *ODNB* under father.
Gentleman: 03.210, 03.416

Sandys, Edwin (c.1517–1588) Bishop of Worcester 1559–1570, Bishop of London 1570–1577, Archbishop of York 1577–1588. *ODNB*.
Bishop: 62.24, 62.204, 63.23, 63.195, 64.22, 65.124, 67.24, 67.194, 68.39, 68.208, 71.36, 71.206, 75.44, 75.152, 76.47, 76.242, 77.48, 77.245, 78.45, 78.246, 79.43, 79.250, 81.38, 81.245, 82.38, 82.238, 82.438, 84.35, 84.233, 85.38, 85.229, 88.38, 88.223

Sandys, Elizabeth—see Elizabeth Berkeley

Sapcote, Anne—see Anne [I] Russell

Sarum—see Salisbury

Saules, Saulte—see Nicolas des Gallars

Savage, John (1554–1615) MP; son of John Savage and Elizabeth Manners; brother of Margaret Brereton*; mar 1576 Mary Alington*. Hasler; will PCC 40 Montague.
Sundry Gift: 77.415 (Marriage Gift)

Savage, Margaret—see Margaret Brereton

Savage, Mary—see Mary Alington

Saverne, Monsieur de (fl.1570s) gentleman with Nicholas Martel*, Monsieur de Bacqueville, from the Duke of Anjou*, with Monsieur de Torsac* and Monsieur de Ninsonan*. Nichols, *Progresses*; Dovey.
Sundry Gift: 79.449 (Gift to Envoy)

Savin, Andrei Grigorievich (fl.1580s) Special Ambassador from Ivan IV*, Emperor of Russia, alias Ivan Grigorievich. Madariaga.
Sundry Gift: 71.362 (Gift to Envoy)

Scambler, Edward (c.1510–1594) Bishop of Peterborough 1561–1585, Bishop of Norwich 1585–1594. *ODNB*; will PCC 50 Dixy.
Bishop: 62.34, 62.214, 63.33, 63.205, 64.32, 65.134, 67.34, 67.204, 68.49, 68.218, 71.47, 71.217, 75.56, 75.164, 76.59, 76.254, 77.60, 77.256, 78.60, 78.261, 79.57, 79.264, 81.51, 81.258, 82.49, 82.248, 82.445, 84.44, 84.242, 85.48, 85.238, 88.45, 88.230, 89.40, 89.225, 94.39, 94.223

Scepeaux, François de (1509–1571) Sieur de Vielleville, Maréchal de France, Special Ambassador from Charles IX* of France. Coignet.
Sundry Gift: 63.364 (Gift to Envoy)

Schein, Calixtus (1529–1600) Caloptues Shene, Messenger from Denmark, Secretary to Anne of Denmark*. *CSP Foreign, 1580–81*; Exchequer Rolls of Scotland.
Sundry Gift: 88.396 (Gift to Envoy)

Schenk, Sir Martin (1549–1589) Dutch Colonel, kntd by Earl of Leicester at Utrecht 1586. Collins, *Jewels*; *CSP Foreign, 1579–80*.
Sundry Gift: 89.399 (Gift during Visit to England)

Schetts, Edmund (d.1603) alias Edmund Treasurer, Page of the Chamber, Instrument Maker. related to William Treasurer*, scribal error of Guilliam for Edmund in 1598 and 1599. *RECM*; *BDECM*; BL Sloane MS 814.
Gentleman: 71.166, 71.343, 75.231, 77.195, 79.206, 79.419, 82.201, 82.405, 94.183, 94.375, 98.201, 98.408, 99.194, 99.395
Custody of Gift: 82.256

Schetts—see also William Threasurer

Schuavenius, George, (fl.1580s) alias Master George. Envoy from Duke Charles (later Charles IX* of Sweden) and Christian IV* of Denmark. See also Jacob Rostrup* who received another piece of the chain given. *Collins*, Jewels; *CSP Foreign, 1581–82*.
Gentleman: 88.407, 89.400

709

Scory, John (d.1585) Bishop of Hereford 1559–1585. *ODNB.*
  Bishop: 62.28, 62.208, 63.27, 63.199, 64.28, 65.130, 67.30, 67.200, 68.45, 68.214, 71.43,
  71.213, 75.51, 75.159, 76.54, 76.249, 77.55, 77.251, 78.55, 78.256, 79.53, 79.260, 81.48,
  81.256, 82.46, 82.247, 82.444, 84.43, 84.241, 85.47, 85.237
Scott, Elizabeth—see Elizabeth Drury
Scott, Cuthbert (c.1520–1564) Bishop of Chester 1556–1559 (deprived). *ODNB.*
  Bishop: 59.33, 59.255
Scrope, Lord/Baroness—see Catherine Scrope, née Clifford, 1549–1598; Henry Scrope, 9th,
  1549–1592; Margaret Scrope, née Howard, 1565–1592; Philadelphia Scrope, née Carey,
  1592–1627; Thomas Scrope, 10th, 1592–1609
Scrope, Catherine, née Clifford, Baroness Scrope (d.1598) Daughter of Henry Clifford,
  Earl of Cumberland and Margaret Percy; mar 1st c.1530 John, Lord Scrope, 2nd c.1556
  Sir Richard Cholmley; mother of Henry Scrope*; possible identification, but more
  likely identification is her daughter-in-law, Margaret Howard*. GEC, *Peerage.*
  Baroness: 62.82, 62.262
Scrope, Henry, Lord Scrope (c.1534–1592) KG 1585. Son of John, Lord Scrope and
  Catherine Clifford (Scrope*); mar 1st Mary North, 2nd by 1535 Margaret Howard
  (Scrope*); father of Thomas Scrope*. GEC, *Peerage.*
  Lord: 59.70, 59.291, 62.65, 62.246, 63.66, 63.239, 64.58, 65.160, 67.59, 67.229, 68.57,
  68.226
Scrope, Emmanuel (1584–1630) later Lord Scrope. Son of Thomas, Lord Scrope* and
  Philadelphia Carey (Scrope*). GEC, *Peerage.*
  Sundry Gift: 85.411 (Christening Gift)
Scrope, Margaret, née Howard, Baroness Scrope (1538–1592) Daughter of Henry Howard,
  Earl of Surrey and Frances Vere (Howard*); mar c.1561 Henry, Lord Scrope*; mother
  of Thomas Lord Scrope*; possible identification, but perhaps is her mother-in-law,
  Catherine Clifford (Scrope*). GEC, *Peerage.*
  Baroness: 62.82, 62.262
Scrope, Philadelphia, née Carey, Baroness Scrope (1562–1627) alias Penelope Carew, Lady
  Scrope, Lady of the Privy Chamber. Daughter of Henry Carey* and Anne Morgan
  (Carey*); sister of George Carey*, Catherine [I] Howard*, and Margaret Hoby*; mar
  1583 Thomas Lord Scrope*; mother of Emmanuel Scrope*; godchild of and 1st cousin
  once removed to Queen Elizabeth. GEC, *Peerage*; Hasler.
  Gentlewoman: 82.149, 82.349, 82.619, 84.142, 84.340, 85.127, 85.317
  Lady: 89.99, 89.284
  Baroness: 94.72, 94.256, 97.80, 97.279, 98.79, 98.291, 99.74, 99.269, 00.81, 00.278,
  03.81, 03.295
  Sundry Gift: 63.366 (Christening Gift), 85.411 (Christening Gift for her child)
Scrope, Thomas, Lord Scrope (c.1567–1609) KG 1599, MP. Son of Henry, Lord Scrope*
  and Margaret Howard; mar 1583 Philadelphia Carey (Scrope*); father of Emmanuel
  Scrope*. GEC, *Peerage*; Hasler.
  Sundry Gift: 85.411 (Christening Gift to his child)
Scudamore, John (1542–1623) Gentleman Pensioner, kntd 1592, MP. Son of William
  Scudamore and Ursula Pakington; 1st cousin of Elizabeth [I] Willoughby*; 2nd cousin
  of John Pakington* and Margaret Lichfield*; mar 1st Eleanor Croft, 2nd 1574 Mary
  Shelton*. Hasler; Bindoff; will PCC 84 Swann.
  Gentleman: 82.176, 82.380, 82.586, 84.171, 84.369, 85.167, 85.367, 88.164, 88.355,
  89.162, 89.355
  Knight: 94.119, 94.304, 97.126, 97.323, 98.126, 98.326, 99.118, 99.312, 00.123, 00.319,
  03.125, 03.337

Scudamore, Mary, née Shelton (c.1550–1603) Mistress Shelton, Mistress Scudamore, Lady Scudamore, Gentlewoman of the Bedchamber. Daughter of John Shelton and Margaret Parker; granddaughter of Sir John Shelton and Anne Boleyn; aunt of Elizabeth Shelton*, Amy Shelton*, and Audrey Walsingham*; niece of Mary Heveningham*; 2nd cousin of Queen Elizabeth; mar 1574 John Scudamore*. *ODNB*; PRO LC 5/49.

Gentlewoman: 71.132, 71.302, 75.93, 76.139, 76.334, 77.142, 77.339, 78.145, 78.346, 79.146, 79.353, 81.139, 81.347, 82.133, 82.334, 82.600, 84.133, 84.328, 85.131, 85.325, 88.131, 88.315, 89.130, 89.315

Lady: 94.102, 94.286, 97.101, 97.299, 98.100, 98.300, 99.97, 99.290, 00.102, 00.297, 03.102, 03.315

Custody of Gift: 75.1, 75.21, 75.38, 75.80, 75.84, 75.88, 75.90–91, 75.93, 75.96–97, 75.99, 75.101–109, 75.111–113, 75.115, 75.119, 75.125–127, 76.38, 76.40–41, 76.100–103, 76.106–110, 76.131, 76.139, 76.141–143, 76.145–148, 76.151, 76.153–157, 76.160–162, 76.164–167, 76.175, 76.180–183, 76.185–192, 76.195, 77.2, 77.42, 77.92, 77.100–101, 77.105, 77.114–115, 77.129, 77.141, 77.145, 77.148, 77.150–151, 77.153–157, 77.159–163, 77.165–168, 77.173, 77.183, 77.185–188, 77.191, 77.193, 77.195, 78.27, 78.43, 78.93, 78.101, 78.103–104, 78.112–114, 78.117–118, 78.120, 78.135, 78.146–147, 78.151, 78.154, 78.159–164, 78.166–168, 78.170, 78.176, 78.180, 78.183–187, 78.190, 78.195, 79.98, 79.102, 79.109, 79.112–113, 79.115, 79.118, 79.135, 79.145, 79.147, 79.149, 79.152–153, 79.156–158, 79.161–165, 79.168–170, 79.173, 79.176, 79.188–192, 79.195, 81.88, 81.92, 81.96, 81.100–101, 81.111, 81.114, 81.129, 81.132, 81.141, 81.147, 81.151–152, 81.156–159, 81.181–166, 81.177–180, 81.183, 81.187–195, 82.66, 82.84–85, 82.88–91, 82.93–95, 82.99, 82.102, 82.105, 82.129, 82.131, 82.133–135, 82.139, 82.144, 82.146, 82.149, 82.151–155, 82.157–159, 82.161, 82.163–164, 82.170, 82.173–176, 82.178, 82.182–184, 82.186–190, 82.200, 84.74, 84.79, 84.82–83, 84.85–86, 84.88, 84.90–91, 84.100–103, 84.118, 84.134, 84.140, 84.142–144, 84.147–150, 84.153, 84.155–158, 84.162–163, 84.171, 84.173–174, 84.178–183, 84.186, 85.75, 85.83, 85.87, 85.89–92, 85.94, 85.105, 85.118, 85.127, 85.135–136, 85.140–142, 85.144–146, 85.149–156, 85.172–177, 85.180, 85.190, 88.83, 88.91–92, 88.98, 88.101, 88.106, 88.109, 88.113, 88.130, 88.135, 88.140, 88.144–147, 88.149–154, 88.165–167, 88.171, 88.173, 88.185, 89.69, 89.84, 89.90, 89.93, 89.102, 89.105, 89.129, 89.136–137, 89.139–144, 89.146–151, 89.161, 89.163–164, 89.168–170, 89.172–173, 89.176–177, 94.73, 94.81, 94.88, 94.90, 94.92, 94.96–99, 94.130, 93.133, 94.135, 94.150, 94.154, 94.156–161, 94.168–169, 94.180, 97.20, 97.71, 97.78–79, 97.96, 97.103, 97.107–108, 97.115, 97.143–155, 97.157, 97.163, 97.166, 97.168–173, 97.175–179, 97.192, 97.197–198, 98.18, 98.72, 98.91, 98.98, 98.108–110, 98.128, 98.142–149, 98.151, 98.153–157, 98.161, 98.163, 98.165–170, 98.195, 98.197–199, 99.14, 99.70, 99.79, 99.85, 99.99, 99.105–107, 99.136–140, 99.142–146, 99.149–150, 99.155, 99.159–164, 99.191–193, 00.19, 00.39, 00.90, 00.93, 00.105, 00.109–111, 00.127, 00.138–145, 00.147, 00.151, 00.153, 00.157, 00.165, 00.189–191, 03.20, 03.82, 03.85, 03.96, 03.108, 03.116, 03.141, 03.146–154, 03.156, 03.159, 03.166, 03.170–172, 03.174–176, 03.212

Seckford, Alice, née Bedingfield (1536-c.1583) Mistress Seckford. Daughter of Henry Bedingfield and Claire Townsend, mar 1st c.1554 Thomas Kervill, 2nd 1560 Sir Henry Seckford*. *ODNB* under husband; *Visitations, Suffolk*.

Gentlewoman: 64.123, 64.181, 71.136, 71.306, 75.98, 76.149, 76.350, 77.155, 77.352, 78.156, 78.357, 79.158, 79.365, 81.152, 81.358, 82.147, 82.347, 82.611

Seckford, Henry (c.1522–1610) Groom of the Privy Chamber, Keeper of the Privy Purse to Elizabeth and James I, Master of Tents and Pavilions, kntd 1603. Son of Thomas

Seckford and Margaret Wingfield, mar 1ˢᵗ c.1560 Alice Bedingfield (Seckford*), 2ⁿᵈ 1583 Helen Bird (Seckford*), 3ʳᵈ c.1594 Rebecca Brandon (Seckford*). *ODNB*; will PCC 95 Wingfield.

Gentleman: 97.195, 97.364

Free Gift: 59.446, 62.370, 63.354, 64.208, 67.350, 68.337, 71.350, 75.237, 76.402, 77.404, 78.410, 79.424, 81.424, 82.409, 84.401, 85.394, 88.380, 89.381, 94.380, 97.406, 98.412, 99.400, 00.403, 03.436

Custody of Gift: 59.148, 59.162–163, 59.181, 59.183, 62.158–59, 62.168–69, 64.134–135, 64.139, 64.141, 71.4, 71.6–10, 71.12–17, 71.19–20, 71.22, 71.25–26, 71.28–56, 71.58–60, 71.62–65, 71.68, 71.72–73, 71.76, 71.78, 71.83, 71.85, 71.88, 71.95, 71.97–99, 71.101–111, 71.117–118, 71.128, 71.145–146, 71.150, 75.2–4, 75.6, 75.8–13, 75.16–20, 75.22–23, 75.25–26, 75.29–31, 75.33–34, 75.37, 75.39–62, 75.64–73, 75.75–78, 75.81–82, 75.114, 75.118, 76.3–5, 76.7–13, 76.13–17, 76.19, 76.21, 76.24–25, 76.27–28, 76.31–33, 76.35–36, 76.39, 76.43–64, 76.67–76, 76.79–88, 76.113–119, 76.121–129, 77.4–6, 77.8–9, 77.11–13, 77.17–20, 77.23–24, 77.27, 77.29–30, 78.4–6, 78.8–14, 78.16–19, 78.22, 78.24, 78.26, 78.28, 78.32, 78.35, 78.38–40, 78.44–62, 78.65–76, 78.81–83, 78.85–89, 78.106–109, 78.121–122, 78.124, 78.127–134, 78.171, 78.175, 78.177, 79.2–4, 79.6–10, 79.12, 79.14–18, 79.22, 79.24–25, 79.29, 79.34–37, 79.39, 79.42–61, 79.64–75, 79.79, 79.83, 79.86, 79.91–93, 79.108, 79.119–120, 79.124–126, 79.129–130, 79.133–134, 79.136–137, 79.141, 79.174, 79.179, 81.1–3, 81.6–10, 81.13–15, 81.19–20, 81.22, 81.24, 81.28–29, 81.32–34, 81.37–57, 81.60–61, 81.63–70, 81.72–73, 81.79, 81.81–82, 81.85–87, 81.105, 81.108–110, 81.116–117, 81.120–121, 81.124–125, 81.130, 81.133, 81.154, 81.168, 81.184, 82.2–4, 82.7–9, 82.11–17, 82.19–20, 82.22, 82.24, 82.27, 82.29–30, 82.32–34, 82.36–55, 82.58–59, 82.61–65, 82.67–68, 82.81–83, 82.100, 82.103–104, 82.110–111, 82.115–119, 82.123, 82.127, 82.165, 82.172, 84.1–3, 84.5–8, 84.10–14, 84.17, 84.19, 84.21, 84.23, 84.27–29, 84.31–51, 84.54, 84.56–60, 84.62–63, 84.73–74, 84.77–78, 84.80, 84.95, 84.98–99, 84.107–108, 84.111–112, 84.114–115, 84.117, 84.121, 84.170, 85.1–3, 85.6–9, 85.11–13, 85.15, 85.18–19, 85.21, 85.24, 85.27, 85.29, 85.32–33, 85.35–55, 85.59–63, 85.65–66, 85.76–77, 85.81–82, 85.84, 85.100, 85.103, 85.108–109, 85.112–113, 85.115–116, 85.119, 85.121, 85.163, 88.2–3, 88.6–8, 88.10–11, 88.13–14, 88.16–18, 88.21, 88.25–29, 88.32–34, 88.36–56, 88.58, 88.60–69, 88.78–79, 88.84–85, 88.87, 88.103–88.104, 88.107, 88.114–115, 88.118–120, 88.122–123, 89.2–8, 89.10–12, 89.16, 89.19, 89.22–24, 89.27–29, 89.32–50, 89.53–62, 89.71–73, 89.76–80, 89.95–96, 89.100, 89.107–108, 89.111–113, 89.116–117, 94.2–10, 94.13, 94.18, 94.20, 94.22–23, 94.25–28, 94.31–51, 94.54–57, 94.59–62, 94.64, 94.77–79, 94.94–95, 94.110, 94.114, 97.1–3, 97.5–12, 97.22, 97.24–26, 97.27–29, 97.33, 97.39, 97.41–57, 97.59–66, 97.68, 97.72, 97.87–89, 97.99, 97.112, 97.117, 97.121–122, 98.1–3, 98.6–12, 98.14–15, 98.20–24, 98.26–27, 98.31, 98.38–56, 98.58–64, 98.70, 98.73, 98.85–87, 98.113, 98.118, 98.122–123, 99.3–11, 99.16–18, 99.20–22, 99.26, 99.32–52, 99.54–61, 99.80–82, 99.95–96, 99.112, 99.115–116, 00.2–3, 00.5–11, 00.15, 00.21, 00.23, 00.25–28, 00.32–33, 00.40–60, 00.62–67, 00.69–70, 00.82, 00.88–89, 00.100–101, 00.118, 00.120–121, 03.2, 03.6, 03.8–10, 03.13–16, 03.22–30, 03.34, 03.42–61, 03.64–67, 03.69, 03.73, 03.75, 03.90–92, 03.106–107, 03.120–122, 03.131

Seckford, Helen, née Bird (c.1568–1594) Mistress Seckford; mar 1583 Henry Seckford*; related to William Bird, mercer. *ODNB* under husband; *Visitations, London*; *Visitations, Suffolk*.

   Gentlewoman: 84.145, 84.342, 85.143, 85.334, 88.139, 88.323, 89.135, 89.320

Seckford, Rebecca, née Brandon (d.aft 1619) Mistress Seckford. Daughter of Robert Brandon* and Catherine Barber; mar 1ˢᵗ John Rowe, 2ⁿᵈ c.1594 Henry Seckford*. *ODNB* under 2ⁿᵈ husband.

Gentlewoman: 98.154, 98.357, 99.148, 99.344, 00.149, 00.350, 03.142, 03.3534

Sergeant of the Pastry—see John Betts, John Dudley, Thomas French, Ralph Batty

Seurre, Michel de (fl.1560s) Resident Ambassador from Charles IX* of France, Le Chevalier de Seurre. *CSP Foreign, 1559–60*; Weaver.

Sundry Gift: 62.392 (Gift to Envoy)

Seymour, Anne, née Stanhope, Duchess of Somerset (1510–1587) Daughter of Sir Edward Stanhope and Elizabeth Bourchier; mar 1ˢᵗ 1535 Edward Seymour, Duke of Somerset, 2ⁿᵈ 1558 Francis Newdigate; mother of Edward Seymour*, Henry Seymour*, Lady Jane Seymour*, Lady Mary [II] Seymour*, and Lady Elizabeth Seymour*. *ODNB*; GEC, *Peerage*.

Duchess: 59.38, 59.259, 62.37, 62.217, 63.38, 63.210, 64.38, 65.138, 67.38, 67.208, 68.20, 68.189, 71.18, 71.188, 76.23, 76.218, 77.27, 77.224, 78.24, 78.225, 79.24, 79.231, 81.20, 81.227, 82.20, 82.220, 82.474, 84.19, 84.217, 85.19, 85.210

Seymour, Lady Catherine—see Lady Catherine Grey

Seymour, Edward, Earl of Hertford (1539–1621) son of Edward Seymour, Duke of Somerset and Anne Stanhope (Seymour*); brother of Lady Mary [II] Seymour*, Lady Elizabeth Seymour*, Lord Henry Seymour*, and Lady Jane Seymour*, mar 1ˢᵗ 1560 Lady Catherine Grey*, 2ⁿᵈ 1585 Frances [I] Howard (Seymour)*, 3ʳᵈ 1601 Frances [II] Howard (Seymour)*. *ODNB*; GEC, *Peerage*.

Earl: 59.21, 59.242, 76.18, 76.214, 77.21, 77.218, 78.20, 78.220, 79.19, 79.225, 81.18, 81.225, 82.18, 82.218, 82.432, 84.16, 84.214, 85.15, 85.207, 88.14, 88.198, 89.10, 89.195, 94.9, 94.193, 97.8, 97.208, 98.9, 98.211, 99.9, 99.202, 03.13, 03.226

Seymour, Lady Elizabeth (1550–1602) Daughter of Edward Seymour, Duke of Somerset and Anne Stanhope (Seymour*); sister of Lady Mary [II] Seymour*, Edward Seymour*, Earl of Hertford, Lord Henry Seymour*, and Lady Jane Seymour*; mar 1578 Sir Richard Knightley MP. GEC, *Peerage*; Hasler.

Lady: 79.100, 79.308, 81.96, 81.303, 82.91, 82.291, 82.516, 84.86, 84.284, 85.90, 85.281, 88.93, 88.278, 89.85, 89.270, 94.82, 94.266, 97.92, 97.291, 98.92, 98.293, 99.89, 99.284, 00.94, 00.291

Sundry Gift: 89.401 (Christening Gift for her child)

Seymour, Frances [I], née Howard, Countess of Hertford (1554–1598) Mistress Howard, Gentlewoman of the Privy Chamber. Daughter of William [I], Lord Howard* of Effingham and Margaret Gamage (Howard*); sister of Douglas Sheffield*, Charles Howard*, Mary Sutton*, and Catherine Howard*; half-sister of Anne/Agnes Howard (Paulet*); mar 1585 Edward Seymour*, Earl of Hertford; 1st cousin once removed to Queen Elizabeth. GEC, *Peerage*; *ODNB*.

Gentlewoman: 71.121, 71.291, 75.87, 76.135, 76.329, 77.138, 77.335, 78.142, 78.344, 79.143, 79.350, 81.137, 81.344, 82.131, 82.331, 82.597, 84.129, 84.325, 85.124, 85.315

Countess: 94., 94., 88.34, 88.219, 89.29, 89.214, 97.29, 97.228, 98.27, 98.231

Seymour, Frances [II], née Howard, Countess of Hertford (1578–1639) later Duchess of Richmond and Duchess of Lennox. Daughter of Thomas [I], Lord Howard* of Bindon and Mabel Burton; half-sister of Thomas [III], Lord Howard* of Bindon and Henry [II], Lord Howard* of Bindon; mar 1ˢᵗ 1591 Henry Prannell, 2ⁿᵈ 1601 Edward Seymour*, Earl of Hertford, 3ʳᵈ 1621 Ludovic Stuart, Duke of Lennox; 2ⁿᵈ cousin of Queen Elizabeth. GEC, *Peerage*; *ODNB*.

Countess: 03.29, 03.242

Seymour, Lord Henry (c.1540–aft.1603) Naval Commander. Son of Edward Seymour, Duke of Somerset and Anne Stanhope*; brother of Lady Mary [II] Seymour*, Edward Seymour*, Earl of Hertford, Lady Elizabeth Seymour*, and Lady Jane Seymour*; mar Jane Percy. GEC, *Peerage*; *ODNB* under father.

Lord: 77.79, 77.275, 88.70, 88.255, 89.63, 89.248

Seymour, Lady Jane (1537–1561) Maid of Honour to Mary I and Elizabeth. Daughter of Edward Seymour, Duke of Somerset and Anne Stanhope*; sister of Edward Seymour*, Earl of Hertford, Lord Henry Seymour*, Lady Mary [II] Seymour*, and Lady Elizabeth Seymour*; unmarried. *ODNB*; Mertens.

Maid of Honour: 59.374

Seymour, Mary [I], née Odell (fl.1550s) Mistress Seymour. Daughter of Nicholas Odell MP and Mary Parr; granddaughter of William Parr and Mary Salisbury; mar c.1546 David Seymour MP. Bindoff under husband and father.

Gentlewoman: 59.138, 59.364

Seymour, Lady Mary [II] (b.1542) Daughter of Edward Seymour, Duke of Somerset and Anne Stanhope (Seymour*); sister of Elizabeth Seymour*, Edward Seymour*, Earl of Hertford, Henry, Lord Seymour*, and Jane Seymour*; mar 1st c.1577 Andrew Rogers* MP, 2nd c.1600 Henry Peyton; mother of infant Rogers*. GEC, *Peerage*; Hasler.

Lady: 77.107, 77.304, 78.101, 78.302, 79.99, 79.307, 81.95, 81.302, 82.90, 82.290, 82.514, 84.84, 84.282, 85.89, 85.280, 88.92, 88.277, 89.84, 89.269, 94.84, 94.265, 97.91, 97.290, 98.91, 98.292, 99.88, 99.283, 00.93, 00.290, 03.96, 03.308

Sundry Gift: 79.438 (Christening Gift for her child)

Shandoes, Shandowes, Shandoyes—see Chandos

Shaw, Christopher (d.1618) Embroiderer. Will PCC 95 Meade.

Gentleman: 03.213, 03.432

Sheffield, Lord/Baroness—see Douglas Sheffield, née Howard, 1560–1608; Edmund Sheffield, 3rd, 1568–1646; John Sheffield, 2nd, 1549–1568; Ursula Sheffield, née Tyrwhitt, 1581–1618

Sheffield, Douglas, née Howard, Baroness Sheffield (c.1545–1608) Maid of Honour, alias Baroness Sheffield Stafford. Daughter of William [I], Lord Howard* and Margaret Gamage (Howard*); sister of Frances [I] Seymour*, Charles Howard*, Mary Sutton*, and Catherine Howard*; 1st cousin once removed to Queen Elizabeth; mar 1st 1560 John Sheffield*, 2nd (allegedly) 1573 Robert Dudley*, Earl of Leicester, 3rd 1579 Edward Stafford*; mother of Elizabeth Butler*, Edmund Sheffield*, and unidentified son Stafford*. *ODNB*; GEC, *Peerage*; BL Sloane MS 814.

Maid of Honour: 59.377

Baroness: 62.81, 62.261, 67.79, 67.249, 71.71, 71.241, 76.99, 76.293, 77.99, 77.296, 78.98, 78.298, 79.94, 79.301, 81.89, 81.296, 82.84, 82.284, 82.507, 89.81, 89.268, 94.76, 94.261, 97.86, 97.281, 98.78, 98.281, 99.79, 99.273, 00.87, 00.282, 03.82, 03.297

Sundry Gift: 62.389 (Christening Gift for her child), 81.441 (Christening Gift for her child)

Regifted: 81.89 (Queen regifted gift to Anne Knollys*)

Sheffield, Edmund, Lord Sheffield (1565–1646) KG 1593. Son of John, Lord Sheffield* and Douglas Howard (Sheffield*); brother of Elizabeth Sheffield*; 2nd cousin of Queen Elizabeth; mar 1st 1581 Ursula Tyrwhitt (Sheffield*), 2nd 1619 Mariana Irvin. *ODNB*; GEC, *Peerage*.

Lord: 98.68, 98.271

Sheffield, Elizabeth—see Elizabeth Butler

Sheffield, John, Lord Sheffield (1538–1568) KB 1559. Son of Edmund Sheffield and Anne Vere; 1st cousin of Edward de Vere*; mar c.1560 Douglas Howard (Sheffield*); father of Edmund Sheffield* and Elizabeth Butler*. *ODNB*; GEC, *Peerage*.

Lord: 62.69, 62.249

Sundry Gift 62.389 (Christening Gift for his child)

Sheffield, Ursula, née Tyrwhitt, Baroness Sheffield (d.1618) Daughter of Sir Robert Tyrwhitt and Elizabeth Oxenbridge; mar 1581 Edmund, Lord Sheffield*. *ODNB* and GEC, *Peerage* under husband.
Baroness: 98.84, 98.290

Sheffield Stafford, Douglas—see Douglas Sheffield

Shelley, Mary—see Lister, Mary

Shelton, Amy (d.1579) Mistress Shelton. Daughter of Ralph Shelton and Mary Wodehouse; great-granddaughter of Sir John Shelton and Anne Boleyn; sister of Elizabeth Shelton* and Audrey Walsingham*; 1st cousin once removed to Queen Anne Boleyn; 2nd cousin once removed to Queen Elizabeth, niece of Mary Scudamore*; unmarried. will PCC 42 Bakon.
Gentlewoman: 62.148, 32.330, 63.138, 63.311, 64.126, 64.178, 65.65, 65.231, 67.136, 67.306, 68.136, 68.304, 71.141, 71.311, 75.104, 76.156, 76.356, 77.166, 77.364, 78.167, 78.369, 79.170, 79.377

Shelton, Audrey—see Audrey Walsingham

Shelton, Elizabeth (d.1594) Mistress Shelton, of the Privy Chamber. Daughter of Ralph Shelton and Mary Wodehouse; great-granddaughter of Sir John Shelton and Anne Boleyn; sister of Amy Shelton* and Audrey Walsingham*; 1st cousin once removed to Queen Anne Boleyn; 2nd cousin once removed to Queen Elizabeth, niece of Mary Scudamore*; mar 1575 John Russell.
Gentlewoman: 62.149, 62.331, 63.139, 63.312, 64.127, 64.179, 65.66, 65.232, 67.137, 67.307, 68.137, 68.305

Shelton, Margaret—see Margaret Wodehouse

Shelton, Mary—see Mary Heveningham, Mary Scudamore

Shene, Caloptues—see Calixtus Schein

Sherer, Elizabeth—see Elizabeth Dale

Sheriff, Lawrence (c.1515–1567) Grocer, supplied household of Princess Elizabeth, founder of Rugby School. Mar Elizabeth [née?]. *ODNB*; will PCC 29 Stonard; Rouse; Foxe.
Gentleman: 59.183, 59.407, 62.169, 62.356, 63.158, 63.337

Sherman, unidentified (fl.1580s) Queen's servant.
Custody of Gift: 82.308

Shipman, Elizabeth—see Elizabeth Hyde

Shrewsbury, Earl/Countess—see Elizabeth Hardwick, 1567–1590, dowager 1590–1608; Elizabeth Talbot, née Walden, 1512–1538, dowager 1538–1567; Francis Talbot, 5th, 1538–1560; George Talbot, 6th, 1560–1590; Gertrude Talbot, née Manners, 1539–1567; Gilbert Talbot, 7th, 1590–1616; Mary Talbot, née Cavendish, 1590–1616, dowager 1616–1632; see also Talbot, Lord/Baroness

Shynke, Martin—see Martin Schenk

Sibell, Lucy—see Lucy Morgan

Sidney, Elizabeth—see Elizabeth Manners

Sidney, Frances, née Walsingham, Countess of Essex (1569–1632) later Countess of Clanricarde. Daughter of Francis Walsingham* and Ursula St Barbe (Walsingham*); mar 1st 1583 Philip Sidney*, 2nd 1590 Robert Devereux*, Earl of Essex, 3rd 1603 Richard Bourke*, Earl of Clanricarde; mother of Elizabeth [III] Manners*. *ODNB* under husbands and father; GEC, *Peerage*.
Countess: 03.41, 03.254

Sidney, Frances—see Frances Radcliffe

Sidney, Sir Henry (1529–1586) Lord President of Wales, Lord Deputy of Ireland, Privy Councillor, kntd 1550, KG 1564, MP. Son of William Sidney and Anne Pakington; mar

1551 Mary Dudley (Sidney*); father of Philip Sidney*, Robert Sidney*, and Mary
  Herbert*. *ODNB*; Hasler; will PCC 27 Windsor.
  Knight: 68.118, 68.287, 79.127, 79.334
Sidney, Lady Mary, née Dudley (c.1530/35–1586) Lady of the Privy Chamber. Daughter of
  John Dudley, Duke of Northumberland and Jane Guildford; sister of Robert Dudley*,
  Catherine [II] Hastings*, and Ambrose Dudley*; mar 1551 Sir Henry Sidney*, mother
  of Mary Herbert*, Sir Philip Sidney*, and Sir Robert Sidney*. *ODNB*; GEC, *Peerage*;
  BL Sloane MS 814.
  Lady: 59.96, 59.316, 71.75, 71.245, 76.104, 76.299, 77.103, 77.300, 78.100, 78.301, 79.98,
  79.306, 81.94, 81.301, 84.85, 84.283, 85.91, 85.283
  Baroness: 82.483 [named on Somerset RO DD\MI/19/1, with Ladies, but no gift listed]
Sidney, Mary—see Mary Herbert
Sidney, Sir Philip (1554–1586) Ambassador, Governor of Flushing, courtier poet, soldier,
  kntd 1583, MP. Son of Sir Henry Sidney* and Mary Dudley*; brother of Mary Herbert*
  and Robert Sidney*; mar 1583 Frances Walsingham (Sidney*); father of Elizabeth [III]
  Manners*. *ODNB*; Hasler.
  Gentleman: 78.176, 78.384, 79.176, 79.389, 81.171, 81.385
  Knight: 84.124, 84.322
Sidney, Sir Robert (1563–1626) courtier poet, kntd 1586. Son of Sir Henry Sidney* and
  Mary Dudley (Sidney*); brother of Mary Herbert* and Philip Sidney*; mar 1st 1584
  Barbara Gamage, 2nd 1625 Sarah Blount. possible identification for 'my skimskin for
  my pantables'. May, *Elizabethan Courtier*; *ODNB*; GEC, *Peerage*.
  Knight: 89.115, 89.306, 97.133, 97.138, 97.334, 99.131, 99.321
Skene/Sken, Calixtus—see Calixtus Schein
Sketts—see Schetts
Skidmore—see Scudamore
'my skimskin for my pantables'—see Robert Sidney as probable identification
Skipwith, Bridget—see Bridget Cave
Skipwith, Margaret—see Margaret Tailboys
Skydmor—see Scudamore
Smallpage alias Randall, Elizabeth—see Elizabeth Collier
Smallwood, William (d.1568) Grocer. will PCC 17 Babington.
  Gentleman: 59.181, 59.405
Smith, Alice—see Alice Montague, Anne York
Smith, Charles (d.1587) Groom of the Chamber, Page of the Robes, MP. Mar Catherine
  Harvey. Hasler; will PCC 62 Spencer; BL Sloane MS 814.
  Gentleman: 71.162, 71.345, 75.229, 77.196, 77.397, 78.194, 78.403, 79.201, 79.414,
  81.196, 81.413, 82.193, 82.397, 82.573, 84.184, 84.378, 85.178, 85.377
  Custody of Gift: 77.3, 79.186, 81.80, 81.113, 81.146
  Regifted: 82.193 (Queen gave his gift to Frances Drury*)
Smith, Elizabeth—see Elizabeth Nott
Smith, Richard (d.1599) Physician. Furdell; Naylor; will PCC 51 Kidd.
  Gentleman: 94.156, 94.351, 97.110, 97.372, 98.166, 98.373, 99.160, 99.361
Smith, Sir Thomas [I] (1513–1577) Principal Secretary 1572–1576, Ambassador to France
  1562–1566, Chancellor of the Garter, kntd 1549, MP. Son of John Smith and Agnes
  Charnock; mar 1st 1548 Elizabeth Carkeke, 2nd 1554 Philippa Wilford. *ODNB*; Hasler.
  Knight: 59.130, 59.349, 76.119, 76.314, 77.121, 77.318
Smith, Thomas [II] (c.1522–1591) Customer of London, Skinner, Haberdasher, MP. Son of
  John Smith and Joanne Brouncker; mar c.1554 Alice Judd. Hasler; Bindoff.

Gentleman: 59.185, 59.409, 62.165, 62.353, 63.155, 63.334, 64.138, 64.198, 65.85, 67.159, 67.335, 68.152, 68.324, 71.155, 71.333, 75.120, 75.217, 76.181, 76.383, 77.181, 77.383, 78.197, 78.389, 79.184, 79.396, 81.206, 81.399, 82.177, 82.381, 82.563, 84.175, 84.377, 85.171, 85.370, 88.2159, 88.350, 89.156, 89.348

Smith, William (d.1592) Sergeant of the Scullery. Collins, *Jewels*; PRO E315/1954; will PCC 85 Dixy.

Custody of Gift: 82.302

Smithson, Elizabeth, née Taylor (d.1593) Mistress Smithson, alias Taylor, Laundress. Mar John Smithson*. PRO SP 121/66, LC 5/49; will PCC 2 Dixy; husband's will PCC 72 Spencer.

Gentlewoman: 64.129, 64.182, 65.70, 65.235, 67.134, 67.304, 68.134, 68.302, 71.139, 71.309, 75.102, 76.155, 76.355, 77.160, 77.356, 78.161, 78.362, 79.162, 79.369, 81.156, 81.362, 82.152, 82.352, 82.607, 84.148, 84.345, 85.153, 85.345, 88.144, 88.328, 89.140, 89.325

Smithson, John (d.c.1589) Master Cook, alias Taylor. Mar by 1560 Elizabeth Taylor (Smithson*). Will PCC 72 Spencer 1587, PRO E315/1954, SP 121/66; Collins, *Jewels*.

Gentleman: 75.128, 75.224, 76.190, 76.393, 77.189, 77.390, 78.188, 78.397, 79.193, 79.406, 81.192, 81.406, 82.187, 82.391, 82.561, 84.187, 84.388, 85.181, 85.381, 88.174, 88.366, 89.174, 89.366

Snakenborg, Helena—see Helena Gorges

Snow, Elizabeth, née Cavendish (c.1522–1587) Mistress Snow. Gentlewoman to Princess Elizabeth, Gentlewoman of the Privy Chamber. Daughter of Richard Cavendish and Elizabeth Grimston; mar 1545 Richard Snowe. Will PCC 17 Spencer, PRO LC 2/4, SP 12/175/81; *CPR, 1560–61*; Folger MS X.d.77; *VCH, Bedfordshire*; *CSP Domestic, 1591–94*; Madden; Collins, *Jewels*.

Gentlewoman: 62.146, 62.326, 63.136, 63.309, 65.73, 65.238, 71.134, 71.304, 75.95, 76.147, 76.351, 77.144, 77.341, 78.146, 78.347, 79.147, 79.354, 81.141, 81.348, 82.135, 82.335, 82.596, 84.143, 84.330, 85.140, 85.326

Snow, Nicholas (d.1583) Servant in household of Princess Elizabeth, Keeper of the Queen's Wardrobe at Richmond. Strangford; will PCC 7 Butts.

Custody of Gift: 82.303

Soda, John (d.aft.1571) Apothecary to Catherine of Aragon, Mary I and Elizabeth, MP, alias Sodaye. Son of John Soda; father of Catherine Soda; father-in-law of Sir John White*; mar Ellen [née?]. Siddons; Hasler under son-in-law; Matthews.

Gentleman: 59.195, 59.420, 65.87, 67.163, 67.339, 68.157, 68.329, 71.159, 71.337

Solns-Laubach, Agnes von—see Agnes von Hesse

Somerset, Anne—see Lady Anne Percy, Anne Russell, Lady Anne Winter

Somerset, Lady Catherine—see Lady Catherine Petre

Somerset, Edward, Earl of Worcester (1553–1628) Lord Herbert, Privy Councillor 1601, KG 1593. Son of William Somerset and Christian North; mar 1571 Elizabeth Hastings (Somerset*), father of Lady Anne Winter*, Lady Elizabeth Guildford* and Lady Catherine Petre*; grandson of Elizabeth [I] Somerset*. *ODNB*; GEC, *Peerage*.

Earl: 94.14, 94.197, 00.16, 00.211, 03.5, 03.218

Somerset, Lady Elizabeth—see Lady Elizabeth Guildford

Somerset, Elizabeth [I], née Browne, Countess of Worcester (d.1565) Daughter of Sir Anthony Browne and Lucy Neville; mar 1526 Henry Somerset, Earl of Worcester; mother of Lucy Neville*, Anne Percy* and William Somerset; grandmother of Edward Somerset*, Catherine Percy* and Dorothy Cecil*. GEC, *Peerage*.

Countess: 59.50, 59.271

Somerset, Lady Elizabeth [II], née Hastings (c.1550–1621) Maid of Honour, Countess of Worcester. Daughter of Francis Hastings*, Earl of Huntingdon, and Catherine Pole (Hastings*); sister of Henry Hastings*, Frances Hastings*, and George Hastings*; mar 1571 Edward Somerset, later Earl of Worcester; mother of Lady Anne Winter*, Lady Catherine Petre* and Lady Elizabeth Guildford*. GEC, *Peerage*; *ODNB* under husband.

Maid of Honour: 71.315

Countess: 94.30, 94.214, 00.39, 00.228, 03.39, 03.253

Somerset, Lucy—see Lucy Neville

Sotherman, William—see William Suderman

Southampton, Earl/Countess—see Elizabeth Wriothesley, née Vernon, 1598–1624; Henry [I] Wriothesley, 2nd; 1550–1581; Henry [II] Wriothesley, 3rd, 1581–1601, 1603; Jane Wriothesley, née Cheyne, 1547–1574; Mary Wriothesley, née Browne, 1565–1607

Southwell, Elizabeth [I] (b.1567) Maid of Honour. Daughter of Thomas Southwell* and Nazareth Paget*; half-sister of Sir Robert Southwell*; aunt of Elizabeth [II] Southwell*; 2nd cousin of Anne Southwell; liaison with Robert Devereux*, Earl of Essex; mar 1600 Sir Barentyne Moleyns. probable scribal error of Anne for Elizabeth in 1588. Father's will PCC 13 Babington; *Visitations, Berkshire*; Lambeth Palace MS 651; Hammer; Rickman.

Maid of Honour: 88.344, 89.342, 94.312

Lady: 94.86, 94.270

Sundry Gift: 68.350 (Christening Gift)

Southwell, Elizabeth [II] (1584–1631) Maid of Honour. Daughter of Sir Robert Southwell* and Elizabeth [I] Howard (Southwell*); niece of Elizabeth [I] Southwell*; 2nd cousin once removed to Queen Elizabeth, mar 1605 Robert Dudley. GEC, *Peerage*.

Maid of Honour: 03.376

Sundry Gift: 85.407 (Christening Gift)

Southwell, Mary—see Mary Mansell

Southwell, Nazareth—see Nazareth Paget

Southwell, Sir Richard (1504–1564) Master of the Ordnance, kntd 1542, MP. Son of Francis Southwell and Dorothy Tendring; mar 1st c.1540 Thomasine Darcy, 2nd c.1542 Mary Darcy. *ODNB*; Bindoff.

Knight: 59.122, 59.341, 62.114, 62.294, 63.112, 63.285, 64.105, 64.159

Southwell, Sir Robert (1564–1598) kntd 1585, MP. Son of Thomas Southwell and Mary Mansell*; half-brother of Elizabeth [I] Southwell*; mar 1583 Elizabeth [I] Howard (Southwell*); father of Elizabeth [II] Southwell*. Hasler; will PCC 78 Lewyn.

Gentleman: 84.163, 84.365, 85.160, 85.358

Knight: 89.119, 89.304

Sundry Gift: 85.407 (Christening Gift for his child)

Southwell, Thomas (c.1542–1568) Son of Robert Southwell and Margaret Neville, mar 1st c.1560 Mary Jerningham, 2nd 1563 Mary Mansell*, 3rd c.1565 Nazareth Newton (Paget*); father of Sir Robert Southwell* and Elizabeth [I] Southwell*. will PCC 13 Babington.

Sundry Gift: 68.350 (Christening Gift for his child)

Souza, Juan Rodriguez de (b.c.1548) alias Joao Roiz de Sousa. Envoy from Don António*, Claimant to the Portuguese throne. *CSP Foreign, 1579–80, 1581–82*; *CSP Spanish, 1580–86*.

Sundry Gift: 81.440 (Gift to Envoy)

Speckard, Abraham (fl.1590s–1600s) Silkman, artificer. Mar Dorothy [née?] Speckard*.

Gentleman: 97.179, 97.381, 98.177, 98.382, 99.175, 99.373, 00.175, 00.374

Speckard, Dorothy [née?] (fl.1590s–1600s) Silkwoman. Mar Abraham Speckard*.
  Gentlewoman: 98.157, 98.364, 99.151, 99.351, 00.152, 00.356, 03.156, 03.371

Spencer, Alice—see Alice Stanley

Spencer, Elizabeth—see Elizabeth Carey, Elizabeth Vincent

Spilman, John (c.1552–1626) Goldsmith, Jeweller, Papermaker, kntd 1603. Son of Matthias
  Spilman, mar 1ˢᵗ Elizabeth Mendel, 2ⁿᵈ Katarina Godshalk. *CSP Domestic, 1581–90*;
  Siddons; Shorter; *Index to Privy Bills*.
  Gentleman: 89.167, 89.360, 94.155, 94.348, 97.167, 97.370, 98.164, 98.371, 99.158,
  99.359, 00.160, 00.362, 03.169, 03.390
  Sundry Gift: 89.407 (Goldsmith)

Spinola, Benedict (1519–1580) Merchant, related to Horatio Palavicino*, unmarried.
  ODNB; *CSP Foreign, 1581–82*; Siddons.
  Gentleman: 59.159, 59.383, 62.161, 62.349, 63.152, 63.331, 64.136, 64.196, 65.82, 67.157,
  67.333, 68.151, 68.323, 71.154, 71.332, 75.121, 75.211, 76.382, 77.182, 77.384, 78.181,
  78.390, 79.184, 79.397

Stafford, Lord/Baroness—see Edward Stafford, 3ʳᵈ, 1566–1603; Henry Stafford, 1ˢᵗ, 1547–
  1563; Ursula Stafford, née Pole, 1547–1563, dowager 1563–1570

Stafford, Dorothy, née Stafford (1526–1604) Lady Stafford, Lady of the Bedchamber.
  Daughter of Henry Stafford* and Ursula Pole (Stafford*); mar 1543 Sir William
  Stafford; mother of Elizabeth Drury* and Edward [II] Stafford* MP. Merton; *ODNB*
  and Hasler under son.
  Lady: 64.84, 65.15, 65.182, 67.86, 67.256, 68.79, 68.248, 71.79, 71.249, 76.105, 76.300,
  77.104, 77.301, 78.102, 78.303, 79.101, 79.309, 81.97, 81.304, 82.92, 82.292, 82.548,
  84.87, 84.285, 85.93, 85.286, 88.95, 88.280, 89.87, 89.272, 94.85, 94.269, 97.94, 97.293,
  98.94, 98.296, 99.91, 99.286, 00.96, 00.293, 03.99, 03.311
  Custody of Gift: 78.146, 81.83, 82.120, 82.132, 84.415

Stafford, Douglas—see Douglas Sheffield

Stafford, Edward [I], Lord Stafford (1536–1603) Son of Henry, Lord Stafford* and Ursula
  Pole (Stafford*); brother of Dorothy Stafford*; mar 1566 Mary Stanley (Stafford*);
  nephew of Cardinal Reginald Pole. GEC, *Peerage*; *ODNB* under father and mother.
  Lord: 71.66, 71.235, 75.70, 75.178, 76.73, 76.264, 77.73, 77.270, 78.72, 78.274, 79.70,
  79.277, 81.67, 81.274, 82.63, 82.263, 82.462, 97.72, 97.267, 98.70, 98.268, 03.75, 03.288

Stafford, Edward [II] (c.1552–1605) Gentleman Pensioner, Ambassador to France 1583–
  1589, kntd 1583, MP; possible idenfication for 'unknown person,1584'. Son of Sir
  William Stafford and Dorothy Stafford*; mar 1ˢᵗ Roberta Chapman, 2ⁿᵈ 1579 Douglas
  Howard (Sheffield*); father of infant Stafford*. *ODNB*; Hasler; Tighe; will PCC 107
  Byrde.
  Gentleman: 79.196, 79.409, 81.176, 81.394, 82.171, 82.375, 82.572
  Knight: [84.126, 84.127] , 94.118, 94.302, 97.124, 97.322, 98.124, 98.325, 99.117, 99.311,
  00.122, 00.318, 03.127, 03.339
  Custody of Gift: 79.447, 81.434, 81.436
  Sundry Gift: 81.441 (Christening gift for his child)

Stafford, Elizabeth - see Elizabeth Drury

Stafford, Henry, Lord Stafford (1501–1563) kntd 1553, MP. Son of Edward, Lord Stafford
  and Eleanor Percy; mar 1519 Ursula Pole*; father of Dorothy Stafford* and Edward,
  Lord Stafford*. *ODNB*; Bindoff; GEC, *Peerage*.
  Lord: 59.60, 59.281, 62.59, 62.240, 63.60, 63.233

Stafford, Jane, née Gorges (c.1538–1591) Lady Stafford. Daughter of Edward Gorges and
  Mary Poyntz; sister of Thomas Gorges* and Elizabeth Wake*; sister-in-law of Helena

Gorges*, Lady Marquess of Northampton; mar 1ˢᵗ c.1550 John Ashe, 2ⁿᵈ c.1566 Sir Robert Stafford. PRO E 115; will PCC 10 Harrington.
Lady: 88.113, 88.297
Stafford, Mary—see Mary Stanley
Stafford, unidentified (b.1581) Son of Edward, Lord Stafford* and Douglas Howard (Sheffield*).
Sundry Gift: 81.441 (Christening Gift)
Stafford, Ursula, née Pole, Baroness Stafford (1504–1570) Daughter of Richard Pole and Margaret York, Countess of Salisbury; mar 1519 Henry, Lord Stafford*; mother of Dorothy Stafford*; sister of Cardinal Reginald Pole; 2ⁿᵈ cousin once removed to Queen Elizabeth. *ODNB* under mother; GEC, *Peerage*.
Baroness: 63.98, 63.258
Stanhope, Anne—see Anne Seymour
Stanhope, Frances—see Frances Mewtas
Stanhope, Jane—see Jane Townsend
Stanhope, John (1545–1621) Gentleman of the Privy Chamber, Treasurer of the Chamber 1596, Privy Councillor 1601, Keeper of Eltham Park, Vice Chamberlain 1601, kntd 1596, Lord Stanhope 1605. Son of Sir Michael Stanhope and Anne Rawson; brother of Jane Townsend* and Michael Stanhope*; mar 1ˢᵗ 1557 Mary Knollys, 2ⁿᵈ 1589 Margaret Mackwilliam*. *ODNB*; GEC, *Peerage*.
Gentleman: 75.213, 76.374, 77.178, 77.381, 78.179, 78.387, 79.181, 79.394, 81.178, 81.396, 82.175, 82.379, 82.570, 84.162, 84.364, 85.165, 85.365, 88.163, 88.354, 89.161, 89.353, 94.143, 94.334
Knight: 97.131, 97.321, 98.129, 98.324, 99.121, 99.310, 00.125, 00.317, 03.123, 03.333
Stanhope, Michael (1549–c.1621) Groom of the Privy Chamber, kntd c.1603. Son of Sir Michael Stanhope and Anne Rawson; brother of Jane Townsend* and Sir John Stanhope*; mar Anne Read. *ODNB* under father; will PCC 10 Savile.
Free Gift: 88.388, 89.389, 94.385, 97.410, 98.417, 99.404, 00.407, 03.439
Stanley, Alice, née Spencer, Countess of Derby (1563–1637) alias Countess Derby Egerton, Lady Strange. Daughter of John Spencer and Catherine Kitson; sister of Elizabeth Carey*; mar 1ˢᵗ 1580 Ferdinando Stanley*, Lord Strange, later Earl of Derby, 2ⁿᵈ 1600 Thomas Egerton* MP. *ODNB*; GEC, *Peerage*.
Countess: 94.23, 94.215, 97.32, 97.222, 98.28, 98.224, 99.23, 99.214, 00.29, 00.221, 03.31, 03.245
Stanley, Edward, Earl of Derby (1509–1572) Privy Councillor, KG 1547. Son of Thomas Stanley and Anne Hastings; mar 1ˢᵗ 1530 Dorothy Howard, 2ⁿᵈ c.1558 Margaret Barlow, 3ʳᵈ c.1562 Mary Cotton (Stanley*). *ODNB*; GEC, *Peerage*; BL Additional MS 63742.
Earl: 59.9, 59.230, 62.7, 62.187, 63.10, 63.182, 64.10, 65.109, 67.9, 67.179, 68.12, 68.181, 71.8, 71.178
Stanley, Lady Elizabeth, née Vere, Countess of Derby (1575–1627) Lady of the Privy Chamber. Daughter of Edward de Vere*, Earl of Oxford and Anne Cecil (Vere*); granddaughter of William Cecil*, Lord Burghley and Mildred Cooke (Cecil*), and of John de Vere*, Earl of Oxford and Margaret Golding (Vere*); mar 1595 William Stanley*, Earl of Derby. GEC, *Peerage*; *ODNB*.
Countess: 97.30, 97.223, 98.30, 98.225, 99.24, 99.215, 00.30, 00.222, 03.33, 03.246
Lady: 94.83, 94.267
Sundry Gift: 76.414 (Christening Gift)
Stanley, Elizabeth—see Parker, Elizabeth
Stanley, Ferdinando (1559–1594) Lord Strange, later Earl of Derby, courtier poet. Son of Henry Stanley*, Earl of Derby and Margaret Clifford (Stanley*); brother of William

Stanley*; mar 1580 Alice Spencer (Stanley*), 1ˢᵗ cousin twice removed and 2nd cousin of Queen Elizabeth. *ODNB*; GEC, *Peerage*.
  Lord: 75.74, 75.182, 76.78, 76.273
  Earl: 94.5, 94.189
Stanley, Henry, Earl of Derby (1531–1593) Privy Councillor 1585, KG 1574. Son of Edward Stanley and Dorothy Howard; mar 1555 Margaret Clifford (Stanley*); father of Ferdinando Stanley* and William Stanley*, 1ˢᵗ cousin once removed to Queen Elizabeth. *ODNB*; GEC, *Peerage*.
  Earl: 62.67, 62.247, 63.68, 63.240, 64.56, 65.157, 67.57, 67.227, 68.55, 68.224, 71.53, 71.223, 75.9, 76.9, 76.204, 77.12, 77.209, 78.13, 78.215, 79.8, 79.215, 81.7, 81.214, 82.8, 82.208, 82.423, 84.6, 84.204, 85.7, 85.198, 88.7, 88.192, 89.5, 89.190
Stanley, Joyce—see Joyce Barrett
Stanley, Lady Margaret, née Clifford, Countess of Derby (1540–1596) Lady Strange. Daughter of Henry Clifford, Earl of Cumberland and Eleanor Brandon, 1ˢᵗ cousin once removed to Queen Elizabeth, mar 1555 Henry Stanley*, Earl of Derby; mother of Ferdinando Stanley* and William Stanley*. Name listed with 'X' but no participation for 1582. GEC, *Peerage*; *ODNB* under father and husband; BL Sloane MS 814.
  Primary: 59.3, 59.224, 62.1, 62.181, 63.2, 63.174, 64.2, 65.100, 67.1, 67.171, 68.2, 68.171, 71.2, 71.171, 75.1, 76.2, 76.197, 77.3, 77.200, 78.3, 78.205, 79.1, 79.208, 82.1
Stanley, Mary, née Cotton, Countess of Derby (d.1580) Countess of Kent. Daughter of George Cotton and Mary Onley; niece of Henry Cotton*; sister-in-law of Lady Susan Grey*; mar 1ˢᵗ c.1562 Edward Stanley*, Earl of Derby, 2ⁿᵈ 1575 Henry Grey, Earl of Kent. GEC, *Peerage*.
  Countess: 62.41, 62.221, 63.46, 63.217, 64.45, 65.146, 67.45, 67.215, 68.25, 68.194, 71.21, 71.191, 74.5, 77.41, 77.240, 78.41, 78.243, 79.41, 79.248
Stanley, Thomas (1511–1571) Master of the Mint, MP. Son of Thomas Stanley and Margaret Fleming; mar c.1552 Joyce Barrett (Wilford*). Bindoff.
  Gentleman: 59.161, 59.385, 62.156, 62.343, 63.147, 63.326, 64.133, 64.192, 65.79, 67.152, 67.328, 68.149, 68.321, 71.150, 71.328
Stanley, William, Earl of Derby (c.1561–1642) KG 1601. Son of Henry Stanley* and Margaret Clifford (Stanley*); brother of Ferdinando Stanley*; mar 1595 Lady Elizabeth Vere (Stanley*), 1ˢᵗ cousin twice removed and 2nd cousin of Queen Elizabeth. *ODNB*; GEC, *Peerage*.
  Earl: 97.5, 97.205, 98.6, 98.208, 99.4, 99.199, 00.5, 00.203, 03.7, 03.220
Stewart—see Stuart
Still, John (1543–1608) Bishop of Bath and Wells 1594–1608. *ODNB*.
  Bishop: 94.51, 94.235, 97.54, 97.253, 98.54, 98.256, 99.48, 99.245, 00.47, 00.255, 03.51, 03.264
Stockett, Lewis (1530–1578) Surveyor of the Works. Will PCC 12 Bakon; BL Egerton MS 2723; PRO AO 1/2411/1–8, E 351/3202–3212.
  Gentleman: 65.94
Stokes, Anne—see Anne Carew
Stokes, Frances—see Frances Brandon
Stolberg, Ludwig, Count Stolberg (1509–1572) Ambassador from Emperor Maximilian II*. *CSP Spanish, 1558–67*; *CSP Foreign, 1566–68*.
  Sundry Gift: 68.347 (Gift to Envoy)
Stone the fool (fl.1570s) possible identification. The 1575 gift from Anne Heneage* is a picture of Stone, possibly 'the fool'. Hotson.
  Gentlewomen: 75.89

Stone, William (fl.1570s–1580s) Groom of the Chamber, Footman. BL Stowe MS 155; *CPR, 1575–78*; PRO LC 5/34.
  Custody of Gift: 82.326
Stonor, Cecilia, née Chamberlain (fl.1560s–1570s) Lady Stonor. Daughter of Leonard Chamberlain and Dorothy Newdigate (Chamberlain*); sister of Francis Chamberlain*; mar Francis Stonor. *Visitations, Oxford.*
  Lady: 68.95, 68.264, 71.93, 71.263
Stourton, Lord/Baroness—see John Stourton, 9th, 1557–1588
Stourton, John, Lord Stourton (1553–1588) Son of Charles Stourton and Anne Stanley; grandson of Edward Stanley*; mar 1580 Frances Brooke. GEC, *Peerage.*
  Lord: 75.66, 75.174, 76.68, 76.267
Strange, Lord/Baroness—see Alice Stanley, née Spencer, 1580–1593; Ferdinando Stanley, 13th, 1572–1594; Henry Stanley, 12th, 1559–1572; Margaret Stanley, née Clifford, 1559–1572; see also Derby, Earl/Countess
Strange, Catherine—see Catherine Clarke
Strangeways, Frances, née Newton (b.c.1585) Daughter of Henry Newton* and Catherine Paston (Paston*); mar by 1596 Giles Strangeways; daughter-in-law of Dorothy Thynne*. *Visitations, Dorsetshire*; Davies.
  Gentlewoman: 03.158, 03.372
Strong, Lancelot (fl.1540s–1560s) Mar Margaret [née?] Coldale. PRO C 1/921/24–25, C 1/1088/14, C 4/144/16.
  Gentleman: 59.217, 59.441
Stuart, Lady Arbella (1575–1615) Daughter of Charles Stuart, Earl of Lennox and Elizabeth Cavendish*; 1st cousin of King James VI*; 1st cousin once removed to Queen Elizabeth; granddaughter of Sir William Cavendish and Elizabeth Hardwick*; mar 1609 William Seymour. *ODNB*; GEC, *Peerage.*
  Baroness: 94.73, 94.257, 97.83, 97.280, 98.81, 98.279, 99.76, 99.271, 00.83, 00.280, 03.83, 03.299
Stuart, Elizabeth, née Cavendish, Countess of Lennox (1555–1582) Daughter of Sir William Cavendish and Elizabeth Hardwick*; mar 1574 Charles Stuart, Earl of Lennox; mother of Lady Arbella Stuart*. *ODNB* under daughter; GEC, *Peerage.*
  Countess: 81.36, 81.243, 82.492
Stuart, Henry, Lord Darnley (1545–1567) Son of Matthew Stuart*, Earl of Lennox and Margaret Douglas*; mar 1565 Mary Stuart*, Queen of Scots; father of King James VI*. *ODNB.*
  Sundry Gift: 67.362 (Christening Gift for his child)
Stuart, James—see James VI of Scotland
Stuart, Margaret, née Douglas, Countess of Lennox (1515–1578) daughter of Archibald Douglas, Earl of Angus and Margaret Tudor, Queen of Scots; granddaughter of Henry VII and Elizabeth of York; 1st cousin of Queen Elizabeth; mar 1544 Matthew Stuart, Earl of Lennox; grandmother of James VI*. *ODNB*; GEC, *Peerage*; BL Sloane MS 814.
  Primary: 59.2, 59.223, 65.99, 68.1, 68.170, 71.1, 71.170, 77.1, 77.198, 78.1, 78.202
Stuart, Mary, Queen of Scots (1542–1587) Gifts to her envoys William Maitland*, James Melville*, and Robert Melville*. Daughter of James V of Scotland and Mary de Guise, great-granddaughter of Henry VII; 1st cousin once removed of Elizabeth; mar 1st 1558 François II of France, 2nd 1565 Henry Stuart*, Lord Darnley, 3rd 1567 James Hepburn Earl of Bothwell; mother of King James VI*. *ODNB.*
  Sundry Gift: 63.363, 64.218, 67.360, 68.346 (Sovereign sending Envoy to England), 67.362 (Christening Gift for her son, James)

Stuart, Matthew, Earl of Lennox (1516–1571) Son of John Stuart and Elizabeth Stuart; grandfather of King James VI*; mar 1544 Margaret Douglas (Stuart*); father of Henry Stuart,* and Charles Stuart. *ODNB*; GEC, *Peerage*.
> **Earl**: 59.15, 59.236, 68.17, 68.186

Stumpe, James (d.1563) kntd 1549, MP. Son of William Stumpe and Joyce Barkeley; mar Bridget Baynton; grandfather of Catherine [III] Knyvett (Howard*). Bindoff.
> **Knight**: 62.127, 62.306

Suarez de Figueroa—see Figueroa

Suderman, William (fl.1580s) Captain Guilham Suderman or Sotherman. Envoy from William Blois van Treslong* Admiral of the Dutch States General, Captain. *CSP Foreign, 1588*.
> **Sundry Gift**: 85.412 (Gift to Envoy)

Suffolk, Duchess—see Frances Grey, née Brandon, 1551–1559; Catherine Bertie, née Willoughby, 1534–1545, dowager 1545–1580

Sussex, Earl/Countess—see Bridget Radcliffe, née Morrison, 1592–1623; Frances Radcliffe, née Sidney, 1557–1583, dowager 1583–1589; Henry Radcliffe, 4th, 1583–1593; Honor Radcliffe, née Pound, 1583–1593; Robert Radcliffe, 5th, 1593–1629; Thomas Radcliffe, 3rd, 1557–1583

Sutton, Edward, Lord Dudley (c.1515–1586) Son of John Sutton alias Dudley and Cecily Grey; mar 1st 1556 Catherine Brydges, 2nd 1566 Jane Stanley, 3rd 1571 Mary Howard (Sutton*); 3rd cousin of Robert Dudley*, Earl of Leicester. Name listed with 'X', but no gift recorded for 1582. *ODNB*.
> **Lord**: 75.76, 75.184, 81.70, 81.277

Sutton, Mary, née Howard, Baroness Dudley (c.1540–1600) Maid of Honour. Daughter of William, Lord Howard* and Margaret [I] Gamage (Howard*); sister of Charles Howard*, Douglas Sheffield*, Martha Howard*, Frances [I] Howard*, and Catherine Howard*; 1st cousin once removed to Queen Elizabeth; mar 1st 1571 Edward Sutton*, Lord Dudley, 2nd 1587 Richard Mompesson. *ODNB* under 1st husband; GEC, *Peerage*.
> **Maid of Honour**: 59.376, 62.332, 63.315, 64.183, 67.317, 68.308, 71.317
> **Baroness**: 81.88, 81.295, 82.510, 88.81, 88.267, 89.74, 89.259, 94.80, 94.260, 97.90, 97.284, 98.88, 98.284, 99.83, 99.276

Sutton—see Dudley (or Sutton of Dudley), Lord/Baroness

Swetheland—variant of Sweden

Sweveghem, Seigneur de—see François Halewyn

Swigo, Lucretia (fl.1560s) Daughter of Baptist Borona, mar John Swigo. Merchant of Milan, Italian protestant who worked with Benedict Spinola* and Horatio Palavicino*. *CPR, 1558–1560; Visitations, London*; Lang; Siddons.
> **Gentlewoman**: 65.72, 65.237

Swooke, George (fl.1580s) Envoy from Frederick II* of Denmark.
> **Gentleman**: 81.442

Tailboys, Baroness—see Margaret Tailboys, née Skipwith, 1539–1583

Tailboys, Elizabeth—see Elizabeth Dudley

Tailboys, Margaret, née Skipwith, Baroness Tailboys (d.1583) Daughter of William Skipwith and Alice Dymoke; sister of Bridget Cave* and Henry Skipwith*; 1st cousin once removed to Edward Dymoke*; mar 1st George, Lord Tailboys, 2nd 1547 Sir Peter Carew*, 3rd 1579 Sir John Clifton. GEC, *Peerage*.
> **Baroness**: 59.97, 59.317, 62.78, 62.260, 63.77, 63.249, 64.79, 65.9, 65.176, 67.76, 67.246, 68.72, 68.241, 71.72, 71.242, 75.190, 76.88, 76.286, 77.87, 77.284, 78.83, 78.287, 79.83, 79.290, 81.86, 81.284, 82.82, 82.274, 82.502

Talbot, *styled* Lord/Baroness—see Anne Talbot, née Herbert, 1563–1593; Francis Talbot, 1560–1582; Gilbert Talbot, 1582–1590; Mary Talbot, née Cavendish, 1582–1590

Talbot, Lady Alethea (1584–1654) later Countess of Arundel. Daughter of Gilbert Talbot*, Earl of Shrewbury and Mary Cavendish*; sister of Elizabeth [II] Grey*; mar 1606 Thomas Howard. GEC, *Peerage*; *ODNB* under husband.
Sundry Gift: 85.413 (Christening Gift)

Talbot, Anne, Baroness Talbot (c.1548–1593) Daughter of William [I] Herbert*, Earl of Pembroke and Anne Parr; sister of Henry Herbert*; niece of Catherine Parr; mar 1563 Francis, Lord Talbot*. GEC, *Peerage*.
Baroness: 76.96, 76.289, 78.97, 78.295, 82.85, 82.285, 85.88, 85.273, 88.89, 88.276, 89.83, 89.264

Talbot, Anne—see Anne [I] Herbert

Talbot, Catherine—see Catherine Herbert

Talbot, Elizabeth, née Walden, Countess of Shrewsbury (d.1567) Daughter of Richard Walden and Margery Wogan; mar 1512 George Talbot, 4ᵗʰ Earl of Shrewsbury; mother of Anne [I] Herbert*, step-mother of Francis Talbot* and Gilbert Talbot*. GEC, *Peerage*; will PCC 21 Stonarde.
Countess: 59.45, 59.266, 62.43, 62.223, 63.44, 63.215, 64.43, 65.144, 67.43, 67.213

Talbot, Elizabeth—see Elizabeth Grey, Elizabeth Hardwick

Talbot, Francis [I], Earl of Shrewsbury (1500–1560) Privy Councillor 1549, KG 1545. Son of George Talbot and Anne Hastings; mar 1ˢᵗ c.1522 Mary Dacre, 2ⁿᵈ 1553 Grace Shackerly; father of George Talbot*. GEC, *Peerage*; *ODNB*.
Earl: 59.8, 59.229

Talbot, Francis [II], Lord Talbot (1550–1582) Son of George Talbot* and Gertrude Manners (Talbot*); brother of Gilbert Talbot* and Catherine Talbot*; mar 1563 Anne [I] Herbert*. GEC, *Peerage*.
Lord: 76.76, 76.266, 82.70, 82.270, 82.473

Talbot, George, Earl of Shrewsbury (c.1522–1590) Lord Talbot, Privy Councillor 1571, Keeper of Queen of Scots 1568–1584, KG 1561. Son of Francis Talbot* and Mary Dacre; mar 1ˢᵗ 1539 Gertrude Manners (Talbot*), 2ⁿᵈ c.1568 Elizabeth Hardwick*; father of Catherine Talbot*, Francis [II] Talbot*, and Gilbert Talbot*. *ODNB*; GEC, *Peerage*.
Earl: 62.6, 62.185, 63.9, 63.181, 64.9, 65.108, 67.8, 67.178, 68.11, 68.180, 71.7, 71.177, 75.8, 76.8, 76.203, 77.11, 77.208, 78.12, 78.214, 79.7, 79.214, 81.6, 81.213, 82.7, 82.207, 82.424, 84.5, 84.203, 85.6, 85.197, 88.6, 88.191, 89.4, 89.189

Talbot, Gertrude, née Manners, Countess of Shrewsbury (c.1523–1567) Daughter of Thomas Manners and Eleanor Paston; sister of Henry Manners* and Frances Neville*; mar 1539 George Talbot*, Earl of Shrewsbury; mother of Catherine Herbert*, Francis [II] Talbot*, and Gilbert Talbot*. GEC, *Peerage*; *ODNB*.
Countess: 62.44, 62.224, 63.45, 63.216, 64.44, 65.145, 67.44, 67.215

Talbot, Gilbert, Earl of Shrewsbury (1552–1616) Lord Talbot, courtier poet, Privy Councillor 1601, KG 1592. Son of George Talbot* and Gertrude Manners*; brother of Catherine Talbot* and Francis [II] Talbot*; mar 1568 Mary Cavendish*; father of Alethea Talbot* and Elizabeth [II] Grey*. *ODNB*; GEC, *Peerage*.
Lord: 84.55, 84.253, 85.68, 85.259, 88.59, 88.244
Earl: 94.4, 94.188, 97.4, 97.204, 98.14, 98.207, 99.3, 99.198, 00.13, 00.202, 03.6, 03.219
Sundry Gift: 85.413 (Christening Gift for his child)

Talbot, Mary, née Cavendish, Countess of Shrewsbury (1556–1632) Baroness Talbot. Daughter of William Cavendish and Elizabeth Hardwick*; mar 1568 Gilbert Talbot*;

mother of Alethea Talbot* and Elizabeth [II] Grey*; sister of Elizabeth Stuart*. *ODNB*; GEC, *Peerage*.

Baroness: 88.86, 88.271

Countess: 94.19, 94.203, 97.23, 97.221, 98.21, 98.223, 99.17, 99.212, 00.22, 00.219, 03.23, 03.236

Sundry Gift: 85.413 (Christening Gift for her child)

Tamworth, John (c.1524–1569) Keeper of the Privy Purse, Groom of the Privy Chamber, Master of the Toils, MP. Son of Thomas Tamworth and Elizabeth Denkaring; brother-in-law of Sir Francis Walsingham*; mar 1562 Christian Walsingham. Hasler; Collins, *Jewels*; BL Harleian Roll MS AA 23; PRO AO 1/2302/1, C 43/5/18; will PCC 8 Lyon.

Free Gift: 59.452, 62.368, 63.352, 64.206, 67.349, 68.336

Custody of Gift: 62.84, 62.132, 62.158–59, 62.168–69, 63.173, 64.3–13, 64.15–38, 64.40–49, 64.51–67, 64.69, 64.71–72, 64.74–76, 64.78–80, 64.82–83, 64.85–86, 64.89–90, 64.93–107, 64.110–112, 64.114–115, 64.132–133, 65.1, 65.3, 65.5–9, 65.14, 65.16–18, 65.20–21, 65.24, 65.29–41, 65.44–45, 65.48–52, 65.78–79, 65.96–97, 67.2–4, 67.6–13, 67.16–19, 67.27–28, 67.31, 67.37, 67.39–45, 67.47–50, 67.52, 67.54–67, 67.69–72, 67.74–76, 67.80–82, 67.88–89, 67.99–112, 67.119–121, 67.123, 67.149–152, 68.1, 68.3–5, 68.7–14, 68.17–18, 68.21–23, 68.25–28, 68.31–66, 68.68–70, 68.72, 68.74, 68.76–78, 68.84–87, 68.89–90, 68.93, 68.98–111, 68.114, 68.141–142, 68.147–149, 68.168

Tartarian, Ipolyta—see Ipolyta the Tartarian

Taylor, Elizabeth—see Elizabeth Smithson

Tedeschi, Lucretia de—see Lucretia de Conti

Teerlinc, Levina, née Benninck (c.1519–1576) Mistress Levina Teerlinc, Miniature Painter. Daughter of Simon Benninck and Katherine Scroo; niece of Lucas Hornebolte; mar by 1564 George Teerlinc. *ODNB*; Bergmans; James.

Gentlewoman: 59.149, 59.360, 62.147, 62.329, 63.137, 63.310, 64.125, 64.177, 65.64, 65.230, 67.135, 67.305, 68.135, 68.301, 71.140, 71.310, 75.103, 76.168, 76.362

Teligny, Charles de (c.1535–1572) Messenger from Gaspard de Coligny*, Admiral of France his father-in-law; possible identification for 'unknown Frenchman, 1568'. Mar Louise Coligny who married as 2nd husband William of Orange*. *CSP Foreign, 1563*.

[Gentleman: 68.169]

Sundry Gift: 64.219 (Gift to Envoy)

Thomas, Jane—see Jane Harvey

Thomasine de Paris (d.aft.1603) Gentlewoman, Queen's dwarf. sister of Prudence de Paris. Arnold, *QE Wardrobe*; Merten; Stopes, *Shakespeare's*.

Gentlewoman: 81.167, 81.373, 82.163, 82.361, 82.622, 84.158, 84.351, 85.152, 85.344, 88.153, 88.332, 89.150, 89.335, 94.138, 94.330, 97.149, 97.353, 98.146, 98.354, 99.141, 99.341, 00.142, 00.347, 03.154, 03.368

Thornborough, John (1551–1641) Chaplain, Clerk of the Closet, Master of the Savoy, Dean of York. *ODNB*; BL Lansdowne MS 75.

Chaplain: 88.125, 88.309, 89.123, 89.308

Thorne, Mary—see Mary Huggins/Hogan

Throckmorton, Anne, née Carew (1519–1586) Lady Throckmorton. Daughter of Sir Nicholas Carew and Elizabeth Bryan, mar 1st by 1541 Sir Nicholas Throckmorton*, 2nd 1572 Adrian Stokes; mother of Elizabeth Throckmorton* and Sir Arthur Throckmorton*; 1st cousin of Griselda Butler*. *ODNB* under husband; Hasler under father; Merten.

Lady: 59.93, 59.313, 63.97, 63.270, 65.26, 65.193, 67.93, 67.263, 68.91, 68.265, 71.89, 71.259, 76.112, 76.309, 77.116, 77.315, 78.115, 78.316, 79.113, 79.321, 81.111, 81.317, 82.106, 82.305, 82.552, 84.103, 84.300, 85.107, 85.298

Sundry Gift: 64.221 (Christening Gift for her child).

Throckmorton, Sir Arthur (c.1557–1626) kntd 1596, MP. Son of Sir Nicholas Throckmorton* and Anne Carew (Throckmorton*); brother of Elizabeth Throckmorton*; mar 1586 Anne Lucas; 1st cousin once removed of Griselda Butler*. Hasler; PRO PROB 11/149.
    Gentleman: 85.164, 85.363
    Sundry Gift: 77.419 (Gift on his Departure to France with Sir Amias Paulet)

Throckmorton, Elizabeth (1566–1647) Gentlewoman of the Privy Chamber. Daughter of Sir Nicholas Throckmorton* and Anne Carew (Throckmorton*), sister of Arthur Throckmorton*, 1st cousin once removed of Griselda Butler*, mar 1591 Sir Walter Ralegh* MP. *ODNB* under husband.
    Gentlewoman: 85.142, 85.338, 88.133, 88.317, 89.128, 89.313

Throckmorton, Sir Nicholas (c.1516–1571) Chief Butler of England at Coronation, kntd 1551. Son of George Throckmorton and Catherine Vaux; brother of George Throckmorton; 1st cousin of Catherine Parr; mar 1541 Anne Carew*; father of Sir Arthur Throckmorton*, unidentified Throckmorton*, and Elizabeth Throckmorton*. *ODNB*; Hasler; Bindoff.
    Knight: 65.47, 65.214, 67.117, 67.287, 68.115, 68.284, 71.114, 71.284
    Sundry Gift: 64.221 (Christening Gift for his child)

Throckmorton, unidentified (b.1564) child of Sir Nicholas Throckmorton* and Anne Carew*
    Sundry Gift: 64.221 (Christening Gift)

Thynne, Catherine—see Catherine Long

Thynne, Dorothy, née Wroughton (d.1616) Lady Thynne. Daughter of William Wroughton and Eleanor Lewknor; mar 1st c.1567 John Thynne*, MP, 2nd c.1580 Carew Ralegh*; mother of Catherine Long*, Gresham Thynne*, and infant Ralegh*. *Hasler* under 1st and 2nd husband; *ODNB* under 1st husband.
    Lady: 84.106, 84.304
    Sundry Gift: 84.420 (Christening Gift for her child)

Thynne, Gresham (b.c.1585) Maid of Honour. Daughter of Sir John Thynne* and Dorothy Wroughton (Thynne*); sister of Catherine Long*. PRO LC 2/4/4; Merton; Longleat House: Thynne Family Papers, TH/BOOK/170.
    Maid of Honour: 03.378

Thynne, Sir John (1522–1580) Comptroller of Household under Princess Elizabeth, kntd 1547, MP. Son of Thomas Thynne and Margaret Haynes; mar 1st 1548 Christian Gresham, 2nd c.1567 Dorothy Wroughton (Thynne*); father of Catherine Long* and Gresham Thynne*. *ODNB*; Hasler; Bindoff; *Visitations, Wiltshire*; BL Sloane MS 814.
    Knight: 59.127, 59.346, 62.117, 62.295, 63.113, 63.286, 64.106, 64.160, 65.40, 65.207, 67.108, 67.278, 68.111, 68.280, 71.111, 71.281, 75.82, 76.129, 76.326, 77.132, 77.329, 78.135, 78.337, 79.137, 79.344

Todd, Richard (d.1583) Keeper of Standing Wardrobe at Hampton Court. PRO E 115; *CPR, 1575–78*.
    Custody of Gift: 65.83, 68.133, 71.18, 71.94, 71.167, 75.32, 76.1, 76.22–23, 76.90, 76.110, 76.112, 76.152, 76.180, 78.23, 78.119, 82.31, 82.86, 82.91, 82.101, 82.126, 82.136, 82.139, 82.176, 82.201, 82.263

Tomisen/Tomysen the dwarf—see Thomasine de Paris

Torsac, Monsieur de (fl.1570s) Gentleman with Nicholas Martel*, Monsieur de Bacqueville, from the Duke of Anjou*, with Monsieur de Saverne* and Monsieur de Ninsonan*. Nichols, *Progresses*; Dovey.
    Sundry Gift: 79.449 (Gift to Envoy)

Touchet—see Tuchet

Townsend, Jane, née Stanhope (1541–1618) Mistress Townsend, Lady Townsend, Baroness Berkeley. Daughter of Sir Michael Stanhope and Anne Rawson; sister of Michael Stanhope* and Sir John Stanhope*; mar 1ˢᵗ c.1567 Sir Roger Townsend, 2ⁿᵈ 1598 Henry, Lord Berkeley*. Hasler; GEC, *Peerage*; will PCC 24 Meade.
    Gentlewoman: 75.110, 76.150, 76.344, 77.152, 77.349, 78.153, 78.354, 79.155, 79.362, 81.149, 81.356, 82.144, 82.344, 82.614, 84.141, 84.330, 85.140, 85.326, 88.137, 88.321
    Lady: 89.106, 89.291, 94.100, 94.284, 97.110, 97.311, 98.111, 98.312
    Baroness: 99.86, 99.281, 00.91, 00.288, 03.86, 03.301

Trafford, Henry (d.1585) Chief Clerk of the Spicery, Clerk of Green Cloth. Son of Edmund Trafford and Anne Radcliffe. Will PCC 15 Brudenell.
    Gentleman: 62.175, 62.362, 63.162, 63.341, 64.141, 64.201, 67.161, 67.337

Tramane—see Tremayne

Treasurer, William/Guilliam (d.1584) Musician, Instrument Maker, alias William Schetts. related to Edmund Schetts* alias Treasurer. *BDECM*; *RECM*.
    Gentleman: 59.204, 59.428, 75.232

Tremayne, Edmund (c.1525–1582) Clerk of the Privy Council. Son of Thomas Tremayne and Philippa Grenville; mar 1576 Eulalia St Leger (Tremayne*). *ODNB*; Hasler; *CPR, 1575–78*; will PCC 45 Tirwhite.
    Sundry Gift: 77.418 (Marriage Gift)

Tremayne, Eulalia (fl.1570s–1580s) Daughter of Sir John St Leger and Catherine Neville; niece of Henry Neville*, Lord Abergavenny; mar 1576 Edmund Tremayne*. *ODNB* and Hasler under husband; husband's will PCC 45 Tirwhite.
    Sundry Gift: 77.418 (Marriage Gift)

Trentham, Elizabeth—see Vere, Elizabeth

Treslong, William Blois van (1529–1594) Admiral of the States General. Gift to his envoy William Suderman*. *CSP Foreign, 1577–78, 1584–85*.
    Sundry Gift: 85.412 (Official sending Envoy to England)

Trimmell, Walter (fl.1580s) Groom of Chamber. *CPR, 1575–78*.
    Custody of Gift: 82.96, 82.166

Troches, Henry (c.1541–1617) Musician, Sackbut. Son of Guilliam Troches; son-in-law of Mark Anthony Galliardello*, brother-in-law of John Lanier* and Caesar Galliardello*. *RECM*; *BDECM*.
    Gentleman: 98.188, 98.394, 99.186, 99.386, 00.186, 00.389, 03.200, 03.425

Tuchet, George, Lord Audley (1551–1617) later Earl of Castlehaven. Son of Henry Tuchet and Elizabeth Sneed; mar 1ˢᵗ c.1578 Lucy Marvyn (Tuchet*), 2ⁿᵈ 1611 Elizabeth Noel; father of Maria Tuchet*. GEC, *Peerage*.
    Lord: 99.64, 99.260, 00.71, 00.268
    Sundry Gift: 79.453 (Christening Gift for child)

Tuchet, Lucy, née Marvyn, Baroness Audley, (d.c.1610) later Countess of Castlehaven. Daughter of James Marvyn and Amy Clarke (Marvyn*); mar c. 1578 George Tuchet*, Lord Audley; mother of Maria Tuchet*. GEC, *Peerage*.
    Baroness: 77.95, 77.292, 78.86, 78.294, 79.90, 78.297, 99.78, 99.270, 00.86, 00.279;
    Sundry Gift: 79.453 (Christening Gift for her child)

Tuchet, Maria (1579–1611) Maid of Honour. Daughter of George Tuchet*, Lord Audley and Lucy Marvyn (Tuchet*); godchild of Queen Elizabeth; mar 1594 Thomas Thynne. GEC, *Peerage*.
    Maid of Honour: 94.311
    Sundry Gift: 79.453 (Christening Gift)

Tunstall, Cuthbert (1474–1559) Bishop of Durham 1530–1559 (deprived). *ODNB*; will PCC 10 Mellershe.
Bishop: 59.25, 59.246
Turberville, James (1494-c.1570) Bishop of Exeter 1555–1559 (deprived). *ODNB*.
Bishop: 59.26, 59.247
Twist, Anne [née?] (d.1612) Mistress Twist, Laundress. Mar Thomas Twist; mother of Lucy Twist*. Will PCC 57 Byrde.
Gentlewoman: 76.166, 76.360, 77.159, 77.357, 78.160, 78.363, 79.163, 79.370, 81.157, 81.363, 82.153, 82.353, 82.593, 84.149, 84.346, 85.154, 85.342, 89.141, 89.326, 94.133, 94.325, 97.145, 97.346, 98.142, 98.348, 99.137, 99.336, 00.138, 00.341, 03.148, 03.360
Twist, Lucy—see Lucy Alley
Tyrrell, Margaret—see Margaret Golding
Tyrwhitt, Ursula—see Ursula Sheffield
Tyrwhitt, Elizabeth—see Elizabeth Manners
Ubaldini, Petruccio (c.1524-c.1599) Calligrapher, Author, Schoolmaster to Henchmen. Mar 1566 Anne Lawrence. *ODNB*; Pelligrini.
Gentleman: 64.145, 64.204, 65.92, 67.167, 67.343, 68.166, 68.334, 71.167, 71.344, 75.228, 76.194, 76.397, 77.194, 77.396, 78.193, 78.403, 79.200, 79.413, 81.200, 81.411, 82.194, 82.398, 82.569, 84.194, 84.392, 85.185, 85.388, 88.179, 88.373, 89.179, 89.371, 94.178, 94.373, 97.191, 97.391, 98.190, 98.393, 99.188, 99.385
'unknown person' (fl.1570s) unidentified, following 'Gentlemen', as 'Jewels brought into the New Years gift chamber without report made by whom they were given'; possible identification: François*, Duc de Anjou; gifts listed on BL Sloane MS 814.
Gentlemen: 78.198, 78.199, 78.200, 78.201
'unknown person' (fl.1580s) unidentified, listed with 'Knights', as 'no report made who gave them', gifts listed on BL Sloane MS 814. Possible identification: Edward [II] Stafford*.
Knight: 84.126, 84.127
'unknown Gentleman' [Chudleigh, John?] (fl. late 1580s) probable identification; John Chudleigh*, appears on 1588 roll in similar location as 1589 roll, between Henry [I] Brooke* and John Stanhope*
Gentleman: 89.160, 89.352
'unknown Frenchman' (fl.1560s) blank space provided on gift roll to fill in name, but information was never added. Does not appear on 'To list'; possible identification: Charles de Teligny*.
Gentleman: 68.169
Unton, Edward (1534–1582) Knight of the Bath 1559, MP. Son of Alexander Unton and Cecily Bulstrode; mar 1555 Anne Seymour, Countess of Warwick. Hasler; will PCC 35 Tirwhite; BL Sloane MS 814.
Knight: 81.134, 81.341, 82.540
Upiam, Adam - see Adam Viman
Urseau, Nicholas (d.c.1577) Keeper of the Queen's Great Clocks at Westminster. *CPR, 1575–78*; *VCH, Middlesex*.
Gentleman: 59.208, 59.432
Vane—see Fane
Vannes, Peter (c.1488–1563) Diplomat, Dean of Salisbury. *ODNB*, will PCC 21 and 22 Chayre.
Chaplain: 59.136, 59.355, 62.130, 62.310, 63.123, 63.296
Vaughan, Frances—see Frances Burgh
Vaughan, Margaret—see Margaret Hawkins

Vaughan, Richard (c.1550–1607) Bishop of Chester 1597–1604, later Bishop of London 1604–1607. Related to John Aylmer*. *ODNB*; will PCC 32 Huddlestone.
   Bishop: 98.56, 98.250, 99.50, 99.239, 00.59, 00.249, 03.56, 03.269

Vavasour, Anne [I] (c.1561–1627) Maid of Honour. Daughter of Henry Vavasour and Margaret Knyvett; sister of Frances Vavasour; aunt of Anne [II] Vavasour*; niece of Catherine [I] Knyvett*; liaison with Edward de Vere*, Earl of Oxford and lived with Sir Henry Lee*; mar 1st John Finch, 2nd John Richardson. *ODNB*; Merton; *HMC Hastings*.
   Maid of Honour: 81.380

Vavasour [II], Anne (fl.1600s) Gentlewoman of the Bedchamber. Daughter of Thomas Vavasour and Mary Dodge; niece of Anne [I] Vavasour*; mar 1603 Sir Richard Warburton*. *ODNB* under Anne [I] Vavasour*; PRO LC 5/49.
   Gentlewoman: 03.141, 03.356

Velleville—see Scepeaux

Veneur, Taneguy le (fl.1580s) Sieur de Carrouges, French Commissioner for marriage settlement between Elizabeth and the Duke of Anjou*. Holt; *CSP Foreign, 1581–82*.
   Sundry Gift: 81.448 (Gift to Envoy)

Venice—see Albert Kellim, Francis Kellim

Vere, Anne, née Cecil, Countess of Oxford (1556–1588) Daughter of William Cecil*, Lord Burghley and Mildred Cooke (Cecil*); mar 1571 Edward de Vere*, Earl of Oxford; mother of Lady Elizabeth Stanley* and Lady Susan Vere*; sister of Robert Cecil*; half-sister of Thomas Cecil*. *ODNB*; GEC, *Peerage*.
   Countess: 75.28, 75.135, 76.29, 76.224, 77.44, 77.234, 78.33, 78.234, 79.33, 79.240, 81.25, 81.232, 82.25, 82.225, 82.487, 84.24, 84.222, 85.22, 85.214, 88.22, 88.207
   Sundry Gift: 64.231 (Gift from Queen), 76.414 (Christening Gift for her child)

Vere, Edward de, Earl of Oxford (1550–1604) courtier poet. Son of John de Vere*, Earl of Oxford, and Margery Golding (Vere*); mar 1st 1571 Anne Cecil (Vere*), 2nd 1591 Elizabeth Trentham (Vere*); father of Lady Elizabeth Stanley* and Lady Susan Vere*. Name listed with 'X' and no participation for 1582. *ODNB*; GEC, *Peerage*; Nelson.
   Earl: 75.7, 79.13, 79.219, 81.12, 81.217
   Sundry Gift: 76.414 (Christening Gift for his child)

Vere, Elizabeth, née Trentham, Countess of Oxford (1570–1613) Maid of Honour. Daughter of Thomas Trentham and Jane Sneed; mar 1591 Edward de Vere*, Earl of Oxford. *ODNB*; GEC, *Peerage*; BL Additional MS 5751A, RP 7288; will PCC 10 Capell.
   Maid of Honour: 82.367, 84.359, 85.352, 88.342, 89.340
   Countess: 94.17, 94.201, 97.21, 97.219, 98.19, 98.220, 99.15, 99.210, 00.20, 00.216, 03.21, 03.234

Vere, Lady Elizabeth—see Elizabeth Stanley

Vere, Frances—see Frances [I] Howard

Vere, John de, Earl of Oxford (c.1516–1562) Chief Ewer at Coronation. Son of John de Vere and Elizabeth Trussell; brother of Frances [I] Howard*; mar 1st 1536 Dorothy Neville, 2nd 1548 Margery Golding (Vere*); father of Edward de Vere*, Earl of Oxford and Lady Mary Vere (Bertie*). *ODNB*; GEC, *Peerage*; Nelson.
   Earl: 59.12, 59.233, 62.13, 62.194

Vere, Margery, née Golding, Countess of Oxford (c.1526–1568) Household of Princess Elizabeth. Daughter of John Golding and Elizabeth Tonge; mar 1st 1548 John de Vere*, Earl of Oxford, 2nd c.1563 Charles Tyrrell; mother of Edward de Vere*, Earl of Oxford and Lady Mary Bertie*. GEC, *Peerage*; Nelson.
   Countess: 59.44, 59.265, 62.42, 62.222, 63.41, 63.213, 64.41, 65.141, 67.40, 67.210, 68.22, 68.191

Vere, Lady Mary—see Lady Mary Bertie

Vere, Lady Susan (1587–1629) Lady of the Privy Chamber, later Countess of Montgomery and Pembroke. Daughter of Edward de Vere*, Earl of Oxford and Anne Cecil (Vere*); mar 1604 Philip Herbert. GEC, *Peerage*.
Lady: 03.95, 03.313

Verenne—see Fouquet de la Verenne

Verney, Anne—see Anne Poyntz

Verney, Richard (1563–1630) Servant to Vice Chamberlain Christopher Hatton*, MP. Son of George Verney and Jane Lucy; mar 1582 Margaret Greville; brother-in-law of Fulke Greville*. Hasler.
Sundry Gift: 81.438 (Gift from the Queen)

Vernon, Elizabeth (1569–1655) Maid of Honour, Countess of Southampton. Daughter of John Vernon and Elizabeth Devereux; niece of Walter Devereux*; 1st cousin of Robert Devereux*, Earl of Essex; mar 1598 Henry Wriothesley*, Earl of Southampton. *ODNB* under husband.
Maid of Honour: 94.315, 97.337, 98.338

Vezelmo—see Manucci, Jacomo

Vidame/Vidam of Chartres—see Jean de Ferrières, Prégent de la Fin

Vielleville, François—see François Scepeaux

Viman, Adam (fl.1590s) Envoy from Friedrich I*, Duke of Wurttemberg, alias Upiam.
Sundry Gift: 98.429 (Gift to Envoy)

Vincent, David (c.1524–1565) Keeper of Standing Wardrobe at Hampton Court, MP. Mar 1538 Elizabeth Spencer (Vincent*). Will PCC 29 Crymes; Hasler under sons, Henry and Thomas.
Custody of Gift: 59.1

Vincent, Elizabeth, [née Spencer] (fl.1550s) Mistress Vincent. Mar c.1538 David Vincent*. husband's will PCC 29 Crymes; Hasler under sons.
Gentlewoman: 59.150, 59.361

Vinton, Anne—see Anne Burton

Violins, 1559—see Innocent Comey, Mark Anthony Galliardello, Paul Galliardello, Albert Kellim, Francis Kellim, Ambrose Lupo; (George Comey has separate entry for this year)

von Hesse—see Hesse

Vpiam—see Viman

Vray, Jacques du (fl.1570s–1580s) Sieur de Fontorte, Envoy from Duke of Anjou*, French Commissioner for marriage settlement between Elizabeth and the Duke of Anjou*. Holt; *CSP Foreign, 1581–82*.
Sundry Gift: 79.443, 81.436, 81.452 (Gift to Envoy)

Vrsue—see Urseau

Waad, Armigal (c.1510–1568) Clerk of the Privy Council, MP. Mar 1st c.1545 Alice Patten, 2nd c.1559 Anne Marbury. *ODNB*; Bindoff; will PCC 6 Lyon.
Gentleman: 59.167, 59.390, 62.166, 62.354, 63.156, 63.335, 65.93

Waineman—see Wenman

Wake, Elizabeth, née Gorges (b.1526) Mistress Wake. Daughter of Edward Gorges and Mary Poyntz; sister of Thomas Gorges* and Jane Stafford*; sister-in-law of Helena Gorges*, Lady Marquess of Northampton; mar c.1540 John Wake.
Gentlewoman: 03.155, 03.369

Waldegrave, Sir Edward (1517–1561) Master of the Great Wardrobe 1553, Chancellor of the Duchy of Lancaster 1557, kntd 1553. Son of John Waldegrave and Laura Rochester; mar 1548 Frances Neville. *ODNB*.
Knight: 59.119, 59.338

Walden, Elizabeth—see Elizabeth Talbot

Wall, Hugh—see Hugh Keall

Walsingham, Audrey, née Shelton (1568–1624) Mistress Shelton, Lady Walsingham, Lady of the Privy Chamber, Lady of the Bedchamber, later Joint Keeper of Queen Anne's Wardrobe with husband. Daughter of Ralph Shelton and Mary Wodehouse; great-granddaughter of Sir John Shelton and Anne Boleyn; sister of Amy Shelton* and Elizabeth Shelton*; niece of Mary Scudamore*, 1st cousin once removed to Queen Anne Boleyn; 2nd cousin once removed to Queen Elizabeth; mar 1590/91 Thomas Walsingham* MP. *ODNB* and Hasler under husband.

    Gentlewoman: 88.143, 88.327, 94.134, 94.322, 97.143, 97.347

    Lady: 98.105, 98.309, 99.103, 99.298, 00.114, 00.305, 03.103, 03.319

Walsingham, Frances—see Frances Sidney

Walsingham, Francis (1530–1590) Principal Secretary 1573, Privy Councillor 1573, Chancellor of the Duchy of Lancaster 1587, kntd 1577, Ambassador to France 1570–73, 1581. Son of William Walsingham and Joyce Denny; 1st cousin once removed to Thomas Walsingham*; mar 1st 1562 Anne Barne, 2nd 1567 Ursula St Barbe (Walsingham*); father of Frances Sidney*; brother-in-law of John Tamworth* and Walter Mildmay*. *ODNB*; will PCC 33 Drury.

    Knight: 76.120, 76.315, 77.122, 77.319, 78.125, 78.326, 79.122, 79.329, 81.119, 81.326, 82.112, 82.313, 82.524, 84.110, 84.308, 85.111, 85.303, 88.116, 88.301, 89.109, 89.294

Walsingham, Thomas (1563–1630) kntd 1597, MP, later joint Keeper of Queen Anne's Wardrobe with wife. Son of Thomas Walsingham and Dorothy Guildford, 1st cousin once removed to Frances Sidney*, mar 1590/91 Audrey Shelton*. *ODNB*; Hasler.

    Knight: 99.129, 99.326, 00.130, 00.328, 03.132, 03.345

Walsingham, Ursula, née St Barbe (d.1602) Mistress Walsingham, Lady Walsingham. Daughter of Henry St Barbe and Eleanor Lewknor; niece of William St Barbe*; mar 1567 Francis Walsingham*; mother of Frances Sidney*. *ODNB*; will PCC 55 Montague.

    Gentlewoman: 77.143, 77.340

    Lady: 78.112, 78.309, 79.106, 79.314, 81.98, 81.305, 82.93, 82.293, 82.545, 84.88, 84.286, 85.94, 85.285, 88.96, 88.281, 89.88, 89.273, 94.108, 94.292, 97.105, 97.307, 98.106, 98.306, 99.102, 99.297, 00.107, 00.304

Warburton, Richard (d.1610) Gentleman Pensioner, MP. Son of Peter Warburton and Elizabeth Winnington; mar 1603 Anne [II] Vavasour*. Hasler; Tighe; *Visitations, Cheshire*.

    Gentleman: 94.181, 94.344, 97.193, 97.398, 98.192, 98.399, 99.171, 99.371

Ware, John (d.1592) Sergeant of the Pantry. Collins, *Jewels*; PRO E315/1954; will PCC 91 Cobham; Tighe.

    Custody of Gift : 82.311

Warner, Edward (1511–1565) Lieutenant of the Tower of London 1558, kntd 1544, MP. Son of Henry Warner and Mary Blennerhasset; mar 1st 1542 Elizabeth Brooke, 2nd 1560 Audrey Hare. *ODNB*; Hasler.

    Knight: 59.125, 59.344, 62.112, 62.292, 63.110, 63.283, 64.103, 64.157, 65.38, 65.205

Warner, Margaret—see Margaret Hunnis

Warren, Joan—see Joan Cromwell

Warren, William (d.1611) Musician, Violin. Ashbee; *BDECM*; *RECM*.

    Gentleman: 97.183, 97.385, 98.181, 98.386, 99.179, 99. 377, 00.179, 00.379, 03.199, 03.413

Warwick, Earl/Countess—see Ambrose Dudley, 1561–1590; Anne Dudley, née Russell, 1565–1604; Elizabeth Dudley, née Tailboys, 1561–1563

Watkins, Maurice (fl.1570s) unidentified.
   Gentleman: 79.207, 79.436 (Reward)
Watson, Anthony (d.1605) Bishop of Chichester 1596–1605, Queen's Almoner 1596. *ODNB*.
   Bishop: 97.50, 97.249, 98.49, 98.251, 99.43, 99.241, 00.54, 00.251, 03.55, 03.268
Watson, John (1521–1584) Bishop of Winchester 1580–1584. *ODNB*; White, *Lives*.
   Bishop: 81.41, 81.250, 82.40, 82.242, 82.440, 84.39, 84.237
Watson, Thomas (1513–1584) Bishop of Lincoln 1556–1559 (deprived). *ODNB*.
   Bishop: 59.30, 59.251
Watson, William (d.1559) Merchant. *Visitations, London*.
   Gentleman: 59.164, 59.388
Webster, George (d.1574) Master Cook, succeeded by John Smithson*. PRO E 115; LC 5/33; *CSP Domestic, 1547–1580*; will PCC 37 Martyn.
   Gentleman: 62.179, 62.366, 63.163, 63.342, 64.142, 64.202, 65.88, 67.165, 67.341, 68.159, 68.331, 71.160, 71.339
Wendy, Thomas (c.1500–1560) Physician to Henry VIII, Catherine Parr, Edward VI and Elizabeth. *ODNB*; will PCC 35 Mellershe.
   Gentleman: 59.162, 59.386
Wenman, Elizabeth (b.1575) Daughter of Thomas Wenman* and Jane West (Wenman*).
   Sundry Gift: 76.417 (Christening Gift)
Wenman, Jane, née West (1550–1621) Mistress Wenman. Daughter of William West and Elizabeth Strange; mar 1st 1572 Thomas Wenman*, 2nd 1578 James Cress; mother of Elizabeth Wenman*. PRO LC 2/4/3; *HMC Salisbury*, vol. II p. 157; *VCH, Buckinghamshire*.
   Sundry Gift: 76.417 (Christening Gift for her child)
Wenman, Thomas (1548–1577) MP. Son of Richard Wenman and Isabel Williams; mar 1572 Jane West (Wenman*); father of Elizabeth Wenman*. Hasler; *VCH, Buckinghamshire*.
   Sundry Gift: 76.417 (Christening Gift for his child)
Wentworth, Lord/Baroness—Anne Wentworth, nee Hopton, c.1589–1625
Wentworth, Anne—see Anne Hopton
Wentworth, Elizabeth—see Elizabeth Cecil
Wentworth, Jane—see Jane Cheyne
Wentworth, Margery—see Margery Williams
Wessenberg—see Wissenburg
West, Anne, née Knollys, Baroness de la Warr (1550–1603) Mistress West, Lady West. Daughter of Sir Francis Knollys* and Catherine Carey (Knollys*); sister of William Knollys*, Lettice Devereux*, and Elizabeth Leighton*, 1st cousin once removed to Queen Elizabeth, mar 1571 Thomas West*, Lord de la Warr. GEC, *Peerage*.
   Gentlewoman: 75.97, 76.148, 76.352, 77.146, 77.343, 78.148, 78.349, 79.150 79.357, 81.143, 81.350, 82.137, 82.337, 82.606, 84.134, 84.332, 85.129, 85.321
   Lady: 88.110, 88.296, 89.103, 89.288
   Baroness: 94.92, 94.276, 97.81, 97.289, 98.80, 98.280, 99.75, 99.272, 00.82, 00.281, 03.85, 03.300;
   Regifted: 81.89 (Queen regifted gift from Douglas Howard*)
West, Catherine (fl.1580s) Gentlewoman of the Privy Chamber, unidentified. Collins, *Jewels*.
   Gentlewoman: 88.154, 88.339, 89.151, 89.336
West, Jane—see Jane Wenman

West, Thomas, Lord de la Warr (1550–1602) Son of William West, Lord de la Warr and Elizabeth Strange; mar 1571 Anne Knollys (West*). GEC, *Peerage*.
Lord: 00.70, 00.272

Westfaling, Herbert (1532–1602) Bishop of Hereford 1586–1602. Son-in-law of William Barlow*; brother-in-law of Tobie Matthew*, William Day*, William Overton*, and William Wickham*. *ODNB*; will PCC 12 Montague.
Bishop: 88.55, 88.240, 89.50, 89.235, 94.49, 94.232, 97.53, 97.252, 98.53, 98.255, 99.47, 99.244, 00.57, 00.254

Westmorland, Earl/Countess—see Charles Neville, 6th, 1564–1601; Henry [II] Neville, 5th, 1549–1564; Jane Neville, née Howard, 1564–1593

Weston, Elizabeth, née Lovett (1521–1577) Mistress Weston. Daughter of Thomas Lovett; mar 1st 1541 Anthony Cave, 2nd John Newdigate, 3rd 1566 Judge Richard Weston; mother of Anne Hampden*. *ODNB* and Hasler under 3rd husband; *CPR, 1574–1575*.
Sundry Gift: 76.415 (Gift given on Progress)

Weston, William (fl.1590s–1600s) Apothecary to Queen Elizabeth. PRO E 179/70/115, LC 2/4(4); Matthews.
Gentleman: 94.160, 94.355, 97.173, 97.376, 98.170, 98.377, 99.164, 99.365, 00.165, 00.367, 03.175, 03.397

Whalley, Eleanor—see Zouche, Eleanor

Wharton, Lord/Baroness—see Frances Wharton, née Clifford, 1577–1592; Philip Wharton, 3rd, 1572–1625

Wharton, Lady Frances, née Clifford, Baroness Wharton (1556–1592) Daughter of Henry Clifford*, Earl of Cumberland, and Anne Dacre (Clifford*); sister of George Clifford, Earl of Cumberland; mar 1577 Philip, Lord Wharton*; mother of Margaret Wharton*. GEC, *Peerage*; *ODNB* under husband.
Baroness: 79.97, 79.304, 81.91, 81.298, 82.80, 82.281, 82.509, 84.77, 84.275, 85.80, 85.271, 88.83, 88.268, 89.76, 89.261

Wharton, Margaret (c.1583–1659) Maid of Honour. Daughter of Philip, Lord Wharton* and Lady Frances Clifford (Wharton*); mar 1603 Sir Edward Wotton MP. *ODNB*; Hasler under husband.
Maid of Honour: 03.374

Wharton, Philip, Lord Wharton (1555–1625) Son of Thomas Wharton and Anne Radcliffe; mar 1st 1577 Frances Clifford (Wharton*), 2nd by 1597 Dorothy Colby. GEC, *Peerage*; *ODNB*.
Lord: 77.78, 77.274, 78.76, 78.279, 79.74, 79.282, 81.73, 81.280, 82.68, 82.268, 82.469, 84.63, 84.259, 85.66, 85.257, 88.65, 88.250, 89.59, 89.244, 94.61, 94.245, 97.64, 97.265, 98.62, 98.266, 99.58, 99.256, 00.65, 00.264, 03.66, 03.279

Wheeler, John (fl.1580s) Queen's servant.
Custody of Gift: 82.376

Whitchurch, Edward (d.1562) Printer, Bookseller. Mar 1st unidentified, 2nd c.1557 Margaret [née?], widow of Thomas Cranmer, Archbishop of Canterbury. *ODNB*.
Gentleman: 59.173, 59.396

White, Sir John [I] (1502–1573) Sewer, Merchant. Brother of John [II] White*; mar 1st Sybil White, 2nd 1558 Catherine Soda; son-in-law of John Soda*. Beaven; *ODNB* under brother; Siddons.
Gentleman: 59.193, 59.418

White, John [II] (1510–1560) Bishop of Winchester 1556–1559 (deprived). Son of Richard White and Catherine Wells; brother of John [I] White*. *ODNB*.
Bishop: 59.36, 59.257

Whitgift, John (c.1530–1604) Bishop of Worcester 1577–1583, Archbishop of Canterbury 1583–1604, Privy Councillor 1586. *ODNB*.
 Bishop: 78.53, 78.254, 79.51, 79.258, 81.46, 81.253, 82.45, 82.245, 82.454, 84.34, 84.232, 85.37, 85.228, 88.37, 88.222, 89.33, 89.218, 94.33, 94.217, 97.41, 97.239, 98.39, 98.240, 99.33, 99.228, 00.41, 00.238, 03.43, 03.256

Wickham, William (1539–1595) Bishop of Lincoln 1584–1595, Bishop of Winchester 1595. Son-in-law of William Barlow*; brother-in-law of Tobie Matthew*, William Day*, William Overton*, and Herbert Westfaling*. *ODNB*.
 Bishop: 85.43, 85.234, 88.42, 88.229, 89.37, 89.222, 94.40, 94.224

Wilbraham, Richard (c.1504–1559) Clerk Comptroller, served in household of Princess Mary and Queen Catherine Parr; Master of the Jewelhouse under Mary I, MP. Son of William Wilbraham and Ellen Egerton; mar Dorothy Grosvenor. Bindoff; *LP Henry VIII*.
 Sundry Gift : 59.453, 59.454, 59.455, 59.456, 59.458, 59.459 (Coronation Fees taken from his Charge)

Wilford, Joyce, née Barrett (1520–1580) Lady Wilford. Daughter of John Barrett and Phyllis Bamfield, mar 1st c.1541 Sir James Wilford MP; 2nd c.1552 Thomas Stanley*. Bindoff under 1st husband.
 Lady: 67.96, 67.266, 68.93, 68.262, 71.91, 71.261, 76.113, 76.310, 77.117, 77.314, 78.117, 78.318, 79.115, 79.322

William of Orange (1533–1584) Stadtholder (Governor) of the provinces of Holland, Zeeland, and Utrecht, alias William the Silent. Gift to his envoy: Charles de Lieven*. *ODNB*.
 Sundry Gift: 77.424 (Gift to his Envoy)

Williams of Thame, Lord/Baroness—see John Williams, 1554–1559; Margery Williams, née Wentworth, 1557–1588

Williams, Elizabeth (1559–1559) Infant daughter of John Williams* and Margery Wentworth (Williams*); half-sister of Margery Norris*.
 Sundry Gift: 59.458 (Christening Gift)

Williams, John, Lord Williams of Thame (1500–1559) Master of the Jewels under Henry VIII, MP. Son of Sir John Williams and Isabel More; mar 1st by 1524 Elizabeth Bletsoe, 2nd 1557 Margery Wentworth (Williams*); father of Margery Norris* and Elizabeth Williams*. GEC, *Peerage*; *ODNB*; Hasler; Bindoff.
 Lord: 59.57, 59.278
 Sundry Gift: 59.458 (Christening Gift for his child)

Williams, John (fl.1600s–1620s) alias 'J W', Goldsmith. Sitwell.
 Sundry Gift: 03.450 (Goldsmith)

Williams, Margery, née Wentworth, Lady Williams of Thame (1528–1588). Daughter of Thomas Wentworth and Margaret Fortescue; sister of Jane Wentworth*; mar 1st 1557 John Williams*, Lord Williams of Thame, MP, 2nd 1560 William Drury* MP, 3rd James Croft, MP; mother of Elizabeth Williams*, step-mother of Margery Norris*. GEC, *Peerage*; *ODNB*; Hasler and Bindoff under husbands.
 Lady: 63.80, 63.252, 64.80
 Sundry Gift: 59.458 (Christening Gift for her child)

Williams, Margery—see Margery Norris

Willoughby de Broke, Baroness—see Anne Greville, née Neville, 1562–1583

Willoughby de Eresby, Lord/Baroness—see Catherine Brandon, later Bertie, née Willoughby, *de jure*, 1526–1580; Mary Bertie, née Vere, 1580–1624; Peregrine Bertie, 1580–1601

Willoughby of Parham, Lord/Baroness—see Margaret Devereux, née Garnish, Viscountess Hereford 1559–1599; Charles Willoughby, 2nd, 1570–1610

Willoughby, Catherine—see Catherine Bertie

Willoughby, Elizabeth [I], née Lyttleton (d.1595) Lady Willoughby. Daughter of John Lyttleton and Bridget Pakington; 1st cousin of John Scudamore*; mar c.1564 Francis Willoughby. *ODNB* under husband; BL Additional MS 22607.

> **Lady**: 78.113, 78.312, 79.109, 79.317, 81.107, 81.313, 82.102, 82.301, 82.554, 84.97, 84.296, 85.102, 85.290, 88.106, 88.290, 89.98, 89.283

Willoughby, Elizabeth [II], née Hildyard (d.1601) Lady Willoughby. Daughter of Christopher Hildyard and Frances Constable; mar 1582 William, Lord Willoughby of Parham. GEC, *Peerage*.

> **Lady**: 94.96, 94.280, 97.115, 97.314, 98.116, 98.317, 99.107, 99.304, 00.111, 00.311

Willoughby, Margaret—see Margaret Devereux; Margaret Arundell

Wilson, Thomas (1524–1581) Master of Requests, Principal Secretary 1571, Privy Councillor 1577, Dean of Durham 1579, courtier poet. Son of Thomas Wilson and Anne Cumberworth; mar 1st c.1560 Agnes Winter, 2nd c.1576 Jane Empson. *ODNB*; BL Royal MS 12: 'A New-Year Address', in Latin, to Queen Elizabeth 1 Jan. 1567.

> **Chaplain**: 75.115, 75.201
>
> **Knight**: 78.126, 78.328, 79.123, 79.330, 81.122, 81.327

Winchester, Bishop—see John White, 1556–1559; Robert Horne, 1561–1580; John Watson, 1580–1584; Thomas Cooper, 1584–1594; William Wickham, 1595; William Day, 1596; Thomas Bilson, 1597–1616

Winchester, Marquess/Lady Marquess—see Anne/Agnes Paulet, née Howard, 1551–1601; John Paulet, 2nd, 1572–1576; Lucy Paulet, née Cecil, 1587–1614; William [I] Paulet, 1st, 1551–1572; William [II] Paulet, 3rd, 1576–1598; William [III] Paulet, 4th, 1598–1629; Winifred Paulet, née Brydges, 1568–1586

Windsor, Lord/Baroness—see Anne [II] Windsor, née Rivett, 1586–1615; Edward Windsor, 3rd, 1558–1575; Frederick Windsor, 4th, 1575–1585; Henry Windsor, 5th, 1575–1605

Windsor, Anne [I] (1549–1605) Maid of Honour, later Baroness Grey of Groby. Daughter of Thomas Windsor and Dorothy Dacre; mar 1572 Henry Grey*; mother of Elizabeth [I] Grey*. GEC, *Peerage*; Merton.

> **Maid of Honour**: 62.335, 63.316, 64.184, 67.318, 68.309
>
> **Sundry Gift**: 75.249 (Christening Gift for her child)

Windsor, Anne [II], née Rivett (d.1615) Baroness Windsor. Daughter of Thomas Rivett* and Griselda Paget; mar c.1586 Henry, Lord Windsor*; mother of Elizabeth Windsor*.

> **Sundry Gift**: 98.430 (Christening Gift for her child)

Windsor, Edward, Lord Windsor (1532–1575) Son of William Windsor and Margaret Samborne; mar 1555 Catherine Vere; father of Frederick Windsor* and Henry Windsor*. GEC, *Peerage*.

> **Lord**: 59.61, 59.282, 62.60, 62.241, 63.61, 63.235, 64.61, 65.163, 67.61, 67.231, 68.59, 68.228, 71.65, 71.236

Windsor, Elizabeth (b.1598) Daughter of Henry Windsor* and Anne [II] Rivett (Windsor*).

> **Sundry Gift**: 98.430 (Christening Gift)

Windsor, Frederick, Lord Windsor (1559–1585) Son of Edward Windsor* and Catherine Vere; brother of Henry Windsor*, unmarried, nephew of Edward de Vere*, Earl of Oxford. GEC, *Peerage*.

> **Lord**: 81.71, 81.278, 82.66, 82.266, 82.471, 84.61, 84.257, 85.64, 85.255

Windsor, Henry, Lord Windsor (1562–1605) Gentleman Pensioner. Son of Edward Windsor* and Catherine Vere; brother of Frederick Windsor*; mar c.1585 Anne Rivett

(Windsor*), father of Elizabeth Windsor*, nephew of Edward de Vere*, Earl of Oxford. GEC, *Peerage*; Tighe.

Lord: 88.69, 88.254

Sundry Gift: 98.430 (Christening Gift for his child)

Wineyard—see Wynyard

Wingfield, Anne (fl.1560s–1570s) Mistress Wingfield, Gentlewoman of the Privy Chamber. Daughter of Sir Anthony Wingfield (d.1552) and Elizabeth Vere; sister-in-law of Elizabeth Leake (Wingfield*); unmarried. *Visitations, Suffolk; Visitations, Cheshire*.

Gentlewoman: 67.128, 67.298, 71.126, 71.296

Wingfield, Anthony (1506–1593) Gentleman Usher, Gentleman of the Black Rod. Son of Sir Anthony Wingfield (d.1552) and Elizabeth Vere; brother-in-law of Elizabeth Hardwick*; mar 1st Margaret Blennerhasset, 2nd c.1559 Jane Purpett, 3rd c.1562 Elizabeth Leake (Wingfield*). *Visitations, Suffolk*; Folger MS X.d.428; will PCC 49 Nevell.

Custody of Gift: 82.216

Wingfield, Elizabeth, née Leake (b.c.1530) Mistress Wingfield, Gentlewoman of the Privy Chamber, Mother of the Maids (1597–1600). Daughter of Ralph Leake and Elizabeth Leake; half-sister of Elizabeth Hardwick*; mar c.1562 Anthony Wingfield*. Mertens; Folger MS X.d.428; husband's will PCC 49 Nevell.

Gentlewoman: 63.132, 63.305, 65.74, 65.239, 67.143, 67.313, 68.132, 68.300, 75.108, 76.152, 76.354, 77.156, 77.353, 78.158, 78.360, 79.160, 79.367, 81.154, 81.360, 82.150, 82.350, 82.599, 84.146, 84.343, 85.144, 85.335, 88.140, 88.324, 89.136, 89.321, 94.141, 94.327, 97.152, 97.356, 98.149, 98.360, 99.144, 99.347, 00.145, 00.353 [designated as 'Mother of the Maids', although listed with Gentlewomen, 1597–1600]

Winter, Lady Anne (b.c.1581) Daughter of Edward Somerset*, Earl of Worcester and Elizabeth Hastings (Somerset*); sister of Lady Catherine Petre* and Lady Elizabeth Guildford*; great-niece of Lady Anne Percy*; mar 1595 Edward Winter* MP; mother of infant daughter Winter*. *ODNB*; Hasler; *Visitations, Glocestershire*.

Sundry Gift: 97.421 (Christening Gift for her child)

Winter, Edward (c.1560–1619) Son of Admiral William Winter and Mary Loughton; mar 1595 Lady Anne Somerset (Winter*). *ODNB* under father; Hasler; *Visitations, Gloucestershire*.

Gentleman: 94.180, 94.343

Sundry Gift: 97.421 (Christening Gift for his child)

Winter, unidentified (b.1596) Infant daughter of Sir Edward Winter* and Lady Anne Somerset (Winter*); granddaughter of Edward Somerset*, Earl of Worcester, and Elizabeth Hastings*.

Sundry Gift: 97.421 (Christening Gift)

Winton—see Winchester

Wissenburg, Ericson, Count Wissenberg (c.1560–1619) Ambassador along with Andrew Keith* from John III*, King of Sweden. *CSP Foreign, 1577–78*.

Sundry Gift: 84.417 (Gift to Envoy)

Witfeldt, Arnold—see Arild Huitfeldt

Wodehouse, Elizabeth—see Elizabeth Jones

Wodehouse, Margaret, née Shelton (b.1522) Lady Wodehouse. Daughter of John Shelton and Anne Boleyn (aunt of Queen Anne Boleyn); sister of Mary Scudamore*; 1st cousin of Queen Anne Boleyn; 1st cousin once removed of Queen Elizabeth; mar 1539 Thomas Wodehouse; mother of Thomas [I] Wodehouse* and Elizabeth Jones*; great-grand-mother of Thomas [II] Wodehouse*. Husband's will PCC 18 Daper, BL Sloane MS 814

Lady: 62.95, 62.276, 63.92, 63.256, 64.82, 65.12, 65.180, 67.84, 67.254, 68.81, 68.250, 71.81, 71.251, 76.111, 76.302, 77.106, 77.303, 78.104, 78.305

Wodehouse, Thomas [I] (fl.1580s) Son of Thomas Wodehouse and Margaret Shelton (Wodehouse*); brother of Elizabeth Jones*; great uncle of Thomas [II] Wodehouse*; 2nd cousin of Queen Elizabeth. *Visitations, Norfolk*.

Gentleman: 84.173, 84.374, 94.151, 94.342

Wodehouse, Thomas [II] (b.1583) Son of Philip Wodehouse and Grisell Yelverton; great-nephew to Thomas [I] Wodehouse* and Elizabeth Jones*; 2nd cousin twice removed to Queen Elizabeth; mar 1605 Blanche Carey. *Visitations, Norfolk*; Middlesex Session Records.

Gentleman: 03.212, 03.429

Wolfe, Ellen—see Helena Gorges

Wolfe, Peter—see Peter Lupo

Wolfe, Reyner (d.c.1574) Printer, King's Printer to Edward VI. *ODNB*; will PCC 1 Martyn.

Gentleman: 59.219, 59.395

Wolley, Elizabeth, née More (1552–1600) Mistress Wolley, Lady Wolley, Lady Egerton. Daughter of William More and Margaret Daniel; related by marriage to Richard Carmarden*; mar 1st 1567 Richard Polsted, 2nd 1577 John Wolley* MP, 3rd 1598 Sir Thomas Egerton* MP; mother of Francis Wolley*. McCutcheon; *ODNB* under husband.

Gentlewoman: 85.133, 85.323, 88.132, 88.316, 89.131, 89.316

Lady: 94.103, 94.287, 97.102, 97.300, 98.101, 98.301, 99.98, 99.292, 00.102, 00.299

Wolley, Francis (1583–1609) kntd 1603, MP. Son of Sir John Wolley* and Elizabeth More (Wolley*); mar 1594 Mary Hawtrey. Hasler; will PCC 118 Dorset.

Gentleman: 97.200, 97.398, 98.197, 98.403, 99.172, 99.372, 00.170, 00.373, 03.165, 03.387

Wolley, Sir John (d.1596) Latin Secretary, Chancellor of the Garter, courtier poet, Privy Councillor 1586, kntd 1592, MP. Son of John Wolley and Edith Buckley; mar 1st Jane Sanderson, 2nd 1583 Elizabeth More (Wolley*); father of Francis Wolley*. *ODNB*; Hasler.

Knight: 79.185, 79.398, 81.177, 81.392, 82.168, 82.373, 82.576, 84.160, 84.362, 85.158, 85.357, 88.156, 88.347, 89.153, 89.345, 94.124, 94.297

Wood, George (fl.1570s) Sergeant of the Buckhounds. PRO LC 5/49.

Gentleman: 71.169, 71.347

Wood, Henry (fl.1580's) Queen's servant.

Custody of Gift: 82.261

Wood, William—see William Byllyard

Woodgate, Joan—see Joan Allen

Woolton, James (fl.1580's) Queen's servant, possible relative of John Woolton*.

Custody of Gift: 82.252

Woolton, John (1535–1594) Bishop of Exeter 1579–1594. *ODNB*.

Bishop: 81.53, 81.262, 82.50, 82.252, 82.442, 84.47, 84.245, 85.51, 85.240, 88.50, 88.236, 89.46, 89.231, 94.50, 94.233

Worcester, Bishop—see Richard Pates, 1555–1559; Edwin Sandys, 1559–1570; Nicholas Bullingham, 1571–1576; John Whitgift, 1577–1583; Edmond Freake, 1584–1591; Thomas Bilson, 1596–1597; Gervase Babington, 1597–1620

Worcester, Earl/Countess—see Edward Somerset, 4th, 1589–1628; Elizabeth [I] Somerset, née Browne, 1549–1565; Elizabeth [II] Somerset, née Hastings, 1589–1621

Wotton, Edward (1548–1628) Comptroller of the Household 1602, Privy Councillor 1602, kntd 1592, MP. Son of Thomas Wotton and Elizabeth Rudston; mar 1st 1575 Hester

Pickering (Wotton*), 2nd 1603 Margaret Wharton*; son-in-law of William Pickering*; father of infant son Wotton*. *ODNB*; GEC, *Peerage*; Hasler.

Knight: 03.118, 03.331

Sundry Gift: 79.444 (Christening Gift for his child)

Wotton, Hester, née Pickering (d.1592) Illegitimate daughter of William Pickering*; mar 1575 Edward Wotton*; mother of infant son. *ODNB* under father and husband.

Sundry Gift: 79.444 (Christening Gift for her child)

Wotton, unidentified (b.1578) Infant son of Edward Wotton* and Hester Pickering (Wotton*).

Sundry Gift: 79.444 (Christening Gift)

Wotton, Margaret—see Margaret Wharton

Wotton, Nicholas (c.1497–1567) Diplomat, Dean of Canterbury, Dean of York, Privy Councillor, Special Ambassador. Son of Robert Wotton and Anne Belknap; brother-in-law of Sir Gawain Carew*, uncle of Lord John Grey*. Ficaro.

Chaplain: 62.129, 62.309, 63.122, 63.295, 64.115, 64.169, 65.52, 65.219, 67.119, 67.289

Wriothesley, Lady Catherine—see Lady Catherine Cornwallis

Wriothesley, Henry [I], Earl of Southampton (1545–1581) Son of Thomas Wriothesley, Earl of Southampton and Jane Cheyne (Wriothesley*); mar 1565 Mary Browne (Wriothesley*), father of Henry [II] Wriothesley*, Earl of Southampton. *ODNB*; GEC, *Peerage*.

Earl: 71.14, 71.184, 75.18, 76.19, 76.213, 77.23, 77.219, 78.19, 78.221, 79.18, 79.226

Wriothesley, Henry [II], Earl of Southampton (1573–1624) Son of Henry [I] Wriothesley*, Earl of Southampton and Mary Browne (Wriothesley*); mar 1598 Elizabeth Vernon*. *ODNB*; GEC, *Peerage*.

Earl: 89.12, 97.14, 97.214, 98.16, 98.216

Wriothesley, Jane, née Cheyne, Countess of Southampton (c.1509–1574) Daughter of William Cheyne and Emma Walwyn; mar 1534 Thomas Wriothesley, Earl of Southampton; mother of Lady Catherine Cornwallis* and Lady Mary Lister*. GEC, *Peerage*.

Countess: 71.28, 71.198

Wriothesley, Lady Mary—see Lady Mary Lister

Wriothesley, Lady Mary, née Browne, Countess of Southampton (c.1554–1607) Daughter of Anthony Browne*, Viscount Montagu and Jane Radcliffe; mar 1st 1565 Henry [I] Wriothesley*, Earl of Southampton, 2nd 1594 Sir Thomas Heneage* MP, 3rd 1599 Sir William Harvey, MP; mother of Henry [II] Wriothesley*, Earl of Southampton. GEC, *Peerage*; *ODNB* under husbands.

Countess: 71.29, 71.199, 75.34, 75.141, 76.36, 76.231, 77.38, 77.237, 78.39, 78.240, 79.37, 79.244, 81.33, 81.240, 82.33, 82.233, 82.485, 84.31, 84.229, 85.32, 85.223, 88.32, 88.217, 89.27, 89.212, 94.25, 94.208, 97.35, 97.226, 98.34, 98.229, 99.29, 99.219, 00.36, 00.226, 03.40, 03.250

Wroughton, Dorothy—see Dorothy Thynne

Wynyard, John (d.1606) Yeoman of the Removing Wardrobe of Beds. Will PCC 10 Stafford.

Custody of Gift: 78.182, 82.109, 89.120, 94.101, 94.129, 94.147, 94.149, 99.133

Wynter—see Winter

York, Archbishop—see Nicholas Heath, 1555–1559; Thomas Young, 1561–1568; Edmund Grindal, 1570–1576; Edwin Sandys, 1577–1588; John Piers, 1589–1594; Matthew Hutton, 1595–1606

York, Anne, née Smith (fl.1550s–1570s) Lady York, Gentlewoman of the Privy Chamber. Daughter of Robert Smith; mar 1ˢᵗ by 1542 Sir John York*, 2ⁿᵈ c.1570 Robert Paget. *ODNB* under 1ˢᵗ husband.
> **Lady**: 59.85, 59.305, 62.88, 62.270, 63.84, 63.268, 67.97, 67.267, 68.94, 68.263, 71.92, 71.262

York, Sir John (d.1569) Master of the Mint, kntd 1549. uncle of Martin Frobisher*; mar c.1542 Anne Smith (York*). *ODNB*; will PCC 4 Sheffelde.
> **Knight**: 59.123, 59.342

Young, George (fl.1580s) Clerk of the Council under James VI* of Scotland. Chalmers.
> **Sundry Gift**: 84.414 (Gift to Envoy)

Young, John (c.1519–1589) kntd 1574, MP. Son of Hugh Young; mar c.1569 Joan Wadham. Hasler; Bindoff; will PCC 23 Chayre, 93 Leicester; Bodleian MS Laud 683.
> **Gentleman**: 59.168, 59.392, 62.157, 62.344, 63.148, 63.327

Young, John (1534–1605) Bishop of Rochester 1578–1605. *ODNB*.
> **Bishop**: 79.60, 79.267, 81.56, 81.261, 82.53, 82.251, 82.452, 84.46, 84.244, 85.50, 85.241, 88.51, 88.236, 89.45, 89.230, 94.44, 94.227, 97.49, 97.247, 98.47, 98.249, 99.41, 99.238, 00.53, 00.248, 03.54, 03.267

Young, Thomas (1507–1568) Archbishop of York 1561–1568. *ODNB*.
> **Bishop**: 62.18, 62.198, 63.16, 63.188, 64.17, 65.118, 67.18, 67.188, 68.33, 68.202

Zinzan—see Zinzano

Zinzano, unidentified [née?] (fl. 1550s) Gentlewoman. Mar Alexander Zinzano, alias Alexander; mother of Robert Zinzano* and Alexander Zinzano*. Mother and two sons share gift from the Queen; all are listed under Gentlewomen.
> **Gentlewoman**: 59.145, 59.371

Zinzano, Alexander (fl.1590s–1600s) Yeoman of the Stable. Son of Alexander Zinzan; grandson of Hanibal Zinzano, alias Alexander; listed with mother on 'To list'.
> **Gentleman**: 59.197
> **Gentlewoman**: 59.371

Zinzano, Robert (d.1607) Equerry of the Stable. Son of Alexander Zinzano, grandson of Hanibal Zinzano, alias Alexander, kntd by 1607; listed with mother on 'To list'.
> **Gentleman**: 59.197

Zouche, Eleanor, née Whalley (d.1600) Lady Zouche. Daughter of Richard Whalley; mar 1564 Sir John Zouche*, MP. Hasler under husband; will PCC 29, 30 Wallopp.
> **Lady**: 78.120, 78.321, 79.118, 79.325, 81.114, 81.321, 85.104, 85.299, 88.109, 88.293, 89.102, 89.287, 94.98, 94.281, 97.107, 97.308, 98.108, 98.316, 99.105, 99.291, 00.109, 00.298

Zouche, Sir John (1524–1586) Esquire for the Body Extraordinary to Henry VIII, Gentleman Pensioner, kntd 1559, MP. Son of George Zouche and Anne Gainsford; mar 1564 Eleanor Whalley (Zouche*). Hasler; Bindoff; will PCC 30 Brudenell.
> **Knight**: 82.129, 82.329, 82.541, 84.123, 84.321

Zveneghen, Seigneur de—see Halewyn, François

#672027

390.22094)

(L)